C000185840

Distances an[d]

The mileage chart shows distance[s]
AA-recommended routes. Using [...]
normally the fastest route, though [...]

The journey times are shown in hours and minutes. These times should
be used as a guide only and do not allow for unforeseen traffic delays, rest
breaks or fuel stops.

For example, the 377 miles (607 km) journey between Glasgow and
Norwich should take approximately 7 hours 18 minutes.

Journey times

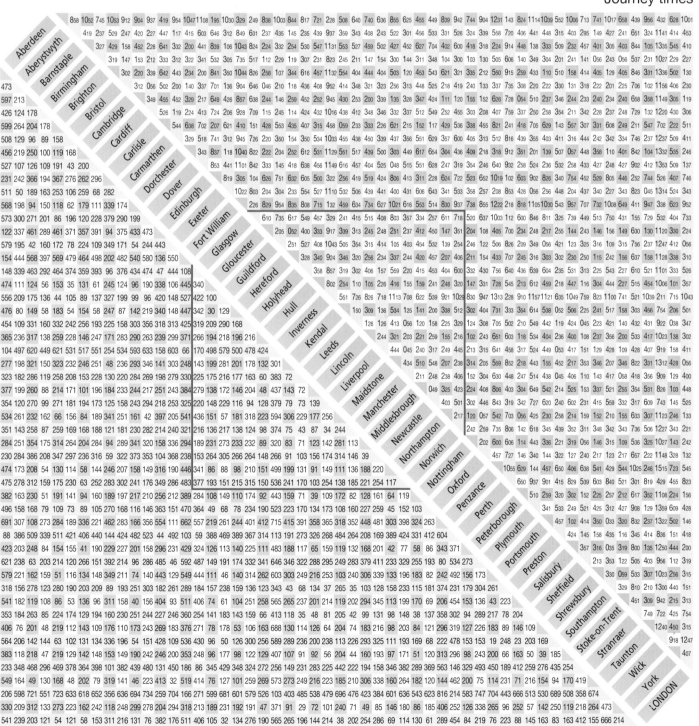

Distances in miles (one mile equals 1.6093 km)

AA

2022
GREAT BRITAIN ROAD ATLAS

Scale 1:200,000
or 3.16 miles to 1 inch

35th edition June 2021 © AA Media Limited 2021
Original edition printed 1986.

All cartography in this atlas edited, designed and produced by the Mapping Services Department of AA Media Limited (A05787).

This atlas contains Ordnance Survey data © Crown copyright and database right 2021 and Royal Mail data © Royal Mail copyright and database right 2021. Contains public sector information licensed under the Open Government Licence v3.0.
Ireland mapping and distance chart contains data available from openstreetmap.org © under the Open Database License found at opendatacommons.org

Published by AA Media Limited, whose registered office is Grove House, Lutyens Close, Basingstoke, Hampshire RG24 8AG, UK. Registered number 06112600

ISBN: 978 0 7495 8268 5 (leather)
ISBN: 978 0 7495 8267 8 (standard)

A CIP catalogue record for this book is available from The British Library.

Disclaimer: The contents of this atlas are believed to be correct at the time of the latest revision, it will not contain any subsequent amended, new or temporary information including diversions and traffic control or enforcement systems. The publishers cannot be held responsible or liable for any loss or damage occasioned to any person acting or refraining from action as a result of any use or reliance on material in this atlas, nor for any errors, omissions or changes in such material. This does not affect your statutory rights.

The publishers would welcome information to correct any errors or omissions and to keep this atlas up to date. Please write to the Atlas Editor, AA Media Limited, Grove House, Lutyens Close, Basingstoke, Hampshire RG24 8AG, UK.
E-mail: *roadatlasfeedback@aamediagroup.co.uk*

Acknowledgements: AA Media Limited would like to thank the following for information used in the creation of this atlas:
Cadw, English Heritage, Forestry Commission, Historic Scotland, National Trust and National Trust for Scotland, RSPB, The Wildlife Trust, Scottish Natural Heritage, Natural England, The Countryside Council for Wales. Award winning beaches from 'Blue Flag' and 'Keep Scotland Beautiful' (summer 2019 data): for latest information visit *www.blueflag.org* and *www.keepscotlandbeautiful.org*. Road signs are © Crown Copyright 2021. Reproduced under the terms of the Open Government Licence. Transport for London (Central London Map), Nexus (Newcastle district map).
Ireland mapping: Republic of Ireland census 2016 © Central Statistics Office and Northern Ireland census 2016 © NISRA (population data); Irish Public Sector Data (CC BY 4.0) (Gaeltacht); Logainm.ie (placenames); Roads Service and Transport Infrastructure Ireland
Printed by 1010 Printing International Ltd

Contents

Map pages and distance chart	inside front cover
Route planning	**II–XVII**
Route planner	II–VII
Ferries and port plans	VIII–XI
Caravan and camping sites in Britain	XII–XV
Traffic signs	XVI–XVII
Motorways	**XVIII–XXV**
Restricted junctions	XVIII–XXI
M25 London Orbital motorway	XXII
M6 Toll motorway	XXIII
Smart motorways	XXIV–XXV
Map pages	**XXVI**
Road map symbols	**1**
Road maps	**2–173**
Britain 1:200,000 scale	2–169
Some islands are shown at slightly smaller scales	
Ireland 1:1,000,000 scale	170–173
District maps	**174–185**
Birmingham	174–175
Glasgow	176–177
London	178–181
Manchester	182–183
Tyne & Wear	184–185
Street map symbols	**186**
Towns, ports and airports	**187–237**
Town plans	188–234
Major airports	235–237
Port plans	VIII–XI
Channel Tunnel terminals	27
Central London street map and index	**238–253**
Index to place names	**254–302**
County, administrative area map	254
Place name index	255–302
Map pages and distance chart	inside back cover

(Mar–Oct)

REPUBLIC
OF
IRELAND

66

Holyhead Anglesey Llandudno Colwyn Bay Rhyl **Birkenhead** **Widnes** Manche
Bangor Conwy Abergele Holywell John Lennon Runcorn Knutsford
Bethesda Denbigh Queensferry **Ellesmere Port** Northwich Maccle
Caernarfon **Chester** Middlewich Cong
Mold Kidsgrove
SNOWDONIA Betws-y-Coed **68** Ruthin **Crewe** **70** Sto
Pwllheli Porthmadog Wrexham Nantwich Newcastle-under-Lyme Sto
Abersoch Bala Llangollen Whitchurch Market Drayton
Oswestry Newport
Barmouth Dolgellau Welshpool **Shrewsbury** **Cannot**
54 **56** Telford **53**
Machynlleth Church Stretton **WOLVERHAMPTON**
Cardigan Bay Newtown Bridgnorth **Dudley**
WALES **Stourbridge**
Aberystwyth **Kidderminster** **Halesowe**
Llangurig Ludlow Bromsgrove
Rhayader Knighton
Aberaeron Leominster **Worcester**
New Quay **42** **44** Llandrindod Wells Kington **46**
Cardigan Tregaron Builth Wells Malvern
Lampeter Hay-on-Wye Hereford Ledbury
Newcastle Emlyn Brecon Tewkesb
St Davids **40** Fishguard Llandovery Ross-on-Wye **Gloucester**
Carmarthen Llandeilo BRECON BEACONS Abergavenny
PEMBROKESHIRE COAST Monmouth Stroud
Haverfordwest St Clears **28** **30** **32**
Milford Haven Llanelli Merthyr Tydfil Chepstow
Pembroke Dock Neath Cwmbran
Pembroke Tenby Swansea Pontypridd **Newport**
Port Talbot Avonmouth **BRISTOL**
Bridgend **CARDIFF** Bath
Cardiff Clevedon **20**
Bristol
Bristol Channel **Weston-super-Mare** Cheddar Frome
18 Minehead Wells Trowb
Ilfracombe Lynton Shepton Mallet War
16 EXMOOR Glastonbury
Lundy Barnstaple Bridgwater Wincanton
Bideford South Molton Taunton Yeovil Shaftesbury
Great Torrington Ilminster Sherborne
Bude **8** Tiverton **10** Chard Crewkerne Blandford Forum
Hatherleigh Crediton Exeter Axminster
Holsworthy Okehampton Honiton Bridport Dorchester
Exeter Lyme Regis Fortuneswell
4 Launceston DARTMOOR Exmouth Weymouth
Tavistock Dawlish
Wadebridge Buckfastleigh Teignmouth Channel Islands inset
Cornwall Newquay Bodmin **6** Newton Abbot Guernsey
Newquay Liskeard Totnes **Torquay** Jersey
Lostwithiel Saltash Paignton St-Malo
2 Isles of Scilly inset Fowey Torpoint **PLYMOUTH** Dartmouth
St Austell Kingsbridge
Redruth Truro
Camborne Roscoff
Penzance Santander (Apr–Oct)
Land's End Helston Falmouth
Lizard **ENGLISH**

Rosslare

Legend:
— Motorway
— Toll motorway
— Primary route dual carriageway
— Primary route single carriageway
— Other A road
Vehicle ferry
Fast vehicle ferry or catamaran
National Park
16 Atlas page number

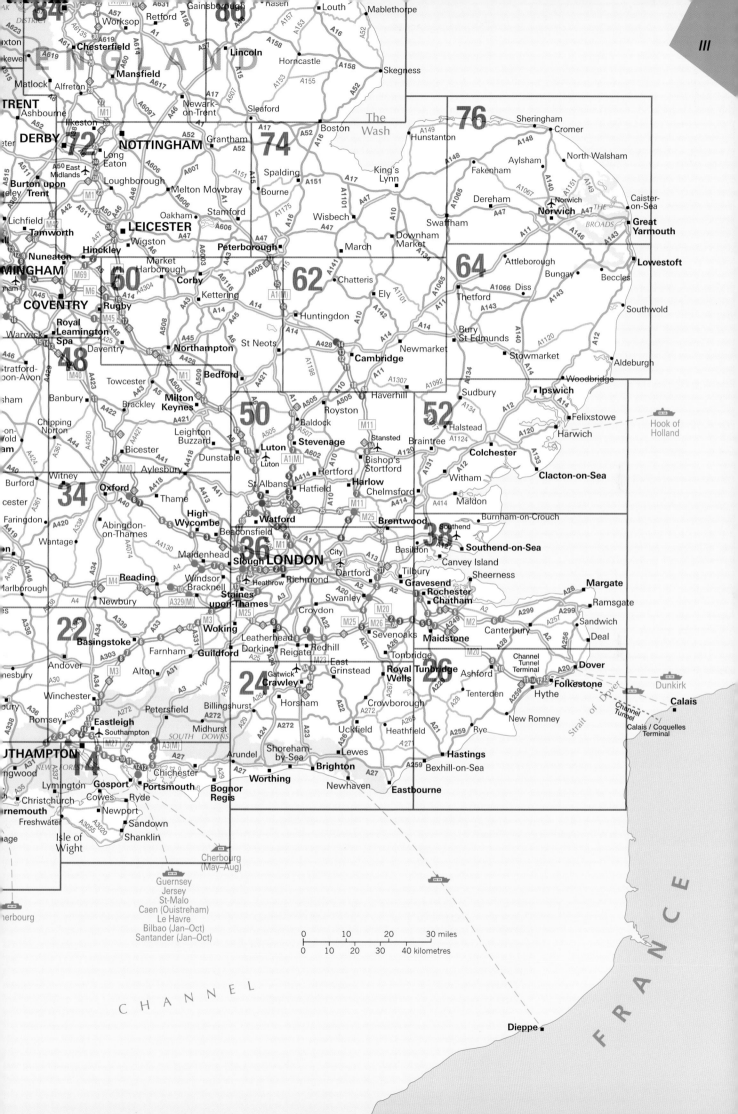

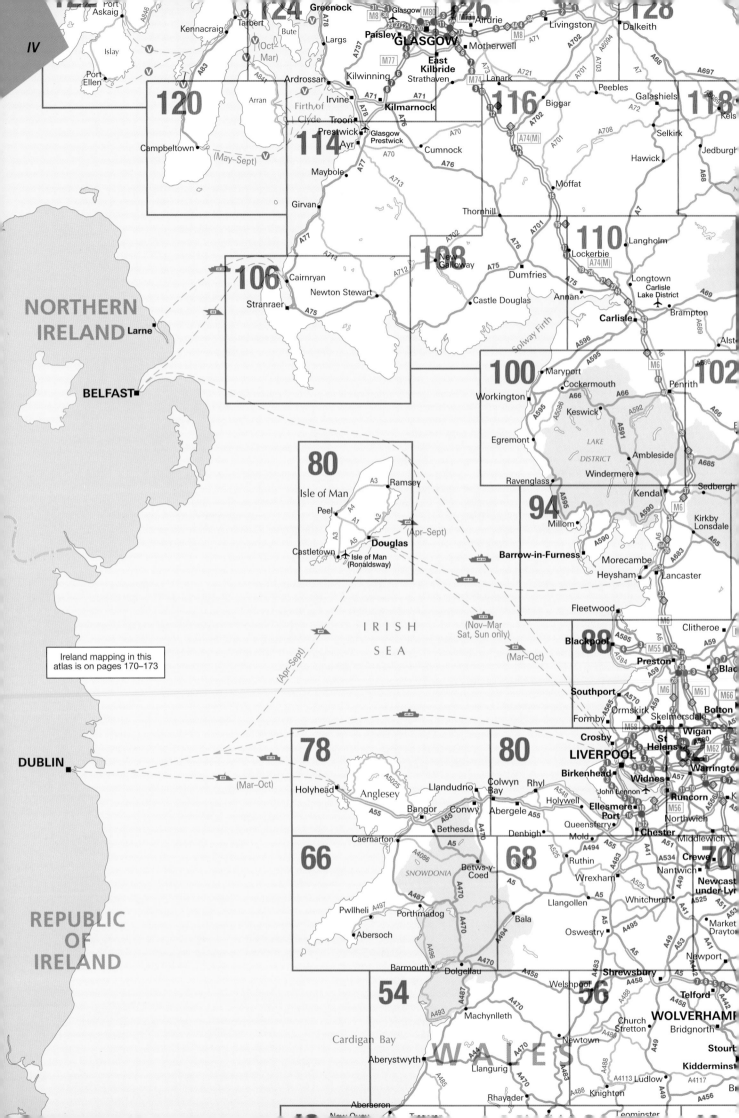

v

Legend

Motorway

Toll motorway

Primary route
dual carriageway

Primary route
single carriageway

Other A road

or V — Vehicle ferry

Fast vehicle ferry
or catamaran

National Park

98 Atlas page number

0   10   20   30 miles
0 10 20 30 40 kilometres

Place names

Eyemouth
Berwick-upon-Tweed
Wooler
Alnwick
Amble
Ashington
Morpeth
Newcastle
North Shields
Tynemouth
South Shields
NEWCASTLE UPON TYNE
Gateshead
SUNDERLAND
Consett
Chester-le-Street
Durham
Bishop Auckland
Barnard Castle
Stockton-on-Tees
Middlesbrough
Hartlepool
Darlington
Durham Tees Valley
Richmond
Guisborough
Whitby
NORTH YORK MOORS
Northallerton
Leyburn
Thirsk
Helmsley
Pickering
Scarborough
Filey
Ripon
Easingwold
Malton
Bridlington
Harrogate
Otley
Leeds Bradford
Wetherby
York
Driffield
Market Weighton
Beverley
BRADFORD
LEEDS
Selby
Halifax
KINGSTON UPON HULL
Withernsea
Huddersfield
Wakefield
Pontefract
Goole
Barnsley
Thorne
Scunthorpe
Immingham
Grimsby
Humberside
Cleethorpes
Doncaster
Brigg
Doncaster Sheffield
MANCHESTER
Glossop
Rotherham
Bawtry
Market Rasen
Louth
Mablethorpe
Stockport
SHEFFIELD
PEAK DISTRICT
Worksop
Retford
Gainsborough
Buxton
Bakewell
Chesterfield
Lincoln
Horncastle
Skegness
Matlock
Alfreton
Mansfield
Leek
Ashbourne
Ilkeston
Newark-on-Trent
Sleaford
The Wash
Sheringham
Cromer
STOKE-ON-TRENT
DERBY
NOTTINGHAM
Grantham
Boston
Hunstanton
North Walsham
Uttoxeter
Long Eaton
East Midlands
Loughborough
Spalding
King's Lynn
Aylsham
Burton upon Trent
Melton Mowbray
Bourne
Fakenham
Dereham
Norwich
Caister-on-Sea
Rugeley
Stafford
Lichfield
Oakham
Stamford
Wisbech
Swaffham
THE BROADS
Walsall
LEICESTER
Wigston
March
Downham Market
Great Yarmouth
Tamworth
Hinckley
Peterborough
Nuneaton
Market Harborough
Attleborough
Lowestoft
BIRMINGHAM
Corby
Chatteris
Bungay
Beccles
Kettering
Ely
Thetford
Diss
COVENTRY
Rugby
Huntingdon
Bury St Edmunds
Southwold
Redditch
Royal Leamington Spa
Warwick
St Neots
Amsterdam (IJmuiden)
Rotterdam (Europoort) Zeebrugge
ENGLAND

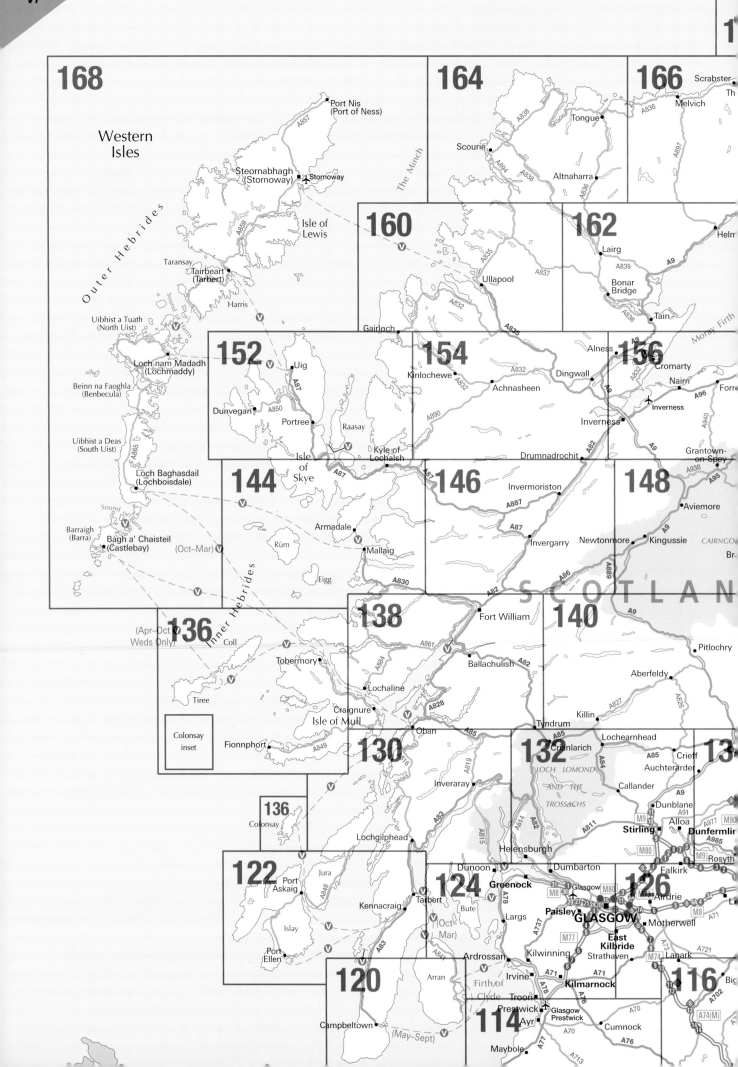

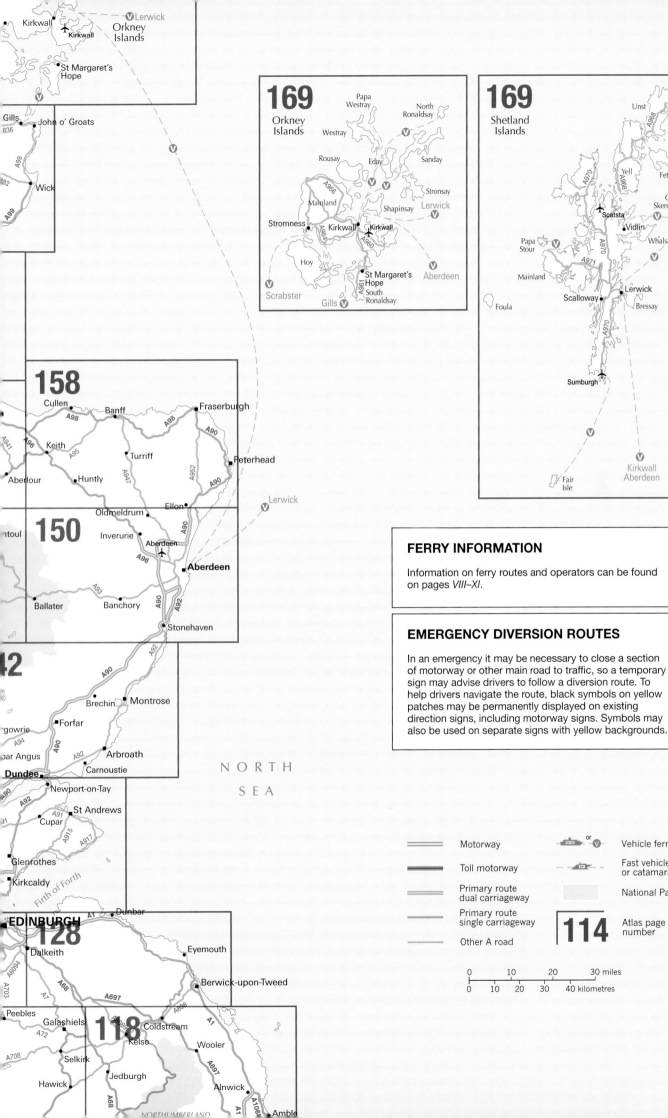

Kirkwall
Orkney Islands
Kirkwall
St Margaret's Hope
Gills
836
John o' Groats
A99
A99
882
Wick
A99

169 Orkney Islands

Papa Westray
North Ronaldsay
Westray
Rousay
Eday
Sanday
Mainland
Stronsay
A966
Shapinsay
Lerwick
Stromness
Kirkwall
Kirkwall
A964
A960
Hoy
A961
St Margaret's Hope
South Ronaldsay
Aberdeen
Scrabster
Gills

169 Shetland Islands

Unst
A968
Yell
A968
Fetlar
A970
A968
Out Skerries
Scatsta
Vidlin
Whalsay
Papa Stour
A970
Mainland
A971
Scalloway
Lerwick
Bressay
A970
Foula
Sumburgh
Fair Isle
Kirkwall Aberdeen

158
Cullen
Banff
Fraserburgh
A98
A98
A90
A941
A96
Keith
A95
Turriff
A952
Peterhead
Aberlour
Huntly
A947
A90
Oldmeldrum
Ellon
Lerwick

150
ntoul
Inverurie
A90
Aberdeen
A96
Aberdeen
A93
Ballater
Banchory
A90
A92
Stonehaven

42
A92
Brechin
Montrose
A90
gowrie
Forfar
A94
ar Angus
A92
Arbroath
90
Carnoustie
Dundee
A92
Newport-on-Tay
St Andrews
A91
Cupar
A915
A917
Glenrothes
Kirkcaldy
Firth of Forth

NORTH
SEA

FERRY INFORMATION

Information on ferry routes and operators can be found on pages *VIII–XI*.

EMERGENCY DIVERSION ROUTES

In an emergency it may be necessary to close a section of motorway or other main road to traffic, so a temporary sign may advise drivers to follow a diversion route. To help drivers navigate the route, black symbols on yellow patches may be permanently displayed on existing direction signs, including motorway signs. Symbols may also be used on separate signs with yellow backgrounds.

Dunbar
A1
EDINBURGH
A1
128
A6094
Dalkeith
Eyemouth
A703
A7
Berwick-upon-Tweed
A68
A697
Peebles
Galashiels
A898
Coldstream
A72
118
Kelso
A1
Selkirk
Wooler
A708
Jedburgh
A697
Hawick
Alnwick
A68
A106
Amble
NORTHUMBERLAND

Motorway
Vehicle ferry
Toll motorway
Fast vehicle ferry or catamaran
Primary route dual carriageway
National Park
Primary route single carriageway
114 Atlas page number
Other A road

0   10   20   30 miles
0   10   20   30   40 kilometres

Channel hopping and the Isle of Wight

For business or pleasure, hopping on a ferry across to France, the Channel Islands or Isle of Wight has never been easier.

The vehicle ferry services listed in the table give you all the options, together with detailed port plans to help you navigate to and from the ferry terminals. Simply choose your preferred route, not forgetting the fast sailings (see 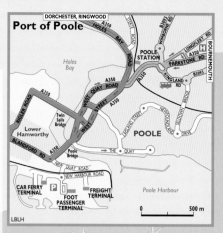). Bon voyage!

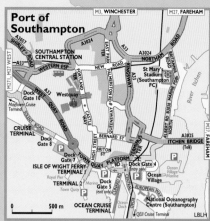
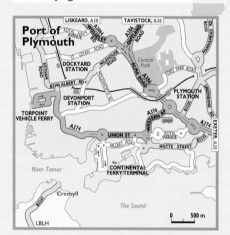
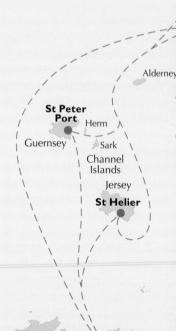

E N G L I S H

ENGLISH CHANNEL AND ISLE OF WIGHT FERRY CROSSINGS

From	To	Journey time	Operator website
Dover	Calais	1 hr 30 mins	dfdsseaways.co.uk
Dover	Calais	1 hr 30 mins	poferries.com
Dover	Dunkirk	2 hrs	dfdsseaways.co.uk
Folkestone	Calais (Coquelles)	35 mins	eurotunnel.com
Lymington	Yarmouth (IOW)	40 mins	wightlink.co.uk
Newhaven	Dieppe	4 hrs	dfdsseaways.co.uk
Plymouth	Roscoff	6–8 hrs	brittany-ferries.co.uk
Poole	Cherbourg	4 hrs 30 mins	brittany-ferries.co.uk
Poole	Guernsey	3 hrs	condorferries.co.uk
Poole	Jersey	4 hrs 30 mins	condorferries.co.uk
Poole	St-Malo	7–12 hrs (via Channel Is.)	condorferries.co.uk
Portsmouth	Caen (Ouistreham)	6–7 hrs	brittany-ferries.co.uk
Portsmouth	Cherbourg	3 hrs (May–Aug)	brittany-ferries.co.uk
Portsmouth	Fishbourne (IOW)	45 mins	wightlink.co.uk
Portsmouth	Guernsey	7 hrs	condorferries.co.uk
Portsmouth	Jersey	8–11 hrs	condorferries.co.uk
Portsmouth	Le Havre	5 hrs 30 mins	brittany-ferries.co.uk
Portsmouth	St-Malo	9–11 hrs	brittany-ferries.co.uk
Southampton	East Cowes (IOW)	1 hr	redfunnel.co.uk

The information listed is provided as a guide only, as services are liable to change at short notice and are weather dependent. Services shown are for vehicle ferries only, operated by conventional ferry unless indicated as a fast ferry service ( ). Please check sailings before planning your journey.

Travelling further afield? For ferry services to Northern Spain see brittany-ferries.co.uk.

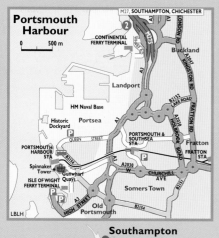

Portsmouth Harbour

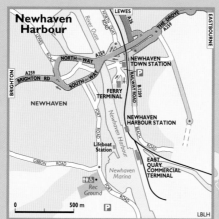

Newhaven Harbour

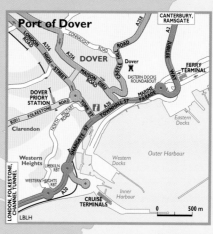

Port of Dover

Poole

Lymington

Southampton

East Cowes

Yarmouth

Fishbourne

Portsmouth

Isle of Wight

GB

Newhaven

Folkestone

Dover

Channel Tunnel

Calais

Calais (Coquelles)

Dunkirk

C H A N N E L

Cherbourg

Dieppe

Le Havre

Caen (Ouistreham)

F

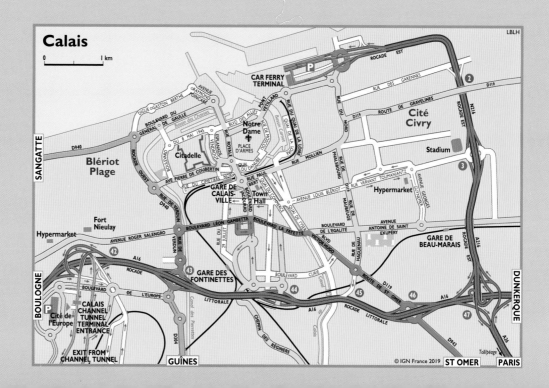

Calais

Ferries to Ireland and the Isle of Man

With so many sea crossings to Ireland and the Isle of Man the information provided in the table to the right will help you make the right choice.

IRISH SEA FERRY CROSSINGS

From	To	Journey time	Operator website
Cairnryan	Belfast	2 hrs 15 mins 🚢	stenaline.co.uk
Cairnryan	Larne	2 hrs	poferries.com
Douglas	Belfast	2 hrs 45 mins (April–Sept) 🚢	steam-packet.com
Douglas	Dublin	2 hrs 55 mins (April–Sept) 🚢	steam-packet.com
Fishguard	Rosslare	3 hrs 15 mins	stenaline.co.uk
Heysham	Douglas	3 hrs 45 mins	steam-packet.com
Holyhead	Dublin	2 hrs (Mar–Oct) 🚢	irishferries.com
Holyhead	Dublin	3 hrs 15 mins	irishferries.com
Holyhead	Dublin	3 hrs 15 mins	stenaline.co.uk
Liverpool	Douglas	2 hrs 45 mins (Mar–Oct) 🚢	steam-packet.com
Liverpool	Dublin	8 hrs–8 hrs 30 mins	poferries.com
Liverpool (Birkenhead)	Belfast	8 hrs	stenaline.co.uk
Liverpool (Birkenhead)	Douglas	4 hrs 15 mins (Nov–Mar Sat, Sun only)	steam-packet.com
Pembroke Dock	Rosslare	4 hrs	irishferries.com

The information listed is provided as a guide only, as services are liable to change at short notice and are weather dependent. Services shown are for vehicle ferries only, operated by conventional ferry unless indicated as a fast ferry service (🚢). Please check sailings before planning your journey.

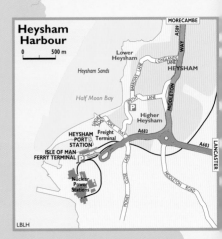

Heysham Harbour

Holyhead Harbour

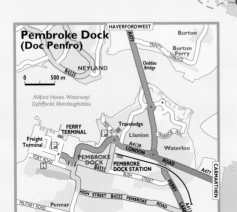

Pembroke Dock (Doc Penfro)

Fishguard Harbour

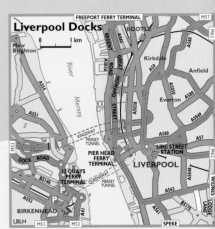

Liverpool Docks

SCOTLAND FERRIES

From	To	Journey time	Operator website
Scottish Islands/west coast of Scotland			
Gourock	Dunoon	20 mins	western-ferries.co.uk
Glenelg	Skye	20 mins (Easter–Oct)	skyeferry.co.uk
Numerous and varied sailings from the west coast of Scotland to Scottish islands are provided by Caledonian MacBrayne. Please visit calmac.co.uk for all ferry information, including those of other operators.			
Orkney Islands			
Aberdeen	Kirkwall	6 hrs	northlinkferries.co.uk
Gills	St Margaret's Hope	1 hr	pentlandferries.co.uk
Scrabster	Stromness	1 hr 30 mins	northlinkferries.co.uk
Lerwick	Kirkwall	5 hrs 30 mins	northlinkferries.co.uk
Inter-island services are operated by Orkney Ferries. Please see orkneyferries.co.uk for details.			
Shetland Islands			
Aberdeen	Lerwick	12 hrs 30 mins	northlinkferries.co.uk
Kirkwall	Lerwick	7 hrs 45 mins	northlinkferries.co.uk
Inter-island services are operated by Shetland Island Council Ferries. Please see shetland.gov.uk/ferries for details.			

Please note that some smaller island services are day and weather dependent and reservations are required for some routes. Book and confirm sailing schedules by contacting the operator.

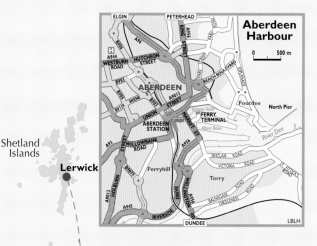

Aberdeen Harbour

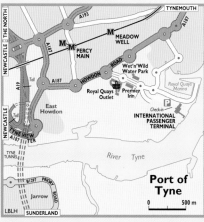

Port of Tyne

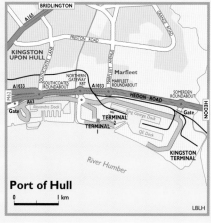

Port of Hull

For a port plan of Harwich see atlas page 53

NORTH SEA FERRY CROSSINGS

From	To	Journey time	Operator website
Harwich	Hook of Holland	7–8 hrs	stenaline.co.uk
Kingston upon Hull	Rotterdam (Europoort)	12 hrs	poferries.com
Kingston upon Hull	Zeebrugge	12 hrs	poferries.com
Newcastle upon Tyne	Amsterdam (IJmuiden)	15 hrs 30 mins	dfdsseaways.co.uk

The information listed on this page is provided as a guide only, as services are liable to change at short notice. Services shown are for vehicle ferries only, operated by conventional ferry. Please check sailings before planning your journey as many are weather dependent.

Caravan and camping sites in Britain

These pages list the top 300 AA-inspected Caravan and Camping (C & C) sites in the Pennant rating scheme. **Five Pennant Premier sites are shown in green,** Four Pennant sites are shown in blue.

Listings include addresses, telephone numbers and websites together with page and grid references to locate the sites in the atlas. The total number of touring pitches is also included for each site, together with the type of pitch available. The following abbreviations are used: **C = Caravan CV = Campervan T = Tent**

To discover AA-rated caravan and camping sites not included on these pages please visit RatedTrips.com

ENGLAND

Alders Caravan Park
Home Farm, Alne, York
YO61 1RY
Tel: 01347 838722   **97 R7**
alderscaravanpark.co.uk
Total Pitches: 91 (C, CV & T)

Andrewshayes Holiday Park
Dalwood, Axminster
EX13 7DY
Tel: 01404 831225   **10 E5**
andrewshayes.co.uk
Total Pitches: 230 (C, CV & T)

Ayr Holiday Park
St Ives, Cornwall
TR26 1EJ
Tel: 01736 795855   **2 E5**
ayrholidaypark.co.uk
Total Pitches: 40 (C, CV & T)

Back of Beyond Touring Park
234 Ringwood Road,
St Leonards, Dorset
BH24 2SB
Tel: 01202 876968   **13 K4**
backofbeyondtouringpark.co.uk
Total Pitches: 83 (C, CV & T)

Bagwell Farm Touring Park
Knights in the Bottom,
Chickerell, Weymouth
DT3 4EA
Tel: 01305 782575   **11 N8**
bagwellfarm.co.uk
Total Pitches: 320 (C, CV & T)

Bardsea Leisure Park
Priory Road, Ulverston
LA12 9QE
Tel: 01229 584712   **94 F5**
bardsealeisure.co.uk
Total Pitches: 171 (C & CV)

**Bath Chew Valley
Caravan Park**
Ham Lane, Bishop Sutton
BS39 5TZ
Tel: 01275 332127   **19 Q3**
bathchewvalley.co.uk
Total Pitches: 45 (C, CV & T)

Bay View Farm C & C Park
Croyde, Devon
EX33 1PN
Tel: 01271 890501   **16 G4**
bayviewfarm.co.uk
Total Pitches: 75 (C, CV & T)

Bay View Holiday Park
Bolton le Sands,
Carnforth
LA5 9TN
Tel: 01524 732854   **95 K7**
holgates.co.uk
Total Pitches: 202 (C, CV & T)

**Beacon Cottage Farm
Touring Park**
Beacon Drive, St Agnes
TR5 0NU
Tel: 01872 552347   **3 J3**
beaconcottagefarmholidays.co.uk
Total Pitches: 70 (C, CV & T)

**Beaconsfield Farm
Caravan Park**
Battlefield, Shrewsbury
SY4 4AA
Tel: 01939 210370   **69 P11**
beaconsfieldholidaypark.co.uk
Total Pitches: 95 (C & CV)

Beech Croft Farm
Beech Croft,
Blackwell in the Peak, Buxton
SK17 9TQ
Tel: 01298 85330   **83 P10**
beechcroftfarm.co.uk
Total Pitches: 30 (C, CV & T)

Beehive Woodland Lakes
Rosliston, Swadlincote,
Derbyshire
DE12 8HZ
Tel: 01283 763981   **71 P11**
beehivefarm-woodlandlakes.co.uk
Total Pitches: 50 (C, CV & T)

Bellingham C & C Club Site
Brown Rigg,
Bellingham
NE48 2JY
Tel: 01434 220175   **112 B4**
campingandcaravanning
club.co.uk/bellingham
Total Pitches: 68 (C, CV & T)

Beverley Park C & C Park
Goodrington Road, Paignton
TQ4 7JE
Tel: 01803 843887   **7 M7**
beverley-holidays.co.uk
Total Pitches: 149 (C, CV & T)

**Blue Rose Caravan
Country Park**
Star Carr Lane, Brandesburton
YO25 8RU
Tel: 01964 543366   **99 N11**
bluerosepark.com
Total Pitches: 114 (C & CV)

**Briarfields Motel &
Touring Park**
Gloucester Road, Cheltenham
GL51 0SX
Tel: 01242 235324   **46 H10**
briarfields.net
Total Pitches: 72 (C, CV & T)

Broadhembury C & C Park
Steeds Lane, Kingsnorth,
Ashford
TN26 1NQ
Tel: 01233 620859   **26 H4**
broadhembury.co.uk
Total Pitches: 120 (C, CV & T)

**Burnham-on-Sea
Holiday Village**
Marine Drive, Burnham-on-Sea
TA8 1LA
Tel: 01278 783391   **19 K5**
haven.com/burnhamonsea
Total Pitches: 781 (C, CV & T)

**Burrowhayes Farm C & C Site
& Riding Stables**
West Luccombe, Porlock,
Minehead
TA24 8HT
Tel: 01643 862463   **18 A5**
burrowhayes.co.uk
Total Pitches: 139 (C, CV & T)

**Burton Constable Holiday Park
& Arboretum**
Old Lodges, Sproatley, Hull
HU11 4LJ
Tel: 01964 562508   **93 L3**
burtonconstableholidaypark.co.uk
Total Pitches: 500 (C, CV & T)

Caister-on-Sea Holiday Park
Ormesby Road, Caister-on-Sea,
Great Yarmouth
NR30 5NH
Tel: 01493 728931   **77 Q9**
haven.com/caister
Total Pitches: 949 (C & CV)

Caistor Lakes Leisure Park
99a Brigg Road, Caistor
LN7 6RX
Tel: 01472 859626   **93 K10**
caistorlakes.co.uk
Total Pitches: 36 (C & CV)

Cakes & Ale
Abbey Lane, Theberton,
Leiston
IP16 4TE
Tel: 01728 831655   **65 N9**
cakesandale.co.uk
Total Pitches: 255 (C, CV & T)

Calloose C & C Park
Leedstown, Hayle
TR27 5ET
Tel: 01736 850431   **2 F7**
calloose.co.uk
Total Pitches: 134 (C, CV & T)

**Camping Caradon
Touring Park**
Trelawne, Looe
PL13 2NA
Tel: 01503 272388   **5 L11**
campingcaradon.co.uk
Total Pitches: 75 (C, CV & T)

Capesthorne Hall
Congleton Road, Siddington,
Macclesfield
SK11 9JY
Tel: 01625 861221   **82 H10**
capesthorne.com/caravan-park
Total Pitches: 50 (C & CV)

Carlyon Bay C & C Park
Bethesda, Cypress Avenue,
Carlyon Bay
PL25 3RE
Tel: 01726 812735   **3 R3**
carlyonbay.net
Total Pitches: 180 (C, CV & T)

Carnon Downs C & C Park
Carnon Downs,
Truro
TR3 6JJ
Tel: 01872 862283   **3 L5**
carnon-downs-caravanpark.co.uk
Total Pitches: 152 (C, CV & T)

Cartref C & C
Cartref, Ford Heath,
Shrewsbury, Shropshire
SY5 9GD
Tel: 01743 821688   **56 G2**
cartrefcaravansite.co.uk
Total Pitches: 44 (C, CV & T)

Carvynick Holiday Park
Summercourt,
Newquay
TR8 5AF
Tel: 01872 510716   **4 D10**
carvynick.co.uk
Total Pitches: 47 (C, CV & T)

Castlerigg Hall C & C Park
Castlerigg Hall, Keswick
CA12 4TE
Tel: 017687 74499   **101 J6**
castlerigg.co.uk
Total Pitches: 105 (C, CV & T)

**Cheddar Mendip Heights
C & C Club Site**
Townsend, Priddy, Wells
BA5 3BP
Tel: 01749 870241   **19 P4**
campingandcaravanning
club.co.uk/cheddar
Total Pitches: 92 (C, CV & T)

Clippesby Hall
Hall Lane, Clippesby,
Great Yarmouth
NR29 3BL
Tel: 01493 367800   **77 N9**
clippesbyhall.com
Total Pitches: 120 (C, CV & T)

Cofton Holidays
Starcross, Dawlish
EX6 8RP
Tel: 01626 890111   **9 N8**
coftonholidays.co.uk
Total Pitches: 532 (C, CV & T)

Concierge Camping
Ratham Estate, Ratham Lane,
West Ashling, Chichester
PO18 8DL
Tel: 01243 573118   **15 M5**
conciergecamping.co.uk
Total Pitches: 15 (C & CV)

Coombe Touring Park
Race Plain, Netherhampton,
Salisbury
SP2 8PN
Tel: 01722 328451   **21 L9**
coombecaravanpark.co.uk
Total Pitches: 56 (C, CV & T)

Corfe Castle C & C Club Site
Bucknowle, Wareham
BH20 5PQ
Tel: 01929 480280   **12 F8**
campingandcaravanning
club.co.uk/corfecastle
Total Pitches: 80 (C, CV & T)

Cornish Farm Touring Park
Shoreditch, Taunton
TA3 7BS
Tel: 01823 327746   **18 H10**
cornishfarm.com
Total Pitches: 50 (C, CV & T)

Cosawes Park
Perranarworthal,
Truro
TR3 7QS
Tel: 01872 863724   **3 K6**
cosawes.co.uk
Total Pitches: 59 (C, CV & T)

Cote Ghyll C & C Park
Osmotherley,
Northallerton
DL6 3AH
Tel: 01609 883425   **104 E11**
coteghyll.com
Total Pitches: 95 (C, CV & T)

Country View Holiday Park
Sand Road, Sand Bay,
Weston-super-Mare
BS22 9UJ
Tel: 01934 627595   **19 K2**
cvhp.co.uk
Total Pitches: 255 (C, CV & T)

Crealy Theme Park & Resort
Sidmouth Road,
Clyst St Mary, Exeter
EX5 1DR
Tel: 01395 234888   **9 P6**
crealy.co.uk
Total Pitches: 127 (C, CV & T)

Crows Nest Caravan Park
Gristhorpe, Filey
YO14 9PS
Tel: 01723 582206   **99 M4**
crowsnestcaravanpark.com
Total Pitches: 263 (C, CV & T)

**Deepdale Backpackers
& Camping**
Deepdale Farm,
Burnham Deepdale
PE31 8DD
Tel: 01485 210256   **75 R2**
deepdalebackpackers.co.uk
Total Pitches: 80 (CV & T)

Diamond C & C Park
Islip Road, Bletchingdon,
Oxfordshire
OX5 3DR
Tel: 01869 350909   **48 F11**
diamondpark.co.uk
Total Pitches: 37 (C, CV & T)

Dibles Park
Dibles Road, Warsash,
Southampton, Hampshire
SO31 9SA
Tel: 01489 575232   **14 F5**
diblespark.co.uk
Total Pitches: 60 (C, CV & T)

Dornafield
Dornafield Farm, Two Mile Oak,
Newton Abbot
TQ12 6DD
Tel: 01803 812732   **7 L5**
dornafield.com
Total Pitches: 135 (C, CV & T)

East Fleet Farm Touring Park
Chickerell, Weymouth
DT3 4DW
Tel: 01305 785768   **11 N9**
eastfleet.co.uk
Total Pitches: 400 (C, CV & T)

Eastham Hall Holiday Park
Saltcotes Road,
Lytham St Annes, Lancashire
FY8 4LS
Tel: 01253 737907   **88 D5**
easthamhall.co.uk
Total Pitches: 274 (C & CV)

Eden Valley Holiday Park
Lanlivery, Nr Lostwithiel
PL30 5BU
Tel: 01208 872277   **4 H10**
edenvalleyholidaypark.co.uk
Total Pitches: 94 (C, CV & T)

Exe Valley Caravan Site
Mill House, Bridgetown,
Dulverton
TA22 9JR
Tel: 01643 851432   **18 B8**
exevalleycamping.co.uk
Total Pitches: 48 (C, CV & T)

Eye Kettleby Lakes
Eye Kettleby, Melton Mowbray
LE14 2TN
Tel: 01664 565900   **73 J7**
eyekettlebylakes.com
Total Pitches: 130 (C, CV & T)

Fen Farm Caravan Site
Moore Lane, East Mersea,
Mersea Island,
Colchester, Essex
CO5 8FE
Tel: 01206 383275   **53 J9**
fenfarm.co.uk
Total Pitches: 180 (C, CV & T)

Fernwood Caravan Park
Lyneal, Ellesmere, Shropshire
SY12 0QF
Tel: 01948 710221   **69 N8**
fernwoodpark.co.uk
Total Pitches: 225 (C & CV)

**Fields End Water
Caravan Park & Fishery**
Benwick Road, Doddington,
March
PE15 0TY
Tel: 01354 740199   **62 E2**
fieldsendwater.co.uk
Total Pitches: 52 (C, CV & T)

Fishpool Farm Caravan Park
Fishpool Road, Delamere,
Northwich, Cheshire
CW8 2HP
Tel: 01606 883970   **82 C11**
fishpoolfarmcaravanpark.co.uk
Total Pitches: 51 (C, CV & T)

Flower of May Holiday Park
Lebberston Cliff, Filey,
Scarborough
YO11 3NU
Tel: 01723 584311   **99 M4**
flowerofmay.com
Total Pitches: 503 (C, CV & T)

**Freshwater Beach
Holiday Park**
Burton Bradstock, Bridport
DT6 4PT
Tel: 01308 897317   **11 K6**
freshwaterbeach.co.uk
Total Pitches: 750 (C, CV & T)

Glenfield Caravan Park
Blackmoor Lane, Bardsey, Leeds
LS17 9DZ
Tel: 01937 574657   **91 J2**
glenfieldcaravanpark.co.uk
Total Pitches: 31 (C, CV & T)

Globe Vale Holiday Park
Radnor, Redruth
TR16 4BH
Tel: 01209 891183   **3 J5**
globevale.co.uk
Total Pitches: 195 (C, CV & T)

Glororum Caravan Park
Glororum Farm, Bamburgh
NE69 7AW
Tel: 01670 860256   **119 N4**
northbrianleisure.co.uk
Total Pitches: 213 (C & CV)

Golden Cap Holiday Park
Seatown, Chideock, Bridport
DT6 6JX
Tel: 01308 422139   **11 J6**
wdlh.co.uk
Total Pitches: 345 (C, CV & T)

Golden Coast Holiday Park
Station Road, Woolacombe
EX34 7HW
Tel: 01271 872302   **16 H3**
woolacombe.com
Total Pitches: 431 (C, CV & T)

Golden Sands Holiday Park
Quebec Road, Mablethorpe
LN12 1QJ
Tel: 01507 477871   **87 N3**
haven.com/goldensands
Total Pitches: 1672 (C, CV & T)

Golden Square C & C Park
Oswaldkirk, Helmsley
YO62 5YQ
Tel: 01439 788269   **98 C5**
goldensquarecaravanpark.com
Total Pitches: 150 (C, CV & T)

Golden Valley C & C Park
Coach Road, Ripley, Derbyshire
DE55 4ES
Tel: 01773 513881   **84 F10**
goldenvalleycaravanpark.co.uk
Total Pitches: 47 (C, CV & T)

Goosewood Holiday Park
Sutton-on-the-Forest, York
YO61 1ET
Tel: 01347 810829   **98 B8**
flowerofmay.com
Total Pitches: 145 (C & CV)

Green Acres Caravan Park
High Knells, Houghton, Carlisle
CA6 4JW
Tel: 01228 675418   **110 H8**
caravanpark-cumbria.com
Total Pitches: 35 (C, CV & T)

Greenhill Farm C & C Park
Greenhill Farm, New Road,
Landford, Salisbury
SP5 2AZ
Tel: 01794 324117   **21 Q11**
greenhillfarm.co.uk
Total Pitches: 160 (C, CV & T)

Greenhills Holiday Park
Crowhill Lane, Bakewell,
Derbyshire
DE45 1PX
Tel: 01629 813052   **84 B7**
greenhillsholidaypark.co.uk
Total Pitches: 245 (C, CV & T)

Grouse Hill Caravan Park
Flask Bungalow Farm,
Fylingdales,
Robin Hood's Bay
YO22 4QH
Tel: 01947 880543   **105 P10**
grousehill.co.uk
Total Pitches: 192 (C, CV & T)

Gunvenna Holiday Park
St Minver, Wadebridge
PL27 6QN
Tel: 01208 862405   **4 F6**
gunvenna.com
Total Pitches: 121 (C, CV & T)

**Haggerston Castle
Holiday Park**
Beal, Berwick-upon-Tweed
TD15 2PA
Tel: 01289 381333   **119 K2**
haven.com/haggerstoncastle
Total Pitches: 1340 (C & CV)

Harbury Fields
Harbury Fields Farm, Harbury,
Nr Leamington Spa
CV33 9JN
Tel: 01926 612457   **48 C2**
harburyfields.co.uk
Total Pitches: 59 (C & CV)

Harford Bridge Holiday Park
Peter Tavy, Tavistock
PL19 9LS
Tel: 01822 810349   **8 D9**
harfordbridge.co.uk
Total Pitches: 198 (C, CV & T)

Haw Wood Farm Caravan Park
Hinton, Saxmundham
IP17 3QT
Tel: 01502 359550   **65 N7**
hawwoodfarm.co.uk
Total Pitches: 115 (C, CV & T)

Heathfield Farm Camping
Heathfield Road,
Freshwater,
Isle of Wight
PO40 9SH
Tel: 01983 407822   **13 P7**
heathfieldcamping.co.uk
Total Pitches: 75 (C, CV & T)

Heathland Beach Holiday Park
London Road,
Kessingland
NR33 7PJ
Tel: 01502 740337   **65 Q4**
heathlandbeach.co.uk
Total Pitches: 263 (C, CV & T)

Hele Valley Holiday Park
Hele Bay,
Ilfracombe
EX34 9RD
Tel: 01271 862460   **17 J2**
helevalley.co.uk
Total Pitches: 133 (C, CV & T)

Hendra Holiday Park
Newquay
TR8 4NY
Tel: 01637 875778   **4 C9**
hendra-holidays.com
Total Pitches: 865 (C, CV & T)

**Herding Hill Farm Touring &
Camping Site**
Shield Hill, Haltwhistle,
Northumberland
NE49 9NW
Tel: 01434 320175   **111 P7**
herdinghillfarm.co.uk
Total Pitches: 22 (C, CV & T)

Highfield Farm Touring Park
Long Road,
Comberton, Cambridge
CB23 7DG
Tel: 01223 262308   **62 E9**
highfieldfarmtouringpark.co.uk
Total Pitches: 120 (C, CV & T)

Highlands End Holiday Park
Eype, Bridport,
Dorset
DT6 6AR
Tel: 01308 422139   **11 K6**
wdlh.co.uk
Total Pitches: 357 (C, CV & T)

Hill of Oaks & Blakeholme
Windermere
LA12 8NR
Tel: 015395 31578   **94 H3**
hillofoaks.co.uk
Total Pitches: 263 (C & CV)

Hillside Caravan Park
Canvas Farm, Moor Road,
Knayton,
Thirsk
YO7 4BR
Tel: 01845 537349   **97 P3**
hillsidecaravanpark.co.uk
Total Pitches: 52 (C & CV)

Holiday Resort Unity
Coast Road, Brean Sands,
Brean
TA8 2RB
Tel: 01278 751235   **19 J4**
hru.co.uk
Total Pitches: 1114 (C, CV & T)

Hollins Farm C & C
Far Arnside, Carnforth
LA5 0SL
Tel: 01524 701767   **95 J5**
holgates.co.uk
Total Pitches: 14 (C, CV & T)

Hylton Caravan Park
Eden Street, Silloth
CA7 4AY
Tel: 016973 32666   **109 P10**
stanwix.com
Total Pitches: 303 (C, CV & T)

Island Lodge C & C Site
Stumpy Post Cross,
Kingsbridge
TQ7 4BL
Tel: 01548 852956   **7 J9**
islandlodgesite.co.uk
Total Pitches: 30 (C, CV & T)

**Isle of Avalon Touring
Caravan Park**
Godney Road,
Glastonbury
BA6 9AF
Tel: 01458 833618   **19 N7**
avaloncaravanpark.co.uk
Total Pitches: 120 (C, CV & T)

Jasmine Caravan Park
Cross Lane, Snainton,
Scarborough
YO13 9BE
Tel: 01723 859240   **99 J4**
jasminepark.co.uk
Total Pitches: 84 (C, CV & T)

**Kennford International
Holiday Park**
Kennford,
Exeter
EX6 7YN
Tel: 01392 833046   **9 M7**
kennfordinternational.co.uk
Total Pitches: 87 (C, CV & T)

King's Lynn C & C Park
New Road, North Runcton,
King's Lynn
PE33 0RA
Tel: 01553 840004   **75 M7**
kl-cc.co.uk
Total Pitches: 170 (C, CV & T)

Kloofs Caravan Park
Sandhurst Lane, Bexhill
TN39 4RG
Tel: 01424 842839   **26 B10**
kloofs.com
Total Pitches: 125 (C, CV & T)

Kneps Farm Holiday Park
River Road, Stanah,
Thornton-Cleveleys,
Blackpool
FY5 5LR
Tel: 01253 823632   **88 D2**
knepsfarm.co.uk
Total Pitches: 86 (C & CV)

**Knight Stainforth Hall
Caravan & Campsite**
Stainforth, Settle
BD24 0DP
Tel: 01729 822200   **96 B7**
knightstainforth.co.uk
Total Pitches: 160 (C, CV & T)

**Ladycross Plantation
Caravan Park**
Egton, Whitby
YO21 1UA
Tel: 01947 895502   **105 M9**
ladycrossplantation.co.uk
Total Pitches: 130 (C & CV)

Lady's Mile Holiday Park
Dawlish, Devon
EX7 0LX
Tel: 01626 863411   **9 N9**
ladysmile.co.uk
Total Pitches: 692 (C, CV & T)

Lakeland Leisure Park
Moor Lane,
Flookburgh
LA11 7LT
Tel: 01539 558556   **94 H6**
haven.com/lakeland
Total Pitches: 977 (C, CV & T)

Lamb Cottage Caravan Park
Dalefords Lane, Whitegate,
Northwich
CW8 2BN
Tel: 01606 882302   **82 D11**
lambcottage.co.uk
Total Pitches: 71 (C & CV)

Langstone Manor C & C Park
Moortown, Tavistock
PL19 9JZ
Tel: 01822 613371   **6 E4**
langstonemanor.co.uk
Total Pitches: 76 (C, CV & T)

Lanyon Holiday Park
Loscombe Lane, Four Lanes,
Redruth
TR16 6LP
Tel: 01209 313474   **2 H6**
lanyonholidaypark.co.uk
Total Pitches: 74 (C, CV & T)

Lickpenny Caravan Site
Lickpenny Lane, Tansley, Matlock
DE4 5GF
Tel: 01629 583040   **84 D9**
lickpennycaravanpark.co.uk
Total Pitches: 80 (C & CV)

Lime Tree Park
Dukes Drive, Buxton
SK17 9RP
Tel: 01298 22988   **83 N10**
limetreeparkbuxton.com
Total Pitches: 149 (C, CV & T)

Lincoln Farm Park Oxfordshire
High Street, Standlake
OX29 7RH
Tel: 01865 300239   **34 C4**
lincolnfarmpark.co.uk
Total Pitches: 90 (C, CV & T)

Littlesea Holiday Park
Lynch Lane, Weymouth
DT4 9DT
Tel: 01305 774414   **11 P9**
haven.com/littlesea
Total Pitches: 861 (C, CV & T)

Long Acres Touring Park
Station Road, Old Leake, Boston
PE22 9RF
Tel: 01205 871555   **87 L10**
long-acres.co.uk
Total Pitches: 40 (C, CV & T)

Long Hazel Park
High Street, Sparkford, Yeovil,
Somerset
BA22 7JH
Tel: 01963 440002   **20 B9**
longhazelpark.co.uk
Total Pitches: 52 (C, CV & T)

Longnor Wood Holiday Park
Newtown, Longnor, Nr Buxton
SK17 0NG
Tel: 01298 83648   **71 K2**
longnorwood.co.uk
Total Pitches: 50 (C, CV & T)

Lowther Holiday Park
Eamont Bridge, Penrith
CA10 2JB
Tel: 01768 863631   **101 P5**
lowther-holidaypark.co.uk
Total Pitches: 180 (C, CV & T)

**Manor Wood Country
Caravan Park**
Manor Wood, Coddington,
Chester
CH3 9EN
Tel: 01829 782990   **69 M4**
cheshire-caravan-sites.co.uk
Total Pitches: 66 (C, CV & T)

Marton Mere Holiday Village
Mythop Road, Blackpool
FY4 4XN
Tel: 01253 767544   **88 C4**
haven.com/martonmere
Total Pitches: 782 (C & CV)

Mayfield Park
Cheltenham Road, Cirencester
GL7 7BH
Tel: 01285 831301   **33 K3**
mayfieldpark.co.uk
Total Pitches: 105 (C, CV & T)

Meadow Lakes Holiday Park
Hewas Water, St Austell,
Cornwall
PL26 7JG
Tel: 01726 882540   **3 P4**
meadow-lakes.co.uk
Total Pitches: 232 (C, CV & T)

Meadowbank Holidays
Stour Way, Christchurch
BH23 2PQ
Tel: 01202 483597   **13 K6**
meadowbank-holidays.co.uk
Total Pitches: 221 (C & CV)

**Middlewood Farm
Holiday Park**
Middlewood Lane, Fylingthorpe,
Robin Hood's Bay, Whitby
YO22 4UF
Tel: 01947 880414   **105 P10**
middlewoodfarm.com
Total Pitches: 144 (C, CV & T)

Mill Park Touring C & C Park
Mill Lane, Berrynarbor,
Ilfracombe, Devon
EX34 9SH
Tel: 01271 882647   **17 K2**
millpark.com
Total Pitches: 160 (C, CV & T)

Minnows Touring Park
Holbrook Lane, Sampford
Peverell
EX16 7EN
Tel: 01884 821770   **18 D11**
minnowstouringpark.co.uk
Total Pitches: 60 (C, CV & T)

Monkey Tree Holiday Park
Hendra Croft, Scotland Road,
Newquay
TR8 5QR
Tel: 01872 572032   **3 L3**
monkeytreeholidaypark.co.uk
Total Pitches: 700 (C, CV & T)

Moon & Sixpence
Newbourn Road,
Waldringfield, Woodbridge
IP12 4PP
Tel: 01473 736650   **53 N2**
moonandsixpence.co.uk
Total Pitches: 275 (C & CV)

Moss Wood Caravan Park
Crimbles Lane,
Cockerham
LA2 0ES
Tel: 01524 791041   **95 K11**
mosswood.co.uk
Total Pitches: 168 (C & CV)

Naburn Lock Caravan Park
Naburn
YO19 4RU
Tel: 01904 728697   **98 C11**
naburnlock.co.uk
Total Pitches: 115 (C, CV & T)

New Lodge Farm C & C Site
New Lodge Farm, Bulwick,
Corby
NN17 3DU
Tel: 01780 450493   **73 P11**
newlodgefarm.com
Total Pitches: 72 (C, CV & T)

Newberry Valley Park
Woodlands, Combe Martin
EX34 0AT
Tel: 01271 882334   **17 K2**
newberryvalleypark.co.uk
Total Pitches: 112 (C, CV & T)

Newlands Holidays
Charmouth, Bridport
DT6 6RB
Tel: 01297 560259   **10 H6**
newlandsholidays.co.uk
Total Pitches: 330 (C, CV & T)

Ninham Country Holidays
Ninham, Shanklin,
Isle of Wight
PO37 7PL
Tel: 01983 864243   **14 G10**
ninham-holidays.co.uk
Total Pitches: 141 (C, CV & T)

North Morte Farm C & C Park
North Morte Road, Mortehoe,
Woolacombe
EX34 7EG
Tel: 01271 870381   **16 H2**
northmortefarm.co.uk
Total Pitches: 253 (C, CV & T)

**Northam Farm Caravan
& Touring Park**
Brean,
Burnham-on-Sea
TA8 2SE
Tel: 01278 751244   **19 K3**
northamfarm.co.uk
Total Pitches: 350 (C, CV & T)

**Oakdown Country
Holiday Park**
Gatedown Lane, Weston,
Sidmouth
EX10 0PT
Tel: 01297 680387   **10 D6**
oakdown.co.uk
Total Pitches: 170 (C, CV & T)

Old Hall Caravan Park
Capernwray,
Carnforth
LA6 1AD
Tel: 01524 733276   **95 L6**
oldhallcaravanpark.co.uk
Total Pitches: 298 (C & CV)

Old Oaks Touring & Glamping
Wick Farm, Wick,
Glastonbury
BA6 8JS
Tel: 01458 831437   **19 P7**
theoldoaks.co.uk
Total Pitches: 100 (C, CV & T)

Orchard Farm Holiday Village
Stonegate, Hunmanby,
Filey, North Yorkshire
YO14 0PU
Tel: 01723 891582   **99 N5**
orchardfarmholidayvillage.co.uk
Total Pitches: 137 (C, CV & T)

Ord House Country Park
East Ord,
Berwick-upon-Tweed
TD15 2NS
Tel: 01289 305288   **129 P9**
maguirescountryparks.co.uk
Total Pitches: 344 (C, CV & T)

Otterington Park
Station Farm,
South Otterington,
Northallerton, North Yorkshire
DL7 9JB
Tel: 01609 780656   **97 N3**
otteringtonpark.com
Total Pitches: 67 (C, CV & T)

Oxon Hall Touring Park
Welshpool Road, Shrewsbury
SY3 5FB
Tel: 01743 340868   **56 H2**
morris-leisure.co.uk
Total Pitches: 165 (C, CV & T)

Park Cliffe C & C Estate
Birks Road, Tower Wood,
Windermere
LA23 3PG
Tel: 015395 31344   **94 H2**
parkcliffe.co.uk
Total Pitches: 126 (C, CV & T)

Parkers Farm Holiday Park
Higher Mead Farm,
Ashburton, Devon
TQ13 7LJ
Tel: 01364 654869   **7 K4**
parkersfarmholidays.co.uk
Total Pitches: 118 (C, CV & T)

Park Foot C & C Park
Howtown Road,
Pooley Bridge
CA10 2NA
Tel: 01768 486309   **101 N6**
parkfootullswater.co.uk
Total Pitches: 454 (C, CV & T)

Parkland C & C Site
Sorley Green Cross,
Kingsbridge
TQ7 4AF
Tel: 01548 852723   **7 J9**
parklandsite.co.uk
Total Pitches: 50 (C, CV & T)

Pebble Bank Caravan Park
Camp Road, Wyke Regis,
Weymouth
DT4 9HF
Tel: 01305 774844   **11 P9**
pebblebank.co.uk
Total Pitches: 120 (C, CV & T)

Perran Sands Holiday Park
Perranporth, Truro
TR6 0AQ
Tel: 01872 573551   **4 B10**
haven.com/perransands
Total Pitches: 1012 (C, CV & T)

Petwood Caravan Park
Off Stixwould Road,
Woodhall Spa
LN10 6QH
Tel: 01526 354799   **86 G8**
petwoodcaravanpark.com
Total Pitches: 98 (C, CV & T)

**Plough Lane Touring
Caravan Site**
Plough Lane, Chippenham,
Wiltshire
SN15 5PS
Tel: 01249 750146   **32 H9**
ploughlane.co.uk
Total Pitches: 52 (C & CV)

Polladras Holiday Park
Carleen, Breage,
Helston
TR13 9NX
Tel: 01736 762220   **2 G7**
polladrasholidaypark.co.uk
Total Pitches: 42 (C, CV & T)

Polmanter Touring Park
Halsetown, St Ives
TR26 3LX
Tel: 01736 795640   **2 E6**
polmanter.com
Total Pitches: 270 (C, CV & T)

Porthtowan Tourist Park
Mile Hill, Porthtowan,
Truro
TR4 8TY
Tel: 01209 890256   **2 H4**
porthtowantouristpark.co.uk
Total Pitches: 80 (C, CV & T)

Primrose Valley Holiday Park
Filey
YO14 9RF
Tel: 01723 513771 **99 N5**
haven.com/primrosevalley
Total Pitches: 1549 (C & CV)

Quantock Orchard Caravan Park
Flaxpool, Crowcombe, Taunton
TA4 4AW
Tel: 01984 618618 **18 F7**
quantock-orchard.co.uk
Total Pitches: 75 (C, CV & T)

Ranch Caravan Park
Station Road, Honeybourne,
Evesham
WR11 7PR
Tel: 01386 830744 **47 M6**
ranch.co.uk
Total Pitches: 338 (C & CV)

Ripley Caravan Park
Knaresborough Road, Ripley,
Harrogate
HG3 3AU
Tel: 01423 770050 **97 L8**
ripleycaravanpark.com
Total Pitches: 135 (C, CV & T)

River Dart Country Park
Holne Park, Ashburton
TQ13 7NP
Tel: 01364 652511 **7 J5**
riverdart.co.uk
Total Pitches: 170 (C, CV & T)

River Valley Holiday Park
London Apprentice,
St Austell
PL26 7AP
Tel: 01726 73533 **3 Q3**
rivervalleyholidaypark.co.uk
Total Pitches: 85 (C, CV & T)

Riverside C & C Park
Marsh Lane,
North Molton Road,
South Molton
EX36 3HQ
Tel: 01769 579269 **17 N6**
exmoorriverside.co.uk
Total Pitches: 61 (C, CV & T)

Riverside Caravan Park
High Bentham,
Lancaster
LA2 7FJ
Tel: 015242 61272 **95 P7**
riversidecaravanpark.co.uk
Total Pitches: 267 (C & CV)

Riverside Meadows Country Caravan Park
Ure Bank Top, Ripon
HG4 1JD
Tel: 01765 602964 **97 M6**
flowerofmay.com
Total Pitches: 349 ( )

Robin Hood C & C Park
Green Dyke Lane,
Slingsby
YO62 4AP
Tel: 01653 628391 **98 E6**
robinhoodcaravanpark.co.uk
Total Pitches: 66 (C, CV & T)

Rose Farm Touring & Camping Park
Stepshort, Belton,
Nr Great Yarmouth
NR31 9JS
Tel: 01493 738292 **77 P11**
rosefarmtouringpark.co.uk
Total Pitches: 147 (C, CV & T)

Rosedale Abbey Caravan Park
Rosedale Abbey,
Pickering
YO18 8SA
Tel: 01751 417272 **105 K11**
rosedaleabbeycaravanpark.co.uk
Total Pitches: 141 (C, CV & T)

Ross Park
Park Hill Farm, Ipplepen,
Newton Abbot
TQ12 5TT
Tel: 01803 812983 **7 L5**
rossparkcaravanpark.co.uk
Total Pitches: 110 (C, CV & T)

Rudding Holiday Park
Follifoot, Harrogate
HG3 1JH
Tel: 01423 870439 **97 M10**
ruddingholidaypark.co.uk
Total Pitches: 143 (C, CV & T)

Run Cottage Touring Park
Alderton Road, Hollesley,
Woodbridge
IP12 3RQ
Tel: 01394 411309 **53 Q3**
runcottage.co.uk
Total Pitches: 47 (C, CV & T)

Rutland C & C
Park Lane, Greetham,
Oakham
LE15 7FN
Tel: 01572 813520 **73 N8**
rutlandcaravanandcamping.co.uk
Total Pitches: 130 (C, CV & T)

St Helens in the Park
Wykeham, Scarborough
YO13 9QD
Tel: 01723 862771 **99 K4**
sthelenscaravanpark.co.uk
Total Pitches: 260 (C, CV & T)

St Ives Bay Holiday Park
73 Loggans Road,
Upton Towans, Hayle
TR27 5BH
Tel: 01736 752274 **2 F6**
stivesbay.co.uk
Total Pitches: 507 (C, CV & T)

Salcombe Regis C & C Park
Salcombe Regis,
Sidmouth
EX10 0JH
Tel: 01395 514303 **10 D7**
salcombe-regis.co.uk
Total Pitches: 110 (C, CV & T)

Sand le Mere Holiday Village
Southfield Lane,
Tunstall
HU12 0JF
Tel: 01964 670403 **93 P4**
sand-le-mere.co.uk
Total Pitches: 89 (C & CV)

Searles Leisure Resort
South Beach Road,
Hunstanton
PE36 5BB
Tel: 01485 534211 **75 N3**
searles.co.uk
Total Pitches: 413 (C, CV & T)

Seaview Gorran Haven Holiday Park
Boswinger,
Mevagissey
PL26 6LL
Tel: 01726 843425 **3 P5**
seaviewinternational.com
Total Pitches: 240 (C, CV & T)

Seaview Holiday Park
Preston, Weymouth
DT3 6DZ
Tel: 01305 832271 **11 Q8**
haven.com/seaview
Total Pitches: 347 (C, CV & T)

Severn Gorge Park
Bridgnorth Road,
Tweedale, Telford
TF7 4JB
Tel: 01952 684789 **57 N3**
severngorgepark.co.uk
Total Pitches: 132 (C & CV)

Shamba Holidays
East Moors Lane,
St Leonards, Ringwood
BH24 2SB
Tel: 01202 873302 **13 K4**
shambaholidays.co.uk
Total Pitches: 150 (C, CV & T)

Shrubbery Touring Park
Rousdon,
Lyme Regis
DT7 3XW
Tel: 01297 442227 **10 F6**
shrubberypark.co.uk
Total Pitches: 122 (C, CV & T)

Silverdale Caravan Park
Middlebarrow Plain,
Cove Road, Silverdale,
Nr Carnforth
LA5 0SH
Tel: 01524 701508 **95 K5**
holgates.co.uk
Total Pitches: 427 (C, CV & T)

Skelwith Fold Caravan Park
Ambleside, Cumbria
LA22 0HX
Tel: 015394 32277 **101 L10**
skelwith.com
Total Pitches: 470 (C & CV)

Skirlington Leisure Park
Driffield, Skipsea
YO25 8SY
Tel: 01262 468213 **99 P10**
skirlington.com
Total Pitches: 930 (C & CV)

Sleningford Watermill Caravan Camping Park
North Stainley,
Ripon
HG4 3HQ
Tel: 01765 635201 **97 L5**
sleningfordwatermill.co.uk
Total Pitches: 135 (C, CV & T)

Somers Wood Caravan Park
Somers Road, Meriden
CV7 7PL
Tel: 01676 522978 **59 K8**
somerswood.co.uk
Total Pitches: 48 (C & CV)

South Lytchett Manor C & C Park
Dorchester Road,
Lytchett Minster, Poole
BH16 6JB
Tel: 01202 622577 **12 G6**
southlytchettmanor.co.uk
Total Pitches: 154 (C, CV & T)

South Meadows Caravan Park
South Road, Belford
NE70 7DP
Tel: 01668 213326 **119 M4**
southmeadows.co.uk
Total Pitches: 186 (C, CV & T)

Stanmore Hall Touring Park
Stourbridge Road,
Bridgnorth
WV15 6DT
Tel: 01746 761761 **57 N6**
morris-leisure.co.uk
Total Pitches: 129 (C, CV & T)

Stanwix Park Holiday Centre
Greenrow, Silloth
CA7 4HH
Tel: 016973 32666 **109 P10**
stanwix.com
Total Pitches: 337 (C, CV & T)

Stowford Farm Meadows
Berry Down,
Combe Martin
EX34 0PW
Tel: 01271 882476 **17 K3**
stowford.co.uk
Total Pitches: 700 (C, CV & T)

Stroud Hill Park
Fen Road, Pidley,
St Ives
PE28 3DE
Tel: 01487 741333 **62 D5**
stroudhillpark.co.uk
Total Pitches: 60 (C, CV & T)

Sumners Ponds Fishery & Campsite
Chapel Road, Barns Green,
Horsham
RH13 0PR
Tel: 01403 732539 **24 D5**
sumnersponds.co.uk
Total Pitches: 90 (C, CV & T)

Swiss Farm Touring & Camping
Marlow Road,
Henley-on-Thames
RG9 2HY
Tel: 01491 573419 **35 L8**
swissfarmhenley.co.uk
Total Pitches: 148 (C, CV & T)

Tanner Farm Touring C & C Park
Tanner Farm, Goudhurst Road,
Marden
TN12 9ND
Tel: 01622 832399 **26 B3**
tannerfarmpark.co.uk
Total Pitches: 122 (C, CV & T)

Tattershall Lakes Country Park
Sleaford Road,
Tattershall
LN4 4LR
Tel: 01526 348800 **86 H9**
awayresorts.co.uk/
tattershall-lakes
Total Pitches: 690 (C, CV & T)

Tehidy Holiday Park
Harris Mill, Illogan, Portreath
TR16 4JQ
Tel: 01209 216489 **2 H5**
tehidy.co.uk
Total Pitches: 52 (C, CV & T)

Tencreek Holiday Park
Polperro Road, Looe
PL13 2JR
Tel: 01503 262447 **5 L11**
dolphinholidays.co.uk
Total Pitches: 355 (C, CV & T)

Teversal C & C Club Site
Silverhill Lane, Teversal
NG17 3JJ
Tel: 01623 551838 **84 G8**
campingandcaravanning
club.co.uk/teversal
Total Pitches: 136 (C, CV & T)

The Laurels Holiday Park
Padstow Road, Whitecross,
Wadebridge
PL27 7JQ
Tel: 01208 813341 **4 F7**
thelaurelsholidaypark.co.uk
Total Pitches: 30 (C, CV & T)

The Old Brick Kilns
Little Barney Lane, Barney,
Fakenham
NR21 0NL
Tel: 01328 878305 **76 E5**
old-brick-kilns.co.uk
Total Pitches: 65 (C, CV & T)

The Orchards Holiday Caravan Park
Main Road, Newbridge,
Yarmouth, Isle of Wight
PO41 0TS
Tel: 01983 531331 **14 D9**
orchards-holiday-park.co.uk
Total Pitches: 225 (C, CV & T)

The Quiet Site
Ullswater, Watermillock
CA11 0LS
Tel: 07768 727016 **101 M6**
thequietsite.co.uk
Total Pitches: 151 (C, CV & T)

Thornwick Bay Holiday Village
North Marine Road, Flamborough
YO15 1AU
Tel: 01262 850569 **99 Q6**
haven.com/parks/yorkshire/
thornwick-bay
Total Pitches: 225 (C, CV & T)

Thorpe Park Holiday Centre
Cleethorpes
DN35 0PW
Tel: 01472 813395 **93 P9**
haven.com/thorpepark
Total Pitches: 1491 (C, CV & T)

Treago Farm Caravan Site
Crantock, Newquay
TR8 5QS
Tel: 01637 830277 **4 B9**
treagofarm.co.uk
Total Pitches: 100 (C, CV & T)

Treloy Touring Park
Newquay
TR8 4JN
Tel: 01637 872063 **4 D9**
treloy.co.uk
Total Pitches: 223 (C, CV & T)

Trencreek Holiday Park
Hillcrest, Higher Trencreek,
Newquay
TR8 4NS
Tel: 01637 874210 **4 C9**
trencreekholidaypark.co.uk
Total Pitches: 200 (C, CV & T)

Trethem Mill Touring Park
St Just-in-Roseland,
Nr St Mawes, Truro
TR2 5JF
Tel: 01872 580504 **3 M6**
trethem.com
Total Pitches: 84 (C, CV & T)

Trevalgan Touring Park
Trevalgan, St Ives
TR26 3BJ
Tel: 01736 791892 **2 D6**
trevalgantouringpark.co.uk
Total Pitches: 135 (C, CV & T)

Trevarth Holiday Park
Blackwater, Truro
TR4 8HR
Tel: 01872 560266 **3 J4**
trevarth.co.uk
Total Pitches: 50 (C, CV & T)

Trevedra Farm C & C Site
Sennen, Penzance
TR19 7BE
Tel: 01736 871818 **2 B8**
trevedrafarm.co.uk
Total Pitches: 100 (C, CV & T)

Trevella Park
Crantock, Newquay
TR8 5EW
Tel: 01637 830308 **4 C10**
trevella.co.uk
Total Pitches: 290 (C, CV & T)

Trevornick
Holywell Bay, Newquay
TR8 5PW
Tel: 01637 830531 **4 B10**
trevornick.co.uk
Total Pitches: 600 (C, CV & T)

Truro C & C Park
Truro
TR4 8QN
Tel: 01872 560274 **3 K4**
trurocaravanandcampingpark.co.uk
Total Pitches: 100 (C, CV & T)

Tudor C & C
Shepherds Patch, Slimbridge,
Gloucester
GL2 7BP
Tel: 01453 890483 **32 D4**
tudorcaravanpark.com
Total Pitches: 75 (C, CV & T)

Twitchen House Holiday Park
Mortehoe Station Road,
Mortehoe, Woolacombe
EX34 7ES
Tel: 01271 872302 **16 H3**
woolacombe.com
Total Pitches: 569 (C, CV & T)

Two Mills Touring Park
Yarmouth Road, North Walsham
NR28 9NA
Tel: 01692 405829 **77 K6**
twomills.co.uk
Total Pitches: 81 (C, CV & T)

Ulwell Cottage Caravan Park
Ulwell Cottage, Ulwell, Swanage
BH19 3DG
Tel: 01929 422823 **12 H8**
ulwellcottagepark.co.uk
Total Pitches: 219 (C, CV & T)

Upper Lynstone Caravan Park
Lynstone, Bude
EX23 0LP
Tel: 01288 352017 **16 C10**
upperlynstone.co.uk
Total Pitches: 106 (C, CV & T)

Vale of Pickering Caravan Park
Carr House Farm, Allerston,
Pickering
YO18 7PQ
Tel: 01723 859280 **98 H4**
valeofpickering.co.uk
Total Pitches: 120 (C, CV & T)

Waldegraves Holiday Park
Mersea Island, Colchester
CO5 8SE
Tel: 01206 382898 **52 H9**
waldegraves.co.uk
Total Pitches: 30 (C, CV & T)

Waleswood C &C Park
Delves Lane, Waleswood,
Wales Bar, Wales, South
Yorkshire
S26 5RN
Tel: 07825 125328 **84 G4**
waleswood.co.uk
Total Pitches: 163 (C, CV & T)

Warcombe Farm C & C Park
Station Road, Mortehoe,
Woolacombe
EX34 7EJ
Tel: 01271 870690 **16 H2**
warcombefarm.co.uk
Total Pitches: 250 (C, CV & T)

Wareham Forest Tourist Park
North Trigon, Wareham
BH20 7NZ
Tel: 01929 551393 **12 E6**
warehamforest.co.uk
Total Pitches: 200 (C, CV & T)

Waren C & C Park
Waren Mill, Bamburgh
NE70 7EE
Tel: 01668 214366 **119 N4**
meadowhead.co.uk
Total Pitches: 458 (C, CV & T)

Warren Farm Holiday Centre
Brean Sands, Brean,
Burnham-on-Sea
TA8 2RP
Tel: 01278 751227 **19 J3**
warrenfarm.co.uk
Total Pitches: 975 (C, CV & T)

Watergate Bay Touring Park
Watergate Bay, Tregurrian
TR8 4AD
Tel: 01637 860387 **4 D8**
watergatebaytouringpark.co.uk
Total Pitches: 173 (C, CV & T)

Waterrow Touring Park
Wiveliscombe, Taunton
TA4 2AZ
Tel: 01984 623464 **18 E9**
waterrowpark.co.uk
Total Pitches: 44 (C, CV & T)

Wayfarers C & C Park
Relubbus Lane, St Hilary,
Penzance
TR20 9EF
Tel: 01736 763326 **2 F7**
wayfarerspark.co.uk
Total Pitches: 35 (C, CV & T)

Wells Touring Park
Haybridge, Wells
BA5 1AJ
Tel: 01749 676869 **19 P5**
wellstouringpark.co.uk
Total Pitches: 84 (C & CV)

Westbrook Park
Little Hereford, Herefordshire
SY8 4AU
Tel: 01584 711280 **57 J11**
westbrookpark.co.uk
Total Pitches: 59 (C, CV & T)

Wheathill Touring Park
Wheathill, Bridgnorth
WV16 6QT
Tel: 01584 823456 **57 L8**
wheathillpark.co.uk
Total Pitches: 50 (C & CV)

Whitefield Forest Touring Park
Brading Road, Ryde,
Isle of Wight
PO33 1QL
Tel: 01983 617069 **14 H9**
whitefieldforest.co.uk
Total Pitches: 90 (C, CV & T)

Whitehill Country Park
Stoke Road, Paignton, Devon
TQ4 7PF
Tel: 01803 782338 **7 M7**
whitehill-park.co.uk
Total Pitches: 325 (C, CV & T)

Whitemead Caravan Park
East Burton Road, Wool
BH20 6HG
Tel: 01929 462241 **12 D7**
whitemeadcaravanpark.co.uk
Total Pitches: 105 (C, CV & T)

**Willowbank Holiday Home
& Touring Park**
Coastal Road, Ainsdale,
Southport
PR8 3ST
Tel: 01704 571566 **88 C8**
willowbankcp.co.uk
Total Pitches: 315 (C & CV)

Willow Valley Holiday Park
Bush, Bude, Cornwall
EX23 9LB
Tel: 01288 353104 **16 C10**
willowvalley.co.uk
Total Pitches: 44 (C, CV & T)

Wilson House Holiday Park
Lancaster Road, Out Rawcliffe,
Preston, Lancashire
PR3 6BN
Tel: 07807 560685 **88 E2**
whhp.co.uk
Total Pitches: 40 (C & CV)

Wolds View Touring Park
115 Brigg Road, Caistor
LN7 6RX
Tel: 01472 851099 **93 K10**
woldsviewtouringpark.co.uk
Total Pitches: 60 (C, CV & T)

Wood Farm C & C Park
Axminster Road, Charmouth
DT6 6BT
Tel: 01297 560697 **10 H6**
woodfarm.co.uk
Total Pitches: 267 (C, CV & T)

Wooda Farm Holiday Park
Poughill, Bude
EX23 9HJ
Tel: 01288 352069 **16 C10**
wooda.co.uk
Total Pitches: 255 (C, CV & T)

Woodclose Caravan Park
High Casterton,
Kirkby Lonsdale
LA6 2SE
Tel: 01524 271597 **95 N5**
woodclosepark.com
Total Pitches: 117 (C & CV)

Woodhall Country Park
Stixwold Road, Woodhall Spa
LN10 6UJ
Tel: 01526 353710 **86 G8**
woodhallcountrypark.co.uk
Total Pitches: 120 (C, CV & T)

**Woodland Springs Adult
Touring Park**
Venton, Drewsteignton
EX6 6PG
Tel: 01647 231695 **8 G6**
woodlandsprings.co.uk
Total Pitches: 81 (C, CV & T)

Woodlands Grove C & C Park
Blackawton, Dartmouth
TQ9 7DQ
Tel: 01803 712598 **7 L8**
woodlandsgrove.com
Total Pitches: 350 (C, CV & T)

Woodovis Park
Gulworthy, Tavistock
PL19 8NY
Tel: 01822 832968 **6 C4**
woodovis.com
Total Pitches: 89 (C, CV & T)

**Yeatheridge Farm
Caravan Park**
East Worlington, Crediton, Devon
EX17 4TN
Tel: 01884 860330 **9 J2**
yeatheridge.co.uk
Total Pitches: 122 (C, CV & T)

York Meadows Caravan Park
York Road, Sheriff Hutton,
York, North Yorkshire
YO60 6QP
Tel: 01347 878508 **98 C7**
yorkmeadowscaravanpark.com
Total Pitches: 60 (C, CV & T)

SCOTLAND

Anwoth Caravan Site
Gatehouse of Fleet,
Castle Douglas,
Dumfries & Galloway
DG7 2JU
Tel: 01557 814333 **108 C9**
swalwellholidaygroup.co.uk
Total Pitches: 72 (C, CV & T)

Auchenlarie Holiday Park
Gatehouse of Fleet
DG7 2EX
Tel: 01556 506200 **107 P7**
swalwellholidaygroup.co.uk
Total Pitches: 451 (C, CV & T)

Banff Links Caravan Park
Inverboyndie, Banff,
Aberdeenshire
AB45 2JJ
Tel: 01261 812228 **158 G5**
banfflinkscaravanpark.co.uk
Total Pitches: 93 (C, CV & T)

Beecraigs C & C Site
Beecraigs Country Park,
The Visitor Centre,
Linlithgow
EH49 6PL
Tel: 01506 284516 **127 J3**
westlothian.gov.uk/
stay-at-beecraigs
Total Pitches: 38 (C, CV & T)

Belhaven Bay C & C Park
Belhaven Bay, Dunbar,
East Lothian
EH42 1TS
Tel: 01368 865956 **128 H4**
meadowhead.co.uk
Total Pitches: 119 (C, CV & T)

Blair Castle Caravan Park
Blair Atholl, Pitlochry
PH18 5SR
Tel: 01796 481263 **141 L4**
blaircastlecaravanpark.co.uk
Total Pitches: 325 (C, CV & T)

Brighouse Bay Holiday Park
Brighouse Bay, Borgue,
Kirkcudbright
DG6 4TS
Tel: 01557 870267 **108 D11**
gillespie-leisure.co.uk
Total Pitches: 418 (C, CV & T)

Cairnsmill Holiday Park
Largo Road, St Andrews
KY16 8NN
Tel: 01334 473604 **135 M5**
cairnsmill.co.uk
Total Pitches: 256 (C, CV & T)

Craig Tara Holiday Park
Ayr
KA7 4LB
Tel: 0800 975 7579 **114 F4**
haven.com/craigtara
Total Pitches: 1144 (C & CV)

**Craigtoun Meadows
Holiday Park**
Mount Melville, St Andrews
KY16 8PQ
Tel: 01334 475959 **135 M4**
craigtounmeadows.co.uk
Total Pitches: 257 (C, CV & T)

Crossburn Caravan Park
Edinburgh Road, Peebles,
Scottish Borders
EH45 8ED
Tel: 01721 720501 **117 J2**
crossburn-caravans.com
Total Pitches: 132 (C, CV & T)

Faskally Caravan Park
Pitlochry
PH16 5LA
Tel: 01796 472007 **141 M6**
faskally.co.uk
Total Pitches: 430 (C, CV & T)

Glen Nevis C & C Park
Glen Nevis, Fort William
PH33 6SX
Tel: 01397 702191 **139 L3**
glen-nevis.co.uk
Total Pitches: 415 (C, CV & T)

Hoddom Castle Caravan Park
Hoddom, Lockerbie
DG11 1AS
Tel: 01576 300251 **110 C6**
hoddomcastle.co.uk
Total Pitches: 265 (C, CV & T)

Huntly Castle Caravan Park
The Meadow, Huntly
AB54 4UJ
Tel: 01466 794999 **158 D9**
huntlycastle.co.uk
Total Pitches: 130 (C, CV & T)

Invercoe C & C Park
Ballachulish,
Glencoe
PH49 4HP
Tel: 01855 811210 **139 K6**
invercoe.co.uk
Total Pitches: 66 (C, CV & T)

Linwater Caravan Park
West Clifton,
East Calder
EH53 0HT
Tel: 0131 333 3326 **127 L4**
linwater.co.uk
Total Pitches: 64 (C, CV & T)

Loch Ken Holiday Park
Parton, Castle Douglas,
Dumfries & Galloway
DG7 3NE
Tel: 01644 470282 **108 E6**
lochkenholidaypark.co.uk
Total Pitches: 75 (C, CV & T)

Lomond Woods Holiday Park
Old Luss Road, Balloch,
Loch Lomond
G83 8QP
Tel: 01389 755000 **132 D11**
woodleisure.co.uk/our-parks/
lomond-woods
Total Pitches: 153 (C & CV)

Milton of Fonab Caravan Park
Bridge Road, Pitlochry
PH16 5NA
Tel: 01796 472882 **141 M6**
fonab.co.uk
Total Pitches: 188 (C, CV & T)

Sands of Luce Holiday Park
Sands of Luce, Sandhead,
Stranraer
DG9 9JN
Tel: 01776 830456 **106 F7**
sandsofluce.com
Total Pitches: 350 (C, CV & T)

**Seal Shore Camping and
Touring Site**
Kildonan, Isle of Arran,
North Ayrshire
KA27 8SE
Tel: 01770 820320 **121 K7**
campingarran.com
Total Pitches: 47 (C, CV & T)

Seaward Holiday Park
Dhoon Bay, Kirkcudbright
DG6 4TJ
Tel: 01557 870267 **108 E11**
gillespie-leisure.co.uk
Total Pitches: 84 (C, CV & T)

Seton Sands Holiday Village
Longniddry
EH32 0QF
Tel: 01875 813333 **128 C4**
haven.com/setonsands
Total Pitches: 640 (C, CV & T)

Shieling Holidays Mull
Craignure,
Isle of Mull,
Argyll & Bute
PA65 6AY
Tel: 01680 812496 **138 C10**
shielingholidays.co.uk
Total Pitches: 106 (C, CV & T)

Silver Sands Holiday Park
Covesea, West Beach,
Lossiemouth
IV31 6SP
Tel: 01343 813262 **157 N3**
silver-sands.co.uk
Total Pitches: 340 (C, CV & T)

Skye C & C Club Site
Loch Greshornish, Borve,
Arnisort, Edinbane,
Isle of Skye
IV51 9PS
Tel: 01470 582230 **152 E7**
campingandcaravanning
club.co.uk/skye
Total Pitches: 107 (C, CV & T)

Thurston Manor Leisure Park
Innerwick, Dunbar
EH42 1SA
Tel: 01368 840643 **129 J5**
thurstonmanor.co.uk
Total Pitches: 690 (C, CV & T)

Witches Craig C & C Park
Blairlogie, Stirling
FK9 5PX
Tel: 01786 474947 **133 N8**
witchescraig.co.uk
Total Pitches: 60 (C, CV & T)

WALES

Bodnant Caravan Park
Nebo Road, Llanrwst,
Conwy Valley, Conwy
LL26 0SD
Tel: 01492 640248 **67 Q2**
bodnant-caravan-park.co.uk
Total Pitches: 56 (C, CV & T)

**Bron Derw Touring
Caravan Park**
Llanrwst
LL26 0YT
Tel: 01492 640494 **67 P2**
bronderw-wales.co.uk
Total Pitches: 48 (C & CV)

Bron-Y-Wendon Caravan Park
Wern Road, Llanddulas,
Colwyn Bay
LL22 8HG
Tel: 01492 512903 **80 C9**
bronywendon.co.uk
Total Pitches: 130 (C & CV)

Bryn Gloch C & C Park
Betws Garmon, Caernarfon
LL54 7YY
Tel: 01286 650216 **67 J3**
campwales.co.uk
Total Pitches: 177 (C, CV & T)

**Caerfai Bay Caravan
& Tent Park**
Caerfai Bay, St Davids,
Haverfordwest
SA62 6QT
Tel: 01437 720274 **40 E6**
caerfaibay.co.uk
Total Pitches: 136 (C, CV & T)

Cenarth Falls Holiday Park
Cenarth, Newcastle Emlyn
SA38 9JS
Tel: 01239 710345 **41 Q2**
cenarth-holipark.co.uk
Total Pitches: 119 (C, CV & T)

Creampots Touring C & C Park
Broadway, Broad Haven,
Haverfordwest,
Pembrokeshire
SA62 3TU
Tel: 01437 781776 **40 G8**
creampots.co.uk
Total Pitches: 73 (C, CV & T)

Daisy Bank Caravan Park
Snead, Montgomery
SY15 6EB
Tel: 01588 620471 **56 E6**
daisy-bank.co.uk
Total Pitches: 87 (C, CV & T)

**Deucoch Touring
& Camping Park**
Sarn Bach, Abersoch,
Gwynedd
LL53 7LD
Tel: 01758 713293 **66 E9**
deucoch.com
Total Pitches: 70 (C, CV & T)

Dinlle Caravan Park
Dinas Dinlle, Caernarfon
LL54 5TW
Tel: 01286 830324 **66 G3**
thornleyleisure.co.uk
Total Pitches: 349 (C, CV & T)

Eisteddfa
Eisteddfa Lodge, Pentrefelin,
Criccieth
LL52 0PT
Tel: 01766 522696 **67 J7**
eisteddfapark.co.uk
Total Pitches: 116 (C, CV & T)

Fforest Fields C & C Park
Hundred House,
Builth Wells
LD1 5RT
Tel: 01982 570406 **44 G4**
fforestfields.co.uk
Total Pitches: 122 (C, CV & T)

Fishguard Bay Resort
Garn Gelli, Fishguard
SA65 9ET
Tel: 01348 811415 **41 J3**
fishguardbay.com
Total Pitches: 102 (C, CV & T)

Greenacres Holiday Park
Black Rock Sands,
Morfa Bychan, Porthmadog
LL49 9YF
Tel: 01766 512781 **67 J7**
haven.com/greenacres
Total Pitches: 945 (C & CV)

Hafan y Môr Holiday Park
Pwllheli
LL53 6HJ
Tel: 01758 612112 **66 G7**
haven.com/hafanymor
Total Pitches: 875 (C & CV)

**Hendre Mynach
Touring C & C Park**
Llanaber Road, Barmouth
LL42 1YR
Tel: 01341 280262 **67 L11**
hendremynach.co.uk
Total Pitches: 241 (C, CV & T)

Home Farm Caravan Park
Marian-glas,
Isle of Anglesey
LL73 8PH
Tel: 01248 410614 **78 H8**
homefarm-anglesey.co.uk
Total Pitches: 186 (C, CV & T)

Islawrffordd Caravan Park
Talybont, Barmouth
LL43 2AQ
Tel: 01341 247269 **67 K10**
islawrffordd.co.uk
Total Pitches: 306 (C & CV)

Kiln Park Holiday Centre
Marsh Road, Tenby
SA70 8RB
Tel: 01834 844121 **41 M10**
haven.com/kilnpark
Total Pitches: 849 (C, CV & T)

Pencelli Castle C & C Park
Pencelli, Brecon
LD3 7LX
Tel: 01874 665451 **44 F10**
pencelli-castle.com
Total Pitches: 80 (C, CV & T)

Penisar Mynydd Caravan Park
Caerwys Road, Rhuallt,
St Asaph
LL17 0TY
Tel: 01745 582227 **80 F9**
penisarmynydd.co.uk
Total Pitches: 71 (C, CV & T)

Plassey Holiday Park
The Plassey, Eyton, Wrexham
LL13 0SP
Tel: 01978 780277 **69 L5**
plassey.com
Total Pitches: 123 (C, CV & T)

Pont Kemys C & C Park
Chainbridge, Abergavenny
NP7 9DS
Tel: 01873 880688 **31 K3**
pontkemys.com
Total Pitches: 65 (C, CV & T)

**Presthaven Sands
Holiday Park**
Gronant, Prestatyn
LL19 9TT
Tel: 01745 856471 **80 F8**
haven.com/presthavensands
Total Pitches: 1102 (C & CV)

Red Kite Touring Park
Van Road, Llanidloes
SY18 6NG
Tel: 01686 412122 **55 L7**
redkitetouringpark.co.uk
Total Pitches: 66 (C & CV)

Riverside Camping
Seiont Nurseries, Pont Rug,
Caernarfon
LL55 2BB
Tel: 01286 678781 **67 J2**
riversidecamping.co.uk
Total Pitches: 73 (C, CV & T)

**The Trotting Mare
Caravan Park**
Overton, Wrexham
LL13 0LE
Tel: 01978 711963 **69 L7**
thetrottingmare.co.uk
Total Pitches: 65 (C, CV & T)

Trawsdir Touring C & C Park
Llanaber, Barmouth
LL42 1RR
Tel: 01341 280999 **67 K11**
barmouthholidays.co.uk
Total Pitches: 80 (C, CV & T)

Tyddyn Isaf Caravan Park
Lligwy Bay, Dulas,
Isle of Anglesey
LL70 9PQ
Tel: 01248 410203 **78 H7**
tyddynisaf.co.uk
Total Pitches: 136 (C, CV & T)

White Tower Caravan Park
Llandwrog, Caernarfon
LL54 5UH
Tel: 01286 830649 **66 H3**
whitetowerpark.co.uk
Total Pitches: 126 (C & CV)

Traffic signs

Signs giving orders

Signs with red circles are mostly prohibitive. Plates below signs qualify their message

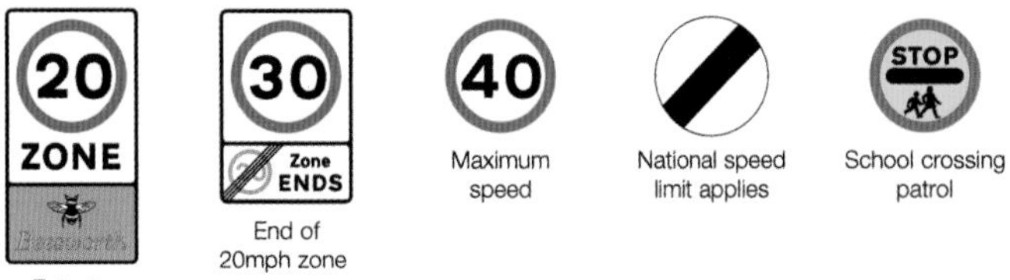

Entry to 20mph zone | End of 20mph zone | Maximum speed | National speed limit applies | School crossing patrol

Stop and give way | Give way to traffic on major road | Manually operated temporary STOP and GO signs | No entry for vehicular traffic

No vehicles except bicycles being pushed | No cycling | No motor vehicles | No buses (over 8 passenger seats) | No overtaking

No towed caravans | No vehicles carrying explosives | No vehicle or combination of vehicles over length shown | No vehicles over height shown | No vehicles over width shown

Give priority to vehicles from opposite direction | No right turn | No left turn | No U-turns | No goods vehicles over maximum gross weight shown (in tonnes) except for loading and unloading

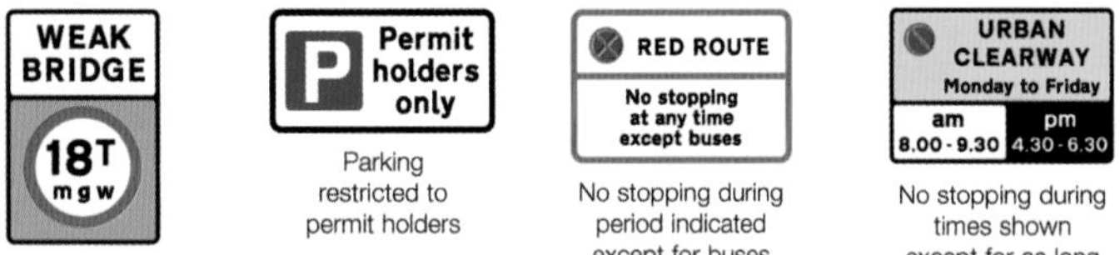

No vehicles over maximum gross weight shown (in tonnes) | Parking restricted to permit holders | No stopping during period indicated except for buses | No stopping during times shown except for as long as necessary to set down or pick up passengers

No waiting | No stopping (Clearway)

Signs with blue circles but no red border mostly give positive instruction.

Ahead only | Turn left ahead (right if symbol reversed) | Turn left (right if symbol reversed) | Keep left (right if symbol reversed) | Vehicles may pass either side to reach same destination

Mini-roundabout (roundabout circulation – give way to vehicles from the immediate right) | Route to be used by pedal cycles only | Segregated pedal cycle and pedestrian route | Minimum speed | End of minimum speed

Buses and cycles only | Trams only | Pedestrian crossing point over tramway | One-way traffic (note: compare circular 'Ahead only' sign)

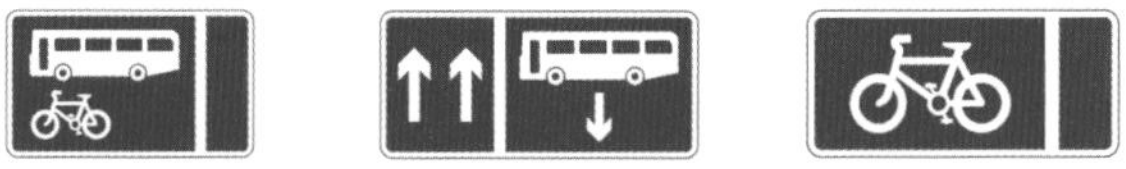

With-flow bus and cycle lane | Contraflow bus lane | With-flow pedal cycle lane

Warning signs

Mostly triangular

Distance to 'STOP' line ahead | Dual carriageway ends | Road narrows on right (left if symbol reversed) | Road narrows on both sides | Distance to 'Give Way' line ahead

Crossroads | Junction on bend ahead | T-junction with priority over vehicles from the right | Staggered junction | Traffic merging from left ahead

The priority through route is indicated by the broader line.

Double bend first to left (symbol may be reversed) | Bend to right (or left if symbol reversed) | Roundabout | Uneven road | Plate below some signs

Two-way traffic crosses one-way road | Two-way traffic straight ahead | Opening or swing bridge ahead | Low-flying aircraft or sudden aircraft noise | Falling or fallen rocks

Traffic signals not in use | Traffic signals | Slippery road | Steep hill downwards | Steep hill upwards

Gradients may be shown as a ratio i.e. 20% = 1:5

Tunnel ahead

Trams crossing ahead

Level crossing with barrier or gate ahead

Level crossing without barrier or gate ahead

Level crossing without barrier

School crossing patrol ahead (some signs have amber lights which flash when crossings are in use)

Frail (or blind or disabled if shown) pedestrians likely to cross road ahead

Pedestrians in road ahead

Zebra crossing

Overhead electric cable; plate indicates maximum height of vehicles which can pass safely

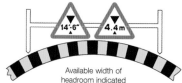 
Available width of headroom indicated

Sharp deviation of route to left (or right if chevrons reversed)

Light signals ahead at level crossing, airfield or bridge

Miniature warning lights at level crossings

Cattle

Wild animals

Wild horses or ponies

Accompanied horses or ponies

Cycle route ahead

Risk of ice

Traffic queues likely ahead

Distance over which road humps extend

Other danger; plate indicates nature of danger

Soft verges

Side winds

Hump bridge

Worded warning sign

Quayside or river bank

Risk of grounding

Direction signs

Mostly rectangular

Signs on motorways - blue backgrounds

At a junction leading directly into a motorway (junction number may be shown on a black background)

On approaches to junctions (junction number on black background)

Route confirmatory sign after junction

Downward pointing arrows mean 'Get in lane'
The left-hand lane leads to a different destination from the other lanes.

The panel with the inclined arrow indicates the destinations which can be reached

Signs on primary routes - green backgrounds

On approaches to junctions

At the junction

Route confirmatory sign after junction

On approaches to junctions

On approach to a junction in Wales (bilingual)

Blue panels indicate that the motorway starts at the junction ahead.
Motorways shown in brackets can also be reached along the route indicated.
White panels indicate local or non-primary routes leading from the junction ahead.
Brown panels show the route to tourist attractions.
The name of the junction may be shown at the top of the sign.
The aircraft symbol indicates the route to an airport.
A symbol may be included to warn of a hazard or restriction along that route.

Signs on non-primary and local routes - black borders

On approaches to junctions

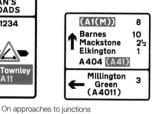

At the junction

Direction to toilets with access for the disabled

Green panels indicate that the primary route starts at the junction ahead.
Route numbers on a blue background show the direction to a motorway.
Route numbers on a green background show the direction to a primary route.

Emergency diversion routes

In an emergency it may be necessary to close a section of motorway or other main road to traffic, so a temporary sign may advise drivers to follow a diversion route. To help drivers navigate the route, black symbols on yellow patches may be permanently displayed on existing direction signs, including motorway signs. Symbols may also be used on separate signs with yellow backgrounds.

Note: The signs shown in this road atlas are those most commonly in use and are not all drawn to the same scale. In Scotland and Wales bilingual versions of some signs are used, showing both English and Gaelic or Welsh spellings. Some older designs of signs may still be seen on the roads. A comprehensive explanation of the signing system illustrating the vast majority of road signs can be found in the AA's handbook *Know Your Road Signs*. Where there is a reference to a rule number, this refers to *The Highway Code*.

Restricted junctions

Motorway and primary route junctions which have access or exit restrictions are shown on the map pages thus:

M1 London - Leeds

Northbound
Access only from A1 (northbound)

Southbound
Exit only to A1 (southbound)

Northbound
Access only from A41 (northbound)

Southbound
Exit only to A41 (southbound)

Northbound
Access only from M25 (no link from A405)

Southbound
Exit only to M25 (no link from A405)

Northbound
Access only from A414

Southbound
Exit only to A414

Northbound
Exit only to M45

Southbound
Access only from M45

Northbound
Exit only to M6 (northbound)

Southbound
Exit only to A14 (southbound)

Northbound
Exit only, no access

Southbound
Access only, no exit

Northbound
No exit, access only

Southbound
Access only from A50 (eastbound)

Northbound
Exit only, no access

Southbound
Access only, no exit

Northbound
Exit only to M621

Southbound
Access only from M621

Northbound
Exit only to A1(M) (northbound)

Southbound
Access only from A1(M) (southbound)

M2 Rochester - Faversham

Westbound
No exit to A2 (eastbound)

Eastbound
No access from A2 (westbound)

M3 Sunbury - Southampton

Northeastbound
Access only from A303, no exit

Southwestbound
Exit only to A303, no access

Northbound
Exit only, no access

Southbound
Access only, no exit

Northeastbound
Access from M27 only, no exit

Southwestbound
No access to M27 (westbound)

M4 London - South Wales

For junctions 1 & 2 see London district map on pages 178–181

Westbound
Exit only to M48

Eastbound
Access only from M48

Westbound
Access only from M48

Eastbound
Exit only to M48

Westbound
Exit only, no access

Eastbound
Access only, no exit

Westbound
Exit only, no access

Eastbound
Access only, no exit

Westbound
Exit only to A48(M)

Eastbound
Access only from A48(M)

Westbound
Exit only, no access

Eastbound
No restriction

Westbound
Access only, no exit

Eastbound
No access or exit

M5 Birmingham - Exeter

Northeastbound
Access only, no exit

Southwestbound
Exit only, no access

Northeastbound
Access only from A417 (westbound)

Southwestbound
Exit only to A417 (eastbound)

Northeastbound
Exit only to M49

Southwestbound
Access only from M49

Northeastbound
No access, exit only

Southwestbound
No exit, access only

Westbound
Exit only to A483

Eastbound
Access only from A483

Westbound
Exit only to A483

Eastbound
Access only from A483

M6 Toll Motorway

See M6 Toll motorway map on page *XXIII*

M6 Rugby - Carlisle

Northbound
Exit only to M6 Toll

Southbound
Access only from M6 Toll

Northbound
Exit only to M42 (southbound) and A446

Southbound
Exit only to A446

Northbound
Access only from M42 (southbound)

Southbound
Exit only to M42

Northbound
Exit only, no access

Southbound
Access only, no exit

Northbound
Exit only to M54

Southbound
Access only from M54

Northbound
Access only from M6 Toll

Southbound
Exit only to M6 Toll

M8 Edinburgh - Bishopton

For junctions 7A to 29A see Glasgow district map on pages 176–177

Westbound
Exit only, no access

Eastbound
Access only, no exit

Westbound
Access only, no exit

Eastbound
Exit only, no access

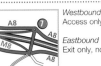
Westbound
Access only, no exit

Eastbound
Exit only, no access

M9 Edinburgh - Dunblane

Northwestbound
Access only, no exit

Southeastbound
Exit only, no access

(Northern section - M6 area, right column)

Northbound
No restriction

Southbound
Access only from M56 (eastbound)

Northbound
Exit only to M56 (westbound)

Southbound
Access only from M56 (eastbound)

Northbound
Access only, no exit

Southbound
Exit only, no access

Northbound
Exit only, no access

Southbound
Access only, no exit

Northbound
Access only from M61

Southbound
Exit only to M61

Northbound
Exit only, no access

Southbound
Access only, no exit

Northbound
Exit only, no access

Southbound
Access only, no exit

Northwestbound
Exit only, no access

Southeastbound
Access only, no exit

Northwestbound
Access only, no exit

Southeastbound
Exit only to A905

Northwestbound
Exit only to M876
(southwestbound)

Southeastbound
Access only from M876
(northeastbound)

M11 London - Cambridge

Northbound
Access only from A406
(eastbound)

Southbound
Exit only to A406

Northbound
Exit only, no access

Southbound
Access only, no exit

Northbound
Exit only, no access

Southbound
No direct access,
use jct 8

Northbound
Exit only to A11

Southbound
Access only from A11

Northbound
Exit only, no access

Southbound
Access only, no exit

Northbound
Exit only, no access

Southbound
Access only, no exit

M20 Swanley - Folkestone

Northwestbound
Staggered junction; follow
signs - access only

Southeastbound
Staggered junction; follow
signs - exit only

Northwestbound
Exit only to M26
(westbound)

Southeastbound
Access only from M26
(eastbound)

Northwestbound
Access only from A20

Southeastbound
For access follow signs -
exit only to A20

Northwestbound
No restriction

Southeastbound
For exit follow signs

Northwestbound
Access only, no exit

Southeastbound
Exit only, no access

M23 Hooley - Crawley

Northbound
Exit only to A23
(northbound)

Southbound
Access only from A23
(southbound)

Northbound
Access only, no exit

Southbound
Exit only, no access

M25 London Orbital Motorway

See M25 London Orbital motorway map on
page *XXII*

M26 Sevenoaks - Wrotham

Westbound
Exit only to clockwise
M25 (westbound)

Eastbound
Access only from
anticlockwise M25
(eastbound)

Westbound
Access only from M20
(northwestbound)

Eastbound
Exit only to M20
(southeastbound)

M27 Cadnam - Portsmouth

Westbound
Staggered junction; follow
signs - access only from
M3 (southbound). Exit
only to M3 (northbound)

Eastbound
Staggered junction; follow
signs - access only from
M3 (southbound). Exit
only to M3 (northbound)

Westbound
Exit only, no access

Eastbound
Access only, no exit

Westbound
Staggered junction; follow
signs - exit only to M275
(southbound)

Eastbound
Staggered junction; follow
signs - access only from
M275 (northbound)

M40 London - Birmingham

Northwestbound
Exit only, no access

Southeastbound
Access only, no exit

Northwestbound
Exit only, no access

Southeastbound
Access only, no exit

Northwestbound
Exit only to M40/A40

Southeastbound
Access only from
M40/A40

Northwestbound
Access only, no exit

Southeastbound
Access only, no exit

Northwestbound
Access only, no exit

Southeastbound
Exit only, no access

Northwestbound
Access only, no exit

Southeastbound
Exit only, no access

M42 Bromsgrove - Measham

See Birmingham district map on pages
174–175

M45 Coventry - M1

Westbound
Access only from A45
(northbound)

Eastbound
Exit only, no access

Westbound
Access only from M1
(northbound)

Eastbound
Exit only to M1
(southbound)

M48 Chepstow

Westbound
Access only from M4
(westbound)

Eastbound
Exit only to M4
(eastbound)

Westbound
No exit to M4 (eastbound)

Eastbound
No access from M4
(westbound)

M53 Mersey Tunnel - Chester

Northbound
Access only from M56
(westbound). Exit only to
M56 (eastbound)

Southbound
Access only from M56
(westbound). Exit only to
M56 (eastbound)

M54 Telford - Birmingham

Westbound
Access only from M6
(northbound)

Eastbound
Exit only to M6
(southbound)

M56 Chester - Manchester

For junctions 1,2,3,4 & 7 see Manchester
district map on pages 182–183

Westbound
Access only, no exit

Eastbound
No access or exit

Westbound
No exit to M6
(southbound)

Eastbound
No access from M6
(northbound)

Westbound
Exit only to M53

Eastbound
Access only from M53

Westbound
No access or exit

Eastbound
No restriction

M57 Liverpool Outer Ring Road

Northwestbound
Access only, no exit

Southeastbound
Exit only, no access

Northwestbound
Access only from A580
(westbound)

Southeastbound
Exit only, no access

M60 Manchester Orbital

See Manchester district map on pages
182–183

M61 Manchester - Preston

Northwestbound
No access or exit

Southeastbound
Exit only, no access

Northwestbound
Exit only to M6
(northbound)

Southeastbound
Access only from M6
(southbound)

M62 Liverpool - Kingston upon Hull

Westbound
Access only, no exit

Eastbound
Exit only, no access

Westbound
No access to A1(M) (southbound)

Eastbound
No restriction

M65 Preston - Colne

Northeastbound
Exit only, no access

Southwestbound
Access only, no exit

Northeastbound
Access only, no exit

Southwestbound
Exit only, no access

M66 Bury

Northbound
Exit only to A56 (northbound)

Southbound
Access only from A56 (southbound)

Northbound
Exit only, no access

Southbound
Access only, no exit

M67 Hyde Bypass

Westbound
Access only, no exit

Eastbound
Exit only, no access

Westbound
Exit only, no access

Eastbound
Access only, no exit

M69 Coventry - Leicester

Northbound
Access only, no exit

Southbound
Exit only, no access

M73 East of Glasgow

Northbound
No exit to A74 and A721

Southbound
No access from A74 and A721

Northbound
No access from or exit to A89. No access from M8 (eastbound)

Southbound
No access from or exit to A89. No exit to M8 (westbound)

M74 and A74(M) Glasgow - Gretna

Northbound
Exit only, no access

Southbound
Access only, no exit

Northbound
Access only, no exit

Southbound
Exit only, no access

Northbound
No access from A74 and A721

Southbound
Access only, no exit to A74 and A721

Northbound
Access only, no exit

Southbound
Exit only, no access

Northbound
No access or exit

Southbound
Exit only, no access

Northbound
No restriction

Southbound
Access only, no exit

Northbound
Access only, no exit

Southbound
Exit only, no access

Northbound
Exit only, no access

Southbound
Access only, no exit

Northbound
Exit only, no access

Southbound
Access only, no exit

M77 Glasgow - Kilmarnock

Northbound
No exit to M8 (westbound)

Southbound
No access from M8 (eastbound)

Northbound
Access only, no exit

Southbound
Exit only, no access

Northbound
Access only, no exit

Southbound
Exit only, no access

Northbound
Access only, no exit

Southbound
No restriction

Northbound
Exit only, no access

Southbound
Exit only, no access

M80 Glasgow - Stirling

For junctions 1 & 4 see Glasgow district map on pages 176–177

Northbound
Exit only, no access

Southbound
Access only, no exit

Northbound
Access only, no exit

Southbound
Exit only, no access

Northbound
Exit only to M876 (northeastbound)

Southbound
Access only from M876 (southwestbound)

M90 Edinburgh - Perth

Northbound
No exit, access only

Southbound
Exit only to A90 (eastbound)

Northbound
Exit only to A92 (eastbound)

Southbound
Access only from A92 (westbound)

Northbound
Access only, no exit

Southbound
Exit only, no access

Northbound
Exit only, no access

Southbound
Access only, no exit

Northbound
No access from A912
No exit to A912 (southbound)

Southbound
No access from A912 (northbound).
No exit to A912

M180 Doncaster - Grimsby

Westbound
Access only, no exit

Eastbound
Exit only, no access

M606 Bradford Spur

Northbound
Exit only, no access

Southbound
No restriction

M621 Leeds - M1

Clockwise
Access only, no exit

Anticlockwise
Exit only, no access

Clockwise
No exit or access

Anticlockwise
No restriction

Clockwise
Access only, no exit

Anticlockwise
Exit only, no access

Clockwise
Exit only, no access

Anticlockwise
Access only, no exit

Clockwise
Exit only to M1 (southbound)

Anticlockwise
Access only from M1 (northbound)

M876 Bonnybridge - Kincardine Bridge

Northeastbound
Access only from M80 (northbound)

Southwestbound
Exit only to M80 (southbound)

Northeastbound
Exit only to M9 (eastbound)

Southwestbound
Access only from M9 (westbound)

A1(M) South Mimms - Baldock

Northbound
Exit only, no access

Southbound
Access only, no exit

Northbound
No restriction

Southbound
Exit only, no access

Northbound
Access only, no exit

Southbound
No access or exit

A1(M) Pontefract - Bedale

Northbound
No access to M62
(eastbound)

Southbound
No restriction

Northbound
Access only from M1
(northbound)

Southbound
Exit only to M1
(southbound)

A1(M) Scotch Corner - Newcastle upon Tyne

Northbound
Exit only to A66(M)
(eastbound)

Southbound
Access only from A66(M)
(westbound)

Northbound
No access. Exit only to
A194(M) & A1
(northbound)

Southbound
No exit. Access only from
A194(M) & A1
(southbound)

A3(M) Horndean - Havant

Northbound
Access only from A3

Southbound
Exit only to A3

Northbound
Exit only, no access

Southbound
Access only, no exit

A38(M) Birmingham
Victoria Road (Park Circus)

Northbound
No exit

Southbound
No access

A48(M) Cardiff Spur

Westbound
Access only from M4
(westbound)

Eastbound
Exit only to M4
(eastbound)

Westbound
Exit only to A48
(westbound)

Eastbound
Access only from A48
(eastbound)

A57(M) Manchester
Brook Street (A34)

Westbound
No exit

Eastbound
No access

A58(M) Leeds
Park Lane and Westgate

Northbound
No restriction

Southbound
No access

A64(M) Leeds
Clay Pit Lane (A58)

Westbound
No exit (to Clay Pit Lane)

Eastbound
No access (from Clay Pit
Lane)

A66(M) Darlington Spur

Westbound
Exit only to A1(M)
(southbound)

Eastbound
Access only from A1(M)
(northbound)

A74(M) Gretna - Abington

Northbound
Exit only, no access

Southbound
Access only, no exit

A194(M)
Newcastle upon Tyne

Northbound
Access only from A1(M)
(northbound)

Southbound
Exit only to A1(M)
(southbound)

A12 M25 - Ipswich

Northeastbound
Access only, no exit

Southwestbound
No restriction

Northeastbound
Exit only, no access

Southwestbound
Access only, no exit

Northeastbound
Exit only, no access

Southwestbound
Access only, no exit

Northeastbound
Access only, no exit

Southwestbound
Exit only, no access

Northeastbound
No restriction

Southwestbound
Access only, no exit

Northeastbound
Exit only, no access

Southwestbound
Access only, no exit

Northeastbound
Access only, no exit

Southwestbound
Exit only, no access

Northeastbound
Exit only, no access

Southwestbound
Access only, no exit

Northeastbound
Exit only (for Stratford
St Mary and Dedham)

Southwestbound
Access only

A14 M1 - Felixstowe

Westbound
Exit only to M6 & M1
(northbound)

Eastbound
Access only from M6 &
M1 (southbound)

Westbound
Exit only, no access

Eastbound
Access only, no exit

Westbound
Access only, no exit

Eastbound
Exit only, no access

Westbound
Exit only, no access

Eastbound
Access only from A1
(southbound)

Westbound
Access only, no exit

Eastbound
Exit only, no access

Westbound
No restriction

Eastbound
Access only, no exit

Westbound
Access only, no exit

Eastbound
Exit only, no access

Westbound
Exit only to A11
Access only from A1303

Eastbound
Access only from A11

Westbound
Access only from A11

Eastbound
Exit only to A11

Westbound
Exit only, no access

Eastbound
Access only, no exit

Westbound
Access only, no exit

Eastbound
Exit only, no access

A55 Holyhead - Chester

Westbound
Exit only, no access

Eastbound
Access only, no exit

Westbound
Access only, no exit

Eastbound
Exit only, no access

Westbound
Exit only, no access

Eastbound
No access or exit.

Westbound
No restriction

Eastbound
No access or exit

Westbound
Exit only, no access

Eastbound
No access or exit

Westbound
Exit only, no access

Eastbound
Access only, no exit

Westbound
Exit only to A5104

Eastbound
Access only from A5104

Refer also to atlas pages 36–37 and 50–51

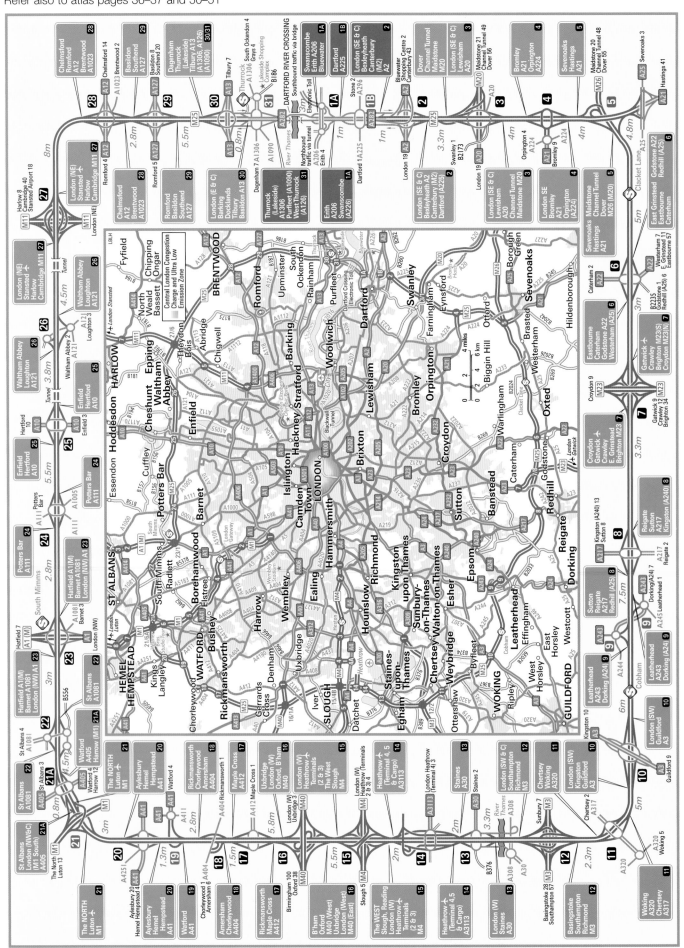

Refer also to atlas pages 58–59

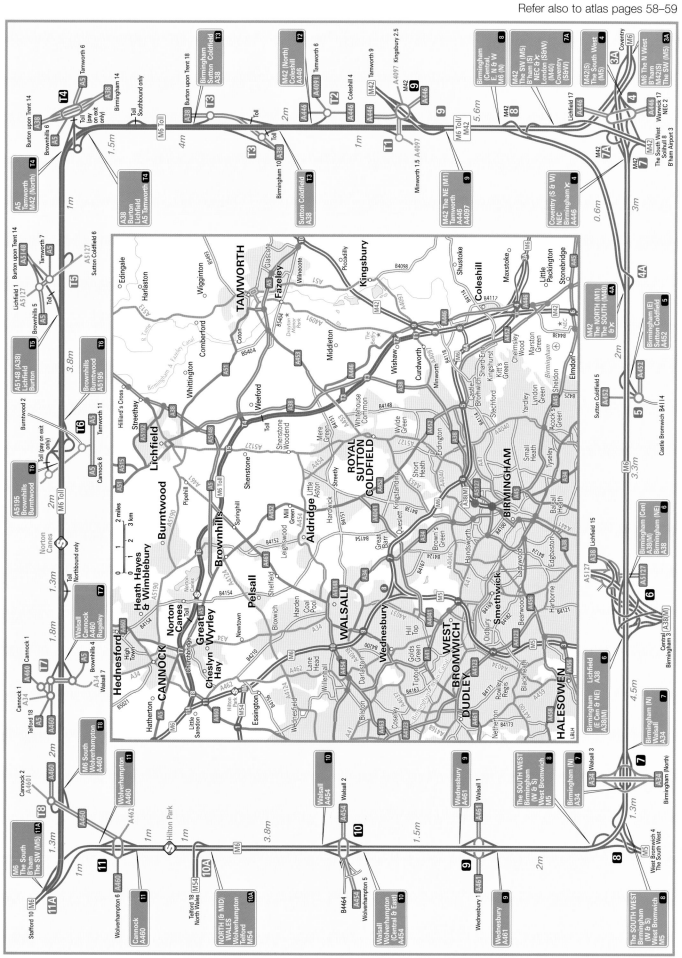

Smart motorways

Since Britain's first motorway (the Preston Bypass) opened in 1958, motorways have changed significantly. A vast increase in car journeys over the last 62 years has meant that motorways quickly filled to capacity. To combat this, the recent development of **smart motorways** uses technology to monitor and actively manage traffic flow and congestion.

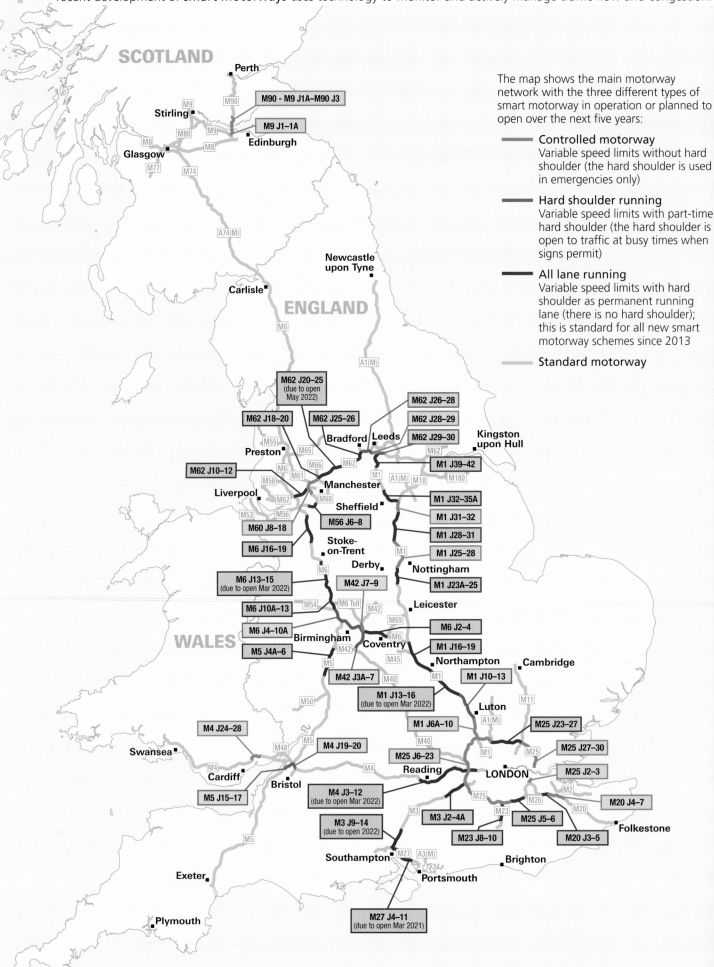

The map shows the main motorway network with the three different types of smart motorway in operation or planned to open over the next five years:

Controlled motorway
Variable speed limits without hard shoulder (the hard shoulder is used in emergencies only)

Hard shoulder running
Variable speed limits with part-time hard shoulder (the hard shoulder is open to traffic at busy times when signs permit)

All lane running
Variable speed limits with hard shoulder as permanent running lane (there is no hard shoulder); this is standard for all new smart motorway schemes since 2013

Standard motorway

SCOTLAND
Perth
M90 - M9 J1A–M90 J3
M9 J1–1A
Stirling
Edinburgh
Glasgow

Newcastle upon Tyne
Carlisle
ENGLAND

M62 J20–25 (due to open May 2022)
M62 J18–20
M62 J25–26
M62 J26–28
M62 J28–29
M62 J29–30
Bradford
Leeds
Kingston upon Hull
M1 J39–42
Preston
M62 J10–12
Liverpool
Manchester
Sheffield
M1 J32–35A
M1 J31–32
M1 J28–31
M56 J6–8
M60 J8–18
Stoke-on-Trent
M1 J25–28
M6 J16–19
Derby
Nottingham
M6 J13–15 (due to open Mar 2022)
M42 J7–9
M1 J23A–25
M6 J10A–13
Leicester
M6 J4–10A
WALES
M6 J2–4
M5 J4A–6
Birmingham
Coventry
M1 J16–19
Northampton
Cambridge
M42 J3A–7
M1 J10–13
M1 J13–16 (due to open Mar 2022)
Luton
M4 J24–28
M1 J6A–10
M25 J23–27
Swansea
M4 J19–20
M25 J6–23
M25 J27–30
Cardiff
Reading
LONDON
M25 J2–3
Bristol
M4 J3–12 (due to open Mar 2022)
M5 J15–17
M20 J4–7
M3 J9–14 (due to open 2022)
M3 J2–4A
M25 J5–6
Folkestone
M23 J8–10
M20 J3–5
Southampton
Brighton
Exeter
Portsmouth
M27 J4–11 (due to open Mar 2021)
Plymouth

How they work

Smart motorways utilise various active traffic management methods, monitored through a regional traffic control centre:

- Traffic flow is monitored using CCTV
- Speed limits are changed to smooth traffic flow and reduce stop-start driving
- Capacity of the motorway can be increased by either temporarily or permanently opening the hard shoulder to traffic

- Warning signs and messages alert drivers to hazards and traffic jams ahead
- Lanes can be closed in the case of an accident or emergency by displaying a red X sign
- Emergency refuge areas are located regularly along the motorway where there is no hard shoulder available

In an emergency

On a smart motorway there is often no hard shoulder so in an emergency you will need to make your way to the nearest **emergency refuge area** or motorway service area.

Emergency refuge areas are lay-bys marked with blue signs featuring an orange SOS telephone symbol. The telephone connects to the regional control centre and pinpoints your location. The control centre will advise you on what to do, send help and assist you in returning to the motorway.

If you are unable to reach an emergency refuge area or hard shoulder (if there is one) move as close to the nearside (left hand) boundary or verge as you can.

If it is not possible to get out of your vehicle safely, or there is no other place of relative safety to wait, stay in your vehicle with your seat-belt on and dial 999 if you have a mobile phone. If you don't have a phone, sit tight and wait to be rescued. Once the regional traffic control centre is aware of your situation, via the police or CCTV, they will use the smart motorway technology to set overhead signs and close the lane to keep traffic away from you. They will also send a traffic officer or the police to help you.

Sign indicating presence of emergency refuge areas ahead

This sign is located at each emergency refuge area

Signs

Motorway signals and messages advise of abnormal traffic conditions ahead and may indicate speed limits. They may apply to individual lanes when mounted overhead or, when located on the central reservation or at the side of the motorway, to the whole carriageway.

Where traffic is allowed to use the hard shoulder as a traffic lane, each lane will have overhead signals and signs. A red cross (with no signals) displayed above the hard shoulder indicates when it is closed. When the hard shoulder is in use as a traffic lane the red cross will change to a speed limit. Should it be necessary to close any lane, a red cross with red lamps flashing in vertical pairs will be shown above that lane. Prior to this, the signal will show an arrow directing traffic into the adjacent lane.

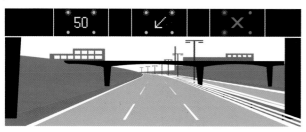

These signals are mounted above the carriageway with a signal for each traffic lane; each signal has two pairs of lamps that flash. You should obey the signal for your lane

Move to adjacent lane (arrow may point downwards to the right)

Leave motorway at next exit

Red lamps flashing from side to side in pairs, together with a red cross, mean 'do not proceed in the traffic lane directly below'. More than one lane may be closed to traffic

Where variable speed limit signs are mounted over individual lanes and the speed limit is shown in a red ring, the limit is mandatory. You will be at risk of a driving offence if you do not keep to the speed limit. Speed limits that do not include the red ring are the maximum speeds advised for the prevailing conditions.

Speed limits of 60, 50 and 40mph are used on all types of smart motorways. When no speed limit is shown the national speed limit of 70mph is in place (this is reduced to 60mph for particular vehicles such as heavy or articulated goods vehicles and vehicles towing caravans or trailers).

Quick tips

- Never drive in a lane closed by a red X
- Keep to the speed limit shown on the gantries
- A solid white line indicates the hard shoulder – do not drive in it unless directed or in the case of an emergency
- A broken white line indicates a normal running lane

- Exit the smart motorway where possible if your vehicle is in difficulty. In an emergency, move onto the hard shoulder where there is one, or the nearest emergency refuge area
- Put on your hazard lights if you break down

Motoring information

M4	Motorway with number	
Toll / T4	Toll motorway with toll station	
6	Motorway junction with and without number	
5	Restricted motorway junctions	
Fleet S R Todhills	Motorway service area, rest area	
	Motorway and junction under construction	
A3	Primary route single/dual carriageway	
1	Primary route junction with and without number	
3	Restricted primary route junctions	

S	Primary route service area
BATH	Primary route destination
A1123	Other A road single/dual carriageway
B2070	B road single/dual carriageway
	Minor road more than 4 metres wide, less than 4 metres wide
	Roundabout
	Interchange/junction
	Narrow primary/other A/B road with passing places (Scotland)
	Road under construction

	Road tunnel
Toll	Road toll, steep gradient (arrows point downhill)
5	Distance in miles between symbols
or V V	Vehicle ferry (all year, seasonal)
	Fast vehicle ferry or catamaran
or P P	Passenger ferry (all year, seasonal)
	Railway line, in tunnel
X	Railway station, tram stop, level crossing
	Preserved or tourist railway

✈ H	Airport (major/minor), heliport
F	International freight terminal
H	24-hour Accident & Emergency hospital
C	Crematorium
P•R	Park and Ride (at least 6 days per week)
	City, town, village or other built-up area
628 ▲ / 637 Lecht Summit	Height in metres, mountain pass
	Snow gates (on main routes)
	National boundary, county or administrative boundary

Touring information   To avoid disappointment, check opening times before visiting

	Scenic route	❋	Garden		Waterfall		Motor-racing circuit
i	Tourist Information Centre	♣	Arboretum		Hill-fort		Air show venue
i	Tourist Information Centre (seasonal)	♆	Country park		Roman antiquity		Ski slope (natural, artificial)
V	Visitor or heritage centre		Showground		Prehistoric monument		National Trust site
♣	Picnic site		Theme park	X 1066	Battle site with year		National Trust for Scotland site
🚐	Caravan site (AA inspected)		Farm or animal centre		Preserved or tourist railway		English Heritage site
▲	Camping site (AA inspected)		Zoological or wildlife collection		Cave or cavern		Historic Scotland site
▲🚐	Caravan & camping site (AA inspected)		Bird collection	¥ 1	Windmill, monument or memorial		Cadw (Welsh heritage) site
	Abbey, cathedral or priory		Aquarium		Beach (award winning)	★	Other place of interest
	Ruined abbey, cathedral or priory	RSPB	RSPB site		Lighthouse	□	Boxed symbols indicate attractions within urban area
¥	Castle		National Nature Reserve (England, Scotland, Wales)		Golf course	◉	World Heritage Site (UNESCO)
	Historic house or building		Local nature reserve		Football stadium		National Park and National Scenic Area (Scotland)
M	Museum or art gallery		Wildlife Trust reserve		County cricket ground		Forest Park
	Industrial interest		Forest drive		Rugby Union national stadium		Sandy beach
	Aqueduct or viaduct		National trail		International athletics stadium		Heritage coast
	Vineyard, brewery or distillery	☀	Viewpoint		Horse racing, show jumping		Major shopping centre

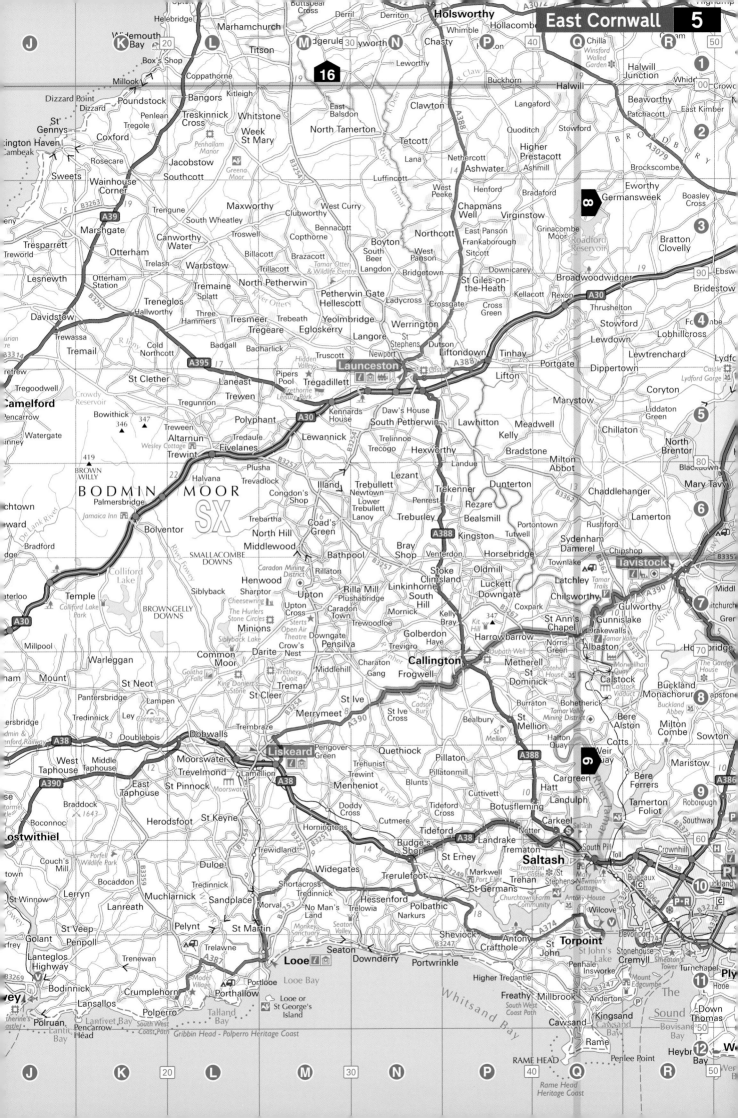

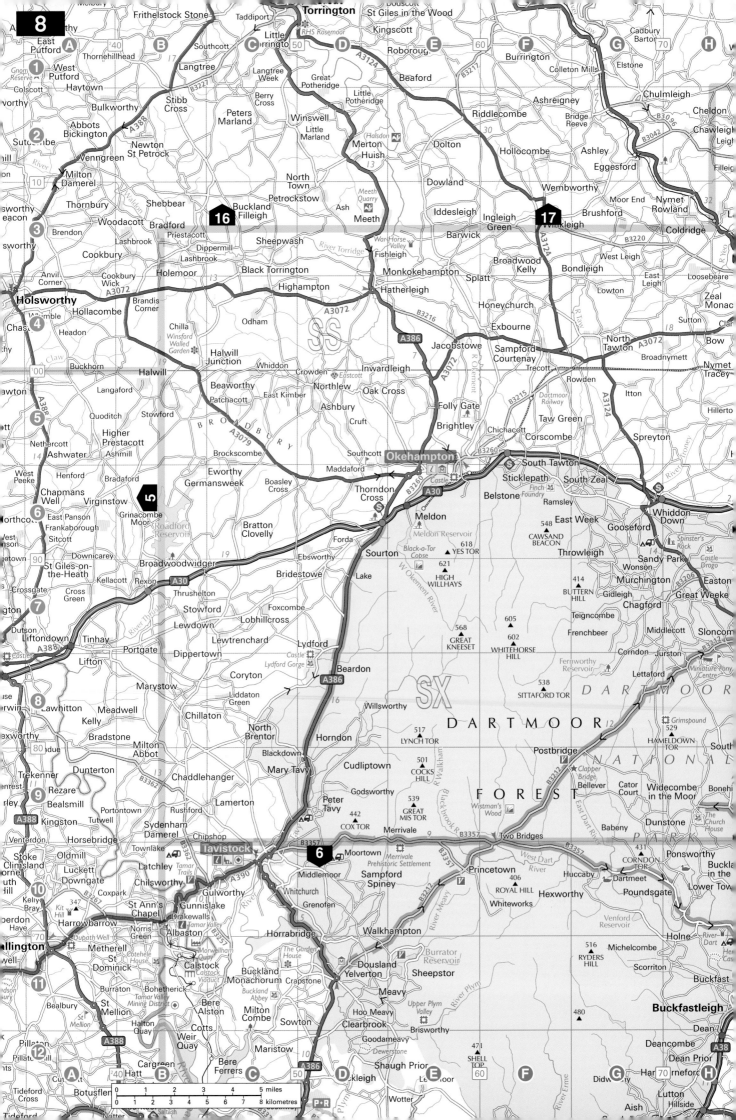

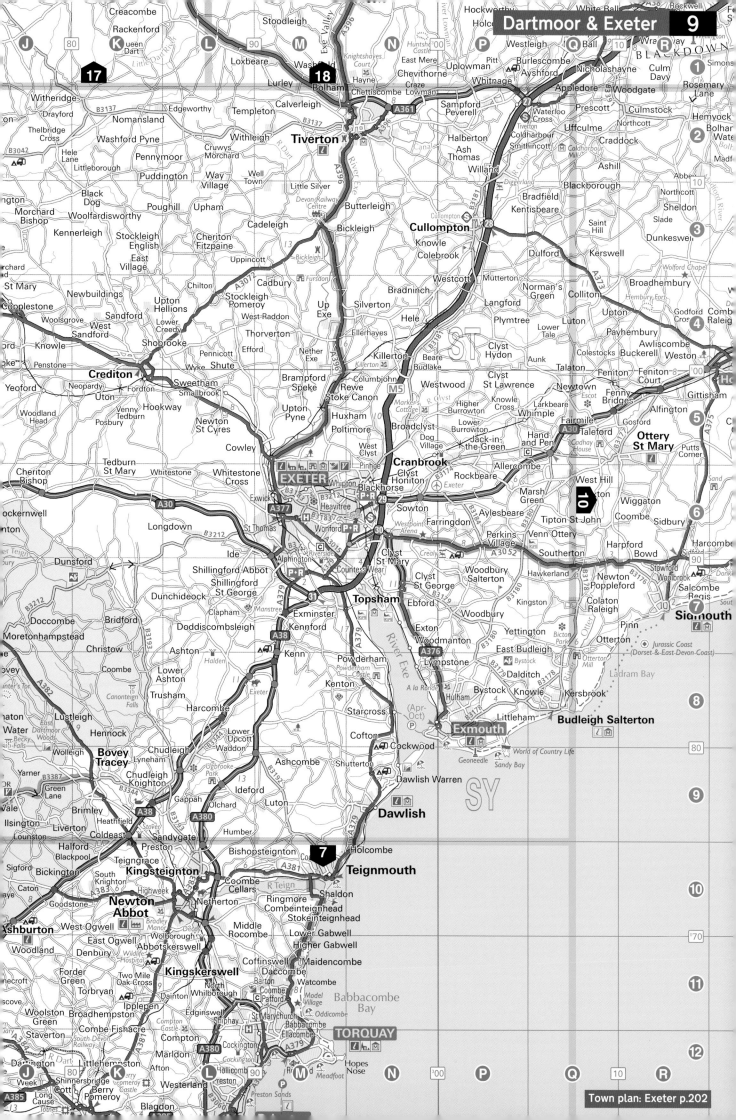

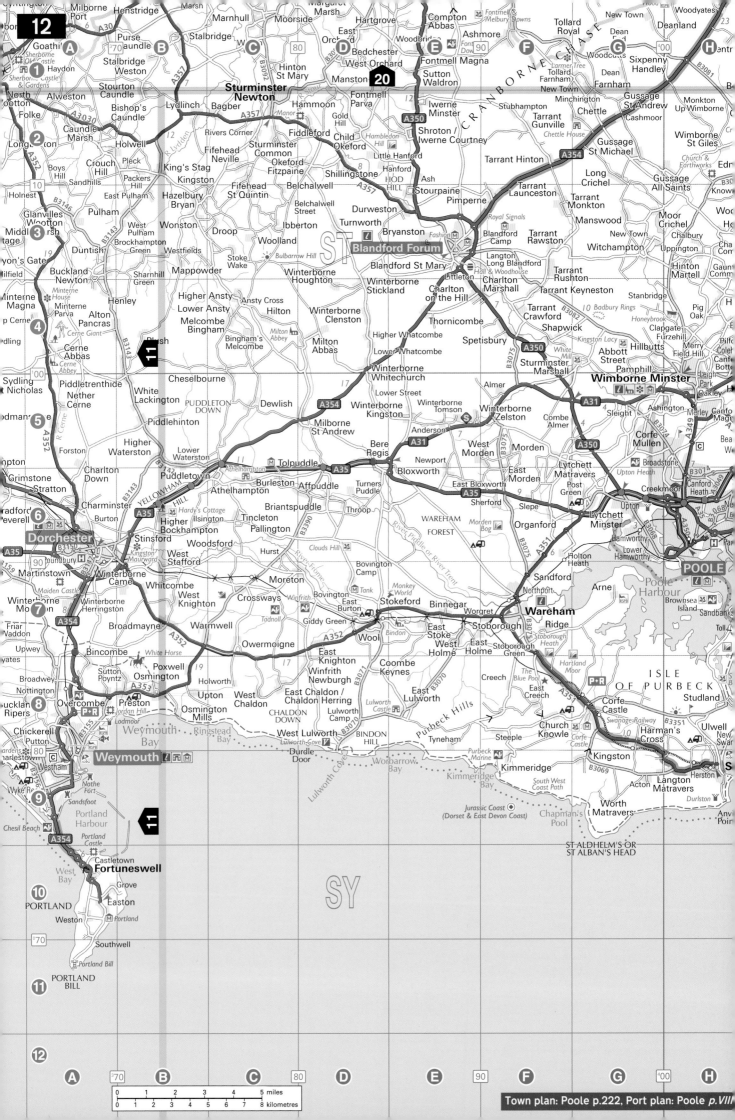

A 20 B 20 C D 30 E F 40 G H

1

50

2

North West
Point

Lundy
Heritage Coast   142   LUNDY

Marine
Reserve   Bideford (Apr-Oct)
Ilfracombe (Apr-Oct)

Shutter Point   Surf Point

3

40

4

5

30

6   SS   HARTLAND POINT   Shipload
Bay

BARNSTAPLE

OR

BIDEFORD BAY

Bull
Point   Lee
Bay
Rockham
Bay   Mortehoe
Morte
Point

Woolacombe   Trims

Morte   Bra
Bay   Chapel Woo

Baggy   Pickwell   North
Point   Putsborough   Buckla   Nethe

Croyde Bay   Georgeham
Croyde Bay   Croyde   Darracott
Saunton   Lobb

Braunton   Wra

Braunton
Burrows

North Devon
Heritage Coast
Lundy   Isley
(Apr-Oct)   Marsh   Yella

Northam   Crow   9
Burrows   Point   Insto
Appledore
Westward Ho!   Northam   Taf

Abbotsham   Eastleigh
Pillhe
The Big   East-the-Water
Sheep

Bideford
Titchberry   Brownsham
Damehole   Hartland Abbey   Velly   Clovelly   Ford   Fairy Cross   Woodtown   Yeo Vale   Landcross
Point   & Gardens   Higher   Buck's   Horns
Stoke   Clovelly   Mills   Cross   Goldworthy   Littleham   We
Hartland Quay   B3248   4   Buck's   A39   10   Saltrens   Gif
Hartland   Cross   Cabbacott   A386
Speke's Mill   Milford   Philham   Woolfardisworthy   Parkham   Buckland   Monkleigh
Mouth   Cranford   Brewer   Taddiport
Elmscott   Edistone   Parkham   Frithelstock   Lit
Hardisworthy   Tosberry   Melbury   Ash   Frithelstock Stone   Torrin
South   Ashmansworthy   Southcott
Hole   Welcombe   Meddon   East   Thornehillhead   Langtree   Langtr
Mead   Darracott   Putford   17   Wee
Gooseham   Woolley   Dinworthy   West   B3227   Berry
Mill   East   Gnome   Putford   Bulkworthy   Stibb   Cross
Gooseham   Eastcott   16   Youlstone   Reserve   Colscott   Haytown   Cross   Peters
Morwenstow   Bradworthy   Abbots   Marland
Higher Sharpnose Point   West Youlstone   A39   Bickington   A388   Newton
South West   Shop   Kimworthy   Sutcombe   Venngreen   St Petrock
Coast Path   Woodford   Alfardisworthy   Milton   River
Lower Sharpnose Point   Tamar   Sutcombemill   Damerel
Lakes   Soldon   Thornbury   Walden   Shebbear   Buckland
Steeple Point   Kilkhampton   Thurdon   Soldon   Holsworthy   Woodacott   Filleigh
Sandy   Stibb   Cross   Beacon   Brendon   Lashbrook   Priestacott   Dippermill   Shee
Mouth   Maer   Poughill   Hersham   Dunsdon   Cookbury   Lashbrook
Northcott   Bush   Lana   Chilsworthy   Anvil   Cookbury   Holemoor   Black To
Mouth   Flexbury   Grimscott   Corner   Wick   A3072   13
Castle Bude   Stratton   Launcells   Kingford   Red Post   A3072   Brandis   Odham
Bude   Launcells   Cross   10   Pancrasweek   Holsworthy   Corner   Chilla
Bay   Lynstone   Upton   Buttsbear   Derril   Hollacombe   Winsford Walled   Halwill
Cross   Derriton   Whimble   Garden   Junction
Widemouth   Helebridge   Marhamchurch   Bridgerule   Pyworthy   Chasty   Headon   Beaworthy
Bay   Box's Shop   Titson   Leworthy   Langaford   Patchacott   Eas
Millook   Coppathorne   R Claw   Buckhorn   Halwill   Whid
Dizzard Point   Bangors   Kitleigh   5   Clawton   Ashmill
Dizzard   Poundstock   East   A388   B
Penlean   Treskinnick   Balsdon   Higher   Brockscombe
St   egole   Cross   Whitstone   North Ta   rton   Tetcott   Quod   40   Sto   d   Prestacott   A3079
Gennys   Coxt   Week   Lana   Nethercott   Ashmill
Crackington Haven   B3   bury   E   Dizzard
Cambeak

0   1   2   3   4   5 miles
0   1   2   3   4   5   6   7   8 kilometres

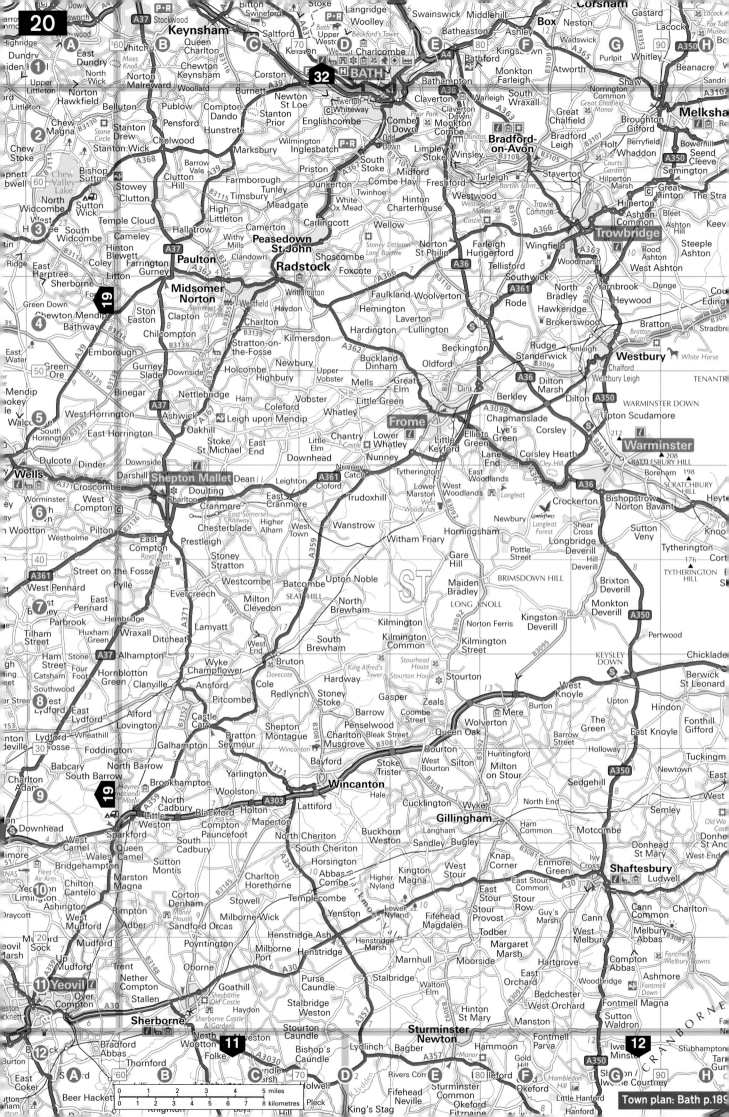

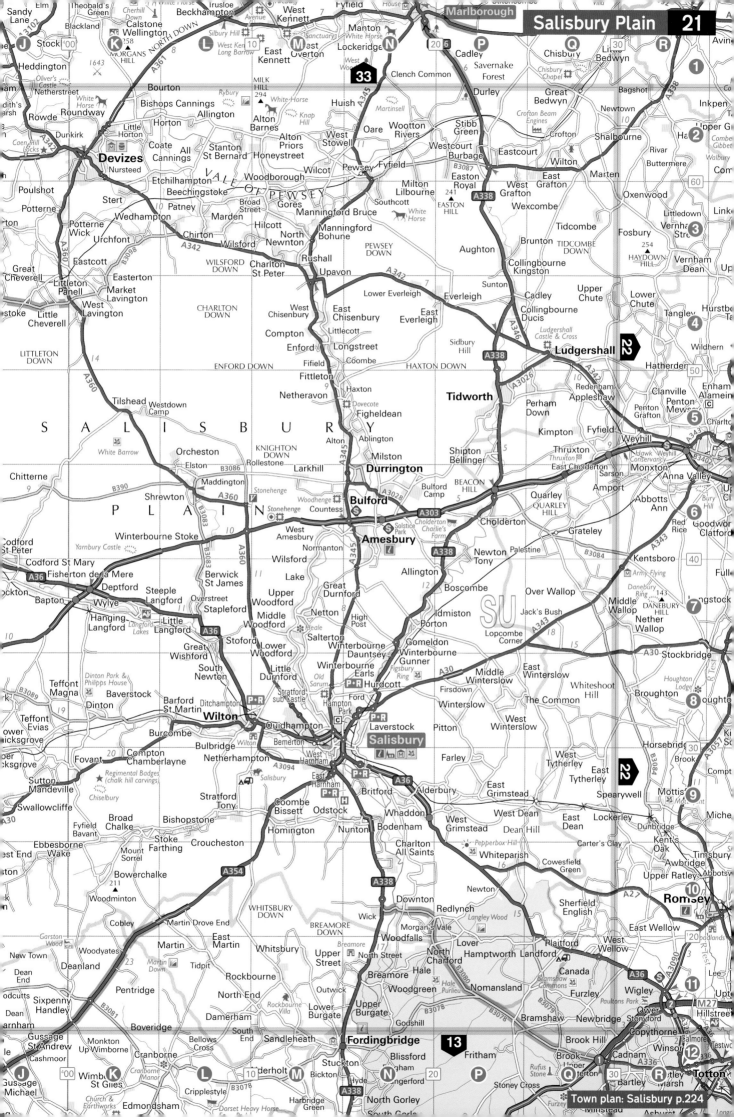

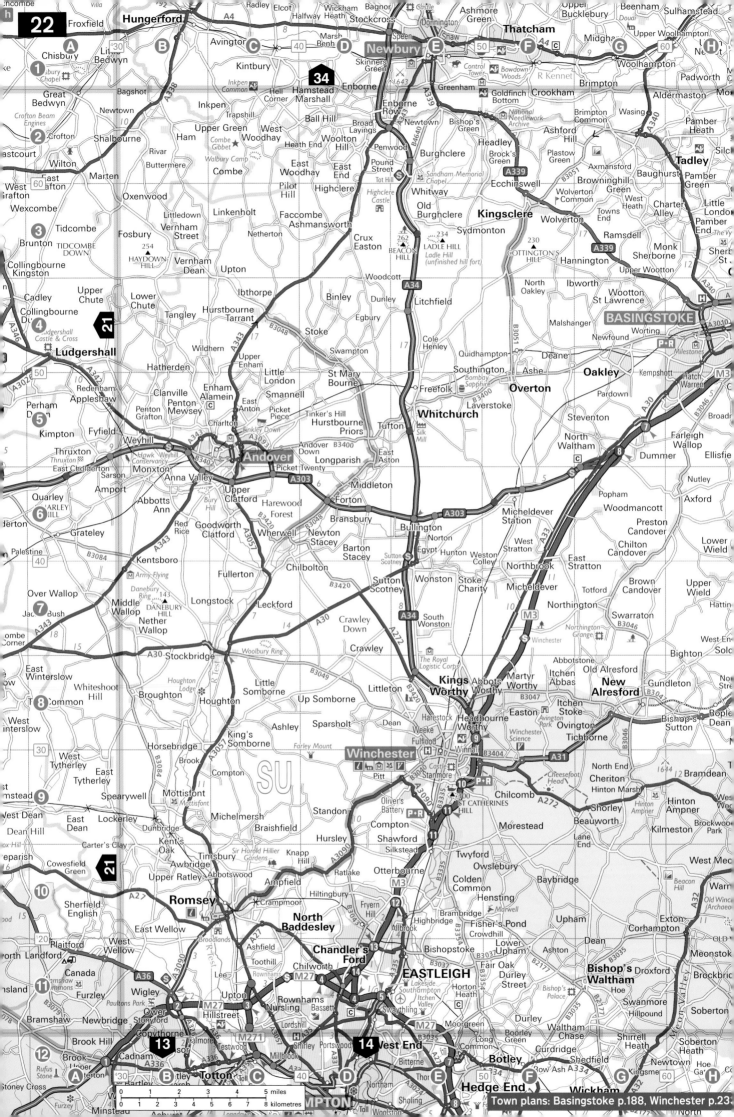

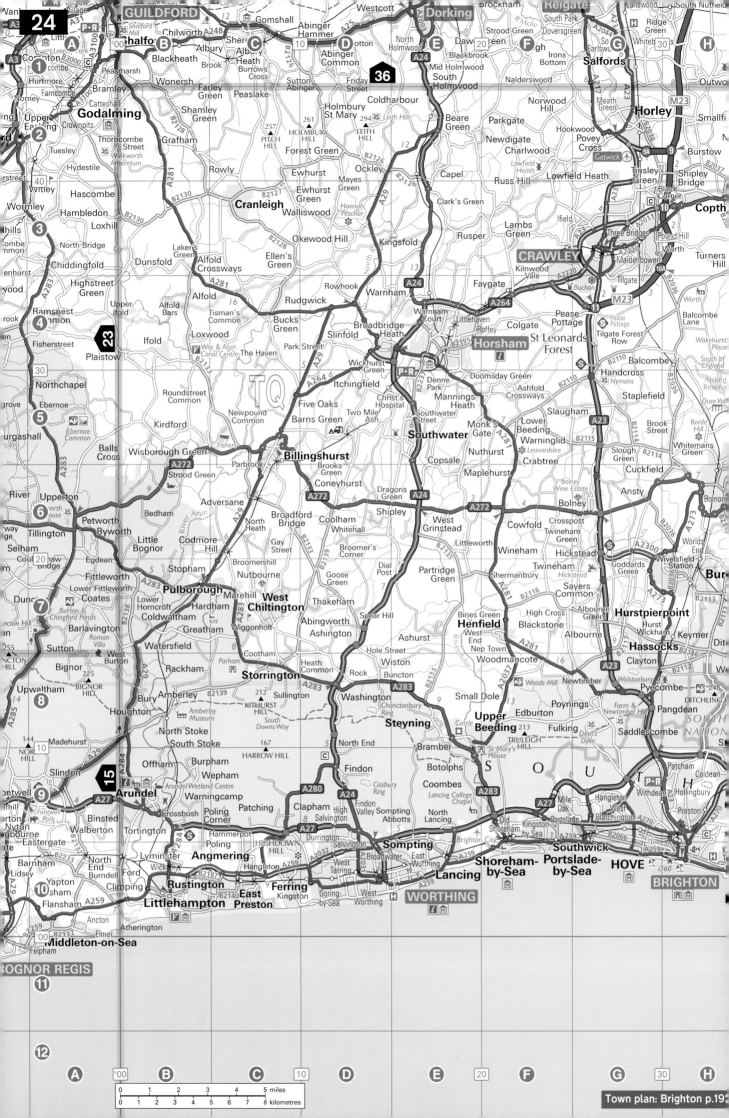

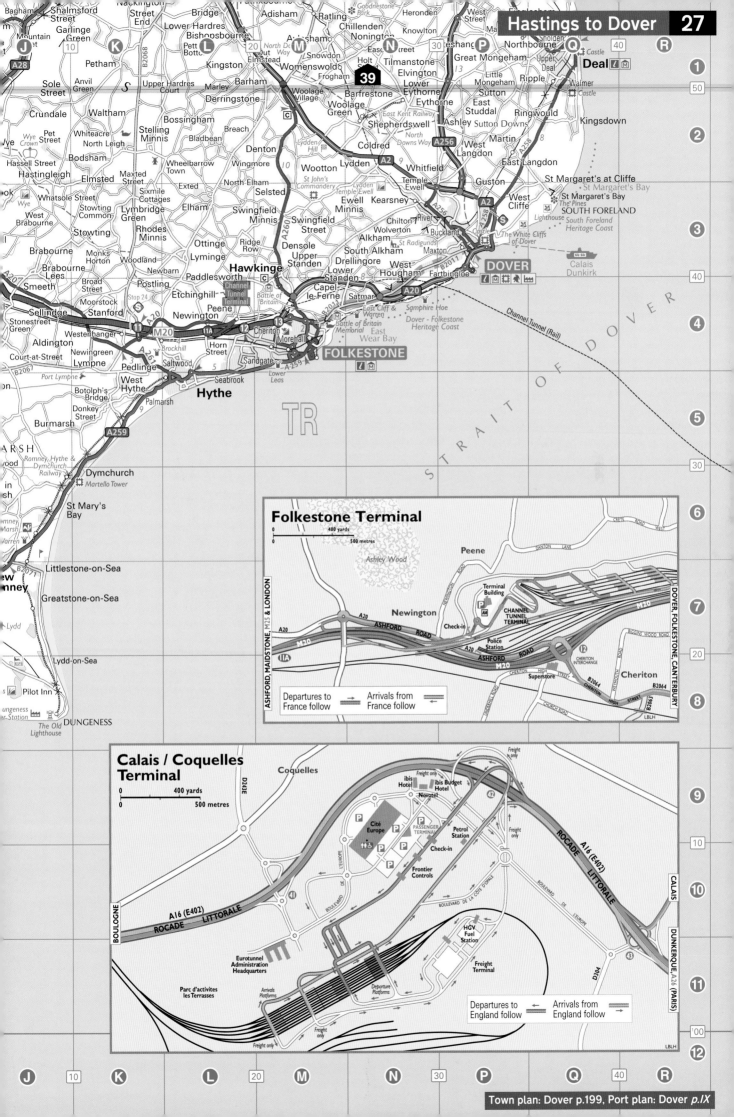

Margate

0   200 m

The Bay

Nayland Rock

Tidal Bathing Pool

Main Sands

LONDON, CANTERBURY
A28

MARGATE STATION

Premier Inn

Hartsdown Leisure Centre

Hartsdown Park

Margate FC

Tivoli Park

All Saints Industrial Estate

Tivoli Industrial Estate

Lifeboat Station

Turner Contemporary Gallery

Police Station

Medical Centre

Winter Gardens

Casino

Tudor House

Clock Tower

Kingdom Hall

Mag & Co Court

Theatre Royal

Royal Mail Depot

Salvation Army

CAB

Holy Trinity & St John's School

Dreamland

War Memorial

Supermarket

College Square

Cecil Square

MARINE TERRACE

BELGRAVE RD

EATON ROAD

HIGH ST

ST PETER'S ROAD

RAMSGATE RD

BROADSTAIRS

RAMSGATE

Ramsgate

0   200 m

BROADSTAIRS

St Ethelbert's School

Chatham House School

St George's

Salvation Army

Kingdom Hall

Priory School

UpDown Gallery

Clarendon House School

Jobcentre Plus

Christ Church School

St Augustine's Abbey

Sports Centre

Police Sta

Granville

Ramsgate Tunnels

Bandstand

Royal Victoria Pavilion

Maritime

Marina

Royal Harbour

Lifeboat Station

MARGATE RD

PARK ROAD

BOUNDARY ROAD

STATION APP

GRANGE ROAD

ROYAL PARADE

LONDON, (M2), CANTERBURY

TR

Herne Bay

Whitstable

Whitstable Bay
Seasalter

Tankerton

Swalecliffe

Greenhill

Chestfield

South Street

Bullockstone

Yorkletts

Highstreet

Dargate

Hernhill
Staplestreet

Denstroude

Blean

Dunkirk

Mount Ephraim

Upper Harbledown

Rough Common

Harbledown

Thanington

Canterbury

Chartham

Chartham Hatch

Old Wives Lees

Shalmsford Street

Garlinge Green

Petham

Sole Street

Crundale

Waltham

Pet Street

North Leigh

Stelling Minnis

Bodsham

Reculver Towers & Roman Fort

Bishopstone

Reculver

Hillborough

Beltinge

Eddington

Broomfield

Highstead

Herne

Maypole

Herne Common

Hoath

Upstreet

Hicks Forstal

Calcott

Broad Oak

Honey Hill

Tyler Hill

Sturry

Hales Place

Fordwich

Ickham

Littlebourne

Bekesbourne Hill

Bekesbourne

Patrixbourne

Bridge

Lower Hardres

Bishopsbourne

Pett Bottom

Kingston

Barham

Derringstone

Womenswold

Nonington

Minnis Bay

Birchington-on-Sea

Westgate-on-Sea

Westbrook

Birchington

Brooks End

Potten Street

St Nicholas-at-Wade

Sarre

Acol

Monkton

Gore Street

Plucks Gutter

West Stourmouth

Grove

East Stourmouth

Westmarsh

Preston

Elmstone

Stodmarsh

Wickhambreaux

Seaton

Wingham

Durlock

Guilton

Marshborough

Ash

Shatterling

Staple

Twitham

Bramling

Goodnestone

Adisham

Ratling

Chillenden

Knowlton

Easole Street

Holt Street

Snowdon

Eythorne

Tilmanstone

Elvington

Lower Eythorne

MARGATE

Main Sands

Cliftonville

Northdown

Westwood

Garlinge

Lydden

Haine

Manston

RAF Manston

Minster

Durlock

Cliffsend

Pegwell

St Augustine's Cross

Viking Ship 'Hugin'

Pegwell Bay

Richborough Roman Fort

Goldstone

Paramour Street

Cop Street

Hoaden

Weddington

Cooper Street

Woodnesborough

Statenborough

Barnsole

Eastry

Heronden

West Street

Betteshanger

Great Mongeham

Ripple

Foreness Point

Botany Bay

Kingsgate

NORTH FORELAND

North Foreland

Reading Street

St Peter's

Stone Bay

Broadstairs

Westwood

Dumpton

Hereson

St Lawrence

Ramsgate

Sandwich Bay

Sandwich

Stone Cross

Great Stonar

Toll

Royal St George's

Sandwich Bay

Ham

Hacklinge

Finglesham

Marley

Northbourne

Upper Deal

The Downs

Castle

Deal

Walmer

Castle

Kingsdown

27

Martin

West Langdon

East Langdon

Shepherdswell

Coldred

Lydden Hill

Wootton

Whitfield

Woolage Village

Woolage Green

Barfrestone

East Kent Railway

Sholden

North Downs Way

Out Elmstead

Nackington

Street End

Town plan: Canterbury p.194

ISLE OF THANET

A '60 B C 70 D E 80 F G 90 H

1
2
40
3
4
30
5
20
6
7
8
10
9
10
'00
11
12

SM

SR

Rosslare

STRUMBLE HEAD

Pen Brush
Garn Fawr
Trefasser

Goodwic
(Wdig)

Pwll·Deri

Pembrokeshire
Coast Path

Manorowen

St Nicholas
Panteg

Ynys
Daullyn

Granston
A42

Carreg Sampson
Abercastle

Llangloffan
Jordan

Porthgain
Trefin
Mathry
Castle
Morris

Abereiddy
16
A487
Llangloffan
Fen
B4331

Llanrhian
Square and
Compass
Letters

Berea
Croes·goch
Treffynnon

Tretio
Treglemais
Cerbyd
Tr

Carnhedryn
River Solva
B4330

ST DAVID'S HEAD
Treleddyd-fawr
Caer
Farchell
Llandeloy
Tancredston
Pont-yr-hafod

Rhodiad-
y-brenin
Middle Mill
Treffgarne
Owen
Hayscastle
Hayscas
Cross

Whitesands
Bay
B4583
Whitchurch
A487
178
DUDWELL
MT
Lew

Bishop's
Palace
St Davids
(Tyddewi)
Nine
Wells
Solva
Penycwn
Roch
Wolfsdale

RAMSEY
ISLAND
Newgale
Roch Gate

'St David's Peninsula
Heritage Coast
PEMBROKESHIRE
COAST
NATIONAL PARK
Simpson
Cross
Keeston
Car

RSPB
Rickets Head
Nolton Haven
Nolton
A487
Pelcomb Cross
Pelcor

St Brides Bay
St Brides Bay
Heritage Coast
Lambston
Pelcomb
Bridge

Druidston
Sutton

Haroldston
West
Portfield
Gate
B4341

Broad Haven
Broadway
B4327
Dreer
Hill

Little Haven
Walton
West
Solbury
4

Pembrokeshire
Coast Path
Talbenny
Tiers
Cross

(Apr-
Sept)
P
Wooltack
Point
St Brides
Walwyn's
Castle

SKOMER
ISLAND
Marloes
B4327
Hasguard
Thornton
3

Broad Sound
St Ishmael's
Sandy
Haven
Herbrandston
Steynto

Marloes & Dale Heritage Coast
Hubberston
Honeybor
Waterst

Dale
Hakin
6
Llanstad

SKOKHOLM
ISLAND
Westdale
Bay
Great Castle
Head
Milford Haven
(Aberdaugleddau)
Per

Dale
Point
Milford Haven

St Ann's Head
Angle
Pwllcrochan
(Do

Angle
Bay
Rhoscrowther

Rosslare
B4320
10

Freshwater
West
Castlemartin Brook
B4

SR
B4319
Castlemartin
Warren

Linney Head
Mer

PEMBROKESHIRE
NATIONAL P

Elegug Stacks
Pembro
Coast

A '60 B 70 C 70 D E 80 F G 90 H

0 1 2 3 4 5 miles
0 1 2 3 4 5 6 7 8 kilometres

Port plan: Pembroke Dock p.

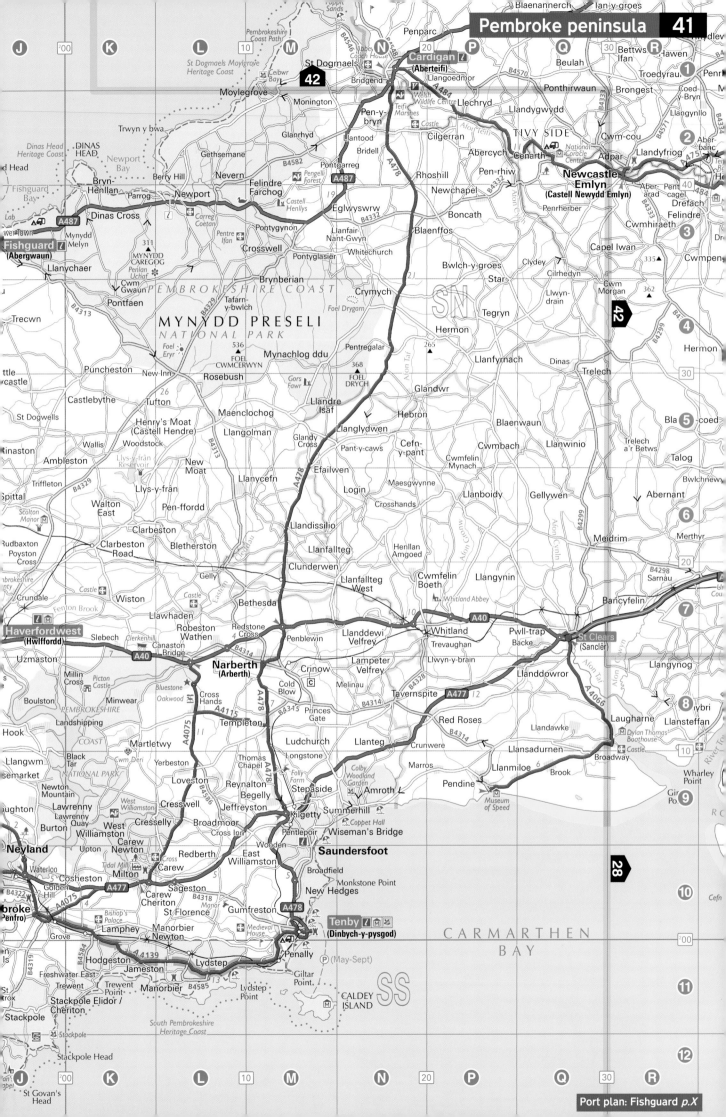

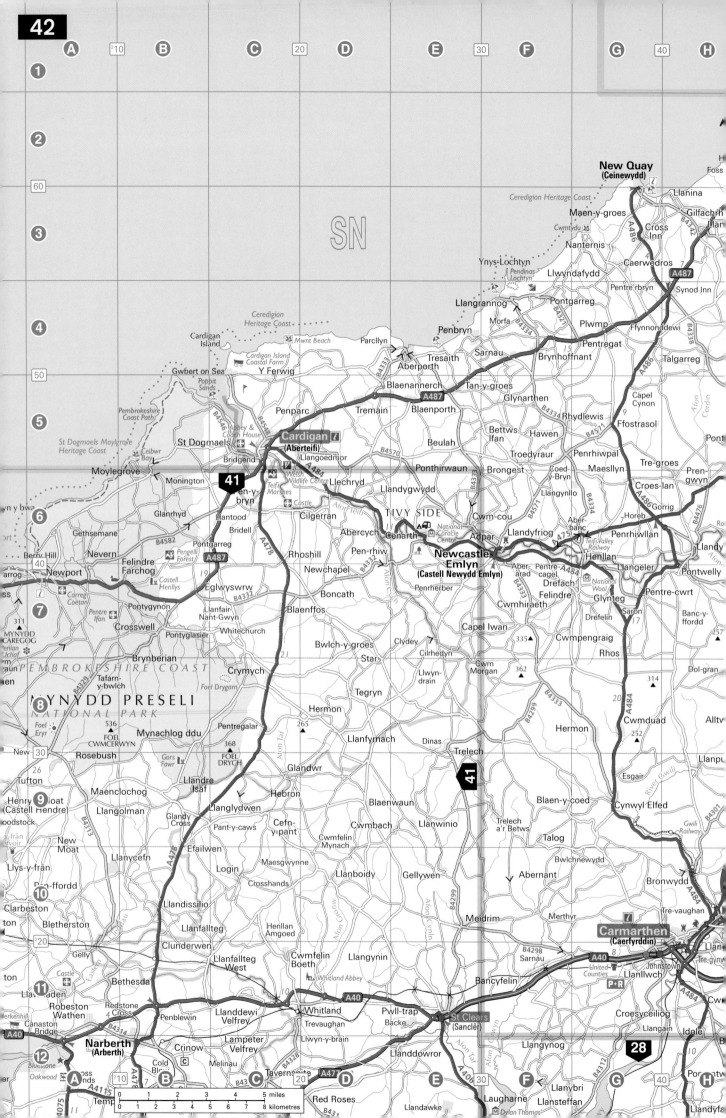

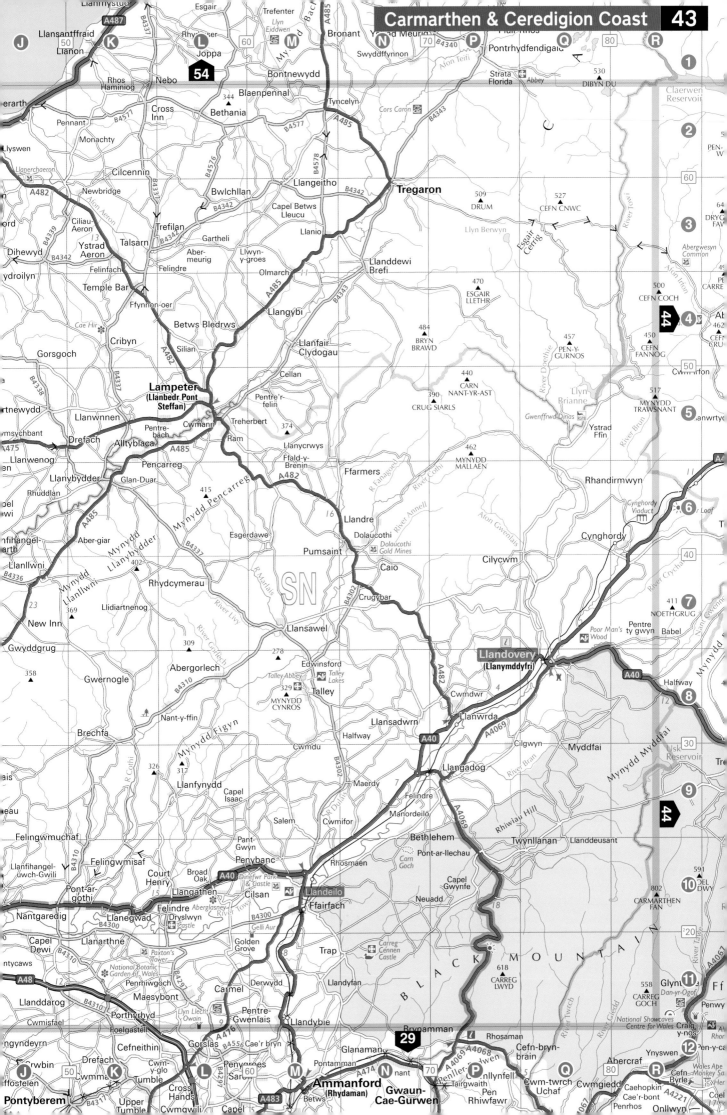

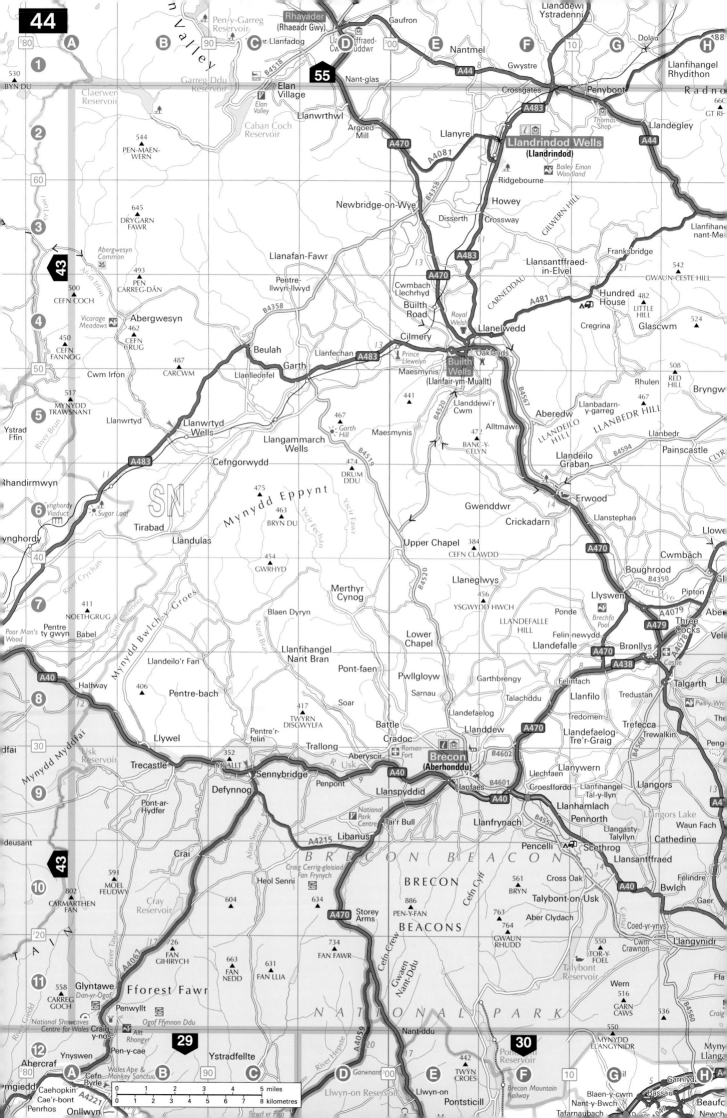

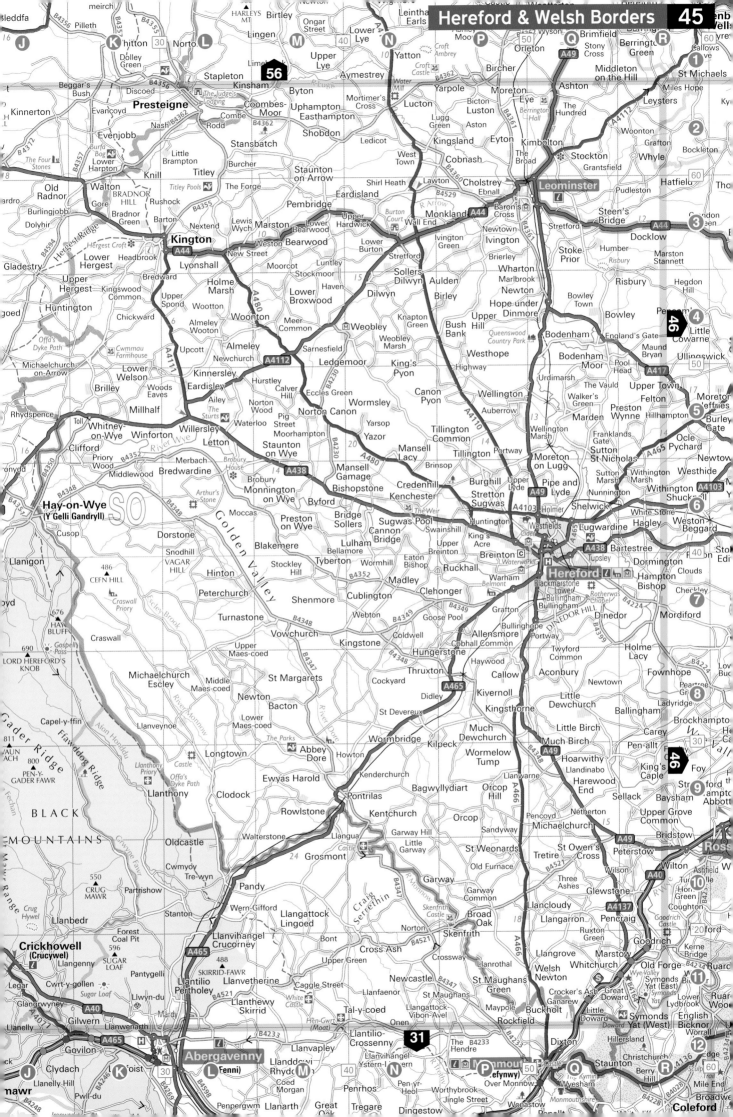

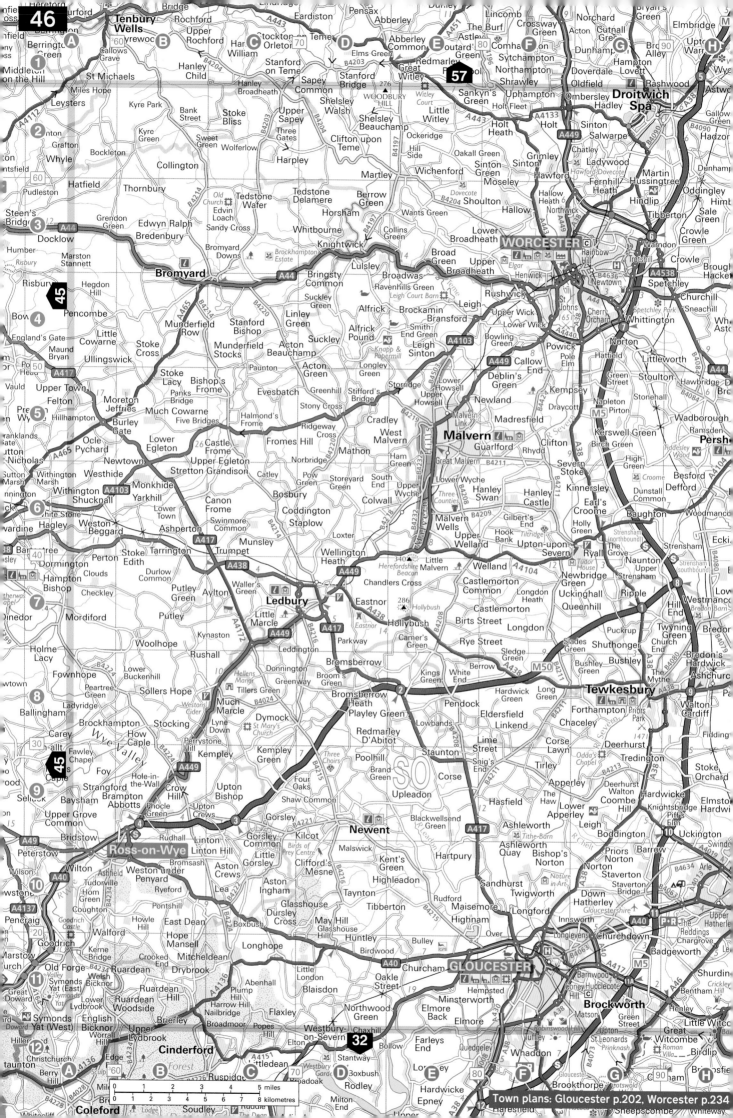

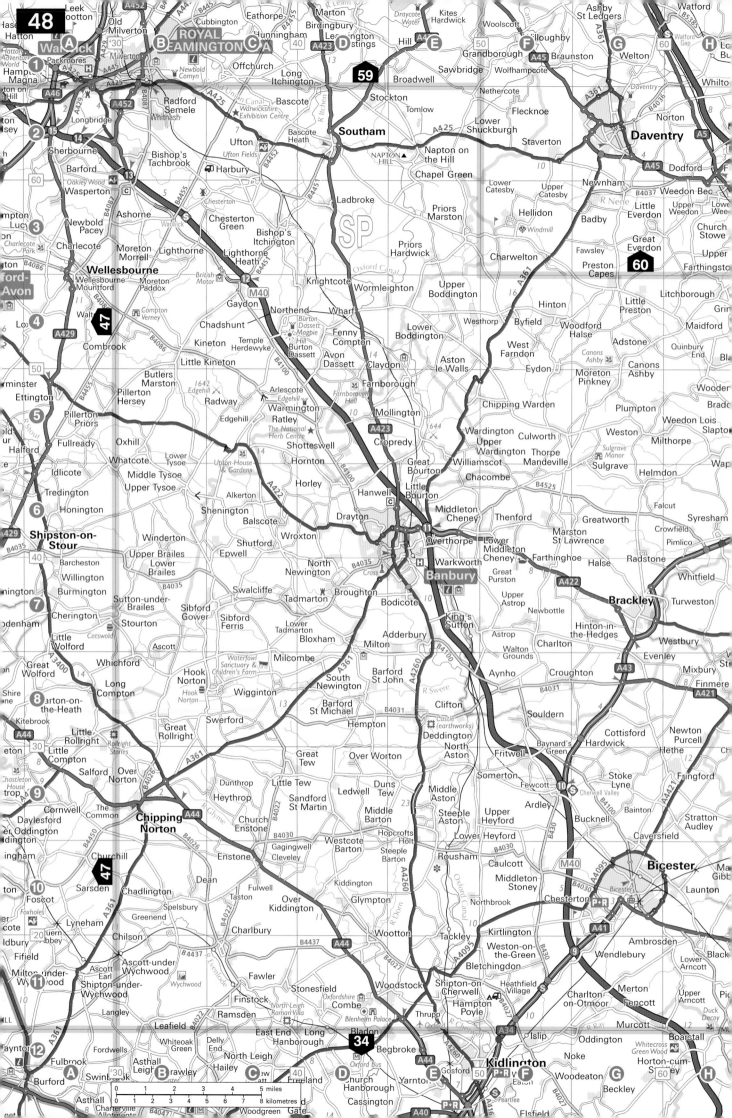

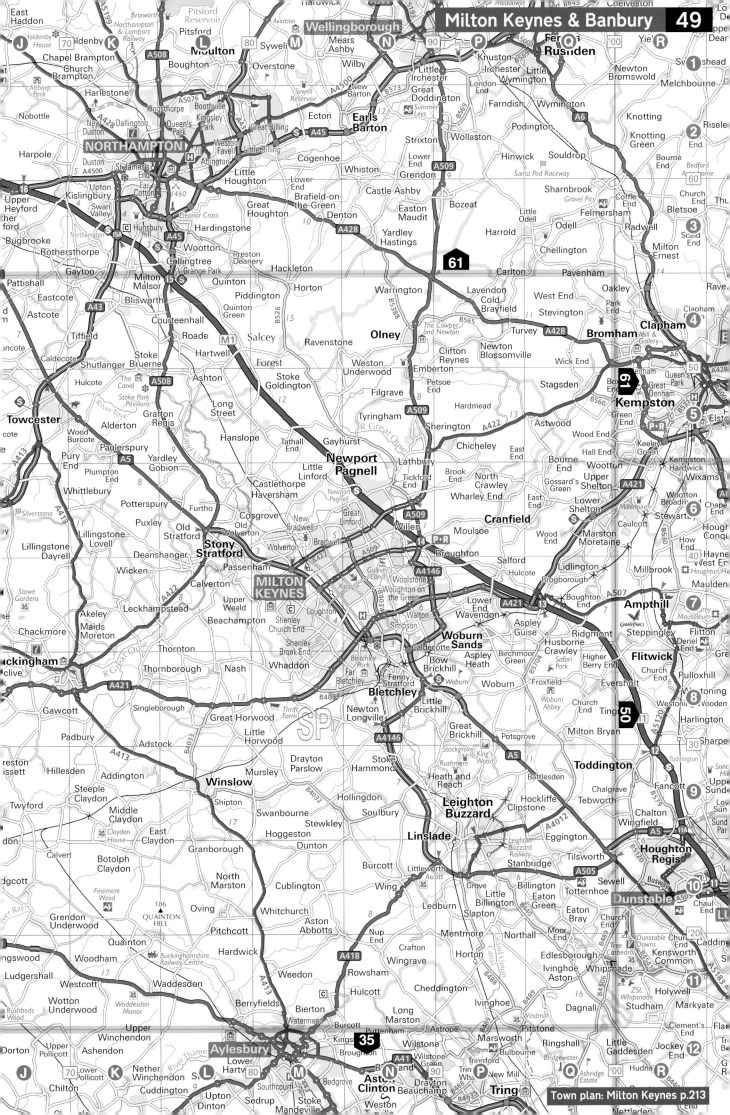

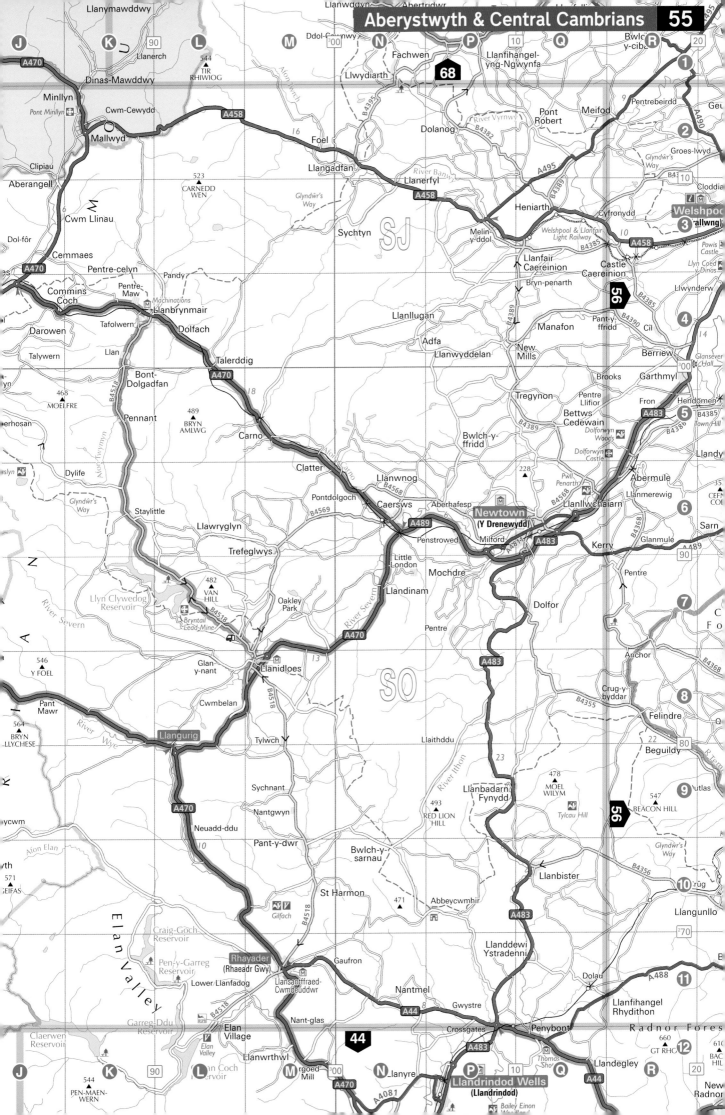

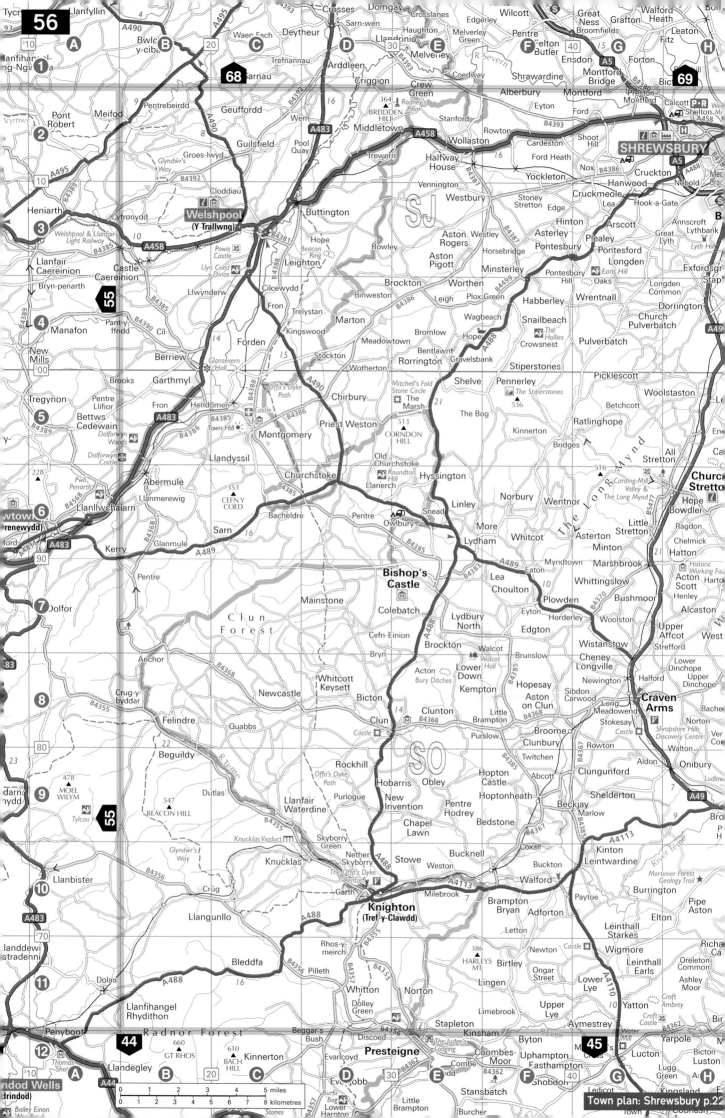

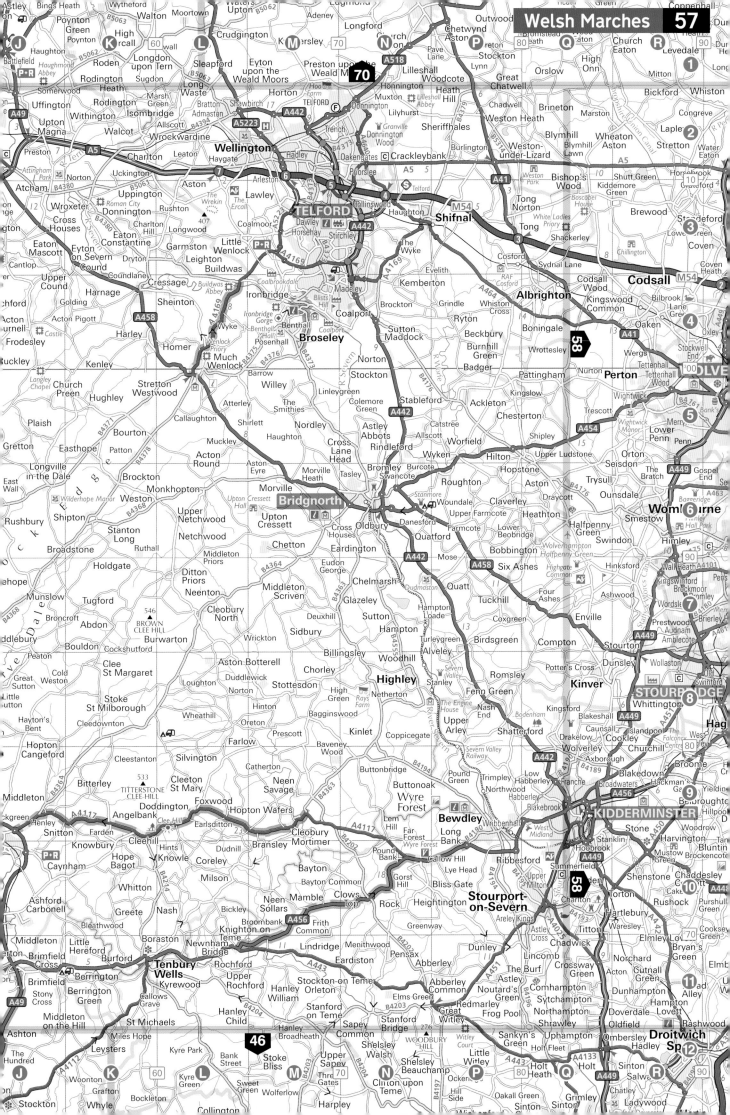

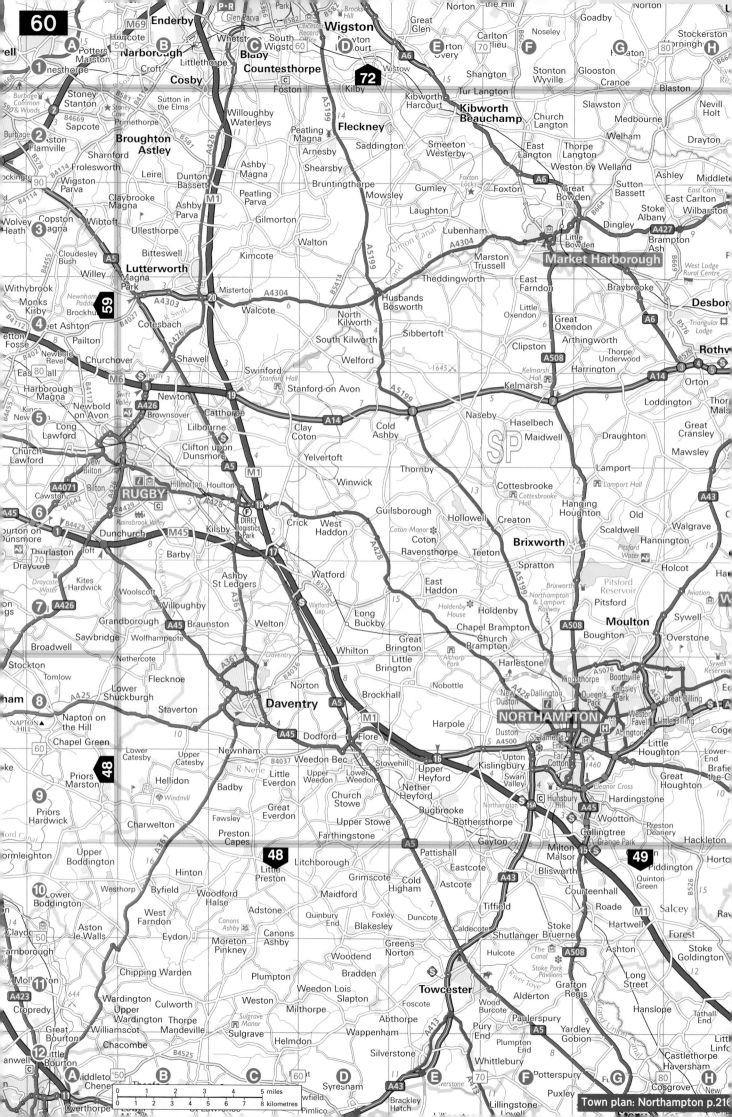

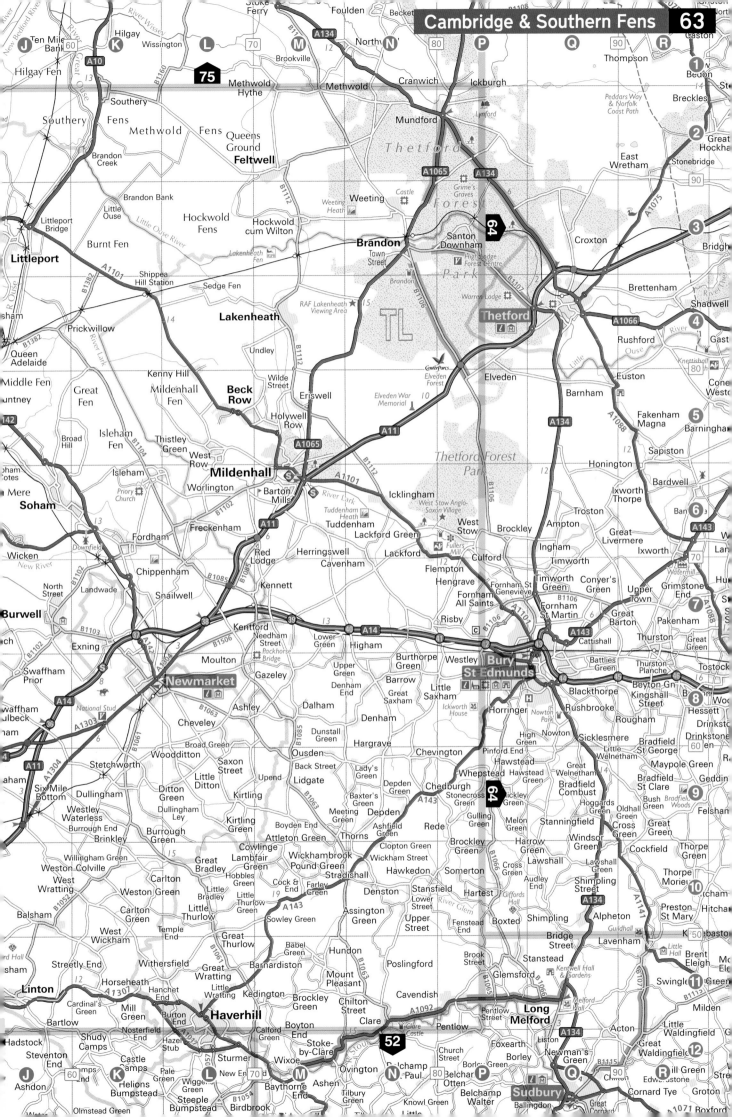

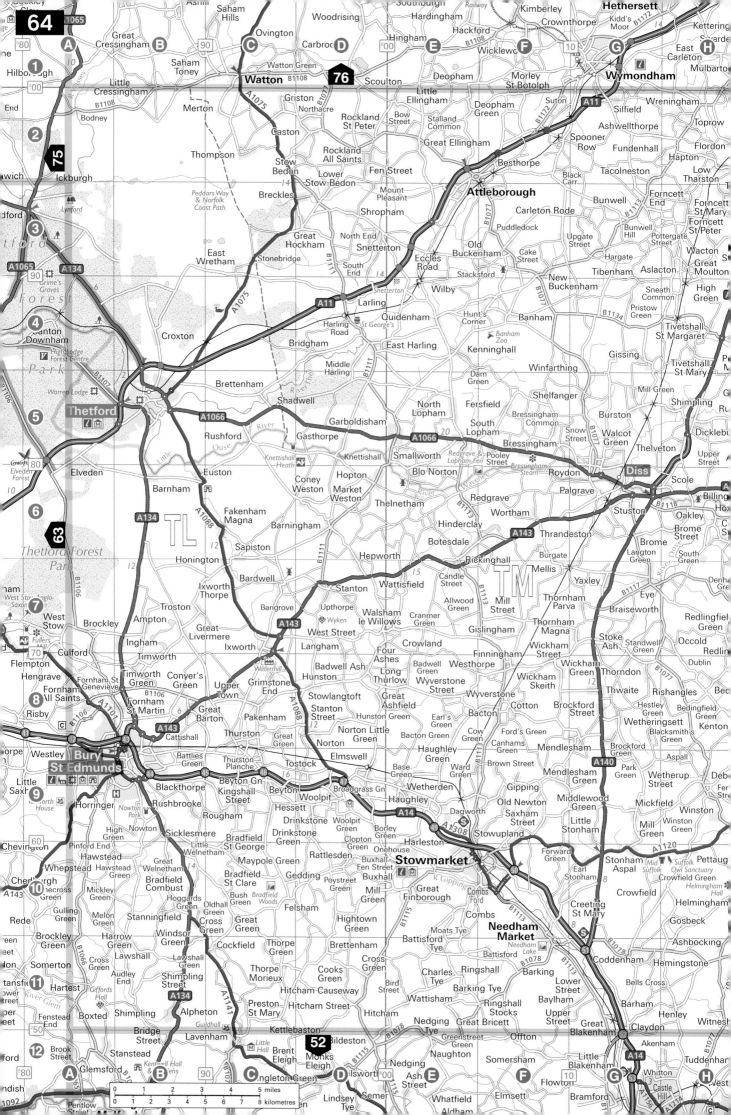

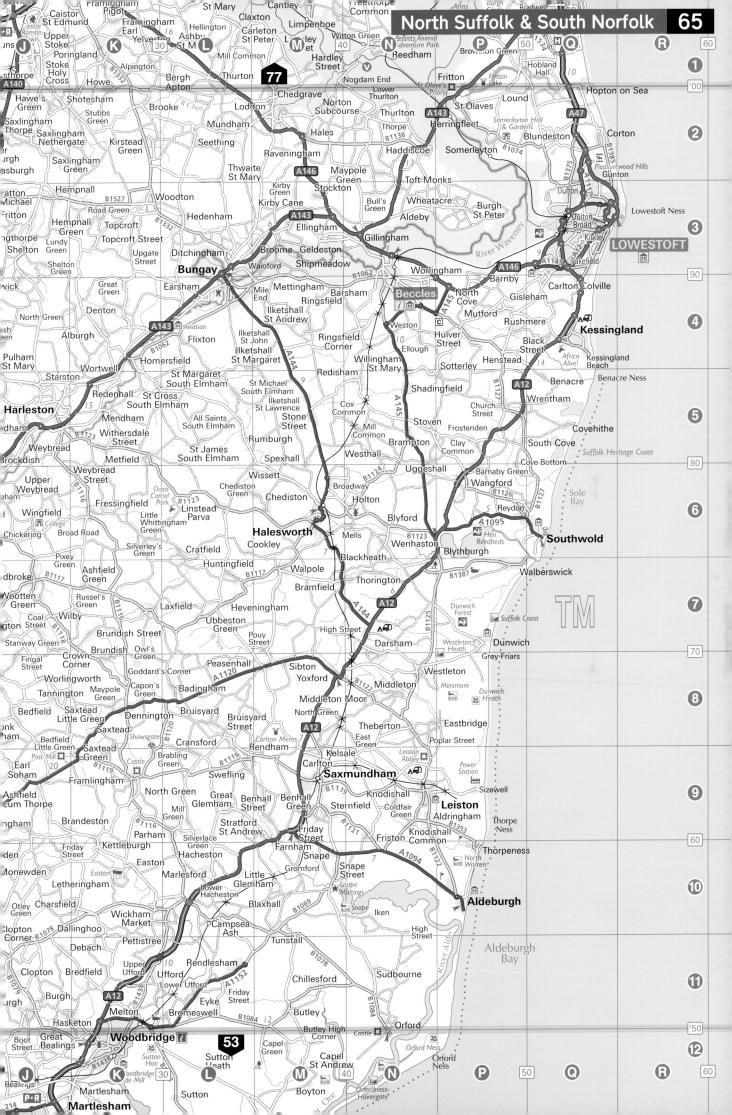

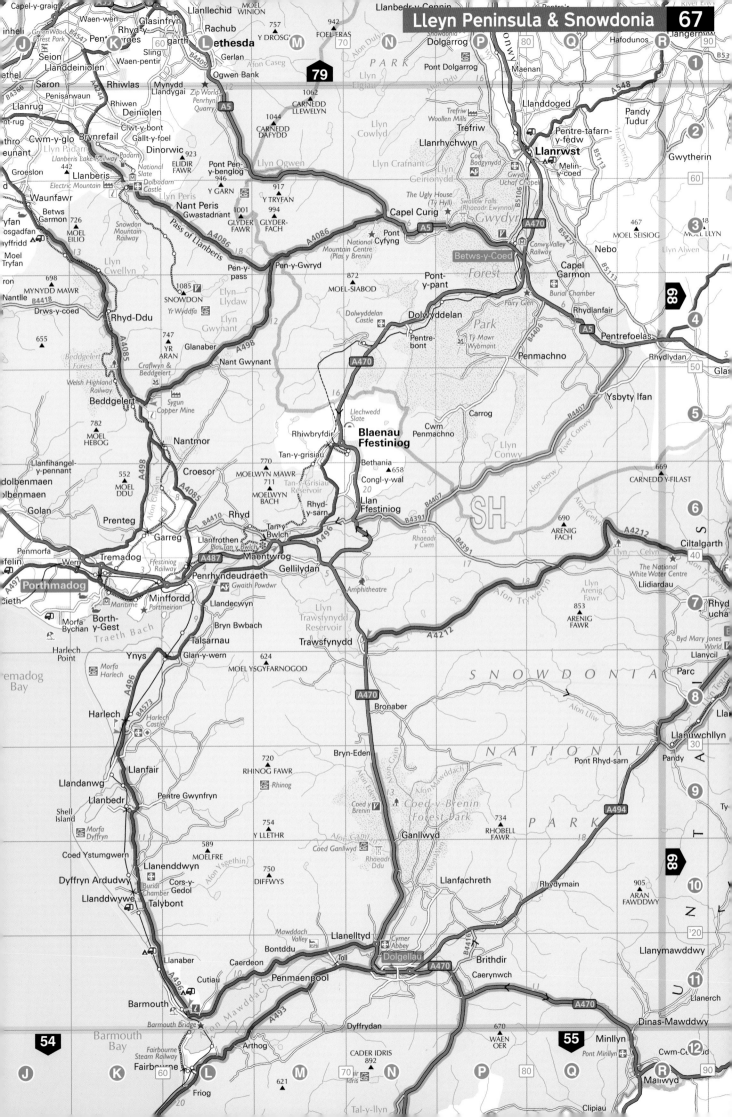

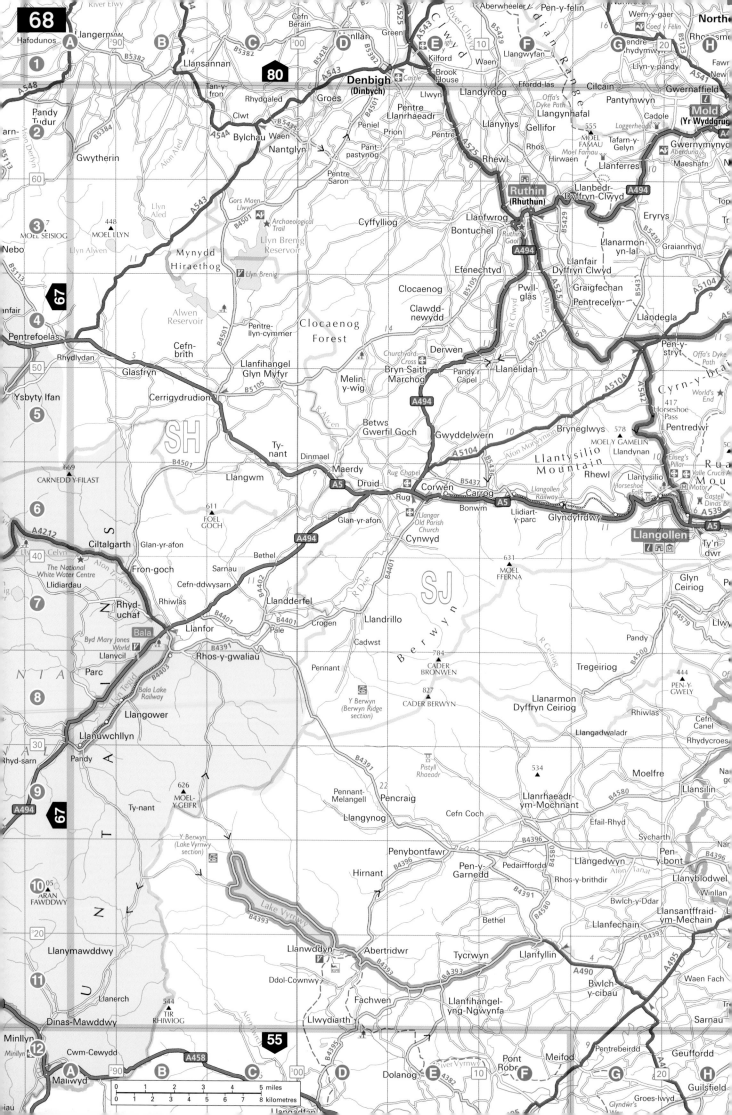

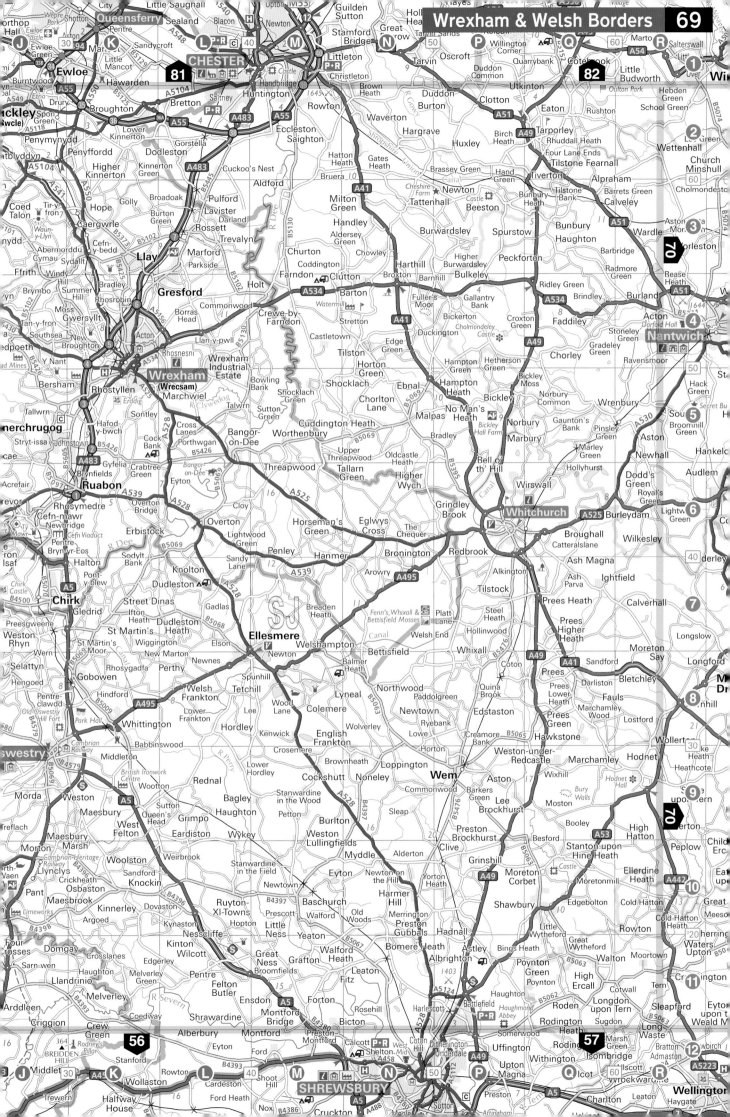

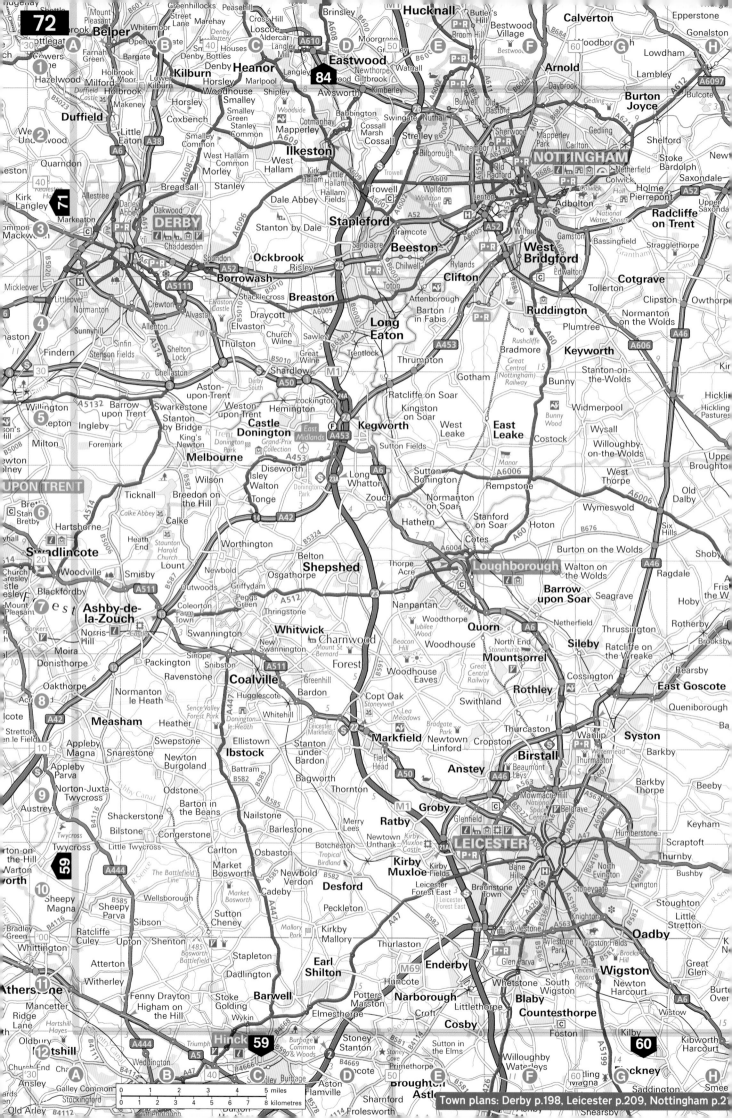

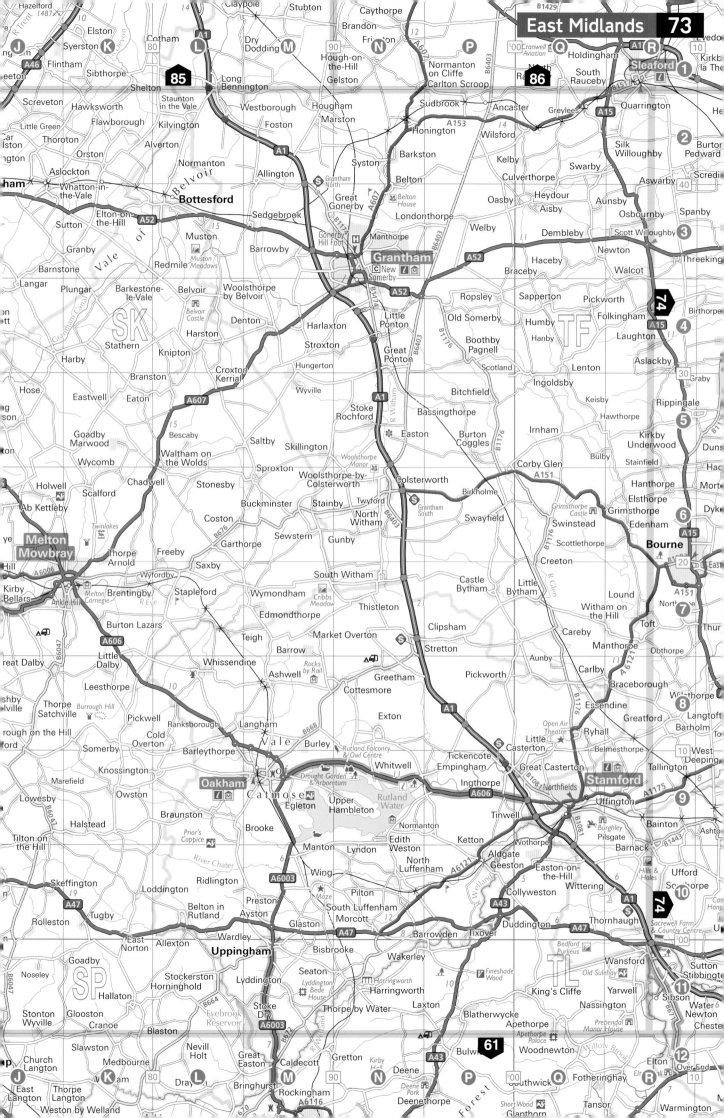

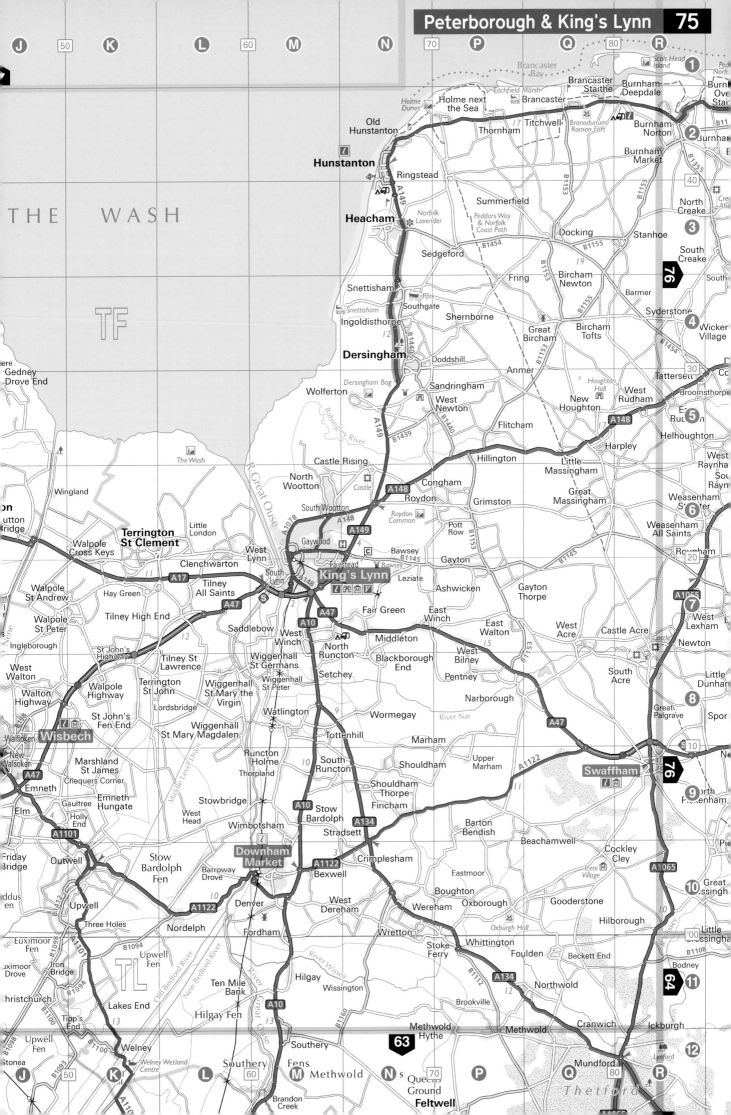

THE WASH

TF

Scolt Head Island

Brancaster Bay
Brancaster Staithe
Brancaster
Burnham Deepdale
Burnham Over Stai
Titchfield Marsh
Holme Dunes
Holme next the Sea
Thornham
Titchwell
Branodunum Roman Fort
Burnham Norton
Burnham
Burnham Market
Old Hunstanton
Summerfield
North Creake
Hunstanton
Ringstead
Norfolk Lavender
Peddars Way & Norfolk Coast Path
Docking
Stanhoe
South Creake
Heacham
Sedgeford
Fring
Bircham Newton
Barmer
Syderstone
Snettisham
Park
Southgate
Shernborne
Great Bircham
Bircham Tofts
Wicker Village
Ingoldisthorpe
Dersingham
Doddshill
Anmer
Houghton Hall
Tattersett
Broomsthorpe
Wolferton
Dersingham Bog
Sandringham
West Newton
Flitcham
New Houghton
West Rudham
Helhoughton
West Raynha
Sou Rayn
Gedney Drove End
The Wash
Castle Rising
Hillington
Little Massingham
Harpley
North Wootton
Castle
Congham
Roydon
Grimston
Great Massingham
Weasenham St's
Wingland
South Wootton
Roydon Common
Pott Row
Weasenham All Saints
Rougham
Walpole Cross Keys
Little London
Gaywood
Bawsey
Gayton
Terrington St Clement
West Lynn
Fairstead
Leziate
Ashwicken
Gayton Thorpe
Clenchwarton
South Lynn
King's Lynn
Walpole St Andrew
Hay Green
Tilney All Saints
Fair Green
East Winch
East Walton
West Acre
Castle Acre
Newton
West Lexham
Tilney High End
Saddlebow
West Winch
Middleton
West Bilney
South Acre
Walpole St Peter
Ingleborough
St John's Highway
North Runcton
Blackborough End
Pentney
Priory
Little Dunhan
West Walton
Tilney St Lawrence
Terrington St John
Wiggenhall St Germans
Setchey
Narborough
Great Palgrave
Walton Highway
Walpole Highway
Lordsbridge
Wiggenhall St Mary the Virgin
Wiggenhall St Peter
Wormegay
Spor
Wisbech
St John's Fen End
Watlington
River Nar
Marshland St James
Chequers Corner
Wiggenhall St Mary Magdalen
Tottenhill
Marham
Upper Marham
Swaffham
New Walsoken
Emneth
Runcton Holme
Shouldham
North Pickenham
Emneth Hungate
Stowbridge
Thorpland
West Head
South Runcton
Shouldham Thorpe
Fincham
Barton Bendish
Beachamwell
Elm
Gaultree
Holly End
Wimbotsham
Stow Bardolph
Stradsett
Cockley Cley
Iceni Village
Friday Bridge
Outwell
Stow Bardolph Fen
Barroway Drove
Bexwell
Crimplesham
Eastmoor
Boughton
Oxborough
Gooderstone
Hilborough
Great essingh
Upwell
Downham Market
Denver
Fordham
West Dereham
Wereham
Oxburgh Hall
Three Holes
Nordelph
Wretton
Whittington
Foulden
Beckett End
Little essingha
Bodney
Euximoor Fen
Iron Bridge
Upwell Fen
Old Bedford River
New Bedford River
River Wissey
Hilgay
Wissington
Stoke Ferry
Northwold
Lakes End
Ten Mile Bank
Hilgay Fen
Brookville
Cranwich
Ickburgh
Tipp's End
Welney
Southery Fens
Methwold Hythe
Methwold
Lynford
Mundford
Stonea
Welney Wetland Centre
Southery
Feltwell
Queens Ground
Brandon Creek
Thetford

Grid references (left to right): J 50, K, L 60, M, N, 70, P, Q, 80, R
Numbers down right: 1, 2, 40, 3, 4, 30, 5, 6, 20, 7, 8, 10, 9, 10, 00, 11, 12

Route markers: 76, 64, 63

Road numbers: A149, A148, A17, A47, A10, A134, A1122, A1065, A1101, A1112, B1153, B1155, B1145, B1439, B1440, B1454, B1355, B1094, B1098, B1100, B1160, B1108

J   K 30   L   M 40   N   P 50   Q   R 60

1
50
2
3
40
4
5
30
6
20
7
8
10
9
10
11
'00
12

Cromer
Overstrand
Sidestrand
Northrepps
Crossdale Street
Trimingham
Southrepps
Gimingham
Mundesley
Stow Mill
Lower Street
Paston
Trunch
Knapton
Bradfield
Old Hall Street
Edingthorpe
Bacton
Walcott
Antingham
Swafield
Pollard Street
North Walsham
Edingthorpe Green
Witton
Ridlington
Happisburgh
Banningham
Spa Common
Ridlington Street
Felmingham
Tungate Norfolk Motorcycle
Meeting House Hill
Crostwight
Happisburgh Common
Whimpwell Green
Eccles on Sea
Hempstead
uttington
Honing
Lessingham
Ingham Corner
Sea Palling
Skeyton Corner
Westwick
Briggate
East Ruston
Ingham
Waxham
rgh next ylsham
Skeyton
Worstead
Calthorpe Street
Swanton Abbott
Sloley
Dilham
Stalham
Stalham Green
Hickling
Horsey Corner
Oxnead Lamas
Scottow
Frankfort
Smallburgh
Low Street
Sutton Fen
Sutton
Hickling Green
Horsey
Buxton
Badersfield Little Hautbois
Fairstead
Pennygate
Barton Turf
Wood Street
Hickling Heath
Hill Common
Horsey Windpump
Stratton Strawless
Sco Ruston
Tunstead
Crowgate Street
Neatishead
Barton Broad
Catfield
Hickling Broad
Martham Broad
St James
Wroxham Barns
Irstead
Catfield Common
Potter Heigham
West Somerton
East Somerton
Horstead
Coltishall
Threehammer Common
Sharp Green
Ludham
Martham
Winterton-on-Sea
Belaugh
Hoveton
RAF Radar
Johnson Street
Bastwick
Cess
Hemsby Hole
Frettenham
Wroxham
BeWILDerwood
Upper Street
Repps
Hemsby
Ormesby Broad
Newport
Newton St Faith
Upper Street
Horning
Thurne
Rollesby
Ormesby St Michael
Scratby
Horsham St Faith
Hillside
Woodbastwick
Bure Marshes
Broads Wildlife Centre
Fleggburgh/ Burgh St Margaret
California
Spixworth
Crostwick
Salhouse
Ranworth
Pilson Green
Clippesby
Ormesby St Margaret
Caister-on-Sea
New Rackheath
Little Plumstead
Ranworth Broad
Fairhaven
Cargate Green
Billockby
Caister Roman Fort
NORWICH
Thorpe End
Great Plumstead
Blofield Heath
Hemblington
South Walsham
Town Green
Upton
Filby
Thrigby
Mautby
West End
West Caister
Thorpe St Andrew
Witton
North Burlingham
Acle
Stokesby
Thrigby Hall
Caister
Runham
Brundall
Postwick
Strumpshaw
Lingwood
Damgate
Stracey Arms Windpump
Runham
Scroby Sands
Kirby Bedon
Surlingham
South Burlingham
Moulton St Mary
Tunstall
Halvergate
THE BROADS
GREAT YARMOUTH
Elizabethan House
Southtown
Trowse Newton
Norfolk Ski Centre
Buckenham
Beighton
Freethorpe
Berney Marshes
Burgh Castle
New Lakenham
Bramerton
Hassingham
Southwood
Freethorpe Common
Wickhampton
Berney Arms Windmill
Burgh Castle
Bradwell
Gorleston-on-Sea
Arminghall
Framingham Pigot
Rockland St Mary
Cantley
Claxton
Limpenhoe
Witton Green
Pettitts Animal Adventure Park
Belton
Caistor Roman Town
Upper Stoke
Framingham Earl Yelverton
Ashby St Mary
Carleton St Peter
Langley Street
Reedham
Browston Green
Hobland Hall
thorpe
Poringland Stoke Holy Cross
Howe
Bergh Apton
Thurton
Hardley Street
Nogdam End
Fritton
Fritton Lake
Hopton on Sea
Hawe's Green
Shotesham
Brooke
Loddon
Chedgrave
Norton Subcourse
Lower Thurlton
St Olave's Priory
St Olaves
Lound
Corton
Saxlingham Nethergate
Stubbs Green
Mundham
Thurlton
Herringfle
Somerleyton Hall & Ga
Blundesto
Saxlingham Green
Kirstead Green
Seething
Hales
Npe
Haddiscoe
Raveningham
Maypole

J   K 30   L   M 40   N   P 50   Q   R 60

Holyhead Harbour

Marina
BEACH ROAD
Maritime
Porth-y-Felin
PORTH-Y-FELIN
PRINCE OF WALES ROAD
WALTHEW AVE
NEW HARBOUR ROAD
PRICE STREET
Salt Island
P+R Long stay
Hertz Car Rental
FERRY TERMINAL
SOUTH STACK ROAD
VICTORIA A5154
TERMINAL BUILDING
P Short stay
HOLYHEAD
Stryd
HOLYHEAD STATION
A5
LLANFAWR ROAD
Môrawelon
H
PLAS ROAD
LONDON ROAD
KINGSLAND ROAD
A55
A5
Kingsland
PORTHDAFARCH
KINGSLAND ROAD
B4545
A55
CITTIR ROAD
A5153
A5
0   500 m
BANGOR
LBLH

North Anglesey Heritage Coast
The Skerries
Wylfa Head
Cemaes Bay
Porth Wen
Bull Bay
Amlwch
Po
Gemlyn Bay
Llanbadrig
Bull Bay
Copper Kingdom
Llaneil
Hen Borth
Cemaes
A5025
Burwen
CARMEL HEAD
Tregele
Pentrefelin
Pengort
Swtan Folk
Rhosbeirio
Penysarn
Llanfairynghornwy
Mynydd Mechell
Llanfechell
Bodewryd
Nebo
Gadfa
A5025
Du
Church Bay
Llanrhyddlad
Llanflewyn
Rhosgoch
Rhosybol
City Dulas
Llanfaethlu
Llanbabo
Carreglefn
Capel Parc
Brynrefail
Holyhead Bay
Llyn Alaw
B5111
Din
Llandyfrydog
Porth Tywynmawr
Llanddeusant
Llynon Mill
Elim
Gwredog
Dublin
Llanfwrog
Llantrisant
Maenaddwy
North Stack
Breakwater
Holyhead Maritime
Stryd-y-Facsen
Llanerchymedd
Hebron Bachau
Dublin (Mar-Oct)
Gogarth Bay
Llaingoch
Holyhead Mountain
Hut Circles
Holyhead (Caergybi)
Pen-llyn
Llanfigael
Llyn Llywenan
B5112
Capel Coch
Brynte
Cors Erddreiniog
South Stack
Ellins Tower
Penrhos Feilw
Llanfachraeth
Penrhos
Llanynghenedl
Presaddfed
B5109
Llechcynfarwy
A N G L E S E Y
Tregaian
Holyhead Mountain Heritage Coast
Kingsland
A5
Trefignath
B4545
Valley
A5025
Bodedern
Trefor
Llanfaes
B5112
Llangwyllog
B5110
Lle
Penrhyn Mawr
A55
Caergeiliog
Bryngwran
Llynfaes
Bodffordd
Cefni Reservoir
Oriel Ynys-Môn
Rhosmeir
Talwrn
Rhosmei
Trearddur Bay
Llanfihangel yn Nhowyn
Gwalchmai
A5
HOLY ISLAND
Four Mile Bridge
Llechylched
Heneglwys
Anglesey
Rhostrehwfa
Llang
Llanfair-yn-Neubwll
Capel Gwyn
A4080
A55
A5114
Valley
Dothan
Rhoscolyn
Plas Cymyran
Ty Newydd
Cerrigceinwen
Llangristiolus
Cein
Rhoscolyn Head
Pencarnisiog
Pentre Berw
Cymyran Bay
Llanfaelog
Bryn Du
Capel Mawr
B4419
Gaerwen
Rhosneigr
A4080
Ty Croes
Bethel
Trefdraeth
Llanddaniel
Barclodiad y Gawres
Henblas
B4422
Llangaffo
Bodowyr Burial Chamber
Porth Trecastell
Aberffraw
Llangadwaladr
Hermon
Malltraeth
A4080
B4421
Caer
Brynsiency
Anglesey Circuit
Bodorgan
Llangaffo
Castell Bryn Gwyn
Dwyran
Anglese Sea Zo
Aberffraw Bay
Newborough
Pen-lôn
Foel Farm Park
M
Aberffraw Bay Heritage Coast
SH
Malltraeth Bay
Newborough W
Caernarfo
Llanddwyn Island
Llanddwyn Bay
Caernarfo Castle
Welsh Highlan
Abermenai
Aberffraw-Be

66

0   1   2   3   4   5 miles
0 1 2 3 4 5 6 7 8 kilometres

Llandudno

0   200 m

Great Orme Tramway
TABOR HILL
Great Orme
Great Orme Station
PLAS-COCH ROAD
Llandudno Pier
HILL TERRACE
PARADE
The Grand Hotel
Victoria
CHURCH WALKS
The Old Bank Gallery
OLD ROAD
TY-COCH ROAD
North Shore Beach
LLEWELYN AVENUE
War Memorial
Llandudno Bay
WHISTON PASSAGE
Travelodge
GLODDAETH STREET
SOUTH PARADE
MOSTYN STREET
TY-YN ROAD
NORTH PARADE
RECTOR LANE
CLIFTON ROAD
A546
DEGANWY
A546
New Street
Town Hall
MARKET STREET
GEORGE STREET
A546
St John's
SOMERSET STREET
The Promenade
Our Lady Star of the Sea
Victoria
CAROLINE ROAD
TRINITY SQUARE
Holy Trinity
BODAFON STREET
CONWEY STREET
THE PARADE
Medical Centre
ADELPHI
A546
CLAREMONT ROAD
Mostyn Gallery
MOSTYN BROADWAY
CLYCH TUDUR
Swimming Pool
B5115
Venue Cymru
St Paul's
LLANDUDNO STATION
Police Station
GARAGE STREET
CONWAY ROAD
A470
Parc Llandudno Retail Park
MOSTYN
MOSTYN AVE
Magistrates' Court
Fire & Ambulance Station
Mostyn Champneys Retail Park
CHARLOTTE ROAD
CRESCENT
CAE CID
CLYD
Ysgol Tudno
AVENUE
NORMAN ROAD
HOWARD ROAD
CLARENCE
CLARENCE DRIVE
Ysgol Craig Y Don
TRINITY
KING'S AVENUE
Superstore
CWM ROAD
BUILDER STREET WEST
FFORDD PENRHYN
B5115
CONWAY ROAD
Ysgol Ffordd Dyffryn
COUNCIL STREET
Llandudno FC
Ysgol Morfa Rhianedd
FFORDD DEWI
FFORDD TUDNO
KINGSWAY
Coach
Ysgol John Bright
A55 **BETWS-Y-COED**
LBLH
A55 A470

Map grid (outer)

SH

Seawatch Centre
Moelfre
nallgo
arian-glas
Benllech
Red Wharf Bay
Goch
Red Wharf Bay
Pentraeth
Llanddona
Glan-yr-afon
Llangoed
Puffin Island
Penmon Priory
Caim
Toll Penmon
Black Point
Conwy Bay
GREAT ORME'S HEAD
Great Orme Heritage Coast
Great Orme Tramway
Toll
Little Ormes Head
Penrhyn Bay
Llandudno
Deganwy
Llanrhos
Penrhynside
Llandrillo-yn-Rhos
Rhôs-on-Sea
Colwyn Bay (Bae Colwyn)
landd
Hafoty Medieval House
Gaol
Beaumaris Castle
B5109
Llandegfan
Llansadwrn
Beaumaris
Courthouse
Dwygyfylchi
Conwy
Conwy Castle
Capelulo
Penmaen
Tywyn
Llandudno Junction
Pydew
Esgyryn
Mochdre
Old Colwyn
Llansanffraid Glan Conwy
Llanelian-yn-Rhos
Bryn-y-Maen
Llysfaen
Rh
Menai Bridge (Porthaethwy)
Bangor
Penrhyn Castle
Llandygai
Penmaenmawr
Llanfairfechan
Nant-y-pandy
Henryd
A470
Dolwen
Betw
n-Rho
Pili Palas
Britannia Bridge
Penrhos garnedd
Anglesey Column
Glasinfryn
Spinnies Abergowen
Gorddinog
Abergwyngregyn
SNOWDONIA
TAL-Y-FAN
610
Rowen
Ty'n-y-Groes
Tal-y-Cafn
Graig
Eglwysbach
Bodnant
Trofarth
Dawn
owllgwyngyll
Capel-y-graig
Waen-wen
Tal-y-bont
Llandygai
Llanllechid
Rachub
Tregarth
Coedydd Aber
Afon Anafon
Afon Aber-Falls
Castell
Llanbedr-y-Cennin
Tal-y-Bont
Cerhun
Adventure Parc Snowdonia
Graig
Pentre'r Felin
River Elwy
Llang
yw
Ta
nheli
GreenWood Forest Park
Rhyd-y-groes
Pentir
MOEL WINION
580
757 Y DROSGL
942 FOEL-FRAS
NATIONAL
Dolgarrog
Vale of Conwy
B5113
Hafodunos
Llang
Bethesda
Gerlan
Ogwen Bank
1062
CARNEDD LLEWELYN
Afon Dulyn
PARK
Pont Dolgarrog
Maenan
Llanddoged
B53
Seion
Llanddeiniolen
Sling
Waen-pentir
Zip World Penrhyn Quarry
923
A5
1044
CARNEDD DAFYDD
70
67
Llyn Cowlyd
Llyn Eigiau
Trefriw Woollen Mills
Tref
Pandy Tudur
Llanrug
Penisarwaun
Rhiwlas
Rhiwen Deiniolen
ELIDIR
442
Cwm-y-glo
Brynrefail
Gallt-y-foel
Dinorwic
Pont Pen
Llyn Ogwen
Llyn Crafnant
Llanrhychwyn
Pen-tafarn-y-fedw
Llanrwst
Gwytherin
Llanberis Lake Railway
B5538
Afon Derfyn
A548

Grid reference letters/numbers (margins)

J K 60 L M 70 N P 80 Q R 90

1 2 10 3 4 '00 5 6 90 7 8 9 10 11 12

J K 60 L M 70 N 80 Q R 90

A55
A5025
B5109
A545
A4087
A5
A4244
A4086
A5025
B4409
A470
A547
A548
B5383
B5113
B5106
B5538

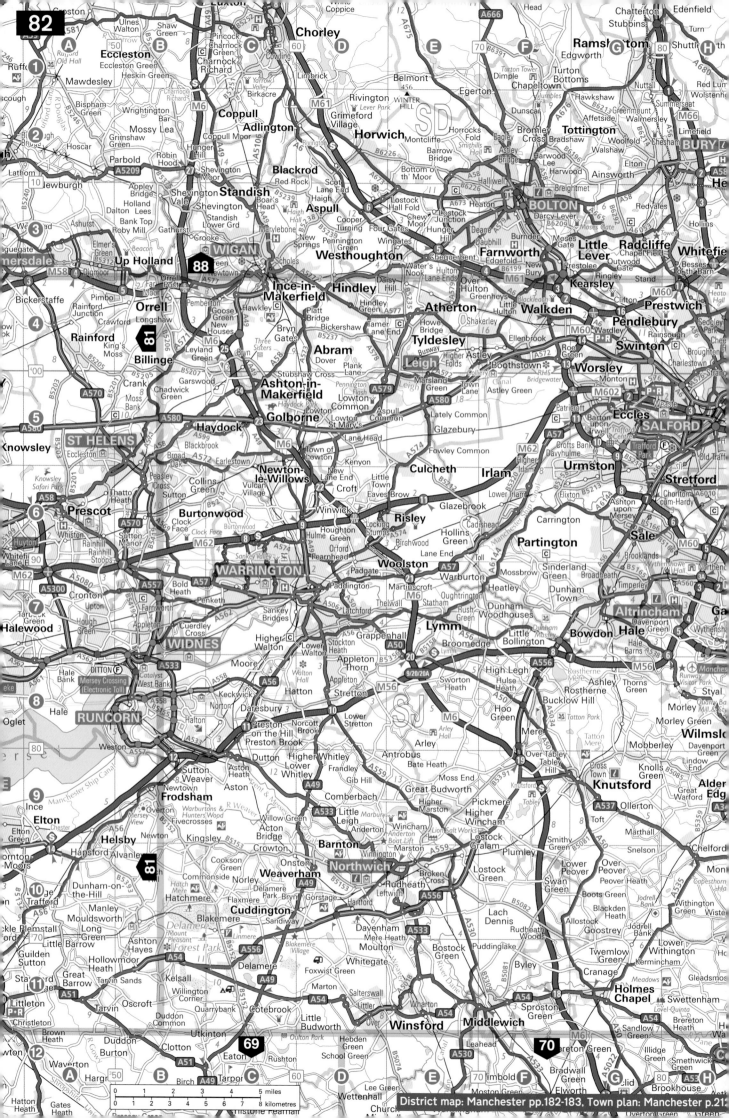

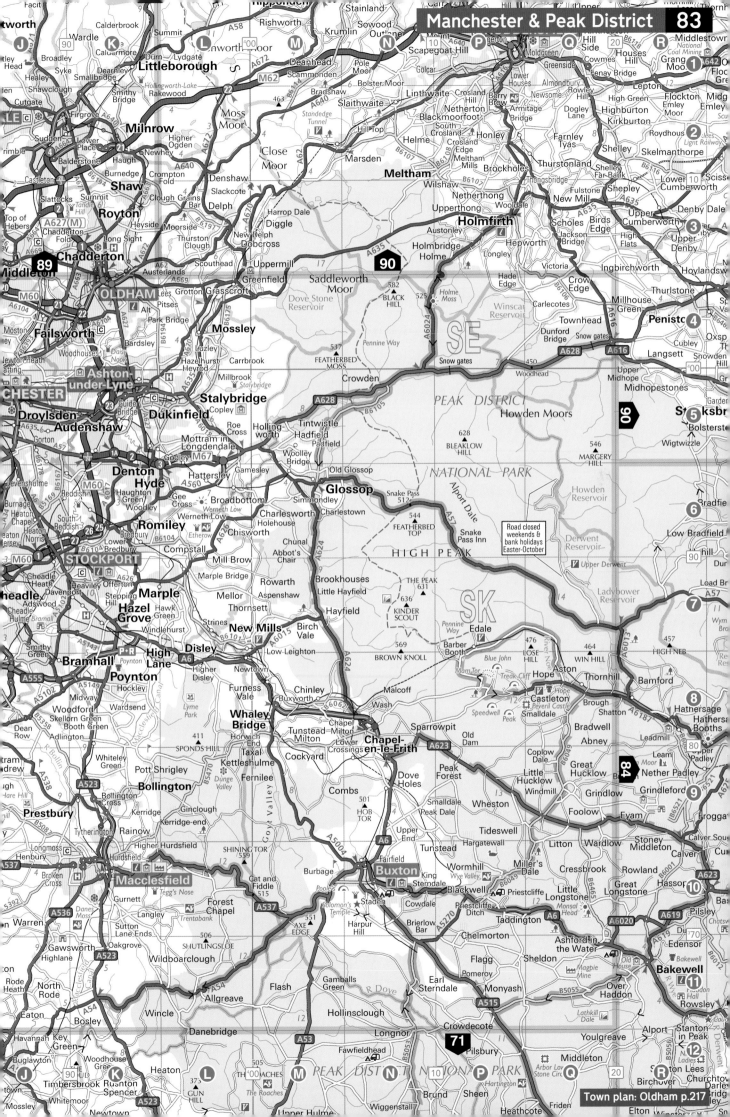

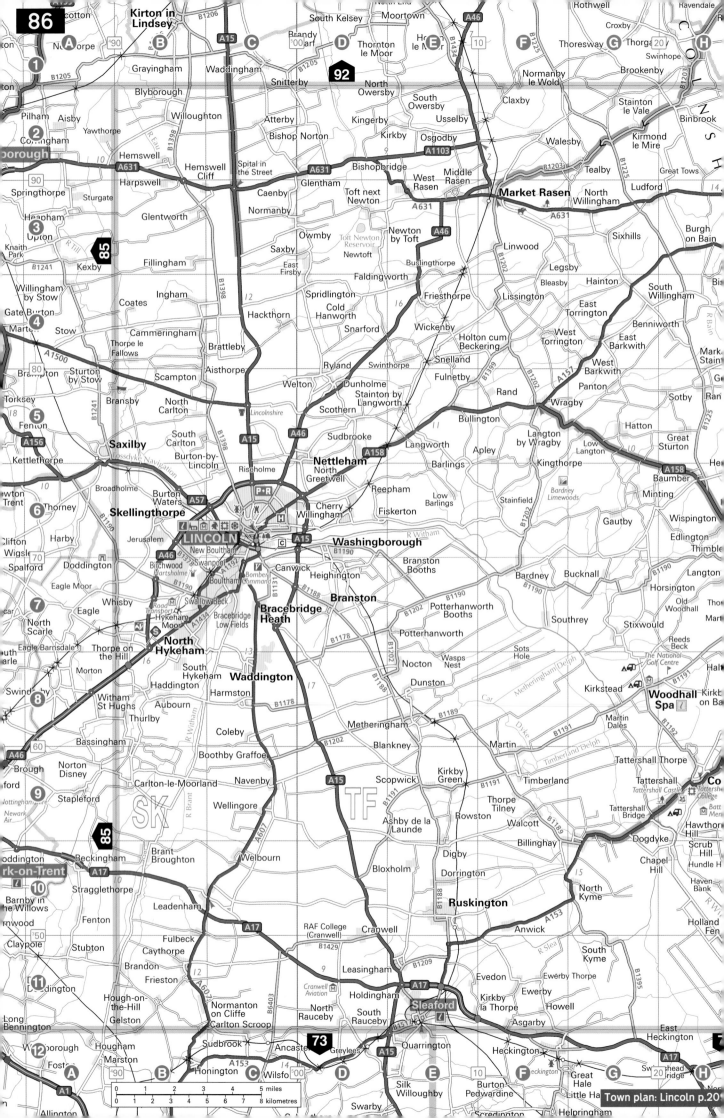

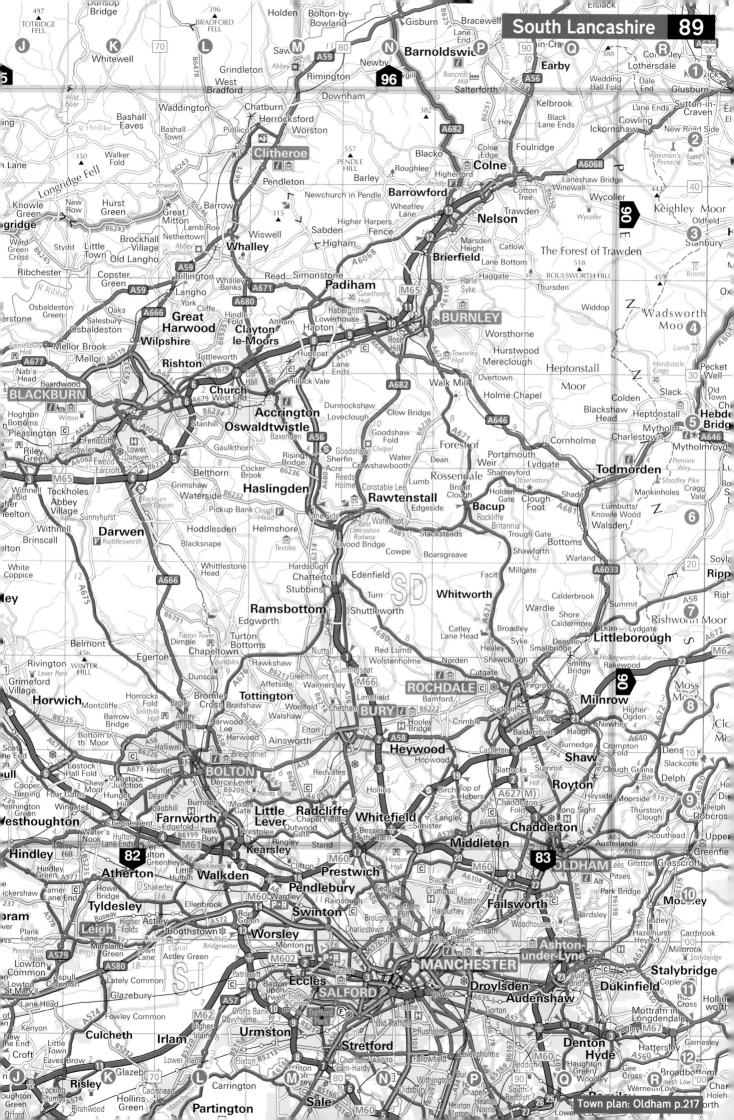

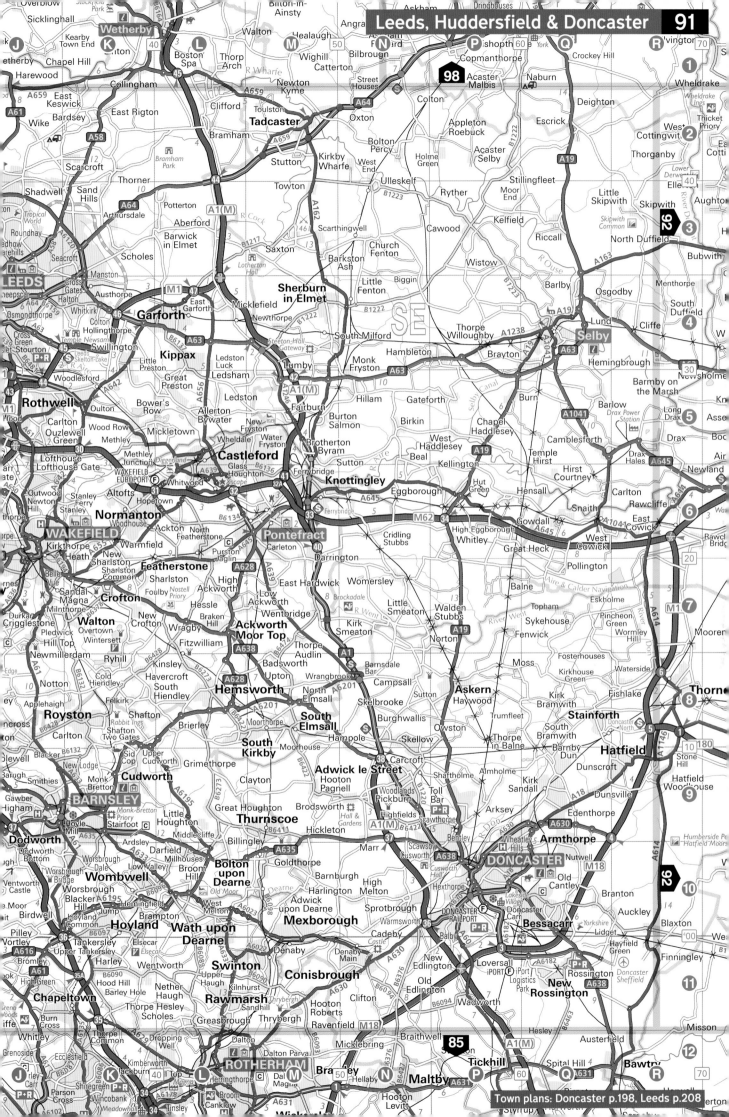

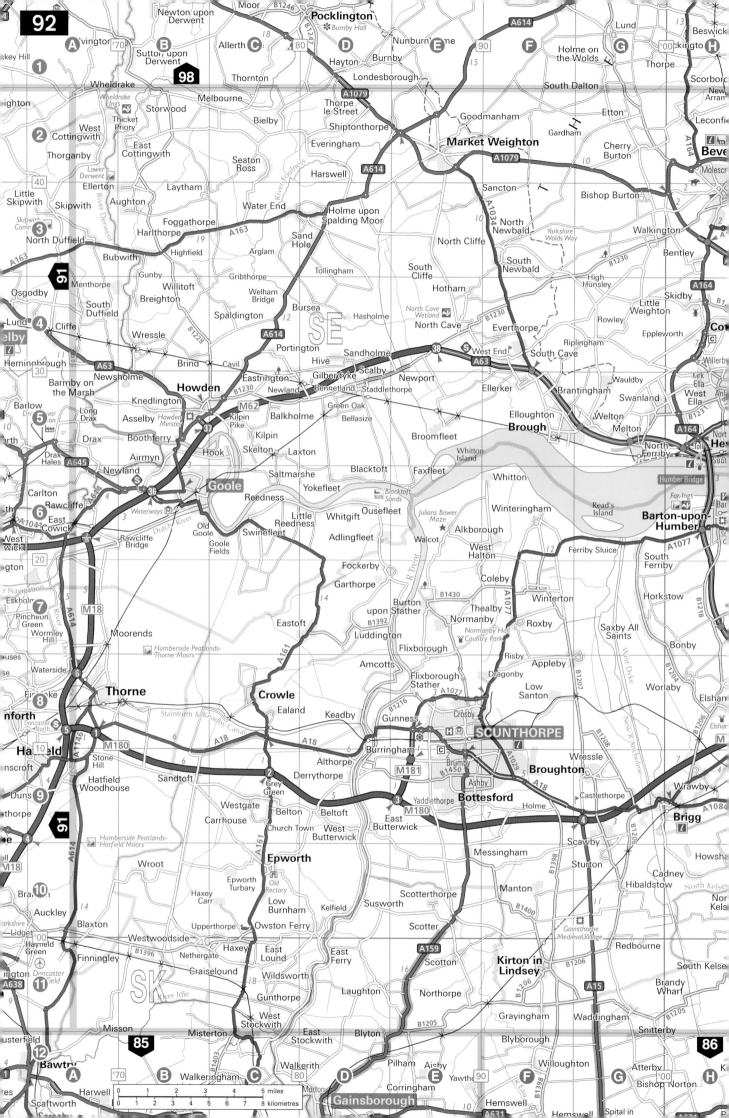

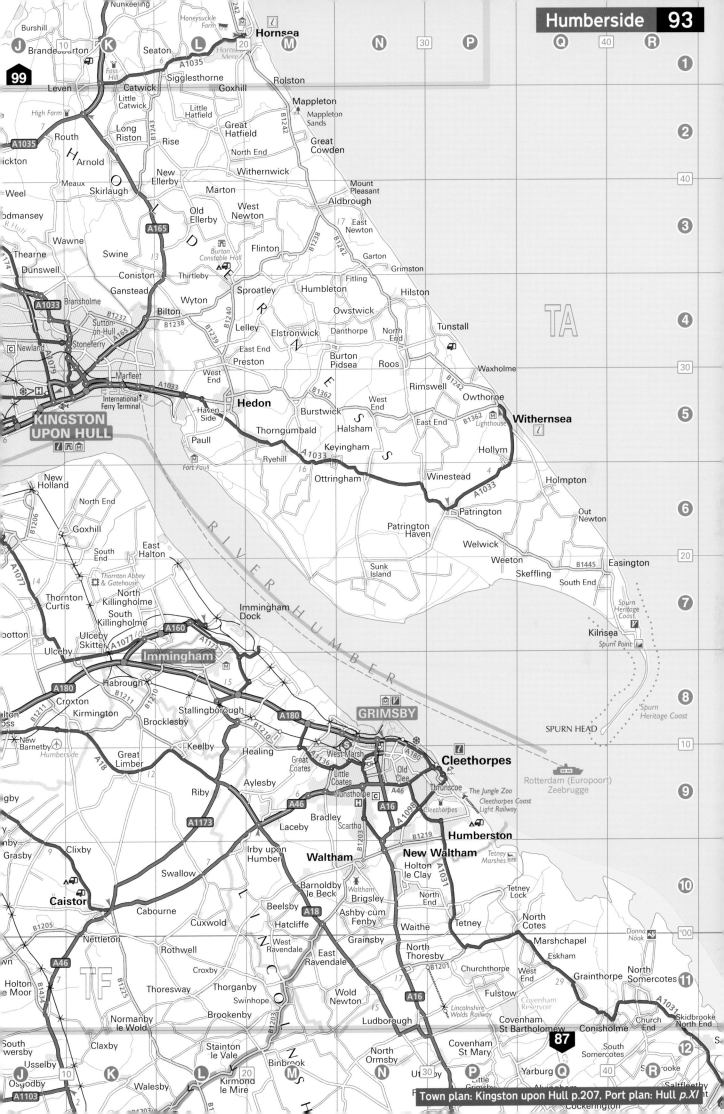

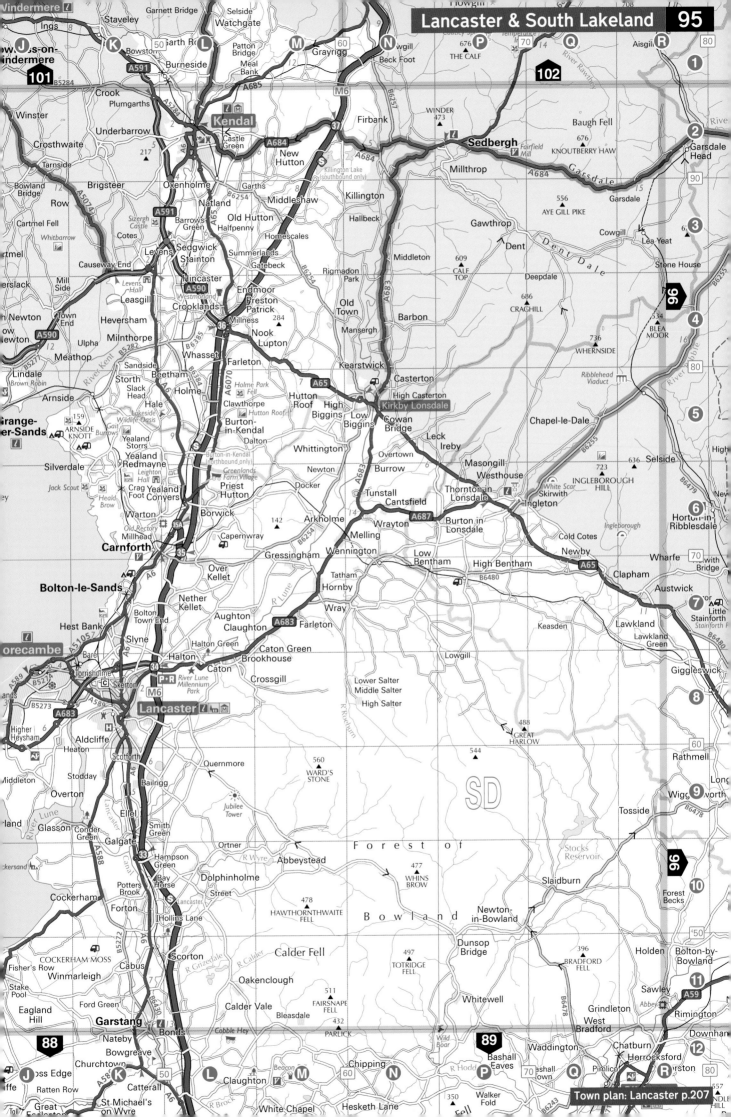

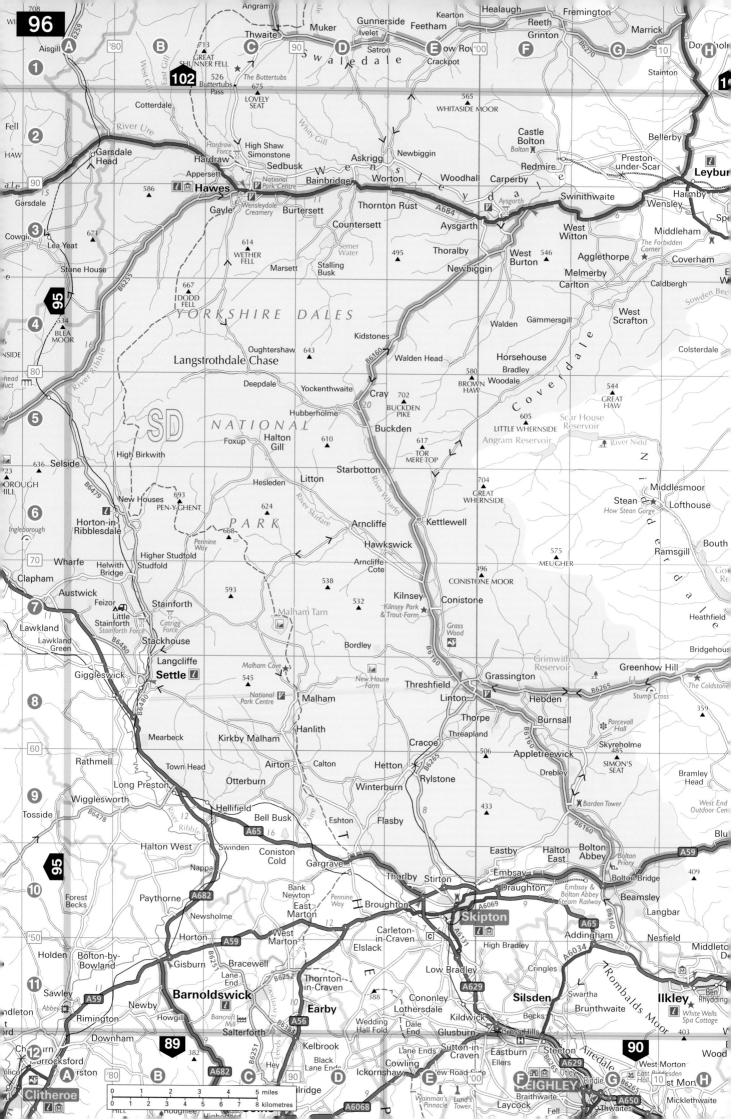

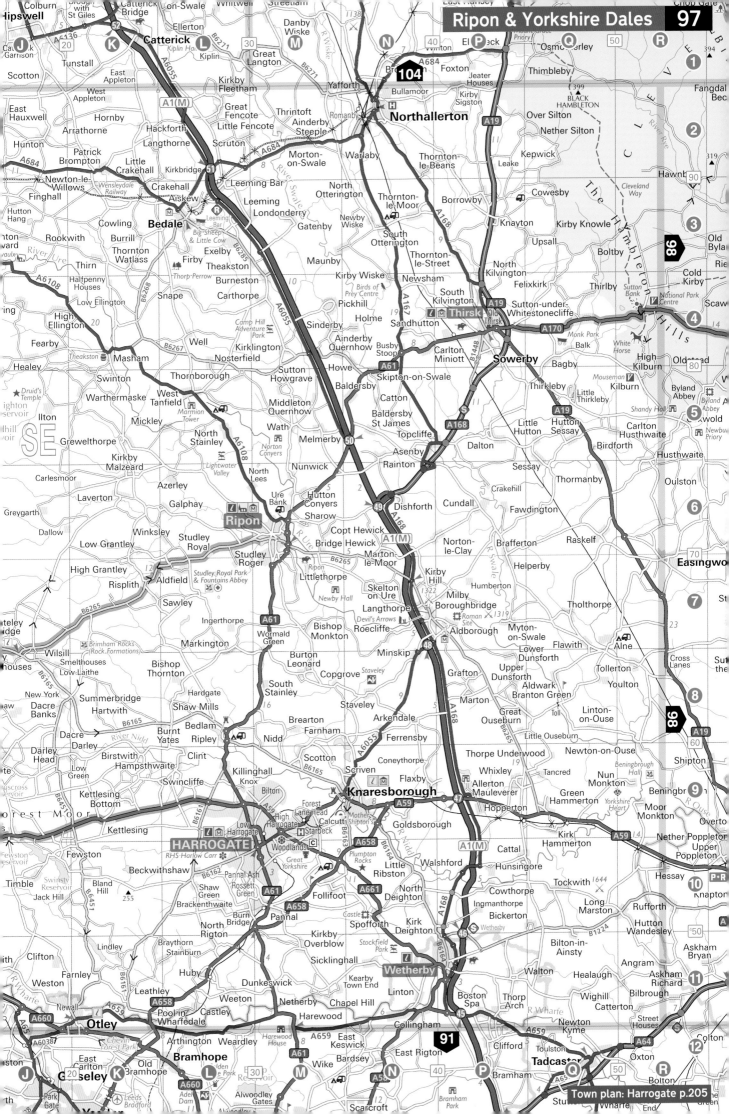

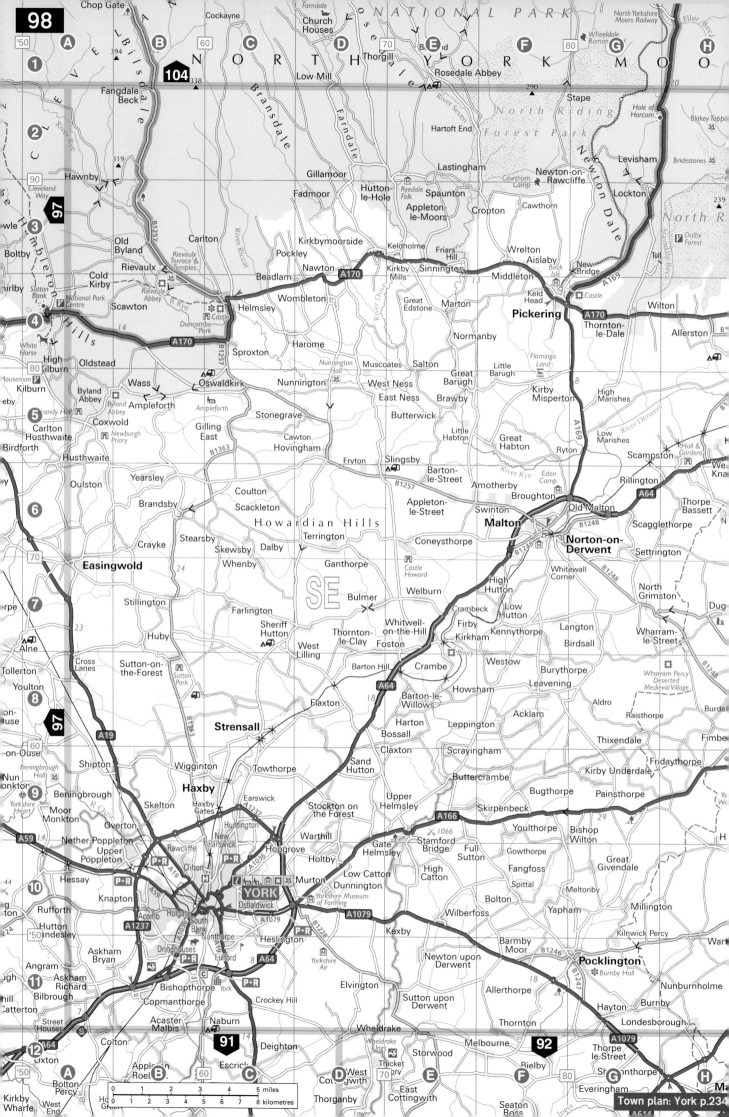

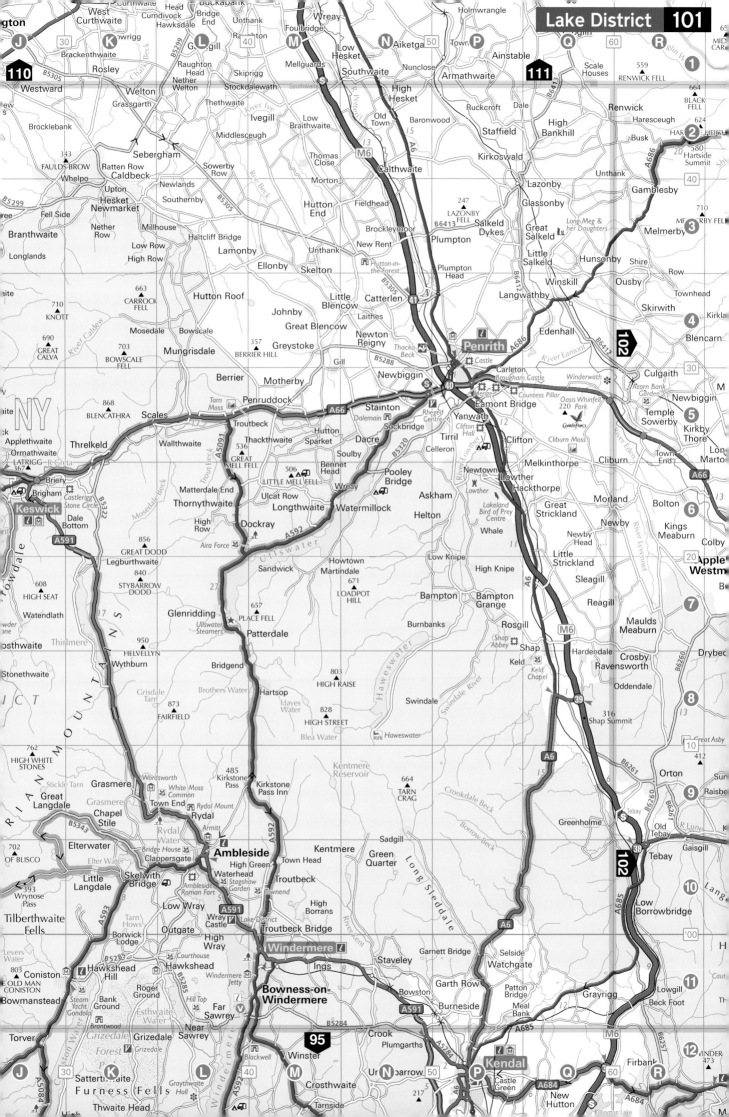

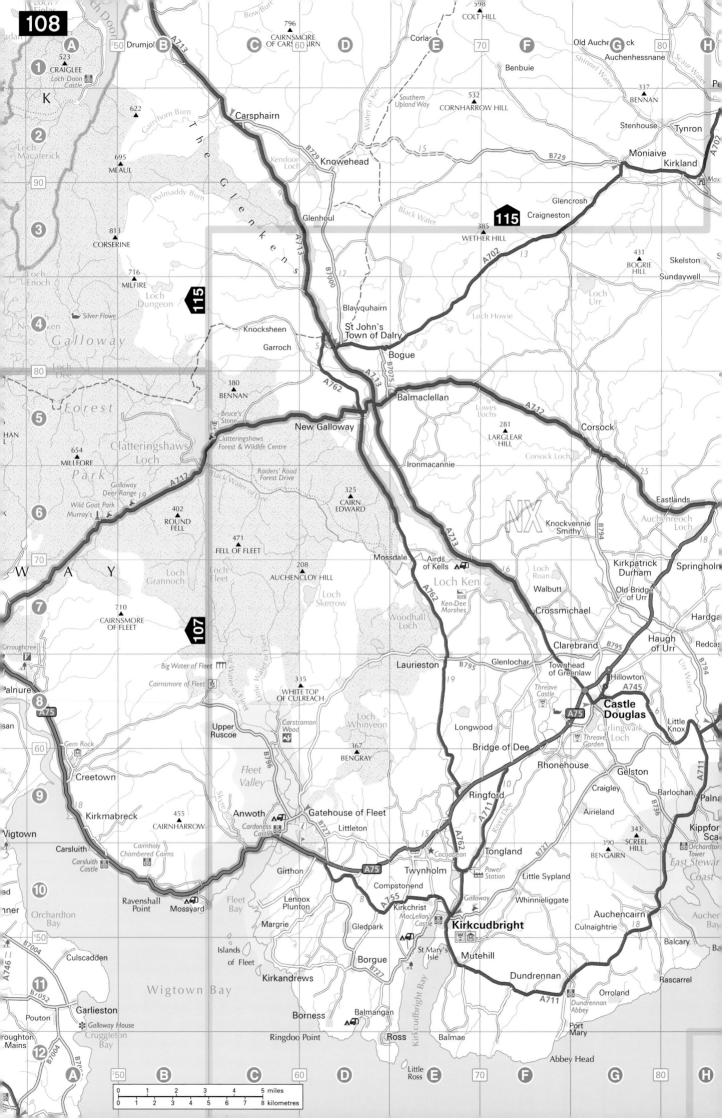

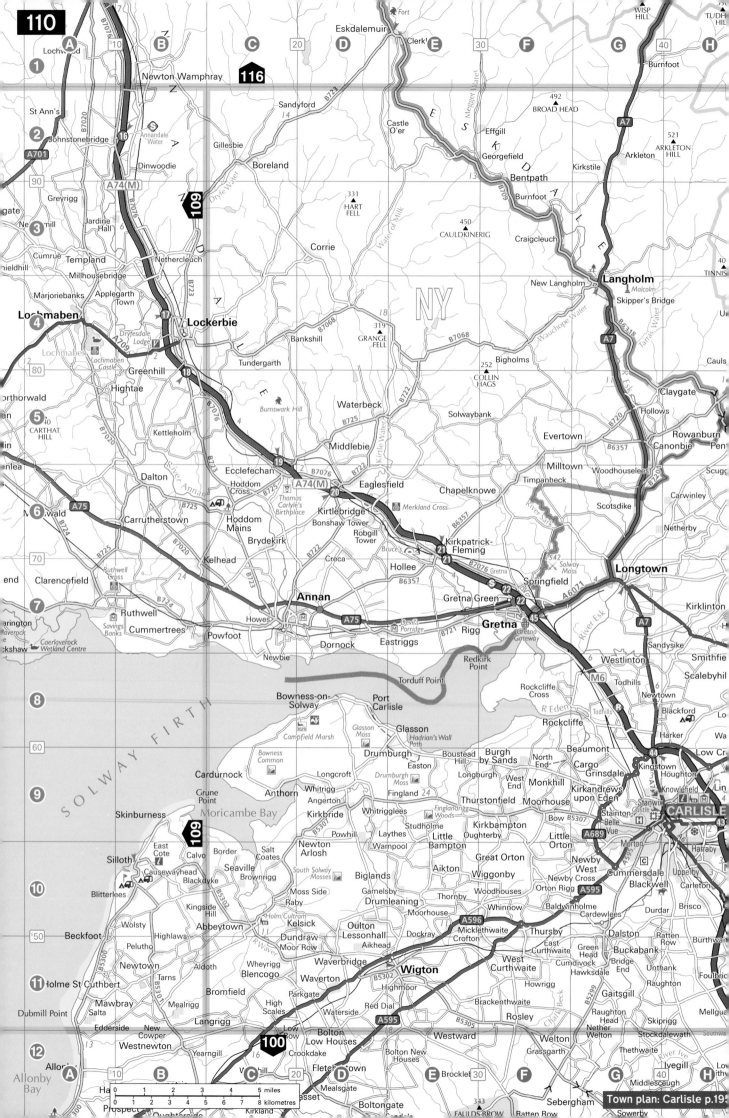

J K L M N P Q R

PEEL FELL
433
SAUGHTREE FELL
Myredykes
Kielderhead
HINDHC LAW
Pennine Way
Camp
Horsley
DE
1

50
Hermitage Castle
Hermitage
Riccarton
60
118
70
Observatory
513
MONKSIDE
80
90
Troughen
2

Newlands
403
LOCH KNOWE
Kielder
Toll
Kielder Castle
397
EARLS SEAT
Highgreen Manor
B6320
3

Steele Road
Skyspace
Black Middens
Bastle House
307
WHITE HILL
Gatehouse
112

Castleton
413
WILSON'S PIKE
Kielder Water
Waterside
Lewis Burn
Falstone
Greenhaugh
4

Newcastleton
513
GLENDHU HILL
Kielder Water
Stannersburn
Tower Knowe
Lanehead
Charlton
Belling
Hott
Dally (ruin)
Hesleyside
Red

275
BLINKBONNY HEIGHT
Kershopefoot
Baileyhead
519
SIGHIY CRAG
492
BLACK KNOWE
395
BOLTS LAW
NORTHUMBERLAND
80
5

Blackpool Gate
Sleetbeck
Oakshaw Ford
Roadhead
Chirdon Burn
WARK FOREST
Wark
Stonehaugh
Park B
Simonb

Haggbeck
Churnsike Lodge
325
ROUND TOP
313
SPY RIGG
Warks Burn
6

Lyneholmford
355
BARRON'S PIKE
Bewcastle
Black Fell
Pennine Way
Greenlee Lough
Broomlee Lough
Hadrian's Path
70
8

Stapleton
265
GREEN RIGG
Crag Lough
Grindon Hill
7
ewbro

Boltonfellend
River Irthing
Walltown Crags
Hadrian's Wall
Cawfields
Housesteads Fort
Vindolanda (Chesterholm)
Once Brewed
The Sill
B6318

Hethersgill
Nickies Hill
Triermain
Gilsland
Roman Army
Birkshaw
Westend Town
Chesterwood
Haydon Bridge

Walton
Banks
Birdoswald Fort
Pike Hill
Upper Denton
Milecastle
Greenhead
Haltwhistle
Henshaw
Westwood
Thorngrafton
8

Newtown
Lanercost
East-Turret
A69
9
Melkridge
Redburn
13
Bardon Mill
Elring
Langley
60
B6305

Brampton
Burtholme
Low Row
255
DENTON FELL
Pennine Way
Plenmeller
Beltingham
Ridley
Allen Banks & Staward Gorge
Deanraw
A686
Casue
B6304

Irthington
Milton
Hallbankgate
Park
Rowfoot
Fellhouse Fell
Whitfield
Catton
9

Low Gettbridge
Kirkhouse
Tindale
A689
Midgeholme
Coanwood
Wolf Hills
Stonehouse
Whitfield Hall
Thornley Gate
Allendale

Farlam
Talkin Tarn
Geltsdale
Halton Lea Gate
Lambley
Eals
Ninebanks
10

Hayton
Talkin
Forest Head
621
COLD FELL
522
GLENDUE FELL
19
Knarsdale
A686
17

How Mill
Fenton
Faugh
Castle Carrock
NY
Slaggyford
11

Cumwhitton
483
CUMREW FELL
521
GELTSDALE MIDDLE
584
THREE PIKES
Kirkhaugh
Ayle
Keirsleywell Row
572
HARTLEY MOOR
Carr Shield
50

Cumrew
Newbiggin
657
MIDDLE CARRICK
Croglin Water
The Hub
Blagill
12

Croglin
559
RENWICK FELL
Alston
102
Nenthall
Nenthead
A689
20

Aiketgate
Towngate
Ainstable
Scale Houses
664
BLACK FELL
624
Gilderdale Forest
Leadgate
Raise
Kill
80
Killhope Mining
Lanehead

High Hesket
Armathwaite
Renwick
Haresough
HARTSIDE HEIGHT
580
Hartside Summit
Alston Moor
Garrigill
R

J K L M N P Q R

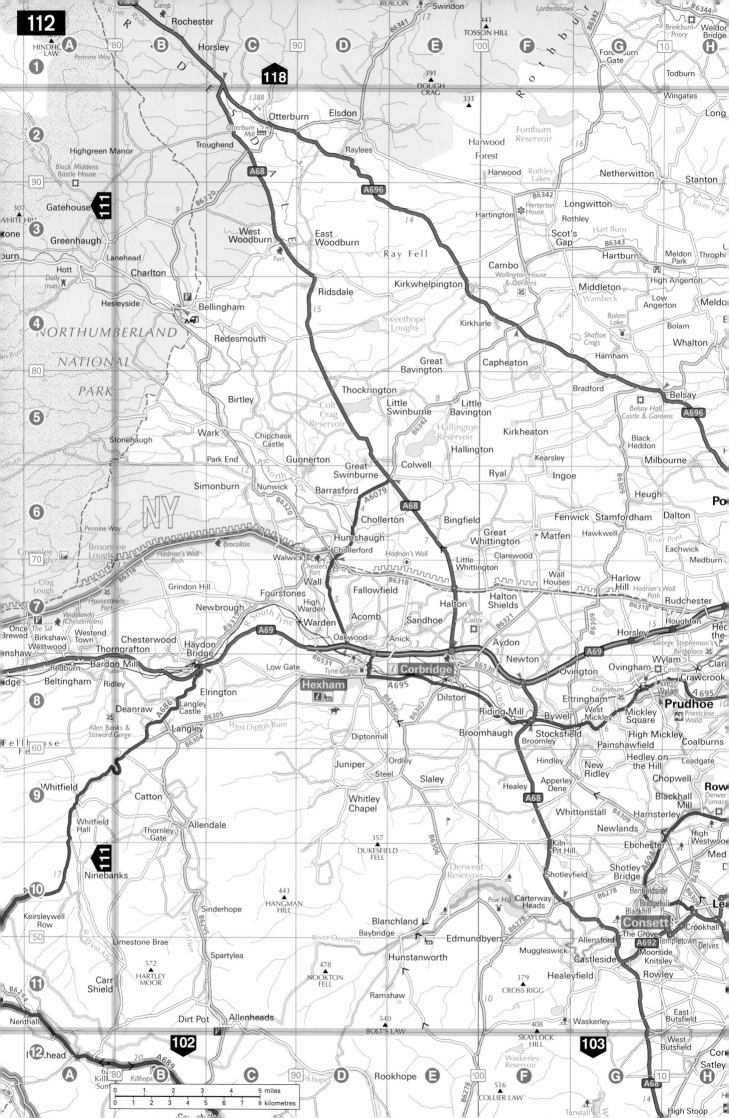

Port of Tyne

0   500 m

NZ

Amsterdam (IJmuiden)

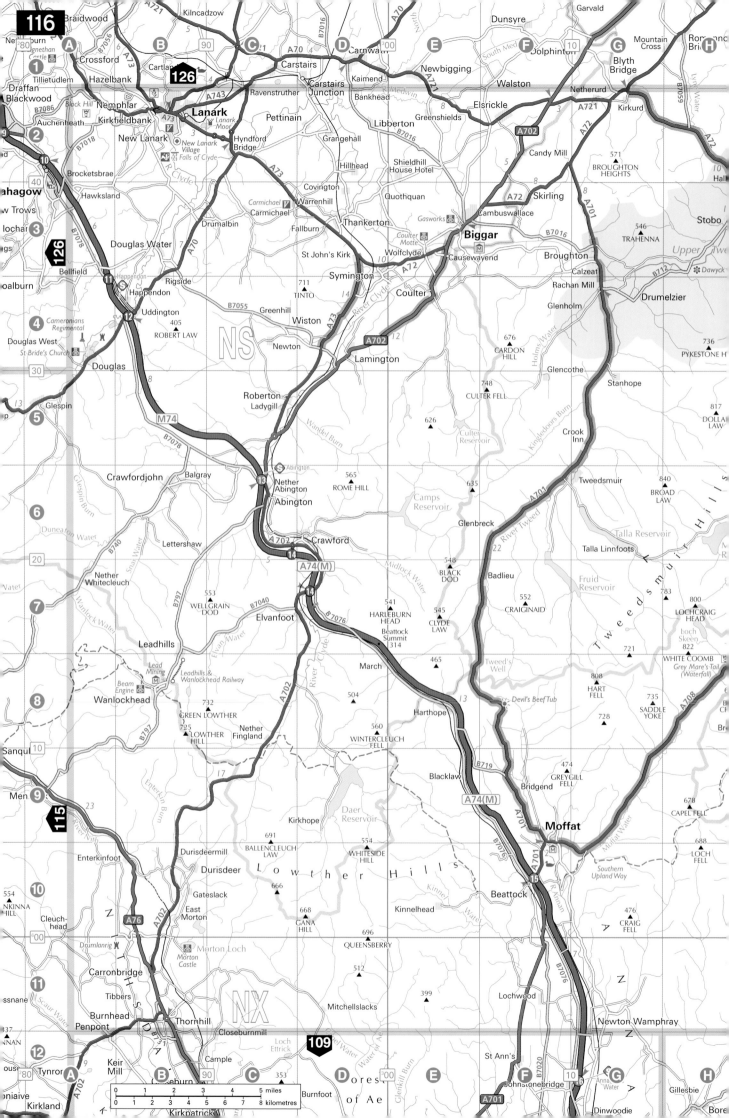

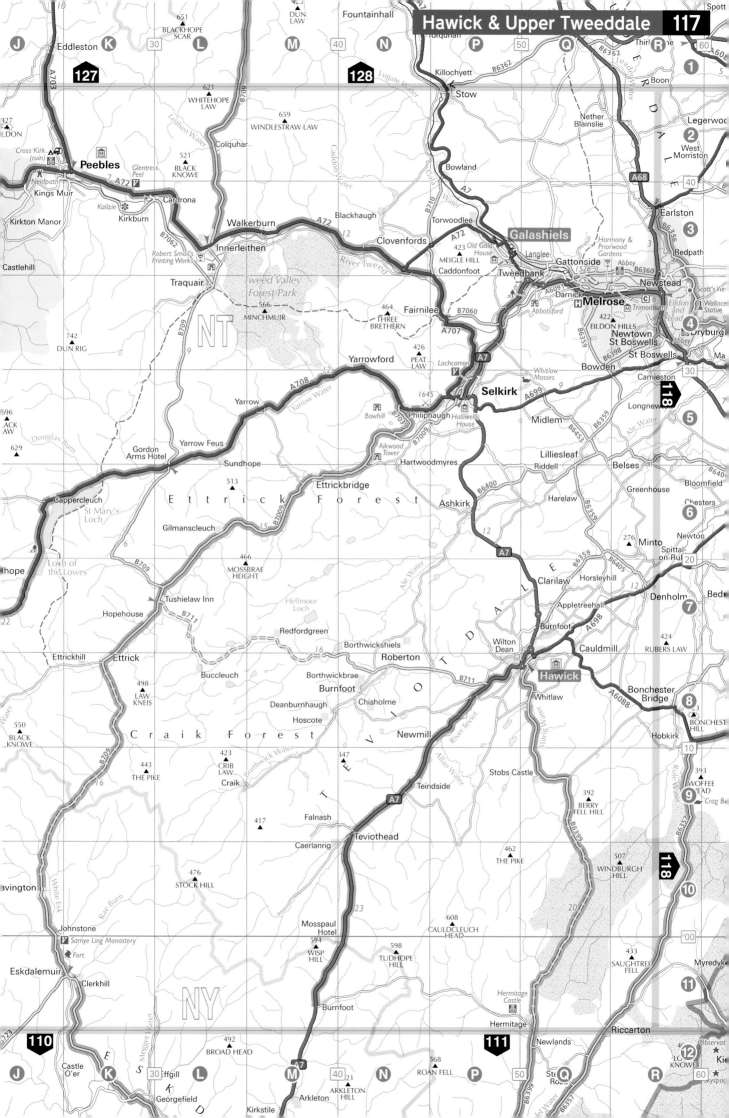

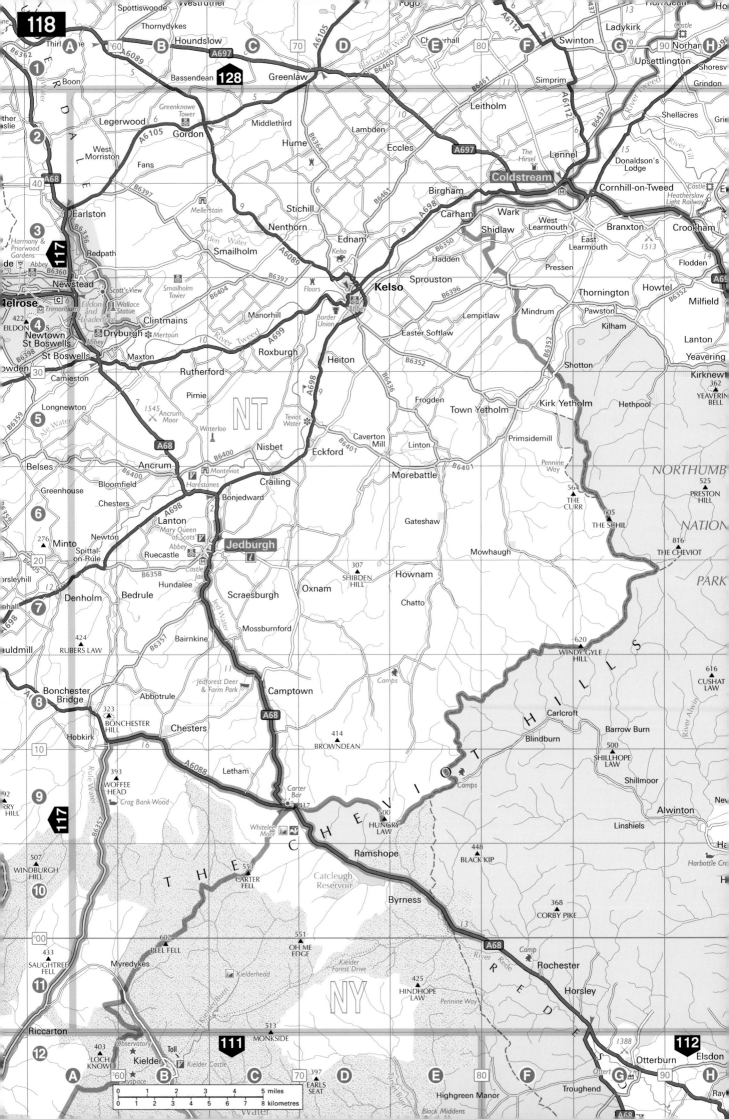

Sound of Bute

St Blane's Church

Fairlie Roads

J

K

L Garrochty
Garroch Head

10

M

Little Cumbrae Island

N

Portencross
Farland Head
B7048

P

Q

R

Kilbirnie
Be

Thon

Highfield

Drakemyre

Dalry

50

Bur

A737

Barr

1

Aucher

2

Munnoch

B780

Hunterston Power Station

20

12

B781

West Kilbride

B7047

Seamill

A78

B780

B714

Dalgarven

Dalgarven Mill

7

B778

Kilwinning

A78

Fergushill

B785

N

A841

124

Sannox

AL ABHAIL

34

Ardrossan
Horse Isle

B780

Stevenston

A738

A78

Eglinton

3

Cunni

Perc

40

Corrie

874
GOATFELL

Saltcoats

Ardeer

B779

Girdle Toll

A78

Irvine
Maritime

Fullarton

Dreghorn

Spring

Glen Rosa

Merkland Point

Brodick Castle, Garden & Country Park

6

Brodick Bay

FIRTH

Dryb

4

RUACH

512

Brodick

Strathwhillan

124

OF

Irvine Bay

Irvine Front Shore

Gailes

Corriegills

CLYDE

V

Castle

Barassie

B746

5

A841

4

H

Clauchlands Point

Lamlash

Margnaheglish

Lamlash Bay

Holy Island

V (May-Sept, Sat only)

A759

Loans

Troon

A78

30

Cordon

Lady Isle

Royal Troon

A79

dale

4

Auchencairn

Kingscross
Knockenkelly

Whiting Bay

M

6

Carn Ban

Whiting Bay

Glenashdale

Largymore

ston

Prestwick

New Prestwick

B743

Whitlet

A71

ory

Dippin

Largybeg
Dippin Head

V (May-Sept)

NS

Ayr Bay

7

Wallace

Bennan

Kildonan

Ayr

Heads of Ayr

Heads of Ayr
Burns Cottage

Doonfoot

20

Belmont

Pladda

A719

Fisherton

Alloway

Robert B Birthplace

8

H

A19

Bennan Head

Dunure

Culroy

B7024

9

B

Drumshang

Croy Brae (Electric Brae)
Knoweside

Minishant

A77

NX

Ailsa Craig

340

Culzean Bay

Culzean Castle & Country Park

Pennyglen

B7023

B71

Whitefaulds

Grimmet

10

Maybole

Maidenhead Bay

114

Maidens

A719

22

Crossraguel Abbey

B7023

Kirkmic

Threave

10

Kirkoswald

Souter Johnnie's Cottage

Crosshill

Turnberry

Turnberry

Turnberry Bay

Roan of Craigoch

Wallacetown

Dipple

Kilgrammie

B741

Dailly

Water of Girvan

11

NX

J

200

K

10

L

M

N **Girvan**

20

Old Dailly

P

B7035

Penkill

B734

Q

30

R

429

12

EFFIN FEL
Linfern Loch

Dounepark

Dalquharran

River Stinchar

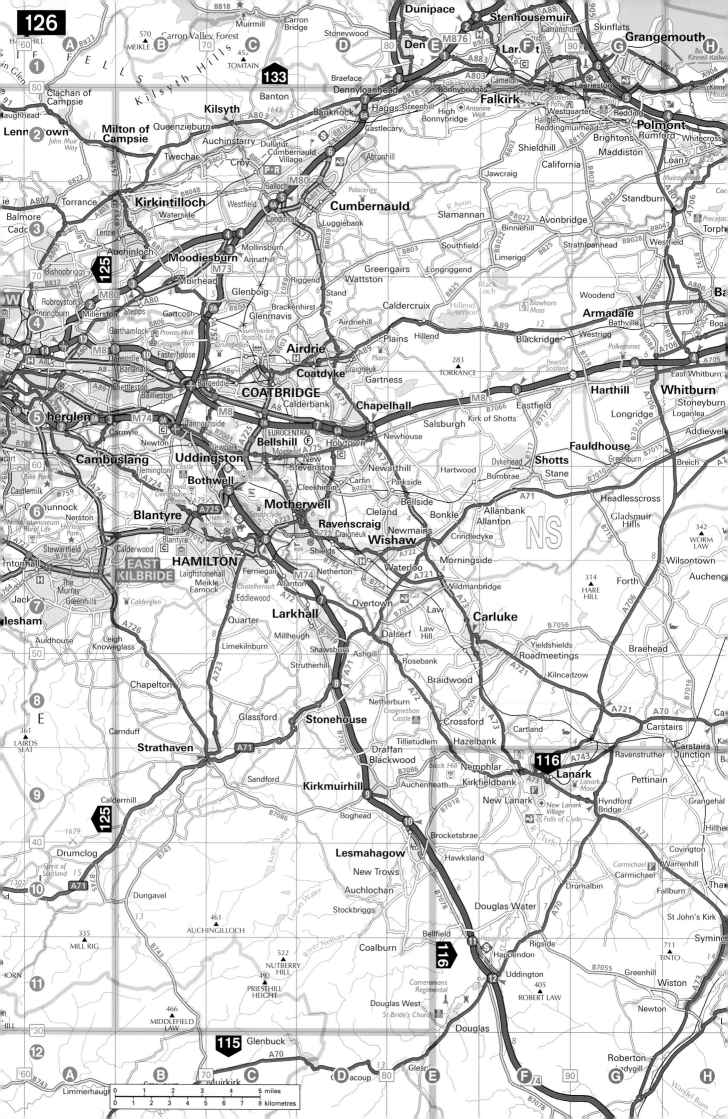

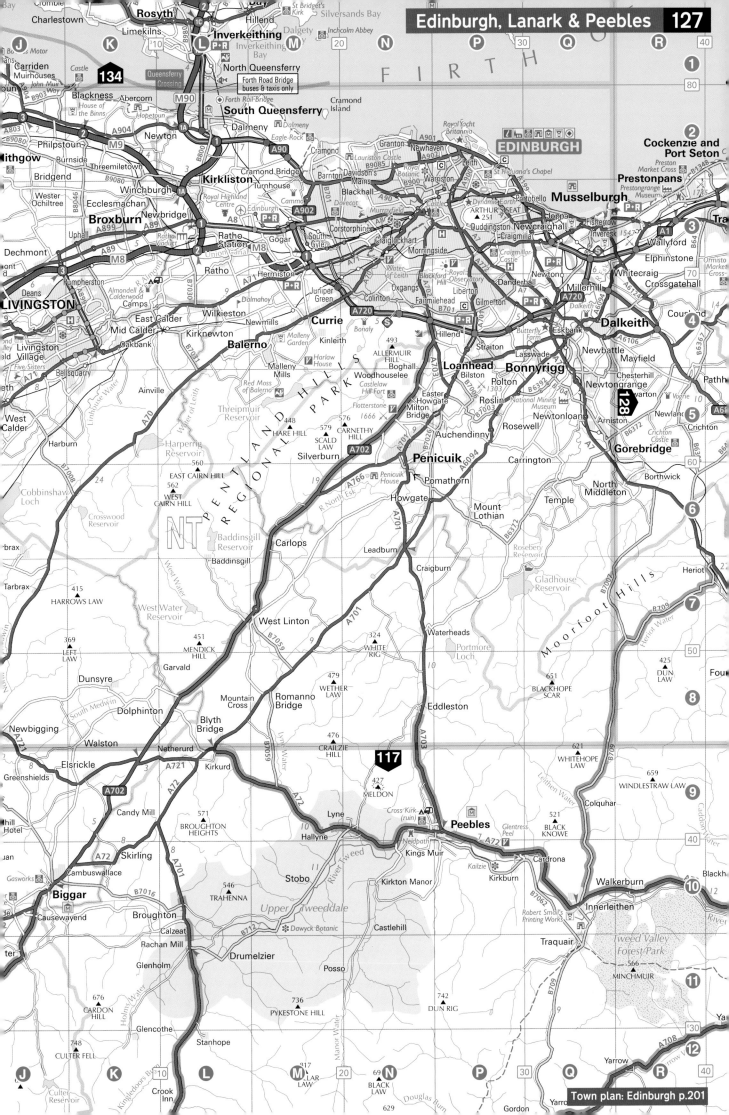

J K 80 L M 90 N P 00 Q R 10

Barns Ness
East Barns
Chapel Point
Skateraw
ick
Crowhill
Torness
Power Station
Thorntonloch
319
COCKLAW
HILL
Reed
Point
Dunglass
Collegiate
Church
Cove
Pease
Bay
Siccar
Point
Fast Castle Head
ldhamstocks
Cockburnspath
A1107
Pease Dean
196
BROWN
RIG
Coldingham
Loch
ST ABB'S HEAD
St Abbs
Coldingham
Bay
Ecclaw
91
ART
AW
Southern
Upland Way
Grantshouse
Eye Water
Butterdean
A1107
22
Eyemouth
Houndwood
Heugh
Head
Cairncross
B6438
A1
Quixwood
262
HORSELEY HILL
Reston
Ayton
Burnmouth
Abbey St Bathans
Edin's
Hall Broch
14
B6438
Auchencrow
B6355
Lamberton
NU
nford
325
COCKBURN
LAW
Marygold
Lintlaw
B6437
Marshall Meadows Bay
Primrosehill
B6355
A6112
Preston
Cumledge
Edrom Church
Chirnside
B6355
Foulden
North Northumberland
Heritage Coast
B6365
Edrom
15
Chirnsidebridge
Foulden
Tithe Barn
1333
Berwick-upon-Tweed
Manderston
Broadhaugh
Edington
Whiteadder Water
A6105
Castle
Town
Ramparts
Barracks &
Main Guard
Duns
A6105
Allanton
Hutton
Paxton
Gavinton
Blackadder
B6460
Paxton
B6461
Tweedmouth
Spittal
A1167
Polwarth
Nisbet
Hill
Sinclair's
Hill
Whitsome
Hilton
Loanend
East
Ord
Huds
Head
Fogo
B6437
B6461
13
Horndean
Horncliffe
Murton
Unthank
Scremerston
A1
Charterhall
A6112
6
Ladykirk
Castle
Norham
Thornton
Cheswick
Swinton
B6470
A698
Causeway
flooded at
high tide
Blackadder Water
B6460
Upsettlington
Shoreswood
West Allerdean
118
B6461
11
Simprim
River Tweed
Grindon
Ancroft
119
Haggerston
Goswick
Lambden
10
Leitholm
Shellacres
Grindonrigg
Felkington
Bowsden
Berrington
Beal
Eccles
A697
The Hirsel
Lennel
Duddo
B6525
15
Fenham
Lindis
Pri
Coldstream
Donaldson's
Lodge
Cornhill-on-Tweed
Castle
Etal
Heatherslaw
Corn Mill
B6353
West
Kyloe
Lowick
Fenwick
Buckton
Birgham
Carham
Wark
hidlaw
West
earmouth
Mxton
90
Crookh
Ford
Holburn
Detchant
Ednam
Kelso
East
Learmouth
1513
N
Flodden
14
Kimmerston
B6350
Hadden

J K 80 L M 90 N P 00 Q R 10

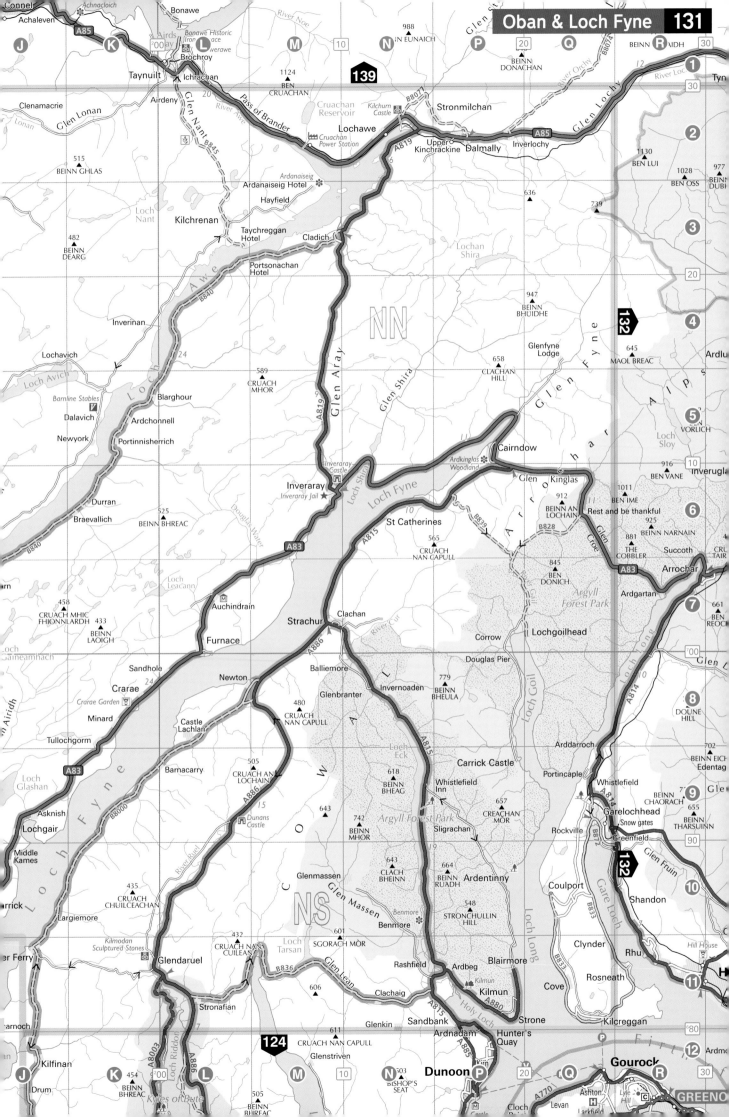

143

128

Town plan: Dundee p.199

A   B   C   D   E   F   G   H

90   '00   10   20

70

1

2

Eilean Mòr

Rubha
Mòr   Rub'
                                    Sgor

3   Cliad   B8072   Bousd   Soris
                                               Bay

                                                        Arnabost
60   Grishipoll   B8071
                                               Clabhach   Loch
                                                               Cliad
                                          Hogh Bay   Ballyhaugh   Arinagour
4   COLL
                                               Totronald
Bàgh a' Chaisteil   Coll
(Castlebay)   Arileod   Acha   B8070
                                        • Feall   Eilean
                                          Bay   Uig   Ornsay

NL   Rubha
5   Calgary Point   Crossapol   Fàsachd
50   Bay
                                          Gunna

                                        Caoles
6   Rubha Port   B8069   Rubha Dubh
         Bhiosd   Clachan   Balephetrish   Ruaig
Hough   Mor   Bay
Bay   B8068
         Ballevullin   Cornoigmore   Kenovay   Gott
                                              Bay
         Kilkenneth   Tiree
                         B8066   B8065   Scarinish
         Middleton   Moss   Heylipoll
7   Crossapol   TIREE
         Barrapoll   B8065   Lunga
                 Loch a'   B8067   Balemartine
                 Phuill   TRESHNISH
40   Rinn   Mannal   ISLES
Thorbhais   Balephuil   Hynish
         Bay
8   Bac Mòr or Dutchma

                                                          Bac Beag

┌───┐
│ **Colonsay**   NM   │
│   │
│ 1   │
│   '00   │
│   Eilean   │
│   Dubh   │
│   │
│   Kiloran Bay   Rubh' a' Geodha   │
│   143   Oban   │
│ 2   COLONSAY   ▲   V   │
│   CARNAN   │
│   EOIN   │
│   Kiloran   │
│   │
│   Kilchattan   B8087   NR   │
│   │
│   Scalasaig   │
│ 30   B8086   │
│ 3   Machrins   │
│   Colonsay   B8085   │
│   Garvard   │
│   '90   │
│   Rubha   │
│   Bàn   │
│   Dubh Eilean   Oronsay   │
│ 4   ORONSAY   Eilean   │
│   Ghaoideamal   │
│   0 1 2 3 miles   │
│   Port Askaig   │
│   0 1 2 3 4 5 kilometres│
│   a   b   '40   c   d   │
└───┘

9   IONA   Iona Ab
30   & Nunn
                                                        Baile Mòr
10   MacLean's Cross

20
11

12
90   '00   10   20

A   B   C   D   E   F   G   H

0 1 2 3 4 5 miles
0 1 2 3 4 5 6 7 8 kilometres

J K 40 L M 50 N P 60 Q R

Eilean
Seven Men
of Moid
Tioram
Kin
Rubha Àird
Druimnich
Ardmolich
1
BEINN
BHREAC 239
Morar, Moidart and
Ardnamurchan
Ockle
Point
Ockle
Kilmory
B8044
Ardtoe Shielfoot
Langa
Sanna Point
Branault
Kentra
Blain
Dalnal
Mingarrypa
Areveraig
A861
2
Sanna
Sanna
Bay
Achnaha
436
MEALL NAN CON
356
BEINN
BHREAC
ARDNAMURCHAN
Acharacle
Salen
Portuairk
Achosnich
Ardnamurchan
Point
B8007
437
Loch
Su
Ormsaigmore
342
BEINN
NA SEILG
Kilchoan
Loch
Mudle
527
BEN
HIANT
Natural
History
Glenbeg
Glenborrodale
512
BEN
LAGA
B8007
3
339
GEARR CH
Mingary
Ardslignish
RSPB
Laga
Carna
60
4
Oronsay
Auliston
Point
571
BEINN
LADAIN
ME
Ardmore
Point
Rubha
nan Gall
138
Sorne
Point
Glengorm Castle
Quinish Point
Tobermory
Loch
Teacuis
5
Loch
Arienas
437
BEINN
BHUIDHE
Drimnin
Acha
292
'S AIRDE
BEINN
P
i
Mull
Calve
Island
Caliach Point
Dervaig
Achnadrish
B8073
5
6
Calgary
Art in
Nature
Calgary Bay
Ensay
nish Point
a' Chaoil
342
CÀRN MÒR
390
CNOC AN
DÀ CHINN
Burg
Fanmore
Ballygown
Eas Fors
Loch
Tuath
Gometra
ULVA
Oskamull
B8073
333
BEINN
NAN CÀRN
Killiechronan
B8035
2
444
SPEINNE MÒR
Loch
Frisa
Glen Aros
Aros
Glenaros House
Salen
A849
Sound
of
Mull
550
SÌTHEAN NA RAPLAICH
Fuinary
A884
Lochaline
Loch
Aline
G-I
Clagga
Larachbeg
Achra
6
Fishnish
Point
Fishnish Pier
7
40
Scamastle Bay
Altcreich
8
Craignur
Little Colonsay
Staffa
Loch na Keal
Isle of Mull
Fingal's
Inch Kenneth
Inchkenneth Chapel
(ruin)
Eorsa
591
BEINN A' GHRÀIG
Loch
na
Keal
Macquarie
Mausoleum
Loch
Bà
408
BEINN
NAN LUS
636
BEINN
MHEADHON
766
DUN DA
GHAOITHE
ISLE
OF
MULL
Lochdo
Loch
9
A849
17
Strathcoil
30
Balnahard
B8035
17
966
BEN
MORE
704
CRUACHAN
DEARG
Glen More
717
BEN
BUIE
698
BEN CREACH
10
Crog
519
BEIN NA
SREINE
491
CREACH BHEINN
Tiroran
Aird of
Kinloch
A849
Pennycross
Pennyghael
503
BEINN NA
CROISE
Lochbuie
Loch
Fuaran
Leidle Water
Loch
Uisg
337
MAOL
BAN
11
Rubha nan Cearc
A849
14
Loch Scridain
Carsaig
Loch
Buie
130
377
DRUIM
FADA
ntra
6
Aridhglas
Bunessan
Loch Assapol
376
CRUACHAN
MIN
376
BEINN
CHREAGACH
Rubha
Dubh
12
ROSS OF MULL
Ardchiavaig
Uisken
Rubh'
Ardalanish
Rubha nam
Bràithrean
Malcolm's
Point
FIRTH

J K 40 L M 50 N P 60 Q R 70

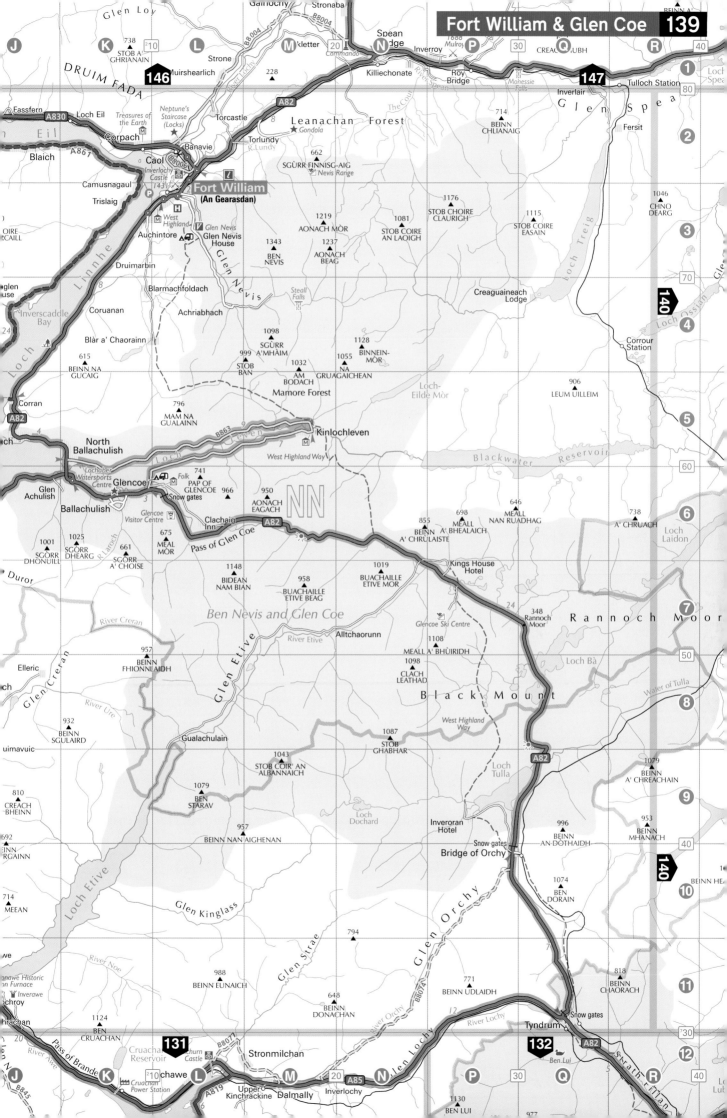

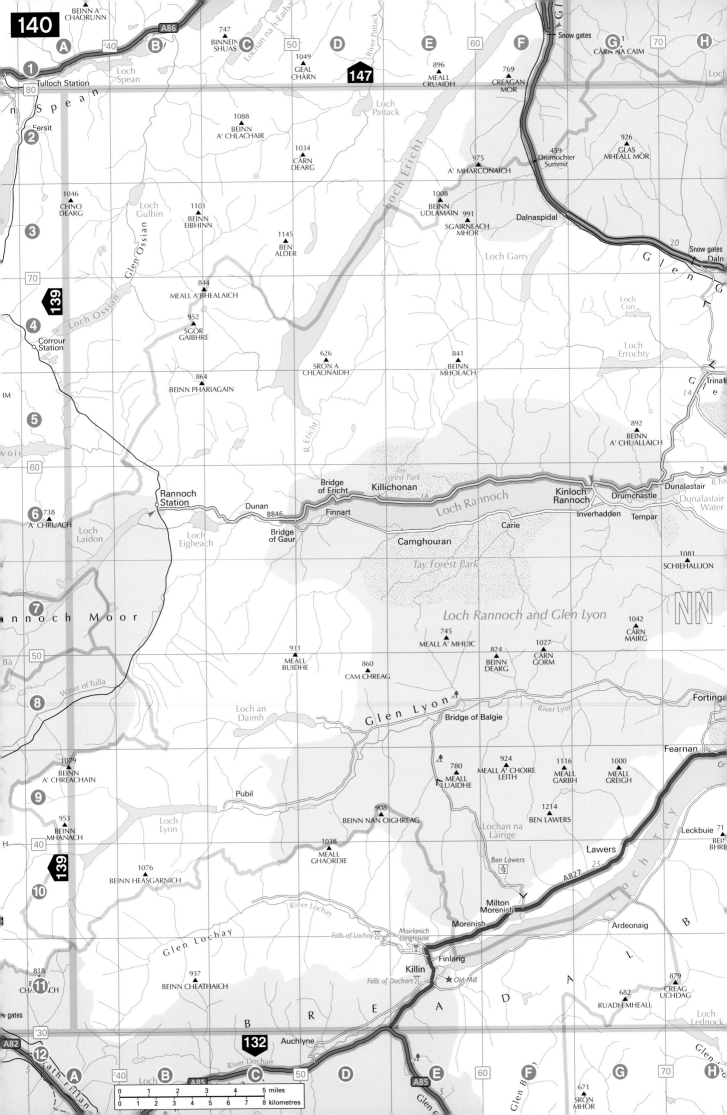

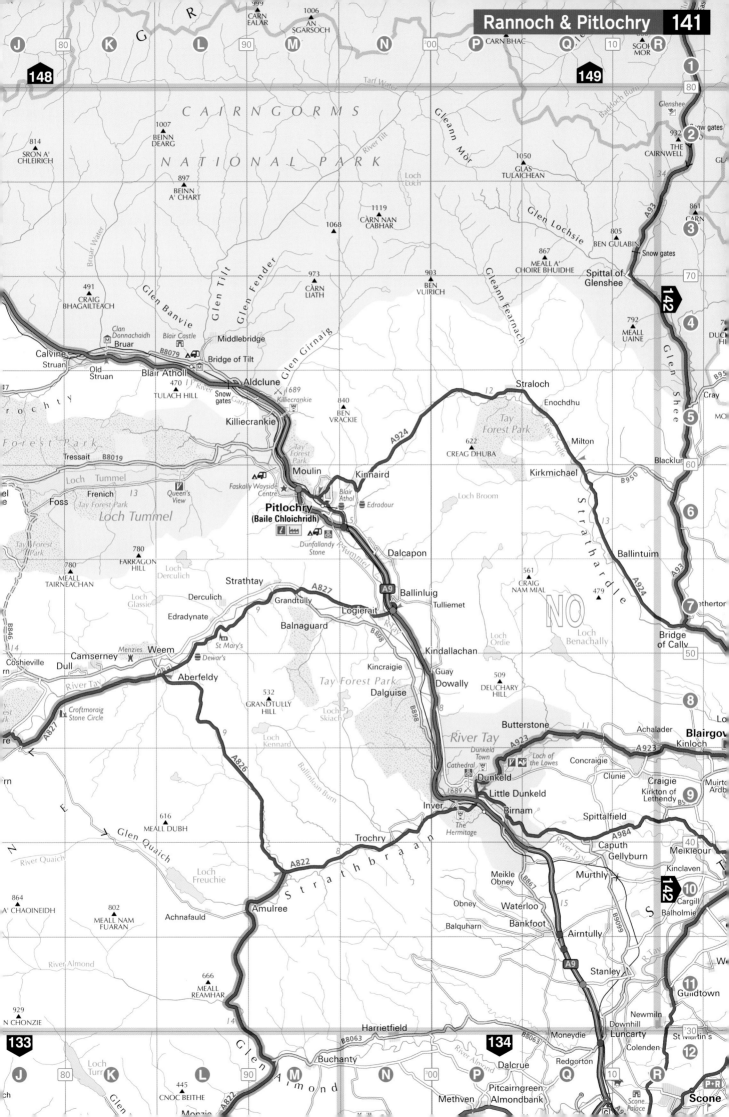

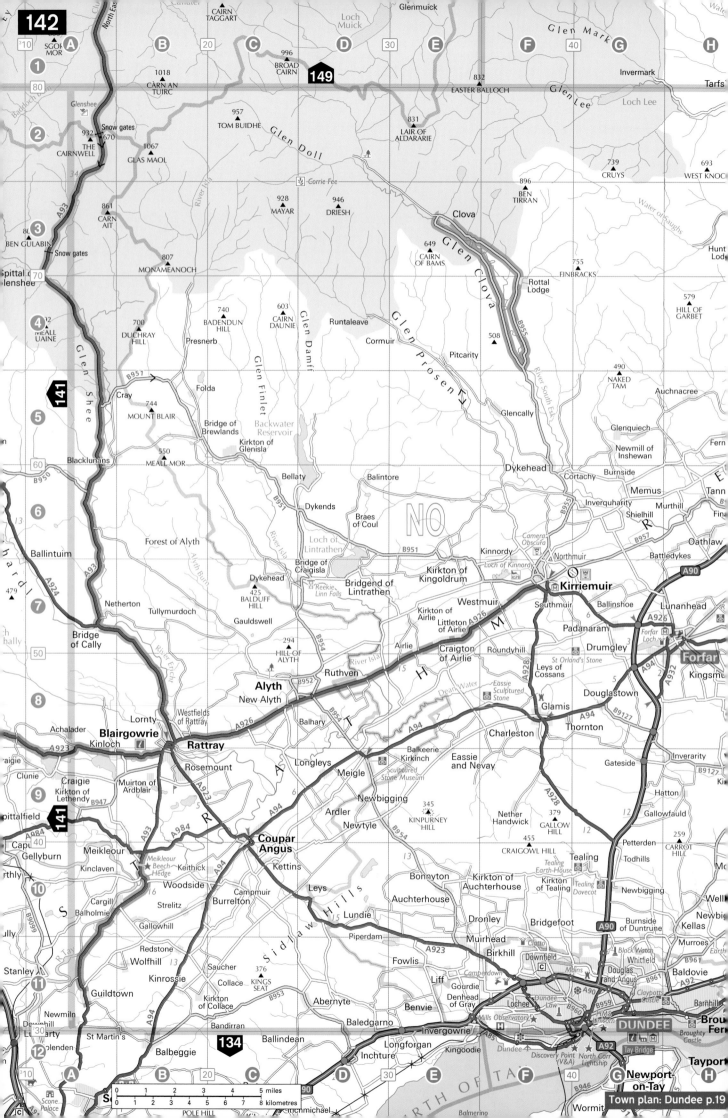

SKYE

B8009

Rubha nan Clach

Fernilea

369
ARNAVAL ▲

Carbost

Talisker 40

Drynoch

A863

Glen Drynoch

Sligachan

444
BEN LEE ▲

conser

50

773
GLAMAIG ▲

A8

152

Talisker
Bay

Merkadale

Glen Eynort

369
BEINN BHREAC ▲

Talisker

Minginish

447
BEINN
BHREAC ▲

Glen
Grula Brittle

Forest

Fairy Pools

965
SGÙRR
NAN GILLEAN ▲

The Cuillin Hills

Loch Eynort

434
AN CRUACHIN ▲

Glenbrittle

Bualintur

974
SGÙRR
A' GHEADAIDH ▲

Cuillin Hills

1009
SGÙRR
ALASDAIR ▲

Loch
Coruisk

927
BLAV ▲

Loch na
Crèithéac

Loch Brittle

894
GARS
BHEINN ▲

225
CEANN NA BEINNE ▲

Rubha an Dùnain

Soay Sound

139
BEINN
BHREAC ▲

Mol-chlach

Loch
Scavaig

Ki

Me

Elg

SOAY

Rubh'
Aonghais

St

Loch Baghasdail
(Lochboisdale)

CUILLIN SOUND

NG

CANNA

210
CÀRN A' GHAILL ▲

A'Chill

Garrisdale Point

Canna
Harbour

Sanday

Kilmory
Bay

Rubha
Shamhnan
Insir

Sound of Canna

302
MULLACH
MÒR ▲

Rubha
na Roinne

800

A' Bhrideanach

570
ORVAL ▲

Kinloch

Loch Scresort

Oigh-sgeir

RÙM

810
ASKIVAL ▲

All vehicles must have
the relevant island
permit prior to travel
to The Small Isles.
Services are seasonal,
day & weather dependent.

Harris
Bay

763
SGÙRR NAN
GILLEAN ▲

The Small Isles

Rubha nam
Meirleach

Sound of Rùm

Bay of
Laig

Cleadale

299
AN
CRUACHAN ▲

NM

Rubha an
Fhasaidh

Laig

EIGG

Kildonnan

393
AN SGÙRR ▲

Galmisdale

Sound of Eigg

Eilean
nan Each

Eilean
Chathastail

MUCK

Port Mòr

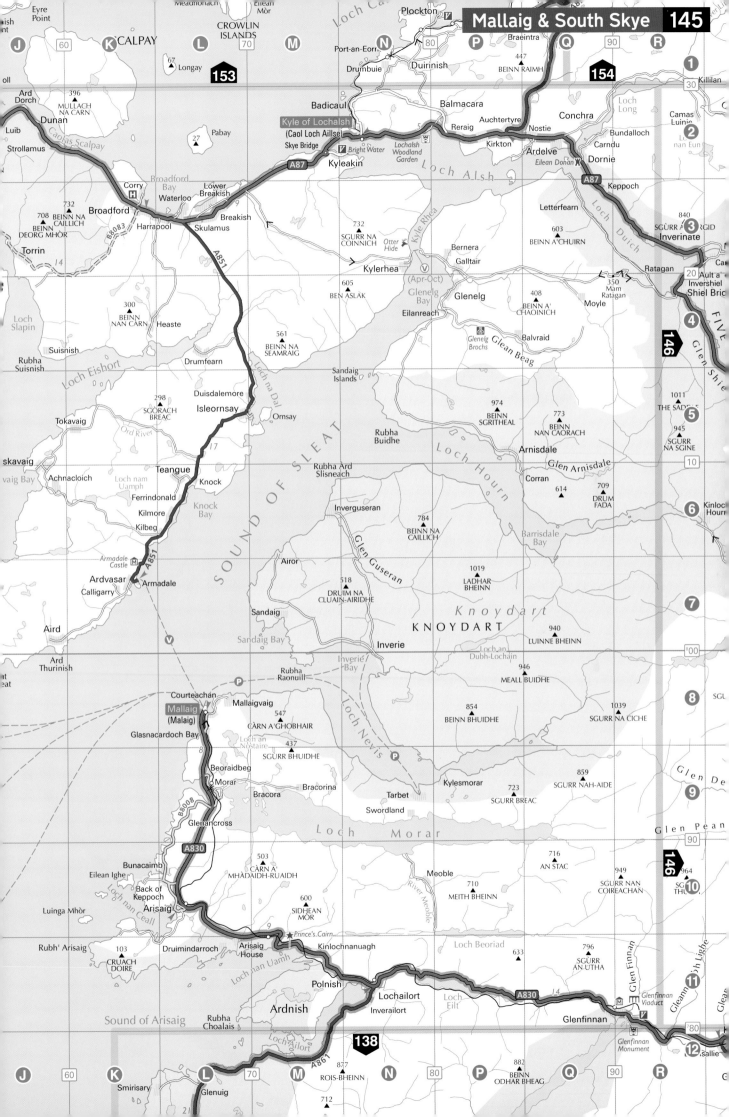

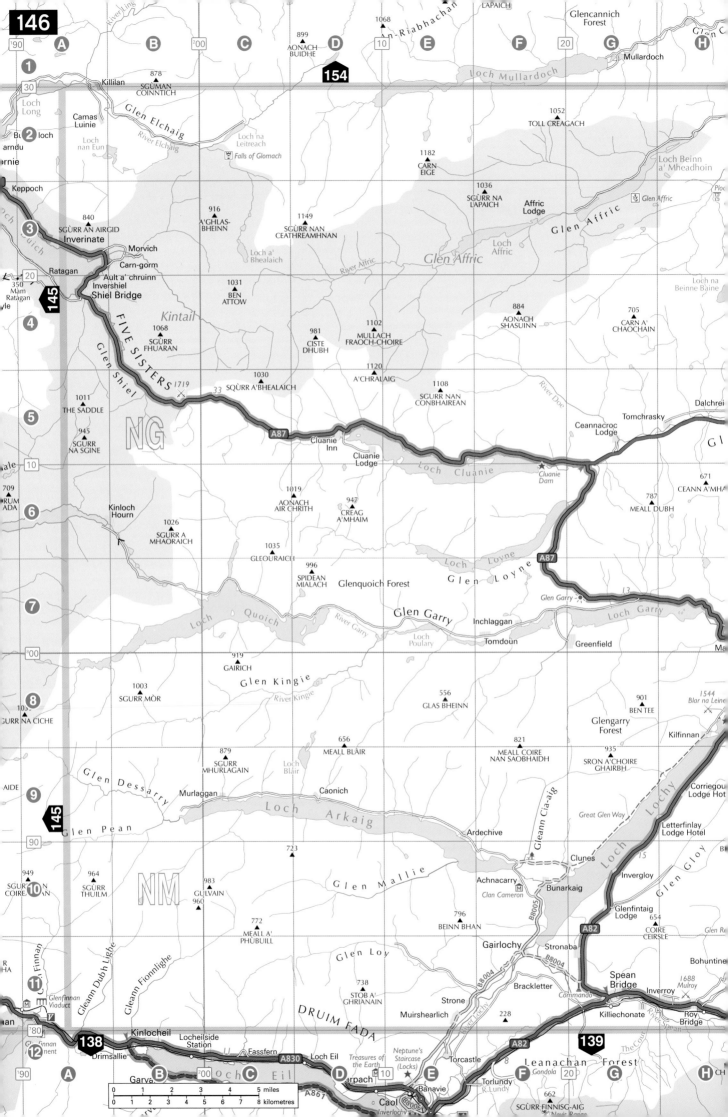

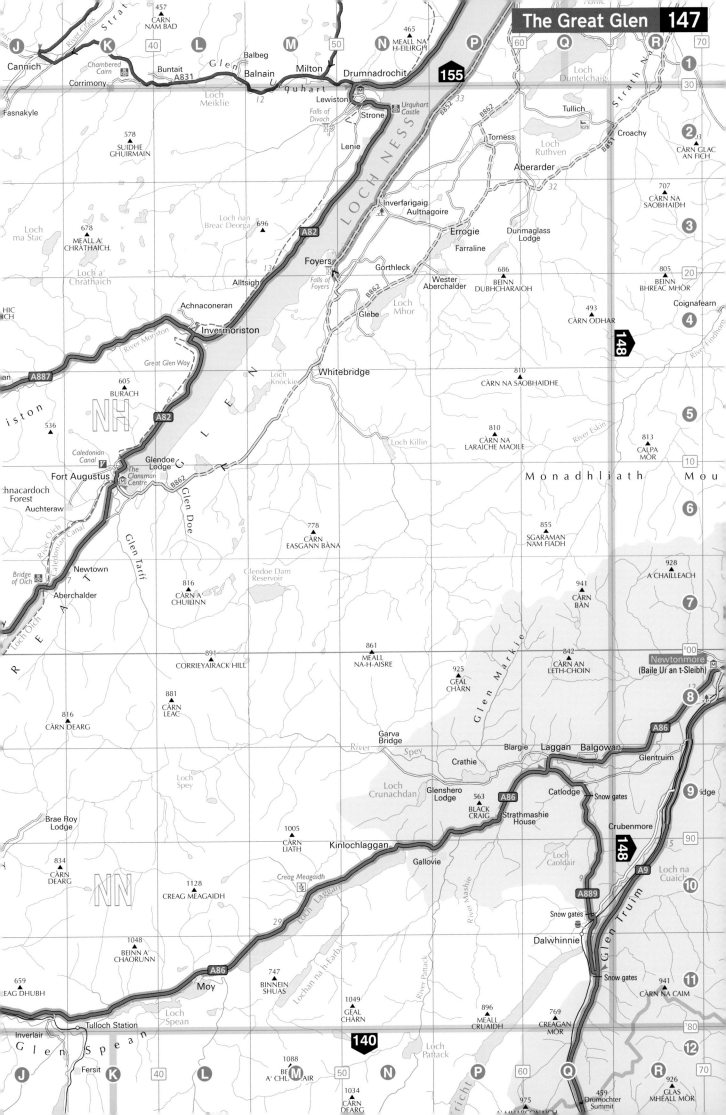

J K L M N P Q R

1
2
3
4
5
6
7
8
9
10
11
12

Cannich
457 CÀRN NAM BAD
Glen Balnain
Balbeg
Milton
Drumnadrochit
465 MEALL NA H-EILIRGH
Loch Duntelchaig
155

Corrimony
Chambered Cairn
Buntait
A831
Lewiston
Strone
Urquhart Castle
B852 33
B862
Tullich
Croachy
30

Fasnakyle
Loch Meiklie
12
Falls of Divach
Strone
Torness
Loch Ruthven
B851
93 CÀRN GLAC AN FICH

578 SUIDHE GHUIRMAIN
Lenie
LOCH NESS
Aberarder
32
707 CÀRN NA SAOBHAIDH

678 MEALL A' CHRÀTHAICH
696
Inverfarigaig
Aultnagoire
Errogie
Dunmaglass Lodge
805 BEINN BHREAC MHÒR
20

Loch ma Stac
Loch nan Breac Deorga
A82
Farraline
686 BEINN DUBHCHARAIOH
493 CÀRN ODHAR
Coignafearn

Loch a' Chràthaich
13
Foyers
Falls of Foyers
Gorthleck
Wester Aberchalder
148

HIC ICH
Achnaconeran
Alltsigh
B862
Glebe
Loch Mhor
810 CÀRN NA SAOBHAIDHE
River Findhorn

iston
A887
Invermoriston
Great Glen Way
Whitebridge
Loch Knockie
810 CÀRN NA LARAICHE MAOILE
River Eskin
813 CALPA MÒR
10

NH
605 BURACH
A82
6
Loch Killin
Monadhliath Mou

536
River Moriston
G
L
E
N
Loch Knockie

Caledonian Canal
Glendoe Lodge
855 SGARAMAN NAM FIADH
928 A CHAILLEACH

Fort Augustus
The Clansman Centre
B862
Glen Doe
941 CÀRN BÀN

chnacardoch Forest
Auchteraw
778 CÀRN EASGANN BÀNA
Glendoe Dam Reservoir
842 CÀRN AN LETH-CHOIN
00

Bridge of Oich
Newtown
816 CÀRN A' CHUILINN
861 MEALL NA-H-AISRE
925 GEAL CHÀRN
Newtonmore (Baile Ur an t-Sleibh)

Aberchalder
Glen Tarff
Loch Oich
891 CORRIEYAIRACK HILL
Glen Markie
8
A86

R E A T
881 CÀRN LEAC
Garva Bridge
Blargie
Laggan
Balgowan
Glentruim

816 CÀRN DEARG
River Spey
Crathie
Loch Crunachdan
Glenshero Lodge
563 BLACK CRAIG
A86
Catlodge
Snow gates
9
idge

Brae Roy Lodge
Loch Spey
Kinlochlaggan
Strathmashie House
Crubenmore
90

834 CÀRN DEARG
NN
1005 CÀRN LIATH
Gallovie
Loch Caoldàir
148
A9
Loch na Cuaich

659 EAG DHUBH
1128 CREAG MEAGAIDH
Creag Meagaidh
River Mashie
Glen Truim
10

1048 BEINN A' CHAORUNN
Loch Laggan
29
A889
Dalwhinnie
Snow gates

A86
Moy
747 BINNEIN SHUAS
Lochan na h-Earba
896 MEALL CRUAIDH
769 CREAGAN MÒR
Snow gates
941 CÀRN NA CAIM
11

Inverlair
Tulloch Station
Loch Spean
1049 GEAL CHÀRN
Loch Pattack
80

Glen Spean
140
1088 BE A' CHL AIR
1034 CÀRN DEARG
975
459 Drumochter Summit
926 GLAS MHÈALL MÒR
12

J K 40 L 50 M N P 60 Q R 70

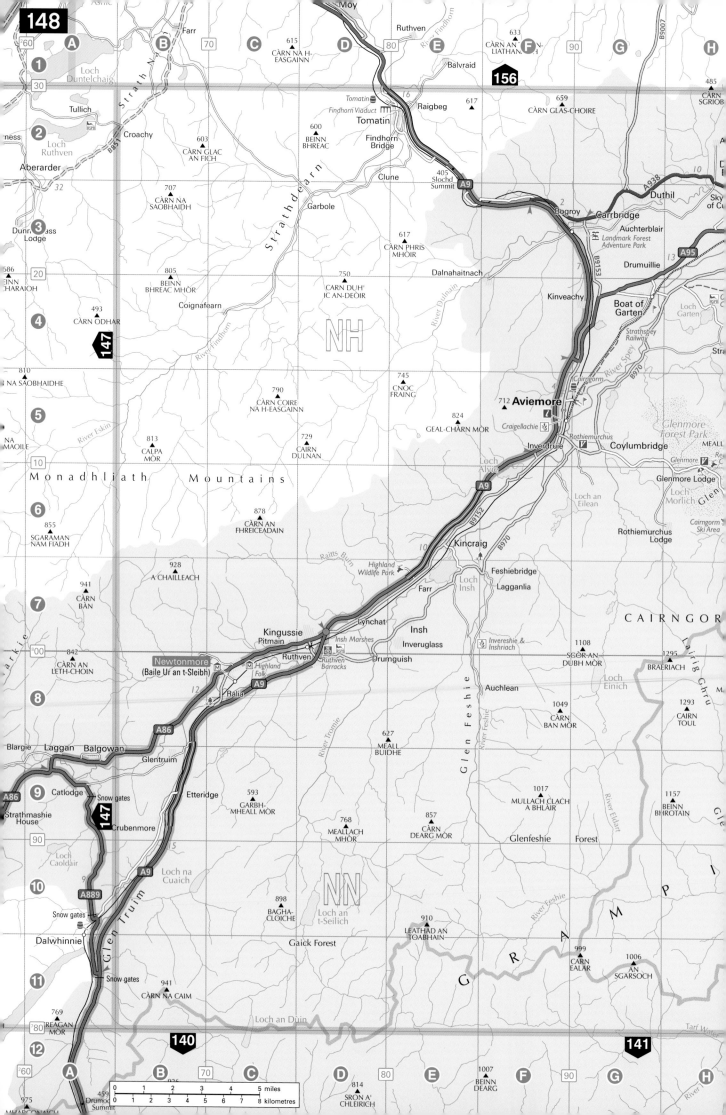

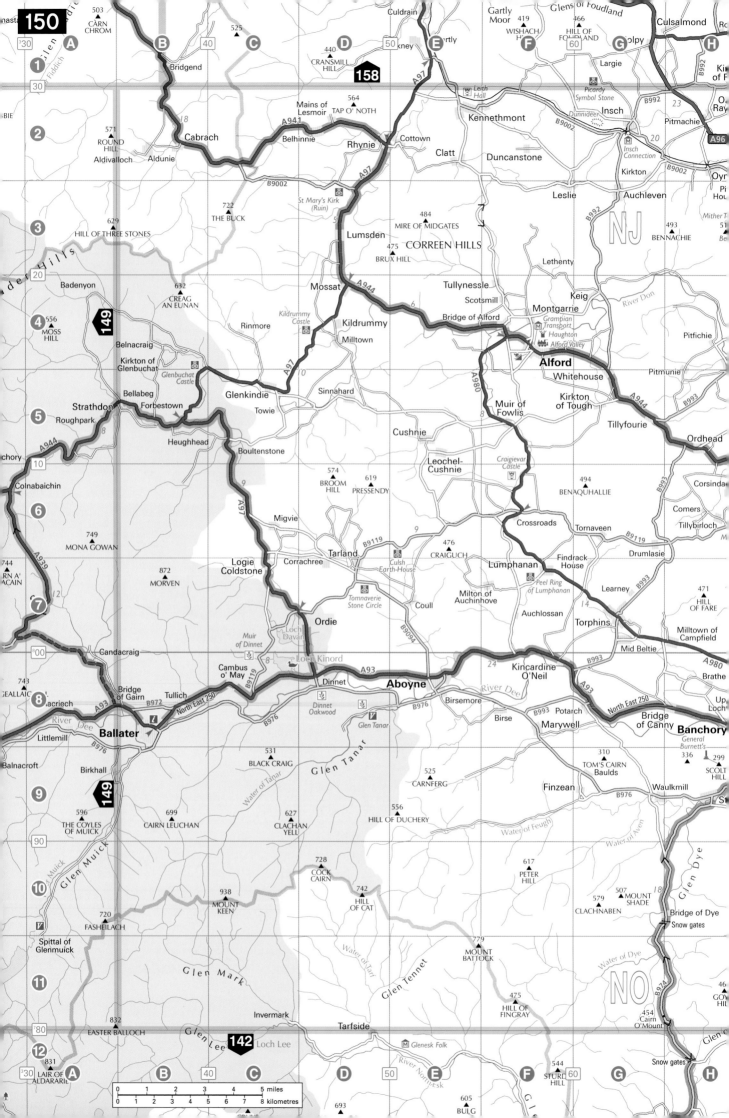

J K L M N P Q R

St Katherines
Barthol Chapel
Earlsford
House
Ythanbank
B9006
Cruden
Folla Rule
Cross of Jackston
Tulloch
Wedderlairs
Ythsiedhedly
Whinnyfold
Tarves
Tomb of William Forbes
Kinharrachie
Ellon
Artrochie
159
Craigdam
Ythsie
Esslemont
Kirkton of Logie Buchan
Collieston
Daviot
Glen Garioch
Oldmeldrum
Tolquhon Castle
Pitmedden Garden
Pitmedden
Logierieve
Kirktown of Slains
Loanhead Stone Circle
Carnbrogie
Udny Green
Housieside
Forvie
NK
Kirktown of Bourtie
Whiterashes
Woodland
Pettymuk
Udny Station
Cultercullen
Foveran
Newburgh
A90
Inverurie
Brandsbutts Symbol Stone
Uryside
Nether Crimond
Straloch
Reisque
Causeyend
Delfrigs
Easter Aquhorthies Stone Circle
Port Elphinstone
Kinmuck
Newmachar
Kingseat
Balmedie
Burnhervie
Kinkell Church
Newmachar
Whitecairns
Balmedie
Thainstone
Hatton of Fintray
Kinmundy
Belhelvie
Kemnay
Kintore
Cothal
R Don
Potterton
Craigearn
Cottown
Dyce Symbol Stones
Blackdog
Leylodge
Blackburn
Overton
Dyce
Castle Fraser
Lyne of Skene
Clinterty
Stoneywood
Middleton Park
Denmore
Bridge of Don
Millbuie
Skene House
Elrick Hill
Bankhead
Botanic
Kirkwall Lerwick
BRIMMOND HILL
Buoksburn
Loch of Skene
Westhill
Kingswells
Northfield
Old Aberdeen
Barmekin
Kirkton of Skene
Elrick
Kingsford
Kittybrewster
Garlogie
Carnie
A944
Countesswells
ABERDEEN
Ruthrieston
Torry
Echt
Redhill
Blacktop
Mannofield
Nigg Bay
Landerberry
Cullerlie
Benthoul
Easter Ord
Cults
Kincorth
Loirston
Hirn
Gullerlie Stone Circle
Bieldside
Banchory-Devenick
Nigg
Altens Haven
Myrebird
West Park
Hardgate
Craigton
Milton of Murtle
Milltimber
Charlestown
Cove Bay
Neuk
Crathes
Drum Castle
Peterculter
Kingcausie
Marywell
Crathes Castle
North East 250
River Dee
Kirkton of Maryculter
The Den & The Glen
A956
Kirkton of Durris
Denside of Durris
Hillside
Findon
Royal Deeside
Woodlands of Durris
Auchlee
Portlethen
Crossroads
Cookney
Cammachmore
Old Portlethen
Cammachmore Bay
Durris Forest
Netherley
Chapelton
Downies
Newtonhill
Skateraw
Muchalls
MONGOUR 376
HILL OF TRUSTA 320
Bridge of Muchalls
Doonie Point
Goosecruives
FETTERESSO FOREST
Garron Point
Stonehaven Bay
LEACHIE HILL 390
New Mill
Temple of Fiddes
Kirktown of Fetteresso
Stonehaven
Tolbooth
Dunnottar
Drumlithie
Tannachie
143
Glenbervie
Mondynes
Crawton
Fowlsheugh
Catterline
Fordoun
Kinneff
Todhead Point
Grassic Gibbon
B967

J K L M N P Q R

Aberdeen Harbour

ELGIN PETERHEAD
WESTBURN ROAD
HUTCHEON STREET
KING STREET
A956
BEACH BOULEVARD
ESPLANADE
ABERDEEN
SKENE ST
UNION STREET
Victoria Dock
FERRY TERMINAL
Foordee
North Pier
Aberdeen Station
Albert Basin
River Dee
WILLOWBANK ROAD
MARKET ST
SINCLAIR ROAD
Ferryhill
VICTORIA ROAD
Torry
HOLBURN STREET
WELLINGTON ROAD
RIVERSIDE DRIVE
BALNAGASK ROAD
GIRDLENESS ROAD
ST FITTICKS ROAD
DUNDEE
LBLH
0 500 m

J K 60 L M 70 N P 80 Q R 90

CNOC
BREAC 293

FALL NA 1
250

Garden 13

North Erradale Londubh

B8021 Poolewe 80

Big Sand A832 2

160 Strath
Smithstown Heritage Auchtercairn
Lonemore Gairloch & Loch Ewe Charlestown MEALL AN 421
DOIREIN

Longa
Island Gairloch 3
Loch
Gairloch Eilean
Horrisdale River Kerry Loch Bad
an Sgalaig

Port
Henderson B8056 Victoria Falls 19
Badachro 70
Opinan

South Erradale 4
Loch Ghaireamhach 154
875 BAOSBHEINN
BEINN
AN EOIN 855

Red Point Loch a'
Ghodhainn 619
BEINN BHREAC Loch a'
Bhealaich 5
Red
Point Craig River 985
BEINN
ALLIGIN BEINN DEARG 914
60

NG Loch
Torridon Lower
Diabaig Alligin Shuas 6
Valtos Rubha
na Fearn Fearnmore Inveralligin 102
Rubha nam Brathairean Fearnbeg Loch
Diabaig Torridon
House
Culnaknock Òb
Chuaig Arrina Ardheslaig Torrid
Kenmore Upper Loch Torridon Deer
Tote Cuaig

RONA Callakille Loch
Shieldaig Shieldaig Annat
Lonbain 492 An Garbh- Croic- 7
Eilean
Tigh Mheall Bheinn 493 A896 Wester oss
North Coast 500

Eilean
Fladday Loch
Damph 902
Manish
Point Loch
Arnish Torran Glenshieldaig Forest B 50
DAMPH
Arnish Loch Lundie 8
Brochel Applecross Loch
Coultrie
Applecross Bay Beinn Bhan 895 SGURR A
GHARAIDH 730
RAASAY Applecross 626 Pass of the Rassal
Milltown Cattle Ashwood 9
444 Bealach na Bà 774 Kirkton
Dùn Caan Camusteel SGURR A CHAORACHAIN A896
Camusterrach Kishorn Lochcarron 40
Aird Dhubh Ardarroch
Culduie Achintraid Slumbay 154 10
Bastianavaig 310 Ardaneaskan 394
Oskaig Beinn na Leac Rubha na' Leac Toscaig Kishorn
Island Bad a
Chreamha Strome Ardnarff
Clachan Ardaneaskan
Inverarish Stromeferry A890
Peinchorran Eilean
Meadhonach Eilean
Mòr Plockton Achmore
Suisnish
Point Eyre
Point Crowlin
Islands Port-an-Eorna Braeintra 11
Drumbuie Duirinish 447
BEINN RAIMH
67 Longay Moll Longay
Ard 396 30
Dorch Mullach Badicaul Balmacara
Dunan Na Carn 145 Kyle of Lochalsh 80 447 Auchtertyre Conchra 12
A87 60 Skye Bridge Nostie
Strollamus Pabay 70 N Loch Aillse Kirkton R 90
564 L K L Bright Water P Rera Q Ardelve
GLAS BHEIN Kyleakin Lochalsh
Woodland
Garden Eilean Donan Dornie

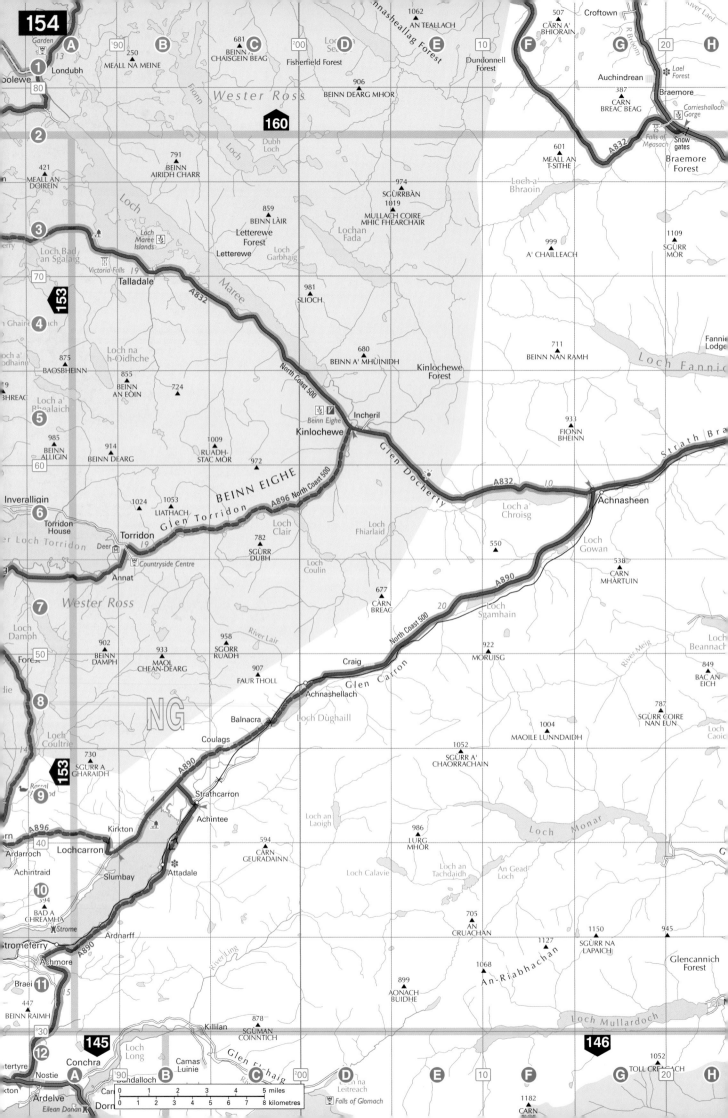

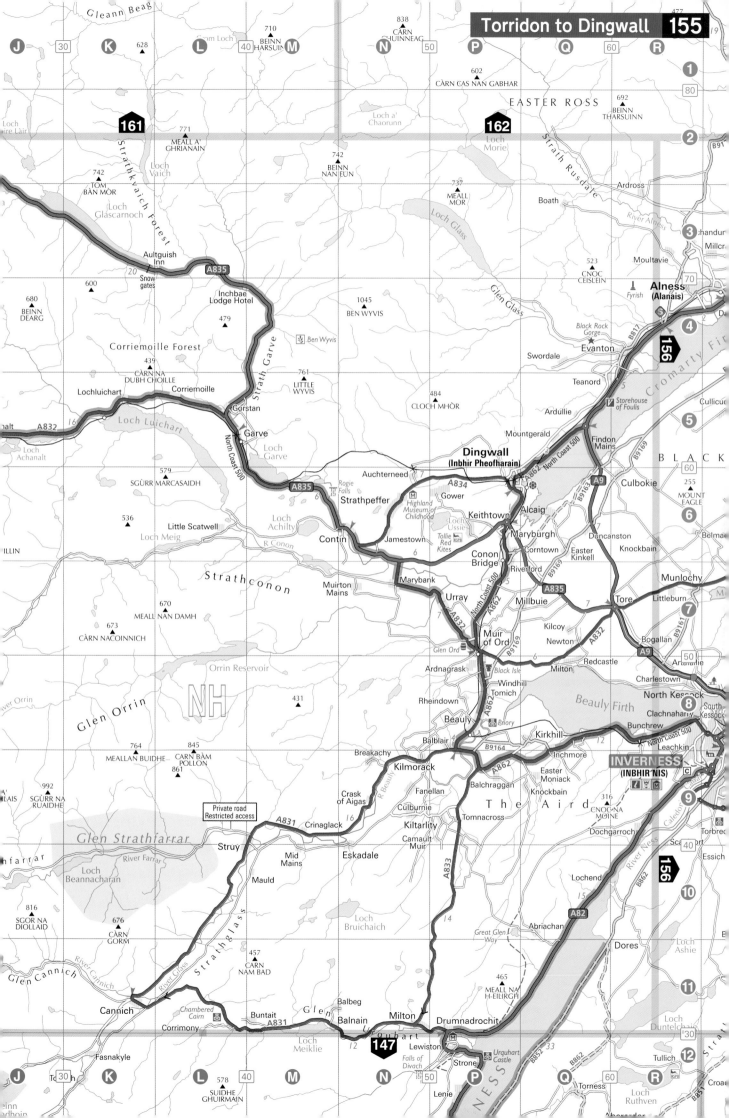

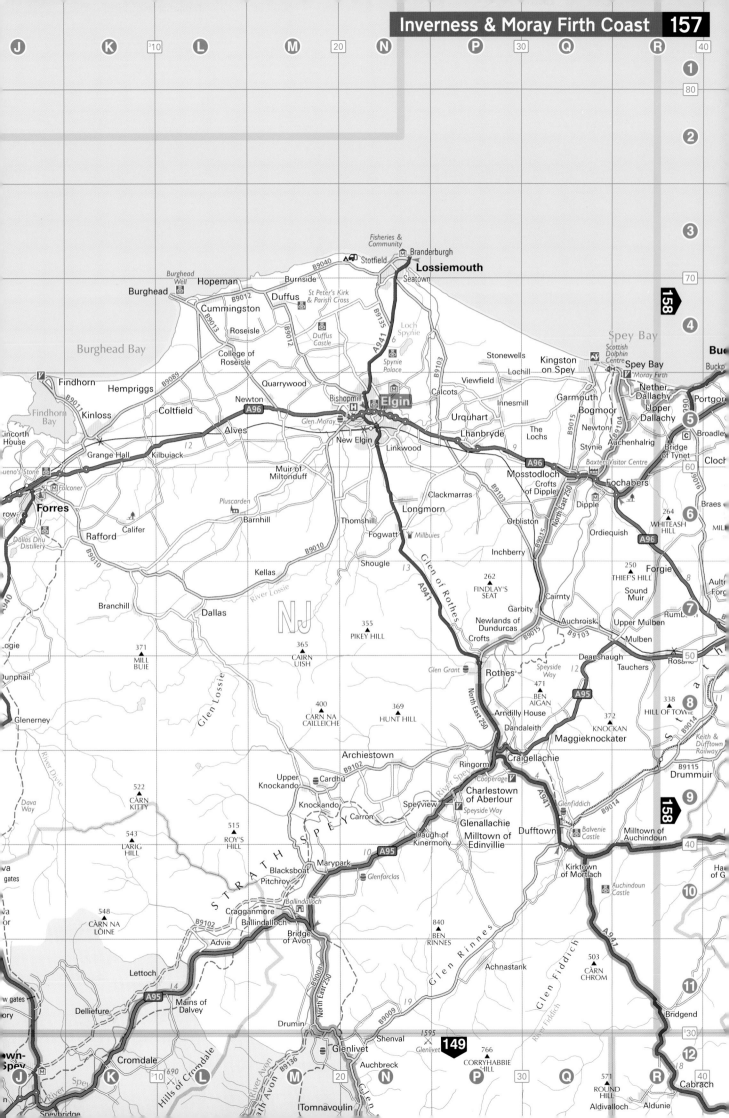

J K L M N P Q R

Fisheries &
Community
Stotfield
Branderburgh
Lossiemouth
Seatow
Burnside

B9040
Hopeman
Burghead
Well
Burghead
Cummingston
Duffus
St Peter's Kirk
& Parish Cross
B9012
Roseisle
Duffus
Castle
Loch
Spynie
B9103

158

Spey Bay
Scottish
Dolphin
Centre
Bu

Findhorn Bay
Spynie
Palace
Stonewells
Kingston
on Spey
Spey Bay
Moray Firth
Buckp

Burghead Bay
College of
Roseisle
Findhorn
Hempriggs
B9089
Quarrywood
Bishopmill
Elgin
Calcots
Viewfield
Lochill
Innesmill
Garmouth
Newton
Nether
Dallachy
Upper
Dallachy
Portgo

Findhorn
Kinloss
Newton
A96
Coltfield
Alves
Glen Moray
New Elgin
Linkwood
Urquhart
Lhanbryde
The
Lochs
Stynie
Auchenhalrig
Bridge
of Tynet
Broadley
Cloch

Cincorth
House
Grange Hall
Kilbuiack
Falconer
Muir of
Miltonduff
Linkwood
A96
Mosstodloch
Crofts
of Dipple
Baxters Visitor Centre
Dipple
Fochabers
Braes
MII

Forres
Bueno's Stone
Pluscarden
Barnhill
Clackmarras
Longmorn
B9103
Orbliston
Ordiequish
264
WHITEASH
HILL
A96

Dallas Dhu
Distillery
Rafford
Califer
Thomshill
Fogwatt
Millbuies
Inchberry
250
THIEF'S HILL
Sound
Muir
Forgie

B9010
Kellas
Shougle
Glen of Rothes
Findlay's
Seat
Cairnty
Garbity
Auchroisk
Upper Mulben
Rumb

Branchill
Glen Lossie
Dallas
355
PIKEY HILL
A941
262
FINDLAY'S
SEAT
Newlands of
Dundurcas
Crofts
B9015
B9103
Mulben
Deanshaugh
Tauchers
Rosa

Glenerney
371
MILL
BUIE
365
CAIRN
UISH
NJ
400
CARN NA
CAILLEICHE
369
HUNT HILL
Glen Grant
Rothes
Speyside
Way
BEN
AIGAN
471
A95
Arndilly House
338
HILL OF TOW
KNOCKAN
372

Dunphail
North East 250
Maggieknockater
Dandaleith
Keith &
Dufftown
Railway

Archiestown
B9102
Cardhu
Upper
Knockando
Ringorm
Cooperage
Charlestown
of Aberlour
Craigellachie
A941
Glenfiddich
B9014
Drummuir
B9115

Dava
Way
522
CARN
KITTY
Knockando
Carron
Speyview
Speyside Way
Glenallachie
Milltown of
Edinvillie
Dufftown
Balvenie
Castle
Milltown of
Auchindoun
158

543
LARIG
HILL
515
ROY'S
HILL
STRATH SPEY
Blacksboat
Pitchroy
Ballindalloch
Maripark
Daugh of
Kinermony
A95
Glenfarclas
A95
Kirktown
of Mortlach
Auchindoun
Castle

River Divie
548
CARN NA
LOINE
B9102
Cragganmore
Ballindalloch
Bridge
of Avon
840
BEN
RINNES
Glen Rinnes
A941
Ha
of G

Lettoch
Advie
B9008
North East 250
Glen Fiddich
River Fiddich
Achnastank
503
CARN
CHROM
Bridgend

A95
Mains of
Dalvey
Drumin
B9009
Glen Rinnes
571
ROUND
HILL
Aldivalloch
Cabrach

Cromdale
Hills of Cromdale
River Avon
B9136
Glenlivet
Shenval
1595
Glenlivet
149
766
CORRYHABBIE
HILL
Aldunie

wn-
Spey
Spey
Tomnavoulin

J K L M N P Q R

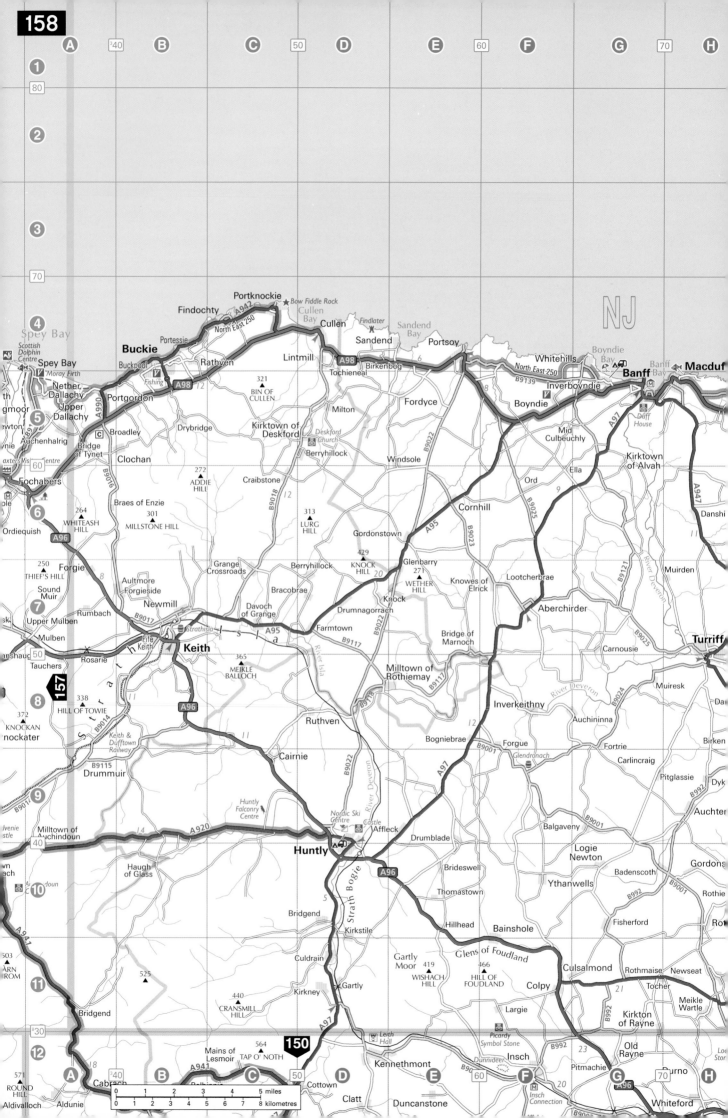

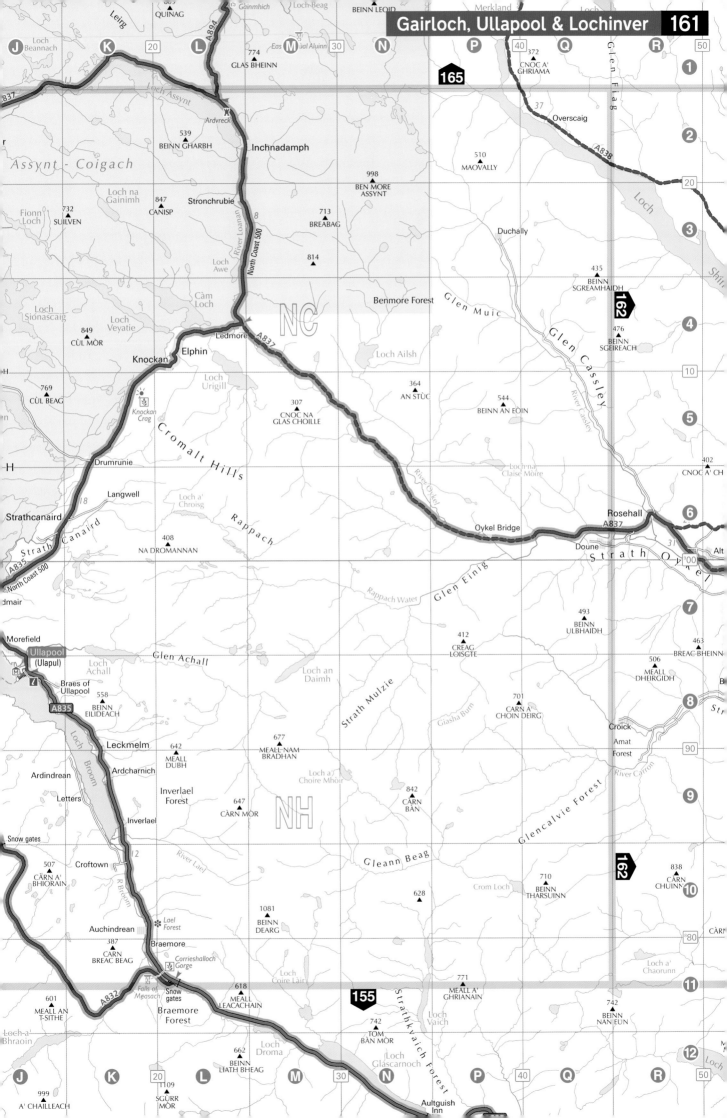

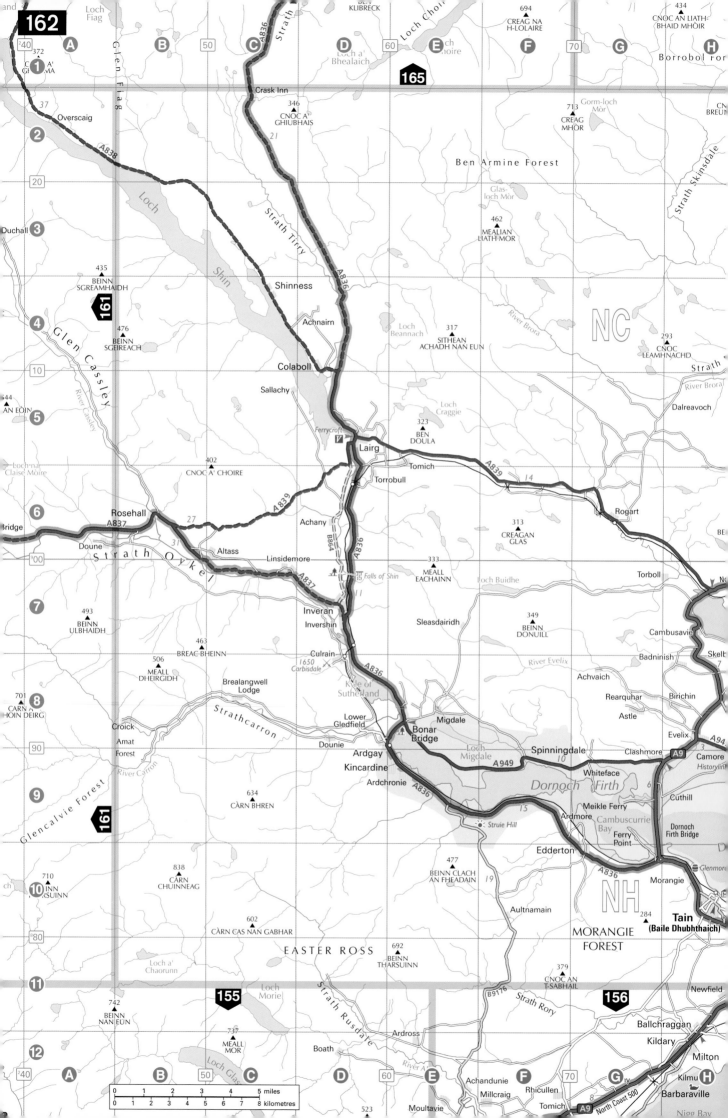

ND

NJ

J **K** **L** **M** **N** **P** **Q** **R**

90 00 10 20

1
2
3
4
5
6
7
8
9
10
11
12

202
CNOC DAIL-
CHAIRN

Strath Free

Loch
Ascaig

90 Suisgill

NA FEARNA

518
CNOC AN
EIREANNAICH

00

705
MORVEN

10

Langwell Forest

167

626
SCARABEN

...mscraigs

Knockally

...n Heritage

10 20

Borgue

Newport

20

388
CREAG NAM FIADH

Learable Hill
Cairns, Stone Row
& Stone Circles

Strath of Kildonan

17

Kildonan Lodge

554
CREAG
SCALABSDALE

North Coast 500

Langwell
House

Berriedale

Kildonan

416
BEINN
DUBHAIN

A897

Torrish

River Helmsdale

401
CNOC NA
MAOILE

404
CREAG
THORARAIDH

A9

Badbea
Historic Village

337
...OC NA H-
SE MOIRE

421
CNOC NAN CRÙBAG MÒR

624
BEINN
DHORAIN

591
BEINN
MHEALAICH

Glen Loth

Navidale

Timespan

Snow gates

West
Helmsdale

Gartymore

Portgower

East Helmsdale

Helmsdale

Ord of Caithness

20

...nacoil

539
COL-
BHEINN

Lothmore

Lothbeg

21

10

Loch
Brora

378
CAGAR
FEOSAIG

Backies

A9

Doll

Clynelish

Dalchalm

Brora

Carn
Liath

Dunrobin
Castle

3
...RAGGIE
...hives

Golspie

00

...eferry

...et
...enny

Embo

... Street

... Dornoch

...och

Firth

...noch
...int

Innis Mhor

Tarbat Ness

Wilkhaven

Portmahomack

Inver

Lower Arboll

B9165

Tarbat Discovery
Centre

Rockfield

90

Toulvaddie

Lochslin

Loch
Eye

Rhynie

Hill of
Fearn

Balmuchy

80

Fearn

Tullich

B9166

Hilton of Cadboll
Chapel (ruin)

Hilton of Cadboll

...abella

Shandwick

Balintore

Shandwick Bay

...ca

J **K** **L** **M** **N** **P** **Q** **R**

90 00 10 20

B9040

A 「00 B C 10 D E 20 F G 30 H

① ② ③ ④ ⑤ ⑥ ⑦ ⑧ ⑨ ⑩ ⑪ ⑫

70
60
50
40
30

CAPE WRATH

Kearvaig
Bay

Cléit
Dhubh

371
SGRIBHIS-
BHEINN

297
CNOC A'
GHIUBHAIS

300
MAOVALLY

THE PARPH

457
FASHVEN

Sandwood
Bay

Sandwood
Loch

485
CREAG
RIABHACH

467
AN GRIANAN

464
MEALL
NA MÒINE

GH
BHE

Rubh' an Fhir Lèithe

Sheigra

521
FARRMHEALL

19

Balchrick   Blairmore

Oldshoremore

355
AN
SOCACH

Kinlochbervie

Loch Clash   Badcall

B801

Achriesgill

North Coast 500

Strath D

Achlyness

Loch Inchard

A838

Rhiconich

Loch na
Claise Càrnaich

Rubha Ruadh

NC

Fanagmore

Skerricha

Loch Laxford

908
FOINAVEN

Tarbet

HANDA
ISLAND

Foindle

North-west Sutherland

Loch na

Scourie Bay

Laxford
Bridge

786
ARKLE

7

Scourie

A894

River Laxford

Loch
Stack

Scourie More

Lower
Badcall

Upper
Badcall

Strath Stack

721
BEN STACK

Badcall Bay

Loch a'
Mhuilinn

386
BEN
AUSKAIRD

Achfary

333
BEN
SCREAVIE

Rubh' a'
Mhucard

North Coast 500

17

A838

Loch A

Point of Stoer

OLDANY
ISLAND

Eddrachillis
Bay

Locha Chàirn Bhàin

419
BEN
STROME

Kylestrome

Loch an
Leathaid Bhuain

Glendhu Forest

Old Man
of Stoer

Culkein

Clashnessie
Bay

Culkein
Drumbeg

Kylesku

Loch Glendhu

Oldany

Drumbeg

B869

Unapool

525
BEINN AIRD
DA LOCH

Achnacarnin

The Rock Stop

Loch Glencoul

Clashmore

Nedd

Glen

Loch
Poll

Clashnessie

Loch an
Leothaid

776
SAIL
GHORM

Leirg

809
QUINAG

Loch na
Gàinmhich

Loch-Beag

792
BEINN LEOID

Stoer

B869

North Coast 500

Loch
Beannach

Eas-a' Chùal Aluinn

774
GLAS BHEINN

Clachtoll

Bay of Clachtoll

Rhicarn

11

A894

Achmelvich
Bay

Achmelvich

A837

Loch Assynt

Ardvreck

161

160

Baddidarrach   10

Lochinver

535
BEINN GHARBH

Inchnadamph

Assynt - Coigach

0 1 2 3 4 5 miles
0 1 2 3 4 5 6 7 8 kilometres

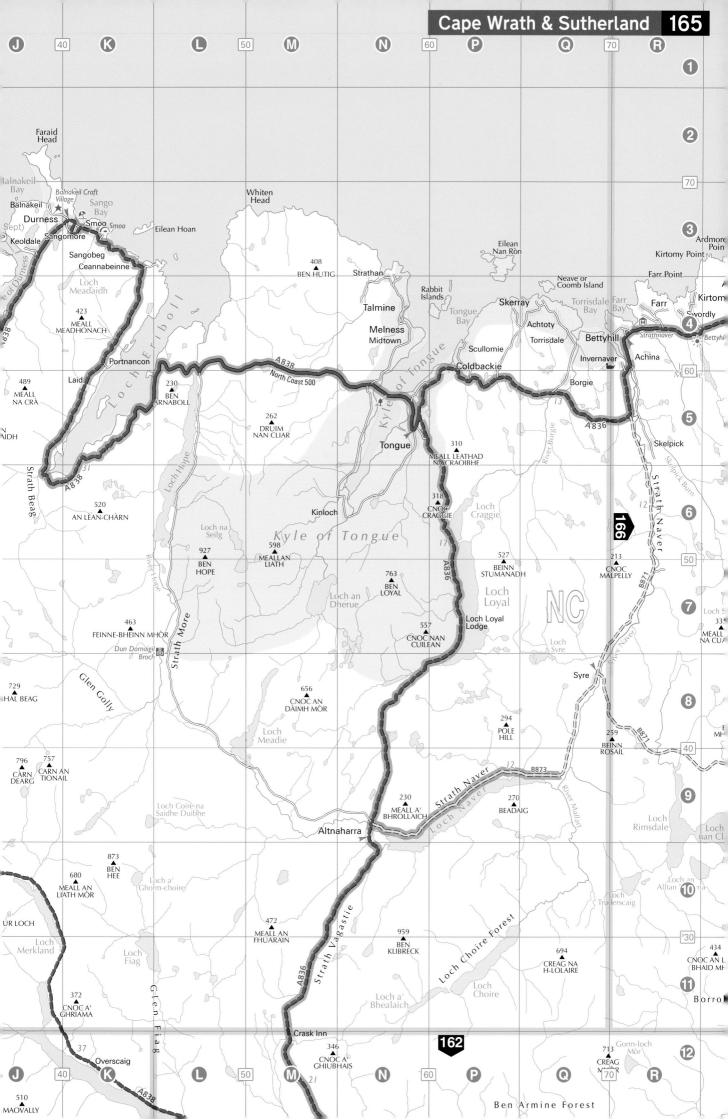

J 40 K L 50 M N 60 P Q 70 R

1
2
70
Ardmore
Poin
Kirtomy Point
Farr Point
Faraid
Head
Balnakeil
Bay
Balnakeil Craft
Village
Sango
Bay
Whiten
Head
Eilean
Nan Ròn
Neave or
Coomb Island
Farr
Kirtom
Balnakeil
Durness
(Sept)
Keoldale
Sangomore
Smoo Smoo
Eilean Hoan
Strathan
Rabbit
Islands
Skerray
Achtoty
Torrisdale
Bettyhill
Invernaver
Swordly
Bettyhi
Strathnaver
Achina
4
Sangobeg
Ceannabeinne
Loch
Meadaidh
408
BEN HUTIG
Talmine
Tongue
Bay
Scullomie
Coldbackie
Skelpick
Strath Naver
423
MEALL
MEADHONACH
Portnancon
Laid
230
BEN
ARNABOLL
A838
North Coast 500
Melness
Midtown
A838
Borgie
13
A836
489
MEALL
NA CRÀ
AIDH
262
DRUIM
NAN CLIAR
Kyle of Tongue
Tongue
310
MEALL LEATHAD
NA CRAOIBHE
5
Strath Beag
A838
31
520
AN LÈAN-CHÀRN
Loch Hope
Kinloch
318
CNOC
CRAGGIE
Loch
Craggie
166
213
CNOC
MALPELLY
B871
6
50
Strath More
Loch na
Seilg
927
BEN
HOPE
598
MEALLAN
LIATH
Kyle of Tongue
A836
17
763
BEN
LOYAL
Loch an
Dherue
527
BEINN
STUMANADH
Loch
Loyal
NC
7
Loch S
MEALL
NA CUA
33
463
FEINNE-BHEINN MHÒR
Dun Dornaigil
Broch
557
CNOC NAN
CUILEAN
Loch Loyal
Lodge
Loch
Syre
Syre
River Naver
729
HAL BEAG
Glen Golly
656
CNOC AN
DÀIMH MÒR
294
POLE
HILL
259
BEINN
ROSAIL
B871
40
MF
8
796
CÀRN AN
DEARG
757
CARN AN
TIONAIL
Loch
Meadie
Strath Naver
Loch Naver
12
B873
River Mallart
9
Loch
Rimsdale
Loch
nan Cl
230
MEALL A'
BHROLLAICH
270
BEADAIG
UR LOCH
Loch
Merkland
873
BEN
HEE
680
MEALL AN
LIATH MÒR
Loch a'
Ghorm-choire
Altnaharra
Loch Coire na
Saidhe Duibhe
Loch an
Alltan
Loch
Truderscaig
30
10
472
MEALL AN
FHUARAIN
959
BEN
KLIBRECK
A836
Strath Vagastie
Loch Choire Forest
694
CREAG NA
H-LOLAIRE
434
CNOC AN L
BHAID MH
11
372
CNOC A'
GHRIAMA
Loch
Fiag
Loch a'
Bhealaich
Loch
Choire
Borro
MAOVALLY
510
37
Overscaig
Glen Fiag
Crask Inn
346
CNOC A'
GHIUBHAIS
162
713
CREAG
M R
Gorm-loch
Mòr
12
J 40 K A838 L 50 M 21 N 60 P Q 70 R

Ben Armine Forest

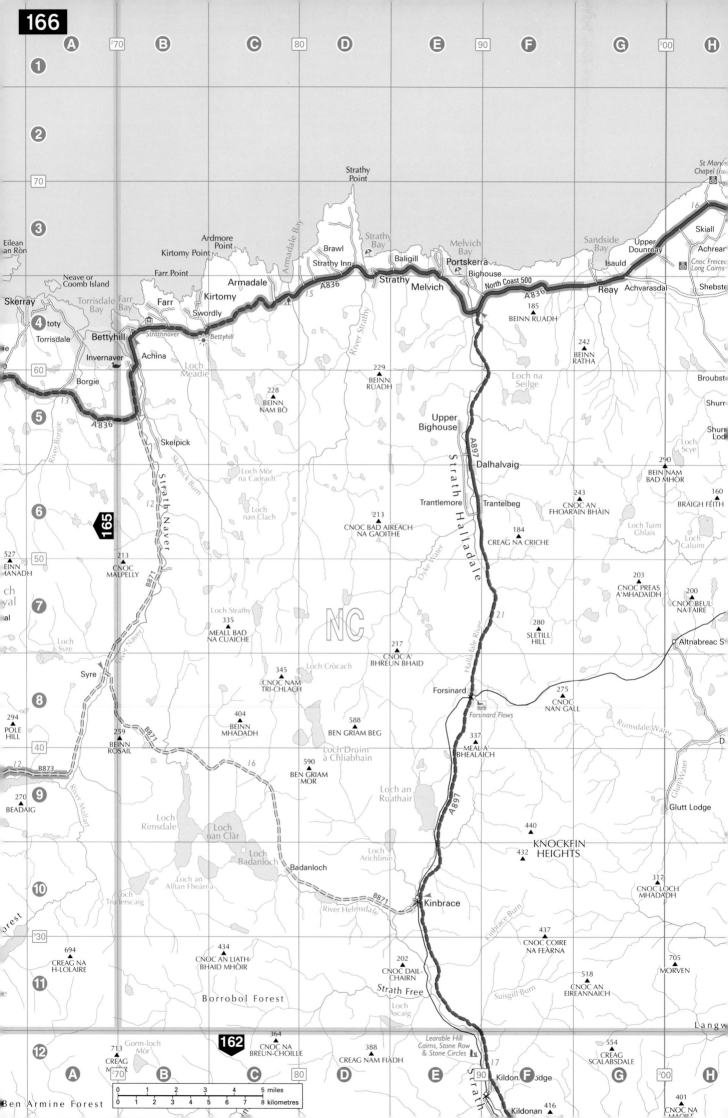

WESTERN ISLES

The Western Isles, na h-Eileanan Siar, stretch for 130 miles along the edge of the Atlantic, fringed on the west by mile after mile of clean, sandy beaches. The islands have a distinctive culture and Gaelic is the first language of the majority of islanders. Roadside place name signs are in Gaelic. Both part of Scotland's largest island, Lewis (in the north) and Harris (in the south) are very different. Lewis is low-lying and covered with bleak peat moors, whereas Harris is rocky and mountainous, with fertile green 'machair' land to the west.

North Uist, Benbecula and South Uist offer beaches and low-lying 'machair' to the west, and mountains and moorland to the east, while Barra has a rocky, broken east coast and fine sandy bays in the west, rising to a summit at Heaval.

For information on ferry services to the Western Isles see page XI.

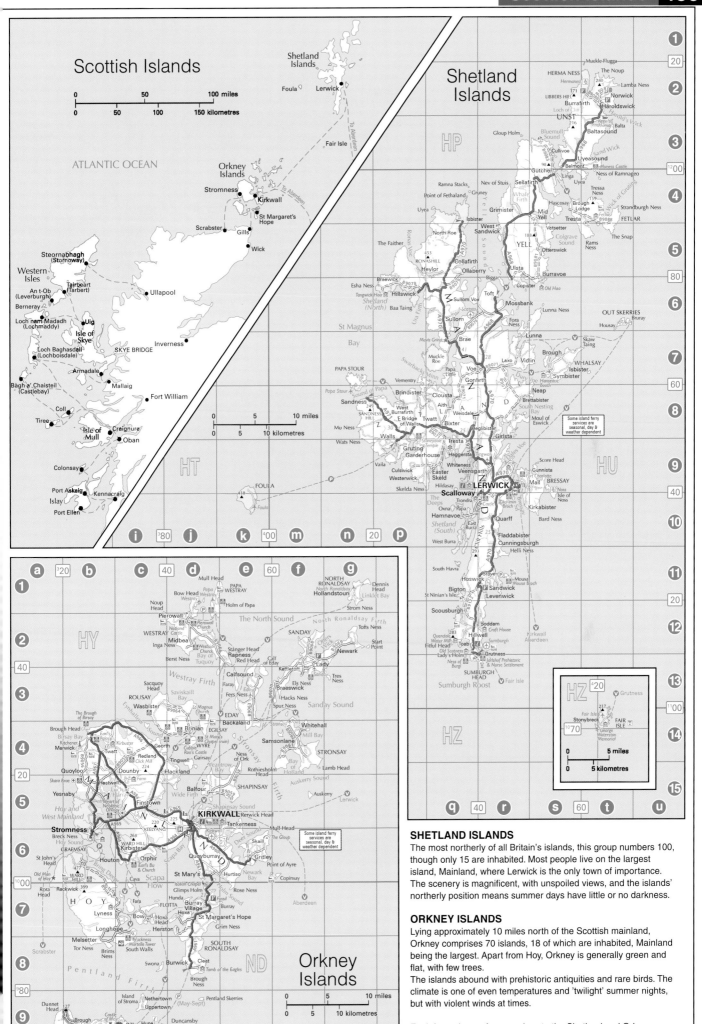

Scottish Islands

ATLANTIC OCEAN

Shetland Islands

Orkney Islands

SHETLAND ISLANDS

The most northerly of all Britain's islands, this group numbers 100, though only 15 are inhabited. Most people live on the largest island, Mainland, where Lerwick is the only town of importance. The scenery is magnificent, with unspoiled views, and the islands' northerly position means summer days have little or no darkness.

ORKNEY ISLANDS

Lying approximately 10 miles north of the Scottish mainland, Orkney comprises 70 islands, 18 of which are inhabited, Mainland being the largest. Apart from Hoy, Orkney is generally green and flat, with few trees.

The islands abound with prehistoric antiquities and rare birds. The climate is one of even temperatures and 'twilight' summer nights, but with violent winds at times.

For information on ferry services to the Shetland and Orkney Islands see page XI.

IRISH SEA

CELTIC SEA

	Toll-free motorway		B road (Northern Ireland)
	Toll motorway and plaza		Distance in miles between symbols (Northern Ireland)
	Motorway junctions with and without number		Minor road
	Restricted motorway junctions		Road tunnel, with toll
	Motorway service area		Road under construction
	National primary route (Republic of Ireland)		Airport (major/minor)
	National secondary route (Republic of Ireland)		International boundary
	Regional route (Republic of Ireland)		Vehicle ferry
	Distance in kilometres between symbols (Republic of Ireland)		Fast vehicle ferry or catamaran
	Primary route (Northern Ireland)		Gaeltacht (Irish language area)
	A road (Northern Ireland)		For key to touring information see page 1

To reflect the distances shown on road signs, distances are shown in miles in Northern Ireland and kilometres in the Republic of Ireland.

16 kilometres = 10 miles

Ireland index

Abbeydorney.............C12
Abbeyfeale.............D12
Abbeyleix.............G11
Adamstown.............H12
Adare.............D12
Adrigole.............C14
Aghalee.............J5
Ahascragh.............E9
Ahoghill.............J4
Allenwood.............H9
Allihies.............B15
An Bun Beag.............E4
An Charraig.............E5
An Cheathrú Rua.............C9
An Clochán Liath.............E4
An Coireán.............B14
An Daingean.............B13
An Fál Carrach.............F3
An Fhairche.............C9
Annahilt.............J6
Annalong.............J7
Annascaul.............B13
Annestown.............G13
An Rinn.............G13
An Spidéal.............D9
Antrim.............J5
Ardagh.............D12
Ardara.............E5
Ardee.............H8
Ardfert.............C12
Ardfinnan.............F12
Ardglass.............K6
Ardgroom.............B14
Ardmore.............F14
Ardnacrusha.............E11
Arklow.............J11
Armagh.............H6
Armoy.............J3
Arvagh.............G7
Ashbourne.............J9
Ashford.............J10
Askeaton.............D12
Athboy.............H8
Athea.............D12
Athenry.............E9
Athleague.............E8
Athlone.............F9
Athy.............H10
Augher.............G6
Aughnacloy.............H6
Aughrim.............E9
Aughrim.............J11
Avoca.............J11

Bagenalstown.............H11
Baile an
   Fheirtéaraigh.............B13
Baile Chláir.............D9
Baile Mhic Íre.............D14
Baile na Finne.............F4
Bailieborough.............H7
Balbriggan.............J8
Balla.............D8
Ballacolla.............G11
Ballaghaderreen.............E7
Ballina.............D7
Ballina.............E11
Ballinafad.............E7
Ballinagar.............G9
Ballinagh.............G7
Ballinamallard.............G6
Ballinamore.............F7
Ballinascarty.............D14
Ballinasloe.............E9
Ballincollig.............E14
Ballindaggan.............H12
Ballindine.............D8
Ballineen.............D14
Ballingarry.............D12
Ballingarry.............G12
Ballingeary.............D14
Ballinlough.............E8
Ballinrobe.............D8
Ballinspittle.............E14
Ballintra.............F5
Ballivor.............H9
Ballon.............H11
Ballybay.............H7
Ballybofey.............F5
Ballybunion.............C12
Ballycanew.............J11
Ballycarry.............K5

Ballycastle.............J3
Ballycastle.............C6
Ballyclare.............J5
Ballyclerahan.............F12
Ballyconneely.............B9
Ballyconnell.............G7
Ballycotton.............F14
Ballycumber.............F9
Ballydehob.............C15
Ballydesmond.............D13
Ballyduff.............C12
Ballyduff.............F14
Ballyfarnon.............E7
Ballyferriter.............B13
Ballygally.............J4
Ballygar.............E9
Ballygawley.............H6
Ballygawley.............E6
Ballygowan.............K5
Ballyhack.............H13
Ballyhaise.............G7
Ballyhalbert.............K5
Ballyhaunis.............E8
Ballyhean.............D8
Ballyheige.............C12
Ballyjamesduff.............G8
Ballylanders.............E12
Ballylickey.............C14
Ballylongford.............C12
Ballylynan.............H10
Ballymacarbry.............F13
Ballymahon.............F8
Ballymakeery.............D14
Ballymena.............J4
Ballymoe.............E8
Ballymoney.............H4
Ballymore.............F9
Ballymore Eustace.............H10
Ballymote.............E7
Ballynacarrigy.............G8
Ballynahinch.............J6
Ballynure.............J5
Ballyporeen.............F13
Ballyragget.............G11
Ballyroan.............G10
Ballysadare.............E6
Ballyshannon.............F5
Ballyvaughan.............D10
Ballywalter.............K5
Balrothery.............J8
Baltimore.............C15
Baltinglass.............H10
Banagher.............F10
Banbridge.............J6
Bandon.............E14
Bangor Erris.............C7
Bansha.............F12
Banteer.............D13
Bantry.............C14
Barna.............D9
Béal an
   Mhuirthead.............B6
Béal Átha an
   Ghaorthaidh.............D14
Bearna.............D9
Belcoo.............F6
Belfast.............J5
Belgooly.............E14
Bellaghy.............H4
Belleek.............F6
Belmullet.............B6
Belturbet.............G7
Benburb.............H6
Bennettsbridge.............H11
Beragh.............G5
Bessbrook.............J6
Bettystown.............J8
Blacklion.............F6
Blackwater.............J12
Blarney.............E14
Blessington.............H10
Boherbue.............D13
Borris.............H12
Borris-in-Ossory.............F10
Borrisokane.............F10
Borrisoleigh.............F11
Boyle.............E7
Bray.............J10
Bridgetown.............H13

Brittas.............J9
Broadford.............E11
Broadford.............D12
Broughshane.............J4
Bruff.............E12
Bunbeg.............E4
Bunclody.............H11
Buncrana.............G3
Bundoran.............E6
Bunmahon.............G13
Bunnyconnellan.............D7
Bushmills.............H3
Buttevant.............E13
Bweeng.............E13

Cadamstown.............F10
Caherconlish.............E12
Caherdaniel.............B14
Cahersiveen.............B14
Cahir.............F12
Caledon.............H6
Callan.............G12
Caltra.............E9
Camp.............B13
Carndonagh.............G3
Carnew.............J11
Carnlough.............J4
Carragh.............H9
Carraig Airt.............F3
Carraroe.............C9
Carrick.............E5
Carrickfergus.............K5
Carrickmacross.............H7
Carrickmore.............G5
Carrick-on-
   Shannon.............F7
Carrick-on-Suir.............G12
Carrigaline.............E14
Carrigallen.............F7
Carriganimmy.............D13
Carrigart.............F3
Carrigtwohill.............E14
Carryduff.............J5
Cashel.............F12
Castlebar.............D8
Castlebellingham.............J7
Castleblakeney.............E9
Castleblayney.............H7
Castlebridge.............J12
Castlecomer.............G11
Castleconnell.............E11
Castlederg.............G5
Castledermot.............H11
Castlegregory.............B13
Castleisland.............C13
Castlemaine.............C13
Castlemartyr.............F14
Castleplunket.............E8
Castlepollard.............G8
Castlerea.............E8
Castlerock.............H3
Castletownbere.............B15
Castletownroche.............E13
Castletownshend.............D15
Castlewellan.............J6
Cathair Dónall.............B14
Causeway.............C12
Cavan.............G7
Celbridge.............H9
Charlestown.............E7
Charleville.............E12
Cill Charthaigh.............E5
Cill Chiaráin.............C9
Clady.............G5
Clane.............H9
Clara.............G9
Claregalway.............D9
Claremorris.............D8
Clashmore.............F13
Claudy.............G4
Cleggan.............B8
Clifden.............B9
Cliffoney.............E6
Cloghan.............F10
Clogheen.............F13
Clogher.............G6

Clogherhead.............J8
Clogh Mills.............J4
Clonakilty.............D15
Clonaslee.............G10
Clonbur.............C9
Clondalkin.............J9
Clonea.............G13
Clones.............G7
Clonmany.............G3
Clonmel.............F12
Clonmellon.............H8
Clonroche.............H12
Clough.............K6
Cloughjordan.............F10
Cloyne.............F14
Coachford.............D14
Coagh.............H5
Coalisland.............H5
Cobh.............E14
Coleraine.............H3
Collinstown.............G8
Collon.............H8
Collooney.............E7
Comber.............K5
Cong.............D9
Convoy.............F4
Cookstown.............H5
Coole.............G8
Cooraclare.............C11
Cootehill.............G7
Cork.............E14
Cornamona.............C9
Corr na Móna.............C9
Corrofin.............D10
Courtmacsherry.............E15
Courtown.............J11
Craigavon.............J6
Craughwell.............E10
Creeslough.............F4
Croithlí.............E4
Crolly.............E4
Crookhaven.............C15
Crookstown.............D14
Croom.............E12
Crossakeel.............H8
Crosshaven.............E14
Crossmaglen.............H7
Crossmolina.............D7
Crumlin.............J5
Crusheen.............D10
Culdaff.............G3
Cullybackey.............J4
Culmore.............G4
Curracloe.............J12
Curry.............E7
Cushendall.............J3
Cushendun.............J3

Daingean.............G9
Daingean Uí
   Chúis.............B13
Delvin.............G8
Derrinturn.............H9
Derry.............G4
Derrygonnelly.............F6
Derrylin.............G6
Dervock.............H3
Dingle.............B13
Doagh.............J5
Donabate.............J9
Donaghadee.............K5
Donaghmore.............H5
Donaghmore.............H8
Donegal.............F5
Donemana.............G4
Doolin.............C10
Doon.............E12
Doonbeg.............C11
Downings.............F3
Downpatrick.............K6
Dowra.............F6
Draperstown.............H5
Drimoleague.............D14
Drogheda.............J8
Droichead Nua.............H10
Dromahair.............E6
Dromara.............J6
Dromcollogher.............D12
Dromiskin.............J7
Drommahane.............E13
Dromod.............F8
Dromore.............J6

Dromore.............G5
Dromore West.............D6
Drumaness.............K6
Drumfries.............G3
Drumkeeran.............F7
Drumlish.............F8
Drumquin.............G5
Drumshanbo.............F7
Drumsna.............F7
Duagh.............C12
Dublin.............J9
Duleek.............J8
Dunboyne.............J9
Dún Chaoin.............A13
Dundalk.............J7
Dundonald.............K5
Dundrum.............F12
Dunfanaghy.............F3
Dungannon.............H5
Dungarvan.............G13
Dungiven.............H4
Dunglow.............E4
Dungourney.............F14
Dunkineely.............E5
Dún Laoghaire.............J9
Dunlavin.............H10
Dunleer.............J8
Dunloy.............J4
Dunmanway.............D14
Dunmore.............E8
Dunmore East.............H13
Dunquin.............A13
Dunshaughlin.............H9
Durrow.............G11
Durrow.............G9
Durrus.............C15
Dysart.............E9

Easky.............D6
Edenderry.............H9
Edgeworthstown.............G8
Eglinton.............H4
Elphin.............F8
Emyvale.............H6
Enfield.............H9
Ennis.............D11
Enniscorthy.............H12
Enniscrone.............D6
Enniskean.............D14
Enniskillen.............G6
Ennistymon.............D10
Eyrecourt.............F10

Fahan.............H4
Falcarragh.............F3
Fanore.............D10
Farranfore.............C13
Feakle.............E11
Fenagh.............F7
Fenit.............C12
Ferbane.............F9
Fermoy.............E13
Ferns.............J12
Fethard.............F12
Fethard.............H13
Fintona.............G6
Fintown.............F4
Fivemiletown.............G6
Foxford.............D7
Foynes.............D12
Freemount.............D13
Frenchpark.............E8
Freshford.............G11

Galbally.............E12
Galway.............D9
Garrison.............F6
Garvagh.............H4
Gilford.............J6
Glandore.............D15
Glanworth.............E13
Glaslough.............H6
Glassan.............F8
Gleann Cholm Cille.............E5
Glenamaddy.............E8
Glenarm.............J4
Glenavy.............J5
Glenbeigh.............B13
Glencolumbkille.............E5
Glenealy.............J10
Glengarriff.............C14
Glenties.............E5

Glin.............D12
Golden.............F12
Goleen.............C15
Goresbridge.............H11
Gorey.............J11
Gort.............D10
Gorteen.............E7
Gortin.............G5
Gowran.............H11
Graiguenamanagh.............H12
Granard.............G8
Grange.............E6
Greencastle.............H3
Greencastle.............G5
Greenore.............J7
Greyabbey.............K5
Greystones.............J10
Gulladuff.............H4

Hacketstown.............H11
Headford.............D9
Hillsborough.............J6
Hilltown.............J6
Holycross.............F11
Holywood.............K5
Hospital.............E12
Howth.............J9

Inagh.............D11
Inch.............B13
Inchigeelagh.............D14
Inishcrone.............D6
Innishannon.............E14
Irvinestown.............F6

Johnstown.............G11

Kanturk.............D13
Keadue.............F7
Keady.............H6
Kealkill.............C14
Keel.............B7
Kells.............J4
Kells.............H5
Kenmare.............C14
Kesh.............F5
Kilbeggan.............G9
Kilcar.............E5
Kilcock.............H9
Kilcolgan.............D10
Kilconnell.............E9
Kilcoole.............J10
Kilcormac.............F10
Kilcullen.............H10
Kildare.............H10
Kildorrery.............E13
Kilfenora.............D10
Kilfinane.............E12
Kilgarvan.............C14
Kilkee.............C11
Kilkenny.............G11
Kilkieran.............C9
Kill.............H9
Kill.............G13
Killadysert.............D11
Killala.............D6
Killaloe.............E11
Killarney.............C13
Killashandra.............G7
Killeagh.............F14
Killenaule.............F12
Killimer.............C11
Killiney.............J9
Killinick.............J13
Killorglin.............C13
Killough.............K6
Killucan.............G9
Killurin.............G10
Killybegs.............E5
Killyleagh.............K6
Kilmacanogue.............J10
Kilmacrenan.............F3
Kilmacthomas.............G13
Kilmaganny.............G12
Kilmaine.............D8
Kilmallock.............E12
Kilmanagh.............G11
Kilmeedy.............D12
Kilmichael.............D14
Kilmihil.............C11
Kilmore Quay.............H13

Kilmuckridge.............J12
Kilpedder.............J10
Kilrea.............H4
Kilrush.............C11
Kilsheelan.............G12
Kiltegan.............H11
Kiltimagh.............D8
Kilworth.............E13
Kingscourt.............H7
Kinlough.............E6
Kinnegad.............G9
Kinnitty.............F10
Kinsale.............E14
Kinvarra.............D10
Kircubbin.............K5
Knock.............D8
Knockcroghery.............F8

Lahinch.............C10
Lanesborough.............F8
Laragh.............J10
Larne.............K4
Lauragh.............C14
Laurencetown.............F10
Leap.............D15
Leenaun.............C8
Leighlinbridge.............H11
Leitrim.............B9
Leitrim.............F7
Leixlip.............H9
Letterfrack.............B8

Letterkenny.............F
Lifford.............G
Limavady.............H
Limerick.............E1
Lisbellaw.............G
Lisburn.............J
Liscarroll.............J
Lisdoonvarna.............D1
Lismore.............F1
Lisnaskea.............G
Listowel.............J
Loghill.............C
Londonderry.............H
Longford.............J
Longwood.............H
Loughbrickland.............J
Loughglinn.............E
Loughrea.............E10
Louisburgh.............C
Lucan.............J
Lurgan.............J
Lusk.............J

Macroom.............D14
Maghera.............H
Magherafelt.............H
Maguiresbridge.............G
Maigh Cuilinn.............D
Malahide.............J
Málainn Mhóir.............E
Malin.............G3

Malin More E5
Mallow E13
Manorhamilton F6
Markethill H6
Martinstown J4
Maynooth H9
Mayobridge J6
Midleton F14
Milford F4
Milltown C13
Milltown Malbay C11
Mitchelstown E13
Moate F9
Mohill F7
Monaghan H6
Monasterevin G10
Moneymore H5
Monivea E9
Mooncoin G13
Mountbellew E9
Mountcharles F5
Mountmellick G10
Mountrath G10
Mountshannon E10
Moville G3
Moy H6
Moycullen D9
Moynalty H8
Mucklagh G9
Muff G4

Muine Bheag H11
Mullagh H8
Mullaghmore E6
Mullinahone G12
Mullinavat G12
Mullingar G9
Mulranny C7
Murrisk C8
Murroe E11
Naas H10
Na Dúnaibh F3
Naul J8
Navan G9
Nenagh E11
Newbawn H12
Newbliss G7
Newbridge H10
Newcastle J6
Newcastle West D12
New Inn E11
Newmarket D13
Newmarket-on-Fergus D11
Newport C7
Newport E11
New Ross H12
Newry J6
Newtownabbey J5
Newtownards K5

Newtownbutler G7
Newtown-cunningham G4
Newtownforbes F8
Newtownhamilton H6
Newtownmount-kennedy J10
Newtownstewart G5
Nobber H8
Ogonnelloe E11
Oilgate H12
Oldcastle G8
Omagh G5
Omeath J7
Oola E12
Oranmore D9
Oughterard D9
Pallasgreen E12
Partry D8
Passage East H13
Passage West E14
Patrickswell E12
Pettigo F5
Piltown G12
Plumbridge G5
Pomeroy H5
Portadown H6
Portaferry K6
Portarlington G10

Portavogie K6
Portballintrae H3
Portglenone H4
Port Laoise G10
Portlaw G13
Portmagee B14
Portmarnock J9
Portnablagh F3
Portnoo E4
Portroe E11
Portrush H3
Portstewart H3
Portumna E10
Poyntzpass J6
Prosperous H9

Quin D11

Raharney G9
Ramelton F4
Randalstown J5
Raphoe G4
Rasharkin J4
Rathangan H10
Rathcoole J9
Rathcormac E13
Rathdowney G11
Rathdrum J10
Rathfriland J6
Rathkeale D12
Ráth Luirc E12

Rathmore D13
Rathmullan G4
Rathnew J10
Rathvilly H11
Ratoath J9
Recess C9
Rhode G9
Ringaskiddy E14
Ringville G13
Riverchapel J11
Riverstick E14
Rochfortbridge G9
Rockcorry H7
Roosky H12
Rosbercon H12
Roscommon F8
Roscrea F10
Rosscarbery D15
Rosses Point E6
Rosslare J13
Rosslare Harbour J13
Rosslea G6
Rossnowlagh E5
Rostrevor J7
Roundstone B9
Roundwood J10
Rush J9

Saintfield K6
St Johnston G4
Sallins H9

Salthill D9
Scarriff E11
Scartaglin C13
Schull C15
Seskinore G5
Shanagarry F14
Shannon D11
Shannonbridge F9
Shercock H7
Shillelagh H11
Shinrone F10
Shrule D9
Silvermines E11
Sion Mills G5
Sixmilebridge D11
Skerries J8
Skibbereen D15
Slane H8
Sligo E6
Smithborough G6
Sneem B14
Spanish Point C11
Spiddal D9
Sraith Salach C9
Stewartstown H5
Stoneyford G12
Strabane G4
Stradbally G10
Stradone G7
Strandhill E6
Strangford K6

Stranorlar F5
Strokestown F8
Summerhill H9
Swan G11
Swanlinbar F6
Swinford D7
Swords J9
Taghmon H12
Tagoat J13
Tallaght J9
Tallow F13
Tandragee J6
Tarbert C12
Templemore F11
Termonfeckin J8
Thomastown G12
Thurles F11
Timahoe G10
Timoleague D15
Tinahely J11
Tipperary F12
Tobercurry E7
Tobermore H4
Toomevara F11
Toomore C15
Tower E14
Tralee C13
Tramore G13
Trim H8
Tuam D9

Tubbercurry E7
Tulla D11
Tullamore G9
Tullow H11
Tulsk E8
Turlough D7

Urlingford G11

Virginia G8

Warrenpoint J7
Waterford G13
Watergrasshill E13
Waterville B14
Wellingtonbridge H13
Westport C8
Wexford J12
Whitegate E14
Whitehead K5
Wicklow J10
Woodenbridge J11
Woodford E10

Youghal F14

Town plan : Central London p.238–247

NORTH

SEA

Street map symbols

Town, port and airport plans

2 Motorway and junction	→ One-way, gated/ closed road	Railway station	Toilet, with facilities for the less able			
4 Primary road single/ dual carriageway and numbered junction	Restricted access road	Preserved or tourist railway	P P Car park, with electric charging point			
37 A road single/ dual carriageway and numbered junction	Pedestrian area	o Light rapid transit system station	P+R Park and Ride (at least 6 days per week)			
B road single/ dual carriageway	Footpath	Level crossing	Bus/coach station			
Local road single/ dual carriageway	Road under construction	Tramway	H H Hospital, 24-hour Accident & Emergency hospital			
Other road single/ dual carriageway, minor road	Road tunnel	Airport, heliport	Beach (award winning)			
Building of interest	Lighthouse	R Railair terminal	City wall			
Ruined building	Castle	Theatre or performing arts centre	Escarpment			
Tourist Information Centre	Castle mound	Cinema	Cliff lift			
Visitor or heritage centre	• Monument, memorial, statue	† Abbey, chapel, church	River/canal, lake			
World Heritage Site (UNESCO)	Post Office	Synagogue	Lock, weir			
Museum	Public library	Mosque	Viewpoint			
English Heritage site	Shopping centre	Golf course	Park/sports ground			
Historic Scotland site	Shopmobility	Racecourse	Cemetery			
Cadw (Welsh heritage) site	Football stadium	Nature reserve	Woodland			
National Trust site	Rugby stadium	Aquarium	Built-up area			
National Trust Scotland site	County cricket ground	Showground	Beach			

Central London street map (see pages 238–247)

London Underground station	London Overground station
Docklands Light Railway (DLR) station	Central London Congestion Charge and Ultra Low Emission boundary*

Royal Parks

Green Park	Park open 5am–midnight. Constitution Hill and The Mall closed to traffic Sundays and public holidays 8am–dusk.
Hyde Park	Park open 5am–midnight. Park roads closed to traffic midnight–5am.
Kensington Gardens	Park open 6am–dusk.
Regent's Park	Park open 5am–dusk. Park roads closed to traffic midnight–7am, except for residents.
St James's Park	Park open 5am–midnight. The Mall closed to traffic Sundays and public holidays 8am–dusk.
Victoria Tower Gardens	Park open dawn–dusk.

Traffic regulations in the City of London include security checkpoints and restrict the number of entry and exit points.

Note: Oxford Street is closed to through-traffic (except buses & taxis) 7am–7pm Monday–Saturday.

Central London Congestion Charge Zone (CCZ)

You need to pay a daily charge for driving or parking a vehicle on public roads in this central London area. Payment permits entry, travel within and exit from the CCZ by the vehicle as often as required on that day.

In June 2020, due to the coronavirus pandemic, temporary changes were made to the charges and times of operation and these continue to be under review. At the time of printing you must pay a £15 daily charge if you drive within the zone 07:00-22:00, every day, except Christmas Day (25 December).

For up to date information on the CCZ, exemptions, discounts or ways to pay, visit **tfl.gov.uk/modes/driving/congestion-charge**

Ultra Low Emission Zone (ULEZ)

Most vehicles in Central London, including cars and vans, need to meet minimum exhaust emission standards or drivers must pay a daily charge to drive within the zone. It applies to the same area covered by the Congestion Charge and operates 24 hours a day, every day of the year, except Christmas Day (25 December). The charge is £12.50 for motorcycles, cars and vans and is in addition to the Congestion Charge.

*From 25th October 2021 the ULEZ boundary will be extended from central London to include the area up to, but not including, the North Circular Road (A406) and South Circular Road (A205).

Please note the maps in this atlas show the zone in operation at the time of going to print.

For further information visit **tfl.gov.uk/ULEZ**

In addition the Low Emission Zone (LEZ) operates across Greater London, 24 hours every day of the year and is aimed at the most heavy-polluting vehicles. It does not apply to cars or motorcycles. For details visit **tfl.gov.uk/LEZ**

Town Plans

Aberdeen 188	Guildford........................ 204	Plymouth 220
Basingstoke................. 188	Harrogate....................... 205	Poole............................ 222
Bath............................. 189	Huddersfield 205	Portsmouth 221
Birmingham 190	Inverness....................... 206	Preston 222
Blackpool..................... 189	Ipswich.......................... 206	Ramsgate...................... 39
Bournemouth................ 191	Kingston upon Hull 207	Reading......................... 223
Bradford....................... 191	Lancaster 207	Royal Tunbridge Wells...... 223
Brighton 192	Leeds............................ 208	Salisbury 224
Bristol 192	Leicester 209	Sheffield........................ 224
Cambridge 193	Lincoln.......................... 209	Shrewsbury 225
Canterbury 194	Liverpool 210	Southampton 226
Cardiff.......................... 194	Llandudno...................... 79	Southend-on-Sea 225
Carlisle........................ 195	LONDON...............238-247	Stirling 227
Cheltenham 195	Luton............................ 211	Stockton-on-Tees............ 227
Chester 196	Maidstone 211	Stoke-on-Trent (Hanley) 228
Colchester 196	Manchester 212	Stratford-upon-Avon 228
Coventry 197	Margate......................... 39	Sunderland.................... 229
Darlington 197	Middlesbrough 214	Swansea........................ 230
Derby 198	Milton Keynes 213	Swindon 230
Doncaster..................... 198	Newcastle upon Tyne 215	Taunton 231
Dover 199	Newport 214	Torquay 231
Dundee 199	Newquay 4	Warwick 232
Durham......................... 200	Northampton 216	Watford 232
Eastbourne................... 200	Norwich 216	Winchester..................... 233
Edinburgh 201	Nottingham.................... 217	Wolverhampton 233
Exeter 202	Oldham 217	Worcester 234
Glasgow 203	Oxford........................... 218	York.............................. 234
Gloucester.................... 202	Perth 219	
Great Yarmouth 204	Peterborough 219	

Central London

Ferry Ports

Aberdeen Harbour	*XI*
Calais	*IX*
Dover, Port of	*IX*
Fishguard Harbour	*X*
Harwich International Port	53
Heysham Harbour	*X*
Holyhead Harbour	*X*
Hull, Port of	*XI*
Liverpool Docks	*X*
Newhaven Harbour	*IX*
Pembroke Dock	*X*
Plymouth, Port of	*VIII*
Poole, Port of	*VIII*
Port of Tyne	*XI*
Portsmouth Harbour	*IX*
Southampton, Port of	*VIII*

Channel Tunnel

Folkestone Terminal	27
Calais / Coquelles Terminal	27

Airports

Aberdeen	237
Birmingham	236
East Midlands	236
Edinburgh	237
Glasgow	237
Leeds Bradford	237
London City	236
London Gatwick	235
London Heathrow	235
London Luton	235
London Stansted	235
Manchester	236

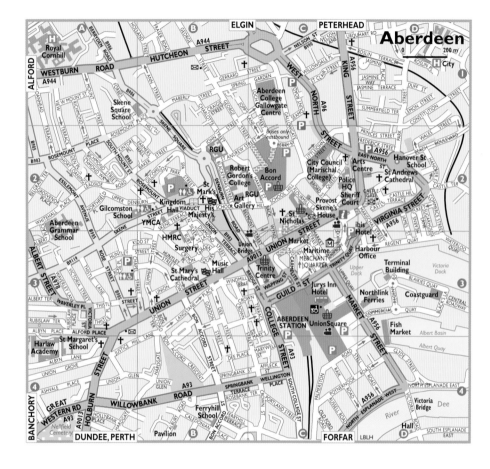

Aberdeen

Aberdeen is found on atlas page **151 N6**

Affleck Street	C4	Maberly Street	
Albert Street	A3	Marischal Street	
Albury Road	B4	Market Street	
Alford Place	A3	Nelson Street	
Ann Street	B1	Palmerston Road	
Beach Boulevard	D2	Park Street	
Belgrave Terrace	A2	Portland Street	
Berryden Road	A1	Poynernook Road	
Blackfriars Street	B2	Regent Quay	
Blaikies Quay	D3	Richmond Street	
Bon Accord Crescent	B4	Rose Place	
Bon Accord Street	B3	Rose Street	
Bridge Street	C3	Rosemount Place	
Caledonian Place	B4	Rosemount Viaduct	
Carmelite Street	C3	St Andrew Street	
Chapel Street	A3	St Clair Street	
Charlotte Street	B1	School Hill	
College Street	C3	Skene Square	
Constitution Street	D1	Skene Street	
Crimon Place	B3	Skene Terrace	
Crown Street	B3	South College Street	
Dee Street	B3	South Esplanade East	
Denburn Road	B2	South Mount Street	
Diamond Street	B3	Spa Street	
East North Street	D2	Springbank Street	
Esslemont Avenue	A2	Springbank Terrace	
Gallowgate	C1	Summer Street	
George Street	B1	Summerfield Terrace	
Gilcomston Park	B2	Thistle Lane	
Golden Square	B3	Thistle Place	
Gordon Street	B3	Thistle Street	
Great Western Road	A4	Trinity Quay	
Guild Street	C3	Union Bridge	
Hadden Street	C3	Union Grove	
Hanover Street	D2	Union Street	
Hardgate	B4	Union Terrace	
Harriet Street	C2	Upper Denburn	
Holburn Street	A4	Victoria Road	
Huntley Street	A3	Victoria Street	
Hutcheon Street	B1	View Terrace	
Jasmine Terrace	D1	Virginia Street	
John Street	B2	Wapping Street	
Justice Mill Lane	A4	Waverley Place	
King Street	C1	Wellington Place	
Langstane Place	B3	West North Street	
Leadside Road	A2	Westburn Road	
Loanhead Terrace	A1	Whitehall Place	
Loch Street	C1	Willowbank Road	

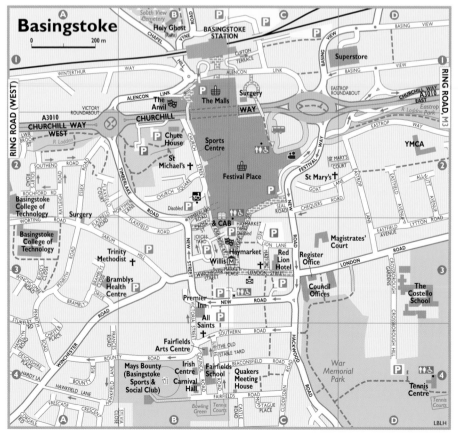

Basingstoke

Basingstoke is found on atlas page **22 H4**

Alencon Link	C1	London Street	
Allnutt Avenue	D2	Lower Brook Street	
Basing View	C1	Lytton Road	
Beaconsfield Road	C4	Market Place	
Bounty Rise	A4	May Place	
Bounty Road	A4	Montague Place	
Bramblys Close	A3	Mortimer Lane	
Bramblys Drive	A3	New Road	
Budd's Close	A3	New Road	
Castle Road	C4	New Street	
Chapel Hill	B1	Penrith Road	
Chequers Road	C2	Rayleigh Road	
Chester Place	A4	Red Lion Lane	
Churchill Way	B2	Rochford Road	
Churchill Way East	D1	St Mary's Court	
Churchill Way West	A2	Sarum Hill	
Church Square	B2	Seal Road	
Church Street	B2	Solby's Road	
Church Street	B3	Southend Road	
Cliddesden Road	C4	Southern Road	
Clifton Terrace	C1	Stukeley Road	
Cordale Road	A4	Sylvia Close	
Council Road	B4	Timberlake Road	
Crossborough Gardens	D3	Victoria Street	
Crossborough Hill	D3	Victory Roundabout	
Cross Street	B3	Vyne Road	
Devonshire Place	A4	Winchcombe Road	
Eastfield Avenue	D2	Winchester Road	
Eastrop Lane	D2	Winchester Street	
Eastrop Roundabout	C1	Winterthur Way	
Eastrop Way	D2	Worting Road	
Essex Road	A2	Wote Street	
Fairfields Road	B4		
Festival Way	C2		
Flaxfield Court	A2		
Flaxfield Road	A3		
Flaxfield Road	B3		
Frances Road	A4		
Frescade Crescent	A4		
Goat Lane	C2		
Hackwood Road	C4		
Hamelyn Road	A4		
Hardy Lane	A4		
Hawkfield Lane	A4		
Haymarket Yard	C3		
Joices Yard	B3		
Jubilee Road	B4		
London Road	D3		

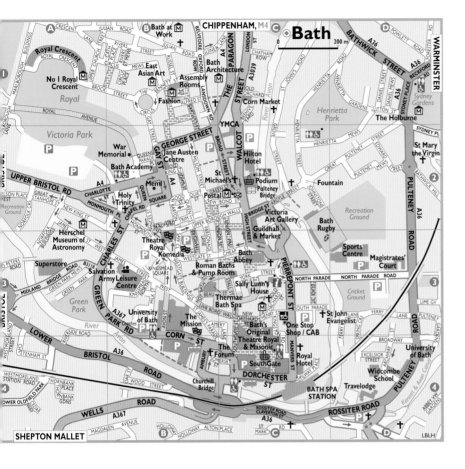

Bath

Bath is found on atlas page **20 D2**

Archway Street	D4	Lower Borough Walls	B3
Argyle Street	C2	Lower Bristol Road	A3
Avon Street	B3	Lower Oldfield Park	A4
Bartlett Street	B1	Manvers Street	C3
Barton Street	B2	Midland Bridge Road	A3
Bathwick Street	D1	Milk Street	B3
Beauford Square	B2	Milsom Street	B2
Beau Street	B3	Monmouth Place	A2
Beckford Road	D1	Monmouth Street	B2
Bennett Street	B1	New Bond Street	B2
Bridge Street	C2	New King Street	A2
Broad Street	C2	New Orchard Street	C3
Broadway	D4	Norfolk Buildings	A3
Brock Street	A1	North Parade	C3
Chapel Road	B2	North Parade Road	D3
Charles Street	A3	Old King Street	B2
Charlotte Street	A2	Oxford Row	B1
Cheap Street	C3	Pierrepont Street	C3
Cheltenham Street	A4	Princes Street	B2
Circus Mews	B1	Pulteney Road	D2
Claverton Street	C4	Queen Square	B2
Corn Street	B4	Queen Street	B2
Daniel Street	D1	Railway Place	C4
Dorchester Street	C4	Rivers Street	B1
Edward Street	D2	Rossiter Road	C4
Ferry Lane	D3	Royal Avenue	A1
Gay Street	B1	Royal Crescent	A1
George Street	B2	St James's Parade	B3
Great Pulteney Street	C2	St John's Road	C1
Great Stanhope Street	A2	Saw Close	B3
Green Park Road	A3	Southgate Street	C4
Green Street	B2	South Parade	C3
Grove Street	C2	Stall Street	C3
Guinea Lane	B1	Sutton Street	D1
Henrietta Gardens	D1	Sydney Place	D1
Henrietta Mews	C2	The Circus	B1
Henrietta Road	C1	The Paragon	C1
Henrietta Street	C2	Thornbank Place	A4
Henry Street	C3	Union Street	B2
High Street	C2	Upper Borough Walls	B2
Hot Bath Street	B3	Upper Bristol Road	A2
James Street West	B3	Upper Church Street	A1
John Street	B2	Walcot Street	C2
Julian Road	B1	Wells Road	A4
Kingsmead North	B3	Westgate Buildings	B3
Kingston Road	C3	Westgate Street	B2
Lansdown Road	B1	Westmoreland Station Road	A4
London Street	C1	York Street	C3

Blackpool

Blackpool is found on atlas page **88 C3**

Abingdon Street	B1	Havelock Street	C4
Adelaide Street	B3	High Street	C1
Albert Road	B3	Hornby Road	B3
Albert Road	C3	Hornby Road	D3
Alfred Street	C2	Hull Road	B3
Ashton Road	D4	Kay Street	C4
Bank Hey Street	B2	Kent Road	C4
Banks Street	B1	King Street	C2
Belmont Avenue	C4	Leamington Road	D2
Bennett Avenue	D3	Leicester Road	D2
Bethesda Road	C4	Leopold Grove	C2
Birley Street	B2	Lincoln Road	D2
Blenheim Avenue	D4	Livingstone Road	C3
Bonny Street	B4	Lord Street	B1
Buchanan Street	C1	Louise Street	C4
Butler Street	C1	Milbourne Street	C1
Caunce Street	D1	Montreal Avenue	D3
Cedar Square	C2	New Bonny Street	B3
Central Drive	C4	New Larkhill Street	C1
Chapel Street	B4	Palatine Road	C4
Charles Street	C1	Palatine Road	D3
Charnley Road	C3	Park Road	D2
Cheapside	B2	Park Road	D4
Church Street	B2	Peter Street	D2
Church Street	C2	Pier Street	B4
Church Street	D2	Princess Parade	B1
Clifton Street	B2	Promenade	A3
Clinton Avenue	D4	Queen Street	B1
Cookson Street	C2	Raikes Parade	D2
Coop Street	B4	Reads Avenue	C3
Coronation Street	C3	Reads Avenue	D3
Corporation Street	B2	Regent Road	C2
Dale Street	B4	Ribble Road	C4
Deansgate	B2	Ripon Road	D3
Dickson Road	B1	Seasiders Way	B4
Edward Street	C2	Selbourne Road	D1
Elizabeth Street	D1	South King Street	C2
Fairhurst Street	D1	Springfield Road	B1
Fisher Street	C1	Stanley Road	C3
Fleet Street	C3	Talbot Road	B2
Foxhall Road	B4	Talbot Road	C1
Freckleton Street	D4	Topping Street	C2
General Street	B1	Vance Road	B3
George Street	C1	Victoria Street	B2
Gorton Street	D1	Victory Road	D1
Granville Road	D2	West Street	B1
Grosvenor Street	C1	Woolman Road	D4
Harrison Street	D4	York Street	B4

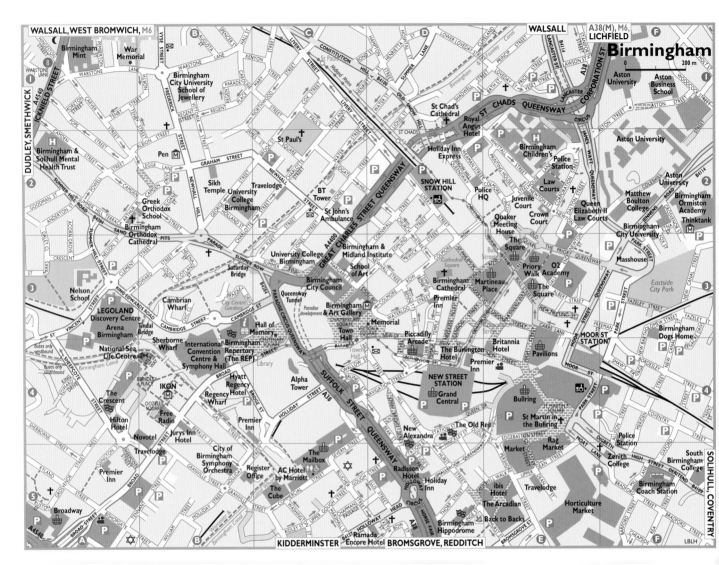

Birmingham

Birmingham is found on atlas page **58 G7**

Acorn Grove.....................A2
Albert Street.....................E3
Albert Street.....................F3
Albion Street....................B2
Allison Street...................F4
Anderton Street...............A2
Arthur Place....................A2
Aston Street.....................F1
Atlas Way........................B4
Banbury Street.................F3
Barford Street..................F5
Bartholomew Street.........F3
Barwick Street.................D3
Bath Street......................E1
Beak Street......................D4
Benacre Drive..................F4
Bennetts Hill...................D3
Berkley Street..................B4
Bishopgate Street............A5
Blucher Street..................C5
Bond Street.....................E1
Bordesley Street..............F4
Bow Street.......................D5
Bradford Street................F5
Bridge Street....................B4
Brindley Drive..................B3
Brindley Place..................B4
Broad Street....................A5
Bromsgrove Street............E5
Brook Street....................C2
Brunel Street...................C4
Bull Street.......................E3
Cambridge Street.............B3
Camden Drive..................B2
Camden Street..................A2
Cannon Street..................D3

Caroline Street.................B1
Carrs Lane.......................E3
Carver Street...................A1
Chamberlain Square.........C3
Chapmans Passage...........C5
Charlotte Street................B3
Cheapside........................F5
Cherry Street....................D3
Church Street...................D2
Civic Close.......................B3
Clement Street..................A3
Cleveland Street...............D1
Coleshill Street.................F2
Colmore Circus Queensway....E2
Colmore Row...................D3
Commercial Street............C5
Constitution Hill...............C1
Cornwall Street................D3
Corporation Street............E1
Corporation Street............E3
Coventry Street................F4
Cox Street........................C1
Dale End.........................E3
Daley Close......................A3
Dalton Street....................E2
Dean Street......................E5
Digbeth...........................E4
Dudley Street..................D4
Eden Place.......................C3
Edgebaston Street.............E4
Edmund Street.................D3
Edward Street..................B3
Ellis Street.......................D5
Essington Street...............A5
Ethel Street......................D4
Etna Street.......................F2

Exeter Street....................D5
Fazeley Street..................F3
Fleet Street......................C3
Fox Street........................F3
Frederick Street...............B1
Freeman Street.................E3
Gas Street........................B4
George Street...................B2
Gloucester Street.............E5
Goodman Street...............A2
Gough Street....................C5
Graham Street..................B2
Granville Street................B5
Great Charles Street
    Queensway..................C3
Grosvenor Street..............F2
Grosvenor Street West.......A5
Hall Street.......................B1
Hampton Street................D1
Helena Street...................B3
Henrietta Street................C1
High Street......................E4
High Street Deritend.........F5
Hill Street.......................C4
Hinckley Street.................D4
Hingeston Street...............A1
Holland Street..................B2
Holliday Street.................B5
Holloway Circus...............D5
Holloway Head.................C5
Holt Street.......................F1
Horse Fair.......................D5
Hospital Street.................D1
Hurst Street.....................D5
Icknield Street..................A1
Inge Street.......................D5
James Street....................B2
James Watt Queensway.....E2
Jennens Road...................F2
John Bright Street............D4
Kenyon Street..................B1

King Edward's Drive...........A4
King Edwards Road............A3
Ladywell Walk..................D5
Lancaster Circus...............E1
Lancaster Street................E1
Lawson Street...................E1
Legge Lane......................B2
Lighthouse Avenue............A3
Lionel Street....................C3
Livery Street....................C1
Louisa Street....................B3
Loveday Street.................E1
Lower Loveday Street.........D1
Lower Temple Street..........D4
Ludgate Hill....................C2
Margaret Street................C3
Marshall Street.................C5
Martineau Way.................E3
Mary Ann Street...............C1
Mary Street......................C1
Meriden Street.................F4
Mill Lane........................F5
Moat Lane.......................E4
Moor Street......................E4
Moor Street Queensway.....E4
Moreton Street.................A1
Navigation Street..............C4
Needless Alley..................D3
Nelson Street...................A3
New Bartholomew Street....F4
New Canal Street..............F4
Newhall Hill....................B2
Newhall Street..................C2
New Meeting Street...........E3
New Street.......................D3
Newton Street..................E2
Northwood Street..............C1
Old Snow Hill...................D1
Old Square......................E3
Oozells Square.................B4
Oxford Street...................F5

Parade..............................B3
Paradise Circus Queensway....C3
Paradise Street.................C4
Park Street.......................E4
Pemberton Street..............A1
Pershore Street.................E5
Pope Street......................A1
Powell Street....................A2
Price Street......................E1
Princip Street...................E1
Printing House Street.........E2
Queens Drive...................D4
Queensway Tunnel............C3
Rea Street........................F5
Regent Parade..................B1
Regent Place....................B1
Regent Street...................B1
Ridley Street....................C5
Ruston Street...................A5
Ryland Street...................A5
St Chads Queensway.........E1
St Jude's Pass..................D5
St Marks Crescent.............A3
St Martin's Square............E4
St Paul's Square................C1
St Philip's Place...............D3
St Vincent Street..............A3
Sand Pitts.......................A2
Saturday Bridge...............B3
Scotland Street.................B3
Severn Street...................C5
Shadwell Street.................D1
Shaw's Passage................F4
Sheepcote Street...............A4
Sherborne Street...............A4
Sloane Street....................B2
Smallbrook Queensway.....D5
Snow Hill Queensway........D2
Spencer Street..................B1
Staniforth Street...............E1
Station Street....................D5

Steelhouse Lane................E2
Stephenson Street.............D4
Suffolk Street Queensway....C4
Summer Hill Road.............A2
Summer Hill Street............A2
Summer Hill Terrace..........A2
Summer Lane...................D1
Summer Row....................B3
Swallow Street..................C4
Temple Row......................D3
Temple Row West..............D3
Temple Street...................D3
Tenby Street.....................A1
Tenby Street North............A1
Tennant Street..................A5
The Priory Queensway.......E3
Thorp Street....................D5
Tindal Bridge...................B3
Trent Street......................F4
Union Street.....................E3
Upper Dean Street............E5
Upper Gough Street...........C5
Vesey Street.....................E1
Victoria Square.................C3
Vittoria Street...................B1
Vyse Street......................B1
Warstone Lane.................A1
Washington Street.............C5
Waterloo Street.................D3
Water Street.....................C2
Weaman Street.................D2
Whittall Street..................E2
William Street..................B5
Woodcock Street...............F1

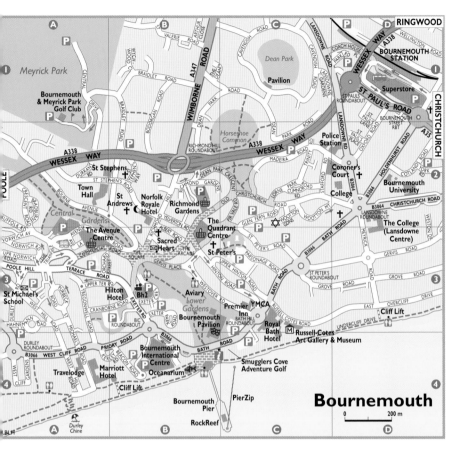

Bournemouth

Bournemouth

Bournemouth is found on atlas page **13 J6**

Albert Road	B3	Old Christchurch Road	C2
Avenue Lane	A3	Orchard Street	A3
Avenue Road	A3	Oxford Road	D2
Bath Hill Roundabout	C3	Park Road	D1
Bath Road	B4	Parsonage Road	C3
Beacon Road	B4	Poole Hill	A3
BIC Roundabout	B3	Poole Road	A3
Bodorgan Road	B2	Priory Road	A4
Bourne Avenue	A2	Purbeck Road	A3
Bournemouth Street		Richmond Gardens	B2
Roundabout	D1	Richmond Hill	B3
Bradburne Road	A2	Richmond Hill Roundabout	B2
Braidley Road	B1	Russell Cotes Road	C3
Cavendish Road	C1	St Michael's Road	A3
Central Drive	A1	St Paul's Lane	D1
Christchurch Road	D2	St Paul's Place	D2
Coach House Place	D1	St Paul's Road	D1
Commercial Road	A3	St Pauls Roundabout	D1
Cotlands Road	D2	St Peter's Road	C3
Cranborne Road	A3	St Peter's Roundabout	C3
Crescent Road	A2	St Stephen's Road	A2
Cumnor Road	C2	St Stephen's Way	B2
Dean Park Crescent	B2	St Valerie Road	B1
Dean Park Road	B2	Stafford Road	C2
Durley Road	A3	Suffolk Road	A2
Durley Roundabout	A4	Terrace Road	A3
Durrant Road	A2	The Arcade	B3
East Overcliff Drive	D3	The Deans	B1
Exeter Crescent	B3	The Square	B3
Exeter Park Road	B3	The Triangle	A3
Exeter Road	B3	Tregonwell Road	A3
Fir Vale Road	C2	Trinity Road	C2
Gervis Place	B3	Undercliff Drive	D3
Gervis Road	D3	Upper Hinton Road	C3
Glen Fern Road	C2	Upper Norwich Road	A3
Grove Road	C3	Upper Terrace Road	A3
Hahnemann Road	A3	Wellington Road	D1
Hinton Road	B3	Wessex Way	A2
Holdenhurst Road	D2	West Cliff Gardens	A4
Kerley Road	A4	West Cliff Road	A4
Lansdowne Gardens	C1	West Hill Road	A3
Lansdowne Road	C1	Weston Drive	D2
Lansdowne Roundabout	D2	Westover Road	B3
Lorne Park Road	C2	Wimborne Road	B1
Madeira Road	C2	Wootton Gardens	C2
Meyrick Road	D3	Wootton Mount	C2
Norwich Avenue	A3	Wychwood Close	B1
Norwich Road	A3	Yelverton Road	B2
		York Road	D2

Bradford

Bradford is found on atlas page **90 F4**

Aldermanbury	B3	Lower Kirkgate	C2
Bank Street	B2	Lumb Lane	A1
Barkerend Road	D2	Manchester Road	B4
Barry Street	B2	Manningham Lane	A1
Bolling Road	C4	Manor Row	B1
Bolton Road	C2	Market Street	B3
Bridge Street	C3	Midland Road	B1
Broadway	C3	Morley Street	A4
Burnett Street	D2	Neal Street	B4
Canal Road	C1	Nelson Street	B4
Carlton Street	A3	North Brook Street	C1
Centenary Square	B3	Northgate	B2
Chandos Street	C4	North Parade	B1
Chapel Street	D3	North Street	C2
Cheapside	B2	North Wing	D1
Chester Street	A4	Otley Road	D1
Church Bank	C2	Paradise Street	A2
Claremont	A4	Peckover Street	D2
Croft Street	C4	Piccadilly	B2
Darfield Street	A1	Pine Street	C2
Darley Street	B2	Princes Way	B3
Drewton Road	A2	Randall Well Street	A3
Dryden Street	D4	Rawson Road	A2
Duke Street	B2	Rawson Square	B2
East Parade	D3	Rebecca Street	A2
Edmund Street	A4	St Blaise Way	C1
Edward Street	C4	St Thomas's Road	A2
Eldon Place	A1	Sawrey Place	A4
Filey Street	D3	Senior Way	B4
George Street	C3	Shipley Airedale Road	C1
Godwin Street	B2	Stott Hill	C2
Grattan Road	A2	Sunbridge Road	A2
Great Horton Road	A4	Tetley Street	A3
Grove Terrace	A4	Thornton Road	A3
Hallfield Road	A1	Trafalgar Street	B1
Hall Ings	B4	Tyrrel Street	B3
Hammerton Street	D3	Upper Park Gate	D2
Hamm Strasse	B1	Upper Piccadilly	B2
Holdsworth Street	C1	Valley Road	C1
Houghton Place	A1	Vicar Lane	C3
Howard Street	A4	Wakefield Road	D4
Hustlergate	B3	Wapping Road	D1
Infirmary Street	A1	Water Lane	A2
John Street	B2	Wellington Street	C2
Lansdowne Place	A4	Westgate	A2
Leeds Road	D3	Wharf Street	C1
Little Horton	A4	Wigan Street	A3
Little Horton Lane	B4	Wilton Street	A4

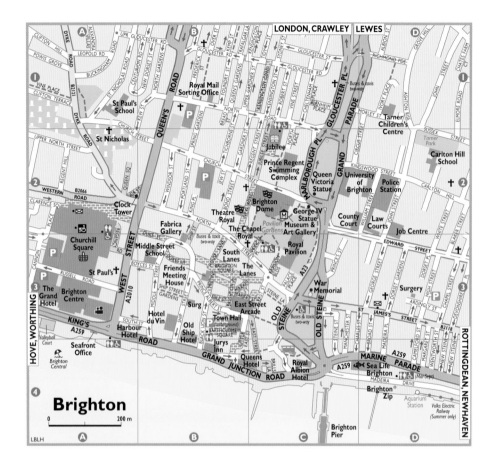

Brighton

Brighton is found on atlas page **24 H10**

Ardingly Street	D3	Madeira Place	D
Ashton Rise	D1	Manchester Street	C
Bartholomew Square	B3	Margaret Street	D
Black Lion Street	B3	Marine Parade	C
Blaker Street	D3	Market Street	B
Bond Street	B2	Marlborough Place	C
Boyces Street	A3	Meeting House Lane	B
Brighton Place	B3	Middle Street	B
Broad Street	D4	Morley Street	B
Buckingham Road	A1	New Dorset Street	B
Camelford Street	D4	New Road	B
Cannon Place	A3	New Steine	D
Carlton Hill	D2	Nile Street	B
Centurion Road	A1	North Gardens	B
Chapel Street	D3	North Place	C
Charles Street	C4	North Road	B
Cheltenham Place	C1	North Street	B
Church Street	A1	Old Steine	C
Church Street	B2	Portland Street	B
Circus Street	C2	Powis Grove	A
Clifton Hill	A1	Prince Albert Street	B
Clifton Terrace	A1	Prince's Street	C
Devonshire Place	D3	Queen's Gardens	C
Dukes Lane	B3	Queen Square	A
Duke Street	B2	Queen's Road	A
East Street	C3	Regency Road	A
Edward Street	D3	Regent Hill	A
Elmore Road	D1	Regent Street	C
Foundry Street	B1	Robert Street	C
Frederick Street	B1	St James's Street	D
Gardner Street	B2	St Nicholas Road	A
George Street	D3	Ship Street	B
Gloucester Place	C1	Spring Gardens	B
Gloucester Road	B1	Steine Street	D
Gloucester Street	C1	Sussex Street	C
Grand Junction Road	B4	Sydney Street	B
Grand Parade	C2	Tichborne Street	B
High Street	D3	Tidy Street	B
Ivory Place	D1	Upper Gardner Street	B
John Street	D2	Upper Gloucester Road	A
Jubilee Street	C2	Upper North Street	A
Kensington Gardens	C1	Vine Street	C
Kensington Street	C1	Wentworth Street	D
Kew Street	B1	Western Road	A
King's Road	A3	West Street	A
Kingswood Street	C2	White Street	D
Leopold Road	A1	William Street	D
Little East Street	B4	Windsor Street	B

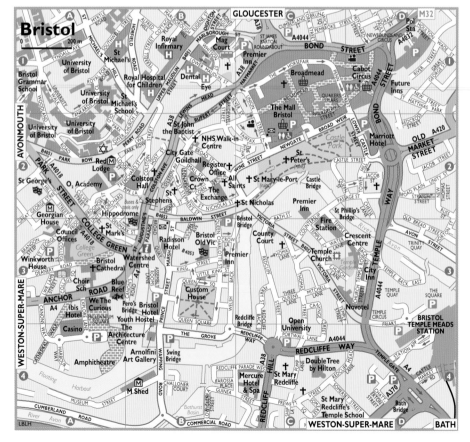

Bristol

Bristol is found on atlas page **31 Q10**

Anchor Road	A3	Passage Street	C
Avon Street	D3	Pembroke Street	C
Baldwin Street	B2	Penn Street	C
Bath Bridge	D4	Pero's Bridge	B
Bond Street	C1	Perry Road	A
Bond Street	D2	Philadelphia Street	C
Broadmead	C1	Portwall Lane	C
Broad Plain	D2	Prewett Street	C
Broad Quay	B3	Prince Street	B
Broad Street	B2	Queen Charlotte Street	B
Broad Weir	C2	Queen Square	B
Canons Way	A3	Redcliffe Parade West	B
Canynge Street	C3	Redcliffe Way	C
Castle Street	C2	Redcliff Hill	C
College Green	A3	Redcliff Mead Lane	C
Colston Avenue	B2	Redcliff Street	C
Colston Street	B2	Royal Fort Road	A
Commercial Road	B4	Rupert Street	B
Corn Street	B2	St Augustine's Parade	B
Countership	C3	St George's Road	A
Cumberland Road	A4	St Matthias Park	D
Deanery Road	A3	St Michael's Hill	A
Denmark Street	A3	St Stephen's Street	B
Explore Lane	A3	St Thomas Street	B
Fairfax Street	C2	Small Street	B
Ferry Street	C3	Somerset Street	A
Friary	D3	Southwell Street	A
Frogmore Street	A2	Tankards Close	A
Great George Street	A3	Telephone Avenue	B
Great George Street	D1	Temple Back	C
Guinea Street	B4	Temple Back East	D
Haymarket	C1	Temple Gate	D
Hill Street	A2	Temple Street	C
Horfield Road	B1	Temple Way	D
Jacob Street	D2	The Grove	B
King Street	B3	The Horsefair	C
Lewins Mead	B2	The Pithay	B
Lodge Street	A2	Tower Hill	C
Lower Castle Street	D2	Trenchard Street	A
Lower Church Lane	A2	Tyndall Avenue	A
Lower Maudlin Street	B1	Union Street	B
Marlborough Hill	B1	Upper Maudlin Street	A
Marlborough Street	B1	Victoria Street	C
Marsh Street	B3	Wapping Road	A
Museum Street	A4	Welsh Back	B
Newgate	C2	Whitson Street	C
Old Market Street	D2	Wine Street	B
Park Street	A2	Woodland Road	A

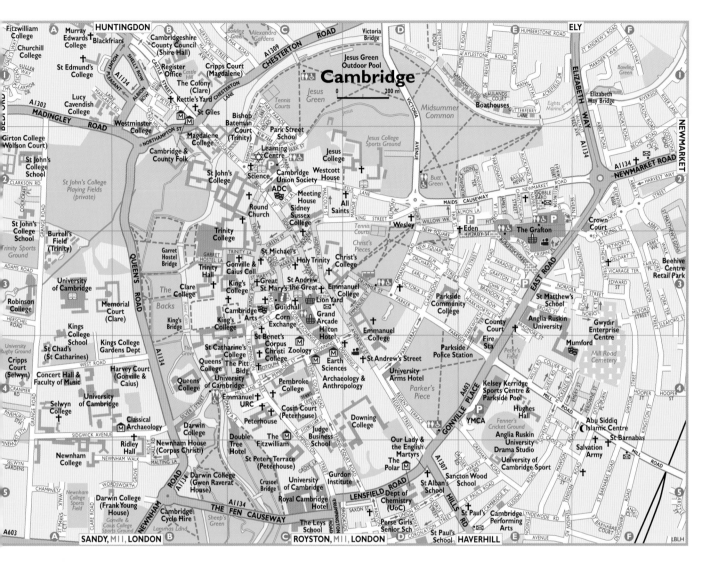

Cambridge

ambridge is found on atlas page **62 G9**

Abbey Road	F1	Collier Road	E4
Abbey Street	F2	Corn Exchange Street	C3
Abbey Walk	F3	Coronation Street	D5
Acrefield Drive	E1	Covent Garden	E4
Adam and Eve Street	E3	Crispin Place	E3
Albion Row	B1	Cross Street	E4
Alpha Road	C1	Crusoe Bridge	B5
Auckland Road	E2	Cutler Ferry Close	E1
Aylestone Road	E1	Cutterferry Lane	E1
Bailey Mews	E2	De Freville Avenue	E1
Banhams Close	D1	Devonshire Road	F5
Beaulands Court	E1	Ditchburn Place	F4
Beche Road	F2	Downing Place	C4
Belmont Place	D2	Downing Street	C4
Belvoir Road	E1	Drosier Road	D5
Bene't Street	C3	Drummer Street	D3
Bloom Street	F3	Earl Street	D3
Bradmore Street	E3	East Road	E3
Brandon Place	E3	Eden Street	E3
Bridge Street	C2	Eden Street Back	E3
Broad Street	E3	Edward Street	F3
Brookside	D5	Elizabeth Way	F1
Brunswick Gardens	E2	Elm Street	D3
Brunswick Terrace	E2	Emery Street	F4
Burleigh Place	E3	Emmanuel Road	D3
Burleigh Street	E3	Emmanuel Street	D3
Cambridge Place	E5	Evening Court	E2
Castle Row	B1	Fairsford Place	F3
Castle Street	B1	Fair Street	D2
Champneys Walk	A5	Fitzroy Lane	E2
Chesterton Lane	B1	Fitzroy Street	E3
Chesterton Road	C1	Fitzwilliam Street	C4
Christchurch Street	E2	Garret Hostel Bridge	B3
City Road	E3	Garret Hostel Lane	B3
Clarendon Street	D3	Geldart Street	F3
Cobble Yard	E2	George IV Street	D5
Glisson Road	E5	Milford Street	F3
Godstone Road	F2	Mill Lane	C4
Gonville Place	D4	Mill Road	E4
Grange Road	A3	Mill Street	E4
Grange Road	A4	Mortimer Road	E4
Granta Place	B4	Mount Pleasant	B1
Green Street	C3	Napier Street	E2
Gresham Road	E5	Newmarket Road	E2
Gwydir Street	F4	Newnham Road	B5
Harvest Way	F2	Newnham Walk	A5
Harvey Road	E5	New Park Street	C2
Hertford Street	B1	New Square	D3
Hills Road	D5	New Street	F2
Hobson Street	C3	Norfolk Street	E3
Humberstone Road	E1	Norfolk Terrace	F3
James Street	E2	Northampton Street	B2
Jesus Lane	C2	Occupation Road	F2
Jesus Terrace	D3	Orchard Street	D3
John Street	E3	Panton Street	D5
Kimberley Road	E1	Paradise Street	E3
King's Bridge	B3	Parker Street	D3
King's Parade	C3	Park Parade	C1
Kingston Street	F4	Parkside	D3
King Street	D2	Park Street	C2
Lady Margaret Road	A1	Park Terrace	D4
Lensfield Road	D5	Parsonage Street	E2
Logan's Way	F1	Peas Hill	C3
Lwr Park Street	C2	Pembroke Street	C4
Lyndewode Road	E5	Perowne Street	F4
Mackenzie Road	E4	Petworth Street	F3
Madingley Road	A1	Pound Hill	B1
Magdalene Street	B2	Priory Road	F1
Magrath Avenue	B1	Prospect Row	E3
Maids Causeway	D2	Queen's Road	B3
Malcolm Street	C2	Regent Street	D4
Malting Lane	B5	Regent Terrace	D4
Manhattan Drive	E1	River Lane	F1
Manor Street	D2	Riverside	F1
Mariner's Way	F1	St Andrew's Road	F1
Market Street	C3	St Andrew's Street	D3
Mawson Road	E5	St Barnabas Road	F5
St Mary's Street	C3
St Matthew's Gardens	F2
St Matthew's Street	F3
St Paul's Road	E5
St Peter's Street	B1
Salmon Lane	E2
Saxon Road	F1
Saxon Street	D5
Severn Place	F2
Shelly Row	B1
Short Street	D2
Sidgwick Avenue	A4
Sidney Street	C2
Silver Street	B4
Staffordshire Street	F3
Sturton Street	F3
Sussex Street	C3
Tenison Avenue	E5
Tenison Road	E4
Tennis Court Road	C4
Tennis Court Terrace	C4
The Fen Causeway	B5
Thompson's Lane	C2
Trinity Lane	C3
Trinity Street	C2
Trumpington Road	C5
Trumpington Street	C4
Union Road	D5
Vicarage Terrace	F4
Victoria Avenue	D1
Victoria Bridge	D1
Victoria Street	D3
Warkworth Street	E4
Warkworth Terrace	E4
Wellington Street	E2
West Road	A4
Wilkin Street	E5
Willis Road	E4
Willow Walk	D2
Wordsworth Grove	A5
Young Street	F3

University Colleges

Christ's College	C3
Clare College	A3
Clare College	B1
Clare College	B3
Corpus Christi College	C4
Darwin College	B4
Downing College	D4
Emmanuel College	D3
Emmanuel College	D3
Fitzwilliam College	A1
Girton College (Wolfson Court)	A2
Gonville & Caius College	C3
Gonville & Caius College	B4
Jesus College	C2
King's College	C3
Lucy Cavendish College	A1
Magdalene College	B2
Murray Edwards College	A1
Newnham College	A5
Pembroke College	C4
Peterhouse	C4
Queens' College	B4
Robinson College	A3
St Catharine's College	C3
St Edmund's College	A1
St John's College	B2
Selwyn College	A4
Sidney Sussex College	C2
Trinity College	B3
Westminster College	B1

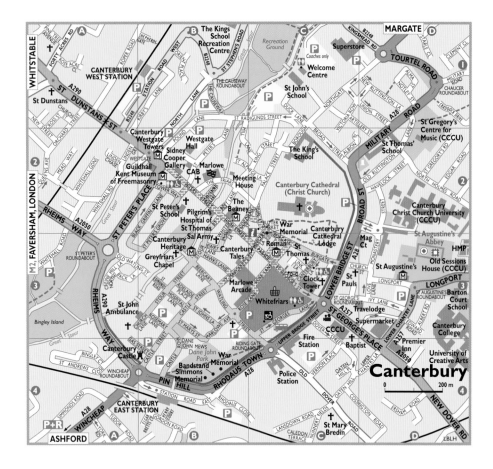

Canterbury

Canterbury is found on atlas page **39 K10**

Adelaide Place	B3	Nunnery Fields	C
Albion Place	C2	Oaten Hill	C
Alma Street	D1	Old Dover Road	C
Artillery Street	C1	Old Ruttington Lane	C
Beercart Lane	B3	Orchard Street	A
Best Lane	B2	Palace Street	C
Black Griffin Lane	A3	Parade	C
Borough	C2	Pin Hill	B
Broad Street	D2	Pound Lane	B
Burgate	C3	Queens Avenue	A
Butter Market	C2	Rheims Way	A
Canterbury Lane	C3	Rhodaus Town	B
Castle Row	B4	Rose Lane	B
Castle Street	B3	Rosemary Lane	B
Cossington Road	C4	St Alphege Lane	B
Dover Street	C3	St Dunstans Street	A
Duck Lane	C1	St Edmunds Road	A
Edgar Road	D2	St George's Lane	B
Edward Road	D3	St George's Place	C
Ersham Road	D4	St George's Street	C
Gas Street	A4	St Gregory's Road	B
Gordon Road	B4	St Johns Lane	B
Guildhall Street	B2	St Margaret's Street	B
Havelock Street	D2	St Marys Street	B
Hawks Lane	B3	St Peter's Grove	A
High Street	B2	St Peter's Lane	B
Hospital Lane	B3	St Peter's Place	A
Ivy Lane	C3	St Peters Street	B
Jewry Lane	B3	St Radigunds Street	B
King Street	C2	Station Road East	A
Kirby's Lane	B1	Station Road West	A
Lansdown Road	C4	Stour Street	B
Linden Grove	A2	Sturry Road	D
Longport	D3	Sun Street	B
Love Lane	D3	The Causeway	A
Lower Bridge Street	C3	The Friars	B
Lower Chantry Lane	D4	Tourtel Road	C
Marlowe Avenue	B3	Tower Way	A
Mead Way	A2	Tudor Road	A
Mercery Lane	C3	Union Street	D
Military Road	D2	Upper Bridge Street	C
Mill Lane	B1	Vernon Place	C
Monastery Street	D3	Victoria Row	C
New Dover Road	D4	Watling Street	A
New Ruttington Lane	D1	Whitehall Gardens	A
North Lane	B1	Whitehall Road	A
Northgate	C1	Wincheap	A
Notley Street	D1	York Road	A

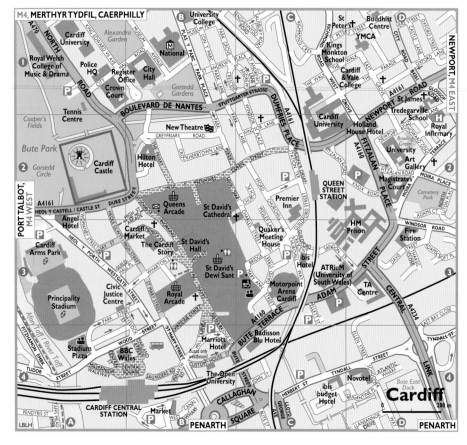

Cardiff

Cardiff is found on atlas page **30 G9**

Adam Street	C3	Museum Avenue	B
Adams Court	D2	Museum Place	B
Adamscroft Place	D3	Newport Road	D
Atlantic Wharf	D4	Newport Road Lane	D
Boulevard de Nantes	B1	North Luton Place	D
Bridge Street	C3	North Road	A
Brigantine Place	D4	Oxford Lane	D
Bute Street	C4	Oxford Street	D
Bute Terrace	C3	Park Grove	B
Callaghan Square	B4	Park Lane	B
Caroline Street	B3	Park Place	B
Castle Lane	D1	Park Street	A
Castle Street	A2	Pellett Street	C
Central Link	D3	Pendyris Street	A
Charles Street	B2	Quay Street	B
Churchill Way	C2	Queen Street	B
City Hall Road	A1	Richmond Crescent	C
City Road	D1	Richmond Road	C
Crockherbtown Lane	B2	St Andrew's Crescent	B
Custom House Street	B4	St Andrew's Lane	B
David Street	C3	St Andrew's Place	B
Davis Street	D3	St John Street	B
Duke Street	A2	St Mary Street	B
Dumfries Place	C2	St Peter's Street	D
East Bay Close	D3	Salisbury Road	C
East Grove	D1	Sandon Street	C
Fford Churchill	C2	Saunders Road	B
Fitzalan Place	D2	Schooner Way	C
Fitzalan Road	D2	Stuttgarter Strasse	B
Fitzhamon Embankment	A4	The Friary	B
Glossop Road	D1	The Hayes	B
Greyfriars Road	B2	The Parade	D
Guildford Street	C3	The Walk	C
Guildhall Place	A3	Trinity Street	B
Havelock Street	B3	Tudor Street	A
Hayes Bridge Road	B3	Tyndall Street	D
Heol Siarl	B2	Vere Street	D
Herbert Street	C4	Wesley Lane	B
High Street	B3	West Canal Wharf	B
High Street Arcade	B2	West Grove	C
Hills Street	B3	Westgate Street	A
King Edward VII Avenue	A1	Wharton Street	B
Knox Road	D2	Windsor Lane	C
Lloyd George Avenue	C4	Windsor Place	C
Mary Ann Street	C3	Windsor Road	D
Mill Lane	B4	Womanby Street	A
Moira Place	D2	Wood Street	A
Moira Terrace	D2	Working Street	B

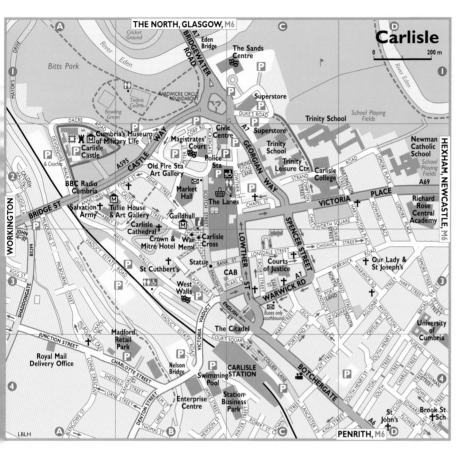

Carlisle

Carlisle is found on atlas page **110 G9**

Abbey Street	A2	Howard Place	D2
Aglionby Street	D3	Howe Street	D4
Annetwell Street	A2	James Street	B4
Bank Street	B3	John Street	A3
Blackfriars Street	B3	Junction Street	A4
Blencowe Street	A4	King Street	C4
Botchergate	C4	Lancaster Street	C4
Bridge Lane	A2	Lime Street	B4
Bridge Street	A2	Lismore Place	D2
Bridgewater Road	B1	Lismore Street	D3
Broad Street	D3	Lonsdale Street	C3
Brunswick Street	C3	Lorne Crescent	A4
Caldew Maltings	A2	Lorne Street	A4
Castle Street	B2	Lowther Street	C3
Castle Way	B2	Mary Street	C3
Cecil Street	C3	Mayor's Drive	A1
Chapel Place	A3	Milbourne Crescent	A3
Chapel Street	C2	Milbourne Street	A3
Charles Street	D4	Myddleton Street	D3
Charlotte Street	B4	North Alfred Street	D3
Chatsworth Square	C2	Orfeur Street	D3
Chiswick Street	C3	Peter Street	B2
Close Street	D4	Petteril Street	D3
Collier Lane	C4	Portland Place	C4
Compton Street	C2	Portland Square	C3
Corp Road	B2	Randall Street	B4
Court Square	B4	Rickergate	B2
Crosby Street	C3	Rigg Street	A3
Crown Street	C4	Robert Street	C4
Currie Street	C3	Rydal Street	D4
Dacre Road	A1	Scotch Street	B2
Denton Street	B4	Shaddongate	A3
Devonshire Walk	A2	Sheffield Street	A4
Duke's Road	C1	South Alfred Street	D3
Edward Street	D4	South Henry Street	D4
Elm Street	B4	Spencer Street	C2
English Street	B3	Spring Gardens Lane	C2
Finkle Street	B2	Strand Road	C2
Fisher Street	B2	Tait Street	C4
Flower Street	D4	Thomas Street	B4
Friars Court	C3	Viaduct Estate Road	A3
Fusehill Street	D4	Victoria Place	C2
Georgian Way	C2	Victoria Viaduct	B4
Grey Street	D4	Warwick Road	D3
Hartington Place	D2	Warwick Square	D3
Hartington Street	D2	Water Street	C4
Hart Street	D3	West Tower Street	B2
Hewson Street	B4	West Walls	B3

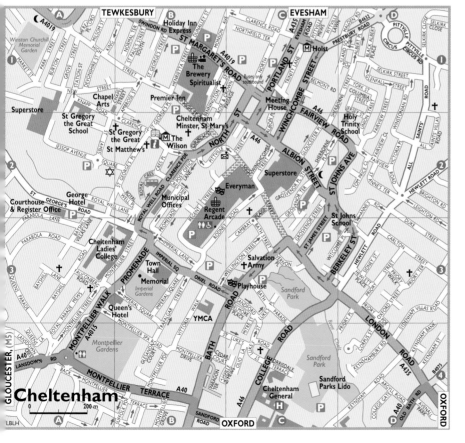

Cheltenham

Cheltenham is found on atlas page **46 H10**

Albion Street	C2	Montpellier Parade	B4
All Saints' Road	D2	Montpellier Spa Road	B4
Ambrose Street	B1	Montpellier Street	A4
Argyll Road	D4	Montpellier Terrace	A4
Back Montpellier Terrace	A4	Montpellier Walk	A4
Bath Road	B4	New Street	A1
Bath Street	C3	North Street	B2
Bayshill Road	A3	Old Bath Road	D4
Bayshill Villas Lane	A3	Oriel Road	B3
Bennington Street	B1	Parabola Lane	A3
Berkeley Street	C3	Parabola Road	A3
Burton Street	A1	Park Street	A1
Carlton Street	D3	Pittville Circus	D1
Church Street	B2	Pittville Circus Road	D1
Clarence Parade	B2	Pittville Street	B2
Clarence Road	C1	Portland Street	C1
Clarence Street	B2	Prestbury Road	C1
College Road	C4	Priory Street	D3
Crescent Terrace	B2	Promenade	B3
Devonshire Street	A1	Queens Parade	A3
Duke Street	D3	Regent Street	B2
Dunalley Street	B1	Rodney Road	B3
Evesham Road	C1	Royal Well Lane	A2
Fairview Road	C2	Royal Well Road	B2
Fairview Street	D2	St Anne's Road	D2
Fauconberg Road	A3	St Anne's Terrace	D2
Glenfall Street	D1	St George's Place	B2
Grosvenor Street	C3	St George's Road	A2
Grove Street	A1	St George's Street	B1
Henrietta Street	B1	St James' Square	A2
Hewlett Road	D3	St James Street	C3
High Street	A1	St Johns Avenue	C2
High Street	C2	St Margaret's Road	B1
Imperial Lane	B3	St Paul's Street South	B1
Imperial Square	B3	Sandford Street	C3
Jersey Street	D1	Selkirk Street	D1
Jessop Avenue	A2	Sherborne Street	C2
Keynsham Road	D4	Station Street	A1
King Street	A1	Suffolk Parade	B4
Knapp Road	A1	Swindon Road	B1
Lansdown Road	A4	Sydenham Villas Road	D3
Leighton Road	D2	Trafalgar Street	B4
London Road	D3	Union Street	D2
Malden Road	D1	Wellington Street	C3
Market Street	A1	Winchcombe Street	C2
Milsom Street	A1	Winstonian Road	D2
Monson Avenue	B1	Witcombe Place	C3
Montpellier Grove	B4	York Street	D1

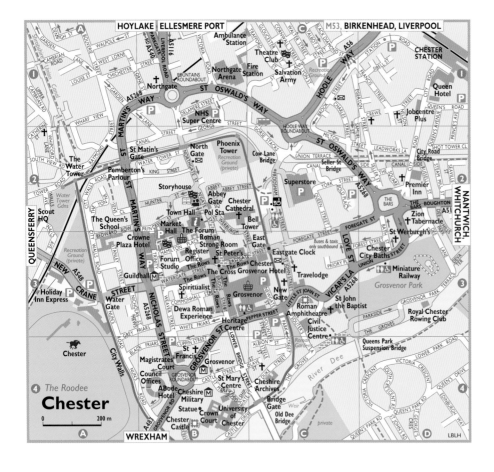

Chester

Chester is found on atlas page **81 N11**

Albion Street	C4	Nicholas Street	B3
Bath Street	D2	Northgate Street	B2
Black Diamond Street	C1	Nun's Road	A3
Boughton	D2	Parkgate Road	B1
Bouverie Street	A1	Park Street	C3
Bridge Street	B3	Pepper Street	C3
Brook Street	C1	Princess Street	C3
Canal Side	C2	Priory Place	C3
Castle Street	B4	Queen's Park Road	C4
Charles Street	C1	Queen's Road	D1
Chichester Street	A1	Queen Street	C2
City Road	D2	Raymond Street	A2
City Walls Road	A2	Russell Street	D2
Commonhall Street	B3	St Anne Street	C1
Cornwall Street	C1	St John's Road	D4
Crewe Street	D1	St John Street	C3
Cuppin Street	B4	St Martin's Way	A2
Dee Hills Park	D2	St Mary's Hill	B4
Dee Lane	D2	St Olave Street	C4
Delamere Street	B1	St Oswald's Way	B1
Duke Street	C4	St Werburgh Street	B2
Eastgate Street	B3	Samuel Street	C2
Egerton Street	C1	Seller Street	C2
Foregate Street	C2	Shipgate Street	B4
Forest Street	C3	Souter's Lane	C3
Francis Street	D1	South View Road	A2
Frodsham Street	C2	Stanley Street	A3
Garden Lane	A1	Station Road	D1
George Street	B2	Steam Mill Street	D2
Gloucester Street	C1	Steele Street	C4
Gorse Stacks	C2	Talbot Street	C1
Grosvenor Park Terrace	D3	Tower Road	A2
Grosvenor Road	B4	Trafford Street	C1
Grosvenor Street	B4	Trinity Street	B3
Hamilton Place	B3	Union Street	C2
Hoole Way	C1	Union Terrace	C2
Hunter Street	B2	Upper Cambrian Road	A1
King Street	B2	Vicar's Lane	C3
Leadworks Lane	D2	Victoria Crescent	D4
Little St John Street	C3	Victoria Road	B1
Liverpool Road	B1	Volunteer Street	C3
Lorne Street	A1	Walpole Street	A1
Love Street	C3	Walter Street	C1
Lower Bridge Street	B4	Watergate Street	B3
Lower Park Road	D4	Water Tower Street	B2
Milton Street	C2	Weaver Street	B3
New Crane Street	A3	White Friars	B3
Newgate Street	C3	York Street	C2

Colchester

Colchester is found on atlas page **52 G6**

Abbey Gates	C3	Middleborough	B1
Alexandra Road	A3	Middleborough Roundabout	A1
Alexandra Terrace	A4	Military Road	D4
Balkerne Hill	A3	Mill Street	D4
Beaconsfield Avenue	A4	Napier Road	C4
Burlington Road	A3	Nicholsons Green	D3
Butt Road	A4	North Bridge	B1
Castle Road	D1	Northgate Street	B1
Cedar Street	B3	North Hill	B1
Chapel Street North	B3	North Station Road	B1
Chapel Street South	B3	Nunn's Road	B1
Church Street	B3	Osborne Street	C3
Church Walk	B3	Papillon Road	A3
Circular Road East	C4	Pope's Lane	A3
Circular Road North	B4	Portland Road	C4
Creffield Road	A4	Priory Street	D3
Cromwell Road	C4	Queen Street	C3
Crouch Street	A3	Rawstorn Road	A2
Crouch Street	B3	Roman Road	D1
Crowhurst Road	A2	St Alban's Road	A3
Culver Street East	C2	St Augustine Mews	D2
Culver Street West	B2	St Botolph's Circus	C3
East Hill	D2	St Botolph's Street	C3
East Stockwell Street	C2	St Helen's Lane	C2
Essex Street	B3	St John's Avenue	B3
Fairfax Road	C4	St John's Street	B3
Flagstaff Road	C4	St Julian Grove	D3
Garland Road	A4	St Mary's Fields	A2
George Street	C2	St Peter's Street	B2
Golden Noble Hill	D4	Salisbury Avenue	A4
Gray Road	A3	Sheepen Place	A1
Headgate	B3	Sheepen Road	A1
Head Street	B2	Short Wyre Street	C3
Henry Laver Court	A2	Sir Isaac's Walk	B3
High Street	B2	South Street	B4
Hospital Road	A4	Southway	A3
Hospital Lane	A3	Stanwell Street	B3
Land Lane	D2	Trinity Street	B2
Lewis Gardens	D2	Walsingham Road	B4
Lexden Road	A3	Wellesley Road	A4
Lincoln Way	D1	Wellington Street	A4
Long Wyre Street	C2	West Stockwell Street	B1
Lucas Road	C4	West Street	B4
Magdalen Street	D3	Westway	A1
Maidenburgh Street	C1	Whitewell Road	B3
Maldon Road	A4	Wickham Road	A4
Manor Road	A3	William's Walk	C1
Mersea Road	C4	Winnock Road	C4

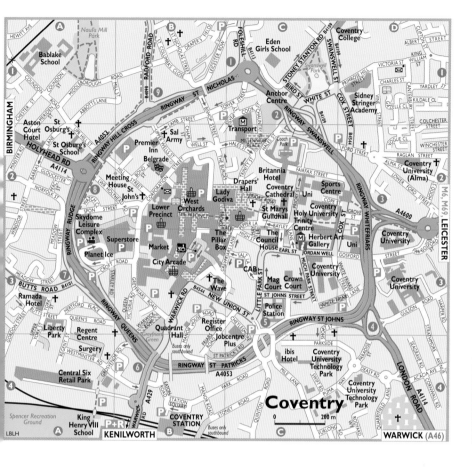

Coventry

Coventry is found on atlas page **59 M9**

Abbotts Lane	A1	Much Park Street	C3
Acacia Avenue	D4	New Union Street	B3
Alma Street	D2	Norfolk Street	A2
Barras Lane	A2	Park Road	B4
Bayley Lane	C2	Parkside	C4
Bird Street	C1	Primrose Hill Street	D1
Bishop Street	B1	Priory Row	C2
Broadgate	B2	Priory Street	C2
Butts Road	A3	Puma Way	C4
Butts Street	A3	Quarryfield Lane	D4
Canterbury Street	D1	Queen's Road	A3
Chester Street	A2	Queen Victoria Road	B3
Cheylesmore	C3	Quinton Road	C4
Cornwall Road	D4	Radford Road	B1
Corporation Street	B2	Raglan Street	D2
Coundon Road	A1	Regent Street	A4
Cox Street	D1	Ringway Hill Cross	A2
Cox Street	D2	Ringway Queens	A3
Croft Road	A3	Ringway Rudge	A3
Earl Street	C3	Ringway St Johns	C3
Eaton Road	B4	Ringway St Nicholas	B1
Fairfax Street	C2	Ringway St Patricks	B4
Foleshill Road	C1	Ringway Swanswell	C1
Gloucester Street	A2	Ringway Whitefriars	D2
Gosford Street	D3	St Johns Street	C3
Greyfriars Lane	B3	St Nicholas Street	B1
Greyfriars Road	B3	Salt Lane	C3
Grosvenor Road	A4	Seagrave Road	D4
Gulson Road	D3	Spon Street	A2
Hales Street	C2	Starley Road	A3
Hertford Place	A3	Stoney Road	B4
High Street	C3	Stoney Stanton Road	C1
Hill Street	B2	Strathmore Avenue	D3
Holyhead Road	A2	Swanswell Street	C1
Jordan Well	C3	The Burges	B2
Lamb Street	B2	Tower Street	B1
Leicester Row	B1	Trinity Street	C2
Little Park Street	C3	Upper Hill Street	B2
London Road	D4	Upper Wells Street	A4
Lower Ford Street	D2	Victoria Street	D1
Lower Holyhead Road	A2	Vine Street	D1
Manor House Road	B4	Warwick Road	B3
Manor Road	B4	Warwick Road	B4
Meadow Street	A3	Westminster Road	A4
Meriden Street	A1	White Friars Street	D3
Middleborough Road	A1	White Street	C1
Mile Lane	C4	Windsor Street	A3
Mill Street	A1	Yardley Street	D1

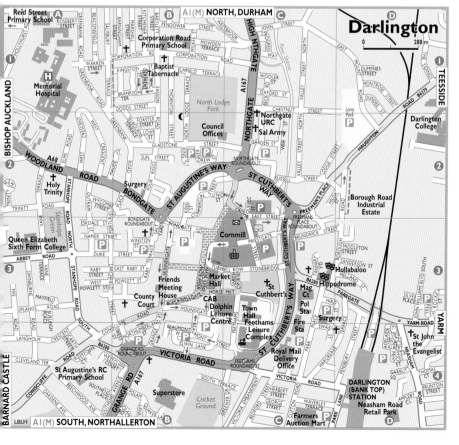

Darlington

Darlington is found on atlas page **103 Q8**

Abbey Road	A3	Maude Street	A2
Albert Street	D4	Melland Street	D3
Appleby Close	D4	Neasham Road	D4
Barningham Street	B1	Northgate	C2
Bartlett Street	B1	North Lodge Terrace	B2
Beaumont Street	B3	Northumberland Street	B4
Bedford Street	C4	Oakdene Avenue	A4
Beechwood Avenue	A4	Outram Street	A2
Blackwellgate	B3	Parkgate	D3
Bondgate	B2	Park Lane	D4
Borough Road	D3	Park Place	C4
Brunswick Street	C3	Pendower Street	B1
Brunton Street	D4	Pensbury Street	D4
Chestnut Street	C1	Polam Lane	B4
Cleveland Terrace	A4	Portland Place	A3
Clifton Road	C4	Powlett Street	B3
Commercial Street	B2	Priestgate	C3
Coniscliffe Road	A4	Raby Terrace	B3
Corporation Road	B1	Russell Street	C2
Crown Street	C2	St Augustine's Way	B2
Dodds Street	B1	St Cuthbert's Way	C2
Duke Street	A3	St Cuthbert's Way	C4
Easson Road	B1	St James Place	D4
East Mount Road	D1	Salisbury Terrace	A1
East Raby Street	B3	Salt Yard	B3
East Street	C3	Scarth Street	A4
Elms Road	A2	Skinnergate	B3
Elwin Lane	B4	Southend Avenue	A4
Feethams	C4	Stanhope Road North	A2
Fife Road	A3	Stanhope Road South	A3
Four Riggs	B2	Stonebridge	C3
Freeman's Place	C2	Sun Street	B2
Gladstone Street	B2	Swan Street	C4
Grange Road	B4	Swinburne Road	A3
Greenbank Road	A1	Trinity Road	A2
Greenbank Road	B2	Tubwell Row	B3
Hargreave Terrace	C4	Uplands Road	A3
Haughton Road	D2	Valley Street North	C2
High Northgate	C1	Vane Terrace	A2
High Row	B3	Victoria Embankment	C4
Hollyhurst Road	A1	Victoria Road	B4
Houndgate	B3	Victoria Road	C4
John Street	C1	West Crescent	A2
John Williams Boulevard	D3	West Powlett Street	A3
Kendrew Street	B2	West Row	B3
Kingston Street	B1	West Street	B4
Langholm Crescent	A4	Woodland Road	A2
Larchfield Street	A3	Yarm Road	D3

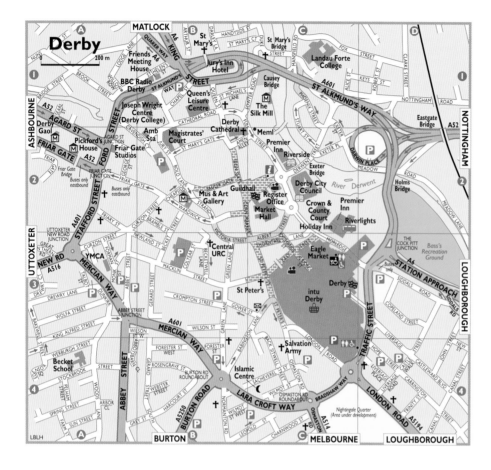

Derby

Derby is found on atlas page **72 B3**

Abbey Street	A4	King Alfred Street	A...
Agard Street	A1	King Street	B
Albert Street	C3	Lara Croft Way	B
Babington Lane	B4	Leopold Street	B
Back Sitwell Street	C4	Liversage Road	D
Becket Street	B3	Liversage Street	D
Bold Lane	B2	Lodge Lane	A
Bradshaw Way	C4	London Road	C
Bramble Street	B2	Macklin Street	B
Bridge Street	A1	Mansfield Road	C
Brook Street	A1	Meadow Lane	C
Burton Road	B4	Meadow Road	C
Canal Street	D4	Mercian Way	B
Carrington Street	D4	Morledge	C
Cathedral Road	B1	Newland Street	A
Cavendish Court	A2	New Road	A
Chapel Street	B1	New Street	D
Clarke Street	D1	Nottingham Road	C
Copeland Street	D3	Osmaston Road	C
Corn Market	B2	Phoenix Street	C
Crompton Street	B3	Queen Street	C
Curzon Street	A2	Robert Street	D
Curzon Street	A3	Rosengrave Street	B
Darwin Place	C2	Sacheverel Street	C
Derwent Street	C2	Sadler Gate	B
Drewry Lane	A3	St Alkmund's Way	B
Duke Street	C1	St Helen's Street	B
Dunkirk	A3	St Mary's Gate	B
East Street	C3	St Peter's Street	C
Exchange Street	C3	Siddals Road	D
Exeter Place	C2	Sowter Road	B
Exeter Street	C2	Spring Street	C
Ford Street	A2	Stafford Street	A
Forester Street West	B4	Station Approach	D
Forman Street	A3	Stockbrook Street	A
Fox Street	C1	Strand	B
Friary Street	A2	Stuart Street	C
Full Street	B1	Sun Street	C
Gerard Street	B3	The Cock Pitt	C
Gower Street	B3	Thorntree Lane	C
Green Lane	B3	Traffic Street	C
Grey Street	A4	Trinity Street	C
Handyside Street	B1	Victoria Street	B
Harcourt Street	B4	Wardwick	B
Iron Gate	B2	Werburgh Street	A
John Street	D4	Wilmot Street	A
Jury Street	B2	Wolfa Street	A
Keys Street	D1	Woods Lane	A

Doncaster

Doncaster is found on atlas page **91 P10**

Alderson Drive	D3	Nelson Street	B
Apley Road	B3	Nether Hall Road	B
Balby Road Bridge	A4	North Bridge Road	A
Beechfield Road	B3	North Street	A
Broxholme Lane	C1	Osborne Road	D
Carr House Road	C4	Palmer Street	C
Carr Lane	B4	Park Road	B
Chamber Road	B3	Park Terrace	B
Chequer Avenue	C4	Prince's Street	B
Chequer Road	C3	Priory Road	C
Childers Street	C4	Prospect Place	B
Christ Church Road	B1	Queen's Road	B
Church View	A1	Rainton Road	C
Church Way	B1	Ravensworth Road	C
Clark Avenue	C4	Rectory Gardens	C
Cleveland Street	A4	Regent Square	C
College Road	B3	Roman Road	D
Cooper Street	C4	Royal Avenue	C
Coopers Terrace	B2	St Georges Gate	B
Copley Road	B1	St James Street	B
Cunningham Road	B3	St Mary's Road	C
Danum Road	D3	St Sepulchre Gate	A
Dockin Hill Road	B1	St Sepulchre Gate West	A
Duke Street	A2	St Vincent Avenue	C
East Laith Gate	B2	St Vincent Road	C
Elmfield Road	C3	Scot Lane	B
Firbeck Road	D3	Silver Street	B
Frances Street	B2	Somerset Road	B
Glyn Avenue	C1	South Parade	C
Green Dyke Lane	A4	South Street	C
Grey Friars' Road	A1	Spring Gardens	A
Hall Cross Hill	C2	Stirling Street	A
Hall Gate	B2	Stockil Road	A
Hamilton Road	D4	Theobald Avenue	D
Harrington Street	B1	Thorne Road	C
High Street	A2	Town Fields	D
Highfield Road	C1	Town Moor Avenue	D
Jarratt Street	B4	Trafford Way	A
King's Road	C1	Vaughan Avenue	C
Lawn Avenue	C2	Waterdale	B
Lawn Road	C2	Welbeck Road	D
Lime Tree Avenue	D4	Welcome Way	A
Manor Drive	D3	West Laith Gate	B
Market Place	A2	West Street	A
Market Road	B1	Whitburn Road	D
Milbanke Street	B1	White Rose Way	A
Milton Walk	B4	Windsor Road	D
Montague Street	B1	Wood Street	B

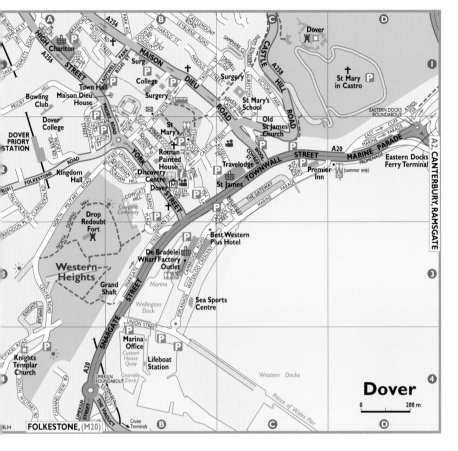

Dover

Dover is found on atlas page **27 P3**

Adrian Street	B3	Marine Parade	D2
Albany Place	B2	Military Road	B2
Ashen Tree Lane	C1	Mill Lane	B2
Athol Terrace	D1	New Street	B2
Biggin Street	B2	Norman Street	A2
Cambridge Road	B3	North Downs Way	A3
Camden Crescent	C2	North Military Road	A3
Castle Hill Road	C1	Park Avenue	B1
Castlemount Road	B1	Park Street	B1
Castle Street	B2	Pencester Road	B2
Centre Road	A3	Peter Street	A1
Channel View Road	A4	Priory Gate Road	A2
Church Street	B2	Priory Hill	A1
Citadel Road	A4	Priory Road	A1
Clarendon Place	A3	Priory Street	B2
Clarendon Road	A2	Promenade	D2
Cowgate Hill	B2	Queen's Gardens	B2
Crafford Street	A1	Queen Street	B2
De Burgh Hill	A1	Russell Street	B2
Douro Place	C2	Samphire Close	C1
Dour Street	A1	Saxon Street	A2
Durham Close	B2	Snargate Street	A4
Durham Hill	B2	South Military Road	A4
East Cliff	D2	Stembrook	B2
Eastern Docks		Taswell Close	C1
Roundabout	D2	Taswell Street	B1
Effingham Street	A2	Templar Street	A1
Elizabeth Street	A4	The Viaduct	A4
Esplanade	B3	Tower Hamlets Road	A1
Folkestone Road	A2	Townwall Street	C2
Godwyne Close	B1	Union Street	B3
Godwyne Road	B1	Victoria Park	C1
Harold Street	B1	Waterloo Crescent	B3
Harold Street	B1	Wellesley Road	C2
Heritage Gardens	C1	Wood Street	A1
Hewitt Road	A1	Woolcomber Street	C2
High Street	A1	York Street	B2
King Street	B2		
Knights Templar	A3		
Ladywell	A1		
Lancaster Road	B2		
Laureston Place	C1		
Leyburne Road	B1		
Limekiln Roundabout	A4		
Limekiln Street	A4		
Maison Dieu Road	B1		
Malvern Road	A2		
Marine Parade	C2		

Dundee

Dundee is found on atlas page **142 G11**

Albert Square	B2	Laurel Bank	B1
Bank Street	B2	Lochee Road	A1
Barrack Road	A1	McDonald Street	D2
Barrack Road	B2	Meadowside	B2
Bell Street	B2	Miln Street	A2
Blackscroft	D1	Murraygate	C2
Blinshall Street	A1	Nethergate	A4
Blinshall Street	A2	North Lindsay Street	B2
Bonnybank Road	C1	North Marketgait	B1
Brown Street	A2	North Victoria Road	C1
Candle Lane	C2	Old Hawkhill	A1
Castle Street	C2	Panmure Street	B2
Chapel Street	C2	Perth Road	A4
City Square	C3	Princes Street	D1
Commercial Street	C2	Prospect Place	B1
Constable Street	D1	Queen Street	C1
Constitution Crescent	A1	Reform Street	B2
Constitution Road	A1	Riverside Drive	B4
Constitution Road	B2	Riverside Esplanade	C3
Court House Square	A2	Roseangle	A4
Cowgate	C1	St Andrews Street	C1
Cowgate	D1	Scrimgeour Place	A1
Crichton Street	C3	Seabraes Lane	A4
Dock Street	C3	Seagate	C2
Douglas Street	A2	Session Street	A2
Dudhope Street	B1	South Castle Street	C3
East Dock Street	D2	South Commercial Street	D3
East Marketgait	C1	South Crichton Street	C3
East Whale Lane	D1	South Marketgait	B3
Euclid Crescent	B2	South Tay Street	B3
Euclid Street	B2	South Union Street	C3
Exchange Street	C3	South Victoria Dock Road	D3
Forebank Road	C1	South Ward Road	B2
Foundry Lane	D1	Sugarhouse Wynd	C1
Gellatly Street	C2	Tay Road Bridge	D3
Greenmarket	B4	Tay Square	B3
Guthrie Street	A2	Thomson Avenue	C3
Hawkhill	A3	Trades Lane	C2
High Street	C3	Union Street	B3
Hilltown	B1	Union Terrace	B1
Hilltown Terrace	B1	Ward Road	B2
Hunter Street	A3	Weavers Yard	D1
Infirmary Brae	A1	West Marketgait	A2
Johnston Street	B2	West Port	A3
King Street	C1	West Victoria Dock Road	D2
Kirk Lane	C1	Whitehall Crescent	C3
Laburn Street	A1	Whitehall Street	C3
Ladywell Avenue	C1	Yeaman Shore	B3

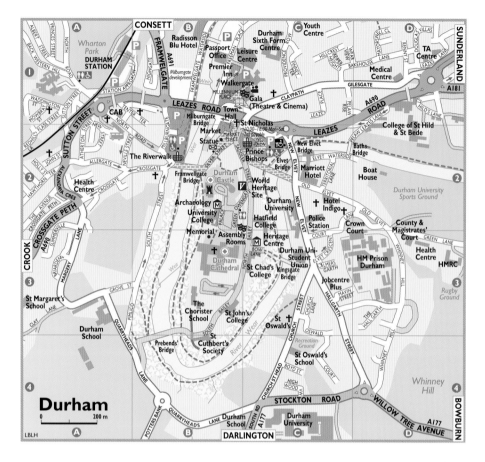

Durham

Durham is found on atlas page **103 Q2**

Albert Street A1	Millburngate..........................
Alexandria Crescent...............A2	Millennium Place ....
Allergate A2	Mowbray Street....................
Atherton Street......................A2	Neville Street.......................
Back Western Hill...................A1	New Elvet ....
Bakehouse Lane C1	New Elvet Bridge ....
Baths Bridge..........................C2	New Street...........................
Bow Lane C3	North Bailey ....
Boyd Street C4	North Road ....
Briardene A3	Old Elvet ....
Church Lane...........................C3	Oswald Court ....
Church Street C4	Owengate............................
Church Street Head C4	Palace Green........................
Clay Lane A3	Palmers Garth ....
Claypath................................C1	Pelaw Leazes Lane ....
Court Lane C3	Pelaw Rise...........................
Crossgate...............................A2	Pimlico................................
Crossgate Peth........................A3	Potters Bank........................
Douglas Villas.........................D1	Prebends' Bridge..................
Elvet Bridge...........................C2	Princes' Street ....
Elvet Crescent........................C3	Providence Row ....
Elvet Waterside.......................C2	Quarryheads Lane ....
Finney Terrace C1	Redhills Lane ....
Flass Street A2	Renny Street........................
Framwelgate..........................B1	Saddler Street.......................
Framwelgate Bridge...............B2	St Hild's Lane.......................
Framwelgate Waterside B1	Silver Street ....
Freeman Place B1	South Bailey ....
Gilesgate................................C1	South Road ....
Green Lane D3	South Street ....
Grove Street............................A3	Station Approach.................
Hallgarth Street......................C3	Stockton Road ....
Hawthorn Terrace...................A2	Summerville.........................
Highgate.................................B1	Sutton Street ....
High Road View.......................C4	Tenter Terrace ....
High Street C2	Territorial Lane....................
Hillcrest C1	The Avenue..........................
Holly Street............................A2	The Hall Garth ....
John Street.............................A2	Waddington Street ....
Keiper Heights C1	Wear View...........................
Kingsgate Bridge....................C3	Whinney Hill ....
Leazes Place C1	Willow Tree Avenue.............
Leazes Road B1	
Margery Lane..........................A3	
Market Square B2	
Mavin Street C3	
Mayorswell Close D1	
Milburngate Bridge B1	

Eastbourne

Eastbourne is found on atlas page **25 P11**

Arlington Road.......................A2	Langney Road.......................
Ashford Road B2	Langney Road ....
Ashford Road C1	Lascelles Terrace..................
Ashford Square B1	Latimer Road ....
Avenue Lane A1	Leaf Road ....
Belmore Road C1	Lismore Road ....
Blackwater Road A4	Longstone Road....................
Bolton Road B3	Lushington Road ....
Bourne Street..........................C1	Marine Parade......................
Burlington Place......................B3	Marine Road ....
Burlington Road......................C3	Mark Lane ....
Camden Road A3	Meads Road ....
Carew Road B1	Melbourne Road...................
Carlisle Road...........................A4	Old Orchard Road ....
Carlisle Road...........................B4	Old Wish Road ....
Cavendish Avenue C1	Pevensey Road.....................
Cavendish Place.......................C1	Promenade..........................
Ceylon Place C2	Queen's Gardens..................
Chiswick Place B3	Saffrons Road ....
College Road...........................B3	St Anne's Road ....
Colonnade Gardens................ D2	St Aubyn's Road ....
Commercial Road B1	St Leonard's Road.................
Compton Street B4	Seaside................................
Compton Street C3	Seaside Road ....
Cornfield Lane.........................B3	Southfields Road..................
Cornfield Road........................B2	South Street ....
Cornfield Terrace.....................B3	South Street ....
Devonshire Place.....................B3	Spencer Road.......................
Dursley Road...........................C1	Station Parade ....
Elms Road C3	Station Street ....
Enys Road A1	Susan's Road ....
Eversfield Road A1	Sutton Road ....
Furness Road A3	Sydney Road ....
Gildredge Road B2	Terminus Road......................
Grand Parade C3	Terminus Road......................
Grange Road A3	The Avenue..........................
Grassington Road A3	Tideswell Road......................
Grove Road A3	Trinity Place ....
Hardwick Road B3	Trinity Trees.........................
Hartfield Lane A1	Upper Avenue.......................
Hartfield Road A1	Upperton Gardens................
Hartington Place......................C3	Upperton Road.....................
Howard Square C4	West Street ....
Hyde Gardens B2	West Terrace ....
Hyde Road A2	Willowfield Road ....
Ivy Terrace A2	Wilmington Square ....
Jevington Gardens...................A4	Wish Road............................
Junction Road.........................B2	York Road ....

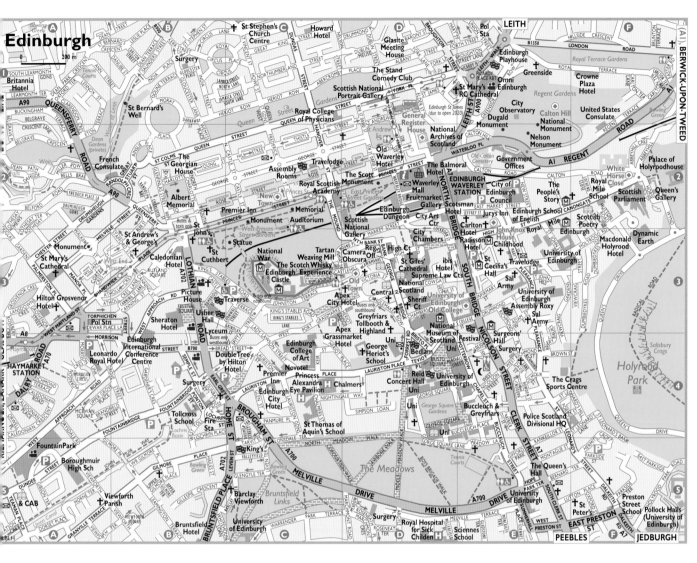

Edinburgh

Edinburgh is found on atlas page **127 P3**

Abbeyhill.....................F2	Chapel Street.....................E4	Gardener's Crescent................B4	Jeffrey Street.....................E2	New Street.....................E2	St Patrick Street.....................E4
Abercromby Place................C1	Charlotte Square................B2	George IV Bridge.................D3	Johnston Terrace...................C3	Nicolson Square.....................E4	St Stephen Street.................B1
Adam Street.....................E3	Chester Street Gardens.........A3	George Square.................D4	Keir Street.....................C4	Nicolson Street.....................E4	St Vincent Street...................C1
Albany Street.....................D1	Circus Lane.....................B1	George Square Lane..........D5	Kerr Street.....................B1	Nightingale Way.....................C4	Saunders Street.....................B1
Ann Street.....................A1	Circus Place.....................B1	George Street.....................B2	King's Stables Road.............B3	North Bridge.....................D2	Sciennes E5
Argyle Place.....................D5	Clarendon Crescent A1	George Street.....................C2	Lady Lawson Street...........C3	North Castle Street.................C2	Semple Street.....................B4
Atholl Crescent Lane.........A3	Clerk Street.....................E4	Gifford Park.....................E5	Lansdowne Crescent.........A3	North St Andrew Street........D1	Shandwick Place................A3
Bank Street.....................D3	Cockburn Street..................D2	Gillespie Crescent.............B5	Lauriston Gardens..............C4	North St David Street.........D1	Simpson Loan.....................D4
Barclay Terrace................C5	Coronation Walk C5	Gilmore Park.....................A5	Lauriston Place.................C4	Northumberland Street.........C1	South Bridge.....................E3
Belford Road.....................A2	Cowan's Close.....................E4	Gilmore Place.....................B5	Lauriston Street................C4	Oxford Street.....................F5	South Charlotte Street...........B2
Belgrave Crescent.............A2	Cowgate.....................D3	Gilmour Street.....................E4	Lawnmarket.....................D3	Palmerston Place.................A3	South Clerk Street...............E5
Bernard Terrace................E5	Dalkeith Road.....................F5	Glenfinlas Street................B2	Leamington Terrace............B5	Panmure Place.....................C4	South Learmonth Gardens.....A1
Boys Brigade Walk............D5	Dalry Road.....................A4	Gloucester Lane................B1	Leith Street.....................E1	Pleasance.....................E3	South St Andrew Street.......D2
Brandfield Street..............A4	Danube Street.....................B1	Granville Terrace...............A5	Leith Walk.....................E1	Ponton Street.....................B4	South St David Street.........D2
Bread Street.....................B4	Davie Street.....................E4	Great King Street...............C1	Lennox Street.....................A1	Potterrow.....................E4	Spittal Street.....................C4
Bristo Place.....................D4	Dean Park Crescent A1	Great Stuart Street............B2	Leven Place.....................C5	Princes Street.....................C2	Stafford Street.....................B3
Brougham Street C4	Dean Street.....................A1	Greenmarket.....................C3	Lochrin Place.....................B4	Queens Drive.....................F3	Tarvit Street.....................C5
Broughton Street D1	Dewar Place Lane A3	Greenside Row...................E1	Lochrin Street.....................B4	Queensferry Road A1	The Mound.....................C2
Broughton Street Lane.......E1	Douglas Gardens................A3	Grindlay Street.....................B3	London Road.....................E1	Queensferry Street...............B2	Thistle Street.....................C2
Brunton Terrace................F1	Doune Terrace.....................B1	Grosvenor Street.................A3	Lothian Road.....................B3	Queen Street.....................B2	Torphichen Street A3
Bruntsfield Place...............B5	Drummond Street................E3	Grove Street.....................A4	Lower Gilmore Place............B5	Radical Road.....................F3	Union Street.....................E1
Buccleuch Place................D4	Dublin Street.....................D1	Haddon's Court.................E4	Lutton Place.....................E5	Ramsay Lane.....................C3	Upper Gilmore Place............B5
Buccleuch Street...............E4	Dumbiedykes Road............F3	Hanover Street..................C2	Lynedoch Place Lane...........A2	Randolph Crescent.............B2	Victoria Street.....................D3
Caledonian Place..............A4	Dunbar Street.....................B4	Haymarket Terrace.............A4	Manor Place.....................A3	Randolph Lane.....................B2	Viewcraig Gardens...............E4
Caledonian Road...............A4	Dundas Street.....................C1	Heriot Row.....................C1	Marchmont Crescent..........D5	Rankeillor Street................E5	Viewcraig Street.................F3
Caledonian Street.............A4	Dundee Street.....................A5	Hermits Croft.....................F5	Marchmont Road.................D5	Regent Road.....................E2	Viewforth A5
Calton Road.....................E2	Earl Grey Street.................B4	High Street.....................D3	Market Street.....................D2	Richmond Place.................E3	Walker Street.....................A3
Candlemaker Row..............D3	Easter Road.....................F1	High Street.....................E3	Meadow Lane.....................E5	Rose Street.....................C2	Warrender Park Terrace.......C5
Canning Street.................B3	East Market Street..............E2	Hillside Crescent................E1	Melville Drive.....................C5	Roseneath Place D5	Waterloo Place.....................D2
Canongate.....................E2	East Parkside F5	Hill Street.....................C2	Melville Street.....................A3	Rothesay Place A3	Waverley Bridge................D2
Carlton Terrace................F1	East Preston Street.............F5	Holyrood Park Road............F5	Melville Terrace.................D5	Royal Circus.....................B1	West Approach Road............A5
Castle Hill.....................C3	Elder Street.....................D1	Holyrood Road.................E3	Middle Meadow Walk..........D5	Royal Terrace.....................E1	West Maitland Street............A3
Castle Street.....................C2	Forrest Road.....................D4	Home Street.....................C4	Millerfield Place.................D5	St Andrew Square...............D1	West Nicolson Street............E4
Castle Terrace.................B3	Forth Street.....................D1	Hope Street.....................B2	Miller Row.....................A2	St Bernard's Crescent A1	West Port.....................C4
Chalmers Street................C4	Fountainbridge.....................A4	Horse Wynd.....................F2	Moncrieff Terrace...............E5	St Colme Street.................B2	West Richmond Street...........E4
Chambers Street................D3	Frederick Street.................C2	Howden Street...................E4	Montague Street.................E5	St James Place.................D1	West Toll Cross.................B4
		Howe Street.....................C1	Moray Place.....................B1	St Leonard's Bank...............F4	William Street.....................A3
		India Place.....................B1	Morrison Link.....................A4	St Leonard's Hill...............E4	Yeaman Place.....................A5
		India Street.....................B1	Morrison Street................A4	St Leonard's Lane...............F4	York Lane.....................D1
		Jamaica Street South Lane...B1	Mound Place.....................D3	St Leonard's Street..............E4	York Place.....................D1
		Jawbone Walk.....................D5	Nelson Street.....................C1		Young Street.....................B2

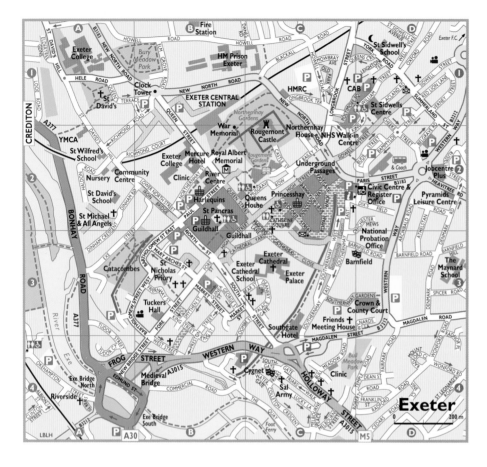

Exeter

Exeter is found on atlas page **9 M6**

Acland Road	D1	King Street	
Archibald Road	D3	King William Street	
Athelstan Road	D3	Longbrook Street	
Bailey Street	C2	Lower North Street	
Bampfylde Lane	C2	Magdalen Road	
Bampfylde Street	D2	Magdalen Street	
Barnfield Road	D3	Market Street	
Bartholomew Street East	B3	Martins Lane	
Bartholomew Street West	B3	Mary Arches Street	
Bear Street	C3	Musgrave Row	
Bedford Street	C2	New Bridge Street	
Belgrave Road	D2	New North Road	
Blackall Road	C1	Northernhay Street	
Bonhay Road	A2	North Street	
Bude Street	D2	Old Park Road	
Bull Meadow Road	C4	Oxford Road	
Castle Street	C2	Palace Gate	
Cathedral Close	C3	Paris Street	
Cathedral Yard	B3	Paul Street	
Cedars Road	D4	Preston Street	
Cheeke Street	D1	Princesshay	
Chichester Mews	C3	Queens Crescent	
Commercial Road	B4	Queen's Terrace	
Coombe Street	B3	Queen Street	
Deanery Place	C3	Radford Road	
Dean Street	D4	Richmond Court	
Denmark Road	D3	Richmond Road	
Dinham Crescent	A3	Roberts Road	
Dinham Road	A2	Roman Walk	
Dix's Field	D2	St David's Hill	
Eastgate	C2	Sidwell Street	
Edmund Street	A4	Sidwell Street	
Elm Grove Road	B1	Smythen Street	
Exe Street	A3	Southernhay East	
Fairpark Road	D4	Southernhay Gardens	
Fore Street	B3	Southernhay West	
Franklin Street	D4	South Street	
Friernhay Street	B3	Spicer Road	
Frog Street	A4	Summerland Street	
George Street	B3	Temple Road	
Guinea Street	B3	Tudor Court	
Haldon Road	A2	Tudor Street	
Heavitree Road	D2	Verney Street	
Hele Road	A1	Well Street	
High Street	C2	Western Way	
Holloway Street	C4	West Street	
Howell Road	B1	Wonford Road	
Iron Bridge	B2	York Road	

Gloucester

Gloucester is found on atlas page **46 F11**

Albert Street	D4	Millbrook Street	
Albion Street	B4	Montpellier	
All Saints' Road	D4	Napier Street	
Alvin Street	C2	Nettleton Road	
Archdeacon Street	B2	New Inn Lane	
Arthur Street	C4	Norfolk Street	
Barbican Road	B3	Northgate Street	
Barrack Square	B3	Old Tram Road	
Barton Street	D4	Over Causeway	
Bedford Street	C3	Oxford Road	
Belgrave Road	C4	Oxford Street	
Berkeley Street	B3	Park Road	
Black Dog Way	C2	Park Street	
Blenheim Road	D4	Parliament Street	
Brunswick Road	B4	Pembroke Street	
Brunswick Square	B4	Pitt Street	
Bruton Way	D3	Priory Road	
Bull Lane	B3	Quay Street	
Castle Meads Way	A2	Royal Oak Road	
Clarence Street	C3	Russell Street	
Clare Street	B2	St Aldate Street	
College Court	B2	St Catherine Street	
Commercial Road	B3	St John's Lane	
Cromwell Street	C4	St Mark Street	
Cross Keys Lane	B3	St Mary's Square	
Deans Walk	C1	St Mary's Street	
Eastgate Street	C3	St Michael's Square	
Gouda Way	B1	St Oswald's Road	
Great Western Road	D2	Sebert Street	
Greyfriars	B3	Severn Road	
Hampden Way	C3	Sherborne Street	
Hare Lane	C2	Sinope Street	
Heathville Road	D2	Southgate Street	
Henry Road	D1	Spa Road	
Henry Street	D2	Station Road	
High Orchard Street	A4	Swan Road	
Honyatt Road	D1	Sweetbriar Street	
Kings Barton Street	C4	The Cross	
Kingsholm Road	C1	The Oxebode	
King's Square	C3	The Quay	
Ladybellegate Street	B3	Union Street	
Llanthony Road	A4	Upper Quay Street	
London Road	D2	Vauxhall Road	
Longsmith Street	B3	Wellington Street	
Market Parade	C3	Westgate Street	
Merchants' Road	A4	Widden Street	
Mercia Road	B1	Worcester Parade	
Metz Way	D3	Worcester Street	

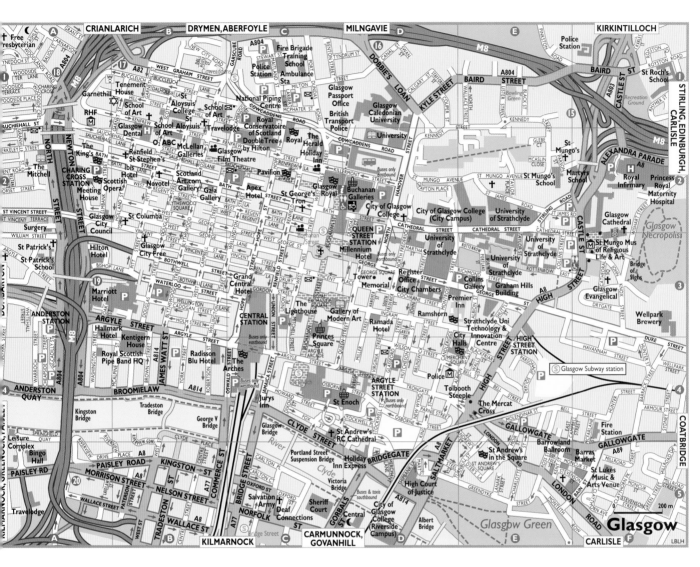

Glasgow

lasgow is found on atlas page **125 P4**

Albert Bridge	D5	
Albion Street	D4	
Albion Street	E3	
Alexandra Parade	F2	
Anderston Quay	A4	
Argyle Arcade	C4	
Argyle Street	A3	
Armour Street	F4	
Ashley Street	A1	
Bain Street	F5	
Baird Street	E1	
Baliol Street	A1	
Barrack Street	F4	
Bath Lane	B2	
Bath Street	A2	
Bell Street	E4	
Berkeley Street	A2	
Blackfriars Street	E4	
Black Street	E1	
Blythswood Square	B2	
Blythswood Street	B3	
Bothwell Lane	B3	
Bothwell Street	B3	
Bridgegate	D5	
Bridge of Sighs	F3	
Bridge Street	C5	
Broomielaw	B4	
Brown Street	B4	
Brunswick Street	D4	
Buccleuch Lane	B1	
Buccleuch Street	B1	
Buchanan Street	C4	
Cadogan Street	B3	
Calgary Street	D1	
Cambridge Street	C1	
Canal Street	D1	
Candleriggs	D4	
Carlton Place	C5	
Carnarvon Street	A1	
Castle Street	F1	
Castle Street	F2	
Cathedral Square	F3	
Cathedral Street	D2	
Centre Street	B5	
Chalmer Street	F5	
Charing Cross	A1	
Charles Street	F1	
Charlotte Street	E5	
Cheapside Street	A4	
Claythorn Avenue	F5	
Claythorn Park	F5	
Clyde Place	B4	
Clyde Street	C4	
Cochrane Street	D3	
Collins Street	E3	
Commerce Street	B5	
Couper Street	D1	
Cowcaddens Road	C1	
Dalhousie Lane	B1	
Dixon Street	C4	
Dobbie's Loan	D1	
Dorset Street	A2	
Douglas Street	B3	
Drury Street	C3	
Drygate	F3	
Duke Street	F4	
Dundas Street	D3	
Dunlop Street	D4	
Dyer's Lane	E5	
East Campbell Street	E4	
Elmbank Street	A2	
Fox Street	C4	
Gallowgate	E4	
Garnethill Street	B1	
Garnet Street	B2	
Garscube Road	C1	
Garth Street	D3	
George Square	D3	
George Street	E3	
George V Bridge	B4	
Glasgow Bridge	C5	
Glassford Street	D4	
Glebe Court	E2	
Gorbals Street	C5	
Gordon Street	C3	
Grafton Place	D2	
Granville Street	A2	
Greendyke Street	E5	
Green Street	F5	
Hanover Street	D3	
High Street	E4	
Hill Street	B1	
Holland Street	B2	
Holm Street	B3	
Hope Street	C3	
Howard Street	C4	
Hunter Street	F4	
Hutcheson Street	D4	
Hydepark Street	A4	
Ingram Street	D3	
Jamaica Street	C4	
James Watt Street	B4	
John Knox Street	F3	
John Street	D3	
Kennedy Street	D2	
Kennedy Street	E1	
Kent Road	A2	
Kent Street	E5	
Killermont Street	C2	
Kingston Bridge	A5	
Kingston Street	B5	
King Street	D4	
Kyle Street	D1	
Lanark Street	E5	
Larbert Street	C1	
Lister Street	E1	
London Road	E4	
Maitland Street	C1	
Martha Street	D3	
Mart Street	D5	
Maxwell Street	C4	
McAlpine Street	B4	
McAslin Close	E2	
McFarlane Street	F4	
McPhater Street	C1	
Merchant Lane	D5	
Miller Street	D4	
Millroad Drive	F5	
Millroad Street	F5	
Milton Street	C1	
Mitchell Street	C4	
Moir Street	E5	
Molendinar Street	E4	
Moncur Street	E5	
Monteith Row	E5	
Montrose Street	D3	
Morrison Street	A5	
Nelson Street	B5	
New City Road	B1	
Newton Street	A2	
New Wynd	D4	
Norfolk Street	C5	
North Frederick Street	D3	
North Hanover Street	D3	
North Portland Street	E3	
North Street	A2	
North Wallace Street	E1	
Osborne Street	C4	
Oswald Street	C4	
Oxford Street	C5	
Paisley Road	A5	
Parnie Street	D4	
Parsonage Square	E4	
Parson Street	E2	
Paterson Street	B5	
Pinkston Road	E1	
Pitt Street	B2	
Port Dundas Road	C1	
Portland Street Suspension Bridge	C5	
Queen Street	C4	
Renfield Lane	C3	
Renfield Street	C3	
Renfrew Lane	C2	
Renfrew Street	B1	
Renton Street	C1	
Rhymer Street	F1	
Richmond Street	E3	
Riverview Drive	A4	
Robertson Street	B4	
Rose Street	B2	
Ross Street	E5	
Rottenrow	E3	
Rottenrow East	E3	
Royal Exchange Square	C3	
Royston Road	F1	
Royston Square	F1	
St Andrew's Square	E5	
St Andrew's Street	E4	
St James Road	E2	
St Mungo Avenue	D2	
St Vincent Lane	B3	
St Vincent Place	C3	
St Vincent Street	A2	
St Vincent Terrace	A2	
Saltmarket	D5	
Sauchiehall Lane	A2	
Sauchiehall Street	A1	
Sauchiehall Street	B2	
Scott Street	B1	
Shipbank Lane	D5	
Shuttle Street	E3	
South Frederick Street	D3	
Springfield Quay	A4	
Stafford Street	D1	
Steel Street	D5	
Stevenson Street	F5	
Stewart Street	C1	
Stirling Road	E2	
Stockwell Place	D4	
Stockwell Street	D4	
Suffolk Street	E5	
Sydney Street	F4	
Taylor Place	E2	
Taylor Street	E2	
Tradeston Bridge	B4	
Tradeston Street	B5	
Trongate	D4	
Turnbull Street	D5	
Tyndrum Street	C1	
Union Street	C3	
Virginia Street	D4	
Wallace Street	A5	
Walls Street	E4	
Warroch Street	A4	
Washington Street	A4	
Waterloo Street	B3	
Wellington Lane	B3	
Wellington Street	B3	
Wellpark Street	F4	
West Campbell Street	B3	
West George Lane	B2	
West George Street	B2	
West Graham Street	B1	
West Nile Street	C3	
West Regent Lane	C2	
West Regent Street	B2	
West Street	B5	
William Street	A3	
Wilson Street	D4	
Wishart Street	F3	
Woodlands Road	A1	
Woodside Crescent	A1	
Woodside Terrace	A1	
Woodside Terrace Lane	A1	
York Street	B4	

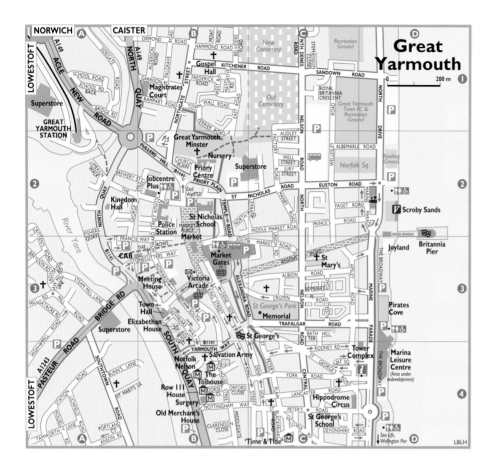

Great Yarmouth

Great Yarmouth is found on atlas page **77 Q10**

Acle New Road...............A1	North Drive.....................D
Albemarle Road C2	North Market Road ....D
Albion Road C3	North Quay.....................A
Alderson Road B1	Northgate Street................B
Alexandra Road B3	Nottingham Way.................B
Apsley Road C3	Ormond Road...................B
Belvidere Road B1	Paget Road ....B
Blackfriars Road C4	Palgrave Road..................B
Brewery Street A2	Pasteur Road ....A
Breydon Road A3	Prince's Road C
Bridge Road A1	Priory Plain ....B
Bridge Road A3	Queen Street...................B
Bunn's Lane A4	Rampart Road..................A
Church Plain B2	Regent Road...................B
Critten's Road A3	Rodney Road...................B
Crown Road C3	Russell Road ....B
Dene Side B3	St Francis Way ....A
Devonshire Road...............C4	St George's Road C
East Road B1	St Nicholas Road ....B
Euston Road C2	St Peter's Plain C
Factory Road C2	St Peter's Road C
Ferrier Road B1	Sandown Road C
Fishers Quay A2	Saw Mill Lane..................B
Frederick Road B1	School Road....................B
Fullers Hill....................B2	School Road Back...............B
Garrison Road B1	Sidegate Road..................A
Gatacre Road A3	South Market Road ....B
George Street A2	South Quay ....A
Greyfriars Way B3	Southtown Road ....A
Hammond Road B1	Station Road ....A
High Mill Road A3	Steam Mill Lane................A
Howard Street North B2	Stephenson Close ....B
Howard Street South B3	Stonecutters Way ....A
King Street B3	Tamworth Lane ....A
Kitchener Road B1	Temple Road...................B
Ladyhaven Road A3	The Broadway ....D
Lancaster Road C4	The Conge ....B
Lichfield Road A4	The Rows ....B
Limekiln Walk A2	Tolhouse Street.................B
Manby Road C2	Town Wall Road ....B
Marine Parade..................D3	Trafalgar Road..................C
Maygrove Road B1	Union Road C
Middle Market Road............C2	Victoria Road C
Middlegate B4	Wellesley Road ....D
Moat Road B1	West Road ....B
Nelson Road Central C3	Wolseley Road C
Nelson Road North C1	Yarmouth Way ....A
North Denes Road C1	York Road C

Guildford

Guildford is found on atlas page **23 Q5**

Abbot Road C4	Millmead......................B
Angel Gate B3	Millmead Terrace...............B
Artillery Road B1	Mount Pleasant................A
Artillery Terrace................C1	Nightingale Road ....D
Bedford Road A2	North Street....................C
Bridge Street A3	Onslow Road ....B
Bright Hill.....................C3	Onslow Street ....B
Brodie Road D3	Oxford Road C
Bury Fields B4	Pannells Court C
Bury Street....................B4	Park Street.....................B
Castle Hill C4	Pewley Bank ....D
Castle Street C3	Pewley Fort Inner Court ....D
Chapel Street B3	Pewley Hill C
Chertsey Street C2	Pewley Way ....D
Cheselden Road D2	Phoenix Court C
Church Road B1	Porridge Pot Alley ....B
College Road...................B2	Portsmouth Road...............D
Commercial Road B2	Poyle Road.....................D
Dene Road D2	Quarry Street C
Drummond Road B1	Sandfield Terrace...............D
Eagle Road C1	Semaphore Road ....D
Eastgate Gardens..............D2	South Hill ....D
Epsom Road D2	Springfield Road ....D
Falcon Road C1	Station Approach................B
Farnham Road A3	Station View ....B
Fort Road C4	Stoke Fields C
Foxenden Road D1	Stoke Grove C
Friary Bridge A3	Stoke Road C
Friary Street...................B3	Swan Lane ....B
George Road B1	Sydenham Road...............C
Guildford Park Road............A2	Testard Road ....A
Harvey Road D3	The Bars C
Haydon Place C2	The Mount ....A
High Pewley D4	The Shambles C
High Street C3	Tunsgate......................C
Jeffries Passage................C2	Upperton Road ....A
Jenner Road D2	Victoria Road C
Laundry Road..................B2	Walnut Tree Close ....A
Leapale Lane B2	Ward Street C
Leapale Road B2	Warwicks Bench C
Leas Road B1	Wherwell Road ....A
London Road D2	William Road ....B
Mareschal Road A4	Wodeland Avenue..............A
Market Street C3	Woodbridge Road ....B
Martyr Road C2	York Road C
Mary Road A1	
Millbrook......................B3	
Mill Lane B3	

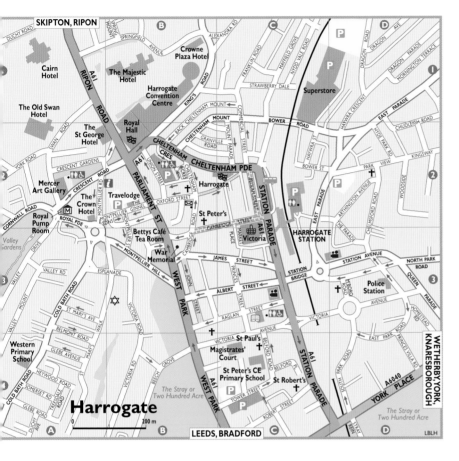

Harrogate

Harrogate is found on atlas page **97 M9**

Albert Street	C3	Montpellier Hill	B3
Alexandra Road	B1	Montpellier Road	A2
Arthington Avenue	D2	Montpellier Street	B2
Back Cheltenham Mount	B2	Mornington Terrace	D1
Beech Grove	B4	Mount Parade	C2
Belford Place	C4	North Park Road	D3
Belford Road	C4	Nydd Vale Road	C1
Belmont Road	A3	Oxford Street	B2
Beulah Street	C2	Park View	D2
Bower Road	C1	Parliament Street	B2
Bower Street	C2	Princes Street	C3
Cambridge Road	B3	Princes Villa Road	D4
Cambridge Street	C2	Queen Parade	D3
Chelmsford Road	D3	Raglan Street	C3
Cheltenham Crescent	B2	Ripon Road	A1
Cheltenham Mount	B2	Robert Street	C4
Cheltenham Parade	B2	Royal Parade	A2
Chudleigh Road	D2	St Mary's Avenue	A3
Cold Bath Road	A3	St Mary's Walk	A4
Commercial Street	C1	Somerset Road	A4
Cornwall Road	A2	South Park Road	D4
Crescent Gardens	A2	Springfield Avenue	B1
Crescent Road	A2	Spring Mount	B1
Dragon Avenue	D1	Station Avenue	D3
Dragon Parade	D1	Station Bridge	C3
Dragon Road	D1	Station Parade	C2
Duchy Avenue	A4	Strawberry Dale	C1
Duchy Road	A1	Stray Rein	D4
East Parade	C2	Swan Road	A2
East Park Road	D4	The Ginnel	B2
Esplanade	A3	The Parade	D2
Franklin Road	C1	Tower Street	C4
Glebe Avenue	A4	Treesdale Road	A4
Glebe Road	A4	Union Street	B2
Granville Road	B2	Valley Drive	A3
Haywra Street	C2	Valley Mount	A3
Heywood Road	A4	Valley Road	A3
Homestead Road	D3	Victoria Avenue	B4
Hyde Park Road	D2	Victoria Road	B3
Hywra Crescent	D2	West Park	B3
James Street	B3	West Park Street	B4
John Street	B3	Woodside	D2
King's Road	B1	York Place	D4
Kingsway	D2	York Road	A2
Market Place	C3		
Marlborough Road	D3		
Mayfield Grove	C1		
Montpellier Gardens	B2		

Huddersfield

Huddersfield is found on atlas page **90 E7**

Albion Street	B4	New North Road	A2
Alfred Street	C4	New Street	B4
Back Union Street	C1	Northgate	C1
Bankfield Road	A4	Northumberland Street	C2
Bath Street	B1	Old Leeds Road	D2
Belmont Street	A1	Old South Street	B3
Brook Street	C2	Outcote Bank	B4
Byram Street	C2	Oxford Street	C1
Cambridge Road	B1	Page Street	C4
Carforth Street	D4	Park Avenue	A2
Castlegate	B1	Park Drive South	A2
Chancery Lane	B3	Peel Street	C4
Chapel Hill	B4	Portland Street	A2
Chapel Street	B4	Princess Street	B4
Church Street	C2	Prospect Street	A4
Clare Hill	B1	Quay Street	D2
Claremont Street	B1	Queen Street	C3
Cloth Hall Street	B3	Queen Street South	C4
Cross Church Street	C3	Queensgate	C4
Dundas Street	B3	Railway Street	B2
Elizabeth Queen Gardens	A2	Ramsden Street	B3
Elmwood Avenue	A1	Rook Street	B1
Firth Street	D4	St Andrew's Road	D2
Fitzwilliam Street	A2	St George's Square	B2
Fitzwilliam Street	B2	St John's Road	B1
Gasworks Street	D1	St Peter's Street	C2
Great Northern Street	C1	Southgate	C2
Greenhead Road	A3	Spring Grove Street	A4
Half Moon Street	B3	Spring Street	A3
High Street	B3	Springwood Avenue	A3
Highfields Road	A1	Stadium Way	D1
John William Street	B2	Station Street	B2
King Street	C3	Trinity Street	A2
King's Mill Lane	D4	Turnbridge Road	D2
Kirkgate	C3	Union Street	C1
Leeds Road	C2	Upper George Street	A3
Lincoln Street	D3	Upperhead Row	B3
Lord Street	C2	Viaduct Street	B2
Lower Fitzwilliam Street	C1	Victoria Lane	C3
Lynton Avenue	A3	Wakefield Road	D3
Manchester Road	A4	Water Street	A3
Market Place	C3	Watergate	D2
Market Street	B3	Waverley Road	A2
Merton Street	A3	Wentworth Street	A2
Milford Street	B4	Westgate	B3
Mountjoy Road	A1	William Street	C1
New North Parade	B2	Wood Street	C2
New North Road	A1	Zetland Street	C3

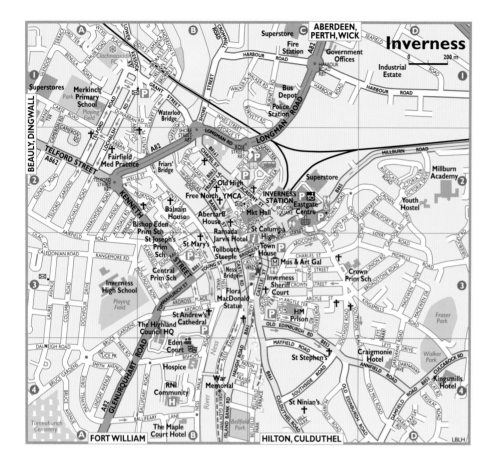

Inverness

Inverness is found on atlas page **156 B8**

Abertaff Road	D2	Glenurquhart Road	
Academy Street	B2	Gordon Terrace	
Anderson Street	B1	Grant Street	
Annfield Road	D4	Great Glen Way	
Ardconnel Terrace	C3	Harbour Road	
Ardross Street	B3	Harris Road	
Argyle Street	C3	Harrowden Road	
Argyle Terrace	C3	Haugh Road	
Ballifeary Lane	A4	High Street	
Ballifeary Road	B4	Hill Park	
Bank Street	B2	Hill Street	
Bellfield Terrace	C4	Huntly Street	
Benula Road	A1	Innes Street	
Birnie Terrace	A1	Kenneth Street	
Bishops Road	B4	King Street	
Bridge Street	B3	Kingsmills Road	
Broadstone Road	D3	Laurel Avenue	
Bruce Gardens	A4	Lindsay Avenue	
Bruce Park	A4	Lochalsh Road	
Burnett Road	C1	Longman Road	
Caledonian Road	A3	Lovat Road	
Cameron Road	A2	Lower Kessock Street	
Cameron Square	A2	Maxwell Drive	
Carse Road	A1	Mayfield Road	
Castle Road	B3	Midmills Road	
Castle Street	C3	Millburn Road	
Chapel Street	B2	Mitchell's Lane	
Charles Street	C3	Muirfield Road	
Columba Road	A3	Ness Bank	
Crown Circus	C2	Old Edinburgh Road	
Crown Drive	D2	Park Road	
Crown Road	C2	Planefield Road	
Crown Street	C3	Porterfield Road	
Culcabock Road	D4	Raasay Road	
Culduthel Road	C4	Rangemore Road	
Dalneigh Road	A4	Ross Avenue	
Damfield Road	D4	Seafield Road	
Darnaway Road	D4	Shore Street	
Denny Street	C3	Smith Avenue	
Dochfour Drive	A3	Southside Place	
Dunabban Road	A1	Southside Road	
Dunain Road	A2	Telford Gardens	
Duncraig Street	B3	Telford Road	
Eriskay Road	D4	Telford Street	
Fairfield Road	A3	Tomnahurich Street	
Falcon Square	C2	Union Road	
Friars' Lane	B2	Walker Road	
Glendoe Terrace	A1	Young Street	

Ipswich

Ipswich is found on atlas page **53 L3**

Alderman Road	A3	Key Street	
Anglesea Road	B1	King Street	
Argyle Street	D2	London Road	
Austin Street	C4	Lower Brook Street	
Barrack Lane	A1	Lower Orwell Street	
Belstead Road	B4	Museum Street	
Berners Street	B1	Neale Street	
Black Horse Lane	B2	Neptune Quay	
Blanche Street	D2	New Cardinal Street	
Bolton Lane	C1	Newson Street	
Bond Street	D3	Northgate Street	
Bramford Road	A1	Norwich Road	
Bridge Street	C4	Old Foundry Road	
Burlington Road	A2	Orchard Street	
Burrell Road	B4	Orford Street	
Cardigan Street	A1	Orwell Place	
Carr Street	C2	Orwell Quay	
Cecil Road	B1	Portman Road	
Cemetery Road	D1	Princes Street	
Chancery Road	A4	Quadling Street	
Charles Street	B1	Queen Street	
Christchurch Street	D1	Ranelagh Road	
Civic Drive	B2	Russell Road	
Clarkson Street	A1	St George's Street	
Cobbold Street	C2	St Helen's Street	
College Street	C3	St Margaret's Street	
Commercial Road	A4	St Matthews Street	
Constantine Road	A3	St Nicholas Street	
Crown Street	B2	St Peter's Street	
Cumberland Street	A1	Silent Street	
Dalton Road	A2	Sir Alf Ramsey Way	
Dock Street	C4	Soane Street	
Duke Street	D4	South Street	
Eagle Street	C3	Star Lane	
Elm Street	B2	Stoke Quay	
Falcon Street	B3	Suffolk Road	
Fonnereau Road	B1	Tacket Street	
Foundation Street	C3	Tavern Street	
Franciscan Way	B3	Tower Ramparts	
Geneva Road	A1	Tuddenham Avenue	
Grafton Way	B3	Turret Lane	
Great Gipping Street	A2	Upper Orwell Street	
Great Whip Street	C4	Vernon Street	
Grey Friars Road	B3	West End Road	
Grimwade Street	D3	Westgate Street	
Handford Road	A2	Willoughby Road	
Hervey Street	D1	Wolsey Street	
High Street	B1	Woodbridge Road	

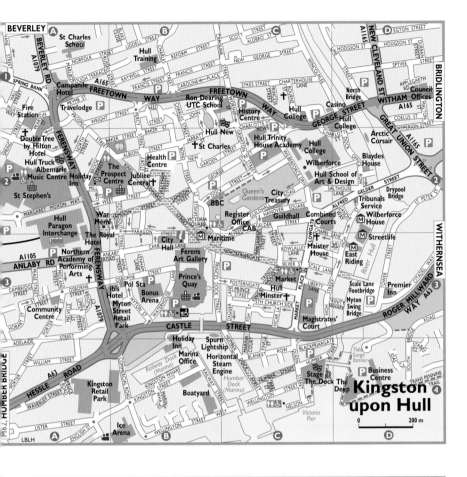

Kingston upon Hull

Kingston upon Hull is found on atlas page **93 J5**

Adelaide Street	A4	Market Place	C3
Albion Street	B2	Mill Street	A2
Alfred Gelder Street	C2	Myton Street	B3
Anlaby Road	A3	New Cleveland Street	D1
Baker Street	B2	New Garden Street	B2
Beverley Road	A1	New George Street	C1
Blackfriargate	C4	Norfolk Street	A1
Blanket Row	C4	Osborne Street	B3
Bond Street	B2	Osborne Street	A3
Brook Street	A2	Paragon Street	B2
Caroline Street	B1	Percy Street	B1
Carr Lane	B3	Porter Street	A3
Castle Street	B3	Portland Place	A2
Chapel Lane	C2	Portland Street	A2
Charles Street	B1	Postergate	C3
Charterhouse Lane	C1	Princes Dock Street	B3
Citadel Way	D3	Prospect Street	A1
Commercial Road	B4	Queen Street	C4
Dagger Lane	C3	Railway Street	B4
Dock Office Row	D2	Raywell Street	B1
Dock Street	B2	Reform Street	B1
Durban Street	D1	Russell Street	A1
Egginton Street	B1	St Luke's Street	A3
Ferensway	A2	St Peter Street	D2
Freetown Way	A1	Saville Street	B2
Gandhi Way	D2	Scale Lane	C3
Garrison Road	D3	Scott Street	C1
George Street	B2	Silver Street	C3
George Street	D1	South Bridge Road	D4
Great Union Street	D1	South Church Side	C3
Grimston Street	C2	South Street	B2
Guildhall Road	C2	Spring Bank	A1
Hanover Square	C2	Spyvee Street	D1
Hessle Road	A4	Sykes Street	C1
High Street	C3	Tower Street	D3
Hodgson Street	D1	Upper Union Street	A3
Humber Dock Street	C4	Victoria Square	B2
Humber Street	C4	Waterhouse Lane	B3
Hyperion Street	D1	Wellington Street	C4
Jameson Street	B2	Wellington Street West	B4
Jarratt Street	B2	West Street	A2
King Edward Street	B2	Whitefriargate	C3
Kingston Street	B4	Wilberforce Drive	C2
Liddell Street	B1	William Street	A4
Lime Street	C1	Wincolmlee	C1
Lister Street	A4	Witham	D1
Lowgate	C3	Worship Street	C1
Margaret Moxon Way	A2	Wright Street	A1

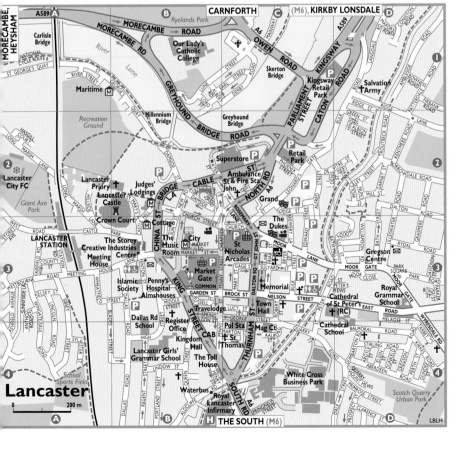

Lancaster

Lancaster is found on atlas page **95 K8**

Aberdeen Road	D4	Lincoln Road	A3
Aldcliffe Road	B4	Lindow Street	B4
Alfred Street	C2	Lodge Street	C2
Ambleside Road	D1	Long Marsh Lane	A2
Balmoral Road	D4	Lune Street	B1
Bath Street	D3	Market Street	B3
Blades Street	A3	Meeting House Lane	A3
Bond Street	D3	Middle Street	B3
Borrowdale Road	D2	Moor Gate	D3
Brewery Lane	C3	Moor Lane	C3
Bridge Lane	B2	Morecambe Road	B1
Brock Street	B3	Nelson Street	C3
Bulk Road	D2	North Road	C2
Bulk Street	C3	Owen Road	C1
Cable Street	B2	Park Road	D3
Castle Hill	B3	Parliament Street	C2
Castle Park	A3	Patterdale Road	D2
Caton Road	C2	Penny Street	B4
Cheapside	C3	Portland Street	B4
China Street	B3	Primrose Street	D4
Church Street	B2	Prospect Street	D4
Common Garden Street	B3	Quarry Road	C4
Dale Street	D4	Queen Street	B4
Dallas Road	B3	Regent Street	A4
Dalton Road	D2	Ridge Lane	D1
Dalton Square	C3	Ridge Street	D1
Damside Street	B2	Robert Street	C3
Derby Road	C1	Rosemary Lane	C2
De Vitre Street	C2	St George's Quay	A1
Dumbarton Road	D4	St Leonard's Gate	C2
East Road	D3	St Peter's Road	C4
Edward Street	C3	Sibsey Street	A3
Fairfield Road	A3	South Road	C4
Fenton Street	B3	Station Road	A3
Gage Street	C3	Stirling Road	D4
Garnet Street	D2	Sulyard Street	C3
George Street	C3	Sun Street	B3
Grasmere Road	D3	Thurnham Street	C4
Great John Street	C3	Troutbeck Road	D2
Gregson Road	D4	Ulleswater Road	D3
Greyhound Bridge Road	B1	West Road	A3
High Street	B4	Westbourne Road	A3
Kelsey Street	A3	Wheatfield Street	A3
Kentmere Road	D2	Williamson Road	D3
King Street	B3	Wingate-Saul Road	A3
Kingsway	C1	Wolseley Street	D2
Kirkes Road	D4	Woodville Street	D3
Langdale Road	D1	Wyresdale Road	D3

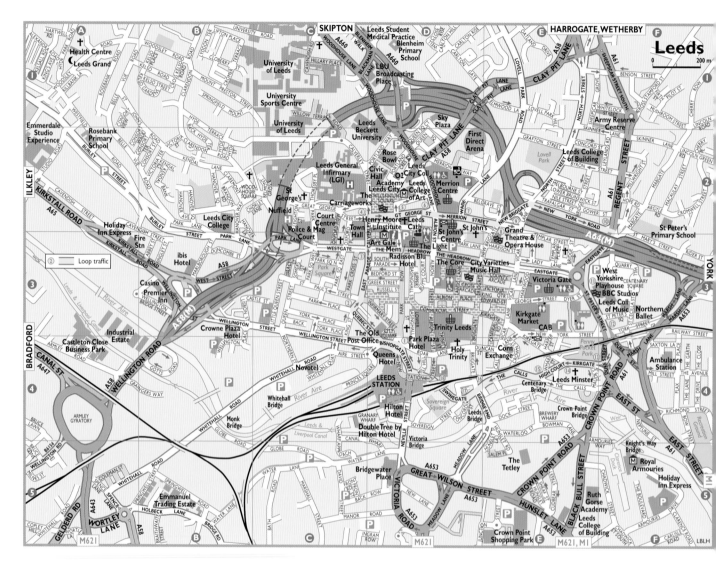

Leeds

Leeds is found on atlas page **90 H4**

Abbey Street.............B3	Calverley Street.............C2	Duke Street.............F4	King's Avenue.............A1	Northern Street.............C4	Springfield Mount.............B1
Aire Street.............C4	Canal Street.............A4	Duncan Street.............D4	King Street.............C3	North Street.............E2	Springwell Road.............B5
Albion Place.............D3	Canal Wharf.............C4	Duncombe Street.............B3	Kirkgate.............E3	Oxford Place.............C3	Springwell Street.............B5
Albion Street.............D2	Carlton Hill.............D1	Dyer Street.............E3	Kirkstall Road.............A2	Oxford Row.............C3	Studio Road.............A2
Alexandra Road.............A1	Carlton Rise.............D1	Eastgate.............E3	Lady Lane.............E3	Park Cross Street.............C3	Swinegate.............D4
Argyle Road.............F2	Castle Street.............B3	East Parade.............C3	Lands Lane.............D3	Park Lane.............B2	Templar Street.............E3
Armley Gyratory.............A4	Cavendish Road.............C1	East Street.............F4	Leighton Street.............C2	Park Place.............C3	The Avenue.............E4
Armley Road.............A4	Cavendish Street.............A2	Elmwood Lane.............E1	Leylands Road.............F2	Park Row.............D3	The Boulevard.............F5
Back Hyde Terrace.............B2	Centenary Square.............F3	Flax Place.............F4	Lifton Place.............B1	Park Square East.............C3	The Calls.............E4
Back Row.............C5	Central Road.............E3	Front Street.............C5	Lincoln Green Road.............F2	Park Square North.............C3	The Headrow.............D3
Bath Road.............C5	Chadwick Street.............F5	Gelderd Road.............A5	Lisbon Street.............B3	Park Square West.............C3	Thoresby Place.............C2
Bedford Street.............D3	Cherry Row.............F1	George Street.............E3	Little Queen Street.............C3	Park Street.............C3	Trafalgar Street.............E2
Belgrave Street.............D2	Chorley Lane.............B2	Globe Road.............B4	Lovell Park Hill.............E1	Pilot Street.............F1	Upper Basinghall Street.............D3
Belle Vue Road.............A1	City Square.............D3	Gotts Road.............B4	Lovell Park Road.............E1	Portland Crescent.............D2	Vicar Lane.............E3
Belmont Grove.............C2	Claremont.............B2	Gower Street.............E2	Lower Basinghall Street.............D3	Portland Way.............D2	Victoria Road.............D5
Benson Street.............F1	Clarence Road.............F5	Grace Street.............C3	Lower Brunswick Street.............E2	Princes Square.............C4	Victoria Street.............B2
Bingley Street.............B3	Clarendon Road.............B1	Grafton Street.............E2	Lyddon Terrace.............B1	Quarry Hill.............F3	Victoria Terrace.............B2
Bishopgate Street.............D4	Clay Pit Lane.............D2	Graingers Way.............A4	Mabgate.............F2	Quebec Street.............C3	Wade Lane.............D2
Black Bull Street.............E5	Cloberry Street.............B1	Great George Street.............C2	Macaulay Street.............F2	Queen Square.............D2	Water Lane.............B5
Blackman Lane.............C1	Commercial Street.............D3	Great Wilson Street.............D5	Manor Road.............C5	Queen Square Court.............D2	Waterloo Street.............E4
Blenheim Walk.............C1	Concordia Street.............D4	Greek Street.............D3	Mark Lane.............D3	Queen Street.............C3	Wellington Bridge Street.............B3
Boar Lane.............D4	Concord Street.............E2	Hanover Avenue.............B2	Marlborough Street.............B3	Railway Street.............F3	Wellington Road.............A4
Bowman Lane.............E4	Consort Street.............B2	Hanover Lane.............B2	Marshall Street.............C5	Regent Street.............F2	Wellington Road.............A5
Bow Street.............F4	Consort View.............A1	Hanover Square.............B2	Marsh Lane.............F4	Richmond Street.............F4	Wellington Street.............B3
Brandon Road.............B2	County Arcade.............E3	Harewood Street.............E3	Maude Street.............E4	Rider Street.............F3	Westfield Road.............A1
Bridge End.............D4	Cromer Terrace.............B1	Harper Street.............E4	Meadow Lane.............D5	Rillbank Lane.............A1	Westgate.............C3
Bridge Road.............B5	Cromwell Street.............F2	Harrison Street.............E3	Melbourne Street.............E2	Rosebank Road.............A1	West Street.............B3
Bridge Street.............E2	Cross Arcade.............E3	Hartwell Road.............A1	Merrion Street.............D2	St Cecilla Street.............F3	Wharf Approach.............C4
Bridge Street.............E3	Cross Kelso Road.............B1	High Court.............E4	Merrion Way.............D2	St John's Road.............A1	Wharf Street.............E4
Briggate.............D4	Cross Stamford Street.............F1	Holbeck Lane.............B5	Millennium Square.............D2	St Mary's Street.............F3	Whitehall Quay.............C4
Burley Street.............A2	Crown Point Road.............E5	Hope Road.............F2	Mill Street.............F3	St Paul's Street.............C3	Whitehall Road.............A5
Butts Court.............D3	Crown Street.............E4	Hunslet Road.............E4	Millwright Street.............F2	St Peter's Square.............E3	Whitehall Road.............A5
Byron Street.............E2	Cudbear Street.............E5	Hunslet Road.............E5	Mount Preston Street.............B1	St Peter's Street.............E3	Whitelock Street.............F1
Call Lane.............E4	David Street.............C5	Hyde Park Road.............A1	Mushroom Street.............F1	Salem Place.............E5	Willow Terrace Road.............C1
	Dock Street.............E4	Hyde Street.............B2	Neptune Street.............F4	Saxton Lane.............F4	Woodhouse Lane.............C1
	Duke Street.............F4	Hyde Terrace.............B1	Neville Street.............D4	Sheepscar Grove.............E1	Woodhouse Square.............B2
		Infirmary Street.............D3	New Briggate.............E3	Sheepscar Street South.............F1	Woodsley Road.............B2
		Junction Street.............D5	New Lane.............D5	Skinner Lane.............E1	Wortley Lane.............B5
		Kelso Road.............B1	New Station Street.............D4	South Parade.............D3	Wortley Lane.............A5
		Kendal Lane.............B2	New York Road.............E2	Sovereign Street.............D4	York Place.............C3
		King Edward Street.............E3	New York Street.............E3	Spence Lane.............A5	York Street.............F3

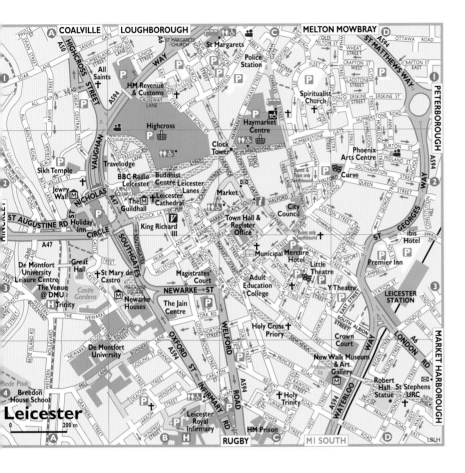

Leicester

Leicester is found on atlas page **72 F10**

Albion Street	C3	Infirmary Road	B4
All Saints Road	A1	Jarrom Street	B4
Bath Lane	A2	Jarvis Street	A1
Bedford Street	C1	King Street	C3
Belgrave Gate	C1	Lee Street	C1
Belvoir Street	C3	London Road	D3
Bishop Street	C3	Lower Brown Street	B3
Bonners Lane	B4	Magazine Square	B3
Bowling Green Street	C3	Mansfield Street	B1
Burgess Street	B1	Market Place South	B2
Burton Street	D2	Market Street	C3
Calais Hill	C3	Mill Lane	A4
Campbell Street	D3	Morledge Street	D1
Cank Street	B2	Newarke Street	B3
Castle Street	A3	New Walk	C3
Charles Street	C1	Oxford Street	B3
Chatham Street	C3	Peacock Lane	B2
Cheapside	C2	Pocklingtons Walk	B3
Church Gate	B1	Princess Road East	D4
Clyde Street	D1	Princess Road West	C4
Colton Street	C2	Queen Street	D2
Conduit Street	D3	Regent Road	C4
Crafton Street West	D1	Regent Street	D4
Deacon Street	B4	Richard III Road	A2
De Montfort Street	D4	Rutland Street	C2
Dover Street	C3	St Augustine Road	A2
Duke Street	C3	St George Street	D2
Duns Lane	A3	St Georges Way	D2
East Bond Street Lane	B1	St James Street	C1
Erskine Street	D1	St Matthews Way	D1
Fleet Street	C1	St Nicholas Circle	A2
Friar Lane	B3	Sanvey Gate	A1
Gallowtree Gate	C2	Soar Lane	A1
Gateway Street	A3	South Albion Street	D3
Granby Street	C2	Southampton Street	D2
Grasmere Street	A4	Southgates	B3
Gravel Street	B1	Station Street	D3
Great Central Street	A1	The Newarke	A3
Greyfriars	B2	Tower Street	C4
Halford Street	C2	Vaughan Way	A2
Haymarket	C2	Waterloo Way	D4
Highcross Street	A1	Welford Road	C4
Highcross Street	B2	Welles Street	A2
High Street	B2	Wellington Street	C3
Hill Street	C1	Western Boulevard	A4
Horsefair Street	B3	West Street	C4
Humberstone Gate	C2	Wharf Street South	D1
Humberstone Road	D1	Yeoman Street	C2

Lincoln

Lincoln is found on atlas page **86 C6**

Alexandra Terrace	B2	Montague Street	D3
Arboretum Avenue	D2	Motherby Lane	B2
Baggholme Road	D3	Nelson Street	A2
Bailgate	C1	Newland	B3
Bank Street	C3	Newland Street West	A2
Beaumont Fee	B3	Northgate	C1
Belle Vue Terrace	A1	Orchard Street	B3
Brayford Way	A4	Oxford Street	C4
Brayford Wharf East	B4	Park Street	B3
Brayford Wharf North	A3	Pelham Street	C4
Broadgate	C3	Pottergate	D2
Burton Road	B1	Queen's Crescent	A1
Carholme Road	A2	Richmond Road	A1
Carline Road	A1	Rope Walk	A4
Cathedral Street	C2	Rosemary Lane	D3
Chapel Lane	B1	Rudgard Lane	A2
Charles Street West	A2	St Hugh Street	D3
Cheviot Street	D2	St Mark Street	B4
City Square	C3	St Martin's Street	C2
Clasketgate	C3	St Mary's Street	B4
Cornhill	B4	St Rumbold's Street	C3
Croft Street	D3	Saltergate	C3
Danesgate	C2	Silver Street	C3
Depot Street	A3	Sincil Street	C4
Drury Lane	B2	Spring Hill	B2
East Bight	C1	Steep Hill	C2
Eastgate	C1	Swan Street	C3
Free School Lane	C3	Tentercroft Street	B4
Friars Lane	C3	The Avenue	A2
Grantham Street	C2	The Sidings	A4
Greetwellgate	D1	Thorngate	C3
Gresham Street	A2	Triton Road	A4
Guildhall Street	B3	Union Road	B1
Hampton Street	A1	Unity Square	C3
High Street	B3	Victoria Street	B2
Hungate	B3	Victoria Terrace	A2
John Street	D3	Vine Street	D2
Langworthgate	D1	Waterside North	C3
Lindum Road	C2	Waterside South	C3
Lindum Terrace	D2	Westgate	B1
Lucy Tower Street	B3	West Parade	A2
May Crescent	A1	Whitehall Grove	A2
Melville Street	C4	Wigford Way	B3
Michaelgate	C2	Winnow Sty Lane	D1
Minster Yard	C2	Winn Street	D3
Mint Lane	B3	Wragby Road	D2
Mint Street	B3	Yarborough Terrace	A1
Monks Road	D3	York Avenue	A1

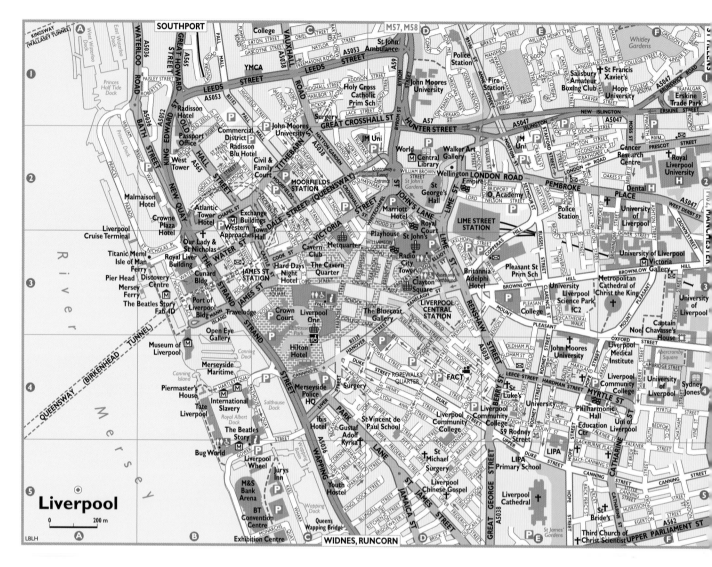

Liverpool

Liverpool is found on atlas page **81 L6**

Addison Street C1
Anson Street E2
Argyle Street C4
Arrad Street F4
Ashton Street F2
Audley Street E2
Back Canning Street E5
Baltimore Street E4
Bath Street B2
Beckwith Street C4
Bedford Street South F5
Benson Street E3
Berry Street E4
Bidder Street E1
Birkett Street D1
Bixteth Street B2
Blackburne Place E5
Blundell Street C5
Bold Street D3
Bosnett Street D3
Bridgewater Street D5
Bridport Street E2
Brook Street B2
Brownlow Hill E3
Brownlow Street F3
Brunswick Road F1
Brunswick Street B3
Byrom Street D1
Cambridge Street F4
Camden Street D2
Canning Place C4
Canning Street E5
Canterbury Street E1
Carver Street E1
Castle Street C3
Catharine Street F5

Cathedral Walk E3
Chapel Street B2
Chatham Street F4
Cheapside C2
Christian Street D1
Churchill Way D2
Church Street C3
Clarence Street E3
Cockspur Street C1
College Lane C3
College Street North F1
College Street South F1
Colquitt Street D4
Constance Street E2
Cook Street C3
Copperas Hill E3
Cornhill C5
Cornwallis Street D5
Craven Street E2
Cropper Street D3
Crosshall Street C2
Crown Street F2
Dale Street (Queensway) C2
Dansie Street E3
Daulby Street F2
Derby Square C3
Devon Street E2
Dover Street F3
Drury Lane B3
Duke Street D4
East Street B1
Eaton Street B1
Edmund Street B2
Egerton Street F5
Elliot Street D3
Epworth Street F1

Erskine Street F1
Falkner Street E4
Fazakerley Street B2
Fenwick Street B3
Fleet Street D3
Fontenoy Street D1
Fraser Street E2
Gascoyne Street B1
Gilbert Street D4
Gildart Street E2
Gill Street E2
Gower Street B5
Gradwell Street D4
Great Crosshall Street C1
Great George Street E5
Great Howard Street B1
Great Newton Street E2
Greek Street E2
Gregson Street F1
Grenville Street South D5
Hackins Hey C2
Hanover Street C4
Hardman Street E4
Harker Street E1
Hartley Quay B4
Hart Street E2
Hatton Garden C2
Hawke Street E3
Henry Street D4
Highfield Street B1
Hood Street D2
Hope Place E4
Hope Street E5
Hotham Street E2
Hunter Street D1
Huskisson Street F5
Islington E2
Jamaica Street D5
James Street B3
Johnson Street C2
Keel Wharf C5

Kempston Street E2
Kent Street D5
Kinder Street F1
King Edward Street B2
Kingsway (Wallasey Tunnel) ... A1
Kitchen Street D5
Knight Street E4
Lace Street C1
Langsdale Street E1
Leece Street E4
Leeds Street B1
Lime Street D2
Liver Street C4
London Road D2
London Road D2
Lord Nelson Street D2
Lord Street C3
Lydia Ann Street D4
Mann Island B3
Mansfield Street E1
Marybone C1
Maryland Street E4
Midghall Street B1
Moorfields B2
Moor Street B3
Moss Street F1
Mount Pleasant E3
Mount Street E4
Mulberry Street E4
Myrtle Street F4
Naylor Street C1
Nelson Street D5
Newington D4
New Islington E1
New Quay B2
North John Street C3
Norton Street E2
Old Hall Street B1
Oldham Street E4
Old Haymarket C2
Old Leeds Street B1

Ormond Street B2
Oxford Street F4
Paisley Street B1
Pall Mall B1
Paradise Street C3
Parker Street D3
Park Lane C4
Parr Street D4
Peech Street F3
Pembroke Place E2
Pembroke Street F2
Percey Street E5
Pilgrim Street E4
Pleasant Street E3
Pomona Street E3
Prescot Street F2
Princes Parade A2
Prospect Street F1
Queensway
   (Birkenhead Tunnel) A4
Ranelagh Street D3
Redcross Street C3
Renshaw Street D3
Richmond Lane C3
Rigby Street B2
Rodney Street E4
Roscoe Street E4
Rose Hill D1
Russell Street E3
St Anne Street D1
St James Street D5
St John's Lane D2
St Josephs Crescent D1
St Nicholas Place B3
St Paul's Street B2
Salisbury Street E1
Salthouse Quay C4
Sandon Street F5
School Lane C3
Seel Street D4
Seymour Street E2

Shaw Street .... F[?]
Sir Thomas Street .... C[?]
Skelhorne Street .... D[?]
Slater Street .... D[?]
Soho Street .... E[?]
Sparling Street .... C[?]
Springfield .... E[?]
Stafford Street .... E[?]
Stanley Street .... C[?]
Strand Street .... B[?]
Suffolk Street .... D[?]
Tabley Street .... C[?]
Tarleton Street .... D[?]
Temple Street .... C[?]
The Strand .... B[?]
Tithe Barn Street .... C[?]
Trafalgar Way .... B[?]
Trowbridge Street .... E[?]
Trueman Street .... C[?]
Upper Duke Street .... E[?]
Upper Frederick Street .... D[?]
Upper Parliament Street .... F[?]
Upper Pitt Street .... D[?]
Vauxhall Road .... C[?]
Vernon Street .... C[?]
Victoria Street .... C[?]
Wakefield Street .... E[?]
Wall Street .... B[?]
Wapping .... B[?]
Waterloo Road .... A[?]
Water Street .... B[?]
West Derby Street .... F[?]
Westmorland Drive .... C[?]
Whitechapel .... C[?]
William Brown Street .... C[?]
William Henry Street .... E[?]
William Jessop Way .... A[?]
Williamson Square .... C[?]
Williamson Street .... C[?]
Wood Street .... D[?]
York Street .... C[?]

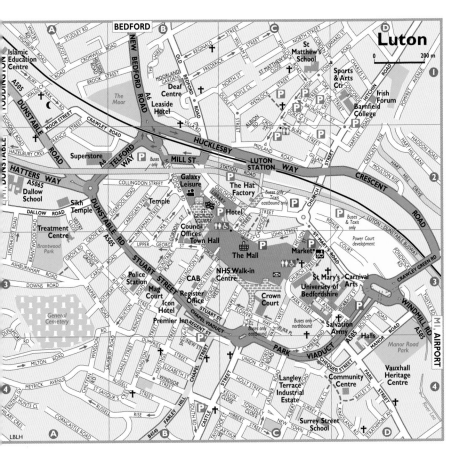

Luton

Luton is found on atlas page **50 C6**

Adelaide Street......................B3	Hibbert Street...........................C4
Albert Road...........................C4	Highbury Road..........................A1
Alma Street...........................B2	High Town Road.......................C1
Arthur Street.........................C4	Hitchin Road............................D1
Ashburnham Road.................A3	Holly Street.............................C4
Biscot Road...........................A1	Hucklesby Way........................B2
Brantwood Road....................A3	Inkerman Street.......................B3
Brunswick Street...................C1	John Street..............................C3
Burr Street............................C2	King Street..............................B3
Bury Park Road.....................A1	Latimer Road...........................C4
Bute Street............................C2	Liverpool Road.........................B2
Buxton Road..........................B3	Manor Road.............................D4
Cardiff Road..........................A3	Meyrick Avenue.......................A4
Cardigan Street......................B2	Midland Road...........................C2
Castle Street..........................B4	Mill Street...............................B2
Chapel Street.........................B4	Milton Road.............................A4
Chapel Viaduct......................B3	Moor Street.............................A1
Charles Street........................D1	Napier Road.............................A3
Chequer Street......................C4	New Bedford Road...................B1
Church Street.........................C2	New Town Street......................C4
Church Street.........................C3	Old Bedford Road.....................B1
Cobden Street........................C1	Park Street..............................C3
Collingdon Street...................B2	Park Street West......................C3
Concorde Street D1	Park Viaduct............................C4
Crawley Green Road..............D3	Princess Street........................B3
Crawley Road........................A1	Regent Street..........................B3
Crescent Road........................D2	Reginald Street.........................B1
Cromwell Road.......................A1	Rothesay Road.........................A3
Cumberland Street..................C4	Russell Rise.............................A4
Dallow Road...........................A2	Russell Street..........................B4
Dudley Street.........................C1	St Mary's Road.........................C3
Dumfries Street......................B4	St Saviour's Crescent..............A4
Dunstable Road......................A1	Salisbury Road.........................A4
Farley Hill.............................B4	Stanley Street..........................B4
Flowers Way..........................C3	Station Road............................C2
Frederick Street......................B1	Strathmore Avenue..................D4
George Street.........................B3	Stuart Street............................B3
George Street West................B3	Surrey Street...........................C4
Gordon Street........................B3	Tavistock Street.......................B4
Grove Road............................A3	Telford Way.............................B2
Guildford Street.....................B2	Upper George Street................B3
Hart Hill Drive.......................D2	Vicarage Street........................C1
Hart Hill Lane........................D2	Waldeck Road..........................A1
Hartley Road..........................D2	Wellington Street.....................B4
Hastings Street.......................B4	Wenlock Street........................C1
Hatters Way...........................A2	Windmill Road..........................D3
Havelock Road........................C1	Windsor Street..........................B4
Hazelbury Crescent...............A2	Winsdon Road..........................A4

Maidstone

Maidstone is found on atlas page **38 C10**

Albany Street......................... D1	Market Buildings.....................B2
Albion Place........................... D2	Marsham Street.......................C2
Allen Street........................... D1	Meadow Walk..........................D4
Ashford Road......................... D3	Medway Street.........................B3
Bank Street........................... B3	Melville Road...........................C4
Barker Road B4	Mill Street...............................B3
Bedford Place........................ A3	Mote Avenue...........................D3
Bishops Way.......................... B3	Mote Road...............................D3
Brewer Street......................... C2	Old School Place......................D2
Broadway A3	Orchard Street.........................C4
Broadway B3	Padsole Lane...........................C2
Brunswick Street.................... C4	Palace Avenue.........................B3
Buckland Hill......................... A2	Princes Street..........................D1
Buckland Road....................... A2	Priory Road.............................C4
Camden Street....................... C1	Pudding Lane...........................B2
Chancery Lane....................... D3	Queen Anne Road....................D2
Charles Street........................ A4	Reginald Road..........................A4
Church Street......................... C2	Rocky Hill...............................A3
College Avenue...................... B4	Romney Place..........................C3
College Road.......................... C4	Rose Yard...............................B2
County Road.......................... C1	Rowland Close.........................A4
Crompton Gardens................. D4	St Anne Court..........................A2
Cromwell Road....................... D2	St Faith's Street.......................B2
Douglas Road......................... A4	St Luke's Avenue.....................D1
Earl Street............................. B2	St Luke's Road........................D1
Elm Grove............................. D4	St Peters Street.......................A2
Fairmeadow........................... B1	Sandling Road..........................B1
Florence Road........................ A4	Sittingbourne Road..................D1
Foley Street........................... D1	Square Hill Road......................D3
Foster Street.......................... C4	Staceys Street..........................B1
Gabriel's Hill......................... C3	Station Approach......................A4
George Street......................... C4	Station Road............................B1
Greenside.............................. D4	Terrace Road...........................A3
Hart Street............................ A4	Tonbridge Road........................A4
Hastings Road........................ D4	Tufton Street...........................C2
Hayle Road............................ C4	Union Street............................C2
Heathorn Street..................... D1	Upper Stone Street...................C4
Hedley Street......................... C1	Victoria Street.........................A3
High Street............................ B3	Vinters Road............................D2
Holland Road......................... D1	Wat Tyler Way.........................C3
James Street.......................... C1	Week Street.............................B1
Jeffrey Street......................... C1	Well Road...............................C1
King Street............................ C2	Westree Road..........................A4
Kingsley Road........................ D4	Wheeler Street.........................C1
Knightrider Street.................. C4	Woollett Street.........................C1
Lesley Place.......................... A1	Wyatt Street...........................C2
London Road......................... A3	
Lower Stone Street................ C3	

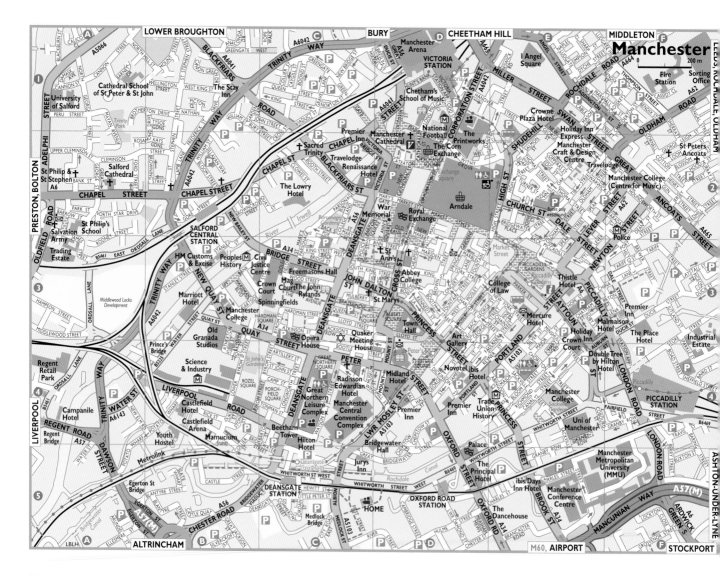

Manchester

Manchester is found on atlas page **82 H5**

Abingdon Street.....................E4
Addington Street.....................E1
Adelphi Street.......................A2
Albion Street..........................C5
Angel Street...........................E1
Ardwick Green South.............F5
Artillery Street.......................C4
Atherton Street......................B4
Atkinson Street......................C3
Auburn Street........................E4
Aytoun Street.........................E3
Back Piccadilly.......................E3
Bank Street.............................A2
Baring Street..........................F4
Barton Street..........................C4
Berry Street............................F4
Blackfriars Road.....................B1
Blackfriars Street....................C2
Blantyre Street.......................B5
Bloom Street..........................B2
Bloom Street..........................E2
Blossom Street.......................F2
Boad Street............................F4
Boond Street..........................C1
Booth Street...........................D3
Bootle Street..........................C4
Brancaster Road.....................E5
Brazennose Street..................C3
Brewer Street..........................F3
Bridge Street..........................C3
Bridgewater Place..................E2
Bridgewater Street.................B4
Bridgewater Viaduct..............B5
Brook Street...........................E5
Brotherton Drive....................A1
Browncross Street..................B2

Browning Street.....................B2
Brown Street..........................D3
Bury Street.............................B1
Byrom Street..........................B4
Cable Street...........................E1
Cambridge Street...................D5
Camp Street...........................C4
Canal Street...........................E4
Cannon Street........................A1
Canon Green Drive................B1
Castle Street..........................B5
Cathedral Street.....................D2
Chadderton Street.................F1
Chapel Street.........................A2
Charles Street.........................E5
Charlotte Street......................D3
Chatham Street......................E3
Cheapside..............................D3
Chester Road..........................B5
China Lane.............................E3
Chorlton Street......................E4
Church Street.........................E2
City Road East........................C5
Cleminson Street....................A2
College Land..........................C2
Collier Street..........................C1
Commercial Street..................C5
Copperas Street.....................E2
Cornell Street.........................F2
Corporation Street.................D2
Cotton Street.........................F2
Crosskeys Street.....................F1
Cross Street............................C2
Cross Street............................D3
Dale Street.............................E2
Dantzic Street........................D2

Dawson Street........................A5
Deansgate..............................C4
Dickinson Street.....................D4
Duke Street............................B4
Dulcie Street...........................F3
East Ordsall Lane...................A3
Egerton Street........................A5
Exchange Square....................D2
Fairfield Street........................F4
Faulkner Street.......................D4
Fennel Street..........................D1
Ford Street.............................A2
Fountain Street.......................D3
Frederick Street......................B2
Garden Lane...........................B1
Gartside Street.......................B3
George Leigh Street...............F2
George Street.........................D4
Gore Street.............................B2
Granby Row............................E5
Gravel Lane............................C1
Great Ancoats Street..............F2
Great Bridgewater Street.......C5
Great Ducie Street.................D1
Great George Street...............A2
Great Jackson Street..............B5
Great John Street...................B4
Greengate..............................C1
Greengate West......................B1
Gun Street..............................F2
Hanover Street.......................D1
Hardman Street......................C3
Hewitt Street..........................C5
High Street.............................E2
Hood Street...........................F2
Hope Street............................E3
Houndsworth Street...............F2
Hulme Street..........................D5
James Street...........................A3
Jersey Street...........................F2
John Dalton Street.................C3

John Street..............................D1
John Street..............................E2
Joiner Street...........................E2
Jutland Street.........................F3
Kennedy Street.......................D3
King Street..............................C1
King Street..............................C3
King Street West.....................C3
Lamb Lane..............................B2
Laystall Street.........................F3
Left Bank................................B3
Lena Street.............................F3
Lever Street............................E2
Little Lever Street...................E3
Little Peter Street...................C5
Liverpool Road.......................B4
Lloyd Street............................C3
London Road..........................F4
Long Millgate.........................D1
Longworth Street....................C4
Lower Byrom Street................B4
Lower Mosley Street...............C4
Lower Ormond Street.............D5
Ludgate Street........................E1
Major Street............................E4
Mancunian Way.....................E5
Marble Street..........................D3
Market Street..........................D2
Marsden Street.......................D3
Marshall Street.......................E1
Mason Street..........................E1
Mayan Avenue.......................A1
Medlock Street.......................C5
Middlewood Street.................A3
Miller Street...........................E1
Minshull Street.......................E3
Mirabel Street........................C1
Mosley Street.........................D3
Mount Street..........................B1
Mount Street..........................D4
Museum Street......................C4

Nathan Drive..........................B1
New Bailey Street....................B2
New Bridge Street...................C1
New Cathedral Street.............D2
New Elm Road........................A4
New George Street..................E2
New Quay Street.....................B3
Newton Street........................E3
New York Street.......................E3
Nicholas Street.......................D3
North George Street...............A1
North Hill Street......................A1
North Star Drive......................A2
Norton Street..........................C1
Oldfield Road..........................A3
Oldham Road..........................F1
Oldham Street........................E2
Ordsall Lane...........................A4
Oxford Road...........................D5
Oxford Street..........................D4
Pall Mall.................................D3
Parker Street..........................E3
Peru Street..............................A1
Peter Street............................C4
Piccadilly................................E3
Piccadilly Gardens..................E3
Portland Street.......................D4
Port Street..............................F3
Potato Wharf..........................A5
Princess Street........................D3
Quay Street.............................B3
Queen Street..........................C1
Queen Street..........................C3
Redhill Street.........................F2
Regent Road...........................A4
Reyner Street..........................D4
Rice Street..............................B4
Richmond Street.....................E4
Rochdale Road.......................E1
Rodney Street.........................A3
Rosamond Drive....................A2

Sackville Street.......................E4
St Anns Square.......................C2
St Ann Street...........................D2
St James Square.....................D4
St James Street.......................D4
St Mary's Parsonage...............C3
St Stephen Street....................B2
Store Street.............................F3
Sharp Street............................E1
Shudehill................................D2
Silk Street...............................F1
Simpson Street.......................E1
South King Street....................C3
Spear Street............................E2
Spring Gardens......................D3
Station Approach....................F3
Swan Street............................E1
Tariff Street.............................F2
Thomas Street........................E2
Thompson Street.....................F1
Tib Lane.................................D3
Tib Street...............................E2
Todd Street.............................D2
Tonman Street........................C4
Travis Street...........................F4
Trinity Way.............................A4
Turner Street..........................E2
Victoria Bridge Street.............C2
Victoria Station Approach......E1
Victoria Street........................C2
Warwick Street.......................E1
Watson Street.........................C4
Well Street..............................E1
West King Street.....................B2
West Mosley Street.................D3
Whitworth Street....................D5
Whitworth Street West............C5
Windmill Street......................C4
Withy Grove...........................D2
Wood Street...........................C3
York Street..............................E4

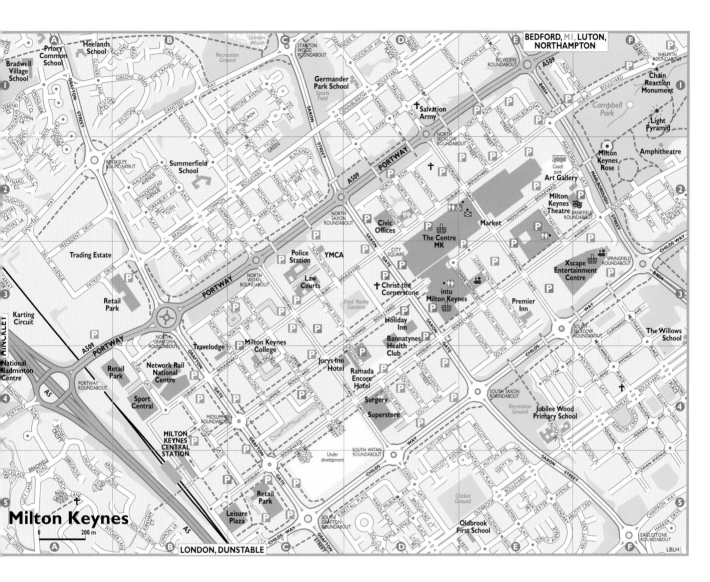

LONDON, DUNSTABLE

Milton Keynes

Milton Keynes is found on atlas page **49 N7**

Adelphi Street	E1	Cranesbill Place	D1
Albion Place	F2	Cresswell Lane	D3
All Saints View	A5	Dalgin Place	F2
Arbrook Avenue	C2	Dansteed Way	A2
Ardys Court	A5	Dansteed Way	B1
Arlott Crescent	F5	Deltic Avenue	A3
Atkins Close	A2	Dexter Avenue	E5
Audley Mews	A2	Douglas Place	D5
Avebury Boulevard	C5	Eaglestone Roundabout	F5
Bankfield Roundabout	E2	Ebbsgrove	A5
Belvedere Roundabout	E1	Edrich Avenue	E5
Bignell Croft	A4	Eelbrook Avenue	B3
Blackheath Crescent	C2	Elder Gate	B4
Booker Avenue	C1	Evans Gate	D5
Boycott Avenue	D5	Falmouth Place	E4
Boycott Avenue	E4	Fennel Drive	D1
Bradwell Common Boulevard	B2	Fishermead Boulevard	F4
Bradwell Road	A4	Forrabury Avenue	B2
Bradwell Road	A5	Fosters Lane	A2
Bridgeford Court	D5	Garrat Drive	A3
Brill Place	B2	Germander Place	C1
Burnham Drive	B1	Gibsons Green	B1
Chaffron Way	F5	Glovers Lane	A1
Childs Way	C5	Grace Avenue	D5
Childs Way	F3	Grafton Gate	B4
Church Lane	A5	Grafton Street	A1
City Square	D3	Grafton Street	C5
Cleavers Avenue	D1	Gurnards Avenue	F3
Coleshill Place	B1	Hadley Place	B2
Coltsfoot Place	C1	Hampstead Gate	B2
Columbia Place	F2	Harrier Drive	F5
Common Lane	B5	Helford Place	F4
Conniburrow Boulevard	C1	Helston Place	F4
Coppin Lane	A2	Holy Close	A1
Craddocks Close	A1	Hutton Avenue	E5
		Ibistone Avenue	C1

Kellan Drive	F4	North Secklow Roundabout	D1
Kernow Crescent	F4	North Second Street	B3
Kirkham Court	B5	North Sixth Street	C3
Kirkstall Place	C5	North Tenth Street	D2
Larwood Place	E5	North Third Street	C3
Leasowe Place	B2	North Thirteenth Street	E1
Linceslade Grove	A5	North Twelfth Street	E1
Loughton Road	A2	North Witan Roundabout	C3
Lower Fourth Street	C4	Oldbrook Boulevard	E5
Lower Ninth Street	E3	Overend Close	A1
Lower Tenth Street	E3	Padstow Avenue	E4
Lower Twelfth Street	E2	Patriot Drive	A3
Lucy Lane	A5	Pencarrow Place	F3
Maidenhead Avenue	B2	Pentewan Gate	F4
Mallow Gate	D1	Perran Avenue	F4
Marigold Place	D1	Pitcher Lane	A5
Marlborough Gate	E1	Plumstead Avenue	C2
Marlborough Gate	E2	Polruan Place	F4
Marlborough Street	F2	Porthleven Place	F3
Mayditch Place	B2	Portway	A4
Maynard Close	A2	Portway Roundabout	A4
Midsummer Boulevard	C4	Precedent Drive	A3
Midsummer Boulevard	E2	Quinton Drive	A2
Midsummer Roundabout	B4	Ramsay Close	A2
Milburn Avenue	D5	Ramsons Avenue	E1
Mitcham Place	C2	Redland Drive	B5
Mullion Place	F4	Rooksley Roundabout	A2
North Eighth Street	D2	Rylstone Close	B1
North Eleventh Street	E1	Saxon Gate	D2
North Fourth Street	C3	Saxon Street	C1
North Grafton Roundabout	B3	Secklow Gate	D2
North Ninth Street	D2	Shackleton Place	E5
North Row	B3	Sheldon Roundabout	F1
North Row	D2	Silbury Boulevard	B4
North Saxon Roundabout	C2	Silbury Roundabout	B4

North Secklow Roundabout	D1	Simons Lea	A1
		Skeldon Gate	F1
		South Eighth Street	E3
		South Fifth Street	D4
		South Fourth Street	C4
		South Grafton Roundabout	C5
		South Ninth Street	E3
		South Row	D4
		South Saxon Roundabout	E4
		South Secklow Roundabout	E3
		South Second Street	C5
		South Seventh Street	D4
		South Sixth Street	D4
		South Tenth Street	D4
		South Witan Roundabout	D5
		Speedwell Place	D1
		Springfield Roundabout	F3
		Stainton Drive	B1
		Stanton Wood Roundabout	C1
		Statham Place	E5
		Stokenchurch Place	C1
		Stonecrop Place	D1
		Streatham Place	B3
		Strudwick Drive	E5
		Sutcliffe Avenue	D4
		Talland Avenue	F4
		The Boundary	E5
		The Close	A1
		The Craven	B1
		The Green	A5
		Towan Avenue	F5
		Tranlands Brigg	B1
		Trueman Place	E5
		Turvil End	A5
		Tylers Green	C2

Tyson Place	D5
Ulyett Place	D5
Upper Fifth Street	C3
Upper Fourth Street	C4
Upper Second Street	C4
Upper Third Street	C4
Verity Place	E5
Walgrave Drive	A1
Walkhampton Avenue	B2
Wandsworth Place	F2
Wardle Place	D5
Whetstone Close	A1
Wimbledon Place	C2
Wisely Avenue	C2
Witan Gate	C3
Woodruff Avenue	D1
Yarrow Place	E1

Middlesbrough

Middlesbrough is found on atlas page **104 E7**

Acklam Road	A4	Heywood Street	
Acton Street	C3	Ironmasters Way	
Aire Street	B4	Kensington Road	
Albert Road	C2	Kildare Street	
Amber Street	C2	Laurel Street	
Athol Street	B3	Lees Road	
Aubrey Street	D3	Linthorpe Road	
Ayresome Park Road	B4	Longford Street	
Ayresome Street	A4	Lorne Street	
Borough Road	C2	Lothian Road	
Bretnall Street	B2	Marsh Street	
Bridge Street East	C1	Marton Road	
Bridge Street West	C1	Melrose Street	
Bush Street	B4	Metz Bridge Road	
Cadogen Street	B3	Myrtle Street	
Camden Street	D2	Newlands Road	
Cannon Park Road	A2	Newport Road	
Cannon Park Way	A2	Palm Street	
Cannon Street	A2	Park Lane	
Carlow Street	A3	Park Road North	
Centre Square	C2	Park Vale Road	
Clairville Road	D4	Parliament Road	
Clarendon Road	C3	Pearl Street	
Clifton Street	B3	Pelham Street	
Corporation Road	D1	Portman Street	
Costa Street	B4	Princes Road	
Craven Street	B3	Riverside Park Road	
Crescent Road	A3	Ruby Street	
Croydon Road	D3	Russell Street	
Derwent Street	A2	St Pauls Road	
Diamond Road	B3	Southfield Road	
Egmont Road	D4	Station Street	
Emily Street	C2	Stowe Street	
Errol Street	D3	Tavistock Street	
Essex Street	A4	Tennyson Street	
Fairbridge Street	C2	Union Street	
Falmouth Street	D3	Victoria Road	
Finsbury Street	B3	Victoria Street	
Fleetham Street	B2	Warren Street	
Garnet Street	B2	Waterloo Road	
Glebe Road	B3	Waverley Street	
Grange Road	B2	Wembley Street	
Grange Road	D2	Wilson Street	
Granville Road	C3	Wilton Street	
Gresham Road	B3	Windsor Street	
Harewood Street	B3	Woodlands Road	
Harford Street	B4	Worcester Street	
Hartington Road	B2	Zetland Road	

Newport

Newport is found on atlas page **31 K7**

Albert Terrace	B3	Jones Street	
Allt-Yr-Yn Avenue	A2	Keynsham Avenue	
Bailey Street	B3	King Street	
Bedford Road	D2	Kingsway	
Blewitt Street	B3	Kingsway	
Bond Street	C1	Llanthewy Road	
Bridge Street	B2	Locke Street	
Bryngwyn Road	A3	Lower Dock Street	
Brynhyfryd Avenue	A4	Lucas Street	
Brynhyfryd Road	A4	Market Street	
Caerau Crescent	A4	Mellon Street	
Caerau Road	A3	Mill Street	
Cambrian Road	B2	North Street	
Caroline Street	D3	Oakfield Road	
Cedar Road	D2	Park Square	
Charles Street	C3	Queen's Hill	
Chepstow Road	D1	Queen's Hill Crescent	
Clarence Place	C1	Queen Street	
Clifton Place	B4	Queensway	
Clifton Road	B4	Risca Road	
Clyffard Crescent	A3	Rodney Road	
Clytha Park Road	A2	Rudry Street	
Clytha Square	C4	Ruperra Lane	
Colts Foot Close	A1	Ruperra Street	
Commercial Street	C3	St Edward Street	
Corelli Street	D1	St Julian Street	
Corn Street	C2	St Mark's Crescent	
Corporation Road	D2	St Mary Street	
Devon Place	B2	St Vincent Road	
Dewsland Park Road	B4	St Woolos Road	
Dumfries Place	D4	School Lane	
East Street	B3	Serpentine Road	
East Usk Road	C1	Skinner Street	
Factory Road	B1	Sorrel Drive	
Fields Road	A2	Spencer Road	
Friars Field	B4	Stow Hill	
Friars Road	B4	Stow Hill	
Friar Street	C3	Stow Park Avenue	
George Street	D4	Talbot Lane	
Godfrey Road	A2	Tregare Street	
Gold Tops	A2	Tunnel Terrace	
Grafton Road	C2	Upper Dock Street	
Granville Lane	D4	Upper Dock Street	
Granville Street	D4	Usk Way	
High Street	B2	Victoria Crescent	
Hill Street	C3	West Street	
John Frost Square	C3	Wyndham Stret	
John Street	D4	York Place	

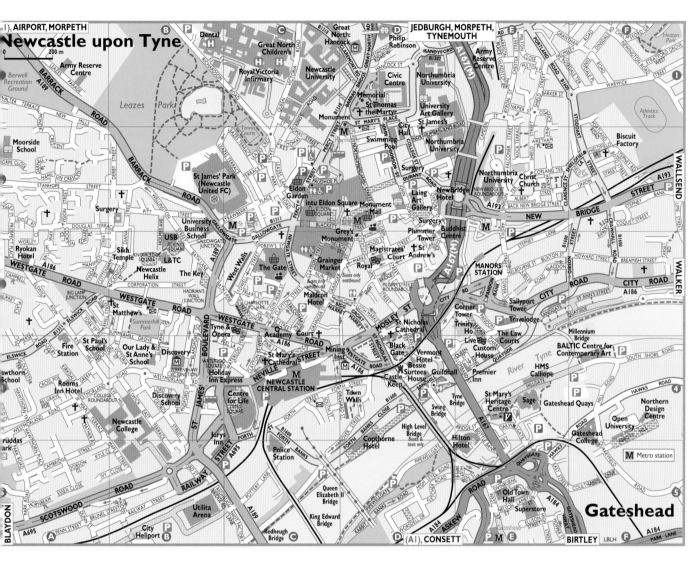

ewcastle upon Tyne

wcastle upon Tyne is found on atlas page **113 K8**

Abbots Hill F4
Albert Street E2
Argyle Street E2
Askew Road D5
Avision Street A2
Back New Bridge Street E2
Barker Street E1
Barrack Road A1
Barras Bridge D1
Bath Lane B3
Belgrave Parade A4
Big Lamp Junction A3
Blackett Street C2
Blagdon Street E3
Blandford Square B4
Blandford Street B4
Bottle Bank E4
Boyd Street F2
Breamish Street F3
Bridge Street E4
Broad Chare E3
Brunel Street A5
Buckingham Street B3
Buxton Street E3
Byron Street E1
Cambridge Street A5
Camden Street E2
Campbell Place A3
Carliol Square D3
Charlotte Square C3
Chelmsford Grove F1
Chester Street E1
City Road E3
Claremont Road D1
Clarence Street E2
Clayton Street C3

Clayton Street West C4
Cloth Market D3
Colby Court A4
College Roundabout A4
College Street D2
Cookson Close A3
Copland Terrace E2
Coppice Way E1
Coquet Street F2
Corporation Street B3
Cottenham Street A3
Coulthards Lane F5
Crawhall Road F2
Cross Parade A4
Cross Street C3
Darnell Place A2
Dean Street D3
Derby Street B2
Diana Street B3
Dinsdale Place F1
Dinsdale Road F1
Dobson Close A5
Douglas Terrace A2
Duke Street B4
Dunn Street A5
Durant Road D2
East Street E5
Edward Place A3
Eldon Square C2
Ellison Street E5
Elswick East Terrace B4
Elswick Road A3
Elswick Row A3
Essex Close A5
Falconar's Court C3
Falconer Street E2

Fenkle Street C3
Field Close F2
Fletcher Road D5
Forth Banks C4
Forth Banks Close D5
Forth Street C4
Friars Street C3
Gallowgate B2
Gallowgate Junction B3
Gateshead Highway E5
George Street B4
Gibson Street F3
Gladstone Terrace E1
Gloucester Terrace A4
Grainger Street C3
Grantham Road E1
Great North Road D1
Grey Street D3
Groat Market C3
Hamilton Crescent A2
Hanover Street C5
Harrison Place E1
Hawks Road E5
Hawthorn Place A4
Hawthorn Terrace A4
Helmsley Road E1
Henry Square E2
High Bridge D3
High Level Road D5
High Street E5
Hillgate E4
Hood Street D3
Hopper Street E5
Hornbeam Place A5
Houston Street A4
Howard Street F3
Hudson Street E5
Ivy Close A5
Jesmond Road West D1
John Dobson Street D2
Jubilee Road E3

King Edward Bridge C5
King Street E4
Kirkdale Green A4
Kyle Close A5
Lambton Street E5
Leazes Crescent C2
Leazes Lane C2
Leazes Park Road C2
Leazes Terrace C2
Liddle Road A2
Lime Street F2
Lombard Street E4
Longley Street A2
Lord Street B4
Low Friar Street C3
Maiden Street B5
Mansfield Street A3
Maple Street B5
Maple Terrace A4
Market Street D3
Mather Road A4
Melbourne Street E3
Mill Road F4
Milton Close E1
Milton Place E1
Monday Crescent A1
Mosley Street D3
Napier Street E1
Nelson Street C3
Nelson Street E5
Neville Street C4
New Bridge Street E2
Newgate Street C3
Newington Road F1
New Mills A1
Northumberland Road D2
Northumberland Street D2
Nun Street C3
Oakwellgate E4
Orchard Street C4
Ord Street B5

Oxford Street D2
Pandon E3
Pandon Bank E3
Park Lane F5
Park Road A5
Peel Lane B4
Penn Street A5
Percy Street C2
Pilgrim Street D2
Pink Lane C4
Pipewellgate D5
Pitt Street B2
Portland Road E1
Portland Road F1
Pottery Lane C5
Prospect Place A2
Prudhoe Place C2
Quarryfield Road F5
Quaysgate E5
Quayside F3
Quayside E4
Queen Street E4
Queen Victoria Road C1
Rabbit Banks Road D5
Railway Street B5
Red Barnes F2
Redheugh Bridge Road B5
Richardson Road B1
Rock Terrace E2
Rosedale Terrace E1
Rye Hill A4
St Andrew's Street C3
St Ann's Street F3
St James' Boulevard B4
St Mary's Place D1
St Nicholas Street D4
St Thomas' Crescent C2
St Thomas' Street C1
Sandgate E3
Sandhill D4
Sandyford Road D1

Scotswood Road A5
Shieldfield Lane F2
Shield Street E2
Shot Factory Lane C5
Simpson Terrace E2
Somerset Place A4
South Shore Road F4
South Street C4
Stanhope Street A2
Stepney Bank F2
Stepney Lane E3
Stepney Road F2
Stoddart Street F1
Stowell Street C3
Stratford Grove West F1
Strawberry Place C2
Summerhill Grove B3
Summerhill Street A3
Summerhill Terrace B4
Swinburne Street E5
Tarset Road F3
Terrace Place C2
Tindal Street A3
Tower Street E3
Tyne Bridge E4
Union Street F2
Vallum Way A3
Victoria Street B4
Walter Street A1
Warwick Street F1
Waterloo Square B4
Waterloo Street C4
Wellington Street B2
Westgate Road A3
Westmorland Road A4
West Street E5
West Walls C3
Worley Close A3
Worsdell Drive D5
Wretham Place E2
York Street A3

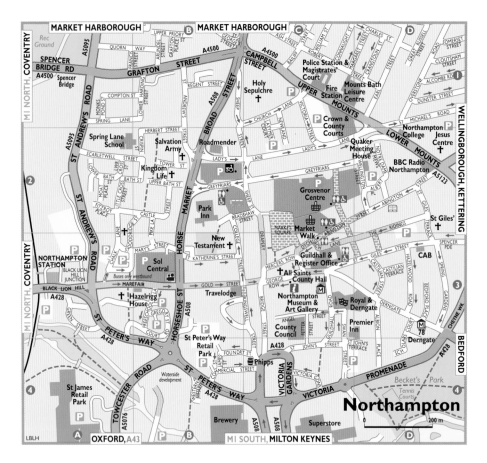

Northampton

Northampton is found on atlas page **60 G8**

Abington Street	C2
Albert Place	D2
Albion Place	D3
Angel Street	C3
Arundel Street	B1
Ash Street	C1
Bailiff Street	C1
Black Lion Hill	A3
Bradshaw Street	B2
Bridge Street	C3
Broad Street	B1
Campbell Street	C1
Castilian Street	D3
Castle Street	B2
Chalk Lane	A3
Cheyne Walk	D3
Church Lane	C1
College Street	B2
Commercial Street	B4
Connaught Street	C1
Court Road	B3
Cranstoun Street	D1
Crispin Street	B2
Derngate	D3
Doddridge Street	A3
Drapery	C3
Dunster Street	D1
Dychurch Lane	C3
Earl Street	D1
Fetter Street	C3
Fitzroy Place	A2
Foundry Street	B4
Francis Street	A1
Freeschool Lane	B2
George Row	C3
Gold Street	B3
Grafton Street	A1
Great Russell Street	D1
Green Street	A3
Gregory Street	B3
Greyfriars	B2
Guildhall Road	C3
Hazelwood Road	D3
Herbert Street	B2
Horse Market	B3
Horseshoe Street	B3
Kingswell Street	C3
Lady's Lane	B2

Little Cross Street	
Lower Bath Street	
Lower Cross Street	
Lower Harding Street	
Lower Mounts	
Marefair	
Margaret Street	
Market Square	
Mercers Row	
Moat Place	
Monkspond Street	
Newland	
Notredame Mews	
Overstone Road	
Pike Lane	
Quorn Way	
Regent Street	
Robert Street	
St Andrew's Road	
St Andrew's Street	
St Giles' Street	
St Giles' Terrace	
St John's Street	
St Katherine's Street	
St Mary's Street	
St Michael's Road	
St Peter's Way	
Scarletwell Street	
Scholars Court	
Sheep Street	
Sheep Street	
Spencer Bridge Road	
Spencer Parade	
Spring Gardens	
Spring Lane	
Swan Street	
Tanner Street	
The Ridings	
Towcester Road	
Tower Street	
Upper Bath Street	
Upper Mounts	
Upper Priory Street	
Victoria Gardens	
Victoria Promenade	
Victoria Street	
Wellington Street	
Western Wharf	

Norwich

Norwich is found on atlas page **77 J10**

All Saints Green	B4
Bank Plain	C2
Barn Road	A1
Bedding Lane	C1
Bedford Street	B2
Ber Street	C4
Bethel Street	A3
Bishopgate	D1
Brigg Street	B3
Calvert Street	B1
Castle Meadow	C3
Cathedral Street	D2
Cattle Market Street	C3
Chantry Road	B3
Chapelfield East	A3
Chapelfield North	A3
Chapelfield Road	A3
Cleveland Road	A3
Colegate	B1
Convent Road	A3
Coslany Street	B2
Cow Hill	A2
Davey Place	B3
Dove Street	B2
Duke Street	B1
Elm Hill	C2
Exchange Street	B2
Farmers Avenue	C3
Ferry Lane	D2
Fishergate	C1
Friars Quay	B1
Gaol Hill	B3
Gentlemans Walk	B3
Goldenball Street	C3
Grapes Hill	A2
Haymarket	B3
Heigham Street	A1
King Street	C2
London Street	B2
Lower Goat Lane	B2
Magdalen Street	C1
Market Avenue	C3
Mountergate	D3
Music House Lane	D4
Muspole Street	B1
New Mills Yard	A1
Oak Street	A1
Palace Street	C1

Pottergate	
Prince of Wales Road	
Princes Street	
Quay Side	
Queens Road	
Queen Street	
Rampant Horse Street	
Recorder Road	
Red Lion Street	
Riverside Road	
Riverside Walk	
Rose Lane	
Rouen Road	
Rupert Street	
St Andrews Street	
St Benedicts Street	
St Faiths Lane	
St Georges Street	
St Giles Street	
St Julians Alley	
St Marys Plain	
St Peters Street	
St Stephens Road	
St Stephens Square	
St Stephens Street	
St Swithins Road	
St Verdast Street	
Surrey Street	
Ten Bell Lane	
Theatre Street	
Thorn Lane	
Tombland	
Unicorn Yard	
Union Street	
Unthank Road	
Upper Goat Lane	
Upper King Street	
Upper St Giles Street	
Vauxhall Street	
Walpole Street	
Wensum Street	
Wessex Street	
Westlegate	
Westwick Street	
Wherry Road	
Whitefriars	
White Lion Street	
Willow Lane	

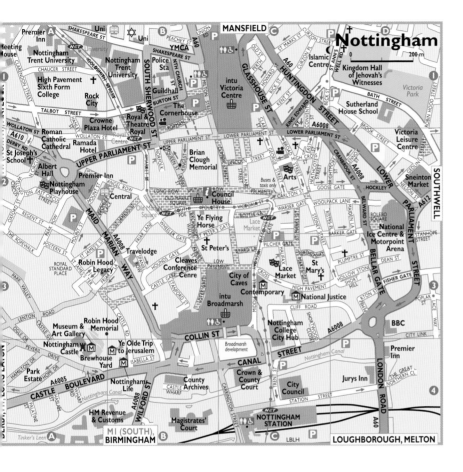

Nottingham

Nottingham is found on atlas page **72 F3**

Albert Street	B3	King Street	B2
Angel Row	B2	Lenton Road	A3
Barker Gate	D2	Lincoln Street	C2
Bath Street	D1	Lister Gate	B3
Bellar Gate	D3	London Road	D4
Belward Street	D2	Long Row	B2
Broad Street	C2	Lower Parliament Street	C2
Broadway	C3	Low Pavement	B3
Bromley Place	A2	Maid Marian Way	A2
Brook Street	D1	Market Street	B2
Burton Street	B1	Middle Hill	C3
Canal Street	C4	Milton Street	B1
Carlton Street	C2	Mount Street	A3
Carrington Street	C4	Norfolk Place	B2
Castle Boulevard	A4	North Circus Street	A2
Castle Gate	B3	Park Row	A3
Castle Road	B3	Pelham Street	C2
Chaucer Street	A1	Peveril Drive	A4
City Link	D3	Pilcher Gate	C3
Clarendon Street	A1	Popham Street	C3
Cliff Road	C3	Poultry	B2
Collin Street	B4	Queen Street	B2
Cranbrook Street	D2	Regent Street	A2
Cumber Street	C2	St Ann's Well Road	D1
Curzon Place	C1	St James's Street	A3
Derby Road	A2	St Marks Gate	C3
Exchange Walk	B2	St Marks Street	C1
Fisher Gate	D3	St Mary's Gate	C3
Fletcher Gate	C3	St Peter's Gate	B3
Forman Street	B1	Shakespeare Street	A1
Friar Lane	A3	Smithy Row	B2
Gedling Street	D2	South Parade	B2
George Street	C2	South Sherwood Street	B1
Glasshouse Street	C1	Spaniel Row	B3
Goldsmith Street	A1	Station Street	C4
Goose Gate	C2	Stoney Street	C2
Halifax Place	C3	Talbot Street	A1
Heathcote Street	C2	Thurland Street	C2
High Cross Street	C2	Trent Street	C4
High Pavement	C3	Upper Parliament Street	A2
Hockley	D2	Victoria Street	C2
Hollow Stone	D3	Warser Gate	C2
Hope Drive	A4	Weekday Cross	C3
Hounds Gate	B3	Wellington Circus	A2
Howard Street	C1	Wheeler Gate	B2
Huntingdon Street	C1	Wilford Street	B4
Kent Street	C1	Wollaton Street	A1
King Edward Street	C1	Woolpack Lane	C2

Oldham

Oldham is found on atlas page **83 K4**

Ascroft Street	B3	Napier Street East	A4
Bar Gap Road	B1	New Radcliffe Street	A2
Barlow Street	D4	Oldham Way	A3
Barn Street	B3	Park Road	B4
Beever Street	D2	Park Street	A4
Bell Street	D2	Peter Street	B3
Belmont Street	B1	Prince Street	D3
Booth Street	A3	Queen Street	C3
Bow Street	C3	Radcliffe Street	B1
Brook Street	D2	Ramsden Street	A1
Brunswick Street	B3	Regent Street	D2
Cardinal Street	C2	Rhodes Bank	C3
Chadderton Way	A1	Rhodes Street	C2
Chaucer Street	B3	Rifle Street	B1
Clegg Street	C3	Rochdale Road	A1
Coldhurst Road	B1	Rock Street	B2
Crossbank Street	B4	Roscoe Street	C3
Curzon Street	B2	Ruskin Street	A1
Dunbar Street	B2	St Hilda's Drive	A1
Eden Street	B2	St Marys Street	B1
Egerton Street	C2	St Mary's Way	B2
Emmott Way	C4	Shaw Road	D1
Firth Street	C3	Shaw Street	C1
Fountain Street	B2	Shore Street	D1
Franklin Street	B1	Siddall Street	C1
Gower Street	D2	Silver Street	B3
Grange Street	A2	Southgate Street	C3
Greaves Street	C3	South Hill Street	D4
Greengate Street	D4	Spencer Street	B3
Hardy Street	D4	Sunfield Road	B1
Harmony Street	C4	Thames Street	D1
Henshaw Street	B2	Trafalgar Street	A1
Higginshaw Road	C1	Trinity Street	B1
Highfield Street	A2	Tulbury Street	A1
High Street	B3	Union Street	B3
Hobson Street	B3	Union Street West	A4
Norsedge Street	C1	Union Street West	B3
John Street	A3	University Way	B4
King Street	B3	Wallshaw Street	D2
Lemnos Street	D2	Wall Street	B4
Malby Street	C1	Ward Street	A1
Malton Street	A4	Waterloo Street	C3
Manchester Street	A3	Wellington Street	B4
Market Place	B3	West End Street	A2
Marlborough Street	C4	West Street	B3
Middleton Road	A3	Willow Street	D2
Mortimer Street	D1	Woodstock Street	C4
Mumps	D2	Yorkshire Street	C3

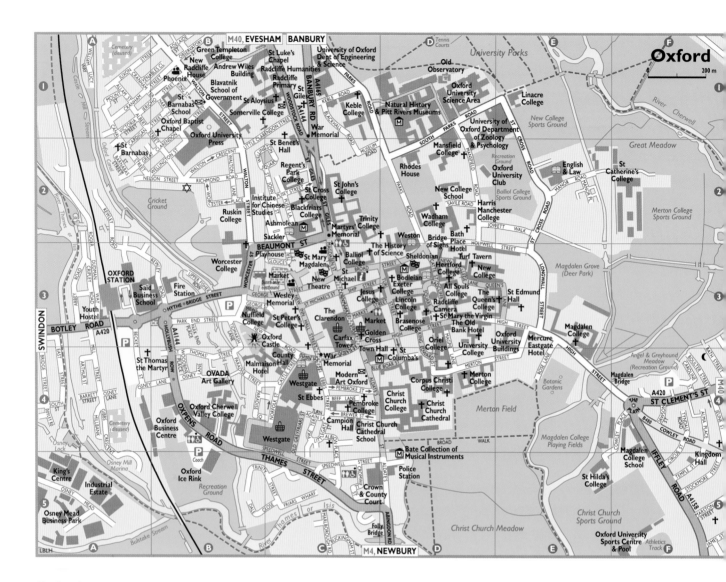

Oxford

Oxford is found on atlas page **34 F3**

Abbey Road	A3	Cromwell Street	C5
Abingdon Road	D5	Dale Close	B5
Adelaide Street	B1	Dawson Street	F4
Albert Street	A1	East Street	A4
Albion Place	C4	Folly Bridge	C5
Allam Street	A1	Friars Wharf	C5
Alma Place	F4	George Street	B3
Arthur Street	A4	George Street Mews	B3
Banbury Road	C1	Gibbs Crescent	A4
Barrett Street	A4	Gloucester Street	C3
Bath Street	F4	Great Clarendon Street	A2
Beaumont Street	C3	Hart Street	B1
Becket Street	A3	High Street	D3
Beef Lane	C4	High Street	E4
Blackhall Road	C1	Hollybush Row	B3
Blue Boar Street	C4	Holywell Street	D2
Bonn Square	C4	Hythe Bridge Street	B3
Botley Road	A3	Iffley Road	F4
Boulter Street	F4	James Street	F5
Brewer Street	C4	Jericho Street	A1
Bridge Street	A4	Jowett Walk	D2
Broad Street	C3	Juxon Street	A1
Broad Walk	D4	Keble Road	C1
Buckingham Street	C5	King Edward Street	D3
Canal Street	A1	King Street	B1
Cardigan Street	A2	Little Clarendon Street	B2
Caroline Street	F4	Littlegate Street	C4
Castle Street	C4	Longwall Street	E3
Catte Street	D3	Magdalen Bridge	E4
Circus Street	F5	Magdalen Street	C3
Cornmarket Street	C3	Magpie Lane	D3
Cowley Place	F4	Manor Place	E2
Cowley Road	F4	Manor Road	E2
Cranham Street	A1	Mansfield Road	D2
Cranham Terrace	A1	Market Street	C3
Cripley Road	A3	Marlborough Road	C5

Marston Street	F5	St Barnabas Street	A2
Merton Street	D4	St Clement's Street	F4
Millbank	A4	St Cross Road	E1
Mill Street	A4	St Cross Road	E2
Mount Street	A1	St Ebbes Street	C4
Museum Road	C2	St Giles	C2
Nelson Street	A2	St John Street	C2
New College Lane	D3	St Michael's Street	C3
New Road	B3	St Thomas' Street	B4
Norfolk Street	C4	Savile Road	D2
Observatory Street	B1	Ship Street	C3
Old Greyfriars Street	C4	South Parks Road	D2
Osney Lane	A4	South Street	A4
Osney Lane	B4	Speedwell Street	C5
Osney Mead	A5	Stockmore Street	F5
Oxpens Road	B4	Temple Street	F5
Paradise Square	B4	Thames Street	C5
Paradise Street	B4	The Plain	F4
Park End Street	B3	Tidmarsh Lane	B3
Parks Road	C1	Trinity Street	B5
Parks Road	D2	Turl Street	D3
Pembroke Street	C4	Turn Again Lane	C4
Pike Terrace	C4	Tyndale Road	F4
Pusey Lane	C2	Upper Fisher Row	B3
Pusey Street	C2	Venables Close	A1
Queen's Lane	D3	Victoria Street	A1
Queen Street	C4	Walton Crescent	B2
Radcliffe Square	D3	Walton Lane	B2
Rewley Road	A2	Walton Street	B1
Rewley Road	B3	Wellington Square	B2
Richmond Road	B2	Wellington Street	B2
Roger Dudman Way	A3	William Lucy Way	A1
Rose Lane	E4	Woodbine Place	B4
St Aldate's	C4	Woodstock Road	C1
St Aldate's	D5	Worcester Place	B2
		Worcester Street	B3

University Colleges

All Souls College	D3
Balliol College	C3
Brasenose College	D3
Christ Church College	D4
Corpus Christi College	D4
Exeter College	D3
Harris Manchester College	D2
Hertford College	D3
Jesus College	C3
Keble College	C1
Linacre College	E1
Lincoln College	D3
Magdalen College	E3
Mansfield College	D2
Merton College	D4
New College	D3
Nuffield College	B3
Oriel College	D3
Pembroke College	C4
Ruskin College	B2
St Catherine's College	F2
St Cross College	C2
St Hilda's College	E5
St John's College	C2
St Peter's College	C3
Somerville College	B1
The Queen's College	D3
Trinity College	C2
University College	D3
Wadham College	D2
Worcester College	B3

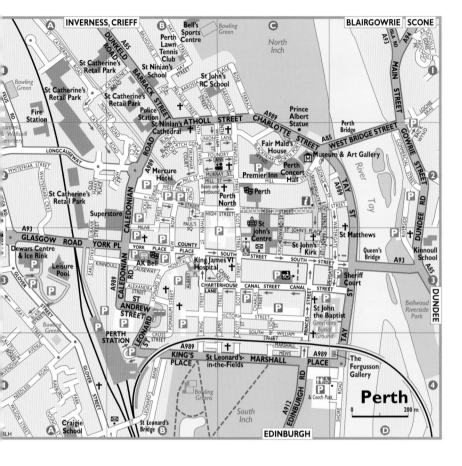

Perth

Perth is found on atlas page **134 E3**

Albert Place	B3	Melville Street	B1
Alexandra Street	B3	Mill Street	B2
Atholl Street	B1	Mill Street	C2
Back Wynd	D2	Milne Street	B2
Balhousie Street	B1	Monart Road	A1
Barossa Place	B1	Murray Street	B2
Barrack Street	B1	Needless Road	A4
Blackfriars Wynd	C2	New Row	B3
Black Watch Garden	B2	North Methven Street	B2
Caledonian Road	B2	North Port	C2
Caledonian Road	B3	North William Street	B2
Canal Street	C3	Old Market Place	A2
Cavendish Avenue	A4	Paul Street	B2
Charles Street	C3	Perth Bridge	D2
Charlotte Street	C2	Pickletullum Road	A4
Charterhouse Lane	B3	Pomarium Street	B3
Commercial Street	D2	Princes Street	C3
County Place	B3	Queen's Bridge	D3
Cross Street	B4	Raeburn Park	A4
Dundee Road	D3	Riggs Road	A2
Dunkeld Road	B1	Riverside	D3
Earls Dykes	A3	Rose Terrace	C1
Edinburgh Road	C4	St Andrew Street	B3
Elibank Street	A3	St Catherine's Road	A1
Feus Road	A1	St John's Place	C3
Foundry Lane	B2	St John Street	C3
George Street	C2	St Leonard's Bank	B4
Glasgow Road	A3	St Paul's Square	B2
Glover Street	A3	Scott Street	C3
Glover Street	A4	Shore Road	D4
Gowrie Street	D2	Skinnergate	C2
Gray Street	A3	South Methven Street	B2
Hay Street	B1	South Street	C3
High Street	B2	South William Street	C4
High Street	C2	Speygate	D3
Hospital Street	B3	Stormont Street	B1
Isla Road	D1	Tay Street	D2
James Street	C3	Tay Street	D4
King Edward Street	C3	Union Lane	B2
King's Place	B4	Victoria Street	C3
King Street	B3	Watergate	D2
Kinnoull Causeway	A3	West Bridge Street	D2
Kinnoull Street	C2	West Mill Wynd	B2
Leonard Street	B3	Whitefriars Crescent	A2
Lochie Brae	D1	Whitefriar Street	A2
Longcauseway	A2	Wilson Street	A4
Main Street	D1	York Place	A3
Marshall Place	C4	York Place	B3

Peterborough

Peterborough is found on atlas page **74 C11**

Albert Place	B3	New Road	C1
Bishop's Road	C3	Northminster	C1
Boongate	D1	North Street	B1
Bourges Boulevard	A1	Oundle Road	B4
Bridge Street	B3	Park Road	B1
Bright Street	A1	Pipe Lane	D2
Broadway	B2	Priestgate	A2
Brook Street	C1	Rivergate	B3
Cathedral Square	B2	River Lane	A2
Cattle Market Street	B1	Russell Street	A1
Chapel Street	C1	St John's Street	C2
Church Street	B2	St Peters Road	B3
Church Walk	C1	South Street	D2
City Road	C2	Star Road	D2
Cowgate	B2	Station Road	A2
Craig Street	B1	Thorpe Lea Road	A3
Crawthorne Road	C1	Thorpe Road	A2
Cromwell Road	A1	Trinity Street	B3
Cross Street	B2	Viersen Platz	B3
Cubitt Way	B4	Vineyard Road	C3
Deacon Street	A1	Wake Road	D2
Dickens Street	D1	Wareley Road	D1
Eastfield Road	D1	Wellington Street	D1
Eastgate	D2	Wentworth Street	B3
East Station Road	C4	Westgate	A1
Embankment Road	C3		
Exchange Street	B2		
Fengate Close	D2		
Field Walk	D1		
Fitzwilliam Street	B1		
Frank Perkins Parkway	D4		
Geneva Street	B1		
Gladstone Street	A1		
Granby Street	C2		
Hawksbill Way	B4		
Hereward Close	D2		
Hereward Road	D2		
King Street	B2		
Laxton Square	C2		
Lea Gardens	A3		
Lincoln Road	B1		
London Road	B4		
Long Causeway	B2		
Manor House Street	B1		
Mayor's Walk	A1		
Midgate	B2		
Morris Street	D1		
Nene Street	D2		

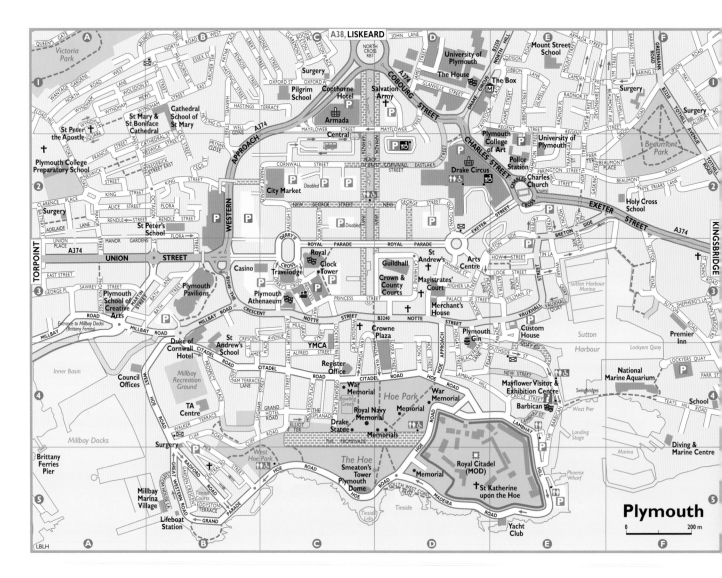

Plymouth

Plymouth is found on atlas page **6 D8**

Addison Road.....E1	Clarence Place.....A2	Great Western Road.....B5	Mayflower Street.....D1	Radnor Place.....E1	Western Approach.....B
Adelaide Lane.....A2	Cliff Road.....B4	Greenbank Road.....F1	May Terrace.....F1	Radnor Street.....E1	West Hoe Road.....A
Alfred Street.....C4	Cobourg Street.....D1	Hampton Street.....E2	Melbourne Street.....B1	Raleigh Street.....C2	Wharf Quay.....E
Alice Street.....A2	Cornwall Street.....C2	Harwell Street.....B1	Millbay Road.....A3	Regent Street.....E1	Whimple Street.....D
Anstis Street.....A2	Courtenay Street.....C3	Hastings Street.....B1	Moon Street.....E2	Rendle Street.....A2	White Friars Lane.....F
Archer Terrace.....B1	Crescent Avenue.....B3	Hastings Terrace.....B1	Mount Street.....E1	Royal Parade.....C3	Windsor Place.....C
Armada Street.....E1	Custom House Lane.....B5	Hawkers Avenue.....E2	Mulgrave Street.....C3	St James Place.....B4	Wolsdon Street.....A
Armada Way.....C2	Derry's Cross.....C3	Hetling Close.....B1	Neswick Street.....A2	St John's Bridge Road.....F3	Wyndham Lane.....A
Armada Way.....C4	Devonshire Street.....E1	Hicks Lane.....E3	New George Street.....C2	St John's Road.....F3	Wyndham Mews.....A
Arundel Crescent.....A1	Drake Circus.....D1	Higher Lane.....D3	New Street.....E4	Salisbury Road.....F1	Wyndham Square.....A
Athenaeum Street.....C3	Eastlake Street.....D2	Hill Street.....E2	North Cross Roundabout.....C1	Sawrey Street.....A3	Wyndham Street East.....A
Baring Street.....F1	East Street.....A3	Hoe Approach.....D4	North Hill.....E1	Shepherd's Lane.....F3	Zion Street.....D
Bath Lane.....B3	Ebrington Street.....E2	Hoegate Street.....D3	North Road West.....A1	Southside Street.....D4	
Bath Street.....B3	Eldad Hill.....A1	Hoe Road.....C5	North Street.....E2	South West Coast Path.....D5	
Batter Street.....E3	Elliot Street.....C4	Hoe Street.....D3	Notte Street.....C3	Stillman Street.....E3	
Battery Street.....A2	Elliot Terrace.....C4	Holyrood Place.....C4	Octagon Street.....B2	Stoke Road.....A2	
Beaumont Avenue.....F1	Essex Street.....B1	How Street.....E3	Old Town Street.....D2	Sussex Street.....D3	
Beaumont Place.....E2	Eton Avenue.....C1	Ilbert Street.....B1	Osborne Place.....C4	Sutton Road.....F3	
Beaumont Road.....F2	Eton Place.....C1	James Street.....D1	Oxford Street.....C1	Sydney Street.....B1	
Bilbury Street.....E2	Exeter Street.....D2	John Lane.....D1	Palace Street.....D3	Tavistock Place.....D1	
Blackfriars Lane.....D4	Exeter Street.....E2	King Street.....A2	Park Terrace.....E2	Teats Hill Road.....F4	
Boon's Place.....C1	Flora Court.....B2	Ladywell Place.....F1	Parr Street.....F4	The Barbican.....E4	
Breton Side.....D3	Flora Street.....B2	Lambhay Hill.....D4	Patna Place.....B1	The Crescent.....B3	
Buckwell Street.....D3	Francis Street.....A2	Lambhay Street.....E4	Peacock Lane.....D3	The Esplanade.....C4	
Camden Street.....E1	Frederick Street East.....B2	Leigham Street.....B4	Penrose Street.....B1	The Promenade.....C4	
Castle Street.....E4	Friar's Parade.....D4	Leigham Terrace Lane.....B4	Phoenix Street.....A3	Tin Lane.....E3	
Cathedral Street.....A2	Garden Crescent.....B5	Lipson Road.....F1	Pier Street.....B5	Tothill Avenue.....F1	
Catherine Street.....D3	Gasking Street.....E2	Lockyers Quay.....F4	Place de Brest.....C2	Tothill Road.....F2	
Cecil Street.....B1	George Place.....A3	Lockyer Street.....C3	Plym Street.....F1	Trafalgar Street.....E2	
Central Road.....B5	Gibbon Lane.....E1	Looe Street.....E3	Princess Street.....C3	Union Place.....A3	
Chapel Street.....E1	Gibbons Street.....E1	Madeira Road.....D5	Princess Way.....C3	Union Street.....A3	
Charles Cross.....E2	Gilwell Street.....E1	Manor Gardens.....A3	Prospect Place.....B4	Vauxhall Quay.....E3	
Charles Street.....D2	Glanville Street.....D1	Manor Street.....A2	Prynne Close.....B2	Vauxhall Street.....E3	
Citadel Road.....B4	Grand Hotel Road.....C4	Market Avenue.....C2	Quay Road.....E4	Walker Terrace.....B4	
Citadel Road.....C4	Grand Parade.....B5	Martin Street.....A3	Queen's Gate.....A1	Wantage Gardens.....A1	
Claremont Street.....C1		Mayflower Street.....C1	Radford Road.....B5	Well Gardens.....B1	

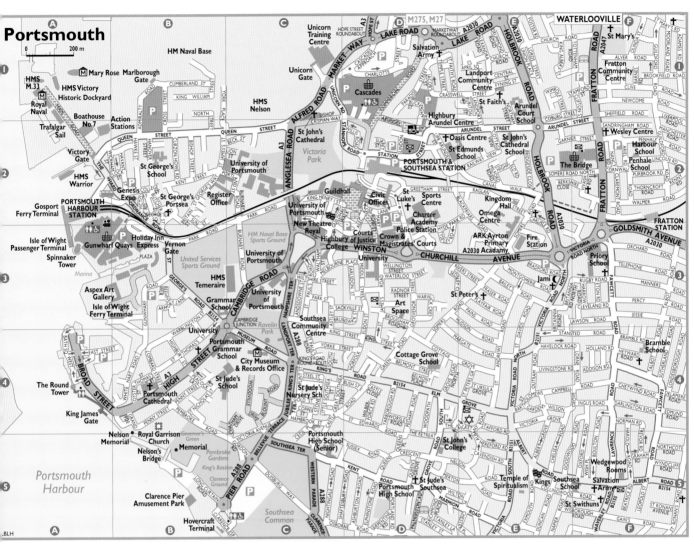

Portsmouth

Portsmouth is found on atlas page **14 H7**

Admiralty Road	B2	Cavendish Road	E5	Foster Road	E1	Lake Road	D1	Palmerston Road	D5	Stamford Street	E1
Albany Road	E5	Central Street	E1	Fratton Road	F2	Landport Street	E1	Paradise Street	D1	Stanhope Road	D2
Albert Grove	E5	Charlotte Street	D1	Gain's Road	F5	Landport Terrace	C3	Park Road	B3	Stansted Road	E4
Albert Road	E5	Chelsea Road	E5	Garnier Street	E2	Landsdowne Street	C3	Pelham Road	D4	Station Street	D2
Alec Rose Lane	D3	Chester Place	E5	Goldsmith Avenue	F3	Lawrence Road	F5	Pembroke Road	B4	Steel Street	C4
Alexandra Road	E1	Chetwynd Road	F4	Gold Street	C4	Lawson Road	F3	Penhale Road	F2	Stone Street	C4
Alfred Road	C1	Churchill Avenue	D3	Goodwood Road	E5	Leopold Street	F5	Penny Street	B4	Sussex Road	D5
Alver Road	F1	Church Road	E1	Gordon Road	C5	Lincoln Road	F2	Percy Road	F3	Sutherland Road	F4
Anglesea Road	C2	Claremont Road	F2	Great Southsea Street	C4	Little Southsea Street	C4	Pier Road	C5	Talbot Road	F4
Ariel Road	F2	Clarence Parade	C5	Green Road	D4	Livingstone Road	E4	Playfair Road	E3	Telephone Road	F3
Armory Lane	B3	Cleveland Road	F3	Greetham Street	D2	Lombard Street	B4	Portland Road	D5	Temple Street	D1
Arundel Street	D2	Clive Road	F1	Grosvenor Street	D3	Londesborough Road	F4	Purbrook Road	F2	The Hard	A2
Arundel Street	E2	Clock Street	B2	Grove Road North	D4	Lords Street	E1	Queens Crescent	D5	The Retreat	D5
Ashburton Road	D5	College Street	B2	Grove Road South	D5	Lorne Road	F4	Queen Street	B2	The Thicket	F2
Bailey's Road	E3	Collingwood Road	E5	Guildford Road	F1	Main Road	A1	Raglan Street	E2	Thorncroft Road	F2
Bath Square	A4	Commercial Road	D1	Guildhall Walk	C2	Manners Road	F3	Railway View	E2	Tottenham Road	F1
Bellevue Terrace	C5	Cornwall Road	F2	Gunwharf Road	B3	Margate Road	D4	Richmond Place	D5	Trevor Road	F3
Belmont Place	D4	Cottage Grove	D4	Hambrook Street	C4	Market Way	C1	Rivers Street	D3	Unicorn Road	C1
Bishop Crispian Way	C2	Cottage View	E2	Hampshire Terrace	C3	Marmion Road	D5	Rugby Road	F3	Upper Arundel Street	D2
Bishop Street	B2	Crasswell Street	D1	Harold Road	F5	Mary Rose Street	D2	Sackville Street	C3	Victoria Avenue	C5
Blackfriars Road	E2	Cross Street	B2	Havant Street	B2	Melbourne Place	C3	St Andrews Road	E4	Victoria Grove	E4
Blount Road	C4	Cumberland Street	B1	Havelock Road	E4	Merton Road	D5	St Bartholomews Gardens	E4	Victoria Road North	E4
Boulton Road	F5	Curzon Howe Road	B2	Hawke Street	B2	Middle Street	D3	St Davids Road	E4	Victoria Road North	F3
Bramble Road	F4	Darlington Road	F4	Hereford Road	E5	Milford Road	E2	St Edwards Road	D4	Victoria Road South	F4
Bridgeside Close	E2	Drummond Road	E1	Highbury Street	B4	Montgomerie Road	E3	St Faith's Road	D1	Vivash Road	F2
Britain Street	B2	Duisburg Way	C5	High Street	B4	Moorland Road	F1	St George's Road	B3	Walmer Road	F2
Broad Street	A4	Duncan Road	E5	Holbrook Road	E1	Museum Road	C4	St George's Square	B2	Warblington Street	B4
Brookfield Road	F1	Earlsdon Street	D3	Holland Road	F4	Napier Road	E5	St George's Way	B2	Warwick Crescent	D3
Brunswick Street	C3	East Street	A4	Hudson Road	E3	Nelson Road	D5	St James's Road	D3	Waterloo Road	D3
Buckingham Street	D1	Eldon Street	D4	Hyde Park Road	D3	Newcome Road	F1	St James's Street	D2	Waverley Road	F5
Cambridge Road	C3	Elm Grove	D4	Inglis Road	F4	Nightingale Road	C5	St Nicholas Street	B4	Western Parade	C5
Campbell Road	E4	Elphinstone Road	D5	Jessie Road	F3	Norfolk Street	D4	St Paul's Road	C3	West Street	A4
Canal Walk	E2	Exmouth Road	E5	Jubilee Terrace	C4	Norman Road	F4	St Peters Grove	F3	White Hart Road	B4
Carlisle Road	E2	Fawcett Road	F3	Kent Road	D5	Olinda Street	F1	St Thomas's Street	B4	Wilson Grove	E5
Cascades Approach	D1	Fawcett Road	F4	Kent Street	B2	Orchard Road	F3	Sandringham Road	E4	Wiltshire Street	C3
Castle Road	C4	Flint Street	C4	King Albert Street	E1	Ordnance Row	B2	Shaftesbury Road	C5	Winston Churchill Avenue	D3
				King Henry I Street	C2	Osborne Road	C5	Somers Road	D4	Wisborough Road	E5
				King's Road	C4	Outram Road	E4	Somers Road	D5	Woodpath	D4
				King's Terrace	C4	Oxford Road	F5	Somers Road North	E2	Woodville Drive	C4
				King Street	C4	Oyster Street	B4	Southsea Terrace	C5	Yarborough Road	D4
				King William Street	B1	Pains Road	E3	Stafford Road	E4	Yorke Street	C4

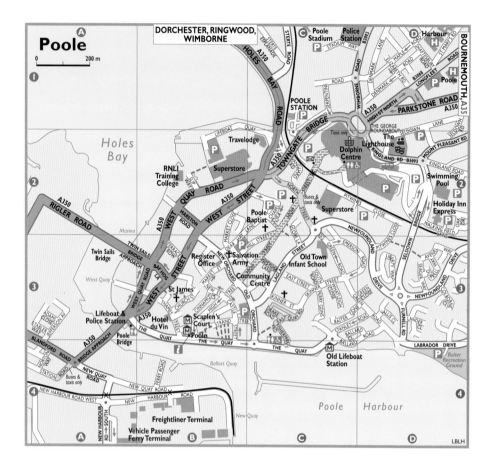

Poole

Poole is found on atlas page **12 H6**

Adams Close	A3	New Harbour Road West
Avenel Way	D3	New Orchard
Baiter Gardens	C3	New Quay Road
Ballard Close	C3	New Street
Ballard Road	C4	North Street
Bay Hog Lane	B3	Norton Way
Blandford Road	A3	Oak Drive
Bridge Approach	A4	Old Orchard
Castle Street	B3	Parkstone Road
Chapel Lane	C2	Perry Gardens
Church Street	B3	Pitwines Close
Cinnamon Lane	B3	Poole Bridge
Colborne Close	D3	Rigler Road
Dear Hay Lane	B3	St Mary's Road
Denmark Lane	D1	Seager Way
Denmark Road	D1	Seldown Bridge
Drake Road	C3	Seldown Lane
Durrell Way	D3	Seldown Road
East Quay Road	C3	Serpentine Road
East Street	C3	Shaftesbury Road
Elizabeth Road	D1	Skinner Street
Emerson Road	C3	Slip Way
Ferry Road	B4	South Road
Fisherman's Road	C3	Stabler Way
Furnell Road	D3	Stadium Way
Globe Lane	C2	Stanley Road
Green Close	D3	Sterte Esplanade
Green Road	C3	Sterte Road
High Street	B3	Strand Street
High Street North	D1	Terrace Row
Hill Street	C3	Thames Street
Holes Bay Road	C1	The Quay
Jefferson Avenue	A3	Towngate Bridge
Kingland Road	D2	Twin Sails Bridge Approach
Labrador Drive	D4	Twin Sails Bridge
Lagland Street	C3	Vallis Close
Lander Close	D3	Vanguard Road
Liberty Way	D3	Walking Field Lane
Lifeboat Quay	B2	Westons Lane
Longfleet Road	D1	West Quay Road
Maple Road	D1	West Street
Market Close	B2	Whatleigh Close
Market Street	B3	Wimborne Road
Marston Road	B2	
Mount Pleasant Road	D2	
Newfoundland Drive	C2	
New Harbour Road	A4	
New Harbour Road South	A4	

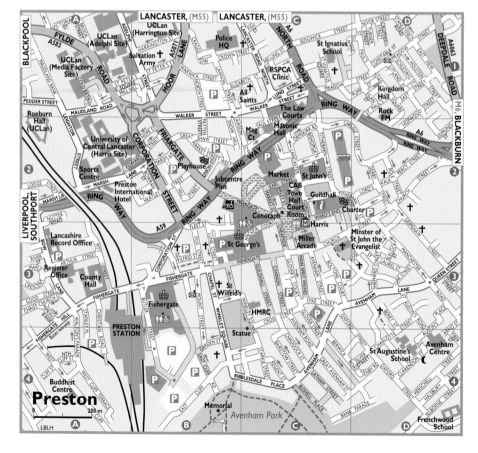

Preston

Preston is found on atlas page **88 G5**

Adelphi Street	A1	Holstein Street
Arthur Street	A3	Hopwood Street
Avenham Lane	C4	Jutland Street
Avenham Road	C3	Lancaster Road
Avenham Street	C3	Lancaster Road North
Berwick Road	C4	Latham Street
Birley Street	C2	Lawson Street
Boltons Court	C3	Leighton Street
Bow Lane	A3	Lund Street
Butler Street	B3	Lune Street
Cannon Street	C3	Main Sprit Weind
Carlisle Street	C2	Manchester Road
Chaddock Street	C4	Market Street
Chapel Street	B3	Market Street West
Charlotte Street	D4	Marsh Lane
Cheapside	C3	Maudland Road
Christ Church Street	A3	Meadow Street
Church Street	C3	Moor Lane
Clarendon Street	D4	Mount Street
Corporation Street	B2	North Road
Corporation Street	B3	Oak Street
Craggs Row	B1	Ormskirk Road
Cross Street	C3	Oxford Street
Crown Street	B1	Pedder Street
Deepdale Road	D1	Percy Street
Derby Street	D2	Pitt Street
Earl Street	C2	Pole Street
East Cliff	B4	Pump Street
East Street	D1	Queen Street
Edmund Street	D2	Ribblesdale Place
Edward Street	A2	Ring Way
Elizabeth Street	B1	Rose Street
Fishergate	B3	St Austin's Road
Fishergate Hill	A4	St Paul's Road
Fleet Street	B3	St Paul's Square
Fox Street	B3	St Peter's Street
Friargate	B2	Sedgwick Street
Friargate	B2	Selborne Street
Fylde Road	A1	Shepherd Street
Glover's Court	C3	Snow Hill
Glover Street	C3	Syke Street
Great Avenham Street	C4	Tithebarn Street
Great Shaw Street	B2	Walker Street
Grimshaw Street	D2	Walton's Parade
Guildhall Street	C3	Ward's End
Harrington Street	B1	Warwick Street
Heatley Street	B2	West Cliff
Herschell Street	D4	Winkley Square

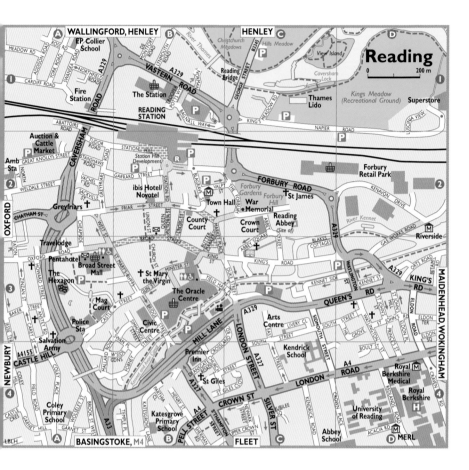

Reading

Reading is found on atlas page **35 K10**

Abbey Square...............C3	King's Meadow Road..............C1
Abbey Street.................C2	King's Road.........................D3
Addison Road................A1	King Street..........................B3
Anstey Road..................A3	Livery Close........................C3
Baker Street...................A3	London Road.......................C4
Blagrave Street..............B2	London Street......................C3
Blakes Cottages.............C3	Mallard Row........................A4
Boult Street...................D4	Market Place.......................B2
Bridge Street.................B3	Mill Lane............................B4
Broad Street..................B3	Minster Street.....................B3
Brook Street West..........A4	Napier Road........................C1
Buttermarket.................B3	Newark Street......................C4
Cardiff Road..................A1	Northfield Road....................A1
Carey Street..................A3	Oxford Road........................A3
Castle Hill.....................A4	Parthia Close......................B4
Castle Street..................A3	Pell Street..........................B4
Caversham Road............A2	Prince's Street.....................D3
Chatham Street..............A2	Queen's Road......................C3
Cheapside.....................A2	Queen Victoria Street...........B2
Church Street.................B3	Redlands Road....................D4
Church Street.................B4	Ross Road...........................A1
Coley Place...................A4	Sackville Street...................A2
Craven Road..................D4	St Giles Close.....................B4
Crossland Road..............B4	St John's Road.....................D3
Cross Street...................B2	St Mary's Butts...................B3
Crown Street..................C4	Sidmouth Street..................C3
Deansgate Road.............B4	Silver Street........................C4
Duke Street....................C3	Simmonds Street.................B3
East Street....................C3	Southampton Street.............B4
Eldon Road....................D3	South Street.......................C3
Field Road.....................A4	Station Hill.........................B2
Fobney Street.................B4	Station Road........................B2
Forbury Road..................C2	Swan Place.........................B3
Friar Street....................B2	Swansea Road.....................A1
Garnet Street.................A4	The Forbury.........................C2
Garrard Street................B2	Tudor Road..........................A2
Gas Works Road.............D3	Union Street........................B2
George Street.................C1	Upper Crown Street..............C4
Great Knollys Street.........A2	Vachel Road........................A2
Greyfriars Road..............A2	Valpy Street........................B2
Gun Street.....................B3	Vastern Road.......................B1
Henry Street..................B4	Watlington Street.................D3
Howard Street................A3	Weldale Street....................A2
Katesgrove Lane.............B4	West Street.........................A2
Kenavon Drive................D2	Wolseley Street...................A4
Kendrick Road................C4	Yield Hall Place...................B3
Kennet Side...................C3	York Road...........................A1
Kennet Street.................D3	Zinzan Street......................A3

Royal Tunbridge Wells

Royal Tunbridge Wells is found on atlas page **25 N3**

Albert Street.................C1	Lansdowne Road..................C2
Arundel Road................C4	Lime Hill Road B1
Bayhall Road.................D2	Linden Park Road.................A4
Belgrave Road................C1	Little Mount Sion.................B4
Berkeley Road................B4	London Road.......................A2
Boyne Park...................A1	Lonsdale Gardens................B2
Buckingham Road...........C4	Madeira Park.......................B4
Calverley Park...............C2	Major York's Road...............A4
Calverley Park Gardens.... D2	Meadow Road......................B1
Calverley Road..............C2	Molyneux Park Road............A1
Calverley Street..............C2	Monson Road.......................C2
Cambridge Gardens.........D4	Monson Way........................B2
Cambridge Street............D3	Mount Edgcumbe Road A3
Camden Hill..................D3	Mount Ephraim....................A2
Camden Park.................D3	Mount Ephraim Road...........B1
Camden Road.................C1	Mountfield Gardens..............C3
Carlton Road.................D2	Mountfield Road..................C3
Castle Road....................A2	Mount Pleasant Avenue........B2
Castle Street..................B3	Mount Pleasant Road...........B2
Chapel Place.................B4	Mount Sion.........................B4
Christchurch Avenue B3	Nevill Street.......................B4
Church Road..................A2	Newton Road.......................B1
Civic Way......................B2	Norfolk Road.......................C4
Claremont Gardens.........C4	North Street.........................D2
Claremont Road..............C4	Oakfield Court Road.............D3
Clarence Road................B2	Park Street..........................D3
Crescent Road................C2	Pembury Road.....................D2
Culverden Street.............B1	Poona Road.........................C4
Dale Street....................C1	Prince's Street.....................D3
Dudley Road..................B1	Prospect Road.....................D3
Eden Road.....................B4	Rock Villa Road...................B1
Eridge Road...................A4	Royal Chase........................A1
Farmcombe Lane.............C4	St James' Road....................D1
Farmcombe Road............C4	Sandrock Road....................D1
Ferndale.......................D1	Somerville Gardens..............A1
Frant Road....................A4	South Green........................B3
Frog Lane......................B4	Station Approach..................B3
Garden Road..................C1	Stone Street........................D1
Garden Street.................C1	Sussex Mews......................A4
George Street.................D3	Sutherland Road..................C3
Goods Station Road.........B1	Tunnel Road........................C1
Grecian Road.................C4	Upper Grosvenor Road B1
Grosvenor Road..............B1	Vale Avenue........................B3
Grove Hill Gardens..........C3	Vale Road...........................B3
Grove Hill Road..............C3	Victoria Road.......................C1
Guildford Road...............C3	Warwick Park......................B4
Hanover Road.................B1	Wood Street........................C1
High Street....................B4	York Road...........................B2

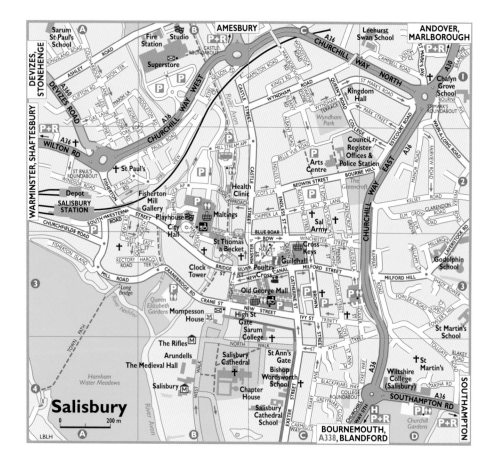

Salisbury

Salisbury is found on atlas page **21 M9**

Albany Road	C1	Kingsland Road	A
Ashley Road	A1	King's Road	C
Avon Approach	B2	Laverstock Road	D
Bedwin Street	C2	Malthouse Lane	B
Belle Vue Road	C2	Manor Road	D
Blackfriars Way	C4	Marlborough Road	C
Blue Boar Row	C3	Meadow Road	A
Bourne Avenue	D1	Middleton Road	A
Bourne Hill	C2	Milford Hill	D
Bridge Street	B3	Milford Street	C
Brown Street	C3	Mill Road	C
Campbell Road	D1	Minster Street	C
Castle Street	B1	Nelson Road	B
Catherine Street	C3	New Canal	C
Chipper Lane	C2	New Street	B
Churchfields Road	A2	North Street	D
Churchill Way East	D3	Park Street	D
Churchill Way North	C1	Pennyfarthing Street	C
Churchill Way South	C4	Queen's Road	B
Churchill Way West	B2	Queen Street	C
Clarendon Road	D2	Rampart Road	D
Clifton Road	A1	Rectory Road	A
Coldharbour Lane	A1	Rollestone Street	C
College Street	C1	St Ann Street	C
Cranebridge Road	B3	St Edmund's Church Street	D
Crane Street	B3	St Mark's Avenue	D
Devizes Road	A1	St Mark's Road	C
Dew's Road	A3	St Paul's Road	B
East Street	B3	Salt Lane	C
Elm Grove	D2	Scots Lane	C
Elm Grove Road	D2	Sidney Street	A
Endless Street	C2	Silver Street	C
Estcourt Road	D2	Southampton Road	D
Exeter Street	C4	South Street	A
Eyres Way	D4	South Western Road	A
Fairview Road	D2	Spire View	B
Fisherton Street	A2	Summerlock Approach	D
Fowler's Road	D3	Tollgate Road	D
Friary Lane	C4	Trinity Street	C
Gas Lane	A1	Wain-A-Long Road	D
George Street	A1	Wessex Road	A
Gigant Street	C3	West Street	A
Greencroft Street	C2	Wilton Road	A
Guilder Lane	C3	Winchester Street	C
Hamilton Road	C1	Windsor Road	A
High Street	B3	Woodstock Road	C
Ivy Street	C3	Wyndham Road	A
Kelsey Road	D2	York Road	A

Sheffield

Sheffield is found on atlas page **84 E3**

Angel Street	C2	Howard Street	C
Arundel Gate	C3	Hoyle Street	A
Arundel Street	C4	King Street	C
Backfields	B3	Lambert Street	B
Bailey Street	A2	Leopold Street	B
Balm Green	B3	Mappin Street	A
Bank Street	C2	Meetinghouse Lane	C
Barkers Pool	B3	Mulberry Street	C
Broad Lane	A2	Newcastle Street	A
Broad Street	D2	New Street	C
Brown Street	C4	Norfolk Street	C
Cambridge Street	B3	North Church Street	B
Campo Lane	B2	Orchard Street	B
Carver Street	B3	Paradise Street	B
Castlegate	C1	Pinstone Street	B
Castle Street	C2	Pond Hill	C
Charles Street	B4	Pond Street	C
Charter Row	B4	Portobello Street	A
Church Street	B2	Queen Street	B
Commercial Street	C2	Rockingham Street	A
Corporation Street	B1	St James Street	B
Cross Burgess Street	B3	Scargill Croft	C
Cutlers Gate	D1	Scotland Street	B
Derek Dooley Way	D1	Sheaf Street	D
Devonshire Street	A3	Shoreham Street	C
Division Street	A3	Shrewsbury Road	D
Dixon Lane	C2	Silver Street	B
Duke Street	D2	Smithfield	B
Exchange Street	D2	Snig Hill	C
Eyre Street	B4	Solly Street	A
Fig Tree Lane	C2	South Street Park	C
Fitzwilliam Street	A4	Suffolk Road	C
Flat Street	C3	Surrey Street	B
Furnace Hill	B1	Talbot Street	D
Furnival Gate	B4	Tenter Street	B
Furnival Road	D1	Townhead Street	B
Furnival Street	C4	Trafalgar Street	A
Garden Street	A2	Trippet Lane	A
George Street	C2	Union Street	B
Gibralter Street	B1	Vicar Lane	B
Harmer Lane	C3	Victoria Station Road	D
Harts Head	C2	Waingate	C
Hawley Street	B2	Wellington Street	A
Haymarket	C2	West Bar	B
High Street	C2	West Bar Green	B
Holland Street	A3	West Street	A
Hollis Croft	A2	White Croft	A
Holly Street	B3	York Street	C

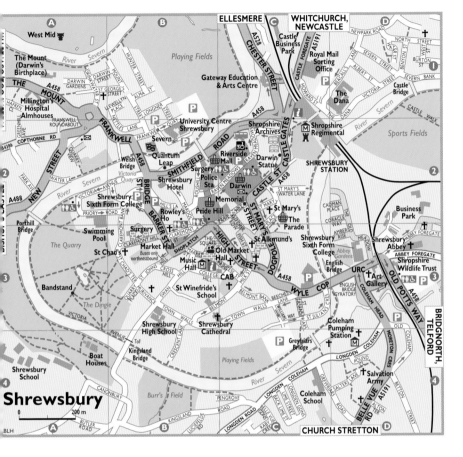

Shrewsbury

Shrewsbury is found on atlas page **56 H2**

Abbey Foregate	D3	Mardol	B2
Albert Street	D1	Market Street	B3
Alma Street	B1	Milk Street	C3
Amber Rise	D3	Moreton Crescent	D4
Barker Street	B2	Mount Street	B1
Beacall's Lane	D1	Murivance	B3
Beeches Lane	C3	Nettles Lane	B1
Belle Vue Gardens	C4	Newpark Road	D1
Belle Vue Road	D4	New Street	A2
Belmont	B3	North Street	D1
Belmont Bank	C3	Old Coleham	D3
Benyon Street	D1	Old Potts Way	D3
Betton Street	D4	Park Avenue	A2
Bridge Street	B2	Pengrove	C4
Burton Street	D1	Pound Close	D4
Butcher Row	C2	Pride Hill	C2
Canonbury	A4	Princess Street	B3
Castle Foregate	C1	Priory Road	A2
Castle Gates	C2	Quarry Place	B3
Castle Street	C2	Quarry View	A2
Chester Street	C1	Raven Meadows	B2
Claremont Bank	B3	Roushill	B2
Claremont Hill	B3	St Chad's Terrace	B3
Claremont Street	B3	St George's Street	A1
Coleham Head	D3	St Johns Hill	B3
College Hill	B3	St Julians Crescent	C3
Copthorne Road	A2	St Julians Friars	C3
Coracle Way	D2	St Mary's Place	C2
Crescent Lane	B4	St Mary's Street	C2
Cross Hill	B3	St Mary's Water Lane	C2
Darwin Gardens	A1	Salters Lane	D4
Darwin Street	A1	Severn Bank	D1
Dogpole	C3	Severn Street	D1
Drinkwater Street	A1	Shoplatch	B3
Fish Street	C3	Smithfield Road	B2
Frankwell	A2	Swan Hill	B3
Frankwell Quay	B2	The Dana	D1
Greenhill Avenue	A2	The Mount	A1
Greyfriars Road	C4	The Old Meadow	D3
High Street	C3	The Square	B3
Hill's Lane	B2	Town Walls	B3
Howard Street	C1	Victoria Avenue	A2
Hunter Street	B1	Victoria Street	D1
Kingsland Road	B4	Water Lane	A2
Lime Street	C4	Water Street	D1
Longden Coleham	C4	West Street	D1
Longden Road	C4	Williams Way	C3
Longner Street	B1	Wyle Cop	C3

Southend-on-Sea

Southend-on-Sea is found on atlas page **38 E4**

Albert Road	C3	Lancaster Gardens	C2
Alexandra Road	A3	Leamington Road	D2
Alexandra Street	A3	London Road	A2
Ambleside Drive	D2	Lucy Road	C4
Ashburnham Road	A2	Luker Road	A2
Baltic Avenue	B3	Marine Parade	C4
Baxter Avenue	A1	Milton Street	B1
Beach Road	D4	Napier Avenue	A2
Boscombe Road	C1	Nelson Street	A3
Bournemouth Park Road	D1	Oban Road	D1
Cambridge Road	A3	Old Southend Road	D3
Capel Terrace	A3	Outing Close	D3
Chancellor Road	B3	Pitmans Close	B2
Cheltenham Road	D2	Pleasant Road	C3
Chichester Road	B1	Portland Avenue	B3
Christchurch Road	D1	Princes Street	A2
Church Road	B3	Prittlewell Square	A3
Clarence Road	A3	Quebec Avenue	B2
Clarence Street	B3	Queen's Road	A2
Clifftown Parade	A4	Queensway	A1
Clifftown Road	B3	Queensway	C3
Coleman Street	B1	Royal Terrace	B4
Cromer Road	C2	Runwell Terrace	A3
Devereux Road	A4	St Ann's Road	B1
Eastern Esplanade	D4	St Leonard's Road	C3
Elmer Approach	A2	Scratton Road	A3
Elmer Avenue	A2	Short Street	B1
Essex Street	B1	Southchurch Avenue	D2
Ferndown Close	D1	Southchurch Road	B2
Fowler Close	D2	Stanier Close	D2
Gordon Place	A2	Stanley Road	C3
Gordon Road	A2	Sutton Road	C1
Grange Gardens	C2	Swanage Road	C1
Grover Street	B3	Toledo Road	C2
Guildford Road	B1	Tylers Avenue	B3
Hamlet Road	A3	Tyrrel Drive	C2
Hartington Place	C4	Victoria Avenue	A1
Hartington Road	C3	Warrior Square East	B2
Hastings Road	C2	Warrior Square North	B2
Hawtree Close	D4	Warrior Square	B2
Herbert Grove	C3	Wesley Road	C3
Heygate Avenue	B3	Western Esplanade	A4
High Street	B2	Weston Road	B3
Hillcrest Road	C2	Whitegate Road	B2
Honiton Road	D2	Wimborne Road	C1
Horace Road	C3	Windermere Road	D3
Kilworth Avenue	C2	Woodgrange Drive	D3
Kursaal Way	D4	York Road	B3

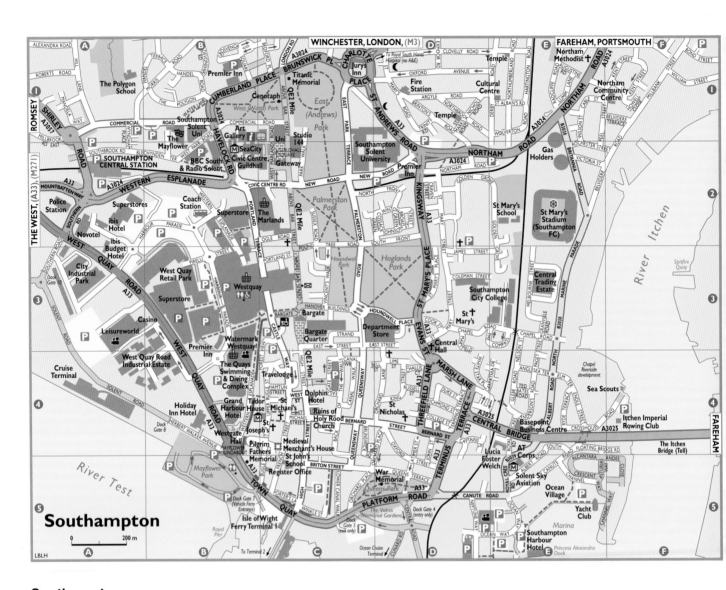

Southampton

Southampton is found on atlas page **14 D4**

Above Bar Street.................C1	Channel Way.........................E5	Hartington Road E1	Northumberland Road E1	South Front...........................C2
Albert Road North.................E4	Chapel Road..........................D3	Havelock Road B1	Ocean Way............................ D5	Strand C3
Albert Road South.................E5	Charlotte Place C1	Herbert Walker Avenue B4	Ogle Road..............................C2	Sussex Road..........................C2
Alcantara Crescent...............E5	Civic Centre Road..................B2	High Street.............................C4	Orchard Place........................C5	Ted Bates Road E4
Alexandra Road.....................A1	Clovelly Road.........................D1	Hill Lane................................A1	Oxford Avenue.......................D1	Terminus Terrace...................D5
Anderson's Road...................E4	Coleman Street......................D3	Houndwell Place D3	Oxford Street..........................D4	The Compass.........................D3
Andes Close..........................F5	College Street........................D4	Howell Close..........................F1	Paget Street...........................E4	The Polygon...........................B1
Anglesea Terrace...................E4	Commercial Road...................A1	Itchen Bridge.........................F4	Palmerston Road....................C2	Threefield Lane......................D4
Argyle Road...........................D1	Cook Street............................D3	James Street..........................D3	Park Walk...............................C2	Town Quay.............................B5
Asturias Way.........................E5	Cossack Green.......................D2	Johnson Street.......................D2	Peel Street..............................E1	Trinity Road............................D1
Augustine Road......................E1	Craven Street.........................D2	John Street.............................D5	Pirelli Street...........................B3	Upper Bugle Street.................C4
Back Of The Walls.................C4	Crosshouse Road...................E4	Kent Street.............................F1	Platform Road.........................C5	Victoria Street........................E2
Bargate Street.......................C3	Cumberland Place..................B1	King Street.............................D4	Porter's Lane..........................C5	Vincent's Walk.......................C3
Bedford Place........................C1	Cunard Road..........................D5	Kingsway................................D2	Portland Street.......................C3	Water Lane.............................B1
Bell Street.............................D4	Derby Road............................E1	Latimer Street........................D5	Portland Terrace.....................B2	Western Esplanade................A2
Belvidere Road.......................E2	Devonshire Road....................B1	Lime Street.............................D4	Pound Tree Road....................C3	Western Esplanade................B4
Belvidere Terrace...................F1	Duke Street............................D4	London Road...........................C1	Queens Terrace......................D5	West Marlands Road...............C2
Bernard Street.......................C4	Eastgate Street......................C4	Lower Canal Walk...................C5	Queensway.............................C4	West Park Road......................B2
Blechynden Terrace...............B2	East Park Terrace...................C1	Lumpy Lane............................E1	Radcliffe Road........................E1	West Quay Road.....................A2
Bond Street............................F1	East Street.............................C3	Mandela Way..........................A1	Richmond Street.....................D4	West Street............................C4
Brinton's Road.......................D1	Elm Terrace............................E4	Marine Parade........................E3	Roberts Road..........................A1	White Star Place.....................D4
Britannia Road.......................E1	Endle Street...........................E4	Marsh Lane............................D4	Rochester Street.....................E2	William Street.........................F1
Briton Street..........................C5	Evans Street...........................D3	Maryfield................................D3	Royal Crescent Road..............E5	Wilson Street..........................E1
Broad Green...........................D2	Exmoor Road..........................D1	Mayflower Roundabout...........B4	Russell Street.........................D4	Winkle Street..........................C5
Brunswick Place.....................C1	Floating Bridge Road E4	Melbourne Street....................E3	Ryde Terrace..........................E4	Winton Street.........................D2
Brunswick Square..................C4	Forest View............................C4	Millbank Street.......................F1	St Alban's Road......................E1	Wolverton Road......................E1
Bugle Street..........................C5	French Street..........................C5	Millbrook Road East...............A1	St Andrews Road....................D1	Wyndham Place......................A1
Cable Street...........................E1	Glebe Road............................E4	Morris Road............................B1	St Marks Road........................D1	
Canal Walk............................C4	Golden Grove.........................D2	Mountbatten Way....................A2	St Mary's Place.......................D3	
Canute Road D5	Granville Road E3	Nelson Street..........................E4	St Mary's Road.......................D1	
Captains Place.......................D4	Grosvenor Square...................B1	Neptune Way..........................D5	St Mary Street.........................D2	
Carpathia Drive......................D4	Hamtun Street........................C4	New Road................................C2	St Michael Street....................C4	
Castle Way.............................C3	Handel Road...........................B1	Nichols Road...........................D1	Shirley Road............................A1	
Central Bridge........................D4	Handel Terrace.......................B1	Northam Road.........................D2	Solent Road............................A3	
Central Road..........................D5	Hanover Buildings...................C3	Northbrook Road.....................D1	Southbrook Road.....................A2	
Challis Court..........................D4	Harbour Parade......................B2	North Front............................C2	Southern Road.........................A2	

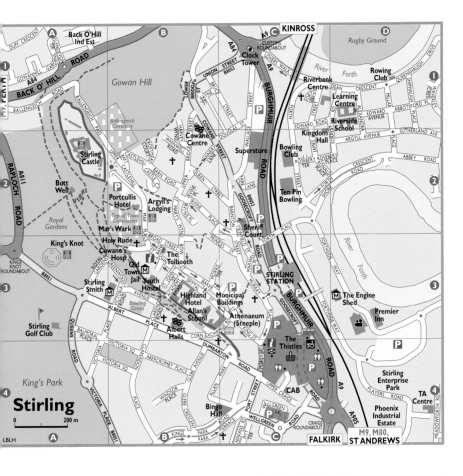

Stirling

Stirling is found on atlas page **133 M9**

Abbey Road	D2	James Street	C2
Abbotsford Place	D1	Kings Knot Roundabout	A3
Abercromby Place	B4	Kings Park Road	B4
Academy Road	B3	King Street	C3
Albert Place	A3	Lovers Walk	C1
Alexandra Place	D1	Lower Bridge Street	B1
Allan Park	B4	Lower Castlehill	B2
Argyll Avenue	D2	Mar Place	B2
Back O' Hill Road	A1	Maxwell Place	C3
Baker Street	B3	Meadowforth Road	D4
Ballengeich Road	A1	Millar Place	D1
Ballengeich Pass	A1	Morris Terrace	B3
Balmoral Place	A3	Murray Place	C3
Bank Street	B3	Ninians Road	C4
Barn Road	B2	Park Lane	C2
Barnton Street	C2	Park Terrace	B4
Bayne Street	B1	Players Road	D4
Bow Street	B3	Port Street	C4
Broad Street	B3	Princes Street	B3
Bruce Street	B1	Queenshaugh Drive	D1
Burghmuir Road	C1	Queens Road	A3
Castle Court	B2	Queen Street	B2
Clarendon Place	B4	Raploch Road	A2
Clarendon Road	B3	Ronald Place	C2
Corn Exchange Road	B3	Rosebery Place	C2
Cowane Street	B1	Rosebery Terrace	C2
Craigs Roundabout	C4	Royal Gardens	A3
Crofthead Court	B2	St John Street	B3
Customs Roundabout	C1	St Mary's Wynd	B2
Dean Crescent	D1	Shiphaugh Place	D1
Douglas Street	C2	Shore Road	C2
Dumbarton Road	B4	Spittal Street	B3
Edward Avenue	D1	Sutherland Avenue	D2
Edward Road	C1	Tannery Lane	B2
Forrest Road	D2	Union Street	B1
Forth Crescent	C2	Upper Bridge Street	B2
Forthside Way	C3	Upper Castlehill	A2
Forth Street	C1	Upper Craigs	C4
Forth Place	C3	Victoria Place	A4
Forth View	C1	Victoria Road	B3
Glebe Avenue	B4	Victoria Square	A4
Glebe Crescent	B4	Viewfield Street	C2
Glendevon Drive	A1	Wallace Street	C2
Goosecroft Road	C2	Waverley Crescent	D1
Gowanhill Gardens	A1	Wellgreen Lane	C4
Greenwood Avenue	A3	Wellgreen Road	C4
Harvey Wynd	B1	Whinwell Road	B2
Irvine Place	B2	Windsor Place	B4

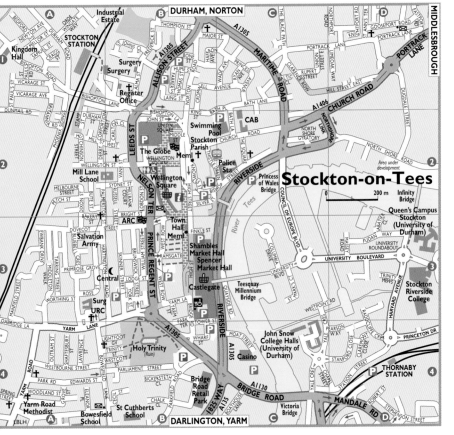

Stockton-on-Tees

Stockton-on-Tees is found on atlas page **104 D7**

1825 Way	B4	Massey Road	D3
Allison Street	B1	Melbourne Street	A2
Alma Street	B1	Middle Street	B2
Bath Lane	C1	Mill Street West	A2
Bedford Street	A1	Nelson Terrace	B2
Bishop Street	B2	North Shore Road	D2
Bishopton Lane	A1	Northport Road	D1
Bishopton Road	A1	Northshore Link	C2
Bowesfield Lane	A4	Norton Road	B1
Bridge Road	B3	Palmerston Street	A2
Bridge Road	C4	Park Road	A4
Bright Street	B2	Park Terrace	B4
Britannia Road	A1	Parkfield Road	B4
Brunswick Street	B3	Parliament Street	B4
Bute Street	A2	Portrack Lane	D1
Church Road	D1	Prince Regent Street	B3
Clarence Row	C1	Princess Avenue	C1
Corportion Street	A2	Princeton Drive	D4
Council of Europe		Quayside Road	C1
Boulevard	C2	Raddcliffe Crescent	D3
Cromwell Avenue	B1	Ramsgate	B3
Dixon Street	A2	Riverside	C3
Dovecot Street	A3	Russell Street	B2
Dugdale Street	D1	St Paul's Street	A1
Durham Road	A1	Silver Street	B2
Durham Street	A2	Skinner Street	B3
Edwards Street	A4	Station Street	D4
Farrer Street	B1	Sydney Street	B2
Finkle Street	B3	The Square	C2
Frederick Street	B1	Thistle Green	C2
Fudan Way	D3	Thomas Street	B1
Gooseport Road	D1	Thompson Street	B1
Hartington Road	A3	Tower Street	B4
Harvard Avenue	D3	Union Street East	C1
High Street	B2	University Boulevard	C3
Hill Street East	D1	Vane Street	B2
Hume Street	B2	Vicarage Street	A1
Hutchinson Street	A2	Wellington Street	A2
John Street	B2	West Row	B3
King Street	B2	Westbourne Street	A4
Knightport Road	D1	Westpoint Road	C3
Knowles Street	C2	Wharf Street	B4
Laing Street	B1	William Street	B3
Leeds Street	B2	Woodland Street	A4
Lobdon Street	B2	Worthing Street	A3
Lodge Street	B3	Yale Crescent	C4
Mandale Road	D4	Yarm Lane	A4
Maritime Road	C1	Yarm Road	A4

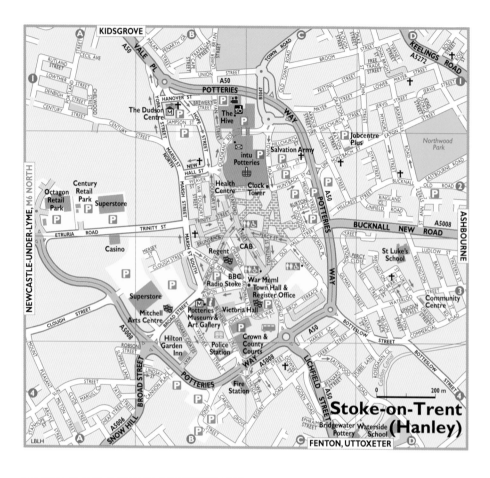

Stoke-on-Trent (Hanley)

Stoke-on-Trent (Hanley) is found on atlas page **70**

Albion Street................B3	Linfield Road................
Bagnall Street...............B3	Lower Mayer Street............
Balfour Street...............D3	Lowther Street................
Baskerville Road.............D1	Ludlow Street................
Bathesda Street..............B4	Malam Street................
Bernard Street...............C4	Marsh Street................
Bethesda Street..............B3	Marsh Street North............
Birch Terrace................C3	Marsh Street South............
Botteslow Street.............C3	Mayer Street................
Broad Street.................B4	Mersey Street................
Broom Street.................C1	Milton Street................
Brunswick Street.............B3	Mount Pleasant................
Bryan Street.................B1	Mynors Street................
Bucknall New Road............C2	New Hall Street................
Bucknall Old Road............D2	Ogden Road................
Cardiff Grove................B4	Old Hall Street................
Century Street...............A1	Old Town Road................
Charles Street...............C3	Pall Mall................
Cheapside....................B3	Percy Street................
Chelwood Street..............A1	Piccadilly................
Clough Street................A3	Portland Street................
Clyde Street.................A4	Potteries Way................
Commercial Road..............D3	Potteries Way................
Denbigh Street...............A1	Quadrant Road................
Derby Street.................C4	Regent Road................
Dyke Street..................D2	Rutland Street................
Eastwood Road................C4	St John Street................
Eaton Street.................D2	St Luke Street................
Etruria Road.................A2	Sampson Street................
Foundry Street...............B2	Sheaf Street................
Garth Street.................C2	Slippery Lane................
Gilman Street................C3	Snow Hill................
Goodson Street...............C2	Stafford Street................
Grafton Street...............C1	Sun Street................
Hanover Street...............B1	Tontine Street................
Harley Street................C4	Town Road................
Hillchurch...................C2	Trafalgar Street................
Hillcrest Street.............C2	Trinity Street................
Hinde Street.................B4	Union Street................
Hope Street..................B1	Upper Hillchurch Street........
Hordley Street...............C3	Upper Huntbach Street..........
Huntbach Street..............C2	Warner Street................
Jasper Street................C4	Waterloo Street................
Jervis Street................D1	Well Street................
John Street..................B3	Wellington Road................
Keelings Road................D1	Wellington Street................
Lichfield Street.............C3	Yates Street................
Lidice Way...................C3	York Street................

Stratford-upon-Avon

Stratford-upon-Avon is found on atlas page **47 P3**

Albany Road..................A3	New Broad Street................
Alcester Road................A2	New Street................
Arden Street.................B2	Old Red Lion Court............
Avenue Road..................C1	Old Town................
Bancroft Place...............C2	Orchard Way................
Birmingham Road..............B1	Payton Street................
Brewery Street...............B1	Percy Street................
Bridge Foot..................D2	Rother Street................
Bridge Street................C2	Rowley Crescent................
Bridgeway....................D2	Ryland Street................
Broad Street.................B4	St Andrew's Crescent............
Brookvale Road...............A4	St Gregory's Road............
Brunel Way...................A2	St Martin's Close............
Bull Street..................B4	Sanctus Drive................
Cedar Close..................D1	Sanctus Road................
Chapel Lane..................C3	Sanctus Street................
Chapel Street................C3	Sandfield Road................
Cherry Orchard...............A4	Scholars Lane................
Cherry Street................B4	Seven Meadows Road............
Chestnut Walk................B3	Shakespeare Street............
Church Street................B3	Sheep Street................
Clopton Bridge...............D3	Shipston Road................
Clopton Road.................B1	Shottery Road................
College Lane.................B4	Shrieves Walk................
College Mews.................B4	Southern Lane................
College Street...............B4	Swan's Nest................
Ely Gardens..................B3	The Willows................
Ely Street...................B3	Tiddington Road................
Evesham Place................B3	Town Square................
Evesham Road.................A4	Tramway Bridge................
Garrick Way..................A4	Tyler Street................
Great William Street.........C1	Union Street................
Greenhill Street.............B2	Warwick Court................
Grove Road...................B3	Warwick Crescent................
Guild Street.................C2	Warwick Road................
Henley Street................C2	Waterside................
High Street..................C3	Welcombe Road................
Holtom Street................B4	Wellesbourne Grove............
John Street..................C2	Western Road................
Kendall Avenue...............B1	West Street................
Lock Close...................C2	Willows Drive North............
Maidenhead Road..............C1	Windsor Street................
Mansell Street...............B2	Wood Street................
Mayfield Avenue..............C1	
Meer Street..................B2	
Mill Lane....................C4	
Mulberry Street..............C1	
Narrow Lane..................B4	

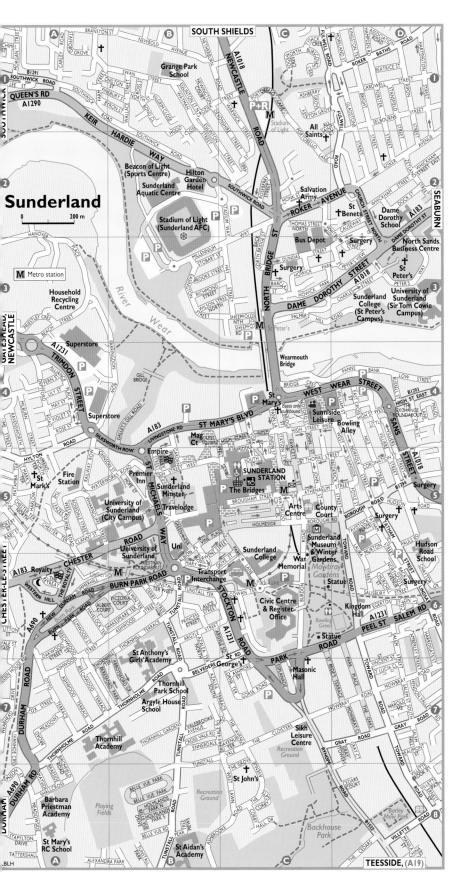

Sunderland

Sunderland is found on atlas page **113 N9**

Abbotsford Green	B7	Milburn Street	A4
Abbs Street	C2	Millennium Way	B3
Albion Place	B6	Monk Street	C2
Alice Street	B6	Moreland Street	D1
Alliance Place	A4	Morgan Street	A1
Amberley Street	D6	Mowbray Road	D7
Argyle Square	B6	Netherburn Road	B1
Argyle Street	B6	Newbold Avenue	B1
Ashbrooke Road	B8	Newcastle Road	C1
Ashmore Street	C7	New Durham Road	A6
Ashwood Street	A7	Nile Street	D4
Ashwood Terrace	A7	Norfolk Street	D5
Association Road	D1	North Bridge Street	C3
Athenaeum Street	C5	Northcote Avenue	D6
Azalea Terrace North	B6	North Street	B1
Azalea Terrace South	B7	Oakwood Street	A6
Back North Bridge Street	C3	Olive Street	B6
Beach Street	A3	Otto Terrace	A7
Bedford Street	C4	Palmer's Hill Road	C3
Beechwood Street	A6	Panns Bank	D4
Beechwood Terrace	A7	Park Lane	C5
Belvedere Road	B7	Park Place	D6
Beresford Park	A7	Park Road	C6
Birchfield Road	A7	Pauls Road	D5
Borough Road	D5	Peel Street	D6
Bridge Crescent	C4	Portobello Lane	C1
Bridge Street	C4	Queen's Road	A1
Briery Vale Road	C7	Railway Row	A5
Bright Street	D1	Ravensworth Street	A4
Brooke Street	B3	Richmond Street	B3
Brougham Street	C5	Ripon Street	D1
Burdon Road	C5	Roker Avenue	C2
Burn Park Road	B6	Roker Baths Road	D1
Cardwell Street	D1	Rosedale Street	A5
Carley Road	A1	Ross Street	B1
Charles Street	D3	Russell Street	D4
Chester Road	A6	Ryhope Road	C7
Churchill Street	D6	St Bede's Terrace	D7
Church Street North	D2	St Mary's Boulevard	B4
Clanny Street	A5	St Michaels Way	B5
Cork Street	D4	St Peter's View	C3
Coronation Street	D5	St Thomas' Street	C5
Cowan Terrace	C6	St Vincent Street	D7
Cross Vale Road	B7	Salem Road	D6
Crozier Street	B1	Salem Street	D6
Dame Dorothy Street	C3	Salem Street South	D7
Deptford Road	A4	Salisbury Street	D6
Derby Street	B6	Sans Street	D4
Derwent Street	B6	Selbourne Street	D1
Devonshire Street	B1	Shakespeare Terrace	A6
Dock Street	D2	Shallcross	A8
Dundas Street	C3	Sheepfolds Road	C3
Durham Road	A7	Silksworth Row	A4
Easington Street	B3	South Street	C5
East Cross Street	D4	Southwick Road	A1
Eden House Road	A7	Southwick Road	C2
Egerton Street	D6	Stadium Way	C2
Eglinton Street	B1	Stansfield Street	D1
Eglinton Street North	B1	Station Street	C4
Elmwood Street	A6	Stobart Street	B3
Ennerdale	B7	Stockton Road	C6
Farm Street	A1	Swan Street	B1
Farringdon Row	B4	Tatham Street	D5
Fawcett Street	C4	Tatham Street Back	D5
Forster Street	D1	The Avenue	C7
Fox Street	A7	The Cloisters	C7
Foyle Street	D5	The Royalty	A6
Frederick Street	D5	Thomas Street North	C2
Fulwell Road	C1	Thornhill Terrace	B6
Galley's Gill Road	B4	Thornholme Road	A7
Gladstone Street	D1	Toward Road	D5
Gorse Road	C7	Trimdon Street	A4
Gray Road	D7	Tunstall Road	B7
Green Terrace	B5	Tunstall Terrace	B6
Hampden Road	D1	Tunstall Terrace West	B6
Hanover Place	A2	Tunstall Vale	B8
Harlow Street	A5	Union Street	C4
Harrogate Street	D6	Valebrooke Avenue	B7
Hartington Street	D1	Villette Road	D8
Havelock Terrace	A6	Villiers Street	D4
Hay Street	C3	Vine Place	B5
Hendon Valley Road	D7	Wallace Street	B1
High Street East	D4	Warwick Street	C1
High Street West	B5	Waterloo Place	C5
Holmeside	C5	Waterworks Road	A5
Hope Street	B5	Wayman Street	B1
Howick Park	C3	Wearhead Drive	A7
Hudson Road	D5	Westbourne Road	A5
Hylton Road	A5	Western Hill	A6
Johnson Street	A5	West Lawn	C8
John Street	C4	West Street	C5
Keir Hardie Way	A1	West Sunniside	D4
Laura Street	D5	West Wear Street	C4
Lindsay Road	D4	Wharncliffe Street	A5
Little Villiers Street	D4	Whickham Street	D2
Livingstone Road	B4	Whickham Street East	D2
Low Street	D4	Whitburn Street	D3
Mary Street	B6	William Street	D4
Mauds Lane	D4	Wilson Street North	B3
Meadowside	A8	York Street	C4
Middle Street	C5	Zetland Street	D2

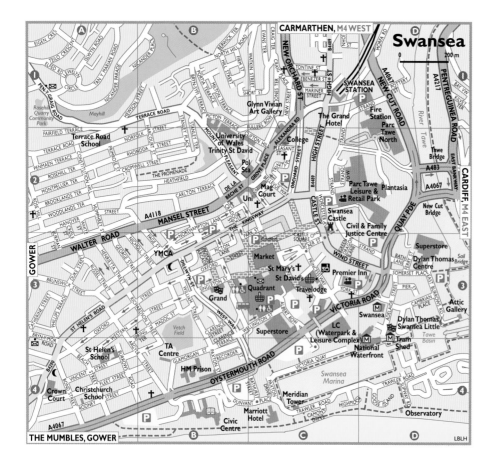

Swansea

Swansea is found on atlas page **29 J6**

Adelaide Street	D3	New Orchard Street	
Alexandra Road	C2	New Street	
Argyle Street	A4	Nicander Parade	
Bath Lane	D3	Nicholl Street	
Beach Street	A4	Norfolk Street	
Bond Street	A4	North Hill Road	
Brunswick Street	A3	Northampton Lane	
Burrows Road	A4	Orchard Street	
Caer Street	C3	Oxford Street	
Carlton Terrace	B2	Oystermouth Road	
Castle Street	C2	Page Street	
Catherine Street	A3	Park Street	
Clarence Street	B3	Paxton Street	
Clifton Hill	C2	Pentreguinea Road	
Constituion Hill	A2	Pen-Y-Graig Road	
Cradock Street	B2	Picton Lane	
Craig Place	C1	Pier Street	
Cromwell Street	A2	Primrose Street	
De La Beche Street	B2	Princess Way	
Dillwyn Street	B3	Quay Parade	
Duke Street	A3	Recorder Street	
Dunvant Place	B4	Rhondda Street	
East Bank Way	D2	Richardson Street	
East Burrows Road	D3	Rodney Street	
Ebenezer Street	C1	Rose Hill	
Elfed Road	A1	Russel Street	
Ferry Street	D3	St Helen's Road	
Firm Street	B1	Short Street	
Fleet Street	A4	Singleton Street	
George Street	A3	Somerset Place	
Glamorgan Street	B4	Strand	
Green Dragon Lane	C3	Tan Y Marian Road	
Grove Place	C2	Teilo Crescent	
Hanover Street	A2	Terrace Road	
Harcourt Street	B2	The Kingsway	
Heathfield	B2	Tontine Street	
Henrietta Street	A3	Trawler Road	
Hewson Street	A1	Victoria Quay	
High Street	C2	Victoria Road	
Hill Street	B1	Vincent Street	
Humphrey Street	A2	Walter Road	
Islwyn Road	A1	Watkin Street	
Llewelyn Circle	A1	Wellington Street	
Madoc Street	B3	West Way	
Mansel Street	B2	Western Street	
Mariner Street	C1	William Street	
Mount Pleasant	B2	Wind Street	
New Cut Road	D1	York Street	

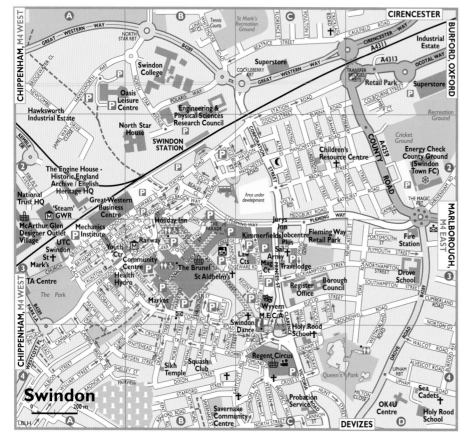

Swindon

Swindon is found on atlas page **33 M8**

Albion Street	A4	Islington Street	
Alfred Street	C2	John Street	
Ashford Road	B4	King Street	
Aylesbury Street	B2	London Street	
Bathurst Road	C2	Manchester Road	
Beckhampton Street	C3	Market Street	
Bridge Street	B2	Maxwell Street	
Bristol Street	A3	Medgbury Road	
Broad Street	C2	Milford Street	
Cambria Bridge Road	A4	Milton Road	
Canal Walk	B3	Morley Street	
Carr Street	B3	Morse Street	
Chester Street	A3	Newcastle Street	
Church Place	A3	Newcombe Drive	
Cirencester Way	D1	Newhall Street	
Clarence Street	C3	Northampton Street	
College Street	B3	North Star Avenue	
Commercial Road	B3	Ocotal Way	
Corporation Street	C2	Park Lane	
County Road	D2	Plymouth Street	
Crombey Street	B4	Polaris Way	
Curtis Street	A4	Ponting Street	
Deacon Street	B4	Portsmouth Street	
Dixon Street	B4	Princes Street	
Dover Street	C4	Prospect Hill	
Dowling Street	B4	Queen Street	
Drove Road	D4	Radnor Street	
Dryden Street	A4	Regent Place	
Eastcott Hill	C4	Regent Street	
East Street	B2	Rosebery Street	
Edgeware Road	B3	Salisbury Street	
Elmina Road	C1	Sanford Street	
Emlyn Square	A3	Sheppard Street	
Euclid Street	C3	Southampton Street	
Faringdon Road	A3	Stafford Street	
Farnsby Street	B3	Stanier Street	
Fire Fly Avenue	A2	Station Road	
Fleet Street	B2	Swindon Road	
Fleming Way	C3	Tennyson Street	
Gladstone Street	C2	Theobald Street	
Gooch Street	C2	Victoria Road	
Graham Street	C2	Villett Street	
Great Western Way	A1	Westcott Place	
Groundwell Road	C3	Western Street	
Havelock Street	B3	Whitehead Street	
Hawksworth Way	A1	Whitney Street	
Haydon Street	C2	William Street	
Holbrook Way	B2	York Road	

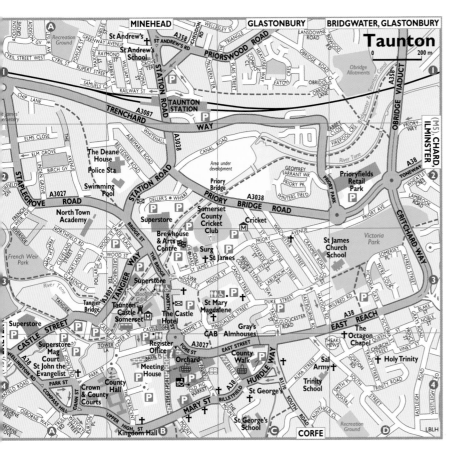

Taunton

Taunton is found on atlas page **18 H10**

Abbey Close	D2	Middle Street	B3
Albemarle Road	B2	Northfield Road	A3
Alfred Street	D3	North Street	B3
Alma Street	C4	Obridge Road	C1
Belvedere Road	B2	Obridge Viaduct	D2
Billetfield	C4	Old Pig Market	B4
Billet Street	C4	Parkfield Road	A4
Bridge Street	B2	Park Street	A4
Canal Road	B2	Paul Street	B4
Cann Street	A4	Plais Street	C1
Canon Street	C3	Portland Street	A3
Castle Street	A4	Priorswood Road	B1
Cheddon Road	B1	Priory Avenue	C3
Chip Lane	A1	Priory Bridge Road	B2
Church Street	D4	Queen Street	D4
Clarence Street	A3	Railway Street	B1
Cleveland Street	A3	Raymond Street	A1
Compass Hill	A4	Rupert Street	A1
Cranmer Road	C3	St Andrew's Road	B1
Critchard Way	D2	St Augustine Street	C3
Cyril Street	A1	St James Street	B3
Deller's Wharf	B2	St John's Road	A4
Duke Street	C3	Samuels Court	A1
Eastbourne Road	C3	South Road	C4
Eastleigh Road	D4	South Street	D4
East Reach	D3	Staplegrove Road	A2
East Street	C4	Station Road	B2
Fore Street	B4	Stephen Street	C3
Fowler Street	A1	Stephen Way	C3
French Weir Avenue	A2	Tancred Street	C3
Gloucester Road	C3	The Avenue	A2
Grays Road	D3	The Bridge	B3
Greenway Avenue	A1	The Crescent	B4
Gyffarde Street	C3	The Triangle	C1
Hammet Street	B4	Thomas Street	B1
Haydon Road	C3	Toneway	D2
Herbert Street	B1	Tower Street	B4
High Street	B4	Trenchard Way	B1
Hugo Street	C3	Trinity Street	D4
Hurdle Way	C4	Upper High Street	B4
Laburnum Street	C3	Victoria Gate	D3
Lansdowne Road	C1	Victoria Street	D4
Leslie Avenue	A1	Viney Street	D4
Linden Grove	A2	Wellington Road	A4
Lower Middle Street	B3	Wilfred Road	C3
Magdalene Street	B3	William Street	B1
Mary Street	B4	Winchester Street	C2
Maxwell Street	A1	Wood Street	B3

Torquay

Torquay is found on atlas page **7 N6**

Abbey Road	B1	Middle Warbury Road	D1
Alexandra Road	C1	Mill Lane	A1
Alpine Road	C2	Montpellier Road	D3
Ash Hill Road	C1	Morgan Avenue	B1
Avenue Road	A1	Palm Road	B1
Bampfylde Road	A2	Parkhill Road	D4
Beacon Hill	D4	Pembroke Road	C1
Belgrave Road	A1	Pennsylvania Road	D1
Braddons Hill Road East	D3	Pimlico	C2
Braddons Hill Road West	C2	Potters Hill	C1
Braddons Street	D2	Princes Road	C1
Bridge Road	A1	Queen Street	C2
Camden Road	D1	Rathmore Road	A2
Cary Parade	C3	Rock Road	C2
Cary Road	C3	Rosehill Road	D1
Castle Lane	C1	St Efride's Road	A1
Castle Road	C1	St Luke's Road	B2
Cavern Road	D1	St Marychurch Road	C1
Chestnut Avenue	A2	Scarborough Road	B2
Church Lane	A1	Seaway Lane	A4
Church Street	A1	Shedden Hill Road	B3
Cleveland Road	A1	Solbro Road	A3
Croft Hill	B2	South Hill Road	D3
Croft Road	B2	South Street	A1
East Street	A1	Stentiford Hill Road	C2
Ellacombe Road	C1	Strand	D3
Falkland Road	A2	Sutherland Road	D1
Fleet Street	C3	Temperance Street	C2
Grafton Road	D2	The King's Drive	A3
Hennapyn Road	A4	The Terrace	D3
Higher Union Lane	B1	Torbay Road	A4
Hillesdon Road	D2	Tor Church Road	A1
Hoxton Road	D1	Tor Hill Road	B1
Hunsdon Road	D3	Torwood Street	D3
Laburnum Street	A1	Trematon Ave	B1
Lime Avenue	A2	Trinity Hill	D3
Lower Ellacombe Church Road	D1	Union Street	B1
Lower Union Lane	C2	Upper Braddons Hill	D2
Lower Warbury Road	D2	Vanehill Road	D4
Lucius Street	A1	Vansittart Road	A1
Lymington Road	B1	Vaughan Parade	C3
Magdalene Road	B1	Victoria Parade	D4
Market Street	C2	Victoria Road	C1
Marion View	D3	Vine Road	A2
Meadfoot Lane	D4	Walnut Road	A2
Melville Lane	C2	Warberry Road West	C1
Melville Street	C2	Warren Road	B2
		Wellington Road	C1

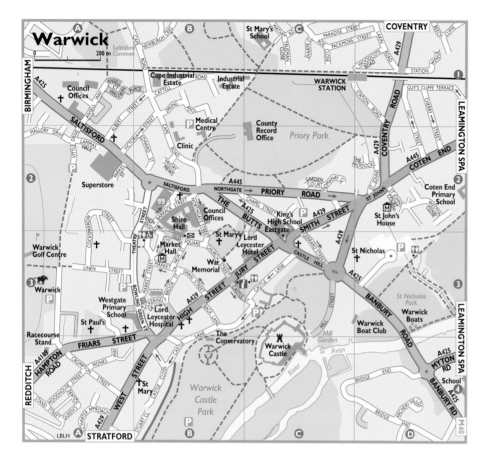

Warwick

Warwick is found on atlas page **59 L11**

Albert Street	A2	Old Square
Ansell Court	A1	Packmore Street
Ansell Way	A1	Paradise Street
Archery Fields	D4	Parkes Street
Back Lane	B3	Priory Mews
Banbury Road	D3	Priory Road
Barrack Street	B2	Puckering's Lane
Beech Cliffe	D1	Queen's Square
Bowling Green Street	B3	Roe Close
Bridge End	D4	St Johns
Brook Street	B3	St Johns Court
Cape Road	B1	Saltisford
Castle Close	B4	Sharpe Close
Castle Hill	C3	Smith Street
Castle Lane	B4	Spring Pool
Castle Street	B3	Stand Street
Cattell Road	B1	Station Avenue
Chapel Street	C2	Station Road
Charter Approach	A4	Stuart Close
Cherry Street	D1	Swan Street
Church Street	B3	Theatre Street
Cocksparrow Street	A3	The Butts
Coten End	D2	The Paddocks
Coventry Street	D2	Trueman Close
Crompton Street	A4	Victoria Street
Edward Street	B2	Vittle Drive
Friars Street	A4	Wallwin Place
Garden Court	C2	Wathen Road
Gerrard Street	C3	Weston Close
Guy's Cliffe Terrace	D1	West Street
Guy Street	D1	Woodcote Road
Hampton Road	A4	Woodhouse Street
High Street	B3	Yeomanry Close
Jury Street	B3	
Lakin Road	D1	
Lammas Walk	A2	
Linen Street	A3	
Mallory Drive	A2	
Market Place	B3	
Market Street	B3	
Mill Street	C3	
Monks Way	A4	
Myton Road	D4	
New Bridge	B2	
Newburgh Crescent	B1	
New Street	B3	
Northgate	B2	
Northgate Street	B2	

Watford

Watford is found on atlas page **50 D11**

Addiscombe Road	B3	Merton Road
Albert Road North	B2	Mildred Avenue
Albert Road South	B2	Monica Close
Alexandra Road	A1	Nascot Street
Anglian Close	D1	New Road
Beechen Grove	C3	New Street
Brocklesbury Close	D2	Orphanage Road
Burton Avenue	A4	Park Avenue
Cassiobury Drive	A2	Peace Drive
Cassio Road	A3	Peace Prospect
Chester Road	A4	Percy Road
Clarendon Road	C1	Pretoria Road
Cross Street	C2	Prince Street
Denmark Street	A1	Queen's Road
Derby Road	C3	Queen Street
Duke Street	C2	Radlett Road
Durban Road East	A4	Raphael Drive
Durban Road West	A4	Reeds Crescent
Earl Street	C3	Rickmansworth Road
Ebury Road	D2	Rosslyn Road
Essex Road	A1	St Albans Road
Estcourt Road	C2	St John's Road
Exchange Road	B3	St Mary's Road
Farraline Road	B4	St Pauls Way
Feranley Street	B4	Shady Lane
Francis Road	B3	Shaftesbury Road
Franklin Road	B1	Smith Street
Gartlet Road	C2	Sotheron Road
Gaumont Approach	B2	Southsea Avenue
George Street	C4	Stanley Road
Gladstone Road	D3	Station Road
Granville Road	C4	Stephenson Way
Grosvenor Road	C3	Sutton Road
Halsey Road	B2	The Avenue
Harwoods Road	A4	The Broadway
Hempstead Road	A1	The Crescent
High Street	C3	The Parade
Hyde Road	A2	Upton Road
Keele Close	C1	Vicarage Road
King Street	C4	Victoria Passage
Lady's Close	C4	Water Lane
Link Road	D1	Wellington Road
Loates Lane	C3	Wellstones
Lord Street	C3	Westland Road
Lower High Street	D4	West Street
Malden Road	A1	Whippendell Road
Market Street	B4	Wiggenhall Road
Marlborough Road	B3	Woodford Road

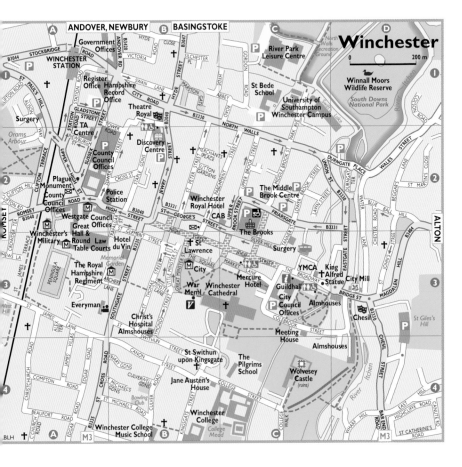

Winchester

Winchester is found on atlas page **22 E9**

Alex Terrace	A3	Market Lane	C3
Alison Way	A1	Marston Gate	B1
Andover Road	B1	Merchants Place	B2
Archery Lane	A3	Mews Lane	A3
Bar End Road	D4	Middle Brook Street	C2
Beaufort Road	A4	Minster Lane	B3
Beggar's Lane	D2	Newburgh Street	A2
Blue Ball Hill	D2	North Walls	C1
Bridge Street	D3	Parchment Street	B2
Canon Street	B4	Park Avenue	C2
Canute Road	D4	Romsey Road	A2
Chesil Street	D3	St Clement Street	B2
Chester Road	D2	St Cross Road	A4
Christchurch Road	A4	St George's Street	B2
City Road	B1	St James' Lane	A3
Clifton Hill	A2	St James Terrace	A3
Clifton Road	A1	St James' Villas	A4
Clifton Terrace	A2	St John's Street	D3
Colebrook Street	C3	St Martin's Close	D2
College Street	B4	St Michael's Gardens	B4
College Walk	C4	St Michael's Road	B4
Colson Road	D1	St Paul's Hill	A1
Compton Road	A4	St Peter Street	B2
Cross Street	B2	St Swithun Street	B3
Crowder Terrace	A3	St Thomas Street	B3
Culver Road	B4	Silchester Place	B1
Culverwell Gardens	B4	Silver Hill	C3
Durngate Place	D2	Southgate Street	B3
Durngate Terrace	D2	Staple Gardens	B2
Eastgate Street	D3	Station Road	A1
East Hill	D4	Stockbridge Road	A1
Edgar Road	A4	Sussex Street	A2
Friarsgate	C2	Sutton Gardens	B2
Friary Gardens	B4	Swan Lane	B1
Gladstone Street	A1	Symonds Street	B3
Gordon Road	C1	Tanner Street	C3
Great Minster Street	B3	The Broadway	C3
Highcliffe Road	D4	The Square	B3
High Street	B2	Tower Road	A1
Hyde Abbey Road	B1	Tower Street	B2
Hyde Close	B1	Trafalgar Street	B3
Hyde Street	B1	Union Street	C2
Jewry Street	B2	Upper Brook Street	C2
Kingsgate Street	B4	Upper High Street	A2
Lawn Street	C2	Victoria Road	B1
Little Minster Street	B3	Wales Street	D2
Lower Brook Street	C2	Water Lane	D3
Magdalen Hill	D3	Wharf Hill	D4

Wolverhampton

Wolverhampton is found on atlas page **58 D5**

Bath Avenue	A1	Peel Street	B3
Bath Road	A2	Penn Road	B4
Bell Street	B3	Piper's Row	D2
Berry Street	C2	Pitt Street	B3
Bilston Road	D3	Powlett Street	D4
Bilston Street	C3	Princess Street	C2
Birch Street	B2	Queen Square	B2
Broad Street	C2	Queen Street	C2
Castle Street	C3	Raby Street	D4
Chapel Ash	A3	Raglan Street	A3
Church Lane	B4	Red Lion Street	B2
Church Street	B4	Retreat Street	A4
Clarence Road	B2	Ring Road St Andrews	A2
Clarence Street	B2	Ring Road St Davids	D2
Cleveland Road	D4	Ring Road St Georges	C4
Cleveland Street	B3	Ring Road St Johns	B4
Corn Hill	D2	Ring Road St Marks	B3
Culwell Street	D1	Ring Road St Patricks	C1
Dale Street	A4	Ring Road St Peters	B2
Darlington Street	B3	Russell Street	A4
Dudley Road	C4	St George's Parade	C3
Dudley Street	C2	St John's Square	C4
Fold Street	B3	St Mark's Road	A3
Fryer Street	C2	St Mark's Street	A3
Garrick Street	C3	Salop Street	B3
Graiseley Street	A4	School Street	B3
Great Brickkiln Street	A4	Skinner Street	B3
Great Western Street	C1	Snow Hill	C3
Grimstone Street	D1	Stafford Street	C1
Horseley Fields	D2	Stephenson Street	A3
Hospital Street	D4	Stewart Street	B4
Lansdown Road	A1	Summer Row	B3
Lever Street	C4	Tempest Street	C3
Lichfield Street	C2	Temple Street	B3
Little's Lane	C1	Thomas Street	B4
Long Street	C2	Tower Street	C3
Lord Street	A3	Vicarage Road	D4
Mander Street	A4	Victoria Street	B3
Market Street	C3	Walsall Street	D3
Merridale Street	A4	Warwick Street	D3
Middle Cross	D3	Waterloo Road	B1
Mitre Fold	B2	Wednesfield Road	D1
Molineux Street	B1	Westbury Street	C2
New Hampton Road East	A1	Whitmore Hill	B1
North Street	B2	Whitmore Street	C2
Park Avenue	A1	Worcester Street	B4
Park Road East	B1	Wulfruna Street	C2
Park Road West	A2	Zoar Street	A4

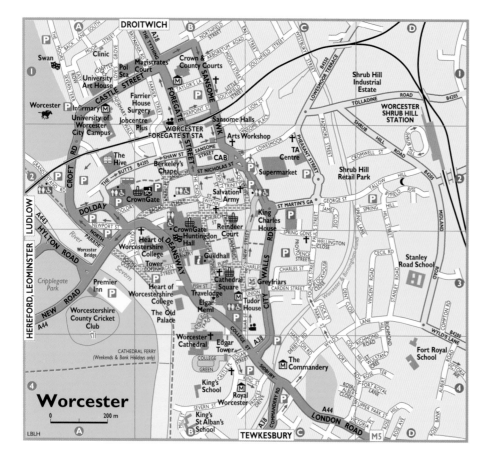

Worcester

Worcester is found on atlas page **46 G4**

Albert Road	D4	Middle Street	B
Angel Street	B2	Midland Road	D
Arboretum Road	B1	Mill Street	D
Back Lane South	A1	Moor Street	B
Blockhouse Close	C3	Newport Street	B
Britannia Road	A1	New Road	B
Broad Street	B2	New Street	C
Byfield Rise	D2	Northfield Street	B
Carden Street	C3	North Parade	B
Castle Street	A1	Padmore Street	D
Cathedral Ferry	A4	Park Street	C
Cecil Road	D3	Pheasant Street	B
Charles Street	C3	Pierpoint Street	B
Charter Place	A1	Providence Street	C
Church Street	B2	Pump Street	B
City Walls Road	C3	Quay Street	B
Cole Hill	C4	Queen Street	B
College Street	B3	Richmond Road	D
Commandery Road	C4	Rose Hill	D
Compton Road	D3	Rose Terrace	D
Copenhagen Street	B3	St Martin's Gate	C
Croft Road	A2	St Nicholas Street	B
Cromwell Street	D2	St Paul's Street	C
Deansway	B3	St Swithin Street	B
Dent Close	C3	Sansome Walk	B
Derby Road	C4	Severn Street	C
Dolday	A2	Severn Terrace	A
East Street	B1	Shaw Street	B
Edgar Street	B4	Shrub Hill Road	D
Farrier Street	B1	Sidbury	C
Fish Street	B3	Southfield Street	B
Foregate Street	B1	Spring Hill	D
Fort Royal Hill	C4	Stanley Road	D
Foundry Street	C3	Tallow Hill	D
Friar Street	C3	Taylor's Lane	B
George Street	C2	The Butts	B
Grandstand Road	A2	The Cross	B
Hamilton Road	C3	The Moors	B
High Street	B3	The Shambles	B
Hill Street	D2	The Tything	B
Hylton Road	A3	Tolladine Road	D
King Street	B4	Trinity Street	B
Little Southfield Street	B1	Union Street	C
Lock Street	C3	Upper Park Street	C
London Road	C4	Vincent Road	D
Love's Grove	A1	Wellington Close	D
Lowesmoor	C2	Westbury Street	C
Lowesmoor Terrace	C1	Wyld's Lane	D

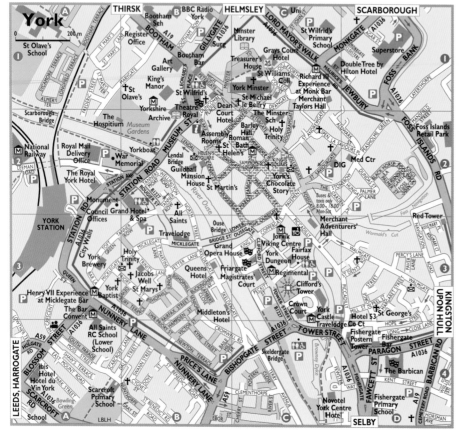

York

York is found on atlas page **98 C10**

Aldwark	C2	Lower Ousegate	C
Barbican Road	D4	Lower Priory Street	B
Bishopgate Street	B4	Low Petergate	C
Bishophill Senior	B3	Margaret Street	D
Black Horse Lane	D2	Market Street	C
Blake Street	B2	Micklegate	B
Blossom Street	A4	Minster Yard	C
Bootham	B1	Monkgate	C
Bridge Street	B3	Museum Street	B
Buckingham Street	B3	Navigation Road	D
Cemetery Road	D4	New Street	B
Church Street	C2	North Street	B
Clifford Street	C3	Nunnery Lane	A
College Street	C1	Ogleforth	C
Colliergate	C2	Palmer Lane	C
Coney Street	B2	Palmer Street	D
Coppergate	C3	Paragon Street	C
Cromwell Road	B4	Parliament Street	C
Davygate	B2	Pavement	C
Deangate	C1	Peasholme Green	D
Dove Street	B4	Percy's Lane	D
Duncombe Place	B2	Piccadilly	C
Dundas Street	D2	Price's Lane	B
Fairfax Street	B3	Priory Street	B
Fawcett Street	D4	Queen Street	A
Feasegate	C2	Rougier Street	B
Fetter Lane	B3	St Andrewgate	C
Finkle Street	C2	St Denys' Road	D
Fishergate	D4	St Leonard's Place	B
Foss Bank	D1	St Martins Lane	B
Fossgate	C2	St Maurice's Road	D
Foss Islands Road	D2	St Saviourgate	C
George Street	D3	St Saviours Place	C
Gillygate	B1	Scarcroft Road	A
Goodramgate	C2	Shambles	C
Hampden Street	B4	Skeldergate	B
High Ousegate	C3	Spen Lane	C
High Petergate	B1	Spurriergate	C
Holgate Road	A4	Station Road	A
Hope Street	D4	Stonegate	B
Hungate	D2	Swinegate	C
Jewbury	D1	The Stonebow	C
Kent Street	D4	Toft Green	A
King Street	C3	Tower Street	C
Kyme Street	B4	Trinity Lane	B
Lendal	B2	Victor Street	B
Long Close Lane	D4	Walmgate	D
Lord Mayor's Walk	C1	Wellington Road	A

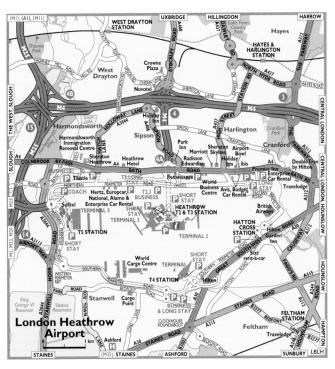

London Heathrow Airport – 17 miles west of central London, M25 junction 14 and M4 junction 4A

Satnav Location: TW6 1EW (Terminal 2), TW6 1QG (T3), TW6 3XA (T4), TW6 2GA (T5)
Information: visit *www.heathrow.com*
Parking: short-stay, long-stay and business parking is available.
Public Transport: coach, bus, rail and London Underground.
There are several 4-star and 3-star hotels within easy reach of the airport.
Car hire facilities are available.

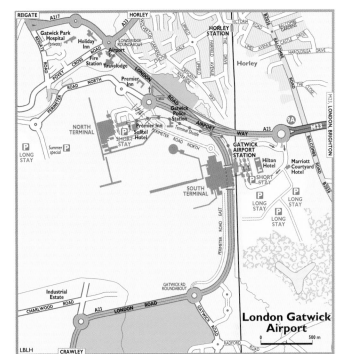

London Gatwick Airport – 29 miles south of central London, M23 junction 9A

Satnav Location: RH6 0NP (South terminal), RH6 0PJ (North terminal)
Information: visit *www.gatwickairport.com*
Parking: short and long-stay parking is available at both the North and South terminals.
Public Transport: coach, bus and rail.
There are several 4-star and 3-star hotels within easy reach of the airport.
Car hire facilities are available.

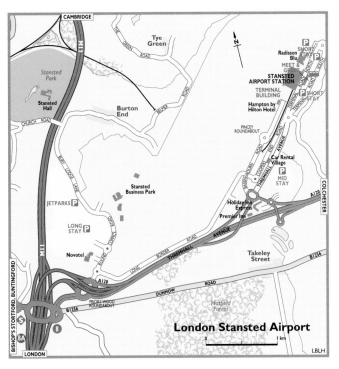

London Stansted Airport – 36 miles north-east of central London, M11 junction 8/8A

Satnav Location: CM24 1RW
Information: visit *www.stanstedairport.com*
Parking: short, mid and long-stay open-air parking is available.
Public Transport: coach, bus and direct rail link to London (Liverpool Street Station) on the Stansted Express.
There are several hotels within easy reach of the airport.
Car hire facilities are available.

London Luton Airport – 34 miles north of central London

Satnav Location: LU2 9QT
Information: visit *www.london-luton.co.uk*
Parking: short-term, mid-term and long-stay parking is available.
Public Transport: coach, bus and rail.
There are several 3-star hotels within easy reach of the airport.
Car hire facilities are available.

London City Airport – 8 miles east of central London

Satnav Location: E16 2PX
Information: visit www.londoncityairport.com
Parking: short and long-stay open-air parking is available.
Public Transport: easy access to the rail network, Docklands Light Railway and the London Underground.
There are 5-star, 4-star and 3-star hotels within easy reach of the airport.
Car hire facilities are available.

Birmingham Airport – 10 miles east of Birmingham, M42 junction 6

Satnav Location: B26 3QJ
Information: visit www.birminghamairport.co.uk
Parking: short and long-stay parking is available.
Public Transport: Monorail service (Air-Rail Link) operates to and from Birmingham International Railway Station.
There are several 4-star and 3-star hotels within easy reach of the airport.
Car hire facilities are available.

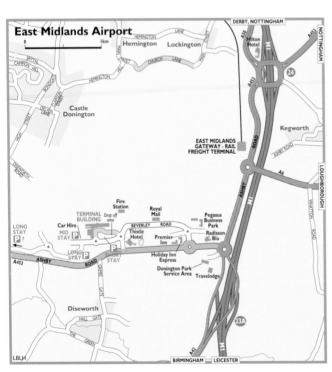

East Midlands Airport – 14 miles south-west
of Nottingham, M1 junction 23A/24

Satnav Location: DE74 2SA
Information: visit www.eastmidlandsairport.com
Parking: short-term, mid-term and long-stay parking is available.
Public Transport: bus and coach services to major towns and cities in the East Midlands.
There are several 4-star and 3-star hotels within easy reach of the airport.
Car hire facilities are available.

Manchester Airport – 10 miles south of Manchester,
M56 junction 5

Satnav Location: M90 1QX
Information visit www.manchesterairport.co.uk
Parking: short-term, mid-term and long-stay parking is available.
Public Transport: coach, bus, rail and tram (Metrolink).
There are several 4-star and 3-star hotels within easy reach of the airport.
Car hire facilities are available.

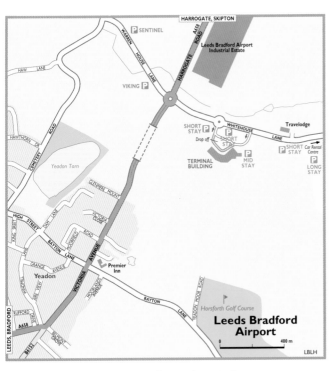

Leeds Bradford Airport – 8 miles north-east of Bradford and 8 miles north-west of Leeds

Satnav Location: LS19 7TU
Information: visit *www.leedsbradfordairport.co.uk*
Parking: short, mid-term and long-stay parking is available.
Public Transport: regular bus services to Bradford, Leeds and Harrogate.
There are several 4-star and 3-star hotels within easy reach of the airport.
Car hire facilities are available.

Aberdeen Airport – 7 miles north-west of Aberdeen

Satnav Location: AB21 7DU
Information: visit *www.aberdeenairport.com*
Parking: short and long-stay parking is available.
Public Transport: regular bus services to central Aberdeen.
There are several 4-star and 3-star hotels within easy reach of the airport.
Car hire facilities are available.

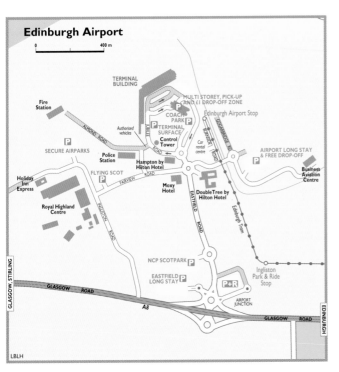

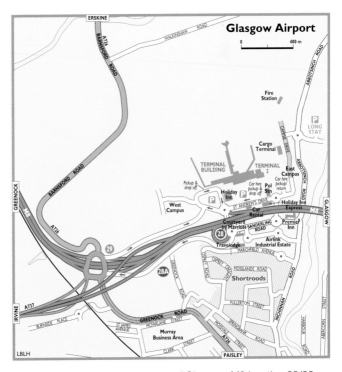

Edinburgh Airport – 9 miles west of Edinburgh

Satnav Location: EH12 9DN
Information: visit *www.edinburghairport.com*
Parking: short and long-stay parking is available.
Public Transport: regular bus services to Scottish cities including central Edinburgh, Glasgow, Dundee and Fife and a tram service to central Edinburgh.
There are several 4-star and 3-star hotels within easy reach of the airport.
Car hire and valet parking facilities are available.

Glasgow Airport – 10 miles west of Glasgow, M8 junction 28/29

Satnav Location: PA3 2SW
Information: visit *www.glasgowairport.com*
Parking: short and long-stay parking is available.
Public Transport: regular direct bus services to central Glasgow.
There are several 3-star hotels within easy reach of the airport.
Car hire facilities are available.

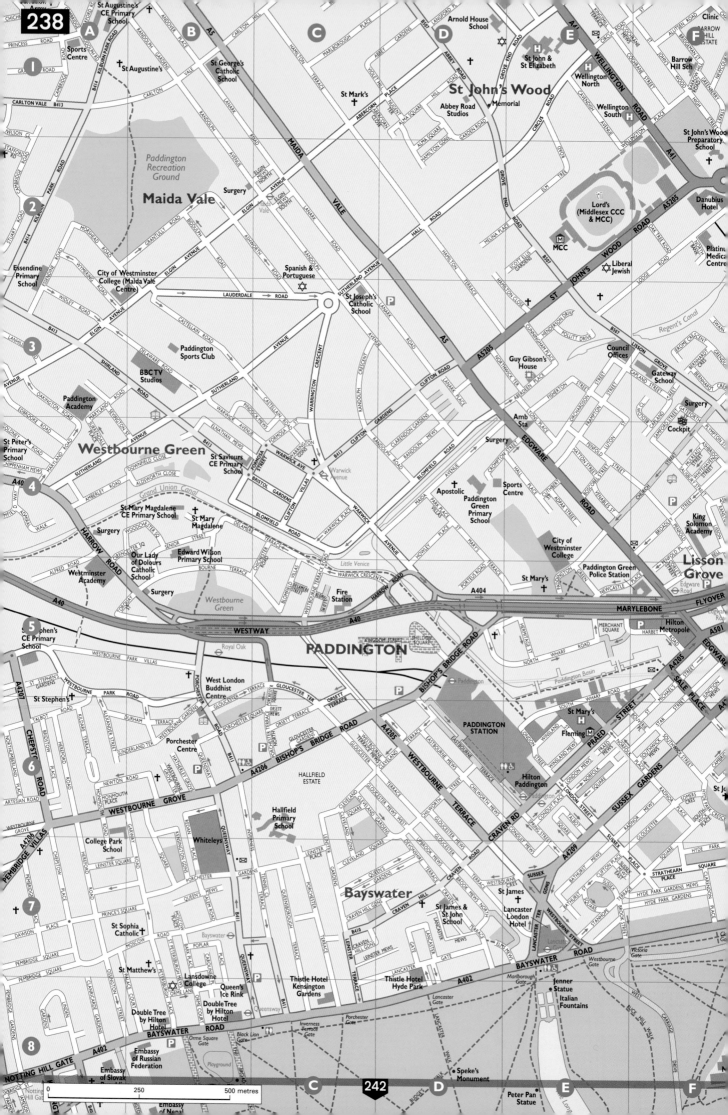

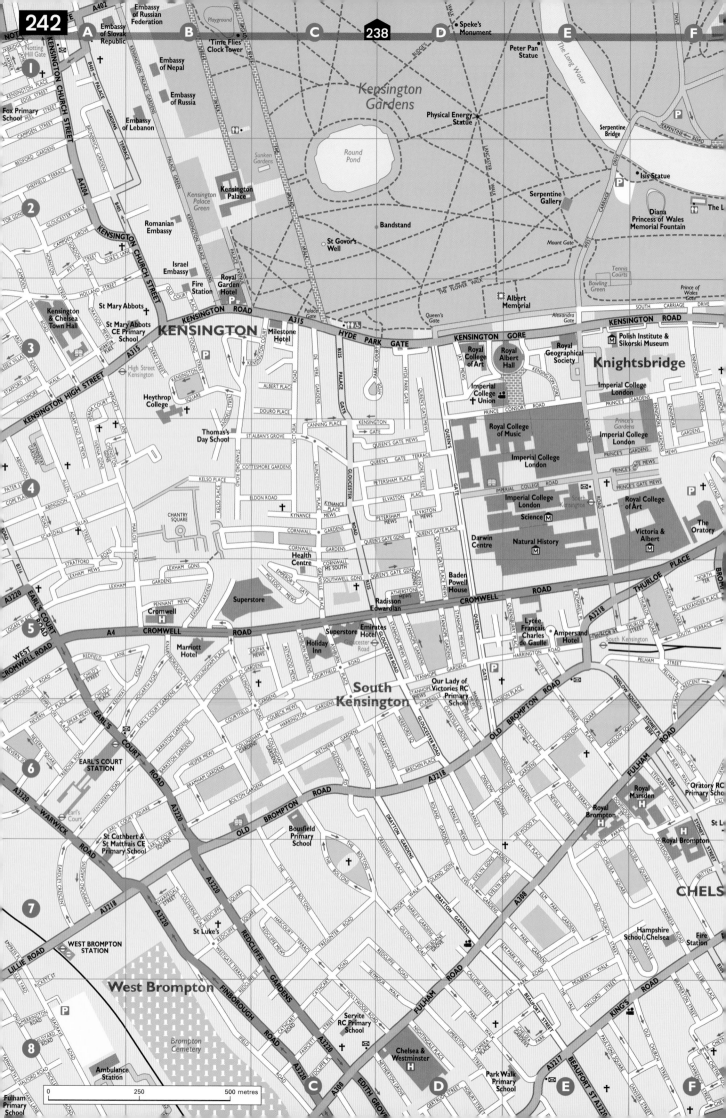

This index lists street and station names, and top places of tourist interest shown in red. Names are listed in alphabetical order and written in full, but may be abbreviated on the map. Each entry is followed by its Postcode District and then the page number and grid reference to the square in which the name is found. Names are asterisked (*) in the index where there is insufficient space to show them on the map.

A

Abbey Gardens NW8................238 C1
Abbey Orchard Street SW1P......244 B4
Abbey Road NW8....................238 D1
Abbey Street SE1...................246 B7
Abchurch Lane EC4N...............241 L7
Abercorn Close NW8................238 C1
Abercorn Place NW8................238 C1
Aberdeen Place NW8...............238 E3
Aberdour Street SE1...............245 M5
Abingdon Road W8..................242 A4
Abingdon Street SW1P.............244 C3
Abingdon Villas W8.................242 A4
Ackroyd Drive E3....................247 L1
Acorn Walk SE16....................247 K5
Acton Street WC1X..................240 E2
Adam and Eve Mews W8...........242 A4
Adam's Row W1K.....................239 K8
Adam Street WC2N..................240 D8
Addington Street SE1...............240 E3
Addle Hill EC4V......................241 H7
Adelina Grove E1...................246 F1
Adeline Place WC1B.................240 B5
Adler Street E1.......................246 D2
Admiral Place SE16..................247 K5
Admiral Walk W9....................238 A4
Adpar Street W2.....................238 E4
Agar Street WC2N...................240 D8
Agdon Street EC1V..................241 H3
Agnes Street E14....................247 L2
Ainsty Street SE16..................247 G6
Air Street W1B.......................240 A8
Alaska Street SE1...................244 F2
Albany Road SE5....................245 L8
Albany Street NW1..................239 L1
Albemarle Street W1S..............239 L8
Albemarle Way EC1V...............241 H4
Alberta Street SE17.................245 H6
Albert Bridge SW3..................243 G8
Albert Embankment SE1...........244 D7
Albert Gardens E1..................247 H3
Albert Gate SW1X...................243 H2
Albert Place W8.....................242 C3
Albion Gate W2......................239 G7
Albion Place EC1M..................241 H4
Albion Street SE16..................247 H4
Albion Street W2....................239 G7
Aldenham Street NW1...............240 A1
Aldermanbury EC2V.................241 K6
Alderney Mews SE1.................245 K4
Alderney Street SW1V..............243 L6
Aldersgate Street EC1A............241 J4
Aldford Street W1K..................239 J8
Aldgate ↔ EC3N.....................246 B3
Aldgate ↔ EC3N.....................246 B3
Aldgate East ↔ E1..................246 C2
Aldgate High Street EC3N.........246 B3
Aldgate Square EC3N...............246 B3
Aldsworth Close W9.................238 B4
Aldwych WC2E.......................240 E7
Alexander Place SW7...............242 F5
Alexander Street W2................238 A6
Alexandra Gate SW7................242 E3
Alfred Mews WC1E..................240 B4
Alfred Place WC1E..................240 B4
Alfred Road W2......................238 A5
Alice Street SE1.....................245 M4
Alie Street E1........................246 C3
Allen Street W8......................242 A4
Allhallows Lane EC4R..............241 L8
Allington Street SW1E.............243 M4
Allitsen Road NW8..................238 F1
Allsop Place NW1...................239 H4
Alma Square NW8...................238 D1
Alpha Place SW3....................243 G8
Alsace Road SE17...................245 M7
Alscot Road * SE1..................246 C8
Alvey Street SE17...................245 M6
Ambergate Street SE17............245 H7
Amberley Road W9..................238 A4
Ambrosden Avenue SW1P.........244 A4
Amelia Street SE17.................245 J6
America Square EC3N...............246 B3
America Street SE1..................245 J2
Ampton Place WC1X................240 E2
Amwell Street EC1R.................240 F2
Anchorage Point E14................247 M6
Andover Place NW6.................238 B1
Angel ↔ N1..........................241 G1
Angela Hooper Place * SW1E....244 A4
Angel Junction N1...................241 G1
Angel Lane EC4R....................241 L8
Angel Street EC1A...................241 J6
Ann Moss Way SE16.................246 F8
Ann's Close SW1X...................243 J3
Ansdell Street W8...................242 B4
Antill Terrace E1....................247 H2
Antizan Street E1...................246 B2
Apple Tree Yard SW1Y.............240 A8
Appold Street EC2A.................241 M4
Apsley Gate W1J....................243 J2
Apsley House & Wellington
  Museum SW1A....................243 K2
Aquinas Street SE1.................245 G1
Arbour Square E1...................247 H2
Archangel Street SE16.............247 J7
Archer Street W1B..................240 B7
Arch Street SE1.....................245 J4
Arden Estate N1.....................241 M1
Argyle Square WC1H...............240 D2
Argyle Street WC1H................240 D2
Argyll Road W8.....................242 A3
Argyll Street W1F...................239 M6
Arlington Street SW1A.............243 M1
Arlington Way EC1R................241 G2
Arne Street WC2H..................240 D6
Arneway Street SW1P..............244 B5
Arnhem Place E14..................247 M8
Arnold Estate SE1..................246 C7
Arnside Street SE17................245 K8
Artesian Road W11.................238 A6
Arthur Street EC4V..................241 L7
Artichoke Hill E1W.................246 E4
Artillery Lane E1....................246 A1
Artillery Row SW1P.................244 B4
Arundel Street WC2R...............240 F7

Ashbridge Street NW8.............238 F4
Ashburn Gardens SW7.............242 C5
Ashburn Place SW7.................242 C5
Ashby Street EC1V..................241 H2
Asher Way E1W......................246 D4
Ashfield Street E1...................246 E2
Ashford Street N1...................241 M2
Ashley Place SW1P.................243 M4
Ashmill Street NW1.................238 F4
Ashmole Street SW8................244 F8
Ashworth Road W9.................238 B2
Assam Street E1.....................246 C2
Assembly Passage E1..............247 G1
Astell Street SW3...................243 G6
Aston Street E14.....................247 K1
Astwood Mews SW7................242 C5
Atherstone Mews SW7.............242 D5
Atterbury Street SW1P.............244 C6
Attneave Street WC1X.............240 F3
Augustus Street NW1..............239 L1
Aulton Place SE11...................245 G7
Austin Friars EC2N..................241 L6
Australia Gate SW1A................243 M3
Austral Street SE11.................245 H5
Ave Maria Lane EC1A...............241 H6
Aveline Street SE11.................244 F7
Avenue Dock Hill SE16.............247 J6
Avery Farm Row SW1W............243 K6
Avery Row W1K......................239 L7
Aybrook Street W1U.................239 J5
Aylesbury Road SE17...............245 L7
Aylesbury Street EC1R.............241 H4
Aylesford Street SW1V.............244 B7
Aylward Street E1...................247 G2
Ayres Street SE1.....................245 K2

B

Babmaes Street SW1Y..............240 B8
Bache's Street N1....................241 L2
Back Church Lane E1...............246 D3
Back Hill EC1R.......................241 G4
Bacon Grove SE1....................246 B8
Bainbridge Street WC1A..........240 C6
Bakers Mews W1U...................239 J6
Baker's Row EC1R...................241 G4
Baker Street NW1...................239 H4
Baker Street W1U....................239 J5
Baker Street ↔ NW1...............239 H4
Balcombe Street NW1..............239 G3
Balderton Street W1K..............239 J7
Baldwin's Gardens EC1N..........240 F5
Baldwin Street EC1V................241 L2
Bale Road E1.........................247 J1
Balfe Street N1.......................240 D1
Balfour Mews W1K..................239 K8
Balfour Place W1K..................239 J8
Balfour Street SE17.................245 K5
Baltic Street East EC1Y............241 J3
Baltic Street West EC1Y...........241 J4
Balvaird Place SW1V...............244 C7
Bank ↔ EC2R.......................241 L6
Bank End SE1........................245 K1
Bankside SE1.........................241 J8
Banner Street EC1Y.................241 K3
Banqueting House SW1A...........244 C2
Banyard Road SE16.................246 E8
Barbican Estate EC2Y..............241 J5
Barbican ↔ EC1A...................241 J5
Barge House Street SE1............245 G1
Bark Place W2.......................238 B7
Barkston Gardens SW5............242 B6
Barley Corn Way E14...............247 L4
Barlow/Congreve Estate SE17...245 M5
Barlow Place W1J...................239 L7
Barlow Street SE17..................245 L5
Barnardo Street E1..................247 H3
Barnby Street NW1.................240 A1
Barnes Street E14...................247 J2
Barnham Street SE1.................246 A6
Baron's Place SE1...................245 G3
Baron Street N1......................241 G1
Barrett Street W1U..................239 K6
Barrow Hill Estate NW8............238 F1
Barrow Hill Road NW8.............238 F1
Barter Street WC1A.................240 D5
Bartholomew Close EC1A.........241 J5
Bartholomew Lane EC2R...........241 L6
Bartholomew Street SE1...........245 L5
Bartlett Court EC4A.................241 G6
Barton Street SW1P.................244 C4
Basil Street SW3....................243 H4
Basin Approach E14.................247 K3
Basinghall Avenue EC2V...........241 K5
Basinghall Street EC2V.............241 K5
Bastwick Street EC1V...............241 J3
Bateman's Buildings W1D.........240 B6
Bateman Street W1D................240 B6
Bath Street EC1V....................241 K2
Bath Terrace SE1....................245 J4
Bathurst Mews W2..................238 E7
Bathurst Street W2..................238 E7
Battle Bridge Lane SE1.............246 M1
Batty Street E1.......................246 D2
Bayley Street WC1B.................240 B5
Baylis Road SE1.....................244 F3
Bayswater ↔ W2...................238 B7
Bayswater Road W2.................238 E7
Baythorne Street E3.................247 L1
Beaconsfield Road SE17...........245 M7
Beak Street W1F.....................240 A7
Bear Gardens SE1...................241 J8
Bear Lane SE1.......................245 H1
Beauchamp Place SW3............243 G4
Beaufort Gardens SW3............243 G4
Beaufort Street SW3................242 E8
Beaumont Place W1T...............240 A3
Beaumont Street W1G..............239 K4
Beccles Street E14...................247 M3
Beckett Street SE1...................245 L3
Beckway Street SE17...............245 M6
Bedale Street SE1...................245 L1
Bedford Avenue WC1B.............240 C5
Bedfordbury WC2N.................240 C7
Bedford Gardens W8...............242 A2
Bedford Place WC1N................240 D4

Bedford Row WC1R..................240 E4
Bedford Square WC1B..............240 B5
Bedford Street WC2E...............240 D7
Bedford Way WC1H..................240 C3
Bedlow Close NW8..................238 F3
Beech Street EC2Y...................241 J4
Beeston Place SW1W...............243 L4
Belgrave Mews North * SW1X....243 J3
Belgrave Mews South * SW1X....243 K4
Belgrave Place SW1X...............243 J4
Belgrave Road SW1V...............243 L5
Belgrave Road SW1V...............244 A6
Belgrave Square SW1X.............243 J3
Belgrave Street WC1H..............247 J2
Belgrove Street WC1H..............240 D2
Bell Lane E1..........................246 B1
Bell Street NW1......................238 F4
Bell Yard WC2A......................240 F6
Belvedere Road SE1................244 E2
Benjamin Street EC1M.............241 H4
Ben Jonson Road E1................247 J1
Bennett Street SW1A...............243 M1
Ben Smith Way SE16................246 D7
Benson Quay E1W...................246 F4
Bentinck Mews W1U................239 K6
Bentinck Street W1U................239 K6
Bere Street E1W.....................247 H3
Bergen Square SE16................247 K8
Berkeley Mews W1H................239 H6
Berkeley Square W1J...............239 L8
Berkeley Street W1J.................239 L8
Bermondsey ↔ ↔ SE16..........246 E7
Bermondsey Spa SE16.............246 C8
Bermondsey Square SE1...........246 A8
Bermondsey Street SE1............246 A6
Bermondsey Wall East SE16......246 E7
Bermondsey Wall West SE16.....246 C6
Bernard Street WC1N...............240 D4
Berners Mews W1T..................240 A5
Berners Place W1F...................240 A6
Berners Street W1T..................240 A5
Bernhardt Crescent NW8..........238 F3
Berryfield Road SE17................245 J6
Berry Street EC1V...................241 H3
Berwick Street W1F.................240 A6
Bessborough Gardens SW1V......244 C6
Bessborough Street SW1V.........244 B6
Betterton Street WC2H.............240 D6
Bevenden Street N1.................241 L2
Bevin Close SE16....................247 J5
Bevington Street SE16.............246 D7
Bevin Way WC1X....................240 F1
Bevis Marks EC3A...................246 A2
Bewley Street E1....................246 F3
Bickenhall Street W1U..............239 H4
Bidborough Street WC1H..........240 C2
Biddulph Road W9...................238 B2
Big Ben (Elizabeth Tower) SW1A..244 D3
Bigland Street E1....................246 E3
Billiter Square EC3M................246 A3
Billiter Street EC3M.................246 A3
Bina Gardens SW5..................242 C6
Bingham Place W1U.................239 J4
Binney Street W1K..................239 K7
Birchfield Street E14................247 M3
Birchin Lane EC3V...................241 L7
Birdcage Walk SW1H...............244 A3
Birde Lane EC4Y.....................241 H6
Bird Street W1C......................239 K6
Birkenhead Street N1...............240 D1
Bishop's Bridge Road W2.........238 C6
Bishopsgate EC2M...................246 A2
Bishops Square E1..................246 B1
Bishop's Terrace SE11.............245 G5
Bittern Street SE1....................245 J3
Blackall Street EC2A................241 M3
Blackburne's Mews W1K..........239 J7
Blackfriars ↔ EC4V................241 H7
Blackfriars Bridge SE1.............241 H8
Blacklands Terrace SW3...........243 H6
Black Friars Lane EC4V............241 H7
Blackfriars Road SE1...............245 H3
Blackhorse Court SE1..............245 L4
Black Lion Gate W2.................238 B8
Black Prince Road SE11............244 E6
Blackwood Street SE17............245 K6
Blandford Street W1U..............239 H5
Blenheim Street W1S...............239 L7
Bletchley Street N1..................241 K1
Blomfield Mews W2.................238 C5
Blomfield Road W9..................238 C4
Blomfield Street EC2M.............241 M5
Blomfield Villas W2..................238 C5
Bloomfield Terrace SW1W.........243 J6
Bloomsbury Square WC1A.........240 D5
Bloomsbury Street WC1B..........240 C5
Bloomsbury Way WC1A............240 C5
Blount Street E14....................247 K2
Blue Ball Yard SW1A...............243 M1
Bohn Road E1........................247 J1
Bolsover Street W1W...............239 L4
Bolton Gardens SW5................242 B6
Bolton Street W1J...................243 L1
Bond Street ↔ W1C................239 K6
Bonding Yard Walk SE16...........247 J7
Bonhill Street EC2A.................241 L4
Bonnington Square SW8...........244 E8
Boot Street N1.......................241 M2
Borough ↔ SE1.....................245 K3
Borough High Street SE1...........245 K3
Borough Road SE1..................245 H3
Boscobel Place SW1W.............243 K5
Boscobel Street NW8...............238 E4
Boss Street SE1......................246 B6
Boston Place NW1...................239 G3
Botolph Lane EC3R..................241 M7
Boundary Lane SE17................245 K8
Boundary Row SE1..................245 H2
Bourdon Street W1K................239 L7
Bourne Estate EC1N................240 F4
Bourne Street SW1W...............243 J6
Bourne Terrace W2..................238 B5
Bouverie Place W2..................238 F6
Bouverie Street EC4Y...............241 G6
Bowland Yard * SW1X.............243 J3
Bow Lane EC4M.....................241 K6

Bowling Green Lane EC1R.........241 G3
Bowling Green Place SE1..........245 L2
Bowling Green Street SE11........244 F8
Bowling Green Walk N1...........241 M2
Bowsell Street WC1N...............240 D4
Boyd Street E1.......................246 D7
Boyfield Street SE1..................245 H3
Boyle Street W1S...................239 M7
Boyson Road SE17..................245 K8
Brackley Street EC1Y...............241 J4
Bradenham Close SE17.............245 K8
Brad Street SE1......................245 G2
Braganza Street SE17...............245 H7
Braham Street E1....................246 C3
Bramerton Street SW3.............242 F7
Bramham Gardens SW5............242 B6
Branch Road E14.....................247 J3
Brandon Estate SE17...............245 H8
Brandon Street SE17................245 K6
Brangton Road SE11................244 F7
Bray Crescent SE16.................247 H6
Bray Place SW3......................243 H6
Bread Street EC4M..................241 K7
Bream's Buildings EC4A...........240 F6
Brechin Place SW7..................242 D6
Breezer's Hill E1W...................246 D4
Brendon Street W1H................239 G5
Bressenden Place SW1W..........243 L4
Brettell Street SE17.................245 L7
Brewers Green SW1H...............244 A3
Brewer Street W1F..................240 A7
Brewhouse Lane E1W..............246 E4
Brewhouse Walk SE16.............247 J5
Brick Court WC2R....................240 F7
Brick Lane E1........................246 C1
Bridewell Place EC4V...............241 H7
Bridgeman Street NW8.............238 F1
Bridge Place SW1V..................243 L5
Bridgeport Place E1W..............246 D4
Bridge Street SW1A................244 D3
Bridgewater Street EC2Y...........241 J4
Bridgeway Street NW1.............240 A1
Bridle Lane W1F.....................240 A7
Bridstow Place W2..................238 A6
Brightlingsea Place E14............247 L4
Brill Place NW1......................240 C1
Briset Street EC1M..................241 H4
Bristol Gardens W9..................238 B4
Britannia Street WC1X.............240 E2
Britannia Walk N1...................241 L2
Britannia Way N1....................241 K1
Britten Street SW3..................242 F7
Britton Street EC1M.................241 H4
Broadbent Street W1U..............239 H4
Broadgate Circle EC2M............241 M5
Broadley Street NW8...............238 F4
Broadley Terrace NW1.............238 F3
Broadstone Place W1U.............239 J5
Broad Walk NW1....................239 K1
Broad Walk W2......................239 H7
Broadwall SE1........................245 G1
Broadway SW1H.....................244 A3
Broadwick Street W1F..............240 A7
Brockham Street SE1...............245 K4
Brodlove Lane E1W.................247 H3
Bromley Street E1...................247 J2
Brompton Place SW3...............243 G4
Brompton Road SW3................243 G4
Brompton Road SW3................242 F5
Brompton Square SW3.............242 F4
Bronti Close SE17...................245 K7
Brook Drive SE11....................245 G5
Brooke Street EC1N.................240 F5
Brook Gate W2.......................239 H8
Brook Mews North W2..............238 D7
Brook's Mews W1K..................239 K7
Brook Street W1K...................239 K7
Brook Street W2.....................238 E7
Brown Heart Gardens W1K........239 K7
Browning Mews W1G...............239 K5
Browning Street SE17...............245 K6
Brownlow Mews WC1N............240 E3
Brownlow Street WC1V............240 E5
Brown Street W1H...................239 G6
Brunel Road SE16...................247 G6
Brune Street E1......................246 B1
Brunswick Close SE1...............245 M4
Brunswick Gardens W8............242 A6
Brunswick Place N1.................241 L2
Brunswick Quay SE16..............247 J8
Brunswick Square WC1N..........240 D3
Brunswick Street WC1N...........240 D3
Brunton Place E14...................247 K3
Brushfield Street E1.................246 B1
Bruton Lane W1J....................239 L8
Bruton Place W1J....................239 L7
Bruton Street W1J...................239 L8
Bryan Road SE16....................247 K6
Bryanston Mews West W1H.......239 G5
Bryanston Mews East W1H........239 H5
Bryanston Place W1H...............239 G5
Bryanston Square W1H.............239 H5
Bryanston Street W1C..............239 H6
Buck Hill Walk W2..................238 E8
Buckingham Gate SW1E...........243 L3
Buckingham Mews SW1E..........243 M3
Buckingham Palace SW1A.........243 L3
Buckingham Palace Road SW1W..243 L5
Buckingham Place SW1E..........243 M4
Buckland Street N1..................241 L1
Buckle Street E1.....................246 C2
Bucknall Street WC2H..............240 C6
Buckters Rents SE16................247 J5
Budge's Walk W2....................242 D2
Bulleid Way SW1V..................243 L6
Bulstrode Street W1U..............239 K5
Bunhill Row EC1Y...................241 L3
Burdett Estate E14..................247 M1
Burdett Road E14...................247 L2
Burdett Street SE1..................244 F3
Burgess Street E14..................247 M1
Burge Street SE1....................245 L4
Burlington Arcade W1J.............239 M8
Burlington Gardens W1S...........239 M8
Burnhouse Place SW1W...........243 J6
Burnsall Street SW3................243 G7

Burnside Close SE16................247 J
Burrell Street SE1...................245 H
Burslem Street E1...................246 D
Burton Grove SE17..................245 L
Burton Street WC1H................240 C
Burwood Place W2..................239 G
Bury Close SE16....................247 J
Bury Court EC3A.....................246 A
Bury Street EC3A....................246 A
Bury Street SW1Y...................244 A
Bury Walk SW3......................242 F
Bushell Street E1W.................246 D
Bush Lane EC4V......................241 L
Butcher Row E1......................247 J
Bute Street SW7.....................242 E
Butler Place SW1H..................244 B
Butler's Wharf SE1..................246 C
Buttesland Street N1...............241 L
Byefield Close SE16.................247 K
Bylands Close SE16.................247 J
Byng Place WC1E...................240 B
Byng Street E14.....................247 M
Byward Street EC3R.................246 A
Bywater Place SE16.................247 K
Bywater Street SW3................243 G

C

Cabbell Street NW1.................238 F
Cable Street E1.......................246 F
Cadiz Street SE17...................245 K
Cadogan Gardens SW3.............243 G
Cadogan Gate SW1X...............243 J
Cadogan Lane SW1X...............243 J
Cadogan Place SW1X..............243 J
Cadogan Square SW1X............243 H
Cadogan Street SW3................243 G
Caledonian Road N1................240 D
Caledonia Street N1................240 D
Cale Street SW3.....................242 F
Callow Street SW3..................242 D
Calshot Street N1....................240 E
Calthorpe Street WC1X............240 E
Cambridge Circus WC2H..........240 C
Cambridge Gardens NW6.........238 A
Cambridge Gate NW1..............239 L
Cambridge Road NW6..............238 A
Cambridge Square W2.............238 F
Cambridge Street SW1V...........243 L
Cambridge Terrace NW1...........239 L
Cambridge Terrace Mews NW1..239 L
Camdenhurst Street E14...........247 K
Camera Square SW10..............242 D
Camomile Street EC3A.............246 A
Campden Grove W8.................242 A
Campden Hill Road W8.............242 A
Campden Street W8.................242 A
Camperdown Street E1.............246 C
Canada Estate SE16.................247 G
Canada Gate SW1A.................243 M
Canada Street SE16.................247 J
Canada Water ↔ ↔ SE16........247 H
Canada Wharf SE16.................247 K
Canal Street SE5.....................245 L
Canary Riverside E14...............247 L
Candle Street E1.....................247 K
Canning Place W8...................242 C
Cannon Drive E14...................247 M
Cannon Street ↔ EC4N...........241 K
Cannon Street EC4R.................241 K
Cannon Street ↔ EC4R...........241 L
Cannon Street Road E1.............246 E
Cannon Beck Road SE16...........247 G
Canon Row SW1A...................244 D
Canton Street E14...................247 M
Capeners Close * SW1X...........243 J
Capland Street NW8................238 E
Capper Street WC1E................240 A
Capstan Way SE16..................247 K
Carbis Road E14.....................247 L
Carburton Street W1W.............239 L
Cardigan Street SE11...............244 F
Cardington Street NW1............240 A
Carey Street WC2A..................240 F
Carlisle Avenue EC3N..............246 B
Carlisle Lane SE1...................244 F
Carlisle Place SW1P................243 M
Carlisle Street W1D.................240 B
Carlos Place W1K...................239 K
Carlton Gardens SW1Y............244 B
Carlton Hill NW6....................238 B
Carlton House Terrace SW1Y....244 B
Carlton Street W1J..................243 L
Carlton Vale NW6...................238 A
Carlton Vale NW6...................238 A
Carlyle Square SW3.................242 F
Carmelite Street EC4Y.............241 G
Carnaby Street W1F.................239 M
Caroline Place W2...................238 B
Caroline Street E1...................247 H
Caroline Terrace SW1W............243 J
Carpenter Street W1K..............239 K
Carrington Street W1J..............243 K
Carr Street E14......................247 J
Carteret Street SW1H...............244 B
Carter Lane EC4V....................241 H
Carter Place SE17...................245 K
Carter Street SE17...................245 J
Carthusian Street EC1M...........241 J
Carting Lane WC2R.................240 D
Cartwright Gardens WC1H........240 C
Cartwright Street E1................246 C
Casey Close NW8...................238 E
Casson Street E1....................246 C
Castellain Road W9.................238 B
Castlebrook Close SE11............245 G
Castle Lane SW1E...................243 M
Catesby Street SE17................245 L
Cathay Street SE16..................246 F
Cathcart Road SW10................242 C
Cathedral Walk SW1E..............243 M
Catherine Place SW1E.............243 M
Catherine Street WC2E............240 E
Cato Street W1H.....................239 G
Causton Street SW1P...............244 C

Cavell Street E1 ... 246 F1
Cavendish Avenue NW8 ... 238 E1
Cavendish Place W1G ... 239 L6
Cavendish Square W1G ... 239 L6
Cavendish Street N1 ... 241 L1
Caversham Street SW3 ... 243 G8
Caxton Street SW1H ... 244 B4
Cayton Street EC1V ... 241 K2
Centaur Street SE1 ... 244 F4
Central Street EC1V ... 241 J2
Chadwell Street EC1R ... 241 G1
Chadwick Street SW1P ... 244 B4
Chagford Street NW1 ... 239 H4
Chalton Street NW1 ... 240 B1
Chambers Street SE16 ... 246 D7
Chamber Street E1 ... 246 C3
Chambers Wharf SE16 ... 246 D6
Chancel Street SE1 ... 245 H1
Chancery Lane WC2A ... 240 F5
Chancery Lane ⊖ WC1V ... 240 F5
Chandos Place WC2N ... 240 C8
Chandos Street W1G ... 239 L5
Chantry Square W8 ... 242 B4
Chapel Market N1 ... 240 F1
Chapel Street NW1 ... 238 F5
Chapel Street SW1X ... 243 K3
Chaplin Close SE1 ... 245 G3
Chapman Street E1 ... 246 E3
Chapter Road SE17 ... 245 H7
Chapter Street SW1P ... 244 B6
Chargrove Close SE16 ... 247 H6
Charing Cross ⇄ ⊖ WC2N ... 244 D1
Charing Cross Road WC2H ... 240 B6
Charing Cross Road WC2N ... 240 C7
Charlbert Street NW8 ... 238 F1
Charles II Street SW1Y ... 240 B8
Charles Square N1 ... 241 M2
Charles Street W1J ... 243 K1
Charleston Street SE17 ... 245 K6
Charlotte Road EC2A ... 241 M3
Charlotte Street W1T ... 240 A4
Charlwood Place SW1V ... 244 A6
Charlwood Street SW1V ... 243 M7
Charlwood Street SW1V ... 244 A6
Charrington Street NW1 ... 240 B1
Charterhouse Square EC1M ... 241 H4
Charterhouse Street EC1M ... 241 G5
Chart Street N1 ... 241 L2
Chaseley Street E14 ... 247 J2
Chatham Street SE17 ... 245 L5
Cheapside EC2V ... 241 K6
Chelsea Bridge SW1W ... 243 K8
Chelsea Bridge Road SW1W ... 243 J7
Chelsea Embankment SW3 ... 243 G8
Chelsea Manor Gardens SW3 ... 242 F7
Chelsea Manor Street SW3 ... 243 G7
Chelsea Park Gardens SW3 ... 242 E8
Chelsea Physic Garden SW3 ... 243 H8
Chelsea Square SW3 ... 242 E7
Cheltenham Terrace SW3 ... 243 H6
Chenies Mews WC1E ... 240 B4
Chenies Street WC1E ... 240 B4
Cheniston Gardens W8 ... 242 A4
Chepstow Place W2 ... 238 A7
Chepstow Road W2 ... 238 A6
Chequer Street EC1Y ... 241 K3
Cherbury Street N1 ... 241 L1
Cherry Garden Street SE16 ... 246 E7
Chesham Close SW1X ... 243 J4
Chesham Place SW1X ... 243 J4
Chesham Street SW1X ... 243 J4
Chester Close SW1X ... 243 K3
Chester Close North NW1 ... 239 L2
Chester Close South NW1 ... 239 L2
Chesterfield Gardens W1J ... 243 K1
Chesterfield Hill W1J ... 239 K8
Chesterfield Street W1J ... 243 K1
Chester Gate NW1 ... 239 L2
Chester Mews SW1X ... 243 K3
Chester Place NW1 ... 239 L1
Chester Road NW1 ... 239 K2
Chester Row SW1W ... 243 K5
Chester Square SW1W ... 243 K5
Chester Square Mews SW1W ... 243 K4
Chester Street SW1X ... 243 K4
Chester Terrace NW1 ... 239 L2
Chester Way SE11 ... 245 G6
Cheval Place SW7 ... 243 G4
Cheval Street E14 ... 247 M7
Cheyne Gardens SW3 ... 243 G8
Cheyne Row SW3 ... 242 F8
Cheyne Walk SW3 ... 242 F8
Chicheley Street SE1 ... 244 E2
Chichester Road NW6 ... 238 A1
Chichester Road W2 ... 238 C6
Chichester Street SW1V ... 244 A7
Chicksand Street E1 ... 246 C1
Chigwell Hill E1W ... 246 E4
Child's Place SW5 ... 242 A5
Child's Street SW5 ... 242 A5
Chiltern Street W1U ... 239 J4
Chilworth Mews W2 ... 238 D6
Chilworth Street W2 ... 238 D6
China Hall Mews SE16 ... 247 H6
Chinatown W1D ... 240 B7
Chippenham Mews W9 ... 238 A4
Chiswell Street EC1Y ... 241 K4
Chitty Street W1T ... 240 A4
Christchurch Street SW3 ... 243 G8
Christian Street E1 ... 246 D3
Christina Street EC2A ... 241 M3
Christopher Close SE16 ... 247 H6
Christopher Street EC2A ... 241 L4
Chudleigh Street E1 ... 247 H2
Chumleigh Street SE5 ... 245 M8
Churchill Gardens Road SW1V ... 243 L7
Churchill War Rooms SW1A ... 244 C3
Church Street NW8 ... 238 F4
Church Way NW1 ... 240 B2
Churchyard Row SE1 ... 245 H5
Churton Place SW1V ... 244 A6
Churton Street SW1V ... 244 A6
Circus Road NW8 ... 238 E1
Cirencester Square W2 ... 238 A5
City Garden Row N1 ... 241 J1
City Road EC1V ... 241 J1
City Road EC1Y ... 241 L3
City Thameslink ⇄ EC4M ... 241 H6
Clabon Mews SW1X ... 243 H5
Clack Street SE16 ... 247 G7
Clanricarde Gardens W2 ... 238 A8
Clarkson Row NW1 ... 239 M1
Claremont Square N1 ... 240 F1
Clarence Gardens NW1 ... 239 L2
Clarence Mews SE16 ... 247 G6
Clarendon Gardens W9 ... 238 D4

Clarendon Gate W2 ... 238 F7
Clarendon Place W2 ... 238 F7
Clarendon Street SW1V ... 243 L6
Clareville Grove SW7 ... 242 D6
Clareville Street SW7 ... 242 D6
Clarges Mews W1J ... 243 L1
Clarges Street W1J ... 243 L1
Clark Street E1 ... 246 F2
Carkson Row NW1 ... 239 M1
Claverton Street SW1V ... 244 A7
Clave Street E1W ... 246 F5
Clay Street W1U ... 239 H5
Clayton Street SE11 ... 244 F8
Cleaver Square SE11 ... 245 G7
Cleaver Street SE11 ... 245 G7
Clegg Street E1W ... 246 F5
Clemence Street E14 ... 247 L2
Clements Lane EC4N ... 241 L7
Clement's Road SE16 ... 246 E8
Clenston Mews W1H ... 239 H6
Clere Street EC2A ... 241 L3
Clerkenwell Close EC1R ... 241 G3
Clerkenwell Green EC1R ... 241 G4
Clerkenwell Road EC1M ... 241 G4
Cleveland Gardens W2 ... 238 C6
Cleveland Mews W1T ... 239 M4
Cleveland Place W2 ... 244 A1
Cleveland Row SW1A ... 244 A2
Cleveland Square W2 ... 238 C6
Cleveland Street W1T ... 239 M4
Cleveland Terrace W2 ... 238 D6
Clifford Street W1S ... 239 M7
Clifton Gardens W9 ... 238 C4
Clifton Place SE16 ... 247 G6
Clifton Place W2 ... 238 E7
Clifton Road W9 ... 238 D3
Clifton Street EC2A ... 241 M3
Clifton Villas W9 ... 238 C4
Clink Street SE1 ... 245 K1
Clipper Close SE16 ... 247 H6
Clipstone Mews W1W ... 239 M4
Clipstone Street W1W ... 239 L4
Cliveden Place SW1W ... 243 J5
Cloak Lane EC4R ... 241 K7
Cloth Fair EC1A ... 241 J5
Cloth Street EC1A ... 241 J5
Cluny Place SE1 ... 246 A8
Cobb Street E1 ... 246 B2
Cobourg Street NW1 ... 240 A2
Coburg Close SW1P ... 244 A5
Cochrane Mews NW8 ... 238 E1
Cochrane Street NW8 ... 238 E1
Cock Lane EC1A ... 241 H5
Cockspur Street SW1Y ... 244 C1
Codling Close * E1W ... 246 D5
Coin Street SE1 ... 245 G1
Coke Street E1 ... 246 D2
Colbeck Mews SW7 ... 242 C6
Colebrook Row N1 ... 241 H1
Coleherne Road SW10 ... 242 B7
Coleman Street EC2R ... 241 L6
Cole Street SE1 ... 245 K3
Coley Street WC1X ... 240 F3
College Hill EC4R ... 241 K7
College Street EC4R ... 241 K7
Collett Road SE16 ... 246 D8
Collier Street N1 ... 240 E1
Collingham Gardens SW5 ... 242 B6
Collingham Place SW5 ... 242 B5
Collingham Road SW5 ... 242 B5
Colnbrook Street SE1 ... 245 H4
Colombo Street SE1 ... 245 H1
Colonnade WC1N ... 240 D4
Coltman Street E14 ... 247 K2
Commercial Road E1 ... 246 D2
Commercial Road E14 ... 247 K3
Commercial Street E1 ... 246 B1
Compton Street EC1V ... 241 H3
Concert Hall Approach SE1 ... 244 E2
Conder Street E14 ... 247 K2
Conduit Mews W2 ... 238 E6
Conduit Place W2 ... 238 E6
Conduit Street W1S ... 239 L7
Congreve Street SE17 ... 245 M5
Connaught Close W2 ... 238 F7
Connaught Place W2 ... 239 G7
Connaught Square W2 ... 239 G6
Connaught Street W2 ... 239 G6
Cons Street SE1 ... 245 G2
Constitution Hill SW1A ... 243 L3
Content Street SE17 ... 245 K5
Conway Street W1T ... 239 M4
Cookham Crescent SE16 ... 247 H6
Cook's Road SE17 ... 245 H8
Coombs Street N1 ... 241 J1
Cooper's Lane Estate NW1 ... 240 B1
Cooper's Row EC3N ... 246 B3
Copenhagen Place E14 ... 247 L2
Cope Place W8 ... 242 A4
Copley Court SE17 ... 245 J8
Copley Street E1 ... 247 H2
Copperfield Road E3 ... 247 K1
Copperfield Street SE1 ... 245 J2
Copthall Avenue EC2R ... 241 L6
Coptic Street WC1A ... 240 C5
Coral Street SE1 ... 245 G3
Coram Street WC1H ... 240 C3
Cork Square E1W ... 246 E5
Cork Street W1S ... 239 M8
Corlett Street NW1 ... 238 F5
Cornhill EC3V ... 241 L6
Cornwall Gardens SW7 ... 242 C4
Cornwall Mews South SW7 ... 242 C5
Cornwall Road SE1 ... 244 F1
Cornwall Road SE1 ... 245 G2
Cornwall Street E1 ... 246 E3
Cornwall Terrace Mews NW1 ... 239 H4
Cornwood Drive E1 ... 247 G2
Coronet Street N1 ... 241 M2
Corporation Row EC1R ... 241 G3
Corsham Street N1 ... 241 L2
Cosser Street SE1 ... 244 F4
Cosway Street NW1 ... 239 G4
Cottage Place SW3 ... 242 F4
Cottesmore Gardens W8 ... 242 B4
Cottons Lane SE1 ... 245 M1
Coulson Street SW3 ... 243 H6
Counter Street SE1 ... 245 M1
County Street SE1 ... 245 K5
Courtenay Square SE11 ... 244 F7
Courtenay Street SE11 ... 244 F6
Courtfield Gardens SW5 ... 242 B5
Courtfield Mews * SW5 ... 242 C5
Courtfield Road SW7 ... 242 C5
Court Street E1 ... 246 E1
Cousin Lane SE1 ... 241 K8

Covent Garden ⊖ WC2E ... 240 D7
Covent Garden WC2E ... 240 D7
Coventry Street W1D ... 240 B8
Cowcross Street EC1M ... 241 H4
Cowper Street EC2A ... 241 L3
Crail Row SE17 ... 245 L5
Cramer Street W1U ... 239 J5
Crampton Street SE17 ... 245 J6
Cranbourn Street WC2H ... 240 C7
Cranleigh Street NW1 ... 240 A1
Cranley Gardens SW7 ... 242 D6
Cranley Mews SW7 ... 242 D6
Cranley Place SW7 ... 242 E6
Cranston Estate N1 ... 241 L1
Cranwood Street EC1V ... 241 L2
Craven Hill W2 ... 238 D7
Craven Hill Gardens W2 ... 238 C7
Craven Road W2 ... 238 D7
Craven Street WC2N ... 244 D1
Craven Terrace W2 ... 238 D7
Crawford Passage EC1R ... 241 G3
Crawford Place W1H ... 239 G5
Crawford Street W1H ... 239 G5
Creechurch Lane EC3A ... 246 A3
Creed Lane EC4V ... 241 H7
Cresswell Place SW10 ... 242 D6
Cressy Place E1 ... 247 G1
Crestfield Street WC1H ... 240 D2
Crimscott Street SE1 ... 246 A8
Crispin Street E1 ... 246 B1
Cromer Street WC1H ... 240 D2
Crompton Street W2 ... 238 D4
Cromwell Mews * SW7 ... 242 E5
Cromwell Place SW7 ... 242 E5
Cromwell Road SW7 ... 242 B5
Cromwell Road SW5 ... 242 E5
Crondall Court N1 ... 241 M1
Crondall Street N1 ... 241 L1
Cropley Street N1 ... 241 K1
Crosby Row SE1 ... 245 L3
Cross Lane EC3R ... 246 A4
Crosswall EC3N ... 246 B3
Crowder Street E1 ... 246 E3
Crucifix Lane SE1 ... 246 A6
Cruikshank Street WC1X ... 240 F1
Crutched Friars EC3N ... 246 A3
Cuba Street E14 ... 247 M6
Cubitt Street WC1X ... 240 E2
Culford Gardens SW3 ... 243 H6
Culling Road SE16 ... 246 F7
Cullum Street EC3M ... 241 M7
Culross Street W1K ... 239 J8
Culworth Street NW8 ... 238 F1
Cumberland Gardens WC1X ... 240 F2
Cumberland Gate W2 ... 239 H7
Cumberland Market NW1 ... 239 L2
Cumberland Street SW1V ... 243 L6
Cumberland Terrace NW1 ... 239 K1
Cumberland Terrace Mews NW1 ... 239 L1
Cumberland Wharf SE16 ... 247 G6
Cumming Street N1 ... 240 F1
Cundy Street SW1W ... 243 K6
Cunningham Place NW8 ... 238 E3
Cureton Street SW1P ... 244 C6
Curlew Street SE1 ... 246 B6
Cursitor Street EC4A ... 240 F6
Curtain Road EC2A ... 241 M3
Curtain Road EC2A ... 241 M4
Curzon Gate W2 ... 243 K2
Curzon Street W1J ... 243 K1
Cuthbert Street W2 ... 238 E4
Cutler Street EC3A ... 246 A2
Cynthia Street N1 ... 240 F1
Cypress Place W1T ... 240 A4
Cyrus Street EC1V ... 241 H3

D

Dacre Street SW1H ... 244 B3
Dakin Place E1 ... 247 J1
Dallington Street EC1V ... 241 H3
Damien Street E1 ... 246 F2
Dane Street WC1R ... 240 E5
Dansey Place W1D ... 240 B7
Dante Road SE11 ... 245 H5
Danvers Street SW3 ... 242 F8
D'Arblay Street W1F ... 240 A6
Dartford Street SE17 ... 245 K8
Dartmouth Street SW1H ... 244 B3
Darwin Street SE17 ... 245 L5
Date Street SE17 ... 245 K7
Davenant Street E1 ... 246 D1
Daventry Street NW1 ... 238 F4
Davidge Street SE1 ... 245 H3
Davies Mews W1K ... 239 K7
Davies Street W1K ... 239 K7
Dawes Street SE17 ... 245 L6
Dawson Place W2 ... 238 A7
Deal Porters Way SE16 ... 247 G8
Deal Street E1 ... 246 D1
Dean Bradley Street SW1P ... 244 C5
Dean Close SE16 ... 247 H6
Deancross Street E1 ... 246 F3
Deanery Street W1K ... 243 K1
Dean Farrar Street SW1H ... 244 B3
Dean Ryle Street SW1P ... 244 C5
Dean's Buildings SE17 ... 245 L6
Dean Stanley Street SW1P ... 244 C4
Dean Street W1D ... 240 B6
Dean's Yard SW1P ... 244 C4
Decima Street SE1 ... 245 M4
Deck Close SE16 ... 247 J6
Defoe Close SE16 ... 247 K7
Delamere Street W2 ... 238 C5
Delamere Terrace W2 ... 238 B4
De Laune Street SE17 ... 245 H7
Delaware Road W9 ... 238 B3
Dellow Street E1 ... 246 F3
Delverton Road SE17 ... 245 H7
Denbigh Place SW1V ... 243 M6
Denbigh Street SW1V ... 243 M6
Denbigh Street SW1V ... 244 A6
Denman Street W1D ... 240 B7
Denmark Street WC2H ... 240 C6
Denny Close SE11 ... 245 G6
Denny Street SE11 ... 245 G6
Denyer Street SW3 ... 243 G5
Derby Gate SW1A ... 244 D3
Derby Street W1J ... 243 K1
Dering Street W1S ... 239 L6
Derry Street W8 ... 242 B3
De Vere Gardens W8 ... 242 C3
Deverell Street SE1 ... 245 L4
Devonport Street E1 ... 247 G3

Devonshire Close W1G ... 239 K4
Devonshire Mews South W1G ... 239 K4
Devonshire Mews West W1G ... 239 K4
Devonshire Place W1G ... 239 K4
Devonshire Place Mews W1G ... 239 K4
Devonshire Row EC2M ... 246 A2
Devonshire Square EC2M ... 246 A2
Devonshire Street W1G ... 239 K4
Devonshire Terrace W2 ... 238 D7
De Walden Street W1G ... 239 K5
Dickens Estate SE16 ... 246 D7
Dickens Square SE1 ... 245 K4
Dilke Street SW3 ... 243 H8
Dingley Place EC1V ... 241 K2
Dingley Road EC1V ... 241 J2
Disney Place SE1 ... 245 K2
Distaff Lane EC4V ... 241 J7
Distin Street SE11 ... 244 F6
Dockhead SE1 ... 246 C7
Dockley Road SE16 ... 246 D8
Dock Street E1 ... 246 D4
Doddington Grove SE17 ... 245 H7
Doddington Place SE17 ... 245 H8
Dodson Street SE1 ... 245 G3
Dod Street E14 ... 247 M2
Dolben Street SE1 ... 245 H2
Dolland Street SE11 ... 244 F7
Dolphin Square SW1V ... 244 A7
Dolphin Street SW1V ... 244 A7
Dombey Street WC1N ... 240 E4
Dominion Drive SE16 ... 247 H7
Dominion Street EC2A ... 241 L5
Donegal Street N1 ... 240 F1
Dongola Road E1 ... 247 J1
Donne Place SW3 ... 243 G5
Doon Street SE1 ... 244 F1
Dora Street E14 ... 247 L2
Doric Way NW1 ... 240 B2
Dorset Rise EC4Y ... 241 G7
Dorset Square NW1 ... 239 H4
Dorset Street W1U ... 239 H5
Doughty Mews WC1N ... 240 E3
Doughty Street WC1N ... 240 E3
Douglas Street SW1P ... 244 B6
Douro Place W8 ... 242 C3
Douthwaite Square * E1W ... 246 D5
Dovehouse Street SW3 ... 242 E6
Dover Street W1J ... 243 L1
Dover Street W1S ... 239 L8
Dowgate Hill EC4R ... 241 K7
Downfield Close W9 ... 238 B4
Downing Street SW1A ... 244 C2
Down Street W1J ... 243 K2
Downtown Road SE16 ... 247 K6
D'Oyley Street SW1X ... 243 J5
Draco Street SE17 ... 245 J8
Drake Close SE16 ... 247 H6
Draycott Avenue SW3 ... 243 G5
Draycott Place SW3 ... 243 H6
Draycott Terrace SW3 ... 243 H5
Drayson Mews W8 ... 242 A3
Drayton Gardens SW10 ... 242 D6
Druid Street SE1 ... 246 A6
Druid Street SE1 ... 246 B6
Drummond Crescent NW1 ... 240 B2
Drummond Gate * SW1V ... 244 B6
Drummond Road SE16 ... 246 E8
Drummond Street NW1 ... 240 A3
Drury Lane WC2B ... 240 D6
Dryden Court SE11 ... 245 G5
Dryden Street WC2B ... 240 D6
Duchess Mews W1G ... 239 L5
Duchess Street W1B ... 239 L5
Duchy Street SE1 ... 245 G1
Duckett Street E1 ... 247 J1
Duck Lane W1F ... 240 B6
Dufferin Street EC1Y ... 241 K4
Duke of Wellington Place SW1W ... 243 K3
Duke of York Square SW3 ... 243 H6
Duke of York Street SW1Y ... 244 A1
Duke Shore Wharf E14 ... 247 K4
Duke's Lane W8 ... 242 A2
Duke's Place EC3A ... 246 B2
Duke's Road WC1H ... 240 C2
Duke Street W1K ... 239 K7
Duke Street W1U ... 239 J6
Duke Street Hill SE1 ... 245 L1
Duke Street St James's SW1Y ... 244 A1
Dunbar Wharf E14 ... 247 L4
Duncannon Street WC2N ... 240 C8
Duncan Terrace N1 ... 241 H1
Dundee Street E1W ... 246 F5
Dundee Wharf E14 ... 247 L4
Dunelm Street E1 ... 247 H2
Dunlop Place SE16 ... 246 C8
Dunraven Street W1K ... 239 H7
Dunster Court EC3R ... 246 A3
Duplex Ride SW1X ... 243 H3
Durand's Wharf SE16 ... 247 L6
Durham Row E1 ... 247 J1
Durham Street SE11 ... 244 E7
Durham Terrace W2 ... 238 A6
Dyott Street WC1A ... 240 C6
Dysart Street EC2A ... 241 M4

E

Eagle Court EC1M ... 241 H4
Eagle Street WC1R ... 240 E5
Eamont Street NW8 ... 239 G1
Eardley Crescent SW5 ... 242 A7
Earlham Street WC2H ... 240 C7
Earl's Court ⇄ ⊖ SW5 ... 242 A6
Earl's Court Gardens SW5 ... 242 B6
Earl's Court Road SW5 ... 242 A6
Earl's Court Square SW5 ... 242 A6
Earlstoke Street EC1V ... 241 H2
Earl Street EC2A ... 241 M4
Earnshaw Street WC2H ... 240 C6
East Arbour Street E1 ... 247 H2
Eastbourne Mews W2 ... 238 D6
Eastbourne Terrace W2 ... 238 D6
Eastcastle Street W1W ... 240 A6
Eastcheap EC3M ... 241 M7
Eastfield Street E14 ... 247 K1
East India Dock Road E14 ... 247 M3
East Lane SE16 ... 246 D6
Easton Street WC1X ... 240 F3
East Poultry Avenue EC1A ... 241 H5
East Road N1 ... 241 L2
East Smithfield E1W ... 246 C4
East Street SE17 ... 245 L6
East Tenter Street E1 ... 246 C3
Eaton Close SW1W ... 243 J5

Eaton Gate SW1W ... 243 J5
Eaton Lane SW1W ... 243 L4
Eaton Mews North SW1W ... 243 J5
Eaton Mews South SW1W ... 243 K5
Eaton Mews West SW1W ... 243 K5
Eaton Place SW1X ... 243 J4
Eaton Row SW1W ... 243 K4
Eaton Square SW1W ... 243 K5
Eaton Terrace SW1W ... 243 J5
Ebbisham Drive SW8 ... 244 E8
Ebury Bridge SW1W ... 243 K6
Ebury Bridge Road SW1W ... 243 K7
Ebury Mews SW1W ... 243 K5
Ebury Square SW1W ... 243 K5
Ebury Street SW1W ... 243 K5
Eccleston Bridge SW1W ... 243 L5
Eccleston Mews SW1X ... 243 K4
Eccleston Place SW1W ... 243 L5
Eccleston Square SW1V ... 243 L6
Eccleston Street SW1X ... 243 K4
Edbrooke Road W9 ... 238 A3
Edge Street W8 ... 242 A1
Edgware Road W2 ... 238 F5
Edgware Road ⊖ NW1 ... 238 F5
Edinburgh Gate SW1X ... 243 H3
Edith Grove SW10 ... 242 C8
Edwards Mews W1H ... 239 J6
Egerton Crescent SW3 ... 242 F5
Egerton Gardens SW3 ... 242 F5
Egerton Terrace SW3 ... 243 G4
Eglington Court SE17 ... 245 J7
Elba Place SE17 ... 245 K5
Eldon Road W8 ... 242 B4
Eldon Street EC2M ... 241 L5
Eleanor Close SE16 ... 247 H6
Elephant & Castle SE1 ... 245 J4
Elephant & Castle ⇄ ⊖ SE1 ... 245 J5
Elephant Lane SE16 ... 246 F6
Elephant Road SE17 ... 245 J5
Elf Row E1W ... 247 G3
Elgar Street SE16 ... 247 K7
Elgin Avenue W9 ... 238 B2
Elgin Mews North W9 ... 238 C2
Elgin Mews South W9 ... 238 C2
Elia Mews N1 ... 241 H1
Elia Street N1 ... 241 H1
Elim Estate SE1 ... 245 M3
Elim Street SE1 ... 245 M3
Elizabeth Bridge SW1V ... 243 L6
Elizabeth Street SW1W ... 243 K5
Ellen Street E1 ... 246 D3
Elliott's Row SE11 ... 245 H5
Ellis Street SW1X ... 243 J5
Elmfield Way W9 ... 238 A4
Elm Park Gardens SW10 ... 242 E7
Elm Park Lane SW3 ... 242 E7
Elm Park Road SW3 ... 242 E8
Elm Place SW7 ... 242 E7
Elms Mews W2 ... 238 D7
Elm Street WC1X ... 240 F4
Elm Tree Road NW8 ... 238 E2
Elnathan Mews W9 ... 238 B4
Elsa Street E1 ... 247 J1
Elsted Street SE17 ... 245 L6
Elvaston Mews SW7 ... 242 D4
Elvaston Place SW7 ... 242 D4
Elverton Street SW1P ... 244 B5
Ely Place EC1N ... 241 G5
Elystan Place SW3 ... 243 G6
Elystan Street SW3 ... 242 F6
Embankment ⊖ WC2N ... 244 D1
Embankment Gardens SW3 ... 243 H8
Embankment Place WC2N ... 244 D1
Emba Street SE16 ... 246 D7
Emerald Street WC1N ... 240 E4
Emerson Street SE1 ... 245 J1
Emery Hill Street SW1P ... 244 A4
Emery Street SE1 ... 245 G3
Emperor's Gate SW7 ... 242 C5
Empire Square SE1 ... 245 L3
Empress Place SW6 ... 242 A7
Endell Street WC2H ... 240 C6
Endsleigh Gardens WC1H ... 240 B3
Endsleigh Place WC1H ... 240 B3
Endsleigh Street WC1H ... 240 B3
Enford Street W1H ... 239 G5
English Grounds SE1 ... 245 M1
Enid Street SE16 ... 246 C8
Ennismore Gardens SW7 ... 242 F3
Ennismore Gardens Mews SW7 ... 242 F3
Ennismore Mews SW7 ... 242 F3
Ennismore Street SW7 ... 242 F4
Ensign Street E1 ... 246 D4
Epworth Street EC2A ... 241 L3
Erasmus Street SW1P ... 244 C6
Errol Street EC1Y ... 241 K4
Essendine Road W9 ... 238 A3
Essex Street WC2R ... 240 F7
Essex Villas W8 ... 242 A3
Europa Place EC1V ... 241 J2
Euston ⇄ ⊖ NW1 ... 240 B2
Euston Road NW1 ... 240 B3
Euston Square NW1 ... 240 B2
Euston Square ⊖ NW1 ... 240 A3
Euston Street NW1 ... 240 A3
Evelyn Gardens SW7 ... 242 D7
Evelyn Walk N1 ... 241 L1
Evershott Street NW1 ... 240 A1
Everton Mews NW1 ... 239 M2
Ewer Street SE1 ... 245 J2
Ewhurst Close E1 ... 247 G1
Exchange Square EC2A ... 241 M4
Exeter Street WC2E ... 240 D7
Exhibition Road SW7 ... 242 E3
Exmouth Market EC1R ... 241 G3
Exon Street SE17 ... 245 M6
Exton Street SE1 ... 244 F2
Eyre Street Hill EC1R ... 240 F4

F

Fairclough Street E1 ... 246 D3
Fair Street SE1 ... 246 B6
Falmouth Road SE1 ... 245 K4
Fann Street EC1M ... 241 J4
Fanshaw Street N1 ... 241 M1
Farmer Street W8 ... 242 A1
Farm Lane SW6 ... 242 A8
Farm Street W1K ... 239 K8
Farnham Place SE1 ... 245 J1
Farrance Street E14 ... 247 M3
Farringdon ⇄ ⊖ EC1M ... 241 G4
Farringdon Lane EC1R ... 241 G4
Farringdon Road EC1R ... 240 F3

Farringdon Street EC1M....241 H5
Farrins Rents SE16....247 J5
Farrow Place SE16....247 K7
Farthing Fields * E1W....246 F5
Fashion Street E1....246 B1
Faunce Street SE17....245 H7
Fawcett Street SW10....242 C8
Featherstone Street EC1Y....241 L3
Fenchurch Avenue EC3M....246 A3
Fenchurch Buildings EC3M....246 A3
Fenchurch Place EC3M....246 A3
Fenchurch Street EC3M....246 A3
Fenchurch Street ⇌ EC3M....246 A3
Fendall Street SE1....246 B8
Fenning Street SE1....245 M2
Fentiman Road SW8....244 D8
Fernsbury Street WC1X....240 F2
Fetter Lane EC4A....241 G6
Fieldgate Street E1....246 D2
Fielding Street SE17....245 J7
Field Street WC1X....240 E1
Finborough Road SW10....242 B8
Finch Lane EC3V....241 L6
Finland Street SE16....247 K8
Finsbury Circus EC2M....241 L5
Finsbury Estate EC1R....241 G3
Finsbury Market E1....241 M4
Finsbury Square EC2A....241 L4
Finsbury Street EC2Y....241 L4
First Street SW3....243 G5
Fishermans Drive SE16....247 J6
Fisher Street WC1R....240 D5
Fisherton Street NW8....238 E3
Fish Street Hill EC3R....241 L7
Fitzalan Street SE11....244 F5
Fitzhardinge Street W1H....239 J6
Fitzroy Square W1T....239 M4
Fitzroy Street W1T....239 M4
Flamborough Street E14....247 J3
Flank Street E1....246 C4
Flaxman Terrace WC1H....240 C3
Fleet Street EC4A....241 G6
Fleming Road SE17....245 H8
Fletcher Street E1....246 D3
Flint Street SE17....245 L6
Flitcroft Street WC2H....240 C6
Flockton Street SE16....246 D7
Flood Street SW3....243 G7
Flood Walk SW3....243 G7
Floral Street WC2E....240 D7
Foley Street W1W....239 M5
Forbes Street E1....246 D3
Fordham Street E1....246 D2
Ford Square E1....246 F2
Fore Street EC2Y....241 K5
Formosa Street W9....238 C4
Forset Street W1H....239 G6
Forsyth Gardens SE17....245 H8
Fort Street E1....246 B1
Fortune Street EC1Y....241 K4
Forum Magnum Square SE1....244 E3
Foster Lane EC2V....241 J6
Foulis Terrace SW7....242 E6
Foundry Close SE16....247 J5
Fournier Street E1....246 B1
Fowey Close E1W....246 E5
Frampton Street NW8....238 E4
Francis Street SW1P....244 A5
Franklin's Row SW3....243 H6
Frazier Street SE1....245 G3
Frean Street SE16....246 C8
Frederick Close W2....239 G7
Frederick Street WC1X....240 E2
Frederic Mews * SW1X....243 J3
Freemantle Street SE17....245 M6
Friday Street EC4V....241 J7
Friend Street EC1V....241 H2
Frith Street W1D....240 B6
Fulbourne Street E1....246 E1
Fulford Street SE16....246 F7
Fulham Road SW10....242 D8
Fulham Road SW3....242 F6
Furnival Street EC4A....240 F5
Fynes Street SW1P....244 B5

G

Gabriel's Wharf SE1....245 G1
Gainsford Street SE1....246 B6
Galleon Close SE16....247 G6
Galsworthy Avenue E14....247 K2
Galway Street EC1V....241 K2
Gambia Street SE1....245 H2
Garden Road NW8....238 D1
Garden Row SE1....245 H4
Garden Street E1....246 F1
Garden Terrace * SW1V....244 B6
Garden Walk EC2A....241 M3
Gard Street EC1V....241 J2
Garford Street E14....247 M4
Garnault Place EC1R....241 G3
Garnet Street E1W....246 F4
Garrett Street EC1Y....241 K3
Garrick Street WC2E....240 C7
Garterway SE16....247 H7
Garway Road W2....238 B6
Gaspar Mews SW7....242 C5
Gataker Street * SE16....246 E8
Gate Mews SW7....242 F3
Gateforth Street NW8....238 F3
Gate Mews NW1....239 L3
Gatesborough Street * EC2A....241 M3
Gate Street WC2A....240 E5
Gatliff Road SW1W....243 K7
Gaunt Street SE1....245 J4
Gayfere Street SW1P....244 C4
Gaywood Street SE1....245 H4
Gaza Street SE17....245 H7
Gedling Place SE1....246 C7
Gee Street EC1V....241 J3
George Mathers Road SE11....245 H5
George Row SE16....246 C7
George Street W1H....239 H6
George Yard W1K....239 K7
Geraldine Street SE11....245 H4
Gerald Road SW1W....243 K5
Gerrard Street W1D....240 B7
Gerridge Street SE1....245 G3
Gertrude Street SW10....242 D8
Gibson Road SE11....244 E5
Gilbert Place WC1A....240 C5
Gilbert Road SE11....245 G5
Gilbert Street W1K....239 K7
Gildea Street W1W....239 L5

Gillingham Street SW1V....243 M5
Gill Street E14....247 L3
Gilston Road SW10....242 D7
Giltspur Street EC1A....241 H5
Gladstone Street SE1....245 H4
Glamis Place E1W....247 G4
Glamis Road E1W....247 G4
Glasgow Terrace SW1V....243 M7
Glasshill Street SE1....245 J3
Glasshouse Street W1B....240 A8
Glasshouse Walk SE11....244 D7
Glasshouse Yard EC1....241 J4
Glebe Place SW3....242 F7
Gledhow Road SW5....242 C6
Glentworth Street NW1....239 H4
Globe Pond Road SE16....247 J5
Globe Street SE1....245 K3
Gloucester Court * EC3R....246 A4
Gloucester Gardens W2....238 C6
Gloucester Mews W2....238 D6
Gloucester Mews West W2....238 C6
Gloucester Place NW1....239 H3
Gloucester Place W1U....239 H5
Gloucester Place Mews W1U....239 H5
Gloucester Road SW7....242 C4
Gloucester Road SW7....242 D6
Gloucester Road ⊖ SW7....242 C5
Gloucester Square W2....238 F6
Gloucester Street SW1V....243 M7
Gloucester Terrace W2....238 B5
Gloucester Terrace W2....238 D6
Gloucester Walk W8....242 A2
Gloucester Way EC1R....241 G2
Glyn Street SE11....244 E7
Godfrey Street SW3....243 G6
Goding Street SE11....244 D7
Godliman Street EC4V....241 J7
Godwin Close N1....241 K1
Golden Hinde II SE1....245 L1
Golden Jubilee Bridge WC2N....244 D1
Golden Lane EC1Y....241 J4
Golden Square W1F....240 A7
Golding Street E1....246 E3
Goldney Road W9....238 A4
Goldsmith Street EC2V....241 K6
Gomm Road SE16....247 G8
Goodge Place W1T....240 A5
Goodge Street W1T....240 A5
Goodge Street ⊖ W1T....240 B5
Goodwin Close SE16....246 C8
Gordon Place W8....242 A2
Gordon Square WC1H....240 B3
Gordon Street WC1H....240 B3
Gore Street SW7....242 D4
Goring Street * EC3A....246 A2
Gosfield Street W1W....239 L5
Goslett Yard WC2H....240 B6
Goswell Road EC1V....241 H1
Gough Street WC1X....240 F3
Goulston Street E1....246 B2
Gower Mews WC1E....240 B5
Gower Place NW1....240 A3
Gower Street WC1E....240 B3
Gower's Walk E1....246 D2
Gracechurch Street EC3V....241 M7
Grafton Mews W1T....239 M4
Grafton Place NW1....240 B2
Grafton Street W1S....239 L8
Grafton Way W1T....240 A4
Graham Street N1....241 J1
Graham Terrace SW1W....243 J6
Granby Terrace NW1....239 M1
Grand Avenue EC1A....241 H5
Grange Road SE1....246 B8
Grange Walk SE1....246 A8
Grange Yard SE1....246 B8
Grantully Road W9....238 B2
Granville Place W1H....239 J6
Granville Road NW6....238 A1
Granville Square WC1X....240 F2
Grape Street WC2H....240 C6
Gravel Lane E1....246 B2
Gray's Inn Road WC1X....240 D2
Gray's Inn Square WC1R....240 F5
Gray Street SE1....245 G3
Great Castle Street W1G....239 L6
Great Central Street NW1....239 G4
Great Chapel Street W1D....240 B6
Great College Street SW1P....244 C4
Great Cumberland Place W1H....239 H6
Great Dover Street SE1....245 K3
Great Eastern Street EC2A....241 M3
Great George Street SW1P....244 C3
Great Guildford Street SE1....245 J1
Great James Street WC1N....240 E4
Great Marlborough Street W1F....239 M7
Great Maze Pond SE1....245 L2
Great Newport Street WC2H....240 C7
Greatorex Street E1....246 D1
Great Ormond Street WC1N....240 D4
Great Percy Street WC1X....240 F2
Great Peter Street SW1P....244 B4
Great Portland Street W1W....239 L4
Great Portland Street ⊖ W1W....239 L4
Great Pulteney Street W1F....240 A7
Great Queen Street WC2B....240 D6
Great Russell Street WC1B....240 C5
Great Scotland Yard SW1A....244 C1
Great Smith Street SW1P....244 C4
Great Suffolk Street SE1....245 H2
Great Sutton Street EC1V....241 H4
Great Swan Alley EC2R....241 L6
Great Titchfield Street W1W....239 M4
Great Tower Street EC3M....246 A3
Great Tower Street EC3R....246 A4
Great Winchester Street EC2N....241 L6
Great Windmill Street W1D....240 B7
Greek Street W1D....240 B6
Greenacre Square SE16....247 J6
Green Bank E1W....246 E5
Greenberry Street NW8....238 F1
Greencoat Place SW1P....244 A5
Green Coat Row SW1P....244 A4
Greenfield Road E1....246 D2
Greenham Close SE1....244 F3
Green Park ⊖ W1J....243 M1
Greenwell Street W1W....239 L4
Greet Street SE1....245 G2
Grenade Street E14....247 L4
Grendon Street NW8....238 F3
Grenville Place SW7....242 C5
Gresham Street EC2V....241 J6
Gresse Street W1T....240 B5
Greville Street EC1N....241 G5

Greycoat Place SW1P....244 B4
Greycoat Street SW1P....244 B4
Grigg's Place SE1....246 A8
Grosvenor Bridge SW8....243 L8
Grosvenor Crescent SW1X....243 J3
Grosvenor Crescent Mews SW1X....243 J3
Grosvenor Gardens SW1W....243 L4
Grosvenor Gardens Mews East SW1W....243 L4
Grosvenor Gardens Mews North SW1W....243 L4
Grosvenor Gardens Mews South * SW1W....243 L4
Grosvenor Gate W2....239 H8
Grosvenor Hill W1K....239 L7
Grosvenor Place SW1X....243 K3
Grosvenor Road SW1V....243 L8
Grosvenor Square W1K....239 J7
Grosvenor Street W1K....239 K7
Grosvenor Terrace SE5....245 J8
Grove End Road NW8....238 D2
Guildhouse Street SW1V....243 M5
Guinness Square SE1....245 M5
Gulliver Street SE16....247 K8
Gun Street E1....246 B1
Gunthorpe Street E1....246 C2
Gutter Lane EC2V....241 J6
Guy Street SE1....245 L3

H

Haberdasher Street N1....241 L2
Haddonhall Estate SE1....245 M4
Hainton Close E1....246 F3
Halcrow Street * E1....246 E2
Half Moon Street W1J....243 L1
Halford Road SW6....242 A8
Halkin Place SW1X....243 J4
Halkin Street SW1X....243 K3
Hallam Street W1W....239 L5
Halley Street E14....247 K1
Hall Place W2....238 E4
Hall Road NW8....238 D2
Hall Street EC1V....241 H2
Halpin Place SE17....245 M6
Halsey Street SW3....243 G5
Hamilton Close NW8....238 D2
Hamilton Close SE16....247 K7
Hamilton Gardens NW8....238 D2
Hamilton Place W1J....243 K2
Hamilton Terrace NW8....238 C1
Hamlet Way SE1....245 L3
Hammett Street EC3N....246 B4
Hampden Close NW1....240 B1
Hampden Gurney Street W2....239 H6
Hampstead Road NW1....239 M2
Hampton Street SE17....245 J6
Hanbury Street E1....246 C1
Hand Court WC1V....240 E5
Handel Street WC1N....240 D3
Hankey Place SE1....245 L3
Hannibal Road E1....247 G1
Hanover Square W1S....239 L6
Hanover Street W1S....239 L7
Hans Crescent SW3....243 H3
Hanson Street W1W....239 M4
Hans Place SW1X....243 H4
Hans Road SW3....243 G4
Hans Street SW1X....243 H4
Hanway Place W1T....240 B6
Hanway Street W1T....240 B6
Harbet Road W2....238 E5
Harcourt Street W1H....239 G5
Harcourt Terrace SW10....242 C7
Hardinge Street E1W....247 G3
Hardwick Street EC1R....241 G2
Hardwidge Street SE1....245 M2
Hardy Close SE16....247 H6
Harewood Place W1G....239 L6
Harewood Row NW1....239 G4
Harford Street E1....247 J1
Harleyford Road SE11....244 E8
Harley Gardens SW10....242 D7
Harley Place W1G....239 K5
Harley Street W1G....239 K4
Harmsworth Street SE17....245 G7
Harold Estate SE1....246 A8
Harper Road SE1....245 K4
Harpour Street WC1N....240 E4
Harriet Street SW1X....243 H3
Harriet Walk SW1X....243 H3
Harrington Gardens SW7....242 C6
Harrington Road SW7....242 E5
Harrington Square NW1....239 M1
Harrington Street NW1....239 M2
Harrison Street WC1H....240 D2
Harrods SW1X....243 G4
Harrowby Street W1H....239 G6
Harrow Place E1....246 B2
Harrow Road W2....238 A4
Hart Street EC3R....246 A3
Hasker Street SW3....243 G5
Hastings Street WC1H....240 C2
Hatfields SE1....245 G1
Hatherley Grove W2....238 B6
Hatteraick Road SE16....247 G6
Hatton Garden EC1N....241 G5
Hatton Street W2....238 E4
Hatton Wall EC1N....241 G4
Havering Street E1....247 H3
Haverstock Street N1....241 J1
Hawke Place * SE16....247 H6
Haydon Street EC3N....246 B3
Hayes Place NW1....239 G4
Hay Hill W1J....239 L8
Hayles Street SE11....245 H5
Haymarket SW1Y....240 B8
Hayne Street EC1A....241 J4
Hay's Lane SE1....245 M1
Hay's Mews W1J....239 L8
Headfort Place SW1X....243 K3
Head Street E1....247 H2
Hearnshaw Street E14....247 K2
Hearn Street EC2A....241 M4
Heathcote Street WC1N....240 E3
Heddon Street W1B....239 M7
Hedger Street SE11....245 H5
Heiron Street SE17....245 J8

Hellings Street E1W....246 D5
Helmet Row EC1V....241 K3
Helsinki Square SE16....247 L8
Henderson Drive NW8....238 E3
Heneage Lane EC3A....246 A3
Heneage Street E1....246 C1
Henrietta Place W1G....239 L6
Henrietta Street WC2E....240 D7
Henriques Street E1....246 D2
Henshaw Street SE17....245 L5
Herbal Hill EC1R....241 G4
Herbert Crescent SW1X....243 H4
Herbrand Street WC1H....240 C3
Hercules Road SE1....244 F4
Hereford Road W2....238 A6
Hereford Square SW7....242 D6
Hermitage Street W2....238 E5
Hermitage Wall E1W....246 D5
Hermit Street EC1V....241 H2
Heron Place SE16....247 K5
Heron Quay E14....247 M5
Herrick Street SW1P....244 C5
Hertford Street W1J....243 K2
Hertsmere Road E14....247 M4
Hesper Mews SW5....242 B6
Hessel Street E1....246 E3
Hewett Street EC2A....241 M3
Heygate Street SE17....245 J5
Hide Place SW1P....244 B6
High Holborn WC1V....240 C6
High Street Kensington ⊖ W8....242 A3
Hildyard Road SW6....242 A8
Hilliards Court E1W....246 F5
Hillingdon Street SE17....245 J8
Hill Road NW8....238 D1
Hills Place W1F....239 M6
Hill Street W1J....239 K8
Hinde Street W1U....239 K6
Hind Grove E14....247 M3
Hindgrove Area E14....247 M3
Hithe Grove SE16....247 G8
HMS Belfast SE1....246 A5
Hobart Place SW1W....243 K4
Hobury Street SW10....242 D8
Hogarth Road SW5....242 B6
Holbein Mews SW1W....243 J6
Holbein Place SW1W....243 J6
Holborn EC1N....241 G5
Holborn ⊖ WC2B....240 E5
Holborn Circus EC1N....241 G5
Holborn Viaduct EC1A....241 G5
Holford Street WC1X....240 F2
Holland Street SE1....245 H1
Holland Street W8....242 A3
Hollen Street W1F....240 A6
Holles Street W1C....239 L6
Hollywood Road SW10....242 C8
Holyoak Road SE11....245 H5
Holyrood Street SE1....245 M2
Holyrood Street SE1....246 A6
Holywell Row EC2A....241 M4
Homefield Street * N1....241 M1
Homer Row W1H....239 G5
Homer Street W1H....239 G5
Hooper Street E1....246 D3
Hopetown Street E1....246 C1
Hopkins Street W1F....240 A7
Hopton Street SE1....245 H1
Hopwood Road SE17....245 L8
Hornton Place W8....242 A3
Hornton Street W8....242 A2
Horse & Dolphin Yard W1D....240 B7
Horseferry Road E14....247 J3
Horseferry Road SW1P....244 B4
Horse Guards Avenue SW1A....244 C2
Horse Guards Parade SW1A....244 C2
Horse Guards Road SW1A....244 C2
Horselydown Lane SE1....246 B6
Horsley Street SE17....245 K8
Hosier Lane EC1A....241 H5
Hothfield Place SE16....247 G8
Hotspur Street SE11....244 F6
Houghton Street WC2A....240 E6
Houndsditch EC3A....246 A2
Houses of Parliament SW1A....244 D3
Howick Place SW1E....244 A4
Howland Street W1T....240 A4
Howley Place W2....238 D5
Hoxton Square N1....241 M2
Hoxton Street N1....241 M1
Hudson's Place SW1V....243 M5
Hugh Mews SW1V....243 L6
Hugh Street SW1V....243 L6
Hull Close SE16....247 J6
Hull Street EC1V....241 J2
Hungerford Bridge SE1....244 E1
Hunter Close SE1....245 M4
Hunter Street WC1N....240 D3
Huntley Street WC1E....240 A4
Huntsman Street SE17....245 M6
Huntsworth Mews NW1....239 H3
Hurley Crescent SE16....247 H6
Hutching's Street E14....247 M7
Hutton Street EC4Y....241 G6
Hyde Park W2....243 G1
Hyde Park Corner W1J....243 K2
Hyde Park Corner ⊖ W1J....243 K2
Hyde Park Court SW7....242 D3
Hyde Park Crescent W2....238 F6
Hyde Park Gardens W2....238 F7
Hyde Park Gardens Mews W2....238 F7
Hyde Park Gate SW7....242 C3
Hyde Park Gate SW7....242 D3
Hyde Park Square W2....238 F7
Hyde Park Street W2....238 F7

I

Idol Lane EC3R....241 M7
Ifield Road SW10....242 B8
Iliffe Street SE17....245 J6
Iliffe Yard SE17....245 J6
Imperial College Road SW7....242 D4
Imperial War Museum SE1....245 G4
India Street EC3N....246 B3
Ingestre Place W1F....240 A7
Inglebert Street EC1R....240 F2
Ingram Close SE11....244 E5
Inner Circle NW1....239 J2
Inverness Street NW1....239 L1
Inverness Terrace W2....238 C6
Inverness Terrace Gate W2....238 C8
Invicta Plaza SE1....245 H1

Inville Road SE17....245 L
Ironmonger Lane EC2V....241 K
Ironmonger Row EC1V....241 K
Irving Street WC2N....240 C
Isambard Place SE16....247 G
Island Row E14....247 K
Iverna Court W8....242 A
Iverna Gardens W8....242 A
Ives Street SW3....243 G
Ivor Place NW1....239 G
Ixworth Place SW3....242 F

J

Jacob Street SE1....246 C
Jamaica Gate SE16....246 F
Jamaica Road SE1....246 C
Jamaica Road SE16....246 F
Jamaica Street E1....247 G
Jamaica Wharf SE1....246 C
James Street W1U....239 K
James Street WC2E....240 D
Jameson Street W8....242 A
Jamuna Close E14....247 K
Janeway Street SE16....246 D
Jardine Road E1W....247 J
Java Wharf SE1....246 C
Jay Mews SW7....242 D
Jermyn Street SW1Y....240 A
Jerome Crescent NW8....238 F
Jewery Street EC3N....246 B
Joan Street SE1....245 G
Jockey's Fields WC1R....240 E
Johanna Street SE1....244 F
John Adam Street WC2N....240 D
John Carpenter Street EC4Y....241 G
John Fisher Street E1....246 C
John Islip Street SW1P....244 C
John Prince's Street W1G....239 L
John Roll Way SE16....246 D
John Ruskin Street SE5....245 J
John's Mews WC1N....240 E
Johnson's Place SW1V....244 A
Johnson Street E1....247 G
John Street WC1N....240 E
Joiner Street SE1....245 L
Jonathan Street SE11....244 E
Jubilee Place SW3....243 G
Jubilee Street E1....247 G
Jubilee Walk W8....242 B
Judd Street WC1H....240 C
Junction Mews W2....238 F
Juxon Street SE11....244 E

K

Katherine Close SE16....247 H5
Kean Street WC2B....240 E
Keel Close SE16....247 J
Keeley Street WC2B....240 E
Keeton's Road SE16....246 E
Kell Street SE1....245 H
Kelso Place W8....242 B
Kemble Street WC2B....240 E
Kempsford Gardens SW5....242 A
Kempsford Road SE11....245 G
Kendall Place W1U....239 J
Kendal Street W2....239 G
Kennet Street E1W....246 D
Kenning Street SE16....247 H
Kennings Way SE11....245 G
Kennington ⊖ SE11....245 H
Kennington Lane SE11....244 E
Kennington Oval SE11....244 E
Kennington Park Gardens SE11....245 G
Kennington Park Place SE11....245 G
Kennington Park Road SE11....245 G
Kennington Road SE1....244 F
Kennington Road SE11....245 G
Kennnington Oval SE11....244 E
Kenrick Place W1U....239 J
Kensington Church Street W8....242 A
Kensington Court W8....242 B
Kensington Gardens W2....242 C
Kensington Gardens Square W2....238 B
Kensington Gate W8....242 C
Kensington Gore SW7....242 E
Kensington High Street W8....242 A
Kensington Palace W8....242 B
Kensington Palace Gardens W8....242 B
Kensington Palace Gardens W8....242 B
Kensington Place W8....242 A
Kensington Road SW7....243 G
Kensington Road W8....242 B
Kensington Square W8....242 C
Kenton Street WC1H....240 C
Kenway Road SW5....242 B
Keystone Close N1....240 D
Keyworth Street SE1....245 H
Kia Oval (Surrey County Cricket Ground) SE11....244 F
Kilburn Park Road NW6....238 A
Kildare Terrace W2....238 A
Killick Street N1....240 E
Kinburn Street SE16....247 H
Kinder Street E1....246 E
King & Queen Wharf SE16....247 K
King and Queen Street SE17....245 K
King Charles Street SW1A....244 C
King David Lane E1....247 G
Kingdom Street W2....238 C
King Edward Street EC1A....241 J
King Edward Walk SE1....245 G
King James Street SE1....245 H
Kingly Street W1F....239 M
King's Arms Yard EC2R....241 L
King's Bench Street SE1....245 H
Kingscote Street EC4V....241 H
King's Cross ⇌ N1C....240 D
King's Cross Road WC1X....240 E
King's Cross Square N1C....240 D
King's Cross St Pancras ⊖ N1C....240 D
Kingsgate Walk * SW1E....244 A
King's Head Yard * SE1....245 L
King's Mews WC1N....240 E
Kingsmill Terrace NW8....238 E
King Square EC1V....241 J
King's Road SW3....243 G
King's Scholars Passage SW1P....243 M
King's Stairs Close SE16....246 F
King Street EC2V....241 K
King Street SW1Y....244 A

King Street EC2V................241 K6
Kingsway WC2B................240 E6
King William Street EC4N........241 L7
Kinnerton Place North * SW1X 243 J3
Kinnerton Place South * SW1X 243 J3
Kinnerton Street SW1X............243 J3
Kinnerton Yard * SW1X...........243 J3
Kipling Estate SE1..............245 L3
Kipling Street SE1..............245 L3
Kirby Estate SE16...............246 D7
Kirby Grove SE1................245 M3
Kirby Street EC1N...............241 G4
Knaresborough Place SW5.........242 B5
Knightrider Street EC4V..........241 H7
Knightsbridge SW1X.............243 H3
Knightsbridge SW3..............243 H3
Knox Street W1H................239 H4
Kynance Mews SW7..............242 C4
Kynance Place SW7..............242 C4

L

Lackington Street EC2A...........241 L4
Lafone Street SE1...............246 B6
Lagado Mews SE16..............247 H3
Lambeth Bridge SW1P............244 D5
Lambeth High Street SE1..........244 E5
Lambeth Hill EC4V..............241 J7
Lambeth North ⊖ SE1............244 F3
Lambeth Palace Road SE1.........244 E4
Lambeth Road SE1...............244 F4
Lambeth Walk SE11.............244 F5
Lamb's Conduit Street WC1N.......240 E4
Lamb's Passage EC1Y............241 K4
Lamb Street E1.................246 B1
Lamb Way SE1..................246 A7
Lamlash Street SE11.............245 H5
Lanark Place W9................238 D3
Lanark Road W9.................238 B1
Lancaster Gate W2..............238 D7
Lancaster Gate ⊖ W2............238 D8
Lancaster Mews W2.............238 D7
Lancaster Place WC2E...........240 E7
Lancaster Street SE1............245 H3
Lancaster Terrace W2............238 E7
Lancaster Walk W2..............238 D8
Lancelot Place SW7.............243 G3
Lancing Street NW1.............240 B2
Lanesborough Place * SW1X........243 J3
Langdale Street E1..............246 E3
Langford Place NW8.............238 D1
Langham Place W1B..............239 L5
Langham Street W1W............239 L5
Langham Street W1W............239 M5
Langley Lane SW8...............244 D8
Langley Street WC2H.............240 C7
Langton Close WC1X.............240 E3
Lanhill Road W9................238 A3
Lansdowne Place SE1............245 L4
Lant Street SE1................245 J3
Larcom Street SE17.............245 K6
Lauderdale Road W9.............238 B3
Laud Street SE11...............244 E7
Launcelot Street SE1............244 F3
Launceston Place W8.............242 C4
Laurence Pountney Lane EC4V......241 L7
Lavender Road SE16.............247 K5
Lavender Wharf SE16............247 K4
Lavington Street SE1............245 J1
Lawn Lane SW8.................244 D8
Lawrence Street SW3............242 F8
Lawrence Wharf SE16............247 L6
Law Street SE1.................245 L4
Laxton Place NW1...............239 L3
Laystall Street EC1R.............240 F4
Leadenhall Street EC3A...........246 A3
Leadenhall Street EC3V...........241 M6
Leake Street SE1................244 E2
Leather Lane EC1N..............241 G4
Leathermarket Street SE1.........245 M3
Luke Street WC1X...............240 E2
Lees Place W1K.................239 J7
Leicester Square ⊖ WC2H.........240 C7
Leicester Square WC2E...........240 C7
Leicester Street WC2H...........240 B7
Leigh Street WC1H..............240 C3
Leinster Gardens W2............238 C6
Leinster Mews W2...............238 C7
Leinster Place W2...............238 C7
Leinster Square W2..............238 A7
Leinster Terrace W2.............238 C7
Leman Street E1................246 C3
Lennox Gardens SW1X............243 G4
Lennox Gardens Mews SW1X.......243 G5
Leonard Street EC2A.............241 L3
Leopold Estate E3..............247 M1
Leopold Street E3...............247 L1
Leroy Street SE1...............245 M5
Lever Street EC1V...............241 J2
Lewisham Street SW1H...........244 B3
Lexham Gardens W8..............242 A5
Lexham Mews W8................242 A5
Lexington Street W1F............240 A7
Leyden Street E1...............246 B2
Leydon Close SE16..............247 H5
Library Street SE1..............245 H3
Lidlington Place NW1............240 A1
Lilestone Street NW8............238 F3
Lilley Close E1W................246 D5
Lillie Road SW6................242 A7
Lillie Yard SW6................242 A7
Limeburner Lane EC4M...........241 H6
Lime Close E1W................246 D5
Limehouse Causeway E14.........247 L4
Limehouse Link E14.............247 L3
Limehouse ⊖ E14..............247 J3
Limerston Street SW10...........242 D8
Lime Street EC3M...............241 M7
Lincoln's Inn Fields WC2A........240 E6
Linden Gardens W2..............238 A8
Lindley Street E1...............246 F1
Lindsay Square SW1V............244 B7
Lindsey Street EC1A.............241 H4
Linsey Street SE16.............246 D8
Linhope Street NW1.............239 G3
Lisle Street WC2H..............240 B7
Lisson Green Estate NW8.........238 F3
Lisson Grove W1...............239 G4
Lisson Grove NW8..............238 F3
Lisson Street NW1..............238 F4
Litchfield Street WC2H...........240 C7
Little Argyll Street W1F..........239 M6
Little Britain EC1A..............241 J5

Little Chester Street SW1X........243 K4
Little George Street SW1P........244 C3
Little Marlborough Street W1F......240 A7
Little New Street EC4A...........241 G6
Little Portland Street W1G........239 L6
Little Russell Street WC1A........240 C5
Little St James's Street SW1A......243 M2
Little Sanctuary SW1A...........244 C3
Little Somerset Street E1.........246 B3
Little Titchfield Street W1W.......239 M5
Liverpool Grove SE17............245 K7
Liverpool Street EC2M...........241 M5
Liverpool Street ⊖ ≥ EC2M......241 M5
Lizard Street EC1V..............241 K3
Llewellyn Street SE16............246 D7
Lloyd Baker Street WC1X..........240 F2
Lloyd's Avenue EC3N............246 B3
Lloyd Square WC1X.............240 F2
Lloyds Row EC1R...............241 G2
Lloyd Street WC1X..............240 F2
Locksley Estate E14.............247 L2
Locksley Street E14.............247 L1
Lockyer Street SE1..............245 L3
Lodge Road NW8...............238 F3
Loftie Street SE16..............246 D7
Logan Place W8................242 A5
Lolesworth Close E1.............246 B1
Lollard Street SE11.............244 F5
Lollard Street SE11.............244 F6
Loman Street SE1...............245 J2
Lomas Street E1................246 D1
Lombard Lane EC4Y.............241 G6
Lombard Street EC3V............241 L7
London Bridge EC4R............241 L8
London Bridge ⊖ ≥ SE1.........245 L1
London Bridge Street SE1.........245 L1
London Dungeon SE1............244 E2
London Eye SE1................244 E2
London Mews W2...............238 E6
London Road SE1...............245 H4
London Street EC3R.............246 A3
London Street W2...............238 E6
London Transport
  Museum WC2E...............240 D7
London Wall EC2V..............241 K5
London Zoo ZSL NW1...........239 J1
Longford Street NW1............239 L3
Long Lane EC1A................241 J5
Long Lane SE1.................245 L3
Longmoore Street SW1V..........243 M5
Longridge Road SW5............242 A5
Longville Road SE11............245 H5
Long Walk SE1.................246 A8
Long Yard WC1N...............240 E4
Lord North Street SW1P..........244 C4
Lorenzo Street WC1X............240 E1
Lorrimore Road SE17............245 J8
Lorrimore Square SE17...........245 H8
Lothbury EC2R................241 L6
Loughborough Street SE11........244 F7
Lovat Lane EC3R...............241 M7
Love Lane EC2V................241 K6
Lovell Place SE16..............247 K7
Lowell Street E14..............247 L2
Lower Belgrave Street SW1W......243 K4
Lower Grosvenor Place SW1W......243 L4
Lower James Street W1F..........240 A7
Lower John Street W1F...........240 A7
Lower Marsh SE1...............244 F3
Lower Road SE16...............247 G7
Lower Sloane Street SW1W........243 J6
Lower Thames Street EC3R........246 A4
Lower Thames Street EC3R........241 M8
Lowndes Close * SW1X...........243 J4
Lowndes Place SW1X............243 J4
Lowndes Square SW1X...........243 H3
Lowndes Street SW1X............243 J4
Lucan Place SW3...............242 F5
Lucey Road SE16...............246 C8
Ludgate Circus EC4M............241 H6
Ludgate Hill EC4M..............241 H6
Luke Street EC2A...............241 M3
Lukin Street E1................247 G3
Lupus Street W1K..............239 K7
Lupus Street SW1V.............243 L7
Lupus Street SW1V.............244 B7
Luton Street NW8..............238 E4
Luxborough Street W1U..........239 J4
Lyall Mews SW1X..............243 J4
Lyall Street SW1X..............243 J4
Lyons Place NW8...............238 E3
Lytham Street SE17.............245 K7

M

Macclesfield Road EC1V..........241 J2
Macclesfield Street * W1D........240 B7
Mace Close E1W...............246 E5
Macklin Street WC2B............240 D6
Mackworth Street NW1..........239 M2
Macleod Street SE17............245 K7
Madame Tussauds NW1..........239 J4
Maddox Street W1S.............239 M7
Magdalen Street SE1............245 M2
Magee Street SE11.............244 F8
Maguire Street SE1.............246 C6
Maida Avenue W9..............238 D4
Maida Vale W9................238 C2
Maida Vale ⊖ W9..............238 C2
Maiden Lane SE1..............245 K1
Maiden Lane WC2E.............240 D7
Major Road SE16..............246 D7
Makins Street SW3.............243 G6
Malet Street WC1E.............240 B4
Mallord Street SW3.............242 E8
Mallory Street NW8.............238 F3
Manette Street W1D............240 B6
Manilla Street E14.............247 M6
Manningford Close EC1V.........241 H2
Manor Place SE17..............245 J7
Manresa Road SW3.............242 F7
Mansell Street E1..............246 C3
Mansfield Mews W1G...........239 L5
Mansfield Street W1G...........239 L5
Mansion House ⊖ EC4V.........241 K7

Manson Mews SW7.............242 D5
Manson Place SW7.............242 D6
Mapleleaf Square SE16...........247 J6
Maples Place E1...............246 F1
Maple Street W1T..............239 M4
Marble Arch W1C..............239 H7
Marchmont Street WC1H.........240 C3
Margaret Street W1W...........239 L6
Margaretta Terrace SW3.........242 F7
Margery Street WC1X...........240 F3
Marigold Street SE16...........246 E7
Marine Street SE16.............246 C7
Market Mews W1J..............243 K1
Market Place W1W.............239 M6
Markham Square SW3...........243 G6
Markham Street SW3...........243 G6
Mark Lane EC3R...............246 A4
Marlborough Gate W2...........238 E7
Marlborough Place NW8.........238 C1
Marlborough Road SW1A........244 A2
Marlborough Street SW3..........242 F6
Marloes Road W8..............242 B4
Marlow Way SE16.............247 H6
Maroon Street E14.............247 K2
Marshall Street W1F............240 A7
Marshalsea Road SE1...........245 K2
Marsham Street SW1P..........244 C5
Marsh Wall E14................247 M5
Martha's Buildings EC1V.........241 K3
Martha Street E1...............246 F3
Martin Lane EC4V..............241 L7
Maryland Road W9.............238 A4
Marylands Road W9............238 A4
Marylebone ⊖ ≥ NW1.........239 G4
Marylebone Flyover W2.........238 E5
Marylebone High Street W1U......239 K5
Marylebone Lane W1U..........239 K6
Marylebone Road NW1..........239 G4
Marylebone Street W1G..........239 K5
Marylee Way SE11.............244 F6
Masjid Lane E14...............247 M2
Mason Street SE17.............245 M5
Massinger Street SE17...........245 M6
Masters Street E1..............247 J1
Matlock Street E14.............247 J2
Matthew Parker Street SW1H......244 C3
Maunsel Street SW1P...........244 B5
Mayfair Place W1J..............243 L1
Mayflower Street SE16...........246 F7
Mayford Estate NW1............240 A1
Maynards Quay E1W............246 F4
May's Court WC2N.............240 C8
McAuley Close SE1.............244 F4
McLeod's Mews SW7............242 C5
Meadcroft Road SE11...........245 G8
Meadcroft Road SE11...........245 H8
Meadow Road SW8.............244 E8
Meadow Row SE1..............245 J5
Meakin Estate SE1.............245 M4
Mecklenburgh Square WC1N.....240 D3
Medway Street SW1P............244 B5
Meeting House Alley E1W........246 E5
Melcombe Place NW1...........239 G4
Melcombe Street W1U...........239 H4
Melina Place NW8.............238 D2
Melior Street SE1..............245 M2
Melton Street NW1.............240 A2
Memorial Gates SW1W..........243 K3
Mepham Street SE1.............244 F2
Mercer Street WC2H............240 C7
Merchant Square W2............238 E5
Mermaid Court SE1.............245 K2
Merlin Street EC1R.............240 F2
Merrick Square SE1............245 K4
Merrington Road SW6...........242 A8
Merrow Street SE17............245 L7
Methley Street SE11............245 G7
Meymott Street SE1.............245 G2
Micawber Street N1.............241 K1
Micklethwaite Road SW6.........242 A8
Middlesex Street E1............246 A1
Middlesex Street E1............246 B1
Middle Street EC1A.............241 J5
Middle Temple EC4Y............240 F7
Middle Temple Lane EC4Y........240 F7
Middleton Drive SE16...........247 H6
Midland Road NW1.............240 C1
Midship Close SE16............247 H6
Milborne Grove SW10...........242 D7
Milcote Street SE1.............245 H3
Miles Street SW8...............244 D8
Milford Lane WC2R.............240 F7
Milk Street EC2V...............241 K6
Milk Yard E1W................247 G4
Millbank SW1P................244 C4
Millennium Bridge SE1..........241 J8
Millennium Harbour E14.........247 M6
Milligan Street E14.............247 L4
Millman Mews WC1N...........240 E4
Millman Street WC1N...........240 E4
Mill Place E14................247 K3
Millstream Road SE1............246 B7
Mill Street SE1................246 C6
Mill Street W1S...............239 L7
Milner Street SW3.............243 G5
Milton Street EC2Y.............241 K4
Milverton Street SE11...........245 G7
Mincing Lane EC3M............246 A4
Minera Mews SW1W............243 J5
Minories EC3N................246 B3
Mitchell Street EC1V...........241 J3
Mitre Road SE1...............245 G2
Mitre Street EC3A.............246 A3
Molyneux Street W1H..........239 G5
Monck Street SW1P............244 C4
Monkton Street SE11...........245 G6
Monkwell Square EC2Y..........241 K5
Monmouth Place W2............238 A6
Monmouth Road W2............238 A6
Monmouth Street WC2H.........240 C6
Montague Close SE1............245 L1
Montague Place WC1B..........240 C5
Montague Street WC1B..........240 C5
Montagu Mansions W1U.........239 H5
Montagu Mews North W1H.......239 H5
Montagu Mews West W1H.......239 H6
Montagu Place W1H............239 H5
Montagu Row W1U.............239 H5
Montagu Square W1H...........239 H5
Montagu Street W1H............239 H6
Montford Place SE11............245 G7
Monthorpe Road E1.............246 C1
Montpelier Place SW7...........242 F3
Montpelier Street SW7...........243 G3
Montpelier Walk SW7...........242 G3

Montrose Place SW1X...........243 K3
Monument ⊖ EC4R.............241 L7
Monument Street EC3R..........241 L7
Monument Street EC3R..........241 M7
Monza Street E1W.............247 G4
Moodkee Street SE16...........247 G7
Moore Street SW3.............243 H5
Moorfields EC2Y...............241 L5
Moorgate EC2R................241 L6
Moorgate ⊖ ≥ EC2Y...........241 L5
Moor Lane EC2Y...............241 K5
Moor Street W1D..............240 C7
Mora Street EC1V..............241 K2
Morecambe Street SE17..........245 K6
Moreland Street EC1V...........241 H2
More London SE1..............246 A5
Moreton Place SW1V............244 A6
Moreton Street SW1V...........244 B6
Moreton Terrace SW1V..........244 A6
Morgan's Lane SE1.............245 M2
Morgan's Lane SE1.............246 A5
Morley Street SE1..............245 G3
Mornington Crescent NW1........239 M1
Mornington Place NW1..........239 L1
Mornington Terrace NW1........239 L1
Morocco Street SE1.............246 A7
Morpeth Terrace SW1P..........243 M5
Morris Street E1...............246 F3
Morshead Road W9.............238 A2
Mortimer Market WC1E..........240 A4
Mortimer Street W1T............240 A5
Mortimer Street W1W...........239 M5
Morton Place SE1..............244 F4
Morwell Street WC1B...........240 B5
Moscow Place W2..............238 B7
Moscow Road W2..............238 B7
Mossop Street SW3.............243 G5
Motcomb Street SW1X...........243 J4
Mount Gate W2................242 E2
Mount Mills EC1V..............241 J3
Mount Pleasant WC1X...........240 F4
Mount Row W1K...............239 K8
Mount Street W1K..............239 K8
Mount Street Mews W1K........239 K8
Mount Terrace E1..............246 E1
Moxon Street W1U.............239 J5
Mulberry Street E1.............246 D2
Mulberry Walk SW3............242 E8
Mulready Street NW8...........238 F4
Mundy Street N1..............241 M2
Munster Square NW1...........239 L3
Munton Road SE17.............245 K5
Murphy Street SE1.............244 F3
Murray Grove N1..............241 K1
Musbury Street E1.............247 G2
Muscovy Street EC3N...........246 A4
Museum of London EC2Y.........241 J5
Museum Street WC1A...........240 C5
Myddelton Passage EC1R........241 G2
Myddelton Square EC1R.........241 G1
Myddelton Street EC1R..........241 G3
Myrdle Street E1...............246 D2

N

Naoroji Street WC1X............240 F2
Napier Grove N1...............241 K1
Narrow Street E14..............247 K4
Nash Street NW1...............239 L2
Nassau Street W1W............239 M5
Nathaniel Close * E1............246 C2
National Portrait
  Gallery WC2H................240 C8
Natural History Museum SW7......242 E4
Neal Street WC2H..............240 C6
Neathouse Place * SW1V.........243 M5
Neckinger SE1................246 C8
Needleman Street SE16..........247 H7
Nelson Close NW6.............238 A1
Nelson Place N1...............241 H1
Nelson's Column WC2N..........240 C8
Nelson Square SE1.............245 H2
Nelson Street E1...............246 E2
Nelson Terrace N1.............241 H1
Neptune Street SE16............247 G7
Nesham Street E1W.............246 D4
Netherton Grove SW10..........242 D8
Netley Street NW1.............239 M2
Nevern Place SW5.............242 A6
Nevern Square SW5............242 A6
Neville Street SW7.............242 E6
Newark Street E1..............246 E2
New Atlas Wharf E14...........247 M8
New Bond Street W1S...........239 L7
New Bond Street W1S...........239 L8
New Bridge Street EC4V.........241 H6
New Broad Street EC2M.........241 M5
New Burlington Street W1S.......239 M7
Newburn Street SE11...........244 F7
Newbury Street EC1A...........241 J5
Newcastle Place W2............238 E5
New Cavendish Street W1G.......239 L5
New Change EC4M.............241 J6
New Church Road SE5..........245 L8
Newcomen Street SE1...........245 K2
New Compton Street WC2H.......240 C6
Newcourt Street NW8...........238 F1
Newell Street E14..............247 L3
New Fetter Lane EC4A...........241 G6
Newgate Street EC1A...........241 H6
New Globe Walk SE1............241 J8
New Goulston Street E1..........246 B2
Newham's Row SE1.............246 A7
Newington Butts SE1...........245 H5
Newington Causeway SE1........245 J4
New Kent Road SE1............245 K5
Newlands Quay E1W............246 F4
Newman Street W1T............240 A5
New North Place EC2A..........241 M3
New North Road N1............240 D4
New North Road N1............241 L1
New Oxford Street WC1A........240 C6
Newport Street SE11............244 E5
New Quebec Street W1H.........239 H6
New Ride SW7................242 E3
New Road E1.................246 E2
New Row WC2N...............240 C7
New Spring Gardens Walk SE1....244 D7
New Square WC2A.............240 F6
New Street EC2M..............246 A2
New Street Square EC4A.........241 G6
Newton Road W2..............238 A6
Newton Street WC2B............240 D5
New Union Street EC2Y..........241 K5

Nicholas Lane EC3V............241 L7
Nicholson Street SE1...........245 H1
Nightingale Place SW10.........242 D8
Nile Street N1................241 K2
Nine Elms Lane SW8............244 C8
Noble Street EC2V.............241 J6
Noel Road N1.................241 J1
Noel Street W1F...............240 A6
Norbiton Road E14.............247 L2
Norfolk Crescent W2............239 G6
Norfolk Place W2..............238 E6
Norfolk Square W2.............238 E6
Norman Street EC1V............241 J3
Norris Street SW1Y............240 B8
Northampton Road EC1R.........241 G3
Northampton Square EC1V........241 H2
North Audley Street W1K.........239 J7
North Bank NW8..............238 F2
Northburgh Street EC1V.........241 H3
North Carriage Drive W2.........238 F7
Northdown Street N1...........240 D1
Northey Street E14.............247 K4
North Gower Street NW1........240 A2
Northington Street WC1N........240 E4
North Mews WC1N.............240 E4
North Ride W2................239 G7
North Row W1K...............239 J7
North Terrace SW3.............242 F5
Northumberland Alley EC3N......246 B3
Northumberland
  Avenue WC2N...............244 C1
Northumberland Place W2........238 A6
Northumberland Street WC2N.....244 C1
North Wharf Road W2...........238 E5
Northwick Terrace NW8.........238 D3
Norway Gate SE16.............247 K7
Norway Place E14.............247 L3
Norwich Street EC4A...........240 F5
Nottingham Place W1U..........239 J4
Nottingham Street W1U.........239 J4
Notting Hill Gate W11..........238 A8
Notting Hill Gate ⊖ W11........242 A1
Nugent Terrace NW8...........238 D1
Nutford Place W1H.............239 G5

O

Oakden Street SE11............245 G5
Oakington Road W9............238 A3
Oak Lane E14.................247 L3
Oakley Close EC1V.............241 H1
Oakley Gardens SW3............243 G8
Oakley Square NW1............240 A1
Oakley Street SW3.............242 F8
Oak Tree Road NW8...........238 F2
Oat Lane EC2V................241 J5
Occupation Road SE17..........245 J6
Ocean Square E1..............247 J1
Ocean Street E1...............247 J1
Odessa Street SE16............247 L7
Ogle Street W1W..............239 M5
Old Bailey EC4M..............241 H6
Old Barrack Yard SW1X.........243 J3
Old Bond Street W1S...........239 M8
Old Broad Street EC2N..........241 M6
Old Brompton Road SW5........242 B6
Old Brompton Road SW7........242 D6
Old Burlington Street W1S........239 M7
Oldbury Place W1U.............239 J4
Old Castle Street E1............246 B2
Old Cavendish Street W1G.......239 L6
Old Church Road E1............247 H2
Old Church Street SW3..........242 E7
Old Compton Street W1D........240 B7
Old Court Place W8............242 B3
Old Gloucester Street WC1N......240 D4
Old Jamaica Road SE16.........246 C7
Old Jewry EC2R...............241 K6
Old Kent Road SE1.............245 M5
Old Marylebone Road NW1.......239 G5
Old Montague Street E1.........246 C1
Old North Street WC1X..........240 E5
Old Paradise Street SE11........244 E5
Old Park Lane W1J.............243 K2
Old Pye Street SW1P............244 B4
Old Queen Street SW1H.........244 B3
Old Square WC2A..............240 F6
Old Street EC1V...............241 K3
Old Street ≥ ⊖ EC1Y...........241 L3
Old Street Junction EC1Y........241 L3
Oliver's Yard EC1Y.............241 L3
Olney Road SE17..............245 J8
O'Meara Street SE1............245 K2
Omega Place N1...............240 D1
Onega Gate SE16..............247 K8
Ongar Road SW6..............242 A8
Onslow Gardens SW7...........242 D6
Onslow Square SW7............242 E5
Onslow Square SW7............242 E6
Ontario Street SE1.............245 J4
Ontario Way E14..............247 M4
Opal Street SE11..............245 H6
Orange Place SE16.............247 G8
Orange Square SW1W...........243 K6
Orange Street E1W.............246 D5
Orange Street WC2H............240 B8
Orb Street SE17...............245 L6
Orchardson Street NW8.........238 E4
Orchard Street W1H............239 J6
Orde Hall Street WC1N..........240 E4
Orient Street SE11.............245 H5
Orme Court W2................238 B8
Orme Lane W2................238 B8
Orme Square Gate W2...........238 B8
Ormond Close W1.............240 D4
Ormonde Gate SW3.............243 H7
Ormond Yard SW1Y............240 A8
Orsett Mews W2...............238 C6
Orsett Street SE11.............244 E6
Orsett Terrace W2.............238 C5
Orton Street E1W..............246 D5
Osbert Street SW1V............244 B6
Osborn Street E1..............246 C2
Oslo Square SE16.............247 K7
Osnaburgh Street NW1..........239 L3
Osnaburgh Terrace NW1.........239 L3
Ossington Buildings W1U........239 J5
Ossington Street W2............238 A7
Ossulston Street NW1...........240 B1
Oswin Street SE11.............245 H5
Othello Close SE11.............245 H6
Otto Street SE17...............245 H8
Outer Circle NW1.............239 H3
Outer Circle NW1.............239 K1

Oval ⊖ SE11 .... 244 F8
Oval Way SE11 .... 244 E7
Ovington Square SW3 .... 243 G4
Ovington Street SW3 .... 243 G5
Owen Street EC1V 241 G1
Oxendon Street SW1Y 240 B8
Oxford Circus ⊖ W1B 239 M6
Oxford Road NW6 .... 238 A1
Oxford Square W2 .... 238 F6
Oxford Street W1C 239 L6
Oxford Street WC1A 240 A6

P

Pace Place E1 .... 246 E3
Pacific Wharf SE16 .... 247 H5
Paddington ⇄⊖ W2 .... 238 D6
Paddington Green W2 .... 238 E5
Paddington Street W1U 239 J5
Pageant Crescent SE16 .... 247 K5
Page Street SW1P 244 B5
Paget Street EC1V 241 H2
Pakenham Street WC1X 240 E3
Palace Avenue W8 .... 242 B2
Palace Court W2 .... 238 A7
Palace Gardens Terrace W8 .... 242 A1
Palace Gate W8 .... 242 C3
Palace Green W8 .... 242 B2
Palace of Westminster SW1A 244 D3
Palace Place SW1E 243 M4
Palace Street SW1E 243 M4
Pall Mall SW1Y 244 A1
Pall Mall East SW1Y 244 B1
Palmer Street SW1H 244 B3
Pancras Lane EC4N 241 K6
Pancras Road N1C 240 C1
Panton Street SW1Y 240 B8
Paradise Street SE16 .... 246 E7
Paradise Walk SW3 .... 243 H8
Pardoner Street SE1 .... 245 L4
Pardon Street EC1V 241 H3
Parfett Street E1 .... 246 D2
Paris Garden SE1 .... 245 G1
Park Crescent W1B 239 K4
Park Crescent Mews West W1G 239 K4
Parker's Row SE1 .... 246 C7
Parker Street WC2B 240 D6
Park Lane W1K 239 H7
Park Lane W1 .... 243 J1
Park Place SW1A 243 M1
Park Place Villas W2 .... 238 D4
Park Road NW1 .... 238 H3
Park Square East NW1 .... 239 L3
Park Square Mews NW1 .... 239 K3
Park Square West NW1 .... 239 K3
Park Street SE1 .... 245 K1
Park Street W1K 239 J7
Park Village East NW1 .... 239 L1
Park Walk SW10 .... 242 D8
Park West Place W2 .... 239 G6
Parliament Street SW1A 244 C2
Parry Street SW8 .... 244 D8
Passmore Square SW1W 243 J6
Pater Street W8 .... 242 A4
Pattina Walk SE16 .... 247 K5
Paul Street EC2A 241 M3
Paultons Square SW3 .... 242 E8
Paveley Street NW1 .... 239 G3
Pavilion Road SW1X 243 H3
Pavilion Street SW1X 243 H4
Paxton Terrace SW1V 243 L7
Peabody Avenue SW1V 243 L7
Peabody Estate SE1 .... 245 J1
Peacock Street SE17 .... 245 J6
Pearl Street E1W 246 F5
Pearman Street SE1 .... 245 G3
Pear Tree Court EC1R 241 G3
Peartree Lane E1W 247 G4
Pear Tree Street EC1V 241 J3
Peel Street W8 .... 242 A1
Peerless Street EC1V 241 K2
Pelham Crescent SW7 .... 242 F6
Pelham Place SW7 .... 242 F5
Pelham Street SW7 .... 242 F5
Pelier Street SE17 .... 245 K8
Pemberton Row EC4A 241 G6
Pembridge Gardens W2 .... 238 A8
Pembridge Place W2 .... 238 A7
Pembridge Square W2 .... 238 A7
Pembridge Villas W11 .... 238 A7
Pembroke Close SW1X 243 J3
Penang Street E1W 246 F5
Penfold Place NW8 .... 238 F5
Penfold Street NW8 .... 238 E4
Pennant Mews W8 .... 242 B5
Pennington Street E1W 246 D4
Pennyfields E14 .... 247 M1
Penrose Grove SE17 .... 245 J7
Penrose Street SE17 .... 245 J7
Penton Place SE17 .... 245 H6
Penton Rise WC1X 240 E2
Penton Street N1 .... 240 F1
Pentonville Road N1 .... 240 D1
Penywern Road SW5 .... 242 A6
Pepper Street SE1 .... 245 J2
Pepys Street EC3N 246 A4
Percival Street EC1V 241 H3
Percy Circus WC1X 240 E2
Percy Street W1T 240 B5
Perkin's Rents SW1P 244 B4
Perryn Road SE16 .... 246 E7
Petersham Mews SW7 .... 242 D4
Petersham Place SW7 .... 242 C4
Peter Street W1F 240 B7
Peto Place NW1 .... 239 L3
Petticoat Lane E1 .... 246 B2
Petty France SW1H 244 A3
Petty Wales EC3R 246 A4
Petyward SW3 .... 243 G6
Phelp Street SE17 .... 245 L7
Phene Street SW3 .... 243 G8
Phillimore Walk W8 .... 242 A3
Philpot Lane EC3M 241 M7
Philpot Street E1 .... 246 E2
Phipp's Mews SW1W 243 L5
Phipp Street EC2A 241 M3
Phoenix Place WC1X 240 F3
Phoenix Road NW1 .... 240 B1
Phoenix Street WC2H 240 C6
Piccadilly W1J 243 L2
Piccadilly Arcade SW1Y 243 M1
Piccadilly Circus W1B 240 A8
Piccadilly Circus ⊖ W1J 240 B8

Pickard Street EC1V 241 J2
Picton Place W1U 239 K6
Pier Head E1W 246 E6
Pigott Street E14 .... 247 M3
Pilgrimage Street SE1 .... 245 L3
Pilgrim Street ⊖ SW1V 244 B6
Pimlico Road SW1W 243 J6
Pinchin Street E1 .... 246 D3
Pindar Street EC2A 241 M4
Pindock Mews W9 .... 238 B3
Pine Street EC1R 240 F3
Pitfield Street N1 .... 241 M1
Pitsea Street E1 .... 247 H3
Pitt's Head Mews W1J 243 K2
Pitt Street W8 .... 242 A2
Pixley Street E14 .... 247 L2
Platina Street * EC2A 241 L3
Plover Way SE16 .... 247 K8
Plumbers Row E1 .... 246 D2
Plumtree Court EC4A 241 G6
Plympton Street NW8 .... 238 F4
Pocock Street SE1 .... 245 H2
Poland Street W1F 240 A6
Pollen Street W1S 239 L7
Pollitt Drive NW8 .... 238 E3
Polperro Mews SE11 .... 245 G5
Polygon Road NW1 .... 240 B1
Pond Place SW3 .... 242 F6
Ponler Street E1 .... 246 E3
Ponsonby Place SW1P 244 C6
Ponsonby Terrace SW1P 244 C6
Ponton Road SW1V 244 B8
Pont Street SW1X 243 H4
Poolmans Street SE16 .... 247 H6
Pope Street SE1 .... 246 B7
Poplar Place W2 .... 238 B7
Poppin's Court EC4A 241 H6
Porchester Gardens W2 .... 238 B7
Porchester Gate W2 .... 238 C8
Porchester Place W2 .... 239 G6
Porchester Road W2 .... 238 B5
Porchester Square W2 .... 238 B6
Porchester Terrace W2 .... 238 C7
Porchester Terrace North W2 .... 238 C6
Porlock Street SE1 .... 245 L3
Porter Street NW1 .... 239 H4
Porteus Road W2 .... 238 D5
Portland Place W1B 239 L4
Portland Place W1B 239 L5
Portland Square E1W 246 E5
Portland Street SE17 .... 245 L7
Portman Close W1H 239 J6
Portman Mews South W1H 239 J6
Portman Square W1H 239 J6
Portman Street W1H 239 J6
Portpool Lane EC1N 240 F4
Portsea Place W2 .... 239 G6
Portsmouth Street WC2A 240 E6
Portsoken Street E1 .... 246 B3
Potier Street SE1 .... 245 L4
Potters Fields SE1 .... 246 B6
Pottery Street SE16 .... 246 F7
Poultry EC2V 241 K6
Powis Place WC1N 240 D4
Praed Mews W2 .... 238 E6
Praed Street W2 .... 238 E6
Pratt Walk SE1 .... 244 E5
Premier Place E14 .... 247 M4
Prescot Street E1 .... 246 C3
Preston Close SE1 .... 245 M5
Price's Street SE1 .... 245 H1
Prideaux Place WC1X 240 F2
Primrose Street EC2A 246 A1
Prince Albert Road NW8 .... 238 F1
Prince Consort Road SW7 .... 242 D3
Princelet Street E1 .... 246 C1
Prince of Wales Gate SW7 .... 242 F3
Princes Arcade SW1Y 240 A8
Prince's Gardens SW7 .... 242 E3
Prince's Gate Mews SW7 .... 242 E4
Princes Riverside Road SE16 .... 247 H5
Prince's Road SW1V 238 A7
Princess Road NW6 .... 238 A1
Princess Street SE1 .... 245 H4
Prince's Street W1B 239 L6
Prince's Street EC2R 241 L6
Princeton Street WC1R 240 E5
Prioress Street SE1 .... 245 L4
Priory Green Estate N1 .... 240 E1
Priory Walk SW10 .... 242 D7
Proctor Street WC1V 240 E5
Prospect Place E1W 247 G5
Prospect Street SE16 .... 246 F7
Provident Court W1K 239 J7
Provost Street N1 .... 241 L1
Prusom Street E1W 246 F5
Pudding Lane EC3R 241 M7
Pumphouse Mews E1 .... 246 D3
Purbrook Street SE1 .... 246 A7
Purcell Street N1 .... 241 M1
Purchese Street NW1 .... 240 B1

Q

Quebec Way SE16 .... 247 J7
Queen Anne's Gate SW1H 244 B3
Queen Anne Street W1G 239 K5
Queen Elizabeth Street SE1 .... 246 B6
Queen Mother Gate W2 .... 243 J2
Queensborough Terrace W2 .... 238 C7
Queensbury Place SW7 .... 242 E5
Queen's Gardens W2 .... 238 C7
Queen's Gate SW7 .... 242 D3
Queen's Gate SW7 .... 242 D4
Queen's Gate Gardens SW7 .... 242 D5
Queen's Gate Mews SW7 .... 242 D4
Queen's Gate Place SW7 .... 242 D4
Queen's Gate Place Mews SW7 .... 242 D4
Queen's Gate Terrace SW7 .... 242 C4
Queen's Mews W2 .... 238 B7
Queen Square WC1N 240 D4
Queen's Row SE17 .... 245 K7
Queen Street EC4N 241 K7
Queen Street W1J 243 L1
Queen Street Place EC4R 241 K7
Queen's Walk SE1 .... 246 A5
Queen's Walk SW1A 243 M2
Queensway W2 .... 238 B6
Queensway ⊖ W2 .... 238 B6
Queen Victoria Street EC4V 241 J7
Quick Street N1 .... 241 H1

R

Raby Street E14 .... 247 K2
Radcliffe Road SE1 .... 246 B8
Radcot Street SE11 .... 245 G7
Radnor Mews W2 .... 238 E6
Radnor Place W2 .... 238 F6
Radnor Street EC1V 241 K3
Radnor Walk SW3 .... 243 G7
Railway Approach SE1 .... 245 L1
Railway Avenue SE16 .... 247 G6
Railway Street N1 .... 240 D1
Raine Street E1W 246 F5
Ralston Street SW3 .... 243 H7
Ramillies Place W1F 239 M6
Ramillies Street W1F 239 M6
Rampart Street E1 .... 246 E2
Rampayne Street SW1V 244 B6
Randall Road SE11 .... 244 D6
Randall Row SE11 .... 244 D6
Randolph Avenue W9 .... 238 B1
Randolph Crescent W9 .... 238 C3
Randolph Gardens NW6 .... 238 B1
Randolph Mews W9 .... 238 D4
Randolph Road W9 .... 238 C4
Ranelagh Grove SW1W 243 K6
Ranelagh Road SW1V 244 A7
Rangoon Street * EC3N 246 B3
Ranston Street NW8 .... 238 F4
Raphael Street SW7 .... 243 G3
Ratcliffe Cross Street E1W 247 J3
Ratcliffe Lane E14 .... 247 J3
Rathbone Place W1T 240 B5
Rathbone Street W1T 240 A5
Raven Row E1 .... 246 F1
Ravensdon Street SE11 .... 245 G7
Ravey Street EC2A 241 M3
Rawlings Street SW3 .... 243 G5
Rawstorne Street EC1V 241 H2
Ray Street EC1R 241 G4
Reardon Place E1W 246 E5
Reardon Street E1W 246 E5
Rectory Square E1 .... 247 H1
Redan Place W2 .... 238 B6
Redburn Street SW3 .... 243 G7
Redcastle Close E1W 247 G4
Redcliffe Gardens SW10 .... 242 B7
Redcliffe Mews SW10 .... 242 C7
Redcliffe Place SW10 .... 242 C8
Redcliffe Road SW10 .... 242 C7
Redcliffe Square SW10 .... 242 B7
Redcliffe Street SW10 .... 242 B8
Redcross Way SE1 .... 245 K2
Redesdale Street SW3 .... 243 G7
Redfield Lane SW5 .... 242 A5
Redhill Street NW1 .... 239 L1
Red Lion Row SE5 .... 245 K8
Red Lion Square WC1R 240 E5
Red Lion Street WC2B 240 E5
Redman's Road E1 .... 247 G1
Red Place W1K 239 J7
Redriff Road SE16 .... 247 J8
Reedworth Street SE11 .... 245 G5
Reeves Mews W1K 239 J8
Regal Close E1 .... 246 D1
Regan Way N1 .... 241 M1
Regency Street SW1P 244 B5
Regent Place W1B 240 A7
Regent's Park ⊖ W1B 239 L4
Regent's Park NW1 .... 239 J1
Regent's Park Estate NW1 .... 239 L2
Regent Square WC1H 240 D2
Regent Street SW1Y 240 B8
Regent Street W1S 239 M7
Relton Mews SW7 .... 243 G4
Remington Street N1 .... 241 H1
Remnant Street WC2A 240 E6
Renforth Street SE16 .... 247 G7
Renfrew Road SE11 .... 245 H5
Rennie Street SE1 .... 245 H1
Rephidim Street SE1 .... 245 M4
Repton Street E14 .... 247 K2
Reveley Square SE16 .... 247 K7
Rex Place W1K 239 J8
Rhodeswell Road E14 .... 247 L2
Rich Street E14 .... 247 M3
Rickett Street SW6 .... 242 A8
Ridgemount Street WC1E 240 B4
Ridgemount Gardens WC1E 240 B4
Riding House Street W1W 239 M5
Riley Road SE1 .... 246 B7
Ripley's Believe It or Not! W1J 240 B8
Risborough Street SE1 .... 245 J2
Risdon Street SE16 .... 247 G7
Rissinghill Street N1 .... 240 F1
River Street EC1R 240 F2
Rivington Street EC2A 241 M3
Robert Adam Street W1U 239 J6
Roberts Close SE16 .... 247 J7
Robert Street NW1 .... 239 L2
Rochester Row SW1P 244 A5
Rochester Street SW1P 244 B5
Rockingham Street SE1 .... 245 J4
Rocliffe Street N1 .... 241 H1
Roding Mews E1W 246 D5
Rodmarton Street W1U 239 H5
Rodney Place SE17 .... 245 K5
Rodney Road SE17 .... 245 K5
Rodney Street N1 .... 240 E1
Roger Street WC1N 240 E4
Roland Gardens SW7 .... 242 D6
Roland Way SE17 .... 245 L7
Romford Street E1 .... 246 E2
Romilly Street W1D 240 C7
Romney Street SW1P 244 C5
Rood Lane EC3M 241 M7
Ropemaker Road SE16 .... 247 K7
Ropemaker Street EC2Y 241 L5
Roper Lane SE1 .... 246 B7
Rope Street SE16 .... 247 K8
Rope Walk Gardens E1 .... 246 E2
Rosary Gardens SW7 .... 242 D6
Roscoe Street EC1Y 241 K3
Rose Alley SE1 .... 245 K1
Rosebery Avenue EC1R 240 F3
Rosemoor Street SW3 .... 243 G6
Rose Street WC2E 240 C7
Rossmore Road NW1 .... 239 G3
Rotary Street SE1 .... 245 H3
Rotherhithe ⊖ SE16 .... 247 G6
Rotherhithe Street SE16 .... 247 G6
Rotherhithe Street SE16 .... 247 J4
Rotherhithe Tunnel E1 .... 247 H4
Rothsay Street SE1 .... 245 M4
Rotten Row W2 .... 242 F2

Rouel Road SE16 .... 246 C8
Roupell Street SE1 .... 245 G2
Royal Albert Hall SW7 .... 242 E3
Royal Avenue SW3 .... 243 H6
Royal Hospital Road SW3 .... 243 H7
Royal Mint Street E1 .... 246 C4
Royal Oak ⊖ W2 .... 238 B5
Royal Oak Yard SE1 .... 246 A7
Royal Opera House WC2E 240 D7
Royal Road SE17 .... 245 H8
Royal Street SE1 .... 244 E4
Rudolph Road NW6 .... 238 A1
Rugby Street WC1N 240 E4
Rum Close E1W 246 F4
Rupack Street SE16 .... 246 F7
Rupert Street W1D 240 B7
Rushworth Street SE1 .... 245 H2
Russell Court SW1A 244 A2
Russell Square WC1B 240 C4
Russell Square ⊖ WC1B 240 D4
Russell Street WC2B 240 D7
Russia Dock Road SE16 .... 247 K6
Rutherford Street SW1P 244 B5
Rutland Gardens SW7 .... 243 G3
Rutland Gate SW7 .... 242 F3
Rutland Mews SW7 .... 242 F4
Rutland Street SW7 .... 242 F4
Ryder Street SW1Y 244 A1

S

Sackville Street W1S 240 A8
Saffron Hill EC1N 241 G4
Saffron Street EC1N 241 G4
Sail Street SE11 .... 244 F5
St Agnes Place SE11 .... 245 G8
St Alban's Grove W8 .... 242 B4
St Alban's Street SW1Y 240 B8
St Alphage Garden EC2Y 241 K5
St Andrews Hill EC4V 241 H7
St Andrew's Place NW1 .... 239 L3
St Andrew Street EC4A 241 G5
St Anne's Court W1F 240 B6
St Ann's Street SW1P 244 C4
St Anselm's Place W1K 239 K7
St Barnabas Street SW1W 243 K6
St Botolph Street EC3N 246 B2
St Bride Street EC4A 241 G6
St Chad's Street WC1H 240 D2
St Clare Street EC3N 246 B3
St Clements Lane WC2A 240 E6
St Cross Street EC1N 241 G4
St Dunstan's Hill EC3R 241 M8
St Dunstan's Lane EC3R 241 M7
St Elmos Road SE16 .... 247 J7
St Ermin's Hill SW1H 244 B3
St George's Circus SE1 .... 245 H3
St George's Drive SW1V 243 M6
St George's Estate E1 .... 246 D3
St George's Lane * EC3R 241 M7
St George's Road SE1 .... 245 G4
St George's Square SW1V 244 B7
St George Street W1S 239 L7
St Giles High Street WC2H 240 C6
St Helen's Place EC3A 241 M6
St James Market * SW1Y 240 B8
St James's Park ⊖ SW1H 244 B3
St James's Park SW1A 244 B3
St James's Place SW1A 243 M2
St James's Road SE16 .... 246 D8
St James's Square SW1Y 240 A8
St James's Street SW1A 243 M1
St James Walk EC1R 241 G3
St John's Lane EC1M 241 H4
St John's Place EC1M 241 H4
St John's Square EC1V 241 H4
St John Street EC1V 241 H2
St John's Wood High Street NW8 .... 238 F1
St John's Wood Road NW8 .... 238 E3
St Katharine's Way E1W 246 C5
St Leonard's Terrace SW3 .... 243 H7
St Loo Avenue SW3 .... 243 G8
St Luke's Close EC1V 241 K3
St Luke's Street SW3 .... 242 F6
St Manningtree E1 .... 246 C2
St Mark Street E1 .... 246 C3
St Martin's Lane WC2N 240 C7
St Martin's le Grand EC1A 241 J6
St Martin's Place WC2N 240 C8
St Mary at Hill EC3R 241 M8
St Mary Axe EC3A 246 A3
St Marychurch Street SE16 .... 246 F7
St Mary's Gardens SE11 .... 245 G5
St Mary's Terrace W2 .... 238 D4
St Mary's Walk SE11 .... 245 G5
St Matthew Street SW1P 244 B4
St Michael's Street W2 .... 238 E6
St Olav's Square SE16 .... 246 F7
St Oswald's Place SE11 .... 244 E7
St Oswulf Street * SW1P 244 C6
St Pancras International ⇄ N1C 240 C1
St Paul's ⊖ EC1A 241 J6
St Paul's Avenue SE16 .... 247 J5
St Paul's Cathedral EC4M 241 J6
St Paul's Churchyard EC4M 241 J6
St Paul's Way E3 .... 247 L1
St Petersburgh Mews W2 .... 238 B7
St Petersburgh Place W2 .... 238 B7
St Saviours Wharf SE1 .... 246 C6
St Stephen's Gardens W2 .... 238 A5
St Swithin's Lane EC4N 241 L7
St Thomas Street SE1 .... 245 L2
St Vincent Street W1U 239 J5
Salamanca Street SE1 .... 244 D6
Salem Road W2 .... 238 B7
Sale Place W2 .... 238 F5
Salisbury Court EC4Y 241 G6
Salisbury Place W1H 239 H4
Salisbury Street NW8 .... 238 F4
Salmon Lane E14 .... 247 J2
Salter Road SE16 .... 247 J5
Salter Street E14 .... 247 M4
Samford Street NW8 .... 238 F4
Sampson Street E1W 246 D5
Sancroft Street SE11 .... 244 F6
Sandland Street WC1R 240 E5
Sandpiper Close SE16 .... 247 L6
Sandwich Street WC1H 240 C2
Sandy's Row E1 .... 246 B1
Sans Walk EC1R 241 G3
Sardinia Street WC2A 240 E6
Savage Gardens EC3N 246 B3
Savile Row W1S 239 M7
Savoy Hill WC2R 240 E8

Savoy Place WC2R 240 D8
Savoy Street WC2E 240 D8
Sawyer Street SE1 .... 245 J2
Scala Street W1T 240 A5
Scandrett Street E1W 246 E5
Scarborough Street E1 .... 246 C3
Scarsdale Villas W8 .... 242 A4
Schooner Close * SE16 .... 247 H6
Science Museum SW7 .... 242 E4
Scoresby Street SE1 .... 245 H2
Scotch House Junction SW1X 243 G3
Scotland Place SW1A 244 C1
Scott Ellis Gardens NW8 .... 238 E3
Scott Lidgett Crescent SE16 .... 246 D7
Scrutton Street EC2A 241 M4
Seaford Street WC1H 240 D2
Seagrave Road SW6 .... 242 A8
Sea Life London Aquarium SE1 .... 244 E3
Searles Road SE1 .... 245 L5
Sebastian Street EC1V 241 H2
Secker Street SE1 .... 244 F2
Sedan Way SE17 .... 245 M6
Sedding Street SW1X 243 J5
Seddon Street WC1X 240 E3
Seething Lane EC3N 246 A4
Sekforde Street EC1R 241 H3
Selfridges W1A 239 J6
Selsey Street E14 .... 247 M1
Selwood Place SW7 .... 242 E6
Semley Place SW1W 243 K6
Senior Street W2 .... 238 B4
Senrab Street E1 .... 247 H2
Serle Street WC2A 240 F6
Serpentine Bridge W2 .... 242 E1
Serpentine Road W2 .... 242 F2
Seth Street SE16 .... 247 G7
Settles Street E1 .... 246 D2
Seven Dials WC2H 240 C6
Seville Street SW1X 243 H3
Sevington Street W9 .... 238 A3
Seward Street EC1V 241 J3
Seymour Mews W1H 239 J6
Seymour Place W1H 239 J5
Seymour Street W1H 239 H6
Seymour Street W2 .... 239 G7
Seymour Walk SW10 .... 242 C7
Shad Thames SE1 .... 246 B6
Shad Thames SE1 .... 246 C6
Shadwell ⊖ E1 .... 246 F3
Shadwell Gardens E1 .... 246 F3
Shaftesbury Avenue W1D 240 B7
Shaftesbury Avenue WC2H 240 C6
Shaftesbury Street N1 .... 241 K1
Shakespeare's Globe SE1 .... 241 J8
Shand Street SE1 .... 246 A6
Sharsted Street SE17 .... 245 H7
Shaw Crescent E14 .... 247 K2
Shawfield Street SW3 .... 243 G7
Sheffield Terrace W8 .... 242 A2
Sheldon Square W2 .... 238 D5
Shelmerdine Close E3 .... 247 M1
Shelton Street WC2H 240 D6
Shepherdess Walk N1 .... 241 K1
Shepherd Street W1J 243 K1
Sheraton Street W1F 240 B6
Sherborne Lane EC4N 241 L7
Sherwood Street W1D 240 A7
Ship and Mermaid Row SE1 .... 245 M2
Shipwright Road SE16 .... 247 K7
Shirland Road W9 .... 238 A3
Shoe Lane EC4A 241 G5
Shorter Street EC3N 246 B4
Shorts Gardens WC2H 240 C6
Short Street SE1 .... 245 G2
Shoulder of Mutton Alley E14 .... 247 K4
Shouldham Street W1H 239 G5
Shroton Street NW1 .... 238 F4
Siddons Lane W1H 239 H4
Sidmouth Street WC1N 240 D3
Sidney Square E1 .... 246 F2
Sidney Street E1 .... 246 F1
Silex Street SE1 .... 245 H3
Silk Street EC2Y 241 K4
Silver Walk SE16 .... 247 K5
Silvester Street SE1 .... 245 K3
Singer Street EC2A 241 L3
Sir John Soane's Museum WC2A 240 E5
Sir Simon Milton Square SW1V 243 L4
Skinner Place * SW1W 243 J6
Skinners Lane EC4V 241 K7
Skinner Street EC1R 241 G3
Slippers Place SE16 .... 246 F8
Sloane Avenue SW3 .... 243 G6
Sloane Court East SW3 .... 243 J6
Sloane Court West SW3 .... 243 J6
Sloane Gardens SW1W 243 J6
Sloane Square SW1W 243 J6
Sloane Square ⊖ SW1W 243 J5
Sloane Street SW1X 243 H3
Sloane Terrace SW1X 243 J5
Smeaton Street E1W 246 E5
Smithfield Street EC1A 241 H5
Smith Square SW1P 244 C4
Smith Street SW3 .... 243 G7
Smith Terrace SW3 .... 243 G7
Smithy Street E1 .... 247 G1
Snowden Street EC2A 241 M4
Snow Hill EC1A 241 H5
Snowsfields SE1 .... 245 L2
Soho Square W1D 240 B6
Soho Street W1D 240 B6
Somerford Way SE16 .... 247 K7
Somers Crescent W2 .... 238 F6
Somerset House WC2R 240 E7
Somerstown Estate NW1 .... 240 A1
Sondes Street SE17 .... 245 L7
South & West Africa Gate SW1A 244 A3
Southall Place SE1 .... 245 L3
Southampton Buildings WC2A 240 F5
Southampton Place WC1A 240 D5
Southampton Row WC1B 240 D4
Southampton Street WC2E 240 D8
South Audley Street W1K 239 K8
South Carriage Drive SW1X 243 H3
South Carriage Drive SW7 .... 242 F3
South Eaton Place SW1W 243 J5
Southern Street N1 .... 240 E1
South Kensington ⊖ SW7 .... 242 E5
South Kensington ⊖ SW7 .... 242 E5
South Lambeth Road SW8 .... 244 D8
South Molton Lane W1K 239 K6
South Molton Street W1K 239 K6
South Parade SW3 .... 242 E6
South Place EC2M 241 L5
South Sea Street SE16 .... 247 L8
South Square WC1R 240 F5

South Street W1K.....243 J1
South Tenter Street E1.....246 C3
South Terrace SW7.....242 F5
Southwark ⊖ SE1.....245 H2
Southwark Bridge SE1.....241 K8
Southwark Bridge Road SE1.....245 J3
Southwark Park Road SE16.....246 E8
Southwark Street SE1.....245 H1
Southwell Gardens SW7.....242 C5
South Wharf Road W2.....238 E6
Southwick Mews W2.....238 F6
Southwick Place W2.....238 F6
Southwick Street W2.....238 F6
Sovereign Close E1W.....246 F4
Sovereign Crescent SE16.....247 J4
Spanish Place W1U.....239 J5
Spa Road SE16.....246 C8
Spear Mews SW5.....242 A6
Spelman Street E1.....246 C1
Spence Close SE16.....247 K7
Spencer Street EC1V.....241 H2
Spenser Street SW1E.....244 A4
Spert Street E14.....247 J4
Spital Square E1.....246 A1
Spring Gardens SW1A.....244 C1
Spring Street W2.....238 E6
Spurgeon Street SE1.....245 L4
Spur Road SE1.....244 F3
Stables Way SE11.....244 F7
Stable Yard Road SW1A.....244 A2
Stacey Street WC2H.....240 C6
Stafford Place SW1.....243 M3
Stafford Road NW6.....238 A2
Stafford Street W1S.....239 M8
Stafford Terrace W8.....242 A3
Stainer Street SE1.....245 L2
Staining Lane EC2V.....241 K6
Stainsby Road E14.....247 M2
Stalham Street SE16.....246 F8
Stamford Street SE1.....245 G1
Stanford Place SE1.....245 M6
Stanford Road W8.....242 B4
Stanford Street * SW1V.....244 B6
Stanhope Close * SE16.....247 H6
Stanhope Gardens SW7.....242 D5
Stanhope Gate W1K.....243 K1
Stanhope Mews SW7.....242 D5
Stanhope Mews East SW7.....242 D5
Stanhope Mews West SW7.....242 D5
Stanhope Place W2.....239 G7
Stanhope Place Gate W2.....239 G7
Stanhope Row W1J.....243 K1
Stanhope Street NW1.....239 M1
Stanhope Terrace W2.....238 E7
Stannary Street SE11.....245 G7
Staples Close SE16.....247 J5
Staple Street SE1.....245 L3
Starcross Street NW1.....240 A2
Star Street W2.....238 F6
Station Approach SE1.....244 F3
Stave Yard Road SE16.....247 K6
Stead Street SE17.....245 K6
Steedman Street SE17.....245 J5
Steel's Lane E1.....247 G3
Steeres Way SE16.....247 K7
Stephenson Way NW1.....240 A3
Stephen Street W1T.....240 B5
Stepney Green E1.....247 H1
Stepney High Street E1.....247 J1
Stepney Way E1.....246 E1
Sterling Street SW7.....243 G3
Stevedore Street E1W.....246 E5
Stevens Street SE1.....246 A7
Steward Street * E1.....246 B1
Stewart's Grove SW3.....242 F6
Stew Lane EC4V.....241 J7
Stillington Street SW1P.....244 A5
Stockholm Way E1W.....246 D5
Stocks Place E14.....247 M3
Stone Buildings WC2A.....240 F5
Stonecutter Street EC4A.....241 G6
Stoney Lane E1.....246 B2
Stoney Street SE1.....245 K1
Stopford Road SE17.....245 J7
Store Street WC1E.....240 B5
Storey's Gate SW1H.....244 C3
Storks Road SE16.....246 D8
Stoughton Close SE11.....244 E6
Stourcliffe Street W1H.....239 G6
Strafford Street E14.....247 M6
Strand WC2R.....240 D8
Stratford Place W1C.....239 K6
Stratford Road W8.....242 A5
Strathearn Place W2.....238 F7
Stratton Street W1J.....243 L1
Strutton Ground SW1P.....244 B4
Strype Street E1.....246 B2
Stuart Road NW6.....238 A2
Stukeley Street WC2B.....240 D6
Sturgeon Road SE17.....245 J7
Sturge Street SE1.....245 J3
Sturt Street N1.....241 K1
Stutfield Street E1.....246 D3
Sudley Street N1.....241 H1
Sudrey Street SE1.....245 J3
Suffolk Lane EC4V.....241 L2
Suffolk Street SW1Y.....240 B8
Sugar Lane SE16.....246 D7
Sugar Quay Walk EC3R.....246 A4
Sullivan Road SE11.....245 G5
Summercourt Road E1.....247 G2
Summers Street EC1R.....240 F4
Sumner Place SW7.....242 E6
Sumner Street SE1.....245 J1
Sunderland Terrace W2.....238 A6
Sun Passage SE16.....246 D8
Sun Street EC2M.....241 M4
Sun Street Passage EC2M.....241 M5
Surrendale Place W9.....238 A4
Surrey Quays Road SE16.....247 H7
Surrey Row SE1.....245 H2
Surrey Square SE17.....245 M6
Surrey Street WC2E.....240 E7
Surrey Water Road SE16.....247 H6
Sussex Gardens W2.....238 E6
Sussex Mews East W2.....238 E7
Sussex Place NW1.....239 H3
Sussex Place W2.....238 E6
Sussex Square W2.....238 E7
Sussex Street SW1V.....243 L7
Sutherland Avenue W9.....238 A4
Sutherland Row SW1V.....243 L6
Sutherland Square SE17.....245 J7
Sutherland Street SW1V.....243 L7
Sutton Row W1D.....240 B6
Sutton Street E1.....247 G3

Suttons Way EC1Y.....241 K4
Swain Street NW8.....238 F3
Swallow Place W1B.....239 L6
Swallow Street W1B.....240 A8
Swan Lane EC4R.....241 L8
Swan Mead SE1.....245 M4
Swan Road SE16.....247 G6
Swan Street SE1.....245 K3
Swan Walk SW3.....243 H8
Swedenborg Gardens E1.....246 E4
Sweeney Crescent SE1.....246 C7
Swinton Street WC1X.....240 E2
Sydney Place SW7.....242 F6
Sydney Street SW3.....242 F6
Symons Street SW3.....243 H6

T
Tabard Gardens Estate SE1.....245 L3
Tabard Street SE1.....245 L3
Tabernacle Street EC2A.....241 L3
Tachbrook Street SW1V.....244 A6
Talbot Road W2.....238 A6
Talbot Square W2.....238 E6
Talbot Yard SE1.....245 L2
Tallis Street EC4Y.....241 G7
Tamworth Street SW6.....242 A8
Tanner Street SE1.....246 A7
Taplow Street N1.....241 K1
Tarling Street E1.....246 F3
Tarver Road SE17.....245 H7
Tatum Street SE17.....245 M6
Taunton Place NW1.....239 G3
Tavistock Place WC1H.....240 C3
Tavistock Square WC1H.....240 C3
Tavistock Street WC2E.....240 D7
Taviton Street WC1H.....240 B3
Teak Close SE16.....247 K6
Tedworth Square SW3.....243 G7
Telford Terrace SW1V.....243 M7
Temeraire Street SE16.....247 G6
Temple ⊖ WC2R.....240 F7
Temple Avenue EC4Y.....241 G7
Temple Lane EC4Y.....241 G7
Temple Place WC2R.....240 F7
Templeton Place SW5.....242 A5
Tench Street E1W.....246 E5
Tenniel Close SW2.....238 C7
Tennis Street SE1.....245 L2
Tenterden Street W1S.....239 L6
Tenterground E1.....246 B1
Teredo Street SE16.....247 J8
Terminus Place SW1V.....243 L4
Thame Road SE16.....247 H6
Thanet Street WC1H.....240 C2
Thavies Inn EC4A.....241 G6
Thayer Street W1U.....239 K5
The Arches WC2N.....240 D8
The Boltons SW10.....242 C7
The British Library NW1.....240 C2
The British Museum WC1B.....240 C5
The Broad Walk W2.....238 B8
The Broad Walk W8.....242 C2
The Cut SE1.....245 G2
Theed Street SE1.....245 G2
The Flower Walk W2.....242 D3
The Grange SE1.....246 B8
The Highway E1W.....246 E4
The Little Boltons SW10.....242 C7
The Mall SW1A.....244 B2
The Mitre E14.....247 L3
The Monument EC3R.....241 L7
The National Gallery WC2N.....240 C8
Theobald's Road WC1X.....240 E4
Theobald Street SE1.....245 L5
The Oval (Surrey County
Cricket Ground) SE11.....244 F8
The Shard SE1.....245 L2
The Vale SW3.....242 E8
Thirleby Road SW1P.....244 A4
Thomas More Street E1W.....246 D4
Thomas Road E14.....247 M2
Thoresby Street N1.....241 K1
Thorney Street SW1P.....244 C5
Thornton Place W1H.....239 H4
Thrale Street SE1.....245 K1
Thrawl Street E1.....246 C1
Threadneedle Street EC2R.....241 L6
Three Colt Street E14.....247 L3
Three Oak Lane SE1.....246 B6
Throgmorton Avenue EC2N.....241 L6
Throgmorton Street EC2N.....241 L6
Thurland Road SE16.....246 D8
Thurloe Place SW7.....242 F5
Thurloe Square SW7.....242 F5
Thurloe Street SW7.....242 E5
Thurlow Street SE17.....245 M7
Tichbourne Row W2.....238 F6
Tiller Road E14.....247 M8
Tillman Street E1.....246 E3
Tilney Street W1J.....243 K1
Timber Pond Road SE16.....247 J6
Tinsley Road E1.....247 G1
Tinworth Street SE11.....244 D6
Tisdall Place SE17.....245 L6
Tite Street SW3.....243 H8
Tiverton Street SE1.....245 J4
Token House Yard EC2R.....241 L6
Tolmer's Square NW1.....240 A3
Tomlin's Terrace E14.....247 K2
Tonbridge Street WC1H.....240 D2
Tooley Street SE1.....245 L1
Tooley Street SE1.....246 B6
Tor Gardens W8.....242 A2
Torquay Street W2.....238 A5
Torrens Street EC1V.....241 G1
Torrington Place WC1E.....240 B4
Torrington Square WC1E.....240 B4
Tothill Street SW1H.....244 B3
Tottenham Court Road W1T.....240 A4
Tottenham Court Road ⊖ W1D.....240 C5
Tottenham Street W1T.....240 A5
Toulmin Street SE1.....245 J3
Tower Bridge E1.....246 B5
Tower Bridge Approach EC3N.....246 B5
Tower Bridge Road SE1.....246 A7
Tower Bridge Wharf E1W.....246 C5
Tower Gateway ⊖ EC3N.....246 B4
Tower Hill EC3N.....246 B4
Tower Hill ⊖ EC3N.....246 B4
Tower of London EC3N.....246 B4

Tower Place EC3R.....246 A4
Tower Street WC2H.....240 C7
Townsend Street SE17.....245 M5
Toynbee Street E1.....246 B1
Trafalgar Gardens E1.....247 H1
Trafalgar Square WC2N.....240 C8
Trafalgar Street SE17.....245 L7
Transept Street NW1.....238 F5
Trebeck Street W1J.....243 L1
Trebovir Road SW5.....242 A6
Tregunter Road SW10.....242 C7
Trenton Road SE16.....246 E8
Tresham Crescent NW8.....238 F3
Trevor Place SW7.....243 G3
Trevor Square SW7.....243 G3
Trevor Street SW7.....243 G3
Trinidad Street E14.....247 M4
Trinity Church Square SE1.....245 K3
Trinity Square EC3N.....246 B4
Trinity Street SE1.....245 K3
Trump Street EC2V.....241 K6
Tudor Street EC4Y.....241 G7
Tufton Street SW1P.....244 C4
Tunnel Road SE16.....247 G6
Turks Row SW3.....243 J6
Turner's Road E1.....247 L2
Turner Street E1.....246 E2
Turnmill Street EC1N.....241 G4
Turpentine Lane SW1V.....243 L7
Turquand Street SE17.....245 K6
Tyers Gate SE1.....245 M3
Tyers Street SE11.....244 E7
Tyers Terrace SE11.....244 E7
Tyron Street SW3.....243 H6
Tysoe Street EC1R.....241 G3

U
Udall Street SW1P.....244 A5
Ufford Street SE1.....245 G2
Ulster Place NW1.....239 K4
Umberston Street E1.....246 E2
Undershaft EC3A.....246 A2
Underwood Road N1.....241 K2
Underwood Street N1.....241 K1
Union Street SE1.....245 H2
University Street WC1E.....240 A4
Upbrook Mews W2.....238 D6
Upper Belgrave Street SW1X.....243 K4
Upper Berkeley Street W1H.....239 H6
Upper Brook Street W1K.....239 J7
Upper Cheyne Row SW3.....242 F8
Upper Grosvenor Street W1K.....239 J8
Upper Ground SE1.....244 F1
Upper Harley Street NW1.....239 K3
Upper James Street W1F.....240 A7
Upper John Street W1F.....240 A7
Upper Marsh SE1.....244 E3
Upper Montagu Street W1H.....239 H5
Upper St Martin's WC2H.....240 C7
Upper Tachbrook Street SW1V.....244 A5
Upper Thames Street EC4V.....241 J7
Upper Wimpole Street W1G.....239 K4
Upper Woburn Place WC1H.....240 B2
Urlwin Street SE5.....245 J8
Uxbridge Street W8.....242 A1

V
Valentine Place SE1.....245 G3
Vandon Passage SW1H.....244 A3
Vandon Street SW1H.....244 A4
Varden Street E1.....246 E2
Varndell Street NW1.....239 M2
Vauban Street SE16.....246 C8
Vaughan Street SE16.....247 L7
Vaughan Way E1W.....246 D5
Vauxhall ⊖ SW8.....244 D7
Vauxhall Bridge SW1V.....244 C7
Vauxhall Bridgefoot SE1.....244 D7
Vauxhall Bridge Road SW1V.....243 M5
Vauxhall Cross SE1.....244 D7
Vauxhall Grove SW8.....244 D8
Vauxhall Street SE11.....244 E6
Vauxhall Walk SE11.....244 E6
Venables Street W2.....238 E4
Vere Street W1G.....239 K6
Vernon Place WC1A.....240 D5
Vernon Rise WC1X.....240 E2
Verulam Street WC1X.....240 F4
Vestry Street N1.....241 L2
Victoria ⊖≷ SW1V.....243 L5
Victoria & Albert Museum SW7.....242 F4
Victoria Embankment SW1A.....244 D2
Victoria Embankment WC2R.....240 F7
Victoria Gate W2.....238 F7
Victoria Road W8.....242 C4
Victoria Square SW1W.....243 L4
Victoria Street SW1E.....243 L4
Victory Place SE17.....245 K5
Victory Way SE16.....247 K7
Vigo Street W1S.....239 M8
Villa Street SE17.....245 L7
Villiers Street WC2N.....240 D8
Vincent Close SE16.....247 K7
Vincent Square SW1P.....244 B5
Vincent Street SW1P.....244 B5
Vincent Terrace N1.....241 H1
Vince Street EC1V.....241 L2
Vine Court E1.....246 D1
Vinegar Street E1W.....246 E5
Vine Hill EC1R.....240 F4
Vine Lane SE1.....246 A6
Vine Street EC3N.....246 B3
Violet Hill NW8.....238 C1
Virgil Street SE1.....244 F4
Virginia Street E1W.....246 D4
Viscount Street EC2Y.....241 J4

W
Wadding Street SE17.....245 K6
Wakefield Street WC1H.....240 D3
Wakeling Street E14.....247 K2
Wakley Street EC1V.....241 H2
Walbrook EC4N.....241 L7
Walcorde Avenue SE17.....245 K6
Walcot Square SE11.....245 G5
Walden Street E1.....246 E2
Waley Street E1.....247 J1

Wallwood Street E14.....247 M1
Walnut Tree Walk SE11.....244 F5
Walpole Street SW3.....243 H6
Walter Terrace E1.....247 H2
Walton Place SW3.....243 H4
Walton Street SW3.....243 G4
Walworth Place SE17.....245 K7
Walworth Road SE17.....245 K5
Wandsworth Road SW8.....244 C8
Wansey Street SE17.....245 K6
Wapping ⊖ E1W.....246 F5
Wapping High Street E1W.....246 E6
Wapping Lane E1W.....246 F4
Wapping Wall E1W.....247 G5
Warden's Grove SE1.....245 J2
Wardour Street W1F.....240 B6
Warner Street EC1R.....240 F4
Warren Street W1T.....239 M4
Warren Street ⊖ NW1.....239 M3
Warrington Crescent W9.....238 C3
Warrington Gardens W9.....238 C4
Warwick Avenue W9.....238 B3
Warwick Avenue ⊖ W9.....238 C4
Warwick Crescent W2.....238 C5
Warwick House Street SW1Y.....244 B1
Warwick Lane EC4M.....241 H6
Warwick Place W9.....238 C4
Warwick Road SW5.....242 A6
Warwick Row SW1E.....243 L4
Warwick Square SW1V.....243 M6
Warwick Street W1B.....240 A7
Warwick Way SW1V.....243 L6
Waterhouse Square EC1N.....241 G5
Waterloo ⊖≷ SE1.....244 F2
Waterloo Bridge SE1.....244 E1
Waterloo Bridge WC2R.....240 E8
Waterloo East ≷ SE1.....245 G2
Waterloo Place SW1Y.....244 B1
Waterloo Road SE1.....244 F1
Waterloo Road SE1.....245 G2
Waterman Way E1W.....246 E5
Waterside Close SE16.....246 D7
Watling Street EC4N.....241 K7
Watney Street E1.....246 F3
Watts Street E1.....246 E5
Waveney Close E1W.....246 D5
Waverton Street W1J.....239 K8
Weavers Lane SE1.....246 A6
Webber Row SE1.....245 G3
Webber Street SE1.....245 H3
Webb Street SE1.....246 A8
Webster Road SE16.....246 D8
Weighhouse Street W1K.....239 K7
Welbeck Street W1G.....239 K5
Welbeck Way W1G.....239 K6
Welland Mews E1W.....246 E5
Wellclose Square E1.....246 D4
Wellesley Street E1.....247 H2
Wellesley Terrace N1.....241 K2
Wellington Arch W1J.....243 K2
Wellington Place NW8.....238 E2
Wellington Road NW8.....238 E1
Wellington Street WC2E.....240 D7
Wells Mews W1T.....240 A5
Wells Street W1T.....240 A5
Wells Way SE5.....245 M8
Wenlock Road N1.....241 K1
Wenlock Street N1.....241 K1
Wentworth Street E1.....246 B2
Werrington Street NW1.....240 A1
Wesley Street W1G.....239 K5
West Arbour Street E1.....247 G2
Westbourne Crescent W2.....238 D7
Westbourne Gardens W2.....238 B6
Westbourne Gate W2.....238 E7
Westbourne Grove W2.....238 A6
Westbourne Grove Terrace W2.....238 B6
Westbourne Park Road W2.....238 A5
Westbourne Park Villas W2.....238 A5
Westbourne Street W2.....238 E7
Westbourne Terrace W2.....238 D6
Westbourne Terrace Mews W2.....238 C6
Westbourne Terrace Road W2.....238 C5
West Brompton ⊖≷ SW5.....242 A7
West Carriage Drive W2.....242 E2
Westcott Road SE17.....245 H8
West Cromwell Road SW5.....242 A5
Western Place SE16.....247 G6
Westferry ⊖ E14.....247 M4
Westferry Circus E14.....247 M5
Westferry Road E14.....247 M5
West Gardens E1W.....246 F4
Westgate Terrace SW10.....242 B7
West Halkin Street SW1X.....243 J4
West Harding Street EC4A.....241 G6
West India Avenue E14.....247 M5
West India Dock Road E14.....247 M3
Westland Place N1.....241 K2
West Lane SE16.....246 E7
Westminster ⊖ SW1A.....244 D3
Westminster Abbey SW1P.....244 C3
Westminster Bridge SE1.....244 D3
Westminster Bridge Road SE1.....244 F3
Westmoreland Place SW1V.....243 L7
Westmoreland Road SE17.....245 K8
Westmoreland Street W1G.....239 K5
Westmoreland Terrace SW1V.....243 L7
Weston Rise WC1X.....240 E1
Weston Street SE1.....245 M3
Weston Street SE1.....245 M2
Westport Street E1.....247 H2
West Poultry Avenue EC1A.....241 H5
West Road SW3.....243 H7
West Smithfield EC1A.....241 H5
West Square SE11.....245 H4
West Street WC2H.....240 C7
West Tenter Street E1.....246 C3
West Warwick Place SW1V.....243 M6
Westway W2.....238 B5
Wetherby Gardens SW5.....242 C6
Weyhill Road E1.....246 D2
Weymouth Mews W1G.....239 L5
Weymouth Street W1G.....239 K5
Wharfdale Road N1.....240 D1
Wharfedale Street SW10.....242 B7
Wharf Road N1.....241 J1
Wharton Street WC1X.....240 F2
Wheatley Street W1G.....239 K5
Whetstone Park WC2A.....240 E5
Whidborne Street WC1H.....240 D2
Whiskin Street EC1R.....241 G2
Whitcomb Street WC2H.....240 B8
Whitechapel ⊖≷ E1.....246 E1
Whitechapel Estate E1.....246 C4
Whitechapel High Street E1.....246 C2

Whitechapel Road E1.....246 D1
Whitecross Street EC1Y.....241 K3
Whitefriars Street EC4Y.....241 G6
Whitehall SW1A.....244 C2
Whitehall Court SW1A.....244 D2
Whitehall Place SW1A.....244 D1
White Hart Street SE11.....245 G6
White Hart Yard SE1.....245 L2
Whitehaven Street NW8.....238 F4
Whitehead's Grove SW3.....243 G6
White Horse Lane E1.....247 H1
Whitehorse Road E1.....247 J1
Whitehorse Road E1.....247 J3
White Horse Street W1J.....243 L1
White Kennett Street E1.....246 B2
White Lion Hill EC4V.....241 H7
White Lion Street N1.....240 F1
White's Grounds SE1.....246 A7
White's Row E1.....246 B1
White Tower Way E1.....247 J1
Whitfield Place W1T.....240 A4
Whitfield Street W1T.....240 A4
Whitgift Street SE11.....244 E5
Whittaker Street SW1W.....243 J6
Whittlesey Street SE1.....245 G2
Wicker Street E1.....246 E3
Wickham Close E1.....247 G1
Wickham Street SE11.....244 E7
Wicklow Street WC1X.....240 E2
Widegate Street E1.....246 A1
Widley Road W9.....238 A3
Wigmore Place W1G.....239 K5
Wigmore Street W1U.....239 K6
Wigton Place SE11.....245 G7
Wilbraham Place SW1X.....243 J5
Wilcox Place * SW1E.....244 A4
Wild Court WC2B.....240 E6
Wild's Rents SE1.....245 M4
Wild Street WC2B.....240 D6
Wilfred Street SW1E.....243 M4
Wilkes Street E1.....246 B1
William IV Street WC2N.....240 C8
William Mews SW1X.....243 H3
William Road NW1.....239 M3
Willow Place SW1P.....244 A5
Willow Street EC2A.....241 M3
Wilmington Square WC1X.....240 F3
Wilmington Street WC1X.....240 F2
Wilson Grove SE16.....246 E7
Wilson Street EC2A.....241 L4
Wilton Crescent SW1X.....243 J3
Wilton Mews SW1X.....243 K4
Wilton Place SW1X.....243 J3
Wilton Road SW1V.....243 M5
Wilton Row SW1X.....243 J3
Wilton Street SW1X.....243 K4
Wimpole Mews W1G.....239 K5
Wimpole Street W1G.....239 K5
Winchester Street SW1V.....243 L6
Winchester Walk SE1.....245 K1
Wincott Street SE11.....245 G5
Windmill Road SE11.....244 F7
Windmill Street W1T.....240 B5
Windrose Close SE16.....247 H6
Windsor Terrace N1.....241 K1
Wine Close E1W.....246 F5
Winnett Street W1D.....240 B7
Winsland Mews W2.....238 E6
Winsland Street W2.....238 E6
Winsley Street W1W.....240 A6
Winthrop Street E1.....246 E1
Woburn Place WC1H.....240 C3
Woburn Square WC1H.....240 C4
Wodeham Gardens E1.....246 E1
Wolfe Crescent SE16.....247 H7
Wolseley Street SE1.....246 C6
Woodbridge Street EC1R.....241 G3
Woodchester Square W9.....238 A4
Woodfall Street SW3.....243 H7
Woodland Crescent SE16.....247 H7
Woodseer Street E1.....246 C1
Woods Mews W1K.....239 J7
Woods Place SE1.....246 A8
Woodstock Street W1C.....239 K6
Wood Street EC2V.....241 K6
Woolaston Close SE1.....245 J5
Wooler Street SE17.....245 L7
Wootton Street SE1.....245 G2
Worgan Street SE11.....244 E6
Worgan Street SE16.....247 H8
Wormwood Street EC2M.....241 M5
Worship Street EC2A.....241 M4
Wren Street WC1X.....240 E3
Wright's Lane W8.....242 A3
Wyatt Close SE16.....247 L7
Wyclif Street EC1V.....241 H2
Wymering Road W9.....238 A2
Wynard Terrace SE11.....244 F7
Wyndham Place W1H.....239 H5
Wyndham Street W1H.....239 G4
Wynnstay Gardens W8.....242 A4
Wynyatt Street EC1V.....241 H2
Wythburn Place W1H.....239 H6

Y
Yalding Road * SE16.....246 C8
Yardley Street WC1X.....240 F2
Yeoman's Row SW3.....243 G4
York Boulevard WC2N.....240 D8
York Bridge NW1.....239 J3
York Gate NW1.....239 J4
York Road SE1.....244 E2
Yorkshire Road E14.....247 K3
York Square E14.....247 J2
York Street W1U.....239 G5
York Street W1U.....239 H5
York Terrace East NW1.....239 J4
York Terrace West NW1.....239 J4
York Way N1.....240 D1
Young Street W8.....242 B3

Z
Zoar Street SE1.....245 J1
ZSL London Zoo NW1.....239 J1

This index lists places appearing in the main map section of the atlas in alphabetical order. The reference following each name gives the atlas page number and grid reference of the square in which the place appears. The map shows counties, unitary authorities and administrative areas, together with a list of the abbreviated name forms used in the index. The top 100 places of tourist interest are indexed in **red**, World Heritage sites in **green**, motorway service areas in **blue**, airports in blue *italic* and National Parks in green *italic*.

Scotland

Abers	Aberdeenshire
Ag & B	Argyll and Bute
Angus	Angus
Border	Scottish Borders
C Aber	City of Aberdeen
C Dund	City of Dundee
C Edin	City of Edinburgh
C Glas	City of Glasgow
Clacks	Clackmannanshire (1)
D & G	Dumfries & Galloway
E Ayrs	East Ayrshire
E Duns	East Dunbartonshire (2)
E Loth	East Lothian
E Rens	East Renfrewshire (3)
Falk	Falkirk
Fife	Fife
Highld	Highland
Inver	Inverclyde (4)
Mdloth	Midlothian (5)
Moray	Moray
N Ayrs	North Ayrshire
N Lans	North Lanarkshire (6)
Ork	Orkney Islands
P & K	Perth & Kinross
Rens	Renfrewshire (7)
S Ayrs	South Ayrshire
S Lans	South Lanarkshire
Shet	Shetland Islands
Stirlg	Stirling
W Duns	West Dunbartonshire (8)
W Isls	Western Isles (Na h-Eileanan an Iar)
W Loth	West Lothian

Wales

Blae G	Blaenau Gwent (9)
Brdgnd	Bridgend (10)
Caerph	Caerphilly (11)
Cardif	Cardiff
Carmth	Carmarthenshire
Cerdgn	Ceredigion
Conwy	Conwy
Denbgs	Denbighshire
Flints	Flintshire
Gwynd	Gwynedd
IoA	Isle of Anglesey
Mons	Monmouthshire
Myr Td	Merthyr Tydfil (12)
Neath	Neath Port Talbot (13)
Newpt	Newport (14)
Pembks	Pembrokeshire
Powys	Powys
Rhondd	Rhondda Cynon Taf (15)
Swans	Swansea
Torfn	Torfaen (16)
V Glam	Vale of Glamorgan (17)
Wrexhm	Wrexham

Channel Islands & Isle of Man

Guern	Guernsey
Jersey	Jersey
IoM	Isle of Man

England

BaNES	Bath & N E Somerset (18)
Barns	Barnsley (19)
BCP	Bournemouth, Christchurch and Poole (20)
Bed	Bedford
Birm	Birmingham
Bl w D	Blackburn with Darwen (21)
Bolton	Bolton (22)
Bpool	Blackpool
Br & H	Brighton & Hove (23)
Br For	Bracknell Forest (24)
Bristl	City of Bristol
Bucks	Buckinghamshire
Bury	Bury (25)
C Beds	Central Bedfordshire
C Brad	City of Bradford
C Derb	City of Derby
C KuH	City of Kingston upon Hull
C Leic	City of Leicester
C Nott	City of Nottingham

C Pete	City of Peterborough
C Plym	City of Plymouth
C Port	City of Portsmouth
C Sotn	City of Southampton
C Stke	City of Stoke-on-Trent
C York	City of York
Calder	Calderdale (26)
Cambs	Cambridgeshire
Ches E	Cheshire East
Ches W	Cheshire West and Chester
Cnwll	Cornwall
Covtry	Coventry
Cumb	Cumbria
Darltn	Darlington (27)
Derbys	Derbyshire
Devon	Devon
Donc	Doncaster (28)
Dorset	Dorset
Dudley	Dudley (29)
Dur	Durham
E R Yk	East Riding of Yorkshire
E Susx	East Sussex
Essex	Essex
Gatesd	Gateshead (30)
Gloucs	Gloucestershire
Gt Lon	Greater London
Halton	Halton (31)
Hants	Hampshire
Hartpl	Hartlepool (32)
Herefs	Herefordshire
Herts	Hertfordshire
IoS	Isles of Scilly
IoW	Isle of Wight
Kent	Kent
Kirk	Kirklees (33)
Knows	Knowsley (34)
Lancs	Lancashire
Leeds	Leeds
Leics	Leicestershire
Lincs	Lincolnshire
Lpool	Liverpool
Luton	Luton

M Keyn	Milton Keynes
Manch	Manchester
Medway	Medway
Middsb	Middlesbrough
N Linc	North Lincolnshire
N Som	North Somerset
N Tyne	North Tyneside (35)
N u Ty	Newcastle upon Tyne
N York	North Yorkshire
NE Lin	North East Lincolnshire
Nhants	Northamptonshire
Norfk	Norfolk
Notts	Nottinghamshire
Nthumb	Northumberland
Oldham	Oldham (36)
Oxon	Oxfordshire
R & Cl	Redcar & Cleveland
Readg	Reading
Rochdl	Rochdale (37)
Rothm	Rotherham (38)
Rutlnd	Rutland
S Glos	South Gloucestershire (39)
S on T	Stockton-on-Tees (40)
S Tyne	South Tyneside (41)
Salfd	Salford (42)
Sandw	Sandwell (43)
Sefton	Sefton (44)
Sheff	Sheffield
Shrops	Shropshire
Slough	Slough (45)
Solhll	Solihull (46)
Somset	Somerset
St Hel	St Helens (47)
Staffs	Staffordshire
Sthend	Southend-on-Sea
Stockp	Stockport (48)
Suffk	Suffolk
Sundld	Sunderland
Surrey	Surrey
Swindn	Swindon
Tamesd	Tameside (49)
Thurr	Thurrock (50)
Torbay	Torbay
Traffd	Trafford (51)
W & M	Windsor & Maidenhead (52)
W Berk	West Berkshire
W Susx	West Sussex
Wakefd	Wakefield (53)
Warrtn	Warrington (54)
Warwks	Warwickshire
Wigan	Wigan (55)
Wilts	Wiltshire
Wirral	Wirral (56)
Wokham	Wokingham (57)
Wolves	Wolverhampton (58)
Worcs	Worcestershire
Wrekin	Telford & Wrekin (59)
Wsall	Walsall (60)

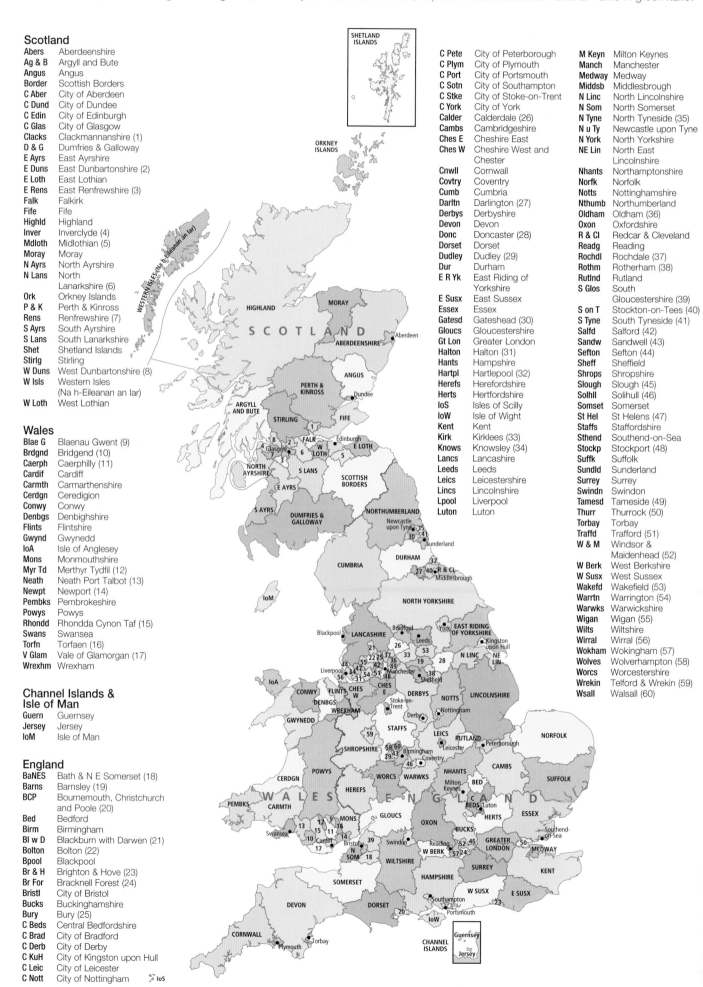

Abbas Combe – Ansley 255

A

Abbas Combe Somset 20 D10
Abberley Worcs 57 P11
Abberley Common Worcs 57 N11
Abberton Essex 52 H8
Abberton Worcs 47 J4
Abberwick Nthumb 119 M8
Abbess Roding Essex 51 N8
Abbey Devon 10 C2
Abbeycwmhir Powys 55 P10
Abbeydale Sheff 84 D4
Abbey Dore Herefs 45 M8
Abbey Green Staffs 70 H3
Abbey Hill Somset 19 J11
Abbey St Bathans Border 129 K7
Abbeystead Lancs 95 M10
Abbeytown Cumb 110 C10
Abbey Village Lancs 89 J6
Abbey Wood Gt Lon 37 L5
Abbotrule Border 118 B8
Abbots Bickington Devon 16 F9
Abbots Bromley Staffs 71 K10
Abbotsbury Dorset 11 M7
Abbot's Chair Derbys 83 M6
Abbots Deuglie P & K 134 E5
Abbotsham Devon 16 G6
Abbotskerswell Devon 7 M5
Abbots Langley Herts 50 C10
Abbotsleigh Devon 7 L9
Abbots Leigh N Som 31 P10
Abbotsley Cambs 62 B9
Abbots Morton Worcs 47 K3
Abbots Ripton Cambs 62 B5
Abbot's Salford Warwks 47 L4
Abbotstone Hants 22 G8
Abbotswood Hants 22 C10
Abbots Worthy Hants 22 E8
Abbotts Ann Hants 22 B6
Abbott Street Dorset 12 G4
Abcott Shrops 56 F9
Abdon Shrops 57 K7
Abenhall Gloucs 46 C11
Aberaeron Cerdgn 43 J2
Aberaman Rhondd 30 D4
Aberangell Gwynd 55 J2
Aber-arad Carmth 42 F6
Aberarder Highld 147 Q2
Aberargie P & K 134 F4
Aberarth Cerdgn 43 J2
Aberavon Neath 29 K7
Aber-banc Cerdgn 42 G6
Aberbargoed Caerph 30 G4
Aberbeeg Blae G 30 H4
Abercanaid Myr Td 30 E4
Abercarn Caerph 30 H6
Abercastle Pembks 40 G4
Abercegir Powys 55 J4
Aberchalder Highld 147 J7
Aberchirder Abers 158 F7
Aber Clydach Powys 44 G10
Abercorn W Loth 127 K2
Abercraf Powys 29 M2
Abercregan Neath 29 M5
Abercwmboi Rhondd 30 D5
Abercych Pembks 41 P2
Abercynon Rhondd 30 E6
Aberdalgie P & K 134 D3
Aberdare Rhondd 30 D4
Aberdaron Gwynd 66 B9
Aberdeen C Aber 151 N6
Aberdeen Airport C Aber 151 M5
Aberdesach Gwynd 66 G4
Aberdour Fife 134 F10
Aberdulais Neath 29 L5
Aberdyfi Gwynd 54 E5
Aberedw Powys 44 F5
Abereiddy Pembks 40 E4
Abererch Gwynd 66 F7
Aberfan Myr Td 30 E4
Aberfeldy P & K 141 L8
Aberffraw IoA 78 F11
Aberffrwd Cerdgn 54 F9
Aberford Leeds 91 L3
Aberfoyle Stirlg 132 G7
Abergarw Brdgnd 29 P8
Abergarwed Neath 29 M4
Abergavenny Mons 31 J2
Abergele Conwy 80 C9
Aber-giar Carmth 43 K6
Abergorlech Carmth 43 L8
Abergwesyn Powys 44 B4
Abergwili Carmth 42 H10
Abergwydol Powys 54 H4
Abergwynfi Neath 29 N5
Abergwyngregyn Gwynd 79 M10
Abergynolwyn Gwynd 54 F3
Aberhafesp Powys 55 P6
Aberhosan Powys 55 J5
Aberkenfig Brdgnd 29 N8
Aberlady E Loth 128 D4
Aberlemno Angus 143 J6
Aberllefenni Gwynd 54 H3
Aberllynfi Powys 44 H7
Aberlour, Charlestown of Moray 157 P9
Abermagwr Cerdgn 54 F10
Aber-meurig Cerdgn 43 L3
Abermorddu Flints 69 K3
Abermule Powys 56 B6
Abernant Carmth 42 F10
Abernant Rhondd 30 D4
Abernethy P & K 134 F4
Abernyte P & K 142 D11
Aberporth Cerdgn 42 E4
Abersoch Gwynd 66 E9
Abersychan Torfn 31 J4
Aberthin V Glam 30 D10
Abertillery Blae G 30 H4
Abertridwr Caerph 30 F7
Abertridwr Powys 68 D11
Abertysswg Caerph 30 F3
Aberuthven P & K 134 B4
Aberwheeler Denbgs 80 F11
Aberyscir Powys 44 D9
Aberystwyth Cerdgn 54 D8
Abingdon-on-Thames Oxon 34 E5
Abinger Common Surrey 36 D11
Abinger Hammer Surrey 36 C11
Abington Nhants 60 G8
Abington S Lans 116 C6
Abington Pigotts Cambs 50 H2
Abington Services S Lans 116 C6
Abingworth W Susx 24 D7
Ab Kettleby Leics 73 J6
Ab Lench Worcs 47 K4
Ablington Gloucs 33 M3
Ablington Wilts 21 N5
Abney Derbys 83 Q8
Above Church Staffs 71 J4
Aboyne Abers 150 E8
Abhainn Suidhe W Isls 168 f7
Abram Wigan 82 D4
Abriachan Highld 155 Q10
Abridge Essex 51 L11
Abronhill N Lans 126 D2
Abson S Glos 32 D10
Abthorpe Nhants 48 H5
Aby Lincs 87 M5
Acaster Malbis C York 98 B11
Acaster Selby N York 91 P2
Accrington Lancs 89 M5
Acha Ag & B 136 F5
Achahoish Ag & B 123 N4
Achalader P & K 141 R8
Achaleven Ag & B 138 G11
Acha Mor W Isls 168 i5
Achanalt Highld 155 J5
Achandunie Highld 156 A3
Achany Highld 162 D6
Acharacle Highld 138 B4
Acharn Highld 138 C7
Acharn P & K 141 J9
Achavanich Highld 167 L8
Achduart Highld 160 G6
Achfary Highld 164 G9
Achgarve Highld 160 D8
A'Chill Highld 144 C6
Achiltibuie Highld 160 G5
Achina Highld 166 B4
Achinhoan Ag & B 120 E8
Achintee Highld 154 B9
Achintraid Highld 153 Q10
Achlyness Highld 164 F6
Achmelvich Highld 160 H2
Achmore Highld 153 R11
Achmore W Isls 168 i5
Achnacarnin Highld 164 B10
Achnacarry Highld 146 F10
Achnacloich Highld 145 J6
Achnaconeran Highld 147 L4
Achnacroish Ag & B 138 F9
Achnadrish Ag & B 137 M5
Achnafauld P & K 141 L10
Achnagarron Highld 156 B3
Achnaha Highld 137 M2
Achnahaird Highld 160 G4
Achnahannet Highld 148 H2
Achnairn Highld 162 D4
Achnalea Highld 138 F5
Achnamara Ag & B 130 F10
Achnasheen Highld 154 G6
Achnashellach Highld 154 D8
Achnastank Moray 157 P11
Achosnich Highld 137 L2
Achranich Highld 138 C8
Achreamie Highld 166 H3
Achriabhach Highld 139 L4
Achriesgill Highld 164 G6
Achtoty Highld 165 Q4
Achurch Nhants 61 M4
Achvaich Highld 162 G8
Achvarasdal Highld 166 G4
Ackergill Highld 167 Q6
Acklam Middsb 104 E7
Acklam N York 98 F8
Ackleton Shrops 57 P5
Acklington Nthumb 119 P10
Ackton Wakefd 91 L6
Ackworth Moor Top Wakefd 91 L7
Acle Norfk 77 N9
Acock's Green Birm 58 H8
Acol Kent 39 P8
Acomb C York 98 B10
Acomb Nthumb 112 D7
Acombe Somset 10 D2
Aconbury Herefs 45 Q8
Acre Lancs 89 M6
Acrefair Wrexhm 69 J6
Acresford Derbys 59 L2
Acton Ches E 70 A4
Acton Dorset 12 G9
Acton Gt Lon 36 F4
Acton Shrops 56 E8
Acton Staffs 70 E6
Acton Suffk 52 E2
Acton Worcs 58 B11
Acton Wrexhm 69 K4
Acton Beauchamp Herefs 46 C4
Acton Bridge Ches W 82 C9
Acton Burnell Shrops 57 J4
Acton Green Herefs 46 C4
Acton Pigott Shrops 57 J4
Acton Round Shrops 57 L5
Acton Scott Shrops 56 H7
Acton Trussell Staffs 70 G11
Acton Turville S Glos 32 F8
Adbaston Staffs 70 D9
Adber Dorset 19 Q10
Adbolton Notts 72 F3
Adderbury Oxon 48 E7
Adderley Shrops 70 B7
Adderstone Nthumb 119 M4
Addiewell W Loth 126 H5
Addingham C Brad 96 G11
Addington Bucks 49 K9
Addington Gt Lon 37 J8
Addington Kent 37 Q9
Addiscombe Gt Lon 36 H7
Addlestone Surrey 36 C8
Addlestonemoor Surrey 36 C7
Addlethorpe Lincs 87 P7
Adeney Wrekin 70 B11
Adeyfield Herts 50 C9
Adfa Powys 55 P4
Adforton Herefs 56 G10
Adisham Kent 39 M11
Adlestrop Gloucs 47 P9
Adlingfleet E R Yk 92 D6
Adlington Ches E 83 K8
Adlington Lancs 89 J8
Admaston Staffs 71 J10
Admaston Wrekin 57 L2
Admington Warwks 47 P5
Adpar Cerdgn 42 F6
Adsborough Somset 19 J9
Adscombe Somset 18 G7
Adstock Bucks 49 K9
Adstone Nhants 48 G4
Adswood Stockp 83 J7
Adversane W Susx 24 C6
Advie Highld 157 L11
Adwalton Leeds 90 G5
Adwell Oxon 35 J5
Adwick le Street Donc 91 N9
Adwick upon Dearne Donc 91 M10
Ae D & G 109 L3
Ae Bridgend D & G 109 M3
Afan Forest Park Neath 29 N5
Affetside Bury 89 M8
Affleck Abers 158 E9
Affpuddle Dorset 12 D6
Affric Lodge Highld 146 F3
Afon-wen Flints 80 G10
Afon Wen Gwynd 66 G7
Afton Devon 7 L6
Afton IoW 13 P7
Agglethorpe N York 96 G3
Aigburth Lpool 81 M7
Aike E R Yk 99 L11
Aiketgate Cumb 111 J11
Aikhead Cumb 110 D11
Aikton Cumb 110 E10
Ailby Lincs 87 M5
Ailey Herefs 45 L5
Ailsworth C Pete 74 B11
Ainderby Quernhow N York 97 M4
Ainderby Steeple N York 97 M2
Aingers Green Essex 53 K7
Ainsdale Sefton 88 C8
Ainsdale-on-Sea Sefton 88 B8
Ainstable Cumb 111 K11
Ainsworth Bury 89 M8
Ainthorpe N York 105 K9
Aintree Sefton 81 M5
Ainville W Loth 127 L5
Aird Ag & B 130 F7
Aird D & G 106 E5
Aird Highld 145 J7
Aird W Isls 168 k4
Àird a' Mhulaidh W Isls 168 g6
Aird Asaig W Isls 168 g7
Aird Dhubh Highld 153 N9
Airdeny Ag & B 131 K2
Airdrie N Lans 126 D4
Airdriehill N Lans 126 D4
Airds of Kells D & G 108 E6
Àird Uig W Isls 168 f4
Airidh a bhruaich W Isls 168 h6
Airieland D & G 108 G9
Airlie Angus 142 E7
Airmyn E R Yk 92 B6
Airntully P & K 141 Q10
Airor Highld 145 M6
Airth Falk 133 Q10
Airton N York 96 D9
Aisby Lincs 73 Q3
Aisby Lincs 85 Q2
Aisgill Cumb 102 E11
Aish Devon 6 H6
Aish Devon 7 L7
Aisholt Somset 18 G7
Aiskew N York 97 L3
Aislaby N York 98 F3
Aislaby N York 105 N9
Aislaby S on T 104 D8
Aisthorpe Lincs 86 B4
Aith Shet 169 q8
Akeld Nthumb 119 J5
Akeley Bucks 49 K7
Akenham Suffk 53 L2
Albaston Cnwll 5 Q7
Alberbury Shrops 56 F2
Albourne W Susx 24 G7
Albourne Green W Susx 24 G7
Albrighton Shrops 57 Q4
Albrighton Shrops 69 N11
Alburgh Norfk 65 K4
Albury Herts 51 K6
Albury Oxon 35 J3
Albury Surrey 36 B11
Albury End Herts 51 K6
Albury Heath Surrey 36 C11
Alby Hill Norfk 76 H5
Alcaig Highld 155 Q6
Alcaston Shrops 56 H7
Alcester Warwks 47 L3
Alciston E Susx 25 M9
Alcombe Somset 18 C5
Alcombe Wilts 32 F11
Alconbury Cambs 61 Q5
Alconbury Weald Cambs 62 B5
Alconbury Weston Cambs 61 Q5
Aldborough N York 97 P7
Aldborough Norfk 76 H5
Aldbourne Wilts 33 Q9
Aldbrough E R Yk 93 M3
Aldbrough St John N York 103 P8
Aldbury Herts 35 Q2
Aldcliffe Lancs 95 K8
Aldclune P & K 141 L5
Aldeburgh Suffk 65 P10
Aldeby Norfk 65 N3
Aldenham Herts 50 D11
Alderbury Wilts 21 N9
Aldercar Derbys 84 F11
Alderford Norfk 76 G8
Alderholt Dorset 13 K2
Alderley Gloucs 32 E6
Alderley Edge Ches E 82 H9
Aldermans Green Covtry 59 N8
Aldermaston W Berk 34 G11
Alderminster Warwks 47 P5
Alder Moor Staffs 71 N9
Aldersey Green Ches W 69 N3
Aldershot Hants 23 N4
Alderton Gloucs 47 K8
Alderton Nhants 49 K5
Alderton Shrops 69 N10
Alderton Suffk 53 P3
Alderton Wilts 32 F8
Alderwasley Derbys 71 Q4
Aldfield N York 97 L7
Aldford Ches W 69 M3
Aldgate Rutlnd 73 P10
Aldham Essex 52 F6
Aldham Suffk 52 J2
Aldingbourne W Susx 15 P5
Aldingham Cumb 94 F6
Aldington Kent 27 J4
Aldington Worcs 47 L6
Aldington Corner Kent 27 J4
Aldivalloch Moray 150 B2
Aldochlay Ag & B 132 D9
Aldon Shrops 56 G9
Aldoth Cumb 109 P11
Aldreth Cambs 62 F6
Aldridge Wsall 58 G4
Aldringham Suffk 65 N9
Aldro N York 98 G8
Aldsworth Gloucs 33 N3
Aldsworth W Susx 15 L5
Aldunie Moray 150 B2
Aldwark Derbys 84 B9
Aldwark N York 97 Q8
Aldwick W Susx 15 P7
Aldwincle Nhants 61 M4
Aldworth W Berk 34 G9
Alexandria W Duns 125 K2
Aley Somset 18 G7
Alfardisworthy Devon 16 D9
Alfington Devon 10 C5
Alfold Surrey 24 B4
Alfold Bars W Susx 24 B4
Alfold Crossways Surrey 24 B3
Alford Abers 150 F4
Alford Lincs 87 N5
Alford Somset 20 B8
Alfreton Derbys 84 F9
Alfrick Worcs 46 D4
Alfrick Pound Worcs 46 D4
Alfriston E Susx 25 M10
Algarkirk Lincs 74 E3
Alhampton Somset 20 B8
Alkborough N Linc 92 E6
Alkerton Gloucs 32 E3
Alkerton Oxon 48 C6
Alkham Kent 27 N3
Alkington Shrops 69 P7
Alkmonton Derbys 71 M7
Allaleigh Devon 7 L8
Allanaquoich Abers 149 L9
Allanbank N Lans 126 E6
Allanton Border 129 M9
Allanton N Lans 126 E6
Allanton S Lans 126 C7
Allaston Gloucs 32 B4
Allbrook Hants 22 E10
All Cannings Wilts 21 L2
Allendale Nthumb 112 B9
Allen End Warwks 59 J5
Allenheads Nthumb 112 C11
Allensford Dur 112 G10
Allen's Green Herts 51 L7
Allensmore Herefs 45 P7
Allenton C Derb 72 B4
Aller Devon 17 P6
Aller Somset 19 M9
Allerby Cumb 100 E3
Allercombe Devon 9 P6
Aller Cross Devon 17 N6
Allerford Somset 18 B5
Allerston N York 98 H4
Allerthorpe E R Yk 98 F11
Allerton C Brad 90 E4
Allerton Highld 156 D4
Allerton Lpool 81 M7
Allerton Bywater Leeds 91 L5
Allerton Mauleverer N York 97 P9
Allesley Covtry 59 M8
Allestree C Derb 72 A3
Allet Common Cnwll 3 K4
Allexton Leics 73 L10
Allgreave Ches E 83 L11
Allhallows Medway 38 D6
Allhallows-on-Sea Medway 38 D6
Alligin Shuas Highld 153 Q6
Allimore Green Staffs 70 F11
Allington Dorset 11 K6
Allington Kent 38 C10
Allington Lincs 73 M2
Allington Wilts 21 L2
Allington Wilts 21 P7
Allington Wilts 32 G9
Allithwaite Cumb 94 H5
Alloa Clacks 133 P9
Allonby Cumb 100 E2
Allostock Ches W 82 F10
Alloway S Ayrs 114 F4
Allowenshay Somset 10 H2
All Saints South Elmham Suffk 65 L5
Allscott Shrops 57 N5
Allscott Wrekin 57 L2
All Stretton Shrops 56 H5
Alltami Flints 81 K11
Alltchaorunn Highld 139 M7
Alltmawr Powys 44 F5
Alltsigh Highld 147 M4
Alltwalis Carmth 42 H8
Alltwen Neath 29 K4
Alltyblaca Cerdgn 43 K5
Allwood Green Suffk 64 E7
Almeley Herefs 45 L4
Almeley Wooton Herefs 45 L4
Almer Dorset 12 F5
Almholme Donc 91 P9
Almington Staffs 70 C8
Almodington W Susx 15 M7
Almondbank P & K 134 D2
Almondbury Kirk 90 F8
Almondsbury S Glos 32 B8
Alne N York 97 Q7
Alness Highld 156 B4
Alnham Nthumb 119 J8
Alnmouth Nthumb 119 P8
Alnwick Nthumb 119 N8
Alperton Gt Lon 36 E4
Alphamstone Essex 52 E4
Alpheton Suffk 64 B11
Alphington Devon 9 M6
Alpington Norfk 77 K11
Alport Derbys 84 B8
Alpraham Ches E 69 Q3
Alresford Essex 53 J7
Alrewas Staffs 59 J2
Alsager Ches E 70 D3
Alsagers Bank Staffs 70 D5
Alsop en le Dale Derbys 71 M4
Alston Cumb 111 P11
Alston Devon 10 G4
Alstone Gloucs 47 J8
Alstone Somset 19 K5
Alstonefield Staffs 71 L3
Alston Sutton Somset 19 M4
Alswear Devon 17 N7
Alt Oldham 83 K4
Altandhu Highld 160 F4
Altarnun Cnwll 5 L5
Altass Highld 162 C6
Altcreich Ag & B 138 B10
Altgaltraig Ag & B 124 C3
Altham Lancs 89 M4
Althorne Essex 38 F2
Althorpe N Linc 92 D9
Altnabreac Station Highld 166 H7
Altnaharra Highld 165 N9
Altofts Wakefd 91 K6
Alton Derbys 84 E8
Alton Hants 23 K7
Alton Staffs 71 K6
Alton Wilts 21 N5
Alton Barnes Wilts 21 M2
Alton Pancras Dorset 11 Q4
Alton Priors Wilts 21 M2
Alton Towers Staffs 71 K6
Altrincham Traffd 82 G7
Altskeith Hotel Stirlg 132 F7
Alva Clacks 133 P8
Alvanley Ches W 81 P10
Alvaston C Derb 72 B4
Alvechurch Worcs 58 F10
Alvecote Warwks 59 K4
Alvediston Wilts 21 J10
Alveley Shrops 57 P8
Alverdiscott Devon 17 J6
Alverstoke Hants 14 H7
Alverstone IoW 14 G9
Alverthorpe Wakefd 91 J6
Alverton Notts 73 K2
Alves Moray 157 L5
Alvescot Oxon 33 Q4
Alveston S Glos 32 B7
Alveston Warwks 47 P3
Alvingham Lincs 87 L2
Alvington Gloucs 32 B4
Alwalton C Pete 74 B11
Alweston Dorset 11 P2
Alwinton Nthumb 118 H9
Alwoodley Leeds 90 H2
Alwoodley Gates Leeds 91 J2
Alyth P & K 142 C8
Am Bàgh a Tuath W Isls 168 c17
Ambergate Derbys 84 D10
Amber Hill Lincs 86 H11
Amberley Gloucs 32 G4
Amberley W Susx 24 B8
Amber Row Derbys 84 E9
Amberstone E Susx 25 N8
Amble Nthumb 119 Q10
Amblecote Dudley 58 C7
Ambler Thorn C Brad 90 D5
Ambleside Cumb 101 L10
Ambleston Pembks 41 K5
Ambrosden Oxon 48 H11
Amcotts N Linc 92 E8
America Cambs 62 F5
Amersham Bucks 35 Q5
Amersham Common Bucks 35 Q5
Amersham Old Town Bucks 35 Q5
Amersham on the Hill Bucks 35 Q5
Amerton Staffs 70 H9
Amesbury Wilts 21 N6
Amhuinnsuidhe W Isls 168 f7
Amington Staffs 59 K4
Amisfield D & G 109 M4
Amlwch IoA 78 G6
Ammanford Carmth 28 H2
Amotherby N York 98 E6
Ampfield Hants 22 D10
Ampleforth N York 98 B5
Ampney Crucis Gloucs 33 L4
Ampney St Mary Gloucs 33 L4
Ampney St Peter Gloucs 33 L4
Amport Hants 22 B6
Ampthill C Beds 50 B3
Ampton Suffk 64 B7
Amroth Pembks 41 N9
Amulree P & K 141 L10
Amwell Herts 50 E8
Anaheilt Highld 138 E5
Ancaster Lincs 73 P2
Ancells Farm Hants 23 M3
Anchor Shrops 56 B7
Ancroft Nthumb 129 P11
Ancrum Border 118 B6
Ancton W Susx 15 Q6
Anderby Lincs 87 P5
Anderby Creek Lincs 87 Q5
Andersea Somset 19 K8
Andersfield Somset 18 H8
Anderson Dorset 12 E5
Anderton Ches W 82 D9
Anderton Cnwll 6 C8
Andover Hants 22 C5
Andover Down Hants 22 C5
Andoversford Gloucs 47 K11
Andreas IoM 80 f2
Anelog Gwynd 66 B9
Anerley Gt Lon 36 H7
Anfield Lpool 81 M6
Angarrack Cnwll 2 F6
Angarrick Cnwll 3 K6
Angelbank Shrops 57 K9
Angersleigh Somset 18 G11
Angerton Cumb 110 D9
Angle Pembks 40 G10
Anglesey IoA 78 G8
Anglesey Abbey Cambs 62 H8
Angmering W Susx 24 C10
Angram N York 97 R11
Angram N York 102 G11
Angrouse Cnwll 2 H10
Anick Nthumb 112 D7
Ankerville Highld 156 E3
Ankle Hill Leics 73 K7
Anlaby E R Yk 92 H5
Anmer Norfk 75 P5
Anmore Hants 15 J4
Annan D & G 110 C7
Annandale Water Services D & G 109 P2
Annaside Cumb 94 B3
Annat Highld 154 A7
Annathill N Lans 126 C3
Anna Valley Hants 22 C6
Annbank S Ayrs 114 H3
Anne Hathaway's Cottage Warwks 47 N4
Annesley Notts 84 H10
Annesley Woodhouse Notts 84 G10
Annfield Plain Dur 113 J10
Anniesland C Glas 125 N4
Annitsford N Tyne 113 L6
Annscroft Shrops 56 H3
Ansdell Lancs 88 C5
Ansford Somset 20 B8
Ansley Warwks 59 M6

Place	County	Page	Grid
Anslow	Staffs	71	N9
Anslow Gate	Staffs	71	M10
Anslow Lees	Staffs	71	N10
Ansteadbrook	Surrey	23	P8
Anstey	Hants	23	K6
Anstey	Herts	51	K4
Anstey	Leics	72	F9
Anstruther	Fife	135	P7
Ansty	W Susx	24	G6
Ansty	Warwks	59	P8
Ansty	Wilts	21	J9
Ansty Cross	Dorset	12	C4
An Tairbeart	W Isls	168	g7
Anthill Common	Hants	14	H4
Anthonys	Surrey	36	B8
Anthorn	Cumb	110	C9
Antingham	Norfk	77	K5
An t-Òb	W Isls	168	f9
Antonine Wall		126	E2
Anton's Gowt	Lincs	87	K11
Antony	Cnwll	5	Q11
Antrobus	Ches W	82	D9
Anvil Corner	Devon	16	F11
Anvil Green	Kent	27	K2
Anwick	Lincs	86	F10
Anwoth	D & G	108	C9
Aperfield	Gt Lon	37	K9
Apes Dale	Worcs	58	E10
Apethorpe	Nhants	73	Q11
Apeton	Staffs	70	F11
Apley	Lincs	86	F5
Apperknowle	Derbys	84	E5
Apperley	Gloucs	46	G9
Apperley Bridge	C Brad	90	F3
Apperley Dene	Nthumb	112	G9
Appersett	N York	96	C2
Appin	Ag & B	138	G8
Appleby	N Linc	92	G8
Appleby-in-Westmorland	Cumb	102	C6
Appleby Magna	Leics	59	M3
Appleby Parva	Leics	59	M3
Appleby Street	Herts	50	H10
Applecross	Highld	153	N9
Appledore	Devon	9	Q2
Appledore	Devon	16	H5
Appledore	Kent	26	G6
Appledore Heath	Kent	26	G5
Appleford	Oxon	34	F6
Applegarth Town	D & G	109	P4
Applehaigh	Wakefd	91	K8
Applemore	Hants	14	C5
Appleshaw	Hants	22	B5
Applethwaite	Cumb	101	J5
Appleton	Halton	81	Q7
Appleton	Oxon	34	D4
Appleton	Warrtn	82	D8
Appleton-le-Moors	N York	98	E3
Appleton-le-Street	N York	98	E6
Appleton Roebuck	N York	91	P2
Appleton Thorn	Warrtn	82	D8
Appleton Wiske	N York	104	C10
Appletreehall	Border	117	Q7
Appletreewick	N York	96	G8
Appley	Somset	18	E10
Appley Bridge	Lancs	88	G9
Apse Heath	IoW	14	G10
Apsley End	C Beds	50	D4
Apuldram	W Susx	15	M6
Arabella	Highld	156	E2
Arbirlot	Angus	143	L9
Arborfield	Wokham	35	L11
Arborfield Cross	Wokham	35	L11
Arborfield Green	Wokham	35	L11
Arbourthorne	Sheff	84	E3
Arbroath	Angus	143	L9
Arbuthnott	Abers	143	P3
Arcadia	Kent	26	E4
Archddu	Carmth	28	D4
Archdeacon Newton	Darltn	103	Q7
Archencarroch	W Duns	132	E11
Archiestown	Moray	157	N9
Archirondel	Jersey	11	c1
Arclid	Ches E	70	D2
Ardallie	Abers	159	P10
Ardanaiseig Hotel	Ag & B	131	M3
Ardaneaskan	Highld	153	Q10
Ardarroch	Highld	153	Q10
Ardcharnich	Highld	161	K9
Ardchiavaig	Ag & B	137	K12
Ardchonnell	Ag & B	131	K5
Ardchronie	Highld	162	E9
Ardchullarie More	Stirlg	132	H5
Arddarroch	Ag & B	131	Q9
Arddleen	Powys	69	J11
Ard Dorch	Highld	145	J2
Ardechive	Highld	146	E9
Ardeer	N Ayrs	124	H9
Ardeley	Herts	50	H5
Ardelve	Highld	145	Q2
Arden	Ag & B	132	D11
Ardens Grafton	Warwks	47	M4
Ardentallen	Ag & B	130	G3
Ardentinny	Ag & B	131	P10
Ardentraive	Ag & B	124	C3
Ardeonaig	Stirlg	140	G10
Ardersier	Highld	156	D7
Ardessie	Highld	160	H9
Ardfern	Ag & B	130	G2
Ardfernal	Ag & B	123	J5
Ardgartan	Ag & B	132	B7
Ardgay	Highld	162	D8
Ardgour	Highld	139	J3
Ardgowan	Inver	124	G3
Ardhallow	Ag & B	124	F3
Ardhasig	W Isls	168	g7
Ardheslaig	Highld	153	P6
Ardindrean	Highld	161	K9
Ardingly	W Susx	24	H5
Ardington	Oxon	34	D7
Ardington Wick	Oxon	34	D7
Ardlamont	Ag & B	124	B4
Ardleigh	Essex	53	J6
Ardleigh Heath	Essex	52	H5
Ardler	P & K	142	D9
Ardley	Oxon	48	F9
Ardley End	Essex	51	M8
Ardlui	Ag & B	132	C4
Ardlussa	Ag & B	130	C10
Ardmair	Highld	161	J7
Ardmaleish	Ag & B	124	D4
Ardminish	Ag & B	123	K10
Ardmolich	Highld	138	C3
Ardmore	Ag & B	125	J2
Ardmore	Highld	162	G9
Ardnadam	Ag & B	131	P11
Ardnagrask	Highld	155	P8
Ardnamurchan	Highld	137	P2
Ardnarff	Highld	154	A10
Ardnastang	Highld	138	E5
Ardpatrick	Ag & B	123	N8
Ardrishaig	Ag & B	130	H10
Ardross	Highld	155	R3
Ardrossan	N Ayrs	124	G9
Ardsley	Barns	91	K9
Ardslignish	Highld	137	P3
Ardtalla	Ag & B	122	G9
Ardtoe	Highld	138	A3
Arduaine	Ag & B	130	F5
Ardullie	Highld	155	Q5
Ardvasar	Highld	145	K7
Ardvorlich	P & K	133	J3
Ardvourlie	W Isls	168	g6
Ardwell	D & G	106	F8
Ardwick	Manch	83	J5
Areley Kings	Worcs	57	P10
Arevegaig	Highld	138	B3
Arford	Hants	23	M7
Argoed	Caerph	30	G5
Argoed	Shrops	69	K10
Argoed Mill	Powys	44	D2
Argos Hill	E Susx	25	N5
Argyll Forest Park	Ag & B	131	Q7
Aribruach	W Isls	168	h6
Aridhglas	Ag & B	137	J11
Arileod	Ag & B	136	F5
Arinagour	Ag & B	136	G4
Ariogan	Ag & B	130	H2
Arisaig	Highld	145	L10
Arisaig House	Highld	145	L11
Arkendale	N York	97	N8
Arkesden	Essex	51	L4
Arkholme	Lancs	95	M6
Arkleby	Cumb	100	F3
Arkleton	D & G	110	H3
Arkle Town	N York	103	K10
Arkley	Gt Lon	50	F11
Arksey	Donc	91	P9
Arkwright Town	Derbys	84	F6
Arle	Gloucs	46	H10
Arlecdon	Cumb	100	D7
Arlescote	Warwks	48	C5
Arlesey	C Beds	50	E3
Arleston	Wrekin	57	M2
Arley	Ches E	82	E8
Arlingham	Gloucs	32	D2
Arlington	Devon	17	L3
Arlington	E Susx	25	M9
Arlington	Gloucs	33	M3
Arlington Beccott	Devon	17	L3
Armadale	Highld	145	K7
Armadale	Highld	166	C4
Armadale	W Loth	126	G4
Armaside	Cumb	100	G5
Armathwaite	Cumb	111	K11
Arminghall	Norfk	77	K11
Armitage	Staffs	71	K11
Armitage Bridge	Kirk	90	E8
Armley	Leeds	90	H4
Armscote	Warwks	47	P6
Armshead	Staffs	70	G5
Armston	Nhants	61	N3
Armthorpe	Donc	91	Q10
Arnabost	Ag & B	136	G3
Arnaby	Cumb	94	D4
Arncliffe	N York	96	D6
Arncliffe Cote	N York	96	D6
Arncroach	Fife	135	N6
Arndilly House	Moray	157	P8
Arne	Dorset	12	G7
Arnesby	Leics	60	D2
Arngask	P & K	134	E5
Arnisdale	Highld	145	M5
Arnish	Highld	153	K8
Arniston	Mdloth	127	Q5
Arnol	W Isls	168	i3
Arnold	E R Yk	93	K11
Arnold	Notts	85	J11
Arnprior	Stirlg	133	J9
Arnside	Cumb	95	K5
Aros	Ag & B	137	P6
Arowry	Wrexhm	69	N7
Arrad Foot	Cumb	94	G4
Arram	E R Yk	92	H2
Arran	N Ayrs	120	H4
Arrathorne	N York	97	K2
Arreton	IoW	14	F9
Arrina	Highld	153	N5
Arrington	Cambs	62	D10
Arrochar	Ag & B	132	B7
Arrow	Warwks	47	L3
Arrowfield Top	Worcs	58	F10
Arscott	Shrops	56	G3
Artafallie	Highld	156	A8
Arthington	Leeds	90	H2
Arthingworth	Nhants	60	G4
Arthog	Gwynd	54	E2
Arthrath	Abers	159	N10
Arthursdale	Leeds	91	K3
Artrochie	Abers	159	P11
Arundel	W Susx	24	B9
Asby	Cumb	100	E6
Ascog	Ag & B	124	E5
Ascot	W & M	35	Q10
Ascott	Warwks	48	B8
Ascott Earl	Oxon	48	B10
Ascott-under-Wychwood	Oxon	48	B11
Asenby	N York	97	N5
Asfordby	Leics	73	J7
Asfordby Hill	Leics	73	J7
Asgarby	Lincs	86	F11
Asgarby	Lincs	87	K7
Ash	Devon	7	L9
Ash	Devon	17	J10
Ash	Dorset	12	D2
Ash	Kent	37	P8
Ash	Kent	39	N10
Ash	Somset	19	J10
Ash	Somset	19	N10
Ash	Surrey	23	N4
Ashampstead	W Berk	34	G9
Ashampstead Green	W Berk	34	G9
Ashbocking	Suffk	64	H11
Ashbourne	Derbys	71	M5
Ashbrittle	Somset	18	E10
Ashburnham Place	E Susx	25	Q8
Ashburton	Devon	7	K4
Ashbury	Devon	8	D5
Ashbury	Oxon	33	Q7
Ashby	N Linc	92	E9
Ashby by Partney	Lincs	87	M7
Ashby cum Fenby	NE Lin	93	N10
Ashby de la Launde	Lincs	86	D9
Ashby Folville	Leics	73	J8
Ashby Magna	Leics	60	C2
Ashby Parva	Leics	60	B3
Ashby Puerorum	Lincs	87	K7
Ashby St Ledgers	Nhants	60	C7
Ashby St Mary	Norfk	77	L11
Ashchurch	Gloucs	46	H8
Ashcombe	Devon	9	M9
Ashcombe	N Som	19	K2
Ashcott	Somset	19	M7
Ashdon	Essex	51	N2
Ashdown Forest	E Susx	25	L4
Ashe	Hants	22	F4
Asheldham	Essex	52	G11
Ashen	Essex	52	B3
Ashendon	Bucks	35	K2
Asheridge	Bucks	35	P4
Asherton	Surrey	23	P5
Ashfield	Hants	22	C11
Ashfield	Herefs	46	A10
Ashfield	Stirlg	133	M7
Ashfield cum Thorpe	Suffk	65	J9
Ashfield Green	Suffk	63	N9
Ashfield Green	Suffk	65	K7
Ashfold Crossways	W Susx	24	F5
Ashford	Devon	6	H9
Ashford	Devon	17	J4
Ashford	Kent	26	H3
Ashford	Surrey	36	C6
Ashford Bowdler	Shrops	57	J10
Ashford Carbonell	Shrops	57	J10
Ashford Hill	Hants	22	G2
Ashford in the Water	Derbys	83	Q11
Ashgill	S Lans	126	D7
Ash Green	Surrey	23	P5
Ash Green	Warwks	59	M8
Ashill	Devon	10	B2
Ashill	Norfk	76	B11
Ashill	Somset	19	L11
Ashingdon	Essex	38	E3
Ashington	BCP	12	H5
Ashington	Nthumb	113	L3
Ashington	Somset	19	Q10
Ashington	W Susx	24	D7
Ashkirk	Border	117	P6
Ashlett	Hants	14	E6
Ashleworth	Gloucs	46	F9
Ashleworth Quay	Gloucs	46	F9
Ashley	Cambs	63	L8
Ashley	Ches E	82	G8
Ashley	Devon	17	M9
Ashley	Dorset	13	K4
Ashley	Gloucs	32	H6
Ashley	Hants	13	N5
Ashley	Hants	22	C8
Ashley	Kent	27	P2
Ashley	Nhants	60	G2
Ashley	Staffs	70	D7
Ashley	Wilts	32	F11
Ashley Green	Bucks	35	Q3
Ashleyhay	Derbys	71	P4
Ashley Heath	Dorset	13	K4
Ashley Moor	Herefs	56	H11
Ash Magna	Shrops	69	Q7
Ashmansworth	Hants	22	D3
Ashmansworthy	Devon	16	E8
Ashmead Green	Gloucs	32	E5
Ashmill	Devon	5	P2
Ash Mill	Devon	17	P7
Ashmore	Dorset	20	H11
Ashmore Green	W Berk	34	F11
Ashorne	Warwks	48	B3
Ashover	Derbys	84	D8
Ashover Hay	Derbys	84	D8
Ashow	Warwks	59	M10
Ash Parva	Shrops	69	Q7
Ashperton	Herefs	46	B6
Ashprington	Devon	7	L7
Ash Priors	Somset	18	G9
Ashreigney	Devon	17	L9
Ash Street	Suffk	52	H2
Ashtead	Surrey	36	E9
Ash Thomas	Devon	9	P2
Ashton	C Pete	74	B9
Ashton	Cnwll	2	G8
Ashton	Devon	9	L8
Ashton	Hants	22	F11
Ashton	Herefs	45	Q2
Ashton	Inver	124	G3
Ashton	Nhants	49	L5
Ashton	Nhants	61	N3
Ashton	Somset	19	M5
Ashton Common	Wilts	20	G3
Ashton Hayes	Ches W	81	Q11
Ashton Hill	Wilts	20	H3
Ashton-in-Makerfield	Wigan	82	C5
Ashton Keynes	Wilts	33	K6
Ashton under Hill	Worcs	47	J7
Ashton-under-Lyne	Tamesd	83	K5
Ashton upon Mersey	Traffd	82	G6
Ashton Vale	Bristl	31	Q10
Ashurst	Hants	13	P2
Ashurst	Kent	25	M3
Ashurst	Lancs	88	F7
Ashurst	W Susx	24	E7
Ashurst Wood	W Susx	25	K3
Ash Vale	Surrey	23	N4
Ashwater	Devon	5	P2
Ashwell	Herts	50	G3
Ashwell	Rutlnd	73	M8
Ashwell	Somset	19	L11
Ashwell End	Herts	50	G2
Ashwellthorpe	Norfk	64	G2
Ashwick	Somset	20	B5
Ashwicken	Norfk	75	P7
Ashwood	Staffs	58	C7
Askam in Furness	Cumb	94	E5
Askern	Donc	91	P8
Askerswell	Dorset	11	L6
Askett	Bucks	35	M3
Askham	Cumb	101	P6
Askham	Notts	85	M6
Askham Bryan	C York	98	B11
Askham Richard	C York	98	A11
Asknish	Ag & B	131	J9
Askrigg	N York	96	D2
Askwith	N York	97	J11
Aslackby	Lincs	74	A4
Aslacton	Norfk	64	H3
Aslockton	Notts	73	J3
Asney	Somset	19	N7
Aspall	Suffk	64	H9
Aspatria	Cumb	100	F2
Aspenden	Herts	51	J5
Aspenshaw	Derbys	83	M7
Asperton	Lincs	74	E3
Aspley	Staffs	70	E8
Aspley Guise	C Beds	49	P7
Aspley Heath	C Beds	49	P8
Aspley Heath	Warwks	58	G10
Aspull	Wigan	89	J9
Aspull Common	Wigan	82	D5
Asselby	E R Yk	92	B5
Asserby	Lincs	87	N5
Asserby Turn	Lincs	87	N5
Assington	Suffk	52	F4
Assington Green	Suffk	63	N10
Astbury	Ches E	70	E2
Astcote	Nhants	49	J4
Asterby	Lincs	87	J5
Asterley	Shrops	56	F3
Asterton	Shrops	56	F6
Asthall	Oxon	33	Q2
Asthall Leigh	Oxon	34	B2
Astle	Highld	162	G8
Astley	Shrops	69	P11
Astley	Warwks	59	M7
Astley	Wigan	82	F4
Astley	Worcs	57	P11
Astley Abbots	Shrops	57	N5
Astley Bridge	Bolton	89	L8
Astley Cross	Worcs	57	Q11
Astley Green	Wigan	82	F5
Aston	Birm	58	G7
Aston	Ches E	69	R5
Aston	Ches W	82	C9
Aston	Derbys	83	Q8
Aston	Flints	81	L11
Aston	Herefs	45	P2
Aston	Herts	50	G6
Aston	Oxon	34	B4
Aston	Rothm	84	G3
Aston	Shrops	69	P9
Aston	Staffs	70	D6
Aston	Staffs	70	F10
Aston	Wokham	35	L8
Aston	Wrekin	57	L3
Aston Abbotts	Bucks	49	M10
Aston Botterell	Shrops	57	L8
Aston-by-Stone	Staffs	70	G8
Aston Cantlow	Warwks	47	M2
Aston Clinton	Bucks	35	N2
Aston Crews	Herefs	46	C10
Aston Cross	Gloucs	46	H8
Aston End	Herts	50	G6
Aston-Eyre	Shrops	57	M6
Aston Fields	Worcs	58	E11
Aston Flamville	Leics	59	Q6
Aston Heath	Ches W	82	C9
Aston Ingham	Herefs	46	C10
Aston juxta Mondrum	Ches E	70	A3
Aston le Walls	Nhants	48	E4
Aston Magna	Gloucs	47	N7
Aston Munslow	Shrops	57	J7
Aston-on-Carrant	Gloucs	46	H8
Aston on Clun	Shrops	56	F8
Aston Pigott	Shrops	56	E3
Aston Rogers	Shrops	56	E3
Aston Rowant	Oxon	35	K4
Aston Sandford	Bucks	35	L3
Aston Somerville	Worcs	47	K7
Aston-sub-Edge	Gloucs	47	M6
Aston Tirrold	Oxon	34	G7
Aston-upon-Trent	Derbys	72	C5
Aston Upthorpe	Oxon	34	G7
Astrop	Nhants	48	F7
Astrope	Herts	35	N2
Astwick	C Beds	50	F3
Astwith	Derbys	84	F8
Astwood	M Keyn	49	Q5
Astwood	Worcs	58	D11
Astwood Bank	Worcs	47	K2
Aswarby	Lincs	73	R3
Aswardby	Lincs	87	L6
Atcham	Shrops	57	J3
Atch Lench	Worcs	47	K4
Athelhampton	Dorset	12	C6
Athelington	Suffk	65	J7
Athelney	Somset	19	K9
Athelstaneford	E Loth	128	E4
Atherfield Green	IoW	14	E11
Atherington	Devon	17	K7
Atherington	W Susx	24	B10
Atherstone	Somset	19	L11
Atherstone	Warwks	59	M5
Atherstone on Stour	Warwks	47	P4
Atherton	Wigan	82	E4
Atley Hill	N York	103	Q10
Atlow	Derbys	71	N5
Attadale	Highld	154	B10
Attenborough	Notts	72	E4
Atterby	Lincs	86	C2
Attercliffe	Sheff	84	E3
Atterley	Shrops	57	L5
Atterton	Leics	72	B11
Attingham Park	Shrops	57	J2
Attleborough	Norfk	64	E2
Attleborough	Warwks	59	N6
Attlebridge	Norfk	76	H8
Attleton Green	Suffk	63	M10
Atwick	E R Yk	99	P11
Atworth	Wilts	32	G11
Auberrow	Herefs	45	P5
Aubourn	Lincs	86	B8
Auchbreck	Moray	149	N9
Auchedly	Abers	159	L11
Auchenblae	Abers	143	N2
Auchenbowie	Stirlg	133	N9
Auchencairn	D & G	108	G10
Auchencairn	D & G	109	L4
Auchencairn	N Ayrs	121	K6
Auchencrow	Border	129	M7
Auchendinny	Mdloth	127	P5
Auchengray	S Lans	126	H7
Auchenhalrig	Moray	157	R5
Auchenheath	S Lans	126	E8
Auchenhessnane	D & G	115	R8
Auchenlochan	Ag & B	124	B3
Auchenmade	N Ayrs	125	K8
Auchenmalg	D & G	106	H7
Auchentiber	N Ayrs	125	K8
Auchindrain	Ag & B	131	L7
Auchindrean	Highld	161	K10
Auchininna	Abers	158	G8
Auchinleck	E Ayrs	115	L3
Auchinloch	N Lans	126	B3
Auchinstarry	N Lans	126	C2
Auchintore	Highld	139	K3
Auchiries	Abers	159	Q10
Auchlean	Highld	148	E9
Auchlee	Abers	151	M8
Auchleven	Abers	150	G3
Auchlochan	S Lans	126	E10
Auchlossan	Abers	150	F7
Auchlyne	Stirlg	140	F2
Auchmillan	E Ayrs	115	L3
Auchmithie	Angus	143	M9
Auchmuirbridge	Fife	134	G7
Auchnacree	Angus	142	H5
Auchnagatt	Abers	159	M9
Auchnarrow	Moray	149	N3
Auchnotteroch	D & G	106	C5
Auchroisk	Moray	157	Q7
Auchterarder	P & K	133	Q5
Auchteraw	Highld	147	K6
Auchterblair	Highld	148	G3
Auchtercairn	Highld	153	Q2
Auchterderran	Fife	134	G7
Auchterhouse	Angus	142	E10
Auchterless	Abers	158	H9
Auchtermuchty	Fife	134	G5
Auchterneed	Highld	155	N6
Auchtertool	Fife	134	G9
Auchtertyre	Highld	145	P2
Auchtubh	Stirlg	132	H3
Auckengill	Highld	167	Q4
Auckley	Donc	91	Q10
Audenshaw	Tamesd	83	K5
Audlem	Ches E	70	B4
Audley	Staffs	70	D4
Audley End	Essex	51	M3
Audley End	Essex	52	D4
Audley End	Suffk	64	B11
Audley End House & Gardens	Essex	51	M3
Audmore	Staffs	70	E10
Audnam	Dudley	58	C7
Aughertree	Cumb	101	J3
Aughton	E R Yk	92	B3
Aughton	Lancs	88	D9
Aughton	Lancs	95	M7
Aughton	Rothm	84	G3
Aughton	Wilts	21	P3
Aughton Park	Lancs	88	E8
Auldearn	Highld	156	G6
Aulden	Herefs	45	P4
Auldgirth	D & G	109	K3
Auldhouse	S Lans	125	Q7
Ault a' chruinn	Highld	146	A3
Aultbea	Highld	160	A9
Aultgrishin	Highld	160	A9
Aultguish Inn	Highld	155	J4
Ault Hucknall	Derbys	84	G7
Aultmore	Moray	158	B7
Aultnagoire	Highld	147	N3
Aultnamain	Highld	162	F10
Aunby	Lincs	73	Q8
Aunk	Devon	9	P4
Aunsby	Lincs	73	Q3
Aust	S Glos	31	Q7
Austendike	Lincs	74	E6
Austerfield	Donc	85	L2
Austerlands	Oldham	90	B9
Austhorpe	Leeds	91	K4
Austonley	Kirk	90	E9
Austrey	Warwks	59	L3
Austwick	N York	95	R7
Authorpe	Lincs	87	L4
Authorpe Row	Lincs	87	P6
Avebury	Wilts	33	M11
Avebury	Wilts	33	M11
Avebury Trusloe	Wilts	33	L11
Aveley	Thurr	37	N4
Avening	Gloucs	32	G5
Averham	Notts	85	N10
Aveton Gifford	Devon	6	H9
Aviemore	Highld	148	F5
Avington	W Berk	34	C11
Avoch	Highld	156	C6
Avon	Hants	13	K5
Avonbridge	Falk	126	G3
Avon Dassett	Warwks	48	D4
Avonmouth	Bristl	31	P9
Avonwick	Devon	7	J7
Awbridge	Hants	22	B10
Awkley	S Glos	31	Q8
Awliscombe	Devon	10	C4
Awre	Gloucs	32	D3
Awsworth	Notts	72	D2
Axborough	Worcs	58	C9
Axbridge	Somset	19	M4
Axford	Hants	22	H4
Axford	Wilts	33	P10
Axmansford	Hants	22	G2
Axminster	Devon	10	F5
Axmouth	Devon	10	E6
Axton	Flints	80	G8
Aycliffe	Dur	103	Q6
Aydon	Nthumb	112	H7
Aylburton	Gloucs	32	B4
Ayle	Nthumb	111	P11
Aylesbeare	Devon	9	P6
Aylesbury	Bucks	35	M2
Aylesby	NE Lin	93	M9
Aylesford	Kent	38	B10
Aylesham	Kent	39	M11
Aylestone	C Leic	72	F10
Aylestone Park	C Leic	72	F10
Aylmerton	Norfk	76	H4
Aylsham	Norfk	76	H6
Aylton	Herefs	46	C7
Aylworth	Gloucs	47	M10
Aymestrey	Herefs	56	G11
Aynho	Nhants	48	F8
Ayot Green	Herts	50	F8
Ayot St Lawrence	Herts	50	E7
Ayot St Peter	Herts	50	F7
Ayr	S Ayrs	114	F3
Aysgarth	N York	96	H3
Ayshford	Devon	18	D11
Ayside	Cumb	94	H4
Ayston	Rutlnd	73	M10
Aythorpe Roding	Essex	51	N8
Ayton	Border	129	N7
Azerley	N York	97	L8

B

abbacombe Torbay 7 N5
abbington Notts 72 D2
abbinswood Shrops 69 K9
abbs Green Herts 51 J7
abcarry Somset 19 Q9
abel Carmth 44 A7
abel Green Suffk 63 M11
abell Flints 80 H10
abeny Devon 8 G9
ablock Hythe Oxon 34 D4
abraham Cambs 62 H10
abworth Notts 85 L4
achau IoA 78 G8
ache Shrops 56 H8
acheldre Powys 56 C9
achelor's Bump E Susx 26 D9
ackaland Cumb 169 e3
ackbarrow Cumb 94 H4
acke Carmth 41 Q7
ackfolds Abers 159 P7
ackford Ches W 81 M10
ackford Cross Ches W 81 M10
ackies Highld 163 J6
ack of Keppoch Highld 145 L10
ack o' th' Brook Staffs 71 K4
ack Street Suffk 63 M9
ackwell N Som 31 N11
ackworth N Tyne 113 M4
acon's End Nhants 59 J7
aconsthorpe Norfk 76 G4
acton Herefs 45 M8
acton Norfk 77 L5
acton Suffk 64 F8
acton Green Suffk 64 E8
acup Lancs 89 P6
adachro Highld 153 P3
adanloch Highld 166 C10
adbury Swindn 33 N8
adby Nhants 60 C9
adcall Highld 164 F5
adcaul Highld 160 G8
addeley Edge C Stke 70 G4
addeley Green C Stke 70 G4
addesley Clinton Warwks 59 K10
addesley Ensor Warwks 59 L5
addidarrach Highld 160 H2
addingsill Border 127 L7
adenscoth Abers 158 G10
adentarbet Highld 160 G5
adenyon Abers 149 Q4
adersfield Norfk 77 K7
adgall Cnwll 5 L4
adgeney Cambs 74 H11
adger Shrops 57 P5
adger's Cross Cnwll 2 D7
adgers Mount Kent 37 L8
adgworth Gloucs 46 H11
adgworth Somset 19 L4
adharlick Cnwll 5 M4
adicaul Highld 145 N2
adingham Suffk 65 L8
adlesmere Kent 38 H11
adlieu Border 116 F7
adlipster Highld 167 M7
adluarach Highld 160 F8
adninish Highld 162 H8
adrallach Highld 160 H8
adsey Worcs 47 L6
adshot Lea Surrey 23 N5
adsworth Wakefd 91 M8
adwell Ash Suffk 64 D8
adwell Green Suffk 64 E8
agber Dorset 12 C2
agby N York 97 Q4
ag Enderby Lincs 87 L6
agendon Gloucs 33 K3
agginswood Shrops 57 M8
aggrow Cumb 100 G2
agh a' Chaisteil W Isls 168 b18
agham Kent 39 J11
agillt Flints 81 J9
aginton Warwks 59 M10
aglan Neath 29 K6
agley Leeds 90 G3
agley Shrops 69 M9
agley Somset 19 N5
agmore Hants 23 J4
agnall Staffs 70 G4
agnor W Berk 34 E11
agshot Surrey 23 P2
agshot Wilts 34 B11
agstone S Glos 32 C7
agthorpe Notts 84 Q10
agworth Leics 72 C9
agwyllydiart Herefs 45 N9
aildon C Brad 90 F3
aildon Green C Brad 90 F3
aile Ailein W Isls 168 h5
aile a' Mhanaich W Isls 168 c12
aile Mòr Ag & B 136 H11
ailey Green Hants 23 J9
aileyhead Cumb 111 K5
ailiff Bridge Calder 90 E5
aillieston C Glas 126 B5
ailrigg Lancs 95 K9
ainbridge N York 96 D2
ainshole Abers 158 F10
ainton C Pete 74 A9
ainton E R Yk 99 K10
ainton Oxon 48 G9
aintown Fife 135 K7
airnkine Border 118 C7
aker's End Herts 51 J7
aker Street Thurr 37 P4
akewell Derbys 84 B7
ala Gwynd 68 B7
alallan W Isls 168 h5
albeg Highld 155 M11
albeggie P & K 134 F2
alblair Highld 155 P8
alblair Highld 156 C4
alby Donc 91 P10
alcary D & G 108 H11
alchraggan Highld 155 P9
alchrick Highld 164 E4
alcombe W Susx 24 H4
alcombe Lane W Susx 24 H4
alcomie Links Fife 135 Q6
aldersby N York 97 N5
aldersby St James N York 97 N5
alderstone Lancs 89 J4
alderstone Rochdl 89 Q8
alderton Notts 85 P10

Baldhu Cnwll 3 K5
Baldinnie Fife 135 L5
Baldinnies P & K 134 C4
Baldock Herts 50 F4
Baldock Services Herts 50 F3
Baldovie C Dund 142 H11
Baldrine IoM 80 f5
Baldslow E Susx 26 D9
Baldwin IoM 80 e5
Baldwinholme Cumb 110 F10
Baldwin's Gate Staffs 70 D7
Baldwin's Hill W Susx 25 K2
Bale Norfk 76 E4
Baledgarno P & K 142 D11
Balemartine Ag & B 136 B7
Balerno C Edin 127 M4
Balfarg Fife 134 H7
Balfield Angus 143 J4
Balfour Ork 169 d5
Balfron Stirlg 132 G10
Balgaveny Abers 158 G9
Balgonar Fife 134 C9
Balgowan D & G 106 F9
Balgowan Highld 147 Q9
Balgown Highld 152 F4
Balgracie D & G 106 C5
Balgray S Lans 116 B6
Balham Gt Lon 36 G6
Balhary P & K 142 D8
Balholmie P & K 142 A10
Baligill Highld 166 E3
Balintore Angus 142 D6
Balintore Highld 156 F2
Balintraid Highld 156 C3
Balivanich W Isls 168 c12
Balk N York 97 Q4
Balkeerie Angus 142 E9
Balkholme E R Yk 92 C5
Ballabeg IoM 80 c7
Ballachulish Highld 139 K6
Ballafesson IoM 80 b7
Ballajora IoM 80 g3
Ballakilpheric IoM 80 b7
Ballamodha IoM 80 c7
Ballantrae S Ayrs 114 A11
Ballards Gore Essex 38 F3
Ballards Green Warwks 59 L6
Ballasalla IoM 80 c7
Ballater Abers 149 B8
Ballaugh IoM 80 d3
Ballchraggan Highld 156 D2
Ballencrieff E Loth 128 D4
Ballevulin Ag & B 136 B6
Ball Green C Stke 70 F4
Ball Haye Green Staffs 70 H3
Ball Hill Hants 22 D2
Ballianlay Ag & B 124 C5
Ballidon Derbys 71 N4
Balliekine N Ayrs 120 G4
Balliemore Ag & B 131 N8
Balligmorrie S Ayrs 114 D9
Ballimore Stirlg 132 G4
Ballindalloch Moray 157 M10
Ballindean P & K 134 H2
Ballingdon Suffk 52 E3
Ballinger Common Bucks 35 P4
Ballingham Herefs 46 A8
Ballingry Fife 134 F8
Ballinluig P & K 141 N7
Ballinshoe Angus 142 G7
Ballintuim P & K 141 R6
Balloch Highld 156 C8
Balloch N Lans 126 C3
Balloch P & K 133 N4
Balloch S Ayrs 114 F8
Balloch W Duns 132 D11
Balls Cross W Susx 23 Q4
Balls Green E Susx 25 L3
Ball's Green Gloucs 32 G5
Ballygown Ag & B 137 L7
Ballygrant Ag & B 122 E6
Ballyhaugh Ag & B 136 F4
Balmacara Highld 145 P2
Balmaclellan D & G 108 E5
Balmae D & G 108 E12
Balmaha Stirlg 132 E9
Balmalcolm Fife 135 J6
Balmangan D & G 108 D11
Balmedie Abers 151 P4
Balmer Heath Shrops 69 M8
Balmerino Fife 135 K3
Balmerlawn Hants 13 P4
Balmichael N Ayrs 120 H5
Balmore E Duns 125 P3
Balmuchy Highld 163 K11
Balmule Fife 134 G10
Balmullo Fife 135 L3
Balnacoil Highld 163 J4
Balnacra Highld 154 C8
Balnacroft Abers 149 P9
Balnafoich Highld 156 B10
Balnaguard P & K 141 M7
Balnahard Ag & B 137 M9
Balnain Highld 155 M11
Balnakeil Highld 165 J3
Balne N York 91 P7
Balquharn P & K 141 P10
Balquhidder Stirlg 132 G3
Balsall Common Solhll 59 K9
Balsall Heath Birm 58 G8
Balsall Street Solhll 59 K9
Balscote Oxon 48 C6
Balsham Cambs 63 J10
Baltasound Shet 169 t3
Balterley Staffs 70 D4
Balterley Green Staffs 70 D4
Balterley Heath Staffs 70 C4
Baltersan D & G 107 M5
Balthangie Abers 159 K7
Baltonsborough Somset 19 P8
Balvicar Ag & B 130 F4
Balvraid Highld 145 P4
Balvraid Highld 156 E11
Balwest Cnwll 2 F9
Bamber Bridge Lancs 88 H5
Bamber's Green Essex 51 N6
Bamburgh Nthumb 119 N4
Bamburgh Castle Nthumb 119 N3
Bamford Derbys 84 B4
Bamford Rochdl 89 P8
Bampton Cumb 101 P7
Bampton Devon 18 C10
Bampton Oxon 34 B4
Bampton Grange Cumb 101 P7
Banavie Highld 139 L2
Banbury Oxon 48 E6

Bancffosfelen Carmth 28 E2
Banchory Abers 150 H8
Banchory-Devenick Abers 151 N7
Bancycapel Carmth 28 D2
Bancyfelin Carmth 42 F11
Banc-y-ffordd Carmth 42 H7
Bandirran P & K 142 C11
Bandrake Head Cumb 94 G3
Banff Abers 158 G5
Bangor Gwynd 79 K10
Bangor-on-Dee Wrexhm 69 L5
Bangors Cnwll 5 L2
Bangor's Green Lancs 88 D9
Bangrove Suffk 64 C7
Banham Norfk 64 F4
Bank Hants 13 N3
Bankend D & G 109 M7
Bankfoot P & K 141 Q10
Bankglen E Ayrs 115 L5
Bank Ground Cumb 101 K11
Bankhead C Aber 151 N6
Bankhead S Lans 116 D2
Bank Newton N York 96 D10
Banknock Falk 126 D2
Banks Cumb 111 L8
Banks Lancs 88 D6
Banks Green Worcs 58 E11
Bankshill D & G 110 C4
Bank Street Worcs 46 B2
Bank Top Calder 90 E6
Bank Top Lancs 88 G9
Banningham Norfk 77 J6
Bannister Green Essex 51 Q6
Bannockburn Stirlg 133 N9
Banstead Surrey 36 G9
Bantham Devon 6 H10
Banton N Lans 126 C2
Banwell N Som 19 L3
Bapchild Kent 38 F9
Bapton Wilts 21 J7
Barabhas W Isls 168 i3
Barassie S Ayrs 125 J11
Barbaraville Highld 156 C3
Barber Booth Derbys 83 P8
Barber Green Cumb 94 H4
Barbieston S Ayrs 114 H4
Barbon Cumb 95 N4
Barbridge Ches E 69 R3
Barbrook Devon 17 N2
Barby Nhants 60 B6
Barcaldine Ag & B 138 H4
Barcheston Warwks 47 Q7
Barclose Cumb 110 H8
Barcombe E Susx 25 K8
Barcombe Cross E Susx 25 K7
Barcroft C Brad 90 C3
Barden N York 96 H2
Barden Park Kent 37 N11
Bardfield End Green Essex 51 P4
Bardfield Saling Essex 51 Q5
Bardney Lincs 86 F7
Bardon Leics 72 C8
Bardon Mill Nthumb 111 Q8
Bardowie E Duns 125 P3
Bardown E Susx 25 Q5
Bardrainney Inver 125 J3
Bardsea Cumb 94 G6
Bardsey Leeds 91 K2
Bardsey Island Gwynd 66 A10
Bardsley Oldham 83 K4
Bardwell Suffk 64 C7
Bare Lancs 95 K8
Bareppa Cnwll 3 K8
Barfad D & G 107 K4
Barford Norfk 76 G10
Barford Warwks 47 Q2
Barford St John Oxon 48 D8
Barford St Martin Wilts 21 L8
Barford St Michael Oxon 48 D8
Barfrestone Kent 39 N11
Bargate Derbys 84 E11
Bargeddie N Lans 126 B5
Bargoed Caerph 30 G5
Bargrennan D & G 107 L2
Barham Cambs 61 P5
Barham Kent 39 M11
Barham Suffk 64 G11
Bar Hill Cambs 62 E8
Barholm Lincs 74 A8
Barkby Leics 72 G9
Barkby Thorpe Leics 72 G9
Barkers Green Shrops 69 P9
Barkestone-le-Vale Leics 73 K4
Barkham Wokham 35 L11
Barking Gt Lon 37 K4
Barking Suffk 64 F11
Barkingside Gt Lon 37 K3
Barking Tye Suffk 64 F11
Barkisland Calder 90 D7
Barkla Shop Cnwll 3 J4
Barkston Lincs 73 N2
Barkston Ash N York 91 M3
Barkway Herts 51 J3
Barlanark C Glas 126 B5
Barlaston Staffs 70 F7
Barlavington W Susx 23 Q11
Barlborough Derbys 84 G5
Barlby N York 91 Q4
Barlestone Leics 72 C9
Barley Herts 51 K3
Barley Lancs 89 N2
Barleycroft End Herts 51 K5
Barley Hole Rothm 91 K11
Barleythorpe Rutlnd 73 L9
Barling Essex 38 F4
Barlings Lincs 86 E6
Barlochan D & G 108 H9
Barlow Derbys 84 D6
Barlow Gatesd 113 J8
Barlow N York 91 Q5
Barmby Moor E R Yk 98 F11
Barmby on the Marsh E R Yk 92 A5
Barmer Norfk 75 R4
Barming Heath Kent 38 B10
Barmollack Ag & B 120 F3
Barmouth Gwynd 67 L11
Barmpton Darltn 104 B7
Barmston E R Yk 99 P9
Barnaby Green Suffk 65 P5
Barnacarry Ag & B 131 J5
Barnack C Pete 74 A9
Barnacle Warwks 59 N8
Barnard Castle Dur 103 L7
Barnard Gate Oxon 34 D2
Barnardiston Suffk 63 M11

Barnbarroch D & G 108 H9
Barnburgh Donc 91 M10
Barnby Suffk 65 P4
Barnby Dun Donc 91 Q9
Barnby in the Willows Notts 85 Q10
Barnby Moor Notts 85 L4
Barncorkrie D & G 106 E10
Barnehurst Gt Lon 37 L5
Barnes Gt Lon 36 F5
Barnes Street Kent 37 P11
Barnet Gt Lon 50 F11
Barnetby le Wold N Linc 93 J9
Barnet Gate Gt Lon 50 F11
Barney Norfk 76 D5
Barnham Suffk 64 B6
Barnham W Susx 15 Q6
Barnham Broom Norfk 76 F10
Barnhead Angus 143 M6
Barnhill C Dund 142 H11
Barnhill Ches W 69 N4
Barnhill Moray 157 L6
Barnhills D & G 106 C3
Barningham Dur 103 L8
Barningham Suffk 64 D6
Barnoldby le Beck NE Lin 93 M10
Barnoldswick Lancs 96 C11
Barnsdale Bar Donc 91 N8
Barns Green W Susx 24 D5
Barnsley Barns 91 J9
Barnsley Gloucs 33 L4
Barnsole Kent 39 N10
Barnstaple Devon 17 K5
Barnston Essex 51 P7
Barnston Wirral 81 K8
Barnstone Notts 73 J3
Barnt Green Worcs 58 F10
Barnton C Edin 127 M3
Barnton Ches W 82 D10
Barnwell All Saints Nhants 61 M4
Barnwell St Andrew Nhants 61 N4
Barnwood Gloucs 46 G11
Baron's Cross Herefs 45 P3
Baronwood Cumb 101 P2
Barr S Ayrs 114 E9
Barra W Isls 168 b17
Barra Airport W Isls 168 c17
Barrachan D & G 107 L8
Barraigh W Isls 168 b17
Barrananaoil Ag & B 130 G6
Barrapoll Ag & B 136 A7
Barras Cumb 102 F8
Barrasford Nthumb 112 D6
Barregarrow IoM 80 d4
Barrets Green Ches E 69 Q3
Barrhead E Rens 125 M6
Barrhill S Ayrs 114 D11
Barrington Cambs 62 E11
Barrington Somset 19 L11
Barripper Cnwll 2 G6
Barrmill N Ayrs 125 K7
Barrock Highld 167 N2
Barrow Gloucs 46 G10
Barrow Lancs 89 L3
Barrow Rutlnd 73 M7
Barrow Shrops 57 M4
Barrow Somset 20 D8
Barrow Suffk 63 N8
Barroway Drove Norfk 75 L10
Barrow Bridge Bolton 89 K8
Barrow Burn Nthumb 118 G8
Barrowby Lincs 73 M3
Barrow Common N Som 31 P11
Barrowden Rutlnd 73 N10
Barrowford Lancs 89 P3
Barrow Gurney N Som 31 P11
Barrow Haven N Linc 93 J6
Barrow Hill Derbys 84 F5
Barrow-in-Furness Cumb 94 E7
Barrow Island Cumb 94 D7
Barrow Nook Lancs 81 N4
Barrow's Green Ches E 70 B3
Barrows Green Cumb 95 L3
Barrow Street Wilts 20 F8
Barrow-upon-Humber N Linc 93 J6
Barrow upon Soar Leics 72 F7
Barrow upon Trent Derbys 72 B5
Barrow Vale BaNES 20 B2
Barry Angus 143 J11
Barry V Glam 30 F11
Barry Island V Glam 30 F11
Barsby Leics 72 H8
Barsham Suffk 65 M4
Barston Solhll 59 K9
Bartestree Herefs 45 R6
Barthol Chapel Abers 159 K11
Bartholomew Green Essex 52 B7
Barthomley Ches E 70 D4
Bartley Hants 13 P2
Bartley Green Birm 58 F8
Bartlow Cambs 63 J11
Barton Cambs 62 F9
Barton Ches W 69 M4
Barton Gloucs 47 L9
Barton Herefs 45 K3
Barton Lancs 88 D9
Barton Lancs 88 G3
Barton N York 103 P9
Barton Oxon 34 G3
Barton Torbay 7 N5
Barton Warwks 47 M4
Barton Bendish Norfk 75 P9
Barton End Gloucs 32 F5
Barton Green Staffs 71 M11
Barton Hartshorn Bucks 48 H8
Barton Hill N York 98 E8
Barton in Fabis Notts 72 E4
Barton in the Beans Leics 72 B9
Barton-le-Clay C Beds 50 C4
Barton-le-Street N York 98 E6
Barton-le-Willows N York 98 E8
Barton Mills Suffk 63 M6
Barton-on-Sea Hants 13 M6
Barton-on-the-Heath Warwks 47 Q8
Barton Park Services N York 103 P9
Barton St David Somset 19 P8
Barton Seagrave Nhants 61 J5
Barton Stacey Hants 22 D6
Barton Town Devon 17 M3
Barton Turf Norfk 77 M7
Barton-under-Needwood Staffs 71 M11
Barton-upon-Humber N Linc 92 H6
Barton upon Irwell Salfd 82 G5

Barton Waterside N Linc 92 H6
Barugh Barns 91 J9
Barugh Green Barns 91 J9
Barvas W Isls 168 i3
Barway Cambs 63 J5
Barwell Leics 72 C11
Barwick Devon 17 K10
Barwick Herts 51 J7
Barwick Somset 11 M2
Barwick in Elmet Leeds 91 L3
Baschurch Shrops 69 M10
Bascote Warwks 48 D2
Bascote Heath Warwks 48 C2
Base Green Suffk 64 E9
Basford Green Staffs 70 H4
Bashall Eaves Lancs 89 K2
Bashall Town Lancs 89 L2
Bashley Hants 13 M5
Basildon Essex 38 B4
Basingstoke Hants 22 H4
Baslow Derbys 84 C6
Bason Bridge Somset 19 K5
Bassaleg Newpt 31 J7
Bassendean Border 128 G10
Bassenthwaite Cumb 100 H4
Bassett C Sotn 22 D11
Bassingbourn-cum-Kneesworth Cambs 50 H2
Bassingfield Notts 72 G3
Bassingham Lincs 86 B9
Bassingthorpe Lincs 73 P5
Bassus Green Herts 50 H5
Basted Kent 37 P9
Baston Lincs 74 B8
Bastwick Norfk 77 N8
Batch Somset 19 K3
Batchworth Herts 36 C2
Batchworth Heath Herts 36 C2
Batcombe Dorset 11 N4
Batcombe Somset 20 C7
Bate Heath Ches E 82 E9
Batford Herts 50 D7
Bath BaNES 20 D2
Bath BaNES 20 E2
Bathampton BaNES 32 E11
Bathealton Somset 18 E10
Batheaston BaNES 32 E11
Bathford BaNES 32 E11
Bathgate W Loth 126 H4
Bathley Notts 85 N9
Bathpool Cnwll 5 M7
Bathpool Somset 19 J9
Bath Side Essex 53 N5
Bathville W Loth 126 G4
Bathway Somset 19 Q4
Batley Kirk 90 G6
Batsford Gloucs 47 N8
Batson Devon 7 J11
Battersby N York 104 G9
Battersea Gt Lon 36 G5
Battisborough Cross Devon 6 F9
Battisford Suffk 64 F11
Battisford Tye Suffk 64 E11
Battle E Susx 26 C8
Battle Powys 44 E8
Battleborough Somset 19 K4
Battledown Gloucs 47 J10
Battledykes Angus 142 H6
Battlefield Shrops 69 P11
Battlesbridge Essex 38 C3
Battlesden C Beds 49 Q9
Battleton Somset 18 B9
Battles Green Suffk 64 C9
Battram Leics 72 C9
Battramsley Cross Hants 13 P5
Batt's Corner Hants 23 M6
Baughton Worcs 46 G6
Baughurst Hants 22 G2
Baulds Abers 150 G9
Baulking Oxon 34 B6
Baumber Lincs 86 H6
Baunton Gloucs 33 K4
Baveney Wood Shrops 57 M9
Baverstock Wilts 21 K8
Bawburgh Norfk 76 H10
Bawdeswell Norfk 76 E7
Bawdrip Somset 19 K7
Bawdsey Suffk 53 P3
Bawsey Norfk 75 N6
Bawtry Donc 85 K2
Baxenden Lancs 89 M5
Baxterley Warwks 59 L5
Baxter's Green Suffk 63 N9
Bay Highld 152 D7
Bayble W Isls 168 k4
Baybridge Hants 22 F10
Baybridge Nthumb 112 E10
Baycliff Cumb 94 F6
Baydon Wilts 33 Q9
Bayford Herts 50 H9
Bayford Somset 20 D9
Bayhead W Isls 168 c11
Bay Horse Lancs 95 K10
Bayley's Hill Kent 37 M10
Baylham Suffk 64 G11
Baynard's Green Oxon 48 F9
Baysdale Abbey N York 104 H9
Baysham Herefs 45 R9
Bayston Hill Shrops 56 H3
Baythorne End Essex 52 B3
Bayton Worcs 57 M10
Bayton Common Worcs 57 N10
Bayworth Oxon 34 E4
Beach S Glos 32 D10
Beachampton Bucks 49 L7
Beachamwell Norfk 75 Q9
Beachley Gloucs 31 Q6
Beachy Head E Susx 25 N11
Beacon Devon 10 D3
Beacon End Essex 52 G7
Beacon Hill Essex 26 D5
Beacon Hill Notts 85 P10
Beacon Hill Surrey 23 N7
Beacon's Bottom Bucks 35 L5
Beaconsfield Bucks 35 P6
Beaconsfield Services Bucks 35 Q7
Beadlam N York 98 D4
Beadlow C Beds 50 D3
Beadnell Nthumb 119 P5
Beaford Devon 17 K8
Beal N York 91 N5
Beal Nthumb 119 L2
Bealbury Cnwll 5 P8
Bealsmill Cnwll 5 P6
Beam Hill Staffs 71 N9

Beamhurst Staffs......71 K7
Beaminster Dorset......11 K4
Beamish Dur......113 K10
Beamish Open Air Museum Dur......113 K10
Beamsley N York......96 G10
Bean Kent......37 N6
Beanacre Wilts......32 H11
Beanley Nthumb......119 L7
Beardon Devon......8 D8
Beardwood Bl w D......89 K5
Beare Devon......9 N4
Beare Green Surrey......24 E2
Bearley Warwks......47 N2
Bearley Cross Warwks......47 N2
Bearpark Dur......103 P2
Bearsden E Duns......125 N3
Bearsted Kent......38 D10
Bearstone Shrops......70 C7
Bearwood BCP......12 H5
Bearwood Birm......58 F7
Bearwood Herefs......45 M3
Beattock D & G......116 F10
Beauchamp Roding Essex......51 N9
Beauchief Sheff......84 D4
Beaudesert Warwks......59 J11
Beaufort Blae G......30 G4
Beaulieu Essex......52 B10
Beaulieu Hants......14 C6
Beaulieu Road Station Hants......13 P3
Beauly Highld......155 P8
Beaumaris IoA......79 L9
Beaumaris Castle IoA......79 L9
Beaumont Cumb......110 F9
Beaumont Essex......53 L7
Beaumont Jersey......11 b2
Beaumont Hill Darltn......103 Q7
Beaumont Leys C Leic......72 F9
Beausale Warwks......59 K10
Beauworth Hants......22 G9
Beaworthy Devon......8 C5
Beazley End Essex......52 B6
Bebington Wirral......81 L8
Bebside Nthumb......113 L4
Beccles Suffk......65 N4
Becconsall Lancs......88 F6
Beckbury Shrops......57 P4
Beckenham Gt Lon......37 J7
Beckermet Cumb......100 D9
Beckett End Norfk......75 Q11
Beckfoot Cumb......94 D3
Beckfoot Cumb......100 G10
Beck Foot Cumb......102 B11
Beckfoot Cumb......109 N11
Beckford Worcs......47 J7
Beckhampton Wilts......33 L11
Beck Hole N York......105 M10
Beckingham Lincs......85 Q10
Beckingham Notts......85 N3
Beckington Somset......20 F4
Beckjay Shrops......56 F9
Beckley E Susx......26 E7
Beckley Hants......13 M5
Beckley Oxon......34 G2
Beck Row Suffk......63 L5
Becks C Brad......96 F11
Beck Side Cumb......94 E4
Beck Side Cumb......94 H4
Beckton Gt Lon......37 K4
Beckwithshaw N York......97 L10
Becontree Gt Lon......37 L3
Becquet Vincent Jersey......11 b1
Bedale N York......97 L3
Bedburn Dur......103 L4
Bedchester Dorset......20 G11
Beddau Rhondd......30 E7
Beddgelert Gwynd......67 K5
Beddingham E Susx......25 K9
Beddington Gt Lon......36 H7
Beddington Corner Gt Lon......36 G7
Bedfield Suffk......65 J8
Bedfield Little Green Suffk......65 J8
Bedford Bed......61 M11
Bedgebury Cross Kent......26 B5
Bedgrove Bucks......35 M2
Bedham W Susx......24 B6
Bedhampton Hants......15 K5
Bedingfield Suffk......64 H8
Bedingfield Green Suffk......64 H8
Bedlam N York......97 L8
Bedlington Nthumb......113 L4
Bedlinog Myr Td......30 E4
Bedminster Bristl......31 Q10
Bedminster Down Bristl......31 Q10
Bedmond Herts......50 C10
Bednall Staffs......70 H11
Bedrule Border......118 B7
Bedstone Shrops......56 F9
Bedwas Caerph......30 G7
Bedwellty Caerph......30 G4
Bedworth Warwks......59 N7
Bedworth Woodlands Warwks......59 M7
Beeby Leics......72 H9
Beech Hants......23 J7
Beech Staffs......70 F7
Beech Hill W Berk......23 J2
Beechingstoke Wilts......21 L3
Beedon W Berk......34 E9
Beedon Hill W Berk......34 E9
Beeford E R Yk......99 N10
Beeley Derbys......84 C7
Beelsby NE Lin......93 M10
Beenham W Berk......34 G11
Beenham's Heath W & M......35 M9
Beeny Cnwll......5 J3
Beer Devon......10 E7
Beer Somset......19 M8
Beercrocombe Somset......19 K10
Beer Hackett Dorset......11 N2
Beesands Devon......7 L10
Beesby Lincs......87 N4
Beeson Devon......7 L10
Beeston C Beds......61 Q11
Beeston Ches W......69 P3
Beeston Leeds......90 H4
Beeston Norfk......76 C8
Beeston Notts......72 E3
Beeston Regis Norfk......76 H3
Beeswing D & G......109 J7
Beetham Cumb......95 K5
Beetley Norfk......76 D8
Began Cardif......30 H8
Begbroke Oxon......34 E2

Begdale Cambs......75 J9
Begelly Pembks......41 M9
Beggarington Hill Leeds......90 H6
Beggar's Bush Powys......45 K2
Beguildy Powys......56 B9
Beighton Norfk......77 M10
Beighton Sheff......84 F4
Beinn Na Faoghla W Isls......168 d12
Beith N Ayrs......125 K7
Bekesbourne Kent......39 L10
Bekesbourne Hill Kent......39 L10
Belaugh Norfk......77 K8
Belbroughton Worcs......58 D9
Belchalwell Dorset......12 C3
Belchalwell Street Dorset......12 C3
Belchamp Otten Essex......52 D3
Belchamp St Paul Essex......52 C3
Belchamp Walter Essex......52 D3
Belchford Lincs......87 J5
Belgrave C Leic......72 F9
Belhaven E Loth......128 H4
Belhelvie Abers......151 N4
Belhinnie Abers......150 D2
Bellabeg Abers......150 B5
Bellamore Herefs......45 M6
Bellanoch Ag & B......130 F9
Bellasize E R Yk......92 D5
Bellaty Angus......142 C6
Bell Bar Herts......51 G9
Bell Busk N York......96 D9
Belleau Lincs......87 M5
Bell End Worcs......58 D9
Bellerby N York......96 H2
Bellever Devon......8 G9
Belle Vue Cumb......110 G9
Belle Vue Wakefd......91 J7
Bellfield S Lans......126 E11
Bellfields Surrey......23 Q4
Bell Heath Worcs......58 D9
Bell Hill Hants......23 K10
Bellingdon Bucks......35 P3
Bellingham Nthumb......112 B4
Belloch Ag & B......120 C4
Bellochantuy Ag & B......120 C5
Bell o' th' Hill Ches W......69 P5
Bellows Cross Dorset......13 J2
Bells Cross Suffk......64 H11
Bellshill N Lans......126 C5
Bellshill Nthumb......119 M4
Bellside N Lans......126 E6
Bellsquarry W Loth......127 K4
Bells Yew Green E Susx......25 P3
Belluton BaNES......20 B2
Belmaduthy Highld......156 A6
Belmesthorpe Rutlnd......73 Q8
Belmont Bl w D......89 K7
Belmont Gt Lon......36 G8
Belmont S Ayrs......114 F4
Belmont Shet......169 s3
Belnacraig Abers......150 B4
Belowda Cnwll......4 F9
Belper Derbys......84 D11
Belper Lane End Derbys......84 D11
Belph Derbys......84 H5
Belsay Nthumb......112 G5
Belses Border......117 R5
Belsford Devon......7 K7
Belsize Herts......50 B10
Belstead Suffk......53 K3
Belstone Devon......8 F6
Belthorn Bl w D......89 L6
Beltinge Kent......39 L8
Beltingham Nthumb......111 Q8
Beltoft N Linc......92 D9
Belton Leics......72 C6
Belton Lincs......73 N3
Belton N Linc......92 C9
Belton Norfk......77 P11
Belton House Lincs......73 N3
Belton in Rutland Rutlnd......73 L10
Beltring Kent......37 Q11
Belvedere Gt Lon......37 L5
Belvoir Leics......73 L4
Bembridge IoW......14 H9
Bemerton Wilts......21 M8
Bempton E R Yk......99 P6
Benacre Suffk......65 Q5
Benbecula W Isls......168 d12
Benbecula Airport W Isls......168 c12
Benbuie D & G......115 P8
Benderloch Ag & B......138 G10
Benenden Kent......26 D5
Benfieldside Dur......112 G10
Bengate Norfk......77 L6
Bengeo Herts......50 H8
Bengeworth Worcs......47 K6
Benhall Green Suffk......65 M9
Benhall Street Suffk......65 M9
Benholm Abers......143 Q4
Beningbrough N York......98 A9
Benington Herts......50 G6
Benington Lincs......87 L11
Benington Sea End Lincs......87 M11
Benllech IoA......79 J8
Benmore Ag & B......131 N10
Bennacott Cnwll......5 M3
Bennan N Ayrs......121 J7
Bennet Head Cumb......101 M6
Bennetland E R Yk......92 D5
Bennett End Bucks......35 L5
Ben Nevis Highld......139 M3
Benniworth Lincs......86 H4
Benover Kent......26 B2
Ben Rhydding C Brad......96 H11
Benslie N Ayrs......125 J9
Benson Oxon......34 H6
Bentfield Green Essex......51 M5
Benthall Shrops......57 M4
Bentham Gloucs......46 H11
Benthoul C Aber......151 L7
Bentlawnt Shrops......56 E4
Bentley Donc......91 P9
Bentley E R Yk......92 H3
Bentley Hants......23 L6
Bentley Suffk......53 K4
Bentley Warwks......59 L5
Bentley Heath Herts......50 G11
Bentley Heath Solhll......59 J9
Benton Devon......17 M4
Bentpath D & G......110 F2
Bentwichen Devon......17 N5
Bentworth Hants......23 J6
Benvie Angus......142 E11
Benville Dorset......11 L4
Benwick Cambs......62 D2

Beoley Worcs......58 G11
Beoraidbeg Highld......145 L9
Bepton W Susx......23 N11
Berden Essex......51 L5
Berea Pembks......40 E4
Bere Alston Devon......6 C5
Bere Ferrers Devon......6 D6
Berepper Cnwll......2 H9
Bere Regis Dorset......12 D6
Bergh Apton Norfk......77 L11
Berhill Somset......19 M7
Berinsfield Oxon......34 G5
Berkeley Gloucs......32 C5
Berkeley Heath Gloucs......32 C5
Berkeley Road Gloucs......32 C4
Berkhamsted Herts......35 Q3
Berkley Somset......20 F5
Berkswell Solhll......59 K9
Bermondsey Gt Lon......36 H5
Bermuda Warwks......59 N7
Bernera Highld......145 P3
Bernisdale Highld......152 G7
Berrick Prior Oxon......34 H6
Berrick Salome Oxon......34 H6
Berriedale Highld......163 Q2
Berrier Cumb......101 L5
Berriew Powys......56 B4
Berrington Nthumb......119 K2
Berrington Shrops......57 J3
Berrington Worcs......57 K11
Berrington Green Worcs......57 K11
Berrow Somset......19 J4
Berrow Worcs......46 E8
Berrow Green Worcs......46 D3
Berry Brow Kirk......90 E8
Berry Cross Devon......16 H9
Berry Down Cross Devon......17 K3
Berryfield Wilts......20 H1
Berryfields Bucks......49 L11
Berry Hill Gloucs......31 Q2
Berry Hill Pembks......41 L2
Berryhillock Moray......158 D5
Berryhillock Moray......158 D7
Berrynarbor Devon......17 K2
Berry Pomeroy Devon......7 L6
Berry's Green Gt Lon......37 K9
Bersham Wrexhm......69 K5
Bersted W Susx......15 P6
Berthengam Flints......80 G9
Berwick E Susx......25 M9
Berwick Bassett Wilts......33 L10
Berwick Hill Nthumb......113 J5
Berwick St James Wilts......21 L7
Berwick St John Wilts......20 H10
Berwick St Leonard Wilts......20 H8
Berwick Station E Susx......25 M9
Berwick-upon-Tweed Nthumb......129 P9
Bescaby Leics......73 L6
Bescar Lancs......88 D8
Besford Shrops......69 P9
Besford Worcs......46 H6
Bessacarr Donc......91 Q10
Bessels Leigh Oxon......34 E4
Besses o' th' Barn Bury......89 N9
Bessingby E R Yk......99 P7
Bessingham Norfk......76 H4
Bestbeech Hill E Susx......25 P4
Besthorpe Norfk......64 F2
Besthorpe Notts......85 P8
Bestwood Village Notts......85 J11
Beswick E R Yk......99 L11
Betchcott Shrops......56 G5
Betchworth Surrey......36 F10
Bethania Cerdgn......43 L2
Bethania Gwynd......67 N6
Bethel Gwynd......68 C7
Bethel Gwynd......79 J11
Bethel IoA......78 F10
Bethel Powys......68 F10
Bethersden Kent......26 F3
Bethesda Gwynd......79 L11
Bethesda Pembks......41 L7
Bethlehem Carmth......43 N9
Bethnal Green Gt Lon......36 H4
Betley Staffs......70 D5
Betsham Kent......37 P6
Betteshanger Kent......39 P11
Bettiscombe Dorset......10 H4
Bettisfield Wrexhm......69 N7
Betton Shrops......70 B7
Betton Strange Shrops......57 J3
Bettws Brdgnd......29 P7
Bettws Newpt......31 J6
Bettws Cedewain Powys......55 Q5
Bettws Ifan Cerdgn......42 F5
Bettws-Newydd Mons......31 L3
Bettws Gwerfil Goch Denbgs......68 D5
Betws-y-Coed Conwy......67 P3
Betws-yn-Rhos Conwy......80 C10
Beulah Cerdgn......42 E5
Beulah Powys......44 C4
Bevendean Br & H......24 H9
Bevercotes Notts......85 L6
Beverley E R Yk......92 H3
Beverston Gloucs......32 G5
Bevington Gloucs......32 C5
Bewaldeth Cumb......100 H4
Bewcastle Cumb......111 L6
Bewdley Worcs......57 P9
Bewerley N York......97 J7
Bewholme E R Yk......99 P11
Bewlbridge Kent......25 Q4
Bexhill-on-Sea E Susx......26 B10
Bexley Gt Lon......37 L5
Bexleyheath Gt Lon......37 L5
Bexleyhill W Susx......23 P9
Bexon Kent......38 E10
Beyton Suffk......64 C9
Beyton Green Suffk......64 C9
Bhaltos W Isls......168 f4
Bharatsaigh W Isls......168 b18
Bibstone S Glos......32 C6
Bibury Gloucs......33 M3
Bicester Oxon......48 G10
Bickenhill Solhll......59 J8
Bicker Lincs......74 D3
Bicker Bar Lincs......74 D3
Bicker Gauntlet Lincs......74 D3
Bickershaw Wigan......82 D4
Bickerstaffe Lancs......81 N4

Bickerton Ches E......69 P4
Bickerton Devon......7 L11
Bickerton N York......97 Q10
Bickerton Nthumb......119 J10
Bickford Staffs......58 C2
Bickington Devon......7 L4
Bickington Devon......17 J5
Bickleigh Devon......6 D6
Bickleigh Devon......9 M3
Bickleton Devon......17 J5
Bickley Ches W......69 P5
Bickley Gt Lon......37 K7
Bickley Worcs......57 L10
Bickley Moss Ches W......69 P5
Bicknacre Essex......52 C11
Bicknoller Somset......18 F7
Bicknor Kent......38 E10
Bickton Hants......13 K2
Bicton Herefs......45 P2
Bicton Shrops......56 D8
Bicton Shrops......69 M11
Bidborough Kent......25 N2
Bidden Hants......23 K5
Biddenden Kent......26 E4
Biddenden Green Kent......26 E3
Biddenham Bed......61 M10
Biddestone Wilts......32 G10
Biddisham Somset......19 L4
Biddlesden Bucks......48 H7
Biddlestone Nthumb......119 J9
Biddulph Staffs......70 F3
Biddulph Moor Staffs......70 G3
Bideford Devon......16 H6
Bidford-on-Avon Warwks......47 M4
Bidston Wirral......81 K6
Bielby E R Yk......92 C2
Bieldside C Aber......151 M7
Bierley IoW......14 F11
Bierton Bucks......49 M11
Big Balcraig D & G......107 L9
Bigbury Devon......6 H9
Bigbury-on-Sea Devon......6 H10
Bigby Lincs......93 J9
Biggar Cumb......94 D7
Biggar S Lans......116 E3
Biggin Derbys......71 M3
Biggin Derbys......71 P5
Biggin N York......91 N4
Biggin Hill Gt Lon......37 K9
Biggleswade C Beds......50 E2
Bigholms D & G......110 F4
Bighouse Highld......166 E4
Bighton Hants......22 H8
Biglands Cumb......110 E10
Bignor W Susx......15 Q4
Bigrigg Cumb......100 D8
Big Sand Highld......160 B11
Bigton Shet......169 q11
Bilborough C Nott......72 F2
Bilbrook Somset......18 D6
Bilbrook Staffs......58 C4
Bilbrough N York......98 A11
Bilbster Highld......167 N6
Bildershaw Dur......103 P6
Bildeston Suffk......52 G2
Billacott Cnwll......5 M4
Billericay Essex......37 Q2
Billesdon Leics......73 J10
Billesley Warwks......47 M3
Billingborough Lincs......74 B4
Billinge St Hel......82 B4
Billingford Norfk......64 H6
Billingford Norfk......76 E7
Billingham S on T......104 E6
Billinghay Lincs......86 G10
Billingley Barns......91 L10
Billingshurst W Susx......24 C5
Billingsley Shrops......57 N8
Billington C Beds......49 Q10
Billington Lancs......89 L3
Billington Staffs......70 F10
Billockby Norfk......77 N9
Billy Row Dur......103 N3
Bilsborrow Lancs......88 G3
Bilsby Lincs......87 N5
Bilsham W Susx......15 Q6
Bilsington Kent......26 H5
Bilsthorpe Notts......85 K8
Bilsthorpe Moor Notts......85 L8
Bilston Mdloth......127 P5
Bilston Wolves......58 D5
Bilstone Leics......72 B9
Bilting Kent......27 J2
Bilton E R Yk......93 K3
Bilton N York......97 M9
Bilton Nthumb......119 P8
Bilton Warwks......59 Q10
Bilton Banks Nthumb......119 P8
Bilton-in-Ainsty N York......97 Q11
Binbrook Lincs......86 H2
Binchester Blocks Dur......103 P3
Bincombe Dorset......11 P8
Binegar Somset......20 B5
Bines Green W Susx......24 E7
Binfield Br For......35 M10
Binfield Heath Oxon......35 K9
Bingfield Nthumb......112 E6
Bingham Notts......73 J3
Bingham's Melcombe Dorset......12 C4
Bingley C Brad......90 E3
Bings Heath Shrops......69 P11
Binham Norfk......76 D4
Binley Covtry......59 N9
Binley Hants......22 D4
Binley Woods Warwks......59 N9
Binnegar Dorset......12 E7
Binniehill Falk......126 F3
Binscombe Surrey......23 Q5
Binsted Hants......23 L6
Binsted W Susx......15 Q5
Binton Warwks......47 M4
Bintree Norfk......76 E7
Binweston Shrops......56 E4
Birch Essex......52 F8
Birch Rochdl......89 P9
Birchall Staffs......70 H4
Bircham Newton Norfk......75 P4
Bircham Tofts Norfk......75 Q4
Birchanger Essex......51 M6
Birchanger Green Services Essex......51 M6
Birch Cross Staffs......71 L8

Birchencliffe Kirk......90 E6
Bircher Herefs......56 H1
Birchett's Green E Susx......25 Q4
Birchfield Birm......58 G6
Birch Green Essex......52 F7
Birch Green Herts......50 G8
Birch Green Worcs......46 G5
Birchgrove Cardif......30 G7
Birchgrove Swans......29 L6
Birchgrove W Susx......25 K4
Birch Heath Ches W......69 P2
Birch Hill Ches W......81 P11
Birchington-on-Sea Kent......39 N8
Birchley Heath Warwks......59 L6
Birchmoor Warwks......59 L4
Birchmoor Green C Beds......49 Q7
Birchover Derbys......84 B8
Birch Services Rochdl......89 N9
Birch Vale Derbys......83 L7
Birchwood Lincs......86 C8
Birch Wood Somset......10 E2
Birchwood Warrtn......82 E5
Bircotes Notts......85 K3
Birdbrook Essex......52 B3
Birdforth N York......97 Q5
Birdham W Susx......15 N6
Birdingbury Warwks......59 P11
Birdlip Gloucs......32 H2
Birdoswald Cumb......111 M8
Birdsall N York......98 G8
Birds Edge Kirk......90 G9
Birds Green Essex......51 N9
Birdsgreen Shrops......57 N7
Birdsmoorgate Dorset......10 H4
Bird Street Suffk......64 F10
Birdwell Barns......91 J10
Birdwood Gloucs......46 D11
Birgham Border......118 E3
Birichin Highld......162 H6
Birkacre Lancs......88 H7
Birkby N York......104 D9
Birkdale Sefton......88 C8
Birkenbog Abers......158 D4
Birkenhead Wirral......81 K7
Birkenhead (Queensway) Tunnel Lpool......81 L7
Birkenhills Abers......158 H8
Birkenshaw Kirk......90 G5
Birkhall Abers......149 Q5
Birkhill Angus......142 F11
Birkhill D & G......117 J2
Birkholme Lincs......73 N6
Birkin N York......91 N5
Birks Leeds......90 H4
Birkshaw Nthumb......111 P8
Birley Herefs......45 P3
Birley Carr Sheff......84 D3
Birling Kent......37 Q8
Birling Nthumb......119 P9
Birling Gap E Susx......25 N11
Birlingham Worcs......46 H6
Birmingham Birm......58 G7
Birmingham Airport Solhll......59 J8
Birnam P & K......141 P9
Birness Abers......159 N11
Birse Abers......150 F8
Birsemore Abers......150 F8
Birstall Leics......72 F9
Birstall Kirk......90 G5
Birstwith N York......97 L9
Birthorpe Lincs......74 B4
Birtley Gatesd......113 L9
Birtley Herefs......56 F11
Birtley Nthumb......112 C4
Birts Street Worcs......46 E7
Bisbrooke Rutlnd......73 M11
Biscathorpe Lincs......86 H4
Biscovey Cnwll......3
Bisham W & M......35 M7
Bishampton Worcs......47 J4
Bish Mill Devon......17 N6
Bishop Auckland Dur......103 P5
Bishopbridge Lincs......86 D2
Bishopbriggs E Duns......125 Q3
Bishop Burton E R Yk......92 G2
Bishop Middleham Dur......104 B4
Bishopmill Moray......157 M5
Bishop Monkton N York......97 M7
Bishop Norton Lincs......86 C2
Bishopsbourne Kent......39 L11
Bishops Cannings Wilts......21 L2
Bishop's Castle Shrops......56 F6
Bishop's Caundle Dorset......11 P2
Bishop's Cleeve Gloucs......47 J9
Bishop's Frome Herefs......46 C5
Bishops Gate Surrey......35 Q11
Bishop's Green Essex......51 P7
Bishop's Green Hants......22 F2
Bishop's Hull Somset......18 H10
Bishop's Itchington Warwks......48 C3
Bishops Lydeard Somset......18 G9
Bishop's Norton Gloucs......46 F10
Bishop's Nympton Devon......17 N7
Bishop's Offley Staffs......70 D9
Bishop's Stortford Herts......51 L6
Bishop's Sutton Hants......22 H8
Bishop's Tachbrook Warwks......48 B2
Bishop's Tawton Devon......17 K6
Bishopsteignton Devon......7 N3
Bishopstoke Hants......22 E10
Bishopston Swans......28 G7
Bishopstone Bucks......35 M2
Bishopstone E Susx......25 L10
Bishopstone Herefs......45 N5
Bishopstone Kent......39 M8
Bishopstone Swindn......33 P8
Bishopstone Wilts......21 L9
Bishopstrow Wilts......20 G7
Bishop Sutton BaNES......19 Q3
Bishop's Waltham Hants......22 G10
Bishopswood Somset......10 E2
Bishop's Wood Staffs......58 C3
Bishopsworth Bristl......31 Q10
Bishop Thornton N York......97 L7
Bishopthorpe C York......98 B11
Bishopton Darltn......104 C6
Bishopton Rens......125 L3
Bishopton Warwks......47 P3
Bishop Wilton E R Yk......98 E9
Bishton Newpt......31 L7
Bishton Staffs......71 J9
Bisley Gloucs......32 H3
Bisley Surrey......23 Q3
Bisley Camp Surrey......23 Q3
Bispham Bpool......88 C2

Bispham Green – Boxbush 259

ispham Green Lancs 88 F8
issoe Cnwll 3 K5
isterne Hants 13 K4
itchet Green Kent 37 N10
itchfield Lincs 73 P5
ittadon Devon 17 J3
ittaford Devon 6 H7
ittering Norfk 76 C8
itterley Shrops 57 K9
itterne C Sotn 14 E4
itteswell Leics 60 B3
itton S Glos 32 C11
ix Oxon 35 K8
ixter Shet 169 q8
laby Leics 72 F11
lackadder Border 129 L9
lackawton Devon 7 L8
lackbeck Cumb 100 D9
lackborough Devon 10 B3
lackborough End Norfk 75 N7
lack Bourton Oxon 33 Q4
lackboys E Susx 25 M6
lackbrook Derbys 84 D11
lackbrook St Hel 82 B5
lackbrook Staffs 70 D7
lackbrook Surrey 36 E11
lackburn Abers 151 L5
lackburn Bl w D 89 K5
lackburn Rothm 84 E2
lackburn W Loth 126 H4
lackburn with Darwen Services Bl w D 89 K6
lack Callerton N u Ty 113 J7
lack Carr Norfk 64 F2
lack Corner W Susx 24 G3
lackcraig E Ayrs 115 M6
lack Crofts Ag & B 138 G11
lack Cross Cnwll 4 E9
lackden Heath Ches E 82 G10
lackdog Abers 151 P5
lack Dog Devon 9 K3
lackdown Devon 8 D9
lackdown Dorset 10 H4
lackdyke Cumb 109 P10
lacker Barns 91 J9
lacker Hill Barns 91 K10
lackfen Gt Lon 37 L6
lackfield Hants 14 D6
lackford Cumb 110 G8
lackford P & K 133 P6
lackford Somset 19 M5
lackford Somset 20 C9
lackfordby Leics 72 A7
lackgang IoW 14 E11
lackhall C Edin 127 N3
lackhall Colliery Dur 104 E3
lackhall Mill Gatesd 112 H9
lackhall Rocks Dur 104 E3
lackham E Susx 25 L2
lackhaugh Border 117 N3
lackheath Essex 52 H7
lackheath Gt Lon 37 J5
lackheath Sandw 58 E7
lackheath Suffk 65 N7
lackheath Surrey 36 B11
lack Heddon Nthumb 112 G5
lackhill Abers 159 Q6
lackhill Abers 159 Q9
lackhill Dur 112 G10
lackhill of Clackriach Abers 159 M8
lackhorse Devon 9 N6
lackjack Lincs 74 E3
lackland Wilts 33 K11
lack Lane Ends Lancs 89 Q2
lacklaw D & G 116 E9
lackley Manch 83 J4
lacklunans P & K 142 A5
lackmarstone Herefs 45 Q7
lackmill Brdgnd 29 P7
lackmoor Hants 23 L8
lack Moor Leeds 90 H3
lackmoor N Som 19 N2
lackmoorfoot Kirk 90 D8
lackmoor Gate Devon 17 L3
lackmore Essex 51 P10
lackmore End Essex 52 B5
lackmore End Herts 50 E7
lack Mountains 45 K9
lackness Falk 127 K2
lacknest Hants 23 L6
lacknest W & M 35 Q11
lack Notley Essex 52 C7
lacko Lancs 89 P2
lack Pill Swans 28 H6
lackpool Bpool 88 C3
lackpool Devon 7 L4
lackpool Devon 7 M9
lackpool Gate Cumb 111 K5
lackpool Zoo Bpool 88 C3
lackridge W Loth 126 F4
lackrock Cnwll 2 H7
lackrock Mons 30 H2
lackrod Bolton 89 J8
lacksboat Moray 157 M10
lackshaw D & G 109 M7
lackshaw Head Calder 90 B5
lacksmith's Green Suffk 64 G8
lacksnape Bl w D 89 L6
lackstone W Susx 24 F7
lack Street Suffk 65 Q4
lack Tar Pembks 41 J9
lackthorn Oxon 48 H11
lackthorpe Suffk 64 C9
lacktoft E R Yk 92 D6
lacktop C Aber 151 M7
lack Torrington Devon 8 C3
lackwall Derbys 71 P5
lackwall Tunnel Gt Lon 37 J4
lackwater Cnwll 3 J4
lackwater Hants 23 M3
lackwater IoW 14 F9
lackwater Somset 19 J11
lackwaterfoot N Ayrs 120 H6
lackwell Cumb 110 H10
lackwell Darltn 103 Q8
lackwell Derbys 83 P10
lackwell Derbys 84 F9
lackwell Warwks 47 P6
lackwell Worcs 58 E10
lackwellsend Green Gloucs 46 E9
lackwood Caerph 30 G5
lackwood D & G 109 K3
lackwood S Lans 126 D9
lackwood Hill Staffs 70 G3
lacon Ches W 81 M11
Bladbean Kent 27 L2
Bladnoch D & G 107 M7
Bladon Oxon 34 E2
Bladon Somset 19 M10
Blaenannerch Cerdgn 42 D5
Blaenau Ffestiniog Gwynd 67 N5
Blaenavon Torfn 31 J3
Blaenavon Industrial Landscape Torfn 30 H3
Blaencwm Rhondd 29 P5
Blaen Dyryn Powys 44 C7
Blaenffos Pembks 41 N3
Blaengarw Brdgnd 29 P6
Blaengeuffordd Cerdgn 54 E8
Blaengwrach Neath 29 N3
Blaengwynfi Neath 29 N5
Blaenllechau Rhondd 30 D5
Blaenpennal Cerdgn 43 M2
Blaenplwyf Cerdgn 54 D9
Blaenporth Cerdgn 42 E5
Blaenrhondda Rhondd 29 P5
Blaenwaun Carmth 41 P5
Blaen-y-coed Carmth 42 F9
Blaen-y-cwm Blae G 30 F2
Blaenycwm Cerdgn 55 J9
Blagdon N Som 19 P3
Blagdon Somset 18 H11
Blagdon Torbay 7 M6
Blagdon Hill Somset 18 H11
Blagill Cumb 111 P11
Blaguegate Lancs 88 F9
Blaich Highld 139 J2
Blain Highld 138 B4
Blaina Blae G 30 H3
Blair Atholl P & K 141 L4
Blair Drummond Stirlg 133 L8
Blairgowrie P & K 142 B8
Blairhall Fife 134 B10
Blairingone P & K 134 B8
Blairlogie Stirlg 133 N8
Blairmore Ag & B 131 P11
Blairmore Highld 164 E5
Blair's Ferry Ag & B 124 B4
Blaisdon Gloucs 46 D11
Blakebrook Worcs 57 Q9
Blakedown Worcs 58 C9
Blake End Essex 52 B7
Blakeley Lane Staffs 70 H5
Blakemere Ches W 82 C10
Blakemere Herefs 45 M6
Blakemore Devon 7 K6
Blakenall Heath Wsall 58 F4
Blakeney Gloucs 32 C3
Blakeney Norfk 76 E3
Blakenhall Ches E 70 C5
Blakenhall Wolves 58 D5
Blakeshall Worcs 58 B8
Blakesley Nhants 48 H4
Blanchland Nthumb 112 E10
Blandford Camp Dorset 12 F3
Blandford Forum Dorset 12 E3
Blandford St Mary Dorset 12 E3
Bland Hill N York 97 K10
Blanefield Stirlg 125 N2
Blankney Lincs 86 E8
Blantyre S Lans 126 B6
Blàr a' Chaorainn Highld 139 L4
Blarghour Ag & B 131 K5
Blargie Highld 147 Q9
Blarmachfoldach Highld 139 K4
Blashford Hants 13 L3
Blaston Leics 73 L11
Blatherwycke Nhants 73 P11
Blawith Cumb 94 F3
Blawquhairn D & G 108 D4
Blaxhall Suffk 65 M10
Blaxton Donc 91 R10
Blaydon Gatesd 113 J8
Bleadney Somset 19 N5
Bleadon N Som 19 K3
Bleak Street Somset 20 E8
Blean Kent 39 K9
Bleasby Lincs 86 F4
Bleasby Notts 85 M11
Bleasdale Lancs 95 M11
Bleatarn Cumb 102 D8
Bleathwood Herefs 57 K10
Blebocraigs Fife 135 L4
Bleddfa Powys 56 C11
Bledington Gloucs 47 P10
Bledlow Bucks 35 L4
Bledlow Ridge Bucks 35 L5
Bleet Wilts 20 G3
Blegbie E Loth 128 D7
Blencarn Cumb 102 B4
Blencogo Cumb 110 C11
Blendworth Hants 15 K4
Blenheim Palace Oxon 48 D11
Blennerhasset Cumb 100 G2
Bletchingdon Oxon 48 F11
Bletchingley Surrey 36 H10
Bletchley M Keyn 49 N8
Bletchley Shrops 69 R8
Bletchley Park Museum M Keyn 49 N8
Bletherston Pembks 41 L6
Bletsoe Bed 61 M9
Blewbury Oxon 34 F7
Blickling Norfk 76 H6
Blidworth Notts 85 J9
Blidworth Bottoms Notts 85 J10
Blindburn Nthumb 118 F8
Blindcrake Cumb 100 F4
Blindley Heath Surrey 37 J11
Blisland Cnwll 5 J7
Blissford Hants 13 L2
Bliss Gate Worcs 57 N10
Blisworth Nhants 49 K4
Blithbury Staffs 71 K11
Blitterlees Cumb 109 P10
Blockley Gloucs 47 N7
Blofield Norfk 77 L10
Blofield Heath Norfk 77 L9
Blo Norton Norfk 64 E6
Bloomfield Border 118 A6
Blore Staffs 70 C8
Blore Staffs 71 L5
Blounce Hants 23 K5
Blounts Green Staffs 71 K8
Blowick Sefton 88 D7
Bloxham Oxon 48 D7
Bloxholm Lincs 86 E10
Bloxwich Wsall 58 E4
Bloxworth Dorset 12 E6
Blubberhouses N York 97 J9
Blue Anchor Cnwll 4 E10
Blue Anchor Somset 18 D6
Blue Bell Hill Kent 38 B9
Blue John Cavern Derbys 83 P8
Blundellsands Sefton 81 L5
Blundeston Suffk 65 Q2
Blunham C Beds 61 Q10
Blunsdon St Andrew Swindn 33 M7
Bluntington Worcs 58 D10
Bluntisham Cambs 62 E6
Blunts Cnwll 5 N9
Blunts Green Warwks 58 H11
Blurton C Stke 70 F6
Blyborough Lincs 86 B2
Blyford Suffk 65 N6
Blymhill Staffs 57 Q2
Blymhill Lawn Staffs 57 Q2
Blyth Notts 85 K3
Blyth Nthumb 113 M4
Blyth Bridge Border 127 L8
Blythburgh Suffk 65 N6
Blythe Border 128 F10
Blythe Bridge Staffs 70 H6
Blythe End Warwks 59 K6
Blythe Marsh Staffs 70 H6
Blyth Services Notts 85 K3
Blyton Lincs 85 Q2
Boarhills Fife 135 P5
Boarhunt Hants 14 H5
Boarley Kent 38 C10
Boarsgreave Lancs 89 N6
Boarshead E Susx 25 M4
Boar's Head Wigan 88 H9
Boars Hill Oxon 34 E4
Boarstall Bucks 34 H2
Boasley Cross Devon 8 D6
Boath Highld 155 Q3
Boat of Garten Highld 148 G4
Bobbing Kent 38 E8
Bobbington Staffs 57 Q6
Bobbingworth Essex 51 M9
Bocaddon Cnwll 5 K10
Bocking Essex 52 C7
Bocking Churchstreet Essex 52 C6
Bockleton Worcs 46 A2
Boconnoc Cnwll 5 J9
Boddam Abers 159 R9
Boddam Shet 169 q12
Boddington Gloucs 46 G9
Bodedern IoA 78 E8
Bodelwyddan Denbgs 80 E9
Bodenham Herefs 45 Q4
Bodenham Wilts 21 N9
Bodenham Moor Herefs 45 Q4
Bodewryd IoA 78 G6
Bodfari Denbgs 80 F10
Bodffordd IoA 78 G9
Bodham Norfk 76 G3
Bodiam E Susx 26 C6
Bodicote Oxon 48 E7
Bodieve Cnwll 4 F7
Bodinnick Cnwll 5 J11
Bodle Street Green E Susx 25 Q8
Bodmin Cnwll 4 H8
Bodmin Moor Cnwll 5 K6
Bodney Norfk 64 A2
Bodorgan IoA 78 F11
Bodsham Kent 27 K2
Boduan Gwynd 66 E7
Bodwen Cnwll 4 G9
Bodymoor Heath Warwks 59 J5
Bogallan Highld 156 A7
Bogbrae Abers 159 P10
Bogend S Ayrs 125 L11
Boggs Holdings E Loth 128 C5
Boghall Mdloth 127 N4
Boghall W Loth 126 H4
Boghead S Lans 126 D9
Bogmoor Moray 157 R5
Bogmuir Abers 143 L3
Bogniebrae Abers 158 E8
Bognor Regis W Susx 15 P7
Bogroy Highld 148 G3
Bogue D & G 108 D4
Bohetherick Cnwll 5 Q8
Bohortha Cnwll 3 M7
Bohuntine Highld 146 H11
Bojewyan Cnwll 2 B7
Bokiddick Cnwll 4 H9
Bolam Dur 103 N6
Bolam Nthumb 112 H4
Bolberry Devon 6 H11
Bold Heath St Hel 82 B7
Boldmere Birm 58 H6
Boldon Colliery S Tyne 113 M8
Boldre Hants 13 P5
Boldron Dur 103 K8
Bole Notts 85 N3
Bolehill Derbys 84 C9
Bole Hill Derbys 84 D6
Bolenowe Cnwll 2 H6
Bolham Devon 18 C11
Bolham Water Devon 10 D2
Bolingey Cnwll 3 K3
Bollington Ches E 83 K9
Bollington Cross Ches E 83 K9
Bollow Gloucs 32 D2
Bolney W Susx 24 G6
Bolnhurst Bed 61 N9
Bolnore W Susx 24 H6
Bolshan Angus 143 L7
Bolsover Derbys 84 G6
Bolster Moor Kirk 90 D7
Bolsterstone Sheff 90 H11
Boltby N York 97 Q3
Bolter End Bucks 35 L6
Bolton Bolton 89 L9
Bolton Cumb 102 B6
Bolton E Loth 128 E6
Bolton E R Yk 98 F10
Bolton Nthumb 119 M8
Bolton Abbey N York 96 G10
Bolton Bridge N York 96 G10
Bolton-by-Bowland Lancs 96 A11
Boltonfellend Cumb 111 J7
Boltongate Cumb 100 H2
Bolton-le-Sands Lancs 95 K7
Bolton Low Houses Cumb 100 H2
Bolton New Houses Cumb 100 H2
Bolton-on-Swale N York 103 Q11
Bolton Percy N York 91 N2
Bolton Town End Lancs 95 K7
Bolton upon Dearne Barns 91 M10
Bolventor Cnwll 5 K6
Bomarsund Nthumb 113 L4
Bomere Heath Shrops 69 N11
Bonar Bridge Highld 162 E8
Bonawe Ag & B 139 J11
Bonby N Linc 92 H7
Boncath Pembks 41 P3
Bonchester Bridge Border 118 A8
Bonchurch IoW 14 G11
Bondleigh Devon 8 G4
Bonds Lancs 88 F2
Bonehill Devon 8 H9
Bonehill Staffs 59 J4
Bo'ness Falk 134 C11
Boney Hay Staffs 58 F2
Bonhill W Duns 125 K2
Boningale Shrops 57 Q4
Bonjedward Border 118 C6
Bonkle N Lans 126 E6
Bonnington Angus 143 K10
Bonnington Kent 27 J4
Bonnybank Fife 135 K7
Bonnybridge Falk 126 E2
Bonnykelly Abers 159 L7
Bonnyrigg Mdloth 127 Q4
Bonnyton Angus 142 E10
Bonsall Derbys 84 C9
Bonshaw Tower D & G 110 D6
Bont Mons 45 M11
Bontddu Gwynd 67 M11
Bont-Dolgadfan Powys 55 K4
Bont-goch Cerdgn 54 F7
Bonthorpe Lincs 87 N6
Bontnewydd Cerdgn 54 E11
Bontnewydd Gwynd 66 H3
Bontuchel Denbgs 68 E3
Bonvilston V Glam 30 E10
Bonwm Denbgs 68 F6
Bon-y-maen Swans 29 J5
Boode Devon 17 J4
Booker Bucks 35 M6
Booley Shrops 69 Q9
Boon Border 128 F10
Boon Hill Staffs 70 E4
Boorley Green Hants 14 F4
Boosbeck R & Cl 105 J7
Boose's Green Essex 52 D5
Boot Cumb 100 G10
Booth Calder 90 C5
Boothby Graffoe Lincs 86 C9
Boothby Pagnell Lincs 73 P4
Boothferry E R Yk 92 B5
Booth Green Ches E 83 K8
Boothstown Salfd 82 F4
Boothtown Calder 90 D5
Boothville Nhants 60 G8
Bootle Cumb 94 C3
Bootle Sefton 81 L5
Boots Green Ches W 82 G10
Boot Street Suffk 53 M2
Booze N York 103 K10
Boraston Shrops 57 L11
Bordeaux Guern 10 c1
Borden Kent 38 E9
Borden W Susx 23 M10
Border Cumb 110 C10
Bordley N York 96 D7
Bordon Hants 23 L7
Boreham Essex 52 C10
Boreham Wilts 20 G6
Boreham Street E Susx 25 Q8
Borehamwood Herts 50 E11
Boreland D & G 110 C2
Boreraig Highld 152 B7
Boreton Shrops 57 J3
Borgh W Isls 168 b17
Borgh W Isls 168 j2
Borgie Highld 165 Q5
Borgue D & G 108 D11
Borgue Highld 167 K11
Borley Essex 52 D3
Borley Green Essex 52 D3
Borley Green Suffk 64 D9
Borneskitaig Highld 152 F3
Borness D & G 108 D11
Boroughbridge N York 97 N7
Borough Green Kent 37 P9
Borras Head Wrexhm 69 L4
Borrowash Derbys 72 C4
Borrowby N York 97 P3
Borrowby N York 105 L7
Borrowdale Cumb 101 J7
Borrowstoun Falk 134 B11
Borstal Medway 38 B8
Borth Cerdgn 54 E6
Borthwick Mdloth 128 B8
Borthwickbrae Border 117 N8
Borthwickshiels Border 117 N7
Borth-y-Gest Gwynd 67 K7
Borve Highld 152 G8
Borve W Isls 168 b17
Borve W Isls 168 f8
Borve W Isls 168 j2
Borwick Lancs 95 L6
Borwick Lodge Cumb 101 K11
Borwick Rails Cumb 94 D5
Bosavern Cnwll 2 B7
Bosbury Herefs 46 C6
Boscarne Cnwll 4 G8
Boscastle Cnwll 4 H3
Boscombe BCP 13 K6
Boscombe Wilts 21 P7
Boscoppa Cnwll 3 Q3
Bosham W Susx 15 M6
Bosham Hoe W Susx 15 M6
Bosherston Pembks 41 J12
Boskednan Cnwll 2 C7
Boskenna Cnwll 2 C9
Bosley Ches E 83 K11
Bosoughan Cnwll 4 D9
Bossall N York 98 E8
Bossiney Cnwll 4 H4
Bossingham Kent 27 L2
Bossington Somset 18 A5
Bostock Green Ches W 82 E11
Boston Lincs 74 F2
Boston Spa Leeds 97 P11
Boswarthan Cnwll 2 C7
Boswinger Cnwll 3 P5
Botallack Cnwll 2 B7
Botany Bay Gt Lon 50 G11
Botcheston Leics 72 D10
Botesdale Suffk 64 E6
Bothal Nthumb 113 K3
Bothampstead W Berk 34 F9
Bothamsall Notts 85 L6
Bothel Cumb 100 G3
Bothenhampton Dorset 11 K6
Bothwell S Lans 126 C6
Bothwell Services (southbound) S Lans 126 C6
Botley Bucks 35 Q4
Botley Hants 14 F4
Botley Oxon 34 E3
Botolph Claydon Bucks 49 K10
Botolphs W Susx 24 E9
Botolph's Bridge Kent 27 K5
Bottesford Leics 73 L3
Bottesford N Linc 92 E9
Bottisham Cambs 62 H8
Bottomcraig Fife 135 K3
Bottom of Hutton Lancs 88 F5
Bottom o' th' Moor Bolton 89 K8
Bottoms Calder 89 Q6
Bottoms Cnwll 2 B9
Botts Green Warwks 59 K6
Botusfleming Cnwll 5 Q9
Botwnnog Gwynd 66 D8
Bough Beech Kent 37 L11
Boughrood Powys 44 G7
Boughspring Gloucs 31 Q5
Boughton Nhants 60 G7
Boughton Norfk 75 P10
Boughton Notts 85 L7
Boughton Aluph Kent 26 H2
Boughton End C Beds 49 Q7
Boughton Green Kent 38 C11
Boughton Lees Kent 26 H2
Boughton Malherbe Kent 26 E2
Boughton Monchelsea Kent 38 C11
Boughton Street Kent 39 J10
Boulby R & Cl 105 L7
Boulder Clough Calder 90 C6
Bouldnor IoW 14 C9
Bouldon Shrops 57 J7
Boulmer Nthumb 119 Q8
Boulston Pembks 41 J8
Boultenstone Abers 150 C5
Boultham Lincs 86 C7
Boundary Staffs 70 H6
Bourn Cambs 62 D9
Bournbrook Birm 58 F8
Bourne Lincs 74 A6
Bournebridge Essex 37 M2
Bourne End Bed 61 M8
Bourne End Bucks 35 N7
Bourne End C Beds 49 Q6
Bourne End Herts 50 B9
Bournemouth BCP 13 J6
Bournemouth Airport BCP 13 K5
Bournes Green Gloucs 32 H4
Bournes Green Sthend 38 F4
Bournheath Worcs 58 E10
Bournmoor Dur 113 M10
Bournstream Gloucs 32 D6
Bournville Birm 58 F8
Bourton Dorset 20 E8
Bourton N Som 19 L2
Bourton Oxon 33 P7
Bourton Shrops 57 K5
Bourton Wilts 21 K2
Bourton on Dunsmore Warwks 59 P10
Bourton-on-the-Hill Gloucs 47 N8
Bourton-on-the-Water Gloucs 47 N10
Bousd Ag & B 136 H3
Boustead Hill Cumb 110 E9
Bouth Cumb 94 G3
Bouthwaite N York 96 H6
Bouts Worcs 47 K3
Boveney Bucks 35 P9
Boveridge Dorset 13 J2
Bovey Tracey Devon 9 K9
Bovingdon Herts 50 B10
Bovingdon Green Bucks 35 M7
Bovinger Essex 51 M9
Bovington Dorset 12 D7
Bovington Camp Dorset 12 D7
Bow Cumb 110 F9
Bow Devon 7 L7
Bow Devon 8 H4
Bow Gt Lon 37 J4
Bow Ork 169 c7
Bowbank Dur 102 H6
Bow Brickhill M Keyn 49 P8
Bowbridge Gloucs 32 G3
Bowburn Dur 104 B3
Bowcombe IoW 14 E9
Bowd Devon 10 C6
Bowden Border 117 R4
Bowden Devon 7 L9
Bowden Hill Wilts 32 H11
Bowdon Traffd 82 G7
Bower Highld 167 M4
Bowerchalke Wilts 21 K10
Bowerhill Wilts 20 H2
Bower Hinton Somset 19 N11
Bower House Tye Suffk 52 G3
Bowermadden Highld 167 M4
Bowers Staffs 70 E7
Bowers Gifford Essex 38 C4
Bowershall Fife 134 D9
Bower's Row Leeds 91 L5
Bowes Dur 103 J8
Bowgreave Lancs 88 F2
Bowhouse D & G 109 M7
Bowithick Cnwll 5 K5
Bowker's Green Lancs 81 N4
Bowland Border 117 P2
Bowland Bridge Cumb 95 J3
Bowley Herefs 45 Q4
Bowley Town Herefs 45 Q4
Bowlhead Green Surrey 23 P7
Bowling C Brad 90 F4
Bowling W Duns 125 L3
Bowling Bank Wrexhm 69 L5
Bowling Green Worcs 46 F4
Bowmanstead Cumb 101 K11
Bowmore Ag & B 122 D8
Bowness-on-Solway Cumb 110 D8
Bowness-on-Windermere Cumb 101 M11
Bow of Fife Fife 135 J5
Bowriefauld Angus 143 J8
Bowscale Cumb 101 L4
Bowsden Nthumb 119 J2
Bowston Cumb 101 N11
Bow Street Cerdgn 54 E7
Bow Street Norfk 64 E2
Bowthorpe Norfk 76 H10
Box Gloucs 32 G4
Box Wilts 32 F11
Boxbush Gloucs 32 D2
Boxbush Gloucs 46 C10

260 Box End – Brocton

Box End Bed 61 M11
Boxford Suffk 52 G3
Boxford W Berk 34 D10
Boxgrove W Susx 15 P5
Box Hill Surrey 36 E10
Boxley Kent 38 C10
Boxmoor Herts 50 B9
Box's Shop Cnwll 16 C11
Boxted Essex 52 G5
Boxted Essex 52 H5
Boxted Suffk 64 A11
Boxted Cross Essex 52 H5
Boxwell Gloucs 32 F6
Boxworth Cambs 62 D8
Boyden End Suffk 63 M9
Boyden Gate Kent 39 M8
Boylestone Derbys 71 M7
Boyndie Abers 158 F5
Boyndlie Abers 159 M5
Boynton E R Yk 99 N7
Boysack Angus 143 L8
Boys Hill Dorset 11 P2
Boythorpe Derbys 84 E7
Boyton Cnwll 5 N3
Boyton Suffk 53 Q2
Boyton Wilts 21 J7
Boyton Cross Essex 51 P9
Boyton End Suffk 52 B3
Bozeat Nhants 61 K9
Braaid IoM 80 d6
Brabling Green Suffk 65 K9
Brabourne Kent 27 K3
Brabourne Lees Kent 27 J3
Brabstermire Highld 167 P3
Bracadale Highld 152 F10
Braceborough Lincs 74 A8
Bracebridge Heath Lincs 86 C7
Bracebridge Low Fields Lincs 86 C7
Braceby Lincs 73 Q3
Bracewell Lancs 96 C11
Brackenfield Derbys 84 E9
Brackenhirst N Lans 126 C4
Brackenthwaite Cumb 110 E11
Brackenthwaite N York 97 L10
Brackla Brdgnd 29 P9
Bracklesham W Susx 15 M7
Brackletter Highld 146 F11
Brackley Nhants 48 G7
Brackley Hatch Nhants 48 H6
Bracknell Br For 35 N11
Braco P & K 133 N6
Bracobrae Moray 158 D7
Bracon Ash Norfk 64 H2
Bracora Highld 145 M9
Bracorina Highld 145 M9
Bradaford Devon 5 P3
Bradbourne Derbys 71 N4
Bradbury Dur 104 B5
Bradden Nhants 48 H5
Braddock Cnwll 5 K9
Bradeley C Stke 70 F4
Bradenham Bucks 35 M5
Bradenstoke Wilts 33 K9
Bradfield Devon 9 Q3
Bradfield Essex 53 K5
Bradfield Norfk 77 K5
Bradfield Sheff 84 C2
Bradfield W Berk 34 H10
Bradfield Combust Suffk 64 B10
Bradfield Green Ches E 70 B3
Bradfield Heath Essex 53 K5
Bradfield St Clare Suffk 64 C10
Bradfield St George Suffk 64 C10
Bradford C Brad 90 F4
Bradford Cnwll 5 J6
Bradford Devon 16 G10
Bradford Nthumb 112 G5
Bradford Nthumb 119 N4
Bradford Abbas Dorset 11 M2
Bradford Leigh Wilts 20 F2
Bradford-on-Avon Wilts 20 F2
Bradford-on-Tone Somset 18 G10
Bradford Peverell Dorset 11 P6
Bradiford Devon 17 K5
Brading IoW 14 H9
Bradley Ches W 69 P5
Bradley Derbys 71 N5
Bradley Hants 22 H6
Bradley Kirk 90 F6
Bradley N York 96 F4
Bradley NE Lin 93 M9
Bradley Staffs 70 F11
Bradley Wolves 58 E5
Bradley Worcs 47 J2
Bradley Wrexhm 69 K4
Bradley Green Somset 19 J7
Bradley Green Warwks 59 L4
Bradley Green Worcs 47 J2
Bradley in the Moors Staffs 71 K6
Bradley Stoke S Glos 32 B8
Bradmore Notts 72 F4
Bradney Somset 19 K7
Bradninch Devon 9 N4
Bradninch Devon 17 L5
Bradnop Staffs 71 J3
Bradnor Green Herefs 45 K3
Bradpole Dorset 11 K6
Bradshaw Bolton 89 L8
Bradshaw Calder 90 D5
Bradshaw Kirk 90 D8
Bradstone Devon 5 P5
Bradwall Green Ches E 70 D2
Bradwell Derbys 83 Q8
Bradwell Devon 17 J3
Bradwell Essex 52 D7
Bradwell M Keyn 49 M6
Bradwell Norfk 77 Q11
Bradwell-on-Sea Essex 52 H10
Bradwell Waterside Essex 52 G10
Bradworthy Devon 16 E9
Brae Highld 156 B5
Brae Shet 169 q7
Braeface Falk 133 M11
Braehead Angus 143 M7
Braehead D & G 107 M7
Braehead S Lans 126 H7
Braeintra Highld 153 R11
Braemar Abers 149 M9
Braemore Highld 161 K11
Braemore Highld 167 J11
Brae Roy Lodge Highld 147 J9
Braeside Inver 124 G3
Braes of Coul Angus 142 D6
Braes of Enzie Moray 158 A6
Braes of Ullapool Highld 161 J8
Braeswick Ork 169 f3
Braevallich Ag & B 131 K6
Braewick Shet 169 p6
Brafferton Darltn 103 Q6
Brafferton N York 97 P6
Brafield-on-the-Green Nhants 60 H9
Bragar W Isls 168 h3
Bragbury End Herts 50 G6
Braidwood S Lans 126 E8
Brailsford Derbys 71 P6
Brailsford Green Derbys 71 P6
Brain's Green Gloucs 32 C3
Braintree Essex 52 C7
Braiseworth Suffk 64 G7
Braishfield Hants 22 C9
Braiswick Essex 52 G6
Braithwaite C Brad 90 C2
Braithwaite Cumb 100 H6
Braithwell Donc 84 H2
Braken Hill Wakefd 91 L7
Bramber W Susx 24 E8
Brambridge Hants 22 E10
Bramcote Notts 72 E3
Bramcote Warwks 59 P7
Bramdean Hants 22 H9
Bramerton Norfk 77 K11
Bramfield Herts 50 G7
Bramfield Suffk 65 M7
Bramford Suffk 53 K2
Bramhall Stockp 83 J8
Bramham Leeds 91 L2
Bramhope Leeds 90 H2
Bramley Hants 23 J3
Bramley Leeds 90 G3
Bramley Rothm 84 G2
Bramley Surrey 24 B2
Bramley Corner Hants 22 H3
Bramley Green Hants 23 J3
Bramley Head N York 96 H9
Bramling Kent 39 M10
Brampford Speke Devon 9 M5
Brampton Cambs 62 B6
Brampton Cumb 102 C6
Brampton Cumb 111 K8
Brampton Lincs 85 P5
Brampton Norfk 77 J7
Brampton Rothm 91 L10
Brampton Suffk 65 N5
Brampton Abbotts Herefs 46 B9
Brampton Ash Nhants 60 G3
Brampton Bryan Herefs 56 F10
Brampton-en-le-Morthen Rothm 84 G3
Bramshall Staffs 71 K8
Bramshaw Hants 21 Q11
Bramshill Hants 23 K2
Bramshott Hants 23 M8
Bramwell Somset 19 M9
Branault Highld 137 N2
Brancaster Norfk 75 Q2
Brancaster Staithe Norfk 75 Q2
Brancepeth Dur 103 P3
Branchill Moray 157 K7
Brand End Lincs 87 L11
Branderburgh Moray 157 N3
Brandesburton E R Yk 99 N11
Brandeston Suffk 65 J9
Brand Green Gloucs 46 D9
Brandis Corner Devon 16 G11
Brandiston Norfk 76 G7
Brandon Dur 103 P2
Brandon Lincs 86 B11
Brandon Nthumb 119 K7
Brandon Suffk 63 N3
Brandon Warwks 59 P9
Brandon Bank Norfk 63 K3
Brandon Creek Norfk 63 K2
Brandon Parva Norfk 76 F10
Brandsby N York 98 B6
Brandy Wharf Lincs 92 H11
Brane Cnwll 2 C8
Bran End Essex 51 Q5
Branksome BCP 12 H6
Branksome Park BCP 13 J6
Bransbury Hants 22 D6
Bransby Lincs 85 Q5
Branscombe Devon 10 D7
Bransford Worcs 46 E4
Bransgore Hants 13 L5
Bransholme C KuH 93 K4
Bransley Shrops 57 M9
Branson's Cross Worcs 58 G10
Branston Leics 73 L5
Branston Lincs 86 D7
Branston Staffs 71 N10
Branston Booths Lincs 86 E7
Branstone IoW 14 G10
Brant Broughton Lincs 86 B10
Brantham Suffk 53 K5
Branthwaite Cumb 100 E6
Branthwaite Cumb 101 J3
Brantingham E R Yk 92 F5
Branton Donc 91 Q10
Branton Nthumb 119 K7
Branton Green N York 97 P8
Branxton Nthumb 118 G3
Brassey Green Ches W 69 P2
Brasside Dur 113 L11
Brassington Derbys 71 N4
Brasted Kent 37 L9
Brasted Chart Kent 37 L10
Brathens Abers 150 H8
Bratoft Lincs 87 N8
Brattleby Lincs 86 B4
Bratton Somset 18 B5
Bratton Wilts 20 H4
Bratton Wrekin 57 L2
Bratton Clovelly Devon 8 C6
Bratton Fleming Devon 17 L4
Bratton Seymour Somset 20 C9
Braughing Herts 51 J5
Braughing Friars Herts 51 K6
Braunston Nhants 60 B7
Braunston Rutlnd 73 L9
Braunstone Town Leics 72 F10
Braunton Devon 16 H4
Brawby N York 98 E5
Brawl Highld 166 D3
Braworth N York 104 F9
Bray W & M 35 P9
Braybrooke Nhants 60 G4
Braydon Wilts 33 L7
Braydon Brook Wilts 33 J6
Braydon Side Wilts 33 K7
Brayford Devon 17 M5
Bray's Hill E Susx 25 Q8
Bray Shop Cnwll 5 N7
Braystones Cumb 100 D9
Braythorn N York 97 K11
Brayton N York 91 Q4
Braywick W & M 35 N9
Braywoodside W & M 35 N9
Brazacott Cnwll 5 M3
Breach Kent 27 L2
Breach Kent 38 D8
Breachwood Green Herts 50 E6
Breacleit W Isls 168 g4
Breaclete W Isls 168 g4
Breaden Heath Shrops 69 M7
Breadsall Derbys 72 B3
Breadstone Gloucs 32 D4
Breage Cnwll 2 G8
Breakachy Highld 155 N9
Breakish Highld 145 L3
Brealangwell Lodge Highld 162 C8
Bream Gloucs 32 B3
Breamore Hants 21 N11
Brean Somset 19 J3
Breanais W Isls 168 e5
Brearley Calder 90 C5
Brearton N York 97 M8
Breascleit W Isls 168 h4
Breasclete W Isls 168 h4
Breaston Derbys 72 D4
Brechfa Carmth 43 K8
Brechin Angus 143 L5
Breckles Norfk 64 D3
Brecon Powys 44 E9
Brecon Beacons National Park 44 E10
Bredbury Stockp 83 K6
Brede E Susx 26 D8
Bredenbury Herefs 46 B3
Bredfield Suffk 65 K11
Bredgar Kent 38 E9
Bredhurst Kent 38 C9
Bredon Worcs 46 H7
Bredon's Hardwick Worcs 46 H7
Bredon's Norton Worcs 46 H7
Bredward Herefs 45 K4
Bredwardine Herefs 45 L6
Breedon on the Hill Leics 72 C6
Breich W Loth 126 H5
Breightmet Bolton 89 L9
Breighton E R Yk 92 B4
Breinton Herefs 45 P7
Bremhill Wilts 33 J10
Bremridge Devon 17 M6
Brenchley Kent 25 Q2
Brendon Devon 16 F10
Brendon Devon 17 P2
Brendon Hill Somset 18 D8
Brenfield Ag & B 123 P3
Brenish W Isls 168 e5
Brenkley N u Ty 113 K5
Brent Cross Gt Lon 36 F3
Brent Eleigh Suffk 52 F2
Brentford Gt Lon 36 E5
Brentingby Leics 73 K7
Brent Knoll Somset 19 K4
Brent Mill Devon 6 H7
Brent Pelham Herts 51 K4
Brentwood Essex 37 N2
Brenzett Kent 26 H6
Brenzett Green Kent 26 H6
Brereton Staffs 71 K11
Brereton Green Ches E 70 D2
Brereton Heath Ches E 82 H11
Brereton Hill Staffs 71 K11
Bressay Shet 169 s9
Bressingham Norfk 64 F5
Bressingham Common Norfk 64 F5
Bretby Derbys 71 P10
Bretford Warwks 59 P9
Bretforton Worcs 47 L6
Bretherton Lancs 88 F6
Brettabister Shet 169 r8
Brettenham Norfk 64 C5
Brettenham Suffk 64 D11
Bretton C Pete 74 C10
Bretton Derbys 84 B5
Bretton Flints 69 L2
Brewers End Essex 51 N6
Brewer Street Surrey 36 H10
Brewood Staffs 58 C3
Briantspuddle Dorset 12 D6
Brick End Essex 51 N5
Brickendon Herts 50 H9
Bricket Wood Herts 50 D10
Brick Houses Sheff 84 D4
Brickkiln Green Essex 52 B5
Bricklehampton Worcs 47 J6
Bride IoM 80 f1
Bridekirk Cumb 100 F4
Bridell Pembks 41 N2
Bridestowe Devon 8 D7
Brideswell Abers 158 E10
Bridford Devon 9 K7
Bridge Kent 39 L11
Bridge End Cumb 94 D4
Bridge End Cumb 110 G11
Bridge End Devon 6 H9
Bridge End Dur 103 K3
Bridge End Essex 51 Q4
Bridge End Lincs 74 B3
Bridgefoot Angus 142 F10
Bridgefoot Cumb 100 E5
Bridge Green Essex 51 L3
Bridgehampton Somset 19 Q10
Bridge Hewick N York 97 M6
Bridgehill Dur 112 G10
Bridgehouse Gate N York 97 J7
Bridgemary Hants 14 G6
Bridgemere Ches E 70 C5
Bridgend Abers 158 D10
Bridgend Ag & B 120 E4
Bridgend Ag & B 122 D7
Bridgend Angus 143 J4
Bridgend Brdgnd 29 P9
Bridgend Cerdgn 42 C5
Bridgend Cumb 101 M8
Bridgend D & G 116 F9
Bridgend Devon 6 F9
Bridgend Fife 135 K5
Bridgend Moray 158 A11
Bridgend P & K 134 E3
Bridgend W Loth 127 J2
Bridgend of Lintrathen Angus 142 D7
Bridge of Alford Abers 150 F4
Bridge of Allan Stirlg 133 M8
Bridge of Avon Moray 149 M4
Bridge of Avon Moray 157 M10
Bridge of Balgie P & K 140 E8
Bridge of Brewlands Angus 142 B5
Bridge of Brown Highld 149 L3
Bridge of Cally P & K 142 A7
Bridge of Canny Abers 150 H8
Bridge of Craigisla Angus 142 D7
Bridge of Dee D & G 108 F9
Bridge of Don C Aber 151 N6
Bridge of Dun Angus 143 M6
Bridge of Dye Abers 150 H10
Bridge of Earn P & K 134 E4
Bridge of Ericht P & K 140 D6
Bridge of Feugh Abers 151 J8
Bridge of Gairn Abers 150 B8
Bridge of Gaur P & K 140 D6
Bridge of Marnoch Abers 158 E7
Bridge of Muchalls Abers 151 M9
Bridge of Orchy Ag & B 139 P10
Bridge of Tilt P & K 141 L4
Bridge of Tynet Moray 158 A5
Bridge of Walls Shet 169 p8
Bridge of Weir Rens 125 K4
Bridge Reeve Devon 17 M9
Bridgerule Devon 16 D11
Bridges Shrops 56 F5
Bridge Sollers Herefs 45 N6
Bridge Street Suffk 52 E2
Bridgetown Cnwll 5 N4
Bridgetown Somset 18 B8
Bridge Trafford Ches W 81 P10
Bridge Yate S Glos 32 C10
Bridgham Norfk 64 D4
Bridgnorth Shrops 57 N6
Bridgwater Somset 19 J7
Bridgwater Services Somset 19 K8
Bridlington E R Yk 99 P7
Bridport Dorset 11 K6
Bridstow Herefs 46 A10
Brierfield Lancs 89 N3
Brierley Barns 91 L8
Brierley Gloucs 46 B11
Brierley Herefs 45 P3
Brierley Hill Dudley 58 D7
Brierlow Bar Derbys 83 N11
Brierton Hartpl 104 E4
Briery Cumb 101 J6
Brigg N Linc 92 H9
Briggate Norfk 77 L6
Briggswath N York 105 N9
Brigham Cumb 100 E4
Brigham Cumb 101 J6
Brigham E R Yk 99 M10
Brighouse Calder 90 E6
Brighstone IoW 14 D10
Brightgate Derbys 84 C9
Brighthampton Oxon 34 C4
Brightholmlee Sheff 90 H11
Brightley Devon 8 F5
Brightling E Susx 25 Q6
Brightlingsea Essex 53 J8
Brighton Br & H 24 H10
Brighton Cnwll 3 N3
Brighton City Airport W Susx 24 E9
Brighton le Sands Sefton 81 L5
Brightons Falk 126 G2
Brightwalton W Berk 34 D9
Brightwalton Green W Berk 34 D9
Brightwalton Holt W Berk 34 D9
Brightwell Suffk 53 N3
Brightwell Baldwin Oxon 35 J5
Brightwell-cum-Sotwell Oxon 34 G6
Brightwell Upperton Oxon 35 J6
Brignall Dur 103 L8
Brig o'Turk Stirlg 132 G6
Brigsley NE Lin 93 N10
Brigsteer Cumb 95 K3
Brigstock Nhants 61 K3
Brill Bucks 35 J2
Brill Cnwll 3 J8
Brilley Herefs 45 K5
Brimfield Herefs 57 J11
Brimfield Cross Herefs 57 J11
Brimington Derbys 84 F6
Brimley Devon 9 K9
Brimpsfield Gloucs 32 H2
Brimpton W Berk 22 G2
Brimpton Common W Berk 22 G2
Brimscombe Gloucs 32 G4
Brimstage Wirral 81 L8
Brincliffe Sheff 84 D4
Brind E R Yk 92 B4
Brindham Somset 19 P7
Brindister Shet 169 p8
Brindle Lancs 88 H6
Brindley Ches E 69 Q4
Brineton Staffs 57 Q2
Bringhurst Leics 60 H2
Bringsty Common Herefs 46 D3
Brington Cambs 61 N5
Brinian Ork 169 d4
Briningham Norfk 76 E5
Brinkely Notts 85 M10
Brinkhill Lincs 87 L6
Brinkley Cambs 63 K10
Brinklow Warwks 59 P9
Brinkworth Wilts 33 K8
Brinscall Lancs 89 J6
Brinscombe Somset 19 M4
Brinsea N Som 19 M2
Brinsley Notts 84 G11
Brinsop Herefs 45 N6
Brinsworth Rothm 84 F3
Brinton Norfk 76 E4
Brisco Cumb 110 H10
Brisley Norfk 76 C7
Brislington Bristl 32 B10
Brissenden Green Kent 26 F4
Bristol Bristl 31 Q10
Bristol Airport N Som 31 P11
Bristol Zoo Gardens Bristl 31 Q10
Briston Norfk 76 F5
Brisworthy Devon 6 F5
Britannia Lancs 89 P6
Britford Wilts 21 N9
Brithdir Caerph 30 F4
Brithdir Gwynd 67 P11
British Legion Village Kent 38 B10
Briton Ferry Neath 29 K6
Britwell Salome Oxon 35 J6
Brixham Torbay 7 N7
Brixton Devon 6 F8
Brixton Gt Lon 36 H5
Brixton Deverill Wilts 20 G7
Brixworth Nhants 60 F6
Brize Norton Oxon 33 Q3
Brize Norton Airport Oxon 33 Q3
Broad Alley Worcs 58 C11
Broad Blunsdon Swindn 33 M6
Broadbottom Tamesd 83 L6
Broadbridge W Susx 15 M5
Broadbridge Heath W Susx 24 D4
Broad Campden Gloucs 47 N7
Broad Carr Calder 90 D7
Broad Chalke Wilts 21 K9
Broad Clough Lancs 89 P6
Broadclyst Devon 9 N5
Broadfield Inver 125 J3
Broadfield Pembks 41 M10
Broadford Highld 145 K3
Broad Ford Kent 26 B4
Broadford Bridge W Susx 24 C6
Broadgairhill Border 117 J8
Broadgrass Green Suffk 64 D9
Broad Green Cambs 63 L8
Broad Green Essex 52 E7
Broad Green Worcs 46 E3
Broad Green Worcs 58 E10
Broadhaugh Border 129 M9
Broad Haven Pembks 40 G8
Broadheath Traffd 82 G7
Broadhembury Devon 10 C4
Broadhempston Devon 7 L5
Broad Hill Cambs 63 J5
Broad Hinton Wilts 33 M9
Broadholme Lincs 85 Q6
Broadland Row E Susx 26 D8
Broadlay Carmth 28 C3
Broad Layings Hants 22 D2
Broadley Essex 51 K9
Broadley Lancs 89 P7
Broadley Moray 158 A5
Broadley Common Essex 51 K9
Broad Marston Worcs 47 M5
Broadmayne Dorset 12 B7
Broad Meadow Staffs 70 E5
Broadmere Hants 22 H5
Broadmoor Gloucs 46 B11
Broadmoor Pembks 41 L9
Broadnymett Devon 8 H4
Broad Oak Carmth 43 L10
Broad Oak Cumb 94 C2
Broadoak Dorset 11 J5
Broad Oak E Susx 25 P6
Broad Oak E Susx 26 D8
Broadoak Gloucs 32 C2
Broad Oak Hants 23 L4
Broad Oak Herefs 45 P10
Broad Oak Kent 39 L9
Broad Oak St Hel 82 B5
Broadoak Wrexhm 69 L3
Broad Road Suffk 65 K6
Broadsands Torbay 7 M7
Broad's Green Essex 51 Q8
Broadstairs Kent 39 Q8
Broadstone BCP 12 H5
Broadstone Mons 31 P4
Broadstone Shrops 57 J7
Broad Street E Susx 26 E8
Broad Street Essex 51 N7
Broad Street Kent 27 K3
Broad Street Kent 38 D10
Broad Street Medway 38 C7
Broad Street Wilts 21 M3
Broad Street Green Essex 52 E10
Broad Town Wilts 33 L9
Broadwas Worcs 46 E3
Broadwater Herts 50 F6
Broadwater W Susx 24 D10
Broadwaters Worcs 58 B9
Broadway Carmth 28 C3
Broadway Carmth 41 Q8
Broadway Pembks 40 G8
Broadway Somset 19 K11
Broadway Suffk 65 M6
Broadway Worcs 47 L7
Broadwell Gloucs 31 Q2
Broadwell Gloucs 47 P9
Broadwell Oxon 33 Q4
Broadwell Warwks 59 Q11
Broadwey Dorset 11 P8
Broadwindsor Dorset 11 J4
Broadwood Kelly Devon 8 F3
Broadwoodwidger Devon 5 Q4
Brobury Herefs 45 L6
Brochel Highld 153 K8
Brochroy Ag & B 139 J11
Brock Lancs 88 G2
Brockamin Worcs 46 E4
Brockbridge Hants 22 H11
Brockdish Norfk 65 J6
Brockencote Worcs 58 C10
Brockenhurst Hants 13 P4
Brocketsbrae S Lans 126 E10
Brockford Green Suffk 64 G8
Brockford Street Suffk 64 G8
Brockhall Nhants 60 D8
Brockhall Village Lancs 89 L3
Brockham Surrey 36 E11
Brockhampton Gloucs 46 H9
Brockhampton Gloucs 47 K10
Brockhampton Hants 15 K5
Brockhampton Herefs 46 A8
Brockhampton Green Dorset 11 Q3
Brockholes Kirk 90 F8
Brockhurst Derbys 84 D8
Brockhurst Warwks 59 Q8
Brocklebank Cumb 101 K2
Brocklesby Lincs 93 K8
Brockley N Som 31 N11
Brockley Suffk 64 A7
Brockley Green Suffk 63 M11
Brockley Green Suffk 64 A11
Brockleymoor Cumb 101 N3
Brockmoor Dudley 58 D7
Brockscombe Devon 8 C5
Brock's Green Hants 22 F2
Brockton Shrops 56 E4
Brockton Shrops 56 E7
Brockton Shrops 57 K6
Brockton Shrops 57 N4
Brockton Staffs 70 E8
Brockweir Gloucs 31 P4
Brockwood Park Hants 22 H9
Brockworth Gloucs 46 G11
Brocton Cnwll 4 G8
Brocton Staffs 70 H11

Brodick N Ayrs 121 K4
Brodie Moray 156 H6
Brodsworth Donc 91 N9
Brogaig Highld 152 H4
Brogborough C Beds 49 Q7
Brokenborough Wilts 32 H7
Broken Cross Ches E 83 J10
Broken Cross Ches W 82 E10
Brokerswood Wilts 20 F4
Bromborough Wirral 81 M8
Brome Suffk 64 G6
Brome Street Suffk 64 H6
Bromeswell Suffk 65 L11
Bromfield Cumb 110 C8
Bromfield Shrops 56 H9
Bromham Bed 61 M10
Bromham Wilts 33 J11
Bromley Barns 91 J11
Bromley Dudley 58 D7
Bromley Gt Lon 37 K7
Bromley Shrops 57 N5
Bromley Common Gt Lon 37 K7
Bromley Cross Bolton 89 L8
Bromley Cross Essex 53 J6
Bromley Green Kent 26 G4
Bromlow Shrops 56 E4
Brompton Medway 38 C8
Brompton N York 104 C11
Brompton-by-Sawdon N York 99 J4
Brompton-on-Swale N York 103 P11
Brompton Ralph Somset 18 E8
Brompton Regis Somset 18 C8
Bromsash Herefs 46 C10
Bromsberrow Gloucs 46 D8
Bromsberrow Heath Gloucs 46 D8
Bromsgrove Worcs 58 E10
Bromstead Heath Staffs 70 D11
Bromyard Herefs 46 C4
Bromyard Downs Herefs 46 C3
Bronaber Gwynd 67 N8
Bronant Cerdgn 54 E11
Broncroft Shrops 57 J7
Brongest Cerdgn 42 F5
Bronington Wrexhm 69 N7
Bronllys Powys 44 G8
Bronwydd Carmth 42 H10
Bronydd Powys 45 J5
Bronygarth Shrops 69 J7
Brook Carmth 41 Q9
Brook Hants 13 N2
Brook Hants 22 B9
Brook IoW 14 C10
Brook Kent 27 J3
Brook Surrey 23 P7
Brook Surrey 36 C11
Brooke Norfk 65 K2
Brooke Rutlnd 73 L9
Brookenby Lincs 93 M11
Brook End Bed 61 N8
Brook End C Beds 61 Q11
Brook End Cambs 61 N6
Brook End M Keyn 49 P6
Brookfield Rens 125 L5
Brookhampton Oxon 34 H5
Brookhampton Somset 20 B9
Brook Hill Hants 13 N2
Brookhouse Lancs 95 L8
Brookhouse Nthumb 84 H3
Brookhouse Green Ches E 70 E2
Brookhouses Derbys 83 M7
Brookland Kent 26 G6
Brooklands Traffd 82 G6
Brookmans Park Herts 50 F10
Brooks Powys 55 Q5
Brooksby Leics 72 H7
Brooks End Kent 39 N8
Brooks Green W Susx 24 C6
Brook Street Essex 37 N2
Brook Street Kent 26 F5
Brook Street Suffk 52 D2
Brook Street W Susx 24 H5
Brookthorpe Gloucs 32 F2
Brookville Norfk 75 P11
Brookwood Surrey 23 Q3
Broom C Beds 50 E2
Broom Rothm 84 F2
Broom Warwks 47 L4
Broombank Worcs 57 M10
Broome Devon 17 M3
Broome Shrops 56 G8
Broome Worcs 58 D9
Broomedge Warrtn 82 F7
Broome Park Nthumb 119 M8
Broomer's Corner W Susx 24 D6
Broomershill W Susx 24 C7
Broomfield Essex 52 B9
Broomfield Kent 38 D11
Broomfield Kent 39 L8
Broomfield Somset 18 H8
Broomfields Shrops 69 M11
Broomfleet E R Yk 92 E5
Broom Green Norfk 76 D7
Broomhall W & M 35 Q11
Broomhaugh Nthumb 112 F8
Broom Hill Barns 91 L10
Broom Hill Dorset 12 H4
Broom Hill Notts 84 H11
Broomhill Nthumb 119 P10
Broom Hill Worcs 58 D9
Broomhill Green Ches E 70 A5
Broomley Nthumb 112 F8
Broompark Dur 103 P2
Broom's Green Worcs 46 D8
Broomsthorpe Norfk 76 A6
Broom Street Kent 38 H9
Brora Highld 163 L6
Broseley Shrops 57 M4
Brotherhouse Bar Lincs 74 L8
Brotherlee Dur 102 H3
Brothertoft Lincs 87 J11
Brotherton N York 91 M5
Brotton R & Cl 105 J7
Broubster Highld 166 H5
Brough Cumb 102 M8
Brough Derbys 83 Q8
Brough E R Yk 92 F5
Brough Highld 167 M2
Brough Notts 85 P9
Brough Shet 169 s6
Broughall Shrops 69 Q6
Brough Lodge Shet 169 s4
Brough Sowerby Cumb 102 M8
Broughton Border 116 G3
Broughton Bucks 35 M2

Broughton Cambs 62 C5
Broughton Flints 69 K2
Broughton Hants 22 B8
Broughton Lancs 88 G4
Broughton M Keyn 49 N7
Broughton N Linc 92 G9
Broughton N York 96 D10
Broughton N York 96 F6
Broughton Nhants 60 H5
Broughton Oxon 48 D7
Broughton Salfd 82 H4
Broughton Staffs 70 D8
Broughton V Glam 29 P10
Broughton Astley Leics 60 B2
Broughton Beck Cumb 94 F4
Broughton Gifford Wilts 20 G2
Broughton Green Worcs 47 J2
Broughton Hackett Worcs 46 H4
Broughton-in-Furness Cumb 94 E3
Broughton Mains D & G 107 N8
Broughton Mills Cumb 94 E2
Broughton Moor Cumb 100 E4
Broughton Poggs Oxon 33 P4
Broughton Tower Cumb 94 E3
Broughty Ferry C Dund 142 H11
Brough with St Giles N York 103 P11
Brow End Cumb 94 F6
Brownber Cumb 102 D9
Brown Candover Hants 22 G7
Brown Edge Lancs 88 D8
Brown Edge Staffs 70 G4
Brown Heath Ches W 69 N2
Brownheath Shrops 69 N9
Brownhill Abers 159 L4
Brownhills Fife 135 N4
Brownhills Wsall 58 F3
Brownieside Nthumb 119 N6
Browninghill Green Hants 22 G3
Brown Lees Staffs 70 F3
Brownlow Heath Ches E 70 E2
Brownrigg Cumb 100 D6
Brownrigg Cumb 110 C10
Brownsea Island Dorset 12 H4
Brown's Green Birm 58 G6
Brownsham Devon 16 D6
Browns Hill Gloucs 32 G4
Brownsover Warwks 60 B5
Brownston Devon 6 H8
Brown Street Suffk 64 F9
Browston Green Norfk 77 P11
Broxa N York 99 J2
Broxbourne Herts 51 J9
Broxburn E Loth 128 H4
Broxburn W Loth 127 K3
Broxfield Nthumb 119 P7
Broxted Essex 51 N5
Broxton Ches W 69 N4
Broyle Side E Susx 25 L8
Bruan Highld 167 P9
Bruar P & K 141 K4
Bruchag Ag & B 124 E6
Bruera Ches W 69 M2
Bruern Abbey Oxon 47 Q10
Bruichladdich Ag & B 122 C7
Bruisyard Suffk 65 L8
Bruisyard Street Suffk 65 L8
Brumby N Linc 92 E9
Brund Staffs 71 L2
Brundall Norfk 77 L10
Brundish Suffk 65 K8
Brundish Street Suffk 65 K7
Brunery Highld 138 C3
Brunnion Cnwll 2 E6
Brunslow Shrops 56 F8
Brunswick Village N u Ty 113 K6
Bruntcliffe Leeds 90 H5
Brunthwaite C Brad 96 G11
Bruntingthorpe Leics 60 D3
Brunton Fife 135 J3
Brunton Nthumb 119 P6
Brunton Wilts 21 P3
Brushford Devon 17 M10
Brushford Somset 18 B9
Bruton Somset 20 C7
Bryan's Green Worcs 58 C11
Bryanston Dorset 12 E3
Bryant's Bottom Bucks 35 N5
Brydekirk D & G 110 C6
Bryher IoS 2 b2
Brymbo Wrexhm 69 J4
Brympton Somset 19 P11
Bryn Carmth 28 F4
Bryn Ches W 82 D10
Bryn Neath 29 M6
Bryn Shrops 56 D7
Bryn Wigan 82 C4
Brynamman Carmth 29 K2
Brynberian Pembks 41 M3
Brynbryddan Neath 29 L6
Bryn Bwbach Gwynd 67 L7
Bryncae Rhondd 30 C8
Bryncethin Brdgnd 29 P8
Bryncir Gwynd 66 H6
Bryn-côch Neath 29 K5
Bryncroes Gwynd 66 C8
Bryncrug Gwynd 54 E4
Bryn Du IoA 78 E10
Bryn-Eden Gwynd 67 N9
Bryneglwys Denbgs 68 F5
Brynfields Wrexhm 69 K6
Brynford Flints 80 H10
Bryn Gates Wigan 82 C4
Bryn Golau Rhondd 30 D7
Bryngwran IoA 78 F9
Bryngwyn Mons 31 L3
Bryngwyn Powys 44 H5
Bryn-Henllan Pembks 41 K3
Brynhoffnant Cerdgn 42 F5
Bryning Lancs 88 E4
Brynithel Blae G 30 H4
Brynmawr Blae G 30 G3
Bryn-mawr Gwynd 66 C8
Brynmenyn Brdgnd 29 P8
Brynmill Swans 28 H6
Brynna Rhondd 30 C8
Brynnau Gwynion Rhondd 30 C8
Bryn-penarth Powys 55 Q4
Brynrefail Gwynd 67 K2
Brynrefail IoA 78 H7
Brynsadler Rhondd 30 D8
Bryn Saith Marchog Denbgs 68 E4
Brynsiencyn IoA 78 H11
Brynteg IoA 78 H8
Bryn-y-bal Flints 69 J2
Bryn-y-Maen Conwy 79 Q9

Bryn-yr-Eos Wrexhm 69 J6
Bualintur Highld 144 F3
Buarth-draw Flints 80 H9
Bubbenhall Warwks 59 N10
Bubwith E R Yk 92 B3
Buccleuch Border 117 L8
Buchanan Smithy Stirlg 132 F10
Buchanhaven Abers 159 R8
Buchanty P & K 133 Q2
Buchany Stirlg 133 L7
Buchlyvie Stirlg 132 H9
Buckabank Cumb 110 G11
Buckden Cambs 61 Q7
Buckden N York 96 D5
Buckenham Norfk 77 M10
Buckerell Devon 10 C4
Buckfast Devon 7 J5
Buckfastleigh Devon 7 J5
Buckhaven Fife 135 K8
Buckholt Mons 45 Q11
Buckhorn Devon 5 P2
Buckhorn Weston Dorset 20 E10
Buckhurst Hill Essex 37 K2
Buckie Moray 158 B4
Buckingham Bucks 49 J8
Buckland Bucks 35 N2
Buckland Devon 6 H10
Buckland Gloucs 47 L7
Buckland Hants 13 P5
Buckland Herts 51 J4
Buckland Kent 27 P3
Buckland Oxon 34 B5
Buckland Surrey 36 F10
Buckland Brewer Devon 16 G7
Buckland Common Bucks 35 P3
Buckland Dinham Somset 20 E4
Buckland Filleigh Devon 16 H10
Buckland in the Moor Devon 7 J4
Buckland Monachorum Devon 6 D5
Buckland Newton Dorset 11 P3
Buckland Ripers Dorset 11 P8
Buckland St Mary Somset 10 F2
Buckland-Tout-Saints Devon 7 K9
Bucklebury W Berk 34 G10
Bucklers Hard Hants 14 D6
Bucklesham Suffk 53 M3
Buckley Flints 69 J2
Buckley Green Warwks 59 J11
Bucklow Hill Ches E 82 F8
Buckminster Leics 73 M6
Bucknall C Stke 70 G5
Bucknall Lincs 86 G7
Bucknell Oxon 48 G9
Bucknell Shrops 56 F10
Buckpool Moray 158 B4
Bucksburn C Aber 151 M6
Buck's Cross Devon 16 F7
Bucks Green W Susx 24 C4
Buckshaw Village Lancs 88 H6
Bucks Hill Herts 50 C10
Bucks Horn Oak Hants 23 M6
Buck's Mills Devon 16 F7
Buckton E R Yk 99 P6
Buckton Herefs 56 F10
Buckton Nthumb 119 L3
Buckworth Cambs 61 P5
Budby Notts 85 K7
Buddileigh Staffs 70 C5
Bude Cnwll 16 C10
Budge's Shop Cnwll 5 N10
Budlake Devon 9 N4
Budle Nthumb 119 N3
Budleigh Salterton Devon 9 Q8
Budlett's Common E Susx 25 L6
Budock Water Cnwll 3 K7
Buerton Ches E 70 B6
Bugbrooke Nhants 60 E9
Bugford Devon 7 L8
Buglawton Ches E 70 F2
Bugle Cnwll 4 G10
Bugley Dorset 20 E10
Bugthorpe E R Yk 98 F9
Buildwas Shrops 57 L4
Builth Road Powys 44 E4
Builth Wells Powys 44 E4
Bulbourne Herts 35 P2
Bulbridge Wilts 21 L8
Bulby Lincs 73 R5
Bulcote Notts 72 H2
Bulford Wilts 21 N6
Bulford Camp Wilts 21 N6
Bulkeley Ches E 69 P4
Bulkington Warwks 59 N7
Bulkington Wilts 20 H3
Bulkworthy Devon 16 F9
Bullamoor N York 97 N2
Bull Bay IoA 78 G6
Bullbridge Derbys 84 E10
Bullbrook Br For 35 N11
Bullen's Green Herts 50 F9
Bulley Gloucs 46 E11
Bullgill Cumb 100 E3
Bullingham Herefs 45 Q7
Bullinghope Herefs 45 Q7
Bullington Hants 22 E6
Bullington Lincs 86 E5
Bullockstone Kent 39 L8
Bull's Green Herts 50 G7
Bull's Green Norfk 65 N3
Bulmer Essex 52 D3
Bulmer N York 98 D7
Bulmer Tye Essex 52 D4
Bulphan Thurr 37 P3
Bulstone Devon 10 D7
Bulstrode Herts 50 B10
Bulverhythe E Susx 26 C10
Bulwark Abers 159 M8
Bulwell C Nott 72 E2
Bulwick Nhants 61 L2
Bumble's Green Essex 51 K9
Bunacaimb Highld 145 L10
Bunarkaig Highld 146 F10
Bunbury Ches E 69 Q3
Bunbury Heath Ches E 69 Q3
Bunchrew Highld 155 R8
Buncton W Susx 24 D8
Bundalloch Highld 145 Q2
Bunessan Ag & B 137 K11
Bungay Suffk 65 L4
Bunker's Hill Lincs 87 J10
Bunnahabhain Ag & B 122 F5
Bunny Notts 72 F5
Buntait Highld 155 M11

Buntingford Herts 51 J5
Bunwell Norfk 64 G3
Bunwell Hill Norfk 64 G3
Bupton Derbys 71 N7
Burbage Derbys 83 M10
Burbage Leics 59 P6
Burbage Wilts 21 P2
Burcher Herefs 45 L2
Burchett's Green W & M 35 M8
Burcombe Wilts 21 L8
Burcot Oxon 34 G5
Burcot Worcs 58 E10
Burcote Shrops 57 N5
Burcott Bucks 49 M11
Burcott Bucks 49 N10
Burdale N York 98 H8
Bures Essex 52 F5
Burford Oxon 33 Q2
Burford Shrops 57 K11
Burg Ag & B 137 K6
Burgate Suffk 64 F6
Burgates Hants 23 L9
Burge End Herts 50 D4
Burgess Hill W Susx 24 H7
Burgh Suffk 65 J11
Burgh by Sands Cumb 110 F9
Burgh Castle Norfk 77 P10
Burghclere Hants 22 E2
Burghead Moray 157 L4
Burghfield W Berk 35 J11
Burghfield Common W Berk 35 J11
Burgh Heath Surrey 36 F9
Burgh Hill E Susx 26 B6
Burghill Herefs 45 P6
Burgh Island Devon 6 G10
Burgh le Marsh Lincs 87 P7
Burgh next Aylsham Norfk 77 J6
Burgh on Bain Lincs 86 H3
Burgh St Margaret Norfk 77 N9
Burgh St Peter Norfk 65 P3
Burghwallis Donc 91 N8
Burham Kent 38 B9
Buriton Hants 23 K11
Burland Ches E 69 R4
Burlawn Cnwll 4 F7
Burleigh Gloucs 32 G4
Burlescombe Devon 18 E11
Burleston Dorset 12 C6
Burlestone Devon 7 L9
Burley Hants 13 M4
Burley Rutlnd 73 M8
Burley Shrops 56 H8
Burleydam Ches E 69 R6
Burley Gate Herefs 46 A5
Burley in Wharfedale C Brad 97 J11
Burley Lawn Hants 13 M4
Burley Street Hants 13 M4
Burley Wood Head C Brad 90 F2
Burlingham Green Norfk 77 M9
Burlingjobb Powys 45 K3
Burlington Shrops 57 P2
Burlton Shrops 69 N9
Burmarsh Kent 27 K5
Burmington Warwks 47 Q7
Burn N York 91 P5
Burnage Manch 83 J6
Burnaston Derbys 71 P8
Burnbanks Cumb 101 P7
Burnbrae N Lans 126 F3
Burn Bridge N York 97 L10
Burnby E R Yk 98 G11
Burn Cross Sheff 91 J11
Burndell W Susx 15 Q6
Burnden Bolton 89 L9
Burnedge Rochdl 89 Q8
Burneside Cumb 101 P11
Burneston N York 97 M4
Burnett BaNES 32 C11
Burnfoot Border 117 N8
Burnfoot Border 117 Q7
Burnfoot D & G 109 L2
Burnfoot D & G 110 F3
Burnfoot D & G 117 M11
Burnfoot P & K 134 B7
Burnham Bucks 35 P8
Burnham N Linc 93 J7
Burnham Deepdale Norfk 75 R2
Burnham Green Herts 50 G7
Burnham Market Norfk 76 A3
Burnham Norton Norfk 76 A3
Burnham-on-Crouch Essex 38 F2
Burnham-on-Sea Somset 19 K5
Burnham Overy Norfk 76 A3
Burnham Overy Staithe Norfk 76 A3
Burnham Thorpe Norfk 76 B3
Burnhead D & G 116 B11
Burnhervie Abers 151 J4
Burnhill Green Staffs 57 P4
Burnhope Dur 113 J11
Burnhouse N Ayrs 125 K7
Burniston N York 99 L2
Burnley Lancs 89 N4
Burnmouth Border 129 P7
Burn Naze Lancs 88 C2
Burn of Cambus Stirlg 133 L7
Burnopfield Dur 113 J9
Burnrigg Cumb 111 J9
Burnsall N York 96 F8
Burnside Angus 142 G6
Burnside Angus 143 J7
Burnside Fife 134 F4
Burnside Moray 157 M4
Burnside W Loth 127 K2
Burnside of Duntrune Angus 142 G11
Burntcommon Surrey 36 B10
Burntheath Derbys 71 N8
Burnt Heath Essex 53 J6
Burnt Hill W Berk 34 G10
Burnthouse Cnwll 3 K6
Burnt Houses Dur 103 M6
Burntisland Fife 134 G10
Burnt Oak E Susx 25 M5
Burnton E Ayrs 115 J4
Burntwood Flints 69 J2
Burntwood Staffs 58 G3
Burntwood Green Staffs 58 G3
Burnt Yates N York 97 L8
Burnworthy Somset 18 G11
Burpham Surrey 36 B10
Burpham W Susx 24 B9
Burradon Nthumb 119 L6
Burradon N Tyne 113 L6
Burrafirth Shet 169 t2
Burras Cnwll 2 H7

Burraton Cnwll 5 Q8
Burravoe Shet 169 s5
Burray Village Ork 169 d7
Burrells Cumb 102 C7
Burrelton P & K 142 C10
Burridge Devon 10 G3
Burridge Devon 17 K4
Burridge Hants 14 F4
Burrill N York 97 K3
Burringham N Linc 92 D9
Burrington Devon 17 L8
Burrington Herefs 56 G10
Burrington N Som 19 N3
Burrough End Cambs 63 K9
Burrough Green Cambs 63 K9
Burrough on the Hill Leics 73 K8
Burrow Lancs 95 N6
Burrow Somset 18 B6
Burrow Bridge Somset 19 L8
Burrowhill Surrey 23 Q2
Burrows Cross Surrey 36 C11
Burry Swans 28 E6
Burry Green Swans 28 E6
Burry Port Carmth 28 D4
Burscough Lancs 88 E8
Burscough Bridge Lancs 88 E8
Bursea E R Yk 92 D4
Burshill E R Yk 99 M11
Bursledon Hants 14 E5
Burslem C Stke 70 F5
Burstall Suffk 53 J3
Burstock Dorset 11 J4
Burston Norfk 64 G5
Burston Staffs 70 G8
Burstow Surrey 24 H2
Burstwick E R Yk 93 M5
Burtersett N York 96 C3
Burtholme Cumb 111 K8
Burthorpe Green Suffk 63 N8
Burthwaite Cumb 110 H11
Burthy Cnwll 4 E10
Burtle Somset 19 L6
Burtle Hill Somset 19 L6
Burtoft Lincs 74 E3
Burton BCP 13 L6
Burton Ches W 69 P2
Burton Ches W 81 L10
Burton Dorset 11 P6
Burton Nthumb 119 N4
Burton Pembks 41 J9
Burton Somset 11 L2
Burton Somset 18 G6
Burton Wilts 20 F8
Burton Wilts 32 F9
Burton Agnes E R Yk 99 N8
Burton Bradstock Dorset 11 K7
Burton-by-Lincoln Lincs 86 C6
Burton Coggles Lincs 73 P5
Burton Dassett Warwks 48 C4
Burton End Essex 51 M6
Burton End Suffk 63 L11
Burton Fleming E R Yk 99 M6
Burton Green Warwks 59 L9
Burton Green Wrexhm 69 K3
Burton Hastings Warwks 59 P7
Burton Hill Wilts 32 H7
Burton-in-Kendal Cumb 95 L5
Burton-in-Kendal Services Cumb 95 L5
Burton in Lonsdale N York 95 P6
Burton Joyce Notts 72 G2
Burton Latimer Nhants 61 K6
Burton Lazars Leics 73 K7
Burton Leonard N York 97 M8
Burton on the Wolds Leics 72 F6
Burton Overy Leics 72 H11
Burton Pedwardine Lincs 74 B2
Burton Pidsea E R Yk 93 M4
Burton Salmon N York 91 M5
Burton's Green Essex 52 D6
Burton upon Stather N Linc 92 E7
Burton upon Trent Staffs 71 N10
Burton Waters Lincs 86 B6
Burtonwood Warrtn 82 C6
Burtonwood Services Warrtn 82 C6
Burwardsley Ches W 69 P3
Burwarton Shrops 57 L7
Burwash E Susx 25 Q6
Burwash Common E Susx 25 P6
Burwash Weald E Susx 25 Q6
Burwell Cambs 63 J7
Burwell Lincs 87 L5
Burwen IoA 78 G6
Burwick Ork 169 d8
Bury Bury 89 N8
Bury Cambs 62 C4
Bury Somset 18 B9
Bury W Susx 24 B8
Bury End C Beds 50 D3
Bury Green Herts 51 L6
Bury St Edmunds Suffk 64 B9
Burythorpe N York 98 F8
Busby E Rens 125 P6
Busby Stoop N York 97 N4
Buscot Oxon 33 P5
Bush Abers 143 P4
Bush Cnwll 16 C10
Bush Bank Herefs 45 P4
Bushbury Wolves 58 D4
Bushby Leics 72 H10
Bushey Herts 50 D11
Bushey Heath Herts 36 D2
Bush Green Norfk 65 J4
Bush Green Suffk 64 C10
Bush Hill Park Gt Lon 50 H11
Bushley Worcs 46 G8
Bushley Green Worcs 46 G8
Bushmead Bed 61 P8
Bushmoor Shrops 56 G7
Bushton Wilts 33 L9
Busk Cumb 102 B2
Buslingthorpe Lincs 86 E3
Bussage Gloucs 32 G4
Bussex Somset 19 L7
Butcher's Cross E Susx 25 N5
Butcombe N Som 19 P2
Bute Ag & B 124 C4
Butleigh Somset 19 P8
Butleigh Wootton Somset 19 P7
Butler's Cross Bucks 35 M3
Butler's Hill Notts 84 H11
Butlers Marston Warwks 48 C4
Butley Suffk 65 M11
Butley High Corner Suffk 53 Q2
Buttercrambe N York 98 E9

Butterdean Border 129 K7
Butterknowle Dur 103 M5
Butterleigh Devon 9 N3
Butterley Derbys 84 F10
Buttermere Cumb 100 G7
Buttermere Wilts 22 B2
Butters Green Staffs 70 E4
Buttershaw C Brad 90 E5
Butterstone P & K 141 Q8
Butterton Staffs 70 E6
Butterton Staffs 71 K3
Butterwick Dur 104 C4
Butterwick Lincs 87 L11
Butterwick N York 98 E5
Butterwick N York 99 K6
Butt Green Ches E 70 B4
Buttington Powys 56 C3
Buttonbridge Shrops 57 N9
Buttonoak Shrops 57 P9
Buttsash Hants 14 D5
Buttsbear Cross Cnwll 16 D11
Butt's Green Essex 52 C11
Buxhall Suffk 64 E10
Buxhall Fen Street Suffk 64 E10
Buxted E Susx 25 L6
Buxton Derbys 83 N10
Buxton Norfk 77 J2
Buxton Heath Norfk 76 H7
Buxworth Derbys 83 M8
Bwlch Powys 44 H10
Bwlchgwyn Wrexhm 69 J4
Bwlchllan Cerdgn 43 L3
Bwlchnewydd Carmth 42 G10
Bwlchtocyn Gwynd 66 E9
Bwlch-y-cibau Powys 68 G11
Bwlch-y-Ddar Powys 68 G10
Bwlchyfadfa Cerdgn 42 H5
Bwlch-y-ffridd Powys 55 P5
Bwlch-y-groes Pembks 41 P3
Bwlchymynydd Swans 28 G5
Bwlch-y-sarnau Powys 55 N10
Byermoor Gatesd 113 J9
Byers Green Dur 103 P4
Byfield Nhants 48 F4
Byfleet Surrey 36 C8
Byford Herefs 45 M6
Bygrave Herts 50 G3
Byker N u Ty 113 L8
Byland Abbey N York 98 A5
Bylaugh Norfk 76 F6
Bylchau Conwy 68 C2
Byley Ches W 82 F11
Bynea Carmth 28 F5
Byram N York 91 M5
Byrness Nthumb 118 E10
Bystock Devon 9 P8
Bythorn Cambs 61 N5
Byton Herefs 45 M2
Bywell Nthumb 112 F8
Byworth W Susx 23 Q10

C

Cabbacott Devon 16 G7
Cabourne Lincs 93 K10
Cabrach Ag & B 122 G7
Cabrach Moray 150 B2
Cabus Lancs 95 K11
Cackle Street E Susx 25 L5
Cackle Street E Susx 25 Q7
Cackle Street E Susx 26 D8
Cadbury Devon 9 M3
Cadbury Barton Devon 17 M8
Cadbury World Birm 58 F8
Cadder E Duns 125 Q3
Caddington C Beds 50 C7
Caddonfoot Border 117 P3
Cadeby Donc 91 N10
Cadeby Leics 72 C10
Cadeleigh Devon 9 M3
Cade Street E Susx 25 P6
Cadgwith Cnwll 3 J11
Cadham Fife 134 H7
Cadishead Salfd 82 F6
Cadle Swans 28 H5
Cadley Lancs 88 G4
Cadley Wilts 21 P4
Cadley Wilts 33 P11
Cadmore End Bucks 35 L6
Cadnam Hants 13 P2
Cadney N Linc 92 H10
Cadole Flints 68 H2
Cadoxton V Glam 30 F11
Cadoxton Juxta-Neath
        Neath 29 L5
Cadwst Denbgs 68 D7
Caeathro Gwynd 67 J2
Caehopkin Powys 29 M2
Caenby Lincs 86 C3
Caerau Brdgnd 29 N6
Caerau Cardif 30 F9
Cae'r-bont Powys 29 M2
Cae'r bryn Carmth 28 G2
Caerdeon Gwynd 67 M11
Caer Farchell Pembks 40 E5
Caergeiliog IoA 78 E9
Caergwrle Flints 69 K3
Caerhun Conwy 79 P10
Caerlanrig Border 117 M10
Caerleon Newpt 31 K6
Caernarfon Gwynd 66 H2
Caernarfon Castle Gwynd 66 H2
Caerphilly Caerph 30 G7
Caersws Powys 55 N6
Caerwedros Cerdgn 42 G3
Caerwent Mons 31 N6
Caerwys Flints 80 G10
Caerynwch Gwynd 67 P11
Caggle Street Mons 45 M11
Caim IoA 79 L8
Cairinis W Isls 168 d11
Cairnbaan Ag & B 130 G9
Cairnbulg Abers 159 P4
Cairncross Border 129 M7
Cairncurran Inver 125 J3
Cairndow Ag & B 131 P5
Cairneyhill Fife 134 C10
Cairngarroch D & G 106 E8
Cairngorms National Park 149 K7
Cairnie Abers 158 C9
Cairnorrie Abers 159 L9
Cairnryan D & G 106 E4
Cairnty Moray 157 Q7

Caister-on-Sea Norfk 77 Q9
Caistor Lincs 93 K10
Caistor St Edmund Norfk 77 J11
Cakebole Worcs 58 C10
Cake Street Norfk 64 F3
Calais Street Suffk 52 G4
Calanais W Isls 168 h4
Calbourne IoW 14 D9
Calceby Lincs 87 L5
Calcoed Flints 80 H10
Calcot Gloucs 33 L2
Calcot V Berk 35 J10
Calcot Row W Berk 35 J10
Calcots Moray 157 P5
Calcott Kent 39 L9
Calcott Shrops 56 G2
Calcutt N York 97 M9
Calcutt Wilts 33 M6
Caldback Cumb 101 K2
Caldbergh N York 96 G3
Caldecote Cambs 61 P3
Caldecote Cambs 62 D9
Caldecote Herts 50 F3
Caldecote Nhants 49 J4
Caldecott Nhants 61 L7
Caldecott Oxon 34 E5
Caldecott Rutlnd 61 J2
Caldecotte M Keyn 49 N7
Calder Cumb 100 D10
Calderbank N Lans 126 D5
Calder Bridge Cumb 100 D9
Calderbrook Rochdl 89 Q7
Caldercruix N Lans 126 E4
Calder Grove Wakefd 91 J7
Caldermill S Lans 126 B9
Caldermore Rochdl 89 Q7
Calder Vale Lancs 95 L11
Calderwood S Lans 126 B6
Caldey Island Pembks 41 M11
Caldicot Mons 31 N7
Caldmore Wsall 58 F5
Caldwell N York 103 N8
Caldy Wirral 81 J7
Calenick Cnwll 3 L5
Calf of Man IoM 80 a8
Calford Green Suffk 63 M11
Calfsound Ork 169 e3
Calgary Ag & B 137 K5
Califer Moray 157 K6
California Falk 126 G2
California Norfk 77 Q8
California Cross Devon 7 J8
Calke Derbys 72 B6
Calke Abbey Derbys 72 B6
Callakille Highld 153 M6
Callander Stirlg 133 J6
Callanish W Isls 168 h4
Callaughton Shrops 57 L5
Callerton N u Ty 113 J7
Callestick Cnwll 3 K3
Calligarry Highld 145 K7
Callington Cnwll 5 P8
Callingwood Staffs 71 M10
Callow Herefs 45 N8
Callow End Worcs 46 F4
Callow Hill Wilts 33 K8
Callow Hill Worcs 47 K2
Callow Hill Worcs 57 N10
Callows Grave Worcs 57 K11
Calmore Hants 13 P2
Calmsden Gloucs 33 K3
Calne Wilts 33 J10
Calow Derbys 84 F6
Calshot Hants 14 E6
Calstock Cnwll 6 C5
Calstone Wellington
        Wilts 33 K11
Calthorpe Norfk 76 H5
Calthorpe Street Norfk 77 N6
Calthwaite Cumb 101 N2
Calton N York 96 D9
Calton Staffs 71 L5
Calveley Ches E 69 Q3
Calver Derbys 84 B6
Calverhall Shrops 69 R7
Calver Hill Herefs 45 M5
Calverleigh Devon 9 M2
Calverley Leeds 90 G3
Calver Sough Derbys 84 B6
Calvert Bucks 49 J10
Calverton M Keyn 49 L7
Calverton Notts 85 K11
Calvine P & K 141 K4
Calvo Cumb 109 P10
Calzeat Border 116 G3
Cam Gloucs 32 E5
Camasachoirce Highld 138 D5
Camasine Highld 138 D5
Camas Luinie Highld 146 A2
Camastianavaig Highld 153 J10
Camault Muir Highld 155 P9
Camber E Susx 26 G8
Camberley Surrey 23 N2
Camberwell Gt Lon 36 H5
Camblesforth N York 91 N5
Cambo Nthumb 112 F3
Cambois Nthumb 113 M4
Camborne Cnwll 2 G5
Camborne & Redruth
        Mining District Cnwll 2 G5
Cambourne Cambs 62 D9
Cambridge Cambs 62 G9
Cambridge Gloucs 32 D4
Cambridge Airport Cambs 62 G9
Cambrose Cnwll 2 H4
Cambus Clacks 133 P9
Cambusavie Highld 162 H7
Cambusbarron Stirlg 133 M9
Cambuskenneth Stirlg 133 N9
Cambuslang S Lans 125 Q5
Cambus o' May Abers 150 C8
Cambuswallace S Lans 116 E3
Camden Town Gt Lon 36 G4
Cameley BaNES 20 B3
Camelford Cnwll 5 J5
Camelon Falk 133 P11
Camerory Highld 157 J11
Camer's Green Worcs 46 E7
Camerton BaNES 20 C3
Camerton Cumb 100 D4
Camghouran P & K 140 E6
Camieston Border 117 R4
Cammachmore Abers 151 N8
Cammeringham Lincs 86 B4
Camore Highld 162 H9
Campbeltown Ag & B 120 D7

Campbeltown Airport
        Ag & B 120 C7
Camperdown N Tyne 113 L6
Cample D & G 109 J2
Campmuir P & K 142 C10
Camps W Loth 127 K4
Campsall Donc 91 N8
Campsea Ash Suffk 65 L10
Camps End Cambs 51 P2
Campton C Beds 50 D3
Camptown Border 118 C8
Camrose Pembks 40 H6
Camserney P & K 141 K8
Camusnagaul Highld 139 K3
Camusnagaul Highld 160 H9
Camusteel Highld 153 M9
Camusterrach Highld 153 N9
Canada Hants 21 Q11
Canal Foot Cumb 94 G5
Canaston Bridge Pembks 41 L7
Candacraig Abers 149 Q8
Candlesby Lincs 87 N7
Candle Street Suffk 64 E7
Candover Green Shrops 57 J3
Candy Mill Border 116 F2
Cane End Oxon 35 J9
Canewdon Essex 38 F3
Canford Bottom Dorset 12 H4
Canford Cliffs BCP 13 J7
Canford Heath BCP 12 H6
Canford Magna BCP 12 H5
Canhams Green Suffk 64 F8
Canisbay Highld 167 P2
Canklow Rothm 84 F2
Canley Covtry 59 M9
Cann Dorset 20 G6
Cann Common Dorset 20 G10
Canna Highld 144 B6
Cannich Highld 155 K11
Cannington Somset 19 J7
Canning Town Gt Lon 37 K4
Cannock Staffs 58 E2
Cannock Chase Staffs 70 H11
Cannock Wood Staffs 58 F2
Canon Bridge Herefs 45 N6
Canonbie D & G 110 G5
Canon Frome Herefs 46 B6
Canon Pyon Herefs 45 P5
Canons Ashby Nhants 48 G4
Canonstown Cnwll 2 E6
Canterbury Kent 39 K10
Canterbury Cathedral Kent ...39 L10
Cantley Norfk 77 M11
Cantlop Shrops 57 J3
Canton Cardif 30 G9
Cantraywood Highld 156 D8
Cantsfield Lancs 95 N6
Canvey Island Essex 38 C5
Canwick Lincs 86 C7
Canworthy Water Cnwll 5 L3
Caol Highld 139 L2
Caolas Scalpaigh W Isls 168 h8
Caoles Ag & B 136 D6
Caonich Highld 146 D9
Capel Kent 25 P2
Capel Surrey 24 E2
Capel Bangor Cerdgn 54 F8
Capel Betws Lleucu Cerdgn ...43 M3
Capel Coch IoA 78 H8
Capel Curig Gwynd 67 N3
Capel Cynon Cerdgn 42 G5
Capel Dewi Carmth 43 J10
Capel Dewi Cerdgn 43 J6
Capel-Dewi Cerdgn 54 E7
Capel Garmon Conwy 67 Q3
Capel Green Suffk 53 Q2
Capel Gwyn Carmth 43 J10
Capel Gwyn IoA 78 E9
Capel Gwynfe Carmth 43 P10
Capel Hendre Carmth 28 G2
Capel Isaac Carmth 43 L9
Capel Iwan Carmth 41 Q3
Capel-le-Ferne Kent 27 N4
Capelles Guern 10 c1
Capel Llanilltern Cardif 30 E9
Capel Mawr IoA 78 G10
Capel Parc IoA 78 G6
Capel St Andrew Suffk 53 Q2
Capel St Mary Suffk 53 J4
Capel Seion Cerdgn 54 E9
Capel Trisant Cerdgn 54 G9
Capeluchaf Gwynd 66 G5
Capelulo Conwy 79 N9
Capel-y-ffin Powys 45 K8
Capel-y-graig Gwynd 79 J11
Capenhurst Ches W 81 M10
Capernwray Lancs 95 L6
Cape Wrath Highld 164 G1
Capheaton Nthumb 112 F4
Caplaw E Rens 125 L6
Capon's Green Suffk 65 K8
Capstone Medway 38 C7
Capton Devon 7 L8
Capton Somset 18 E7
Caputh P & K 141 Q9
Caradon Mining District
        Cnwll 5 M7
Caradon Town Cnwll 5 M7
Carbeth Stirlg 125 N2
Carbis Cnwll 4 G6
Carbis Bay Cnwll 2 E6
Carbost Highld 152 F11
Carbost Highld 152 G8
Carbrook Sheff 84 E3
Carbrooke Norfk 76 C11
Carburton Notts 85 K6
Carclaze Cnwll 3 Q3
Car Colston Notts 73 J2
Carcroft Donc 91 N9
Cardenden Fife 134 G8
Cardeston Shrops 56 F2
Cardewlees Cumb 110 G10
Cardhu Moray 157 M9
Cardiff Cardif 30 G9
Cardiff Airport V Glam 30 E11
Cardiff Gate Services Cardif ...30 H8
Cardiff West Services Cardif ..30 E9
Cardigan Cerdgn 42 C5
Cardinal's Green Cambs 63 K11
Cardington Bed 61 N11
Cardington Shrops 57 J5
Cardinham Cnwll 5 J8
Cardrain D & G 106 F11
Cardrona Border 117 L3
Cardross Ag & B 125 J2

Cardryne D & G 106 F11
Cardurnock Cumb 110 C9
Careby Lincs 73 Q7
Careston Angus 143 J5
Carew Pembks 41 K10
Carew Cheriton Pembks 41 K10
Carew Newton Pembks 41 K10
Carey Herefs 45 R8
Carfin N Lans 126 D6
Carfraemill Border 128 D3
Cargate Green Norfk 77 M9
Cargenbridge D & G 109 L6
Cargill P & K 142 B10
Cargo Cumb 110 G9
Cargreen Cnwll 6 C6
Cargurrel Cnwll 3 M6
Carham Nthumb 118 E3
Carhampton Somset 18 D6
Carharrack Cnwll 3 J5
Carie P & K 140 F6
Carinish W Isls 168 d11
Carisbrooke IoW 14 E9
Cark Cumb 94 H5
Carkeel Cnwll 5 Q9
Càrlabhagh W Isls 168 h3
Carland Cross Cnwll 3 M3
Carlbury Darltn 103 P7
Carlby Lincs 73 Q8
Carlcroft Nthumb 118 F8
Carlecotes Barns 83 Q4
Carleen Cnwll 2 G7
Carlesmoor N York 97 K6
Carleton Cumb 100 D9
Carleton Cumb 101 P5
Carleton Cumb 110 H10
Carleton Lancs 88 C3
Carleton Wakefd 91 M6
Carleton Forehoe Norfk 76 F10
Carleton-in-Craven N York 96 E11
Carleton Rode Norfk 64 G3
Carleton St Peter Norfk 77 L11
Carlidnack Cnwll 3 K8
Carlincraig Abers 158 G9
Carlingcott BaNES 20 C3
Carlin How R & Cl 105 K7
Carlisle Cumb 110 H9
Carlisle Lake District
        Airport Cumb 111 J8
Carloggas Cnwll 4 E8
Carlops Border 127 M6
Carloway W Isls 168 h3
Carlton Barns 91 K8
Carlton Bed 61 L9
Carlton Cambs 63 K10
Carlton Leeds 91 J5
Carlton Leics 72 B10
Carlton N York 91 Q5
Carlton N York 96 G4
Carlton N York 98 C3
Carlton Notts 72 G2
Carlton S on T 104 C6
Carlton Suffk 65 M9
Carlton Colville Suffk 65 Q4
Carlton Curlieu Leics 72 H11
Carlton Green Cambs 63 K10
Carlton Husthwaite N York 97 Q5
Carlton-in-Cleveland
        N York 104 F9
Carlton in Lindrick Notts 85 J4
Carlton-le-Moorland Lincs 86 B9
Carlton Miniott N York 97 N4
Carlton-on-Trent Notts 85 N8
Carlton Scroop Lincs 86 B11
Carluke S Lans 126 E7
Carlyon Bay Cnwll 3 R3
Carmacoup S Lans 115 Q2
Carmarthen Carmth 42 H10
Carmel Carmth 43 L11
Carmel Flints 80 H9
Carmel Gwynd 66 H4
Carmichael S Lans 116 C3
Carmunnock C Glas 125 P6
Carmyle C Glas 125 Q5
Carmyllie Angus 143 J9
Carnaby E R Yk 99 N7
Carnbee Fife 135 N6
Carnbo P & K 134 D7
Carn Brea Cnwll 2 H5
Carnbrogie Abers 151 M2
Carndu Highld 145 Q2
Carnduff S Lans 126 B8
Carne Cnwll 3 L5
Carne Cnwll 3 N6
Carne Cnwll 3 M6
Carnell E Ayrs 125 M11
Carnewas Cnwll 4 D7
Carnforth Lancs 95 K6
Carn-gorm Highld 146 B3
Carnhedryn Pembks 40 F5
Carnhell Green Cnwll 2 G6
Carnie Abers 151 L6
Carnkie Cnwll 2 H5
Carnkie Cnwll 3 J7
Carnkief Cnwll 3 K3
Carno Powys 55 M5
Carnock Fife 134 C10
Carnon Downs Cnwll 3 K5
Carnousie Abers 158 G7
Carnoustie Angus 143 K9
Carnsmerry Cnwll 4 G10
Carnwath S Lans 126 H8
Carnyorth Cnwll 2 B7
Carol Green Solhll 59 L9
Carpalla Cnwll 3 P3
Carperby N York 96 F3
Carr Rothm 84 H2
Carradale Ag & B 120 E5
Carradale Village Ag & B 120 E6
Carrbridge Highld 148 G3
Carrbrook Tamesd 83 L4
Carrefour Jersey 11 b1
Carreglefn IoA 78 F7
Carr Gate Wakefd 91 J6
Carrhouse N Linc 92 C9
Carrick Ag & B 131 J10
Carrick Castle Ag & B 131 P9
Carriden Falk 134 C11
Carrington Lincs 87 K9
Carrington Mdloth 127 Q5
Carrington Traffd 82 F6
Carrog Conwy 67 P2
Carrog Denbgs 68 F6
Carron Falk 133 P11
Carron Moray 157 N9
Carronbridge D & G 116 B11
Carron Bridge Stirlg 133 L11

Carronshore Falk 133 P11
Carrow Hill Mons 31 M6
Carr Shield Nthumb 112 B11
Carrutherstown D & G 109 P6
Carruth House Inver 125 K4
Carr Vale Derbys 84 G7
Carrville Dur 104 B2
Carsaig Ag & B 137 N11
Carseriggan D & G 107 K4
Carsethorn D & G 109 L9
Carshalton Gt Lon 36 G8
Carsington Derbys 71 P4
Carskey Ag & B 120 C10
Carsluith D & G 107 N7
Carsphairn D & G 115 L9
Carstairs S Lans 126 G8
Carstairs Junction S Lans 126 H8
Carswell Marsh Oxon 34 B5
Carter's Clay Hants 22 B10
Carters Green Essex 51 M8
Carterton Oxon 33 Q3
Carterway Heads Nthumb 112 F10
Carthew Cnwll 4 G10
Carthorpe N York 97 M4
Cartington Nthumb 119 K10
Cartland S Lans 126 F8
Cartledge Derbys 84 D5
Cartmel Cumb 94 H5
Cartmel Fell Cumb 95 J3
Carway Carmth 28 E3
Carwinley Cumb 110 H6
Cashe's Green Gloucs 32 F3
Cashmoor Dorset 12 G2
Cassington Oxon 34 E2
Cassop Dur 104 B3
Castallack Cnwll 2 D8
Castel Guern 10 b2
Castell Conwy 79 P11
Castell-y-bwch Torfn 31 J6
Casterton Cumb 95 N5
Castle Cnwll 4 H10
Castle Acre Norfk 75 R7
Castle Ashby Nhants 61 J9
Castlebay W Isls 168 b18
Castle Bolton N York 96 F2
Castle Bromwich Solhll 58 H7
Castle Bytham Lincs 73 P7
Castle Caereinion Powys 56 B3
Castle Camps Cambs 51 P2
Castle Carrock Cumb 111 K9
Castlecary Falk 126 D2
Castle Cary Somset 20 B8
Castle Combe Wilts 32 F9
Castlecraig Highld 156 E4
Castle Donington Leics 72 C5
Castle Douglas D & G 108 G8
Castle Eaton Swindn 33 M5
Castle Eden Dur 104 D3
Castle End C Pete 74 B9
Castleford Wakefd 91 L5
Castle Frome Herefs 46 C7
Castle Gate Cnwll 2 D7
Castle Green Cumb 95 L2
Castle Green Surrey 23 Q2
Castle Gresley Derbys 71 P11
Castle Hedingham Essex 52 C4
Castlehill Border 117 J3
Castlehill Highld 167 L3
Castle Hill Kent 25 Q2
Castle Hill Suffk 53 K2
Castlehill W Duns 125 K2
Castle Howard N York 98 E6
Castle Kennedy D & G 106 F6
Castle Lachlan Ag & B 131 L8
Castlemartin Pembks 40 H11
Castlemilk C Glas 125 P6
Castle Morris Pembks 40 H4
Castlemorton Worcs 46 E7
Castlemorton Common
        Worcs 46 E7
Castle O'er D & G 110 D2
Castle Rising Norfk 75 N6
Castleside Dur 112 G11
Castle Stuart Highld 156 C8
Castlethorpe M Keyn 49 M6
Castlethorpe N Linc 92 G9
Castleton Border 111 K3
Castleton Derbys 83 Q8
Castleton N York 105 J9
Castleton Newpt 31 J8
Castleton Rochdl 89 P8
Castletown Ches W 69 M4
Castletown Dorset 11 P10
Castletown Highld 167 L3
Castletown IoM 80 c8
Castletown Sundld 113 N9
Castley N York 97 L11
Caston Norfk 64 C2
Castor C Pete 74 B11
Caswell Bay Swans 28 G7
Cat and Fiddle Derbys 83 M10
Catbrain S Glos 31 Q8
Catbrook Mons 31 P4
Catch Flints 81 J10
Catchall Cnwll 2 C8
Catchem's Corner Solhll 59 L9
Catchgate Dur 113 J10
Catcliffe Rothm 84 F3
Catcomb Wilts 33 K9
Catcott Somset 19 L7
Caterham Surrey 36 H9
Catfield Norfk 77 N7
Catfield Common Norfk 77 N7
Catford Gt Lon 37 J6
Catforth Lancs 88 F4
Cathcart C Glas 125 P5
Cathedine Powys 44 G8
Catherine-de-Barnes Solhll 59 J8
Catherine Slack C Brad 90 D5
Catherington Hants 15 J4
Catherston Leweston
        Dorset 10 H6
Catherton Shrops 57 M9
Catisfield Hants 14 G5
Catley Herefs 46 C6
Catley Lane Head Rochdl 89 P7
Catlodge Highld 147 N9
Catlow Lancs 89 P3
Catlowdy Cumb 111 J6
Catmere End Essex 51 L4
Catmore W Berk 34 E8
Caton Devon 7 K4
Caton Lancs 95 L8

aton Green Lancs...95 M7
ator Court Devon...8 G9
atrine E Ayrs...115 K2
at's Ash Newpt...31 L6
atsfield E Susx...26 B9
atsfield Stream E Susx...26 B9
atsgore Somset...19 P9
atsham Somset...19 Q8
atshill Worcs...58 E10
atstree Shrops...57 N5
attadale Ag & B...120 C9
attal N York...97 P10
attawade Suffk...53 K5
atterall Lancs...88 F2
atteralslane Shrops...69 Q6
atterick N York...103 P11
atterick Bridge N York...103 P11
atterick Garrison N York...103 N11
atterlen Cumb...101 N4
atterline Abers...143 R2
atterton N York...97 R11
atteshall Surrey...23 Q6
atthorpe Leics...60 C5
attishall Suffk...64 B8
attistock Dorset...11 M5
atton N York...97 N5
atton Nthumb...112 B9
atwick E R Yk...99 N11
atworth Cambs...61 N6
audle Green Gloucs...32 H2
aulcott C Beds...50 B2
aulcott Oxon...48 F10
auldcots Angus...143 M8
auldhame Stirlg...133 J9
auldmill Border...117 Q7
auldon Staffs...71 K5
auldon Lowe Staffs...71 K5
auldwell Derbys...71 P11
aulkerbush D & G...109 K9
aulside D & G...110 H4
aundle Marsh Dorset...11 P2
aunsall Worcs...58 C8
aunton Notts...85 M8
auseway Hants...23 K10
auseway End Cumb...95 K3
auseway End D & G...107 M6
auseway End Essex...51 Q7
ausewayend S Lans...116 E3
ausewayhead Cumb...109 P10
ausewayhead Stirlg...133 N8
ausey Abers...151 N4
ausey Park Nthumb...113 J2
ausey Park Bridge Nthumb...113 J2
avendish Suffk...63 P11
avenham Suffk...63 N6
aversfield Oxon...48 G9
aversham Readg...35 K10
averswall Staffs...70 H6
averton Mill Border...118 D5
avil E R Yk...92 C4
awdor Highld...156 E7
awkwell Lincs...87 J5
awood N York...91 P3
awsand Cnwll...6 C8
awston Norfk...76 G7
awston Warwks...59 Q10
awthorn N York...98 F3
awthorne Barns...90 H9
awton N York...98 C5
axton Cambs...62 D9
axton End Cambs...62 D9
axton Gibbet Cambs...62 C8
aynham Shrops...57 K10
aythorpe Lincs...86 B11
aythorpe Notts...85 L11
ayton N York...99 M4
eannabeinne Highld...165 K3
eann a Bhaigh W Isls...168 c11
earsiadar W Isls...168 i6
eciliford Mons...31 P4
efn Newpt...31 J7
efn Berain Conwy...80 D11
efn-brith Conwy...68 B4
efn-bryn-brain Carmth...29 K2
efn Byrle Powys...29 M2
efn Canel Powys...68 H8
efn Coch Powys...68 F9
efn-coed-y-cymmer Myr Td...30 D3
efn Cribwr Brdgnd...29 N8
efn Cross Brdgnd...29 N8
efn-ddwysarn Gwynd...68 C7
efn-Einion Shrops...56 D7
efneithin Carmth...28 G2
efngorwydd Powys...44 C5
efn-mawr Wrexhm...69 J6
efnpennar Rhondd...30 D4
efn-y-bedd Flints...69 K3
efn-y-pant Carmth...41 L9
eint IoA...78 H9
ellan Cerdgn...43 M5
ellardyke Fife...135 P7
ellarhead Staffs...70 H5
elleron Cumb...101 N5
elynen Caerph...30 H5
emaes IoA...78 F6
emmaes Powys...55 J3
emmaes Road Powys...55 J4
enarth Cerdgn...41 Q2
erbyd Pembks...40 F5
eres Fife...135 L5
erne Abbas Dorset...11 N4
erney Wick Gloucs...33 L5
errigceinwen IoA...78 G10
errigdrudion Conwy...68 C5
ess Norfk...77 N8
eunant Gwynd...67 J2
haceley Gloucs...46 G8
hacewater Cnwll...3 J6
hackmore Bucks...49 J7
hacombe Nhants...48 B6
hadbury Worcs...47 K5
hadderton Oldham...89 Q9
hadderton Fold Oldham...89 Q9
haddesden C Derb...72 B3
haddesley Corbett Worcs...58 C10
haddlehanger Devon...8 C9
haddleworth W Berk...34 D9
hadlington Oxon...48 B10
hadshunt Warwks...48 B4
hadwell Leics...73 K6
hadwell Shrops...57 P2
hadwell End Bed...61 N7
hadwell Heath Gt Lon...37 L3
hadwell St Mary Thurr...37 P5

Chadwick Worcs...58 B11
Chadwick End Solhll...59 K10
Chadwick Green St Hel...82 B5
Chaffcombe Somset...10 H2
Chafford Hundred Thurr...37 P5
Chagford Devon...8 H7
Chailey E Susx...25 J7
Chainbridge Cambs...74 H10
Chainhurst Kent...26 B2
Chalbury Dorset...12 H3
Chalbury Common Dorset...12 H3
Chaldon Surrey...36 H9
Chaldon Herring Dorset...12 C8
Chale IoW...14 E11
Chale Green IoW...14 E11
Chalfont Common Bucks...36 B2
Chalfont St Giles Bucks...35 Q6
Chalfont St Peter Bucks...36 B2
Chalford Gloucs...32 G4
Chalford Oxon...35 K4
Chalford Wilts...20 G4
Chalgrave C Beds...50 B5
Chalgrove Oxon...34 H5
Chalk Kent...37 Q6
Chalk End Essex...51 P8
Chalkhouse Green Oxon...35 K9
Chalkway Somset...10 H3
Chalkwell Kent...38 E9
Challaborough Devon...6 H10
Challacombe Devon...17 M3
Challoch D & G...107 L4
Challock Kent...38 H11
Chalmington Dorset...11 M4
Chalton C Beds...50 B5
Chalton C Beds...61 P10
Chalton Hants...23 K11
Chalvey Slough...35 Q9
Chalvington E Susx...25 M9
Chambers Green Kent...26 F3
Chandler's Cross Herts...50 C11
Chandlers Cross Worcs...46 E7
Chandler's Ford Hants...22 D11
Channel's End Bed...61 P9
Channel Tunnel Terminal Kent...27 L4
Chantry Somset...20 D5
Chantry Suffk...53 K3
Chapel Cumb...100 H4
Chapel Fife...134 H9
Chapel Allerton Leeds...91 J3
Chapel Allerton Somset...19 M4
Chapel Amble Cnwll...4 F6
Chapel Brampton Nhants...60 F7
Chapelbridge Cambs...62 C2
Chapel Chorlton Staffs...70 E7
Chapel Cross E Susx...25 P6
Chapel End Bed...61 P9
Chapel End C Beds...50 C2
Chapel End Cambs...62 P4
Chapel End Warwks...59 M6
Chapelend Way Essex...52 B4
Chapel-en-le-Frith Derbys...83 N8
Chapel Field Bury...89 M9
Chapelgate Lincs...74 H6
Chapel Green Warwks...48 E2
Chapel Green Warwks...59 L7
Chapel Haddlesey N York...91 P5
Chapelhall N Lans...126 D5
Chapel Hill Abers...159 Q10
Chapel Hill Lincs...86 H10
Chapel Hill Mons...31 P5
Chapel Hill N York...97 M11
Chapelhope Border...117 J7
Chapelknowe D & G...110 H4
Chapel Lawn Shrops...56 E9
Chapel-le-Dale N York...95 Q5
Chapel Leigh Somset...18 F9
Chapel Milton Derbys...83 N8
Chapel of Garioch Abers...151 J3
Chapel Rossan D & G...106 F9
Chapel Row E Susx...25 P8
Chapel Row Essex...52 C11
Chapel Row W Berk...34 G11
Chapels Cumb...94 E4
Chapel St Leonards Lincs...87 Q6
Chapel Stile Cumb...101 K9
Chapelton Abers...151 M9
Chapelton Angus...143 L8
Chapelton Devon...17 K6
Chapelton S Lans...126 B8
Chapeltown Bl w D...89 L7
Chapel Town Cnwll...4 D10
Chapeltown Moray...149 N3
Chapeltown Sheff...91 K11
Chapmanslade Wilts...20 F5
Chapmans Well Devon...5 P3
Chapmore End Herts...50 H7
Chappel Essex...52 E6
Charaton Cnwll...5 N8
Chard Somset...10 G3
Chard Junction Somset...10 G4
Chardleigh Green Somset...10 G2
Chardstock Devon...10 G4
Charfield S Glos...32 D6
Chargrove Gloucs...46 H11
Charing Kent...26 G2
Charing Heath Kent...26 F2
Charing Hill Kent...38 G11
Charingworth Gloucs...47 N7
Charlbury Oxon...48 C11
Charlcombe BaNES...32 D11
Charlcutt Wilts...33 J9
Charlecote Warwks...47 Q3
Charlemont Sandw...58 F6
Charles Devon...17 M5
Charleshill Surrey...23 N6
Charleston Angus...142 F8
Charlestown C Aber...151 N7
Charlestown C Brad...90 F3
Charlestown Calder...90 B5
Charlestown Cnwll...3 Q3
Charlestown Cnwll...3 Q3
Charlestown Derbys...83 M6
Charlestown Dorset...11 P9
Charlestown Fife...134 D11
Charlestown Highld...153 Q3
Charlestown Highld...156 A8
Charlestown Salfd...82 H4
Charlestown of Aberlour Moray...157 P9
Charles Tye Suffk...64 E11
Charlesworth Derbys...83 M6
Charlinch Somset...18 H7
Charlottetown Fife...134 H5
Charlton Gt Lon...37 K5
Charlton Hants...22 C5

Charlton Herts...50 E5
Charlton Nhants...48 F7
Charlton Nthumb...112 B4
Charlton Oxon...34 D7
Charlton Somset...19 J9
Charlton Somset...20 B6
Charlton Somset...20 C4
Charlton Somset...20 C7
Charlton Surrey...36 C7
Charlton W Susx...15 N4
Charlton Wilts...20 H10
Charlton Wilts...33 J7
Charlton Worcs...47 K5
Charlton Worcs...58 B10
Charlton Wrekin...57 K2
Charlton Abbots Gloucs...47 K10
Charlton Adam Somset...19 P9
Charlton All Saints Wilts...21 N10
Charlton Down Dorset...11 P5
Charlton Hill Shrops...57 K3
Charlton Horethorne Somset...20 C10
Charlton Kings Gloucs...47 J10
Charlton Mackrell Somset...19 P9
Charlton Marshall Dorset...12 F4
Charlton Musgrove Somset...20 D9
Charlton-on-Otmoor Oxon...48 G11
Charlton on the Hill Dorset...12 E4
Charlton St Peter Wilts...21 M3
Charlwood Hants...23 J8
Charlwood Surrey...24 F2
Charminster Dorset...11 P6
Charmouth Dorset...10 H6
Charndon Bucks...49 J10
Charney Bassett Oxon...34 C6
Charnock Green Lancs...88 H7
Charnock Richard Lancs...88 H7
Charnock Richard Services Lancs...88 G7
Charsfield Suffk...65 K10
Chart Corner Kent...38 C11
Charter Alley Hants...22 G3
Charterhall Border...129 K10
Charterhouse Somset...19 N3
Charterville Allotments Oxon...34 B2
Chartham Kent...39 K11
Chartham Hatch Kent...39 K10
Chart Hill Kent...26 C2
Chartridge Bucks...35 P4
Chart Sutton Kent...26 D2
Chartway Street Kent...38 D11
Charvil Wokham...35 L9
Charwelton Nhants...60 B9
Chase Terrace Staffs...58 F3
Chasetown Staffs...58 F3
Chastleton Oxon...47 P9
Chasty Devon...16 E11
Chatburn Lancs...89 M2
Chatcull Staffs...70 D8
Chatham Caerph...30 H7
Chatham Medway...38 C8
Chatham Green Essex...52 B8
Chathill Nthumb...119 N5
Chatley Worcs...46 G2
Chattenden Medway...38 C7
Chatter End Essex...51 L5
Chatteris Cambs...62 E3
Chatterton Lancs...89 M7
Chatsworth House Derbys...84 C6
Chattisham Suffk...53 J3
Chatto Border...118 E7
Chatton Nthumb...119 L5
Chaul End C Beds...50 C6
Chawleigh Devon...8 H2
Chawley Oxon...34 E4
Chawston Bed...61 Q9
Chawton Hants...23 K7
Chaxhill Gloucs...32 D2
Chazey Heath Oxon...35 J9
Cheadle Staffs...71 J6
Cheadle Stockp...83 J7
Cheadle Heath Stockp...83 J7
Cheadle Hulme Stockp...83 J7
Cheam Gt Lon...36 F8
Cheapside W & M...35 P11
Chearsley Bucks...35 K2
Chebsey Staffs...70 F9
Checkendon Oxon...35 J8
Checkley Ches E...70 C5
Checkley Herefs...46 A7
Checkley Staffs...71 J7
Checkley Green Ches E...70 C5
Chedburgh Suffk...63 N9
Cheddar Somset...19 N4
Cheddington Bucks...49 P11
Cheddleton Staffs...70 H4
Cheddleton Heath Staffs...70 H4
Cheddon Fitzpaine Somset...18 H9
Chedglow Wilts...32 H6
Chedgrave Norfk...65 M2
Chedington Dorset...11 K3
Chediston Suffk...65 M6
Chediston Green Suffk...65 M6
Chedworth Gloucs...33 L2
Chedzoy Somset...19 K7
Cheeseman's Green Kent...26 H4
Cheetham Hill Manch...82 H4
Cheldon Devon...8 H2
Chelford Ches E...82 H10
Chellaston C Derb...72 B4
Chellington Bed...61 L9
Chelmarsh Shrops...57 N7
Chelmer Village Essex...52 B10
Chelmick Shrops...56 H6
Chelmondiston Suffk...53 M4
Chelmorton Derbys...83 P11
Chelmsford Essex...52 B10
Chelmsley Wood Solhll...59 J7
Chelsea Gt Lon...36 G5
Chelsfield Gt Lon...37 L8
Chelsham Surrey...37 J9
Chelston Somset...18 G10
Chelsworth Suffk...52 G2
Cheltenham Gloucs...46 H10
Chelveston Nhants...61 L7
Chelvey N Som...31 N11
Chelwood BaNES...20 B2
Chelwood Common E Susx...25 K5
Chelwood Gate E Susx...25 K4
Chelworth Wilts...33 J6
Chelworth Lower Green Wilts...33 L6
Chelworth Upper Green Wilts...33 L6
Cheney Longville Shrops...56 G8

Chenies Bucks...50 B11
Chepstow Mons...31 P6
Chequerbent Bolton...89 K9
Chequers Corner Norfk...75 J9
Cherhill Wilts...33 K10
Cherington Gloucs...32 H5
Cherington Warwks...47 Q7
Cheriton Devon...17 N2
Cheriton Hants...22 G9
Cheriton Kent...27 M4
Cheriton Pembks...41 J11
Cheriton Swans...28 E6
Cheriton Bishop Devon...9 J6
Cheriton Fitzpaine Devon...9 L3
Cherrington Wrekin...70 B11
Cherry Burton E R Yk...92 G2
Cherry Hinton Cambs...62 G9
Cherry Orchard Worcs...46 G4
Cherry Willingham Lincs...86 D6
Chertsey Surrey...36 B7
Cherwell Valley Services Oxon...48 F9
Cheselbourne Dorset...12 C5
Chesham Bucks...35 Q4
Chesham Bury...89 N8
Chesham Bois Bucks...35 Q5
Cheshunt Herts...51 J10
Chesil Beach Dorset...11 N9
Chesley Kent...38 E9
Cheslyn Hay Staffs...58 E3
Chessetts Wood Warwks...59 J10
Chessington Gt Lon...36 E8
Chessington World of Adventures Gt Lon...36 E8
Chester Ches W...81 N11
Chesterblade Somset...20 C6
Chesterfield Derbys...84 E6
Chesterfield Staffs...58 G3
Chesterhill Mdloth...128 B7
Chester-le-Street Dur...113 L10
Chester Moor Dur...113 L11
Chesters Border...118 B6
Chesters Border...118 B8
Chester Services Ches W...81 P9
Chesterton Cambs...62 G8
Chesterton Cambs...74 B11
Chesterton Gloucs...33 K4
Chesterton Oxon...48 G10
Chesterton Shrops...57 P5
Chesterton Staffs...70 E5
Chesterton Green Warwks...48 C3
Chesterwood Nthumb...112 B7
Chester Zoo Ches W...81 N10
Chestfield Kent...39 K8
Chestnut Street Kent...38 E9
Cheston Devon...6 H7
Cheswardine Shrops...70 C8
Cheswick Nthumb...129 Q10
Cheswick Green Solhll...58 H9
Chetnole Dorset...11 N3
Chettiscombe Devon...9 N2
Chettisham Cambs...62 H4
Chettle Dorset...12 G2
Chetton Shrops...57 M6
Chetwode Bucks...48 H9
Chetwynd Wrekin...70 C10
Chetwynd Aston Wrekin...70 D11
Cheveley Cambs...63 L8
Chevening Kent...37 L9
Cheverton IoW...14 E10
Chevington Suffk...63 N9
Cheviot Hills...118 E9
Chevithorne Devon...18 C11
Chew Magna BaNES...19 Q2
Chew Moor Bolton...89 K9
Chew Stoke BaNES...19 Q2
Chewton Keynsham BaNES...32 C11
Chewton Mendip Somset...19 Q4
Chichacott Devon...8 F5
Chicheley M Keyn...49 P5
Chichester W Susx...15 N6
Chickerell Dorset...11 N8
Chickering Suffk...65 J6
Chicklade Wilts...20 H8
Chicksands C Beds...50 D3
Chickward Herefs...45 K4
Chidden Hants...23 J11
Chiddingfold Surrey...23 Q7
Chiddingly E Susx...25 M8
Chiddingstone Kent...25 M2
Chiddingstone Causeway Kent...37 M11
Chiddingstone Hoath Kent...25 L2
Chideock Dorset...11 J6
Chidham W Susx...15 L6
Chidswell Kirk...90 H6
Chieveley W Berk...34 E10
Chieveley Services W Berk...34 E10
Chignall St James Essex...51 Q8
Chignall Smealy Essex...51 Q8
Chigwell Essex...37 K2
Chigwell Row Essex...37 L2
Chilbolton Hants...22 C6
Chilcomb Hants...22 F9
Chilcombe Dorset...11 L6
Chilcompton Somset...20 B4
Chilcote Leics...59 L2
Childer Thornton Ches W...81 M9
Child Okeford Dorset...12 D2
Childrey Oxon...34 C7
Child's Ercall Shrops...70 B9
Childswickham Worcs...47 L7
Childwall Lpool...81 N7
Childwick Bury Herts...50 D8
Childwick Green Herts...50 D8
Chilfrome Dorset...11 M5
Chilgrove W Susx...15 M4
Chilham Kent...39 J11
Chilla Devon...8 B3
Chillaton Devon...8 B8
Chillenden Kent...39 N11
Chillerton IoW...14 E10
Chillesford Suffk...65 M11
Chillingham Nthumb...119 L5
Chillington Devon...7 K10
Chillington Somset...10 H2
Chilmark Wilts...21 J8
Chilmington Green Kent...26 G3
Chilson Oxon...48 B11
Chilsworthy Cnwll...5 Q7
Chilsworthy Devon...16 E10
Chiltern Green C Beds...50 D7
Chiltern Hills...35 L5
Chilthorne Domer Somset...19 P11
Chilton Bucks...35 J2
Chilton Devon...9 L4

Chilton Dur...103 Q5
Chilton Kent...27 N3
Chilton Oxon...34 E7
Chilton Suffk...52 E3
Chilton Candover Hants...22 G6
Chilton Cantelo Somset...19 Q10
Chilton Foliat Wilts...34 B10
Chilton Polden Somset...19 L6
Chilton Street Suffk...63 N11
Chilton Trinity Somset...19 J7
Chilwell Notts...72 E3
Chilworth Hants...22 D11
Chilworth Surrey...36 B11
Chimney Oxon...34 C4
Chineham Hants...23 J3
Chingford Gt Lon...37 J2
Chinley Derbys...83 M8
Chinnor Oxon...35 L4
Chipchase Castle Nthumb...112 C5
Chipnall Shrops...70 C8
Chippenham Cambs...63 L7
Chippenham Wilts...32 H10
Chipperfield Herts...50 B10
Chipping Herts...51 J4
Chipping Lancs...89 J2
Chipping Campden Gloucs...47 N7
Chipping Hill Essex...52 D8
Chipping Norton Oxon...48 B9
Chipping Ongar Essex...51 N10
Chipping Sodbury S Glos...32 D8
Chipping Warden Nhants...48 E5
Chipshop Devon...8 B9
Chipstable Somset...18 D9
Chipstead Kent...37 M9
Chipstead Surrey...36 G9
Chirbury Shrops...56 D5
Chirk Wrexhm...69 J7
Chirnside Border...129 M8
Chirnsidebridge Border...129 M8
Chirton Wilts...21 L3
Chisbury Wilts...33 Q11
Chiselborough Somset...11 K2
Chiseldon Swindn...33 N8
Chislehampton Oxon...34 G5
Chiserley Calder...90 C5
Chisholme Border...117 N8
Chislehurst Gt Lon...37 K6
Chislet Kent...39 M9
Chiswell Green Herts...50 D10
Chiswick Gt Lon...36 F5
Chiswick End Cambs...62 E11
Chisworth Derbys...83 L6
Chitcombe E Susx...26 D7
Chithurst W Susx...23 M10
Chittering Cambs...62 G7
Chitterne Wilts...21 J6
Chittlehamholt Devon...17 M7
Chittlehampton Devon...17 L6
Chittoe Wilts...33 J11
Chivelstone Devon...7 K11
Chivenor Devon...17 J5
Chiverton Cross Cnwll...3 J4
Chlenry D & G...106 F5
Chobham Surrey...23 Q2
Cholderton Wilts...21 P6
Cholesbury Bucks...35 P3
Chollerford Nthumb...112 D6
Chollerton Nthumb...112 D6
Cholmondeston Ches E...70 A3
Cholsey Oxon...34 G7
Cholstrey Herefs...45 P3
Chop Gate N York...104 G11
Choppington Nthumb...113 L4
Chopwell Gatesd...112 H9
Chorley Ches E...69 Q4
Chorley Lancs...88 H7
Chorley Shrops...57 M8
Chorley Staffs...58 G2
Chorleywood Herts...50 B11
Chorleywood West Herts...50 B11
Chorlton Ches E...70 C4
Chorlton-cum-Hardy Manch...82 H6
Chorlton Lane Ches W...69 N5
Choulton Shrops...56 G6
Chowley Ches W...69 N3
Chrishall Essex...51 K3
Chrisswell Inver...124 G3
Christchurch BCP...13 L6
Christchurch Cambs...75 J11
Christchurch Gloucs...31 Q2
Christchurch Newpt...31 K7
Christian Malford Wilts...33 J9
Christleton Ches W...81 N11
Christmas Common Oxon...35 K6
Christmas Pie Surrey...23 P5
Christon N Som...19 L3
Christon Bank Nthumb...119 P6
Christow Devon...9 K7
Christ's Hospital W Susx...24 D5
Chuck Hatch E Susx...25 L4
Chudleigh Devon...9 L9
Chudleigh Knighton Devon...9 K9
Chulmleigh Devon...17 M9
Chunal Derbys...83 M6
Church Lancs...89 L5
Churcham Gloucs...46 E11
Church Aston Wrekin...70 C11
Church Brampton Nhants...60 F7
Church Brough Cumb...102 E8
Church Broughton Derbys...71 N8
Church Cove Cnwll...3 J11
Church Crookham Hants...23 M4
Churchdown Gloucs...46 G11
Church Eaton Staffs...70 E11
Church End Bed...61 N9
Church End Bed...61 P9
Church End Bucks...35 K3
Church End C Beds...49 Q10
Church End C Beds...49 Q8
Church End C Beds...50 B4
Church End C Beds...50 B7
Church End C Beds...50 D5
Church End C Beds...61 Q10
Church End Cambs...61 N6
Church End Cambs...62 B4
Church End Cambs...62 D5
Churchend Essex...38 H3
Church End Essex...51 P6
Church End Essex...52 B6
Church End Essex...52 B8
Church End Gt Lon...36 F2
Church End Herts...50 D8
Church End Herts...50 G4
Church End Herts...51 K6
Church End Lincs...74 D4

Church End Lincs 93 R11
Church End Suffk 53 M4
Church End Warwks 59 K6
Church End Warwks 59 L6
Church Enstone Oxon 48 C9
Church Fenton N York 91 N3
Churchfield Sandw 58 F6
Churchgate Herts 50 H10
Churchgate Street Essex 51 L8
Church Green Devon 10 D5
Church Gresley Derbys 71 P11
Church Hanborough Oxon 34 D2
Church Hill Staffs 58 F2
Church Houses N York 105 J11
Churchill Devon 10 F4
Churchill Devon 17 K3
Churchill N Som 19 M3
Churchill Oxon 47 Q10
Churchill Worcs 46 H4
Churchill Worcs 58 C9
Churchinford Somset 10 E2
Church Knowle Dorset 12 H4
Church Laneham Notts 85 P5
Church Langton Leics 60 F2
Church Lawford Warwks 59 Q9
Church Lawton Ches E 70 E3
Church Leigh Staffs 71 J7
Church Lench Worcs 47 K4
Church Mayfield Staffs 71 M6
Church Minshull Ches E 70 B2
Church Norton W Susx 15 N7
Churchover Warwks 60 B4
Church Preen Shrops 57 J5
Church Pulverbatch Shrops ...56 G4
Churchstanton Somset 10 D2
Churchstoke Powys 56 D6
Churchstow Devon 7 J9
Church Stowe Nhants 60 D9
Church Street Essex 52 C3
Church Street Kent 38 B7
Church Street Suffk 65 P5
Church Stretton Shrops 56 H6
Churchthorpe Lincs 93 P11
Churchtown Bpool 88 C2
Churchtown Cnwll 4 H6
Churchtown Derbys 84 C8
Churchtown Devon 17 M3
Churchtown IoM 80 f3
Churchtown Lancs 88 F2
Church Town N Linc 92 C9
Churchtown Sefton 88 D7
Church Village Rhondd 30 E7
Church Warsop Notts 85 J7
Church Wilne Derbys 72 C4
Churnsike Lodge Nthumb 111 N5
Churston Ferrers Torbay 7 N7
Churt Surrey 23 N7
Churton Ches W 69 M3
Churwell Leeds 90 H5
Chwilog Gwynd 66 G7
Chyandour Cnwll 2 D7
Chyanvounder Cnwll 2 H9
Chyeowling Cnwll 3 K5
Chyvarloe Cnwll 2 H9
Cil Powys 56 B4
Cilcain Flints 80 H11
Cilcennin Cerdgn 43 K2
Cilcewydd Powys 56 C4
Cilfrew Neath 29 L4
Cilfynydd Rhondd 30 E6
Cilgerran Pembks 41 N2
Cilgwyn Carmth 43 P9
Cilgwyn Gwynd 66 H4
Ciliau-Aeron Cerdgn 43 K3
Cilmaengwyn Neath 29 K3
Cilmery Powys 44 E4
Cilrhedyn Pembks 41 Q4
Cilsan Carmth 43 L10
Ciltalgarth Gwynd 68 A6
Cilycwm Carmth 43 Q7
Cimla Neath 29 L5
Cinderford Gloucs 32 C2
Cinder Hill Wolves 58 D6
Cippenham Slough 35 Q8
Cirencester Gloucs 33 K4
Citadilla N York 103 P11
City Gt Lon 36 H4
City V Glam 30 C9
City Airport Gt Lon 37 K4
City Dulas IoA 78 H7
Clabhach Ag & B 136 F4
Clachaig Ag & B 131 N11
Clachaig Inn Highld 139 L6
Clachan Ag & B 123 N8
Clachan Ag & B 130 F4
Clachan Ag & B 131 M7
Clachan Ag & B 138 F9
Clachan Highld 153 J10
Clachan-a-Luib W Isls 168 d11
Clachan Mor Ag & B 136 B6
Clachan na Luib W Isls 168 d11
Clachan of Campsie E Duns ..125 Q2
Clachan-Seil Ag & B 130 F4
Clachnaharry Highld 156 A8
Clachtoll Highld 164 B11
Clacket Lane Services
  Surrey 37 K10
Clackmannan Clacks 133 Q9
Clackmannanshire Bridge
  Fife 133 Q10
Clackmarras Moray 157 N6
Clacton-on-Sea Essex 53 L8
Cladich Ag & B 131 M3
Cladswell Worcs 47 L3
Claggan Highld 138 C8
Claigan Highld 152 C7
Clandown BaNES 20 C3
Clanfield Hants 23 J11
Clanfield Oxon 33 Q4
Clannaborough Devon 8 H4
Clanville Hants 22 B5
Clanville Somset 20 B8
Claonaig Ag & B 123 Q8
Clapgate Dorset 12 H4
Clapgate Herts 51 K6
Clapham Bed 32 M10
Clapham Devon 9 L7
Clapham Gt Lon 36 G5
Clapham N York 95 Q7
Clapham W Susx 24 C9
Clapham Green Bed 32 M10
Clap Hill Kent 27 J4
Clappersgate Cumb 101 L10
Clapton Somset 11 J3
Clapton Somset 20 B4
Clapton-in-Gordano N Som ...31 N10

Clapton-on-the-Hill Gloucs ...47 N11
Clapworthy Devon 17 M7
Clarach Cerdgn 54 E8
Claravale Gatesd 112 H8
Clarbeston Pembks 41 L6
Clarbeston Road Pembks 41 K6
Clarborough Notts 85 M4
Clare Suffk 63 N11
Clarebrand D & G 108 G7
Clarencefield D & G 109 N7
Clarewood Nthumb 112 F7
Clarilaw Border 117 Q7
Clark's Green Surrey 24 E3
Clarkston E Rens 125 P6
Clashmore Highld 162 G9
Clashmore Highld 164 B10
Clashnessie Highld 164 C10
Clashnoir Moray 149 N3
Clathy P & K 134 B3
Clathymore P & K 134 C3
Clatt Abers 150 E2
Clatter Powys 55 M6
Clatterford End Essex 51 P8
Clatworthy Somset 18 E8
Claughton Lancs 88 G2
Claughton Lancs 95 M7
Claughton Wirral 81 L7
Clavelshay Somset 19 J8
Claverdon Warwks 59 J11
Claverham N Som 31 N11
Clavering Essex 51 L4
Claverley Shrops 57 P6
Claverton BaNES 20 E2
Claverton Down BaNES 20 E2
Clawdd-coch V Glam 30 E9
Clawdd-newydd Denbgs 68 E4
Clawthorpe Cumb 95 L5
Clawton Devon 5 P2
Claxby Lincs 86 F2
Claxby Lincs 87 N6
Claxton N York 98 D9
Claxton Norfk 77 L11
Claybrooke Magna Leics 59 Q7
Clay Common Suffk 65 P5
Clay Coton Nhants 60 C5
Clay Cross Derbys 84 E8
Claydon Oxon 48 E5
Claydon Suffk 53 K2
Clay End Herts 50 H6
Claygate D & G 110 G5
Claygate Kent 26 B3
Claygate Surrey 36 E8
Claygate Cross Kent 37 P9
Clayhall Gt Lon 37 K2
Clayhanger Devon 18 D10
Clayhanger Wsall 58 F4
Clayhidon Devon 18 G11
Clayhill E Susx 26 D7
Clayhill Hants 13 P3
Clayhithe Cambs 62 H8
Clayock Highld 167 L5
Claypit Hill Cambs 62 E10
Claypits Gloucs 32 E3
Claypole Lincs 85 P11
Claythorpe Lincs 87 M5
Clayton C Brad 90 E4
Clayton Donc 91 M9
Clayton W Susx 24 G8
Clayton Green Lancs 88 H6
Clayton-le-Moors Lancs 89 M4
Clayton-le-Woods Lancs 88 H6
Clayton West Kirk 90 H8
Clayworth Notts 85 M3
Cleadale Highld 144 G10
Cleadon S Tyne 113 N8
Cleadon Park S Tyne 113 N8
Clearbrook Devon 6 E5
Clearwell Gloucs 31 Q3
Cleasby N York 103 Q8
Cleat Ork 169 d8
Cleatlam Dur 103 M7
Cleator Cumb 100 D8
Cleator Moor Cumb 100 D7
Cleckheaton Kirk 90 F5
Cleedownton Shrops 57 K8
Cleehill Shrops 57 K9
Cleekhimin N Lans 126 D6
Clee St Margaret Shrops 57 K8
Cleestanton Shrops 57 K9
Cleethorpes NE Lin 93 P9
Cleeton St Mary Shrops 57 L9
Cleeve N Som 31 N11
Cleeve Oxon 34 H8
Cleeve Hill Gloucs 47 J9
Cleeve Prior Worcs 47 L5
Cleghornie E Loth 128 F3
Clehonger Herefs 45 N7
Cleish P & K 134 D8
Cleland N Lans 126 D6
Clement's End C Beds 50 B8
Clement Street Kent 37 M6
Clenamacrie Ag & B 131 J2
Clench Common Wilts 33 N11
Clenchwarton Norfk 75 L6
Clenerty Abers 159 J5
Clent Worcs 58 D9
Cleobury Mortimer Shrops 57 M9
Cleobury North Shrops 57 L7
Cleongart Ag & B 120 C5
Clephanton Highld 156 E7
Clerkhill D & G 117 K11
Clevancy Wilts 33 L9
Clevedon N Som 31 M10
Cleveley Oxon 48 C10
Cleveleys Lancs 88 C2
Cleverton Wilts 33 J7
Clewer Somset 19 M4
Cley next the Sea Norfk 76 E3
Cliburn Cumb 101 Q6
Cliddesden Hants 22 H5
Cliff Warwks 59 K5
Cliffe Lancs 89 L4
Cliffe Medway 38 B6
Cliffe N York 91 R4
Cliffe N York 103 P7
Cliff End E Susx 26 E9
Cliffe Woods Medway 38 B7
Clifford Herefs 45 J5
Clifford Leeds 91 L2
Clifford Chambers Warwks 47 M4
Clifford's Mesne Gloucs 46 D10
Cliffsend Kent 39 P9
Clifton Bristl 31 Q7
Clifton C Beds 50 E3
Clifton C Nott 72 F4

Clifton C York 98 B10
Clifton Calder 90 F6
Clifton Cumb 101 P5
Clifton Derbys 71 M6
Clifton Devon 17 L3
Clifton Donc 91 N11
Clifton Lancs 88 F4
Clifton N York 97 J11
Clifton Nthumb 113 K4
Clifton Oxon 48 E4
Clifton Salfd 82 G4
Clifton Worcs 46 F5
Clifton Campville Staffs 59 L2
Clifton Hampden Oxon 34 F5
Clifton Reynes M Keyn 49 P4
Clifton upon Dunsmore
  Warwks 60 B5
Clifton upon Teme Worcs 46 D2
Cliftonville Kent 39 Q7
Climping W Susx 15 Q6
Clink Somset 20 E5
Clint N York 97 L9
Clinterty C Aber 151 L5
Clint Green Norfk 76 E9
Clintmains Border 118 B4
Clipiau Gwynd 55 J2
Clippesby Norfk 77 N9
Clipsham Rutlnd 73 P7
Clipston Nhants 60 F4
Clipston Notts 72 G4
Clipstone C Beds 49 P9
Clipstone Notts 85 J8
Clitheroe Lancs 89 L2
Clive Shrops 69 P10
Clivocast Shet 169 s3
Clixby Lincs 93 J10
Cloatley Wilts 33 J6
Clocaenog Denbgs 68 E4
Clochan Moray 158 B5
Clock Face St Hel 82 B6
Cloddiau Powys 56 C3
Clodock Herefs 45 L9
Cloford Somset 20 D6
Clola Abers 159 P9
Clophill C Beds 50 C3
Clopton Nhants 61 N4
Clopton Suffk 65 J11
Clopton Corner Suffk 65 J11
Clopton Green Suffk 63 N10
Clopton Green Suffk 64 D10
Clos du Valle Guern 10 c1
Closeburn D & G 109 J2
Closeburnmill D & G 109 K2
Closeclark IoM 80 c6
Closworth Somset 11 M2
Clothall Herts 50 G4
Clotton Ches W 69 P2
Cloudesley Bush Warwks 59 Q6
Clouds Herefs 46 A7
Clough Oldham 89 Q9
Clough Foot Calder 89 Q6
Clough Head Calder 90 D7
Cloughton N York 99 L2
Cloughton Newlands N York ..105 R11
Clousta Shet 169 q8
Clova Angus 142 E3
Clovelly Devon 16 E7
Clovenfords Border 117 P3
Clovulin Highld 139 J5
Clow Bridge Lancs 89 N5
Clowne Derbys 84 G5
Clows Top Worcs 57 N10
Cloy Wrexhm 69 L6
Cluanie Inn Highld 146 D5
Cluanie Lodge Highld 146 D5
Clubworthy Cnwll 5 M3
Clugston D & G 107 L6
Clun Shrops 56 F8
Clunas Highld 156 F8
Clunbury Shrops 56 F8
Clunderwen Carmth 41 M7
Clune Highld 148 D2
Clunes Highld 146 F10
Clungunford Shrops 56 F9
Clunie P & K 141 R9
Clunton Shrops 56 F8
Cluny P & K 134 G8
Clutton BaNES 20 B3
Clutton Ches W 69 N4
Clutton Hill BaNES 20 B3
Clwt Conwy 68 C2
Clwt-y-bont Gwynd 67 K2
Clydach Mons 30 H3
Clydach Swans 29 J4
Clydach Vale Rhondd 30 C6
Clydebank W Duns 125 M3
Clydey Pembks 41 Q3
Clyffe Pypard Wilts 33 L9
Clynder Ag & B 131 Q11
Clyne Neath 29 M4
Clynnog Fawr Gwynd 66 G5
Clyro Powys 45 J5
Clyst Honiton Devon 9 N6
Clyst Hydon Devon 9 N5
Clyst St George Devon 9 N7
Clyst St Lawrence Devon 9 N5
Clyst St Mary Devon 9 N6
Cnoc W Isls 168 j4
Cnwch Coch Cerdgn 54 F10
Coad's Green Cnwll 5 M6
Coal Aston Derbys 84 E5
Coalbrookvale Blae G 30 G3
Coalburn S Lans 126 E11
Coalburns Gatesd 112 H8
Coaley Gloucs 32 E4
Coalhill Essex 38 C2
Coalmoor Wrekin 57 M3
Coalpit Heath S Glos 32 C8
Coal Pool Wsall 58 F4
Coalport Wrekin 57 N4
Coalsnaughton Clacks 133 Q8
Coal Street Suffk 65 J7
Coaltown of Balgonie Fife 134 H8
Coaltown of Wemyss Fife 135 J8
Coalville Leics 72 C8
Coanwood Nthumb 111 N9
Coat Somset 19 N10
Coatbridge N Lans 126 C4
Coatdyke N Lans 126 C4
Coate Swindn 33 N8
Coate Wilts 21 K2
Coates Cambs 74 F11
Coates Gloucs 33 J4
Coates Lincs 86 B4
Coates Notts 85 P4
Coates W Susx 23 Q11

Coatham R & Cl 104 G5
Coatham Mundeville Darltn ..103 Q6
Cobbaton Devon 17 L6
Coberley Gloucs 47 J11
Cobhall Common Herefs 45 P7
Cobham Kent 37 Q7
Cobham Surrey 36 D8
Cobham Services Surrey 36 D9
Coblers Green Essex 51 Q7
Cobley Dorset 21 K10
Cobnash Herefs 45 P2
Cobo Guern 10 b1
Cobridge C Stke 70 F5
Coburby Abers 159 M5
Cockayne N York 104 H11
Cockayne Hatley C Beds 62 C11
Cock Bank Wrexhm 69 L5
Cock Bevington Warwks 47 L4
Cock Bridge Abers 149 P6
Cockburnspath Border 129 K5
Cock Clarks Essex 52 D11
Cock & End Suffk 63 M10
Cockenzie and Port Seton
  E Loth 128 C4
Cocker Bar Lancs 88 G5
Cocker Brook Lancs 89 L5
Cockerham Lancs 95 K10
Cockermouth Cumb 100 F4
Cockernhoe Herts 50 D6
Cockersdale Leeds 90 G5
Cockett Swans 28 G5
Cockfield Dur 103 M6
Cockfield Suffk 64 C11
Cockfosters Gt Lon 50 G11
Cock Green Essex 51 Q7
Cocking W Susx 23 N11
Cocking Causeway W Susx 23 N11
Cockington Torbay 7 M6
Cocklake Somset 19 M5
Cockley Beck Cumb 100 H10
Cockley Cley Norfk 75 Q10
Cock Marling E Susx 26 E8
Cockpole Green Wokham 35 L8
Cocks Cnwll 3 K3
Cockshutford Shrops 57 K7
Cockshutt Shrops 69 M9
Cock Street Kent 38 C11
Cockthorpe Norfk 76 D3
Cockwells Cnwll 2 E7
Cockwood Devon 9 N8
Cockwood Somset 18 H6
Cockyard Herefs 45 N8
Cockyard Herefs 64 C11
Coddenham Suffk 64 C11
Coddington Ches W 69 N3
Coddington Herefs 46 D6
Coddington Notts 85 P10
Codford St Mary Wilts 21 J7
Codford St Peter Wilts 21 J7
Codicote Herts 50 F7
Codmore Hill W Susx 24 C6
Codnor Derbys 84 F11
Codrington S Glos 32 D9
Codsall Staffs 58 C4
Codsall Wood Staffs 58 B4
Coed Darcy Neath 29 K5
Coedely Rhondd 30 D7
Coed Hirwaun Neath 29 M8
Coed Morgan Mons 31 L2
Coedpoeth Wrexhm 69 J4
Coed Talon Flints 69 J3
Coedway Powys 69 K11
Coed-y-Bryn Cerdgn 42 G5
Coed-y-caerau Newpt 31 L7
Coed-y-Cwm Rhondd 30 D6
Coed-y-paen Mons 31 K5
Coed-yr-ynys Powys 44 H10
Coed Ystumgwern Gwynd 67 K10
Coelbren Powys 29 N2
Coffinswell Devon 7 M5
Coffle End Bed 61 M9
Cofton Devon 9 N8
Cofton Hackett Worcs 58 F9
Cogan V Glam 30 G10
Cogenhoe Nhants 60 H8
Cogges Oxon 34 C3
Coggeshall Essex 52 E7
Coggin's Mill E Susx 25 N5
Coignafearn Highld 148 C3
Coilacriech Abers 149 Q8
Coilantogle Stirlg 132 H6
Coillore Highld 152 F10
Coity Brdgnd 29 P8
Col W Isls 168 j4
Colaboll Highld 162 F4
Colan Cnwll 4 D9
Colaton Raleigh Devon 10 B7
Colbost Highld 152 C8
Colburn N York 103 N11
Colby Cumb 102 C6
Colby IoM 80 b7
Colby Norfk 77 J5
Colchester Essex 52 G6
Colchester Zoo Essex 52 G7
Cold Ash W Berk 34 F11
Cold Ashby Nhants 60 E5
Cold Ashton S Glos 32 D10
Cold Aston Gloucs 47 M11
Coldbackie Highld 165 P4
Coldbeck Cumb 102 D10
Cold Blow Pembks 41 M8
Cold Brayfield M Keyn 49 P4
Cold Cotes N York 95 Q6
Coldeast Devon 7 L4
Colden Calder 90 B5
Colden Common Hants 22 E10
Coldfair Green Suffk 65 N9
Coldham Cambs 74 H10
Cold Hanworth Lincs 86 D4
Coldharbour Cnwll 3 J5
Coldharbour Devon 9 Q2
Coldharbour Gloucs 31 Q4
Cold Harbour Oxon 34 H9
Coldharbour Surrey 24 D2
Cold Hatton Wrekin 70 A10
Cold Hatton Heath Wrekin 70 A10
Cold Hesledon Dur 113 P11
Cold Hiendley Wakefd 91 K8
Cold Higham Nhants 49 J4
Coldingham Border 129 N6
Cold Kirby N York 98 A4
Coldmeece Staffs 70 F8

Cold Newton Leics ....73 L...
Cold Northcott Cnwll ....5 L...
Cold Norton Essex ....52 E...
Cold Overton Leics ....73 L...
Coldred Kent ....27 N...
Coldridge Devon ....17 M1...
Coldstream Border ....118 E...
Coldwaltham W Susx ....24 B...
Coldwell Herefs ....45 N...
Coldwells Abers 159 N11
Cold Weston Shrops ....57 K...
Cole Somset ....20 C...
Colebatch Shrops ....56 E...
Colebrook C Plym ....6 E...
Colebrook Devon ....9 N...
Colebrooke Devon ....9 J...
Coleby Lincs ....86 C...
Coleby N Linc ....92 F...
Cole End Warwks ....59 K...
Coleford Devon ....9 J...
Coleford Gloucs ....31 Q...
Coleford Somset ....20 D...
Coleford Water Somset ....18 F...
Colegate End Norfk ....64 H...
Cole Green Herts 50 G7
Cole Green Herts ....51 J...
Cole Henley Hants ....22 D...
Colehill Dorset ....12 H...
Coleman Green Herts ....50 E...
Coleman's Hatch E Susx ....25 L...
Colemere Shrops ....69 M...
Colemore Hants ....23 K...
Colemore Green Shrops ....57 N...
Colenden P & K ....134 E...
Coleorton Leics ....72 C...
Colerne Wilts ....32 F1...
Colesbourne Gloucs ....33 K...
Cole's Cross Devon ....7 K...
Coles Cross Dorset ....10 H...
Colesden Bed ....61 M...
Coles Green Suffk ....53 J...
Coleshill Bucks ....35 Q...
Coleshill Oxon ....33 Q...
Coleshill Warwks ....59 K...
Colestocks Devon ....10 B...
Coley BaNES ....19 P...
Colgate W Susx ....24 E...
Colinsburgh Fife ....135 L...
Colinton C Edin ....127 N...
Colintraive Ag & B ....124 C...
Colkirk Norfk ....76 C...
Coll Ag & B ....136 D...
Coll W Isls 168 j4
Collace P & K ....142 C1...
Collafirth Shet ....169 q...
Coll Airport Ag & B ....136 ...
Collaton Devon ....7 J1...
Collaton St Mary Torbay ....7 M...
College of Roseisle Moray .....157 M...
College Town Br For ....23 N...
Collessie Fife ....134 ...
Collier Row Gt Lon ....37 M...
Collier's End Herts ....51 J...
Collier's Green E Susx ....26 C...
Colliers Green Kent ....26 C...
Collier Street Kent ....26 B...
Colliery Row Sundld ....113 M1...
Collieston Abers ....151 P...
Collin D & G ....109 M...
Collingbourne Ducis Wilts .....21 P...
Collingbourne Kingston
  Wilts ....21 P...
Collingham Leeds ....97 N1...
Collingham Notts ....85 P...
Collington Herefs ....46 C...
Collingtree Nhants ....60 G...
Collins Green Warrtn ....82 C...
Collins Green Worcs ....46 D...
Colliston Angus ....143 L...
Colliton Devon ....10 B...
Collyweston Nhants ....73 P...
Colmonell S Ayrs ....114 B1...
Colmworth Bed ....61 P...
Colnabaichin Abers ....149 P...
Colnbrook Slough ....36 B...
Colne Cambs ....62 E...
Colne Lancs ....89 P...
Colne Bridge Kirk ....90 F...
Colne Edge Lancs ....89 P...
Colne Engaine Essex ....52 D...
Colney Norfk ....76 H1...
Colney Heath Herts ....50 E...
Colney Street Herts ....50 D1...
Coln Rogers Gloucs ....33 M...
Coln St Aldwyns Gloucs ....33 M...
Coln St Dennis Gloucs ....33 M...
Colonsay Ag & B ....136 ...
Colonsay Airport Ag & B ....136 ...
Colpy Abers ....158 F...
Colquhar Border ....117 ...
Colquite Cnwll ....4 ...
Colscott Devon ....16 ...
Colsterdale N York ....96 ...
Colsterworth Lincs ....73 N...
Colston Bassett Notts ....73 ...
Coltfield Moray ....157 M...
Colt Hill Hants ....23 J...
Coltishall Norfk ....77 K...
Colton Cumb ....94 G...
Colton Leeds ....91 L...
Colton N York ....91 N...
Colton Norfk ....76 H...
Colton Staffs ....71 J1...
Colt's Hill Kent ....25 P...
Columbjohn Devon ....9 M...
Colva Powys ....44 G...
Colvend D & G ....109 J...
Colwall Herefs ....46 E...
Colworth W Susx ....15 P...
Colwyn Bay Conwy ....80 B...
Colyford Devon ....10 E...
Colyton Devon ....10 E...
Combe Devon ....7 J...
Combe Herefs ....45 L...
Combe Oxon ....48 C...
Combe W Berk ....22 B...
Combe Almer Dorset ....12 F...
Combe Common Surrey ....23 P...
Combe Down BaNES ....20 E...
Combe Fishacre Devon ....7 L...
Combe Florey Somset ....18 F...

Combe Hay BaNES 20 D3
Combeinteignhead Devon 7 N4
Combe Martin Devon 17 K2
Combe Raleigh Devon 10 D4
Comberbach Ches W 82 D9
Comberford Staffs 59 J3
Comberton Cambs 62 E9
Comberton Herefs 56 H11
Combe St Nicholas Somset 10 G2
Combpyne Devon 10 F6
Combridge Staffs 71 K7
Combrook Warwks 48 B4
Combs Derbys 83 M9
Combs Suffk 64 E10
Combs Ford Suffk 64 E10
Combwich Somset 19 J6
Comers Abers 150 H6
Comeytrowe Somset 18 H10
Comhampton Worcs 58 B11
Commercial End Cambs 63 J8
Commins Coch Powys 55 J4
Commondale N York 105 J8
Common Edge Bpool 88 C4
Common End Cumb 100 D6
Common Moor Cnwll 5 L8
Common Platt Wilts 33 M7
Commonside Ches W 82 B10
Commonside Derbys 71 N6
Common Side Derbys 84 D5
Commonwood Shrops 69 N9
Commonwood Wrexhm 69 L4
Compass Somset 19 J8
Compstall Stockp 83 L6
Compton Devon 7 M6
Compton Hants 22 C9
Compton Hants 22 E9
Compton Staffs 57 Q8
Compton Surrey 23 Q5
Compton W Berk 34 F8
Compton W Susx 15 L4
Compton Wilts 21 M4
Compton Abbas Dorset 20 G11
Compton Abdale Gloucs 47 L11
Compton Bassett Wilts 33 K10
Compton Beauchamp Oxon 33 Q7
Compton Bishop Somset 19 L3
Compton Chamberlayne Wilts 21 K9
Compton Dando BaNES 20 B2
Compton Dundon Somset 19 N8
Compton Durville Somset 19 M11
Compton Greenfield S Glos 31 Q8
Compton Martin BaNES 19 P3
Compton Pauncefoot Somset 20 B9
Compton Valence Dorset 11 M6
Comrie Fife 134 C10
Comrie P & K 133 M3
Conaglen House Highld 139 J4
Conchra Highld 145 Q2
Concraigie P & K 141 Q9
Conder Green Lancs 95 K9
Conderton Worcs 47 J7
Condicote Gloucs 47 N9
Condorrat N Lans 126 C3
Condover Shrops 56 H3
Coney Hill Gloucs 46 G11
Coneyhurst W Susx 24 D6
Coneysthorpe N York 98 E6
Coneythorpe N York 97 N9
Coney Weston Suffk 64 D6
Conford Hants 23 M8
Congdon's Shop Cnwll 5 M6
Congerstone Leics 72 B9
Congham Norfk 75 P6
Congleton Ches E 70 F2
Congl-y-wal Gwynd 67 N6
Congresbury N Som 19 M2
Congreve Staffs 58 D2
Conheath D & G 109 L7
Conicavel Moray 156 H7
Coningsby Lincs 86 H9
Conington Cambs 61 Q3
Conington Cambs 62 D7
Conisbrough Donc 91 N11
Conisholme Lincs 93 R11
Coniston Cumb 101 K11
Coniston E R Yk 93 L3
Coniston Cold N York 96 D10
Conistone N York 96 E7
Connah's Quay Flints 81 K11
Connel Ag & B 138 G11
Connel Park E Ayrs 115 M5
Connor Downs Cnwll 2 F6
Cononley N York 96 E11
Conon Bridge Highld 155 P6
Cononsyth Angus 143 K8
Consall Staffs 70 H5
Consett Dur 112 H10
Constable Burton N York 97 J2
Constable Lee Lancs 89 N6
Constantine Cnwll 3 J8
Constantine Bay Cnwll 3 D7
Contin Highld 155 N6
Conwy Conwy 79 P9
Conwy Castle Conwy 79 P9
Conyer Kent 38 G9
Conyer's Green Suffk 64 B8
Cooden E Susx 26 B10
Cookbury Devon 16 G10
Cookbury Wick Devon 16 F10
Cookham W & M 35 N7
Cookham Dean W & M 35 N7
Cookham Rise W & M 35 N7
Cookhill Worcs 47 L3
Cookley Suffk 65 L6
Cookley Worcs 58 B8
Cookley Green Oxon 35 J6
Cookney Abers 151 M9
Cooksbridge E Susx 25 K8
Cooksey Green Worcs 58 D11
Cook's Green Essex 53 L8
Cooks Green Suffk 64 D11
Cookshill Staffs 70 G6
Cooksland Cnwll 4 H8
Cooksmill Green Essex 51 P9
Cookson Green Ches W 82 C10
Coolham W Susx 24 D6
Cooling Medway 38 C7
Cooling Street Medway 38 B7
Cooling Cnwll 2 L5
Coombe Cnwll 3 L5
Coombe Cnwll 3 N3
Coombe Devon 7 N4
Coombe Devon 9 K8
Coombe Devon 10 C6

Coombe Gloucs 32 E6
Coombe Hants 23 J10
Coombe Wilts 21 M4
Coombe Bissett Wilts 21 M9
Coombe Cellars Devon 7 N4
Coombe Cross Hants 23 J10
Coombe Hill Gloucs 46 G9
Coombe Keynes Dorset 12 D8
Coombe Pafford Torbay 7 N5
Coombes W Susx 24 E9
Coombes-Moor Herefs 45 M2
Coombe Street Somset 20 E8
Coombeswood Dudley 58 E7
Coopersale Common Essex 51 L10
Coopersale Street Essex 51 L10
Cooper's Corner Kent 37 L11
Coopers Green E Susx 25 L6
Coopers Green Herts 50 E9
Cooper Street Kent 39 P9
Cooper Turning Bolton 89 J9
Cootham W Susx 24 C8
Copdock Suffk 53 K3
Copford Green Essex 52 F7
Copgrove N York 97 M8
Copister Shet 169 r6
Cople Bed 61 P11
Copley Calder 90 D6
Copley Dur 103 L5
Copley Tamesd 83 L5
Coplow Dale Derbys 83 Q9
Copmanthorpe C York 98 B11
Copmere End Staffs 70 E3
Copp Lancs 88 E3
Coppathorne Cnwll 16 C11
Coppenhall Staffs 70 G11
Coppenhall Moss Ches E 70 C3
Copperhouse Cnwll 2 F6
Coppicegate Shrops 57 N8
Coppingford Cambs 61 Q5
Coppins Corner Kent 26 F2
Copplestone Devon 9 J4
Coppull Lancs 88 H8
Coppull Moor Lancs 88 H8
Copsale W Susx 24 E6
Copster Green Lancs 89 K4
Copston Magna Warwks 59 Q7
Cop Street Kent 39 N9
Copthall Green Essex 51 K10
Copt Heath Solhll 59 J9
Copt Hewick N York 97 M6
Copthorne Cnwll 5 M5
Copthorne W Susx 24 H3
Copt Oak Leics 72 D8
Copy's Green Norfk 76 C4
Copythorne Hants 13 P2
Coram Street Suffk 52 H3
Corbets Tey Gt Lon 37 N3
Corbière Jersey 11 a2
Corbridge Nthumb 112 E8
Corby Nhants 61 J3
Corby Glen Lincs 73 Q6
Corby Hill Cumb 111 Q9
Cordon N Ayrs 121 K5
Cordwell Derbys 84 D5
Coreley Shrops 57 L10
Cores End Bucks 35 P7
Corfe Somset 18 H11
Corfe Castle Dorset 12 G8
Corfe Mullen Dorset 12 G5
Corfton Shrops 56 H7
Corgarff Abers 149 P6
Corhampton Hants 22 H10
Corks Pond Kent 25 Q2
Corlae D & G 115 N8
Corley Warwks 59 M7
Corley Ash Warwks 59 L7
Corley Moor Warwks 59 L8
Corley Services Warwks 59 M7
Cormuir Angus 142 E4
Cornard Tye Suffk 52 F3
Corndon Devon 8 E4
Corner Row Lancs 88 E4
Corney Cumb 94 C2
Cornforth Dur 104 B4
Cornhill Abers 158 E6
Cornhill-on-Tweed Nthumb 118 D3
Cornholme Calder 89 Q5
Cornish Hall End Essex 51 Q3
Cornoigmore Ag & B 136 B6
Cornriggs Dur 102 F2
Cornsay Dur 103 M2
Cornsay Colliery Dur 103 N2
Corntown Highld 155 Q6
Corntown V Glam 29 P9
Cornwall Airport Newquay Cnwll 4 D9
Cornwood Oxon 47 Q9
Cornwood Devon 6 G7
Cornworthy Devon 7 L7
Corpach Highld 139 K2
Corpusty Norfk 76 G6
Corrachree Abers 150 D7
Corran Highld 139 J5
Corran Highld 145 P6
Corrany IoM 80 g4
Corrie N Ayrs 121 K3
Corrie D & G 110 D3
Corrie N Ayrs 121 K3
Corriecravie N Ayrs 120 H7
Corriegills N Ayrs 121 K4
Corriegour Lodge Hotel Highld 146 H9
Corriemoille Highld 155 L5
Corrimony Highld 155 L11
Corringham Lincs 85 Q2
Corringham Thurr 38 B5
Corris Gwynd 54 H3
Corris Uchaf Gwynd 54 G3
Corrow Ag & B 131 P2
Corry Highld 145 K3
Corscombe Devon 8 E4
Corscombe Dorset 11 L3
Corse Gloucs 46 E9
Corse Lawn Gloucs 46 F8
Corsham Wilts 32 G10
Corsindae Abers 150 H6
Corsley Wilts 20 F5
Corsley Heath Wilts 20 F5
Corsock D & G 108 G5
Corston BaNES 32 C11
Corston Wilts 32 H8
Corstorphine C Edin 127 M3
Cors-y-Gedol Gwynd 67 L10
Cortachy Angus 142 F6
Corton Suffk 65 Q2
Corton Wilts 20 H6
Corton Denham Somset 20 B10

Coruanan Highld 139 K4
Corwen Denbgs 68 E6
Coryates Dorset 11 N7
Coryton Devon 8 C8
Coryton Thurr 38 B5
Cosby Leics 72 E11
Coseley Dudley 58 D6
Cosford Shrops 57 Q3
Cosgrove Nhants 49 L6
Cosham C Port 15 J5
Cosheston Pembks 41 K10
Coshieville P & K 141 J8
Cossall Notts 72 D2
Cossall Marsh Notts 72 D2
Cossington Leics 72 G8
Cossington Somset 19 L6
Costessey Norfk 76 H9
Costock Notts 72 F5
Coston Leics 73 L6
Coston Norfk 76 F10
Cote Oxon 34 C4
Cote Somset 19 K6
Cotebrook Ches W 82 C11
Cotehill Cumb 111 J10
Cotes Cumb 95 K3
Cotes Leics 72 F6
Cotes Staffs 70 E8
Cotesbach Leics 60 B4
Cotes Heath Staffs 70 E8
Cotford St Luke Somset 18 G9
Cotgrave Notts 72 G3
Cothal Abers 151 M4
Cotham Notts 85 N11
Cothelstone Somset 18 G8
Cotherstone Dur 103 K7
Cothill Oxon 34 E5
Cotleigh Devon 10 E4
Cotmanhay Derbys 72 D2
Coton Cambs 62 F9
Coton Nhants 60 E6
Coton Shrops 69 P8
Coton Staffs 59 J4
Coton Staffs 70 E10
Coton Staffs 70 H8
Coton Clanford Staffs 70 F10
Coton Hayes Staffs 70 H8
Coton Hill Shrops 56 H2
Coton in the Clay Staffs 71 M9
Coton in the Elms Derbys 71 N11
Coton Park Derbys 71 P11
Cotswold Airport Wilts 33 J5
Cotswolds 33 J3
Cotswold Wildlife Park & Gardens Oxon 33 P3
Cott Devon 7 K6
Cottam E R Yk 99 K7
Cottam Lancs 88 G4
Cottam Notts 85 P5
Cottenham Cambs 62 F7
Cotterdale N York 96 B2
Cottered Herts 50 H5
Cotteridge Birm 58 F8
Cotterstock Nhants 61 M2
Cottesbrooke Nhants 60 F6
Cottesmore Rutlnd 73 N8
Cottingham E R Yk 92 H4
Cottingham Nhants 60 H2
Cottingley C Brad 90 E3
Cottisford Oxon 48 G8
Cotton Suffk 64 F8
Cotton End Bed 61 N11
Cotton Tree Lancs 89 Q3
Cottown Abers 150 E2
Cottown Abers 151 K4
Cottown of Gight Abers 159 K9
Cotts Devon 6 C5
Cotwall Wrekin 69 R11
Cotwalton Staffs 70 G8
Couch's Mill Cnwll 5 J10
Coughton Herefs 46 A10
Coughton Warwks 47 L2
Coulaghailtro Ag & B 123 M6
Coulags Highld 154 C9
Coulby Newham Middsb 104 F8
Coulderton Cumb 100 C9
Coull Abers 150 E7
Coulport Ag & B 131 Q10
Coulsdon Gt Lon 36 G9
Coulston Wilts 21 J4
Coulter S Lans 116 E4
Coultershaw Bridge W Susx 23 Q11
Coultings Somset 18 H6
Coulton N York 98 C6
Coultra Fife 135 K3
Cound Shrops 57 K3
Coundlane Shrops 57 K3
Coundon Dur 103 P5
Coundon Grange Dur 103 P5
Countersett N York 96 D3
Countess Wilts 21 N6
Countess Cross Essex 52 E5
Countess Wear Devon 9 M7
Countesswells C Aber 151 M7
Countesthorpe Leics 72 F11
Countisbury Devon 17 N2
Coupar Angus P & K 142 C10
Coupe Green Lancs 88 H5
Coupland Cumb 102 D7
Coupland Nthumb 118 H4
Cour Ag & B 123 P10
Court-at-Street Kent 27 J4
Courteachan Highld 145 L4
Courteenhall Nhants 49 L4
Court Henry Carmth 43 L10
Courtsend Essex 38 H3
Courtway Somset 18 H8
Cousland Mdloth 128 B6
Cousley Wood E Susx 25 Q4
Cove Ag & B 131 Q11
Cove Border 129 K5
Cove Devon 18 C11
Cove Hants 23 N3
Cove Highld 160 C8
Cove Bay C Aber 151 P7
Cove Bottom Suffk 65 P6
Covehithe Suffk 65 Q5
Coven Staffs 58 D3
Coveney Cambs 62 G4
Covenham St Bartholomew Lincs 87 K2
Covenham St Mary Lincs 87 K2
Coven Heath Staffs 58 D3
Coventry Covtry 59 M9
Coverack Cnwll 3 K10
Coverack Bridges Cnwll 2 H7
Coverham N York 96 H3

Covington Cambs 61 N6
Covington S Lans 116 D3
Cowan Bridge Lancs 95 N5
Cowbeech E Susx 25 P8
Cowbit Lincs 74 E7
Cowbridge V Glam 30 C10
Cowdale Derbys 83 N10
Cowden Kent 25 L2
Cowdenbeath Fife 134 F9
Cowden Pound Kent 25 L2
Cowden Station Kent 25 L2
Cowers Lane Derbys 71 Q5
Cowes IoW 14 E7
Cowesby N York 97 Q3
Cowesfield Green Wilts 21 Q10
Cowfold W Susx 24 F6
Cowgill Cumb 95 R3
Cow Green Suffk 64 F8
Cowhill S Glos 32 B6
Cowie Stirlg 133 N10
Cowlam E R Yk 99 K7
Cowley Devon 9 M5
Cowley Gloucs 33 J2
Cowley Gt Lon 36 C4
Cowley Oxon 34 F4
Cowling Lancs 88 H7
Cowling N York 90 B2
Cowling N York 97 K3
Cowlinge Suffk 63 M10
Cowmes Kirk 90 F7
Cowpe Lancs 89 N6
Cowpen Nthumb 113 L4
Cowpen Bewley S on T 104 E6
Cowplain Hants 15 J4
Cowshill Dur 102 G2
Cowslip Green N Som 19 N2
Cowthorpe N York 97 P10
Coxall Herefs 56 F10
Coxbank Ches E 70 B6
Coxbench Derbys 72 B2
Coxbridge Somset 19 P7
Cox Common Suffk 65 N5
Coxford Cnwll 5 K2
Coxford Norfk 76 B6
Coxgreen Staffs 57 Q7
Coxheath Kent 38 B11
Coxhoe Dur 104 B3
Coxley Somset 19 P6
Coxley Wakefd 90 H7
Coxley Wick Somset 19 P6
Coxpark Cnwll 5 Q7
Coxtie Green Essex 51 N11
Coxwold N York 98 A5
Coychurch Brdgnd 29 P9
Coylton S Ayrs 114 H4
Coylumbridge Highld 148 G5
Coytrahen Brdgnd 29 N7
Crabbs Cross Worcs 58 F11
Crab Orchard Dorset 13 J3
Crabtree W Susx 24 F5
Crabtree Green Wrexhm 69 K6
Crackenthorpe Cumb 102 C6
Crackington Haven Cnwll 5 J2
Crackley Staffs 70 E4
Crackley Warwks 59 L10
Crackleybank Shrops 57 P2
Crackpot N York 103 J11
Cracoe N York 96 E8
Craddock Devon 10 B2
Cradle End Herts 51 L6
Cradley Dudley 58 D7
Cradley Herefs 46 D5
Cradley Heath Sandw 58 D7
Cradoc Powys 44 E8
Crafthole Cnwll 5 P11
Crafton Bucks 49 N11
Crag Foot Lancs 95 K6
Craggan Highld 149 J2
Cragganmore Moray 157 M10
Cragg Hill Leeds 90 G3
Cragg Vale Calder 90 C6
Craghead Dur 113 K10
Cragside House & Garden Nthumb 119 L10
Crai Powys 44 B10
Craibstone Moray 158 C6
Craichie Angus 143 J8
Craig Angus 143 M6
Craig Highld 154 D8
Craigbank E Ayrs 115 L5
Craigburn Border 127 N7
Craig-cefn-parc Swans 29 J4
Craigcleuch D & G 110 F3
Craigdam Abers 159 K11
Craigdhu Ag & B 130 G6
Craigearn Abers 151 J5
Craigellachie Moray 157 P9
Craigend P & K 134 E2
Craigend Rens 125 M3
Craigendoran Ag & B 132 C11
Craigends Rens 125 L4
Craighlaw D & G 107 K5
Craighouse Ag & B 122 H6
Craigie P & K 141 R9
Craigie S Ayrs 125 L11
Craigiefold Abers 159 M4
Craigley D & G 108 G9
Craig Llangiwg Neath 29 K4
Craiglockhart C Edin 127 N3
Craigmillar C Edin 127 Q3
Craignant Shrops 69 J7
Craigneston D & G 115 Q10
Craigneuk N Lans 126 D4
Craigneuk N Lans 126 D6
Craignure Ag & B 138 C10
Craigo Angus 143 M5
Craig Penllyn V Glam 30 C9
Craigrothie Fife 135 K5
Craigruie Stirlg 132 F3
Craig's End Essex 52 B4
Craigton Angus 143 J10
Craigton C Aber 151 L7
Craigton E Rens 125 M7
Craigton of Airlie Angus 142 E7
Craig-y-Duke Neath 29 K4
Craig-y-nos Powys 44 A11
Craik Border 117 L9
Crail Fife 135 Q6
Crailing Border 118 C6
Craiselound N Linc 92 C11
Crakehall N York 97 K3
Crakehill N York 97 P6
Crakemarsh Staffs 71 K7
Crambe N York 98 E8
Crambeck N York 98 E7
Cramlington Nthumb 113 L5

Cramond C Edin 127 M2
Cramond Bridge C Edin 127 M2
Crampmoor Hants 22 C10
Cranage Ches E 82 G11
Cranberry Staffs 70 E7
Cranborne Dorset 13 J2
Cranbourne Br For 35 P10
Cranbrook Devon 9 N6
Cranbrook Kent 26 C4
Cranbrook Common Kent 26 C4
Crane Moor Barns 91 J10
Crane's Corner Norfk 76 C9
Cranfield C Beds 49 Q6
Cranford Devon 16 E7
Cranford Gt Lon 36 D5
Cranford St Andrew Nhants 61 K5
Cranford St John Nhants 61 K5
Cranham Gloucs 32 G2
Cranham Gt Lon 37 N3
Cranhill Warwks 47 M4
Crank St Hel 81 Q5
Cranleigh Surrey 24 C3
Cranmer Green Suffk 64 E7
Cranmore IoW 14 C8
Cranmore Somset 20 C6
Cranoe Leics 73 K11
Cransford Suffk 65 L9
Cranshaws Border 128 H7
Cranstal IoM 80 g1
Cranswick E R Yk 99 L10
Crantock Cnwll 4 B9
Cranwell Lincs 86 D11
Cranwich Norfk 63 N2
Cranworth Norfk 76 D11
Craobh Haven Ag & B 130 F6
Crapstone Devon 6 E5
Crarae Ag & B 131 K8
Crask Inn Highld 162 C2
Crask of Aigas Highld 155 N9
Craster Nthumb 119 Q7
Craswall Herefs 45 K7
Crateford Staffs 58 D3
Cratfield Suffk 65 L6
Crathes Abers 151 K8
Crathie Abers 149 P8
Crathie Highld 147 P9
Crathorne N York 104 D9
Craven Arms Shrops 56 G8
Crawcrook Gatesd 112 H8
Crawford Lancs 81 P4
Crawford S Lans 116 D6
Crawfordjohn S Lans 116 B6
Crawley Hants 22 D8
Crawley Oxon 34 B2
Crawley W Susx 24 G3
Crawley Down W Susx 24 H3
Crawleyside Dur 103 J2
Crawshawbooth Lancs 89 N5
Crawton Abers 143 R2
Craxe's Green Essex 52 F8
Cray N York 96 D5
Cray P & K 142 A5
Crayford Gt Lon 37 M5
Crayke N York 98 B6
Craymere Beck Norfk 76 F5
Crays Hill Essex 38 B3
Cray's Pond Oxon 34 H8
Craythorne Staffs 71 N9
Craze Lowman Devon 9 N2
Crazies Hill Wokhm 35 L8
Creacombe Devon 17 Q8
Creagan Inn Ag & B 138 H9
Creag Ghoraidh W Isls 168 c13
Creagorry W Isls 168 c13
Creaguaineach Lodge Highld 139 Q4
Creamore Bank Shrops 69 P8
Creaton Nhants 60 F6
Creca D & G 110 D6
Credenhill Herefs 45 P6
Crediton Devon 9 K4
Creebank D & G 107 K2
Creebridge D & G 107 M4
Creech Dorset 12 F8
Creech Heathfield Somset 19 J9
Creech St Michael Somset 19 J9
Creed Cnwll 3 N4
Creekmoor BCP 12 H6
Creekmouth Gt Lon 37 L4
Creeksea Essex 38 F2
Creeting St Mary Suffk 64 F10
Creeton Lincs 73 Q6
Creetown D & G 107 N6
Cregneash IoM 80 a8
Creg ny Baa IoM 80 e5
Cregrina Powys 44 G4
Creich Fife 135 J3
Creigiau Cardif 30 E8
Cremyll Cnwll 6 D8
Cressage Shrops 57 K4
Cressbrook Derbys 83 Q10
Cresselly Pembks 41 L9
Cressex Bucks 35 M6
Cressing Essex 52 C7
Cresswell Nthumb 113 L2
Cresswell Pembks 41 L9
Cresswell Staffs 70 H7
Creswell Derbys 84 H6
Creswell Green Staffs 58 G2
Cretingham Suffk 65 J9
Cretshengan Ag & B 123 M6
Crewe Ches E 70 C3
Crewe-by-Farndon Ches W 69 M4
Crewe Green Ches E 70 C3
Crew Green Powys 69 K11
Crewkerne Somset 11 J3
Crews Hill Gt Lon 50 H11
Crewton C Derb 72 B4
Crianlarich Stirlg 132 D2
Cribyn Cerdgn 43 K4
Criccieth Gwynd 66 H7
Crich Derbys 84 D10
Crich Carr Derbys 84 D10
Crichton Mdloth 128 B7
Crick Mons 31 N6
Crick Nhants 60 C6
Crickadarn Powys 44 F6
Cricket St Thomas Somset 10 H3
Crickheath Shrops 69 J11
Crickhowell Powys 45 J11
Cricklade Wilts 33 L6
Cricklewood Gt Lon 36 F3
Cridling Stubbs N York 91 N6
Crieff P & K 133 P3
Criggan Cnwll 4 G9
Criggion Powys 69 J11

Crigglestone Wakefd ...91 J7
Crimble Rochdl ...89 P8
Crimond Abers ...159 Q6
Crimplesham Norfk ...75 N10
Crimscote Warwks ...47 P5
Crinaglack Highld ...155 M9
Crinan Ag & B ...130 F9
Crindledyke N Lans ...126 K6
Cringleford Norfk ...76 H10
Cringles C Brad ...96 F11
Crinow Pembks ...41 M8
Crippleseace Cnwll ...2 E6
Cripplestyle Dorset ...13 J2
Cripp's Corner E Susx ...26 C7
Croachy Highld ...148 B2
Croanford Cnwll ...4 G7
Crockenhill Kent ...37 M7
Crocker End Oxon ...35 K7
Crockerhill W Susx ...15 P5
Crockernwell Devon ...9 J6
Crocker's Ash Herefs ...45 Q11
Crockerton Wilts ...20 G6
Crocketford D & G ...108 H6
Crockey Hill C York ...98 C11
Crockham Hill Kent ...37 K10
Crockhurst Street Kent ...37 P11
Crockleford Heath Essex ...52 H6
Crock Street Somset ...10 G2
Croeserw Neath ...29 N5
Croes-goch Pembks ...40 F4
Croes-lan Cerdgn ...42 G6
Croesor Gwynd ...67 L6
Croesyceiliog Carmth ...42 H11
Croesyceiliog Torfn ...31 K5
Croes-y-mwyalch Torfn ...31 K6
Croes-y-pant Mons ...31 K4
Croft Leics ...72 E11
Croft Lincs ...87 P8
Croft Warrtn ...82 D6
Croftamie Stirlg ...132 F10
Croft Mitchell Cnwll ...2 H6
Crofton Cumb ...110 F10
Crofton Wakefd ...91 K7
Crofton Wilts ...21 Q2
Croft-on-Tees N York ...103 Q9
Croftown Highld ...161 K10
Crofts Moray ...157 P7
Crofts Bank Traffd ...82 G5
Crofts of Dipple Moray ...157 Q6
Crofts of Haddo Abers ...159 K10
Crofts of Savoch Abers ...159 P5
Crofty Swans ...28 F6
Crogen Gwynd ...68 D7
Croggan Ag & B ...130 E2
Croglin Cumb ...111 L11
Croick Highld ...162 B8
Cromarty Highld ...156 D4
Crombie Fife ...134 D11
Cromdale Highld ...149 K2
Cromer Herts ...50 G5
Cromer Norfk ...77 J3
Cromford Derbys ...84 C9
Cromhall S Glos ...32 C6
Cromhall Common S Glos ...32 C7
Cromor W Isls ...168 j5
Cromore W Isls ...168 j5
Crompton Fold Oldham ...89 Q9
Cromwell Notts ...85 N8
Cronberry E Ayrs ...115 M3
Crondall Hants ...23 L5
Cronkbourne IoM ...80 e6
Cronk-y-Voddy IoM ...80 d4
Cronton Knows ...81 P7
Crook Cumb ...101 N11
Crook Dur ...103 N3
Crookdake Cumb ...100 G2
Crooke Wigan ...88 H9
Crooked End Gloucs ...46 B11
Crookedholm E Ayrs ...125 M10
Crooked Soley Wilts ...34 B10
Crookes Sheff ...84 D3
Crookhall Dur ...112 H10
Crookham Nthumb ...118 H3
Crookham W Berk ...22 F2
Crookham Village Hants ...23 L4
Crook Inn Border ...116 G5
Crooklands Cumb ...95 L4
Crook of Devon P & K ...134 C7
Cropper Derbys ...71 N7
Cropredy Oxon ...48 E5
Cropston Leics ...72 F8
Cropthorne Worcs ...47 J5
Cropton N York ...98 F3
Cropwell Bishop Notts ...72 H3
Cropwell Butler Notts ...72 H3
Cros W Isls ...168 k1
Crosbost W Isls ...168 i5
Crosby Cumb ...100 E3
Crosby IoM ...80 d6
Crosby N Linc ...92 E8
Crosby Sefton ...81 L5
Crosby Garret Cumb ...102 D9
Crosby Ravensworth Cumb ...102 B8
Crosby Villa Cumb ...100 E3
Croscombe Somset ...19 Q6
Crosemere Shrops ...69 M9
Crosland Edge Kirk ...90 E8
Crosland Hill Kirk ...90 E8
Cross Somset ...19 M4
Crossaig Ag & B ...123 P9
Crossapol Ag & B ...136 B7
Cross Ash Mons ...45 N11
Cross-at-Hand Kent ...26 C2
Crossbost W Isls ...168 i5
Crossbush W Susx ...24 B9
Crosscanonby Cumb ...100 E3
Cross Coombe Cnwll ...3 J3
Crossdale Street Norfk ...77 J4
Cross End Bed ...61 N9
Cross End Essex ...52 E5
Crossens Sefton ...88 D6
Cross Flatts C Brad ...90 E2
Crossford Fife ...134 D10
Crossford S Lans ...126 E8
Crossgate Cnwll ...5 N4
Crossgate Lincs ...74 D5
Crossgate Staffs ...70 G7
Crossgatehall E Loth ...128 B6
Crossgates E Ayrs ...125 K9
Crossgates Fife ...134 E10
Crossgates N York ...99 L4
Crossgates Powys ...44 F2
Crossgill Lancs ...95 M8
Cross Gates Leeds ...91 K4
Cross Green Devon ...5 P4
Cross Green Leeds ...91 J4

Cross Green Staffs ...58 D3
Cross Green Suffk ...64 A11
Cross Green Suffk ...64 B10
Cross Green Suffk ...64 D11
Cross Hands Carmth ...28 G2
Crosshands Carmth ...41 N6
Crosshands E Ayrs ...125 M11
Cross Hands Pembks ...41 L8
Cross Hill Derbys ...84 F11
Crosshill Fife ...134 F8
Crosshill S Ayrs ...114 F6
Cross Hills N York ...96 F11
Crosshouse E Ayrs ...125 K10
Cross Houses Shrops ...57 J3
Cross Houses Shrops ...57 M6
Cross in Hand E Susx ...25 N6
Cross Inn Cerdgn ...42 G3
Cross Inn Cerdgn ...43 K2
Cross Inn Pembks ...41 M9
Cross Inn Rhondd ...30 E8
Cross Keys Ag & B ...132 C10
Crosskeys Caerph ...30 H6
Cross Keys Wilts ...32 G10
Crosslands Cumb ...94 G3
Cross Lane IoW ...14 F9
Cross Lane Head Shrops ...57 N5
Cross Lanes Cnwll ...2 H9
Cross Lanes Cnwll ...3 K5
Cross Lanes N York ...98 A8
Crosslanes Shrops ...69 K11
Cross Lanes Wrexhm ...69 L5
Crosslee Rens ...125 L4
Crossley Kirk ...90 G6
Crossmichael D & G ...108 F7
Cross Oak Powys ...44 G10
Cross o' th' hands Derbys ...71 P5
Crosspost W Susx ...24 G6
Crossroads Abers ...150 F6
Crossroads Abers ...151 K9
Cross Roads C Brad ...90 D3
Cross Street Suffk ...64 H6
Crosston Angus ...143 J6
Cross Town Ches E ...82 G9
Crossway Mons ...45 N11
Crossway Powys ...44 F3
Crossway Green Mons ...31 P6
Crossway Green Worcs ...58 B11
Crossways Dorset ...12 C7
Crosswell Pembks ...41 M3
Crosthwaite Cumb ...95 J2
Croston Lancs ...88 F7
Crostwick Norfk ...77 K8
Crostwight Norfk ...77 L6
Crouch Kent ...37 P9
Crouch Kent ...39 J10
Crouch End Gt Lon ...36 H3
Croucheston Wilts ...21 L9
Crouch Hill Dorset ...11 Q2
Crough House Green Kent ...37 K11
Croughton Nhants ...48 F8
Crovie Abers ...159 K4
Crow Hants ...13 L4
Crowan Cnwll ...2 G7
Crowborough E Susx ...25 M4
Crowborough Warren E Susx ...25 M4
Crowcombe Somset ...18 F7
Crowdecote Derbys ...83 P11
Crowden Derbys ...83 N5
Crowden Devon ...8 C5
Crowdhill Hants ...22 E10
Crowdleham Kent ...37 N9
Crow Edge Barns ...83 Q4
Crowell Oxon ...35 K5
Crow End Cambs ...62 D9
Crowfield Nhants ...48 H6
Crowfield Suffk ...64 G10
Crowfield Green Suffk ...64 G10
Crowgate Street Norfk ...77 L7
Crow Green Essex ...51 N11
Crowhill E Loth ...129 J5
Crow Hill Herefs ...46 B9
Crowhole Derbys ...84 D5
Crowhurst E Susx ...26 C9
Crowhurst Surrey ...37 J11
Crowhurst Lane End Surrey ...37 J11
Crowland Lincs ...74 D8
Crowland Suffk ...64 E7
Crowlas Cnwll ...2 E8
Crowle N Linc ...92 C8
Crowle Worcs ...46 H3
Crowle Green Worcs ...46 H3
Crowmarsh Gifford Oxon ...34 H7
Crown Corner Suffk ...65 K7
Crownhill C Plym ...6 D7
Crownpits Surrey ...23 Q6
Crownthorpe Norfk ...76 F11
Crowntown Cnwll ...2 G7
Crows-an-Wra Cnwll ...2 B8
Crow's Green Essex ...51 Q5
Crowshill Norfk ...76 D10
Crow's Nest Cnwll ...5 M8
Crowsnest Shrops ...56 F4
Crowthorne Wokam ...23 M2
Crowton Ches W ...82 C10
Croxall Staffs ...59 J2
Croxby Lincs ...93 L11
Croxdale Dur ...103 Q3
Croxden Staffs ...71 K7
Croxley Green Herts ...50 C11
Croxton Cambs ...62 B8
Croxton N Linc ...93 J8
Croxton Norfk ...64 B4
Croxton Norfk ...76 D3
Croxton Staffs ...70 D8
Croxton Green Ches E ...69 Q4
Croxton Kerrial Leics ...73 L5
Croy Highld ...156 D8
Croy N Lans ...126 C2
Croyde Devon ...16 G4
Croyde Bay Devon ...16 G4
Croydon Cambs ...62 D11
Croydon Gt Lon ...36 H7
Crubenmore Highld ...148 B9
Cruckmeole Shrops ...56 G3
Cruckton Shrops ...56 G2
Cruden Bay Abers ...159 Q8
Crudgington Wrekin ...70 A11
Crudie Abers ...159 J6
Crudwell Wilts ...33 J6
Cruft Devon ...8 D5
Crüg Powys ...56 B10

Crugmeer Cnwll ...4 E6
Crugybar Carmth ...43 N7
Crug-y-byddar Powys ...56 B8
Crumlin Caerph ...30 H5
Crumplehorn Cnwll ...5 L11
Crumpsall Manch ...82 H4
Crundale Kent ...27 J2
Crundale Pembks ...41 J7
Crunwere Pembks ...41 N8
Cruwys Morchard Devon ...9 L2
Crux Easton Hants ...22 D3
Cruxton Dorset ...11 N5
Crwbin Carmth ...28 E2
Cryers Hill Bucks ...35 N5
Crymych Pembks ...41 N4
Crynant Neath ...29 L4
Crystal Palace Gt Lon ...36 H6
Cuaig Highld ...153 N6
Cuan Ag & B ...130 F5
Cubbington Warwks ...59 M11
Cubert Cnwll ...4 B10
Cubley Barns ...90 G10
Cublington Bucks ...49 M10
Cublington Herefs ...45 N7
Cuckfield W Susx ...24 H5
Cucklington Somset ...20 E9
Cuckney Notts ...85 J6
Cuckoo Bridge Lincs ...74 D6
Cuckoo's Corner Hants ...23 K6
Cuckoo's Nest Ches W ...69 L2
Cuddesdon Oxon ...34 G4
Cuddington Bucks ...35 K2
Cuddington Ches W ...82 C10
Cuddington Heath Ches W ...69 N5
Cuddy Hill Lancs ...88 F3
Cudham Gt Lon ...37 K9
Cudliptown Devon ...8 D9
Cudnell BCP ...13 J5
Cudworth Barns ...91 K9
Cudworth Somset ...10 H2
Cuerdley Cross Warrtn ...82 C7
Cufaude Hants ...23 J3
Cuffley Herts ...50 H10
Cuil Highld ...138 H6
Culbokie Highld ...155 R6
Culbone Somset ...17 Q2
Culburnie Highld ...155 N9
Culcabock Highld ...156 B9
Culcharry Highld ...156 F7
Culcheth Warrtn ...82 E6
Culdrain Abers ...158 D11
Culduie Highld ...153 N9
Culford Suffk ...64 A7
Culgaith Cumb ...102 B5
Culham Oxon ...34 F5
Culkein Highld ...164 B10
Culkein Drumbeg Highld ...164 D10
Culkerton Gloucs ...32 H5
Cullen Moray ...158 D4
Cullercoats N Tyne ...113 N6
Cullerlie Abers ...151 K7
Cullicudden Highld ...156 A5
Cullingworth C Brad ...90 D3
Cuillin Hills Highld ...144 G3
Cullipool Ag & B ...130 E5
Cullivoe Shet ...169 s3
Culloden Highld ...156 C8
Cullompton Devon ...9 P3
Cullompton Services Devon ...9 P3
Culm Davy Devon ...18 F11
Culmington Shrops ...56 H8
Culmstock Devon ...10 C2
Culnacraig Highld ...160 H6
Culnaightrie D & G ...108 G10
Culnaknock Highld ...153 J5
Culpho Suffk ...53 M2
Culrain Highld ...162 C5
Culross Fife ...134 B10
Culroy S Ayrs ...114 F5
Culsalmond Abers ...158 G11
Culscadden D & G ...107 N8
Culshabbin D & G ...107 K7
Culswick Shet ...169 p9
Cultercullen Abers ...151 N3
Cults C Aber ...151 M7
Culverstone Green Kent ...37 P8
Culverthorpe Lincs ...73 Q2
Culworth Nhants ...48 F5
Culzean Castle & Country Park S Ayrs ...114 D5
Cumbernauld N Lans ...126 D3
Cumbernauld Village N Lans ...126 D2
Cumberworth Lincs ...87 P6
Cumdivock Cumb ...110 F11
Cuminestown Abers ...159 K7
Cumledge Border ...129 K8
Cummersdale Cumb ...110 G10
Cummertrees D & G ...109 P7
Cummingston Moray ...157 L4
Cumnock E Ayrs ...115 L3
Cumnor Oxon ...34 E4
Cumrew Cumb ...111 L10
Cumrue D & G ...109 N3
Cumwhinton Cumb ...111 J10
Cumwhitton Cumb ...111 K10
Cundall N York ...97 P6
Cunninghamhead N Ayrs ...125 K9
Cunningsburgh Shet ...169 r10
Cupar Fife ...135 K5
Cupar Muir Fife ...135 K5
Curbar Derbys ...84 C6
Curbridge Hants ...14 F4
Curbridge Oxon ...34 B3
Curdridge Hants ...14 F4
Curdworth Warwks ...59 J6
Curland Somset ...19 J11
Curridge W Berk ...34 E10
Currie C Edin ...127 N4
Curry Mallet Somset ...19 K10
Curry Rivel Somset ...19 L9
Curteis Corner Kent ...26 E4
Curtisden Green Kent ...26 B3
Curtisknowle Devon ...7 J8
Cury Cnwll ...2 H9
Cushnie Abers ...150 E5
Cushuish Somset ...18 G8
Cusop Herefs ...45 J6
Cusworth Donc ...91 N10
Cutcloy D & G ...107 N11
Cutcombe Somset ...18 B7
Cutgate Rochdl ...89 P8
Cuthill Highld ...162 H9
Cutiau Gwynd ...67 L11
Cutler's Green Essex ...51 N4
Cutmadoc Cnwll ...4 H9
Cutmere Cnwll ...5 N9

Cutnall Green Worcs ...58 C11
Cutsdean Gloucs ...47 L8
Cutthorpe Derbys ...84 D6
Cuttivett Cnwll ...5 P9
Cuxham Oxon ...35 J5
Cuxton Medway ...38 B8
Cuxwold Lincs ...93 L10
Cwm Blae G ...30 G3
Cwm Denbgs ...80 F9
Cwmafan Neath ...29 L6
Cwmaman Rhondd ...30 D5
Cwmann Carmth ...43 L5
Cwmavon Torfn ...31 J3
Cwmbach Carmth ...28 E4
Cwmbach Carmth ...41 Q5
Cwmbach Powys ...44 H7
Cwmbâch Rhondd ...30 D4
Cwmbach Llechryd Powys ...44 E4
Cwmbelan Powys ...55 L8
Cwmbran Torfn ...31 J6
Cwmbrwyno Cerdgn ...54 G8
Cwm Capel Carmth ...28 E4
Cwmcarn Caerph ...30 H6
Cwmcarvan Mons ...31 N3
Cwm-celyn Blae G ...30 H3
Cwm-Cewydd Gwynd ...55 K2
Cwm-cou Cerdgn ...41 Q2
Cwm Crawnon Powys ...44 G11
Cwmdare Rhondd ...30 C4
Cwmdu Carmth ...43 M8
Cwmdu Powys ...44 H10
Cwmdu Swans ...28 H6
Cwmduad Carmth ...42 G8
Cwm Dulais Swans ...28 H4
Cwmdwr Carmth ...43 P8
Cwmfelin Brdgnd ...29 N7
Cwmfelin Myr Td ...30 E4
Cwmfelin Boeth Carmth ...41 N7
Cwmfelinfach Caerph ...30 G6
Cwmfelin Mynach Carmth ...41 N6
Cwmffrwd Carmth ...42 H11
Cwmgiedd Powys ...29 L2
Cwmgorse Carmth ...29 K2
Cwm Gwaun Pembks ...41 K4
Cwmgwili Carmth ...28 G2
Cwmgwrach Neath ...29 N4
Cwmhiraeth Carmth ...42 F7
Cwmifor Carmth ...43 N9
Cwm Irfon Powys ...44 B5
Cwmisfael Carmth ...43 J11
Cwm Llinau Powys ...55 J3
Cwmllynfell Neath ...29 K2
Cwm Morgan Carmth ...41 Q4
Cwmparc Rhondd ...29 P5
Cwmpengraig Carmth ...42 G7
Cwm Penmachno Conwy ...67 P5
Cwmpennar Rhondd ...30 D4
Cwmrhos Powys ...44 H10
Cwmrhydyceirw Swans ...29 J5
Cwmsychbant Cerdgn ...43 J5
Cwmtillery Blae G ...30 H3
Cwm-twrch Isaf Powys ...29 L2
Cwm-twrch Uchaf Powys ...29 L2
Cwm-y-glo Carmth ...28 G2
Cwm-y-glo Gwynd ...67 K2
Cwmyoy Mons ...45 K10
Cwmystwyth Cerdgn ...54 H10
Cwrt Gwynd ...54 F5
Cwrtnewydd Cerdgn ...43 J5
Cwrt-y-gollen Powys ...45 J11
Cyfarthfa Castle Museum Myr Td ...30 D3
Cyffylliog Denbgs ...68 E3
Cyfronydd Powys ...55 Q3
Cylibebyll Neath ...29 K4
Cymau Flints ...69 J3
Cymer Neath ...29 N5
Cymmer Rhondd ...30 D6
Cyncoed Cardif ...30 G8
Cynghordy Carmth ...43 R6
Cynheidre Carmth ...28 E3
Cynonville Neath ...29 M5
Cynwyd Denbgs ...68 E6
Cynwyl Elfed Carmth ...42 G9

D

Daccombe Devon ...7 N5
Dacre Cumb ...101 N5
Dacre N York ...97 J8
Dacre Banks N York ...97 J8
Daddry Shield Dur ...102 G3
Dadford Bucks ...49 J7
Dadlington Leics ...72 C11
Dafen Carmth ...28 F4
Daffy Green Norfk ...76 D10
Dagenham Gt Lon ...37 M4
Daglingworth Gloucs ...33 J3
Dagnall Bucks ...49 Q11
Dagworth Suffk ...64 E9
Dail bho Dheas W Isls ...168 j1
Dailly S Ayrs ...114 E7
Dainton Devon ...7 M5
Dairsie Fife ...135 L4
Daisy Hill Bolton ...82 E4
Daisy Hill Leeds ...90 H5
Dalabrog W Isls ...168 c15
Dalavich Ag & B ...131 K5
Dalbeattie D & G ...108 H7
Dalbury Derbys ...71 P8
Dalby IoM ...80 b6
Dalby Lincs ...87 M7
Dalby N York ...98 C7
Dalcapon P & K ...141 Q4
Dalchalm Highld ...163 L5
Dalchreichart Highld ...146 H5
Dalchruin P & K ...133 L4
Dalcrue P & K ...134 C2
Dalderby Lincs ...87 J7
Dalditch Devon ...9 P8
Dale Cumb ...101 P2
Dale Pembks ...40 F8
Dale Abbey Derbys ...72 C3
Dale Bottom Cumb ...101 J6
Dale End Derbys ...84 B8
Dale End N York ...96 E11
Dale Hill E Susx ...26 B5
Dalehouse N York ...105 K7
Dalelia Highld ...138 C4
Dalgarven N Ayrs ...124 H9
Dalgety Bay Fife ...134 F11
Dalgig E Ayrs ...115 L5
Dalginross P & K ...133 M3

Dalguise P & K ...141 L6
Dalhalvaig Highld ...166 H6
Dalham Suffk ...63 M9
Daliburgh W Isls ...168 c15
Dalkeith Mdloth ...127 Q4
Dallas Moray ...157 L7
Dallinghoo Suffk ...65 K10
Dallington E Susx ...25 Q8
Dallington Nhants ...60 F8
Dallow N York ...97 J6
Dalmally Ag & B ...131 K2
Dalmary Stirlg ...132 G8
Dalmellington E Ayrs ...115 L6
Dalmeny C Edin ...127 L2
Dalmore Highld ...156 B5
Dalmuir W Duns ...125 M3
Dalnabreck Highld ...138 C4
Dalnacardoch P & K ...140 H2
Dalnahaitnach Highld ...148 E5
Dalnaspidal P & K ...140 F3
Dalnawillan Lodge Highld ...166 H6
Dalqueich P & K ...134 D6
Dalquhairn S Ayrs ...114 F8
Dalreavoch Highld ...162 H5
Dalry N Ayrs ...124 H9
Dalserf S Lans ...126 D7
Dalsmeran Ag & B ...120 B9
Dalston Cumb ...110 G10
Dalston Gt Lon ...36 H4
Dalswinton D & G ...109 K3
Dalton Cumb ...95 L6
Dalton D & G ...109 N5
Dalton Lancs ...88 G9
Dalton N York ...97 P5
Dalton N York ...103 N8
Dalton Nthumb ...112 H6
Dalton Rothm ...84 G2
Dalton-in-Furness Cumb ...94 E6
Dalton-le-Dale Dur ...113 P11
Dalton Magna Rothm ...84 G2
Dalton-on-Tees N York ...103 P8
Dalton Parva Rothm ...84 G2
Dalton Piercy Hartpl ...104 E4
Dalveich Stirlg ...133 J2
Dalwhinnie Highld ...147 Q11
Dalwood Devon ...10 E4
Damask Green Herts ...50 F5
Damerham Hants ...21 M11
Damgate Norfk ...77 N10
Dam Green Norfk ...64 E4
Damnaglaur D & G ...106 F11
Danaway Kent ...38 E9
Danbury Essex ...52 C10
Danby N York ...105 K9
Danby Bottom N York ...105 J10
Danby Wiske N York ...104 F9
Dandaleith Moray ...157 P9
Danderhall Mdloth ...127 Q4
Danebridge Ches E ...83 J11
Dane End Herts ...50 H6
Danegate E Susx ...25 N4
Danehill E Susx ...25 K5
Dane Hills C Leic ...72 F10
Danemoor Green Norfk ...76 F10
Danesford Shrops ...57 N6
Danesmoor Derbys ...84 F8
Dane Street Kent ...39 J11
Daniel's Water Kent ...26 G3
Danshillock Abers ...158 H6
Danskine E Loth ...128 F5
Danthorpe E R Yk ...93 M3
Danzey Green Warwks ...58 H11
Dapple Heath Staffs ...71 J8
Darby Green Hants ...23 M3
Darcy Lever Bolton ...89 L9
Dardy Powys ...45 J11
Darenth Kent ...37 N6
Daresbury Halton ...82 C8
Darfield Barns ...91 L10
Darfoulds Notts ...85 J5
Dargate Kent ...39 J9
Dargavel Rens ...125 L3
Darite Cnwll ...5 M8
Darland Medway ...38 C8
Darland Wrexhm ...69 L3
Darlaston Wsall ...58 E5
Darlaston Green Wsall ...58 E5
Darley N York ...97 J9
Darley Abbey C Derb ...72 B3
Darley Bridge Derbys ...84 C8
Darley Dale Derbys ...84 C8
Darley Green Solhll ...59 J10
Darleyhall Herts ...50 D6
Darley Head N York ...97 J9
Darlingscott Warwks ...47 P6
Darlington Darltn ...103 P8
Darliston Shrops ...69 P8
Darlton Notts ...85 M6
Darnford Staffs ...58 H3
Darnick Border ...117 P3
Darowen Powys ...55 K4
Darra Abers ...158 H8
Darracott Devon ...16 H7
Darracott Devon ...16 H4
Darras Hall Nthumb ...113 J6
Darrington Wakefd ...91 M6
Darsham Suffk ...65 N8
Darshill Somset ...20 C6
Dartford Kent ...37 N6
Dartford Crossing Kent ...37 N5
Dartington Devon ...7 K6
Dartmeet Devon ...6 H6
Dartmoor National Park Devon ...8 G9
Dartmouth Devon ...7 M8
Darton Barns ...91 J9
Darvel E Ayrs ...125 M11
Darwell Hole E Susx ...25 Q7
Darwen Bl w D ...89 K6
Datchet W & M ...35 Q9
Datchworth Herts ...50 F7
Datchworth Green Herts ...50 F7
Daubhill Bolton ...89 L9
Daugh of Kinnermony Moray ...157 P9
Dauntsey Wilts ...33 J8
Dava Highld ...157 J9
Davenham Ches W ...82 D10
Davenport Stockp ...83 J7
Davenport Green Ches E ...82 H9
Davenport Green Traffd ...82 G7
Daventry Nhants ...60 C8
Davidson's Mains C Edin ...127 N2
Davidstow Cnwll ...5 K4
David Street Kent ...37 P7
Davington D & G ...117 J8

Davington Hill Kent......38 H9
Daviot Abers......151 J2
Daviot Highld......156 C10
Daviot House Highld......156 C9
Davis's Town E Susx......25 M7
Davoch of Grange Moray......158 C7
Davyhulme Traffd......82 G5
Daw End Wsall......58 F4
Dawesgreen Surrey......36 F11
Dawley Wrekin......57 M3
Dawlish Devon......9 N9
Dawlish Warren Devon......9 N9
Dawn Conwy......80 B10
Daws Green Somset......18 G10
Daws Heath Essex......38 D4
Daw's House Cnwll......5 N5
Dawsmere Lincs......74 H4
Daybrook Notts......85 J11
Dayhills Staffs......70 H8
Dayhouse Bank Worcs......58 E9
Daylesford Gloucs......47 P9
Ddol Flints......80 G10
Ddol-Cownwy Powys......68 D11
Deal Kent......39 Q11
Dean Cumb......100 E5
Dean Devon......7 J6
Dean Devon......17 L2
Dean Devon......17 N2
Dean Dorset......21 J11
Dean Hants......22 D8
Dean Hants......22 G11
Dean Lancs......89 P5
Dean Oxon......48 B10
Dean Somset......20 C6
Dean Bottom Kent......37 N7
Deanburnhaugh Border......117 M8
Deancombe Devon......7 J6
Dean Court Oxon......34 E3
Deane Bolton......89 K9
Deane Hants......22 F4
Dean End Dorset......21 J11
Dean Head Barns......90 H10
Deanhead Kirk......90 C7
Deanland Dorset......21 J11
Deanlane End W Susx......15 K4
Dean Prior Devon......7 J6
Deanraw Nthumb......112 B8
Dean Row Ches E......83 J8
Deans W Loth......127 J4
Deanscales Cumb......100 E5
Deanshanger Nhants......49 L7
Deanshaugh Moray......157 R7
Deanston Stirlg......133 L7
Dean Street Kent......38 B11
Dearham Cumb......100 E3
Dearnley Rochdl......89 Q7
Debach Suffk......65 J11
Debden Essex......51 K11
Debden Essex......51 N4
Debden Green Essex......51 N4
Debenham Suffk......64 H9
Deblin's Green Worcs......46 F5
Dechmont W Loth......127 J3
Dechmont Road W Loth......127 J4
Deddington Oxon......48 E8
Dedham Essex......53 J5
Dedham Heath Essex......53 J5
Dedworth W & M......35 P9
Deene Nhants......61 K2
Deenethorpe Nhants......61 L2
Deepcar Sheff......90 H11
Deepcut Surrey......23 P3
Deepdale Cumb......95 Q4
Deepdale N York......96 C5
Deeping Gate C Pete......74 B9
Deeping St James Lincs......74 C9
Deeping St Nicholas Lincs......74 D7
Deerhurst Gloucs......46 G8
Deerhurst Walton Gloucs......46 G9
Deerton Street Kent......38 G9
Defford Worcs......46 H6
Defynnog Powys......44 C9
Deganwy Conwy......79 P9
Degnish Ag & B......130 F5
Deighton C York......91 Q2
Deighton N York......104 C10
Deiniolen Gwynd......67 K2
Delabole Cnwll......4 H5
Delamere Ches W......82 C11
Delamere Park Ches W......82 C10
Delfrigs Abers......151 P3
Delley Devon......17 J7
Dellieure Highld......157 K11
Dell Quay W Susx......15 M6
Delly End Oxon......34 C2
Delnabo Moray......149 M4
Delny Highld......156 C3
Delph Oldham......90 B9
Delves Dur......112 H11
Delvin End Essex......52 C4
Dembleby Lincs......73 Q3
Demelza Cnwll......4 F9
Denaby Donc......91 M11
Denaby Main Donc......91 M11
Denbies Surrey......36 D10
Denbigh Denbgs......80 F11
Denbrae Fife......135 K4
Denbury Devon......7 L5
Denby Derbys......84 E11
Denby Bottles Derbys......84 E11
Denby Dale Kirk......90 G9
Denchworth Oxon......34 C6
Dendron Cumb......94 E6
Denel End C Beds......50 B4
Denfield P & K......134 B4
Denford Nhants......61 L5
Dengie Essex......52 G11
Denham Bucks......36 B3
Denham Suffk......63 N8
Denham Suffk......64 H7
Denham End Suffk......63 N8
Denham Green Bucks......36 B3
Denham Green Suffk......64 H7
Denhead Abers......159 N7
Denhead Fife......135 M5
Denhead of Gray C Dund......142 F11
Denholm Border......117 R7
Denholme C Brad......90 D4
Denholme Clough C Brad......90 D4
Denio Gwynd......66 E7
Denmead Hants......15 J4
Denmore C Aber......151 N5
Denne Park W Susx......24 E5
Dennington Suffk......65 K8
Denny Falk......133 N11

Dennyloanhead Falk......133 N11
Den of Lindores Fife......134 H4
Denshaw Oldham......90 B8
Denside of Durris Abers......151 L8
Densole Kent......27 M3
Denston Suffk......63 N10
Denstone Staffs......71 K6
Denstroude Kent......39 K9
Dent Cumb......95 Q3
Denton Cambs......61 Q3
Denton Darltn......103 P7
Denton E Susx......25 L10
Denton Kent......27 M2
Denton Kent......37 Q6
Denton Lincs......73 M4
Denton N York......96 H11
Denton Nhants......60 H9
Denton Norfk......65 K4
Denton Oxon......34 G4
Denton Tamesd......83 K5
Denver Norfk......75 M10
Denwick Nthumb......119 P8
Deopham Norfk......76 E11
Deopham Green Norfk......64 E2
Depden Suffk......63 N9
Depden Green Suffk......63 N9
Deptford Gt Lon......37 J5
Deptford Wilts......21 K7
Derby C Derb......72 B3
Derby Devon......17 K5
Derbyhaven IoM......80 c8
Dereham Norfk......76 D9
Deri Caerph......30 F4
Derril Devon......16 E11
Derringstone Kent......27 M2
Derrington Staffs......70 F10
Derriton Devon......16 E11
Derry Hill Wilts......33 J10
Derrythorpe N Linc......92 D9
Dersingham Norfk......75 N4
Derwen Denbgs......68 E4
Derwenlas Powys......54 G5
Derwent Valley Mills Derbys......84 D9
Derwent Water Cumb......101 J6
Derwydd Carmth......43 M11
Desborough Nhants......60 H4
Desford Leics......72 D10
Detchant Nthumb......119 L3
Detling Kent......38 C10
Deuxhill Shrops......57 M7
Devauden Mons......31 N5
Devil's Bridge Cerdgn......54 G9
Devitts Green Warwks......59 L6
Devizes Wilts......21 K2
Devonport C Plym......6 D8
Devonside Clacks......133 Q8
Devoran Cnwll......3 K6
Devoran & Perran Cnwll......3 K6
Dewarton Mdloth......128 B7
Dewlish Dorset......12 C5
Dewsbury Kirk......90 G6
Dewsbury Moor Kirk......90 G6
Deytheur Powys......68 H11
Dial N Som......31 P11
Dial Green W Susx......23 P9
Dial Post W Susx......24 E7
Dibberford Dorset......11 K4
Dibden Hants......14 D5
Dibden Purlieu Hants......14 D5
Dickens Heath Solhll......58 H9
Dickleburgh Norfk......64 H5
Didbrook Gloucs......47 L8
Didcot Oxon......34 F6
Diddington Cambs......61 Q7
Diddlebury Shrops......57 J7
Didley Herefs......45 P8
Didling W Susx......23 M11
Didmarton Gloucs......32 F7
Didsbury Manch......82 H6
Didworthy Devon......6 H6
Digby Lincs......86 E10
Digg Highld......152 H4
Diggle Oldham......90 C9
Digmoor Lancs......88 F9
Digswell Herts......50 F7
Digswell Water Herts......50 G8
Dihewyd Cerdgn......43 J3
Dilham Norfk......77 L6
Dilhorne Staffs......70 H6
Dill Hall Lancs......89 M5
Dillington Cambs......61 P7
Dilston Nthumb......112 E8
Dilton Wilts......20 G5
Dilton Marsh Wilts......20 F5
Dilwyn Herefs......45 N4
Dimple Bolton......89 L7
Dimple Derbys......84 C8
Dinas Carmth......41 Q4
Dinas Cnwll......4 E7
Dinas Gwynd......66 D7
Dinas Gwynd......66 H3
Dinas Rhondd......30 D6
Dinas Cross Pembks......41 K3
Dinas Dinlle Gwynd......66 G3
Dinas-Mawddwy Gwynd......67 M3
Dinas Powys V Glam......30 G10
Dinder Somset......19 Q6
Dinedor Herefs......45 Q7
Dingestow Mons......31 N2
Dingle Lpool......81 M7
Dingleden Kent......26 D5
Dingley Nhants......60 G3
Dingwall Highld......155 P6
Dinmael Conwy......68 D6
Dinnet Abers......150 D8
Dinnington N u Ty......113 K6
Dinnington Rothm......84 H3
Dinnington Somset......11 J2
Dinorwic Gwynd......67 K2
Dinton Bucks......35 L2
Dinton Wilts......21 K8
Dinwoodie D & G......109 P2
Dinworthy Devon......16 E8
Dipford Somset......18 H10
Dipley Hants......23 K3
Dippen Ag & B......120 F4
Dippenhall Surrey......23 M5
Dippermill Devon......8 D7
Dippertown Devon......8 B8
Dippin N Ayrs......121 K7
Dipple Moray......157 Q9
Dipple S Ayrs......114 D7
Diptford Devon......7 J7
Dipton Dur......113 J10

Diptonmill Nthumb......112 D8
Dirleton E Loth......128 E3
Dirt Pot Nthumb......112 C11
Discoed Powys......45 K2
Diseworth Leics......72 D6
Dishforth N York......97 N6
Disley Ches E......83 L8
Diss Norfk......64 G5
Disserth Powys......44 E3
Distington Cumb......100 D6
Ditcham Wilts......21 L8
Ditcheat Somset......20 B7
Ditchingham Norfk......65 L3
Ditchling E Susx......24 H7
Ditherington Shrops......57 J2
Ditteridge Wilts......32 F11
Dittisham Devon......7 M7
Ditton Kent......38 B10
Ditton Green Cambs......63 L9
Ditton Priors Shrops......57 L7
Dixton Gloucs......47 J8
Dixton Mons......31 P2
Dizzard Cnwll......5 K2
Dobcross Oldham......90 B9
Dobwalls Cnwll......5 L8
Doccombe Devon......9 J7
Dochgarroch Highld......155 R9
Dockenfield Surrey......23 M6
Docker Lancs......95 M6
Docking Norfk......75 Q3
Docklow Herefs......45 R3
Dockray Cumb......101 L6
Dockray Cumb......110 E11
Dodbrooke Devon......7 J10
Doddinghurst Essex......51 N11
Doddington Cambs......62 F2
Doddington Kent......38 F10
Doddington Lincs......85 Q6
Doddington Nthumb......119 J4
Doddington Shrops......57 L9
Doddiscombsleigh Devon......9 L7
Dodd's Green Ches E......69 R6
Doddshill Norfk......75 N4
Doddy Cross Cnwll......5 N9
Dodford Nhants......60 D8
Dodford Worcs......58 D10
Dodington S Glos......32 E8
Dodington Somset......18 G6
Dodleston Ches W......69 L2
Dodscott Devon......17 J8
Dodside E Rens......125 N7
Dod's Leigh Staffs......71 J8
Dodworth Barns......91 J9
Dodworth Bottom Barns......91 J10
Dodworth Green Barns......91 J10
Doe Bank Birm......58 H5
Doe Lea Derbys......84 G7
Dogdyke Lincs......86 H9
Dogley Lane Kirk......90 F8
Dogmersfield Hants......23 L4
Dogridge Wilts......33 L7
Dogsthorpe C Pete......74 C10
Dog Village Devon......9 N5
Dolanog Powys......55 P2
Dolau Powys......55 Q11
Dolaucothi Carmth......43 N6
Dolbenmaen Gwynd......67 J6
Doley Staffs......70 C9
Dolfach Powys......55 L4
Dol-fôr Powys......55 J3
Dolfor Powys......55 Q7
Dolgarrog Conwy......79 P11
Dolgellau Gwynd......67 N11
Dolgoch Gwynd......54 F4
Dol-gran Carmth......42 H8
Doll Highld......163 K6
Dollar Clacks......134 B8
Dollarfield Clacks......134 B8
Dolley Green Powys......56 D11
Dollwen Cerdgn......54 F8
Dolphin Flints......80 H10
Dolphinholme Lancs......95 L10
Dolphinton S Lans......127 L8
Dolton Devon......17 K9
Dolwen Conwy......80 B10
Dolwyddelan Conwy......67 N4
Dolybont Cerdgn......54 E7
Dolyhir Powys......45 J3
Domgay Powys......69 J11
Donaldson's Lodge Nthumb......118 G2
Doncaster Donc......91 P10
Doncaster Carr Donc......91 P10
Doncaster North Services
    Donc......91 R8
Doncaster Sheffield
    Airport Donc......91 R11
Donhead St Andrew Wilts......20 H10
Donhead St Mary Wilts......20 H10
Donibristle Fife......134 F10
Doniford Somset......18 E6
Donington Lincs......74 D3
Donington on Bain Lincs......86 H4
Donington Park Services
    Leics......72 D5
Donington Southing Lincs......74 D4
Donisthorpe Leics......59 M2
Donkey Street Kent......27 K5
Donkey Town Surrey......23 P2
Donnington Gloucs......47 N9
Donnington Herefs......46 D8
Donnington Shrops......57 K3
Donnington W Berk......34 E11
Donnington W Susx......15 N6
Donnington Wrekin......57 N2
Donnington Wood Wrekin......57 N2
Donyatt Somset......10 G2
Doomsday Green W Susx......24 E5
Doonfoot S Ayrs......114 F4
Dora's Green Hants......23 M5
Dorback Lodge Highld......149 K4
Dorchester Dorset......11 P6
Dorchester-on-Thames
    Oxon......34 G6
Dordon Warwks......59 L4
Dore Sheff......84 D4
Dores Highld......155 Q10
Dorking Surrey......36 E11
Dorking Tye Suffk......52 F4
Dormansland Surrey......25 K2
Dormans Park Surrey......25 J2
Dormington Herefs......46 A6
Dormston Worcs......47 J3
Dorn Gloucs......47 P8
Dorney Bucks......35 P9
Dorney Reach Bucks......35 P9
Dornie Highld......145 Q2

Dornoch Highld......162 H9
Dornock D & G......110 D7
Dorrery Highld......167 J6
Dorridge Solhll......59 J10
Dorrington Lincs......86 E10
Dorrington Shrops......56 H4
Dorrington Shrops......70 C6
Dorsington Warwks......47 M5
Dorstone Herefs......45 L5
Dorton Bucks......35 J2
Dosthill Staffs......59 K5
Dothan IoA......78 F10
Dottery Dorset......11 K5
Doublebois Cnwll......5 K9
Doughton Gloucs......32 G6
Douglas S Lans......116 A4
Douglas IoM......80 e6
Douglas and Angus C Dund......142 G11
Douglas Pier Ag & B......131 P8
Douglastown Angus......142 G8
Douglas Water S Lans......116 B3
Douglas West S Lans......126 E11
Doulting Somset......20 B6
Dounby Ork......169 b4
Doune Highld......161 Q6
Doune Stirlg......133 L7
Dounepark S Ayrs......114 C8
Dounie Highld......162 D8
Dousland Devon......6 F4
Dovaston Shrops......69 L10
Dove Dale Derbys......71 L4
Dove Green Notts......84 G10
Dove Holes Derbys......83 N9
Dovenby Cumb......100 E4
Dover Kent......27 P3
Dover Wigan......82 D4
Dover Castle Kent......27 P3
Dovercourt Essex......53 M5
Doverdale Worcs......58 C11
Doveridge Derbys......71 L8
Doversgreen Surrey......36 G11
Dowally P & K......141 P6
Dowbridge Lancs......88 E4
Dowdeswell Gloucs......47 K11
Dowlais Myr Td......30 E3
Dowland Devon......17 K9
Dowlish Ford Somset......10 H2
Dowlish Wake Somset......10 H2
Down Ampney Gloucs......33 L5
Downderry Cnwll......5 N11
Downe Gt Lon......37 K8
Downend Gloucs......32 F5
Downend IoW......14 F9
Downend S Glos......32 C9
Downend W Berk......34 E9
Downfield C Dund......142 F11
Downgate Cnwll......5 N7
Downgate Cnwll......5 P7
Downham Essex......38 B2
Downham Gt Lon......37 J6
Downham Lancs......89 M2
Downham Market Norfk......75 M10
Down Hatherley Gloucs......46 G10
Downhead Somset......19 Q9
Downhead Somset......20 C5
Downhill Cnwll......4 D8
Downhill P & K......134 D2
Downholland Cross Lancs......88 D9
Downholme N York......103 M11
Downicarey Devon......5 P3
Downies Abers......151 N9
Downing Flints......80 H9
Downley Bucks......35 M5
Down St Mary Devon......8 H4
Downside Somset......20 B4
Downside Somset......20 B6
Downside Surrey......36 D9
Down Thomas Devon......6 E8
Downton Hants......13 N6
Downton Wilts......21 N10
Dowsby Lincs......74 B5
Dowsdale Lincs......74 C8
Doxey Staffs......70 F10
Doxford Nthumb......119 N6
Doynton S Glos......32 D10
Draethen Caerph......30 H7
Draffan S Lans......126 D8
Dragonby N Linc......92 F8
Dragons Green W Susx......24 D6
Drakeholes Notts......85 M2
Drakelow Worcs......57 Q8
Drakemyre N Ayrs......124 H7
Drakes Broughton Worcs......46 H5
Drakewalls Cnwll......6 C4
Draughton N York......96 F10
Draughton Nhants......60 G5
Drax N York......92 A5
Drax Hales N York......91 R5
Draycote Warwks......59 P10
Draycot Foliat Swindn......33 N9
Draycott Derbys......72 C4
Draycott Gloucs......47 N7
Draycott Shrops......57 Q6
Draycott Somset......19 N4
Draycott Somset......19 Q10
Draycott Worcs......46 G5
Draycott in the Clay Staffs......71 M9
Draycott in the Moors
    Staffs......70 H6
Drayford Devon......9 J2
Drayton C Port......15 J5
Drayton Leics......60 H2
Drayton Lincs......74 D3
Drayton Norfk......76 H9
Drayton Oxon......34 E6
Drayton Oxon......48 D6
Drayton Somset......19 M10
Drayton Somset......19 N11
Drayton Worcs......58 D9
Drayton Bassett Staffs......59 J4
Drayton Beauchamp Bucks......35 P2
Drayton Manor Park Staffs......59 J4
Drayton Parslow Bucks......49 M9
Drayton St Leonard Oxon......34 G5
Drebley N York......96 G9
Dreemskerry IoM......80 g3
Dreen Hill Pembks......40 H8
Drefach Carmth......28 F2
Drefach Carmth......42 G7
Drefach Cerdgn......43 J5
Drefelin Carmth......42 G7
Dreghorn N Ayrs......125 K4
Drellingore Kent......27 M3
Drem E Loth......128 E4
Dresden C Stke......70 G6
Drewsteignton Devon......8 H6

Driby Lincs......87 L6
Driffield E R Yk......99 L9
Driffield Gloucs......33 L5
Driffield Cross Roads
    Gloucs......33 L5
Drift Cnwll......2 C8
Drigg Cumb......100 E11
Drighlington Leeds......90 G5
Drimnin Highld......137 P5
Drimpton Dorset......11 J4
Drimsallie Highld......138 H2
Dringhouses C York......98 B11
Drinkstone Suffk......64 D9
Drinkstone Green Suffk......64 D9
Drive End Dorset......11 M3
Driver's End Herts......50 F6
Drointon Staffs......71 J9
Droitwich Spa Worcs......46 G2
Dron P & K......134 E4
Dronfield Derbys......84 E5
Dronfield Woodhouse
    Derbys......84 D5
Drongan E Ayrs......114 H4
Dronley Angus......142 E10
Droop Dorset......12 C3
Dropping Well Rothm......84 E2
Droxford Hants......22 H11
Droylsden Tamesd......83 K5
Druid Denbgs......68 D6
Druidston Pembks......40 G7
Druimarbin Highld......139 K3
Druimavuic Ag & B......139 J8
Druimdrishaig Ag & B......123 M5
Druimindarroch Highld......145 L11
Drum Ag & B......124 A2
Drum P & K......134 C7
Drumalbin S Lans......116 C3
Drumbeg Highld......164 D10
Drumblade Abers......158 E9
Drumbreddon D & G......106 E9
Drumbuie Highld......153 P11
Drumburgh Cumb......110 E9
Drumburn D & G......109 J10
Drumburn D & G......109 L8
Drumchapel C Glas......125 N3
Drumchastle P & K......140 G6
Drumclog S Lans......125 Q10
Drumeldrie Fife......135 L7
Drumelzier Border......116 G4
Drumfearn Highld......145 L4
Drumfrennie Abers......151 J8
Drumgley Angus......142 G7
Drumguish Highld......148 D7
Drumin Moray......157 M11
Drumjohn D & G......115 K8
Drumlamford S Ayrs......107 J2
Drumlasie Abers......150 G6
Drumleaning Cumb......110 E10
Drumlemble Ag & B......120 C8
Drumlithie Abers......151 K11
Drummoddie D & G......107 L8
Drummore D & G......106 F10
Drummuir Moray......158 A9
Drumnadrochit Highld......155 P11
Drumnagorrach Moray......158 D7
Drumpark D & G......109 J5
Drumrunie Highld......161 K5
Drumshang S Ayrs......114 E5
Drumuie Highld......152 H8
Drumuillie Highld......148 G3
Drumvaich Stirlg......133 K7
Drunzie P & K......134 E6
Druridge Nthumb......119 Q11
Drury Flints......69 J2
Drws-y-coed Gwynd......67 J4
Drybeck Cumb......102 C7
Drybridge Moray......158 B5
Drybridge N Ayrs......125 K10
Drybrook Gloucs......46 B11
Dryburgh Border......118 A4
Dry Doddington Lincs......85 Q11
Dry Drayton Cambs......62 E8
Dryhill Kent......37 L10
Drymen Stirlg......132 F10
Drymuir Abers......159 M8
Drynoch Highld......152 G11
Dry Sandford Oxon......34 E4
Dryslwyn Carmth......43 L10
Dry Street Essex......37 Q3
Dryton Shrops......57 K3
Dubford Abers......159 J5
Dublin Suffk......64 H8
Duchally Highld......161 P3
Duck End Bed......50 C2
Duck End Cambs......62 B8
Duck End Essex......51 Q4
Duck End Essex......51 Q5
Duckend Green Essex......52 B7
Duckington Ches W......69 N4
Ducklington Oxon......34 C3
Duck's Cross Bed......61 P9
Duddenhoe End Essex......51 L3
Duddington Nhants......73 P3
Duddingston C Edin......127 P3
Duddington Nhants......73 P10
Duddlestone Somset......18 H10
Duddleswell E Susx......25 L5
Duddlewick Shrops......57 M8
Duddo Nthumb......118 H2
Duddon Ches W......69 P2
Duddon Bridge Cumb......94 D3
Duddon Common Ches W......69 Q11
Dudleston Shrops......69 K7
Dudleston Heath Shrops......69 L7
Dudley Dudley......58 D6
Dudley N Tyne......113 L6
Dudley Hill C Brad......90 F4
Dudley Port Sandw......58 E6
Dudnill Shrops......57 L10
Dudsbury Dorset......13 J5
Dudswell Herts......35 Q3
Duffield Derbys......72 A2
Duffryn Neath......29 M5
Dufftown Moray......157 Q9
Duffus Moray......157 M4
Dufton Cumb......102 C5
Duggleby N York......98 H7
Duirinish Highld......153 P11
Duisdalemore Highld......145 M5
Duisky Highld......139 J2
Dukestown Blae G......30 F2
Duke Street Suffk......53 J3
Dukinfield Tamesd......83 K5
Dulas IoA......78 H7
Dulcote Somset......19 Q6
Dulford Devon......9 Q3
Dull P & K......141 K8

268 Dullatur – Eccles Road

Dullatur N Lans 126 C2
Dullingham Cambs 63 K9
Dullingham Ley Cambs 63 K9
Dulnain Bridge Highld 148 H3
Duloe Bed 61 Q8
Duloe Cnwll 5 L10
Dulsie Bridge Highld 156 G9
Dulverton Somset 18 B9
Dulwich Gt Lon 36 H6
Dumbarton W Duns 125 L2
Dumbleton Gloucs 47 K7
Dumfries D & G 109 L5
Dumgoyne Stirlg 132 G11
Dummer Hants 22 G5
Dumpton Kent 39 Q8
Dun Angus 143 M6
Dunalastair P & K 140 H6
Dunan Ag & B 124 F3
Dunan Highld 145 J2
Dunan P & K 140 C6
Dunaverty Ag & B 120 C10
Dunball Somset 19 K6
Dunbar E Loth 128 H4
Dunbeath Highld 167 L11
Dunbeg Ag & B 138 F11
Dunblane Stirlg 133 M7
Dunbog Fife 134 H4
Dunbridge Hants 22 B9
Duncanston Highld 155 Q6
Duncanstone Abers 150 F2
Dunchideock Devon 9 L7
Dunchurch Warwks 59 Q10
Duncote Nhants 49 J4
Duncow D & G 109 L4
Duncrievie P & K 134 E6
Duncton W Susx 23 Q11
Dundee C Dund 142 G11
Dundee Airport C Dund 135 K2
Dundon Somset 19 N8
Dundonald S Ayrs 125 K11
Dundonnell Highld 160 H9
Dundraw Cumb 110 D11
Dundreggan Highld 147 J5
Dundrennan D & G 108 F11
Dundry N Som 31 Q11
Dunecht Abers 151 K6
Dunfermline Fife 134 D10
Dunfield Gloucs 33 M5
Dunford Bridge Barns 83 Q4
Dungate Kent 38 F10
Dungavel S Lans 126 B10
Dunge Wilts 20 G4
Dungeness Kent 27 J8
Dungworth Sheff 84 C3
Dunham Massey Traffd 82 F7
Dunham-on-the-Hill Ches W 81 P10
Dunham-on-Trent Notts 85 P6
Dunhampstead Worcs 46 H2
Dunhampton Worcs 58 B11
Dunham Town Traffd 82 F7
Dunham Woodhouses Traffd 82 F7
Dunholme Lincs 86 D5
Dunino Fife 135 N5
Dunipace Falk 133 N11
Dunkeld P & K 141 P9
Dunkerton BaNES 20 D3
Dunkeswell Devon 10 C3
Dunkeswick N York 97 M11
Dunkirk Ches W 81 M10
Dunkirk Kent 39 J10
Dunkirk S Glos 32 E7
Dunkirk Wilts 21 J2
Dunk's Green Kent 37 P10
Dunlappie Angus 143 K4
Dunley Hants 22 E4
Dunley Worcs 57 P11
Dunlop E Ayrs 125 L8
Dunmaglass Highld 147 P3
Dunmere Cnwll 4 G8
Dunmore Falk 133 P10
Dunnet Highld 167 M2
Dunnichen Angus 143 J8
Dunning P & K 134 C5
Dunnington C York 98 D10
Dunnington E R Yk 99 P10
Dunnington Warwks 47 L4
Dunnockshaw Lancs 89 N5
Dunn Street Kent 38 C9
Dunoon Ag & B 124 F2
Dunphail Moray 157 J8
Dunragit D & G 106 G6
Duns Border 129 K9
Dunsa Derbys 84 B6
Dunsby Lincs 74 B5
Dunscar Bolton 89 L8
Dunscore D & G 109 J4
Dunscroft Donc 91 Q9
Dunsdale R & Cl 104 H7
Dunsden Green Oxon 35 K9
Dunsdon Devon 16 E10
Dunsfold Surrey 24 B3
Dunsford Devon 9 K7
Dunshalt Fife 134 G5
Dunshillock Abers 159 N8
Dunsill Notts 84 G8
Dunsley N York 105 N8
Dunsley Staffs 58 C8
Dunsmore Bucks 35 N3
Dunsop Bridge Lancs 95 P11
Dunstable C Beds 50 B6
Dunstall Staffs 71 M10
Dunstall Common Worcs 46 G6
Dunstall Green Suffk 63 M8
Dunstan Nthumb 119 P7
Dunstan Steads Nthumb 119 P6
Dunster Somset 18 C6
Duns Tew Oxon 48 E9
Dunston Gatesd 113 K8
Dunston Lincs 86 E8
Dunston Norfk 77 J11
Dunston Staffs 70 G11
Dunstone Devon 6 F8
Dunstone Devon 8 H9
Dunston Heath Staffs 70 G11
Dunsville Donc 91 Q9
Dunswell E R Yk 93 J3
Dunsyre S Lans 127 K8
Dunterton Devon 5 P6
Dunthrop Oxon 48 C9
Duntisbourne Abbots Gloucs 33 J3
Duntisbourne Leer Gloucs 33 J3
Duntisbourne Rouse Gloucs 33 J3
Duntish Dorset 11 P3
Duntocher W Duns 125 M3
Dunton Bucks 49 M10
Dunton C Beds 50 F2
Dunton Norfk 76 B5
Dunton Bassett Leics 60 B2
Dunton Green Kent 37 M9
Dunton Wayletts Essex 37 Q2
Duntulm Highld 152 G3
Dunure S Ayrs 114 E4
Dunvant Swans 28 G6
Dunvegan Highld 152 D8
Dunwich Suffk 65 P7
Dunwood Staffs 70 G3
Durdar Cumb 110 H10
Durgan Cnwll 3 K8
Durham Dur 103 Q2
Durham Cathedral Dur 103 Q2
Durham Services Dur 104 B3
Durham Tees Valley Airport S on T 104 C8
Durisdeer D & G 116 B10
Durisdeermill D & G 116 B10
Durkar Wakefd 91 J7
Durleigh Somset 19 J7
Durley Hants 22 F11
Durley Wilts 21 P2
Durley Street Hants 22 F11
Durlock Kent 39 N10
Durlock Kent 39 P9
Durlow Common Herefs 46 B7
Durn Rochdl 89 Q7
Durness Highld 165 K3
Durno Abers 151 J2
Duror Highld 138 H6
Durran Ag & B 131 K6
Durrington W Susx 24 D9
Durrington Wilts 21 N6
Dursley Gloucs 32 E5
Dursley Cross Gloucs 46 C10
Durston Somset 19 J9
Durweston Dorset 12 E3
Duston Nhants 60 F8
Duthil Highld 148 G3
Dutlas Powys 56 C9
Duton Hill Essex 51 P5
Dutson Cnwll 5 N4
Dutton Ches W 82 C9
Duxford Cambs 62 G11
Duxford Oxon 34 C5
Duxford IWM Cambs 62 G11
Dwygyfylchi Conwy 79 N9
Dwyran IoA 78 G11
Dyce C Aber 151 M5
Dyer's End Essex 52 B4
Dyfatty Carmth 28 E4
Dyffrydan Gwynd 54 F2
Dyffryn Brdgnd 29 N6
Dyffryn Myr Td 30 E4
Dyffryn V Glam 30 E10
Dyffryn Ardudwy Gwynd 67 K10
Dyffryn Castell Cerdgn 54 H8
Dyffryn Cellwen Neath 29 N2
Dyke Lincs 74 B6
Dyke Moray 156 H6
Dykehead Angus 142 C7
Dykehead Angus 142 F6
Dykehead N Lans 126 F6
Dykehead Stirlg 132 H8
Dykelands Abers 143 N4
Dykends Angus 142 D6
Dykeside Abers 158 H9
Dylife Powys 55 K6
Dymchurch Kent 27 K6
Dymock Gloucs 46 D8
Dyrham S Glos 32 D9
Dysart Fife 135 J9
Dyserth Denbgs 80 F9

E

Eachway Worcs 58 E9
Eachwick Nthumb 112 H6
Eagland Hill Lancs 95 J11
Eagle Lincs 85 Q7
Eagle Barnsdale Lincs 85 Q7
Eagle Moor Lincs 85 Q7
Eaglescliffe S on T 104 D7
Eaglesfield Cumb 100 E5
Eaglesfield D & G 110 D6
Eaglesham E Rens 125 P7
Eagley Bolton 89 L8
Eairy IoM 80 c6
Eakring Notts 85 L8
Ealand N Linc 92 C8
Ealing Gt Lon 36 E4
Eals Nthumb 111 N9
Eamont Bridge Cumb 101 P5
Earby Lancs 96 D11
Earcroft Bl w D 89 K6
Eardington Shrops 57 N6
Eardisland Herefs 45 N3
Eardisley Herefs 45 L5
Eardiston Shrops 69 L9
Eardiston Worcs 57 M11
Earith Cambs 62 E5
Earle Nthumb 119 J5
Earlestown St Hel 82 C5
Earley Wokham 35 K10
Earlham Norfk 76 H10
Earlish Highld 152 F5
Earls Barton Nhants 61 J8
Earls Colne Essex 52 E6
Earls Common Worcs 47 J3
Earl's Croome Worcs 46 G6
Earlsditton Shrops 57 L9
Earlsdon Covtry 59 M9
Earl's Down E Susx 25 P7
Earlsferry Fife 135 M7
Earlsfield Gt Lon 36 G6
Earlsford Abers 159 K11
Earl's Green Suffk 64 E8
Earlsheaton Kirk 90 H6
Earl Shilton Leics 72 D11
Earl Soham Suffk 65 J9
Earl Sterndale Derbys 83 N11
Earlston Border 117 R3
Earlston E Ayrs 125 L10
Earl Stonham Suffk 64 G10
Earlswood Surrey 36 G11
Earlswood Warwks 58 H10
Earlswood Common Mons 31 N6
Earnley W Susx 15 M7
Earnshaw Bridge Lancs 88 G6
Earsdon N Tyne 113 M6
Earsdon Nthumb 113 J2
Earsham Norfk 65 L4
Earswick C York 98 C9
Eartham W Susx 15 P5
Earthcott S Glos 32 C7
Easby N York 104 G9
Easdale Ag & B 130 E4
Easebourne W Susx 23 N10
Easenhall Warwks 59 Q9
Eashing Surrey 23 P6
Easington Bucks 35 J2
Easington Dur 104 D2
Easington E R Yk 93 Q7
Easington Nthumb 119 M4
Easington Oxon 35 J5
Easington R & Cl 105 K7
Easington Colliery Dur 104 D2
Easington Lane Sundld 113 N11
Easingwold N York 98 A7
Easole Street Kent 39 N11
Eassie and Nevay Angus 142 E9
East Aberthaw V Glam 30 D11
East Allington Devon 7 K9
East Anstey Devon 17 R6
East Anton Hants 22 C5
East Appleton N York 103 P11
East Ardsley Leeds 91 J5
East Ashey IoW 14 G9
East Ashling W Susx 15 M5
East Aston Hants 22 D5
East Ayton N York 99 K3
East Balsdon Cnwll 5 M2
East Bank Blae G 30 H3
East Barkwith Lincs 86 G4
East Barming Kent 38 B11
East Barnby N York 105 M8
East Barnet Gt Lon 50 G11
East Barns E Loth 129 J4
East Barsham Norfk 76 C5
East Beckham Norfk 76 H4
East Bedfont Gt Lon 36 C6
East Bergholt Suffk 53 J5
East Bierley Kirk 90 F5
East Bilney Norfk 76 D8
East Blatchington E Susx 25 L10
East Bloxworth Dorset 12 E6
East Boldon S Tyne 113 N8
East Boldre Hants 14 C6
East Bolton Nthumb 119 M7
Eastbourne Darltn 104 B8
Eastbourne E Susx 25 P11
East Bower Somset 19 K7
East Bradenham Norfk 76 C10
East Brent Somset 19 K4
Eastbridge Suffk 65 P8
East Bridgford Notts 72 H2
East Briscoe Dur 103 J7
Eastbrook V Glam 30 G10
East Buckland Devon 17 M5
East Budleigh Devon 9 Q8
Eastburn C Brad 90 C2
Eastburn E R Yk 99 K9
East Burnham Bucks 35 Q8
East Burton Dorset 12 D7
Eastbury W Berk 34 B9
East Butsfield Dur 112 H11
East Butterwick N Linc 92 D9
Eastby N York 96 F10
East Calder W Loth 127 K4
East Carleton Norfk 76 H11
East Carlton Leeds 90 G2
East Carlton Nhants 60 H3
East Chaldon Dorset 12 C8
East Challow Oxon 34 C7
East Charleton Devon 7 K10
East Chelborough Dorset 11 M3
East Chiltington E Susx 25 J7
East Chinnock Somset 11 K2
East Chisenbury Wilts 21 M4
East Cholderton Hants 21 Q5
Eastchurch Kent 38 G7
East Clandon Surrey 36 C10
East Claydon Bucks 49 K9
East Clevedon N Som 31 M10
East Coker Somset 11 L2
Eastcombe Gloucs 32 G4
Eastcombe Somset 18 G8
East Compton Somset 20 B6
East Cornworthy Devon 7 L7
East Cote Cumb 109 P9
Eastcote Gt Lon 36 D3
Eastcote Nhants 49 J4
Eastcote Solhll 59 J9
Eastcott Cnwll 16 D8
Eastcott Wilts 21 K3
East Cottingwith E R Yk 92 B2
Eastcourt Wilts 21 P2
Eastcourt Wilts 33 J6
East Cowes IoW 14 F7
East Cowick E R Yk 91 R6
East Cowton N York 104 B10
East Cramlington Nthumb 113 L5
East Cranmore Somset 20 C6
East Creech Dorset 12 F8
East Curthwaite Cumb 110 F11
East Dean E Susx 25 N11
East Dean Gloucs 46 C10
East Dean Hants 21 Q9
East Dean W Susx 15 P4
Eastdown Devon 7 L9
East Down Devon 17 L3
East Drayton Notts 85 N5
East Dulwich Gt Lon 36 H5
East Dundry N Som 31 Q11
East Ella C KuH 93 J5
East End Bed 61 P9
East End C Beds 49 Q6
East End E R Yk 93 L4
East End E R Yk 93 N5
Eastend Essex 38 F3
East End Essex 51 K8
East End Hants 14 C7
East End Hants 22 D2
East End Herts 51 L5
East End Kent 26 D4
East End Kent 38 G7
East End M Keyn 49 P6
East End Oxon 48 C11
East End Somset 20 C5
East End Suffk 53 K4
Easter Balmoral Abers 149 P9
Easter Compton S Glos 31 Q8
Easter Dalziel Highld 156 D7
Eastergate W Susx 15 P5
Easterhouse C Glas 126 B4
Easter Howgate Mdloth 127 N5
Easter Kinkell Highld 155 Q6
Easter Moniack Highld 155 Q9
Eastern Green Covtry 59 L9
Easter Ord Abers 151 L7
Easter Pitkierie Fife 135 P6
Easter Skeld Shet 169 q9
Easter Softlaw Border 118 E4
Easterton Wilts 21 K4
Eastertown Somset 19 K4
East Everleigh Wilts 21 P4
East Farleigh Kent 38 B11
East Farndon Nhants 60 F4
East Ferry Lincs 92 D11
Eastfield N Lans 126 F5
Eastfield N York 99 L4
East Firsby Lincs 86 D3
East Fortune E Loth 128 E4
East Garforth Leeds 91 L4
East Garston W Berk 34 C9
Eastgate Dur 103 J3
Eastgate Lincs 74 B7
Eastgate Norfk 76 G7
East Ginge Oxon 34 D7
East Goscote Leics 72 G8
East Grafton Wilts 21 Q2
East Green Suffk 65 N8
East Grimstead Wilts 21 P9
East Grinstead W Susx 25 J3
East Guldeford E Susx 26 F7
East Haddon Nhants 60 E7
East Hagbourne Oxon 34 F7
East Halton N Linc 93 K7
East Ham Gt Lon 37 K4
Eastham Wirral 81 M8
Eastham Ferry Wirral 81 M8
Easthampton Herefs 45 N2
East Hanney Oxon 34 D6
East Hanningfield Essex 52 C11
East Hardwick Wakefd 91 M7
East Harling Norfk 64 D4
East Harlsey N York 104 D11
East Harnham Wilts 21 M9
East Harptree BaNES 19 Q3
East Hartford Nthumb 113 L5
East Harting W Susx 23 L11
East Hatch Wilts 20 H9
East Hatley Cambs 62 C10
East Hauxwell N York 97 J2
East Haven Angus 143 K10
Eastheath Wokham 35 L11
East Heckington Lincs 74 C2
East Hedleyhope Dur 103 N2
East Helmsdale Highld 163 N3
East Hendred Oxon 34 E7
East Heslerton N York 99 J5
East Hewish N Som 19 M2
East Hoathly E Susx 25 M7
East Holme Dorset 12 E7
East Hope Dur 103 K9
Easthope Shrops 57 K5
Easthorpe Essex 52 F7
Easthorpe Notts 85 M10
East Horrington Somset 19 Q5
East Horsley Surrey 36 C10
East Horton Nthumb 119 K4
East Howe BCP 13 J5
East Huntspill Somset 19 K5
East Hyde C Beds 50 D7
East Ilkerton Devon 17 N2
East Ilsley W Berk 34 E8
Eastington Devon 8 H3
Eastington Gloucs 32 E3
Eastington Gloucs 33 M2
East Keal Lincs 87 L8
East Kennett Wilts 33 M11
East Keswick Leeds 91 K2
East Kilbride S Lans 125 Q7
East Kimber Devon 8 C5
East Kirkby Lincs 87 K8
East Knighton Dorset 12 D7
East Knowstone Devon 17 Q7
East Knoyle Wilts 20 G8
East Lambrook Somset 19 M11
Eastlands D & G 108 H6
East Langdon Kent 27 P2
East Langton Leics 60 F2
East Lavant W Susx 15 N5
East Lavington W Susx 23 P11
East Layton N York 103 N9
Eastleach Martin Gloucs 33 P4
Eastleach Turville Gloucs 33 N3
East Leake Notts 72 F5
East Learmouth Nthumb 118 G3
East Leigh Devon 6 H8
East Leigh Devon 7 K7
East Leigh Devon 8 G3
Eastleigh Devon 16 H6
Eastleigh Hants 22 E11
East Lexham Norfk 76 B8
Eastling Kent 38 G10
East Linton E Loth 128 F4
East Liss Hants 23 L9
East Lockinge Oxon 34 D7
East Lound N Linc 92 C11
East Lulworth Dorset 12 E8
East Lutton N York 99 J7
East Lydeard Somset 18 G9
East Lydford Somset 19 Q8
East Malling Kent 38 B10
East Malling Heath Kent 37 Q9
East Marden W Susx 15 M4
East Markham Notts 85 M6
East Martin Hants 21 L11
East Marton N York 96 D10
East Meon Hants 23 J10
East Mere Devon 18 C11
East Mersea Essex 52 H9
East Midlands Airport Leics 72 D5
East Molesey Surrey 36 D7
Eastmoor Norfk 75 P10
East Morden Dorset 12 F6
East Morton C Brad 90 D2
East Morton D & G 116 B10
East Ness N York 98 D5
East Newton E R Yk 93 N3
Eastney C Port 15 J7
Eastnor Herefs 46 D7
East Norton Leics 73 K10
Eastoft N Linc 92 D7
East Ogwell Devon 7 L4
Easton Cambs 61 P6
Easton Cumb 110 E9
Easton Devon 8 H7
Easton Dorset 11 P10
Easton Hants 22 F8
Easton Lincs 73 N5
Easton Norfk 76 G9
Easton Somset 19 P5
Easton Suffk 65 K10
Easton W Berk 34 D10
Easton Wilts 32 G10
Easton Grey Wilts 32 G7
Easton-in-Gordano N Som 31 P9
Easton Maudit Nhants 61 J9
Easton-on-the-Hill Nhants 73 Q10
Easton Royal Wilts 21 P2
East Orchard Dorset 20 F11
East Ord Nthumb 129 P9
East Panson Devon 5 P3
East Parley BCP 13 J5
East Peckham Kent 37 Q11
East Pennard Somset 19 Q7
East Portlemouth Devon 7 K11
East Prawle Devon 7 K11
East Preston W Susx 24 C10
East Pulham Dorset 11 Q3
East Putford Devon 16 F8
East Quantoxhead Somset 18 F6
East Rainham Medway 38 D8
East Rainton Sundld 113 M11
East Ravendale NE Lin 93 M11
East Raynham Norfk 76 B6
Eastrea Cambs 74 E11
Eastriggs D & G 110 D7
East Rigton Leeds 91 K2
Eastrington E R Yk 92 C5
East Rolstone N Som 19 L2
Eastrop Swindn 33 P6
East Rounton N York 104 D10
East Rudham Norfk 76 A6
East Runton Norfk 76 H3
East Ruston Norfk 77 L6
Eastry Kent 39 P11
East Saltoun E Loth 128 D6
Eastshaw W Susx 23 N10
East Sheen Gt Lon 36 F6
East Shefford W Berk 34 C10
East Sleekburn Nthumb 113 L4
East Somerton Norfk 77 P8
East Stockwith Lincs 85 N2
East Stoke Dorset 12 E7
East Stoke Notts 85 N11
East Stour Dorset 20 F10
East Stour Common Dorset 20 F10
East Stourmouth Kent 39 N9
East Stowford Devon 17 L6
East Stratton Hants 22 F6
East Studdal Kent 27 P2
East Sutton Kent 26 D2
East Taphouse Cnwll 5 K9
East-the-Water Devon 16 H6
East Thirston Nthumb 119 N10
East Tilbury Thurr 37 Q5
East Tilbury Village Thurr 37 Q5
East Tisted Hants 23 K8
East Torrington Lincs 86 F4
East Tuddenham Norfk 76 F9
East Tytherley Hants 21 Q9
East Tytherton Wilts 33 J10
East Village Devon 9 K3
Eastville Bristl 32 B10
Eastville Lincs 87 M9
East Wall Shrops 57 J6
East Walton Norfk 75 P7
East Water Somset 19 P4
East Week Devon 8 G6
Eastwell Leics 73 K5
East Wellow Hants 22 B10
East Wemyss Fife 135 J8
East Whitburn W Loth 126 H4
Eastwick Herts 51 K8
East Wickham Gt Lon 37 L5
East Williamston Pembks 41 L10
East Winch Norfk 75 N7
East Winterslow Wilts 21 P8
East Wittering W Susx 15 L7
East Witton N York 96 H3
Eastwood Notts 84 G11
Eastwood Sthend 38 D4
East Woodburn Nthumb 112 D3
Eastwood End Cambs 62 F2
East Woodhay Hants 22 D2
East Woodlands Somset 20 E6
East Worldham Hants 23 L7
East Worthing W Susx 24 E10
East Wretham Norfk 64 C3
East Youlstone Devon 16 D8
Eathorpe Warwks 59 N11
Eaton Ches E 83 J11
Eaton Ches W 69 Q2
Eaton Leics 73 K5
Eaton Norfk 77 J10
Eaton Notts 85 M5
Eaton Oxon 34 D4
Eaton Shrops 56 F7
Eaton Shrops 57 J7
Eaton Bishop Herefs 45 N7
Eaton Bray C Beds 49 Q10
Eaton Constantine Shrops 57 K3
Eaton Ford Cambs 61 Q9
Eaton Green C Beds 49 Q10
Eaton Hastings Oxon 33 Q5
Eaton Mascott Shrops 57 J3
Eaton Socon Cambs 61 Q9
Eaton upon Tern Shrops 70 B10
Eaves Brow Warrtn 82 D6
Eaves Green Solhll 59 L8
Ebberston N York 98 H4
Ebbesborne Wake Wilts 21 J10
Ebbw Vale Blae G 30 G3
Ebchester Dur 112 H9
Ebdon N Som 19 L2
Ebernoe W Susx 23 Q9
Ebford Devon 9 N7
Ebley Gloucs 32 F3
Ebnal Ches W 69 N5
Ebnall Herefs 45 P3
Ebrington Gloucs 47 N6
Ebsworthy Devon 8 D6
Ecchinswell Hants 22 E3
Ecclaw Border 129 K6
Ecclefechan D & G 110 C6
Eccles Border 118 E2
Eccles Kent 38 B9
Eccles Salfd 82 G5
Ecclesall Sheff 84 D4
Ecclesfield Sheff 84 E2
Eccles Green Herefs 45 M5
Eccleshall Staffs 70 E9
Eccleshill C Brad 90 F3
Ecclesmachan W Loth 127 K3
Eccles on Sea Norfk 77 N6
Eccles Road Norfk 64 E4

Eccleston – Farnell 269

ccleston Ches W 69 M2
ccleston Lancs 88 G7
ccleston St Hel 81 P5
ccleston Green Lancs 88 G7
cht Abers 151 J6
ckford Border 118 D5
ckington Derbys 84 F5
ckington Worcs 46 H6
cton Nhants 60 H8
cton Staffs 71 K3
dale Derbys 83 P7
day Ork 169 e3
day Airport Ork 169 e3
dburton W Susx 24 F8
dderside Cumb 109 P11
dderton Highld 162 G10
ddington Cambs 62 F9
ddington Kent 39 L8
ddleston Border 127 N8
ddlewood S Lans 126 C7
denbridge Kent 37 K11
denfield Lancs 89 N7
denhall Cumb 101 Q4
denham Lincs 73 R6
den Mount Cumb 95 J5
den Park Gt Lon 37 J7
den Project Cnwll 3 Q3
densor Derbys 84 B7
dentaggart Ag & B 132 C9
denthorpe Donc 91 Q9
dern Gwynd 66 D7
dgarley Somset 19 P7
dgbaston Birm 58 G8
dgcott Bucks 49 J10
dgcott Somset 17 Q4
dgcumbe Cnwll 3 J7
dge Gloucs 32 F3
dge Shrops 56 F3
dgebolton Shrops 69 Q10
dge End Gloucs 31 Q2
dgefield Norfk 76 F5
dgefield Green Norfk 76 F5
dgefold Bolton 89 L9
dge Green Ches W 69 N4
dgehill Warwks 48 C5
dgerley Shrops 69 L11
dgerton Kirk 90 E7
dgeside Lancs 89 N6
dgeworth Gloucs 32 H3
dgeworthy Devon 9 K2
dginswell Torbay 7 M5
dgiock Worcs 47 K2
dgmond Wrekin 70 C11
dgmond Marsh Wrekin 70 C10
dgton Shrops 56 F7
dgware Gt Lon 36 E2
dgworth Bl w D 89 L7
dinbane Highld 152 E7
dinburgh C Edin 127 P3
Edinburgh Airport C Edin 127 L3
Edinburgh Castle C Edin 127 P3
Edinburgh Old & New Town C Edin 127 P3
Edinburgh Royal Botanic Gardens C Edin 127 N2
Edinburgh Zoo RZSS C Edin 127 N3
Edingale Staffs 59 K2
Edingham D & G 108 H8
Edingley Notts 85 L9
Edingthorpe Norfk 77 L5
Edingthorpe Green Norfk 77 L5
Edington Border 129 M9
Edington Nthumb 113 J4
Edington Somset 19 L7
Edington Wilts 20 H4
Edingworth Somset 19 L4
Edistone Devon 16 D7
Edithmead Somset 19 K5
Edith Weston Rutlnd 73 N9
Edlesborough Bucks 49 Q11
Edlingham Nthumb 119 M9
Edlington Lincs 86 H6
Edmond Castle Cumb 111 J9
Edmondsham Dorset 13 J2
Edmondsley Dur 113 K11
Edmondstown Rhondd 30 D6
Edmondthorpe Leics 73 M7
Edmonton Cnwll 4 F7
Edmonton Gt Lon 36 H2
Edmundbyers Dur 112 F10
Ednam Border 118 D3
Ednaston Derbys 71 N6
Edney Common Essex 51 Q10
Edradynate P & K 141 L7
Edrom Border 129 L8
Edstaston Shrops 69 P8
Edstone Warwks 47 N2
Edvin Loach Herefs 46 C3
Edwalton Notts 72 F3
Edwardstone Suffk 52 F3
Edwardsville Myr Td 30 E5
Edwinsford Carmth 43 M8
Edwinstowe Notts 85 K7
Edworth C Beds 50 F2
Edwyn Ralph Herefs 46 B3
Edzell Angus 143 L4
Edzell Woods Abers 143 L4
Efail-fach Neath 29 L5
Efail Isaf Rhondd 30 E8
Efailnewydd Gwynd 66 F7
Efail-Rhyd Powys 68 G9
Efailwen Carmth 41 M5
Efenechtyd Denbgs 68 F3
Effgill D & G 110 F2
Effingham Surrey 36 D10
Effingham Junction Surrey 36 D9
Efflinch Staffs 71 M11
Efford Devon 9 L4
Egbury Hants 22 D4
Egdean W Susx 23 Q10
Egerton Bolton 89 L8
Egerton Kent 26 F2
Egerton Forstal Kent 26 E2
Eggborough N York 91 P6
Eggbuckland C Plym 6 E7
Eggesford Devon 17 M9
Eggington C Beds 49 Q9
Egginton Derbys 71 P9
Egglescliffe S on T 104 D8
Eggleston Dur 103 J6
Egham Surrey 36 B6
Egham Wick Surrey 35 Q10
Egleton Rutlnd 73 M9
Eglingham Nthumb 119 M7
Egloshayle Cnwll 4 G7
Egloskerry Cnwll 5 M4
Eglwysbach Conwy 79 Q10
Eglwys-Brewis V Glam 30 D11
Eglwys Cross Wrexhm 69 N6
Eglwys Fach Cerdgn 54 F5
Eglwyswrw Pembks 41 M3
Egmanton Notts 85 M7
Egremont Cumb 100 D8
Egremont Wirral 81 L6
Egton N York 105 M9
Egton Bridge N York 105 M10
Egypt Bucks 35 Q7
Egypt Hants 22 E6
Eigg Highld 144 G10
Eight Ash Green Essex 52 F6
Eilanreach Highld 145 P4
Eilean Donan Castle Highld 145 Q2
Eisgein W Isls 168 i6
Eishken W Isls 168 i6
Eisteddfa Gurig Cerdgn 54 H8
Elan Valley Powys 55 K11
Elan Village Powys 44 C2
Elberton S Glos 32 B7
Elbridge W Susx 15 P6
Elburton C Plym 6 E8
Elcombe Swindn 33 M8
Elcot W Berk 34 C11
Eldernell Cambs 74 F11
Eldersfield Worcs 46 E8
Elderslie Rens 125 L5
Elder Street Essex 51 N4
Eldon Dur 103 P5
Eldwick C Brad 90 E2
Elerch Cerdgn 54 F7
Elfhill Abers 151 L10
Elford Nthumb 119 N4
Elford Staffs 59 J2
Elgin Moray 157 N5
Elgol Highld 144 H5
Elham Kent 27 L3
Elie Fife 135 M7
Elilaw Nthumb 119 J9
Elim IoA 78 F8
Eling Hants 14 C4
Elkesley Notts 85 L5
Elkstone Gloucs 33 J2
Ella Abers 158 F6
Ellacombe Torbay 7 N6
Elland Calder 90 E6
Elland Lower Edge Calder 90 E6
Ellary Ag & B 123 M4
Ellastone Staffs 71 L6
Ellel Lancs 95 K9
Ellemford Border 129 J7
Ellenabeich Ag & B 130 E4
Ellenborough Cumb 100 D3
Ellenbrook Salfd 82 F4
Ellenhall Staffs 70 E9
Ellen's Green Surrey 24 C3
Ellerbeck N York 104 D11
Ellerby N York 105 L8
Ellerdine Heath Wrekin 69 R10
Ellerhayes Devon 9 N4
Elleric Ag & B 139 J8
Ellerker E R Yk 92 F5
Ellers N York 90 C2
Ellerton E R Yk 92 B3
Ellerton N York 103 Q11
Ellerton Shrops 70 C9
Ellesborough Bucks 35 M3
Ellesmere Shrops 69 L8
Ellesmere Port Ches W 81 N9
Ellingham Hants 13 K3
Ellingham Norfk 65 M3
Ellingham Nthumb 119 N5
Ellingstring N York 97 J4
Ellington Cambs 61 Q6
Ellington Nthumb 113 L2
Ellington Thorpe Cambs 61 Q6
Elliots Green Somset 20 E5
Ellisfield Hants 22 H5
Ellishader Highld 153 J4
Ellistown Leics 72 C8
Ellon Abers 159 N11
Ellonby Cumb 101 M3
Ellough Suffk 65 N4
Elloughton E R Yk 92 F5
Ellwood Gloucs 31 Q3
Elm Cambs 75 J9
Elmbridge Worcs 58 D11
Elmdon Essex 51 L3
Elmdon Solhll 59 J8
Elmdon Heath Solhll 59 J8
Elmer W Susx 15 Q6
Elmers End Gt Lon 37 J7
Elmer's Green Lancs 88 G9
Elmesthorpe Leics 72 D11
Elm Green Essex 52 C10
Elmhurst Staffs 58 H2
Elmley Castle Worcs 47 J6
Elmley Lovett Worcs 58 C11
Elmore Gloucs 46 E11
Elmore Back Gloucs 46 E11
Elm Park Gt Lon 37 M3
Elmscott Devon 16 C7
Elmsett Suffk 53 J2
Elms Green Worcs 57 N11
Elmstead Heath Essex 53 J7
Elmstead Market Essex 53 J7
Elmstead Row Essex 53 J7
Elmsted Kent 27 K3
Elmstone Kent 39 N9
Elmstone Hardwicke Gloucs 46 H9
Elmswell E R Yk 99 K9
Elmswell Suffk 64 D9
Elmton Derbys 84 H6
Elphin Highld 161 L4
Elphinstone E Loth 128 B6
Elrick Abers 151 L6
Elrig D & G 107 K8
Elrington Nthumb 112 C8
Elsdon Nthumb 112 D2
Elsecar Barns 91 K11
Elsenham Essex 51 M5
Elsfield Oxon 34 F2
Elsham N Linc 92 H8
Elsing Norfk 76 F8
Elslack N York 96 D11
Elson Hants 14 H6
Elson Shrops 69 L7
Elsrickle S Lans 116 F2
Elstead Surrey 23 P6
Elsted W Susx 23 M11
Elsted Marsh W Susx 23 M10
Elsthorpe Lincs 73 R6
Elstob Dur 104 B6
Elston Lancs 88 H4
Elston Notts 85 N11
Elston Wilts 21 L6
Elstone Devon 17 M8
Elstow Bed 61 N11
Elstree Herts 50 E11
Elstronwick E R Yk 93 M4
Elswick Lancs 88 E3
Elswick N u Ty 113 K8
Elsworth Cambs 62 D8
Elterwater Cumb 101 K10
Eltham Gt Lon 37 K6
Eltisley Cambs 62 C9
Elton Bury 89 M8
Elton Cambs 61 N2
Elton Ches W 81 P9
Elton Derbys 84 B8
Elton Gloucs 32 D2
Elton Herefs 56 H10
Elton S on T 104 D7
Elton Green Ches W 81 P10
Elton-on-the-Hill Notts 73 K3
Eltringham Nthumb 112 G8
Elvanfoot S Lans 116 D7
Elvaston Derbys 72 C4
Elveden Suffk 63 P4
Elvetham Heath Hants 23 M3
Elvingston E Loth 128 D5
Elvington C York 98 E11
Elvington Kent 39 N11
Elwell Devon 17 M5
Elwick Hartpl 104 E4
Elwick Nthumb 119 M3
Elworth Ches E 70 C2
Elworthy Somset 18 E8
Ely Cambs 62 H4
Ely Cardif 30 F9
Emberton M Keyn 49 N5
Embleton Cumb 100 G4
Embleton Dur 104 D5
Embleton Nthumb 119 P6
Embo Highld 163 J8
Emborough Somset 20 B4
Embo Street Highld 163 J8
Embsay N York 96 F10
Emery Down Hants 13 N3
Emley Kirk 90 G8
Emley Moor Kirk 90 G8
Emmbrook Wokham 35 M11
Emmer Green Readg 35 K9
Emmett Carr Derbys 84 G5
Emmington Oxon 35 K4
Emneth Norfk 75 J9
Emneth Hungate Norfk 75 K9
Empingham Rutlnd 73 N9
Empshott Hants 23 L8
Empshott Green Hants 23 K8
Emsworth Hants 15 K5
Enborne W Berk 34 D11
Enborne Row W Berk 22 D2
Enchmarsh Shrops 57 J5
Enderby Leics 72 E11
Endmoor Cumb 95 L4
Endon Staffs 70 G4
Endon Bank Staffs 70 G4
Enfield Gt Lon 51 J11
Enfield Lock Gt Lon 51 J11
Enfield Wash Gt Lon 51 J11
Enford Wilts 21 M4
Engine Common S Glos 32 C8
England's Gate Herefs 45 Q4
Englefield W Berk 34 H10
Englefield Green Surrey 35 Q10
Engleseabrook Ches E 70 D4
English Bicknor Gloucs 46 A11
Englishcombe BaNES 20 D2
English Frankton Shrops 69 N9
Engollan Cnwll 4 D7
Enham Alamein Hants 22 C5
Enmore Somset 18 H7
Enmore Green Dorset 20 G10
Ennerdale Bridge Cumb 100 E7
Enniscaven Cnwll 4 F10
Enochdhu P & K 141 Q5
Ensay Ag & B 137 K6
Ensbury BCP 13 J5
Ensdon Shrops 69 M11
Ensis Devon 17 K6
Enson Staffs 70 G9
Enstone Oxon 48 C10
Enterkinfoot D & G 116 B10
Enterpen N York 104 E9
Enville Staffs 58 B7
Eochar W Isls 168 c13
Eòlaigearraidh W Isls 168 c17
Eoligarry W Isls 168 c17
Epney Gloucs 32 E2
Epperstone Notts 85 L11
Epping Essex 51 L10
Epping Green Essex 51 K9
Epping Green Herts 50 G9
Epping Upland Essex 51 K10
Eppleby N York 103 N8
Eppleworth E R Yk 92 H4
Epsom Surrey 36 F8
Epwell Oxon 48 C6
Epworth N Linc 92 C10
Epworth Turbary N Linc 92 C10
Erbistock Wrexhm 69 L6
Erdington Birm 58 H6
Eridge Green E Susx 25 N3
Eridge Station E Susx 25 M4
Erines Ag & B 123 Q4
Eriska Ag & B 138 G9
Eriskay W Isls 168 c17
Eriswell Suffk 63 M5
Erith Gt Lon 37 M5
Erlestoke Wilts 21 J4
Ermington Devon 6 G8
Erpingham Norfk 76 H5
Erriottwood Kent 38 F10
Errogie Highld 147 P3
Errol P & K 134 G3
Erskine Rens 125 M3
Erskine Bridge Rens 125 M3
Ervie D & G 106 D4
Erwarton Suffk 53 M5
Erwood Powys 44 F6
Eryholme N York 104 B9
Eryrys Denbgs 68 H3
Escalls Cnwll 2 B8
Escomb Dur 103 N4
Escott Somset 18 E7
Escrick N York 91 Q2
Esgair Carmth 42 G9
Esgair Cerdgn 54 D11
Esgairgeiliog Powys 54 H3
Esgerdawe Carmth 43 M6
Esgyryn Conwy 79 Q9
Esh Dur 103 N2
Esher Surrey 36 D8
Esholt C Brad 90 F2
Eshott Nthumb 119 P11
Eshton N York 96 D9
Esh Winning Dur 103 N2
Eskadale Highld 155 N9
Eskbank Mdloth 127 Q4
Eskdale Green Cumb 100 F10
Eskdalemuir D & G 117 K11
Eske E R Yk 93 J2
Eskham Lincs 93 Q11
Eskholme Donc 91 Q7
Esperley Lane Ends Dur 103 M6
Esprick Lancs 88 E3
Essendine Rutlnd 73 Q8
Essendon Herts 50 G9
Essich Highld 156 A10
Essington Staffs 58 E4
Esslemont Abers 151 N2
Eston R & Cl 104 F7
Etal Nthumb 118 H3
Etchilhampton Wilts 21 K2
Etchingham E Susx 26 B6
Etchinghill Kent 27 L4
Etchinghill Staffs 71 J11
Etchingwood E Susx 25 M6
Etling Green Norfk 76 E9
Etloe Gloucs 32 C3
Eton W & M 35 Q9
Eton Wick W & M 35 P9
Etruria C Stke 70 F5
Etteridge Highld 148 B9
Ettersgill Dur 102 G5
Ettiley Heath Ches E 70 C2
Ettingshall Wolves 58 D5
Ettington Warwks 47 Q5
Etton C Pete 74 B9
Etton E R Yk 92 G2
Ettrick Border 117 K8
Ettrickbridge Border 117 M6
Ettrickhill Border 117 K8
Etwall Derbys 71 P8
Eudon George Shrops 57 M7
Euston Suffk 64 B6
Euximoor Drove Cambs 75 J11
Euxton Lancs 88 H7
Evancoyd Powys 45 K2
Evanton Highld 155 R4
Evedon Lincs 86 E11
Evelith Shrops 57 N3
Evelix Highld 162 H8
Evenjobb Powys 45 K2
Evenley Nhants 48 G8
Evenlode Gloucs 47 P9
Evenwood Dur 103 N6
Evenwood Gate Dur 103 N6
Evercreech Somset 20 B7
Everingham E R Yk 92 D2
Everleigh Wilts 21 P4
Everley N York 99 K3
Eversholt C Beds 49 Q8
Evershot Dorset 11 M4
Eversley Hants 23 L2
Eversley Cross Hants 23 L2
Everthorpe E R Yk 92 F4
Everton C Beds 62 B10
Everton Hants 13 N6
Everton Lpool 81 L6
Everton Notts 85 L2
Evertown D & G 110 G5
Evesbatch Herefs 46 C5
Evesham Worcs 47 K6
Evington C Leic 72 G10
Ewden Village Sheff 90 H11
Ewell Surrey 36 F8
Ewell Minnis Kent 27 N3
Ewelme Oxon 34 H6
Ewen Gloucs 33 K5
Ewenny V Glam 29 P9
Ewerby Lincs 86 F11
Ewerby Thorpe Lincs 86 F11
Ewhurst Surrey 24 C2
Ewhurst Green E Susx 26 C7
Ewhurst Green Surrey 24 C3
Ewloe Flints 81 L11
Ewloe Green Flints 81 K11
Ewood Bl w D 89 K5
Ewood Bridge Lancs 89 M6
Eworthy Devon 8 B5
Ewshot Hants 23 M5
Ewyas Harold Herefs 45 M9
Exbourne Devon 8 F4
Exbury Hants 14 D6
Exceat E Susx 25 M11
Exebridge Somset 18 B10
Exelby N York 97 L3
Exeter Devon 9 M6
Exeter Airport Devon 9 N6
Exeter Services Devon 9 N6
Exford Somset 17 R4
Exfordsgreen Shrops 56 H3
Exhall Warwks 47 M3
Exhall Warwks 59 N7
Exlade Street Oxon 35 J8
Exley Head C Brad 90 C2
Exminster Devon 9 M7
Exmoor National Park 17 R4
Exmouth Devon 9 P8
Exning Suffk 63 K7
Exted Kent 27 L3
Exton Devon 9 N7
Exton Hants 22 H10
Exton Rutlnd 73 N8
Exton Somset 18 B8
Exwick Devon 9 M6
Eyam Derbys 84 B5
Eydon Nhants 48 F5
Eye C Pete 74 D10
Eye Herefs 45 P2
Eye Suffk 64 G7
Eye Green C Pete 74 D10
Eyemouth Border 129 N7
Eyeworth C Beds 62 C11
Eyhorne Street Kent 38 D11
Eyke Suffk 65 L11
Eynesbury Cambs 61 Q9
Eynsford Kent 37 M7
Eynsham Oxon 34 D3
Eype Dorset 11 J6
Eyre Highld 152 G7
Eythorne Kent 27 N2
Eyton Herefs 45 P2
Eyton Shrops 56 F2
Eyton Shrops 56 F7
Eyton Shrops 69 M10
Eyton Wrexhm 69 L6
Eyton on Severn Shrops 57 K3
Eyton upon the Weald Moors Wrekin 57 M2

F

Faccombe Hants 22 C3
Faceby N York 104 E10
Fachwen Powys 68 D11
Facit Lancs 89 P7
Fackley Notts 84 G8
Faddiley Ches E 69 Q4
Fadmoor N York 98 D3
Faerdre Swans 29 J4
Faifley W Duns 125 M3
Failand N Som 31 P10
Failford S Ayrs 115 J2
Failsworth Oldham 83 J4
Fairbourne Gwynd 54 E2
Fairburn N York 91 M5
Fairfield Derbys 83 N10
Fairfield Kent 26 G6
Fairfield Worcs 58 D9
Fairfield Park Herts 50 F4
Fairford Gloucs 33 N4
Fairford Park Gloucs 33 N4
Fairgirth D & G 109 J9
Fair Green Norfk 75 N7
Fairhaven Lancs 88 C5
Fair Isle Shet 169 t14
Fair Isle Airport Shet 169 t14
Fairlands Surrey 23 Q4
Fairlie N Ayrs 124 G7
Fairlight E Susx 26 E9
Fairlight Cove E Susx 26 E9
Fairmile Devon 10 B5
Fairmile Surrey 36 D8
Fairmilehead C Edin 127 N4
Fairnilee Border 117 P4
Fair Oak Hants 22 E11
Fairoak Staffs 70 D8
Fair Oak Green Hants 23 J2
Fairseat Kent 37 P8
Fairstead Essex 52 C8
Fairstead Norfk 75 M6
Fairstead Norfk 77 K7
Fairwarp E Susx 25 L5
Fairwater Cardif 30 F9
Fairy Cross Devon 16 G7
Fakenham Norfk 76 C6
Fakenham Magna Suffk 64 C6
Fala Mdloth 128 C7
Fala Dam Mdloth 128 C7
Falcut Nhants 48 G6
Faldingworth Lincs 86 E4
Faldouët Jersey 11 c2
Falfield S Glos 32 C6
Falkenham Suffk 53 N4
Falkirk Falk 133 P11
Falkirk Wheel Falk 133 P11
Falkland Fife 134 H6
Fallburn S Lans 116 D3
Fallgate Derbys 84 E8
Fallin Stirlg 133 N9
Fallodon Nthumb 119 N6
Fallowfield Manch 83 J6
Fallowfield Nthumb 112 D7
Falmer E Susx 25 J9
Falmouth Cnwll 3 L7
Falnash Border 117 M9
Falsgrave N York 99 L3
Falstone Nthumb 111 P3
Fanagmore Highld 164 E7
Fancott C Beds 50 B5
Fanellan Highld 155 N9
Fangdale Beck N York 98 B2
Fangfoss E R Yk 98 F10
Fanmore Ag & B 137 L7
Fannich Lodge Highld 154 H4
Fans Border 118 B2
Far Bletchley M Keyn 49 N8
Farcet Cambs 62 B2
Far Cotton Nhants 60 G9
Farden Shrops 57 K9
Fareham Hants 14 G5
Farewell Staffs 58 G2
Far Forest Worcs 57 N9
Farforth Lincs 87 K5
Far Green Gloucs 32 E4
Faringdon Oxon 33 Q5
Farington Lancs 88 G5
Farlam Cumb 111 L9
Farleigh N Som 31 P11
Farleigh Surrey 37 J8
Farleigh Hungerford Somset 20 F3
Farleigh Wallop Hants 22 H5
Farlesthorpe Lincs 87 N6
Farleton Cumb 95 L4
Farleton Lancs 95 M7
Farley Derbys 84 C8
Farley Staffs 71 K6
Farley Wilts 21 P9
Farley Green Suffk 63 M10
Farley Green Surrey 36 C11
Farley Hill Wokham 23 K2
Farleys End Gloucs 32 E2
Farlington C Port 15 J5
Farlington N York 98 C7
Farlow Shrops 57 L8
Farmborough BaNES 20 C2
Farmbridge End Essex 51 P8
Farmcote Gloucs 47 L9
Farmcote Shrops 57 P6
Farmington Gloucs 47 M11
Farmoor Oxon 34 E3
Far Moor Wigan 82 B4
Farms Common Cnwll 2 H7
Farm Town Leics 72 B7
Farmtown Moray 158 D7
Farnah Green Derbys 84 D11
Farnborough Gt Lon 37 K8
Farnborough Hants 23 N4
Farnborough W Berk 34 D8
Farnborough Warwks 48 D5
Farnborough Park Hants 23 N3
Farncombe Surrey 23 Q6
Farndish Bed 61 K8
Farndon Ches W 69 M4
Farndon Notts 85 N10
Farne Islands Nthumb 119 P3
Farnell Angus 143 L6

Farnham Dorset ... 21 J11
Farnham Essex ... 51 L6
Farnham N York ... 97 M8
Farnham Suffk ... 65 M9
Farnham Surrey ... 23 M5
Farnham Common Bucks ... 35 Q7
Farnham Green Essex ... 51 L5
Farnham Royal Bucks ... 35 Q8
Farningham Kent ... 37 M7
Farnley Leeds ... 90 H4
Farnley N York ... 97 K11
Farnley Tyas Kirk ... 90 F8
Farnsfield Notts ... 85 K9
Farnworth Bolton ... 89 L9
Farnworth Halton ... 81 Q7
Far Oakridge Gloucs ... 32 H4
Farr Highld ... 148 E7
Farr Highld ... 156 B11
Farr Highld ... 166 B4
Farraline Highld ... 147 P3
Farringdon Devon ... 9 P6
Farrington Gurney BaNES ... 20 B3
Far Sawrey Cumb ... 101 L11
Farsley Leeds ... 90 G3
Farther Howegreen Essex ... 52 D11
Farthing Green Kent ... 26 D2
Farthinghoe Nhants ... 48 F7
Farthingloe Kent ... 27 N3
Farthingstone Nhants ... 48 H4
Farthing Street Gt Lon ... 37 K8
Fartown Kirk ... 90 F7
Farway Devon ... 10 D5
Fasnacloich Ag & B ... 139 J8
Fasnakyle Highld ... 147 J2
Fassfern Highld ... 139 J2
Fatfield Sundld ... 113 M10
Faugh Cumb ... 111 K10
Fauld Staffs ... 71 M9
Fauldhouse W Loth ... 126 G5
Faulkbourne Essex ... 52 C8
Faulkland Somset ... 20 D4
Fauls Shrops ... 69 Q8
Faversham Kent ... 38 H9
Fawdington N York ... 97 P6
Fawdon N u Ty ... 113 K7
Fawdon Nthumb ... 119 K7
Fawfieldhead Staffs ... 71 K2
Fawkham Green Kent ... 37 N7
Fawler Oxon ... 48 C11
Fawley Bucks ... 35 L7
Fawley Hants ... 14 E6
Fawley W Berk ... 34 C8
Fawley Chapel Herefs ... 46 A9
Fawnog Flints ... 81 J11
Fawsley Nhants ... 60 C9
Faxfleet E R Yk ... 92 E6
Faygate W Susx ... 24 F4
Fazeley Staffs ... 59 K4
Fearby N York ... 97 J4
Fearn Highld ... 156 E2
Fearnan P & K ... 140 H9
Fearnbeg Highld ... 153 N6
Fearnhead Warrtn ... 82 D6
Fearnmore Highld ... 153 N5
Fearnoch Ag & B ... 124 A2
Featherstone Staffs ... 58 D3
Featherstone Wakefd ... 91 L7
Feckenham Worcs ... 47 K2
Feering Essex ... 52 E7
Feetham N York ... 103 J11
Feizor N York ... 96 A7
Felbridge Surrey ... 25 J3
Felbrigg Norfk ... 77 J4
Felcourt Surrey ... 25 J2
Felden Herts ... 50 B10
Felindre Carmth ... 42 G7
Felindre Carmth ... 43 L10
Felindre Carmth ... 43 P9
Felindre Cerdgn ... 43 L3
Felindre Powys ... 44 H10
Felindre Swans ... 28 H4
Felindre Farchog Pembks ... 41 M3
Felinfach Cerdgn ... 43 K3
Felinfach Powys ... 44 F8
Felinfoel Carmth ... 28 F4
Felingwmisaf Carmth ... 43 K10
Felingwmuchaf Carmth ... 43 K10
Felin-newydd Powys ... 44 G7
Felixkirk N York ... 97 Q4
Felixstowe Suffk ... 53 P5
Felixstowe Ferry Suffk ... 53 P4
Felkington Nthumb ... 118 H2
Felling Gatesd ... 113 L8
Fell Lane C Brad ... 90 C3
Fell Side Cumb ... 101 K3
Felmersham Bed ... 61 L9
Felmingham Norfk ... 77 K6
Felpham W Susx ... 15 P7
Felsham Suffk ... 64 C10
Felsted Essex ... 51 Q6
Feltham Gt Lon ... 36 D6
Felthamhill Surrey ... 36 C6
Felthorpe Norfk ... 76 H8
Felton Herefs ... 46 A5
Felton N Som ... 31 P11
Felton Nthumb ... 119 N10
Felton Butler Shrops ... 69 L11
Feltwell Norfk ... 63 M2
Fenay Bridge Kirk ... 90 F7
Fence Lancs ... 89 N3
Fence Rothm ... 84 F3
Fence Houses Sundld ... 113 M11
Fendike Corner Lincs ... 87 N8
Fen Ditton Cambs ... 62 G8
Fen Drayton Cambs ... 62 D7
Fen End Lincs ... 74 D6
Fen End Solhll ... 59 K10
Fenham Nthumb ... 119 L2
Feniscliffe Bl w D ... 89 K5
Feniscowles Bl w D ... 89 K5
Feniton Devon ... 10 B5
Feniton Court Devon ... 10 C5
Fenn Green Shrops ... 57 P8
Fenn Street Medway ... 38 C6
Fenny Bentley Derbys ... 71 M5
Fenny Bridges Devon ... 10 C5
Fenny Compton Warwks ... 48 C4
Fenny Drayton Leics ... 72 B11
Fenny Stratford M Keyn ... 49 N8
Fenrother Nthumb ... 113 J2
Fenstanton Cambs ... 62 D7
Fenstead End Suffk ... 63 P10

Fen Street Norfk ... 64 D2
Fen Street Suffk ... 64 H9
Fenton C Stke ... 70 F6
Fenton Cambs ... 62 D5
Fenton Cumb ... 111 K9
Fenton Lincs ... 85 P5
Fenton Lincs ... 85 Q10
Fenton Notts ... 85 N4
Fenton Nthumb ... 119 J4
Fenton Barns E Loth ... 128 E3
Fenwick Donc ... 91 N6
Fenwick E Ayrs ... 125 M9
Fenwick Nthumb ... 112 G6
Fenwick Nthumb ... 119 L6
Feock Cnwll ... 3 L6
Feolin Ferry Ag & B ... 122 F6
Fergushill N Ayrs ... 125 J9
Feriniquarrie Highld ... 152 B7
Fermain Bay Guern ... 10 c2
Fern Angus ... 142 H5
Ferndale Rhondd ... 30 C5
Ferndown Dorset ... 13 J4
Ferness Highld ... 156 H8
Fernham Oxon ... 33 N4
Fernhill Heath Worcs ... 46 G3
Fernhurst W Susx ... 23 N9
Fernie Fife ... 135 J4
Ferniegair S Lans ... 126 C7
Fernilea Highld ... 152 F11
Fernilee Derbys ... 83 M9
Fernwood Notts ... 85 P10
Ferrensby N York ... 97 N8
Ferriby Sluice N Linc ... 92 G6
Ferrindonald Highld ... 145 L6
Ferring W Susx ... 24 C10
Ferrybridge Wakefd ... 91 M6
Ferrybridge Services
Wakefd ... 91 M6
Ferryden Angus ... 143 N6
Ferryhill Dur ... 103 Q4
Ferryhill Station Dur ... 103 Q4
Ferryside Carmth ... 28 C2
Ferry Point Highld ... 162 G9
Fersfield Norfk ... 64 F5
Fersit Highld ... 139 N2
Feshiebridge Highld ... 148 F5
Fetcham Surrey ... 36 D9
Fetlar Shet ... 169 t4
Fetterangus Abers ... 159 N7
Fettercairn Abers ... 143 M3
Fewcott Oxon ... 48 F9
Fewston N York ... 97 J10
Ffairfach Carmth ... 43 M10
Ffair Rhos Cerdgn ... 54 G11
Ffald-y-Brenin Carmth ... 43 M6
Ffarmers Carmth ... 43 N6
Ffawyddog Powys ... 45 J11
Ffestiniog Railway Gwynd ... 67 L7
Ffordd-las Denbgs ... 68 F2
Fforest Carmth ... 28 G4
Fforest Gôch Neath ... 29 K4
Ffostrasol Cerdgn ... 42 G5
Ffrith Flints ... 69 J3
Ffynnonddewi Cerdgn ... 42 G4
Ffynnongroyw Flints ... 80 G8
Ffynnon-oer Cerdgn ... 43 K4
Fickleshole Surrey ... 37 J8
Fiddington Gloucs ... 46 H8
Fiddington Somset ... 18 H6
Fiddleford Dorset ... 12 D2
Fiddlers Green Cnwll ... 4 C10
Fiddlers Hamlet Essex ... 51 L11
Field Staffs ... 71 J8
Field Broughton Cumb ... 94 H4
Field Dalling Norfk ... 76 E4
Fieldhead Cumb ... 101 N3
Field Head Leics ... 72 D9
Fifehead Magdalen Dorset ... 20 E10
Fifehead Neville Dorset ... 12 C2
Fifehead St Quintin Dorset ... 12 C2
Fife Keith Moray ... 158 B7
Fifield Oxon ... 47 P11
Fifield W & M ... 35 P9
Fifield Wilts ... 21 M4
Figheldean Wilts ... 21 N5
Filands Wilts ... 32 H7
Filby Norfk ... 77 P9
Filey N York ... 99 N4
Filgrave M Keyn ... 49 N5
Filkins Oxon ... 33 P4
Filleigh Devon ... 17 M6
Filleigh Devon ... 8 H2
Fillingham Lincs ... 86 B3
Fillongley Warwks ... 59 L7
Filmore Hill Hants ... 23 J9
Filton S Glos ... 32 B9
Fimber E R Yk ... 98 H8
Finavon Angus ... 142 H6
Finberry Kent ... 26 H4
Fincham Norfk ... 75 N9
Finchampstead Wokham ... 23 L2
Fincharn Ag & B ... 131 J7
Finchdean Hants ... 15 K4
Finchingfield Essex ... 51 Q4
Finchley Gt Lon ... 36 G2
Findern Derbys ... 71 Q8
Findhorn Moray ... 157 J5
Findhorn Bridge Highld ... 148 E2
Findochty Moray ... 158 C4
Findo Gask P & K ... 134 C4
Findon Abers ... 151 N8
Findon W Susx ... 24 D9
Findon Mains Highld ... 155 R5
Findon Valley W Susx ... 24 D9
Findrack House Abers ... 150 G7
Finedon Nhants ... 61 K6
Fingal Street Suffk ... 65 J8
Fingask P & K ... 134 F2
Fingest Bucks ... 35 L6
Finghall N York ... 97 J3
Fingland Cumb ... 110 E9
Fingland D & G ... 115 Q4
Finglesham Kent ... 39 P11
Fingringhoe Essex ... 52 H7
Finkle Green Essex ... 52 B3
Finkle Street Barns ... 91 J11
Finlarig Stirlg ... 140 E11
Finmere Oxon ... 48 H8
Finnart P & K ... 140 D6
Finningham Suffk ... 64 F8
Finningley Donc ... 91 R11
Finsbay W Isls ... 168 f9
Finstall Worcs ... 58 E11
Finsthwaite Cumb ... 94 H3
Finstock Oxon ... 48 C11
Finstown Ork ... 169 c5

Fintry Abers ... 159 J7
Fintry Stirlg ... 133 J10
Finzean Abers ... 150 G9
Fionnphort Ag & B ... 137 J11
Fionnsbhagh W Isls ... 168 f9
Firbank Cumb ... 95 N2
Firbeck Rothm ... 85 J3
Firby N York ... 97 L3
Firby N York ... 98 E7
Firgrove Rochdl ... 89 Q8
Firle E Susx ... 25 L9
Firsby Lincs ... 87 N8
Firsdown Wilts ... 21 P7
Fir Tree Dur ... 103 M4
Fishbourne IoW ... 14 G8
Fishbourne W Susx ... 15 M6
Fishbourne Roman Palace
W Susx ... 15 M6
Fishburn Dur ... 104 C4
Fishcross Clacks ... 133 P8
Fisher W Susx ... 15 N6
Fisherford Abers ... 158 G10
Fisherrow E Loth ... 127 Q3
Fisher's Pond Hants ... 22 E10
Fisherstreet W Susx ... 23 P8
Fisherton Highld ... 156 C7
Fisherton S Ayrs ... 114 E4
Fisherton de la Mere Wilts ... 21 K7
Fisherwick Staffs ... 59 J4
Fishery W & M ... 35 N8
Fishguard Pembks ... 41 J3
Fishlake Donc ... 91 R8
Fishleigh Devon ... 8 D3
Fishmere End Lincs ... 74 E3
Fishnish Pier Ag & B ... 138 B3
Fishpond Bottom Dorset ... 10 H5
Fishponds Bristl ... 32 B9
Fishtoft Lincs ... 74 G2
Fishtoft Drove Lincs ... 87 K11
Fishwick Lancs ... 88 H5
Fiskavaig Highld ... 152 E11
Fiskerton Lincs ... 86 D6
Fiskerton Notts ... 85 M10
Fitling E R Yk ... 93 N4
Fittleton Wilts ... 21 M5
Fittleworth W Susx ... 24 B7
Fitton End Cambs ... 74 H8
Fitz Shrops ... 69 M11
Fitzhead Somset ... 18 F9
Fitzroy Somset ... 18 G9
Fitzwilliam Wakefd ... 91 L7
Five Ash Down E Susx ... 25 L6
Five Ashes E Susx ... 25 N5
Five Bells Somset ... 18 E6
Five Bridges Herefs ... 46 B5
Fivecrosses Ches W ... 82 B9
Fivehead Somset ... 19 L10
Fivelanes Cnwll ... 5 L5
Five Lanes Mons ... 31 M6
Five Oak Green Kent ... 37 P11
Five Oaks Jersey ... 11 c2
Five Oaks W Susx ... 24 C5
Five Roads Carmth ... 28 E3
Five Wents Kent ... 38 D11
Flack's Green Essex ... 52 C9
Flackwell Heath Bucks ... 35 N7
Fladbury Worcs ... 47 J5
Fladdabister Shet ... 169 r10
Flagg Derbys ... 83 N7
Flamborough E R Yk ... 99 Q6
Flamborough Head E R Yk ... 99 R6
Flamingo Land Theme
Park N York ... 98 F5
Flamstead Herts ... 50 C8
Flamstead End Herts ... 50 H10
Flansham W Susx ... 15 Q6
Flanshaw Wakefd ... 91 J6
Flappit Spring C Brad ... 90 D3
Flasby N York ... 96 D9
Flash Staffs ... 83 M11
Flashader Highld ... 152 E7
Flaunden Herts ... 50 B10
Flawborough Notts ... 73 K2
Flawith N York ... 97 Q7
Flax Bourton N Som ... 31 P11
Flaxby N York ... 97 N9
Flaxley Gloucs ... 46 C11
Flaxmere Ches W ... 82 C10
Flaxpool Somset ... 18 F7
Flaxton N York ... 98 D8
Fleckney Leics ... 60 D2
Flecknoe Warwks ... 60 B8
Fledborough Notts ... 85 P6
Fleet Dorset ... 11 N8
Fleet Hants ... 15 N6
Fleet Hants ... 23 M4
Fleet Lincs ... 74 G6
Fleetend Hants ... 14 F5
Fleet Hargate Lincs ... 74 G6
Fleet Services Hants ... 23 L3
Fleetwood Lancs ... 94 G11
Fleggburgh Norfk ... 77 N9
Flemingston V Glam ... 30 D11
Flemington S Lans ... 126 B6
Flempton Suffk ... 63 P7
Fletchersbridge Cnwll ... 5 J8
Fletcher's Green Kent ... 37 M11
Fletchertown Cumb ... 100 H3
Fletching E Susx ... 25 K6
Fleur-de-lis Caerph ... 30 G5
Flexbury Cnwll ... 16 C10
Flexford Surrey ... 23 P4
Flimby Cumb ... 100 D4
Flimwell E Susx ... 26 B5
Flint Flints ... 81 J10
Flintham Notts ... 85 M11
Flint Mountain Flints ... 81 J10
Flinton E R Yk ... 93 M3
Flint's Green Solhll ... 59 L8
Flishinghurst Kent ... 26 C4
Flitcham Norfk ... 75 P5
Flitch Green Essex ... 51 Q6
Flitton C Beds ... 50 C3
Flitwick C Beds ... 50 B4
Flixborough N Linc ... 92 E8
Flixborough Stather N Linc ... 92 E8
Flixton N York ... 99 L5
Flixton Suffk ... 65 L4
Flixton Traffd ... 82 F6
Flockton Kirk ... 90 G8
Flockton Green Kirk ... 90 H7
Flodden Nthumb ... 118 H3
Flodigarry Highld ... 152 H3
Flookburgh Cumb ... 94 H5
Flordon Norfk ... 64 H2

Flore Nhants ... 60 D8
Flotterton Nthumb ... 119 J10
Flowers Green E Susx ... 25 P8
Flowton Suffk ... 64 H6
Flushdyke Wakefd ... 90 H6
Flushing Cnwll ... 3 L6
Fluxton Devon ... 10 B6
Flyford Flavell Worcs ... 47 J3
Fobbing Thurr ... 38 B5
Fochabers Moray ... 157 Q6
Fochriw Caerph ... 30 F3
Fockerby N Linc ... 92 E7
Foddington Somset ... 19 Q9
Foel Powys ... 55 M2
Foelgastell Carmth ... 28 F2
Foel y Dyffryn Brdgnd ... 29 N6
Foggathorpe E R Yk ... 92 D3
Fogo Border ... 129 K10
Fogwatt Moray ... 157 N6
Foindle Highld ... 164 E7
Folda Angus ... 142 B5
Fole Staffs ... 71 J7
Foleshill Covtry ... 59 N8
Folke Dorset ... 11 P2
Folkestone Kent ... 27 M4
Folkingham Lincs ... 73 R4
Folkington E Susx ... 25 N10
Folksworth Cambs ... 61 P3
Folkton N York ... 99 L5
Folla Rule Abers ... 158 H11
Follifoot N York ... 97 M10
Folly Gate Devon ... 8 E5
Folly Hill Surrey ... 23 M5
Fonmon V Glam ... 30 D11
Fonthill Bishop Wilts ... 20 H8
Fonthill Gifford Wilts ... 20 H8
Fontmell Magna Dorset ... 20 G11
Fontmell Parva Dorset ... 12 D2
Fontwell W Susx ... 15 P5
Font-y-gary V Glam ... 30 L11
Foolow Derbys ... 83 Q9
Foots Cray Gt Lon ... 37 L6
Forbestown Abers ... 150 B5
Forcett N York ... 103 N8
Ford Ag & B ... 130 H1
Ford Bucks ... 35 L3
Ford Derbys ... 84 F4
Ford Devon ... 6 G8
Ford Devon ... 7 L9
Ford Devon ... 16 G7
Ford Gloucs ... 47 L9
Ford Nthumb ... 118 H3
Ford Shrops ... 56 G2
Ford Somset ... 18 E9
Ford Somset ... 19 Q4
Ford Staffs ... 71 K4
Ford W Susx ... 15 Q6
Ford Wilts ... 21 N8
Ford Wilts ... 32 F9
Forda Devon ... 8 D6
Fordcombe Kent ... 25 M2
Fordell Fife ... 134 F10
Forden Powys ... 56 C4
Ford End Essex ... 51 Q7
Forder Green Devon ... 7 K5
Ford Green Lancs ... 95 K5
Fordham Cambs ... 63 K6
Fordham Essex ... 52 F6
Fordham Norfk ... 75 M11
Ford Heath Shrops ... 56 G2
Fordingbridge Hants ... 13 K2
Fordon E R Yk ... 99 L5
Fordoun Abers ... 143 N2
Ford's Green Suffk ... 64 F8
Fordstreet Essex ... 52 F6
Ford Street Somset ... 18 G11
Fordton Devon ... 9 K5
Fordwells Oxon ... 34 B2
Fordwich Kent ... 39 L10
Fordyce Abers ... 158 E5
Forebridge Staffs ... 70 G10
Foremark Derbys ... 72 A5
Forest Guern ... 10 b2
Forest N York ... 103 Q10
Forest Becks Lancs ... 96 A10
Forestburn Gate Nthumb ... 119 L11
Forest Chapel Ches E ... 83 L10
Forest Coal Pit Mons ... 45 K10
Forest Gate Gt Lon ... 37 K3
Forest Green Surrey ... 24 D2
Forest Hall N Tyne ... 113 L7
Forest Head Cumb ... 111 L9
Forest Hill Gt Lon ... 37 J6
Forest Hill Oxon ... 34 G3
Forest-in-Teesdale Dur ... 102 G4
Forest Lane Head N York ... 97 M9
Forest Mill Clacks ... 134 B9
Forest of Bowland Lancs ... 95 N10
Forest of Dean Gloucs ... 32 B2
Forest Row E Susx ... 25 K4
Forest Side IoW ... 14 E9
Forestside W Susx ... 15 L4
Forest Town Notts ... 85 J8
Forfar Angus ... 142 H7
Forgandenny P & K ... 134 D4
Forge Powys ... 54 H4
Forge Hammer Torfn ... 31 J5
Forge Side Torfn ... 30 H3
Forgie Moray ... 158 A7
Forgieside Moray ... 158 B7
Forgue Abers ... 158 F8
Forhill Worcs ... 58 G9
Formby Sefton ... 88 C9
Forncett End Norfk ... 64 G3
Forncett St Mary Norfk ... 64 H3
Forncett St Peter Norfk ... 64 H3
Fornham All Saints Suffk ... 64 B8
Fornham St Martin Suffk ... 64 B8
Fornham St Genevieve
Suffk ... 64 A8
Fornighty Highld ... 156 G7
Forres Moray ... 157 J6
Forsbrook Staffs ... 70 H6
Forse Highld ... 167 M10
Forshaw Heath Warwks ... 58 G10
Forsinard Highld ... 166 H8
Forss Highld ... 166 H3
Forston Dorset ... 11 P5
Fort Augustus Highld ... 147 K6
Forteviot P & K ... 134 D4
Forth S Lans ... 126 G7
Forthampton Gloucs ... 46 G8
Fort Hommet Guern ... 10 b1
Forth Rail Bridge C Edin ... 127 L2
Forth Road Bridge Fife ... 127 L2

Fortingall P & K ... 140 H8
Forton Hants ... 22 D6
Forton Lancs ... 95 K10
Forton Shrops ... 69 M11
Forton Somset ... 10 G3
Forton Staffs ... 70 D10
Fort Richmond Guern ... 10 b2
Fortrie Abers ... 158 G8
Fortrose Highld ... 156 C6
Fortuneswell Dorset ... 11 P10
Fort William Highld ... 139 L3
Forty Green Bucks ... 35 P6
Forty Hill Gt Lon ... 50 H11
Forward Green Suffk ... 64 G10
Fosbury Wilts ... 22 B3
Foscot Oxon ... 47 P10
Foscote Nhants ... 49 J5
Fosdyke Lincs ... 74 F4
Fosdyke Bridge Lincs ... 74 F4
Foss P & K ... 141 J6
Fossebridge Gloucs ... 33 L2
Foss-y-ffin Cerdgn ... 42 H2
Fosterhouses Donc ... 91 R6
Foster Street Essex ... 51 L9
Foston Derbys ... 71 M8
Foston Leics ... 60 D2
Foston Lincs ... 73 M2
Foston N York ... 98 D7
Foston on the Wolds E R Yk ... 99 N9
Fotherby Lincs ... 87 K2
Fothergill Cumb ... 100 D4
Fotheringhay Nhants ... 61 N2
Foula Shet ... 169 k10
Foula Airport Shet ... 169 k10
Foul Anchor Cambs ... 75 J7
Foulbridge Cumb ... 110 H11
Foulby Wakefd ... 91 K7
Foulden Border ... 129 N8
Foulden Norfk ... 75 Q11
Foul End Warwks ... 59 K6
Foul Mile E Susx ... 25 P7
Foulness Island Essex ... 38 G3
Foulridge Lancs ... 89 P2
Foulsham Norfk ... 76 E6
Fountainhall Border ... 128 C10
Four Ashes Solhll ... 59 J9
Four Ashes Staffs ... 57 Q7
Four Ashes Staffs ... 58 D3
Four Ashes Suffk ... 64 E7
Four Cabots Guern ... 10 b2
Four Crosses Powys ... 69 J5
Four Crosses Staffs ... 58 E3
Four Elms Kent ... 37 L11
Four Foot Somset ... 19 Q8
Four Forks Somset ... 18 H7
Four Gates Bolton ... 89 J9
Four Gotes Cambs ... 75 J7
Four Lane End Barns ... 90 H10
Four Lane Ends Ches W ... 69 Q2
Four Lanes Cnwll ... 2 H6
Fourlanes End Ches E ... 70 E3
Four Marks Hants ... 23 J7
Four Mile Bridge IoA ... 78 D9
Four Oaks Birm ... 58 H5
Four Oaks E Susx ... 26 E5
Four Oaks Gloucs ... 46 C9
Four Oaks Solhll ... 59 K8
Fourpenny Highld ... 163 J8
Four Points W Berk ... 34 G9
Four Roads Carmth ... 28 D3
Four Shire Stone Warwks ... 47 P8
Fourstones Nthumb ... 112 C6
Four Throws Kent ... 26 C6
Four Wents Kent ... 37 P10
Fovant Wilts ... 21 K9
Foveran Abers ... 151 P2
Fowey Cnwll ... 5 J11
Fowley Common Warrtn ... 82 E5
Fowlhall Kent ... 37 Q11
Fowlis Angus ... 142 E11
Fowlis Wester P & K ... 133 Q3
Fowlmere Cambs ... 62 F11
Fownhope Herefs ... 46 A8
Foxbar Rens ... 125 M5
Foxcombe Devon ... 8 C7
Fox Corner Surrey ... 23 Q4
Foxcote Gloucs ... 47 K11
Foxcote Somset ... 20 D3
Foxdale IoM ... 80 c6
Foxearth Essex ... 52 D3
Foxendown Kent ... 37 P7
Foxfield Cumb ... 94 E3
Foxham Wilts ... 33 J9
Fox Hatch Essex ... 51 N11
Foxhills Hants ... 13 P2
Foxhole Cnwll ... 3 P3
Foxholes N York ... 99 L6
Foxhunt Green E Susx ... 25 M7
Foxley Nhants ... 48 H4
Foxley Norfk ... 76 F7
Foxley Wilts ... 32 G7
Foxlydiate Worcs ... 58 F11
Fox Street Essex ... 53 J6
Foxt Staffs ... 71 J5
Foxton Cambs ... 62 F11
Foxton Dur ... 104 C6
Foxton Leics ... 60 F3
Foxton N York ... 104 D3
Foxup N York ... 96 C6
Foxwist Green Ches W ... 82 D11
Foxwood Shrops ... 57 M9
Foy Herefs ... 46 A9
Foyers Highld ... 147 M3
Foynesfield Highld ... 156 F7
Fraddam Cnwll ... 2 F7
Fraddon Cnwll ... 4 E10
Fradley Staffs ... 59 J2
Fradswell Staffs ... 70 H8
Fraisthorpe E R Yk ... 99 P8
Framfield E Susx ... 25 L6
Framingham Earl Norfk ... 77 K11
Framingham Pigot Norfk ... 77 K11
Framlingham Suffk ... 65 K9
Frampton Dorset ... 11 N5
Frampton Lincs ... 74 F3
Frampton Cotterell S Glos ... 32 C8
Frampton Mansell Gloucs ... 32 H4
Frampton-on-Severn
Gloucs ... 32 D3
Frampton West End Lincs ... 74 F2
Framsden Suffk ... 65 J9
Framwellgate Moor Dur ... 103 Q2
Franche Worcs ... 57 Q9
Frandley Ches W ... 82 D9
Frankaborough Devon ... 5 P3
Frankby Wirral ... 81 J7

Frankfort Norfk 77 L7
Franklands Gate Herefs 45 Q5
Frankley Worcs 58 E8
Frankley Services Worcs 58 E8
Franksbridge Powys 44 G3
Frankton Warwks 59 P10
Frant E Susx 25 N3
Fraserburgh Abers 159 N4
Frating Essex 53 J7
Frating Green Essex 53 J7
Fratton C Port 15 J6
Freathy Cnwll 5 P11
Freckenham Suffk 63 L6
Freckleton Lancs 88 E5
Freebirch Derbys 84 D6
Freeby Leics 73 L6
Freefolk Hants 22 E5
Freehay Staffs 71 J4
Freeland Oxon 34 D2
Freethorpe Norfk 77 N10
Freethorpe Common Norfk 77 N11
Freiston Lincs 74 G2
Fremington Devon 17 J5
Fremington N York 103 K11
Frenchay S Glos 32 B9
Frenchbeer Devon 8 G7
French Street Kent 37 L10
Frenich P & K 141 K6
Frensham Surrey 23 M6
Fresgoe Highld 166 B3
Freshfield Sefton 88 B9
Freshford Wilts 20 E2
Freshwater IoW 13 P7
Freshwater Bay IoW 13 P7
Freshwater East Pembks 41 K11
Fressingfield Suffk 65 K6
Freston Suffk 53 L4
Freswick Highld 167 Q3
Fretherne Gloucs 32 D2
Frettenham Norfk 77 J8
Freuchie Fife 134 H6
Freystrop Pembks 41 J8
Friar Park Sandw 58 F6
Friar's Gate E Susx 25 L4
Friars' Hill N York 98 E3
Friar Waddon Dorset 11 N7
Friday Bridge Cambs 75 J10
Friday Street Suffk 65 J10
Friday Street Suffk 65 L11
Friday Street Suffk 65 M9
Friday Street Surrey 36 D11
Fridaythorpe E R Yk 98 H9
Friden Derbys 71 M2
Friendly Calder 90 D6
Friern Barnet Gt Lon 36 G2
Friesthorpe Lincs 86 E4
Frieston Lincs 86 B11
Frieth Bucks 35 L6
Friezeland Notts 84 G10
Frilford Oxon 34 D5
Frilsham W Berk 34 F10
Frimley Surrey 23 N3
Frimley Green Surrey 23 N3
Frindsbury Medway 38 B8
Fring Norfk 75 P4
Fringford Oxon 48 H9
Frinsted Kent 38 E10
Frinton-on-Sea Essex 53 M7
Friockheim Angus 143 K8
Friog Gwynd 54 E2
Frisby on the Wreake Leics 72 H7
Friskney Lincs 87 N9
Friskney Eaudike Lincs 87 N9
Friston E Susx 25 N11
Friston Suffk 65 N9
Fritchley Derbys 84 E10
Fritham Hants 13 M2
Frith Bank Lincs 87 K11
Frith Common Worcs 57 M11
Frithelstock Devon 16 H8
Frithelstock Stone Devon 16 H8
Frithend Hants 23 M7
Frithsden Herts 50 B9
Frithville Lincs 87 K10
Frittenden Kent 26 D3
Frittiscombe Devon 7 L10
Fritton Norfk 65 J3
Fritton Norfk 77 P11
Fritwell Oxon 48 F9
Frizinghall C Brad 90 E3
Frizington Cumb 100 D7
Frocester Gloucs 32 E4
Frodesley Shrops 57 J4
Frodsham Ches W 81 Q9
Frogden Border 118 E5
Frog End Cambs 62 E11
Frog End Cambs 62 H9
Froggatt Derbys 84 B5
Froghall Staffs 71 J5
Frogham Hants 13 L2
Frogham Kent 39 N11
Frogmore Devon 7 K10
Frognall Lincs 74 C8
Frogpool Cnwll 3 K5
Frog Pool Worcs 57 Q11
Frogwell Cnwll 5 N8
Frolesworth Leics 60 B3
Frome Somset 20 E5
Frome St Quintin Dorset 11 M4
Fromes Hill Herefs 46 C6
Fron Gwynd 66 F7
Fron Gwynd 67 J4
Fron Powys 44 B5
Fron Powys 56 C4
Froncysyllte Wrexhm 69 J6
Fron-goch Gwynd 68 B7
Fron Isaf Wrexhm 69 J6
Frostenden Suffk 65 P5
Frosterley Dur 103 K3
Froxfield C Beds 49 Q8
Froxfield Wilts 33 Q11
Froxfield Green Hants 23 K9
Fryern Hill Hants 22 D10
Fryerning Essex 51 P10
Fryton N York 98 D6
Fuinary Highld 137 M7
Fulbeck Lincs 86 B10
Fulbourn Cambs 62 H9
Fulbrook Oxon 33 Q3
Fulflood Hants 22 E8
Fulford C York 98 C11
Fulford Somset 18 H9
Fulford Staffs 70 H7
Fulham Gt Lon 36 F5
Fulking W Susx 24 F8
Fullaford Devon 17 M4
Fullarton N Ayrs 125 J10

Fuller's End Essex 51 M5
Fuller's Moor Ches W 69 N4
Fuller Street Essex 52 B8
Fuller Street Kent 37 N9
Fullerton Hants 22 C7
Fulletby Lincs 87 J6
Fullready Warwks 47 P8
Full Sutton E R Yk 98 E9
Fullwood E Ayrs 125 L7
Fulmer Bucks 35 Q7
Fulmodeston Norfk 76 D5
Fulnetby Lincs 86 E5
Fulney Lincs 74 E6
Fulstone Kirk 90 F9
Fulstow Lincs 93 P11
Fulwell Oxon 48 C10
Fulwell Sundld 113 N9
Fulwood Lancs 88 G4
Fulwood Notts 84 G9
Fulwood Sheff 84 D3
Fulwood Somset 18 H10
Fundenhall Norfk 64 H2
Funtington W Susx 15 M5
Funtley Hants 14 G5
Funtullich P & K 133 M2
Furley Devon 10 F4
Furnace Ag & B 131 L7
Furnace Carmth 28 F4
Furnace Cerdgn 54 F5
Furnace End Warwks 59 K6
Furner's Green E Susx 25 K5
Furness Vale Derbys 83 M8
Furneux Pelham Herts 51 K5
Further Quarter Kent 26 E4
Furtho Nhants 49 L6
Furzehill Devon 17 N2
Furzehill Dorset 12 H4
Furzehills Lincs 87 J6
Furzeley Corner Hants 15 J4
Furze Platt W & M 35 N8
Furzley Hants 21 Q11
Fyfett Somset 10 E2
Fyfield Essex 51 N9
Fyfield Hants 21 Q5
Fyfield Oxon 34 D5
Fyfield Wilts 21 N2
Fyfield Wilts 33 M11
Fyfield Bavant Wilts 21 K9
Fylingthorpe N York 105 P10
Fyning W Susx 23 M10
Fyvie Abers 159 J10

G

Gabroc Hill E Ayrs 125 M7
Gaddesby Leics 72 H8
Gaddesden Row Herts 50 C8
Gadfa IoA 78 H7
Gadgirth S Ayrs 114 H3
Gadlas Shrops 69 L7
Gaer Powys 44 H10
Gaerllwyd Mons 31 M5
Gaerwen IoA 78 H10
Gagingwell Oxon 48 D9
Gailes N Ayrs 125 J10
Gailey Staffs 58 D2
Gainford Dur 103 N7
Gainsborough Lincs 85 P3
Gainsborough Suffk 53 L3
Gainsford End Essex 52 B4
Gairloch Highld 153 Q2
Gairlochy Highld 146 F11
Gairneybridge P & K 134 E8
Gaisgill Cumb 102 B9
Gaitsgill Cumb 110 G11
Galashiels Border 117 P3
Galgate Lancs 95 K9
Galhampton Somset 20 B9
Gallanachbeg Ag & B 130 G2
Gallanachmore Ag & B 130 G2
Gallantry Bank Ches E 69 P4
Gallatown Fife 134 H9
Galley Common Warwks 59 M6
Galleywood Essex 52 B11
Gallovie Highld 147 P10
Galloway Forest Park 114 H10
Gallowfauld Angus 142 H9
Gallowhill P & K 142 B10
Gallows Green Essex 52 F6
Gallows Green Worcs 46 H2
Gallowstree Common Oxon 35 J8
Galltair Highld 145 P3
Gallt-y-foel Gwynd 67 K2
Gallypot Street E Susx 25 L3
Galmisdale Highld 144 G11
Galmpton Devon 6 H10
Galmpton Torbay 7 M7
Galphay N York 97 L6
Galston E Ayrs 125 N10
Gamballs Green Staffs 83 M11
Gamblesby Cumb 102 B3
Gambles Green Essex 52 C9
Gamelsby Cumb 110 E10
Gamesley Derbys 83 M6
Gamlingay Cambs 62 B10
Gamlingay Cinques Cambs 62 B10
Gamlingay Great Heath
Cambs 62 B10
Gammersgill N York 96 H4
Gamrie Abers 159 J5
Gamston Notts 72 F3
Gamston Notts 85 M5
Ganavan Herefs 45 Q11
Ganavan Bay Ag & B 138 F11
Gang Cnwll 5 N8
Ganllwyd Gwynd 67 N10
Gannachy Angus 143 K3
Ganstead E R Yk 93 K4
Ganthorpe N York 98 D6
Ganton N York 99 K5
Ganwick Corner Herts 50 G11
Gappah Devon 9 C4
Garbity Moray 157 Q7
Garboldisham Norfk 64 E5
Garbole Highld 148 D3
Garchory Abers 149 Q5
Garden City Flints 81 L11
Gardeners Green Wokham 35 M11
Gardenstown Abers 159 K5
Garden Village Sheff 90 H11
Garderhouse Shet 169 q9
Gardham E R Yk 92 G2
Gare Hill Somset 20 E6
Garelochhead Ag & B 131 Q9

Garford Oxon 34 D5
Garforth Leeds 91 L4
Gargrave N York 96 D10
Gargunnock Stirlg 133 L9
Garlic Street Norfk 65 J5
Garlieston D & G 107 N8
Garlinge Kent 39 P8
Garlinge Green Kent 39 K11
Garlogie Abers 151 K6
Garmond Abers 159 K7
Garmouth Moray 157 Q5
Garmston Shrops 57 L3
Garnant Carmth 29 J2
Garndolbenmaen Gwynd 66 H6
Garnett Bridge Cumb 101 P11
Garnfadryn Gwynd 66 D8
Garnkirk N Lans 126 B4
Garnlydan Blae G 30 G2
Garnswllt Swans 28 H3
Garn-yr-erw Torfn 30 H3
Garrabost W Isls 168 k4
Garrallan E Ayrs 115 K4
Garras Cnwll 3 J9
Garreg Gwynd 67 L6
Garrigill Cumb 102 D2
Garriston N York 97 J2
Garroch D & G 108 C4
Garrochtrie D & G 106 F10
Garrochty Ag & B 124 D7
Garros Highld 152 H5
Garsdale Cumb 95 Q3
Garsdale Head Cumb 96 A2
Garsdon Wilts 33 J7
Garshall Green Staffs 70 H8
Garsington Oxon 34 G4
Garstang Lancs 95 K11
Garston Herts 50 D10
Garston Lpool 81 N8
Garswood St Hel 82 C5
Gartachossan Ag & B 122 D7
Gartcosh N Lans 126 B4
Garth Brdgnd 29 N6
Garth Mons 31 K6
Garth Powys 44 D5
Garth Powys 56 D10
Garth Wrexhm 69 J6
Garthamlock C Glas 126 B4
Garthbrengy Powys 44 E8
Gartheli Cerdgn 43 L3
Garthmyl Powys 56 B5
Garthorpe Leics 73 L6
Garthorpe N Linc 92 D7
Garth Row Cumb 101 P11
Garths Cumb 95 L3
Gartly Abers 158 D11
Gartmore Stirlg 132 G8
Gartness N Lans 126 D5
Gartness Stirlg 132 G10
Gartocharn W Duns 132 E10
Garton E R Yk 93 N3
Garton-on-the-Wolds
E R Yk 99 K9
Gartymore Highld 163 N4
Garva Bridge Highld 147 N10
Garvald Border 127 L8
Garvald E Loth 128 F5
Garvan Highld 138 H2
Garvard Ag & B 136 b3
Garve Highld 155 L5
Garvellachs Ag & B 130 D5
Garvestone Norfk 76 E10
Garvock Inver 124 H3
Garway Herefs 45 P10
Garway Common Herefs 45 P10
Garway Hill Herefs 45 N9
Garynahine W Isls 168 h4
Garyvard W Isls 168 i6
Gasper Wilts 20 E8
Gastard Wilts 32 G11
Gasthorpe Norfk 64 D5
Gaston Green Essex 51 L7
Gatcombe IoW 14 E9
Gateacre Lpool 81 N8
Gatebeck Cumb 95 L3
Gate Burton Lincs 85 P4
Gateford Notts 85 J4
Gateforth N York 91 P5
Gatehead E Ayrs 125 K10
Gate Helmsley N York 98 D9
Gatehouse Nthumb 111 Q3
Gatehouse of Fleet D & G 108 C9
Gateley Norfk 76 D7
Gatenby N York 97 M3
Gatesgarth Cumb 100 G7
Gateshaw Border 118 E6
Gateshead Gatesd 113 L8
Gates Heath Ches W 69 N2
Gateside Angus 142 G9
Gateside E Rens 125 M6
Gateside Fife 134 F6
Gateside N Ayrs 125 K7
Gateslack D & G 116 B10
Gathurst Wigan 88 G9
Gatley Stockp 82 H7
Gatton Surrey 36 G10
Gattonside Border 117 Q3
Gatwick Airport W Susx 24 G2
Gaufron Powys 55 M11
Gaulby Leics 72 H10
Gauldry Fife 135 K3
Gauldswell P & K 142 C7
Gaulkthorn Lancs 89 M5
Gaultree Norfk 75 J9
Gaunton's Bank Ches E 69 Q5
Gaunt's Common Dorset 12 H3
Gaunt's End Essex 51 N5
Gautby Lincs 86 G6
Gavinton Border 129 K9
Gawber Barns 91 J9
Gawcott Bucks 49 J8
Gawsworth Ches E 83 J11
Gawthorpe Wakefd 90 H6
Gawthrop Cumb 95 P3
Gawthwaite Cumb 94 F4
Gay Bowers Essex 52 C11
Gaydon Warwks 48 C4
Gayhurst M Keyn 49 M5
Gayle N York 96 C3
Gayles N York 103 M9
Gay Street W Susx 24 C6
Gayton Nhants 49 K4
Gayton Norfk 75 P7
Gayton Staffs 70 H9
Gayton Wirral 81 K8
Gayton le Marsh Lincs 87 M4
Gayton Thorpe Norfk 75 P7
Gaywood Norfk 75 M6
Gazeley Suffk 63 M8

Gear Cnwll 3 J9
Gearraidh Bhaird W Isls 168 i6
Gearraidh na h-Aibhne
W Isls 168 h4
Geary Highld 152 D5
Gedding Suffk 64 C10
Geddington Nhants 61 J4
Gedling Notts 72 G2
Gedney Lincs 74 H6
Gedney Broadgate Lincs 74 H6
Gedney Drove End Lincs 75 J5
Gedney Dyke Lincs 74 H5
Gedney Hill Lincs 74 F8
Gee Cross Tamesd 83 L6
Geeston Rutlnd 73 P10
Geirinis W Isls 168 c13
Geldeston Norfk 65 M3
Gelli Rhondd 30 C6
Gelli Torfn 31 J6
Gellideg Myr Td 30 D3
Gellifor Denbgs 68 F2
Gelligaer Caerph 30 F5
Gelligroes Caerph 30 G6
Gelligron Neath 29 K4
Gellilydan Gwynd 67 M7
Gellinudd Neath 29 K4
Gelly Pembks 41 L7
Gellyburn P & K 141 Q10
Gellywen Carmth 41 Q6
Gelston D & G 108 G9
Gelston Lincs 86 B11
Gembling E R Yk 99 N9
Gentleshaw Staffs 58 G2
Georgefield D & G 110 E2
George Green Bucks 35 Q8
Georgeham Devon 16 H4
Georgemas Junction
Station Highld 167 L5
George Nympton Devon 17 N7
Georgetown Blae G 30 G3
Georgia Cnwll 2 D6
Georth Ork 169 c4
Gerinish W Isls 168 c13
Gerlan Gwynd 79 L11
Germansweek Devon 8 B6
Germoe Cnwll 2 F8
Gerrans Cnwll 3 M6
Gerrards Cross Bucks 36 B3
Gerrick R & Cl 105 K8
Gestingthorpe Essex 52 D4
Gethsemane Pembks 41 L2
Geuffordd Powys 56 C2
Gib Hill Ches W 82 D9
Gibraltar Lincs 87 Q9
Gibsmere Notts 85 M11
Giddeahall Wilts 32 G10
Giddy Green Dorset 12 D7
Gidea Park Gt Lon 37 M2
Gidleigh Devon 8 G7
Giffnock E Rens 125 P6
Gifford E Loth 128 E6
Giffordtown Fife 134 H5
Giggleswick N York 96 B8
Gigha Ag & B 123 K10
Gilberdyke E R Yk 92 D5
Gilbert's End Worcs 46 F6
Gilbert Street Hants 22 H8
Gilchriston E Loth 128 D6
Gilcrux Cumb 100 F3
Gildersome Leeds 90 G5
Gildingwells Rothm 85 J3
Gilesgate Moor Dur 103 Q2
Gileston V Glam 30 D11
Gilfach Caerph 30 G5
Gilfach Goch Brdgnd 30 C6
Gilfachrheda Cerdgn 42 H3
Gilgarran Cumb 100 D6
Gill Cumb 101 M5
Gillamoor N York 98 D3
Gillan Cnwll 3 K8
Gillen Highld 152 D6
Gillesbie D & G 110 C2
Gilling East N York 98 C5
Gillingham Dorset 20 F9
Gillingham Medway 38 C8
Gillingham Norfk 65 N3
Gilling West N York 103 N9
Gillock Highld 167 M5
Gillow Heath Staffs 70 F3
Gills Highld 167 P2
Gill's Green Kent 26 C5
Gilmanscleuch Border 117 L6
Gilmerton C Edin 127 P4
Gilmerton P & K 133 P3
Gilmonby Dur 103 J8
Gilmorton Leics 60 C3
Gilsland Nthumb 111 M7
Gilson Warwks 59 J7
Gilstead C Brad 90 E3
Gilston Border 128 D6
Gilston Herts 51 K8
Gilston Park Herts 51 K8
Giltbrook Notts 84 G11
Gilwern Mons 30 H2
Gimingham Norfk 77 K4
Ginclough Ches E 83 L9
Gingers Green E Susx 25 P8
Gipping Suffk 64 F9
Gipsey Bridge Lincs 87 J11
Girdle Toll N Ayrs 125 J9
Girlington C Brad 90 E4
Girlsta Shet 169 r8
Girsby N York 104 C9
Girtford C Beds 61 Q11
Girthon D & G 108 D10
Girton Cambs 62 F8
Girton Notts 85 P7
Girvan S Ayrs 114 C8
Gisburn Lancs 96 B11
Gisleham Suffk 65 Q4
Gislingham Suffk 64 F7
Gissing Norfk 64 G4
Gittisham Devon 10 C5
Givons Grove Surrey 36 E10
Gladestry Powys 45 J3
Gladsmuir E Loth 128 D5
Glais Swans 29 K4
Glaisdale N York 105 L9
Glamis Angus 142 F8
Glanaber Gwynd 67 L4
Glanaman Carmth 29 J2
Glandford Norfk 76 E3
Glan-Duar Carmth 43 K6
Glandwr Pembks 41 N5
Glan-Dwyfach Gwynd 66 H6
Glandy Cross Carmth 41 M5

Glandyfi Cerdgn 54 F5
Glangrwyney Powys 45 J11
Glanllynfi Brdgnd 29 N6
Glanmule Powys 56 B6
Glanrhyd Pembks 41 M2
Glan-rhyd Powys 29 L3
Glanton Nthumb 119 L8
Glanton Pike Nthumb 119 L8
Glanvilles Wootton Dorset 11 P3
Glan-y-don Flints 80 H9
Glan-y-llyn Rhondd 30 F8
Glan-y-nant Powys 55 L8
Glan-yr-afon Gwynd 68 B6
Glan-yr-afon Gwynd 68 D6
Glan-yr-afon IoA 79 L8
Glan-y-wern Gwynd 67 L8
Glapthorn Nhants 61 M2
Glapwell Derbys 84 G7
Glasbury Powys 44 H7
Glascoed Denbgs 80 D10
Glascoed Mons 31 K4
Glascote Staffs 59 K4
Glascwm Powys 44 H4
Glasfryn Conwy 68 B4
Glasgow C Glas 125 P4
Glasgow Airport Rens 125 M4
Glasgow Prestwick Airport
S Ayrs 114 G2
Glasgow Science Centre
C Glas 125 P4
Glasinfryn Gwynd 79 K11
Glasnacardoch Bay Highld 145 L8
Glasnakille Highld 144 H5
Glasphein Highld 152 B8
Glaspwll Powys 54 G5
Glassenbury Kent 26 C4
Glassford S Lans 126 C8
Glass Houghton Wakefd 91 L6
Glasshouse Gloucs 46 D10
Glasshouse Hill Gloucs 46 D10
Glasshouses N York 97 J8
Glasslaw Abers 159 L6
Glasson Cumb 110 E8
Glasson Lancs 95 J9
Glassonby Cumb 101 Q3
Glasterlaw Angus 143 K7
Glaston Rutlnd 73 M10
Glastonbury Somset 19 P7
Glatton Cambs 61 Q3
Glazebrook Warrtn 82 E6
Glazebury Warrtn 82 E5
Glazeley Shrops 57 N7
Gleadless Sheff 84 E4
Gleadsmoss Ches E 82 H11
Gleaston Cumb 94 F6
Glebe Highld 147 N4
Gledhow Leeds 91 J3
Gledpark D & G 108 D10
Gledrid Shrops 69 K7
Glemsford Suffk 52 D2
Glen Achulish Highld 139 K6
Glenallachie Moray 157 P9
Glenancross Highld 145 L9
Glenaros House Ag & B 137 P4
Glen Auldyn IoM 80 f3
Glenbarr Ag & B 120 C4
Glenbarry Abers 158 E7
Glenbeg Highld 137 P3
Glenbervie Abers 151 K11
Glenboig N Lans 126 C4
Glenborrodale Highld 137 Q3
Glenbranter Ag & B 131 N8
Glenbreck Border 116 F6
Glenbrittle Highld 144 F3
Glenbuck E Ayrs 115 P2
Glencally Angus 142 F5
Glencaple D & G 109 L7
Glencarse P & K 134 F3
Glencoe Highld 139 L6
Glencothe Border 116 F5
Glencraig Fife 134 F9
Glencrosh D & G 115 Q10
Glendale Highld 152 B8
Glendaruel Ag & B 131 K11
Glendevon P & K 134 B7
Glendoe Lodge Highld 147 L6
Glendoick P & K 134 G3
Glenduckie Fife 134 H4
Glenegedale Ag & B 122 D9
Glenelg Highld 145 P4
Glenerney Moray 157 J8
Glenfarg P & K 134 E5
Glenfield Leics 72 E9
Glenfinnan Highld 145 R11
Glenfintaig Lodge Highld 146 G10
Glenfoot P & K 134 F4
Glenfyne Lodge Ag & B 132 Q4
Glengarnock N Ayrs 125 J7
Glengolly Highld 167 K3
Glengorm Castle Ag & B 137 L4
Glengrasco Highld 152 G8
Glenholm Border 116 G4
Glenhoul D & G 115 M10
Glenkin Ag & B 131 N11
Glenkindie Abers 150 C5
Glenlivet Moray 149 M2
Glenlochar D & G 108 F8
Glenlomond P & K 134 F7
Glenluce D & G 106 G6
Glenmassen Ag & B 131 N10
Glenmavis N Lans 126 D4
Glen Maye IoM 80 b6
Glen Mona IoM 80 g4
Glenmore Highld 152 G9
Glenmore Lodge Highld 148 H6
Glen Nevis House Highld 139 L3
Glenochil Clacks 133 P8
Glen Parva Leics 72 F11
Glenquiech Angus 142 G5
Glenralloch Ag & B 123 Q6
Glenridding Cumb 101 L7
Glenrothes Fife 134 H7
Glenshero Lodge Highld 147 P9
Glenstriven Ag & B 124 D2
Glentham Lincs 86 D2
Glentrool D & G 107 L2
Glen Trool Lodge D & G 114 H11
Glentruim Highld 148 B9
Glentworth Lincs 86 B3
Glenuig Highld 138 B2
Glenvarragill Highld 152 H10
Glen Vine IoM 80 d6
Glenwhilly D & G 106 G3
Glespin S Lans 115 R2
Glewstone Herefs 45 R10

Glinton C Pete 74 C9
Glooston Leics 73 K11
Glossop Derbys 83 M6
Gloster Hill Nthumb 119 Q10
Gloucester Gloucs 46 F11
Gloucester Services Gloucs 32 F2
Gloucestershire Airport Gloucs 46 G10
Glusburn N York 96 F11
Glutt Lodge Highld 166 H9
Gluvian Cnwll 4 E9
Glympton Oxon 48 D10
Glynarthen Cerdgn 42 F5
Glyn Ceiriog Wrexhm 68 H7
Glyncoch Rhondd 30 E6
Glyncorrwg Neath 29 N5
Glynde E Susx 25 L9
Glyndebourne E Susx 25 L8
Glyndyfrdwy Denbgs 68 F6
Glynneath Neath 29 N3
Glynogwr Brdgnd 30 C7
Glyntaff Rhondd 30 L7
Glyntawe Powys 44 A11
Glynteg Carmth 42 G7
Gnosall Staffs 70 E10
Gnosall Heath Staffs 70 E10
Goadby Leics 73 K11
Goadby Marwood Leics 73 K5
Goatacre Wilts 33 K9
Goatham Green E Susx 26 D7
Goathill Dorset 20 C11
Goathland N York 105 M10
Goathurst Somset 19 J8
Goathurst Common Kent 37 L10
Goat Lees Kent 26 H2
Gobowen Shrops 69 K8
Godalming Surrey 23 Q6
Goddard's Corner Suffk 65 K8
Goddard's Green Kent 26 D5
Goddards Green W Susx 24 G6
Godden Green Kent 37 N9
Godford Cross Devon 10 C4
Godington Oxon 48 H9
Godley Tamesd 83 L5
Godmanchester Cambs 62 B6
Godmanstone Dorset 11 P5
Godmersham Kent 39 J11
Godney Somset 19 N6
Godolphin Cross Cnwll 2 G7
Godre'r-graig Neath 29 L3
Godshill Hants 21 N11
Godshill IoW 14 F10
Godstone Staffs 71 J8
Godstone Surrey 37 J10
Godsworthy Devon 8 D9
Godwinscroft Hants 13 L5
Goetre Mons 31 K3
Goff's Oak Herts 50 H10
Gogar C Edin 127 M3
Goginan Cerdgn 54 F8
Golan Gwynd 67 J6
Golant Cnwll 5 J11
Golberdon Cnwll 5 N7
Golborne Wigan 82 D5
Golcar Kirk 90 D7
Goldcliff Newpt 31 L8
Golden Cross E Susx 25 M8
Golden Green Kent 37 P11
Golden Grove Carmth 43 L11
Goldenhill C Stke 70 F4
Golden Hill Pembks 41 J10
Golden Pot Hants 23 K6
Golden Valley Derbys 84 F10
Golders Green Gt Lon 36 F3
Goldfinch Bottom W Berk 22 F2
Goldhanger Essex 52 F10
Gold Hill Cambs 62 H2
Gold Hill Dorset 12 D2
Golding Shrops 57 J4
Goldington Bed 61 N10
Goldsborough N York 97 N9
Goldsborough N York 105 M8
Golds Green Sandw 58 E6
Goldsithney Cnwll 2 E9
Goldstone Kent 39 N9
Goldstone Shrops 70 C9
Goldthorpe Barns 91 M10
Goldworthy Devon 16 F7
Golford Kent 26 C4
Golford Green Kent 26 C4
Gollanfield Highld 156 E7
Gollinglith Foot N York 96 H4
Golly Wrexhm 69 K3
Golsoncott Somset 18 D7
Golspie Highld 163 J6
Gomeldon Wilts 21 N7
Gomersal Kirk 90 G5
Gomshall Surrey 36 C11
Gonalston Notts 85 L11
Gonerby Hill Foot Lincs 73 N3
Gonfirth Shet 169 q7
Goodameavy Devon 6 E6
Good Easter Essex 51 P8
Gooderstone Norfk 75 Q10
Goodleigh Devon 17 L5
Goodmanham E R Yk 92 E2
Goodmayes Gt Lon 37 L3
Goodnestone Kent 38 H9
Goodnestone Kent 39 N11
Goodrich Herefs 45 R11
Goodrington Torbay 7 M7
Goodshaw Lancs 89 N5
Goodshaw Fold Lancs 89 N5
Goodstone Devon 7 K4
Goodwick Pembks 40 H3
Goodwood W Susx 15 N5
Goodworth Clatford Hants 22 C6
Goodyers End Warwks 59 M7
Goole E R Yk 92 B6
Goole Fields E R Yk 92 C6
Goom's Hill Worcs 47 K4
Goonbell Cnwll 3 J4
Goonhavern Cnwll 3 K3
Goonvrea Cnwll 3 J4
Goosecruives Abers 151 K11
Gooseford Devon 8 G6
Goose Green Essex 53 K6
Goose Green Kent 26 D4
Goose Green Kent 37 P10
Goose Green S Glos 32 C10
Goose Green W Susx 24 D7
Goose Green Wigan 82 C4
Gooseham Cnwll 16 C8
Gooseham Mill Cnwll 16 C8
Goosehill Green Worcs 46 H2
Goose Pool Herefs 45 P7

Goosey Oxon 34 C6
Goosnargh Lancs 88 H3
Goostrey Ches E 82 G10
Gordano Services N Som 31 P9
Gorddinog Conwy 79 M10
Gordon Border 118 B2
Gordon Arms Hotel Border 117 L5
Gordonstown Abers 158 E6
Gordonstown Abers 158 H10
Gore Powys 45 K3
Gorebridge Mdloth 127 Q5
Gorefield Cambs 74 H8
Gore Pit Essex 52 E8
Gores Wilts 21 M3
Gore Street Kent 39 N8
Gorey Jersey 11 c2
Goring Oxon 34 H8
Goring-by-Sea W Susx 24 D10
Goring Heath Oxon 35 J9
Gorleston-on-Sea Norfk 77 Q11
Gorrachie Abers 158 H6
Gorran Churchtown Cnwll 3 P5
Gorran Haven Cnwll 3 Q5
Gorran High Lanes Cnwll 3 P5
Gorrig Cerdgn 42 H6
Gors Cerdgn 54 E9
Gorsedd Flints 80 H9
Gorse Hill Swindn 33 N7
Gorseinon Swans 28 G5
Gorseybank Derbys 71 P4
Gorsgoch Cerdgn 43 J4
Gorslas Carmth 28 G2
Gorsley Gloucs 46 C9
Gorsley Common Herefs 46 C9
Gorstage Ches W 82 D10
Gorstan Highld 155 J5
Gorstella Ches W 69 L2
Gorsten Ag & B 138 C11
Gorst Hill Worcs 57 N10
Gorsty Hill Staffs 71 L9
Gorthleck Highld 147 N3
Gorton Manch 83 J5
Gosbeck Suffk 64 H10
Gosberton Lincs 74 D4
Gosberton Clough Lincs 74 C5
Gosfield Essex 52 C6
Gosford Devon 10 C5
Gosford Oxon 34 E2
Gosforth Cumb 100 E10
Gosforth N u Ty 113 K7
Gosling Street Somset 19 P8
Gosmore Herts 50 E5
Gospel End Staffs 58 C6
Gospel Green W Susx 23 P8
Gosport Hants 14 H7
Gossard's Green C Beds 49 Q6
Gossington Gloucs 32 D4
Goswick Nthumb 119 L2
Gotham Notts 72 E4
Gotherington Gloucs 47 J9
Gotton Somset 18 H9
Goudhurst Kent 26 B4
Goulceby Lincs 87 J5
Gourdas Abers 159 J9
Gourdie C Dund 142 F11
Gourdon Abers 143 Q3
Gourock Inver 124 G2
Govan C Glas 125 N4
Goveton Devon 7 K9
Govilon Mons 31 J2
Gowdall E R Yk 91 Q6
Gower Highld 155 P6
Gower Swans 28 F6
Gowerton Swans 28 G5
Gowkhall Fife 134 D10
Gowthorpe E R Yk 98 F10
Goxhill E R Yk 93 L2
Goxhill N Linc 93 K6
Goytre Neath 29 L7
Grabhair W Isls 168 i6
Graby Lincs 74 A5
Grade Cnwll 3 J11
Gradeley Green Ches E 69 Q4
Graffham W Susx 23 P11
Grafham Cambs 61 Q7
Grafham Surrey 24 B2
Grafton Herefs 45 P7
Grafton N York 97 P8
Grafton Oxon 33 Q4
Grafton Shrops 69 M11
Grafton Worcs 46 A2
Grafton Worcs 47 J7
Grafton Flyford Worcs 47 J3
Grafton Regis Nhants 49 L5
Grafton Underwood Nhants 61 K4
Grafty Green Kent 26 E2
Graianrhyd Denbgs 68 H3
Graig Conwy 79 Q10
Graig Denbgs 80 F10
Graigfechan Denbgs 68 F4
Grain Medway 38 E6
Grains Bar Oldham 90 B9
Grainsby Lincs 93 N11
Grainthorpe Lincs 93 Q11
Grampound Cnwll 3 N4
Grampound Road Cnwll 3 N3
Gramsdal W Isls 168 d12
Gramsdale W Isls 168 d12
Granborough Bucks 49 L9
Granby Notts 73 K3
Grandborough Warwks 59 Q11
Grand Chemins Jersey 11 c2
Grandes Rocques Guern 10 b1
Grandtully P & K 141 M7
Grange Cumb 101 J7
Grange Medway 38 C8
Grange P & K 134 H2
Grange Villa Dur 113 K10
Gransmoor E R Yk 99 N9
Gransmore Green Essex 51 Q6
Granston Pembks 40 G4
Grantchester Cambs 62 F9

Grantham Lincs 73 N3
Granton C Edin 127 N2
Grantown-on-Spey Highld 149 J2
Grantsfield Herefs 45 Q2
Grantshouse Border 129 L6
Grappenhall Warrtn 82 D7
Grasby Lincs 93 J10
Grasmere Cumb 101 K9
Grasscroft Oldham 83 L4
Grassendale Lpool 81 M7
Grassgarth Cumb 101 K2
Grass Green Essex 52 B4
Grassington N York 96 F8
Grassmoor Derbys 84 F7
Grassthorpe Notts 85 N7
Gratwich Staffs 71 J8
Graveley Cambs 62 C8
Graveley Herts 50 F5
Gravelly Hill Birm 58 H6
Gravelsbank Shrops 56 E4
Graveney Kent 39 J9
Gravesend Kent 37 Q6
Gravir W Isls 168 i6
Grayingham Lincs 92 F11
Grayrigg Cumb 101 Q11
Grays Thurr 37 P5
Grayshott Hants 23 N7
Grayson Green Cumb 100 C5
Grayswood Surrey 23 P8
Graythorpe Hartpl 104 F5
Grazeley Wokham 35 J11
Greasbrough Rothm 91 L11
Greasby Wirral 81 K7
Greasley Notts 84 G11
Great Abington Cambs 62 H11
Great Addington Nhants 61 L5
Great Alne Warwks 47 M3
Great Altcar Lancs 88 C9
Great Amwell Herts 51 J8
Great Asby Cumb 102 C8
Great Ashfield Suffk 64 D8
Great Ayton N York 104 G8
Great Baddow Essex 52 B11
Great Badminton S Glos 32 F8
Great Bardfield Essex 51 Q4
Great Barford Bed 61 P10
Great Barr Sandw 58 F5
Great Barrington Gloucs 33 Q2
Great Barrow Ches W 81 P11
Great Barton Suffk 64 B8
Great Barugh N York 98 E5
Great Bavington Nthumb 112 G4
Great Bealings Suffk 53 M2
Great Bedwyn Wilts 21 Q2
Great Bentley Essex 53 K7
Great Billing Nhants 60 H8
Great Bircham Norfk 75 Q4
Great Blakenham Suffk 64 G10
Great Blencow Cumb 101 N4
Great Bolas Wrekin 70 A10
Great Bookham Surrey 36 D10
Great Bosullow Cnwll 2 C7
Great Bourton Oxon 48 E5
Great Bowden Leics 60 F3
Great Bradley Suffk 63 L10
Great Braxted Essex 52 E9
Great Bricett Suffk 64 E11
Great Brickhill Bucks 49 P8
Great Bridgeford Staffs 70 F9
Great Brington Nhants 60 E7
Great Bromley Essex 53 J6
Great Broughton Cumb 100 E4
Great Broughton N York 104 H9
Great Budworth Ches W 82 E9
Great Burdon Darltn 104 B7
Great Burstead Essex 37 Q2
Great Busby N York 104 F9
Great Canfield Essex 51 N7
Great Carlton Lincs 87 M3
Great Casterton Rutlnd 73 Q9
Great Chalfield Wilts 20 G2
Great Chart Kent 26 G3
Great Chatwell Staffs 57 P2
Great Chell C Stke 70 F4
Great Chesterford Essex 51 M2
Great Chishill Cambs 51 K3
Great Clacton Essex 53 L8
Great Cliffe Wakefd 91 J7
Great Clifton Cumb 100 D5
Great Coates NE Lin 93 M9
Great Comberton Worcs 47 J6
Great Comp Kent 37 P9
Great Corby Cumb 111 J10
Great Cornard Suffk 52 E3
Great Cowden E R Yk 93 M2
Great Coxwell Oxon 33 Q6
Great Cransley Nhants 60 H5
Great Cressingham Norfk 76 B11
Great Crosthwaite Cumb 101 J6
Great Cubley Derbys 71 M7
Great Cumbrae Island N Ayrs 124 F6
Great Dalby Leics 73 J8
Great Denham Bed 61 M11
Great Doddington Nhants 61 J8
Great Doward Herefs 45 Q11
Great Dunham Norfk 76 B9
Great Dunmow Essex 51 P6
Great Durnford Wilts 21 M7
Great Easton Essex 51 P5
Great Easton Leics 60 H2
Great Eccleston Lancs 88 E2
Great Edstone N York 98 E3
Great Ellingham Norfk 64 E2
Great Elm Somset 20 D5
Great Everdon Nhants 60 C9
Great Eversden Cambs 62 E10
Great Fencote N York 97 L2
Greatfield Wilts 33 L7
Great Finborough Suffk 64 D10
Greatford Lincs 74 A8
Great Fransham Norfk 76 B9
Great Gaddesden Herts 50 B8
Greatgate Staffs 71 K5
Great Gidding Cambs 61 P4
Great Givendale E R Yk 98 G10
Great Glemham Suffk 65 L9
Great Glen Leics 72 H11
Great Gonerby Lincs 73 M3
Great Gransden Cambs 62 C9
Great Green Cambs 50 Q2
Great Green Norfk 65 K4
Great Green Suffk 64 C10
Great Green Suffk 64 C8

Great Habton N York 98 F5
Great Hale Lincs 74 B2
Great Hallingbury Essex 51 M7
Greatham Hants 23 L8
Greatham Hartpl 104 E5
Greatham W Susx 24 B7
Great Hampden Bucks 35 M4
Great Harrowden Nhants 61 J6
Great Harwood Lancs 89 L4
Great Haseley Oxon 34 H4
Great Hatfield E R Yk 93 L2
Great Haywood Staffs 70 H10
Great Heck N York 91 P6
Great Henny Essex 52 E4
Great Hinton Wilts 20 H3
Great Hockham Norfk 64 D3
Great Holland Essex 53 M8
Great Hollands Br For 35 N11
Great Horkesley Essex 52 G5
Great Hormead Herts 51 K5
Great Horton C Brad 90 E4
Great Horwood Bucks 49 L8
Great Houghton Barns 91 L9
Great Houghton Nhants 60 G9
Great Hucklow Derbys 83 Q9
Great Kelk E R Yk 99 N9
Great Kimble Bucks 35 M4
Great Kingshill Bucks 35 N5
Great Langdale Cumb 101 J9
Great Langton N York 103 Q11
Great Leighs Essex 52 B8
Great Limber Lincs 93 K9
Great Linford M Keyn 49 N6
Great Livermere Suffk 64 B7
Great Longstone Derbys 84 B6
Great Lumley Dur 113 L11
Great Lyth Shrops 56 H3
Great Malvern Worcs 46 E5
Great Maplestead Essex 52 D5
Great Marton Bpool 88 C3
Great Massingham Norfk 75 Q6
Great Melton Norfk 76 G10
Great Meols Wirral 81 J6
Great Milton Oxon 34 H4
Great Missenden Bucks 35 N4
Great Mitton Lancs 89 L3
Great Mongeham Kent 39 Q11
Great Moulton Norfk 64 H3
Great Munden Herts 51 J6
Great Musgrave Cumb 102 E8
Great Ness Shrops 69 L11
Great Notley Essex 52 B7
Great Oak Mons 31 L2
Great Oakley Essex 53 L6
Great Oakley Nhants 61 J3
Great Offley Herts 50 D5
Great Ormside Cumb 102 D7
Great Orton Cumb 110 F10
Great Ouseburn N York 97 P8
Great Oxendon Nhants 60 F4
Great Oxney Green Essex 51 Q9
Great Palgrave Norfk 76 A9
Great Park N u Ty 113 K6
Great Parndon Essex 51 K9
Great Pattenden Kent 26 B3
Great Paxton Cambs 62 B8
Great Plumpton Lancs 88 D4
Great Plumstead Norfk 77 L9
Great Ponton Lincs 73 N4
Great Potheridge Devon 17 J9
Great Preston Leeds 91 L5
Great Purston Nhants 48 F6
Great Raveley Cambs 62 C4
Great Rissington Gloucs 47 N11
Great Rollright Oxon 48 B8
Great Ryburgh Norfk 76 D6
Great Ryle Nthumb 119 K8
Great Ryton Shrops 56 H4
Great Saling Essex 52 B6
Great Salkeld Cumb 101 Q3
Great Sampford Essex 51 P3
Great Saredon Staffs 58 E3
Great Saughall Ches W 81 M11
Great Saxham Suffk 63 N8
Great Shefford W Berk 34 C9
Great Shelford Cambs 62 G10
Great Smeaton N York 104 B10
Great Snoring Norfk 76 C5
Great Somerford Wilts 33 J8
Great Soudley Shrops 70 C9
Great Stainton Darltn 104 B6
Great Stambridge Essex 38 E3
Great Staughton Cambs 61 P8
Great Steeping Lincs 87 M7
Great Stoke S Glos 32 B8
Great Stonar Kent 39 P10
Greatstone-on-Sea Kent 27 J7
Great Strickland Cumb 101 Q6
Great Stukeley Cambs 62 B6
Great Sturton Lincs 86 H5
Great Sutton Ches W 81 M9
Great Sutton Shrops 57 J8
Great Swinburne Nthumb 112 G5
Great Tew Oxon 48 D9
Great Tey Essex 52 E6
Great Thurlow Suffk 63 L10
Great Torrington Devon 16 H8
Great Tosson Nthumb 119 K10
Great Totham Essex 52 E9
Great Totham Essex 52 E9
Great Tows Lincs 86 H2
Great Urswick Cumb 94 F5
Great Wakering Essex 38 F3
Great Waldingfield Suffk 52 F3
Great Walsingham Norfk 76 C4
Great Waltham Essex 51 Q8
Great Warford Ches E 82 H9
Great Warley Essex 37 N2
Great Washbourne Gloucs 47 J8
Great Weeke Devon 8 H7
Great Welnetham Suffk 64 B10
Great Wenham Suffk 53 J4
Great Whittington Nthumb 112 H6
Great Wigborough Essex 52 G8
Great Wilbraham Cambs 63 J9
Great Wilne Derbys 72 C4
Great Wishford Wilts 21 L7
Great Witchingham Norfk 76 G7
Great Witcombe Gloucs 32 H2
Great Witley Worcs 57 P11
Great Wolford Warwks 47 Q8
Greatworth Nhants 48 G6
Great Wratting Suffk 63 L11
Great Wymondley Herts 50 F5
Great Wyrley Staffs 58 E3
Great Wytheford Shrops 69 Q11

Great Yarmouth Norfk 77 Q10
Great Yeldham Essex 52 C4
Grebby Lincs 87 M7
Greeba IoM 80 d5
Green Denbgs 80 F11
Green Bank Cumb 94 H4
Greenbottom Cnwll 3 K4
Greenburn W Loth 126 G5
Greencroft Hall Dur 113 J11
Green Cross Surrey 23 N7
Green Down Somset 19 Q4
Green End Bed 61 M11
Green End Bed 61 P10
Green End Bed 61 P8
Green End Cambs 62 B6
Green End Cambs 62 E9
Green End Cambs 62 G8
Green End Herts 50 H4
Green End Herts 51 H6
Greenend Oxon 48 B10
Green End Warwks 59 L7
Greenfield Ag & B 131 Q9
Greenfield C Beds 50 C4
Greenfield Flints 80 H9
Greenfield Highld 146 G3
Greenfield Oldham 83 L4
Greenford Gt Lon 36 D4
Greengairs N Lans 126 D3
Greengates C Brad 90 F3
Greengill Cumb 100 F3
Greenhalgh Lancs 88 E3
Greenham Somset 18 E10
Greenham W Berk 34 E11
Green Hammerton N York 97 Q9
Greenhaugh Nthumb 111 Q3
Green Head Cumb 110 G11
Greenhead Nthumb 111 N7
Green Heath Staffs 58 E2
Greenheys Salfd 82 F4
Greenhill D & G 109 P5
Greenhill Falk 126 E2
Greenhill Herefs 46 D5
Greenhill Kent 39 L8
Greenhill Leics 72 C8
Greenhill S Lans 116 C4
Green Hill Wilts 33 L7
Greenhillocks Derbys 84 F11
Greenhills S Lans 125 Q7
Greenhithe Kent 37 N6
Greenholm E Ayrs 125 N10
Greenholme Cumb 101 Q9
Greenhouse Border 117 R6
Greenhow Hill N York 96 H8
Greenland Highld 167 M3
Greenland Sheff 84 E3
Greenlands Bucks 35 L7
Green Lane Devon 9 J7
Green Lane Worcs 47 J2
Greenlaw Border 129 J10
Greenlea D & G 109 M5
Greenloaning P & K 133 N6
Green Moor Barns 90 H11
Greenmount Bury 89 M8
Green Oak E R Yk 92 D5
Greenock Inver 124 F2
Greenodd Cumb 94 G4
Green Ore Somset 19 Q4
Green Park Readg 35 K10
Green Quarter Cumb 101 Q9
Greensgate Norfk 76 G8
Greenshields S Lans 116 C2
Greenside Gatesd 112 H8
Greenside Kirk 90 E7
Greens Norton Nhants 49 J5
Greenstead Green Essex 52 D6
Greensted Essex 51 M10
Green Street E Susx 26 C9
Green Street Gloucs 46 G11
Green Street Herts 50 E11
Green Street Herts 51 L4
Green Street Worcs 46 G5
Green Street Green Gt Lon 37 L6
Green Street Green Kent 37 N6
Greenstreet Green Suffk 52 H2
Green Tye Herts 51 K7
Greenway Gloucs 46 D8
Greenway Somset 19 K10
Greenway V Glam 30 E10
Greenway Worcs 57 N10
Greenwich Gt Lon 37 J5
Greenwich Maritime Gt Lon 37 J5
Greet Gloucs 47 K8
Greete Shrops 57 K9
Greetham Lincs 87 K6
Greetham Rutlnd 73 N8
Greetland Calder 90 D6
Gregson Lane Lancs 88 H5
Greinton Somset 19 M7
Grenaby IoM 80 c7
Grendon Nhants 61 J8
Grendon Warwks 59 L3
Grendon Green Herefs 46 A3
Grendon Underwood Bucks 49 J10
Grenofen Devon 6 D4
Grenoside Sheff 84 D2
Greosabhagh W Isls 168 g8
Gresford Wrexhm 69 K4
Gresham Norfk 76 H4
Greshornish Highld 152 E7
Gressenhall Norfk 76 C8
Gressingham Lancs 95 M8
Gresty Green Ches E 70 C3
Greta Bridge Dur 103 L8
Gretna D & G 110 F7
Gretna Green D & G 110 F7
Gretna Services D & G 110 F7
Gretton Gloucs 47 K8
Gretton Nhants 61 J2
Gretton Shrops 57 J5
Grewelthorpe N York 97 K5
Grey Friars Suffk 65 P7
Greygarth N York 97 K6
Grey Green N Linc 92 D9
Greylake Somset 19 L8
Greylees Lincs 73 Q2
Greyrigg D & G 109 N3
Greys Green Oxon 35 K8
Greysouthen Cumb 100 E5
Greystoke Cumb 101 M4
Greystone Angus 143 J9

Greywell – Harrapool 273

Greywell Hants 23 K4
Gribb Dorset 10 H4
Gribthorpe E R Yk 92 C3
Griff Warwks 59 N7
Griffithstown Torfn 31 J5
Griffydam Leics 72 C7
Griggs Green Hants 23 M8
Grimeford Village Lancs 89 J8
Grimesthorpe Sheff 84 E3
Grimethorpe Barns 91 L9
Grimister Shet 169 r4
Grimley Worcs 46 F2
Grimmet S Ayrs 114 F5
Grimoldby Lincs 87 L3
Grimpo Shrops 69 L9
Grimsargh Lancs 88 H4
Grimsby NE Lin 93 N8
Grimscote Nhants 49 J4
Grimscott Cnwll 16 D10
Grimshader W Isls 168 j5
Grimshaw Bl w D 89 L6
Grimshaw Green Lancs 88 F8
Grimsthorpe Lincs 73 Q6
Grimston E R Yk 93 N3
Grimston Leics 72 H6
Grimston Norfk 75 P6
Grimstone Dorset 11 N6
Grimstone End Suffk 64 C8
Grinacombe Moor Devon 5 Q3
Grindale E R Yk 99 N6
Grindle Shrops 57 P4
Grindleford Derbys 84 B5
Grindleton Lancs 95 R11
Grindley Brook Shrops 69 P6
Grindlow Derbys 83 Q9
Grindon Nthumb 118 H2
Grindon S on T 104 C5
Grindon Staffs 71 K4
Grindon Hill Nthumb 112 B7
Grindonrigg Nthumb 118 H2
Gringley on the Hill Notts 85 M2
Grinsdale Cumb 110 G9
Grinshill Shrops 69 P10
Grinton N York 103 K11
Griomsiadar W Isls 168 j5
Grishipoll Ag & B 136 F4
Grisling Common E Susx 25 K6
Gristhorpe N York 99 M4
Griston Norfk 64 C2
Gritley Ork 169 e6
Grittenham Wilts 33 K8
Grittleton Wilts 32 G8
Grizebeck Cumb 94 E4
Grizedale Cumb 94 G2
Groby Leics 72 E9
Groes Conwy 68 D2
Groes-faen Rhondd 30 E8
Groesffordd Gwynd 66 D7
Groesffordd Powys 44 F9
Groesffordd Marli Denbgs 80 E10
Groeslon Gwynd 66 H3
Groeslon Gwynd 67 J2
Groes-lwyd Powys 56 C2
Groes-Wen Caerph 30 F7
Grogarry W Isls 168 c14
Grogport Ag & B 120 F3
Groigearraidh W Isls 168 c14
Gromford Suffk 65 M10
Gronant Flints 80 F8
Groombridge E Susx 25 M3
Grosebay W Isls 168 g8
Grosmont Mons 45 N10
Grosmont N York 105 M9
Groton Suffk 52 G3
Grotton Oldham 83 L4
Grouville Jersey 11 c2
Grove Bucks 49 P10
Grove Dorset 11 P10
Grove Kent 39 M9
Grove Notts 85 M5
Grove Oxon 34 D6
Grove Pembks 41 J10
Grove Green Kent 38 C10
Grovenhurst Kent 26 B3
Grove Park Gt Lon 37 K6
Grovesend S Glos 32 C7
Grovesend Swans 28 G4
Grubb Street Kent 37 N7
Gruinard Highld 160 E9
Gruinart Ag & B 122 C6
Grula Highld 144 E2
Gruline Ag & B 137 N7
Grumbla Cnwll 2 C8
Grundisburgh Suffk 65 J11
Gruting Shet 169 p9
Grutness Shet 169 r12
Gualachulain Highld 139 L8
Guanockgate Lincs 74 G8
Guardbridge Fife 135 M4
Guarlford Worcs 46 F5
Guay P & K 141 P8
Guernsey Guern 10 b2
Guernsey Airport Guern 10 b2
Guestling Green E Susx 26 E9
Guestling Thorn E Susx 26 E8
Guestwick Norfk 76 F6
Guide Bridge Tamesd 83 K5
Guide Post Nthumb 113 L3
Guilden Morden Cambs 50 G2
Guilden Sutton Ches W 81 N11
Guildford Surrey 23 Q5
Guildstead Kent 38 D9
Guildtown P & K 142 A11
Guilsborough Nhants 60 E6
Guilsfield Powys 56 C2
Guilton Kent 39 N10
Guiltreehill S Ayrs 114 G5
Guineaford Devon 17 K4
Guisborough R & Cl 104 H7
Guiseley Leeds 90 F2
Guist Norfk 76 E6
Guiting Power Gloucs 47 L10
Gullane E Loth 128 D3
Gulling Green Suffk 64 A10
Gulval Cnwll 2 D7
Gulworthy Devon 6 D4
Gumfreston Pembks 41 M10
Gumley Leics 60 E3
Gummow's Shop Cnwll 4 D10
Gunby E R Yk 92 B3
Gunby Lincs 73 N6
Gundleton Hants 22 H8
Gun Green Kent 26 C5
Gun Hill E Susx 25 N8
Gun Hill Warwks 59 L7
Gunn Devon 17 L5
Gunnerside N York 103 J11
Gunnerton Nthumb 112 D6
Gunness N Linc 92 D8
Gunnislake Cnwll 6 C4
Gunnista Shet 169 s9
Gunthorpe C Pete 74 C10
Gunthorpe N Linc 92 D11
Gunthorpe Norfk 76 E5
Gunthorpe Notts 72 H2
Gunton Suffk 65 Q2
Gunwalloe Cnwll 2 H9
Gupworthy Somset 18 C8
Gurnard IoW 14 E7
Gurnett Ches E 83 K10
Gurney Slade Somset 20 B5
Gurnos Powys 29 L3
Gushmere Kent 38 H10
Gussage All Saints Dorset 12 H2
Gussage St Andrew Dorset 12 G2
Gussage St Michael Dorset 12 G2
Guston Kent 27 P3
Gutcher Shet 169 s4
Guthrie Angus 143 K7
Guyhirn Cambs 74 H10
Guyhirn Gull Cambs 74 G10
Guy's Marsh Dorset 20 F10
Guyzance Nthumb 119 P10
Gwaenysgor Flints 80 F8
Gwalchmai IoA 78 F9
Gwastadnant Gwynd 67 L3
Gwaun-Cae-Gurwen Carmth 29 J2
Gwbert on Sea Cerdgn 42 C4
Gwealavellan Cnwll 2 G5
Gweek Cnwll 3 J8
Gwehelog Mons 31 L4
Gwenddwr Powys 44 F6
Gwennap Cnwll 3 J5
Gwennap Mining District Cnwll 3 K5
Gwenter Cnwll 3 J10
Gwernaffield Flints 81 J11
Gwernesney Mons 31 M4
Gwernogle Carmth 43 K8
Gwernymynydd Flints 68 H2
Gwersyllt Wrexhm 69 K4
Gwespyr Flints 80 G8
Gwindra Cnwll 3 P3
Gwinear Cnwll 2 F6
Gwithian Cnwll 2 F5
Gwredog IoA 78 G7
Gwrhay Caerph 30 G5
Gwyddelwern Denbgs 68 E5
Gwyddgrug Carmth 43 J7
Gwynfryn Wrexhm 69 J4
Gwystre Powys 55 P11
Gwytherin Conwy 68 A2
Gyfelia Wrexhm 69 K5
Gyrn Goch Gwynd 66 G5

H

Habberley Shrops 56 F4
Habberley Worcs 57 Q9
Habergham Lancs 89 N4
Habertoft Lincs 87 P7
Habin W Susx 23 M10
Habrough NE Lin 93 K8
Hacconby Lincs 74 B5
Haceby Lincs 73 Q3
Hacheston Suffk 65 L10
Hackbridge Gt Lon 36 G7
Hackenthorpe Sheff 84 F4
Hackford Norfk 76 F11
Hackforth N York 97 K2
Hack Green Ches E 70 A5
Hackland Ork 169 c4
Hackleton Nhants 60 H9
Hacklinge Kent 39 P11
Hackman's Gate Worcs 58 C9
Hackness N York 99 K2
Hackness Somset 19 K5
Hackney Gt Lon 36 H4
Hackthorn Lincs 86 C4
Hackthorpe Cumb 101 P6
Hacton Gt Lon 37 N3
Hadden Border 118 E3
Haddenham Bucks 35 K3
Haddenham Cambs 62 G5
Haddington E Loth 128 E5
Haddington Lincs 86 B8
Haddiscoe Norfk 65 N2
Haddon Cambs 61 P2
Hade Edge Kirk 83 P4
Hadfield Derbys 83 M5
Hadham Cross Herts 51 K7
Hadham Ford Herts 51 K6
Hadleigh Essex 38 D4
Hadleigh Suffk 52 H3
Hadleigh Heath Suffk 52 G3
Hadley Worcs 46 G2
Hadley Wrekin 57 M2
Hadley End Staffs 71 L10
Hadley Wood Gt Lon 50 G11
Hadlow Kent 37 P10
Hadlow Down E Susx 25 M6
Hadnall Shrops 69 P10
Hadrian's Wall 112 E7
Hadstock Essex 51 N2
Hadston Nthumb 119 Q11
Hadzor Worcs 46 H2
Haffenden Quarter Kent 26 E3
Hafodunos Conwy 80 B11
Hafod-y-bwch Wrexhm 69 K5
Hafod-y-coed Blae G 30 H4
Hafodyrynys Caerph 30 H5
Haggate Lancs 89 P3
Haggbeck Cumb 111 J6
Haggersta Shet 169 q9
Haggerston Nthumb 119 K2
Haggington Hill Devon 17 K2
Haggs Falk 126 D2
Hagley Herefs 45 R6
Hagley Worcs 58 D8
Hagmore Green Suffk 52 G4
Hagnaby Lincs 87 K8
Hagnaby Lincs 87 N5
Hagworthingham Lincs 87 K7
Haigh Wigan 89 J9
Haighton Green Lancs 88 H4
Haile Cumb 100 D9
Hailes Gloucs 47 K8
Hailey Herts 51 J8
Hailey Oxon 34 C2
Hailey Oxon 34 H7
Hailsham E Susx 25 N9
Hail Weston Cambs 61 Q8
Hainault Gt Lon 37 L2
Haine Kent 39 Q8
Hainford Norfk 77 J8
Hainton Lincs 86 G4
Hainworth C Brad 90 D3
Haisthorpe E R Yk 99 N8
Hakin Pembks 40 G9
Halam Notts 85 L10
Halbeath Fife 134 E10
Halberton Devon 9 P2
Halcro Highld 167 M4
Hale Cumb 95 L5
Hale Halton 81 P8
Hale Hants 21 N11
Hale Somset 20 D9
Hale Surrey 23 M5
Hale Traffd 82 G7
Hale Bank Halton 81 P8
Hale Barns Traffd 82 G7
Hale Green E Susx 25 N8
Hale Nook Lancs 88 D2
Hales Norfk 65 M2
Hales Staffs 70 C8
Halesgate Lincs 74 F5
Hales Green Derbys 71 M6
Halesowen Dudley 58 E8
Hales Place Kent 39 K10
Hale Street Kent 37 Q11
Halesville Essex 38 F3
Halesworth Suffk 65 M6
Halewood Knows 81 P7
Halford Devon 7 L4
Halford Shrops 56 G8
Halford Warwks 47 Q5
Halfpenny Cumb 95 L3
Halfpenny Green Staffs 58 B6
Halfpenny Houses N York 97 K4
Halfway Carmth 43 M8
Halfway Carmth 44 A8
Halfway Sheff 84 F4
Halfway W Berk 34 D11
Halfway Bridge W Susx 23 P10
Halfway House Shrops 56 E2
Halfway Houses Kent 38 F7
Halifax Calder 90 D5
Halket E Ayrs 125 L7
Halkirk Highld 167 K5
Halkyn Flints 81 J10
Hall E Rens 125 L7
Hallam Fields Derbys 72 D3
Halland E Susx 25 L7
Hallaton Leics 73 K11
Hallatrow BaNES 20 B3
Hallbankgate Cumb 111 L9
Hallbeck Cumb 95 N3
Hall Cliffe Wakefd 90 H7
Hall Cross Lancs 88 E4
Hall Dunnerdale Cumb 100 H11
Hallen S Glos 31 Q8
Hall End Bed 61 M11
Hall End C Beds 50 C3
Hallfield Gate Derbys 84 E9
Hallgarth Dur 104 B2
Hallglen Falk 126 F2
Hall Green Birm 58 H8
Hallin Highld 152 D6
Halling Medway 38 B9
Hallington Lincs 87 K3
Hallington Nthumb 112 E5
Halliwell Bolton 89 K8
Halloughton Notts 85 L10
Hallow Worcs 46 F3
Hallow Heath Worcs 46 F3
Hallsands Devon 7 L11
Hall's Green Essex 51 K9
Hall's Green Herts 50 G5
Hallthwaites Cumb 94 D3
Hallworthy Cnwll 5 K4
Hallyne Border 116 H2
Halmer End Staffs 70 D5
Halmond's Frome Herefs 46 C5
Halmore Gloucs 32 D4
Halnaker W Susx 15 P5
Halsall Lancs 88 D8
Halse Nhants 48 G6
Halse Somset 18 F9
Halsetown Cnwll 2 E6
Halsham E R Yk 93 N5
Halsinger Devon 17 J4
Halstead Essex 52 D5
Halstead Kent 37 L8
Halstead Leics 73 K9
Halstock Dorset 11 L3
Halsway Somset 18 F7
Haltcliff Bridge Cumb 101 L3
Haltham Lincs 86 H8
Haltoft End Lincs 87 L11
Halton Bucks 35 N3
Halton Halton 82 B8
Halton Lancs 95 L8
Halton Leeds 91 K4
Halton Nthumb 112 E7
Halton Wrexhm 69 K7
Halton East N York 96 F10
Halton Fenside Lincs 87 M8
Halton Gill N York 96 C5
Halton Green Lancs 95 L7
Halton Holegate Lincs 87 M7
Halton Lea Gate Nthumb 111 M9
Halton Quay Cnwll 5 Q8
Halton Shields Nthumb 112 F7
Halton West N York 96 B10
Haltwhistle Nthumb 111 P8
Halvana Cnwll 5 L6
Halvergate Norfk 77 N10
Halwell Devon 7 K8
Halwill Devon 8 B5
Halwill Junction Devon 8 B4
Ham Devon 10 E4
Ham Gloucs 32 C5
Ham Gloucs 47 J10
Ham Gt Lon 36 E6
Ham Kent 39 P11
Ham Somset 19 J9
Ham Somset 20 C5
Ham Wilts 22 B2
Hambleden Bucks 35 L7
Hambledon Hants 14 H4
Hambledon Surrey 23 Q7
Hamble-le-Rice Hants 14 E5
Hambleton Lancs 88 D2
Hambleton N York 91 P4
Hambleton Moss Side Lancs 88 D2
Hambridge Somset 19 L10
Hambrook S Glos 32 B9
Hambrook W Susx 15 L5
Ham Common Dorset 20 F9
Hameringham Lincs 87 K7
Hamerton Cambs 61 P5
Ham Green Herefs 46 E6
Ham Green Kent 26 E6
Ham Green Kent 38 D8
Ham Green N Som 31 P9
Ham Green Worcs 47 K2
Ham Hill Kent 37 Q8
Hamilton S Lans 126 C6
Hamilton Services (northbound) S Lans 126 C6
Hamlet Dorset 11 M3
Hammer W Susx 23 N8
Hammerpot W Susx 24 C9
Hammersmith Gt Lon 36 F5
Hammer Vale Hants 23 N8
Hammerwich Staffs 58 G3
Hammerwood E Susx 25 K3
Hammond Street Herts 50 H10
Hammoon Dorset 12 D2
Hamnavoe Shet 169 q10
Hampden Park E Susx 25 P10
Hamperden End Essex 51 N4
Hampnett Gloucs 47 L11
Hampole Donc 91 N8
Hampreston Dorset 13 J5
Hampsfield Cumb 95 J4
Hampson Green Lancs 95 K10
Hampstead Gt Lon 36 G3
Hampstead Norreys W Berk 34 F9
Hampsthwaite N York 97 L9
Hampton C Pete 61 Q2
Hampton Devon 10 F5
Hampton Gt Lon 36 D7
Hampton Kent 39 L8
Hampton Shrops 57 N7
Hampton Swindn 33 N6
Hampton Worcs 47 K6
Hampton Bishop Herefs 45 R7
Hampton Court Palace Gt Lon 36 E7
Hampton Fields Gloucs 32 G5
Hampton Green Ches W 69 P5
Hampton Heath Ches W 69 P5
Hampton-in-Arden Solhll 59 K8
Hampton Loade Shrops 57 N7
Hampton Lovett Worcs 58 C11
Hampton Lucy Warwks 47 Q3
Hampton Magna Warwks 59 L11
Hampton on the Hill Warwks 47 Q2
Hampton Park Wilts 21 N8
Hampton Poyle Oxon 48 F11
Hampton Wick Gt Lon 36 E7
Hamptworth Wilts 21 P11
Hamrow Norfk 76 C7
Hamsey E Susx 25 K8
Hamsey Green Surrey 37 J9
Hamstall Ridware Staffs 71 L11
Hamstead Birm 58 G6
Hamstead IoW 14 D8
Hamstead Marshall W Berk 34 D11
Hamsterley Dur 103 M4
Hamsterley Dur 112 H9
Hamsterley Mill Dur 112 H9
Hamstreet Kent 26 H5
Ham Street Somset 19 Q8
Hamwood N Som 19 L3
Hamworthy BCP 12 G6
Hanbury Staffs 71 M9
Hanbury Worcs 47 J2
Hanby Lincs 73 Q4
Hanchet End Suffk 63 K11
Hanchurch Staffs 70 E6
Handa Island Highld 164 D7
Handale R & Cl 105 K7
Hand and Pen Devon 9 P5
Handbridge Ches W 81 N11
Handcross W Susx 24 G5
Handforth Ches E 83 J8
Hand Green Ches W 69 P2
Handley Ches W 69 N3
Handley Derbys 84 E8
Handley Green Essex 51 Q10
Handsacre Staffs 71 K11
Handsworth Birm 58 F7
Handsworth Sheff 84 F3
Handy Cross Bucks 35 N6
Hanford C Stke 70 F6
Hanford Dorset 12 D2
Hanging Heaton Kirk 90 H6
Hanging Houghton Nhants 60 G6
Hanging Langford Wilts 21 K7
Hangleton Br & H 24 G9
Hangleton W Susx 24 C10
Hanham S Glos 32 B10
Hankelow Ches E 70 B5
Hankerton Wilts 33 J6
Hankham E Susx 25 P9
Hanley C Stke 70 F5
Hanley Broadheath Worcs 57 M11
Hanley Castle Worcs 46 F6
Hanley Child Worcs 57 M11
Hanley Swan Worcs 46 F6
Hanley William Worcs 57 M11
Hanlith N York 96 C8
Hanmer Wrexhm 69 N7
Hannaford Devon 17 L6
Hannah Lincs 87 N5
Hannington Hants 22 F3
Hannington Nhants 60 H6
Hannington Swindn 33 N6
Hannington Wick Swindn 33 N5
Hanscombe End C Beds 50 D4
Hanslope M Keyn 49 M5
Hanthorpe Lincs 74 A6
Hanwell Gt Lon 36 E5
Hanwell Oxon 48 D6
Hanwood Shrops 56 G3
Hanworth Gt Lon 36 D6
Hanworth Norfk 76 H4
Happendon S Lans 116 B4
Happendon Services S Lans 116 B4
Happisburgh Norfk 77 M5
Happisburgh Common Norfk 77 M6
Hapsford Ches W 81 P10
Hapton Lancs 89 M4
Hapton Norfk 64 H2
Harberton Devon 7 K7
Harbertonford Devon 7 K7
Harbledown Kent 39 K10
Harborne Birm 58 F8
Harborough Magna Warwks 59 Q9
Harbottle Nthumb 118 H10
Harbourneford Devon 7 J6
Harbours Hill Worcs 58 E11
Harbridge Hants 13 K2
Harbridge Green Hants 13 K2
Harburn W Loth 127 J5
Harbury Warwks 48 C3
Harby Leics 73 J4
Harby Notts 85 Q6
Harcombe Devon 9 L8
Harcombe Devon 10 D6
Harcombe Bottom Devon 10 G5
Harden C Brad 90 D3
Harden Wsall 58 F4
Hardendale Cumb 101 Q8
Hardenhuish Wilts 32 H10
Hardgate Abers 151 K7
Hardgate D & G 108 H7
Hardgate N York 97 L8
Hardgate W Duns 125 N3
Hardham W Susx 24 B7
Hardhorn Lancs 88 D3
Hardingham Norfk 76 E11
Hardingstone Nhants 60 G9
Hardington Somset 20 D4
Hardington Mandeville Somset 11 L2
Hardington Marsh Somset 11 L3
Hardington Moor Somset 11 L2
Hardisworthy Devon 16 C7
Hardley Hants 14 D6
Hardley Street Norfk 77 M11
Hardmead M Keyn 49 P5
Hardraw N York 96 C2
Hardsough Lancs 89 M6
Hardstoft Derbys 84 F8
Hardway Hants 14 H6
Hardway Somset 20 D8
Hardwick Bucks 49 M11
Hardwick Cambs 62 E9
Hardwick Nhants 60 H7
Hardwick Norfk 65 J4
Hardwick Oxon 34 C3
Hardwick Oxon 48 G9
Hardwick Rothm 84 G3
Hardwick Wsall 58 G5
Hardwicke Gloucs 32 E2
Hardwicke Gloucs 46 H9
Hardwick Hall Derbys 84 G8
Hardwick Village Notts 85 K5
Hardy's Green Essex 52 F7
Harebeating E Susx 25 N8
Hareby Lincs 87 K7
Hare Croft C Brad 90 D3
Harefield Gt Lon 36 C2
Hare Green Essex 53 K6
Hare Hatch Wokham 35 M9
Harehill Derbys 71 M7
Harehills Leeds 91 J4
Harehope Nthumb 119 L6
Harelaw Border 117 Q6
Harelaw D & G 110 H5
Harelaw Dur 113 J10
Hareplain Kent 26 D4
Haresceugh Cumb 102 B2
Harescombe Gloucs 32 F2
Haresfield Gloucs 32 F2
Harestock Hants 22 E8
Hare Street Essex 51 K9
Hare Street Essex 51 M10
Hare Street Herts 51 J5
Harewood Leeds 97 M11
Harewood End Herefs 45 Q9
Harford Devon 6 G7
Hargate Norfk 64 G3
Hargatewall Derbys 83 P9
Hargrave Ches W 69 N2
Hargrave Nhants 61 M6
Hargrave Suffk 63 N9
Harker Cumb 110 G8
Harkstead Suffk 53 L5
Harlaston Staffs 59 K2
Harlaxton Lincs 73 M4
Harlech Gwynd 67 K8
Harlech Castle Gwynd 67 K8
Harlescott Shrops 69 N11
Harlesden Gt Lon 36 F4
Harlesthorpe Derbys 84 G5
Harleston Devon 7 K9
Harleston Norfk 65 J5
Harleston Suffk 64 E9
Harlestone Nhants 60 F8
Harle Syke Lancs 89 P3
Harley Rothm 91 K11
Harley Shrops 57 K4
Harling Road Norfk 64 D4
Harlington C Beds 50 B4
Harlington Donc 91 M10
Harlington Gt Lon 36 C5
Harlosh Highld 152 D9
Harlow Essex 51 K8
Harlow Carr RHS N York 97 L10
Harlow Hill Nthumb 112 G7
Harlthorpe E R Yk 92 B3
Harlton Cambs 62 E10
Harlyn Cnwll 4 D6
Harman's Cross Dorset 12 G8
Harmby N York 96 H3
Harmer Green Herts 50 G7
Harmer Hill Shrops 69 N10
Harmondsworth Gt Lon 36 C5
Harmston Lincs 86 C8
Harnage Shrops 57 K4
Harnham Nthumb 112 G4
Harnhill Gloucs 33 L4
Harold Hill Gt Lon 37 M2
Haroldston West Pembks 40 G7
Haroldswick Shet 169 t2
Harold Wood Gt Lon 37 N2
Harome N York 98 C4
Harpenden Herts 50 D8
Harpford Devon 10 B6
Harpham E R Yk 99 M8
Harpley Norfk 75 Q5
Harpley Worcs 46 C2
Harpole Nhants 60 E8
Harpsdale Highld 167 K5
Harpsden Oxon 35 L8
Harpswell Lincs 86 B3
Harpurhey Manch 83 J4
Harpur Hill Derbys 83 N10
Harraby Cumb 110 H10
Harracott Devon 17 K6
Harrapool Highld 145 L3

Harras Cumb 100 C7
Harrietfield P & K 134 B2
Harrietsham Kent 38 E11
Harrington Cumb 100 C5
Harrington Lincs 87 L6
Harrington Nhants 60 G4
Harringworth Nhants 73 N11
Harris W Isls 168 f8
Harriseahead Staffs 70 F3
Harriston Cumb 100 G2
Harrogate N York 97 M9
Harrold Bed 61 K9
Harrop Dale Oldham 90 C9
Harrow Gt Lon 36 E3
Harrowbarrow Cnwll 5 Q7
Harrowden Bed 61 N11
Harrowgate Village Darltn 103 Q7
Harrow Green Suffk 64 B11
Harrow Hill Gloucs 46 C11
Harrow on the Hill Gt Lon 36 E3
Harrow Weald Gt Lon 36 E2
Harston Cambs 62 F10
Harston Leics 73 L4
Harswell E R Yk 92 D2
Hart Hartpl 104 E3
Hartburn Nthumb 112 G3
Hartburn S on T 104 D7
Hartest Suffk 64 A11
Hartfield E Susx 25 L3
Hartford Cambs 62 C6
Hartford Ches W 82 D10
Hartford Somset 18 C9
Hartfordbridge Hants 23 L3
Hartford End Essex 51 Q7
Harthill Ches W 69 N3
Harthill N Lans 126 G5
Harthill Rothm 84 G4
Harthope D & G 116 E8
Hartington Derbys 71 L2
Hartington Nthumb 112 F3
Hartland Devon 16 D7
Hartland Quay Devon 16 C7
Hartlebury Worcs 58 B10
Hartlepool Hartpl 104 F4
Hartley Cumb 102 E9
Hartley Kent 26 C5
Hartley Kent 37 P7
Hartley Nthumb 113 M5
Hartley Green Kent 37 P7
Hartley Green Staffs 70 H9
Hartley Wespall Hants 23 J3
Hartley Wintney Hants 23 L3
Hartlip Kent 38 D9
Hartoft End N York 98 E2
Harton N York 98 E8
Harton S Tyne 113 N7
Harton Shrops 56 H7
Hartpury Gloucs 46 E10
Hartshead Kirk 90 F6
Hartshead Moor Services Calder 90 F6
Hartshead Moor Top Kirk 90 F5
Hartshill C Stke 70 F5
Hartshill Warwks 59 M6
Hartshorne Derbys 71 Q10
Hartside Nthumb 119 J7
Hartsop Cumb 101 M8
Hart Station Hartpl 104 E3
Hartswell Somset 18 E9
Hartwell Nhants 49 L4
Hartwith N York 97 K8
Hartwood N Lans 126 E6
Hartwoodmyres Border 117 N6
Harvel Kent 37 Q8
Harvington Worcs 47 L5
Harvington Worcs 58 C10
Harwell Notts 85 L2
Harwell Oxon 34 E7
Harwich Essex 53 N5
Harwood Bolton 89 L8
Harwood Dur 102 F4
Harwood Nthumb 112 F2
Harwood Dale N York 105 Q11
Harwood Lee Bolton 89 L8
Harworth Notts 85 K2
Hasbury Dudley 58 E8
Hascombe Surrey 24 B3
Haselbech Nhants 60 F5
Haselbury Plucknett Somset 11 L2
Haseley Warwks 59 K11
Haseley Green Warwks 59 K11
Haseley Knob Warwks 59 K10
Haselor Warwks 47 M3
Hasfield Gloucs 46 F9
Hasguard Pembks 40 G9
Haskayne Lancs 88 D9
Hasketon Suffk 65 J11
Hasland Derbys 84 E7
Haslemere Surrey 23 P8
Haslingden Lancs 89 M6
Haslingfield Cambs 62 F10
Haslington Ches E 70 C3
Hassall Ches E 70 D3
Hassall Green Ches E 70 D3
Hassell Street Kent 27 J2
Hassingham Norfk 77 M10
Hassness Cumb 100 G7
Hassocks W Susx 24 H7
Hassop Derbys 84 B6
Haste Hill Surrey 23 P8
Haster Highld 167 P6
Hasthorpe Lincs 87 N7
Hastingleigh Kent 27 J2
Hastings E Susx 26 D10
Hastings Somset 19 K11
Hastingwood Essex 51 L9
Hastoe Herts 35 P3
Haswell Dur 104 C2
Haswell Plough Dur 104 C2
Hatch C Beds 61 Q11
Hatch Beauchamp Somset 19 K10
Hatch End Bed 61 N8
Hatch End Gt Lon 36 D2
Hatchet Gate Hants 14 C6
Hatching Green Herts 50 D8
Hatchmere Ches W 82 C10
Hatch Warren Hants 22 H5
Hatcliffe NE Lin 93 M10
Hatfield Donc 91 R9
Hatfield Herefs 46 A3
Hatfield Herts 50 F9
Hatfield Worcs 46 G4

Hatfield Broad Oak Essex 51 M7
Hatfield Heath Essex 51 M7
Hatfield Peverel Essex 52 C9
Hatfield Woodhouse Donc 92 A9
Hatford Oxon 34 B6
Hatherden Hants 22 B4
Hatherleigh Devon 8 D4
Hathern Leics 72 E6
Hatherop Gloucs 33 N3
Hathersage Derbys 84 B4
Hathersage Booths Derbys 84 B4
Hatherton Ches E 70 B5
Hatherton Staffs 58 E2
Hatley St George Cambs 62 C10
Hatt Cnwll 5 Q9
Hattersley Tamesd 83 L6
Hattingley Hants 22 H7
Hatton Abers 159 Q10
Hatton Angus 142 H9
Hatton Derbys 71 N8
Hatton Gt Lon 36 C5
Hatton Lincs 86 G5
Hatton Shrops 56 H6
Hatton Warrtn 82 C8
Hatton Warwks 59 K11
Hatton Heath Ches W 69 N2
Hatton of Fintray Abers 151 L4
Haugh E Ayrs 115 J2
Haugh Lincs 87 M5
Haugh Rochdl 89 Q8
Haugham Lincs 87 K4
Haughhead E Duns 125 P2
Haugh Head Nthumb 119 K5
Haughley Suffk 64 E9
Haughley Green Suffk 64 E9
Haugh of Glass Moray 158 B3
Haugh of Urr D & G 108 H7
Haughs of Kinnaird Angus 143 L6
Haughton Ches E 69 Q3
Haughton Notts 85 L6
Haughton Powys 69 K11
Haughton Shrops 57 M5
Haughton Shrops 57 N3
Haughton Shrops 69 L9
Haughton Shrops 69 Q11
Haughton Staffs 70 F10
Haughton Green Tamesd 83 K6
Haughton le Skerne Darltn 104 B7
Haultwick Herts 50 H6
Haunton Staffs 59 K2
Hautes Croix Jersey 11 b1
Hauxton Cambs 62 F10
Havannah Ches E 70 F2
Havant Hants 15 K5
Haven Herefs 45 N4
Haven Bank Lincs 86 H10
Haven Side E R Yk 93 L5
Havenstreet IoW 14 G8
Havercroft Wakefd 91 K8
Haverfordwest Pembks 41 J7
Haverhill Suffk 63 L11
Haverigg Cumb 94 D5
Havering-atte-Bower Gt Lon 37 M2
Haversham M Keyn 49 M6
Haverthwaite Cumb 94 G4
Haverton Hill S on T 104 E6
Havyatt N Som 19 N2
Havyatt Somset 19 P7
Hawarden Flints 81 L11
Hawbridge Worcs 46 H5
Hawbush Green Essex 52 C7
Hawcoat Cumb 94 E6
Hawen Cerdgn 42 F5
Hawes N York 96 C3
Hawe's Green Norfk 65 J2
Hawford Worcs 46 F2
Hawick Border 117 Q8
Hawkchurch Devon 10 G4
Hawkedon Suffk 63 N10
Hawkenbury Kent 26 D2
Hawkeridge Wilts 20 G4
Hawkerland Devon 9 Q7
Hawker's Cove Cnwll 4 E6
Hawkesbury S Glos 32 E7
Hawkesbury Warwks 59 N8
Hawkesbury Upton S Glos 32 E7
Hawkes End Covtry 59 L8
Hawk Green Stockp 83 L7
Hawkhill Nthumb 119 P8
Hawkhurst Kent 26 C5
Hawkhurst Common E Susx 25 M7
Hawkinge Kent 27 M4
Hawkley Hants 23 K9
Hawkley Wigan 82 C4
Hawkridge Somset 17 R5
Hawksdale Cumb 110 G11
Hawkshaw Bury 89 M7
Hawkshead Cumb 101 L11
Hawkshead Hill Cumb 101 K11
Hawksland S Lans 116 A3
Hawkspur Green Essex 51 Q4
Hawkstone Shrops 69 Q8
Hawkswick N York 96 E6
Hawksworth Leeds 90 F2
Hawksworth Notts 73 K2
Hawkwell Essex 38 E3
Hawkwell Nthumb 112 G6
Hawley Hants 23 N3
Hawley Kent 37 M6
Hawling Gloucs 47 L10
Hawnby N York 98 A3
Haworth C Brad 90 C3
Hawridge Bucks 35 P3
Hawstead Suffk 64 B10
Hawstead Green Suffk 64 B10
Hawthorn Dur 113 P11
Hawthorn Hants 23 J8
Hawthorn Rhondd 30 E7
Hawthorn Hill Br For 35 N10
Hawthorn Hill Lincs 86 H9
Hawthorpe Lincs 73 Q5
Hawton Notts 85 N10
Haxby C York 98 C9
Haxby Gates C York 98 C9
Haxey N Linc 92 C11
Haxey Carr N Linc 92 C10
Haxted Surrey 37 K11
Haxton Wilts 21 M5
Hay Cnwll 3 P3
Hay Cnwll 4 H4
Haydock St Hel 82 C5
Haydon BaNES 20 C4
Haydon Dorset 20 C11
Haydon Somset 19 J10
Haydon Bridge Nthumb 112 B8

Haydon Wick Swindn 33 M7
Haye Cnwll 5 P7
Hayes Gt Lon 36 C4
Hayes Gt Lon 37 K7
Hayes End Gt Lon 36 C4
Hayfield Ag & B 131 M3
Hayfield Derbys 83 M7
Hayfield Green Donc 91 R11
Haygate Wrekin 57 L2
Hay Green Norfk 75 K7
Hayhillock Angus 143 J9
Hayle Cnwll 2 E8
Hay Port Cnwll 2 F6
Hayley Green Dudley 58 E8
Haymoor Green Ches E 70 B4
Hayne Devon 9 J7
Hayne Devon 18 C11
Haynes C Beds 50 C2
Haynes Church End C Beds 50 C2
Haynes West End C Beds 50 C2
Hay-on-Wye Powys 45 J2
Hayscastle Pembks 40 G5
Hayscastle Cross Pembks 40 H5
Hay Street Herts 51 J5
Hayton Cumb 100 F2
Hayton Cumb 111 K9
Hayton E R Yk 98 G11
Hayton Notts 85 M4
Hayton's Bent Shrops 57 J8
Haytor Vale Devon 9 J9
Haytown Devon 16 F9
Haywards Heath W Susx 24 H6
Haywood Donc 91 P8
Haywood Herefs 45 P8
Haywood Oaks Notts 85 K9
Hazards Green E Susx 25 Q8
Hazelbank S Lans 126 E3
Hazelbury Bryan Dorset 12 B3
Hazeleigh Essex 52 D11
Hazeley Hants 23 K3
Hazelford Notts 85 M11
Hazel Grove Stockp 83 K7
Hazelhurst Tamesd 83 L4
Hazelslade Staffs 58 F2
Hazel Street Kent 25 Q3
Hazel Stub Suffk 51 Q2
Hazelton Walls Fife 135 J3
Hazelwood Derbys 84 D11
Hazlemere Bucks 35 N5
Hazlerigg N u Ty 113 K6
Hazles Staffs 71 J5
Hazleton Gloucs 47 L11
Heacham Norfk 75 N3
Headbourne Worthy Hants 22 E8
Headbrook Herefs 45 K3
Headcorn Kent 26 D3
Headingley Leeds 90 H3
Headington Oxon 34 F3
Headlam Dur 103 N7
Headless Cross Worcs 58 F11
Headley Hants 22 F2
Headley Hants 23 M7
Headley Surrey 36 F10
Headley Down Hants 23 M7
Headley Heath Worcs 58 G9
Headon Devon 16 D2
Headon Notts 85 M5
Heads Nook Cumb 111 K10
Heage Derbys 84 E10
Healaugh N York 97 R11
Healaugh N York 103 K11
Heald Green Stockp 82 H7
Heale Devon 17 L2
Heale Somset 18 H10
Heale Somset 19 L9
Healey N York 97 J4
Healey Nthumb 112 H9
Healey Rochdl 89 P7
Healey Wakefd 90 H7
Healeyfield Dur 112 G11
Healing NE Lin 93 M8
Heamoor Cnwll 2 D7
Heanor Derbys 84 F11
Heanton Punchardon Devon 17 J4
Heapham Lincs 85 Q3
Hearn Hants 23 M7
Heart of Scotland Services N Lans 126 G5
Hearts Delight Kent 38 E9
Heasley Mill Devon 17 N5
Heaste Highld 145 K4
Heath Derbys 84 F7
Heath Wakefd 91 K6
Heath and Reach C Beds 49 Q9
Heath Common W Susx 24 D7
Heathcote Derbys 71 L2
Heathcote Shrops 70 B9
Heath End Bucks 35 N5
Heath End Hants 22 D2
Heath End Leics 72 B6
Heath End Warwks 47 P2
Heather Leics 72 B8
Heathfield Cambs 62 G11
Heathfield Devon 9 K9
Heathfield E Susx 25 N6
Heathfield N York 96 H7
Heathfield Somset 18 G9
Heathfield Village Oxon 48 F11
Heath Green Worcs 58 G10
Heath Hall D & G 109 L5
Heath Hayes & Wimblebury Staffs 58 F2
Heath Hill Shrops 57 P2
Heath House Somset 19 M5
Heathrow Airport Gt Lon 36 C5
Heathstock Devon 10 C4
Heathton Shrops 57 Q6
Heath Town Wolves 58 D5
Heathwaite N York 104 E10
Heatley Staffs 71 J7
Heaton Bolton 89 K9
Heaton C Brad 90 E3
Heaton Lancs 95 J8
Heaton N u Ty 113 L7
Heaton Staffs 70 H2
Heaton Chapel Stockp 83 J6
Heaton Mersey Stockp 83 J6
Heaton Norris Stockp 83 J6
Heaton's Bridge Lancs 88 E8
Heaverham Kent 37 N9
Heaviley Stockp 83 K7
Heavitree Devon 9 M6
Hebburn S Tyne 113 M8

Hebden N York 96 F8
Hebden Bridge Calder 90 B5
Hebden Green Ches W 82 D11
Hebing End Herts 50 H6
Hebron Carmth 41 N5
Hebron IoA 78 H8
Hebron Nthumb 113 J3
Heckfield Hants 23 K2
Heckfield Green Suffk 64 H6
Heckfordbridge Essex 52 F7
Heckington Lincs 74 B2
Heckmondwike Kirk 90 G6
Heddington Wilts 33 J11
Heddon-on-the-Wall Nthumb 112 H7
Hedenham Norfk 65 L3
Hedge End Hants 14 E4
Hedgerley Bucks 35 Q7
Hedgerley Green Bucks 35 Q7
Hedging Somset 19 K9
Hedley on the Hill Nthumb 112 H9
Hednesford Staffs 58 E2
Hedon E R Yk 93 L5
Hedsor Bucks 35 P7
Heeley Sheff 84 E4
Hegdon Hill Herefs 46 A4
Heglibister Shet 169 q8
Heighington Darltn 103 P6
Heighington Lincs 86 D7
Heightington Worcs 57 P10
Heiton Border 118 D4
Hele Devon 7 J4
Hele Devon 9 N4
Hele Devon 17 J2
Hele Somset 18 G10
Helebridge Cnwll 16 C11
Hele Lane Devon 9 J2
Helensburgh Ag & B 132 B11
Helenton S Ayrs 125 K11
Helford Cnwll 3 K8
Helford Passage Cnwll 3 K8
Helhoughton Norfk 76 B6
Helions Bumpstead Essex 51 Q2
Hellaby Rothm 84 H2
Helland Cnwll 4 H7
Hellandbridge Cnwll 4 H7
Hell Corner W Berk 22 C2
Hellescott Cnwll 5 M4
Hellesdon Norfk 77 J9
Hellesveor Cnwll 2 E5
Hellidon Nhants 60 B9
Hellifield N York 96 C9
Hellingly E Susx 25 N8
Hellington Norfk 77 L11
Helm Nthumb 119 N11
Helmdon Nhants 48 G6
Helme Kirk 90 D8
Helmingham Suffk 64 H10
Helmington Row Dur 103 N3
Helmsdale Highld 163 N3
Helmshore Lancs 89 M6
Helmsley N York 98 C4
Helperby N York 97 P7
Helperthorpe N York 99 K6
Helpringham Lincs 74 B2
Helpston C Pete 74 B9
Helsby Ches W 81 P9
Helsey Lincs 87 P6
Helston Cnwll 2 H8
Helstone Cnwll 4 H5
Helton Cumb 101 P6
Helwith Bridge N York 96 B7
Hemblington Norfk 77 L9
Hembridge Somset 19 Q7
Hemel Hempstead Herts 50 C9
Hemerdon Devon 6 F7
Hemingbrough N York 91 R4
Hemingby Lincs 86 H6
Hemingfield Barns 91 K10
Hemingford Abbots Cambs 62 C6
Hemingford Grey Cambs 62 C6
Hemingstone Suffk 64 G11
Hemington Leics 72 D5
Hemington Nhants 61 N3
Hemington Somset 20 C4
Hemley Suffk 53 N3
Hemlington Middsb 104 F8
Hempholme E R Yk 99 M10
Hempnall Norfk 65 J3
Hempnall Green Norfk 65 J3
Hempriggs Moray 157 J5
Hempstead Essex 51 P3
Hempstead Medway 38 C9
Hempstead Norfk 76 G4
Hempstead Norfk 77 N6
Hempsted Gloucs 46 F11
Hempton Norfk 76 C6
Hempton Oxon 48 D8
Hemsby Norfk 77 P8
Hemswell Lincs 86 B3
Hemswell Cliff Lincs 86 B3
Hemsworth Wakefd 91 L8
Hemyock Devon 10 C2
Henbury Bristl 31 Q9
Henbury Ches E 83 J10
Hendham Devon 7 J8
Hendomen Powys 56 C5
Hendon Gt Lon 36 F3
Hendon Sundld 113 P9
Hendra Cnwll 3 J6
Hendra Cnwll 4 F5
Hendre Brdgnd 29 P8
Hendre Flints 80 H11
Hendy Carmth 28 G4
Heneglwys IoA 78 G9
Henfield W Susx 24 F7
Henford Devon 5 P3
Henfynyw Cerdgn 43 J2
Henghurst Kent 26 G4
Hengoed Caerph 30 G6
Hengoed Powys 45 J4
Hengoed Shrops 69 J8
Hengrave Suffk 63 P9
Henham Essex 51 M5
Heniarth Powys 55 Q3
Henlade Somset 19 J9
Henley Dorset 11 P4
Henley Gloucs 46 H11
Henley Shrops 56 H7
Henley Shrops 57 J9
Henley Somset 19 M8
Henley Suffk 64 H11
Henley W Susx 23 N9
Henley Green Covtry 59 N8
Henley-in-Arden Warwks 59 J11

Henley-on-Thames Oxon 35 L8
Henley Park Surrey 23 P4
Henley's Down E Susx 26 B9
Henley Street Kent 37 Q7
Henllan Cerdgn 42 G6
Henllan Denbgs 80 E11
Henllan Amgoed Carmth 41 N7
Henllys Torfn 31 J6
Henlow C Beds 50 E4
Henlow Camp C Beds 50 E4
Hennock Devon 9 K4
Henny Street Essex 52 E4
Henryd Conwy 79 P10
Henry's Moat (Castell Hendre) Pembks 41 K5
Hensall N York 91 P6
Henshaw Nthumb 111 Q8
Hensingham Cumb 100 C7
Henstead Suffk 65 P4
Hensting Hants 22 E10
Henstridge Somset 20 D11
Henstridge Ash Somset 20 D10
Henstridge Marsh Somset 20 D10
Henton Oxon 35 L4
Henton Somset 19 N5
Henwick Worcs 46 F3
Henwood Cnwll 5 M7
Henwood Oxon 34 E4
Heolgerrig Myr Td 30 D3
Heol-las Swans 29 J5
Heol Senni Powys 44 C10
Heol-y-Cyw Brdgnd 29 P8
Hepburn Nthumb 119 L6
Hepple Nthumb 119 J10
Hepscott Nthumb 113 K4
Heptonstall Calder 90 B5
Hepworth Kirk 90 F9
Hepworth Suffk 64 D7
Herbrandston Pembks 40 G9
Hereford Herefs 45 Q7
Hereson Kent 39 Q8
Heribusta Highld 152 F3
Heriot Border 128 C9
Hermiston C Edin 127 M3
Hermitage Border 117 Q11
Hermitage Dorset 11 P3
Hermitage W Berk 34 F10
Hermitage W Susx 15 L5
Hermit Hill Barns 91 J11
Hermon Carmth 42 G8
Hermon IoA 78 F11
Hermon Pembks 41 P4
Herne Kent 39 L8
Herne Bay Kent 39 L8
Herne Common Kent 39 L8
Herne Hill Gt Lon 36 H6
Herne Pound Kent 37 Q10
Herner Devon 17 K6
Hernhill Kent 39 J9
Herodsfoot Cnwll 5 L9
Heronden Kent 39 N11
Herongate Essex 37 P2
Heronsford S Ayrs 114 B11
Heronsgate Herts 36 B2
Herriard Hants 23 J5
Herringfleet Suffk 65 P2
Herring's Green Bed 50 C2
Herringswell Suffk 63 N6
Herringthorpe Rothm 84 F2
Herrington Sundld 113 N10
Hersden Kent 39 M9
Hersham Cnwll 16 C10
Hersham Surrey 36 D8
Herstmonceux E Susx 25 P8
Herston Dorset 12 H9
Herston Ork 169 d7
Hertford Herts 50 H8
Hertford Heath Herts 51 J8
Hertingfordbury Herts 50 H8
Hesketh Bank Lancs 88 E6
Hesketh Lane Lancs 89 J2
Hesket Newmarket Cumb 101 K3
Heskin Green Lancs 88 G7
Hesleden Dur 104 D3
Hesleden N York 96 D5
Hesley Donc 85 K2
Hesleyside Nthumb 112 C4
Heslington C York 98 C10
Hessay C York 97 R10
Hessenford Cnwll 5 N10
Hessett Suffk 64 C9
Hessle E R Yk 92 H5
Hessle Wakefd 91 L7
Hest Bank Lancs 95 K4
Hestley Green Suffk 64 H8
Heston Gt Lon 36 D5
Heston Services Gt Lon 36 D5
Hestwall Ork 169 b5
Heswall Wirral 81 K8
Hethe Oxon 48 G9
Hethersett Norfk 76 G11
Hethersgill Cumb 111 J7
Hetherside Cumb 110 H6
Hetherson Green Ches W 69 P4
Hethpool Nthumb 118 G5
Hett Dur 103 Q3
Hetton N York 96 E9
Hetton-le-Hole Sundld 113 N11
Hetton Steads Nthumb 119 K3
Heugh Nthumb 112 G6
Heughhead Abers 150 B5
Heugh Head Border 129 M7
Heveningham Suffk 65 L7
Hever Kent 37 L11
Heversham Cumb 95 K4
Hevingham Norfk 76 H7
Hewas Water Cnwll 3 N4
Hewelsfield Gloucs 31 Q4
Hewenden C Brad 90 E3
Hewish N Som 19 M2
Hewish Somset 11 J3
Hewood Dorset 10 H4
Hexham Nthumb 112 D8
Hextable Kent 37 M6
Hexthorpe Donc 91 P10
Hexton Herts 50 D5
Hexworthy Cnwll 5 N3
Hexworthy Devon 6 H4
Hey Lancs 89 P2
Heybridge Essex 51 P11
Heybridge Essex 52 E10
Heybridge Basin Essex 52 E10
Heybrook Bay Devon 6 D9
Heydon Cambs 51 K3
Heydon Norfk 76 H6
Heydour Lincs 73 R3

Hey Houses Lancs ... 88 C5
Heylipoll Ag & B ... 136 B7
Heylor Shet ... 169 p5
Heyrod Tamesd ... 83 L5
Heysham Lancs ... 95 J8
Heyshaw N York ... 97 J8
Heyshott W Susx ... 23 N11
Heyside Oldham ... 89 Q9
Heytesbury Wilts ... 20 H6
Heythrop Oxon ... 48 C9
Heywood Rochdl ... 89 P8
Heywood Wilts ... 20 G4
Hibaldstow N Linc ... 92 G10
Hickleton Donc ... 91 M9
Hickling Norfk ... 77 N7
Hickling Notts ... 72 H5
Hickling Green Norfk ... 77 N7
Hickling Heath Norfk ... 77 N7
Hickling Pastures Notts ... 72 H5
Hickmans Green Kent ... 39 J10
Hicks Forstal Kent ... 39 L9
Hickstead W Susx ... 24 G6
Hidcote Bartrim Gloucs ... 47 N6
Hidcote Boyce Gloucs ... 47 N6
High Ackworth Wakefd ... 91 L7
Higham Barns ... 91 J9
Higham Derbys ... 84 E9
Higham Kent ... 37 P11
Higham Kent ... 38 B7
Higham Lancs ... 89 N3
Higham Suffk ... 52 H4
Higham Suffk ... 63 M7
Higham Dykes Nthumb ... 112 H5
Higham Ferrers Nhants ... 61 L7
Higham Gobion C Beds ... 50 D4
Higham Hill Gt Lon ... 37 J2
Higham on the Hill Leics ... 72 B11
Highampton Devon ... 8 C4
Highams Park Gt Lon ... 37 J2
High Angerton Nthumb ... 112 G3
High Ardwell D & G ... 106 E8
High Auldgirth D & G ... 109 K3
High Bankhill Cumb ... 101 Q2
High Beach Essex ... 51 K11
High Bentham N York ... 95 P7
High Bewaldeth Cumb ... 100 H4
High Bickington Devon ... 17 L7
High Biggins Cumb ... 95 N5
High Birkwith N York ... 96 B5
High Blantyre S Lans ... 126 B6
High Bonnybridge Falk ... 126 E2
High Borrans Cumb ... 101 M10
High Bradley N York ... 96 F11
High Bray Devon ... 17 M5
Highbridge Hants ... 22 E10
Highbridge Somset ... 19 K5
Highbrook W Susx ... 25 J4
High Brooms Kent ... 25 N2
High Bullen Devon ... 17 J7
Highburton Kirk ... 90 F8
Highbury Gt Lon ... 36 H3
Highbury Somset ... 20 C5
High Buston Nthumb ... 119 P9
High Callerton Nthumb ... 113 J6
High Casterton Cumb ... 95 N5
High Catton E R Yk ... 98 E10
Highclere Hants ... 22 D3
Highcliffe BCP ... 13 M6
High Close Dur ... 103 N7
High Cogges Oxon ... 34 C3
High Common Norfk ... 76 D10
High Coniscliffe Darltn ... 103 P7
High Crosby Cumb ... 111 J9
High Cross Cnwll ... 3 J8
High Cross E Ayrs ... 125 L8
High Cross Hants ... 23 K9
High Cross Herts ... 51 J7
Highcross Lancs ... 88 C3
High Cross W Susx ... 24 F7
High Cross Warwks ... 59 K11
High Drummore D & G ... 106 F10
High Dubmire Sundld ... 113 M11
High Easter Essex ... 51 P8
High Eggborough N York ... 91 P6
High Ellington N York ... 97 J9
Higher Alham Somset ... 20 C6
Higher Ansty Dorset ... 12 C4
Higher Ballam Lancs ... 88 D4
Higher Bartle Lancs ... 88 G4
Higher Berry End C Beds ... 49 Q8
Higher Bockhampton
  Dorset ... 12 B6
Higher Brixham Torbay ... 7 N8
Higher Burrowton Devon ... 9 P5
Higher Burwardsley Ches W ... 69 P3
High Ercall Wrekin ... 69 Q11
Higher Chillington Somset ... 10 H2
Higher Clovelly Devon ... 16 E7
Highercombe Somset ... 18 B8
Higher Coombe Dorset ... 11 L6
Higher Disley Ches E ... 83 K8
Higher Folds Wigan ... 82 E4
Higherford Lancs ... 89 P2
Higher Gabwell Devon ... 7 N5
Higher Halstock Leigh
  Dorset ... 11 L3
Higher Harpers Lancs ... 89 N3
Higher Heysham Lancs ... 95 J8
Higher Hurdsfield Ches E ... 83 K10
Higher Irlam Salfd ... 82 F5
Higher Kingcombe Dorset ... 11 L5
Higher Kinnerton Flints ... 69 K2
Higher Marston Ches W ... 82 E9
Higher Muddiford Devon ... 17 K4
Higher Nyland Dorset ... 20 D10
Higher Ogden Rochdl ... 90 B8
Higher Pentire Cnwll ... 2 H8
Higher Penwortham Lancs ... 88 G4
Higher Prestacott Devon ... 5 P2
Higher Studfold N York ... 96 B5
Higher Town Cnwll ... 3 L5
Higher Town Cnwll ... 4 G9
Higher Town IoS ... 2 c1
Higher Tregantle Cnwll ... 5 Q11
Higher Walton Lancs ... 88 H5
Higher Walton Warrtn ... 82 C7
Higher Wambrook Somset ... 10 F3
Higher Waterston Dorset ... 11 Q5
Higher Whatcombe Dorset ... 12 D4
Higher Wheelton Lancs ... 89 J6
Higher Whitley Ches W ... 82 D8
Higher Wincham Ches W ... 82 E9
Higher Wraxall Dorset ... 11 M4
Higher Wych Ches W ... 69 N6
High Etherley Dur ... 103 N5
High Ferry Lincs ... 87 L11

Highfield E R Yk ... 92 B3
Highfield Gatesd ... 112 H9
Highfield N Ayrs ... 125 J7
Highfields Donc ... 91 N9
Highfields Caldecote Cambs ... 62 E9
High Flats Kirk ... 90 G9
High Garrett Essex ... 52 C6
Highgate E Susx ... 25 K4
Highgate Gt Lon ... 36 G3
Highgate Kent ... 26 C5
High Grange Dur ... 103 N4
High Grantley N York ... 97 K7
High Green Cumb ... 101 M10
High Green Kirk ... 90 G8
High Green Norfk ... 64 H4
High Green Norfk ... 76 G10
High Green Sheff ... 91 J11
High Green Shrops ... 57 N8
High Green Suffk ... 64 B9
High Green Worcs ... 46 G5
Highgreen Manor Nthumb ... 112 B2
High Halden Kent ... 26 E4
High Halstow Medway ... 38 C6
High Ham Somset ... 19 M8
High Harrington Cumb ... 100 D5
High Harrogate N York ... 97 M9
High Haswell Dur ... 104 C2
High Hatton Shrops ... 69 R10
High Hauxley Nthumb ... 119 Q10
High Hawsker N York ... 105 P9
High Hesket Cumb ... 101 N2
High Hoyland Barns ... 90 H9
High Hunsley E R Yk ... 92 G3
High Hurstwood E Susx ... 25 L5
High Hutton N York ... 98 F7
High Ireby Cumb ... 100 H3
High Kelling Norfk ... 76 G3
High Kilburn N York ... 97 R5
High Killerby N York ... 99 M4
High Knipe Cumb ... 101 P7
High Lands Dur ... 103 M5
Highlane Ches E ... 83 J11
Highlane Derbys ... 84 F4
High Lane Stockp ... 83 L7
High Lanes Cnwll ... 2 F6
Highlaws Cumb ... 109 P11
Highleadon Gloucs ... 46 E10
High Legh Ches E ... 82 F8
Highleigh W Susx ... 15 M7
High Leven S on T ... 104 E8
Highley Shrops ... 57 N8
High Littleton BaNES ... 20 B3
High Lorton Cumb ... 100 G5
High Marishes N York ... 98 G5
High Marnham Notts ... 85 P6
High Melton Donc ... 91 N10
High Mickley Nthumb ... 112 G8
Highmoor Cumb ... 110 E11
Highmoor Oxon ... 35 K8
Highmoor Cross Oxon ... 35 K8
Highmoor Hill Mons ... 31 N7
High Moorsley Sundld ... 113 M11
Highnam Gloucs ... 46 F10
High Newport Sundld ... 113 N10
High Newton Cumb ... 95 J4
High Newton-by-the-Sea
  Nthumb ... 119 P5
High Nibthwaite Cumb ... 94 F3
High Offley Staffs ... 70 D9
High Ongar Essex ... 51 N10
High Onn Staffs ... 70 E11
High Park Corner Essex ... 52 H7
High Pennyvenie E Ayrs ... 115 J6
High Pittington Dur ... 104 B2
High Post Wilts ... 21 N7
Highridge N Som ... 31 Q1
High Roding Essex ... 51 P7
High Row Cumb ... 101 L3
High Row Cumb ... 101 L6
High Salter Lancs ... 95 N8
High Salvington W Susx ... 24 D9
High Scales Cumb ... 110 C11
High Seaton Cumb ... 100 D4
High Shaw N York ... 96 C2
High Side Cumb ... 100 H4
High Spen Gatesd ... 112 H9
Highstead Kent ... 39 M8
Highsted Kent ... 38 F9
High Stoop Dur ... 103 M2
High Street Cnwll ... 3 P3
High Street Kent ... 26 B5
High Street Kent ... 39 J9
Highstreet Suffk ... 65 N10
High Street Suffk ... 65 N7
Highstreet Green Essex ... 52 C5
Highstreet Green Surrey ... 23 Q7
Hightae D & G ... 109 N5
High Throston Hartpl ... 104 E7
Hightown Ches E ... 70 F2
Hightown Hants ... 13 L4
Hightown Sefton ... 81 L4
High Town Staffs ... 58 E2
Hightown Green Suffk ... 64 D10
High Toynton Lincs ... 87 J7
High Trewhitt Nthumb ... 119 N3
High Urpeth Dur ... 113 K10
High Valleyfield Fife ... 134 C10
High Warden Nthumb ... 112 D7
Highway Herefs ... 45 P5
Highway Wilts ... 33 K10
Highweek Devon ... 7 L4
High Westwood Dur ... 112 H9
Highwood Essex ... 51 P10
Highwood Staffs ... 71 K8
Highwood Hill Gt Lon ... 36 F2
High Woolaston Gloucs ... 31 Q5
High Worsall N York ... 104 C9
Highworth Swindn ... 33 P6
High Wray Cumb ... 101 L11
High Wych Herts ... 51 L8
High Wycombe Bucks ... 35 N6
Hilborough Norfk ... 75 N3
Hilcote Derbys ... 84 G9
Hilcott Wilts ... 21 M3
Hildenborough Kent ... 37 N11
Hilden Park Kent ... 37 N11
Hildersham Cambs ... 62 H11
Hilderstone Staffs ... 70 H8
Hilderthorpe E R Yk ... 99 N7
Hilfield Dorset ... 11 N3
Hilgay Norfk ... 75 N1
Hill S Glos ... 32 B5
Hill Warwks ... 59 Q11
Hillam N York ... 91 N5

Hillbeck Cumb ... 102 E7
Hillborough Kent ... 39 M8
Hill Brow Hants ... 23 L9
Hillbutts Dorset ... 12 G4
Hill Chorlton Staffs ... 70 D7
Hillclifflane Derbys ... 71 P5
Hill Common Norfk ... 77 N7
Hill Common Somset ... 18 F9
Hill Deverill Wilts ... 20 G6
Hilldyke Lincs ... 87 K11
Hill End Dur ... 103 K3
Hill End Fife ... 134 C8
Hillend Fife ... 134 E11
Hill End Gloucs ... 46 H7
Hillend Mdloth ... 127 P4
Hillend N Lans ... 126 E4
Hillend Swans ... 28 D6
Hillersland Gloucs ... 31 Q2
Hillerton Devon ... 8 H5
Hillesden Bucks ... 49 J9
Hillesley Gloucs ... 32 E7
Hillfarrance Somset ... 18 G10
Hill Green Kent ... 38 D9
Hillgrove W Susx ... 23 P9
Hillhampton Herefs ... 46 A5
Hillhead Abers ... 158 E10
Hillhead Devon ... 7 N8
Hill Head Hants ... 14 F6
Hillhead S Lans ... 116 D2
Hillhead of Cocklaw Abers ... 159 Q9
Hilliard's Cross Staffs ... 59 J2
Hilliclay Highld ... 167 L4
Hillingdon Gt Lon ... 36 C4
Hillington C Glas ... 125 N5
Hillington Norfk ... 75 P5
Hillis Corner IoW ... 14 E8
Hillmorton Warwks ... 60 B6
Hillock Vale Lancs ... 89 M5
Hill of Beath Fife ... 134 F9
Hill of Fearn Highld ... 163 J11
Hillowton D & G ... 108 G8
Hillpool Worcs ... 58 C9
Hillpound Hants ... 22 G11
Hill Ridware Staffs ... 71 K11
Hillside Abers ... 151 N8
Hillside Angus ... 143 N5
Hillside Devon ... 7 J6
Hill Side Kirk ... 90 F7
Hill Side Worcs ... 46 E2
Hills Town Derbys ... 84 G7
Hillstreet Hants ... 22 B11
Hillswick Shet ... 169 p6
Hill Top Dur ... 103 J6
Hill Top Hants ... 14 D6
Hill Top Kirk ... 90 D8
Hill Top Rothm ... 84 E2
Hill Top Sandw ... 58 E6
Hill Top Wakefd ... 91 J7
Hillwell Shet ... 169 q12
Hilmarton Wilts ... 33 K9
Hilperton Wilts ... 20 G3
Hilperton Marsh Wilts ... 20 G3
Hilsea C Port ... 15 J6
Hilston E R Yk ... 93 N4
Hiltingbury Hants ... 22 D10
Hilton Border ... 129 M9
Hilton Cambs ... 62 C7
Hilton Cumb ... 102 D6
Hilton Derbys ... 71 N8
Hilton Dorset ... 12 C4
Hilton Dur ... 103 N6
Hilton S on T ... 104 E8
Hilton Shrops ... 57 P5
Hilton of Cadboll Highld ... 156 F2
Hilton Park Services Staffs ... 58 E4
Himbleton Worcs ... 46 H3
Himley Staffs ... 58 C6
Hincaster Cumb ... 95 L4
Hinchley Wood Surrey ... 36 E7
Hinckley Leics ... 59 P6
Hinderclay Suffk ... 64 E6
Hinderwell N York ... 105 L7
Hindford Shrops ... 69 K8
Hindhead Surrey ... 23 N7
Hindhead Tunnel Surrey ... 23 N7
Hindle Fold Lancs ... 89 L4
Hindley Nthumb ... 112 H9
Hindley Wigan ... 82 D4
Hindley Green Wigan ... 82 D4
Hindlip Worcs ... 46 G3
Hindolveston Norfk ... 76 E6
Hindon Wilts ... 20 H8
Hindringham Norfk ... 76 D4
Hingham Norfk ... 76 E11
Hinksford Staffs ... 58 C7
Hinstock Shrops ... 70 B9
Hintlesham Suffk ... 53 J3
Hinton Gloucs ... 32 C4
Hinton Hants ... 13 M5
Hinton Herefs ... 45 L7
Hinton Nhants ... 48 F4
Hinton S Glos ... 32 D9
Hinton Shrops ... 56 G3
Hinton Shrops ... 57 M8
Hinton Admiral Hants ... 13 M5
Hinton Ampner Hants ... 22 H9
Hinton Blewett BaNES ... 19 Q3
Hinton Charterhouse BaNES ... 20 E3
Hinton Cross Worcs ... 47 K6
Hinton-in-the-Hedges
  Nhants ... 48 G7
Hinton Marsh Hants ... 22 G9
Hinton Martell Dorset ... 12 H3
Hinton on the Green Worcs ... 47 K6
Hinton Parva Swindn ... 33 P8
Hinton St George Somset ... 11 J2
Hinton St Mary Dorset ... 20 D11
Hinton Waldrist Oxon ... 34 C5
Hints Shrops ... 57 L10
Hints Staffs ... 59 J4
Hinwick Bed ... 61 K8
Hinxhill Kent ... 26 H3
Hinxton Cambs ... 62 G11
Hinxworth Herts ... 50 F2
Hipperholme Calder ... 90 E5
Hipsburn Nthumb ... 119 P8
Hipswell N York ... 103 N11
Hirn Abers ... 151 J7
Hirnant Powys ... 68 D10
Hirst Nthumb ... 113 L3
Hirst Courtney N York ... 91 Q6
Hirwaun Denbgs ... 68 F2
Hirwaun Rhondd ... 30 C3
Hiscott Devon ... 17 J6
Histon Cambs ... 62 F8
Hitcham Suffk ... 64 D11

Hitcham Causeway Suffk ... 64 D11
Hitcham Street Suffk ... 64 D11
Hitchin Herts ... 50 E5
Hither Green Gt Lon ... 37 J6
Hittisleigh Devon ... 8 H5
Hive E R Yk ... 92 D4
Hixon Staffs ... 71 J9
Hoaden Kent ... 39 N10
Hoar Cross Staffs ... 71 L10
Hoarwithy Herefs ... 45 Q9
Hoath Kent ... 39 M9
Hoathly Kent ... 25 Q3
Hobarris Shrops ... 56 E9
Hobbles Green Suffk ... 63 M10
Hobbs Cross Essex ... 51 L11
Hobbs Cross Essex ... 51 L8
Hobkirk Border ... 118 A8
Hobland Norfk ... 77 Q11
Hobsick Notts ... 84 G11
Hobson Dur ... 113 J9
Hoby Leics ... 72 H7
Hoccombe Somset ... 18 F9
Hockering Norfk ... 76 F9
Hockerton Notts ... 85 M9
Hockley Ches E ... 83 K8
Hockley Covtry ... 59 L9
Hockley Essex ... 38 D3
Hockley Staffs ... 59 K4
Hockley Heath Solhll ... 59 J10
Hockliffe C Beds ... 49 Q9
Hockwold cum Wilton Norfk ... 63 M3
Hockworthy Devon ... 18 D11
Hoddesdon Herts ... 51 J9
Hoddlesden Bl w D ... 89 L6
Hoddom Cross D & G ... 110 C6
Hoddom Mains D & G ... 110 C6
Hodgehill Ches E ... 82 H11
Hodgeston Pembks ... 41 K11
Hodnet Shrops ... 69 R9
Hodsock Notts ... 85 K3
Hodsoll Street Kent ... 37 P8
Hodson Swindn ... 33 N8
Hodthorpe Derbys ... 84 H5
Hoe Hants ... 22 G11
Hoe Norfk ... 76 D8
Hoe Benham W Berk ... 34 D11
Hoe Gate Hants ... 14 H4
Hoff Cumb ... 102 C7
Hogben's Hill Kent ... 38 H10
Hoggards Green Suffk ... 64 B10
Hoggeston Bucks ... 49 M10
Hoggrill's End Warwks ... 59 K6
Hog Hill E Susx ... 26 E8
Hoghton Lancs ... 89 J5
Hoghton Bottoms Lancs ... 89 J5
Hognaston Derbys ... 71 N4
Hogsthorpe Lincs ... 87 P6
Holbeach Lincs ... 74 G6
Holbeach Bank Lincs ... 74 G5
Holbeach Clough Lincs ... 74 G5
Holbeach Drove Lincs ... 74 F8
Holbeach Hurn Lincs ... 74 G5
Holbeach St Johns Lincs ... 74 G7
Holbeach St Mark's Lincs ... 74 G4
Holbeach St Matthew Lincs ... 74 H4
Holbeck Notts ... 84 H6
Holbeck Woodhouse Notts ... 84 H6
Holberrow Green Worcs ... 47 K3
Holbeton Devon ... 6 G8
Holborn Gt Lon ... 36 H4
Holborough Kent ... 37 Q8
Holbrook Derbys ... 72 B2
Holbrook Sheff ... 84 F4
Holbrook Suffk ... 53 L4
Holbrook Moor Derbys ... 84 E11
Holbrooks Covtry ... 59 M8
Holburn Nthumb ... 119 K3
Holbury Hants ... 14 D6
Holcombe Devon ... 7 P4
Holcombe Somset ... 20 C5
Holcombe Rogus Devon ... 18 E11
Holcot Nhants ... 60 G7
Holden Lancs ... 96 A11
Holdenby Nhants ... 60 E7
Holden Gate Calder ... 89 P6
Holder's Green Essex ... 51 P5
Holdgate Shrops ... 57 K7
Holdingham Lincs ... 86 E11
Holditch Dorset ... 10 G4
Holdsworth Calder ... 90 D5
Holehouse Derbys ... 83 M6
Hole-in-the-Wall Herefs ... 46 B9
Holemoor Devon ... 16 G10
Hole Street W Susx ... 24 D8
Holford Somset ... 18 G6
Holgate C York ... 98 B10
Holker Cumb ... 94 H5
Holkham Norfk ... 76 B3
Hollacombe Devon ... 16 F11
Holland Fen Lincs ... 86 H11
Holland Lees Lancs ... 88 G9
Holland-on-Sea Essex ... 53 L8
Hollandstoun Ork ... 169 g1
Hollee D & G ... 110 C2
Hollesley Suffk ... 53 Q3
Hollicombe Torbay ... 7 M6
Hollingbourne Kent ... 38 D10
Hollingbury Br & H ... 24 H9
Hollingdon Bucks ... 49 N9
Hollingrove E Susx ... 25 Q6
Hollingthorpe Leeds ... 91 K4
Hollington Derbys ... 71 N7
Hollington Staffs ... 71 K7
Hollingworth Tamesd ... 83 M5
Hollins Bury ... 89 N9
Hollins Derbys ... 84 D6
Hollins Staffs ... 70 H5
Hollinsclough Staffs ... 83 N11
Hollins End Sheff ... 84 E4
Hollins Green Warrtn ... 82 E6
Hollins Lane Lancs ... 95 K10
Hollinswood Wrekin ... 57 N3
Hollinwood Shrops ... 69 P7
Hollocombe Devon ... 17 L9
Holloway Derbys ... 84 D9
Holloway Gt Lon ... 36 H3
Holloway Wilts ... 20 G8
Hollowell Nhants ... 60 E6
Hollowmoor Heath Ches W ... 81 P11
Hollows D & G ... 110 G5
Hollybush Caerph ... 30 G4
Hollybush E Ayrs ... 114 G4
Hollybush Herefs ... 46 E7
Holly End Norfk ... 75 J9
Holly Green Worcs ... 46 G6
Hollyhurst Ches E ... 69 Q6

Hollym E R Yk ... 93 P5
Hollywood Worcs ... 58 G9
Holmbridge Kirk ... 90 E9
Holmbury St Mary Surrey ... 24 D2
Holmbush Cnwll ... 3 Q3
Holmcroft Staffs ... 70 G10
Holme Cambs ... 61 Q3
Holme Cumb ... 95 L5
Holme Kirk ... 90 E9
Holme N Linc ... 92 F9
Holme N York ... 97 N4
Holme Notts ... 85 P9
Holme Chapel Lancs ... 89 P5
Holme Green N York ... 91 P2
Holme Hale Norfk ... 76 B10
Holme Lacy Herefs ... 45 R7
Holme Marsh Herefs ... 45 L4
Holme next the Sea Norfk ... 75 P2
Holme on the Wolds E R Yk ... 99 K11
Holme Pierrepont Notts ... 72 G3
Holmer Herefs ... 45 Q6
Holmer Green Bucks ... 35 P5
Holme St Cuthbert Cumb ... 109 P11
Holmes Chapel Ches E ... 82 G11
Holmesfield Derbys ... 84 D5
Holmes Hill E Susx ... 25 M8
Holmeswood Lancs ... 88 E7
Holmethorpe Surrey ... 36 G10
Holme upon Spalding
  Moor E R Yk ... 92 D3
Holmewood Derbys ... 84 F7
Holmfield Calder ... 90 D5
Holmfirth Kirk ... 90 E9
Holmgate Derbys ... 84 E8
Holmhead E Ayrs ... 115 L3
Holmpton E R Yk ... 93 Q6
Holmrook Cumb ... 100 E11
Holmshurst E Susx ... 25 P5
Holmside Dur ... 113 K11
Holmwrangle Cumb ... 111 K11
Holne Devon ... 7 J5
Holnest Dorset ... 11 P3
Holnicote Somset ... 18 B5
Holsworthy Devon ... 16 E11
Holsworthy Beacon Devon ... 16 F10
Holt Dorset ... 12 H4
Holt Norfk ... 76 F4
Holt Wilts ... 20 G2
Holt Worcs ... 46 F2
Holt Wrexhm ... 69 M4
Holtby C York ... 98 D10
Holt End Worcs ... 58 G11
Holt Fleet Worcs ... 46 F2
Holt Green Lancs ... 88 D9
Holt Heath Dorset ... 13 J4
Holt Heath Worcs ... 46 F2
Holton Oxon ... 34 H3
Holton Somset ... 20 C9
Holton Suffk ... 65 N6
Holton cum Beckering Lincs ... 86 F6
Holton Heath Dorset ... 12 F6
Holton Hill E Susx ... 25 Q5
Holton le Clay Lincs ... 93 N10
Holton le Moor Lincs ... 93 J11
Holton St Mary Suffk ... 53 J4
Holt Street Kent ... 39 N11
Holtye E Susx ... 25 L3
Holway Flints ... 80 H9
Holwell Dorset ... 11 P2
Holwell Herts ... 50 E4
Holwell Leics ... 73 J6
Holwell Oxon ... 33 P3
Holwick Dur ... 102 H5
Holworth Dorset ... 12 C8
Holybourne Hants ... 23 K6
Holy Cross Worcs ... 58 D9
Holyfield Essex ... 51 J10
Holyhead IoA ... 78 C8
Holy Island IoA ... 78 D8
Holy Island Nthumb ... 119 M2
Holy Island Nthumb ... 119 M2
Holymoorside Derbys ... 84 D7
Holyport W & M ... 35 N9
Holystone Nthumb ... 119 J10
Holytown N Lans ... 126 D5
Holywell C Beds ... 50 B7
Holywell Cambs ... 62 D6
Holywell Cnwll ... 4 B10
Holywell Dorset ... 11 M4
Holywell Flints ... 80 H9
Holywell Nthumb ... 113 M6
Holywell Warwks ... 59 K11
Holywell Green Calder ... 90 D7
Holywell Lake Somset ... 18 F10
Holywell Row Suffk ... 63 M5
Holywood D & G ... 109 K4
Holywood Village D & G ... 109 L5
Homer Shrops ... 57 L4
Homer Green Sefton ... 81 L4
Homersfield Suffk ... 65 K4
Homescales Cumb ... 95 M3
Hom Green Herefs ... 46 A10
Homington Wilts ... 21 M9
Honeyborough Pembks ... 40 H9
Honeybourne Worcs ... 47 M6
Honeychurch Devon ... 8 F4
Honey Hill Kent ... 39 K9
Honeystreet Wilts ... 21 M2
Honey Tye Suffk ... 52 G4
Honiley Warwks ... 59 K10
Honing Norfk ... 77 L6
Honingham Norfk ... 76 G9
Honington Lincs ... 73 N2
Honington Suffk ... 64 C6
Honington Warwks ... 47 Q6
Honiton Devon ... 10 D4
Honley Kirk ... 90 E8
Honnington Wrekin ... 70 C11
Hoo Kent ... 39 N9
Hoobrook Worcs ... 58 B10
Hood Green Barns ... 91 J10
Hood Hill Rothm ... 91 K11
Hooe C Plym ... 6 E8
Hooe E Susx ... 25 Q8
Hoo End Herts ... 50 E6
Hoo Green Ches E ... 82 F8
Hoohill Bpool ... 88 C3
Hook Cambs ... 75 J11
Hook Devon ... 10 G3
Hook E R Yk ... 92 C5
Hook Gt Lon ... 36 E8
Hook Hants ... 14 F5
Hook Hants ... 23 K4
Hook Pembks ... 41 J8
Hook Wilts ... 33 L8
Hook-a-Gate Shrops ... 56 H3

Hook Bank Worcs ... 46 F6
Hooke Dorset ... 11 L4
Hook End Essex ... 51 N10
Hookgate Staffs ... 70 C7
Hook Green Kent ... 25 Q3
Hook Green Kent ... 37 P6
Hook Norton Oxon ... 48 C8
Hook Street Gloucs ... 32 C5
Hook Street Wilts ... 33 L8
Hookway Devon ... 9 L5
Hooley Surrey ... 36 G9
Hooley Bridge Rochdl ... 89 P8
Hoo Meavy Devon ... 6 E5
Hoo St Werburgh Medway ... 38 C7
Hooton Ches W ... 81 M9
Hooton Levitt Rothm ... 84 H2
Hooton Pagnell Donc ... 91 M9
Hooton Roberts Rothm ... 91 M11
Hopcrofts Holt Oxon ... 48 E9
Hope Derbys ... 83 Q8
Hope Devon ... 6 H10
Hope Flints ... 69 K3
Hope Powys ... 56 D3
Hope Shrops ... 56 E4
Hope Staffs ... 71 L4
Hope Bagot Shrops ... 57 K10
Hope Bowdler Shrops ... 56 H6
Hope End Green Essex ... 51 N6
Hopehouse Border ... 117 K7
Hopeman Moray ... 157 L4
Hope Mansell Herefs ... 46 B11
Hopesay Shrops ... 56 F8
Hopetown Wakefd ... 91 K6
Hope under Dinmore Herefs ... 45 Q4
Hopgrove C York ... 98 C10
Hopperton N York ... 97 P9
Hop Pole Lincs ... 74 C8
Hopsford Warwks ... 59 P8
Hopstone Shrops ... 57 P6
Hopton Derbys ... 71 P4
Hopton Shrops ... 69 L10
Hopton Staffs ... 70 G9
Hopton Suffk ... 64 D6
Hopton Cangeford Shrops ... 57 J8
Hopton Castle Shrops ... 56 F9
Hoptonheath Shrops ... 56 F9
Hopton on Sea Norfk ... 65 Q2
Hopton Wafers Shrops ... 57 L9
Hopwas Staffs ... 59 J4
Hopwood Rochdl ... 89 P9
Hopwood Worcs ... 58 F9
Hopwood Park Services Worcs ... 58 F10
Horam E Susx ... 25 N7
Horbling Lincs ... 74 B3
Horbury Wakefd ... 90 H7
Horcott Gloucs ... 33 N4
Horden Dur ... 104 D2
Horderley Shrops ... 56 G7
Hordle Hants ... 13 N5
Hordley Shrops ... 69 L8
Horeb Carmth ... 28 E3
Horeb Cerdgn ... 42 G6
Horfield Bristl ... 31 Q9
Horham Suffk ... 65 J7
Horkesley Heath Essex ... 52 G6
Horkstow N Linc ... 92 G7
Horley Oxon ... 48 D6
Horley Surrey ... 24 G2
Hornblotton Green Somset ... 19 Q8
Hornby Lancs ... 95 M7
Hornby N York ... 97 K2
Hornby N York ... 104 C9
Horncastle Lincs ... 87 J7
Hornchurch Gt Lon ... 37 M3
Horncliffe Nthumb ... 129 N10
Horndean Border ... 129 N10
Horndean Hants ... 15 K4
Horndon Devon ... 8 D8
Horndon on the Hill Thurr ... 37 Q4
Horne Surrey ... 24 H2
Horner Somset ... 18 B5
Horne Row Essex ... 52 C11
Horners Green Suffk ... 52 G3
Horney Common E Susx ... 25 L5
Horn Hill Bucks ... 36 B2
Horning Norfk ... 77 L8
Horninghold Leics ... 73 L11
Horninglow Staffs ... 71 N9
Horningsea Cambs ... 62 G8
Horningsham Wilts ... 20 F6
Horningtoft Norfk ... 76 C7
Horningtops Cnwll ... 5 M9
Hornsbury Somset ... 10 G2
Hornsby Cumb ... 111 K10
Hornsbygate Cumb ... 111 K10
Horns Cross Devon ... 16 F7
Horns Cross E Susx ... 26 D7
Hornsea E R Yk ... 99 P11
Hornsey Gt Lon ... 36 H3
Horn's Green Gt Lon ... 37 L9
Horn Street Kent ... 27 L4
Hornton Oxon ... 48 C5
Horpit Swindn ... 33 P8
Horrabridge Devon ... 6 E5
Horringer Suffk ... 64 A9
Horringford IoW ... 14 F9
Horrocks Fold Bolton ... 89 L8
Horrocksford Lancs ... 89 M2
Horsacott Devon ... 17 J5
Horsebridge Devon ... 5 Q6
Horsebridge E Susx ... 25 N8
Horsebridge Hants ... 22 B8
Horsebridge Shrops ... 56 F3
Horsebridge Staffs ... 70 H4
Horsebrook Staffs ... 58 C2
Horsecastle N Som ... 31 M11
Horsedown Cnwll ... 2 G7
Horsehay Wrekin ... 57 M3
Horseheath Cambs ... 63 K11
Horsehouse N York ... 96 F4
Horsell Surrey ... 23 Q3
Horseman's Green Wrexhm ... 69 M6
Horsenden Bucks ... 35 L4
Horsey Norfk ... 77 P7
Horsey Somset ... 19 K7
Horsey Corner Norfk ... 77 P7
Horsford Norfk ... 76 H8
Horsforth Leeds ... 90 G3
Horsham W Susx ... 24 E4
Horsham Worcs ... 46 D3
Horsham St Faith Norfk ... 77 J8
Horsington Lincs ... 86 G7
Horsington Somset ... 20 D10
Horsley Derbys ... 72 B2

Horsley Gloucs ... 32 F5
Horsley Nthumb ... 112 G7
Horsley Nthumb ... 118 F11
Horsley Cross Essex ... 53 K6
Horsleycross Street Essex ... 53 K6
Horsley-Gate Derbys ... 84 D5
Horsleyhill Border ... 117 Q7
Horsley Woodhouse Derbys ... 72 B2
Horsmonden Kent ... 26 B3
Horspath Oxon ... 34 G3
Horstead Norfk ... 77 K8
Horsted Keynes W Susx ... 25 J5
Horton Bucks ... 49 P11
Horton Dorset ... 12 H3
Horton Lancs ... 96 C10
Horton Nhants ... 49 M4
Horton S Glos ... 32 E8
Horton Shrops ... 69 N9
Horton Somset ... 10 G2
Horton Staffs ... 70 G3
Horton Surrey ... 36 E8
Horton Swans ... 28 E7
Horton W & M ... 36 B5
Horton Wilts ... 21 K7
Horton Wrekin ... 57 M2
Horton Cross Somset ... 19 K11
Horton-cum-Studley Oxon ... 34 G3
Horton Green Ches W ... 69 N5
Horton Heath Hants ... 22 E11
Horton-in-Ribblesdale N York ... 96 B6
Horton Kirby Kent ... 37 N7
Horwich Bolton ... 89 J8
Horwich End Derbys ... 83 M8
Horwood Devon ... 17 J6
Hoscar Lancs ... 88 F7
Hoscote Border ... 117 M8
Hose Leics ... 73 J5
Hosey Hill Kent ... 37 L10
Hosh P & K ... 133 P3
Hoswick Shet ... 169 r11
Hotham E R Yk ... 92 E4
Hothfield Kent ... 26 G3
Hoton Leics ... 72 F6
Hott Nthumb ... 111 Q3
Hough Ches E ... 70 C4
Hough Ches E ... 83 J9
Hougham Lincs ... 73 M2
Hough End Leeds ... 90 G4
Hough Green Halton ... 81 P7
Hough-on-the-Hill Lincs ... 86 B11
Houghton Cambs ... 62 C6
Houghton Cumb ... 110 H9
Houghton Hants ... 22 B8
Houghton Nthumb ... 112 H7
Houghton Pembks ... 41 J9
Houghton W Susx ... 24 B8
Houghton Conquest C Beds ... 50 B2
Houghton Gate Dur ... 113 M10
Houghton Green E Susx ... 26 F7
Houghton Green Warrtn ... 82 D6
Houghton le Side Darltn ... 103 P6
Houghton-le-Spring Sundld ... 113 M11
Houghton on the Hill Leics ... 72 H10
Houghton Regis C Beds ... 50 B6
Houghton St Giles Norfk ... 76 C4
Houlton Warwks ... 60 C6
Hound Green Hants ... 23 K3
Houndslow Border ... 128 G10
Houndsmoor Somset ... 18 F9
Houndwood Border ... 129 L7
Hounslow Gt Lon ... 36 D5
Househill Highld ... 156 F7
Houses Hill Kirk ... 90 F7
Housieside Abers ... 151 M2
Houston Rens ... 125 L4
Houstry Highld ... 167 L10
Houton Ork ... 169 c6
Hove Br & H ... 24 G10
Hove Edge Calder ... 90 E6
Hoveringham Notts ... 85 L11
Hoveton Norfk ... 77 L8
Hovingham N York ... 98 D5
Howbrook Barns ... 91 J11
How Caple Herefs ... 46 B8
Howden E R Yk ... 92 B5
Howden-le-Wear Dur ... 103 N4
Howe Highld ... 167 P4
Howe IoM ... 80 b7
Howe N York ... 97 N4
Howe Norfk ... 65 K2
Howe Bridge Wigan ... 82 E4
Howe Green Essex ... 52 B11
Howegreen Essex ... 52 D11
Howell Lincs ... 86 F11
How End C Beds ... 50 B2
How of Teuchar Abers ... 159 J8
Howes D & G ... 110 C7
Howe Street Essex ... 51 Q4
Howe Street Essex ... 51 Q8
Howey Powys ... 44 F3
Howgate C Cumb ... 100 C6
Howgate Mdloth ... 127 N6
Howgill Lancs ... 96 B11
Howick Nthumb ... 119 Q7
How Wrekin ... 70 B10
Howle Hill Herefs ... 46 B10
Howlett End Essex ... 51 N4
Howley Somset ... 10 F3
How Mill Cumb ... 111 K9
Hownam Border ... 118 E7
Howrigg Cumb ... 110 F11
Howsham N Linc ... 92 H10
Howsham N York ... 98 E8
Howtel Nthumb ... 118 G4
Howt Green Kent ... 38 E8
Howton Herefs ... 45 N9
Howtown Cumb ... 101 M7
How Wood Herts ... 50 D10
Howwood Rens ... 125 K5
Hoxa Ork ... 169 d7
Hoxne Suffk ... 64 H6
Hoy Ork ... 169 b7
Hoylake Wirral ... 81 J7
Hoyland Barns ... 91 K10
Hoyland Common Barns ... 91 K10
Hoylandswaine Barns ... 90 H10
Hoyle W Susx ... 23 P11
Hoyle Mill Barns ... 91 K9
Hubberholme N York ... 96 D5
Hubberston Pembks ... 40 G9
Hubbert's Bridge Lincs ... 74 E2
Huby N York ... 97 L11
Huby N York ... 98 B7

Huccaby Devon ... 6 H4
Hucclecote Gloucs ... 46 G11
Hucking Kent ... 38 D10
Hucknall Notts ... 84 H11
Huddersfield Kirk ... 90 E7
Huddington Worcs ... 46 H3
Hudnall Herts ... 50 B8
Hudswell N York ... 103 M10
Huggate E R Yk ... 98 H9
Hugglescote Leics ... 72 C8
Hughenden Valley Bucks ... 35 N5
Hughley Shrops ... 57 K5
Hugh Town IoS ... 2 c2
Huish Devon ... 17 J9
Huish Wilts ... 21 M2
Huish Champflower Somset ... 18 E9
Huish Episcopi Somset ... 19 M9
Hüisinis W Isls ... 168 e6
Huisinish W Isls ... 168 e6
Hulcote C Beds ... 49 P7
Hulcote Nhants ... 49 K5
Hulcott Bucks ... 49 N11
Hulham Devon ... 9 P8
Hulland Derbys ... 71 N5
Hulland Ward Derbys ... 71 P5
Hullavington Wilts ... 32 G8
Hull Bridge E R Yk ... 93 J2
Hullbridge Essex ... 38 D2
Hull, Kingston upon C KuH ... 93 J5
Hulme Manch ... 82 H5
Hulme Staffs ... 70 G5
Hulme Warrtn ... 82 D6
Hulme End Staffs ... 71 L3
Hulme Walfield Ches E ... 82 H11
Hulse Heath Ches E ... 82 F8
Hulton Lane Ends Bolton ... 89 K9
Hulverstone IoW ... 14 C10
Hulver Street Norfk ... 76 C9
Hulver Street Suffk ... 65 P4
Humber Devon ... 9 J4
Humber Herefs ... 45 Q3
Humber Bridge N Linc ... 92 H6
Humberside Airport N Linc ... 93 J8
Humberston NE Lin ... 93 P9
Humberstone C Leic ... 72 G9
Humberton N York ... 97 P7
Humbie E Loth ... 128 D7
Humbleton E R Yk ... 93 M4
Humbleton Nthumb ... 119 J5
Humby Lincs ... 73 Q4
Hume Border ... 118 D2
Humshaugh Nthumb ... 112 D6
Huna Highld ... 167 Q2
Huncoat Lancs ... 89 M4
Huncote Leics ... 72 E11
Hundalee Border ... 118 B7
Hundall Derbys ... 84 E5
Hunderthwaite Dur ... 103 J6
Hundleby Lincs ... 87 L7
Hundle Houses Lincs ... 86 H10
Hundleton Pembks ... 41 J10
Hundon Suffk ... 63 M11
Hundred End Lancs ... 88 E6
Hundred House Powys ... 44 G4
Hungarton Leics ... 72 H9
Hungerford Hants ... 13 L2
Hungerford Somset ... 18 D6
Hungerford W Berk ... 34 B11
Hungerford Newtown W Berk ... 34 C10
Hunger Hill Bolton ... 89 K9
Hunger Hill Lancs ... 88 H8
Hungerstone Herefs ... 45 N7
Hungerton Lincs ... 73 M5
Hungryhatton Shrops ... 70 B9
Hunmanby N York ... 99 M5
Hunningham Warwks ... 59 N11
Hunnington Worcs ... 58 E8
Hunsbury Hill Nhants ... 60 F9
Hunsdon Herts ... 51 K8
Hunsdonbury Herts ... 51 K8
Hunsingore N York ... 97 P10
Hunslet Leeds ... 91 J4
Hunsonby Cumb ... 101 Q3
Hunspow Highld ... 167 N2
Hunstanton Norfk ... 75 M2
Hunstanworth Dur ... 112 D11
Hunsterson Ches E ... 70 B5
Hunston Suffk ... 64 D8
Hunston W Susx ... 15 N6
Hunston Green Suffk ... 64 D8
Hunstrete BaNES ... 20 B2
Hunsworth Kirk ... 90 F5
Hunt End Worcs ... 47 K2
Hunter's Inn Devon ... 17 M2
Hunter's Quay Ag & B ... 124 F2
Huntham Somset ... 19 K9
Hunthill Lodge Angus ... 142 H3
Huntingdon Cambs ... 62 B6
Huntingfield Suffk ... 65 L7
Huntingford Dorset ... 20 F9
Huntington C York ... 98 C9
Huntington Ches W ... 69 M2
Huntington E Loth ... 128 D5
Huntington Herefs ... 45 K4
Huntington Herefs ... 45 P6
Huntington Staffs ... 58 E2
Huntingtowerfield P & K ... 134 D2
Huntley Gloucs ... 46 D11
Huntly Abers ... 158 D10
Hunton Hants ... 22 E6
Hunton Kent ... 26 B2
Hunton N York ... 97 J2
Hunton Bridge Herts ... 50 C10
Hunt's Corner Norfk ... 64 F4
Huntscott Somset ... 18 B6
Hunt's Cross Lpool ... 81 N7
Hunts Green Bucks ... 35 N4
Hunts Green Warwks ... 59 J5
Huntsham Devon ... 18 D10
Huntshaw Devon ... 17 J7
Huntshaw Cross Devon ... 17 J7
Huntspill Somset ... 19 K6
Huntstile Somset ... 19 J8
Huntworth Somset ... 19 K8
Hunwick Dur ... 103 N4
Hunworth Norfk ... 76 F4
Hurcott Somset ... 19 L11
Hurdcott Wilts ... 21 N8
Hurdsfield Ches E ... 83 K10
Hurley W & M ... 35 M8
Hurley Warwks ... 59 K5
Hurley Bottom W & M ... 35 M8
Hurley Common Warwks ... 59 K5
Hurlford E Ayrs ... 125 M10
Hurlston Green Lancs ... 88 D8
Hurn BCP ... 13 K5

Hurn's End Lincs ... 87 M11
Hursley Hants ... 22 D9
Hurst Dorset ... 12 C6
Hurst N York ... 103 K10
Hurst Somset ... 19 N11
Hurst Wokham ... 35 L10
Hurstbourne Priors Hants ... 22 D5
Hurstbourne Tarrant Hants ... 22 C4
Hurst Green E Susx ... 26 B6
Hurst Green Essex ... 53 J8
Hurst Green Lancs ... 89 K3
Hurst Green Surrey ... 37 K10
Hurst Hill Dudley ... 58 D6
Hurstley Herefs ... 45 M5
Hurstpierpoint W Susx ... 24 G7
Hurst Wickham W Susx ... 24 G7
Hurstwood Lancs ... 89 P4
Hurtiso Ork ... 169 e6
Hurtmore Surrey ... 23 P5
Hurworth Burn Dur ... 104 D4
Hurworth-on-Tees Darltn ... 104 B9
Hurworth Place Darltn ... 103 Q9
Hury Dur ... 103 J7
Husbands Bosworth Leics ... 60 D4
Husborne Crawley C Beds ... 49 Q7
Husthwaite N York ... 97 R6
Hutcherleigh Devon ... 7 K8
Hut Green N York ... 91 P6
Huthwaite Notts ... 84 G9
Huttoft Lincs ... 87 P5
Hutton Border ... 129 N9
Hutton Cumb ... 101 M5
Hutton E R Yk ... 99 L10
Hutton Essex ... 37 P2
Hutton Lancs ... 88 F5
Hutton N Som ... 19 L3
Hutton Bonville N York ... 104 B10
Hutton Buscel N York ... 99 K4
Hutton Conyers N York ... 97 M6
Hutton Cranswick E R Yk ... 99 L10
Hutton End Cumb ... 101 N3
Hutton Hang N York ... 97 J3
Hutton Henry Dur ... 104 D3
Hutton-le-Hole N York ... 98 E2
Hutton Lowcross R & Cl ... 104 G8
Hutton Magna Dur ... 103 M8
Hutton Mulgrave N York ... 105 M9
Hutton Roof Cumb ... 95 M5
Hutton Roof Cumb ... 101 L4
Hutton Rudby N York ... 104 E9
Hutton Sessay N York ... 97 Q5
Hutton Wandesley N York ... 97 R10
Huxham Devon ... 9 M5
Huxham Green Somset ... 19 Q7
Huxley Ches W ... 69 P2
Huyton Knows ... 81 N6
Hycemoor Cumb ... 94 B3
Hyde Gloucs ... 32 G4
Hyde Hants ... 13 L2
Hyde Tamesd ... 83 K6
Hyde Heath Bucks ... 35 P4
Hyde Lea Staffs ... 70 G11
Hydestile Surrey ... 23 Q6
Hykeham Moor Lincs ... 86 B7
Hylands House & Park Essex ... 51 Q3
Hyndford Bridge S Lans ... 116 C2
Hynish Ag & B ... 136 B8
Hyssington Powys ... 56 E6
Hystfield Gloucs ... 32 C5
Hythe Essex ... 52 H6
Hythe Hants ... 14 D5
Hythe Kent ... 27 L5
Hythe Somset ... 19 M4
Hythe End W & M ... 36 B6
Hyton Cumb ... 94 B3

I

Ibberton Dorset ... 12 C3
Ible Derbys ... 84 B9
Ibsley Hants ... 13 L3
Ibstock Leics ... 72 C9
Ibstone Bucks ... 35 L6
Ibthorpe Hants ... 22 C4
Iburndale N York ... 105 N9
Ibworth Hants ... 22 G4
Icelton N Som ... 31 L11
Ichrachan Ag & B ... 139 J11
Ickburgh Norfk ... 75 R11
Ickenham Gt Lon ... 36 C3
Ickford Bucks ... 34 H3
Ickham Kent ... 39 M10
Ickleford Herts ... 50 E4
Icklesham E Susx ... 26 E8
Ickleton Cambs ... 51 L2
Icklingham Suffk ... 63 N6
Ickornshaw N York ... 90 B2
Ickwell Green C Beds ... 61 Q11
Icomb Gloucs ... 47 P10
Idbury Oxon ... 47 P11
Iddesleigh Devon ... 17 K10
Ide Devon ... 9 L6
Ideford Devon ... 9 L9
Ide Hill Kent ... 37 L10
Iden E Susx ... 26 F7
Iden Green Kent ... 26 B4
Iden Green Kent ... 26 D5
Idle C Brad ... 90 F3
Idless Cnwll ... 3 L4
Idlicote Warwks ... 47 Q6
Idmiston Wilts ... 21 N7
Idole Carmth ... 42 H11
Idridgehay Derbys ... 71 P5
Idrigill Highld ... 152 F5
Idstone Oxon ... 33 Q8
Iffley Oxon ... 34 F4
Ifield W Susx ... 24 G3
Ifold W Susx ... 24 B4
Iford BCP ... 13 K6
Iford E Susx ... 25 K9
Ifton Heath Shrops ... 69 K7
Ightfield Shrops ... 70 B6
Ightham Kent ... 37 N9
Iken Suffk ... 65 N10
Ilam Staffs ... 71 L4
Ilchester Somset ... 19 P10
Ilderton Nthumb ... 119 K6
Ilford Gt Lon ... 37 K3
Ilford Somset ... 19 L11
Ilfracombe Devon ... 17 J2
Ilkeston Derbys ... 72 D2
Ilketshall St Andrew Suffk ... 65 M4

Ilketshall St John Suffk ... 65 M4
Ilketshall St Lawrence Suffk ... 65 M4
Ilketshall St Margaret Suffk ... 65 M4
Ilkley C Brad ... 96 H11
Illand Cnwll ... 5 M6
Illey Dudley ... 58 E8
Illidge Green Ches E ... 70 D2
Illingworth Calder ... 90 D5
Illogan Cnwll ... 2 H5
Illston on the Hill Leics ... 73 J10
Ilmer Bucks ... 35 L3
Ilmington Warwks ... 47 P6
Ilminster Somset ... 10 H2
Ilsington Devon ... 9 J9
Ilsington Dorset ... 12 C6
Ilston Swans ... 28 F6
Ilton N York ... 97 J4
Ilton Somset ... 19 L11
Imachar N Ayrs ... 120 G3
Immingham NE Lin ... 93 M8
Immingham Dock NE Lin ... 93 N7
Impington Cambs ... 62 F8
Ince Ches W ... 81 N9
Ince Blundell Sefton ... 81 L4
Ince-in-Makerfield Wigan ... 82 C4
Inchbae Lodge Hotel Highld ... 155 M4
Inchbare Angus ... 143 L4
Inchberry Moray ... 157 Q6
Incheril Highld ... 154 D5
Inchinnan Rens ... 125 M4
Inchlaggan Highld ... 146 F6
Inchmichael P & K ... 134 G2
Inchmore Highld ... 155 Q8
Inchnadamph Highld ... 161 M2
Inchture P & K ... 134 H2
Inchyra P & K ... 134 F3
Indian Queens Cnwll ... 4 E10
Ingatestone Essex ... 51 P11
Ingbirchworth Barns ... 90 G9
Ingerthorpe N York ... 97 L7
Ingestre Staffs ... 70 H10
Ingham Lincs ... 86 B4
Ingham Norfk ... 77 M6
Ingham Suffk ... 64 B7
Ingham Corner Norfk ... 77 M6
Ingleborough Norfk ... 75 J7
Ingleby Derbys ... 72 A5
Ingleby Arncliffe N York ... 104 D10
Ingleby Barwick S on T ... 104 D8
Ingleby Cross N York ... 104 E10
Ingleby Greenhow N York ... 104 G9
Ingleigh Green Devon ... 8 F3
Inglesbatch BaNES ... 20 D2
Inglesham Swindn ... 33 P5
Ingleston D & G ... 109 L7
Ingleton Dur ... 103 N6
Ingleton N York ... 95 P6
Inglewhite Lancs ... 88 G3
Ingmanthorpe N York ... 97 P10
Ingoe Nthumb ... 112 F6
Ingol Lancs ... 88 G4
Ingoldisthorpe Norfk ... 75 N4
Ingoldmells Lincs ... 87 Q7
Ingoldsby Lincs ... 73 Q5
Ingram Nthumb ... 119 K7
Ingrave Essex ... 37 P2
Ingrow C Brad ... 90 D3
Ings Cumb ... 101 M11
Ingst S Glos ... 31 Q7
Ingthorpe Rutlnd ... 73 P9
Ingworth Norfk ... 76 H6
Inkberrow Worcs ... 47 K3
Inkerman Dur ... 103 M3
Inkhorn Abers ... 159 M10
Inkpen W Berk ... 22 C2
Inkstack Highld ... 167 N2
Inmarsh Wilts ... 20 H2
Innellan Ag & B ... 124 F3
Innerleithen Border ... 117 L3
Innerleven Fife ... 135 K7
Innermessan D & G ... 106 E5
Innerwick E Loth ... 129 J4
Innesmill Moray ... 157 P5
Innsworth Gloucs ... 46 G10
Insch Abers ... 150 G2
Insh Highld ... 148 E7
Inshes Highld ... 156 B9
Inskip Lancs ... 88 F3
Inskip Moss Side Lancs ... 88 F3
Instow Devon ... 16 H5
Insworke Cnwll ... 6 C8
Intake Sheff ... 84 E4
Inver Abers ... 149 N9
Inver Highld ... 163 K10
Inver P & K ... 141 P9
Inverailort Highld ... 145 N11
Inveralligin Highld ... 153 Q6
Inverallochy Abers ... 159 P4
Inveran Highld ... 162 D7
Inveraray Ag & B ... 131 M6
Inverarish Highld ... 145 K10
Inverarity Angus ... 142 H9
Inverarnan Stirlg ... 132 C4
Inverasdale Highld ... 160 C10
Inverbeg Ag & B ... 132 C8
Inverbervie Abers ... 143 Q3
Inverboyndie Abers ... 158 G5
Invercreran Lodge Ag & B ... 139 J8
Inverdruie Highld ... 148 F5
Inveresk E Loth ... 127 Q3
Inveresragan Ag & B ... 138 H10
Inverey Abers ... 149 K10
Inverfarigaig Highld ... 147 N3
Inverfolla Highld ... 138 H9
Invergarry Highld ... 147 J2
Invergeldie P & K ... 133 L2
Invergloy Highld ... 146 H9
Invergordon Highld ... 156 C4
Invergowrie P & K ... 142 H11
Inverguseran Highld ... 145 M6
Inverhadden P & K ... 140 G6
Inverie Highld ... 145 M7
Inverinan Ag & B ... 131 K4
Inverinate Highld ... 145 R3
Inverkeilor Angus ... 143 M8
Inverkeithing Fife ... 134 E11
Inverkeithny Abers ... 158 F8
Inverkip Inver ... 124 G3
Inverkirkaig Highld ... 160 H3
Inverlael Highld ... 161 K9
Inverlair Highld ... 146 H11
Inverliever Lodge Ag & B ... 130 H6
Inverlochy Ag & B ... 131 L2
Invermark Angus ... 150 C11
Invermoriston Highld ... 147 L4

Place	County	Page	Grid
Invernaver	Highld	166	B4
Inverneill	Ag & B	123	P3
Inverness	Highld	156	B8
Inverness Airport	Highld	156	D7
Invernettie	Abers	159	R9
Invernoaden	Ag & B	131	N8
Inveroran Hotel	Ag & B	139	P9
Inverquharity	Angus	142	G6
Inverquhomery	Abers	159	P8
Inverroy	Highld	146	H11
Inversanda	Highld	138	G6
Invershiel	Highld	146	A4
Invershin	Highld	162	D7
Invershore	Highld	167	M9
Inversnaid Hotel	Stirlg	132	C6
Inverugie	Abers	159	Q8
Inveruglas	Ag & B	132	C6
Inveruglass	Highld	148	E7
Inverurie	Abers	151	K3
Inwardleigh	Devon	8	E5
Inworth	Essex	52	E8
Iochdar	W Isls	168	c13
Iona	Ag & B	136	H10
Iping	W Susx	23	N10
iPort Logistics Park	Donc	91	Q11
Ipplepen	Devon	7	L5
Ipsden	Oxon	34	H7
Ipstones	Staffs	71	J5
Ipswich	Suffk	53	L3
Irby	Wirral	81	K8
Irby in the Marsh	Lincs	87	N8
Irby upon Humber	NE Lin	93	L10
Irchester	Nhants	61	K7
Ireby	Cumb	100	H3
Ireby	Lancs	95	P5
Ireland	C Beds	50	D2
Ireleth	Cumb	94	E5
Ireshopeburn	Dur	102	G3
Ireton Wood	Derbys	71	P5
Irlam	Salfd	82	F6
Irnham	Lincs	73	Q5
Iron Acton	S Glos	32	C8
Iron Bridge	Cambs	75	J11
Ironbridge	Wrekin	57	M4
Ironbridge Gorge	Wrekin	57	M4
Iron Cross	Warwks	47	L4
Ironmacannie	D & G	108	E5
Irons Bottom	Surrey	36	F11
Ironville	Derbys	84	F10
Irstead	Norfk	77	M7
Irthington	Cumb	111	D9
Irthlingborough	Nhants	61	K6
Irton	N York	99	L4
Irvine	N Ayrs	125	J10
Isauld	Highld	166	G3
Isbister	Shet	169	q4
Isbister	Shet	169	s7
Isfield	E Susx	25	K7
Isham	Nhants	61	J6
Isington	Hants	23	L6
Islandpool	Worcs	58	C8
Islay	Ag & B	122	C6
Islay Airport	Ag & B	122	D9
Isle Abbotts	Somset	19	L10
Isle Brewers	Somset	19	L10
Isleham	Cambs	63	K6
Isle of Dogs	Gt Lon	37	J5
Isle of Grain	Medway	38	E6
Isle of Lewis	W Isls	168	i4
Isle of Man	IoM	80	e4
Isle of Man Ronaldsway Airport	IoM	80	c8
Isle of Mull	Ag & B	137	Q8
Isle of Purbeck	Dorset	12	H8
Isle of Sheppey	Kent	38	G8
Isle of Skye	Highld	152	G10
Isle of Thanet	Kent	39	P8
Isle of Walney	Cumb	94	D7
Isle of Whithorn	D & G	107	N10
Isle of Wight	IoW	14	F9
Isleornsay	Highld	145	M5
Isles of Scilly	IoS	2	c2
Isles of Scilly St Mary's Airport	IoS	2	c2
Islesteps	D & G	109	L6
Islet Village	Guern	10	c1
Isleworth	Gt Lon	36	E5
Isley Walton	Leics	72	C6
Islibhig	W Isls	168	f5
Islington	Gt Lon	36	H4
Islip	Nhants	61	L5
Islip	Oxon	34	F2
Islivig	W Isls	168	f5
Isombridge	Wrekin	57	L2
Istead Rise	Kent	37	P6
Itchen Abbas	Hants	22	F8
Itchen Stoke	Hants	22	G8
Itchingfield	W Susx	24	D5
Itchington	S Glos	32	C8
Itteringham	Norfk	76	G5
Itton	Devon	8	G7
Itton	Mons	31	N5
Itton Common	Mons	31	N5
Ivegill	Cumb	101	M2
Ivelet	N York	102	H11
Iver	Bucks	36	B4
Iver Heath	Bucks	36	B4
Iveston	Dur	112	H10
Ivinghoe	Bucks	49	P11
Ivinghoe Aston	Bucks	49	Q11
Ivington	Herefs	45	P3
Ivington Green	Herefs	45	P3
Ivybridge	Devon	6	G7
Ivychurch	Kent	26	H6
Ivy Cross	Dorset	20	G10
Ivy Hatch	Kent	37	N10
Ivy Todd	Norfk	76	B10
Iwade	Kent	38	F8
Iwerne Courtney	Dorset	12	E2
Iwerne Minster	Dorset	12	E2
Ixworth	Suffk	64	C7
Ixworth Thorpe	Suffk	64	C7

J

Place	County	Page	Grid
Jack Green	Lancs	88	H5
Jack Hill	N York	97	J10
Jack-in-the-Green	Devon	9	P5
Jack's Bush	Hants	21	Q7
Jacksdale	Notts	84	F10
Jackson Bridge	Kirk	90	F7
Jackton	S Lans	125	P7
Jacobstow	Cnwll	5	K2
Jacobstowe	Devon	8	E4
Jacobs Well	Surrey	23	Q4
Jameston	Pembks	41	L11
Jamestown	Highld	155	N6
Jamestown	W Duns	132	D11
Janetstown	Highld	167	L10
Janetstown	Highld	167	Q6
Jardine Hall	D & G	109	P3
Jarrow	S Tyne	113	M8
Jarvis Brook	E Susx	25	M5
Jasper's Green	Essex	52	B6
Jawcraig	Falk	126	E2
Jaywick	Essex	53	L9
Jealott's Hill	Br For	35	N10
Jeater Houses	N York	97	P2
Jedburgh	Border	118	B6
Jeffreyston	Pembks	41	L9
Jemimaville	Highld	156	C4
Jerbourg	Guern	10	c2
Jersey	Jersey	11	b1
Jersey Airport	Jersey	11	a2
Jersey Marine	Neath	29	K6
Jerusalem	Lincs	86	B6
Jesmond	N u Ty	113	L7
Jevington	E Susx	25	N10
Jingle Street	Mons	31	N2
Jockey End	Herts	50	B8
Jodrell Bank	Ches E	82	G10
Jodrell Bank	Ches E	82	G10
Johnby	Cumb	101	M4
John Lennon Airport	Lpool	81	N8
John o' Groats	Highld	167	Q2
Johns Cross	E Susx	26	B7
Johnshaven	Abers	143	P4
Johnson Street	Norfk	77	M8
Johnston	Pembks	40	H8
Johnstone	D & G	117	J10
Johnstone	Rens	125	L5
Johnstonebridge	D & G	109	P2
Johnstown	Carmth	42	G11
Johnstown	Wrexhm	69	K5
Joppa	C Edin	127	Q3
Joppa	Cerdgn	54	D11
Joppa	S Ayrs	114	H4
Jordans	Bucks	35	Q6
Jordanston	Pembks	40	H4
Jordanthorpe	Sheff	84	E4
Joyden's Wood	Kent	37	M6
Jubilee Corner	Kent	26	D2
Jump	Barns	91	K10
Jumper's Town	E Susx	25	L4
Juniper	Nthumb	112	D9
Juniper Green	C Edin	127	N4
Jura	Ag & B	122	H3
Jurassic Coast	Devon	10	G7
Jurby	IoM	80	e2
Jurston	Devon	8	G8

K

Place	County	Page	Grid
Kaber	Cumb	102	E8
Kaimend	S Lans	126	H8
Kames	Ag & B	124	B3
Kames	E Ayrs	115	N2
Kea	Cnwll	3	L5
Keadby	N Linc	92	D8
Keal Cotes	Lincs	87	L8
Kearby Town End	N York	97	M11
Kearsley	Bolton	82	G4
Kearsley	Nthumb	112	F5
Kearsney	Kent	27	N3
Kearstwick	Cumb	95	N5
Kearton	N York	103	J11
Keasden	N York	95	Q7
Keaton	Devon	6	G8
Keckwick	Halton	82	C8
Keddington	Lincs	87	K3
Keddington Corner	Lincs	87	L3
Kedington	Suffk	63	M11
Kedleston	Derbys	71	Q6
Keelby	Lincs	93	L8
Keele	Staffs	70	E5
Keele Services	Staffs	70	E6
Keele University	Staffs	70	E5
Keelham	C Brad	90	D4
Keeres Green	Essex	51	N8
Keeston	Pembks	40	H7
Keevil	Wilts	20	H3
Kegworth	Leics	72	D5
Kehelland	Cnwll	2	G5
Keig	Abers	150	G4
Keighley	C Brad	90	D2
Keilarsbrae	Clacks	133	P9
Keillour	P & K	134	B2
Keiloch	Abers	149	M9
Keils	Ag & B	122	H6
Keinton Mandeville	Somset	19	Q9
Keir Mill	D & G	109	J2
Keirsleywell Row	Nthumb	111	Q10
Keisby	Lincs	73	Q5
Keisley	Cumb	102	D6
Keiss	Highld	167	P4
Keith	Moray	158	B7
Keithick	P & K	142	C10
Keithock	Angus	143	L5
Keithtown	Highld	155	P6
Kelbrook	Lancs	89	Q2
Kelby	Lincs	73	Q2
Keld	Cumb	101	Q8
Keld	N York	102	G10
Keld Head	N York	98	F4
Keldholme	N York	98	E3
Kelfield	N Linc	92	D10
Kelfield	N York	91	P3
Kelham	Notts	85	N9
Kelhead	D & G	109	P7
Kellacott	Devon	5	P3
Kellamergh	Lancs	88	E5
Kellan	Angus	142	H10
Kellas	Moray	157	M7
Kellaton	Devon	7	L11
Kelleth	Cumb	102	C10
Kelling	Norfk	76	F3
Kellingley	N York	91	P6
Kelloe	Dur	104	B3
Kelloholm	D & G	115	P5
Kells	Cumb	100	C7
Kelly	Devon	5	P5
Kelly Bray	Cnwll	5	P5
Kelmarsh	Nhants	60	F5
Kelmscott	Oxon	33	P5
Kelsale	Suffk	65	M8
Kelsall	Ches W	81	Q11
Kelshall	Herts	50	H3
Kelsick	Cumb	110	C10
Kelso	Border	118	D4
Kelstedge	Derbys	84	D8
Kelstern	Lincs	86	H3
Kelsterton	Flints	81	K10
Kelston	BaNES	32	D11
Keltneyburn	P & K	141	J8
Kelton	D & G	109	L6
Kelty	Fife	134	E9
Kelvedon	Essex	52	E8
Kelvedon Hatch	Essex	51	N11
Kelynack	Cnwll	2	B8
Kemacott	Devon	17	M2
Kemback	Fife	135	L5
Kemberton	Shrops	57	N4
Kemble	Gloucs	33	J5
Kemble Wick	Gloucs	33	J5
Kemerton	Worcs	47	J7
Kemeys Commander	Mons	31	K4
Kemnay	Abers	151	H9
Kempe's Corner	Kent	26	H2
Kempley	Gloucs	46	C9
Kempley Green	Gloucs	46	C9
Kempsey	Worcs	46	H5
Kempsford	Gloucs	33	N5
Kemps Green	Warwks	58	H10
Kempshott	Hants	22	H4
Kempston	Bed	61	M11
Kempston Hardwick	Bed	50	B2
Kempton	Shrops	56	F7
Kemp Town	Br & H	24	H10
Kemsing	Kent	37	N9
Kemsley	Kent	38	F8
Kemsley Street	Kent	38	D9
Kenardington	Kent	26	G5
Kenchester	Herefs	45	N4
Kencot	Oxon	33	Q4
Kendal	Cumb	95	L2
Kenderchurch	Herefs	45	M9
Kendleshire	S Glos	32	C9
Kenfig	Brdgnd	29	M8
Kenfig Hill	Brdgnd	29	M8
Kenilworth	Warwks	59	L10
Kenley	Gt Lon	36	H8
Kenley	Shrops	57	K4
Kenmore	Highld	153	P6
Kenmore	P & K	141	J8
Kenn	Devon	9	M7
Kenn	N Som	31	M11
Kennacraig	Ag & B	123	P7
Kennall Vale	Cnwll	3	J6
Kennards House	Cnwll	5	M5
Kennegy	Cnwll	2	F8
Kennerleigh	Devon	9	K3
Kennet	Clacks	133	Q9
Kennethmont	Abers	150	E2
Kennett	Cambs	63	L7
Kennford	Devon	9	M7
Kenninghall	Norfk	64	E4
Kennington	Kent	26	H2
Kennington	Oxon	34	F4
Kennoway	Fife	135	K7
Kenny	Somset	19	K11
Kenny Hill	Suffk	63	L5
Kennythorpe	N York	98	F7
Kenovay	Ag & B	136	B6
Kensaleyre	Highld	152	G7
Kensington	Gt Lon	36	G5
Kensington Palace	Gt Lon	36	G4
Kensworth Common	C Beds	50	B7
Kentallen	Highld	139	J6
Kentchurch	Herefs	45	N9
Kentford	Suffk	63	M7
Kent Green	Ches E	70	E3
Kentisbeare	Devon	9	Q3
Kentisbury	Devon	17	L3
Kentisbury Ford	Devon	17	L3
Kentish Town	Gt Lon	36	G4
Kentmere	Cumb	101	N10
Kenton	Devon	9	N8
Kenton	Gt Lon	36	E3
Kenton	Suffk	65	J8
Kenton	N u Ty	113	K7
Kenton Bankfoot	N u Ty	113	K7
Kentra	Highld	138	B4
Kents Bank	Cumb	94	H5
Kentsboro	Hants	22	B7
Kent's Green	Gloucs	46	D10
Kent's Oak	Hants	22	B10
Kent Street	E Susx	26	C8
Kent Street	Kent	37	Q10
Kenwick	Shrops	69	M8
Kenwyn	Cnwll	3	L4
Kenyon	Warrtn	82	D5
Keoldale	Highld	165	J3
Keppoch	Highld	145	Q3
Keppwick	N York	97	Q2
Keresley	Covtry	59	M8
Kermincham	Ches E	82	H11
Kernborough	Devon	7	K10
Kerne Bridge	Herefs	46	A11
Kerrera	Ag & B	130	G2
Kerridge	Ches E	83	K9
Kerridge-end	Ches E	83	K9
Kerris	Cnwll	2	C8
Kerry	Powys	55	Q6
Kerrycroy	Ag & B	124	C5
Kersall	Notts	85	M8
Kersbrook	Devon	9	Q6
Kerscott	Devon	17	L6
Kersey	Suffk	52	H3
Kersey Tye	Suffk	52	G3
Kersey Upland	Suffk	52	G3
Kershader	W Isls	168	i6
Kershopefoot	Cumb	111	J4
Kersoe	Worcs	47	J5
Kerswell	Devon	10	B3
Kerswell Green	Worcs	46	G5
Kerthen Wood	Cnwll	2	F7
Kesgrave	Suffk	53	M2
Kessingland	Suffk	65	Q4
Kessingland Beach	Suffk	65	Q4
Kestle	Cnwll	3	P4
Kestle Mill	Cnwll	4	C10
Keston	Gt Lon	37	K8
Keswick	Cumb	101	J6
Keswick	Norfk	77	J11
Kettering	Nhants	61	J5
Ketteringham	Norfk	76	H11
Kettins	P & K	142	C10
Kettlebaston	Suffk	64	D11
Kettlebridge	Fife	135	J6
Kettlebrook	Staffs	59	K4
Kettleburgh	Suffk	65	K9
Kettle Green	Herts	51	K7
Kettleholm	D & G	109	P5
Kettleness	N York	105	M7
Kettleshulme	Ches E	83	L9
Kettlesing	N York	97	K9
Kettlesing Bottom	N York	97	K9
Kettlestone	Norfk	76	D5
Kettlethorpe	Lincs	85	P5
Kettletoft	Ork	169	f3
Kettlewell	N York	96	E6
Ketton	Rutlnd	73	P10
Kew	Gt Lon	36	E5
Kew Royal Botanic Gardens	Gt Lon	36	E5
Kewstoke	N Som	19	K2
Kexbrough	Barns	91	J9
Kexby	C York	98	E10
Kexby	Lincs	85	Q3
Key Green	Ches E	70	F2
Key Green	N York	105	M10
Keyham	Leics	72	H9
Keyhaven	Hants	13	P6
Keyingham	E R Yk	93	M5
Keymer	W Susx	24	H7
Keynsham	BaNES	32	C11
Keysoe	Bed	61	N8
Keysoe Row	Bed	61	N8
Keyston	Cambs	61	N5
Key Street	Kent	38	E9
Keyworth	Notts	72	G4
Kibbear	Somset	18	H10
Kibblesworth	Gatesd	113	K9
Kibworth Beauchamp	Leics	60	E2
Kibworth Harcourt	Leics	60	E2
Kidbrooke	Gt Lon	37	K5
Kidburngill	Cumb	100	E6
Kiddemore Green	Staffs	58	C3
Kidderminster	Worcs	58	B9
Kiddington	Oxon	48	D10
Kidd's Moor	Norfk	76	G11
Kidlington	Oxon	34	E2
Kidmore End	Oxon	35	J9
Kidsdale	D & G	107	M10
Kidsgrove	Staffs	70	E4
Kidstones	N York	96	E4
Kidwelly	Carmth	28	D3
Kiel Crofts	Ag & B	138	G10
Kielder	Nthumb	111	M2
Kielder Forest	Nthumb	111	M3
Kiells	Ag & B	122	F6
Kilbarchan	Rens	125	L5
Kilbeg	Highld	145	L6
Kilberry	Ag & B	123	M7
Kilbirnie	N Ayrs	125	J7
Kilbride	Ag & B	123	M4
Kilbride	Ag & B	124	C4
Kilbuiack	Moray	157	K5
Kilburn	Derbys	84	E11
Kilburn	Gt Lon	36	F4
Kilburn	N York	97	R5
Kilby	Leics	72	G11
Kilchamaig	Ag & B	123	P7
Kilchattan	Ag & B	124	E7
Kilchattan	Ag & B	136	b2
Kilcheran	Ag & B	138	G10
Kilchoan	Highld	137	M3
Kilchoman	Ag & B	122	B7
Kilchrenan	Ag & B	131	L3
Kilconquhar	Fife	135	M7
Kilcot	Gloucs	46	C9
Kilcoy	Highld	155	Q7
Kilcreggan	Ag & B	131	Q11
Kildale	N York	104	H9
Kildalloig	Ag & B	120	E8
Kildary	Highld	156	D3
Kildavaig	Ag & B	124	B4
Kildavanan	Ag & B	124	C4
Kildonan	Highld	163	L2
Kildonan	N Ayrs	121	K7
Kildonan Lodge	Highld	163	L2
Kildonnan	Highld	144	G10
Kildrochet House	D & G	106	E6
Kildrummy	Abers	150	D4
Kildwick	N York	96	F11
Kilfinan	Ag & B	124	A2
Kilfinnan	Highld	146	H8
Kilford	Denbgs	80	F11
Kilgetty	Pembks	41	M9
Kilgrammie	S Ayrs	114	E7
Kilgwrrwg Common	Mons	31	N5
Kilham	E R Yk	99	M8
Kilham	Nthumb	118	G4
Kilkenneth	Ag & B	136	A7
Kilkenzie	Ag & B	120	C7
Kilkerran	Ag & B	120	D8
Kilkhampton	Cnwll	16	D9
Killamarsh	Derbys	84	G4
Killay	Swans	28	H6
Killean	Ag & B	120	E8
Killearn	Stirlg	132	G10
Killellan	Ag & B	120	E8
Killen	Highld	156	B6
Killerby	Darltn	103	N7
Killerton	Devon	9	N4
Killichonan	P & K	140	D6
Killiechonate	Highld	146	G11
Killiechronan	Ag & B	137	N7
Killiecrankie	P & K	141	M5
Killilan	Highld	154	B11
Killimster	Highld	167	P5
Killin	Stirlg	140	E11
Killinghall	N York	97	L9
Killington	Cumb	95	N3
Killington	Devon	17	M2
Killington Lake Services	Cumb	95	M2
Killingworth	N Tyne	113	L6
Killiow	Cnwll	3	L5
Killochyett	Border	128	D10
Kilmacolm	Inver	125	K3
Kilmahog	Stirlg	133	J6
Kilmahumaig	Ag & B	130	F9
Kilmaluag	Highld	152	G3
Kilmany	Fife	135	K3
Kilmarnock	E Ayrs	125	L10
Kilmartin	Ag & B	130	G8
Kilmaurs	E Ayrs	125	L9
Kilmelford	Ag & B	130	H5
Kilmersdon	Somset	20	C4
Kilmeston	Hants	22	G9
Kilmichael	Ag & B	120	C7
Kilmichael Glassary	Ag & B	130	H9
Kilmichael of Inverlussa	Ag & B	130	F10
Kilmington	Devon	10	F5
Kilmington	Wilts	20	E7
Kilmington Common	Wilts	20	E7
Kilmington Street	Wilts	20	E7
Kilmorack	Highld	155	N9
Kilmore	Ag & B	130	H2
Kilmore	Highld	145	L6
Kilmory	Ag & B	123	N5
Kilmory	Highld	137	N2
Kilmory	N Ayrs	121	J7
Kilmuir	Highld	152	D8
Kilmuir	Highld	152	F3
Kilmuir	Highld	156	B8
Kilmuir	Highld	156	D3
Kilmun	Ag & B	131	P11
Kilnave	Ag & B	122	C5
Kilncadzow	S Lans	126	F8
Kilndown	Kent	26	B4
Kiln Green	Wokham	35	M9
Kilnhill	Cumb	100	H4
Kilnhurst	Rothm	91	M11
Kilninver	Ag & B	130	G3
Kiln Pit Hill	Nthumb	112	F9
Kilnsea	E R Yk	93	R7
Kilnsey	N York	96	E7
Kilnwick	E R Yk	99	K11
Kilnwick Percy	E R Yk	98	G11
Kilnwood Vale	W Susx	24	F4
Kiloran	Ag & B	136	b2
Kilpatrick	N Ayrs	120	H6
Kilpeck	Herefs	45	N8
Kilpin	E R Yk	92	C5
Kilpin Pike	E R Yk	92	C5
Kilrenny	Fife	135	P7
Kilsby	Nhants	60	C6
Kilspindie	P & K	134	G2
Kilstay	D & G	106	F10
Kilsyth	N Lans	126	C2
Kiltarlity	Highld	155	P9
Kilton	R & Cl	105	K7
Kilton	Somset	18	G6
Kilton Thorpe	R & Cl	105	J7
Kilvaxter	Highld	152	F4
Kilve	Somset	18	F6
Kilvington	Notts	73	L2
Kilwinning	N Ayrs	125	J9
Kimberley	Norfk	76	F11
Kimberley	Notts	72	D2
Kimberworth	Rothm	84	F2
Kimblesworth	Dur	113	L11
Kimble Wick	Bucks	35	M3
Kimbolton	Cambs	61	P7
Kimbolton	Herefs	45	Q2
Kimcote	Leics	60	C3
Kimmeridge	Dorset	12	F9
Kimmerston	Nthumb	119	J3
Kimpton	Hants	21	Q5
Kimpton	Herts	50	E7
Kimworthy	Devon	16	E9
Kinbrace	Highld	166	G10
Kinbuck	Stirlg	133	M6
Kincaple	Fife	135	M4
Kincardine	Fife	133	Q10
Kincardine	Highld	162	E9
Kincardine Bridge	Fife	133	Q10
Kincardine O'Neil	Abers	150	F8
Kinclaven	P & K	142	B10
Kincorth	C Aber	151	N7
Kincorth House	Moray	157	J5
Kincraig	Highld	148	E6
Kincraigie	P & K	141	N8
Kindallachan	P & K	141	N8
Kinerarach	Ag & B	123	L9
Kineton	Gloucs	47	L9
Kineton	Warwks	48	B4
Kinfauns	P & K	134	F3
Kingarth	Ag & B	124	D6
Kingcausie	Abers	151	M8
Kingcoed	Mons	31	M3
Kingerby	Lincs	86	E2
Kingford	Devon	16	D10
Kingham	Oxon	47	Q10
Kingholm Quay	D & G	109	L6
Kinghorn	Fife	134	H10
Kinglassie	Fife	134	G8
Kingoodie	P & K	135	J2
King's Acre	Herefs	45	P6
Kingsand	Cnwll	6	C8
Kingsash	Bucks	35	N3
Kingsbarns	Fife	135	P5
Kingsborough	Kent	38	G7
Kingsbridge	Devon	7	J10
Kingsbridge	Somset	18	C7
Kings Bridge	Swans	28	G5
King's Bromley	Staffs	71	L11
Kingsburgh	Highld	152	F6
Kingsbury	Gt Lon	36	E3
Kingsbury	Warwks	59	K5
Kingsbury Episcopi	Somset	19	M10
King's Caple	Herefs	45	R9
Kingsclere	Hants	22	F3
King's Cliffe	Nhants	73	Q11
Kings Clipstone	Notts	85	K8
Kingscote	Gloucs	32	F5
Kingscott	Devon	17	J8
King's Coughton	Warwks	47	L3
Kingscross	N Ayrs	121	K6
Kingsdon	Somset	19	P9
Kingsdown	Kent	27	Q2
Kingsdown	Swindn	33	N7
Kingsdown	Wilts	32	F11
Kingseat	Abers	151	N4
Kingseat	Fife	134	E9
Kingsey	Bucks	35	K3
Kingsfold	W Susx	24	E3
Kingsford	C Aber	151	M6
Kingsford	E Ayrs	125	L8
Kingsford	Worcs	57	Q8
Kingsgate	Kent	39	Q7
Kingshall Street	Suffk	64	C9
Kingsheanton	Devon	17	K4
King's Heath	Birm	58	G8
Kings Hill	Kent	37	Q9
King's Hill	Wsall	58	E5
Kings House Hotel	Highld	139	P7
Kingshurst	Solhll	59	J7
Kingside Hill	Cumb	110	C10
Kingskerswell	Devon	7	M5
Kingskettle	Fife	135	J6
Kingsland	Dorset	11	K5
Kingsland	Herefs	45	N2
Kingsland	IoA	78	D8
Kings Langley	Herts	50	C10
Kingsley	Ches W	82	C10
Kingsley	Hants	23	L7
Kingsley	Staffs	71	J5
Kingsley Green	W Susx	23	N8
Kingsley Holt	Staffs	71	J5
Kingsley Park	Nhants	60	G8

278 Kingslow – Langley

Kingslow Shrops 57 P5
King's Lynn Norfk 75 M6
Kings Meaburn Cumb 102 B6
Kingsmead Hants 14 G4
King's Mills Guern 10 b2
King's Moss St Hel 81 Q4
Kingsmuir Angus 142 H8
Kings Muir Border 117 K3
Kingsmuir Fife 135 N6
Kings Newnham Warwks 59 Q9
King's Newton Derbys 72 B5
Kingsnorth Kent 26 H4
Kings Norton Birm 58 G9
King's Norton Leics 72 H10
Kings Nympton Devon 17 M8
King's Pyon Herefs 45 N4
Kings Ripton Cambs 62 C5
King's Somborne Hants 22 C8
King's Stag Dorset 11 Q2
King's Stanley Gloucs 32 F4
King's Sutton Nhants 48 E7
Kingstanding Birm 58 G6
Kingsteignton Devon 7 M4
Kingsteps Highld 156 G6
King Sterndale Derbys 83 N10
Kingsthorne Herefs 45 P8
Kingsthorpe Nhants 60 G8
Kingston Cambs 62 D9
Kingston Cnwll 5 P6
Kingston Devon 6 G9
Kingston Devon 9 Q7
Kingston Dorset 12 C3
Kingston Dorset 12 G9
Kingston E Loth 128 E3
Kingston Hants 13 K4
Kingston IoW 14 E10
Kingston Kent 39 L11
Kingston W Susx 24 C10
Kingston Bagpuize Oxon 34 D5
Kingston Blount Oxon 35 K5
Kingston by Sea W Susx 24 F9
Kingston Deverill Wilts 20 F7
Kingstone Herefs 45 N7
Kingstone Somset 10 H2
Kingstone Staffs 71 K9
Kingstone Winslow Oxon 33 Q7
Kingston Lacy House & Gardens Dorset 12 G4
Kingston Lisle Oxon 34 B7
Kingston near Lewes E Susx 25 J9
Kingston on Soar Notts 72 E5
Kingston on Spey Moray 157 Q4
Kingston Russell Dorset 11 M6
Kingston St Mary Somset 18 H9
Kingston Seymour N Som 31 M11
Kingston Stert Oxon 35 K4
Kingston upon Hull C KuH 93 J5
Kingston upon Thames Gt Lon 36 E7
Kingstown Cumb 110 G9
King's Walden Herts 50 E6
Kingswear Devon 7 M8
Kingswells C Aber 151 M6
Kings Weston Bristl 31 P9
Kingswinford Dudley 58 C7
Kingswood Bucks 49 J11
Kingswood Gloucs 32 D6
Kingswood Kent 38 D11
Kingswood Powys 56 C4
Kingswood S Glos 32 B10
Kingswood Somset 18 F7
Kingswood Surrey 36 F9
Kingswood Warwks 59 J10
Kingswood Brook Warwks 59 J10
Kingswood Common Herefs 45 K4
Kingswood Common Staffs 58 B4
Kings Worthy Hants 22 E8
Kingthorpe Lincs 86 F5
Kington Herefs 45 K3
Kington S Glos 32 B6
Kington Worcs 47 J3
Kington Langley Wilts 32 H9
Kington Magna Dorset 20 E10
Kington St Michael Wilts 32 H9
Kingussie Highld 148 D7
Kingweston Somset 19 P8
Kinharrachie Abers 159 M11
Kinharvie D & G 109 K7
Kinkell Bridge P & K 133 Q4
Kinknockie Abers 159 P9
Kinleith C Edin 127 M4
Kinlet Shrops 57 N8
Kinloch Highld 144 F8
Kinloch Highld 164 H10
Kinloch Highld 165 N6
Kinloch P & K 142 A9
Kinlochard Stirlg 132 F7
Kinlochbervie Highld 164 F5
Kinlocheil Highld 138 H2
Kinlochewe Highld 154 D5
Kinloch Hourn Highld 146 B6
Kinlochlaggan Highld 147 N10
Kinlochleven Highld 139 M5
Kinlochmoidart Highld 138 C3
Kinlochnanuagh Highld 145 M11
Kinloch Rannoch P & K 140 G6
Kinloss Moray 157 K5
Kinmel Bay Conwy 80 D8
Kinmuck Abers 151 L4
Kinmundy Abers 151 M4
Kinnabus Ag & B 122 C11
Kinnadie Abers 159 N9
Kinnaird P & K 141 N6
Kinneff Abers 143 Q2
Kinnelhead D & G 116 E10
Kinnell Angus 143 L7
Kinnerley Shrops 69 K10
Kinnersley Herefs 45 L5
Kinnersley Worcs 46 G6
Kinnerton Powys 45 J2
Kinnerton Shrops 56 F5
Kinnerton Green Flints 69 K2
Kinnesswood P & K 134 F7
Kinninvie Dur 103 L6
Kinnordy Angus 142 F6
Kinoulton Notts 72 H4
Kinross P & K 134 E7
Kinrossie P & K 142 B11
Kinross Services P & K 134 E7
Kinsbourne Green Herts 50 D7
Kinsey Heath Ches E 70 B6
Kinsham Herefs 56 F11
Kinsham Worcs 46 H7
Kinsley Wakefd 91 L8
Kinson BCP 13 J5
Kintail Highld 146 B4
Kintbury W Berk 34 C11
Kintessack Moray 157 J5
Kintillo P & K 134 E4
Kinton Herefs 56 G10
Kinton Shrops 69 L11
Kintore Abers 151 K4
Kintour Ag & B 122 G9
Kintra Ag & B 122 D10
Kintra Ag & B 137 J10
Kintraw Ag & B 130 G7
Kintyre Ag & B 120 D4
Kinveachy Highld 148 G4
Kinver Staffs 58 B8
Kiplin N York 103 Q11
Kippax Leeds 91 L4
Kippen Stirlg 133 J9
Kippford D & G 108 H10
Kipping's Cross Kent 25 P2
Kirbister Ork 169 c6
Kirby Bedon Norfk 77 K10
Kirby Bellars Leics 73 J7
Kirby Cane Norfk 65 M3
Kirby Corner Covtry 59 L9
Kirby Cross Essex 53 M7
Kirby Fields Leics 72 E10
Kirby Green Norfk 65 M3
Kirby Grindalythe N York 99 J7
Kirby Hill N York 97 N7
Kirby Hill N York 103 M9
Kirby Knowle N York 97 Q3
Kirby-le-Soken Essex 53 M7
Kirby Misperton N York 98 F5
Kirby Muxloe Leics 72 E10
Kirby Sigston N York 97 P2
Kirby Underdale E R Yk 98 G9
Kirby Wiske N York 97 N4
Kirdford W Susx 24 B5
Kirk Highld 167 N5
Kirkabister Shet 169 r10
Kirkandrews D & G 108 D11
Kirkandrews upon Eden Cumb 110 G9
Kirkbampton Cumb 110 F9
Kirkbean D & G 109 L9
Kirk Bramwith Donc 91 Q8
Kirkbride Cumb 110 D9
Kirkbridge N York 97 L2
Kirkbuddo Angus 143 J9
Kirkburn Border 117 K3
Kirkburn E R Yk 99 K9
Kirkburton Kirk 90 F8
Kirkby Knows 81 N5
Kirkby Lincs 86 E2
Kirkby N York 104 F9
Kirkby Fleetham N York 97 L2
Kirkby Green Lincs 86 E9
Kirkby-in-Ashfield Notts 84 H9
Kirkby-in-Furness Cumb 94 E4
Kirkby la Thorpe Lincs 86 E11
Kirkby Lonsdale Cumb 95 N5
Kirkby Malham N York 96 C8
Kirkby Mallory Leics 72 D10
Kirkby Malzeard N York 97 K6
Kirkby Mills N York 98 E3
Kirkbymoorside N York 98 D3
Kirkby on Bain Lincs 86 H8
Kirkby Overblow N York 97 M11
Kirkby Stephen Cumb 102 E9
Kirkby Thore Cumb 102 B5
Kirkby Underwood Lincs 73 R5
Kirkby Wharf N York 91 N2
Kirkby Woodhouse Notts 84 G10
Kirkcaldy Fife 134 H9
Kirkcambeck Cumb 111 K7
Kirkchrist D & G 108 E10
Kirkcolm D & G 106 D4
Kirkconnel D & G 115 P5
Kirkconnell D & G 109 L7
Kirkcowan D & G 107 K5
Kirkcudbright D & G 108 E10
Kirkdale Lpool 81 L6
Kirk Deighton N York 97 N10
Kirk Ella E R Yk 92 H5
Kirkfieldbank S Lans 116 B2
Kirkgunzeon D & G 109 J7
Kirk Hallam Derbys 72 D2
Kirkham Lancs 88 E4
Kirkham N York 98 E7
Kirkhamgate Wakefd 90 H6
Kirk Hammerton N York 97 Q9
Kirkharle Nthumb 112 F4
Kirkhaugh Nthumb 111 N11
Kirkheaton Kirk 90 F7
Kirkheaton Nthumb 112 F5
Kirkhill Highld 155 Q8
Kirkhope S Lans 116 D9
Kirkhouse Cumb 111 L9
Kirkhouse Green Donc 91 Q8
Kirkibost Highld 145 J4
Kirkinch P & K 142 E9
Kirkinner D & G 107 M7
Kirkintilloch E Duns 126 B3
Kirk Ireton Derbys 71 P4
Kirkland Cumb 100 E7
Kirkland Cumb 102 B4
Kirkland D & G 109 M3
Kirkland D & G 115 P5
Kirkland D & G 115 R9
Kirkland Guards Cumb 100 G2
Kirk Langley Derbys 71 P7
Kirkleatham R & Cl 104 G6
Kirklevington S on T 104 D9
Kirkley Suffk 65 Q3
Kirklington N York 97 M4
Kirklington Notts 85 L9
Kirklinton Cumb 110 H7
Kirkliston C Edin 127 L3
Kirkmabreck D & G 107 N6
Kirkmaiden D & G 106 F10
Kirk Merrington Dur 103 Q4
Kirk Michael IoM 80 d3
Kirkmichael P & K 141 Q6
Kirkmichael S Ayrs 114 F6
Kirkmuirhill S Lans 126 D9
Kirknewton Nthumb 118 H4
Kirknewton W Loth 127 L4
Kirkney Abers 158 D11
Kirk of Shotts N Lans 126 E5
Kirkoswald Cumb 101 Q2
Kirkoswald S Ayrs 114 D6
Kirkpatrick D & G 109 K2
Kirkpatrick Durham D & G 108 G6
Kirkpatrick-Fleming D & G 110 E6
Kirk Sandall Donc 91 Q9
Kirksanton Cumb 94 C4
Kirk Smeaton N York 91 N7
Kirkstall Leeds 90 H3
Kirkstead Lincs 86 G8
Kirkstile Abers 158 D10
Kirkstile D & G 110 G2
Kirkstone Pass Inn Cumb 101 M9
Kirkstyle Highld 167 P2
Kirkthorpe Wakefd 91 K6
Kirkton Abers 150 G2
Kirkton D & G 109 L4
Kirkton Fife 135 K2
Kirkton Highld 145 P2
Kirkton Highld 154 B9
Kirkton P & K 134 B4
Kirkton Manor Border 117 J3
Kirkton of Airlie Angus 142 E7
Kirkton of Auchterhouse Angus 142 E10
Kirkton of Barevan Highld 156 E8
Kirkton of Collace P & K 142 B11
Kirkton of Durris Abers 151 K8
Kirkton of Glenbuchat Abers 150 B4
Kirkton of Glenisla Angus 142 C5
Kirkton of Kingoldrum Angus 142 E6
Kirkton of Lethendy P & K 142 A9
Kirkton of Logie Buchan Abers 151 P2
Kirkton of Maryculter Abers 151 M8
Kirkton of Menmuir Angus 143 J5
Kirkton of Monikie Angus 143 J10
Kirkton of Rayne Abers 158 G11
Kirkton of Skene Abers 151 L6
Kirkton of Tealing Angus 142 G10
Kirkton of Tough Abers 150 G5
Kirktown Abers 159 N4
Kirktown Abers 159 Q7
Kirktown of Alvah Abers 158 G5
Kirktown of Bourtie Abers 151 L2
Kirktown of Deskford Moray 158 D5
Kirktown of Fetteresso Abers 151 M10
Kirktown of Mortlach Moray 157 Q10
Kirktown of Slains Abers 151 Q2
Kirkurd Border 116 G2
Kirkwall Ork 169 d5
Kirkwall Airport Ork 169 d6
Kirkwhelpington Nthumb 112 E4
Kirk Yetholm Border 118 F5
Kirmington N Linc 93 K8
Kirmond le Mire Lincs 86 G2
Kirn Ag & B 124 F2
Kirriemuir Angus 142 F7
Kirstead Green Norfk 65 K2
Kirtlebridge D & G 110 D6
Kirtling Cambs 63 L9
Kirtling Green Cambs 63 L9
Kirtlington Oxon 48 E11
Kirtomy Highld 166 B4
Kirton Lincs 74 F3
Kirton Notts 85 L7
Kirton Suffk 53 N3
Kirton End Lincs 74 E2
Kirtonhill W Duns 125 K3
Kirton Holme Lincs 74 E2
Kirton in Lindsey N Linc 92 F11
Kirwaugh D & G 107 M7
Kishorn Highld 153 Q10
Kislingbury Nhants 60 E9
Kitebrook Warwks 47 P8
Kite Green Warwks 59 J11
Kites Hardwick Warwks 59 Q11
Kitleigh Cnwll 5 L2
Kitt Green Wigan 88 G9
Kittisford Somset 18 E10
Kittle Swans 28 G7
Kitt's Green Birm 59 J7
Kittybrewster C Aber 151 N6
Kitwood Hants 23 J8
Kivernoll Herefs 45 P8
Kiveton Park Rothm 84 G4
Knaith Lincs 85 P4
Knaith Park Lincs 85 P3
Knap Corner Dorset 20 F10
Knaphill Surrey 23 Q3
Knapp Somset 19 K9
Knapp Hill Hants 22 D10
Knapthorpe Notts 85 M9
Knapton C York 98 B10
Knapton N York 98 H5
Knapton Norfk 77 L5
Knapton Green Herefs 45 N4
Knapwell Cambs 62 D8
Knaresborough N York 97 N9
Knarsdale Nthumb 111 N10
Knaven Abers 159 L9
Knayton N York 97 P3
Knebworth Herts 50 G6
Knedlington E R Yk 92 B5
Kneesall Notts 85 M8
Kneeton Notts 85 M11
Knelston Swans 28 E7
Knenhall Staffs 70 G7
Knettishall Suffk 64 D5
Knightacott Devon 17 M4
Knightcote Warwks 48 D4
Knightley Staffs 70 E9
Knightley Dale Staffs 70 E10
Knighton BCP 13 J5
Knighton C Leic 72 G10
Knighton Devon 6 E9
Knighton Dorset 11 N2
Knighton Powys 56 D10
Knighton Somset 18 G6
Knighton Staffs 70 C6
Knighton Staffs 70 D9
Knighton Wilts 33 Q10
Knighton on Teme Worcs 57 L11
Knightsbridge Gloucs 46 G9
Knightsmill Cnwll 4 H5
Knightwick Worcs 46 D3
Knill Herefs 45 K2
Knipoch Ag & B 130 G3
Knipton Leics 73 L4
Knitsley Dur 112 H11
Kniveton Derbys 71 N4
Knock Cumb 102 C5
Knock Highld 145 L6
Knock Moray 158 D7
Knock W Isls 168 j4
Knockally Highld 167 K11
Knockan Highld 161 L4
Knockando Moray 157 M9
Knockbain Highld 155 Q9
Knockbain Highld 156 A6
Knock Castle N Ayrs 124 F5
Knockdee Highld 167 L4
Knockdow Ag & B 124 E3
Knockdown Wilts 32 F7
Knockeen S Ayrs 114 F8
Knockenkelly N Ayrs 121 K6
Knockentiber E Ayrs 125 L10
Knockhall Kent 37 N6
Knockholt Kent 37 L9
Knockholt Pound Kent 37 L9
Knockin Shrops 69 K10
Knockinlaw E Ayrs 125 L10
Knockmill Kent 37 N8
Knocknain D & G 106 C5
Knockrome Ag & B 123 J5
Knocksharry IoM 80 c4
Knocksheen D & G 108 C4
Knockvennie Smithy D & G 108 G6
Knodishall Suffk 65 N9
Knodishall Common Suffk 65 N9
Knole Somset 19 N9
Knole Park S Glos 31 Q8
Knolls Green Ches E 82 H9
Knolton Wrexhm 69 L7
Knook Wilts 20 H6
Knossington Leics 73 L9
Knott End-on-Sea Lancs 94 H11
Knotting Bed 61 M8
Knotting Green Bed 61 M8
Knottingley Wakefd 91 N6
Knotty Ash Lpool 81 N6
Knotty Green Bucks 35 P6
Knowbury Shrops 57 K9
Knowe D & G 107 K3
Knowehead D & G 115 M9
Knoweside S Ayrs 114 E5
Knowes of Elrick Abers 158 F7
Knowle Bristl 32 B10
Knowle Devon 9 J4
Knowle Devon 9 P3
Knowle Devon 9 Q8
Knowle Devon 16 H4
Knowle Shrops 57 K10
Knowle Solhll 59 J9
Knowle Somset 18 C6
Knowle Cross Devon 9 P5
Knowlefield Cumb 110 H9
Knowle Green Lancs 89 J3
Knowle Hill Surrey 35 Q11
Knowle St Giles Somset 10 G2
Knowle Village Hants 14 G5
Knowle Wood Calder 89 Q6
Knowl Green Essex 52 C3
Knowl Hill W & M 35 M9
Knowlton Dorset 12 H3
Knowlton Kent 39 N11
Knowsley Knows 81 N5
Knowsley Safari Park Knows 81 P6
Knowstone Devon 17 Q7
Knox N York 97 L9
Knox Bridge Kent 26 C3
Knoydart Highld 145 P7
Knucklas Powys 56 D10
Knuston Nhants 61 K7
Knutsford Ches E 82 G9
Knutsford Services Ches E 82 F9
Knutton Staffs 70 E5
Krumlin Calder 90 D7
Kuggar Cnwll 3 J10
Kyleakin Highld 145 N2
Kyle of Lochalsh Highld 145 N2
Kylerhea Highld 145 N3
Kylesku Highld 164 F10
Kylesmorar Highld 145 P9
Kyles Scalpay W Isls 168 h8
Kylestrome Highld 164 F10
Kynaston Herefs 46 B7
Kynaston Shrops 69 L10
Kynnersley Wrekin 70 B11
Kyre Green Worcs 46 B2
Kyre Park Worcs 46 B2
Kyrewood Worcs 57 K11
Kyrle Somset 18 E10

L

La Bellieuse Guern 10 b2
Lacasaigh W Isls 168 i5
Lacasdal W Isls 168 j4
Laceby NE Lin 93 M9
Lacey Green Bucks 35 M4
Lach Dennis Ches W 82 F10
Lackenby R & Cl 104 G7
Lackford Suffk 63 N6
Lackford Green Suffk 63 N6
Lacock Wilts 32 H11
Ladbroke Warwks 48 D3
Ladderedge Staffs 70 H4
Laddingford Kent 37 Q11
Lade Bank Lincs 87 L10
Ladock Cnwll 3 M3
Lady Ork 169 f2
Ladybank Fife 135 J6
Ladycross Cnwll 5 N4
Ladygill S Lans 116 C5
Lady Hall Cumb 94 D3
Ladykirk Border 129 M10
Ladyridge Herefs 46 A8
Lady's Green Suffk 63 N9
Ladywood Birm 58 G7
Ladywood Worcs 46 G2
La Fontenelle Guern 10 c1
La Fosse Guern 10 b2
Lag D & G 109 J3
Laga Highld 138 A5
Lagavulin Ag & B 122 F10
Lagg N Ayrs 121 J7
Laggan Highld 146 H8
Laggan Highld 147 Q9
Lagganlia Highld 148 F7
La Greve Guern 10 c1
La Grève de Lecq Jersey 11 a1
La Hougue Bie Jersey 11 c2
La Houguette Guern 10 b2
Laid Highld 165 K5
Laide Highld 160 E8
Laig Highld 144 G10
Laigh Clunch E Ayrs 125 M8
Laigh Fenwick E Ayrs 125 M9
Laigh Glenmuir E Ayrs 115 M3
Laighstonehall S Lans 126 C7
Laindon Essex 37 Q3
Lairg Highld 162 D5
Laisterdyke C Brad 90 F4
Laithes Cumb 101 N4
Lake Devon 8 D7
Lake Devon 17 K5
Lake IoW 14 G10
Lake Wilts 21 M7
Lake District Cumb 100 H8
Lake District National Park Cumb 100 H8
Lakenheath Suffk 63 M4
Laker's Green Surrey 24 B3
Lakes End Norfk 75 K11
Lakeside Cumb 94 H3
Laleham Surrey 36 C7
Laleston Brdgnd 29 N9
Lamanva Cnwll 3 K7
Lamarsh Essex 52 E4
Lamas Norfk 77 J7
Lambden Border 118 D2
Lamberhurst Kent 25 Q3
Lamberhurst Down Kent 25 Q3
Lamberton Border 129 P8
Lambeth Gt Lon 36 H5
Lambfair Green Suffk 63 M10
Lambley Notts 85 K11
Lambley Nthumb 111 N9
Lambourn W Berk 34 B9
Lambourne End Essex 37 L2
Lambourn Woodlands W Berk 34 B9
Lamb Roe Lancs 89 L3
Lambs Green W Susx 24 F3
Lambston Pembks 40 H7
Lamellion Cnwll 5 L9
Lamerton Devon 8 C9
Lamesley Gatesd 113 L9
Lamington S Lans 116 D4
Lamlash N Ayrs 121 K5
Lamonby Cumb 101 M3
Lamorick Cnwll 4 G9
Lamorna Cnwll 2 C9
Lamorran Cnwll 3 M5
Lampen Cnwll 5 K8
Lampeter Cerdgn 43 L5
Lampeter Velfrey Pembks 41 N8
Lamphey Pembks 41 K10
Lamplugh Cumb 100 E6
Lamport Nhants 60 G6
Lamyatt Somset 20 C7
Lana Devon 5 N2
Lana Devon 16 E10
Lanark S Lans 116 B2
Lancaster Lancs 95 K8
Lancaster Services Lancs 95 L10
Lancaut Gloucs 31 P5
Lanchester Dur 113 J11
Lancing W Susx 24 E10
L'Ancresse Guern 10 c1
Landbeach Cambs 62 G7
Landcross Devon 16 H7
Landerberry Abers 151 J7
Landford Wilts 21 Q11
Land-hallow Highld 167 L10
Landimore Swans 28 E6
Landkey Devon 17 K5
Landore Swans 29 J5
Landrake Cnwll 5 P9
Landscove Devon 7 K5
Land's End Cnwll 2 A8
Land's End Airport Cnwll 2 B8
Landshipping Pembks 41 K8
Landue Cnwll 5 P6
Landulph Cnwll 6 C6
Landwade Suffk 63 K7
Lane Cnwll 4 C9
Laneast Cnwll 5 L5
Lane Bottom Lancs 89 P3
Lane End Bucks 35 M6
Lane End Cnwll 4 G8
Lane End Hants 22 G9
Lane End Kent 37 N6
Lane End Lancs 96 C11
Lane End Warrtn 82 E6
Lane End Wilts 20 F5
Lane Ends Derbys 71 N8
Lane Ends Lancs 89 M4
Lane Ends N York 90 B2
Lane Green Staffs 58 C4
Laneham Notts 85 P5
Lanehead Dur 102 F2
Lane Head Dur 103 M8
Lanehead Nthumb 111 Q3
Lane Head Wigan 82 D5
Lane Head Wsall 58 E4
Lane Heads Lancs 88 E3
Lanercost Cumb 111 L8
Laneshaw Bridge Lancs 89 Q2
Lane Side Lancs 89 M6
Langaford Devon 5 Q2
Langal Highld 138 C4
Langaller Somset 19 J9
Langar Notts 73 J4
Langbank Rens 125 K3
Langbar N York 96 G10
Langbaurgh N York 104 G8
Langcliffe N York 96 B8
Langdale End N York 99 J2
Langdon Cnwll 5 N4
Langdon Beck Dur 102 G4
Langdon Hills Essex 37 Q3
Langdown Hants 14 D5
Langdyke Fife 135 J7
Langenhoe Essex 52 H8
Langford C Beds 50 E2
Langford Devon 9 P4
Langford Essex 52 D10
Langford N Som 19 N2
Langford Notts 85 P9
Langford Oxon 33 P4
Langford Budville Somset 18 F10
Langham Dorset 20 E9
Langham Essex 52 H5
Langham Norfk 76 E3
Langham Rutlnd 73 L8
Langham Suffk 64 D8
Langho Lancs 89 L4
Langholm D & G 110 G4
Langland Swans 28 H7
Langlee Border 117 Q3
Langley Ches E 83 K10
Langley Derbys 84 F11
Langley Gloucs 47 K9
Langley Hants 14 D6
Langley Herts 50 F6
Langley Kent 38 D11
Langley Nthumb 112 B8

Langley Oxon 47 Q11
Langley Rochdl 89 P9
Langley Slough 36 B5
Langley W Susx 23 M9
Langley Somset 18 E9
Langley Warwks 47 N2
Langley Burrell Wilts 32 H9
Langley Castle Nthumb 112 B8
Langley Common Derbys 71 P7
Langley Green Derbys 71 P7
Langley Green Essex 52 E7
Langley Green Warwks 47 N2
Langley Heath Kent 38 D11
Langley Lower Green Essex ...51 K4
Langley Marsh Somset 18 E9
Langley Mill Derbys 84 F11
Langley Moor Dur 103 Q2
Langley Park Dur 113 K11
Langley Street Norfk 77 M11
Langley Upper Green Essex ...51 K4
Langley Vale Surrey 36 F9
Langney E Susx 25 P10
Langold Notts 85 J3
Langore Cnwll 5 M4
Langport Somset 19 M9
Langrick Lincs 87 J11
Langridge BaNES 32 D11
Langridgeford Devon 17 K7
Langrigg Cumb 110 C11
Langrish Hants 23 K10
Langsett Barns 90 G10
Langside P & K 133 M5
Langstone Hants 15 K6
Langstone Newpt 31 L7
Langthorne N York 97 K2
Langthorpe N York 97 N7
Langthwaite N York 103 K10
Langtoft E R Yk 99 L7
Langtoft Lincs 74 B8
Langton Dur 103 N7
Langton Lincs 86 H7
Langton Lincs 87 L6
Langton N York 98 F7
Langton by Wragby Lincs 86 F5
Langton Green Kent 25 M3
Langton Green Suffk 64 G7
Langton Herring Dorset 11 N8
Langton Long Blandford
    Dorset 12 F3
Langton Matravers Dorset 12 H9
Langtree Devon 16 H8
Langtree Week Devon 16 H8
Langwathby Cumb 101 Q4
Langwell Highld 161 K6
Langwell House Highld 163 Q2
Langwith Derbys 84 H7
Langwith Junction Derbys 84 H7
Langworth Lincs 86 E5
Lanhydrock House &
    Gardens Cnwll 4 H9
Lanivet Cnwll 4 G9
Lanjeth Cnwll 3 P3
Lank Cnwll 4 H6
Lanlivery Cnwll 4 H10
Lanner Cnwll 3 J6
Lanoy Cnwll 5 M6
Lanreath Cnwll 5 K10
Lansallos Cnwll 5 K11
Lanteglos Cnwll 4 H5
Lanteglos Highway Cnwll 5 J11
Lanton Border 118 B6
Lanton Nthumb 118 H4
La Passee Guern 10 b1
Lapford Devon 8 H3
La Pulente Jersey 11 a2
Lapworth Warwks 59 J10
Larachbeg Highld 138 B8
Larbert Falk 133 P11
Larbreck Lancs 88 E2
Largie Abers 158 F11
Largiemore Ag & B 131 J10
Largoward Fife 135 M6
Largs N Ayrs 124 G6
Largybeg N Ayrs 121 K7
Largymore N Ayrs 121 K7
Larkbeare Devon 9 Q5
Larkfield Inver 124 G2
Larkfield Kent 38 B10
Larkhall S Lans 126 D7
Larkhill Wilts 21 M6
Larling Norfk 64 D4
La Rocque Jersey 11 c2
La Rousaillerie Guern 10 b1
Lartington Dur 103 K7
Lasborough Gloucs 32 F6
Lasham Hants 23 J6
Lashbrook Devon 8 B3
Lashbrook Devon 16 G10
Lashenden Kent 26 D3
Lask Edge Staffs 70 G3
Lasswade Mdloth 127 P4
Lastingham N York 98 E2
Latcham Somset 19 M5
Latchford Herts 51 J6
Latchford Oxon 35 J4
Latchford Warrtn 82 D7
Latchingdon Essex 52 E11
Latchley Cnwll 5 Q7
Lately Common Warrtn 82 E5
Lathbury M Keyn 49 N6
Latheron Highld 167 M10
Latheronwheel Highld 167 L10
Lathom Lancs 88 F8
Lathones Fife 135 M6
Latimer Bucks 50 B11
Latteridge S Glos 32 C8
Lattiford Somset 20 C9
Latton Wilts 33 L5
Lauder Border 128 E10
Laugharne Carmth 28 B2
Laughterton Lincs 85 P5
Laughton E Susx 25 L8
Laughton Leics 60 E3
Laughton Lincs 74 A4
Laughton Lincs 92 D11
Laughton Common Rothm 84 H3
Laughton-en-le-Morthen
    Rothm 84 H3
Launcells Cnwll 16 C10
Launcells Cross Cnwll 16 D10
Launceston Cnwll 5 N5
Launton Oxon 48 H10
Laurencekirk Abers 143 N3
Laurieston D & G 108 E8

Laurieston Falk 126 G2
Lavendon M Keyn 49 P4
Lavenham Suffk 52 F2
Lavernock V Glam 30 G11
Laversdale Cumb 111 J8
Laverstock Wilts 21 N8
Laverstoke Hants 22 F5
Laverton Gloucs 47 L7
Laverton N York 97 K6
Laverton Somset 20 E4
La Villette Guern 10 b2
Lavister Wrexhm 69 L3
Law S Lans 126 E7
Lawers P & K 140 G10
Lawford Essex 53 J5
Lawford Somset 18 F7
Law Hill S Lans 126 E7
Lawhitton Cnwll 5 P5
Lawkland N York 95 R7
Lawkland Green N York 96 A1
Lawley Wrekin 57 M3
Lawnhead Staffs 70 E9
Lawrence Weston Bristl 31 P9
Lawrenny Pembks 41 K9
Lawrenny Quay Pembks 41 K9
Lawshall Suffk 64 B11
Lawshall Green Suffk 64 B11
Lawton Herefs 45 N3
Laxay W Isls 168 i5
Laxdale W Isls 168 j4
Laxey IoM 80 f5
Laxfield Suffk 65 K7
Laxford Bridge Highld 164 F7
Laxo Shet 169 r7
Laxton E R Yk 92 C5
Laxton Nhants 73 P11
Laxton Notts 85 M7
Laycock C Brad 90 C2
Layer Breton Essex 52 F8
Layer-de-la-Haye Essex 52 G7
Layer Marney Essex 52 F8
Layham Suffk 52 H3
Laymore Dorset 10 H4
Layter's Green Bucks 35 Q6
Laytham E R Yk 92 B3
Laythes Cumb 110 D9
Lazenby R & Cl 104 G7
Lazonby Cumb 101 P3
Lea Derbys 84 D9
Lea Herefs 46 C10
Lea Lincs 85 P3
Lea Shrops 56 F7
Lea Shrops 56 G3
Lea Wilts 33 J7
Leachkin Highld 156 A8
Leadburn Border 127 N6
Leadenham Lincs 86 B10
Leaden Roding Essex 51 N8
Leadgate Cumb 102 D2
Leadgate Dur 112 H10
Leadgate Nthumb 112 H9
Leadhills S Lans 116 B7
Leadingcross Green Kent 38 E11
Leadmill Derbys 84 B4
Leafield Oxon 48 B11
Leagrave Luton 50 C6
Leahead Ches W 70 B2
Lea Heath Staffs 71 J9
Leake N York 97 P2
Leake Common Side Lincs 87 L10
Lealholm N York 105 L9
Lealholm Side N York 105 L9
Lealt Highld 153 J5
Leam Derbys 84 B4
Lea Marston Warwks 59 K6
Leamington Hastings
    Warwks 59 P11
Leamington Spa Warwks 59 M11
Leamside Dur 113 M11
Leap Cross E Susx 25 N8
Learney Abers 150 G7
Leasgill Cumb 95 K4
Leasingham Lincs 86 E11
Leasingthorne Dur 103 Q4
Leatherhead Surrey 36 E9
Leathley N York 97 K11
Leaton Shrops 69 N11
Leaton Wrekin 57 L2
Lea Town Lancs 88 F4
Leavenheath Suffk 52 G4
Leavening N York 98 F8
Leaves Green Gt Lon 37 K8
Lea Yeat Cumb 95 R3
Lebberston N York 99 M4
Le Bigard Guern 10 b2
Le Bourg Guern 10 b2
Le Bourg Jersey 11 c2
Lechlade on Thames
    Gloucs 33 P5
Lecht Gruinart Ag & B 122 C6
Leck Lancs 95 N5
Leckbuie P & K 140 H9
Leckford Hants 22 C7
Leckhampstead Bucks 49 K7
Leckhampstead W Berk 34 D9
Leckhampstead Thicket
    W Berk 34 D9
Leckhampton Gloucs 46 H1
Leckmelm Highld 161 K9
Leckwith V Glam 30 G10
Leconfield E R Yk 92 H2
Ledaig Ag & B 138 G10
Ledburn Bucks 49 P10
Ledbury Herefs 46 D7
Leddington Gloucs 46 D7
Ledgemoor Herefs 45 N4
Ledicot Herefs 45 N4
Ledmore Highld 161 L4
Ledsham Ches W 81 M10
Ledsham Leeds 91 M5
Ledston Leeds 91 L5
Ledstone Devon 7 J9
Ledston Luck Leeds 91 L4
Ledwell Oxon 48 D9
Lee Devon 16 H2
Lee Gt Lon 37 J5
Lee Hants 22 C11
Lee Shrops 69 M8
Leebotwood Shrops 56 H5
Lee Brockhurst Shrops 69 P9
Leece Cumb 94 E7
Lee Chapel Essex 37 Q3
Lee Clump Bucks 35 P4
Lee Common Bucks 35 P4
Leeds Kent 38 C11

Leeds Leeds 90 H4
Leeds Bradford Airport
    Leeds 90 G2
Leeds Castle Kent 38 D11
Leeds Skelton Lake
    Services Leeds 91 K4
Leedstown Cnwll 2 H7
Lee Green Ches E 70 B2
Leek Staffs 70 H3
Leek Wootton Warwks 59 L11
Lee Mill Devon 6 F7
Leeming C Brad 90 C4
Leeming N York 97 L3
Leeming Bar N York 97 L3
Leeming Bar Rest Area
    N York 97 L3
Lee Moor Devon 6 F6
Lee-on-the-Solent Hants 14 F6
Lees C Brad 90 C3
Lees Derbys 71 P7
Lees Oldham 83 L4
Lees Green Derbys 71 P7
Leesthorpe Leics 73 K8
Leeswood Flints 69 J2
Leetown P & K 134 G3
Leftwich Ches W 82 E10
Legar Powys 45 J11
Legbourne Lincs 87 L4
Legburthwaite Cumb 101 K7
Legerwood Border 118 A2
Legoland W & M 35 Q10
Le Gron Guern 10 b2
Legsby Lincs 86 F3
Le Haguais Jersey 11 c2
Le Hocq Jersey 11 c2
Leicester C Leic 72 F10
Leicester Forest East Leics ...72 E10
Leicester Forest East
    Services Leics 72 E10
Leigh Devon 17 N9
Leigh Dorset 11 N3
Leigh Gloucs 46 G9
Leigh Kent 37 M11
Leigh Shrops 56 E4
Leigh Surrey 36 F11
Leigh Wigan 82 E5
Leigh Wilts 33 L6
Leigh Worcs 46 E4
Leigh Beck Essex 38 D5
Leigh Delamere Wilts 32 G9
Leigh Delamere Services
    Wilts 32 G9
Leigh Green Kent 26 F5
Leigh Knoweglass S Lans 125 Q7
Leighland Chapel Somset 18 D7
Leigh-on-Sea Sthend 38 D4
Leigh Park Dorset 12 H5
Leigh Park Hants 15 K5
Leigh Sinton Worcs 46 E4
Leighswood Wsall 58 G4
Leighterton Gloucs 32 F6
Leighton N York 97 J5
Leighton Powys 56 C3
Leighton Shrops 57 L3
Leighton Somset 20 D6
Leighton Bromswold Cambs ...61 P5
Leighton Buzzard C Beds 49 P9
Leigh upon Mendip Somset ...20 C5
Leigh Woods N Som 31 Q10
Leinthall Earls Herefs 56 G11
Leinthall Starkes Herefs 56 G11
Leintwardine Herefs 56 G10
Leire Leics 60 B3
Leiston Suffk 65 N9
Leith C Edin 127 P2
Leitholm Border 118 E2
Lelant Cnwll 2 E6
Lelley E R Yk 93 M4
Lem Hill Worcs 57 N9
Lempitlaw Border 118 E4
Lemreway W Isls 168 i6
Lemsford Herts 50 F8
Lenchwick Worcs 47 J4
Lendalfoot S Ayrs 114 B9
Lendrick Stirlg 132 H6
Lendrum Terrace Abers 159 R9
Lenham Kent 38 C11
Lenham Heath Kent 26 F2
Lenie Highld 147 N2
Lennel Border 118 G2
Lennox Plunton D & G 108 D10
Lennoxtown E Duns 125 Q2
Lent Bucks 35 P8
Lenton C Nott 72 F3
Lenton Lincs 73 Q4
Lenwade Norfk 76 F8
Lenzie E Duns 126 B3
Leoch Angus 142 F11
Leochel-Cushnie Abers 150 E5
Leomansley Staffs 58 H3
Leominster Herefs 45 P3
Leonard Stanley Gloucs 32 F4
Leoville Jersey 11 a1
Lepe Hants 14 D7
Lephin Highld 152 B8
Leppington N York 98 F9
Lepton Kirk 90 G7
Lerags Ag & B 130 H2
L'Erée Guern 10 a2
Lerryn Cnwll 5 J10
Lerwick Shet 169 r9
Les Arquêts Guern 10 b2
Lesbury Nthumb 119 P8
Les Hubits Guern 10 c2
Leslie Abers 150 F3
Leslie Fife 134 H7
Les Lohiers Guern 10 b2
Lesmahagow S Lans 126 E10
Les Murchez Guern 10 b2
Lesnewth Cnwll 5 J3
Les Nicolles Guern 10 b2
Les Quartiers Guern 10 c1
Les Sages Guern 10 b2
Lessingham Norfk 77 M6
Lessonhall Cumb 110 D10
Lestowder Cnwll 3 K9
Les Villets Guern 10 b2
Leswalt D & G 106 D5
L'Etacq Jersey 11 a1
Letchmore Heath Herts 50 E11
Letchworth Garden City
    Herts 50 F4
Letcombe Bassett Oxon 34 C7
Letcombe Regis Oxon 34 C7
Letham Angus 143 J9
Letham Border 118 C9

Letham Falk 133 P10
Letham Fife 135 J5
Letham Grange Angus 143 L8
Lethenty Abers 150 F3
Lethenty Abers 159 K9
Letheringham Suffk 65 K10
Letheringsett Norfk 76 F4
Lettaford Devon 8 H8
Letterewe Highld 154 C3
Letterfearn Highld 145 Q3
Letterfinlay Lodge Hotel
    Highld 146 H9
Letters Highld 161 K9
Lettershaw S Lans 116 B4
Letterston Pembks 40 H5
Lettoch Highld 149 J4
Lettoch Highld 157 L11
Letton Herefs 45 L5
Letton Herefs 56 F10
Lett's Green Kent 37 L9
Letty Green Herts 50 G8
Letwell Rothm 85 J3
Leuchars Fife 135 M3
Leumrabhagh W Isls 168 i6
Leurbost W Isls 168 i5
Levalsa Meor Cnwll 3 Q4
Levan Inver 124 G2
Levedale Staffs 70 F11
Level's Green Essex 51 L6
Leven E R Yk 99 N11
Leven Fife 135 K7
Levens Cumb 95 K3
Levens Green Herts 51 J6
Levenshulme Manch 83 J6
Levenwick Shet 169 r11
Leverburgh W Isls 168 f9
Leverington Cambs 74 H8
Leverstock Green Herts 50 C9
Leverton Lincs 87 M11
Le Villocq Guern 10 b1
Levington Suffk 53 M4
Levisham N York 98 G2
Lew Oxon 34 B3
Lewannick Cnwll 5 M5
Lewdown Devon 8 C7
Lewes E Susx 25 K8
Leweston Pembks 40 H6
Lewisham Gt Lon 37 J6
Lewiston Highld 147 N2
Lewistown Brdgnd 29 P7
Lewis Wych Herefs 45 L3
Lewknor Oxon 35 K5
Leworthy Devon 16 H4
Leworthy Devon 17 M4
Lewson Street Kent 38 G9
Lewth Lancs 88 F3
Lewtrenchard Devon 8 C7
Lexden Essex 52 G6
Lexworthy Somset 19 J7
Ley Cnwll 5 K8
Leybourne Kent 37 Q9
Leyburn N York 96 H2
Leycett Staffs 70 D5
Leygreen Herts 50 E6
Ley Hill Bucks 35 Q4
Leyland Lancs 88 G6
Leyland Green St Hel 82 C4
Leylodge Abers 151 K5
Leys Abers 159 P7
Leys P & K 142 D10
Leysdown-on-Sea Kent 38 H7
Leysmill Angus 143 L8
Leys of Cossans Angus 142 F8
Leysters Herefs 45 R2
Leyton Gt Lon 37 J3
Leytonstone Gt Lon 37 J3
Lezant Cnwll 5 N6
Lezerea Cnwll 2 H7
Leziate Norfk 75 N7
Lhanbryde Moray 157 P5
Libanus Powys 44 D9
Libberton S Lans 116 D2
Libbery Worcs 47 J3
Liberton C Edin 127 P4
Lichfield Staffs 58 H3
Lickey Worcs 58 E9
Lickey End Worcs 58 E10
Lickey Rock Worcs 58 E10
Lickfold W Susx 23 N9
Liddaton Green Devon 8 C8
Liddesdale Highld 138 D6
Liddington Swindn 33 P8
Lidgate Derbys 84 D5
Lidgate Suffk 63 M9
Lidget Donc 91 R10
Lidgett Notts 85 K7
Lidham Hill E Susx 26 D8
Lidlington C Beds 49 Q7
Lidsey W Susx 15 P6
Lidsing Kent 38 C9
Liff Angus 142 E11
Lifford Birm 58 G8
Lifton Devon 5 P4
Liftondown Devon 5 P4
Lighthorne Warwks 48 B3
Lighthorne Heath Warwks 48 C3
Lilbourne Nhants 60 C5
Lilburn Tower Nthumb 119 K6
Lilleshall Wrekin 70 C11
Lilley Herts 50 D5
Lilley W Berk 34 D9
Lilliesleaf Border 117 Q5
Lillingstone Dayrell Bucks 49 K7
Lillingstone Lovell Bucks 49 K6
Lillington Dorset 11 N2
Lilliput BCP 12 H7
Lilstock Somset 18 G5
Lilyhurst Shrops 57 N2
Limbrick Lancs 89 J7
Limbury Luton 50 C6
Limebrook Herefs 56 F11
Limefield Bury 89 N8
Limekilnburn S Lans 126 C7
Limekilns Fife 134 D11
Limerigg Falk 126 F3
Limerstone IoW 14 D10
Limestone Brae Nthumb 111 Q11
Limington Somset 19 P10
Limmerhaugh E Ayrs 115 M2

Limpenhoe Norfk 77 M11
Limpley Stoke Wilts 20 E2
Limpsfield Surrey 37 K10
Limpsfield Chart Surrey 37 K10
Linby Notts 84 H10
Linchmere W Susx 23 N8
Lincluden D & G 109 L5
Lincoln Lincs 86 C6
Lincomb Worcs 57 Q11
Lincombe Devon 7 J10
Lincombe Devon 16 H2
Lindale Cumb 94 J4
Lindal in Furness Cumb 94 E5
Lindfield W Susx 24 H5
Lindford Hants 23 M7
Lindley Kirk 90 E7
Lindley N York 97 K11
Lindores Fife 134 H4
Lindow End Ches E 82 H9
Lindridge Worcs 57 M11
Lindsell Essex 51 P5
Lindsey Suffk 52 G2
Lindsey Tye Suffk 52 G2
Liney Somset 19 L7
Linford Hants 13 L3
Linford Thurr 37 Q5
Lingbob C Brad 90 D3
Lingdale R & Cl 105 J7
Lingen Herefs 56 F11
Lingfield Surrey 25 J2
Lingfield Common Surrey 25 J2
Lingwood Norfk 77 M10
Liniclate W Isls 168 c13
Linicro Highld 152 F4
Linkend Worcs 46 F8
Linkenholt Hants 22 C3
Linkhill Kent 26 D6
Linkinhorne Cnwll 5 N7
Linktown Fife 134 H9
Linkwood Moray 157 N5
Linley Shrops 56 F6
Linley Shrops 57 M5
Linley Green Herefs 46 C4
Linleygreen Shrops 57 M5
Linlithgow W Loth 126 H2
Linshiels Nthumb 118 G9
Linsidemore Highld 162 C7
Linslade C Beds 49 P9
Linstead Parva Suffk 65 L6
Linstock Cumb 110 H9
Linthurst Worcs 58 E10
Linthwaite Kirk 90 E8
Lintlaw Border 129 L8
Lintmill Moray 158 D4
Linton Border 118 E5
Linton Cambs 63 J11
Linton Derbys 71 P11
Linton Herefs 46 C9
Linton Kent 38 C11
Linton Leeds 97 N11
Linton N York 96 E8
Linton N York 113 L2
Linton Heath Derbys 71 P11
Linton Hill Herefs 46 C10
Linton-on-Ouse N York 97 Q8
Linwood Hants 13 L3
Linwood Lincs 86 F3
Linwood Rens 125 L5
Lionacleit W Isls 168 c13
Lional W Isls 168 k1
Lions Green E Susx 25 N7
Liphook Hants 23 M8
Lipley Shrops 70 C8
Liscard Wirral 81 K6
Liscombe Somset 18 A8
Liskeard Cnwll 5 M9
Lismore Ag & B 138 E9
Liss Hants 23 L9
Lissett E R Yk 99 N9
Liss Forest Hants 23 L9
Lissington Lincs 86 F4
Liston Essex 52 E3
Lisvane Cardif 30 G8
Liswerry Newpt 31 K7
Litcham Norfk 76 B8
Litchborough Nhants 48 H4
Litchfield Hants 22 E4
Litherland Sefton 81 L5
Litlington Cambs 50 H2
Litlington E Susx 25 M10
Little Abington Cambs 62 H11
Little Addington Nhants 61 L6
Little Airies D & G 107 M8
Little Almshoe Herts 50 F5
Little Alne Warwks 47 M2
Little Altcar Sefton 88 C9
Little Amwell Herts 51 J8
Little Asby Cumb 102 C9
Little Aston Staffs 58 G5
Little Atherfield IoW 14 E11
Little Ayton N York 104 G8
Little Baddow Essex 52 C10
Little Badminton S Glos 32 F8
Little Bampton Cumb 110 E9
Little Bardfield Essex 51 Q4
Little Barford Bed 61 Q9
Little Barningham Norfk 76 G5
Little Barrington Gloucs 33 P2
Little Barrow Ches W 81 P11
Little Barugh N York 98 F5
Little Bavington Nthumb 112 E5
Little Bealings Suffk 53 M2
Littlebeck N York 105 N10
Little Bedwyn Wilts 33 Q11
Little Bentley Essex 53 K6
Little Berkhamsted Herts 50 G9
Little Billing Nhants 60 H8
Little Billington C Beds 49 P10
Little Birch Herefs 45 Q8
Little Bispham Bpool 88 C2
Little Blakenham Suffk 53 K2
Little Blencow Cumb 101 N4
Little Bloxwich Wsall 58 F4
Little Bognor W Susx 24 B6
Little Bolehill Derbys 71 P4
Little Bollington Ches E 82 F7
Little Bookham Surrey 36 D10
Littleborough Devon 17 K2
Littleborough Notts 85 P4
Littleborough Rochdl 89 Q7
Littlebourne Kent 39 M10
Little Bourton Oxon 48 E6
Little Bowden Leics 60 F3
Little Bradley Suffk 63 L10
Little Brampton Herefs 45 L2
Little Brampton Shrops 56 F8
Little Braxted Essex 52 D9

Little Brechin Angus.....143 K5
Littlebredy Dorset.....11 M7
Little Brickhill M Keyn.....49 P8
Little Bridgeford Staffs.....70 F9
Little Brington Nhants.....60 E8
Little Bromley Essex.....53 J6
Little Broughton Cumb.....100 E4
Little Budworth Ches W.....82 C11
Littleburn Highld.....156 A7
Little Burstead Essex.....37 Q2
Littlebury Essex.....51 M3
Littlebury Green Essex.....51 L3
Little Bytham Lincs.....73 Q7
Little Canfield Essex.....51 N6
Little Carlton Lincs.....87 L3
Little Carlton Notts.....85 N9
Little Casterton Rutlnd.....73 Q9
Little Catwick E R Yk.....93 K2
Little Catworth Cambs.....61 P6
Little Cawthorpe Lincs.....87 L4
Little Chalfont Bucks.....35 Q5
Little Chart Kent.....26 F2
Little Chesterford Essex.....51 M2
Little Cheveney Kent.....26 B3
Little Cheverell Wilts.....21 J4
Little Chishill Cambs.....51 K3
Little Clacton Essex.....53 L8
Little Clanfield Oxon.....33 Q4
Little Clifton Cumb.....100 E5
Little Coates NE Lin.....93 M9
Little Comberton Worcs.....47 J6
Little Common E Susx.....26 B10
Little Comp Kent.....37 P9
Little Compton Warwks.....47 Q8
Little Corby Cumb.....111 J9
Little Cornard Suffk.....52 F4
Littlecott Wilts.....21 M4
Little Cowarne Herefs.....46 B4
Little Coxwell Oxon.....33 Q6
Little Crakehall N York.....97 K2
Little Cransley Nhants.....60 H5
Little Cressingham Norfk.....76 B11
Little Crosby Sefton.....81 L4
Little Crosthwaite Cumb.....100 H5
Little Cubley Derbys.....71 M7
Little Dalby Leics.....73 K8
Littledean Gloucs.....32 C2
Little Dewchurch Herefs.....45 Q8
Little Ditton Cambs.....63 L9
Little Doward Herefs.....45 Q11
Littledown Hants.....22 B3
Little Downham Cambs.....62 H4
Little Driffield E R Yk.....99 L9
Little Dunham Norfk.....76 B9
Little Dunkeld P & K.....141 P9
Little Dunmow Essex.....51 Q6
Little Durnford Wilts.....21 M8
Little Easton Essex.....51 P6
Little Eaton Derbys.....72 B2
Little Ellingham Norfk.....64 E2
Little Elm Somset.....20 D5
Little Everdon Nhants.....60 C9
Little Eversden Cambs.....62 E10
Little Faringdon Oxon.....33 P4
Little Fencote N York.....97 L2
Little Fenton N York.....91 N3
Littleferry Highld.....163 J7
Little Fransham Norfk.....76 C9
Little Gaddesden Herts.....35 Q2
Little Garway Herefs.....45 N10
Little Gidding Cambs.....61 P4
Little Glemham Suffk.....65 L10
Little Gorsley Herefs.....46 C10
Little Gransden Cambs.....62 C9
Little Green Notts.....73 J2
Little Green Somset.....20 D5
Little Grimsby Lincs.....87 K2
Little Gringley Notts.....85 M4
Little Habton N York.....98 E5
Little Hadham Herts.....51 K6
Little Hale Lincs.....74 B2
Little Hallam Derbys.....72 D2
Little Hallingbury Essex.....51 M7
Littleham Devon.....9 P8
Littleham Devon.....16 G7
Little Hampden Bucks.....35 N4
Littlehampton W Susx.....24 B10
Little Hanford Dorset.....12 D2
Little Harrowden Nhants.....61 J6
Little Haseley Oxon.....34 H4
Little Hatfield E R Yk.....93 L2
Little Hautbois Norfk.....77 K7
Little Haven Pembks.....40 G8
Littlehaven W Susx.....24 E4
Little Hay Staffs.....58 H4
Little Hayfield Derbys.....83 M4
Little Haywood Staffs.....71 J10
Little Heath Staffs.....70 F11
Little Heath W Berk.....35 J10
Littlehempston Devon.....7 L6
Little Hereford Herefs.....57 K11
Little Horkesley Essex.....52 G5
Little Hormead Herts.....51 K5
Little Horsted E Susx.....25 L7
Little Horton C Brad.....90 F4
Little Horton Wilts.....21 K2
Little Horwood Bucks.....49 L8
Little Houghton Barns.....91 L9
Little Houghton Nhants.....60 H9
Littlehoughton Nthumb.....119 P7
Little Hucklow Derbys.....83 Q9
Little Hulton Salfd.....82 F4
Little Hungerford W Berk.....34 F10
Little Hutton N York.....97 Q5
Little Irchester Nhants.....61 K7
Little Kelk E R Yk.....99 M9
Little Keyford Somset.....20 E5
Little Kimble Bucks.....35 M3
Little Kineton Warwks.....48 B4
Little Kingshill Bucks.....35 N5
Little Knox D & G.....108 H8
Little Langdale Cumb.....101 K10
Little Langford Wilts.....21 K7
Little Laver Essex.....51 M9
Little Leigh Ches W.....82 D9
Little Leighs Essex.....52 B8
Little Lever Bolton.....89 M9
Little Linford M Keyn.....49 M6
Little Load Somset.....19 N10
Little London Bucks.....34 H2
Little London Cambs.....74 H11
Little London E Susx.....25 N6
Little London Essex.....51 L5
Little London Essex.....51 Q3
Little London Gloucs.....46 D11
Little London Hants.....22 C5

Little London Hants.....22 H3
Little London Leeds.....90 G3
Little London Lincs.....74 D6
Little London Lincs.....74 H6
Little London Lincs.....87 K6
Little London Norfk.....75 L6
Little London Powys.....55 N7
Little Longstone Derbys.....83 Q10
Little Madeley Staffs.....70 D5
Little Malvern Worcs.....46 E6
Little Mancot Flints.....81 L11
Little Maplestead Essex.....52 D5
Little Marcle Herefs.....46 C7
Little Marland Devon.....17 J9
Little Marlow Bucks.....35 N7
Little Massingham Norfk.....75 Q6
Little Melton Norfk.....76 H10
Little Mill Mons.....31 K4
Little Milton Oxon.....34 H4
Little Missenden Bucks.....35 P5
Little Mongeham Kent.....39 P11
Littlemoor Derbys.....84 E8
Little Moor Somset.....19 K8
Littlemore Oxon.....34 F4
Little Musgrave Cumb.....102 E8
Little Ness Shrops.....69 M11
Little Neston Ches W.....81 K9
Little Newcastle Pembks.....41 J5
Little Newsham Dur.....103 M7
Little Norton Somset.....19 N11
Little Oakley Essex.....53 M6
Little Oakley Nhants.....61 J3
Little Odell Bed.....61 L9
Little Offley Herts.....50 D5
Little Ormside Cumb.....102 D7
Little Orton Cumb.....110 G9
Little Ouse Cambs.....63 K3
Little Ouseburn N York.....97 P8
Littleover C Derb.....72 A4
Little Oxendon Nhants.....60 H4
Little Packington Warwks.....59 K8
Little Pattenden Kent.....26 B2
Little Paxton Cambs.....61 Q8
Little Petherick Cnwll.....4 E7
Little Plumpton Lancs.....88 D4
Little Plumstead Norfk.....77 L9
Little Ponton Lincs.....73 N4
Littleport Cambs.....63 J3
Littleport Bridge Cambs.....63 J3
Little Posbrook Hants.....14 F6
Little Potheridge Devon.....17 J9
Little Preston Leeds.....91 K4
Little Preston Nhants.....48 G4
Littler Ches W.....82 D11
Little Raveley Cambs.....62 C5
Little Reedness E R Yk.....92 F6
Little Ribston N York.....97 N10
Little Rissington Gloucs.....47 N11
Little Rollright Oxon.....47 Q8
Little Rowsley Derbys.....84 C7
Little Ryburgh Norfk.....76 D6
Little Ryle Nthumb.....119 K8
Little Ryton Shrops.....56 H4
Little Salkeld Cumb.....101 Q3
Little Sampford Essex.....51 Q4
Little Sandhurst Br For.....23 M2
Little Saredon Staffs.....58 D3
Little Saughall Ches W.....81 M11
Little Saxham Suffk.....63 P8
Little Scatwell Highld.....155 L6
Little Shelford Cambs.....62 G10
Little Shrewley Warwks.....59 K11
Little Silver Devon.....9 M3
Little Singleton Lancs.....88 D3
Little Skipwith N York.....91 R3
Little Smeaton N York.....91 N7
Little Snoring Norfk.....76 D5
Little Sodbury S Glos.....32 E8
Little Sodbury End S Glos.....32 E8
Little Somborne Hants.....22 C8
Little Somerford Wilts.....33 J8
Little Soudley Shrops.....70 C9
Little Stainforth N York.....96 B7
Little Stainton Darltn.....104 B6
Little Stanion Nhants.....61 J3
Little Stanney Ches W.....81 N10
Little Staughton Bed.....61 P8
Little Steeping Lincs.....87 M8
Little Stoke Staffs.....70 G8
Littlestone-on-Sea Kent.....27 J7
Little Stonham Suffk.....64 G9
Little Stretton Leics.....72 H10
Little Stretton Shrops.....56 G6
Little Strickland Cumb.....101 Q10
Little Stukeley Cambs.....62 B5
Little Sugnall Staffs.....70 E8
Little Sutton Ches W.....81 M9
Little Sutton Shrops.....57 J8
Little Swinburne Nthumb.....112 D5
Little Sypland D & G.....108 F10
Little Tew Oxon.....48 C9
Little Tey Essex.....52 E7
Little Thetford Cambs.....62 H5
Little Thirkleby N York.....97 Q5
Little Thornage Norfk.....76 F4
Little Thornton Lancs.....88 D2
Little Thorpe Dur.....104 D2
Littlethorpe Leics.....72 E11
Littlethorpe N York.....97 M7
Little Thurlow Suffk.....63 L10
Little Thurlow Green Suffk.....63 L10
Little Thurrock Thurr.....37 P5
Littleton BaNES.....19 Q2
Littleton Ches W.....81 N11
Littleton D & G.....108 D9
Littleton Dorset.....12 E4
Littleton Hants.....22 E8
Littleton Somset.....19 N8
Littleton Surrey.....23 Q5
Littleton Surrey.....36 C7
Littleton Drew Wilts.....32 F8
Littleton of Airlie Angus.....142 E7
Littleton-on-Severn S Glos.....31 Q7
Littleton Panell Wilts.....21 J4
Little Torrington Devon.....16 H8
Little Totham Essex.....52 E9
Little Town Cumb.....100 H7
Littletown Dur.....104 B2
Little Town Lancs.....89 K3
Little Town Warrtn.....82 D6
Little Twycross Leics.....72 A9
Little Urswick Cumb.....94 F5
Little Wakering Essex.....38 F4
Little Walden Essex.....51 M2

Little Waldingfield Suffk.....52 F2
Little Walsingham Norfk.....76 C4
Little Waltham Essex.....52 B9
Little Warley Essex.....37 P2
Little Washbourne Gloucs.....47 J8
Little Weighton E R Yk.....92 G4
Little Welnetham Suffk.....64 B10
Little Welton Lincs.....87 K3
Little Wenham Suffk.....53 J4
Little Wenlock Wrekin.....57 L3
Little Weston Somset.....20 B9
Little Whitefield IoW.....14 G9
Little Whittingham Green Suffk.....65 K6
Little Whittington Nthumb.....112 E7
Littlewick Green W & M.....35 M9
Little Wilbraham Cambs.....62 H9
Littlewindsor Dorset.....11 J4
Little Witcombe Gloucs.....46 H11
Little Witley Worcs.....46 E2
Little Wittenham Oxon.....34 G6
Little Wolford Warwks.....47 Q7
Littlewood Staffs.....58 E3
Little Woodcote Gt Lon.....36 G8
Littleworth Bucks.....49 N10
Littleworth Oxon.....34 B5
Littleworth Staffs.....58 F2
Littleworth Staffs.....70 G10
Littleworth W Susx.....24 E6
Littleworth Worcs.....46 G4
Littleworth Worcs.....47 J2
Littleworth Common Bucks.....35 P7
Little Wratting Suffk.....63 L11
Little Wymington Bed.....61 L8
Little Wymondley Herts.....50 F5
Little Wyrley Staffs.....58 F3
Little Wytheford Shrops.....69 Q11
Little Yeldham Essex.....52 C4
Littley Green Essex.....51 Q7
Litton Derbys.....83 Q9
Litton N York.....96 D6
Litton Somset.....19 Q4
Litton Cheney Dorset.....11 L6
Liurbost W Isls.....168 i5
Liverpool Lpool.....81 L6
Liverpool Maritime Mercantile City Lpool.....81 L7
Liversedge Kirk.....90 F6
Liverton Devon.....9 K9
Liverton R & Cl.....105 K7
Liverton Mines R & Cl.....105 K7
Liverton Street Kent.....38 E11
Livingston W Loth.....127 K4
Livingston Village W Loth.....127 K4
Lixwm Flints.....80 H10
Lizard Cnwll.....3 J11
Llaingoch IoA.....78 C8
Llaithddu Powys.....55 P8
Llan Powys.....55 K4
Llanaber Gwynd.....67 L11
Llanaelhaearn Gwynd.....66 F6
Llanafan Cerdgn.....54 F10
Llanafan-Fawr Powys.....44 D3
Llanallgo IoA.....79 J7
Llanarmon Gwynd.....66 G7
Llanarmon Dyffryn Ceiriog Wrexhm.....68 G8
Llanarmon-yn-Ial Denbgs.....68 G3
Llanarth Cerdgn.....42 H3
Llanarth Mons.....31 L2
Llanarthne Carmth.....43 K11
Llanasa Flints.....80 G8
Llanbabo IoA.....78 F7
Llanbadarn Fawr Cerdgn.....54 E8
Llanbadarn Fynydd Powys.....55 P9
Llanbadarn-y-garreg Powys.....44 G5
Llanbadoc Mons.....31 L5
Llanbadrig IoA.....78 F6
Llanbeder Newpt.....31 L6
Llanbedr Gwynd.....67 K9
Llanbedr Powys.....44 G5
Llanbedr Powys.....45 J10
Llanbedr-Dyffryn-Clwyd Denbgs.....68 F3
Llanbedrgoch IoA.....79 J8
Llanbedrog Gwynd.....66 E8
Llanbedr-y-Cennin Conwy.....79 P11
Llanberis Gwynd.....67 K2
Llanbethèry V Glam.....30 D11
Llanbister Powys.....55 Q10
Llanblethian V Glam.....30 C10
Llanboidy Carmth.....41 P6
Llanbradach Caerph.....30 F6
Llanbrynmair Powys.....55 K4
Llancadle V Glam.....30 D11
Llancarfan V Glam.....30 D10
Llancayo Mons.....31 L4
Llancloudy Herefs.....45 P10
Llancynfelyn Cerdgn.....54 E6
Llandaff Cardif.....30 G9
Llandanwg Gwynd.....67 K9
Llandarcy Neath.....29 K5
Llandawke Carmth.....41 Q8
Llanddaniel Fab IoA.....78 H10
Llanddarog Carmth.....43 K11
Llanddeiniol Cerdgn.....54 D10
Llanddeiniolen Gwynd.....79 J11
Llandderfel Gwynd.....68 C7
Llanddeusant Carmth.....43 Q10
Llanddeusant IoA.....78 E7
Llanddew Powys.....44 F8
Llanddewi Swans.....28 E7
Llanddewi Brefi Cerdgn.....43 N3
Llanddewi'r Cwm Powys.....44 E5
Llanddewi Rhydderch Mons.....31 L2
Llanddewi Velfrey Pembks.....41 M7
Llanddewi Ystradenni Powys.....55 Q10
Llanddoged Conwy.....67 Q2
Llanddona IoA.....79 K9
Llanddowror Carmth.....41 Q8
Llanddulas Conwy.....80 C9
Llanddwywe Gwynd.....67 K10
Llanddyfnan IoA.....79 J9
Llandecwyn Gwynd.....67 L7
Llandefaelog Powys.....44 E8
Llandefaelog-Tre'r-Graig Powys.....44 G9
Llandefalle Powys.....44 G7
Llandegfan IoA.....79 K10
Llandegla Denbgs.....68 G4
Llandegley Powys.....44 G2
Llandegveth Mons.....31 K5
Llandegwning Gwynd.....66 D9
Llandeilo Carmth.....43 M10
Llandeilo Graban Powys.....44 F6

Llandeilo'r Fan Powys.....44 B8
Llandeloy Pembks.....40 G5
Llandenny Mons.....31 M4
Llandevaud Newpt.....31 M6
Llandevenny Mons.....31 M7
Llandinabo Herefs.....45 Q9
Llandinam Powys.....55 N7
Llandissilio Pembks.....41 M6
Llandogo Mons.....31 P4
Llandough V Glam.....30 C10
Llandough V Glam.....30 G10
Llandovery Carmth.....43 Q8
Llandow V Glam.....29 P10
Llandre Carmth.....43 N6
Llandre Cerdgn.....54 E7
Llandre Isaf Pembks.....41 M5
Llandrillo Denbgs.....68 D7
Llandrillo-yn-Rhos Conwy.....79 Q8
Llandrindod Wells Powys.....44 F2
Llandrinio Powys.....69 J11
Llandudno Conwy.....79 P8
Llandudno Junction Conwy.....79 P9
Llandulas Powys.....44 B6
Llandwrog Gwynd.....66 H3
Llandybie Carmth.....43 M10
Llandyfaelog Carmth.....28 D2
Llandyfan Carmth.....43 M10
Llandyfriog Cerdgn.....42 F6
Llandyfrydog IoA.....78 G7
Llandygai Gwynd.....79 K10
Llandygwydd Cerdgn.....41 P2
Llandynan Denbgs.....68 G5
Llandyrnog Denbgs.....80 G11
Llandyssil Powys.....56 B5
Llandysul Cerdgn.....42 H6
Llanedeyrn Cardif.....30 H8
Llanedi Carmth.....28 G3
Llaneglwys Powys.....44 F7
Llanegryn Gwynd.....54 E3
Llanegwad Carmth.....43 K10
Llaneilian IoA.....78 H6
Llanelian-yn-Rhôs Conwy.....80 B9
Llanelidan Denbgs.....68 F4
Llanelieu Powys.....44 H8
Llanellen Mons.....31 K2
Llanelli Carmth.....28 F4
Llanelltyd Gwynd.....67 M11
Llanelly Mons.....30 H2
Llanelly Hill Mons.....30 H2
Llanelwedd Powys.....44 E4
Llanenddwyn Gwynd.....67 K10
Llanengan Gwynd.....66 D9
Llanerch Gwynd.....68 A11
Llanerch Powys.....56 E6
Llanerchymedd IoA.....78 G8
Llanerfyl Powys.....55 N3
Llanfabon Caerph.....30 F6
Llanfachraeth IoA.....78 E8
Llanfachreth Gwynd.....67 P10
Llanfaelog IoA.....78 E10
Llanfaelrhys Gwynd.....66 C9
Llanfaenor Mons.....45 N11
Llanfaes IoA.....79 L9
Llanfaes Powys.....44 E9
Llanfaethlu IoA.....78 E7
Llanfair Gwynd.....67 K9
Llanfair Caereinion Powys.....55 Q3
Llanfair Clydogau Cerdgn.....43 M4
Llanfair Dyffryn Clwyd Denbgs.....68 F3
Llanfairfechan Conwy.....79 M10
Llanfair Kilgeddin Mons.....31 L3
Llanfair-Nant-Gwyn Pembks.....41 N3
Llanfairpwllgwyngyll IoA.....79 J10
Llanfair Talhaiarn Conwy.....80 C10
Llanfair Waterdine Shrops.....56 C9
Llanfairynghornwy IoA.....78 E6
Llanfair-yn-Neubwll IoA.....78 E9
Llanfallteg Carmth.....41 N6
Llanfallteg West Carmth.....41 M7
Llanfarian Cerdgn.....54 D9
Llanfechain Powys.....68 G10
Llanfechan Powys.....44 D4
Llanfechell IoA.....78 F6
Llanferres Denbgs.....68 G2
Llan Ffestiniog Gwynd.....67 N6
Llanfflewyn IoA.....78 F7
Llanfigael IoA.....78 E8
Llanfihangel-ar-arth Carmth.....43 J7
Llanfihangel Glyn Myfyr Conwy.....68 C5
Llanfihangel Nant Bran Powys.....44 C8
Llanfihangel-nant-Melan Powys.....44 H3
Llanfihangel Rhydithon Powys.....56 B11
Llanfihangel Rogiet Mons.....31 N7
Llanfihangel Tal-y-llyn Powys.....44 G9
Llanfihangel-uwch-Gwili Carmth.....43 J10
Llanfihangel-y-Creuddyn Cerdgn.....54 F9
Llanfihangel-yng-Ngwynfa Powys.....68 E11
Llanfihangel yn Nhowyn IoA.....78 E9
Llanfihangel-y-pennant Gwynd.....54 F3
Llanfihangel-y-pennant Gwynd.....67 J6
Llanfilo Powys.....44 G8
Llanfoist Mons.....31 J2
Llanfor Gwynd.....68 B7
Llanfrechfa Torfn.....31 K6
Llanfrothen Gwynd.....67 L6
Llanfrynach Powys.....44 F9
Llanfwrog Denbgs.....68 F3
Llanfwrog IoA.....78 E8
Llanfyllin Powys.....68 F11
Llanfynydd Carmth.....43 L9
Llanfynydd Flints.....69 J3
Llanfyrnach Pembks.....41 P4
Llangadfan Powys.....55 N2
Llangadog Carmth.....28 D3
Llangadog Carmth.....43 P9
Llangadwaladr IoA.....78 F11
Llangadwaladr Powys.....68 G8
Llangaffo IoA.....78 G11
Llangain Carmth.....42 G11
Llangammarch Wells Powys.....44 C5
Llangan V Glam.....30 C9
Llangarron Herefs.....45 Q10
Llangasty-Talyllyn Powys.....44 G9

Llangathen Carmth.....43 L10
Llangattock Powys.....45 J11
Llangattock Lingoed Mons.....45 M10
Llangattock-Vibon-Avel Mons.....45 P11
Llangedwyn Powys.....68 G10
Llangefni IoA.....78 H9
Llangeinor Brdgnd.....29 P7
Llangeitho Cerdgn.....43 M3
Llangeler Carmth.....42 G7
Llangelynin Gwynd.....54 D3
Llangennech Carmth.....28 G4
Llangennith Swans.....28 D6
Llangenny Powys.....45 J11
Llangernyw Conwy.....80 B11
Llangian Gwynd.....66 D9
Llangiwg Neath.....29 K3
Llangloffan Pembks.....40 H4
Llanglydwen Carmth.....41 N5
Llangoed IoA.....79 L9
Llangoedmor Cerdgn.....42 D5
Llangollen Denbgs.....68 H6
Llangolman Pembks.....41 M5
Llangors Powys.....44 G9
Llangorwen Cerdgn.....54 E8
Llangovan Mons.....31 N3
Llangower Gwynd.....68 B8
Llangrannog Cerdgn.....42 F4
Llangristiolus IoA.....78 G10
Llangrove Herefs.....45 Q11
Llangua Mons.....45 M9
Llangunllo Powys.....56 C10
Llangunnor Carmth.....42 H10
Llangurig Powys.....55 L9
Llangwm Conwy.....68 C6
Llangwm Mons.....31 M5
Llangwm Pembks.....41 J9
Llangwnnadl Gwynd.....66 C8
Llangwyfan Denbgs.....80 G11
Llangwyllog IoA.....78 G9
Llangwyryfon Cerdgn.....54 D10
Llangybi Cerdgn.....43 M4
Llangybi Gwynd.....66 G6
Llangybi Mons.....31 L5
Llangyfelach Swans.....28 F5
Llangyndeyrn Carmth.....28 E2
Llangynhafal Denbgs.....68 F2
Llangynidr Powys.....44 H11
Llangynin Carmth.....41 Q7
Llangynllo Cerdgn.....42 G6
Llangynog Carmth.....28 B2
Llangynog Powys.....68 E9
Llangynwyd Brdgnd.....29 N7
Llanhamlach Powys.....44 F9
Llanharan Rhondd.....30 D8
Llanharry Rhondd.....30 D8
Llanhennock Mons.....31 L6
Llanhilleth Blae G.....30 H4
Llanidan IoA.....78 H11
Llanidloes Powys.....55 M8
Llaniestyn Gwynd.....66 D8
Llanigon Powys.....45 J7
Llanilar Cerdgn.....54 E9
Llanilid Rhondd.....30 C8
Llanio Cerdgn.....42 H3
Llanishen Cardif.....30 G8
Llanishen Mons.....31 N4
Llanllechid Gwynd.....79 L11
Llanlleonfel Powys.....44 C4
Llanllowell Mons.....31 L5
Llanllugan Powys.....55 N4
Llanllwch Carmth.....42 G11
Llanllwchaiarn Powys.....55 Q6
Llanllwni Carmth.....43 J7
Llanllyfni Gwynd.....66 H4
Llanmadoc Swans.....28 D6
Llanmaes V Glam.....30 C11
Llanmartin Newpt.....31 L7
Llanmerewig Powys.....56 B6
Llanmihangel V Glam.....30 C10
Llanmiloe Carmth.....41 P9
Llanmorlais Swans.....28 F6
Llannefydd Conwy.....80 D10
Llannon Carmth.....28 F3
Llannor Gwynd.....66 F7
Llanon Cerdgn.....54 C11
Llanover Mons.....31 K3
Llanpumsaint Carmth.....42 H9
Llanrhaeadr-ym-Mochnant Powys.....68 F9
Llanrhian Pembks.....40 F4
Llanrhidian Swans.....28 E6
Llanrhos Conwy.....79 P8
Llanrhychwyn Conwy.....67 P2
Llanrhyddlad IoA.....78 E7
Llanrhystud Cerdgn.....54 C11
Llanrothal Herefs.....45 P11
Llanrug Gwynd.....67 J2
Llanrumney Cardif.....30 H8
Llanrwst Conwy.....67 Q2
Llansadurnen Carmth.....41 N8
Llansadwrn Carmth.....43 N8
Llansadwrn IoA.....79 K9
Llansaint Carmth.....28 C3
Llansamlet Swans.....28 J5
Llansanffraid Glan Conwy Conwy.....79 Q9
Llansannan Conwy.....80 C11
Llansannor V Glam.....30 C9
Llansantffraed Powys.....44 G10
Llansantffraed-Cwmdeuddwr Powys.....55 M11
Llansantffraed-in-Elvel Powys.....44 F4
Llansantffraid Cerdgn.....54 C11
Llansantffraid-ym-Mechain Powys.....68 H10
Llansawel Carmth.....43 M7
Llansilin Powys.....68 H9
Llansoy Mons.....31 M4
Llanspyddid Powys.....44 E9
Llanstadwell Pembks.....40 H10
Llansteffan Carmth.....28 C2
Llanstephan Powys.....44 G6
Llantarnam Torfn.....31 K6
Llanteg Pembks.....41 N8
Llanthewy Skirrid Mons.....31 L11
Llanthony Mons.....45 K9
Llantilio-Crossenny Mons.....45 L2
Llantilio Pertholey Mons.....45 L11
Llantood Pembks.....41 N2
Llantrisant IoA.....78 F8
Llantrisant Mons.....31 L5
Llantrisant Rhondd.....30 D8
Llantrithyd V Glam.....30 D10

Place	County	Page	Grid
Llantwit Fardre	Rhondd	30	E7
Llantwit Major	V Glam	30	C11
Llantysilio	Denbgs	68	G6
Llanuwchllyn	Gwynd	68	A8
Llanvaches	Newpt	31	M6
Llanvair Discoed	Mons	31	M6
Llanvapley	Mons	31	L2
Llanvetherine	Mons	45	M11
Llanveynoe	Herefs	45	L8
Llanvihangel Crucorney	Mons	45	L10
Llanvihangel Gobion	Mons	31	K3
Llanvihangel-Ystern-Llewern	Mons	31	M2
Llanwarne	Herefs	45	Q9
Llanwddyn	Powys	68	D11
Llanwenarth	Mons	31	J2
Llanwenog	Cerdgn	43	J5
Llanwern	Newpt	31	L7
Llanwinio	Carmth	41	Q5
Llanwnda	Gwynd	66	H3
Llanwnda	Pembks	40	H3
Llanwnnen	Cerdgn	43	K5
Llanwnog	Powys	55	N6
Llanwonno	Rhondd	30	D5
Llanwrda	Carmth	43	P8
Llanwrin	Powys	54	H4
Llanwrthwl	Powys	44	D2
Llanwrtyd	Powys	44	B5
Llanwrtyd Wells	Powys	44	B5
Llanwyddelan	Powys	55	P4
Llanyblodwel	Shrops	68	H10
Llanybri	Carmth	28	B2
Llanybydder	Carmth	43	K6
Llanycefn	Pembks	41	L6
Llanychaer	Pembks	41	J3
Llanycil	Gwynd	68	B8
Llanycrwys	Carmth	43	M5
Llanymawddwy	Gwynd	68	B11
Llanymynech	Powys	69	J10
Llanynghenedl	IoA	78	E8
Llanynys	Denbgs	68	F2
Llan-y-pwll	Wrexhm	69	L4
Llanyre	Powys	44	E2
Llanystumdwy	Gwynd	66	H7
Llanywern	Powys	44	G9
Llawhaden	Pembks	41	L7
Llawnt	Shrops	68	H8
Llawryglyn	Powys	55	L6
Llay	Wrexhm	69	K3
Llechfaen	Powys	44	F9
Llechrhyd	Caerph	30	F3
Llechryd	Cerdgn	41	P2
Llechylched	IoA	78	E9
Lledrod	Cerdgn	54	E10
Lleyn Peninsula	Gwynd	66	E7
Llidiardau	Gwynd	68	A7
Llidiartnenog	Carmth	43	K7
Llidiart-y-parc	Denbgs	68	F6
Llithfaen	Gwynd	66	F6
Lloc	Flints	80	G9
Llowes	Powys	44	H6
Llwydcoed	Rhondd	30	C4
Llwydiarth	Powys	68	D11
Llwyn	Denbgs	68	E2
Llwyncelyn	Cerdgn	42	H3
Llwyndafydd	Cerdgn	42	G3
Llwynderw	Powys	56	C4
Llwyn-drain	Pembks	41	Q4
Llwyn-du	Mons	45	K11
Llwyndyrys	Gwynd	66	F6
Llwyngwril	Gwynd	54	D3
Llwynhendy	Carmth	28	F5
Llwynmawr	Wrexhm	68	H7
Llwyn-on	Myr Td	30	D2
Llwyn-y-brain	Carmth	41	N8
Llwyn-y-groes	Cerdgn	43	L3
Llwynypia	Rhondd	30	C6
Llynclys	Shrops	69	J10
Llynfaes	IoA	78	G9
Llyn-y-pandy	Flints	81	J11
Llysfaen	Conwy	80	B9
Llyswen	Cerdgn	43	J2
Llyswen	Powys	44	G7
Llysworney	V Glam	30	C10
Llys-y-frân	Pembks	41	K6
Llywel	Powys	44	B8
Load Brook	Sheff	84	C3
Loan	Falk	126	H2
Loanend	Nthumb	129	N9
Loanhead	Mdloth	127	P4
Loaningfoot	D & G	109	L9
Loans	S Ayrs	125	J11
Lobb	Devon	16	H4
Lobhillcross	Devon	8	C7
Lochailort	Highld	145	N11
Lochaline	Highld	138	B9
Lochans	D & G	106	E6
Locharbriggs	D & G	109	L4
Lochavich	Ag & B	131	J4
Lochawe	Ag & B	131	N2
Loch Baghasdail	W Isls	168	c16
Lochboisdale	W Isls	168	c16
Lochbuie	Ag & B	137	Q10
Lochcarron	Highld	154	A10
Lochdon	Ag & B	138	C11
Lochdonhead	Ag & B	138	C11
Lochead	Ag & B	123	N4
Lochearnhead	Stirlg	132	H3
Lochee	C Dund	142	F11
Loch Eil	Highld	139	K2
Locheilside Station	Highld	138	H2
Lochend	Highld	155	Q10
Lochfoot	D & G	109	J6
Lochgair	Ag & B	131	J9
Lochgelly	Fife	134	F9
Lochgilphead	Ag & B	130	H10
Lochgoilhead	Ag & B	131	Q7
Lochieheads	Fife	134	H5
Lochill	Moray	157	P5
Lochindorb Lodge	Highld	156	H10
Lochinver	Highld	160	H2
Loch Lomond and The Trossachs National Park		132	E5
Loch Loyal Lodge	Highld	165	P7
Lochluichart	Highld	155	K5
Lochmaben	D & G	109	N4
Lochmaddy	W Isls	168	e11
Loch nam Madadh	W Isls	168	e11
Loch Ness	Highld	147	N2
Lochore	Fife	134	F8
Loch Portain	W Isls	168	e10

Place	County	Page	Grid
Lochportain	W Isls	168	e10
Lochranza	N Ayrs	124	A7
Loch Sgioport	W Isls	168	d14
Lochside	Abers	143	N5
Lochside	D & G	109	L5
Lochside	Highld	156	E7
Lochskipport	W Isls	168	d14
Lochslin	Highld	163	J10
Lochton	S Ayrs	107	J2
Lochty	Angus	143	J5
Lochty	Fife	135	N6
Lochuisge	Highld	138	D6
Lochwinnoch	Rens	125	K6
Lochwood	D & G	116	F11
Lockengate	Cnwll	4	G9
Lockerbie	D & G	109	P4
Lockeridge	Wilts	33	M11
Lockerley	Hants	22	B9
Locking	N Som	19	L3
Locking Stumps	Warrtn	82	D6
Lockington	E R Yk	99	K11
Lockington	Leics	72	D5
Locklewood	Shrops	70	B9
Locksbottom	Gt Lon	37	K7
Locksgreen	IoW	14	D8
Locks Heath	Hants	14	F5
Lockton	N York	98	G3
Loddington	Leics	73	K10
Loddington	Nhants	60	H5
Loddiswell	Devon	7	J9
Loddon	Norfk	65	M2
Lode	Cambs	62	H8
Lode Heath	Solhll	59	J8
Loders	Dorset	11	K6
Lodsworth	W Susx	23	P10
Lofthouse	Leeds	91	J5
Lofthouse	N York	96	H6
Lofthouse Gate	Wakefd	91	J6
Loftus	R & Cl	105	K7
Logan	E Ayrs	115	L3
Loganbeck	Cumb	94	D2
Loganlea	W Loth	126	H5
Loggerheads	Staffs	70	C7
Logie	Angus	143	M5
Logie	Fife	135	L3
Logie	Moray	157	J7
Logie Coldstone	Abers	150	C7
Logie Newton	Abers	158	G10
Logie Pert	Angus	143	M5
Logierait	P & K	141	N7
Logierieve	Abers	151	N2
Login	Carmth	41	N6
Lolworth	Cambs	62	E8
Lonbain	Highld	153	M7
Londesborough	E R Yk	98	H11
London	Gt Lon	36	H4
London Apprentice	Cnwll	3	Q4
London Beach	Kent	26	E4
London City Airport	Gt Lon	37	K4
London Colney	Herts	50	E10
Londonderry	N York	97	M3
London End	Nhants	61	K7
London Gateway Services	Gt Lon	36	E2
London Gatwick Airport	W Susx	24	G2
London Heathrow Airport	Gt Lon	36	C5
London Luton Airport	Luton	50	D6
London Oxford Airport	Oxon	48	E11
London Southend Airport	Essex	38	E4
London Stansted Airport	Essex	51	N6
Londonthorpe	Lincs	73	P3
London Zoo ZSL	Gt Lon	36	G4
Londubh	Highld	160	D10
Lonemore	Highld	153	P2
Long Ashton	N Som	31	P10
Long Bank	Worcs	57	P10
Long Bennington	Lincs	73	L2
Longbenton	N Tyne	113	L7
Longborough	Gloucs	47	N9
Long Bredy	Dorset	11	M6
Longbridge	Birm	58	F9
Longbridge	Warwks	47	Q2
Longbridge Deverill	Wilts	20	G6
Long Buckby	Nhants	60	D7
Longburgh	Cumb	110	F9
Longburton	Dorset	11	N2
Long Cause	Devon	7	K6
Long Clawson	Leics	73	J5
Longcliffe	Derbys	84	B9
Longcombe	Devon	7	L7
Long Common	Hants	14	F4
Long Compton	Staffs	70	F10
Long Compton	Warwks	47	Q8
Longcot	Oxon	33	Q6
Long Crendon	Bucks	35	J3
Long Crichel	Dorset	12	G2
Longcroft	Cumb	110	D9
Longcross	Surrey	35	Q11
Longden	Shrops	56	H3
Longden Common	Shrops	56	H3
Long Ditton	Surrey	36	E7
Longdon	Staffs	58	G2
Longdon	Worcs	46	F7
Longdon Green	Staffs	58	G2
Longdon Heath	Worcs	46	F7
Longdon upon Tern	Wrekin	69	R11
Longdown	Devon	9	L6
Longdowns	Cnwll	3	J7
Long Drax	N York	92	A5
Long Duckmanton	Derbys	84	F6
Long Eaton	Derbys	72	D4
Longfield	Kent	37	P7
Longford	Covtry	59	N8
Longford	Derbys	71	N7
Longford	Gloucs	46	F10
Longford	Gt Lon	36	C5
Longford	Kent	37	M9
Longford	Shrops	70	A8
Longford	Wrekin	70	C11
Longforgan	P & K	134	H2
Longformacus	Border	128	H8
Longframlington	Nthumb	119	M10
Long Green	Ches W	81	P10
Long Green	Worcs	46	F8
Longham	Dorset	13	J5
Longham	Norfk	76	C8
Long Hanborough	Oxon	34	D2
Longhaven	Abers	159	R10
Long Hedges	Lincs	87	L11
Longhirst	Nthumb	113	K3
Longhope	Gloucs	46	C11

Place	County	Page	Grid
Longhope	Ork	169	c7
Longhorsley	Nthumb	112	H2
Longhoughton	Nthumb	119	P7
Long Itchington	Warwks	59	P11
Longlands	Cumb	101	J3
Longlane	Derbys	71	N7
Long Lawford	Warwks	59	Q7
Longleat Safari & Adventure Park	Wilts	20	F6
Longlevens	Gloucs	46	G11
Longley	Calder	90	D6
Longley	Kirk	90	E9
Longley Green	Worcs	46	D4
Longleys	P & K	142	D9
Long Load	Somset	19	N10
Longmanhill	Abers	158	H5
Long Marston	Herts	49	N11
Long Marston	N York	97	R10
Long Marston	Warwks	47	N5
Long Marton	Cumb	102	C6
Long Meadowend	Shrops	56	G8
Long Melford	Suffk	52	E2
Longmoor Camp	Hants	23	L8
Longmorn	Moray	157	N6
Longmoss	Ches E	83	J10
Long Newnton	Gloucs	32	H6
Longnewton	Border	118	A5
Long Newton	E Loth	128	E7
Longnewton	S on T	104	C7
Longney	Gloucs	32	E2
Longniddry	E Loth	128	C4
Longnor	Shrops	56	H4
Longnor	Staffs	71	K2
Longparish	Hants	22	D5
Longpark	Cumb	110	H8
Long Preston	N York	96	B9
Longridge	Lancs	89	J3
Longridge	Staffs	70	G11
Longridge	W Loth	126	G5
Longriggend	N Lans	126	E3
Long Riston	E R Yk	93	K2
Longrock	Cnwll	2	D7
Longsdon	Staffs	70	H4
Longshaw	Wigan	82	B4
Longside	Abers	159	P8
Long Sight	Oldham	89	Q9
Longslow	Shrops	70	B7
Longstanton	Cambs	62	E7
Longstock	Hants	22	C7
Longstone	Pembks	41	M9
Longstowe	Cambs	62	D10
Long Stratton	Norfk	64	H3
Long Street	M Keyn	49	L5
Longstreet	Wilts	21	M4
Long Sutton	Hants	23	K5
Long Sutton	Lincs	74	H6
Long Sutton	Somset	19	N9
Longthorpe	C Pete	74	C11
Long Thurlow	Suffk	64	E8
Longthwaite	Cumb	101	M6
Longton	C Stke	70	G6
Longton	Lancs	88	F5
Longtown	Cumb	110	G7
Longtown	Herefs	45	L9
Longueville	Jersey	11	c2
Longville in the Dale	Shrops	57	J6
Long Waste	Wrekin	69	R11
Long Whatton	Leics	72	D6
Longwick	Bucks	35	L3
Long Wittenham	Oxon	34	F6
Longwitton	Nthumb	112	G3
Longwood	D & G	108	F8
Longwood	Shrops	57	L3
Longworth	Oxon	34	C5
Longyester	E Loth	128	E7
Lôn-las	Swans	29	K5
Lonmay	Abers	159	P6
Lonmore	Highld	152	D8
Looe	Cnwll	5	M11
Loose	Kent	38	C11
Loosebeare	Devon	8	H3
Loosegate	Lincs	74	F5
Loosley Row	Bucks	35	M4
Lootcherbrae	Abers	158	F7
Lopcombe Corner	Wilts	21	Q7
Lopen	Somset	11	J2
Loppington	Shrops	69	N9
Lorbottle	Nthumb	119	K9
Lordington	W Susx	15	L5
Lordsbridge	Norfk	75	L8
Lordshill	C Sotn	22	C11
Lords Wood	Medway	38	C9
Lornty	P & K	142	B8
Loscoe	Derbys	84	F11
Loscombe	Dorset	11	K5
Losgaintir	W Isls	168	f8
Lossiemouth	Moray	157	N3
Lostford	Shrops	69	R8
Lostock Gralam	Ches W	82	E10
Lostock Green	Ches W	82	E10
Lostock Hall	Lancs	88	G5
Lostock Hall Fold	Bolton	89	K9
Lostock Junction	Bolton	89	K9
Lostwithiel	Cnwll	5	J10
Lothbeg	Highld	163	L4
Lothersdale	N York	96	E11
Lothmore	Highld	163	M4
Loudwater	Bucks	35	P6
Loughborough	Leics	72	E7
Loughor	Swans	28	G5
Loughton	Essex	51	K11
Loughton	M Keyn	49	M7
Loughton	Shrops	57	L8
Lound	Lincs	73	R7
Lound	Notts	85	L3
Lound	Suffk	65	Q2
Lounston	Devon	9	J9
Lount	Leics	72	B7
Louth	Lincs	87	K3
Loveclough	Lancs	89	N5
Lovedean	Hants	15	J4
Lover	Wilts	21	P10
Loversall	Donc	91	P11
Loves Green	Essex	51	P10
Lovesome Hill	N York	104	C11
Loveston	Pembks	41	L9
Lovington	Somset	19	Q8
Low Ackworth	Wakefd	91	M7
Low Angerton	Nthumb	112	G4
Lowbands	Gloucs	46	E8
Low Barbeth	D & G	106	D4
Low Bell End	N York	105	K11
Low Bentham	N York	95	N7
Low Biggins	Cumb	95	N5
Low Borrowbridge	Cumb	102	B10

Place	County	Page	Grid
Low Bradfield	Sheff	84	C2
Low Bradley	N York	96	F11
Low Braithwaite	Cumb	101	M2
Low Burnham	N Linc	92	C10
Low Buston	Nthumb	119	P8
Lowca	Cumb	100	C6
Low Catton	E R Yk	98	E10
Low Coniscliffe	Darltn	103	Q8
Low Crosby	Cumb	110	H9
Lowdham	Notts	85	L11
Low Dinsdale	Darltn	104	B8
Lowe	Shrops	69	N8
Lowe Hill	Staffs	70	H3
Low Ellington	N York	97	K4
Lower Aisholt	Somset	18	H7
Lower Ansty	Dorset	12	C4
Lower Apperley	Gloucs	46	G9
Lower Arboll	Highld	163	K10
Lower Arncott	Oxon	48	H11
Lower Ashton	Devon	9	K8
Lower Assendon	Oxon	35	K8
Lower Badcall	Highld	164	C8
Lower Ballam	Lancs	88	D4
Lower Bartle	Lancs	88	F4
Lower Basildon	W Berk	34	H9
Lower Bearwood	Herefs	45	M3
Lower Beeding	W Susx	24	F5
Lower Benefield	Nhants	61	L3
Lower Bentley	Worcs	58	E11
Lower Beobridge	Shrops	57	P6
Lower Birchwood	Derbys	84	F10
Lower Boddington	Nhants	48	E4
Lower Boscaswell	Cnwll	2	B7
Lower Bourne	Surrey	23	M6
Lower Brailes	Warwks	48	B7
Lower Breakish	Highld	145	L3
Lower Bredbury	Stockp	83	K6
Lower Broadheath	Worcs	46	F3
Lower Broxwood	Herefs	45	M4
Lower Buckenhill	Herefs	46	B8
Lower Bullingham	Herefs	45	Q7
Lower Burgate	Hants	21	N11
Lower Burrowton	Devon	9	P5
Lower Burton	Herefs	45	N3
Lower Caldecote	C Beds	61	Q11
Lower Cam	Gloucs	32	D4
Lower Canada	N Som	19	L3
Lower Catesby	Nhants	60	B9
Lower Chapel	Powys	44	E7
Lower Chicksgrove	Wilts	21	J9
Lower Chute	Wilts	22	B4
Lower Clapton	Gt Lon	36	H3
Lower Clent	Worcs	58	D9
Lower Common	Hants	23	L2
Lower Compton	Wilts	33	K10
Lower Creedy	Devon	9	K4
Lower Crossings	Derbys	83	M8
Lower Cumberworth	Kirk	90	G9
Lower Darwen	Bl w D	89	K5
Lower Dean	Bed	61	N7
Lower Denby	Kirk	90	G9
Lower Diabaig	Highld	153	P5
Lower Dicker	E Susx	25	N8
Lower Dinchope	Shrops	56	H8
Lower Down	Shrops	56	E8
Lower Dunsforth	N York	97	P8
Lower Egleton	Herefs	46	B5
Lower Elkstone	Staffs	71	K3
Lower Ellastone	Staffs	71	L6
Lower End	Bucks	35	J3
Lower End	M Keyn	49	P7
Lower End	Nhants	60	H9
Lower End	Nhants	61	J8
Lower Everleigh	Wilts	21	N4
Lower Exbury	Hants	14	D7
Lower Eythorne	Kent	27	N2
Lower Failand	N Som	31	P10
Lower Farringdon	Hants	23	K7
Lower Feltham	Gt Lon	36	C6
Lower Fittleworth	W Susx	24	B7
Lower Foxdale	IoM	80	c6
Lower Frankton	Shrops	69	L8
Lower Freystrop	Pembks	41	J8
Lower Froyle	Hants	23	L6
Lower Gabwell	Devon	7	N5
Lower Gledfield	Highld	162	D8
Lower Godney	Somset	19	N6
Lower Gornal	Dudley	58	D6
Lower Gravenhurst	C Beds	50	D3
Lower Green	Herts	50	E4
Lower Green	Herts	51	K4
Lower Green	Kent	25	N2
Lower Green	Kent	25	P2
Lower Green	Norfk	76	D4
Lower Green	Staffs	58	D3
Lower Green	Suffk	63	M7
Lower Hacheston	Suffk	65	L10
Lower Halstock Leigh	Dorset	11	L3
Lower Halstow	Kent	38	E8
Lower Hamworthy	BCP	12	G6
Lower Hardres	Kent	39	L11
Lower Harpton	Herefs	45	K2
Lower Hartlip	Kent	38	D9
Lower Hartshay	Derbys	84	E10
Lower Hartwell	Bucks	35	L2
Lower Hatton	Staffs	70	E7
Lower Hawthwaite	Cumb	94	E3
Lower Haysden	Kent	37	N11
Lower Hergest	Herefs	45	K4
Lower Heyford	Oxon	48	E10
Lower Heysham	Lancs	95	J8
Lower Higham	Kent	38	B7
Lower Holbrook	Suffk	53	L4
Lower Hordley	Shrops	69	L9
Lower Horncroft	W Susx	24	B7
Lowerhouse	Lancs	89	N4
Lower Houses	Kirk	90	F7
Lower Howsell	Worcs	46	E5
Lower Irlam	Salfd	82	F6
Lower Kilburn	Derbys	72	B2
Lower Kilcott	Gloucs	32	E5
Lower Killeyan	Ag & B	122	C11
Lower Kingcombe	Dorset	11	M5
Lower Kingswood	Surrey	36	F10
Lower Kinnerton	Ches W	69	K2
Lower Langford	N Som	19	N2
Lower Largo	Fife	135	L7
Lower Leigh	Staffs	71	J7
Lower Lemington	Gloucs	47	P8
Lower Llanfadog	Powys	55	M11
Lower Lovacott	Devon	17	J6
Lower Loxhore	Devon	17	L4
Lower Lydbrook	Gloucs	46	A11
Lower Lye	Herefs	56	G11
Lower Machen	Newpt	30	H7

Place	County	Page	Grid
Lower Maes-coed	Herefs	45	L8
Lower Mannington	Dorset	13	J4
Lower Marston	Somset	20	E6
Lower Meend	Gloucs	31	Q4
Lower Merridge	Somset	18	H8
Lower Middleton Cheney	Nhants	48	F6
Lower Milton	Somset	19	P5
Lower Moor	Worcs	47	J5
Lower Morton	S Glos	32	B6
Lower Nazeing	Essex	51	J9
Lower Norton	Warwks	47	P2
Lower Nyland	Dorset	20	E10
Lower Oddington	Gloucs	47	P9
Lower Penarth	V Glam	30	G11
Lower Penn	Staffs	58	C5
Lower Pennington	Hants	13	P6
Lower Penwortham	Lancs	88	G5
Lower Peover	Ches E	82	F10
Lower Place	Rochdl	89	Q8
Lower Pollicott	Bucks	35	K2
Lower Quinton	Warwks	47	N5
Lower Rainham	Medway	38	D8
Lower Raydon	Suffk	52	H4
Lower Roadwater	Somset	18	D7
Lower Salter	Lancs	95	N8
Lower Seagry	Wilts	33	J8
Lower Sheering	Essex	51	L8
Lower Shelton	C Beds	49	Q6
Lower Shiplake	Oxon	35	L9
Lower Shuckburgh	Warwks	48	E2
Lower Slaughter	Gloucs	47	N10
Lower Soothill	Kirk	90	H6
Lower Soudley	Gloucs	32	C3
Lower Standen	Kent	27	M3
Lower Stanton St Quintin	Wilts	32	H8
Lower Stoke	Medway	38	D6
Lower Stondon	C Beds	50	E3
Lower Stone	Gloucs	32	C6
Lower Stonnall	Staffs	58	G4
Lower Stow Bedon	Norfk	64	D3
Lower Street	Dorset	12	D5
Lower Street	E Susx	26	B9
Lower Street	Norfk	77	K4
Lower Street	Suffk	63	N10
Lower Street	Suffk	64	G11
Lower Stretton	Warrtn	82	D8
Lower Stroud	Dorset	11	K5
Lower Sundon	C Beds	50	C5
Lower Swanwick	Hants	14	E5
Lower Swell	Gloucs	47	N9
Lower Tadmarton	Oxon	48	D7
Lower Tale	Devon	9	Q4
Lower Tasburgh	Norfk	64	H2
Lower Tean	Staffs	71	J7
Lower Thurlton	Norfk	65	N2
Lower Town	Cnwll	2	H8
Lower Town	Devon	7	J4
Lower Town	Herefs	46	B6
Lower Town	IoS	2	c1
Lower Town	Pembks	41	J3
Lower Trebullett	Cnwll	5	N8
Lower Treluswell	Cnwll	3	K6
Lower Tysoe	Warwks	48	B5
Lower Ufford	Suffk	65	K11
Lower Upcott	Devon		L8
Lower Upham	Hants	22	F11
Lower Upnor	Medway	38	C7
Lower Vexford	Somset	18	F7
Lower Walton	Warrtn	82	D7
Lower Waterston	Dorset	12	B5
Lower Weare	Somset	19	M4
Lower Weedon	Nhants	60	D9
Lower Welson	Herefs	45	K4
Lower Westmancote	Worcs	46	H7
Lower Whatcombe	Dorset	12	D4
Lower Whatley	Somset	20	D5
Lower Whitley	Ches W	82	D9
Lower Wick	Gloucs	32	D5
Lower Wick	Worcs	46	F4
Lower Wield	Hants	22	H6
Lower Willingdon	E Susx	25	N10
Lower Withington	Ches E	82	H11
Lower Woodend	Bucks	35	M7
Lower Woodford	Wilts	21	M7
Lower Wraxhall	Dorset	11	M4
Lower Wyche	Worcs	46	E6
Lower Wyke	C Brad	90	E5
Lowesby	Leics	73	J9
Lowestoft	Suffk	65	Q3
Loweswater	Cumb	100	F6
Low Fell	Gatesd	113	L9
Lowfield Heath	W Susx	24	G3
Low Gartachorrans	Stirlg	132	F10
Low Gate	Nthumb	112	D8
Low Gettbridge	Cumb	111	K9
Lowgill	Cumb	102	B11
Lowgill	Lancs	95	P8
Low Grantley	N York	97	K6
Low Green	N York	97	K9
Low Habberley	Worcs	57	Q9
Low Ham	Somset	19	M9
Low Harrogate	N York	97	L9
Low Hawsker	N York	105	P9
Low Hesket	Cumb	111	J11
Low Hutton	N York	98	F7
Lowick	Cumb	94	F3
Lowick	Nhants	61	L4
Lowick	Nthumb	119	K3
Lowick Bridge	Cumb	94	F3
Lowick Green	Cumb	94	F3
Low Knipe	Cumb	101	P7
Low Laithe	N York	97	J8
Lowlands	Dur	103	M5
Lowlands	Torfn	31	J5
Low Langton	Lincs	86	G5
Low Leighton	Derbys	83	M7
Low Lorton	Cumb	100	G5
Low Marishes	N York	98	G5
Low Marnham	Notts	85	P7
Low Middleton	Nthumb	119	M3
Low Mill	N York	105	J11
Low Moor	C Brad	90	F5
Low Moorsley	Sundld	113	M11
Low Moresby	Cumb	100	C5
Low Newton	Cumb	95	J4
Low Newton-by-the-Sea	Nthumb	119	P6
Low Pittington	Dur	104	B2
Low Row	Cumb	100	G2
Low Row	Cumb	101	L3
Low Row	Cumb	110	L8
Low Row	N York	103	J11
Low Salchrie	D & G	106	D4
Low Santon	N Linc	92	F8

Lowsonford Warwks	59	J11
Low Street Norfk	77	L7
Low Street Thurr	37	Q5
Low Tharston Norfk	64	H2
Lowther Cumb	101	P6
Lowthorpe E R Yk	99	M8
Lowton Devon	8	G4
Lowton Somset	18	G11
Lowton Wigan	82	D5
Lowton Common Wigan	82	D5
Lowton St Mary's Wigan	82	D5
Low Torry Fife	134	C10
Low Toynton Lincs	87	J6
Low Valley Barns	91	L10
Low Wood Cumb	94	G4
Low Worsall N York	104	C9
Low Wray Cumb	101	L10
Loxbeare Devon	18	B11
Loxhill Surrey	24	B3
Loxhore Devon	17	L4
Loxhore Cott Devon	17	L4
Loxley Warwks	47	Q4
Loxley Green Staffs	71	K8
Loxter Herefs	46	D6
Loxton N Som	19	L3
Loxwood W Susx	24	B4
Lubenham Leics	60	F3
Lucasgate Lincs	87	M11
Lucas Green Surrey	23	P2
Luccombe Somset	18	B6
Luccombe Village IoW	14	G11
Lucker Nthumb	119	N4
Luckett Cnwll	5	P7
Lucking Street Essex	52	D5
Luckington Wilts	32	F8
Lucklawhill Fife	135	L3
Lucknam Wilts	32	F10
Luckwell Bridge Somset	18	B7
Lucton Herefs	45	N2
Lucy Cross N York	103	P8
Ludag W Isls	168	c16
Ludborough Lincs	93	N11
Ludbrook Devon	6	H8
Ludchurch Pembks	41	M8
Luddenden Calder	90	C5
Luddenden Foot Calder	90	C5
Luddenham Court Kent	38	G9
Luddesdown Kent	37	Q7
Luddington N Linc	92	D7
Luddington Warwks	47	N4
Luddington in the Brook Nhants	61	P4
Ludford Lincs	86	G3
Ludford Shrops	57	J10
Ludgershall Bucks	49	J11
Ludgershall Wilts	21	Q4
Ludgvan Cnwll	2	E7
Ludham Norfk	77	M8
Ludlow Shrops	57	J9
Ludney Somset	10	H2
Ludwell Wilts	20	H10
Ludworth Dur	104	C2
Luffenhall Herts	50	G5
Luffincott Devon	5	N3
Luffness E Loth	128	D4
Lugar E Ayrs	115	L3
Luggate Burn E Loth	128	K3
Lugg Green Herefs	45	N2
Luggiebank N Lans	126	D3
Lugton E Ayrs	125	L7
Lugwardine Herefs	45	R6
Luib Highld	145	J2
Luing Ag & B	130	E5
Lulham Herefs	45	N6
Lullington Derbys	59	K2
Lullington E Susx	25	M10
Lullington Somset	20	E4
Lulsgate Bottom N Som	31	P11
Lulsley Worcs	46	D3
Lulworth Camp Dorset	12	D8
Lumb Calder	90	C6
Lumb Lancs	89	N6
Lumbutts Calder	90	B6
Lumby N York	91	M4
Lumphanan Abers	150	F7
Lumphinnans Fife	134	F9
Lumsden Abers	150	D3
Lunan Angus	143	M7
Lunanhead Angus	142	H7
Luncarty P & K	134	D2
Lund E R Yk	99	K11
Lund N York	91	N4
Lundie Angus	142	D10
Lundin Links Fife	135	L7
Lundin Mill Fife	135	L7
Lundy Devon	16	A2
Lundy Green Norfk	65	J3
Lunga Ag & B	130	E6
Lunna Shet	169	r7
Lunsford Kent	37	Q9
Lunsford's Cross E Susx	26	B9
Lunt Sefton	81	L4
Luntley Herefs	45	M3
Luppitt Devon	10	D3
Lupridge Devon	7	J8
Lupset Wakefd	91	J7
Lupton Cumb	95	M4
Lurgashall W Susx	23	P9
Lurley Devon	18	B11
Lusby Lincs	87	K7
Luscombe Devon	7	K7
Luson Devon	6	G8
Luss Ag & B	132	D9
Lussagiven Ag & B	130	C10
Lusta Highld	152	D6
Lustleigh Devon	9	J8
Luston Herefs	45	P2
Luthermuir Abers	143	M4
Luthrie Fife	135	J4
Lutley Dudley	58	D8
Luton Devon	9	M9
Luton Devon	10	B4
Luton Luton	50	C6
Luton Medway	38	C8
Luton Airport Luton	50	D6
Lutterworth Leics	60	B4
Lutton Devon	6	F7
Lutton Devon	6	H6
Lutton Lincs	74	H5
Lutton Nhants	61	P3
Luxborough Somset	18	C7
Luxulyan Cnwll	4	H10
Luxulyan Valley Cnwll	4	H10
Luzley Tamesd	83	L4
Lybster Highld	167	M9

Lydbury North Shrops	56	E7
Lydcott Devon	17	M4
Lydd Kent	26	H7
Lydd Airport Kent	27	J7
Lydden Kent	27	N2
Lydden Kent	39	Q8
Lyddington Rutlnd	73	M11
Lydd-on-Sea Kent	27	J8
Lydeard St Lawrence Somset	18	F8
Lyde Green Hants	23	K3
Lydford Devon	8	D7
Lydford on Fosse Somset	19	Q8
Lydgate Calder	89	Q5
Lydgate Rochdl	90	B7
Lydham Shrops	56	E6
Lydiard Green Wilts	33	L7
Lydiard Millicent Wilts	33	L7
Lydiard Tregoze Swindn	33	M8
Lydiate Sefton	81	M4
Lydiate Ash Worcs	58	E9
Lydlinch Dorset	12	B2
Lydney Gloucs	32	B4
Lydstep Pembks	41	L11
Lye Dudley	58	D8
Lye Cross N Som	19	N2
Lye Green Bucks	35	Q4
Lye Green E Susx	25	M4
Lye Green Warwks	59	J11
Lye Head Worcs	57	P10
Lye's Green Wilts	20	F5
Lyford Oxon	34	C6
Lymbridge Green Kent	27	K3
Lyme Regis Dorset	10	G6
Lyminge Kent	27	L3
Lymington Hants	13	P5
Lyminster W Susx	24	B10
Lymm Warrtn	82	E7
Lymm Services Warrtn	82	E8
Lympne Kent	27	K4
Lympsham Somset	19	K4
Lympstone Devon	9	N8
Lynbridge Devon	17	N2
Lynchat Highld	148	D7
Lynch Green Norfk	76	H10
Lyndhurst Hants	13	P3
Lyndon Rutlnd	73	N10
Lyndon Green Birm	58	H7
Lyne Border	117	J2
Lyne Surrey	36	B7
Lyneal Shrops	69	M8
Lyne Down Herefs	46	B8
Lyneham Devon	9	L9
Lyneham Oxon	47	Q10
Lyneham Wilts	33	K9
Lyneholmford Cumb	111	K6
Lynemouth Nthumb	113	L2
Lyne of Skene Abers	151	K5
Lynesack Dur	103	L5
Lyness Ork	169	c7
Lyng Norfk	76	F8
Lyng Somset	19	K9
Lynmouth Devon	17	N2
Lynn Staffs	58	G4
Lynn Wrekin	70	D11
Lynsted Kent	38	F9
Lynstone Cnwll	16	C10
Lynton Devon	17	N2
Lynton Cross Devon	17	J3
Lyon's Gate Dorset	11	P3
Lyonshall Herefs	45	L3
Lytchett Matravers Dorset	12	F5
Lytchett Minster Dorset	12	G6
Lyth Highld	167	N4
Lytham Lancs	88	D5
Lytham St Annes Lancs	88	C5
Lythbank Shrops	56	H3
Lythe N York	105	M8
Lythmore Highld	167	J3

M

Maaruig W Isls	168	h7
Mabe Burnthouse Cnwll	3	K7
Mablethorpe Lincs	87	P4
Macclesfield Ches E	83	K10
Macduff Abers	158	H5
Machan S Lans	126	D10
Macharioch Ag & B	120	D10
Machen Caerph	30	H7
Machrie N Ayrs	120	G5
Machrihanish Ag & B	120	B7
Machrins Ag & B	136	b3
Machroes Gwynd	66	E9
Machynlleth Powys	54	G4
Machynys Carmth	28	F5
Mackworth Derbys	71	Q7
Macmerry E Loth	128	C5
Maddaford Devon	8	D6
Madderty P & K	134	B3
Maddington Wilts	21	L6
Maddiston Falk	126	G2
Madehurst W Susx	15	Q4
Madeley Staffs	70	D6
Madeley Wrekin	57	M4
Madeley Heath Staffs	70	D5
Madeley Park Wood Staffs	70	D6
Madford Devon	10	C2
Madingley Cambs	62	E8
Madley Herefs	45	N7
Madresfield Worcs	46	F5
Madron Cnwll	2	D7
Maenaddwyn IoA	78	H8
Maenan Conwy	79	P11
Maenclochog Pembks	41	L5
Maendy V Glam	30	D9
Maenporth Cnwll	3	K8
Maentwrog Gwynd	67	M6
Maen-y-groes Cerdgn	42	G3
Maer Cnwll	16	C10
Maer Staffs	70	D7
Maerdy Carmth	43	N9
Maerdy Conwy	68	D6
Maerdy Rhondd	30	C5
Maesbrook Shrops	69	K10
Maesbury Shrops	69	K9
Maesbury Marsh Shrops	69	K9
Maes-glas Newpt	31	J7
Maesgwynne Carmth	41	P6
Maeshafn Denbgs	68	H2
Maesllyn Cerdgn	42	G6
Maesmynis Powys	44	E5
Maesmynis Powys	44	E5
Maesteg Brdgnd	29	N6
Maesybont Carmth	43	L11

Maesycwmmer Caerph	30	G6
Magdalen Laver Essex	51	M9
Maggieknockater Moray	157	Q8
Maggots End Essex	51	L5
Magham Down E Susx	25	P8
Maghull Sefton	81	M4
Magna Park Leics	60	B4
Magor Mons	31	M7
Magor Services Mons	31	M7
Maidenbower W Susx	24	G4
Maiden Bradley Wilts	20	F7
Maidencombe Torbay	7	N5
Maidenhayne Devon	10	F5
Maidenhead W & M	35	N8
Maiden Law Dur	113	J11
Maiden Newton Dorset	11	M5
Maidens S Ayrs	114	D6
Maiden's Green Br For	35	P10
Maidenwell Lincs	87	K5
Maiden Wells Pembks	41	J11
Maidford Nhants	48	H4
Maids Moreton Bucks	49	K7
Maidstone Kent	38	C10
Maidstone Services Kent	38	D10
Maidwell Nhants	60	F5
Mail Shet	169	r9
Maindee Newpt	31	K7
Mainland Ork	169	d6
Mainland Shet	169	r8
Mainsforth Dur	104	B4
Mains of Balhall Angus	143	J5
Mains of Balnakettle Abers	143	L3
Mains of Dalvey Highld	157	L11
Mains of Haulkerton Abers	143	N3
Mains of Lesmoir Abers	150	D2
Mains of Melgunds Angus	143	J6
Mainsriddle D & G	109	K9
Mainstone Shrops	56	D7
Maisemore Gloucs	46	F10
Major's Green Worcs	58	H9
Makeney Derbys	72	B2
Malborough Devon	7	J11
Malcoff Derbys	83	M8
Malden Rushett Gt Lon	36	E8
Maldon Essex	52	E10
Malham N York	96	D9
Maligar Highld	152	H5
Mallaig Highld	145	L8
Mallaigvaig Highld	145	L8
Malleny Mills C Edin	127	M4
Mallows Green Essex	51	L5
Malltraeth IoA	78	G11
Mallwyd Gwynd	55	K2
Malmesbury Wilts	32	H7
Malmsmead Devon	17	P2
Malpas Ches W	69	N5
Malpas Cnwll	3	L5
Malpas Newpt	31	K6
Malshanger Hants	22	G4
Malswick Gloucs	46	D10
Maltby Lincs	87	K4
Maltby Rothm	84	H2
Maltby S on T	104	E8
Maltby le Marsh Lincs	87	N4
Malting Green Essex	52	G7
Maltman's Hill Kent	26	F3
Malton N York	98	F6
Malvern Worcs	46	E5
Malvern Hills	46	E6
Malvern Link Worcs	46	E5
Malvern Wells Worcs	46	E6
Mamble Worcs	57	M10
Mamhilad Mons	31	K4
Manaccan Cnwll	3	K9
Manafon Powys	55	Q4
Mànais W Isls	168	g9
Manaton Devon	9	J8
Manby Lincs	87	L3
Mancetter Warwks	59	M5
Manchester Manch	82	H5
Manchester Airport Manch	82	H8
Mancot Flints	81	L11
Mandally Highld	146	H7
Manea Cambs	62	G3
Maney Birm	58	H5
Manfield N York	103	P8
Mangersta W Isls	168	f4
Mangerton Dorset	11	K5
Mangotsfield S Glos	32	C9
Mangrove Green Herts	50	D6
Mangurstadh W Isls	168	f4
Manhay Cnwll	2	H7
Manish W Isls	168	g9
Mankinholes Calder	90	B6
Manley Ches W	81	Q10
Manmoel Caerph	30	G4
Mannal Ag & B	136	B7
Manningford Bohune Wilts	21	M3
Manningford Bruce Wilts	21	M3
Manningham C Brad	90	E4
Mannings Heath W Susx	24	F5
Mannington Dorset	13	J3
Manningtree Essex	53	K5
Mannofield C Aber	151	N7
Manorbier Pembks	41	L11
Manorbier Newton Pembks	41	L11
Manordeilo Carmth	43	N9
Manorhill Border	118	C4
Manorowen Pembks	40	H3
Manor Park Gt Lon	37	K3
Mansell Gamage Herefs	45	M6
Mansell Lacy Herefs	45	N5
Mansergh Cumb	95	N4
Mansfield E Ayrs	115	M5
Mansfield Notts	84	H8
Mansfield Woodhouse Notts	84	H8
Mansriggs Cumb	94	F4
Manston Dorset	20	F11
Manston Kent	39	P8
Manston Leeds	91	K4
Manswood Dorset	12	G3
Manthorpe Lincs	73	N3
Manthorpe Lincs	73	R7
Manton N Linc	92	F10
Manton Notts	85	K5
Manton Rutlnd	73	M10
Manton Wilts	33	N11
Manuden Essex	51	L5
Manwood Green Essex	51	M8
Maperton Somset	20	C9
Maplebeck Notts	85	M8
Maple Cross Herts	36	C2
Mapledurham Oxon	35	J9
Mapledurwell Hants	23	J4
Maplehurst W Susx	24	E6

Maplescombe Kent	37	N8
Mapleton Derbys	71	M5
Mapleton Kent	37	L11
Mapperley Derbys	72	C2
Mapperley Park C Nott	72	F2
Mapperton Dorset	11	L5
Mappleborough Green Warwks	58	G11
Mappleton E R Yk	93	M2
Mapplewell Barns	91	J8
Mappowder Dorset	12	B3
Màraig W Isls	168	h7
Marazanvose Cnwll	3	K3
Marazion Cnwll	2	E7
Marbhig W Isls	168	j6
Marbury Ches E	69	Q5
March Cambs	74	H11
March S Lans	116	D8
Marcham Oxon	34	E5
Marchamley Shrops	69	Q9
Marchamley Wood Shrops	69	Q8
Marchington Staffs	71	L8
Marchington Woodlands Staffs	71	L9
Marchwiel Wrexhm	69	L5
Marchwood Hants	14	C4
Marcross V Glam	29	P11
Marden Herefs	45	Q5
Marden Kent	26	B3
Marden Wilts	21	L3
Marden Ash Essex	51	N10
Marden Beech Kent	26	B3
Marden's Hill E Susx	25	M4
Marden Thorn Kent	26	C3
Mardlebury Herts	50	G7
Mardy Mons	45	J11
Marefield Leics	73	J9
Mareham le Fen Lincs	87	J8
Mareham on the Hill Lincs	87	J7
Marehay Derbys	84	E11
Marehill W Susx	24	C7
Maresfield E Susx	25	L6
Marfleet C KuH	93	K5
Marford Wrexhm	69	L3
Margam Neath	29	L7
Margaret Marsh Dorset	20	F11
Margaret Roding Essex	51	N8
Margaretting Essex	51	Q10
Margaretting Tye Essex	51	Q10
Margate Kent	39	Q7
Margnaheglish N Ayrs	121	K5
Margrie D & G	108	C10
Margrove Park R & Cl	105	J7
Marham Norfk	75	P9
Marhamchurch Cnwll	16	C11
Marholm C Pete	74	B10
Marian-glas IoA	79	J8
Mariansleigh Devon	17	N7
Marine Town Kent	38	F7
Marionburgh Abers	151	J6
Marishader Highld	152	H5
Maristow Devon	6	D6
Mark Somset	19	L5
Markbeech Kent	25	L2
Markby Lincs	87	N5
Mark Causeway Somset	19	L5
Mark Cross E Susx	25	N4
Markeaton C Derb	72	A3
Market Bosworth Leics	72	C10
Market Deeping Lincs	74	B8
Market Drayton Shrops	70	B8
Market Harborough Leics	60	F3
Market Lavington Wilts	21	K4
Market Overton Rutlnd	73	M7
Market Rasen Lincs	86	F3
Market Stainton Lincs	86	H5
Market Warsop Notts	85	J7
Market Weighton E R Yk	92	G3
Market Weston Suffk	64	D6
Markfield Leics	72	D8
Markham Caerph	30	G4
Markham Moor Notts	85	M6
Markinch Fife	134	H7
Markington N York	97	L7
Markle E Loth	128	E4
Marksbury BaNES	20	C2
Mark's Corner IoW	14	E8
Marks Tey Essex	52	F7
Markwell Cnwll	5	P10
Markyate Herts	50	C7
Marlborough Wilts	33	N11
Marlbrook Herefs	45	Q4
Marlbrook Worcs	58	E10
Marlcliff Warwks	47	L4
Marldon Devon	7	M6
Marle Green E Susx	25	N7
Marlesford Suffk	65	L10
Marley Kent	39	L10
Marley Kent	39	P11
Marley Green Ches E	69	Q5
Marley Hill Gatesd	113	K9
Marlingford Norfk	76	G10
Marloes Pembks	40	E9
Marlow Bucks	35	M7
Marlow Herefs	56	G9
Marlow Bottom Bucks	35	M7
Marlpit Hill Kent	37	K11
Marlpits E Susx	25	L5
Marlpits E Susx	26	B9
Marlpool Derbys	84	F11
Marnhull Dorset	20	E11
Marple Stockp	83	L7
Marple Bridge Stockp	83	L7
Marr Donc	91	N9
Marrick N York	103	L9
Marros Carmth	41	P9
Marsden S Tyne	113	N8
Marsden Height Lancs	89	P3
Marsett N York	96	D3
Marsh Bucks	35	M3
Marsh C Brad	90	C3
Marsh Devon	10	D2
Marshall's Heath Herts	50	E8
Marshalswick Herts	50	E9
Marsham Norfk	76	H7
Marshborough Kent	39	P10
Marshbrook Shrops	56	H7
Marshchapel Lincs	93	Q11
Marsh Farm Luton	50	C5
Marshfield Newpt	31	J8
Marshfield S Glos	32	E10
Marshgate Cnwll	5	K3

Marsh Gibbon Bucks	48	H10
Marsh Green Devon	9	P6
Marsh Green Kent	25	K2
Marsh Green Wrekin	57	L2
Marshland St James Norfk	75	K9
Marsh Lane Derbys	84	F5
Marsh Lane Gloucs	31	Q5
Marshside Sefton	88	D7
Marsh Street Somset	18	C6
Marshwood Dorset	10	H5
Marske N York	103	M10
Marske-by-the-Sea R & Cl	104	H6
Marsland Green Wigan	82	E5
Marston Ches W	82	E9
Marston Herefs	45	M3
Marston Lincs	73	M2
Marston Oxon	34	F3
Marston Staffs	58	B2
Marston Staffs	70	G9
Marston Warwks	59	K6
Marston Wilts	21	J3
Marston Green Solhll	59	J7
Marston Jabbet Warwks	59	N7
Marston Magna Somset	20	Q10
Marston Meysey Wilts	33	M8
Marston Montgomery Derbys	71	L7
Marston Moretaine C Beds	49	Q6
Marston on Dove Derbys	71	N9
Marston St Lawrence Nhants	48	F6
Marston Stannett Herefs	45	R3
Marston Trussell Nhants	60	E3
Marstow Herefs	45	R11
Marsworth Bucks	35	P2
Marten Wilts	21	Q2
Marthall Ches E	82	G9
Martham Norfk	77	P8
Martin Hants	21	L11
Martin Kent	27	P2
Martin Lincs	86	F9
Martin Lincs	86	H7
Martindale Cumb	101	M7
Martin Dales Lincs	86	G8
Martin Drove End Hants	21	L10
Martinhoe Devon	17	M2
Martin Hussingtree Worcs	46	G2
Martinscroft Warrtn	82	E7
Martinstown Dorset	11	N7
Martlesham Suffk	53	M2
Martlesham Heath Suffk	53	M2
Martletwy Pembks	41	K8
Martley Worcs	46	E2
Martock Somset	19	N11
Marton Ches E	83	J11
Marton Ches W	82	D11
Marton Cumb	94	E5
Marton E R Yk	93	L3
Marton E R Yk	99	P4
Marton Lincs	85	P4
Marton Middsb	104	F7
Marton N York	97	P7
Marton N York	98	D4
Marton Shrops	56	D4
Marton Warwks	59	P11
Marton-le-Moor N York	97	N6
Martyr's Green Surrey	36	C9
Martyr Worthy Hants	22	F8
Marvig W Isls	168	j6
Marwell Wildlife Hants	22	F10
Marwick Ork	169	b4
Marwood Devon	17	J4
Marybank Highld	155	N7
Maryburgh Highld	155	Q6
Marygold Border	129	L8
Maryhill C Glas	125	P4
Marykirk Abers	143	M4
Maryland Mons	31	P3
Marylebone Gt Lon	36	G4
Marylebone Wigan	88	H9
Marypark Moray	157	M9
Maryport Cumb	100	D3
Maryport D & G	106	F11
Marystow Devon	8	D9
Mary Tavy Devon	8	D9
Maryton Angus	143	M6
Marywell Abers	150	G8
Marywell Abers	151	N8
Marywell Angus	143	M9
Masham N York	97	K4
Mashbury Essex	51	Q8
Mason N u Ty	113	L6
Masongill N York	95	P5
Mastin Moor Derbys	84	G6
Matching Essex	51	M8
Matching Green Essex	51	M8
Matching Tye Essex	51	M8
Matfen Nthumb	112	H6
Matfield Kent	25	Q2
Mathern Mons	31	P6
Mathon Herefs	46	D5
Mathry Pembks	40	G4
Matlask Norfk	76	H5
Matlock Derbys	84	C8
Matlock Bank Derbys	84	D8
Matlock Bath Derbys	84	C9
Matlock Dale Derbys	84	C9
Matson Gloucs	46	G11
Matterdale End Cumb	101	L6
Mattersey Notts	85	L3
Mattersey Thorpe Notts	85	L3
Mattingley Hants	23	K3
Mattishall Norfk	76	F9
Mattishall Burgh Norfk	76	F9
Mauchline E Ayrs	115	J3
Maud Abers	159	M8
Maufant Jersey	11	c1
Maugersbury Gloucs	47	P9
Maughold IoM	80	g3
Mauld Highld	155	M10
Maulden C Beds	50	B4
Maulds Meaburn Cumb	102	B7
Maunby N York	97	N4
Maund Bryan Herefs	45	R4
Maundown Somset	18	E9
Mautby Norfk	77	P9
Mavesyn Ridware Staffs	71	K11
Mavis Enderby Lincs	87	L7
Mawbray Cumb	109	N11
Mawdesley Lancs	88	F8
Mawdlam Brdgnd	29	M8
Mawgan Cnwll	3	J8
Mawgan Porth Cnwll	4	C9
Maw Green Ches E	70	C2
Mawla Cnwll	3	J4
Mawnan Cnwll	3	K8

Place	Location	Page	Grid
Mawnan Smith	Cnwll	3	K8
Mawsley	Nhants	60	H5
Mawthorpe	Lincs	87	N6
Maxey	C Pete	74	B9
Maxstoke	Warwks	59	K7
Maxted Street	Kent	27	K3
Maxton	Border	118	B4
Maxton	Kent	27	P3
Maxwelltown	D & G	109	L5
Maxworthy	Cnwll	5	M3
Mayals	Swans	28	H7
May Bank	Staffs	70	F5
Maybole	S Ayrs	114	E6
Maybury	Surrey	36	B9
Mayes Green	Surrey	24	D3
Mayfield	E Susx	25	N5
Mayfield	Mdloth	128	B7
Mayfield	Staffs	71	M5
Mayford	Surrey	23	Q3
May Hill	Gloucs	46	D10
Mayland	Essex	52	F11
Maylandsea	Essex	52	F11
Maynard's Green	E Susx	25	N7
Maypole	Birm	58	G9
Maypole	Kent	39	M9
Maypole	Mons	45	P11
Maypole Green	Norfk	65	N2
Maypole Green	Suffk	64	C10
Maypole Green	Suffk	65	K8
May's Green	Oxon	35	K8
May's Green	Surrey	36	C9
Mead	Devon	16	C8
Meadgate	BaNES	20	C3
Meadle	Bucks	35	M3
Meadowfield	Dur	103	P3
Meadowtown	Shrops	56	E4
Meadwell	Devon	5	Q5
Meaford	Staffs	70	F7
Mealabost	W Isls	168	j4
Meal Bank	Cumb	101	P11
Mealrigg	Cumb	109	P11
Mealsgate	Cumb	100	H2
Meanwood	Leeds	90	H3
Mearbeck	N York	96	B8
Meare	Somset	19	N6
Meare Green	Somset	19	J10
Meare Green	Somset	19	K9
Mearns	E Rens	125	N6
Mears Ashby	Nhants	60	H7
Measham	Leics	72	A8
Meath Green	Surrey	24	G2
Meathop	Cumb	95	J4
Meaux	E R Yk	93	J3
Meavaig	W Isls	168	f4
Meavy	Devon	6	E5
Medbourne	Leics	60	H2
Medburn	Nthumb	112	H6
Meddon	Devon	16	D8
Meden Vale	Notts	85	J7
Medlam	Lincs	87	K9
Medlar	Lancs	88	E3
Medmenham	Bucks	35	M8
Medomsley	Dur	112	H10
Medstead	Hants	23	J7
Medway Services	Medway	38	D9
Meerbrook	Staffs	70	H2
Meer Common	Herefs	45	M4
Meesden	Herts	51	K4
Meeson	Wrekin	70	A10
Meeth	Devon	17	J10
Meeting Green	Suffk	63	M9
Meeting House Hill	Norfk	77	L6
Meidrim	Carmth	41	Q6
Meifod	Powys	56	B2
Meigle	P & K	142	D9
Meikle Carco	D & G	115	Q5
Meikle Earnock	S Lans	126	C7
Meikle Ferry	Highld	162	G9
Meikle Kilmory	Ag & B	124	D5
Meikle Obney	P & K	141	P10
Meikleour	P & K	142	B10
Meikle Wartle	Abers	158	H11
Meinciau	Carmth	28	E2
Meir	C Stke	70	G6
Meir Heath	Staffs	70	G6
Melbost	W Isls	168	j4
Melbourn	Cambs	51	J2
Melbourne	Derbys	72	B5
Melbourne	E R Yk	92	C2
Melbur	Cnwll	3	N3
Melbury	Devon	16	F8
Melbury Abbas	Dorset	20	G10
Melbury Bubb	Dorset	11	M3
Melbury Osmond	Dorset	11	M3
Melbury Sampford	Dorset	11	M3
Melchbourne	Bed	61	M7
Melcombe Bingham	Dorset	12	C4
Meldon	Devon	8	E6
Meldon	Nthumb	112	H4
Meldon Park	Nthumb	112	H3
Meldreth	Cambs	62	E11
Meldrum	Stirlg	133	L8
Melfort	Ag & B	130	G5
Meliden	Denbgs	80	F8
Melinau	Pembks	41	N8
Melin-byrhedyn	Powys	55	J5
Melincourt	Neath	29	M4
Melin-y-coed	Conwy	67	Q2
Melin-y-ddol	Powys	55	P3
Melin-y-wig	Denbgs	68	D5
Melkinthorpe	Cumb	101	Q5
Melkridge	Nthumb	111	P8
Melksham	Wilts	20	H2
Mellangoose	Cnwll	2	H8
Mell Green	W Berk	34	E9
Mellguards	Cumb	110	H11
Melling	Lancs	95	M6
Melling	Sefton	81	M4
Melling Mount	Sefton	81	N4
Mellis	Suffk	64	F7
Mellon Charles	Highld	160	C8
Mellon Udrigle	Highld	160	D7
Mellor	Lancs	89	K4
Mellor	Stockp	83	L7
Mellor Brook	Lancs	89	J4
Mells	Somset	20	D5
Mells	Suffk	65	N6
Melmerby	Cumb	102	B3
Melmerby	N York	96	G3
Melmerby	N York	97	M5
Melness	Highld	165	N4
Melon Green	Suffk	64	A10
Melplash	Dorset	11	K5
Melrose	Border	117	Q4
Melsetter	Ork	169	b8
Melsonby	N York	103	N9
Meltham	Kirk	90	E8
Meltham Mills	Kirk	90	E8
Melton	E R Yk	92	G5
Melton	Suffk	65	K11
Meltonby	E R Yk	98	F10
Melton Constable	Norfk	76	E5
Melton Mowbray	Leics	73	K7
Melton Ross	N Linc	93	J8
Melvaig	Highld	160	A9
Melverley	Shrops	69	K11
Melverley Green	Shrops	69	K11
Melvich	Highld	166	E4
Membury	Devon	10	F4
Membury Services	W Berk	34	B9
Memsie	Abers	159	N5
Memus	Angus	142	G6
Menabilly	Cnwll	4	H11
Menagissey	Cnwll	3	J4
Menai Bridge	IoA	79	K10
Mendham	Suffk	65	K5
Mendip Hills		19	P4
Mendlesham	Suffk	64	G8
Mendlesham Green	Suffk	64	F9
Menheniot	Cnwll	5	M9
Menithwood	Worcs	57	N11
Menna	Cnwll	3	N3
Mennock	D & G	115	R6
Menston	C Brad	90	F2
Menstrie	Clacks	133	P8
Menthorpe	N York	92	B4
Mentmore	Bucks	49	P11
Meoble	Highld	145	N10
Meole Brace	Shrops	56	H2
Meonstoke	Hants	22	H11
Meon Vale	Warwks	47	N5
Meopham	Kent	37	P7
Meopham Green	Kent	37	P7
Meopham Station	Kent	37	P7
Mepal	Cambs	62	F4
Meppershall	C Beds	50	D3
Merbach	Herefs	45	L5
Mere	Ches E	82	F8
Mere	Wilts	20	F8
Mere Brow	Lancs	88	E7
Mereclough	Lancs	89	P4
Mere Green	Birm	58	H5
Mere Green	Worcs	47	J2
Mere Heath	Ches W	82	E10
Meresborough	Medway	38	D9
Mereworth	Kent	37	Q10
Mergie	Abers	151	F11
Meriden	Solhll	59	K8
Merkadale	Highld	152	F11
Merley	BCP	12	H5
Merlin's Bridge	Pembks	40	H8
Merrington	Shrops	69	N10
Merrion	Pembks	40	H11
Merriott	Somset	11	J2
Merrivale	Devon	8	D9
Merrow	Surrey	36	B10
Merry Field Hill	Dorset	12	H4
Merry Hill	Herts	36	D2
Merryhill	Wolves	58	C5
Merry Lees	Leics	72	D9
Merrymeet	Cnwll	5	M8
Mersea Island	Essex	52	H8
Mersey Crossing	Halton	81	Q8
Mersham	Kent	27	J3
Merstham	Surrey	36	G10
Merston	W Susx	15	N6
Merstone	IoW	14	F9
Merther	Cnwll	3	M5
Merthyr	Carmth	42	G10
Merthyr Cynog	Powys	44	D7
Merthyr Dyfan	V Glam	30	F11
Merthyr Mawr	Brdgnd	29	N9
Merthyr Tydfil	Myr Td	30	D3
Merthyr Vale	Myr Td	30	E5
Merton	Devon	17	J9
Merton	Gt Lon	36	G6
Merton	Norfk	64	C2
Merton	Oxon	48	G11
Meshaw	Devon	17	P8
Messing	Essex	52	E8
Messingham	N Linc	92	E10
Metal Bridge	Dur	103	Q4
Metfield	Suffk	65	K5
Metherell	Cnwll	5	Q8
Metheringham	Lincs	86	E8
Methil	Fife	135	K8
Methilhill	Fife	135	K7
Methley	Leeds	91	K5
Methley Junction	Leeds	91	K5
Methlick	Abers	159	L10
Methven	P & K	134	C2
Methwold	Norfk	63	M2
Methwold Hythe	Norfk	63	M2
Mettingham	Suffk	65	M4
Metton	Norfk	76	J4
Mevagissey	Cnwll	3	Q5
Mexborough	Donc	91	M10
Mey	Highld	167	N2
Meysey Hampton	Gloucs	33	M4
Miabhaig	W Isls	168	f4
Michaelchurch	Herefs	45	Q9
Michaelchurch Escley	Herefs	45	L8
Michaelchurch-on-Arrow	Powys	45	J4
Michaelstone-y-Fedw	Newpt	30	H8
Michaelston-le-Pit	V Glam	30	G10
Michaelstow	Cnwll	4	H6
Michaelwood Services	Gloucs	32	D5
Michelcombe	Devon	6	H5
Micheldever	Hants	22	F7
Micheldever Station	Hants	22	F6
Michelmersh	Hants	22	B9
Mickfield	Suffk	64	G9
Micklebring	Donc	84	H2
Mickleby	N York	105	M8
Micklefield	Leeds	91	L4
Micklefield Green	Herts	50	B11
Mickleham	Surrey	36	E10
Mickleover	C Derb	71	Q8
Micklethwaite	C Brad	90	E2
Micklethwaite	Cumb	110	E10
Mickleton	Dur	103	J6
Mickleton	Gloucs	47	N6
Mickletown	Leeds	91	L5
Mickle Trafford	Ches W	81	N11
Mickley	Derbys	84	D5
Mickley	N York	97	L5
Mickley Green	Suffk	64	A10
Mickley Square	Nthumb	112	G8
Mid Ardlaw	Abers	159	M5
Midbea	Ork	169	d2
Mid Beltie	Abers	150	G7
Mid Bockhampton	BCP	13	L5
Mid Calder	W Loth	127	K4
Mid Clyth	Highld	167	N9
Middle Assendon	Oxon	35	K7
Middle Aston	Oxon	48	E9
Middle Barton	Oxon	48	D9
Middlebie	D & G	110	D5
Middlebridge	P & K	141	L4
Middle Chinnock	Somset	11	K2
Middle Claydon	Bucks	49	K9
Middlecliffe	Barns	91	L9
Middlecott	Devon	8	H7
Middlecroft	Derbys	84	F6
Middle Duntisbourne	Gloucs	33	J3
Middleham	N York	96	H3
Middle Handley	Derbys	84	F5
Middle Harling	Norfk	64	D4
Middlehill	Cnwll	5	M8
Middlehill	Wilts	32	F11
Middlehope	Shrops	56	H7
Middle Kames	Ag & B	131	J3
Middle Littleton	Worcs	47	L5
Middle Madeley	Staffs	70	D5
Middle Maes-coed	Herefs	45	L8
Middlemarsh	Dorset	11	P3
Middle Mayfield	Staffs	71	L6
Middle Mill	Pembks	40	F5
Middlemoor	Devon	6	D4
Middle Quarter	Kent	26	E4
Middle Rasen	Lincs	86	E3
Middle Rocombe	Devon	7	N5
Middle Salter	Lancs	95	N8
Middlesbrough	Middsb	104	E7
Middlescough	Cumb	101	M2
Middleshaw	Cumb	95	M3
Middlesmoor	N York	96	G6
Middle Stoford	Somset	18	G10
Middle Stoke	Medway	38	D6
Middlestone	Dur	103	Q4
Middlestone Moor	Dur	103	P4
Middle Stoughton	Somset	19	M5
Middlestown	Wakefd	90	H7
Middle Street	Gloucs	32	E4
Middle Taphouse	Cnwll	5	K9
Middlethird	Border	118	C2
Middleton	Ag & B	136	A7
Middleton	Cumb	95	N3
Middleton	Derbys	71	M2
Middleton	Derbys	84	C9
Middleton	Essex	52	E4
Middleton	Hants	22	D6
Middleton	Herefs	57	J11
Middleton	Lancs	95	J9
Middleton	Leeds	91	J5
Middleton	N York	96	H11
Middleton	N York	98	F3
Middleton	Nhants	60	H3
Middleton	Norfk	75	N7
Middleton	Nthumb	112	G4
Middleton	Nthumb	119	M3
Middleton	P & K	134	E6
Middleton	Rochdl	89	P9
Middleton	Shrops	57	J9
Middleton	Shrops	69	K9
Middleton	Suffk	65	N8
Middleton	Swans	28	D7
Middleton	Warwks	59	J5
Middleton Cheney	Nhants	48	E6
Middleton Green	Staffs	70	H7
Middleton Hall	Nthumb	119	J5
Middleton-in-Teesdale	Dur	102	H5
Middleton Moor	Suffk	65	N8
Middleton One Row	Darltn	104	C8
Middleton-on-Leven	N York	104	E9
Middleton-on-Sea	W Susx	15	Q6
Middleton on the Hill	Herefs	45	Q2
Middleton on the Wolds	E R Yk	99	J11
Middleton Park	C Aber	151	N5
Middleton Priors	Shrops	57	L6
Middleton Quernhow	N York	97	M5
Middleton St George	Darltn	104	B8
Middleton Scriven	Shrops	57	M7
Middleton Stoney	Oxon	48	F10
Middleton Tyas	N York	103	P9
Middletown	Cumb	100	C9
Middle Town	IoS	2	b3
Middletown	N Som	31	N10
Middletown	Powys	56	E2
Middle Tysoe	Warwks	48	B6
Middle Wallop	Hants	21	Q7
Middlewich	Ches E	82	F11
Middle Winterslow	Wilts	21	P8
Middlewood	Cnwll	5	M6
Middlewood	Herefs	45	K6
Middle Woodford	Wilts	21	M7
Middlewood Green	Suffk	64	F9
Middle Yard	Gloucs	32	F4
Middlezoy	Somset	19	L8
Middridge	Dur	103	P5
Midford	BaNES	20	E2
Midge Hall	Lancs	88	G5
Midgeholme	Cumb	111	M9
Midgham	W Berk	34	G11
Midgley	Calder	90	C5
Midgley	Wakefd	90	H8
Mid Holmwood	Surrey	36	E11
Midhopestones	Sheff	90	G11
Midhurst	W Susx	23	N10
Mid Lavant	W Susx	15	N5
Midlem	Border	117	Q5
Mid Mains	Highld	155	M10
Midney	Somset	19	N9
Midpark	Ag & B	124	C6
Midsomer Norton	BaNES	20	C4
Midtown	Highld	165	N4
Midville	Lincs	87	L9
Midway	Ches E	83	K8
Mid Yell	Shet	169	s4
Migdale	Highld	162	G8
Migvie	Abers	150	C6
Milborne Port	Somset	20	C11
Milborne St Andrew	Dorset	12	D5
Milborne Wick	Somset	20	C10
Milbourne	Nthumb	112	H5
Milburn	Cumb	102	C5
Milbury Heath	S Glos	32	C6
Milby	N York	97	P7
Milcombe	Oxon	48	D8
Milden	Suffk	52	G2
Mildenhall	Suffk	63	M6
Mildenhall	Wilts	33	P11
Milebrook	Powys	56	F10
Milebush	Kent	26	C2
Mile Elm	Wilts	33	J11
Mile End	Essex	52	G6
Mile End	Gloucs	31	Q2
Mile End	Suffk	65	L4
Mileham	Norfk	76	C8
Mile Oak	Br & H	24	F9
Mile Oak	Kent	25	Q2
Mile Oak	Staffs	59	J4
Miles Hope	Herefs	45	R2
Milesmark	Fife	134	D10
Mile Town	Kent	38	F7
Milfield	Nthumb	118	H4
Milford	Derbys	84	E11
Milford	Devon	16	C7
Milford	Powys	55	P6
Milford	Staffs	70	H10
Milford	Surrey	23	P6
Milford Haven	Pembks	40	H9
Milford on Sea	Hants	13	N6
Milkwall	Gloucs	31	Q3
Millais	Jersey	11	a1
Milland	W Susx	23	M9
Milland Marsh	W Susx	23	M9
Mill Bank	Calder	90	C6
Millbeck	Cumb	101	J5
Millbreck	Abers	159	P9
Millbridge	Surrey	23	M6
Millbrook	C Beds	50	B3
Millbrook	C Sotn	14	C4
Millbrook	Cnwll	6	C8
Millbrook	Jersey	11	b2
Millbrook	Tamesd	83	L5
Mill Brow	Stockp	83	L7
Millbuie	Abers	151	K6
Millbuie	Highld	155	Q7
Millcombe	Devon	7	L9
Mill Common	Norfk	77	L11
Mill Common	Suffk	65	N5
Millcorner	E Susx	26	D7
Millcraig	Highld	156	B3
Milldale	Staffs	71	L4
Mill End	Bucks	35	L7
Mill End	Gloucs	32	D5
Mill End	Herts	50	H4
Millerhill	Mdloth	127	Q4
Miller's Dale	Derbys	83	P10
Millers Green	Derbys	71	P4
Miller's Green	Essex	51	N9
Millerston	C Glas	125	Q4
Millgate	Lancs	89	P7
Mill Green	Cambs	63	K11
Mill Green	Essex	51	P10
Mill Green	Herts	50	F8
Mill Green	Lincs	74	D6
Mill Green	Norfk	64	G5
Mill Green	Shrops	70	B9
Mill Green	Staffs	58	G4
Mill Green	Staffs	71	K10
Mill Green	Suffk	52	G3
Mill Green	Suffk	64	D10
Mill Green	Suffk	64	G9
Mill Green	Suffk	65	L9
Millhalf	Herefs	45	K5
Millhayes	Devon	10	E4
Millhead	Lancs	95	K6
Millheugh	S Lans	126	C7
Mill Hill	E Susx	25	P9
Mill Hill	Gt Lon	36	F2
Millhouse	Ag & B	124	B3
Millhouse	Cumb	101	L3
Millhousebridge	D & G	109	P3
Millhouse Green	Barns	90	G10
Millhouses	Barns	91	L10
Millhouses	Sheff	84	D4
Milliken Park	Rens	125	L5
Millin Cross	Pembks	41	J8
Millington	E R Yk	98	G10
Mill Lane	Hants	23	L4
Millmeece	Staffs	70	E8
Millness	Cumb	95	L4
Mill of Drummond	P & K	133	N4
Mill of Haldane	W Duns	132	D11
Millom	Cumb	94	D4
Millook	Cnwll	5	K2
Millpool	Cnwll	2	F7
Millpool	Cnwll	5	J7
Millport	N Ayrs	124	F7
Mill Side	Cumb	95	J4
Mill Street	Kent	37	Q9
Mill Street	Norfk	76	F8
Mill Street	Suffk	64	G7
Millthorpe	Derbys	84	D5
Millthrop	Cumb	95	P2
Milltimber	C Aber	151	M7
Milltown	Abers	149	P6
Milltown	Abers	150	D4
Milltown	Cnwll	5	J10
Milltown	D & G	110	F5
Milltown	Derbys	84	E8
Milltown	Devon	17	K4
Milltown	Highld	153	N9
Milltown of Auchindoun	Moray	157	R9
Milltown of Campfield	Abers	150	H7
Milltown of Edinvillie	Moray	157	P9
Milltown of Rothiemay	Moray	158	D8
Milnathort	P & K	134	E7
Milngavie	E Duns	125	P3
Milnrow	Rochdl	89	Q8
Milnthorpe	Cumb	95	K4
Milnthorpe	Wakefd	91	J7
Milovaig	Highld	152	B8
Milson	Shrops	57	L10
Milstead	Kent	38	F10
Milston	Wilts	21	N5
Milthorpe	Lincs	74	B8
Milthorpe	Nhants	48	G5
Milton	C Stke	70	G4
Milton	Cambs	62	G8
Milton	Cumb	111	L8
Milton	D & G	106	H7
Milton	D & G	108	H6
Milton	Derbys	71	Q9
Milton	Highld	155	N11
Milton	Highld	155	Q8
Milton	Highld	156	D3
Milton	Highld	167	P6
Milton	Inver	125	K4
Milton	Kent	37	Q6
Milton	Moray	149	M4
Milton	Moray	158	D5
Milton	N Som	19	K2
Milton	Newpt	31	L7
Milton	Notts	85	M6
Milton	Oxon	34	E6
Milton	Oxon	48	E7
Milton	P & K	141	Q5
Milton	Pembks	41	K10
Milton	Somset	19	N10
Milton	Stirlg	132	G7
Milton	W Duns	125	L3
Milton Abbas	Dorset	12	D4
Milton Abbot	Devon	5	Q6
Milton Bridge	Mdloth	127	P5
Milton Bryan	C Beds	49	Q8
Milton Clevedon	Somset	20	C7
Milton Combe	Devon	6	D5
Milton Common	Oxon	35	J4
Milton Damerel	Devon	16	F9
Milton End	Gloucs	32	D2
Milton End	Gloucs	33	M4
Milton Ernest	Bed	61	M9
Milton Green	Ches W	69	N3
Milton Hill	Oxon	34	E6
Milton Keynes	M Keyn	49	N7
Milton Lilbourne	Wilts	21	N2
Milton Malsor	Nhants	60	F9
Milton Morenish	P & K	140	F10
Milton of Auchinhove	Abers	150	F7
Milton of Balgonie	Fife	135	J7
Milton of Buchanan	Stirlg	132	E9
Milton of Campsie	E Duns	126	B2
Milton of Finavon	Angus	142	H6
Milton of Leys	Highld	156	B9
Milton of Murtle	C Aber	151	M7
Milton on Stour	Dorset	20	E9
Milton Regis	Kent	38	F9
Milton Street	E Susx	25	M10
Milton-under-Wychwood	Oxon	47	Q11
Milverton	Somset	18	F9
Milverton	Warwks	59	M11
Milwich	Staffs	70	H8
Milwr	Flints	80	H10
Minard	Ag & B	131	K8
Minchington	Dorset	12	G2
Minchinhampton	Gloucs	32	G4
Mindrum	Nthumb	118	F4
Minehead	Somset	18	C5
Minera	Wrexhm	69	J4
Minety	Wilts	33	K6
Minffordd	Gwynd	67	K7
Mingarrypark	Highld	138	B4
Miningsby	Lincs	87	K8
Minions	Cnwll	5	M7
Minishant	S Ayrs	114	F5
Minllyn	Gwynd	55	K2
Minnigaff	D & G	107	M4
Minnonie	Abers	159	J5
Minshull Vernon	Ches E	70	B2
Minskip	N York	97	N8
Minstead	Hants	13	N2
Minsted	W Susx	23	N10
Minster	Kent	39	P9
Minsterley	Shrops	56	F3
Minster Lovell	Oxon	34	B2
Minster-on-Sea	Kent	38	G7
Minsterworth	Gloucs	46	E11
Minterne Magna	Dorset	11	P4
Minterne Parva	Dorset	11	P4
Minting	Lincs	86	G6
Mintlaw	Abers	159	N8
Minto	Border	117	R6
Minton	Shrops	56	G6
Minwear	Pembks	41	K8
Minworth	Birm	59	J6
Mirehouse	Cumb	100	C7
Mireland	Highld	167	P4
Mirfield	Kirk	90	G7
Miserden	Gloucs	32	H3
Miskin	Rhondd	30	D5
Miskin	Rhondd	30	D8
Misson	Notts	85	L2
Misterton	Leics	60	C4
Misterton	Notts	85	N2
Misterton	Somset	11	K3
Mistley	Essex	53	K5
Mistley Heath	Essex	53	K5
Mitcham	Gt Lon	36	G7
Mitcheldean	Gloucs	46	C11
Mitchell	Cnwll	3	M3
Mitchellslacks	D & G	116	D11
Mitchel Troy	Mons	31	N2
Mitford	Nthumb	113	J3
Mithian	Cnwll	3	J3
Mitton	Staffs	70	F11
Mixbury	Oxon	48	H8
Mixenden	Calder	90	D5
Moats Tye	Suffk	64	E10
Mobberley	Ches E	82	G9
Mobberley	Staffs	71	J6
Moccas	Herefs	45	M6
Mochdre	Conwy	79	Q9
Mochdre	Powys	55	P7
Mochrum	D & G	107	K8
Mockbeggar	Hants	13	L3
Mockbeggar	Kent	26	B2
Mockerkin	Cumb	100	E6
Modbury	Devon	6	H8
Moddershall	Staffs	70	G7
Moelfre	IoA	79	J7
Moelfre	Powys	68	F9
Moel Tryfan	Gwynd	67	J3
Moffat	D & G	116	F9
Mogador	Surrey	36	F10
Moggerhanger	C Beds	61	P11
Moira	Leics	71	Q11
Molash	Kent	38	H11
Mol-chlach	Highld	144	G5
Mold	Flints	68	H2
Moldgreen	Kirk	90	F7
Molehill Green	Essex	51	N6
Molehill Green	Essex	52	B7
Molescroft	E R Yk	92	H2
Molesden	Nthumb	112	H4
Molesworth	Cambs	61	N5
Moll	Highld	153	K11
Molland	Devon	17	Q6
Mollington	Ches W	81	M10
Mollington	Oxon	48	D5
Mollinsburn	N Lans	126	C3
Monachty	Cerdgn	43	K2
Mondynes	Abers	143	P2

Monewden Suffk 65 J10
Moneydie P & K 134 D2
Moneyrow Green W & M 35 N9
Moniaive D & G 115 Q9
Monifieth Angus 142 H11
Monikie Angus 142 H10
Monimail Fife 134 H5
Monington Pembks 41 M2
Monk Bretton Barns 91 K9
Monken Hadley Gt Lon 50 F11
Monk Fryston N York 91 N5
Monkhide Herefs 46 B6
Monkhill Cumb 110 F9
Monkhopton Shrops 57 L6
Monkland Herefs 45 P3
Monkleigh Devon 16 H7
Monknash V Glam 29 P10
Monkokehampton Devon 8 E3
Monkseaton N Tyne 113 M6
Monks Eleigh Suffk 52 G2
Monk's Gate W Susx 24 F5
Monks Heath Ches E 82 H10
Monk Sherborne Hants 22 H3
Monks Horton Kent 27 K3
Monksilver Somset 18 E7
Monks Kirby Warwks 59 Q8
Monk Soham Suffk 65 J8
Monkspath Solhll 58 H9
Monks Risborough Bucks 35 M4
Monksthorpe Lincs 87 M7
Monk Street Essex 51 P5
Monkswood Mons 31 K4
Monkton Devon 10 D4
Monkton Kent 39 N9
Monkton S Ayrs 114 G2
Monkton S Tyne 113 M8
Monkton V Glam 29 P10
Monkton Combe BaNES 20 E2
Monkton Deverill Wilts 20 G7
Monkton Farleigh Wilts 32 F11
Monkton Heathfield Somset 19 J9
Monkton Up Wimborne Dorset 12 H2
Monkton Wyld Dorset 10 G5
Monkwearmouth Sundld 113 N9
Monkwood Hants 23 J8
Monmore Green Wolves 58 D5
Monmouth Mons 31 P2
Monnington on Wye Herefs 45 M6
Monreith D & G 107 L9
Montacute Somset 19 N11
Montcliffe Bolton 89 K8
Montford Shrops 56 G2
Montford Bridge Shrops 69 M11
Montgarrie Abers 150 F4
Montgomery Powys 56 C5
Monton Salfd 82 G5
Montrose Angus 143 N6
Mont Saint Guern 10 b2
Monxton Hants 22 B6
Monyash Derbys 83 Q11
Monymusk Abers 150 H4
Monzie P & K 133 P2
Moodiesburn N Lans 126 B3
Moonzie Fife 135 J4
Moor Allerton Leeds 91 J3
Moorbath Dorset 11 J5
Moorby Lincs 87 J8
Moorcot Herefs 45 M3
Moor Crichel Dorset 12 G3
Moordown BCP 13 J6
Moore Halton 82 C8
Moor End C Beds 49 Q10
Moor End Calder 90 D5
Moor End Devon 17 M10
Moorend Gloucs 32 D4
Moor End Lancs 88 D2
Moor End N York 91 Q3
Moorends Donc 92 A7
Moorgreen Hants 22 E11
Moor Green Herts 50 H5
Moorgreen Notts 84 G11
Moorhall Derbys 84 D6
Moorhampton Herefs 45 M5
Moorhead C Brad 90 E3
Moor Head Leeds 90 G5
Moorhouse Cumb 110 E10
Moorhouse Cumb 110 F9
Moorhouse Donc 91 M8
Moorhouse Notts 85 N7
Moorhouse Bank Surrey 37 K10
Moorland Somset 19 K8
Moorlinch Somset 19 L7
Moor Monkton N York 97 R9
Moor Row Cumb 100 D8
Moor Row Cumb 110 D11
Moorsholm R & Cl 105 J8
Moorside Dorset 20 E11
Moorside Dur 112 G11
Moor Side Lancs 88 E4
Moor Side Lancs 88 F3
Moorside Leeds 90 G3
Moor Side Lincs 87 J9
Moorside Oldham 89 Q9
Moorstock Kent 27 K4
Moor Street Medway 38 D8
Moorswater Cnwll 5 L9
Moorthorpe Wakefd 91 M8
Moortown Devon 6 E4
Moortown Hants 13 L4
Moortown IoW 14 D10
Moortown Leeds 90 H3
Moortown Lincs 93 J11
Moortown Wrekin 69 R11
Morangie Highld 162 H10
Morar Highld 145 L9
Morborne Cambs 61 P2
Morchard Bishop Devon 9 J3
Morchard Road Devon 9 J3
Morcombelake Dorset 11 J6
Morcott Rutlnd 73 N10
Morda Shrops 69 J9
Morden Dorset 12 F5
Morden Gt Lon 36 G7
Mordiford Herefs 45 R7
Mordon Dur 104 B5
More Shrops 56 E6
Morebath Devon 18 C9
Morebattle Border 118 E6
Morecambe Lancs 95 J8
Moredon Swindn 33 M7
Morefield Highld 161 J7
Morehall Kent 27 M4
Moreleigh Devon 7 K8
Morenish P & K 140 F10
Moresby Parks Cumb 100 C7

Morestead Hants 22 F9
Moreton Dorset 12 D7
Moreton Essex 51 N9
Moreton Herefs 45 Q3
Moreton Oxon 35 J4
Moreton Staffs 70 D11
Moreton Staffs 71 L9
Moreton Wirral 81 K7
Moreton Corbet Shrops 69 Q10
Moretonhampstead Devon 9 J7
Moreton Jeffries Herefs 46 B5
Moreton-in-Marsh Gloucs 47 P8
Moretonmill Shrops 69 Q10
Moreton Morrell Warwks 48 B3
Moreton on Lugg Herefs 45 Q5
Moreton Paddox Warwks 48 B4
Moreton Pinkney Nhants 48 G5
Moreton Say Shrops 70 A8
Moreton Valence Gloucs 32 E3
Morfa Cerdgn 42 F4
Morfa Bychan Gwynd 67 J7
Morfa Dinlle Gwynd 66 G3
Morfa Glas Neath 29 N3
Morfa Nefyn Gwynd 66 D6
Morganstown Cardif 30 F8
Morgan's Vale Wilts 21 N10
Morham E Loth 128 F5
Moriah Cerdgn 54 E9
Morland Cumb 102 B6
Morley Ches E 82 H8
Morley Derbys 72 B2
Morley Dur 103 M5
Morley Leeds 90 H5
Morley Green Ches E 82 H8
Morley St Botolph Norfk 64 F2
Mornick Cnwll 5 N7
Morningside C Edin 127 N3
Morningside N Lans 126 E6
Morningthorpe Norfk 65 J3
Morpeth Nthumb 113 J3
Morphie Abers 143 N5
Morrey Staffs 71 L11
Morridge Side Staffs 71 J4
Morriston Swans 29 J5
Morston Norfk 76 E3
Mortehoe Devon 16 H2
Morthen Rothm 84 G3
Mortimer W Berk 23 J2
Mortimer Common W Berk 35 J11
Mortimer's Cross Herefs 45 N2
Mortimer West End Hants 22 H2
Mortlake Gt Lon 36 F5
Morton Cumb 101 N3
Morton Cumb 110 G10
Morton Derbys 84 F8
Morton IoW 14 H9
Morton Lincs 74 A6
Morton Lincs 85 P3
Morton Lincs 85 Q8
Morton Notts 85 M10
Morton Shrops 69 J10
Morton-on-Swale N York 97 M2
Morton on the Hill Norfk 76 G8
Morton Tinmouth Dur 103 N6
Morvah Cnwll 2 C6
Morval Cnwll 5 M10
Morvich Highld 146 B3
Morville Shrops 57 M6
Morville Heath Shrops 57 M6
Morwenstow Cnwll 16 C8
Mosborough Sheff 84 F4
Moscow E Ayrs 125 M9
Mose Shrops 57 P6
Mosedale Cumb 101 L4
Moseley Birm 58 G8
Moseley Wolves 58 D5
Moseley Worcs 46 F3
Moses Gate Bolton 89 L9
Moss Ag & B 136 B7
Moss Donc 91 P8
Moss Wrexhm 69 K4
Mossat Abers 150 D4
Mossbank Shet 169 r6
Moss Bank St Hel 81 Q5
Mossbay Cumb 100 C5
Mossblown S Ayrs 114 H3
Mossbrow Traffd 82 F7
Mossburnford Border 118 C7
Mossdale D & G 108 E6
Mossdale E Ayrs 115 J7
Moss Edge Lancs 88 E2
Moss End Ches E 82 E7
Mossend N Lans 126 C5
Mosser Mains Cumb 100 F5
Mossley Ches E 82 F2
Mossley Tamesd 83 L4
Mosspaul Hotel Border 117 M11
Moss Side Cumb 110 C10
Moss-side Highld 156 F6
Moss Side Lancs 88 D4
Moss Side Sefton 81 M4
Mosstodloch Moray 157 Q6
Mossyard D & G 107 P7
Mossy Lea Lancs 88 G8
Mosterton Dorset 11 K3
Moston Manch 83 J4
Moston Shrops 69 Q9
Moston Green Ches E 82 C2
Mostyn Flints 80 H8
Motcombe Dorset 20 G9
Mothecombe Devon 6 G9
Motherby Cumb 101 M5
Motherwell N Lans 126 C6
Motspur Park Gt Lon 36 F7
Mottingham Gt Lon 37 K6
Mottisfont Hants 22 B9
Mottistone IoW 14 D10
Mottram in Longdendale Tamesd 83 L5
Mottram St Andrew Ches E 83 J9
Mouilpied Guern 10 b2
Mouldsworth Ches W 81 Q10
Moulin P & K 141 M6
Moulsecoomb Br & H 24 H9
Moulsford Oxon 34 G8
Moulsoe M Keyn 49 P6
Moultavie Highld 156 A3
Moulton Ches W 82 E11
Moulton Lincs 74 F6
Moulton N York 103 P10
Moulton Nhants 60 G7
Moulton Suffk 63 L8
Moulton V Glam 30 E11
Moulton Chapel Lincs 74 E7
Moulton St Mary Norfk 77 M10

Moulton Seas End Lincs 74 F5
Mount Cnwll 4 B10
Mount Cnwll 5 J8
Mount Kirk 90 D7
Mountain C Brad 90 D4
Mountain Ash Rhondd 30 D5
Mountain Cross Border 127 M8
Mountain Street Kent 39 J11
Mount Ambrose Cnwll 3 J5
Mount Bures Essex 52 F5
Mountfield E Susx 26 B7
Mountgerald Highld 155 Q5
Mount Hawke Cnwll 3 J4
Mount Hermon Cnwll 2 H10
Mountjoy Cnwll 4 D9
Mount Lothian Mdloth 127 P6
Mountnessing Essex 51 P11
Mounton Mons 31 P6
Mount Pleasant Ches E 70 E3
Mount Pleasant Derbys 71 P11
Mount Pleasant Derbys 84 D11
Mount Pleasant Dur 103 Q4
Mount Pleasant E R Yk 93 N3
Mount Pleasant E Susx 25 K7
Mount Pleasant Norfk 64 D3
Mount Pleasant Suffk 63 M11
Mount Pleasant Worcs 47 K2
Mountsorrel Leics 72 F8
Mount Sorrel Wilts 21 K10
Mount Tabor Calder 90 D5
Mousehole Cnwll 2 D8
Mouswald D & G 109 N6
Mow Cop Ches E 70 F3
Mowhaugh Border 118 F6
Mowmacre Hill C Leic 72 F9
Mowsley Leics 60 D3
Moy Highld 147 L11
Moy Highld 156 D11
Moyle Highld 145 Q4
Moylegrove Pembks 41 M2
Muasdale Ag & B 120 C3
Muchalls Abers 151 N9
Much Birch Herefs 45 Q8
Much Cowarne Herefs 46 B5
Much Dewchurch Herefs 45 P8
Muchelney Somset 19 M10
Muchelney Ham Somset 19 M10
Much Hadham Herts 51 K7
Much Hoole Lancs 88 F6
Much Hoole Town Lancs 88 F6
Muchlarnick Cnwll 5 L10
Much Marcle Herefs 46 C8
Much Wenlock Shrops 57 L5
Muck Highld 144 F12
Mucking Thurr 37 Q4
Muckleburgh Collection Norfk 76 G3
Muckleford Dorset 11 N6
Mucklestone Staffs 70 C7
Muckley Shrops 57 L5
Muckton Lincs 87 L4
Muddiford Devon 17 K4
Muddles Green E Susx 25 M8
Mudeford BCP 13 L6
Mudford Somset 19 Q11
Mudford Sock Somset 19 Q11
Mudgley Somset 19 N5
Mud Row Kent 38 H7
Mugdock Stirlg 125 P2
Mugeary Highld 152 G10
Muggington Derbys 71 P6
Muggintonlane End Derbys 71 P6
Muggleswick Dur 112 F11
Muirden Abers 158 H7
Muirdrum Angus 143 K10
Muiresk Abers 158 G8
Muirhead Angus 142 E11
Muirhead Fife 134 H6
Muirhead N Lans 126 B4
Muirhouses Falk 134 C11
Muirkirk E Ayrs 115 N2
Muirmill Stirlg 133 L11
Muir of Fowlis Abers 150 F5
Muir of Miltonduff Moray 157 M6
Muir of Ord Highld 155 P7
Muirshearlich Highld 146 E11
Muirtack Abers 159 N10
Muirton P & K 133 Q5
Muirton Mains Highld 155 N7
Muirton of Ardblair P & K 142 B9
Muker N York 102 H11
Mulbarton Norfk 76 H11
Mulben Moray 157 R7
Mulfra Cnwll 2 D7
Mull Ag & B 137 Q9
Mullacott Cross Devon 17 J3
Mullardoch Highld 154 H11
Mullion Cnwll 2 H10
Mullion Cove Cnwll 2 H10
Mumby Lincs 87 P6
Munderfield Row Herefs 46 B4
Munderfield Stocks Herefs 46 C4
Mundesley Norfk 77 L4
Mundford Norfk 63 P2
Mundham Norfk 65 L2
Mundon Hill Essex 52 E11
Mundy Bois Kent 26 F2
Mungrisdale Cumb 101 L4
Munlochy Highld 156 A7
Munnoch N Ayrs 124 H8
Munsley Herefs 46 C6
Munslow Shrops 57 J7
Murchington Devon 8 G7
Murcot Worcs 47 L6
Murcott Oxon 48 G11
Murcott Wilts 33 J6
Murkle Highld 167 L3
Murlaggan Highld 146 C9
Murrell Green Hants 23 K3
Murroes Angus 142 H10
Murrow Cambs 74 G9
Mursley Bucks 49 M9
Murston Kent 38 F9
Murthill Angus 142 H6
Murthly P & K 141 R10
Murton C York 98 C10
Murton Cumb 102 D6
Murton Dur 113 N11
Murton N Tyne 113 M6
Murton Nthumb 129 P10
Murton Swans 28 G7
Musbury Devon 10 F6
Muscoates N York 98 D5
Musselburgh E Loth 127 Q3
Muston Leics 73 L3
Muston N York 99 M5

Mustow Green Worcs 58 C10
Muswell Hill Gt Lon 36 G3
Mutehill D & G 108 E11
Mutford Suffk 65 P4
Muthill P & K 133 P4
Mutterton Devon 9 P3
Muxton Wrekin 57 N2
Mybster Highld 167 L6
Myddfai Carmth 43 Q8
Myddle Shrops 69 N10
Mydroilyn Cerdgn 43 J3
Myerscough Lancs 88 F3
Mylor Cnwll 3 L6
Mylor Bridge Cnwll 3 L6
Mynachlog ddu Pembks 41 M4
Mynydd-Ilan Flints 80 H10
Myndtown Shrops 56 F7
Mynydd Bach Cerdgn 54 G9
Mynydd-bach Mons 31 N6
Mynydd-Bach Swans 29 J5
Mynyddgarreg Carmth 28 D3
Mynydd Isa Flints 69 J2
Mynydd Llandygai Gwynd 79 L11
Mynydd Mechell IoA 78 F6
Mynytho Gwynd 66 E8
Myrebird Abers 151 J8
Myredykes Border 118 A11
Mytchett Surrey 23 N3
Mytholm Calder 90 B5
Mytholmroyd Calder 90 C5
Mythop Lancs 88 D4
Myton-on-Swale N York 97 P7

N
Naast Highld 160 C10
Nab's Head Lancs 89 J5
Na Buirgh W Isls 168 f8
Naburn C York 98 B11
Naccolt Kent 27 J3
Nackington Kent 39 L11
Nacton Suffk 53 M3
Nafferton E R Yk 99 M9
Nag's Head Gloucs 32 G5
Nailbridge Gloucs 46 B11
Nailsea N Som 31 N10
Nailstone Leics 72 C9
Nailsworth Gloucs 32 F5
Nairn Highld 156 F6
Nalderswood Surrey 36 F11
Nancegollan Cnwll 2 G7
Nancledra Cnwll 2 D6
Nanhoron Gwynd 66 D8
Nannerch Flints 80 H11
Nanpantan Leics 72 E7
Nanpean Cnwll 4 F10
Nanquidno Cnwll 2 B8
Nanstallon Cnwll 4 G8
Nant-ddu Powys 30 D2
Nanternis Cerdgn 42 G3
Nantgaredig Carmth 43 J10
Nantgarw Rhondd 30 F7
Nant-glas Powys 55 M11
Nantglyn Denbgs 68 D2
Nantgwyn Powys 55 M9
Nant Gwynant Gwynd 67 L4
Nantlle Gwynd 67 J4
Nantmawr Shrops 69 J10
Nantmel Powys 55 N11
Nantmor Gwynd 67 L5
Nant Peris Gwynd 67 L3
Nantwich Ches E 70 B4
Nant-y-Bwch Blae G 30 F2
Nantycaws Carmth 43 J11
Nant-y-derry Mons 31 K3
Nant-y-ffin Carmth 43 L8
Nantyffyllon Brdgnd 29 N6
Nantyglo Blae G 30 G2
Nant-y-gollen Shrops 68 H9
Nant-y-moel Brdgnd 29 P6
Nant-y-pandy Conwy 79 M10
Naphill Bucks 35 M5
Napleton Worcs 46 G5
Nappa N York 96 C10
Napton on the Hill Warwks 48 E2
Narberth Pembks 41 M8
Narborough Leics 72 E11
Narborough Norfk 75 P8
Narkurs Cnwll 5 N10
Nasareth Gwynd 66 H5
Naseby Nhants 60 E5
Nash Bucks 49 L8
Nash Gt Lon 37 K8
Nash Herefs 45 L2
Nash Newpt 31 K8
Nash Shrops 57 L10
Nash End Worcs 57 P8
Nashes Green Hants 23 J5
Nash Lee Bucks 35 M3
Nash Street Kent 37 P7
Nassington Nhants 73 R11
Nastend Gloucs 32 E3
Nasty Herts 51 J6
Nateby Cumb 102 E9
Nateby Lancs 88 F2
National Memorial Arboretum Staffs 59 J2
National Motor Museum (Beaulieu) Hants 14 C6
National Space Centre C Leic 72 F9
Natland Cumb 95 L3
Naughton Suffk 52 H2
Naunton Gloucs 47 M10
Naunton Worcs 46 G7
Naunton Beauchamp Worcs 47 J4
Navenby Lincs 86 C9
Navestock Essex 51 M11
Navestock Side Essex 51 N11
Navidale Highld 163 N3
Navity Highld 156 D5
Nawton N York 98 D5
Nayland Suffk 52 G5
Nazeing Essex 51 K9
Nazeing Gate Essex 51 K9
Neacroft Hants 13 L5
Neal's Green Warwks 59 M8
Neap Shet 169 s8
Near Cotton Staffs 71 K5
Near Sawrey Cumb 101 L11
Neasden Gt Lon 36 F3
Neasham Darltn 104 B8
Neath Neath 29 L5

Neatham Hants 23 K6
Neatishead Norfk 77 L7
Nebo Cerdgn 54 C11
Nebo Conwy 67 Q3
Nebo Gwynd 66 H4
Nebo IoA 78 H6
Necton Norfk 76 B10
Nedd Highld 164 D10
Nedderton Nthumb 113 K4
Nedging Suffk 52 G2
Nedging Tye Suffk 52 H2
Needham Norfk 65 J3
Needham Market Suffk 64 F10
Needham Street Suffk 63 M7
Needingworth Cambs 62 D6
Neen Savage Shrops 57 M9
Neen Sollars Shrops 57 M10
Neenton Shrops 57 L7
Nefyn Gwynd 66 E6
Neilston E Rens 125 M6
Nelson Caerph 30 F5
Nelson Lancs 89 P3
Nemphlar S Lans 116 B2
Nempnett Thrubwell BaNES 19 P2
Nenthall Cumb 111 Q10
Nenthead Cumb 102 E2
Nenthorn Border 118 C3
Neopardy Devon 9 J5
Nep Town W Susx 24 F7
Nerabus Ag & B 122 B8
Nercwys Flints 68 H2
Nerston S Lans 125 Q6
Nesbit Nthumb 119 J4
Nesfield N York 96 G11
Ness Ches W 81 L9
Nesscliffe Shrops 69 L11
Neston Ches W 81 K9
Neston Wilts 32 G11
Netchwood Shrops 57 L6
Nether Abington S Lans 116 C6
Nether Alderley Ches E 82 H9
Netheravon Wilts 21 M5
Nether Blainslie Border 117 Q2
Netherbrae Abers 159 J6
Nether Broughton Leics 72 H5
Netherburn S Lans 126 D8
Netherbury Dorset 11 K5
Netherby Cumb 110 G6
Nether Cerne Dorset 11 P5
Nethercleuch D & G 109 P3
Nether Compton Dorset 19 Q11
Nethercote Warwks 60 B8
Nethercott Devon 5 P2
Nethercott Devon 16 H4
Nether Crimond Abers 151 L3
Nether Dallachy Moray 157 R5
Netherend Gloucs 31 Q4
Nether Exe Devon 9 M4
Netherfield E Susx 26 B8
Netherfield Leics 72 C2
Netherfield Notts 85 G2
Nethergate N Linc 92 C10
Nethergate Norfk 76 F6
Netherhampton Wilts 21 M9
Nether Handley Derbys 84 F5
Nether Handwick Angus 142 F9
Nether Haugh Rothm 91 L11
Netherhay Dorset 11 J3
Nether Headon Notts 85 M5
Nether Heage Derbys 84 E10
Nether Heyford Nhants 60 F9
Nether Kellet Lancs 95 L7
Nether Kinmundy Abers 159 Q8
Netherland Green Staffs 71 L8
Nether Langwith Notts 84 H6
Netherley Abers 151 M9
Nethermill D & G 109 M3
Nethermuir Abers 159 M9
Netherne-on-the-Hill Surrey 36 G9
Netheroyd Hill Kirk 90 E7
Nether Padley Derbys 84 B5
Nether Poppleton C York 98 B10
Nether Row Cumb 101 K3
Netherseal Derbys 59 L2
Nether Silton N York 97 Q2
Nether Skyborry Shrops 56 D10
Nether Stowey Somset 18 G7
Nether Street Essex 51 N8
Netherstreet Wilts 21 J2
Netherthong Kirk 90 E9
Netherthorpe Derbys 84 F6
Netherton Angus 143 J6
Netherton Devon 7 M4
Netherton Dudley 58 D7
Netherton Hants 22 C4
Netherton Herefs 45 Q9
Netherton Kirk 90 E8
Netherton N Lans 126 D7
Netherton Nthumb 119 J9
Netherton Oxon 34 D5
Netherton P & K 142 A7
Netherton Sefton 81 M4
Netherton Shrops 57 N8
Netherton Stirlg 125 P2
Netherton Wakefd 90 H7
Netherton Worcs 47 J6
Nethertown Cumb 100 C9
Nethertown Highld 167 P1
Nethertown Lancs 89 L3
Nethertown Staffs 71 L11
Netherurd Border 116 G2
Nether Wallop Hants 22 B7
Nether Wasdale Cumb 100 F11
Nether Welton Cumb 110 G11
Nether Westcote Gloucs 47 P10
Nether Whitacre Warwks 59 K6
Nether Whitecleuch S Lans 116 C4
Nether Winchendon Bucks 35 K2
Netherwitton Nthumb 112 H2
Nethy Bridge Highld 149 J3
Netley Hants 14 E5
Netley Marsh Hants 13 P2
Nettlebed Oxon 35 K8
Nettlebridge Somset 20 B5
Nettlecombe Dorset 11 L5
Nettlecombe IoW 14 F11
Nettleden Herts 35 P2
Nettleham Lincs 86 D5
Nettlestead Kent 37 Q10
Nettlestead Green Kent 37 Q11
Nettlestone IoW 14 H8
Nettlesworth Dur 113 L11
Nettleton Lincs 93 K10

Nettleton Wilts....32 F9
Nettleton Shrub Wilts....32 F9
Netton Devon....6 F9
Netton Wilts....21 M7
Neuadd Carmth....43 P10
Neuadd-ddu Powys....55 L9
Nevendon Essex....38 C3
Nevern Pembks....41 L2
Nevill Holt Leics....60 H2
New Abbey D & G....109 L7
New Aberdour Abers....159 L5
New Addington Gt Lon....37 J8
Newall Leeds....97 J11
New Alresford Hants....22 G8
New Alyth P & K....142 C8
Newark C Pete....74 D10
Newark Ork....169 g2
Newark-on-Trent Notts....85 N10
New Arley Warwks....59 L7
New Arram E R Yk....92 H2
Newarthill N Lans....126 D6
New Ash Green Kent....37 P7
New Balderton Notts....85 P10
New Barn Kent....37 P7
New Barnet Gt Lon....50 G11
New Barnetby N Linc....93 J8
New Barton Nhants....61 J8
Newbattle Mdloth....127 Q4
New Bewick Nthumb....119 L6
Newbie D & G....110 C7
Newbiggin Cumb....94 B2
Newbiggin Cumb....94 F7
Newbiggin Cumb....101 N5
Newbiggin Cumb....102 B5
Newbiggin Cumb....111 L11
Newbiggin Dur....102 H5
Newbiggin Dur....112 H11
Newbiggin N York....96 E2
Newbiggin N York....96 F3
Newbiggin-by-the-Sea Nthumb....113 M3
Newbigging Angus....142 D9
Newbigging Angus....142 G10
Newbigging Angus....142 H10
Newbigging S Lans....127 J8
Newbiggin-on-Lune Cumb....102 D10
New Bilton Warwks....59 Q9
Newbold Derbys....84 E6
Newbold Leics....72 C7
Newbold on Avon Warwks....59 Q9
Newbold on Stour Warwks....47 P5
Newbold Pacey Warwks....47 Q3
Newbold Revel Warwks....59 Q8
Newbold Verdon Leics....72 C10
New Bolingbroke Lincs....87 K9
Newborough C Pete....74 D9
Newborough IoA....78 G11
Newborough Staffs....71 L9
Newbottle Nhants....48 F7
Newbottle Sundld....113 M10
New Boultham Lincs....86 C6
Newbourne Suffk....53 N3
New Bradwell M Keyn....49 M6
New Brampton Derbys....84 E6
New Brancepeth Dur....103 P2
Newbridge C Edin....127 L3
Newbridge Caerph....30 H5
Newbridge Cerdgn....43 K3
Newbridge Cnwll....2 C7
Newbridge Cnwll....3 K5
Newbridge D & G....109 K5
Newbridge Hants....21 Q11
Newbridge IoW....14 D9
New Bridge N York....98 G3
Newbridge Oxon....34 D4
Newbridge Wrexhm....69 J6
Newbridge Green Worcs....46 F7
Newbridge-on-Usk Mons....31 L6
Newbridge-on-Wye Powys....44 E3
New Brighton Flints....81 K11
New Brighton Wirral....81 L6
New Brinsley Notts....84 G10
New Brotton R & Cl....105 J6
Newbrough Nthumb....112 C7
New Broughton Wrexhm....69 K4
New Buckenham Norfk....64 F3
Newbuildings Devon....9 J4
Newburgh Abers....151 P2
Newburgh Abers....159 N6
Newburgh Fife....134 G4
Newburgh Lancs....88 F8
Newburn N u Ty....113 J7
New Bury Bolton....82 F4
Newbury Somset....20 C5
Newbury W Berk....34 E11
Newbury Wilts....20 F6
Newbury Park Gt Lon....37 K3
Newby Cumb....101 Q6
Newby Lancs....96 B11
Newby N York....95 L2
Newby N York....99 L2
Newby N York....104 F8
Newby Bridge Cumb....94 H3
Newby Cross Cumb....110 G10
Newby East Cumb....111 J9
Newby Head Cumb....101 Q6
New Byth Abers....159 K7
Newby West Cumb....110 G10
Newby Wiske N York....97 N3
Newcastle Mons....45 N11
Newcastle Shrops....56 D8
Newcastle Airport Nthumb....113 J6
Newcastle Emlyn Carmth....42 F7
Newcastleton Border....111 J3
Newcastle-under-Lyme Staffs....70 E5
Newcastle upon Tyne N u Ty....113 K8
Newchapel Pembks....41 P3
Newchapel Staffs....70 F4
Newchapel Surrey....25 J2
Newchurch Blae G....30 G4
Newchurch Herefs....45 M4
Newchurch IoW....14 G9
Newchurch Kent....27 J5
Newchurch Mons....31 N5
Newchurch Powys....45 J4
Newchurch Staffs....71 L10
Newchurch in Pendle Lancs....89 N3
New Costessey Norfk....76 H9
New Cowper Cumb....109 P11
Newcraighall C Edin....127 Q3
New Crofton Wakefd....91 K7
New Cross Cerdgn....54 E9
New Cross Gt Lon....37 J5
New Cross Somset....19 M11

New Cumnock E Ayrs....115 M5
New Cut E Susx....26 D8
New Deer Abers....159 L8
New Delaval Nthumb....113 L5
New Delph Oldham....90 B9
New Denham Bucks....36 B4
Newdigate Surrey....24 E2
New Duston Nhants....60 F8
New Earswick C York....98 C9
New Eastwood Notts....84 G11
New Edlington Donc....91 N11
New Elgin Moray....157 N5
New Ellerby E R Yk....93 L3
Newell Green Br For....35 N10
New Eltham Gt Lon....37 K6
New End Worcs....47 L2
Newenden Kent....26 D6
New England C Pete....74 C10
New England Essex....52 B3
Newent Gloucs....46 D9
New Farnley Leeds....90 H4
New Ferry Wirral....81 L7
Newfield Dur....103 P4
Newfield Dur....113 K10
Newfield Highld....156 D2
New Fletton C Pete....74 C11
New Forest National Park....13 N3
Newfound Hants....22 G4
New Fryston Wakefd....91 M5
Newgale Pembks....40 G6
New Galloway D & G....108 D5
Newgate Norfk....76 E3
Newgate Street Herts....50 H9
New Gilston Fife....135 L6
New Grimsby IoS....2 b1
Newhall Ches E....69 R5
Newhall Derbys....71 P10
Newham Nthumb....119 N5
New Hartley Nthumb....113 M5
Newhaven C Edin....127 P2
Newhaven Derbys....71 M2
Newhaven E Susx....25 K10
New Haw Surrey....36 C8
New Hedges Pembks....41 M10
New Herrington Sundld....113 M10
Newhey Rochdl....89 Q8
New Holkham Norfk....76 B4
New Holland N Linc....93 J6
Newholm N York....105 N8
New Houghton Derbys....84 G7
New Houghton Norfk....75 Q5
Newhouse N Lans....126 D5
New Houses N York....96 B6
New Houses Wigan....82 C4
New Hutton Cumb....95 M2
New Hythe Kent....38 B10
Newick E Susx....25 K6
Newingreen Kent....27 K4
Newington Kent....27 L4
Newington Kent....38 E9
Newington Oxon....34 H5
Newington Bagpath Gloucs....32 F6
New Inn Carmth....43 J7
New Inn Pembks....41 L4
New Inn Torfn....31 K5
New Invention Shrops....56 D9
New Lakenham Norfk....77 J10
New Lanark S Lans....116 B2
New Lanark Village S Lans....116 B2
Newland C KuH....93 J4
Newland Cumb....94 G5
Newland E R Yk....92 D5
Newland Gloucs....31 Q3
Newland N York....92 A6
Newland Oxon....34 C3
Newland Somset....17 Q4
Newland Worcs....46 E5
Newlandrig Mdloth....128 B7
Newlands Border....111 K2
Newlands Cumb....101 K3
Newlands Nthumb....112 G9
Newlands of Dundurcas Moray....157 P7
New Lane Lancs....88 E8
New Lane End Warrtn....82 D6
New Langholm D & G....110 G4
New Leake Lincs....87 M9
New Leeds Abers....159 N7
New Lodge Barns....91 K9
New Longton Lancs....88 G5
New Luce D & G....106 G5
Newlyn Cnwll....2 D8
Newmachar Abers....151 M4
Newmains N Lans....126 E6
New Malden Gt Lon....36 F7
Newman's End Essex....51 M8
Newman's Green Suffk....52 E3
Newmarket Suffk....63 K8
Newmarket W Isls....168 j4
New Marske R & Cl....104 H6
New Marston Oxon....34 F3
New Marton Shrops....69 K8
New Mill Abers....151 K11
Newmill Border....117 P8
New Mill Cnwll....2 D7
New Mill Herts....35 P2
New Mill Kirk....90 F9
Newmill Moray....158 B7
Newmillerdam Wakefd....91 J7
Newmill of Inshewan Angus....142 G5
Newmills C Edin....127 M4
New Mills Cnwll....3 M3
New Mills Derbys....83 M7
Newmills Fife....134 C10
Newmills Mons....31 P3
New Mills Powys....55 P4
Newmiln P & K....142 A11
Newmilns E Ayrs....125 N10
New Milton Hants....13 M5
New Mistley Essex....53 M5
New Moat Pembks....41 L5
Newnes Shrops....69 L8
Newney Green Essex....51 Q9
Newnham Hants....23 K4
Newnham Herts....50 F3
Newnham Kent....38 G10
Newnham Nhants....60 C9
Newnham Bridge Worcs....57 L11
Newnham on Severn Gloucs....32 C2
New Ollerton Notts....85 L7
New Oscott Birm....58 G6
New Pitsligo Abers....159 L6
New Polzeath Cnwll....4 E6
Newport Cnwll....5 N4

Newport Dorset....12 E5
Newport E R Yk....92 E4
Newport Essex....51 M4
Newport Gloucs....32 D5
Newport Highld....163 Q2
Newport IoW....14 F9
Newport Newpt....31 K7
Newport Norfk....77 Q8
Newport Pembks....41 L3
Newport Wrekin....70 C11
Newport-on-Tay Fife....135 L2
Newport Pagnell M Keyn....49 N6
Newport Pagnell Services M Keyn....49 N6
Newpound Common W Susx....24 C5
New Prestwick S Ayrs....114 F3
New Quay Cerdgn....42 G3
Newquay Cnwll....4 C9
New Quay Essex....52 H7
Newquay Zoo Cnwll....4 C9
New Rackheath Norfk....77 K9
New Radnor Powys....45 J2
New Rent Cumb....101 N3
New Ridley Nthumb....112 G9
New Road Side N York....90 B2
New Romney Kent....27 J7
New Rossington Donc....91 Q11
New Row Cerdgn....54 G10
New Row Lancs....89 J3
New Sauchie Clacks....133 P9
Newsbank Ches E....82 H11
Newseat Abers....158 H11
Newsham Lancs....88 G3
Newsham N York....97 N4
Newsham N York....103 M8
Newsham Nthumb....113 M5
New Sharlston Wakefd....91 K7
Newsholme E R Yk....92 B5
Newsholme Lancs....96 B10
New Shoreston Nthumb....119 N4
New Silksworth Sundld....113 N10
New Skelton R & Cl....105 J7
Newsome Kirk....90 F8
New Somerby Lincs....73 N3
New Springs Wigan....88 H9
Newstead Border....117 R4
Newstead Notts....84 H10
Newstead Nthumb....119 N5
New Stevenston N Lans....126 D6
New Street Herefs....45 L3
New Swanage Dorset....12 H8
New Swannington Leics....72 C7
Newthorpe N York....91 M4
Newthorpe Notts....84 G11
New Thundersley Essex....38 C4
Newtimber W Susx....24 G8
Newtoft Lincs....86 D3
Newton Ag & B....131 L8
Newton Border....118 B6
Newton Brdgnd....29 M9
Newton C Beds....50 F2
Newton Cambs....62 F11
Newton Cambs....74 H8
Newton Cardif....30 H9
Newton Ches W....69 P3
Newton Ches W....81 N11
Newton Ches W....82 B9
Newton Cumb....94 E6
Newton Derbys....84 F9
Newton Herefs....45 L8
Newton Herefs....56 F11
Newton Highld....155 Q7
Newton Highld....156 C8
Newton Highld....156 D4
Newton Highld....167 P7
Newton Lancs....88 C3
Newton Lancs....95 M6
Newton Lincs....73 Q3
Newton Mdloth....127 Q4
Newton Moray....157 M5
Newton Moray....157 Q5
Newton N York....98 H6
Newton Nhants....61 J4
Newton Norfk....76 A8
Newton Notts....72 H2
Newton Nthumb....112 F8
Newton Nthumb....118 H9
Newton S Lans....116 C4
Newton S Lans....126 B5
Newton Sandw....58 F6
Newton Shrops....69 M8
Newton Somset....18 F7
Newton Staffs....71 J9
Newton Suffk....52 F3
Newton W Loth....127 K2
Newton Warwks....60 B5
Newton Wilts....21 P10
Newton Abbot Devon....7 M4
Newton Arlosh Cumb....110 D9
Newton Aycliffe Dur....103 Q6
Newton Bewley Hartpl....104 E5
Newton Blossomville M Keyn....49 P4
Newton Bromswold Nhants....61 L7
Newton Burgoland Leics....72 B9
Newton by Toft Lincs....86 D3
Newton Ferrers Devon....6 F9
Newton Ferry W Isls....168 d10
Newton Flotman Norfk....65 J2
Newtongrange Mdloth....127 Q5
Newton Green Mons....31 P6
Newton Harcourt Leics....72 G11
Newton Heath Manch....83 J4
Newtonhill Abers....151 N9
Newton Hill Wakefd....91 J6
Newton-in-Bowland Lancs....95 P10
Newton Kyme N York....91 M2
Newton-le-Willows N York....97 K3
Newton-le-Willows St Hel....82 C5
Newtonloan Mdloth....127 Q5
Newton Longville Bucks....49 M8
Newton Mearns E Rens....125 N6
Newtonmill Angus....143 L5
Newtonmore Highld....148 C8
Newton Morrell N York....103 P9
Newton Mountain Pembks....41 J9
Newton Mulgrave N York....105 L7
Newton of Balcanquhal P & K....134 F5
Newton of Balcormo Fife....135 N7
Newton of Belltrees Rens....125 K6
Newton-on-Ouse N York....97 R9
Newton-on-Rawcliffe N York....98 G2
Newton on the Hill Shrops....69 N10

Newton-on-the-Moor Nthumb....119 N9
Newton on Trent Lincs....85 P6
Newton Poppleford Devon....10 B7
Newton Purcell Oxon....48 H8
Newton Regis Warwks....59 L3
Newton Reigny Cumb....101 N4
Newton St Cyres Devon....9 L5
Newton St Faith Norfk....77 J8
Newton St Loe BaNES....20 D2
Newton St Petrock Devon....16 G9
Newton Solney Derbys....71 P9
Newton Stacey Hants....22 D6
Newton Stewart D & G....107 M4
Newton Tony Wilts....21 P6
Newton Tracey Devon....17 J6
Newton under Roseberry R & Cl....104 G8
Newton Underwood Nthumb....112 H3
Newton upon Derwent E R Yk....98 E11
Newton Valence Hants....23 K8
Newton Wamphray D & G....109 P2
Newton with Scales Lancs....88 F4
Newtown BCP....12 H6
Newtown Blae G....30 G3
Newtown Ches W....82 B9
Newtown Cnwll....2 F8
Newtown Cnwll....5 M6
Newtown Cumb....101 P6
Newtown Cumb....109 P11
Newtown Cumb....110 G8
Newtown Cumb....111 K8
Newtown D & G....115 Q5
Newtown Derbys....83 L8
Newtown Devon....9 Q5
Newtown Devon....17 P6
Newtown Dorset....11 K4
Newtown Dorset....12 G3
Newtown Dorset....21 J11
Newtown Dorset....21 J11
Newtown E Susx....25 L6
Newtown Gloucs....32 C4
Newtown Hants....13 N4
Newtown Hants....14 H4
Newtown Hants....22 E2
Newtown Herefs....45 P3
Newtown Herefs....45 Q8
Newtown Herefs....46 B5
Newtown Highld....147 K7
Newtown IoW....14 D8
Newtown Nthumb....119 J4
Newtown Nthumb....119 K10
Newtown Nthumb....119 K5
Newtown Powys....55 Q6
Newtown Rhondd....30 E5
Newtown Shrops....69 M10
Newtown Shrops....69 N8
Newtown Somset....10 F2
Newtown Staffs....58 E4
Newtown Staffs....70 G2
Newtown Wigan....82 C4
Newtown Wilts....20 H9
Newtown Wilts....21 Q2
Newtown Worcs....46 G3
Newtown Worcs....58 D9
Newtown-in-St Martin Cnwll....3 J9
Newtown Linford Leics....72 E9
Newtown St Boswells Border....117 R4
Newtown Unthank Leics....72 D10
New Tredegar Caerph....30 F4
New Trows S Lans....126 E10
New Tupton Derbys....84 E7
Newtyle Angus....142 D9
New Walsoken Cambs....75 J9
New Waltham NE Lin....93 N10
New Whittington Derbys....84 E6
New Winton E Loth....128 C5
New Yatt Oxon....34 C2
Newyears Green Gt Lon....36 C3
Newyork Ag & B....131 K5
New York Lincs....86 H9
New York N Tyne....113 M6
New York N York....97 K3
New Zealand Wilts....33 K9
Nextend Herefs....45 L3
Neyland Pembks....41 J9
Niarbyl IoM....80 b6
Nibley Gloucs....32 C3
Nibley S Glos....32 C8
Nibley Green Gloucs....32 D5
Nicholashayne Devon....18 F7
Nicholaston Swans....28 F7
Nickies Hill Cumb....111 K7
Nidd N York....97 M8
Nigg C Aber....151 N7
Nigg Highld....156 E3
Nigg Ferry Highld....156 D4
Nimlet BaNES....32 D10
Ninebanks Nthumb....111 Q10
Nine Elms Swindn....33 M7
Nine Wells Pembks....40 E6
Ninfield E Susx....26 B9
Ningwood IoW....14 C9
Nisbet Border....118 C5
Nisbet Hill Border....129 K9
Niton IoW....14 F11
Nitshill C Glas....125 N5
Noah's Ark Kent....37 N9
Noak Bridge Essex....37 Q2
Noak Hill Gt Lon....37 M2
Noblethorpe Barns....90 H9
Nobold Shrops....56 H2
Nobottle Nhants....60 E8
Nocton Lincs....86 E8
Nogdam End Norfk....77 M11
Noke Oxon....34 F2
Nolton Pembks....40 G7
Nolton Haven Pembks....40 G7
No Man's Heath Ches W....69 P5
No Man's Heath Warwks....59 L3
No Man's Land Cnwll....5 M10
Nomansland Devon....9 K2
Nomansland Wilts....21 Q11
Noneley Shrops....69 N9
Nonington Kent....39 N11
Nook Cumb....95 L4
Nook Cumb....111 J5
Norbiton Gt Lon....36 E7
Norbreck Bpool....88 C2
Norbridge Herefs....46 D6
Norbury Ches E....69 Q5
Norbury Derbys....71 L6
Norbury Gt Lon....36 H7

Norbury Shrops....56 F6
Norbury Staffs....70 D10
Norbury Common Ches E....69 Q5
Norbury Junction Staffs....70 D10
Norchard Worcs....58 B11
Norcott Brook Ches W....82 D8
Norcross Lancs....88 C2
Nordelph Norfk....75 L10
Norden Rochdl....89 P8
Nordley Shrops....57 M5
Norfolk Broads Norfk....77 P10
Norham Nthumb....129 N10
Norland Town Calder....90 D6
Norley Ches W....82 C10
Norleywood Hants....14 C7
Norlington E Susx....25 K8
Normanby Lincs....86 C3
Normanby N Linc....92 E7
Normanby N York....98 E4
Normanby R & Cl....104 F7
Normanby le Wold Lincs....93 K11
Norman Cross Cambs....61 Q2
Normandy Surrey....23 P4
Normans Bay E Susx....25 Q9
Norman's Green Devon....9 Q4
Normanton C Derb....72 A4
Normanton Leics....73 L2
Normanton Notts....85 M10
Normanton Rutlnd....73 N9
Normanton Wakefd....91 K6
Normanton Wilts....21 M6
Normanton le Heath Leics....72 B8
Normanton on Cliffe Lincs....86 B11
Normanton on Soar Notts....72 E6
Normanton on the Wolds Notts....72 G4
Normanton on Trent Notts....85 N7
Normoss Lancs....88 C3
Norney Surrey....23 P6
Norrington Common Wilts....20 G2
Norris Green Cnwll....5 Q8
Norris Green Lpool....81 M6
Norris Hill Leics....72 A7
Norristhorpe Kirk....90 G6
Northacre Norfk....64 D2
Northall Bucks....49 Q10
Northallerton N York....97 N2
Northall Green Norfk....76 D9
Northam C Sotn....14 D4
Northam Devon....16 H6
Northampton Nhants....60 G8
Northampton Worcs....58 B11
Northants Services Nhants....60 F9
North Anston Rothm....84 H4
North Ascot Br For....35 P11
North Aston Oxon....48 E9
Northaw Herts....50 G10
Northay Somset....10 F2
North Baddesley Hants....22 C10
North Ballachulish Highld....139 K5
North Barrow Somset....20 B9
North Barsham Norfk....76 C4
Northbay W Isls....168 c17
North Benfleet Essex....38 C4
North Berwick E Loth....128 E3
Northbithburn Dur....103 N4
North Blyth Nthumb....113 M4
North Boarhunt Hants....14 H4
North Bockhampton BCP....13 L5
Northborough C Pete....74 C9
Northbourne Kent....39 P11
North Bovey Devon....8 H8
North Bradley Wilts....20 G3
North Brentor Devon....8 C8
North Brewham Somset....20 D7
North Bridge Surrey....23 Q7
Northbridge Street E Susx....26 B7
Northbrook Hants....22 F7
Northbrook Oxon....48 E10
North Brook End Cambs....50 G2
North Buckland Devon....16 H3
North Burlingham Norfk....77 M10
North Cadbury Somset....20 B9
North Carlton Lincs....86 B5
North Carlton Notts....85 J4
North Cave E R Yk....92 E4
North Cerney Gloucs....33 K3
North Chailey E Susx....25 J6
Northchapel W Susx....23 Q9
North Charford Hants....21 N11
North Charlton Nthumb....119 N6
North Cheam Gt Lon....36 F7
North Cheriton Somset....20 C9
North Chideock Dorset....11 J6
Northchurch Herts....35 Q3
North Cliffe E R Yk....92 E3
North Clifton Notts....85 P6
North Close Dur....103 Q4
North Cockerington Lincs....87 L2
North Connel Ag & B....138 G11
North Cornelly Brdgnd....29 M8
North Corner Cnwll....3 K10
North Cotes Lincs....93 P10
Northcott Devon....5 N3
Northcott Devon....10 B2
Northcott Devon....10 C3
North Country Cnwll....2 H5
Northcourt Oxon....34 E5
North Cove Suffk....65 P4
North Cowton N York....103 Q10
North Crawley M Keyn....49 P6
North Cray Gt Lon....37 L6
North Creake Norfk....76 B4
North Curry Somset....19 K9
North Dalton E R Yk....99 J10
North Deighton N York....97 N10
Northdown Kent....39 Q7
North Downs....38 F10
North Duffield N York....92 A3
Northedge Derbys....84 E7
North Elham Kent....27 L3
North Elkington Lincs....87 J2
North Elmham Norfk....76 D7
North Elmsall Wakefd....91 M8
Northend Bucks....35 K6
North End C Port....15 J6
North End Cumb....110 F9
North End Dorset....20 F9
North End E R Yk....93 L2
North End E R Yk....93 N4
North End Essex....51 Q7
North End Essex....38 M11
North End Hants....22 G9
North End Leics....72 F7
North End....74 D2

Place	County	Page	Grid
North End	Lincs	87	M3
North End	Lincs	92	H11
North End	Lincs	93	P10
North End	N Linc	93	K6
North End	N Som	31	M11
North End	Nhants	61	L7
North End	Norfk	64	D3
North End	Nthumb	119	M10
North End	Sefton	81	L4
North End	W Susx	15	Q6
North End	W Susx	24	D9
Northend	Warwks	48	C4
Northenden	Manch	82	H7
Northend Woods	Bucks	35	P7
North Erradale	Highld	160	A10
North Evington	C Leic	72	G10
North Fambridge	Essex	38	E2
North Featherstone	Wakefd	91	L6
North Ferriby	E R Yk	92	G5
Northfield	Birm	58	F9
Northfield	C Aber	151	N6
Northfield	E R Yk	92	H5
Northfields	Lincs	73	Q9
Northfleet	Kent	37	P6
North Frodingham	E R Yk	99	N10
Northgate	Lincs	74	C5
North Gorley	Hants	13	L2
North Green	Norfk	65	J4
North Green	Suffk	65	L9
North Green	Suffk	65	M8
North Greetwell	Lincs	86	D6
North Grimston	N York	98	G7
North Halling	Medway	38	B8
North Hayling	Hants	15	K6
North Hazelrigg	Nthumb	119	L4
North Heasley	Devon	17	N5
North Heath	W Susx	24	C6
North Hele	Devon	18	D10
North Hill	Cnwll	5	M6
North Hillingdon	Gt Lon	36	C4
North Hinksey Village	Oxon	34	E3
North Holmwood	Surrey	36	E11
North Huish	Devon	7	J7
North Hykeham	Lincs	86	B7
Northiam	E Susx	26	D7
Northill	C Beds	61	P11
Northington	Gloucs	32	D3
Northington	Hants	22	G7
North Kelsey	Lincs	92	H10
North Kessock	Highld	156	B8
North Killingholme	N Linc	93	K7
North Kilvington	N York	97	P3
North Kilworth	Leics	60	D4
North Kingston	Hants	13	L4
North Kyme	Lincs	86	G10
North Lancing	W Susx	24	E9
North Landing	E R Yk	99	Q6
Northlands	Lincs	87	K10
Northleach	Gloucs	33	M2
North Lee	Bucks	35	M3
North Lees	N York	97	L6
Northleigh	Devon	10	D5
Northleigh	Devon	17	L5
North Leigh	Kent	27	K2
North Leigh	Oxon	34	C2
North Leverton with Habblesthorpe	Notts	85	N4
Northlew	Devon	8	D5
North Littleton	Worcs	47	L5
Northload Bridge	Somset	19	N7
North Lopham	Norfk	64	E5
North Luffenham	Rutlnd	73	N10
North Marden	W Susx	23	M11
North Marston	Bucks	49	L10
North Middleton	Mdloth	128	B8
North Middleton	Nthumb	119	J6
North Millbrex	Abers	159	K9
North Milmain	D & G	106	E7
North Molton	Devon	17	N6
Northmoor	Oxon	34	D4
North Moreton	Oxon	34	G7
Northmuir	Angus	142	F6
North Mundham	W Susx	15	N6
North Muskham	Notts	85	N9
North Newbald	E R Yk	92	F3
North Newington	Oxon	48	D6
North Newnton	Wilts	21	M3
North Newton	Somset	19	K8
Northney	Hants	15	K6
North Nibley	Gloucs	32	D5
North Oakley	Hants	22	F4
North Ockendon	Gt Lon	37	N3
Northolt	Gt Lon	36	D4
Northolt Airport	Gt Lon	36	C3
Northop	Flints	81	J11
Northop Hall	Flints	81	K11
North Ormesby	Middsb	104	F7
North Ormsby	Lincs	87	J2
Northorpe	Kirk	90	G6
Northorpe	Lincs	74	A7
Northorpe	Lincs	74	D3
Northorpe	Lincs	92	E11
North Otterington	N York	97	N3
Northover	Somset	19	N7
Northover	Somset	19	P10
North Owersby	Lincs	86	E2
Northowram	Calder	90	E5
North Perrott	Somset	11	K3
North Petherton	Somset	19	J8
North Petherwin	Cnwll	5	M4
North Pickenham	Norfk	76	B10
North Piddle	Worcs	47	J4
North Poorton	Dorset	11	L5
Northport	Dorset	12	F7
North Poulner	Hants	13	L3
North Queensferry	Fife	134	E11
North Radworthy	Devon	17	P5
North Rauceby	Lincs	86	D11
Northrepps	Norfk	77	J4
North Reston	Lincs	87	L4
North Rigton	N York	97	L11
North Ripley	Hants	13	L5
North Rode	Ches E	83	J11
North Roe	Shet	169	q5
North Ronaldsay	Ork	169	g1
North Ronaldsay Airport	Ork	169	g1
North Row	Cumb	100	H4
North Runcton	Norfk	75	M7
North Scale	Cumb	94	D7
North Scarle	Lincs	85	P7
North Seaton	Nthumb	113	L4
North Seaton Colliery	Nthumb	113	L3
North Shian	Ag & B	138	G9
North Shields	N Tyne	113	N7
North Shoebury	Sthend	38	F4
North Shore	Bpool	88	C3
North Side	C Pete	74	E11
North Side	Cumb	100	C5
North Skelton	R & Cl	105	J7
North Somercotes	Lincs	93	R11
North Stainley	N York	97	L5
North Stainmore	Cumb	102	F7
North Stifford	Thurr	37	P4
North Stoke	BaNES	32	D11
North Stoke	Oxon	34	H7
North Stoke	W Susx	24	B8
Northstowe	Cambs	62	F7
North Street	Cambs	63	J7
North Street	Hants	21	N11
North Street	Hants	22	H8
North Street	Kent	38	H10
North Street	Medway	38	D7
North Street	W Berk	34	H10
North Sunderland	Nthumb	119	P4
North Tamerton	Cnwll	5	M11
North Tawton	Devon	8	G4
North Third	Stirlg	133	M10
North Thoresby	Lincs	93	N11
North Togston	Nthumb	119	P10
North Tolsta	W Isls	168	k3
Northton	W Isls	168	e9
North Town	Devon	17	J10
North Town	Somset	19	Q6
North Town	W & M	35	N8
North Tuddenham	Norfk	76	E9
North Uist	W Isls	168	c10
Northumberland National Park	Nthumb	111	Q4
North Walbottle	N u Ty	113	J7
North Walsham	Norfk	77	K5
North Waltham	Hants	22	G5
North Warnborough	Hants	23	K4
Northway	Somset	18	F9
North Weald Bassett	Essex	51	L11
North Wheatley	Notts	85	N3
North Whilborough	Devon	7	M5
Northwich	Ches W	82	E10
North Wick	BaNES	31	Q11
Northwick	S Glos	31	Q7
Northwick	Somset	19	L5
Northwick	Worcs	46	F3
North Widcombe	BaNES	19	Q3
North Willingham	Lincs	86	G3
North Wingfield	Derbys	84	F7
North Witham	Lincs	73	N6
Northwold	Norfk	75	Q11
Northwood	C Stke	70	F5
Northwood	Derbys	84	C8
Northwood	Gt Lon	36	C2
Northwood	IoW	14	E8
Northwood	Shrops	69	N8
Northwood	Worcs	57	P9
Northwood Green	Gloucs	46	D11
North Wootton	Dorset	11	P2
North Wootton	Norfk	75	M6
North Wootton	Somset	19	Q6
North Wraxall	Wilts	32	F9
North Wroughton	Swindn	33	M8
North York Moors National Park		105	K10
Norton	Donc	91	N7
Norton	E Susx	25	L10
Norton	Gloucs	46	G10
Norton	Halton	82	C8
Norton	Hants	22	E6
Norton	Herts	50	F4
Norton	IoW	13	P7
Norton	Mons	45	N11
Norton	N Som	19	K2
Norton	Nhants	60	C8
Norton	Notts	85	J6
Norton	Powys	56	E11
Norton	S on T	104	D6
Norton	Sheff	84	E4
Norton	Shrops	56	H8
Norton	Shrops	57	K3
Norton	Shrops	57	L8
Norton	Shrops	57	N4
Norton	Suffk	64	D8
Norton	Swans	28	H7
Norton	W Susx	15	P5
Norton	Wilts	32	G8
Norton	Worcs	46	G4
Norton	Worcs	47	K5
Norton Bavant	Wilts	20	H6
Norton Bridge	Staffs	70	F6
Norton Canes	Staffs	58	F3
Norton Canes Services	Staffs	58	F3
Norton Canon	Herefs	45	M5
Norton Corner	Norfk	76	F6
Norton Disney	Lincs	85	Q9
Norton Ferris	Wilts	20	E7
Norton Fitzwarren	Somset	18	G9
Norton Green	IoW	13	P7
Norton Hawkfield	BaNES	19	Q2
Norton Heath	Essex	51	P10
Norton in Hales	Shrops	70	C7
Norton-Juxta-Twycross	Leics	59	M3
Norton-le-Clay	N York	97	N6
Norton-le-Moors	C Stke	70	F4
Norton Lindsey	Warwks	47	P2
Norton Little Green	Suffk	64	D8
Norton Malreward	BaNES	20	B2
Norton Mandeville	Essex	51	N10
Norton-on-Derwent	N York	98	F6
Norton St Philip	Somset	20	E3
Norton Subcourse	Norfk	65	N2
Norton sub Hamdon	Somset	19	N11
Norton Wood	Herefs	45	M5
Norwell	Notts	85	N8
Norwell Woodhouse	Notts	85	M8
Norwich	Norfk	77	H2
Norwich Airport	Norfk	77	J9
Norwick	Shet	169	t2
Norwood	Clacks	133	P9
Norwood	Derbys	84	G4
Norwood	Kent	27	J5
Norwood End	Essex	51	N9
Norwood Green	Calder	90	E5
Norwood Green	Gt Lon	36	D5
Norwood Hill	Surrey	24	F2
Norwoodside	Cambs	74	H11
Noseley	Leics	73	J11
Noss Mayo	Devon	6	F9
Nosterfield	N York	97	L4
Nosterfield End	Cambs	51	P2
Nostie	Highld	145	Q2
Notgrove	Gloucs	47	M10
Nottage	Brdgnd	29	M9
Notter	Cnwll	5	P9
Nottingham	C Nott	72	F3
Nottington	Dorset	11	P8
Notton	Wakefd	91	J8
Notton	Wilts	32	H11
Nounsley	Essex	52	C9
Noutard's Green	Worcs	57	Q11
Nowton	Suffk	64	B9
Nox	Shrops	56	G2
Nuffield	Oxon	35	J7
Nunburnholme	E R Yk	98	G11
Nuncargate	Notts	84	H10
Nunclose	Cumb	111	J11
Nuneaton	Warwks	59	N6
Nuneham Courtenay	Oxon	34	G5
Nunhead	Gt Lon	36	H5
Nunkeeling	E R Yk	99	N11
Nun Monkton	N York	97	R9
Nunney	Somset	20	D5
Nunnington	Herefs	45	R6
Nunnington	N York	98	D5
Nunsthorpe	NE Lin	93	N9
Nunthorpe	C York	98	C10
Nunthorpe	Middsb	104	F8
Nunthorpe Village	Middsb	104	F8
Nunton	Wilts	21	N9
Nunwick	N York	97	M6
Nunwick	Nthumb	112	C6
Nupdown	S Glos	32	B5
Nup End	Bucks	49	N11
Nupend	Gloucs	32	E3
Nuptown	Br For	35	N10
Nursling	Hants	22	C11
Nursted	Hants	23	L10
Nursteed	Wilts	21	K2
Nurton	Staffs	58	B5
Nutbourne	W Susx	15	L5
Nutbourne	W Susx	24	C7
Nutfield	Surrey	36	H10
Nuthall	Notts	72	E2
Nuthampstead	Herts	51	K4
Nuthurst	W Susx	24	E5
Nutley	E Susx	25	K5
Nutley	Hants	22	H6
Nuttall	Bury	89	M7
Nutwell	Donc	91	Q10
Nybster	Highld	167	Q4
Nyetimber	W Susx	15	N7
Nyewood	W Susx	23	M10
Nymans	W Susx	24	G5
Nymet Rowland	Devon	17	N10
Nymet Tracey	Devon	8	H4
Nympsfield	Gloucs	32	F4
Nynehead	Somset	18	F10
Nythe	Somset	19	M8
Nyton	W Susx	15	P5

O

Place	County	Page	Grid
Oadby	Leics	72	G10
Oad Street	Kent	38	E9
Oakall Green	Worcs	46	F2
Oakamoor	Staffs	71	J6
Oakbank	W Loth	127	K4
Oak Cross	Devon	8	D5
Oakdale	Caerph	30	G5
Oake	Somset	18	G9
Oaken	Staffs	58	C4
Oakenclough	Lancs	95	L11
Oakengates	Wrekin	57	N2
Oakenholt	Flints	81	K10
Oakenshaw	Dur	103	N3
Oakenshaw	Kirk	90	F5
Oakerthorpe	Derbys	84	E10
Oakford	Cerdgn	43	J3
Oakford	Devon	18	B10
Oakfordbridge	Devon	18	B10
Oakgrove	Ches E	83	K11
Oakham	Rutlnd	73	M9
Oakhanger	Ches E	70	D4
Oakhanger	Hants	23	L7
Oakhill	Somset	20	B5
Oakhurst	Kent	37	N10
Oakington	Cambs	62	F8
Oaklands	Herts	50	F7
Oaklands	Powys	44	E4
Oakle Street	Gloucs	46	E11
Oakley	BCP	12	H5
Oakley	Bed	61	M10
Oakley	Bucks	34	H2
Oakley	Fife	134	C10
Oakley	Hants	22	G4
Oakley	Oxon	35	L4
Oakley	Suffk	64	H6
Oakley Green	W & M	35	P9
Oakley Park	Powys	55	M7
Oakridge Lynch	Gloucs	32	H4
Oaks	Lancs	89	K4
Oaks	Shrops	56	G4
Oaksey	Wilts	33	J6
Oaks Green	Derbys	71	M8
Oakshaw Ford	Cumb	111	K5
Oakshott	Hants	23	K9
Oakthorpe	Leics	59	M2
Oak Tree	Darltn	104	C8
Oakwood	C Derb	72	B3
Oakwood	Nthumb	112	D7
Oakworth	C Brad	90	C3
Oare	Kent	38	H9
Oare	Somset	17	P2
Oare	Wilts	21	N2
Oasby	Lincs	73	Q3
Oath	Somset	19	L9
Oathlaw	Angus	142	H6
Oatlands Park	Surrey	36	C7
Oban	Ag & B	130	H2
Oban Airport	Ag & B	138	G10
Obley	Shrops	56	E9
Obney	P & K	141	P10
Oborne	Dorset	20	C11
Obthorpe	Lincs	74	A8
Occold	Suffk	64	H7
Occumster	Highld	167	N9
Ochiltree	E Ayrs	115	K3
Ockbrook	Derbys	72	C3
Ocker Hill	Sandw	58	E6
Ockeridge	Worcs	46	E2
Ockham	Surrey	36	C9
Ockle	Highld	137	P1
Ockley	Surrey	24	D2
Ocle Pychard	Herefs	46	A5
Octon	E R Yk	99	L7
Odcombe	Somset	19	P11
Odd Down	BaNES	20	D2
Oddendale	Cumb	101	Q8
Oddingley	Worcs	46	H3
Oddington	Oxon	48	G11
Odell	Bed	61	L9
Odham	Devon	8	C4
Odiham	Hants	23	K4
Odsal	C Brad	90	F5
Odsey	Cambs	50	G3
Odstock	Wilts	21	M9
Odstone	Leics	72	B9
Offchurch	Warwks	59	N11
Offenham	Worcs	47	L5
Offerton	Stockp	83	K7
Offerton	Sundld	113	M9
Offham	E Susx	25	K8
Offham	Kent	37	Q9
Offham	W Susx	24	B9
Offleymarsh	Staffs	70	D9
Offord Cluny	Cambs	62	B7
Offord D'Arcy	Cambs	62	B7
Offton	Suffk	53	J2
Offwell	Devon	10	D5
Ogbourne Maizey	Wilts	33	N10
Ogbourne St Andrew	Wilts	33	N10
Ogbourne St George	Wilts	33	N10
Ogden	Calder	90	D4
Ogle	Nthumb	112	H5
Oglet	Lpool	81	N8
Ogmore	V Glam	29	N9
Ogmore-by-Sea	V Glam	29	N9
Ogmore Vale	Brdgnd	29	P6
Ogwen Bank	Gwynd	79	L11
Okeford Fitzpaine	Dorset	12	D2
Okehampton	Devon	8	E5
Oker Side	Derbys	84	C8
Okewood Hill	Surrey	24	D3
Olchard	Devon	9	L9
Old	Nhants	60	G6
Old Aberdeen	C Aber	151	N6
Old Alresford	Hants	22	G8
Oldany	Highld	164	C10
Old Arley	Warwks	59	L6
Old Auchenbrack	D & G	115	Q8
Old Basford	C Nott	72	F2
Old Basing	Hants	23	J4
Old Beetley	Norfk	76	D8
Old Bewick	Nthumb	119	L6
Old Bolingbroke	Lincs	87	L7
Old Bramhope	Leeds	90	G2
Old Brampton	Derbys	84	D6
Old Bridge of Urr	D & G	108	G7
Old Buckenham	Norfk	64	F3
Old Burghclere	Hants	22	E3
Oldbury	Kent	37	N9
Oldbury	Sandw	58	E7
Oldbury	Shrops	57	N6
Oldbury	Warwks	59	M6
Oldbury Naite	S Glos	32	B6
Oldbury-on-Severn	S Glos	32	B6
Oldbury on the Hill	Gloucs	32	F7
Old Byland	N York	98	B3
Old Cantley	Donc	91	Q10
Old Cassop	Dur	104	B3
Oldcastle	Mons	45	L10
Oldcastle Heath	Ches W	69	N5
Old Catton	Norfk	77	J9
Old Churchstoke	Powys	56	D6
Old Clee	NE Lin	93	N9
Old Cleeve	Somset	18	D6
Old Colwyn	Conwy	80	B9
Oldcotes	Notts	85	J3
Old Coulsdon	Gt Lon	36	H9
Old Dailly	S Ayrs	114	D8
Old Dalby	Leics	72	H6
Old Dam	Derbys	83	P9
Old Deer	Abers	159	N8
Old Ditch	Somset	19	P5
Old Edlington	Donc	91	N10
Old Eldon	Dur	103	P5
Old Ellerby	E R Yk	93	L3
Old Felixstowe	Suffk	53	P4
Oldfield	C Brad	90	C3
Oldfield	Worcs	46	F2
Old Fletton	C Pete	74	C11
Oldford	Somset	20	E4
Old Forge	Herefs	45	R11
Old Furnace	Herefs	45	P9
Old Glossop	Derbys	83	M6
Old Goole	E R Yk	92	B6
Old Grimsby	IoS	2	b1
Old Hall Green	Herts	51	J6
Old Hall Street	Norfk	77	L5
Oldham	Oldham	83	K4
Oldhamstocks	E Loth	129	J5
Old Harlow	Essex	51	L8
Old Heath	Essex	52	H7
Old Hunstanton	Norfk	75	N2
Old Hurst	Cambs	62	D5
Old Hutton	Cumb	95	M3
Old Inns Services	N Lans	126	D2
Old Kea	Cnwll	3	L5
Old Kilpatrick	W Duns	125	M3
Old Knebworth	Herts	50	F6
Old Lakenham	Norfk	77	J10
Oldland	S Glos	32	C10
Old Langho	Lancs	89	L3
Old Laxey	IoM	80	f5
Old Leake	Lincs	87	M10
Old Malton	N York	98	F6
Oldmeldrum	Abers	151	K2
Oldmill	Cnwll	5	P7
Old Milverton	Warwks	59	L11
Oldmixon	N Som	19	K3
Old Newton	Suffk	64	F9
Old Oxted	Surrey	37	J10
Old Portlethen	Abers	151	N8
Old Quarrington	Dur	104	B3
Old Radford	C Nott	72	F2
Old Radnor	Powys	45	K3
Old Rayne	Abers	150	H2
Old Romney	Kent	26	H7
Old Shoreham	W Susx	24	F9
Oldshoremore	Highld	164	G5
Old Soar	Kent	37	P10
Old Sodbury	S Glos	32	E8
Old Somerby	Lincs	73	P4
Oldstead	N York	98	A5
Old Stratford	Nhants	49	L6
Old Struan	P & K	141	K4
Old Swarland	Nthumb	119	N10
Old Swinford	Dudley	58	D8
Old Tebay	Cumb	102	B9
Old Thirsk	N York	97	P4
Old Town	Calder	90	C5
Old Town	Cumb	95	M4
Old Town	Cumb	101	N2
Old Town	E Susx	25	N11
Old Town	IoS	2	c2
Old Trafford	Traffd	82	H5
Old Tupton	Derbys	84	E7
Oldwall	Cumb	111	J8
Oldwalls	Swans	28	E6
Old Warden	C Beds	50	D2
Oldways End	Somset	17	P7
Old Weston	Cambs	61	N5
Old Wick	Highld	167	Q10
Old Windsor	W & M	35	Q10
Old Wives Lees	Kent	39	J11
Old Woking	Surrey	36	B9
Old Wolverton	M Keyn	49	M6
Old Woodhall	Lincs	86	H7
Old Woods	Shrops	69	N10
Olgrinmore	Highld	167	J6
Olive Green	Staffs	71	L11
Oliver's Battery	Hants	22	E9
Ollaberry	Shet	169	q5
Ollach	Highld	153	J10
Ollerton	Ches E	82	G9
Ollerton	Notts	85	L7
Ollerton	Shrops	70	A9
Olmarch	Cerdgn	43	M3
Olmstead Green	Cambs	51	P2
Olney	M Keyn	49	N4
Olrig House	Highld	167	L3
Olton	Solhll	58	H8
Olveston	S Glos	32	B7
Ombersley	Worcs	46	F2
Ompton	Notts	85	L7
Once Brewed	Nthumb	111	P7
Onchan	IoM	80	e6
Onecote	Staffs	71	J3
Onehouse	Suffk	64	D10
Onen	Mons	31	M2
Ongar Street	Herefs	56	F11
Onibury	Shrops	56	H9
Onich	Highld	139	J5
Onllwyn	Neath	29	M2
Onneley	Staffs	70	D5
Onslow Green	Essex	51	Q7
Onslow Village	Surrey	23	Q5
Onston	Ches W	82	C10
Openwoodgate	Derbys	84	E11
Opinan	Highld	153	N3
Orbliston	Moray	157	Q6
Orbost	Highld	152	D9
Orby	Lincs	87	N7
Orchard Portman	Somset	18	H10
Orcheston	Wilts	21	L5
Orcop	Herefs	45	P9
Orcop Hill	Herefs	45	P9
Ord	Abers	158	F6
Ordhead	Abers	150	H5
Ordie	Abers	150	F7
Ordiequish	Moray	157	Q6
Ordley	Nthumb	112	E8
Ordsall	Notts	85	M5
Ore	E Susx	26	D9
Oreleton Common	Herefs	56	H11
Oreton	Shrops	57	M8
Orford	Suffk	65	N11
Orford	Warrtn	82	D6
Organford	Dorset	12	F6
Orgreave	Staffs	71	L11
Orkney Islands	Ork	169	d6
Orkney Neolithic	Ork	169	c5
Orlestone	Kent	26	H5
Orleton	Herefs	56	H11
Orleton	Worcs	57	N11
Orlingbury	Nhants	61	J6
Ormathwaite	Cumb	101	J5
Ormesby	R & Cl	104	F7
Ormesby St Margaret	Norfk	77	P9
Ormesby St Michael	Norfk	77	P9
Ormiscaig	Highld	160	H9
Ormiston	E Loth	128	C6
Ormsaigmore	Highld	137	M3
Ormsary	Ag & B	123	M5
Ormskirk	Lancs	88	E9
Ornsby Hill	Dur	113	J11
Oronsay	Ag & B	136	b4
Orphir	Ork	169	c5
Orpington	Gt Lon	37	L7
Orrell	Sefton	81	L5
Orrell	Wigan	82	B4
Orrell Post	Wigan	88	G9
Orrisdale	IoM	80	d3
Orroland	D & G	108	G11
Orsett	Thurr	37	P4
Orsett Heath	Thurr	37	P4
Orslow	Staffs	70	E11
Orston	Notts	73	K2
Orthwaite	Cumb	101	J4
Ortner	Lancs	95	L10
Orton	Cumb	102	B9
Orton	Nhants	60	H5
Orton	Staffs	58	C5
Orton Longueville	C Pete	74	C11
Orton-on-the-Hill	Leics	59	M4
Orton Rigg	Cumb	110	F10
Orton Waterville	C Pete	74	C11
Orwell	Cambs	62	E10
Osbaldeston	Lancs	89	J4
Osbaldeston Green	Lancs	89	J4
Osbaldwick	C York	98	C10
Osbaston	Leics	72	C10
Osbaston	Shrops	69	K10
Osborne	IoW	14	F8
Osborne House	IoW	14	F8
Osbournby	Lincs	73	R3
Oscroft	Ches W	81	Q11
Ose	Highld	152	E9
Osgathorpe	Leics	72	C7
Osgodby	Lincs	86	F2
Osgodby	N York	91	Q4
Osgodby	N York	99	M4
Oskaig	Highld	153	J10
Oskamull	Ag & B	137	M7
Osmaston	Derbys	71	N5
Osmington	Dorset	11	Q8
Osmington Mills	Dorset	11	Q8
Osmondthorpe	Leeds	91	J4
Osmotherley	N York	104	E11
Osney	C Oxon	34	F3
Ospringe	Kent	38	H9
Ossett	Wakefd	90	H6
Ossington	Notts	85	N8
Ostend	Essex	38	F2
Osterley	Gt Lon	36	E5

Oswaldkirk – Pentre Bach 287

Oswaldkirk N York 98 C5
Oswaldtwistle Lancs 89 L5
Oswestry Shrops 69 J9
Otairnis W Isls 168 e10
Otford Kent 37 M9
Otham Kent 38 C11
Otham Hole Kent 38 D11
Othery Somset 19 L8
Otley Leeds 97 K11
Otley Suffk 65 J10
Otley Green Suffk 65 J10
Otterbourne Hants 22 E10
Otterburn N York 96 C9
Otterburn Nthumb 112 C2
Otter Ferry Ag & B 131 J11
Otterham Cnwll 5 K3
Otterhampton Somset 18 H6
Otterham Quay Kent 38 D8
Otterham Station Cnwll 5 K4
Otternish W Isls 168 e10
Ottershaw Surrey 36 B8
Otterswick Shet 169 s5
Otterton Devon 10 B7
Otterwood Hants 14 D6
Ottery St Mary Devon 10 C5
Ottinge Kent 27 L3
Ottringham E R Yk 93 N6
Oughterby Cumb 110 E9
Oughtershaw N York 96 C4
Oughterside Cumb 100 F2
Oughtibridge Sheff 84 D2
Oughtrington Warrtn 82 E7
Oulston N York 98 A6
Oulton Cumb 110 D10
Oulton Leeds 91 K5
Oulton Norfk 76 G6
Oulton Staffs 70 D10
Oulton Staffs 70 G7
Oulton Suffk 65 Q3
Oulton Broad Suffk 65 Q3
Oulton Street Norfk 76 H6
Oundle Nhants 61 M3
Ounsdale Staffs 58 C6
Our Dynamic Earth C Edin 127 P3
Ousby Cumb 102 B4
Ousden Suffk 63 M9
Ousefleet E R Yk 92 D6
Ouston Dur 113 L10
Outchester Nthumb 119 M4
Out Elmstead Kent 39 M11
Outgate Cumb 101 L11
Outhgill Cumb 102 E10
Outhill Warwks 58 H11
Outlands Staffs 70 D8
Outlane Kirk 90 D7
Out Newton E R Yk 93 Q6
Out Rawcliffe Lancs 88 E2
Out Skerries Shet 169 t6
Outwell Norfk 75 K10
Outwick Hants 21 M11
Outwood Surrey 36 H11
Outwood Wakefd 91 J6
Outwood Gate Bury 89 M9
Outwoods Leics 72 C7
Outwoods Staffs 70 D11
Ouzlewell Green Leeds 91 J5
Ovenden Calder 90 D5
Over Cambs 62 E6
Over Ches W 82 D11
Over Gloucs 46 F11
Over S Glos 31 Q8
Over Burrows Derbys 71 P7
Overbury Worcs 47 J7
Overcombe Dorset 11 P8
Over Compton Dorset 19 Q11
Over End Cambs 61 N2
Overgreen Derbys 84 D6
Over Green Warwks 59 J6
Over Haddon Derbys 84 B7
Over Hulton Bolton 82 E4
Over Kellet Lancs 95 L7
Over Kiddington Oxon 48 D10
Overleigh Somset 19 N7
Overley Staffs 71 M11
Over Monnow Mons 31 P2
Over Norton Oxon 48 B9
Over Peover Ches E 82 G10
Overpool Ches W 81 M9
Overscaig Highld 161 Q2
Overseal Derbys 71 P11
Over Silton N York 97 P2
Oversland Kent 39 J10
Oversley Green Warwks 47 L3
Overstone Nhants 60 G7
Over Stowey Somset 18 G7
Overstrand Norfk 77 J3
Over Stratton Somset 19 M11
Overstreet Wilts 21 L7
Over Tabley Ches E 82 F9
Overthorpe Nhants 48 E6
Overton C Aber 151 M5
Overton Ches W 81 Q9
Overton Hants 22 F5
Overton Lancs 95 J9
Overton N York 98 B9
Overton Shrops 57 J10
Overton Swans 28 E7
Overton Wakefd 90 H7
Overton Wrexhm 69 L6
Overton Bridge Wrexhm 69 L6
Overton Green Ches E 70 E2
Overtown Lancs 89 P5
Overtown Lancs 95 N5
Overtown N Lans 126 E7
Overtown Swindn 33 N9
Overtown Wakefd 91 K7
Over Wallop Hants 21 Q7
Over Whitacre Warwks 59 L6
Over Woodhouse Derbys 84 G6
Over Worton Oxon 48 D9
Overy Oxon 34 G6
Oving Bucks 49 L10
Oving W Susx 15 P6
Ovingdean Br & H 25 J10
Ovingham Nthumb 112 G8
Ovington Dur 103 M8
Ovington Essex 52 C3
Ovington Hants 22 G8
Ovington Norfk 76 C11
Ovington Nthumb 112 G8
Ower Hants 14 E6
Ower Hants 22 B11
Owermoigne Dorset 12 C7
Owlbury Shrops 56 E6
Owlerton Sheff 84 D3
Owlpen Gloucs 32 E5
Owl's Green Suffk 65 K8
Owlsmoor Br For 23 M2
Owlswick Bucks 35 L3
Owmby Lincs 86 D3
Owmby Lincs 93 J10
Owslebury Hants 22 F10
Owston Donc 91 P8
Owston Leics 73 K9
Owston Ferry N Linc 92 D10
Owstwick E R Yk 93 N4
Owthorne E R Yk 93 P5
Owthorpe Notts 72 H4
Owton Manor Hartpl 104 E5
Oxborough Norfk 75 P10
Oxbridge Dorset 11 K5
Oxcombe Lincs 87 K5
Oxcroft Derbys 84 G6
Oxen End Essex 51 Q5
Oxenholme Cumb 95 L3
Oxenhope C Brad 90 C4
Oxen Park Cumb 94 G3
Oxenpill Somset 19 M6
Oxenton Gloucs 47 J8
Oxenwood Wilts 22 B3
Oxford Oxon 34 F3
Oxford Airport Oxon 48 E11
Oxford Services Oxon 34 H4
Oxgangs C Edin 127 N4
Oxhey Herts 50 D11
Oxhill Dur 113 J10
Oxhill Warwks 48 B5
Oxley Wolves 58 D4
Oxley Green Essex 52 F9
Oxley's Green E Susx 25 Q6
Oxlode Cambs 62 G3
Oxnam Border 118 C7
Oxnead Norfk 77 J7
Oxshott Surrey 36 D8
Oxshott Heath Surrey 36 D8
Oxspring Barns 90 H10
Oxted Surrey 37 J10
Oxton Border 128 D9
Oxton N York 91 N2
Oxton Notts 85 K10
Oxton Wirral 81 L7
Oxwich Swans 28 E7
Oxwich Green Swans 28 E7
Oxwick Norfk 76 C6
Oykel Bridge Highld 161 P6
Oyne Abers 150 H2
Oystermouth Swans 28 H7
Ozleworth Gloucs 32 E6

P

Pabail W Isls 168 k4
Packers Hill Dorset 11 Q2
Packington Leics 72 B8
Packmoor C Stke 70 F4
Packmores Warwks 59 L11
Padanaram Angus 142 G7
Padbury Bucks 49 K8
Paddington Gt Lon 36 G4
Paddington Warrtn 82 D7
Paddlesworth Kent 27 L4
Paddlesworth Kent 37 Q8
Paddock Wood Kent 25 Q2
Paddolgreen Shrops 69 P8
Padfield Derbys 83 M5
Padgate Warrtn 82 D7
Padhams Green Essex 51 P11
Padiham Lancs 89 M4
Padside N York 97 J9
Padstow Cnwll 4 E6
Padworth W Berk 34 H11
Page Bank Dur 103 P3
Pagham W Susx 15 N7
Paglesham Essex 38 F3
Paignton Torbay 7 M6
Pailton Warwks 59 Q8
Paine's Cross E Susx 25 P6
Painleyhill Staffs 71 J8
Painscastle Powys 44 H5
Painshawfield Nthumb 112 G8
Painsthorpe E R Yk 98 G9
Painswick Gloucs 32 G3
Painter's Forstal Kent 38 G10
Paisley Rens 125 M5
Pakefield Suffk 65 Q3
Pakenham Suffk 64 C8
Pale Gwynd 68 C7
Pale Green Essex 51 Q2
Palestine Hants 21 Q6
Paley Street W & M 35 N9
Palfrey Wsall 58 F5
Palgrave Suffk 64 G6
Pallington Dorset 12 C6
Palmarsh Kent 27 K5
Palmersbridge Cnwll 5 K6
Palmers Green Gt Lon 36 H2
Palmerston E Ayrs 115 K4
Palmerstown V Glam 30 F11
Palnackie D & G 108 H9
Palnure D & G 107 N5
Palterton Derbys 84 G7
Pamber End Hants 22 H3
Pamber Green Hants 22 H3
Pamber Heath Hants 22 H2
Pamington Gloucs 46 H8
Pamphill Dorset 12 G4
Pampisford Cambs 62 G11
Panborough Somset 19 N5
Panbride Angus 143 K10
Pancrasweek Devon 16 D10
Pancross V Glam 30 D11
Pandy Caerph 30 G7
Pandy Gwynd 54 E4
Pandy Gwynd 68 A9
Pandy Mons 45 L10
Pandy Powys 55 L4
Pandy Wrexhm 68 G7
Pandy'r Capel Denbgs 68 E4
Pandy Tudur Conwy 67 R2
Panfield Essex 52 B6
Pangbourne W Berk 34 H9
Pangdean W Susx 24 G8
Panks Bridge Herefs 46 B5
Pannal N York 97 M10
Pannal Ash N York 97 L10
Pant Shrops 69 J10
Pantasaph Flints 80 H9
Panteg Pembks 40 H4
Pantersbridge Cnwll 5 K8
Pant-ffrwyth Brdgnd 29 P8
Pant Glas Gwynd 66 H5
Pantglas Powys 54 H5
Pant-Gwyn Carmth 43 L9
Pant-lasau Swans 29 J4
Pant Mawr Powys 55 J8
Panton Lincs 86 G5
Pant-pastynog Denbgs 68 D2
Pantperthog Gwynd 54 G4
Pantside Caerph 30 H5
Pant-y-caws Carmth 41 M5
Pant-y-dwr Powys 55 M10
Pant-y-ffridd Powys 56 B4
Pantyffynnon Carmth 28 H2
Pantygaseg Torfn 31 J5
Pantygelli Mons 45 L11
Pant-y-gog Brdgnd 29 P6
Pantymwyn Flints 68 G2
Panxworth Norfk 77 M9
Papa Stour Shet 169 n7
Papa Stour Airport Shet 169 n8
Papa Westray Ork 169 d1
Papa Westray Airport Ork 169 d1
Papcastle Cumb 100 F4
Papigoe Highld 167 Q6
Papple E Loth 128 F5
Papplewick Notts 84 H10
Papworth Everard Cambs 62 C8
Papworth St Agnes Cambs 62 C8
Par Cnwll 3 R3
Paramour Street Kent 39 N9
Parbold Lancs 88 F8
Parbrook Somset 19 Q7
Parbrook W Susx 24 C5
Parc Gwynd 68 A8
Parcllyn Cerdgn 42 D4
Parc Seymour Newpt 31 M6
Pardown Hants 22 G5
Pardshaw Cumb 100 E6
Parham Suffk 65 L9
Park D & G 109 K2
Park Nthumb 111 N8
Park Bottom Cnwll 2 H5
Park Bridge Tamesd 83 K4
Park Corner E Susx 25 M3
Park Corner Oxon 35 J7
Park Corner W & M 35 N8
Park End Bed 49 Q4
Parkend Gloucs 32 B3
Park End Nthumb 112 C5
Parker's Green Kent 37 P11
Parkeston Essex 53 M5
Parkeston Quay Essex 53 M5
Park Farm Kent 26 H4
Parkgate Ches W 81 K9
Parkgate Cumb 110 D11
Parkgate D & G 109 M3
Parkgate E Susx 26 B9
Parkgate Essex 51 Q5
Park Gate Hants 14 F5
Parkgate Kent 26 E5
Parkgate Kent 37 M8
Park Gate Leeds 90 F2
Parkgate Surrey 24 F2
Park Gate Worcs 58 D10
Park Green Essex 51 L5
Park Green Suffk 64 G9
Parkhall W Duns 125 M3
Parkham Devon 16 F7
Parkham Ash Devon 16 F7
Park Head Derbys 84 E10
Parkhill Dur 104 B3
Park Hill Gloucs 31 Q5
Parkhouse Mons 31 P4
Parkmill Swans 28 F7
Park Royal Gt Lon 36 E4
Parkside Dur 113 P11
Parkside N Lans 126 E6
Parkside Wrexhm 69 L3
Parkstone BCP 12 H6
Park Street Herts 50 D10
Park Street W Susx 24 D4
Parkway Herefs 46 D7
Parley Green BCP 13 K5
Parmoor Bucks 35 L7
Parracombe Devon 17 M2
Parrog Pembks 41 L3
Parsonby Cumb 100 F3
Parson Cross Sheff 84 D2
Parson Drove Cambs 74 G9
Parson's Heath Essex 52 H6
Parson's Hill Derbys 71 P9
Partick C Glas 125 N4
Partington Traffd 82 F6
Partney Lincs 87 M7
Parton Cumb 100 C6
Partridge Green W Susx 24 E7
Partrishow Powys 45 K10
Parwich Derbys 71 M4
Paslow Wood Common Essex 51 N10
Passenham Nhants 49 L7
Passfield Hants 23 M8
Passingford Bridge Essex 51 M11
Paston C Pete 74 C10
Paston Norfk 77 L5
Pasturefields Staffs 70 H10
Patchacott Devon 8 C5
Patcham Br & H 24 H9
Patchetts Green Herts 50 D11
Patching W Susx 24 C9
Patchole Devon 17 L3
Patchway S Glos 32 B8
Pateley Bridge N York 97 J7
Paternoster Heath Essex 52 F8
Pathe Somset 19 L8
Pathhead Fife 134 H9
Pathhead Mdloth 128 B7
Pathlow Warwks 47 N3
Path of Condie P & K 134 D5
Patmore Heath Herts 51 K5
Patna E Ayrs 114 H5
Patney Wilts 21 L3
Patrick IoM 80 b5
Patrick Brompton N York 97 K2
Patricroft Salfd 82 G5
Patrington E R Yk 93 P6
Patrington Haven E R Yk 93 P6
Patrixbourne Kent 39 L10
Patterdale Cumb 101 L7
Pattingham Staffs 57 Q5
Pattishall Nhants 49 J4
Pattiswick Green Essex 52 D7
Patton Shrops 57 K5
Patton Bridge Cumb 101 Q11
Paul Cnwll 2 D8
Paulerspury Nhants 49 K5
Paull E R Yk 93 L5
Paulton BaNES 20 C3
Paultons Park Hants 22 B11
Paunton Herefs 46 C4
Pauperhaugh Nthumb 119 M11
Pave Lane Wrekin 70 D11
Pavenham Bed 61 L9
Pawlett Somset 19 J6
Pawston Nthumb 118 G4
Paxford Gloucs 47 N7
Paxton Border 129 N9
Payden Street Kent 38 F11
Payhembury Devon 10 B4
Paynter's Lane End Cnwll 2 H5
Paythorne Lancs 96 B10
Paytoe Herefs 56 G10
Peacehaven E Susx 25 K10
Peak Dale Derbys 83 N9
Peak District National Park 83 Q6
Peak Forest Derbys 83 P9
Peak Hill Lincs 74 E7
Peakirk C Pete 74 C9
Pearson's Green Kent 25 Q2
Peartree Green Herefs 46 A8
Peasedown St John BaNES 20 D3
Peasehill Derbys 84 F11
Peaseland Green Norfk 76 F8
Peasemore W Berk 34 E9
Peasenhall Suffk 65 M8
Pease Pottage W Susx 24 G4
Pease Pottage Services W Susx 24 G4
Peaslake Surrey 24 C2
Peasley Cross St Hel 81 Q6
Peasmarsh E Susx 26 E7
Peasmarsh Somset 10 G2
Peasmarsh Surrey 23 Q5
Peathill Abers 159 M4
Peat Inn Fife 135 M6
Peatling Magna Leics 60 C2
Peatling Parva Leics 60 C3
Peaton Shrops 57 J7
Pebmarsh Essex 52 E5
Pebsham E Susx 26 C10
Pebworth Worcs 47 M5
Pecket Well Calder 90 B5
Peckforton Ches E 69 P3
Peckham Gt Lon 36 H5
Peckleton Leics 72 D10
Pedairffordd Powys 68 F10
Pedlinge Kent 27 K4
Pedmore Dudley 58 D8
Pedwell Somset 19 M7
Peebles Border 117 K2
Peel IoM 80 b5
Peel Lancs 88 D4
Peel Common Hants 14 G6
Peene Kent 27 L4
Peening Quarter Kent 26 E6
Peggs Green Leics 72 C7
Pegsdon C Beds 50 D4
Pegswood Nthumb 113 K3
Pegwell Kent 39 Q9
Peinchorran Highld 153 J11
Peinlich Highld 152 G6
Pelcomb Pembks 40 H7
Pelcomb Bridge Pembks 40 H7
Pelcomb Cross Pembks 40 H7
Peldon Essex 52 G8
Pell Green E Susx 25 P4
Pelsall Wsall 58 F4
Pelsall Wood Wsall 58 F4
Pelton Dur 113 L10
Pelton Fell Dur 113 L10
Pelutho Cumb 109 P11
Pelynt Cnwll 5 L10
Pemberton Carmth 28 F4
Pemberton Wigan 82 C4
Pembles Cross Kent 26 E2
Pembrey Carmth 28 D4
Pembridge Herefs 45 M3
Pembroke Pembks 41 J10
Pembroke Dock Pembks 41 J10
Pembrokeshire Coast National Park Pembks 40 F6
Pembury Kent 25 P2
Pen-allt Herefs 45 R9
Penallt Mons 31 P2
Penally Pembks 41 M11
Penare Cnwll 3 P5
Penarth V Glam 30 G10
Penblewin Pembks 41 M7
Pen-bont Rhydybeddau Cerdgn 54 F8
Penbryn Cerdgn 42 E4
Pencader Carmth 42 H7
Pencaenewydd Gwynd 66 G6
Pencaitland E Loth 128 C6
Pencarnisiog IoA 78 F10
Pencarreg Carmth 43 K5
Pencarrow Cnwll 5 J5
Pencelli Powys 44 F9
Penclawdd Swans 28 F5
Pencoed Brdgnd 30 C8
Pencombe Herefs 46 A4
Pencoyd Herefs 45 Q9
Pencraig Herefs 45 R10
Pencraig Powys 68 D9
Pendeen Cnwll 2 B7
Penderyn Rhondd 29 P3
Pendine Carmth 41 P9
Pendlebury Salfd 82 G4
Pendleton Lancs 89 M3
Pendock Worcs 46 E8
Pendoggett Cnwll 4 G6
Pendomer Somset 11 L2
Pendoylan V Glam 30 E9
Penegoes Powys 54 H4
Penelewey Cnwll 3 L5
Pen-ffordd Pembks 41 L6
Pengam Caerph 30 G5
Pengam Cardif 30 H9
Penge Gt Lon 37 J6
Pengelly Cnwll 4 H5
Pengenffordd Powys 44 H9
Pengorffwysfa IoA 78 H6
Pengover Green Cnwll 5 M8
Pen-groes-oped Mons 31 K3
Pengwern Denbgs 80 E9
Penhale Cnwll 2 H10
Penhale Cnwll 4 E10
Penhale Cnwll 4 H9
Penhale Cnwll 5 Q11
Penhallow Cnwll 3 K3
Penhalurick Cnwll 3 J6
Penhalvean Cnwll 3 J6
Penhill Swindn 33 N7
Penhow Newpt 31 M6
Penhurst E Susx 25 Q7
Peniarth Gwynd 54 E3
Penicuik Mdloth 127 N6
Peniel Carmth 42 H10
Peniel Denbgs 68 D2
Penifiler Highld 152 H9
Peninver Ag & B 120 E7
Penisarwaun Gwynd 67 K2
Penistone Barns 90 G10
Penjerrick Cnwll 3 K7
Penketh Warrtn 82 C7
Penkill S Ayrs 114 D8
Penkridge Staffs 58 D2
Penlean Cnwll 5 L2
Penleigh Wilts 20 G4
Penley Wrexhm 69 M6
Penllergaer Swans 28 H5
Pen-llyn IoA 78 F8
Penllyn V Glam 30 C9
Pen-lôn IoA 78 G11
Penmachno Conwy 67 P4
Penmaen Caerph 30 G5
Penmaen Swans 28 F7
Penmaenan Conwy 79 N9
Penmaenmawr Conwy 79 N9
Penmaenpool Gwynd 67 M11
Penmark V Glam 30 E11
Penmon IoA 79 L8
Penmorfa Gwynd 67 J6
Penmynydd IoA 79 J10
Penn Bucks 35 P6
Penn Wolves 58 C5
Pennal Gwynd 54 F4
Pennan Abers 159 K4
Pennant Cerdgn 43 K2
Pennant Denbgs 68 D8
Pennant Powys 55 K5
Pennant-Melangell Powys 68 D9
Pennar Pembks 41 J10
Pennard Swans 28 G7
Pennerley Shrops 56 F5
Pennicott Devon 9 L4
Pennines 90 B3
Pennington Cumb 94 F5
Pennington Hants 13 P5
Pennington Green Wigan 89 J9
Pennorth Powys 44 G9
Penn Street Bucks 35 P5
Pennsylvania S Glos 32 D10
Penny Bridge Cumb 94 G4
Pennycross Ag & B 137 N10
Pennygate Norfk 77 L7
Pennyghael Ag & B 137 N10
Pennyglen S Ayrs 114 E5
Penny Green Derbys 84 H5
Penny Hill Lincs 74 G5
Pennymoor Devon 9 L2
Pennywell Sundld 113 N9
Penparc Cerdgn 42 D5
Penparcau Cerdgn 54 D8
Penpedairheol Caerph 30 F5
Penpedairheol Mons 31 K4
Penpergwm Mons 31 K2
Penperlleni Mons 31 K4
Penpethy Cnwll 4 H4
Penpillick Cnwll 4 H10
Penpol Cnwll 3 L6
Penpoll Cnwll 5 J11
Penponds Cnwll 2 G6
Penpont Cnwll 4 H7
Penpont D & G 108 H2
Penpont Powys 44 D9
Penquit Devon 6 G8
Penrest Cnwll 5 N6
Penrherber Carmth 41 Q3
Pen-rhiw Pembks 41 P2
Penrhiwceiber Rhondd 30 E5
Pen Rhiwfawr Neath 29 K2
Penrhiwgoch Carmth 43 L11
Penrhiwllan Cerdgn 42 G6
Penrhiwpal Cerdgn 42 F5
Penrhos Gwynd 66 E8
Penrhos IoA 78 D8
Penrhos Mons 31 M2
Penrhos Powys 29 M2
Penrhos garnedd Gwynd 79 K10
Penrhyn Bay Conwy 79 Q8
Penrhyn-coch Cerdgn 54 E8
Penrhyndeudraeth Gwynd 67 L7
Penrhyn-side Conwy 79 Q8
Penrhys Rhondd 30 D6
Penrice Swans 28 E7
Penrioch N Ayrs 120 G3
Penrith Cumb 101 P4
Penrose Cnwll 4 D7
Penruddock Cumb 101 M5
Penryn Cnwll 3 K7
Pensarn Conwy 80 D9
Pensax Worcs 57 N11
Pensby Wirral 81 K8
Penselwood Somset 20 E8
Pensford BaNES 20 B2
Pensham Worcs 46 H6
Penshaw Sundld 113 M10
Penshurst Kent 25 M2
Penshurst Station Kent 37 M11
Pensilva Cnwll 5 M7
Pensnett Dudley 58 D7
Penstone Devon 9 J4
Penstrowed Powys 55 P6
Pentewan Cnwll 3 Q4
Pentir Gwynd 79 K11
Pentire Cnwll 4 B9
Pentlepoir Pembks 41 M9
Pentlow Essex 52 D3
Pentlow Street Essex 63 P11
Pentney Norfk 75 P8
Pentonbridge Cumb 110 H5
Penton Grafton Hants 22 B5
Penton Mewsey Hants 22 B5
Pentraeth IoA 79 J9
Pentre Denbgs 68 E2
Pentre Flints 81 L11
Pentre Mons 31 K3
Pentre Mons 31 M4
Pentre Powys 55 P7
Pentre Powys 56 B7
Pentre Powys 56 D6
Pentre Rhondd 30 C5
Pentre Shrops 69 L11
Pentre Wrexhm 69 J6
Pentre-bâch Cerdgn 43 L5
Pentre Bach Flints 81 J9

Pentrebach Myr Td 30 E4
Pentre-bach Powys 44 C8
Pentrebeirdd Powys 56 B2
Pentre Berw IoA 78 H10
Pentre-bont Conwy 67 N4
Pentre-cagel Carmth 42 F6
Pentrecelyn Denbgs 67 F4
Pentre-celyn Powys 55 K3
Pentre-chwyth Swans 29 J6
Pentre-clawdd Shrops 69 J8
Pentre-cwrt Carmth 42 G7
Pentredwr Denbgs 68 G5
Pentrefelin Gwynd 67 J7
Pentrefelin IoA 78 L6
Pentre Ffwrndan Flints 81 K10
Pentrefoelas Conwy 67 R4
Pentregalar Pembks 41 N4
Pentregat Cerdgn 42 G4
Pentre-Gwenlais Carmth 43 M11
Pentre Gwynfryn Gwynd 67 K9
Pentre Halkyn Flints 81 J10
Pentre Hodrey Shrops 56 E9
Pentre Isaf Conwy 80 D10
Pentre Llanrhaeadr Denbgs 68 E2
Pentre Llifior Powys 56 B5
Pentre-llwyn-llwyd Powys 44 D4
Pentre-llyn Cerdgn 54 E9
Pentre-llyn-cymmer Conwy 68 C4
Pentre-Maw Powys 55 K4
Pentre Meyrick V Glam 30 C9
Pentre-piod Torfn 31 J4
Pentre-poeth Newpt 31 J7
Pentre'r'bryn Cerdgn 42 G4
Pentre'r-felin Cerdgn 43 M5
Pentre'r Felin Conwy 79 Q11
Pentre'r Felin Powys 44 C8
Pentre Saron Denbgs 68 D2
Pentre-tafarn-y-fedw Conwy 67 Q2
Pentre ty gwyn Carmth 43 R7
Pentrich Derbys 84 E10
Pentridge Dorset 21 K11
Pen-twyn Caerph 30 H4
Pentwyn Cardif 30 H8
Pen-twyn Mons 31 P3
Pen-twyn Torfn 31 J4
Pentwynmaur Caerph 30 G5
Pentyrch Cardif 30 F8
Penwithick Cnwll 4 G10
Penwood Hants 22 D2
Penwyllt Powys 44 B11
Penybanc Carmth 43 M10
Penybont Powys 44 G2
Pen-y-bont Powys 68 H10
Penybontfawr Powys 68 E10
Pen-y-bryn Pembks 41 N2
Pen-y-cae Powys 29 M2
Penycae Wrexhm 69 J5
Pen-y-cae-mawr Mons 31 M5
Penycaerau Gwynd 66 B9
Pen-y-cefn Flints 80 G9
Pen-y-clawdd Mons 31 N3
Pen-y-coedcae Rhondd 30 E7
Penycwn Pembks 40 G6
Pen-y-fai Brdgnd 29 N8
Pen-y-felin Flints 80 H11
Penyffordd Flints 69 K2
Pen-y-ffordd Flints 80 G8
Penyffridd Gwynd 67 J3
Pen-y-garn Cerdgn 54 E7
Pen-y-Garnedd Powys 68 F10
Pen-y-graig Gwynd 66 C8
Penygraig Rhondd 30 D6
Penygroes Carmth 28 G2
Penygroes Gwynd 66 H4
Penygroeslon Gwynd 66 C8
Pen-y-Gwryd Gwynd 67 M3
Pen-y-lan V Glam 30 C9
Pen-y-Mynydd Carmth 28 E4
Penymynydd Flints 69 K2
Pen-y-pass Gwynd 67 L3
Pen-yr-Heol Mons 31 M2
Penysarn IoA 78 H6
Pen-y-stryt Denbgs 68 H4
Penywaun Rhondd 30 C4
Penzance Cnwll 2 D7
Peopleton Worcs 46 H4
Peover Heath Ches E 82 G10
Peper Harow Surrey 23 P6
Peplow Shrops 70 A10
Pepper's Green Essex 51 P8
Pepperstock C Beds 50 C7
Perceton N Ayrs 125 K4
Percyhorner Abers 159 N4
Perelle Guern 10 b2
Perham Down Wilts 21 Q5
Periton Somset 18 C5
Perivale Gt Lon 36 E4
Perkins Village Devon 9 P6
Perkinsville Dur 113 L10
Perlethorpe Notts 85 K6
Perranarworthal Cnwll 3 K5
Perranporth Cnwll 3 K3
Perranuthnoe Cnwll 2 E8
Perranwell Cnwll 3 K3
Perranwell Cnwll 3 K5
Perran Wharf Cnwll 3 K5
Perranzabuloe Cnwll 3 K3
Perrott's Brook Gloucs 33 K3
Perry Birm 58 G6
Perry Cambs 61 P7
Perry Barr Birm 58 G6
Perry Green Essex 52 B2
Perry Green Herts 51 K7
Perry Green Wilts 33 L3
Perrystone Hill Herefs 46 B9
Perry Street Somset 10 H3
Pershall Staffs 70 E9
Pershore Worcs 46 H5
Pertenhall Bed 61 N7
Perth P & K 134 E3
Perthy Shrops 69 L8
Perton Herefs 46 A6
Perton Staffs 58 C5
Pertwood Wilts 20 G7
Peterborough C Pete 74 C11
Peterborough Services Cambs 61 P2
Peterchurch Herefs 45 L7
Peterculter C Aber 151 L7
Peterhead Abers 159 R8
Peterlee Dur 104 D2
Petersfield Hants 23 K10
Peter's Green Herts 50 D7
Petersham Gt Lon 36 E6
Peters Marland Devon 16 H9

Peterstone Wentlooge Newpt 31 J9
Peterston-super-Ely V Glam 30 E9
Peterstow Herefs 45 R10
Peters Village Kent 38 B9
Peter Tavy Devon 8 D9
Petham Kent 39 K11
Petherwin Gate Cnwll 5 M4
Petrockstow Devon 17 J10
Petsoe End M Keyn 49 N5
Pet Street Kent 27 J2
Pett E Susx 26 E9
Pettaugh Suffk 64 H10
Pett Bottom Kent 39 L11
Petterden Angus 142 G10
Pettinain S Lans 116 D2
Pettistree Suffk 65 L10
Petton Devon 18 D10
Petton Shrops 69 M9
Petts Wood Gt Lon 37 L7
Pettycur Fife 134 H10
Petty France S Glos 32 E7
Pettymuk Abers 151 N3
Petworth W Susx 23 Q10
Pevensey E Susx 25 P9
Pevensey Bay E Susx 25 Q10
Pewsey Wilts 21 N2
Pewsham Wilts 32 H10
Pheasant's Hill Bucks 35 L7
Phepson Worcs 46 H3
Philadelphia Sundld 113 M10
Philham Devon 16 D7
Philiphaugh Border 117 N5
Phillack Cnwll 2 F6
Philleigh Cnwll 3 M6
Philpot End Essex 51 P7
Philpstoun W Loth 127 K2
Phocle Green Herefs 46 B9
Phoenix Green Hants 23 L3
Pibsbury Somset 19 M9
Pica Cumb 100 D6
Piccadilly Warwks 59 K5
Piccotts End Herts 50 B9
Pickburn Donc 91 N9
Pickering N York 98 F4
Picket Piece Hants 22 C5
Picket Post Hants 13 L3
Picket Twenty Hants 22 C5
Pickford Covtry 59 L8
Pickford Green Covtry 59 L8
Pickhill N York 97 M4
Picklescott Shrops 56 G4
Pickmere Ches E 82 E9
Pickney Somset 18 G9
Pickstock Wrekin 70 C10
Pickup Bank Bl w D 89 L6
Pickwell Devon 16 H3
Pickwell Leics 73 K8
Pickwick Wilts 32 G10
Pickworth Lincs 73 Q4
Pickworth Rutlnd 73 P8
Picton Ches W 81 N10
Picton Flints 80 G8
Picton N York 104 D9
Piddinghoe E Susx 25 K10
Piddington Bucks 35 M6
Piddington Nhants 49 M4
Piddington Oxon 48 H11
Piddlehinton Dorset 11 Q5
Piddletrenthide Dorset 11 Q5
Pidley Cambs 62 D5
Piercebridge Darltn 103 P7
Pierowall Ork 169 d2
Piff's Elm Gloucs 46 H9
Pigdon Nthumb 113 J3
Pigeon Green Warwks 47 P2
Pig Oak Dorset 12 H4
Pig Street Herefs 45 M5
Pikehall Derbys 71 M3
Pilford Dorset 12 H4
Pilgrims Hatch Essex 51 N11
Pilham Lincs 85 Q2
Pill N Som 31 P9
Pillaton Cnwll 5 P9
Pillatonmill Cnwll 5 P9
Pillerton Hersey Warwks 47 Q5
Pillerton Priors Warwks 47 Q5
Pilleth Powys 56 D11
Pilley Barns 91 J10
Pilley Hants 13 P5
Pilley Bailey Hants 13 P5
Pillgwenlly Newpt 31 K7
Pillhead Devon 16 H6
Pilling Lancs 95 J11
Pilling Lane Lancs 94 H11
Pilning S Glos 31 Q7
Pilot Inn Kent 27 J8
Pilsbury Derbys 71 L2
Pilsdon Dorset 11 J5
Pilsgate C Pete 73 R9
Pilsley Derbys 84 B6
Pilsley Derbys 84 F8
Pilson Green Norfk 77 M9
Piltdown E Susx 25 K6
Pilton Devon 17 K5
Pilton Nhants 61 M4
Pilton Rutlnd 73 N10
Pilton Somset 19 Q6
Pilton Green Swans 28 D7
Pimbo Lancs 81 P4
Pimlico Herts 50 C9
Pimlico Lancs 89 L2
Pimlico Nhants 48 H6
Pimperne Dorset 12 F3
Pinchbeck Lincs 74 D5
Pinchbeck Bars Lincs 74 C5
Pincheon Green Donc 91 R7
Pinchinthorpe R & Cl 104 G8
Pincock Lancs 88 G7
Pinfold Lancs 88 D8
Pinford End Suffk 64 A10
Pinged Carmth 28 D4
Pingewood W Berk 35 J11
Pin Green Herts 50 G5
Pinhoe Devon 9 N6
Pinkett's Booth Covtry 59 L8
Pinkney Wilts 32 G7
Pinkneys Green W & M 35 N8
Pinley Covtry 59 N9
Pinley Green Warwks 59 K11
Pin Mill Suffk 53 M4
Pinminnoch S Ayrs 114 C9
Pinmore S Ayrs 114 D9
Pinn Devon 10 C7
Pinner Gt Lon 36 D3
Pinner Green Gt Lon 36 D2

Pinsley Green Ches E 69 Q5
Pinvin Worcs 47 J5
Pinwherry S Ayrs 114 D10
Pinxton Derbys 84 G10
Pipe and Lyde Herefs 45 Q6
Pipe Aston Herefs 56 H10
Pipe Gate Shrops 70 C6
Pipehill Staffs 58 G3
Piperdam Angus 142 D11
Piperhill Highld 156 F7
Pipers Pool Cnwll 5 M5
Pipewell Nhants 60 H3
Pippacott Devon 17 J4
Pippin Street Lancs 88 H6
Pipton Powys 44 H7
Pirbright Surrey 23 P3
Pirbright Camp Surrey 23 P3
Pirnie Border 118 C5
Pirnmill N Ayrs 120 G3
Pirton Herts 50 D4
Pirton Worcs 46 G5
Pisgah Cerdgn 54 F9
Pishill Oxon 35 K7
Pistyll Gwynd 66 E6
Pitblae Abers 159 N5
Pitcairngreen P & K 134 D2
Pitcalnie Highld 156 E3
Pitcaple Abers 151 J2
Pitcarity Angus 142 E4
Pitchcombe Gloucs 32 G3
Pitchcott Bucks 49 L10
Pitcher Row Lincs 74 E4
Pitchford Shrops 57 J4
Pitch Green Bucks 35 L4
Pitch Place Surrey 23 N7
Pitch Place Surrey 23 Q4
Pitchroy Moray 157 M10
Pitcombe Somset 20 C8
Pitcot V Glam 29 N10
Pitcox E Loth 128 G5
Pitfichie Abers 150 H4
Pitglassie Abers 158 G9
Pitgrudy Highld 162 H8
Pitlessie Fife 135 J6
Pitlochry P & K 141 M6
Pitmachie Abers 150 H2
Pitmain Highld 148 C7
Pitmedden Abers 151 M2
Pitminster Somset 18 H11
Pitmuies Angus 143 K8
Pitmunie Abers 150 H5
Pitney Somset 19 N9
Pitroddie P & K 134 G2
Pitscottie Fife 135 L5
Pitsea Essex 38 B4
Pitses Oldham 83 K4
Pitsford Nhants 60 G7
Pitstone Bucks 49 P11
Pitt Devon 18 D11
Pitt Hants 22 E9
Pittarrow Abers 143 N3
Pitt Court Gloucs 32 D5
Pittenweem Fife 135 P7
Pitteuchar Fife 134 H8
Pittodrie House Hotel Abers 150 H3
Pitton Wilts 21 P8
Pitt's Wood Kent 37 P11
Pittulie Abers 159 N4
Pityme Cnwll 4 F6
Pity Me Dur 113 L11
Pivington Kent 26 F2
Pixey Green Suffk 65 J6
Pixham Surrey 36 E10
Plains N Lans 126 D4
Plain Street Cnwll 4 F6
Plaish Shrops 57 J5
Plaistow Gt Lon 37 K4
Plaistow W Susx 24 B4
Plaitford Hants 21 Q11
Plank Lane Wigan 82 D5
Plas Cymyran IoA 78 D9
Plastow Green Hants 22 F2
Platt Bridge Wigan 82 D4
Platt Lane Shrops 69 P7
Platts Heath Kent 38 E11
Plawsworth Dur 113 L11
Plaxtol Kent 37 P10
Playden E Susx 26 F7
Playford Suffk 53 M2
Play Hatch Oxon 35 K9
Playing Place Cnwll 3 L5
Playley Green Gloucs 46 E8
Plealey Shrops 56 G3
Plean Stirlg 133 N10
Pleasance Fife 134 G5
Pleasington Bl w D 89 J5
Pleasley Derbys 84 H8
Pleasleyhill Notts 84 H8
Pleasurewood Hills Suffk 65 Q2
Pleck Dorset 11 Q2
Pledgdon Green Essex 51 N5
Pledwick Wakefd 91 J7
Pleinheaume Guern 10 b1
Plemont Jersey 11 a1
Plemstall Ches W 81 P10
Plenmeller Nthumb 111 P8
Pleshey Essex 51 Q8
Plockton Highld 153 Q11
Plowden Shrops 56 F7
Plox Green Shrops 56 F4
Pluckley Kent 26 F2
Pluckley Station Kent 26 F3
Pluckley Thorne Kent 26 F3
Plucks Gutter Kent 39 N9
Plumbland Cumb 100 G3
Plumgarths Cumb 95 K2
Plumley Ches E 82 F10
Plump Hill Gloucs 46 C11
Plumpton Cumb 101 N4
Plumpton Cumb 94 D4
Plumpton E Susx 25 J8
Plumpton Nhants 48 G5
Plumpton End Nhants 49 K6
Plumpton Green E Susx 25 J7
Plumpton Head Cumb 101 P3
Plumstead Gt Lon 37 K5
Plumstead Norfk 76 H5
Plumstead Green Norfk 76 G5
Plumtree Notts 72 G4
Plumtree Green Kent 26 D2
Plungar Leics 73 K4
Plurenden Kent 26 F4
Plush Dorset 11 Q4
Plusha Cnwll 5 M5

Plushabridge Cnwll 5 N7
Plwmp Cerdgn 42 G4
Plymouth C Plym 6 D8
Plympton C Plym 6 E7
Plymstock C Plym 6 E8
Plymtree Devon 9 Q4
Pockley N York 98 C3
Pocklington E R Yk 98 G11
Pode Hole Lincs 74 D6
Podimore Somset 19 P10
Podington Bed 61 K8
Podmore Staffs 70 D7
Point Clear Essex 53 K9
Pointon Lincs 74 B4
Pokesdown BCP 13 K6
Polbain Highld 160 F4
Polbathic Cnwll 5 N10
Polbeth W Loth 127 J5
Polbrock Cnwll 4 G8
Poldark Mine Cnwll 2 H7
Polebrook Nhants 61 N3
Pole Elm Worcs 46 F4
Polegate E Susx 25 N10
Pole Moor Kirk 90 D7
Polesden Lacey Surrey 36 D10
Polesworth Warwks 59 L4
Polgigga Cnwll 2 B9
Polglass Highld 160 G5
Polgooth Cnwll 3 P3
Polgown D & G 115 P7
Poling W Susx 24 B10
Poling Corner W Susx 24 B9
Polkerris Cnwll 4 H11
Pollard Street Norfk 77 L5
Pollington E R Yk 91 Q7
Polloch Highld 138 D4
Pollokshaws C Glas 125 P5
Pollokshields C Glas 125 P5
Polmassick Cnwll 3 P4
Polmear Cnwll 4 H11
Polmont Falk 126 G2
Polnish Highld 145 N11
Polperro Cnwll 5 L11
Polruan Cnwll 5 J11
Polsham Somset 19 P6
Polstead Suffk 52 G4
Polstead Heath Suffk 52 G3
Poltalloch Ag & B 130 G8
Poltescoe Cnwll 3 J10
Poltimore Devon 9 N5
Polton Mdloth 127 P5
Polwarth Border 129 J9
Polyphant Cnwll 5 M5
Polzeath Cnwll 4 E6
Pomathorn Mdloth 127 N6
Pomeroy Derbys 83 P11
Ponde Powys 44 G7
Pondersbridge Cambs 62 C2
Ponders End Gt Lon 51 J11
Ponsanooth Cnwll 3 K6
Ponsonby Cumb 100 E9
Ponsongath Cnwll 3 K10
Ponsworthy Devon 7 J4
Pont Abraham Services Carmth 28 G3
Pontac Jersey 11 c2
Pontamman Carmth 28 H2
Pontantwn Carmth 28 D2
Pontardawe Neath 28 K4
Pontarddulais Swans 28 G4
Pont-ar-gothi Carmth 43 K10
Pont-ar-Hydfer Powys 44 B9
Pont-ar-llechau Carmth 43 P10
Pontarsais Carmth 42 H9
Pontblyddyn Flints 69 J2
Pont Cyfyng Conwy 67 N3
Pontcysyllte Aqueduct Wrexhm 69 J6
Pont Dolgarrog Conwy 79 P11
Pontdolgoch Powys 55 N6
Pont-Ebbw Newpt 31 J7
Pontefract Wakefd 91 M6
Ponteland Nthumb 113 J6
Ponterwyd Cerdgn 54 G8
Pontesbury Shrops 56 F3
Pontesbury Hill Shrops 56 F3
Pontesford Shrops 56 G3
Pontfadog Wrexhm 68 H7
Pontfaen Pembks 41 K4
Pont-faen Powys 44 C8
Pontgarreg Cerdgn 42 F4
Pontgarreg Pembks 41 M2
Ponthenri Carmth 28 E3
Ponthir Torfn 31 K6
Ponthirwaun Cerdgn 42 E5
Pontllanfraith Caerph 30 G5
Pontlliw Swans 28 H4
Pontllyfni Gwynd 66 G4
Pontlottyn Caerph 30 F3
Pont Morlais Carmth 28 F3
Pontnêddfèchan Neath 29 P3
Pontnewydd Torfn 31 J5
Pontnewynydd Torfn 31 J4
Pont Pen-y-benglog Gwynd 67 M2
Pontrhydfendigaid Cerdgn 54 G11
Pont Rhyd-sarn Gwynd 67 R9
Pont Rhyd-y-cyff Brdgnd 29 M3
Pontrhydyfen Neath 29 L6
Pont-rhyd-y-groes Cerdgn 54 G10
Pontrhydyrun Torfn 31 J5
Pontrilas Herefs 45 M9
Pont Robert Powys 55 Q2
Pont-rug Gwynd 67 J2
Ponts Green E Susx 25 Q7
Pontshaen Cerdgn 42 H5
Pontshill Herefs 46 B10
Pontsticill Myr Td 30 E2
Pont Walby Neath 29 N3
Pontwelly Carmth 42 H6
Pontyates Carmth 28 E2
Pontyberem Carmth 28 F2
Pont-y-blew Wrexhm 69 K7
Pontybodkin Flints 69 J3
Pontyclun Rhondd 30 D8
Pontycymer Brdgnd 29 P6
Pontyglasier Pembks 41 M3
Pontygwaith Rhondd 30 D6
Pontygynon Pembks 41 M3
Pontymister Caerph 30 H6
Pont-y-pant Conwy 67 P4
Pontypool Torfn 31 J4
Pontypridd Rhondd 30 E7
Pont-yr-hafod Pembks 40 H5
Pont-yr-Rhyl Brdgnd 29 P7
Pontywaun Caerph 30 H5
Pool Cnwll 2 H5

Pool IoS 2 b2
Poole BCP 12 H6
Poole Keynes Gloucs 33 J5
Poolewe Highld 160 D10
Pooley Bridge Cumb 101 N6
Pooley Street Norfk 64 F3
Poolfold Staffs 70 F3
Pool Head Herefs 45 R4
Pool in Wharfedale Leeds 97 L11
Pool of Muckhart Clacks 134 C7
Pool Quay Powys 56 D2
Pool Street Essex 52 C4
Pootings Kent 37 L11
Popes Hill Gloucs 32 C2
Popham Hants 22 G6
Poplar Gt Lon 37 J4
Poplar Street Suffk 65 N8
Porchfield IoW 14 D8
Poringland Norfk 77 K11
Porkellis Cnwll 2 H7
Porlock Somset 18 A5
Porlock Weir Somset 17 R2
Portachoillan Ag & B 123 N11
Port-an-Eorna Highld 153 P11
Port Appin Ag & B 138 G4
Port Askaig Ag & B 122 F6
Portavadie Ag & B 124 C4
Port Bannatyne Ag & B 124 C4
Portbury N Som 31 P9
Port Carlisle Cumb 110 D8
Port Charlotte Ag & B 122 C4
Portchester Hants 14 H5
Port Clarence S on T 104 E6
Port Driseach Ag & B 124 B3
Port Ellen Ag & B 122 E10
Port Elphinstone Abers 151 K3
Portencalzie D & G 106 D3
Portencross N Ayrs 124 C11
Port Erin IoM 80 a8
Portesham Dorset 11 N7
Portessie Moray 158 B4
Port e Vullen IoM 80 e3
Port Eynon Swans 28 E7
Portfield Gate Pembks 40 H5
Portgate Devon 5 Q4
Port Gaverne Cnwll 4 G5
Port Glasgow Inver 125 J3
Portgordon Moray 158 A5
Portgower Highld 163 N4
Porth Cnwll 4 C9
Porth Rhondd 30 D6
Porthallow Cnwll 3 K9
Porthallow Cnwll 5 L11
Porthcawl Brdgnd 29 M9
Porthcothan Cnwll 4 C7
Porthcurno Cnwll 2 B9
Porthdinllaen Gwynd 66 D6
Port Henderson Highld 153 P3
Porthgain Pembks 40 F4
Porthgwarra Cnwll 2 B9
Porthill Staffs 70 F4
Porthkea Cnwll 3 L5
Porthkerry V Glam 30 E11
Porthleven Cnwll 2 G8
Porthmadog Gwynd 67 K7
Porthmeor Cnwll 2 C7
Porth Navas Cnwll 3 K8
Portholland Cnwll 3 P5
Porthoustock Cnwll 3 L9
Porthpean Cnwll 3 Q3
Porthtowan Cnwll 3 H4
Porthwgan Wrexhm 69 L5
Porthyrhyd Carmth 43 K11
Porth-y-Waen Shrops 69 J10
Portincaple Ag & B 131 Q3
Portinfer Jersey 11 a1
Portington E R Yk 92 C4
Portinnisherrich Ag & B 131 K5
Portinscale Cumb 101 J5
Port Isaac Cnwll 4 F5
Portishead N Som 31 N9
Portknockie Moray 158 C4
Portland Dorset 11 P9
Portlethen Abers 151 N8
Portling D & G 109 J9
Portloe Cnwll 3 N6
Port Logan D & G 106 E8
Portlooe Cnwll 5 L11
Portmahomack Highld 163 L8
Port Mary D & G 108 F11
Portmeirion Gwynd 67 K7
Portmellon Cnwll 3 Q5
Port Mòr Highld 144 F12
Portmore Hants 13 P5
Port Mulgrave N York 105 L8
Portnacroish Ag & B 138 G4
Portnaguran W Isls 168 k4
Portnahaven Ag & B 122 A4
Portnalong Highld 152 E11
Portnancon Highld 165 K4
Port nan Giùran W Isls 168 k4
Port nan Long W Isls 168 d10
Port Nis W Isls 168 k1
Portobello C Edin 127 Q3
Portobello Gatesd 113 L9
Portobello Wolves 58 E5
Port of Menteith Stirlg 132 F7
Port of Ness W Isls 168 k1
Porton Wilts 21 N7
Portontown Devon 5 Q6
Portpatrick D & G 106 C7
Port Quin Cnwll 4 F5
Port Ramsay Ag & B 138 F4
Portreath Cnwll 2 H4
Portreath Harbour Cnwll 2 H4
Portree Highld 152 H9
Port Righ Ag & B 120 G4
Port St Mary IoM 80 b8
Portscatho Cnwll 3 M6
Portsea C Port 14 H6
Portskerra Highld 166 E3
Portskewett Mons 31 N7
Portslade Br & H 24 G9
Portslade-by-Sea Br & H 24 G9
Portslogan D & G 106 C6
Portsmouth C Port 14 H7
Portsmouth Calder 89 Q5
Portsmouth Arms Devon 17 L8
Portsmouth Dockyard C Port 14 H6
Port Soderick IoM 80 d7
Port Solent C Port 14 H5
Portsonachan Hotel Ag & B 131 L3
Portsoy Abers 158 E4
Port Sunlight Wirral 81 L8

Portswood – Reisque 289

Portswood C Sotn 14 D4
Port Talbot Neath 29 L7
Port Tennant Swans 29 J6
Portuairk Highld 137 L2
Portway Herefs 45 P6
Portway Herefs 45 P7
Portway Sandw 58 E7
Portway Worcs 58 G10
Port Wemyss Ag & B 122 A9
Port William D & G 107 K9
Portwrinkle Cnwll 5 P11
Portyerrock D & G 107 N10
Posbury Devon 9 K5
Posenhall Shrops 57 M4
Poslingford Suffk 63 N11
Posso Border 117 J4
Postbridge Devon 8 G9
Postcombe Oxon 35 K4
Post Green Dorset 12 G6
Postling Kent 27 K4
Postwick Norfk 77 K10
Potarch Abers 150 G8
Potsgrove C Beds 49 Q8
Potten End Herts 50 B9
Potten Street Kent 39 N8
Potter Brompton N York 99 K5
Pottergate Street Norfk 64 H3
Potterhanworth Lincs 86 E7
Potterhanworth Booths
Lincs 86 E7
Potter Heigham Norfk 77 N8
Potterne Wilts 21 J3
Potterne Wick Wilts 21 J3
Potter Row Bucks 35 P4
Potters Bar Herts 50 F10
Potters Brook Lancs 95 K10
Potters Corner Kent 26 G3
Potter's Cross Staffs 58 B8
Potters Crouch Herts 50 D9
Potter's Forstal Kent 26 E2
Potters Green Covtry 59 N8
Potter's Green E Susx 25 M6
Potter's Green Herts 51 J6
Pottersheath Herts 50 F7
Potters Marston Leics 72 D11
Potter Somersal Derbys 71 L7
Potterspury Nhants 49 L6
Potter Street Essex 51 L9
Potterton Abers 151 N4
Potterton Leeds 91 L3
Potthorpe Norfk 76 C7
Pottle Street Wilts 20 F6
Potto N York 104 E10
Potton C Beds 62 B11
Pott Row Norfk 75 P6
Pott's Green Essex 52 F7
Pott Shrigley Ches E 83 K9
Poughill Cnwll 16 C10
Poughill Devon 9 L3
Poulner Hants 13 L3
Poulshot Wilts 21 J3
Poulton Gloucs 33 L4
Poulton Wirral 81 L6
Poulton-le-Fylde Lancs 88 C3
Poulton Priory Gloucs 33 L5
Pound Bank Worcs 57 N10
Poundbury Dorset 11 P6
Poundffald Swans 28 G6
Poundgate E Susx 25 L5
Pound Green E Susx 25 M6
Pound Green Suffk 63 M10
Pound Green Worcs 57 P9
Pound Hill W Susx 24 G3
Poundon Bucks 48 H9
Poundsbridge Kent 25 M2
Poundsgate Devon 7 J4
Poundstock Cnwll 5 L2
Pound Street Hants 22 E2
Pounsley E Susx 25 M6
Pouton D & G 107 N8
Pouy Street Suffk 65 M7
ovey Cross Surrey 24 G2
owburn Nthumb 119 L7
owderham Devon 9 N8
owerstock Dorset 11 L5
owfoot D & G 109 P7
ow Green Herefs 46 D6
owhill Cumb 110 D9
owick Worcs 46 F4
owmill P & K 134 C8
oxwell Dorset 12 B8
oyle Slough 36 B5
oynings W Susx 24 G8
oyntington Dorset 20 C10
oynton Ches E 83 K8
oynton Wrekin 69 Q11
oynton Green Wrekin 69 Q11
oyston Cross Pembks 41 J7
oystreet Green Suffk 64 D10
Praa Sands Cnwll 2 F8
Pratt's Bottom Gt Lon 37 L8
Praze-an-Beeble Cnwll 2 G6
Predannack Wollas Cnwll 2 H10
Prees Shrops 69 Q8
Preesall Lancs 94 H11
Prees Green Shrops 69 Q8
Preesgweene Shrops 69 J7
Prees Heath Shrops 69 Q7
Prees Higher Heath Shrops 69 Q7
Prees Lower Heath Shrops 69 Q8
Prendwick Nthumb 119 K8
Pren-gwyn Cerdgn 42 H6
Prenteg Gwynd 67 K6
Prenton Wirral 81 L7
Prescot Knows 81 P6
Prescott Devon 10 B2
Prescott Shrops 57 M8
Prescott Shrops 69 M10
Presnerb Angus 142 B4
Pressen Nthumb 118 F3
Prestatyn Denbgs 80 F8
Prestbury Ches E 83 J9
Prestbury Gloucs 47 J10
Presteigne Powys 45 L2
Prestleigh Somset 20 B6
Prestolee Bolton 89 M9
Preston Border 129 K8
Preston Br & H 24 H9
Preston Devon 7 M4
Preston Dorset 11 Q8
Preston E R Yk 93 L4
Preston Gloucs 33 K4
Preston Herts 50 E6
Preston Kent 38 H9
Preston Kent 39 M9
Preston Lancs 88 G5
Preston Nthumb 119 N5
Preston Rutlnd 73 M10
Preston Shrops 57 J2
Preston Somset 18 E7
Preston Torbay 7 M6
Preston Wilts 33 K9
Preston Wilts 33 Q10
Preston Bagot Warwks 59 J11
Preston Bissett Bucks 49 J9
Preston Bowyer Somset 18 F9
Preston Brockhurst Shrops 69 P10
Preston Brook Halton 82 C8
Preston Candover Hants 22 H6
Preston Capes Nhants 48 G4
Preston Crowmarsh Oxon 34 H6
Preston Deanery Nhants 60 G9
Preston Green Warwks 59 J11
Preston Gubbals Shrops 69 N11
Preston Montford Shrops 56 G2
Preston on Stour Warwks 47 P5
Preston on Tees S on T 104 D7
Preston on the Hill Halton 82 C8
Preston on Wye Herefs 45 M6
Prestonpans E Loth 128 B5
Preston Patrick Cumb 95 L4
Preston Plucknett Somset 19 P11
Preston St Mary Suffk 64 C11
Preston Street Kent 39 N9
Preston-under-Scar N York 96 G2
Preston upon the Weald
Moors Wrekin 70 B11
Preston Wynne Herefs 45 R5
Prestwich Bury 82 H4
Prestwick Nthumb 113 J6
Prestwick S Ayrs 114 G2
Prestwick Airport S Ayrs 114 G2
Prestwood Bucks 35 N4
Prestwood Staffs 58 C7
Price Town Brdgnd 29 P6
Prickwillow Cambs 63 J4
Priddy Somset 19 P4
Priestacott Devon 8 B3
Priestcliffe Derbys 83 P10
Priestcliffe Ditch Derbys 83 P10
Priest Hutton Lancs 95 L6
Priestland E Ayrs 125 P10
Priestley Green Calder 90 E5
Priest Weston Shrops 56 D5
Priestwood Green Kent 37 Q8
Primethorpe Leics 60 B2
Primrose Green Norfk 76 F8
Primrosehill Border 129 K8
Primrose Hill Cambs 62 E3
Primrose Hill Derbys 84 F9
Primrose Hill Dudley 58 D7
Primrose Hill Lancs 88 D9
Primsidemill Border 118 F5
Prince of Wales Bridge
Mons 31 P7
Princes Gate Pembks 41 M8
Princes Risborough Bucks 35 M4
Princethorpe Warwks 59 P10
Princetown Devon 6 F4
Prinsted W Susx 15 L5
Prion Denbgs 68 E2
Prior Rigg Cumb 111 J7
Priors Halton Shrops 56 H9
Priors Hardwick Warwks 48 E3
Priorslee Wrekin 57 N2
Priors Marston Warwks 48 E3
Priors Norton Gloucs 46 G10
Priors Park Gloucs 46 G8
Priory Wood Herefs 45 K5
Prisk V Glam 30 D9
Priston BaNES 20 C2
Pristow Green Norfk 64 G4
Prittlewell Sthend 38 E4
Privett Hants 23 J9
Prixford Devon 17 K4
Probus Cnwll 3 M4
Prora E Loth 128 E4
Prospect Cumb 100 F2
Prospidnick Cnwll 2 G7
Protstonhill Abers 159 K5
Prudhoe Nthumb 112 G8
Prussia Cove Cnwll 2 F8
Pubil P & K 140 C9
Publow BaNES 20 B2
Puckeridge Herts 51 J6
Puckington Somset 19 L11
Pucklechurch S Glos 32 C9
Puckrup Gloucs 46 G7
Puddinglake Ches W 82 F11
Puddington Ches W 81 L10
Puddington Devon 9 K2
Puddledock Norfk 64 F3
Puddletown Dorset 12 C6
Pudleston Herefs 45 R3
Pudsey Leeds 90 G4
Pulborough W Susx 24 B7
Puleston Wrekin 70 C10
Pulford Ches W 69 L3
Pulham Dorset 11 Q3
Pulham Market Norfk 64 H4
Pulham St Mary Norfk 65 J4
Pullens Green S Glos 32 B6
Pulloxhill C Beds 50 C4
Pulverbatch Shrops 56 G4
Pumpherston W Loth 127 K4
Pumsaint Carmth 43 N6
Puncheston Pembks 41 K5
Puncknowle Dorset 11 L7
Punnett's Town E Susx 25 P6
Purbrook Hants 15 J5
Purfleet-on-Thames Thurr 37 N5
Puriton Somset 19 K6
Purleigh Essex 52 D11
Purley Gt Lon 36 H8
Purley on Thames W Berk 35 J9
Purlogue Shrops 56 D9
Purlpit Wilts 32 G11
Purls Bridge Cambs 62 G3
Purse Caundle Dorset 20 C11
Purshull Green Worcs 58 C10
Purslow Shrops 56 F8
Purston Jaglin Wakefd 91 L7
Purtington Somset 10 H3
Purton Gloucs 32 C3
Purton Gloucs 32 C4
Purton Wilts 33 L7
Purton Stoke Wilts 33 L6
Pury End Nhants 49 K5
Pusey Oxon 34 C5
Putley Herefs 46 B7
Putley Green Herefs 46 B7
Putloe Gloucs 32 E3
Putney Gt Lon 36 F6
Putsborough Devon 16 G3
Puttenham Herts 35 N2
Puttenham Surrey 23 P5
Puttock End Essex 52 D3
Putton Dorset 11 N8
Putts Corner Devon 10 C5
Puxley Nhants 49 L6
Puxton N Som 19 M2
Pwll Carmth 28 E4
Pwllcrochan Pembks 40 H10
Pwll-du Mons 30 H2
Pwll-glàs Denbgs 68 F4
Pwllgloyw Powys 44 E8
Pwllheli Gwynd 66 F7
Pwllmeyric Mons 31 P6
Pwll-trap Carmth 41 Q7
Pwll-y-glaw Neath 29 L6
Pydew Conwy 79 Q9
Pye Bridge Derbys 84 F10
Pyecombe W Susx 24 G8
Pye Corner Newpt 31 K7
Pye Green Staffs 58 E2
Pyle Brdgnd 29 M8
Pyleigh Somset 18 F8
Pylle Somset 20 B7
Pymoor Cambs 62 G3
Pymore Dorset 11 K6
Pyrford Surrey 36 B9
Pyrton Oxon 35 J5
Pytchley Nhants 61 J6
Pyworthy Devon 16 E11

Q

Quabbs Shrops 56 C8
Quadring Lincs 74 D4
Quadring Eaudike Lincs 74 D4
Quainton Bucks 49 K10
Quaker's Yard Myr Td 30 E5
Quaking Houses Dur 113 J10
Quantock Hills Somset 18 G7
Quarff Shet 169 r10
Quarley Hants 21 Q6
Quarndon Derbys 72 A2
Quarr Hill IoW 14 G8
Quarrier's Village Inver 125 K4
Quarrington Lincs 73 R2
Quarrington Hill Dur 104 B3
Quarrybank Ches W 82 C11
Quarry Bank Dudley 58 D7
Quarrywood Moray 157 M5
Quarter N Ayrs 124 F5
Quarter S Lans 126 C7
Quatford Shrops 57 N6
Quatt Shrops 57 P7
Quebec Dur 103 N2
Quedgeley Gloucs 32 F2
Queen Adelaide Cambs 63 J4
Queenborough Kent 38 F7
Queen Camel Somset 19 Q10
Queen Charlton BaNES 32 B11
Queen Dart Devon 17 Q8
Queen Elizabeth Forest
Park Stirlg 132 G7
Queen Elizabeth II Bridge
Thurr 37 N5
Queenhill Worcs 46 G7
Queen Oak Dorset 20 E8
Queen's Bower IoW 14 G10
Queensbury C Brad 90 E4
Queensferry Flints 81 L11
Queensferry Crossing Fife 134 E11
Queen's Head Shrops 69 K9
Queen's Hills Norfk 76 H9
Queenslie C Glas 126 B4
Queen's Park Bed 61 M11
Queen's Park Essex 51 Q11
Queen's Park Nhants 60 G8
Queen Street Kent 37 Q11
Queen Street Wilts 33 K7
Queenzieburn N Lans 126 B2
Quendon Essex 51 M4
Queniborough Leics 72 G8
Quenington Gloucs 33 M4
Quernmore Lancs 95 L9
Queslett Birm 58 G6
Quethiock Cnwll 5 N9
Quick's Green W Berk 34 G9
Quidenham Norfk 64 E4
Quidhampton Hants 22 F4
Quidhampton Wilts 21 M8
Quina Brook Shrops 69 P8
Quinbury End Nhants 48 H4
Quinton Dudley 58 E8
Quinton Nhants 49 L4
Quinton Green Nhants 49 L4
Quintrell Downs Cnwll 4 C9
Quixhall Staffs 71 L6
Quixwood Border 129 K7
Quoditch Devon 5 Q2
Quoig P & K 133 N3
Quorn Leics 72 F7
Quothquan S Lans 116 D3
Quoyburray Ork 169 e6
Quoyloo Ork 169 b4

R

Raasay Highld 153 K9
Rabbit's Cross Kent 26 C2
Rableyheath Herts 50 F7
Raby Cumb 110 C10
Raby Wirral 81 L9
Rachan Mill Border 116 G4
Rachub Gwynd 79 L11
Rackenford Devon 17 R8
Rackham W Susx 24 B8
Rackheath Norfk 77 K9
Racks D & G 109 M6
Rackwick Ork 169 b7
Radbourne Derbys 71 P7
Radcliffe Bury 89 M9
Radcliffe Nthumb 119 Q10
Radcliffe on Trent Notts 72 G3
Radclive Bucks 49 J8
Radcot Oxon 33 Q5
Raddery Highld 156 C6
Raddington Somset 18 D9
Radernie Fife 135 M6
Radford Covtry 59 M8
Radford Semele Warwks 48 B2
Radlet Somset 18 H7
Radlett Herts 50 E10
Radley Devon 17 N7
Radley Oxon 34 F5
Radley W Berk 34 C11
Radley Green Essex 51 P9
Radmore Green Ches E 69 Q3
Radnage Bucks 35 L5
Radstock BaNES 20 C4
Radstone Nhants 48 G6
Radway Warwks 48 C5
Radwell Bed 61 M9
Radwell Herts 50 F3
Radwinter Essex 51 P3
Radwinter End Essex 51 P3
Radyr Cardif 30 F8
RAF College (Cranwell)
Lincs 86 D11
Rafford Moray 157 K6
RAF Museum Cosford
Shrops 57 P3
RAF Museum Hendon
Gt Lon 36 F2
Ragdale Leics 72 H7
Ragdon Shrops 56 H6
Raginnis Cnwll 2 D8
Raglan Mons 31 M3
Ragnall Notts 85 P6
Raigbeg Highld 148 E2
Rainbow Hill Worcs 46 G3
Rainford St Hel 81 P4
Rainford Junction St Hel 81 P4
Rainham Gt Lon 37 M4
Rainham Medway 38 D8
Rainhill St Hel 81 P6
Rainhill Stoops St Hel 81 Q6
Rainow Ches E 83 K9
Rainsough Bury 82 H4
Rainton N York 97 N5
Rainworth Notts 85 J9
Raisbeck Cumb 102 B9
Raise Cumb 111 P11
Raisthorpe N York 98 H8
Rait P & K 134 G2
Raithby Lincs 87 K4
Raithby Lincs 87 L7
Raithwaite N York 105 N8
Rake Hants 23 M9
Rakewood Rochdl 89 Q8
Ralia Highld 148 C8
Ram Carmth 43 L5
Ramasaig Highld 152 B9
Rame Cnwll 3 J7
Rame Cnwll 6 C9
Ram Hill S Glos 32 C9
Ram Lane Kent 26 G2
Rampisham Dorset 11 M4
Rampside Cumb 94 E7
Rampton Cambs 62 F7
Rampton Notts 85 P5
Ramsbottom Bury 89 M7
Ramsbury Wilts 33 Q10
Ramscraigs Highld 167 K11
Ramsdean Hants 23 K10
Ramsdell Hants 22 G3
Ramsden Oxon 48 C11
Ramsden Worcs 46 H5
Ramsden Bellhouse Essex 38 B3
Ramsden Heath Essex 38 B2
Ramsey Cambs 62 C3
Ramsey Essex 53 M5
Ramsey IoM 80 g3
Ramsey Forty Foot Cambs 62 D3
Ramsey Heights Cambs 62 B4
Ramsey Island Essex 52 F10
Ramsey Island Pembks 40 D6
Ramsey Mereside Cambs 62 C3
Ramsey St Mary's Cambs 62 C3
Ramsgate Kent 39 Q8
Ramsgill N York 96 H6
Ramshaw Dur 103 M5
Ramshaw Dur 112 E11
Ramsholt Suffk 53 P3
Ramshope Nthumb 118 D10
Ramshorn Staffs 71 K5
Ramsley Devon 8 G6
Ramsnest Common Surrey 23 P8
Ranby Lincs 86 H5
Ranby Notts 85 L4
Rand Lincs 86 F5
Randwick Gloucs 32 F3
Ranfurly Rens 125 K4
Rangemore Staffs 71 M10
Rangeworthy S Glos 32 C7
Rankinston E Ayrs 115 J5
Ranksborough Rutlnd 73 L8
Rank's Green Essex 52 B8
Rannoch Station P & K 140 B6
Ranscombe Somset 18 B6
Ranskill Notts 85 L3
Ranton Staffs 70 F10
Ranton Green Staffs 70 E10
Ranworth Norfk 77 M9
Raploch Stirlg 133 M9
Rapness Ork 169 e2
Rapps Somset 19 K11
Rascarrel D & G 108 G11
Rashfield Ag & B 131 N11
Rashwood Worcs 58 D11
Raskelf N York 97 Q6
Rassau Blae G 30 G2
Rastrick Calder 90 E6
Ratagan Highld 145 R4
Ratby Leics 72 E9
Ratcliffe Culey Leics 72 A11
Ratcliffe on Soar Notts 72 D5
Ratcliffe on the Wreake
Leics 72 G8
Rathen Abers 159 N5
Rathillet Fife 135 K3
Rathmell N York 96 B9
Ratho C Edin 127 L3
Ratho Station C Edin 127 L3
Rathven Moray 158 B4
Ratlake Hants 22 D10
Ratley Warwks 48 C5
Ratling Kent 39 M11
Ratlinghope Shrops 56 G5
Rattar Highld 167 N2
Ratten Row Cumb 101 K2
Ratten Row Cumb 110 G11
Ratten Row Lancs 88 E2
Rattery Devon 7 J6
Rattlesden Suffk 64 D10
Ratton Village E Susx 25 N10
Rattray P & K 142 B8
Raughton Cumb 110 G11
Raughton Head Cumb 110 G11
Raunds Nhants 61 L6
Ravenfield Rothm 91 M11
Ravenglass Cumb 100 E11
Ravenhills Green Worcs 46 D4
Raveningham Norfk 65 M2
Ravenscar N York 105 Q10
Ravenscraig N Lans 126 D6
Ravensdale IoM 80 e3
Ravensden Bed 61 N10
Ravenseat N York 102 G10
Ravenshead Notts 85 J10
Ravensmoor Ches E 69 R4
Ravensthorpe Kirk 90 G6
Ravensthorpe Nhants 60 E6
Ravenstone Leics 72 C8
Ravenstone M Keyn 49 M4
Ravenstonedale Cumb 102 D10
Ravenstruther S Lans 126 G8
Ravensworth N York 103 M9
Raw N York 105 P9
Rawcliffe C York 98 B10
Rawcliffe E R Yk 92 A6
Rawcliffe Bridge E R Yk 92 A6
Rawdon Leeds 90 G3
Rawling Street Kent 38 F10
Rawmarsh Rothm 91 L11
Rawnsley Staffs 58 F2
Rawreth Essex 38 C3
Rawridge Devon 10 E3
Rawtenstall Lancs 89 N6
Raydon Suffk 52 H4
Raylees Nthumb 112 D2
Rayleigh Essex 38 D3
Raymond's Hill Devon 10 G5
Rayne Essex 52 B7
Raynes Park Gt Lon 36 F7
Reach Cambs 63 J7
Read Lancs 89 M4
Reading Readg 35 K10
Reading Services W Berk 35 J11
Reading Street Kent 26 F5
Reading Street Kent 39 Q8
Reagill Cumb 102 B7
Rearquhar Highld 162 G8
Rearsby Leics 72 H8
Rease Heath Ches E 70 A4
Reawla Cnwll 2 G6
Reay Highld 166 G4
Reculver Kent 39 M8
Red Ball Devon 18 E11
Redberth Pembks 41 L10
Redbourn Herts 50 D8
Redbourne N Linc 92 G11
Redbrook Gloucs 31 P3
Redbrook Wrexhm 69 P6
Redbrook Street Kent 26 F4
Redburn Highld 156 G8
Redburn Nthumb 111 Q8
Redcar R & Cl 104 H6
Redcastle D & G 108 H7
Redcastle Highld 155 Q8
Red Dial Cumb 110 E11
Redding Falk 126 G2
Reddingmuirhead Falk 126 G2
Reddish Stockp 83 J6
Redditch Worcs 58 F11
Rede Suffk 63 P9
Redenhall Norfk 65 K5
Redenham Hants 22 B5
Redesmouth Nthumb 112 C4
Redford Abers 143 P3
Redford Angus 143 K9
Redford W Susx 23 N9
Redfordgreen Border 117 M7
Redgate Rhondd 30 D7
Redgorton P & K 134 D2
Redgrave Suffk 64 E6
Redhill Abers 151 K7
Red Hill BCP 13 J5
Redhill Herts 50 H4
Redhill N Som 19 N2
Redhill Surrey 36 G10
Red Hill Warwks 47 M3
Redisham Suffk 65 N5
Redland Bristl 31 Q9
Redland Ork 169 c4
Redlingfield Suffk 64 H7
Redlingfield Green Suffk 64 H7
Red Lodge Suffk 63 L6
Red Lumb Rochdl 89 N7
Redlynch Somset 20 D8
Redlynch Wilts 21 P10
Redmain Cumb 100 F4
Redmarley Worcs 57 P11
Redmarley D'Abitot Gloucs 46 E8
Redmarshall S on T 104 C6
Redmile Leics 73 K3
Redmire N York 96 F2
Redmyre Abers 143 P2
Rednal Birm 58 F9
Rednal Shrops 69 L9
Redpath Border 118 A3
Red Point Highld 153 N4
Red Post Cnwll 16 D10
Red Rice Hants 22 B6
Red Rock Wigan 88 H9
Red Roses Carmth 41 P8
Red Row Nthumb 119 Q11
Redruth Cnwll 2 H5
Redstocks Wilts 20 H2
Redstone P & K 142 B11
Redstone Cross Pembks 41 M7
Red Street Staffs 70 E4
Redvales Bury 89 N9
Red Wharf Bay IoA 79 J8
Redwick Newpt 31 M8
Redwick S Glos 31 P7
Redworth Darltn 103 P6
Reed Herts 51 J3
Reedham Norfk 77 N11
Reedness E R Yk 92 C6
Reeds Beck Lincs 86 H7
Reeds Holme Lancs 89 N6
Reepham Lincs 86 D6
Reepham Norfk 76 G7
Reeth N York 103 K11
Reeves Green Solhll 59 L9
Regaby IoM 80 f2
Regil N Som 19 P2
Reiff Highld 160 F4
Reigate Surrey 36 G10
Reighton N York 99 N5
Reinigeadal W Isls 168 h7
Reisque Abers 151 M4

Reiss Highld 167 P6
Rejerrah Cnwll 4 B10
Releath Cnwll 2 H7
Relubbus Cnwll 2 F7
Relugas Moray 156 H8
Remenham Wokam 35 L8
Remenham Hill Wokham 35 L8
Rempstone Notts 72 F6
Rendcomb Gloucs 33 K3
Rendham Suffk 65 L9
Rendlesham Suffk 65 L11
Renfrew Rens 125 N4
Renhold Bed 61 N10
Renishaw Derbys 84 G5
Rennington Nthumb 119 P7
Renton W Duns 125 K2
Renwick Cumb 101 Q2
Repps Norfk 77 N8
Repton Derbys 71 Q9
Reraig Highld 145 P2
Resaurie Highld 156 C8
Rescassa Cnwll 3 P5
Rescorla Cnwll 3 P4
Resipole Burn Highld 138 C5
Reskadinnick Cnwll 2 G5
Resolis Highld 156 B4
Resolven Neath 29 M4
Rest and be thankful Ag & B 131 Q6
Reston Border 129 M7
Restronguet Cnwll 3 L6
Reswallie Angus 143 J7
Reterth Cnwll 4 E9
Retford Notts 85 M4
Retire Cnwll 4 G9
Rettendon Essex 38 C2
Retyn Cnwll 4 D10
Revesby Lincs 87 J8
Rew Devon 7 J11
Rew Devon 7 K4
Rewe Devon 9 M5
Rew Street IoW 14 E8
Rexon Devon 5 Q4
Reydon Suffk 65 P6
Reymerston Norfk 76 E10
Reynalton Pembks 41 L9
Reynoldston Swans 28 E7
Rezare Cnwll 5 P6
Rhadyr Mons 31 L4
Rhandirmwyn Carmth 43 Q6
Rhayader Powys 55 M11
Rheindown Highld 155 P8
Rhenigidale W Isls 168 h7
Rhes-y-cae Flints 80 H10
Rhewl Denbgs 68 F2
Rhewl Denbgs 68 G8
Rhewl Mostyn Flints 80 H8
Rhicarn Highld 164 C11
Rhiconich Highld 164 G6
Rhicullen Highld 156 B3
Rhigos Rhondd 29 P3
Rhives Highld 163 J6
Rhiwbina Cardif 30 G8
Rhiwbryfdir Gwynd 67 M5
Rhiwderyn Newpt 31 J7
Rhiwen Gwynd 67 K2
Rhiwinder Rhondd 30 D7
Rhiwlas Gwynd 68 B7
Rhiwlas Gwynd 79 K11
Rhiwlas Powys 68 G8
Rhiwsaeson Rhondd 30 E8
Rhode Somset 19 J8
Rhoden Green Kent 37 Q11
Rhodesia Notts 85 J5
Rhodes Minnis Kent 27 L3
Rhodiad-y-brenin Pembks 40 E5
Rhonehouse D & G 108 F9
Rhoose V Glam 30 E11
Rhos Carmth 42 G7
Rhos Denbgs 68 F2
Rhos Neath 29 K4
Rhosaman Carmth 29 K2
Rhosbeirio IoA 78 F6
Rhoscefnhir IoA 78 J9
Rhoscolyn IoA 78 D9
Rhoscrowther Pembks 40 H10
Rhosesmor Flints 81 J11
Rhos-fawr Gwynd 66 F7
Rhosgadfan Gwynd 67 J3
Rhosgoch IoA 78 G7
Rhosgoch Powys 44 H5
Rhos Haminiog Cerdgn 43 K2
Rhoshill Pembks 41 N2
Rhoshirwaun Gwynd 66 C9
Rhoslan Gwynd 66 H6
Rhoslefain Gwynd 54 D3
Rhosllanerchrugog Wrexhm 69 J5
Rhôs Lligwy IoA 78 H7
Rhosmaen Carmth 43 M10
Rhosmeirch IoA 78 H9
Rhosneigr IoA 78 E10
Rhosnesni Wrexhm 69 L4
Rhôs-on-Sea Conwy 79 Q8
Rhosrobin Wrexhm 69 K4
Rhossili Swans 28 D7
Rhostrehwfa IoA 78 G10
Rhostryfan Gwynd 66 H3
Rhostyllen Wrexhm 69 K5
Rhosybol IoA 78 G7
Rhos-y-brithdir Powys 68 F10
Rhosygadfa Shrops 69 K8
Rhos-y-garth Cerdgn 54 E10
Rhos-y-gwaliau Gwynd 68 B8
Rhos-y-llan Gwynd 66 C7
Rhosymedre Wrexhm 69 J6
Rhos-y-meirch Powys 56 D11
Rhu Ag & B 132 B11
Rhuallt Denbgs 80 F9
Rhubodach Ag & B 124 C3
Rhuddall Heath Ches W 69 Q2
Rhuddlan Cerdgn 43 J6
Rhuddlan Denbgs 80 E9
Rhue Highld 161 J2
Rhulen Powys 44 G5
Rhunahaorine Ag & B 123 M10
Rhyd Gwynd 67 L6
Rhydargaeau Carmth 42 H9
Rhydcymerau Carmth 43 L7
Rhydd Worcs 46 F5
Rhyd-Ddu Gwynd 67 K4
Rhydding Neath 29 K5
Rhydgaled Cnwll 68 C2
Rhydlanfair Conwy 67 F5
Rhydlewis Cerdgn 42 F5
Rhydlios Gwynd 66 B9
Rhydlydan Conwy 68 A4
Rhydowen Cerdgn 42 H5

Rhydroser Cerdgn 54 D11
Rhydspence Herefs 45 J5
Rhydtalog Flints 68 H4
Rhyd-uchaf Gwynd 68 B7
Rhyd-y-clafdy Gwynd 66 E8
Rhydycroesau Shrops 68 H8
Rhydyfelin Cerdgn 54 D9
Rhydyfelin Rhondd 30 E7
Rhyd-y-foel Conwy 80 C9
Rhydyfro Neath 29 K3
Rhyd-y-groes Gwynd 79 K11
Rhydymain Gwynd 67 Q10
Rhyd-y-meirch Mons 31 K3
Rhydymwyn Flints 81 J11
Rhyd-y-pennau Cerdgn 54 E7
Rhyd-yr-onnen Gwynd 54 E4
Rhyd-y-sarn Gwynd 67 M6
Rhyl Denbgs 80 E8
Rhymney Caerph 30 F3
Rhynd P & K 134 F3
Rhynie Abers 150 D2
Rhynie Highld 163 J11
Ribbesford Worcs 57 P10
Ribbleton Lancs 88 H4
Ribby Lancs 88 E4
Ribchester Lancs 89 K3
Riber Derbys 84 D9
Riby Lincs 93 L9
Riccall N York 91 Q3
Riccarton Border 111 K2
Riccarton E Ayrs 125 L10
Richards Castle Herefs 56 H11
Richings Park Bucks 36 B5
Richmond Gt Lon 36 E6
Richmond N York 103 N10
Richmond Sheff 84 F3
Rich's Holford Somset 18 F8
Rickerscote Staffs 70 G10
Rickford N Som 19 N3
Rickham Devon 7 K11
Rickinghall Suffk 64 E6
Rickling Essex 51 L4
Rickling Green Essex 51 M5
Rickmansworth Herts 36 C2
Riddell Border 117 Q6
Riddings Derbys 84 F10
Riddlecombe Devon 17 L9
Riddlesden C Brad 90 D2
Ridge BaNES 19 Q3
Ridge Dorset 12 F7
Ridge Herts 50 F10
Ridge Wilts 21 J8
Ridgebourne Powys 44 F2
Ridge Green Surrey 36 H11
Ridge Lane Warwks 59 L6
Ridge Row Kent 27 M3
Ridgeway Derbys 84 F4
Ridgeway Worcs 47 K2
Ridgeway Cross Herefs 46 D5
Ridgewell Essex 52 B3
Ridgewood E Susx 25 L7
Ridgmont C Beds 49 Q7
Riding Mill Nthumb 112 F8
Ridley Kent 37 P8
Ridley Nthumb 111 Q8
Ridley Green Ches E 69 Q4
Ridlington Norfk 77 L5
Ridlington Rutlnd 73 L10
Ridlington Street Norfk 77 L5
Ridsdale Nthumb 112 D4
Rievaulx N York 98 B3
Rigg D & G 110 E7
Riggend N Lans 126 D3
Righoul Highld 156 F7
Rigmadon Park Cumb 95 N4
Rigsby Lincs 87 M5
Rigside S Lans 116 B3
Riley Green Lancs 89 J5
Rileyhill Staffs 58 H2
Rilla Mill Cnwll 5 M7
Rillaton Cnwll 5 M7
Rillington N York 98 H6
Rimington Lancs 96 B11
Rimpton Somset 20 B10
Rimswell E R Yk 93 P5
Rinaston Pembks 41 J5
Rindleford Shrops 57 N5
Ringford D & G 108 E9
Ringinglow Sheff 84 C4
Ringland Norfk 76 G9
Ringles Cross E Susx 25 L6
Ringlestone Kent 38 E10
Ringley Bolton 89 M9
Ringmer E Susx 25 K8
Ringmore Devon 6 H9
Ringmore Devon 7 N4
Ringorm Moray 157 P9
Ring's End Cambs 74 G10
Ringsfield Suffk 65 N4
Ringsfield Corner Suffk 65 N4
Ringshall Herts 35 Q2
Ringshall Suffk 64 E11
Ringshall Stocks Suffk 64 F11
Ringstead Nhants 61 L5
Ringstead Norfk 75 P2
Ringwood Hants 13 L3
Ringwould Kent 27 Q2
Rinmore Abers 150 C4
Rinsey Cnwll 2 F8
Rinsey Croft Cnwll 2 G8
Ripe E Susx 25 M8
Ripley Derbys 84 E10
Ripley Hants 13 L5
Ripley N York 97 L8
Ripley Surrey 36 C9
Riplingham E R Yk 92 G4
Riplington Hants 23 J10
Ripon N York 97 M6
Rippingale Lincs 74 A5
Ripple Kent 39 Q11
Ripple Worcs 46 G7
Ripponden Calder 90 C7
Risabus Ag & B 122 D11
Risbury Herefs 45 Q4
Risby N Linc 92 F8
Risby Suffk 63 P7
Risca Caerph 30 H6
Rise E R Yk 93 L2
Riseden E Susx 26 B4
Riseden Kent 26 B4
Risegate Lincs 74 D5
Riseholme Lincs 86 C6
Risehow Cumb 100 D4
Riseley Bed 61 M8
Riseley Wokham 23 K2
Rishangles Suffk 64 H8

Rishton Lancs 89 L4
Rishworth Calder 90 C7
Rising Bridge Lancs 89 M5
Risley Derbys 72 D3
Risley Warrtn 82 E6
Risplith N York 97 K7
Rivar Wilts 22 B2
Rivenhall End Essex 52 D8
River Kent 27 N3
River W Susx 23 P10
River Bank Cambs 62 H7
Riverford Highld 155 P7
Riverhead Kent 37 M9
Rivers Corner Dorset 12 C2
Rivington Lancs 89 J8
Rivington Services Lancs 89 J8
Roachill Devon 17 R7
Roade Nhants 49 L4
Road Green Norfk 65 K3
Roadhead Cumb 111 K6
Roadmeetings S Lans 126 F5
Roadside E Ayrs 115 L4
Roadside Highld 167 L4
Roadwater Somset 18 D7
Roag Highld 152 D9
Roa Island Cumb 94 E7
Roan of Craigoch S Ayrs 114 E7
Roast Green Essex 51 L4
Roath Cardif 30 G9
Roberton Border 117 N8
Roberton S Lans 116 C5
Robertsbridge E Susx 26 B7
Roberttown Kirk 90 F6
Robeston Wathen Pembks 41 L7
Robgill Tower D & G 110 D6
Robin Hill Staffs 70 G3
Robin Hood Lancs 88 G8
Robin Hood Leeds 91 J5
Robinhood End Essex 52 B4
Robin Hood's Bay N York 105 Q9
Roborough Devon 6
Roborough Devon 17 K8
Robroyston C Glas 125 Q4
Roby Knows 81 N6
Roby Mill Lancs 88 G9
Rocester Staffs 71 L7
Roch Pembks 40 G5
Rochdale Rochdl 89 P8
Roche Cnwll 4 F9
Rochester Medway 38 B8
Rochester Nthumb 118 F11
Rochford Essex 38 E3
Rochford Worcs 57 L11
Roch Gate Pembks 40 G6
Rock Cnwll 4 E6
Rock Neath 29 L4
Rock Nthumb 119 P6
Rock W Susx 24 D8
Rock Worcs 57 N10
Rockbeare Devon 9 P6
Rockbourne Hants 21 M11
Rockcliffe Cumb 110 G8
Rockcliffe D & G 108 H10
Rockcliffe Cross Cumb 110 F8
Rock End Staffs 70 F3
Rockend Torbay 7 N6
Rock Ferry Wirral 81 L7
Rockfield Highld 163 L10
Rockfield Mons 31 N2
Rockford Devon 17 N2
Rockford Hants 13 L3
Rockgreen Shrops 57 J9
Rockhampton S Glos 32 C6
Rockhead Cnwll 4 H5
Rockhill Shrops 56 D9
Rock Hill Worcs 58 E11
Rockingham Nhants 61 J2
Rockland All Saints Norfk 64 D2
Rockland St Mary Norfk 77 L11
Rockland St Peter Norfk 64 D2
Rockley Notts 85 M6
Rockley Wilts 33 N10
Rockliffe Lancs 89 P6
Rockville Ag & B 131 Q2
Rockwell End Bucks 35 L7
Rockwell Green Somset 18 F10
Rodborough Gloucs 32 F4
Rodbourne Swindn 33 M7
Rodbourne Wilts 32 H8
Rodd Herefs 45 L2
Roddam Nthumb 119 K6
Rodden Dorset 11 N8
Roddymoor Dur 103 N3
Rode Somset 20 F4
Rode Heath Ches E 70 E3
Rode Heath Ches E 83 J11
Rodel W Isls 168 f9
Roden Wrekin 69 Q11
Rodhuish Somset 18 D7
Rodington Wrekin 57 K2
Rodington Heath Wrekin 57 K2
Rodley Gloucs 32 D2
Rodley Leeds 90 G3
Rodmarton Gloucs 32 H5
Rodmell E Susx 25 K9
Rodmersham Kent 38 F9
Rodmersham Green Kent 38 F9
Rodney Stoke Somset 19 N5
Rodsley Derbys 71 N6
Rodway Somset 19 J6
Roecliffe N York 97 N7
Roe Cross Tamesd 83 L5
Roe Green Herts 50 F9
Roe Green Herts 50 H4
Roe Green Salfd 82 F4
Roffey W Susx 24 E4
Rogart Highld 162 H6
Rogate W Susx 23 M10
Roger Ground Cumb 101 L11
Rogerstone Newpt 31 J7
Roghadal W Isls 168 f9
Rogiet Mons 31 N7
Roke Oxon 34 H6
Roker Sundld 113 P9
Rollesby Norfk 77 N8
Rolleston Leics 73 J10
Rolleston Notts 85 M10
Rolleston on Dove Staffs 71 N9
Rolston E R Yk 93 M2
Rolstone N Som 19 L2
Rolvenden Kent 26 E5
Rolvenden Layne Kent 26 E5
Romaldkirk Dur 103 J6
Romanby N York 97 N2

Romanno Bridge Border 127 M8
Romansleigh Devon 17 N7
Romden Castle Kent 26 E3
Romesdal Highld 152 F7
Romford Dorset 13 J3
Romford Gt Lon 37 M3
Romiley Stockp 83 K6
Romney Street Kent 37 N8
Romsey Cambs 62 G9
Romsey Hants 22 C10
Romsley Shrops 57 P8
Romsley Worcs 58 E8
Rona Highld 153 L6
Rorrington Shrops 56 F4
Rosarie Moray 158 A7
Rose Cnwll 3 K3
Roseacre Lancs 88 E3
Rose Ash Devon 17 P7
Rosebank S Lans 126 E8
Rosebush Pembks 41 L5
Rosecare Cnwll 5 K2
Rosecliston Cnwll 4 C10
Rosedale Abbey N York 105 K11
Rose Green Essex 52 F6
Rose Green Suffk 52 F4
Rose Green Suffk 52 G3
Rose Green W Susx 15 N5
Rosehall Highld 162 B6
Rosehearty Abers 159 M4
Rose Hill E Susx 25 L7
Rose Hill Lancs 89 N4
Rosehill Shrops 69 Q8
Roseisle Moray 157 L4
Roselands E Susx 25 P10
Rosemarket Pembks 41 J8
Rosemarkie Highld 156 C6
Rosemary Lane Devon 10 D2
Rosemount P & K 142 B9
Rosenannon Cnwll 4 F8
Rosenithon Cnwll 3 K8
Roser's Cross E Susx 25 M6
Rosevean Cnwll 4 G10
Rosevine Cnwll 3 M6
Rosewarne Cnwll 2 G6
Rosewell Mdloth 127 P5
Roseworth S on T 104 D6
Roseworthy Cnwll 2 G6
Rosgill Cumb 101 P7
Roskestal Cnwll 2 B9
Roskhill Highld 152 D9
Roskorwell Cnwll 3 K9
Rosley Cumb 110 F11
Roslin Mdloth 127 P5
Rosliston Derbys 71 N11
Rosneath Ag & B 132 B11
Ross D & G 108 D12
Ross Nthumb 119 M3
Rossett Wrexhm 69 L3
Rossett Green N York 97 L10
Rossington Donc 91 Q11
Ross-on-Wye Herefs 46 A10
Roster Highld 167 N9
Rostherne Ches E 82 F8
Rosthwaite Cumb 101 J8
Roston Derbys 71 L6
Rosudgeon Cnwll 2 F8
Rosyth Fife 134 E11
Rothbury Nthumb 119 L10
Rotherby Leics 72 H7
Rotherfield E Susx 25 N5
Rotherfield Greys Oxon 35 K8
Rotherfield Peppard Oxon 35 K8
Rotherham Rothm 84 F2
Rothersthorpe Nhants 60 F9
Rotherwick Hants 23 K3
Rothes Moray 157 P8
Rothesay Ag & B 124 C4
Rothiebrisbane Abers 158 H10
Rothiemurchus Lodge Highld 148 H6
Rothienorman Abers 158 H10
Rothley Leics 72 F8
Rothley Nthumb 112 F3
Rothmaise Abers 158 G10
Rothwell Leeds 91 J5
Rothwell Lincs 93 J11
Rothwell Nhants 60 H4
Rotsea E R Yk 99 M10
Rottal Lodge Angus 142 F4
Rottingdean Br & H 25 J10
Rottington Cumb 100 C8
Roucan D & G 109 M5
Roud IoW 14 F10
Rougham Norfk 76 A7
Rougham Suffk 64 C9
Rough Close Staffs 70 G7
Rough Common Kent 39 K10
Roughlee Lancs 89 N2
Roughpark Abers 149 Q5
Roughton Lincs 86 H8
Roughton Norfk 77 J4
Roughton Shrops 57 P6
Roundbush Essex 52 E11
Round Bush Herts 50 D11
Roundbush Green Essex 51 N8
Round Green Luton 50 D6
Roundham Somset 11 J3
Roundhay Leeds 91 J3
Rounds Green Sandw 58 E7
Round Street Kent 37 Q7
Roundstreet Common W Susx 24 C5
Roundswell Devon 17 J5
Roundway Wilts 21 K2
Roundyhill Angus 142 F7
Rousay Ork 169 c3
Rousdon Devon 10 F6
Rousham Oxon 48 E10

Rous Lench Worcs 47 K4
Routenburn N Ayrs 124 F5
Routh E R Yk 93 J2
Rout's Green Bucks 35 L5
Row Cnwll 4
Row Cumb 95 K4
Row Cumb 102 B4
Rowanburn D & G 110 H5
Rowardennan Stirlg 132 D8
Rowarth Derbys 83 M7
Row Ash Hants 14 F4
Rowberrow Somset 19 N3
Rowborough IoW 14 G10
Rowde Wilts 21 J2
Rowden Devon 8 G5
Rowen Conwy 79 P9
Rowfield Derbys 71 M6
Rowfoot Nthumb 111 N9
Rowford Somset 18 H9
Row Green Essex 52 B7
Rowhedge Essex 52 H7
Rowhook W Susx 24 D4
Rowington Warwks 59 K11
Rowland Derbys 84 B6
Rowland's Castle Hants 15 K4
Rowlands Gill Gatesd 113 J9
Rowledge Surrey 23 M6
Rowley Dur 112 G11
Rowley E R Yk 92 G4
Rowley Shrops 56 F4
Rowley Hill Kirk 90 E7
Rowley Regis Sandw 58 E7
Rowlstone Herefs 45 M8
Rowly Surrey 24 B3
Rowner Hants 14 F5
Rowney Green Worcs 58 F10
Rownhams Hants 22 C11
Rownhams Services Hants 22 C11
Rowrah Cumb 100 D7
Rowsham Bucks 49 M11
Rowsley Derbys 84 C7
Rowstock Oxon 34 E5
Rowston Lincs 86 E9
Rowthorne Derbys 84 F8
Rowton Ches W 69 M2
Rowton Shrops 56 F2
Rowton Shrops 56 G2
Rowton Wrekin 69 R11
Row Town Surrey 36 C8
Roxburgh Border 118 C4
Roxby N Linc 92 F7
Roxby N York 105 K7
Roxton Bed 61 Q10
Roxwell Essex 51 P9
Royal Leamington Spa Warwks 59 M11
Royal Oak Darltn 103 P6
Royal Oak Lancs 81 N4
Royal's Green Ches E 69 R6
Royal Sutton Coldfield Birm 58 H6
Royal Tunbridge Wells Kent 25 N4
Royal Wootton Bassett Wilts 33 L8
Royal Yacht Britannia C Edin 127 P2
Roy Bridge Highld 146 H11
Roydhouse Kirk 90 G8
Roydon Essex 51 K8
Roydon Norfk 64 G5
Roydon Norfk 75 P6
Roydon Hamlet Essex 51 K9
Royston Barns 91 K8
Royston Herts 51 J2
Royton Oldham 89 Q9
Rozel Jersey 11 c1
Ruabon Wrexhm 69 K6
Ruaig Ag & B 136 C6
Ruan High Lanes Cnwll 3 N6
Ruan Lanihorne Cnwll 3 M5
Ruan Major Cnwll 3 J10
Ruan Minor Cnwll 3 J10
Ruardean Gloucs 46 B11
Ruardean Hill Gloucs 46 B11
Ruardean Woodside Gloucs 46 B11
Rubery Birm 58 E8
Rubha Ban W Isls 168 c16
Ruckcroft Cumb 101 P2
Ruckhall Herefs 45 P7
Ruckinge Kent 26 H3
Ruckland Lincs 87 K5
Ruckley Shrops 57 J3
Rudbaxton Pembks 41 K5
Rudby N York 104 E8
Rudchester Nthumb 112 H7
Ruddington Notts 72 F3
Ruddle Gloucs 32 C2
Ruddlemoor Cnwll 3 Q3
Rudford Gloucs 46 E10
Rudge Somset 20 F4
Rudgeway S Glos 32 B7
Rudgwick W Susx 24 C4
Rudhall Herefs 46 B9
Rudheath Ches W 82 E10
Rudheath Woods Ches E 82 F10
Rudley Green Essex 52 D11
Rudloe Wilts 32 F11
Rudry Caerph 30 G6
Rudston E R Yk 99 M7
Rudyard Staffs 70 H3
Ruecastle Border 118 B6
Rufford Lancs 88 F7
Rufford Abbey Notts 85 L8
Rufforth C York 98 A10
Rug Denbgs 68 B5
Rugby Warwks 60 B5
Rugby Services Warwks 60 B5
Rugeley Staffs 71 J11
Ruigh'riabhach Highld 160 H2
Ruisgarry W Isls 168 f6
Ruishton Somset 19 J9
Ruisigearraidh W Isls 168 c16
Ruislip Gt Lon 36 C3
Rùm Highld 144 D11
Rumbach Moray 158 A7
Rumbling Bridge P & K 134 C9
Rumburgh Suffk 65 L5
Rumby Hill Dur 103 N3
Rumford Cnwll 4
Rumford Falk 126 G2
Rumney Cardif 30 H9
Rumwell Somset 18 F10
Runcorn Halton 81 Q8
Runcton W Susx 15 N5
Runcton Holme Norfk 75 N9
Runfold Surrey 23 M4
Runhall Norfk 76 F10
Runham Norfk 77 N9
Runham Norfk 77 P9

Runnington – Scholes 291

Runnington Somset 18 F10
Runsell Green Essex 52 C10
Runshaw Moor Lancs 88 G7
Runswick N York 105 M7
Runtaleave Angus 142 D4
Runwell Essex 38 C3
Ruscombe Wokham 35 L9
Rushall Herefs 46 B7
Rushall Norfk 64 H5
Rushall Wilts 21 M3
Rushall Wsall 58 F4
Rushbrooke Suffk 64 B9
Rushbury Shrops 57 J6
Rushden Herts 50 H4
Rushden Nhants 61 L7
Rushenden Kent 38 F7
Rusher's Cross E Susx 25 P5
Rushford Devon 8 C9
Rushford Norfk 64 C5
Rush Green Essex 53 L8
Rush Green Gt Lon 37 M3
Rush Green Herts 50 F6
Rush Green Warrtn 82 E7
ushlake Green E Susx 25 P7
ushmere Suffk 65 P4
ushmere St Andrew Suffk 53 L2
ushmoor Surrey 23 N6
Rushock Herefs 45 L3
Rushock Worcs 58 C10
usholme Manch 83 J6
ushton Ches W 69 Q2
ushton Nhants 60 H4
ushton Shrops 57 L3
ushton Spencer Staffs 70 G2
ushwick Worcs 46 F4
ushyford Dur 103 Q5
uskie Stirlg 133 J7
uskington Lincs 86 E10
usland Cross Cumb 94 G3
usper W Susx 24 F3
uspidge Gloucs 32 C2
ussell Green Essex 52 B9
ussell's Water Oxon 35 K7
ussel's Green Suffk 65 K7
uss Hill Surrey 24 F2
usthall Kent 25 N3
ustington W Susx 24 B10
uston N York 99 K4
uston Parva E R Yk 99 M8
uswarp N York 105 N9
uthall Shrops 57 K6
Rutherford Border 118 B4
Rutherglen S Lans 125 Q5
uthernbridge Cnwll 4 G8
uthin Denbgs 68 F3
uthrieston C Aber 151 N7
uthven Abers 158 D8
uthven Angus 142 D8
uthven Highld 148 D8
uthven Highld 156 E11
uthvoes Cnwll 4 E9
uthwaite Cumb 100 H3
uthwell D & G 109 N7
Ruxley Gt Lon 37 L6
Ruxton Green Herefs 45 Q11
Ruyton-XI-Towns Shrops 69 L10
yal Nthumb 112 F6
Ryall Dorset 11 J5
Ryall Worcs 46 G6
yarsh Kent 37 Q8
ycote Oxon 35 J3
ydal Cumb 101 L9
yde IoW 14 G8
ye E Susx 26 F7
yebank Shrops 69 P8
yeford Herefs 46 B10
ye Foreign E Susx 26 E7
ye Harbour E Susx 26 F8
yehill E R Yk 93 M5
yeish Green Wokham 35 K11
ye Street Worcs 46 E7
yhall Rutlnd 73 Q8
yhill Wakefd 91 K8
yhope Sundld 113 P10
ylah Derbys 84 G7
yland Lincs 86 D5
ylands Notts 72 E3
ylstone N York 96 E9
yme Intrinseca Dorset 11 M2
yther N York 91 P3
yton Gatesd 113 J8
yton N York 98 F5
yton Shrops 57 P4
yton Warwks 59 P7
yton-on-Dunsmore Warwks 59 N10
yton Woodside Gatesd 112 H8
ZSS Edinburgh Zoo C Edin 127 N3

S

abden Lancs 89 M3
abine's Green Essex 51 M11
acombe Herts 50 H7
acombe Green Herts 50 H7
acriston Dur 113 K11
adberge Darltn 104 B7
addell Ag & B 120 E5
addington Leics 60 E2
addlebow Norfk 75 M7
addlescombe W Susx 24 G8
adgill Cumb 101 N9
affron Walden Essex 51 M3
ageston Pembks 41 L10
aham Hills Norfk 76 C11
aham Toney Norfk 76 B11
aighton Ches W 69 M2
St Abbs Border 129 N6
St Agnes Border 128 H7
St Agnes Cnwll 3 J3
St Agnes IoS 2 b3
St Agnes Mining District Cnwll 3 J4
St Albans Herts 50 D9
St Allen Cnwll 3 L3
St Andrew Guern 10 b2
St Andrews Fife 135 N4
St Andrews Botanic Garden Fife 135 N4
St Andrews Major V Glam 30 F10
St Andrews Well Dorset 11 K6
St Anne's Lancs 88 C5
St Ann's D & G 109 N2
St Ann's Chapel Cnwll 5 Q7
St Ann's Chapel Devon 6 H9
St Anthony-in-Meneage Cnwll 3 K8
St Anthony's Hill E Susx 25 P10
St Arvans Mons 31 P5
St Asaph Denbgs 80 E10
St Athan V Glam 30 D11
St Aubin Jersey 11 b2
St Austell Cnwll 3 Q3
St Bees Cumb 100 C8
St Blazey Cnwll 3 R3
St Blazey Gate Cnwll 3 R3
St Boswells Border 118 A4
St Brelade Jersey 11 a2
St Brelade's Bay Jersey 11 a2
St Breock Cnwll 4 F7
St Breward Cnwll 4 H6
St Briavels Gloucs 31 Q4
St Brides Pembks 40 F8
St Brides Major V Glam 29 N10
St Brides Netherwent Mons 31 M7
St Brides-super-Ely V Glam 30 E9
St Brides Wentlooge Newpt 31 J8
St Budeaux C Plym 6 D7
Saintbury Gloucs 47 M7
St Buryan Cnwll 2 C8
St Catherine BaNES 32 E11
St Catherines Ag & B 131 N6
St Chloe Gloucs 32 F4
St Clears Carmth 41 Q7
St Cleer Cnwll 5 L8
St Clement Cnwll 3 M5
St Clement Jersey 11 c2
St Clether Cnwll 5 L5
St Colmac Ag & B 124 C4
St Columb Major Cnwll 4 E9
St Columb Minor Cnwll 4 C9
St Columb Road Cnwll 4 E10
St Combs Abers 159 Q5
St Cross South Elmham Suffk 65 K5
St Cyrus Abers 143 N5
St David's P & K 133 Q3
St Davids Pembks 40 E5
St Davids Cathedral Pembks 40 E5
St Day Cnwll 3 J5
St Decumans Somset 18 E6
St Dennis Cnwll 4 F10
St Devereux Herefs 45 N8
St Dogmaels Pembks 42 C5
St Dogwells Pembks 41 J5
St Dominick Cnwll 5 Q8
St Donats V Glam 29 P11
St Edith's Marsh Wilts 21 J2
St Endellion Cnwll 4 F6
St Enoder Cnwll 4 D10
St Erme Cnwll 3 L4
St Erney Cnwll 5 P10
St Erth Cnwll 2 F6
St Erth Praze Cnwll 2 F6
St Ervan Cnwll 4 E7
St Eval Cnwll 4 D8
St Ewe Cnwll 3 P4
St Fagans Cardif 30 F9
St Fagans: National History Museum Cardif 30 F9
St Fergus Abers 159 Q7
St Fillans P & K 133 K3
St Florence Pembks 41 L10
St Gennys Cnwll 5 J2
St George Conwy 80 D9
St Georges N Som 19 L2
St George's V Glam 30 F9
St George's Hill Surrey 36 C8
St Germans Cnwll 5 P10
St Giles in the Wood Devon 17 J8
St Giles-on-the-Heath Devon 5 P3
St Gluvia's Cnwll 3 K7
St Harmon Powys 55 M10
St Helen Auckland Dur 103 N5
St Helens Cumb 100 D4
St Helen's E Susx 26 D9
St Helens IoW 14 H9
St Helens St Hel 81 Q5
St Helier Gt Lon 36 G7
St Helier Jersey 11 b2
St Hilary Cnwll 2 E7
St Hilary V Glam 30 D10
Saint Hill Devon 10 B3
Saint Hill W Susx 25 J3
St Illtyd Blae G 30 H4
St Ippolyts Herts 50 E5
St Ishmael's Pembks 40 F9
St Issey Cnwll 4 E7
St Ive Cnwll 5 N8
St Ive Cross Cnwll 5 N8
St Ives Cambs 62 D6
St Ives Cnwll 2 E5
St Ives Dorset 13 K4
St James Norfk 77 K7
St James's End Nhants 60 F8
St James South Elmham Suffk 65 L5
St Jidgey Cnwll 4 E8
St John Cnwll 5 Q11
St John Jersey 11 b1
St Johns Dur 103 L4
St John's E Susx 25 M4
St John's IoM 80 c5
St John's Kent 37 M9
St Johns Surrey 23 Q3
St Johns Worcs 46 F4
St John's Chapel Devon 17 J6
St John's Chapel Dur 102 G3
St John's Fen End Norfk 75 K8
St John's Highway Norfk 75 K8
St John's Kirk S Lans 116 D3
St John's Town of Dalry D & G 108 D4
St John's Wood Gt Lon 36 G4
St Judes IoM 80 e2
St Just Cnwll 2 B7
St Just-in-Roseland Cnwll 3 L6
St Just Mining District Cnwll 2 B7
St Katherines Abers 159 J11
St Keverne Cnwll 3 K9
St Kew Cnwll 4 G6
St Kew Highway Cnwll 4 G6
St Keyne Cnwll 5 L9
St Lawrence Cnwll 4 G8
St Lawrence Essex 52 G11
St Lawrence IoW 14 F11
St Lawrence Jersey 11 b1
St Lawrence Kent 39 Q8
St Leonards Bucks 35 P3
St Leonards Dorset 13 K4
St Leonards E Susx 26 D10
St Leonard's Street Kent 37 Q9
St Levan Cnwll 2 B9
St Lythans V Glam 30 F10
St Mabyn Cnwll 4 G7
St Madoes P & K 134 F3
St Margarets Herefs 45 M8
St Margarets Herts 51 J8
St Margaret's at Cliffe Kent 27 Q3
St Margaret's Hope Ork 169 d7
St Margaret South Elmham Suffk 65 L5
St Marks IoM 80 c7
St Martin Cnwll 3 J9
St Martin Cnwll 5 M10
St Martin Guern 10 b2
St Martin Jersey 11 c1
St Martin's IoS 2 c1
St Martin's P & K 142 B11
St Martin's Shrops 69 K7
St Martin's Moor Shrops 69 K7
St Mary Jersey 11 a1
St Mary Bourne Hants 22 D4
St Marychurch Torbay 7 N5
St Mary Church V Glam 30 D10
St Mary Cray Gt Lon 37 L7
St Mary Hill V Glam 30 C9
St Mary in the Marsh Kent 27 J6
St Mary's IoS 2 c2
St Mary's Ork 169 d6
St Mary's Bay Kent 27 J6
St Mary's Hoo Medway 38 D6
St Mary's Platt Kent 37 P9
St Maughans Mons 45 P11
St Maughans Green Mons 45 P11
St Mawes Cnwll 3 L7
St Mawgan Cnwll 4 D8
St Mellion Cnwll 5 P8
St Mellons Cardif 30 H8
St Merryn Cnwll 4 D7
St Mewan Cnwll 3 P3
St Michael Caerhays Cnwll 3 P5
St Michael Church Somset 19 K8
St Michael Penkevil Cnwll 3 M5
St Michaels Kent 26 E4
St Michaels Worcs 57 K11
St Michael's Mount Cnwll 2 E8
St Michael's on Wyre Lancs 88 F2
St Michael South Elmham Suffk 65 L5
St Minver Cnwll 4 F6
St Monans Fife 135 N7
St Neot Cnwll 5 K8
St Neots Cambs 61 Q8
St Newlyn East Cnwll 4 C10
St Nicholas Pembks 40 H3
St Nicholas V Glam 30 E10
St Nicholas-at-Wade Kent 39 N8
St Ninians Stirlg 133 M9
St Olaves Norfk 65 P2
St Osyth Essex 53 K8
St Ouen Jersey 11 a1
St Owen's Cross Herefs 45 Q10
St Paul's Cray Gt Lon 37 L7
St Paul's Walden Herts 50 E6
St Peter Jersey 11 a1
St Peter Port Guern 10 c2
St Peter's Guern 10 b2
St Peter's Kent 39 Q8
St Peter's Hill Cambs 62 B6
St Petrox Pembks 41 J11
St Pinnock Cnwll 5 L9
St Quivox S Ayrs 114 G3
St Ruan Cnwll 3 J10
St Sampson Guern 10 c1
St Saviour Guern 10 b2
St Saviour Jersey 11 b2
St Stephen Cnwll 3 N3
St Stephens Cnwll 5 N4
St Stephens Cnwll 5 Q10
St Teath Cnwll 4 H5
St Thomas Devon 9 M6
St Margaret's Bay Kent 27 Q3
St Tudy Cnwll 4 H6
St Twynnells Pembks 41 J11
St Veep Cnwll 5 J10
St Vigeans Angus 143 L9
St Wenn Cnwll 4 F9
St Weonards Herefs 45 P10
St Winnow Cnwll 5 J10
St y-Nyll V Glam 30 E9
Salcombe Devon 7 J11
Salcombe Regis Devon 10 D7
Salcott-cum-Virley Essex 52 F9
Sale Traffd 82 G6
Saleby Lincs 87 N5
Sale Green Worcs 46 H3
Salehurst E Susx 26 C7
Salem Carmth 43 M9
Salem Cerdgn 54 F8
Salen Ag & B 137 P7
Salen Highld 138 B5
Salesbury Lancs 89 K4
Salford C Beds 49 P7
Salford Oxon 47 Q9
Salford Salfd 82 H5
Salford Priors Warwks 47 L4
Salfords Surrey 36 G11
Salhouse Norfk 77 L9
Saline Fife 134 C9
Salisbury Wilts 21 M8
Salisbury Plain Wilts 21 L6
Salkeld Dykes Cumb 101 P3
Sallachy Highld 162 C5
Salle Norfk 76 G7
Salmonby Lincs 87 K6
Salperton Gloucs 47 L10
Salph End Bed 61 N10
Salsburgh N Lans 126 E5
Salt Staffs 70 H9
Salta Cumb 109 N11
Saltaire C Brad 90 E3
Saltaire C Brad 90 E3
Saltash Cnwll 6 C7
Saltburn Highld 156 C3
Saltburn-by-the-Sea R & Cl 105 J6
Saltby Leics 73 M5
Salt Coates Cumb 110 C10
Saltcoats Cumb 100 E11
Saltcoats N Ayrs 124 G9
Saltcotes Lancs 88 D5
Saltdean Br & H 25 J10
Salterbeck Cumb 100 C5
Salterforth Lancs 96 C11
Salterswall Ches W 82 D11
Salterton Wilts 21 M7
Saltfleet Lincs 87 N2
Saltfleetby All Saints Lincs 87 N2
Saltfleetby St Clement Lincs 87 N2
Saltfleetby St Peter Lincs 87 M3
Saltford BaNES 32 C11
Salthouse Norfk 76 F3
Saltley Birm 58 H7
Saltmarsh Newpt 31 K8
Saltmarshe E R Yk 92 C6
Saltney Flints 69 L2
Salton N York 98 E5
Saltrens Devon 16 H7
Saltwick Nthumb 113 J4
Saltwood Kent 27 L4
Salvington W Susx 24 D9
Salwarpe Worcs 46 G2
Salway Ash Dorset 11 K5
Sambourne Warwks 47 L2
Sambrook Wrekin 70 C10
Samlesbury Lancs 88 H4
Samlesbury Bottoms Lancs 89 J5
Sampford Arundel Somset 18 F11
Sampford Brett Somset 18 E6
Sampford Courtenay Devon 8 F4
Sampford Moor Somset 18 F11
Sampford Peverell Devon 9 P2
Sampford Spiney Devon 6 E4
Samsonlane Ork 169 f4
Samson's Corner Essex 53 J8
Samuelston E Loth 128 D5
Sanaigmore Ag & B 122 B5
Sancreed Cnwll 2 C8
Sancton E R Yk 92 E3
Sand Somset 19 M5
Sandaig Highld 145 M7
Sandale Cumb 100 H2
Sandal Magna Wakefd 91 J7
Sanday Ork 169 f2
Sanday Airport Ork 169 f2
Sandbach Ches E 70 D2
Sandbach Services Ches E 70 D2
Sandbank Ag & B 131 P11
Sandbanks BCP 12 H7
Sandend Abers 158 E4
Sanderstead Gt Lon 36 H8
Sandford Cumb 102 D7
Sandford Devon 9 K4
Sandford Dorset 12 F7
Sandford Hants 13 L4
Sandford IoW 14 F10
Sandford N Som 19 M3
Sandford S Lans 126 C9
Sandford Shrops 69 K10
Sandford Shrops 69 Q8
Sandford-on-Thames Oxon 34 F4
Sandford Orcas Dorset 20 B10
Sandford St Martin Oxon 48 D9
Sandgate Kent 27 M4
Sandhaven Abers 159 N4
Sandhead D & G 106 E8
Sandhill Rothm 91 L11
Sandhills Dorset 11 M3
Sandhills Dorset 11 P2
Sand Hills Leeds 91 K3
Sandhills Oxon 34 G3
Sandhills Surrey 23 P7
Sandhoe Nthumb 112 E7
Sandhole Ag & B 131 L8
Sand Hole E R Yk 92 D3
Sandholme E R Yk 92 D4
Sandholme Lincs 74 F3
Sandhurst Br For 23 M2
Sandhurst Gloucs 46 F10
Sandhurst Kent 26 D6
Sandhurst Cross Kent 26 C6
Sandhutton N York 97 N4
Sand Hutton N York 98 D9
Sandiacre Derbys 72 D3
Sandilands Lincs 87 P4
Sandiway Ches W 82 D10
Sandleheath Hants 21 M11
Sandleigh Oxon 34 E4
Sandley Dorset 20 E10
Sandling Kent 38 C10
Sandlow Green Ches E 82 G11
Sandness Shet 169 n8
Sandon Essex 52 B11
Sandon Herts 50 H4
Sandon Staffs 70 G9
Sandon Bank Staffs 70 G9
Sandown IoW 14 G10
Sandplace Cnwll 5 M10
Sandridge Herts 50 E8
Sandridge Wilts 32 H11
Sandringham Norfk 75 N5
Sands Bucks 35 M6
Sandsend N York 105 N8
Sand Side Cumb 94 E4
Sandside Cumb 95 K4
Sandtoft N Linc 92 B9
Sandway Kent 38 E11
Sandwich Kent 39 P10
Sandwich Bay Kent 39 Q10
Sandwick Cumb 101 M7
Sandwick Shet 169 r11
Sandwick W Isls 168 j4
Sandwith Cumb 100 C8
Sandwith Newtown Cumb 100 C8
Sandy C Beds 61 Q11
Sandy Bank Lincs 87 J9
Sandycroft Flints 81 L11
Sandy Cross E Susx 25 N6
Sandy Cross Herefs 46 C3
Sandyford D & G 110 D2
Sandygate Devon 7 M4
Sandygate IoM 80 e2
Sandy Haven Pembks 40 G9
Sandyhills D & G 109 J9
Sandylands Lancs 95 J8
Sandy Lane C Brad 90 E3
Sandylane Staffs 70 C7
Sandylane Swans 28 G7
Sandy Lane Wilts 33 J11
Sandy Lane Wrexhm 69 M6
Sandy Park Devon 8 H7
Sandysike Cumb 110 G7
Sandyway Herefs 45 P9
Sangobeg Highld 165 K3
Sangomore Highld 165 K3
Sankey Bridges Warrtn 82 C7
Sankyn's Green Worcs 57 P11
Sanna Highld 137 L2
Sanndabhaig W Isls 168 j4
Sannox N Ayrs 124 C8
Sanquhar D & G 115 Q6
Santon Cumb 100 F10
Santon IoM 80 d7
Santon Bridge Cumb 100 F10
Santon Downham Suffk 63 P3
Sapcote Leics 59 Q6
Sapey Common Herefs 46 D2
Sapiston Suffk 64 C6
Sapley Cambs 62 B6
Sapperton Derbys 71 M8
Sapperton Gloucs 32 H4
Sapperton Lincs 73 Q4
Saracen's Head Lincs 74 F5
Sarclet Highld 167 P8
Sarisbury Hants 14 F5
Sarn Brdgnd 29 P8
Sarn Powys 56 C6
Sarnau Carmth 42 F11
Sarnau Cerdgn 42 F4
Sarnau Gwynd 68 C7
Sarnau Powys 44 E8
Sarnau Powys 68 H11
Sarn Bach Gwynd 66 E9
Sarnesfield Herefs 45 M4
Sarn Mellteyrn Gwynd 66 C8
Sarn Park Services Brdgnd 29 P8
Sarn-wen Powys 69 J11
Saron Carmth 28 H2
Saron Carmth 42 G7
Saron Gwynd 66 H3
Saron Gwynd 79 J11
Sarratt Herts 50 B11
Sarre Kent 39 N8
Sarsden Oxon 47 Q10
Sarson Hants 22 B6
Satley Dur 103 M2
Satmar Kent 27 N4
Satron N York 102 H11
Satterleigh Devon 17 M7
Satterthwaite Cumb 94 G2
Satwell Oxon 35 K8
Sauchen Abers 151 J5
Saucher P & K 142 B11
Sauchieburn Abers 143 M4
Saul Gloucs 32 D3
Saundby Notts 85 N3
Saundersfoot Pembks 41 M10
Saunderton Bucks 35 L4
Saunderton Station Bucks 35 M5
Saunton Devon 16 H4
Sausthorpe Lincs 87 L7
Saverley Green Staffs 70 H7
Savile Town Kirk 90 G6
Sawbridge Warwks 60 B7
Sawbridgeworth Herts 51 L8
Sawdon N York 99 J4
Sawley Derbys 72 D4
Sawley Lancs 96 A11
Sawley N York 97 K7
Sawston Cambs 62 G11
Sawtry Cambs 61 Q4
Saxby Leics 73 L7
Saxby Lincs 86 D3
Saxby All Saints N Linc 92 G7
Saxelbye Leics 72 H6
Saxham Street Suffk 64 F9
Saxilby Lincs 85 Q5
Saxlingham Norfk 76 E4
Saxlingham Green Norfk 65 J2
Saxlingham Nethergate Norfk 65 J2
Saxlingham Thorpe Norfk 65 J2
Saxmundham Suffk 65 M9
Saxondale Notts 72 H3
Saxon Street Cambs 63 L9
Saxtead Suffk 65 K8
Saxtead Green Suffk 65 K9
Saxtead Little Green Suffk 65 J8
Saxthorpe Norfk 76 G5
Saxton N York 91 M3
Sayers Common W Susx 24 G7
Scackleton N York 98 C6
Scadabay W Isls 168 g8
Scadabhagh W Isls 168 g8
Scafell Pike Cumb 100 H9
Scaftworth Notts 85 L2
Scagglethorpe N York 98 G6
Scalasaig Ag & B 136 b3
Scalby E R Yk 92 D5
Scalby N York 99 L2
Scald End Bed 61 M9
Scaldwell Nhants 60 G6
Scaleby Cumb 110 H8
Scalebyhill Cumb 110 H8
Scale Houses Cumb 111 L11
Scales Cumb 94 F6
Scales Cumb 101 K5
Scalesceugh Cumb 110 H11
Scalford Leics 73 K6
Scaling N York 105 K8
Scaling Dam R & Cl 105 K8
Scalloway Shet 169 r10
Scalpay Highld 153 L11
Scalpay W Isls 168 h8
Scamblesby Lincs 87 J5
Scammonden Kirk 90 D7
Scamodale Highld 138 E3
Scampston N York 98 H5
Scampton Lincs 86 C5
Scaniport Highld 156 A10
Scapegoat Hill Kirk 90 D7
Scarba Ag & B 130 D7
Scarborough N York 99 L3
Scarcewater Cnwll 3 N3
Scarcliffe Derbys 84 G7
Scarcroft Leeds 91 K2
Scarfskerry Highld 167 N2
Scargill Dur 103 L8
Scarinish Ag & B 136 C7
Scarisbrick Lancs 88 D8
Scarness Cumb 100 H4
Scarning Norfk 76 D9
Scarrington Notts 73 J2
Scarth Hill Lancs 88 E9
Scarthingwell N York 91 M3
Scartho NE Lin 93 N9
Scatsta Airport Shet 169 q6
Scaur D & G 108 H10
Scawby N Linc 92 G9
Scawsby Donc 91 N10
Scawthorpe Donc 91 P9
Scawton N York 98 A4
Scayne's Hill W Susx 25 J6
Scethrog Powys 44 G9
Scholar Green Ches E 70 E3
Scholes Kirk 90 F5

Scholes Kirk 90 F9
Scholes Leeds 91 K3
Scholes Rothm 91 K11
Scholes Wigan 88 H9
School Aycliffe Dur 103 Q6
School Green C Brad 90 E4
School Green Ches W 70 A2
Schoolgreen Wokam 35 K11
School House Dorset 10 H4
Scissett Kirk 90 G8
Scofton Notts 85 K4
Scole Norfk 64 H6
Scone P & K 134 E12
Sconser Highld 153 J11
Scoonie Fife 135 K7
Scopwick Lincs 86 E9
Scorborough E R Yk 99 J13
Scorrier Cnwll 3 J5
Scorriton Devon 7 J5
Scorton Lancs 95 L11
Scorton N York 103 Q10
Sco Ruston Norfk 77 K7
Scotby Cumb 110 H9
Scotch Corner N York 103 P9
Scotch Corner Rest Area N York 103 P9
Scotforth Lancs 95 K9
Scot Hay Staffs 70 D5
Scothern Lincs 86 D5
Scotland Lincs 73 Q4
Scotland Gate Nthumb 113 L4
Scotlandwell P & K 134 F7
Scot Lane End Bolton 89 J9
Scotscalder Station Highld 167 J5
Scotsdike Cumb 110 G6
Scot's Gap Nthumb 112 F3
Scotsmill Abers 150 F4
Scotstown C Glas 125 N4
Scotswood N u Ty 113 K8
Scotter Lincs 92 E10
Scotterthorpe Lincs 92 E10
Scottish Seabird Centre E Loth 128 F2
Scottish Wool Centre Stirlg 132 G7
Scottlethorpe Lincs 73 R6
Scotton Lincs 92 E11
Scotton N York 97 M9
Scotton N York 103 N11
Scottow Norfk 77 K7
Scott Willoughby Lincs 73 R3
Scoulton Norfk 76 D11
Scounslow Green Staffs 71 K9
Scourie Highld 164 E8
Scourie More Highld 164 D8
Scousburgh Shet 169 q12
Scouthead Oldham 90 B9
Scrabster Highld 167 K2
Scraesburgh Border 118 C7
Scrafield Lincs 87 K7
Scrainwood Nthumb 119 J9
Scrane End Lincs 74 G2
Scraptoft Leics 72 G9
Scratby Norfk 77 Q8
Scrayingham N York 98 E9
Scrays E Susx 26 C8
Scredington Lincs 74 A2
Scremby Lincs 87 M7
Scremerston Nthumb 129 Q10
Screveton Notts 73 J2
Scrivelsby Lincs 87 J7
Scriven N York 97 M9
Scrooby Notts 85 L2
Scropton Derbys 71 M8
Scrub Hill Lincs 86 H9
Scruton N York 97 L2
Scuggate Cumb 110 H6
Scullomie Highld 165 P4
Sculthorpe Norfk 76 B5
Scunthorpe N Linc 92 E8
Scurlage Swans 28 E7
Sea Somset 10 G2
Seaborough Dorset 11 J3
Seabridge Staffs 70 E6
Seabrook Kent 27 L4
Seaburn Sundld 113 P9
Seacombe Wirral 81 L6
Seacroft Leeds 91 K3
Seacroft Lincs 87 Q8
Seadyke Lincs 74 F3
Seafield W Loth 127 J4
Seaford E Susx 25 L11
Seaforth Sefton 81 L5
Seagrave Leics 72 G7
Seagry Heath Wilts 33 J8
Seaham Dur 113 P11
Seahouses Nthumb 119 P4
Seal Kent 37 N9
Sealand Flints 81 M11
Seale Surrey 23 N5
Seamer N York 99 L4
Seamer N York 104 E8
Seamill N Ayrs 124 G8
Sea Palling Norfk 77 N6
Searby Lincs 93 J9
Seasalter Kent 39 J9
Seascale Cumb 100 D10
Seathwaite Cumb 100 H11
Seathwaite Cumb 100 H8
Seatle Cumb 94 H4
Seatoller Cumb 100 H8
Seaton Cnwll 5 N11
Seaton Cumb 100 D4
Seaton Devon 10 E6
Seaton Dur 113 N11
Seaton E R Yk 99 P11
Seaton Kent 39 M10
Seaton Nthumb 113 M5
Seaton Rutlnd 73 N11
Seaton Burn N Tyne 113 K6
Seaton Carew Hartpl 104 F5
Seaton Delaval Nthumb 113 M5
Seaton Ross E R Yk 92 C2
Seaton Sluice Nthumb 113 M5
Seatown Dorset 11 J6
Seatown Moray 157 N3
Seave Green N York 104 G10
Seaview IoW 14 H8
Seaville Cumb 110 C10
Seavington St Mary Somset 11 J2
Seavington St Michael Somset 19 M11
Sebastopol Torfn 31 J5
Sebergham Cumb 101 L2
Seckington Warwks 59 L3

Second Severn Crossing Mons 31 P7
Sedbergh Cumb 95 P2
Sedbury Gloucs 31 P6
Sedbusk N York 96 C2
Sedgeberrow Worcs 47 K7
Sedgebrook Lincs 73 M3
Sedge Fen Suffk 63 L4
Sedgefield Dur 104 C5
Sedgeford Norfk 75 P3
Sedgehill Wilts 20 G9
Sedgemoor Services Somset 19 L4
Sedgley Dudley 58 D6
Sedgley Park Bury 82 H4
Sedgwick Cumb 95 L3
Sedlescombe E Susx 26 C8
Sedrup Bucks 35 M2
Seed Kent 38 F10
Seend Wilts 20 H1
Seend Cleeve Wilts 20 H2
Seer Green Bucks 35 Q6
Seething Norfk 65 L2
Sefton Sefton 81 M4
Seghill Nthumb 113 L6
Seighford Staffs 70 F9
Seion Gwynd 79 J11
Seisdon Staffs 58 B5
Selattyn Shrops 69 J8
Selborne Hants 23 K8
Selby N York 91 Q4
Selham W Susx 23 P10
Selhurst Gt Lon 36 H7
Selkirk Border 117 P5
Sellack Herefs 45 R9
Sellafield Station Cumb 100 D10
Sellafirth Shet 169 s4
Sellan Cnwll 2 C7
Sellick's Green Somset 18 H11
Sellindge Kent 27 J4
Selling Kent 38 H10
Sells Green Wilts 20 H2
Selly Oak Birm 58 F8
Selmeston E Susx 25 M9
Selsdon Gt Lon 37 J8
Selsey W Susx 15 N8
Selsfield Common W Susx 24 H4
Selside Cumb 101 P11
Selside N York 96 A5
Selsley Gloucs 32 F4
Selsted Kent 27 M3
Selston Notts 84 G10
Selworthy Somset 18 B5
Semer Suffk 52 G2
Semington Wilts 20 G2
Semley Wilts 20 G9
Sempringham Lincs 74 B4
Send Surrey 36 B9
Send Marsh Surrey 36 B9
Senghenydd Caerph 30 F6
Sennen Cnwll 2 B8
Sennen Cove Cnwll 2 B8
Sennybridge Powys 44 C9
Serlby Notts 85 K3
Sessay N York 97 Q5
Setchey Norfk 75 M8
Setley Hants 13 P4
Seton Mains E Loth 128 C4
Settle N York 96 B8
Settrington N York 98 G6
Seven Ash Somset 18 G8
Sevenhampton Gloucs 47 K10
Sevenhampton Swindn 33 P6
Seven Kings Gt Lon 37 L3
Sevenoaks Kent 37 M9
Sevenoaks Weald Kent 37 M10
Seven Sisters Neath 29 M3
Seven Springs Gloucs 47 J11
Seven Star Green Essex 52 F6
Severn Beach S Glos 31 P8
Severn Bridge S Glos 31 Q6
Severn Stoke Worcs 46 G6
Severn View Services S Glos 31 Q7
Sevick End Bed 61 N10
Sevington Kent 26 H3
Sewards End Essex 51 N3
Sewardstonebury Essex 51 J11
Sewell C Beds 49 Q10
Sewerby E R Yk 99 P7
Seworgan Cnwll 3 J7
Sewstern Leics 73 M6
Sexhow N York 104 E9
Sgalpaigh W Isls 168 h8
Sgiogarstaigh W Isls 168 k1
Shabbington Bucks 35 J3
Shackerley Shrops 57 Q3
Shackerstone Leics 72 B9
Shacklecross Derbys 72 C4
Shackleford Surrey 23 P5
Shade Calder 89 Q6
Shader W Isls 168 i2
Shadforth Dur 104 B2
Shadingfield Suffk 65 N5
Shadoxhurst Kent 26 H4
Shadwell Leeds 91 J3
Shadwell Norfk 64 C5
Shaftenhoe End Herts 51 K3
Shaftesbury Dorset 20 G10
Shaftholme Donc 91 P9
Shafton Barns 91 K8
Shafton Two Gates Barns 91 K8
Shakerley Wigan 82 E4
Shalbourne Wilts 22 B2
Shalcombe IoW 14 C9
Shalden Hants 23 J6
Shalden Green Hants 23 K6
Shaldon Devon 7 N4
Shalfleet IoW 14 D9
Shalford Essex 52 B6
Shalford Surrey 36 B11
Shalford Green Essex 52 B6
Shallowford Staffs 70 F9
Shalmsford Street Kent 39 J11
Shalstone Bucks 48 H7
Shamley Green Surrey 24 B2
Shandford Angus 142 H5
Shandon Ag & B 132 B10
Shandwick Highld 156 F2
Shangton Leics 73 J11
Shankhouse Nthumb 113 L5
Shanklin IoW 14 G11
Shantron Ag & B 132 C10
Shap Cumb 101 Q7
Shapinsay Ork 169 e5
Shapwick Dorset 12 F4
Shapwick Somset 19 M7

Shard End Birm 59 J7
Shardlow Derbys 72 C4
Shareshill Staffs 58 D3
Sharlston Wakefd 91 K7
Sharlston Common Wakefd 91 K7
Sharmans Cross Solhll 58 H9
Sharnal Street Medway 38 C7
Sharnbrook Bed 61 L9
Sharneyford Lancs 89 P6
Sharnford Leics 59 Q6
Sharnhill Green Dorset 11 P3
Sharoe Green Lancs 88 G4
Sharow N York 97 M6
Sharpenhoe C Beds 50 C4
Sharperton Nthumb 119 J10
Sharp Green Norfk 77 M7
Sharpness Gloucs 32 C4
Sharpthorne W Susx 25 J4
Sharptor Cnwll 5 M7
Sharpway Gate Worcs 58 E11
Sharrington Norfk 76 E4
Shatterford Worcs 57 P8
Shattering Kent 39 N10
Shatton Derbys 84 E6
Shaugh Prior Devon 6 E7
Shave Cross Dorset 11 J5
Shavington Ches E 70 B4
Shaw C Brad 90 C3
Shaw Oldham 89 Q9
Shaw Swindn 33 M7
Shaw W Berk 34 E11
Shaw Wilts 32 G5
Shawbirch Wrekin 57 L2
Shawbost W Isls 168 h3
Shawbury Shrops 69 Q10
Shawclough Rochdl 89 P8
Shaw Common Gloucs 46 C9
Shawdon Hill Nthumb 119 L10
Shawell Leics 60 B4
Shawford Hants 22 E9
Shawforth Lancs 89 P6
Shaw Green Herts 50 H4
Shaw Green Lancs 88 G6
Shaw Green N York 97 L10
Shawhead D & G 109 J5
Shaw Mills N York 97 L8
Shawsburn S Lans 126 D7
Shear Cross Wilts 20 G6
Shearington D & G 109 M7
Shearsby Leics 60 D2
Shearston Somset 19 J9
Shebbear Devon 16 G10
Shebdon Staffs 70 D9
Shebster Highld 166 H4
Shedfield Hants 14 G4
Sheen Staffs 71 L2
Sheepbridge Derbys 84 E6
Sheep Hill Dur 113 J9
Sheepridge Kirk 90 F7
Sheepscar Leeds 91 J4
Sheepscombe Gloucs 32 G2
Sheepstor Devon 6 E7
Sheepwash Devon 8 C3
Sheepwash Nthumb 113 L4
Sheepway N Som 31 N9
Sheepy Magna Leics 72 A10
Sheepy Parva Leics 72 A10
Sheering Essex 51 M8
Sheerness Kent 38 F7
Sheerwater Surrey 36 B8
Sheet Hants 23 L10
Sheffield Cnwll 2 D8
Sheffield Sheff 84 E3
Sheffield Bottom W Berk 34 H11
Sheffield Green E Susx 25 K5
Sheffield Park E Susx 25 K6
Shefford C Beds 50 D3
Shefford Woodlands W Berk 34 C10
Sheigra Highld 164 E4
Sheinton Shrops 57 L4
Shelderton Shrops 56 G9
Sheldon Birm 58 J8
Sheldon Derbys 83 Q11
Sheldon Devon 10 C3
Sheldwich Kent 38 H10
Sheldwich Lees Kent 38 H10
Shelf Calder 90 E5
Shelfanger Norfk 64 G5
Shelfield Warwks 47 M2
Shelfield Wsall 58 F4
Shelfield Green Warwks 47 M2
Shelford Notts 72 H2
Shelford Warwks 59 P7
Shellacres Nthumb 118 G2
Shelley Essex 51 N9
Shelley Kirk 90 G8
Shelley Suffk 52 H4
Shelley Far Bank Kirk 90 G8
Shellingford Oxon 34 B6
Shellow Bowells Essex 51 P9
Shelsley Beauchamp Worcs 46 D2
Shelsley Walsh Worcs 46 D2
Shelton Bed 61 M7
Shelton Norfk 65 J3
Shelton Notts 73 K2
Shelton Shrops 56 H2
Shelton Green Norfk 65 J3
Shelton Lock C Derb 72 B4
Shelton Under Harley Staffs 70 E7
Shelve Shrops 56 F5
Shelwick Herefs 45 Q6
Shenfield Essex 51 P11
Shenington Oxon 48 C6
Shenley Herts 50 E10
Shenley Brook End M Keyn 49 M7
Shenleybury Herts 50 E10
Shenley Church End M Keyn 49 M7
Shenmore Herefs 45 M7
Shennanton D & G 107 K5
Shenstone Staffs 58 H4
Shenstone Worcs 58 C10
Shenstone Woodend Staffs 58 H4
Shenton Leics 72 B11
Shenval Moray 149 N2
Shepeau Stow Lincs 74 F8
Shephall Herts 50 G6
Shepherd's Bush Gt Lon 36 F4
Shepherd's Green Oxon 35 K8
Shepherds Patch Gloucs 32 D3
Shepherdswell Kent 27 N2
Shepley Kirk 90 F8
Shepperdine S Glos 32 B5
Shepperton Surrey 36 C7
Shepperton Green Surrey 36 C7
Shepreth Cambs 62 E11
Shepshed Leics 72 D7

Shepton Beauchamp Somset 19 M11
Shepton Mallet Somset 20 B6
Shepton Montague Somset 20 C8
Shepway Kent 38 C11
Sheraton Dur 104 D2
Sherborne Dorset 20 B11
Sherborne Gloucs 33 N2
Sherborne Somset 19 Q3
Sherborne St John Hants 22 H3
Sherbourne Warwks 47 Q2
Sherburn Dur 104 B2
Sherburn N York 99 K5
Sherburn Hill Dur 104 B2
Sherburn in Elmet N York 91 M4
Shere Surrey 36 C11
Shereford Norfk 76 B6
Sherfield English Hants 21 Q10
Sherfield on Loddon Hants 23 J3
Sherfin Lancs 89 M5
Sherford Devon 6 F11
Sherford Somset 7 K10
Sheriffhales Shrops 57 P2
Sheriff Hutton N York 98 D7
Sheringham Norfk 76 H3
Sherington M Keyn 49 N5
Shermanbury W Susx 24 F7
Shernborne Norfk 75 P4
Sherrington Wilts 21 J7
Sherston Wilts 32 G7
Sherwood C Nott 72 F2
Sherwood Forest Notts 85 K8
Shetland Islands Shet 169 r8
Shettleston C Glas 125 Q5
Shevington Wigan 88 G9
Shevington Moor Wigan 88 G8
Shevington Vale Wigan 88 G9
Sheviock Cnwll 5 P10
Shibden Head C Brad 90 D5
Shide IoW 14 F9
Shidlaw Nthumb 118 F3
Shiel Bridge Highld 146 A4
Shieldaig Highld 153 Q7
Shieldhill D & G 109 M3
Shieldhill Falk 126 F2
Shieldhill House Hotel S Lans 116 E2
Shields N Lans 126 D6
Shielfoot Highld 138 B3
Shielhill Angus 142 G6
Shielhill Inver 124 G3
Shifford Oxon 34 C4
Shifnal Shrops 57 N3
Shilbottle Nthumb 119 N9
Shildon Dur 103 P5
Shillford E Rens 125 M6
Shillingford Devon 18 C10
Shillingford Oxon 34 G6
Shillingford Abbot Devon 9 M7
Shillingford St George Devon 9 M7
Shillingstone Dorset 12 D2
Shillington C Beds 50 D4
Shillmoor Nthumb 118 G9
Shilton Oxon 33 Q3
Shilton Warwks 59 P8
Shimpling Norfk 64 H5
Shimpling Suffk 64 B11
Shimpling Street Suffk 64 B11
Shincliffe Dur 103 Q2
Shiney Row Sundld 113 M10
Shinfield Wokham 35 K11
Shingay Cambs 62 D11
Shingle Street Suffk 53 Q3
Shinnersbridge Devon 7 K6
Shinness Highld 162 C4
Shipbourne Kent 37 N10
Shipdham Norfk 76 D10
Shipham Somset 19 M3
Shiphay Torbay 7 M5
Shiplake Oxon 35 L9
Shiplake Row Oxon 35 K9
Shiplate N Som 19 L3
Shipley C Brad 90 F3
Shipley Derbys 72 C2
Shipley Shrops 57 Q5
Shipley W Susx 24 D6
Shipley Bridge Surrey 24 H2
Shipley Hatch Kent 26 H3
Shipmeadow Suffk 65 M3
Shippea Hill Station Cambs 63 K4
Shippon Oxon 34 E5
Shipston-on-Stour Warwks 47 Q6
Shipton Bucks 49 L9
Shipton Gloucs 47 K11
Shipton N York 98 B9
Shipton Shrops 57 K6
Shipton Bellinger Hants 21 P5
Shipton Gorge Dorset 11 K6
Shipton Green W Susx 15 M7
Shipton Moyne Gloucs 32 G7
Shipton-on-Cherwell Oxon 48 E10
Shiptonthorpe E R Yk 92 E2
Shipton-under-Wychwood Oxon 47 Q11
Shirburn Oxon 35 J5
Shirdley Hill Lancs 88 D8
Shire Cumb 102 B3
Shirebrook Derbys 84 H7
Shiregreen Sheff 84 E2
Shirehampton Bristl 31 P9
Shiremoor N Tyne 113 M6
Shirenewton Mons 31 N5
Shire Oak Wsall 58 G4
Shireoaks Notts 85 K4
Shirkoak Kent 26 H4
Shirland Derbys 84 E9
Shirlett Shrops 57 L5
Shirley C Sotn 14 D4
Shirley Derbys 71 N6
Shirley Gt Lon 37 J7
Shirley Solhll 58 H9
Shirl Heath Herefs 45 N3
Shirrell Heath Hants 14 F3
Shirwell Devon 17 L4
Shiskine N Ayrs 120 H6
Shittlehope Dur 103 K3
Shobdon Herefs 45 M2
Shobley Hants 13 L3
Shobrooke Devon 9 K4
Shoby Leics 72 H6
Shocklach Ches W 69 M5
Shocklach Green Ches W 69 M5
Shoeburyness Sthend 38 F4
Sholden Kent 39 Q11

Sholing C Sotn 14 E4
Shoot Hill Shrops 56 G2
Shop Cnwll 4 D7
Shop Cnwll 16 C9
Shopwyke W Susx 15 N5
Shore Rochdl 89 Q7
Shoreditch Gt Lon 36 H4
Shoreditch Somset 18 H10
Shoreham Kent 37 M8
Shoreham-by-Sea W Susx 24 F9
Shoreswood Nthumb 129 N10
Shorley Hants 22 G9
Shorncote Gloucs 33 K5
Shorne Kent 37 Q6
Shortacross Cnwll 5 M10
Shortbridge E Susx 25 L6
Shortfield Common Surrey 23 N6
Shortgate E Susx 25 L7
Short Heath Birm 58 G6
Shortheath Hants 23 L7
Short Heath Wsall 58 E4
Shortlanesend Cnwll 3 L4
Shortlees E Ayrs 125 L11
Shortstown Bed 61 N11
Shorwell IoW 14 E10
Shoscombe BaNES 20 D3
Shotesham Norfk 65 J2
Shotgate Essex 38 C3
Shotley Suffk 53 M4
Shotley Bridge Dur 112 G10
Shotleyfield Nthumb 112 G10
Shotley Gate Suffk 53 M4
Shottenden Kent 38 H11
Shottermill Surrey 23 N8
Shottery Warwks 47 N4
Shotteswell Warwks 48 D5
Shottisham Suffk 53 P3
Shottle Derbys 71 Q5
Shottlegate Derbys 71 Q5
Shotton Dur 104 C5
Shotton Dur 104 D3
Shotton Flints 81 L11
Shotton Nthumb 113 L5
Shotton Nthumb 118 F4
Shotton Colliery Dur 104 C2
Shotts N Lans 126 F6
Shotwick Ches W 81 L11
Shougle Moray 157 N6
Shouldham Norfk 75 N9
Shouldham Thorpe Norfk 75 N9
Shoulton Worcs 46 F3
Shover's Green E Susx 25 Q4
Shraleybrook Staffs 70 D5
Shrawardine Shrops 69 L11
Shrawley Worcs 57 Q11
Shreding Green Bucks 36 B4
Shrewley Warwks 59 K11
Shrewsbury Shrops 56 H2
Shrewton Wilts 21 L6
Shripney W Susx 15 P6
Shrivenham Oxon 33 Q7
Shropham Norfk 64 D2
Shroton Dorset 12 D2
Shrub End Essex 52 G6
Shucknall Herefs 46 A6
Shudy Camps Cambs 51 P2
Shuna Ag & B 130 F2
Shurdington Gloucs 46 H11
Shurlock Row W & M 35 M10
Shurnock Worcs 47 K2
Shurrery Highld 166 H5
Shurrery Lodge Highld 166 H5
Shurton Somset 18 H6
Shustoke Warwks 59 K6
Shute Devon 9 L4
Shute Devon 10 F5
Shutford Oxon 48 C6
Shut Heath Staffs 70 F10
Shuthonger Gloucs 46 H7
Shutlanger Nhants 49 K5
Shutterton Devon 9 N7
Shutt Green Staffs 58 C3
Shuttington Warwks 59 K4
Shuttlewood Derbys 84 G6
Shuttleworth Bury 89 N7
Siabost W Isls 168 h3
Siadar W Isls 168 i2
Sibbertoft Nhants 60 E4
Sibdon Carwood Shrops 56 H7
Sibford Ferris Oxon 48 C7
Sibford Gower Oxon 48 C7
Sible Hedingham Essex 52 C4
Sibley's Green Essex 51 P5
Siblyback Cnwll 5 L7
Sibsey Lincs 87 L9
Sibsey Fenside Lincs 87 L9
Sibson Cambs 74 A11
Sibson Leics 72 B10
Sibster Highld 167 P5
Sibthorpe Notts 85 M6
Sibthorpe Notts 85 N11
Sibton Suffk 65 M8
Sicklesmere Suffk 64 B9
Sicklinghall N York 97 N11
Sidbrook Somset 19 J9
Sidbury Devon 10 C6
Sidbury Shrops 57 M7
Sid Cop Barns 91 K8
Sidcot N Som 19 M4
Sidcup Gt Lon 37 L6
Siddick Cumb 100 D4
Siddington Ches E 82 H10
Siddington Gloucs 33 K4
Sidemoor Worcs 58 E10
Sidestrand Norfk 77 K4
Sidford Devon 10 C6
Sidlesham W Susx 15 N7
Sidlesham Common W Susx 15 N6
Sidley E Susx 26 C9
Sidmouth Devon 10 C7
Siefton Shrops 56 H6
Sigford Devon 7 K4
Sigglesthorne E R Yk 99 P11
Sigingstone V Glam 30 C10
Signet Oxon 33 P2
Silchester Hants 22 H2
Sileby Leics 72 F7
Silecroft Cumb 94 C4
Silfield Norfk 64 G2
Silian Cerdgn 43 L4
Silkstead Hants 22 D10
Silkstone Barns 90 H8
Silkstone Common Barns 90 H8
Silk Willoughby Lincs 73 R2
Silloth Cumb 109 P11
Silpho N York 105 L10

Silsden C Brad....96 F11
Silsoe C Beds....50 C3
Silton Dorset....20 E9
Silverburn Mdloth....127 N5
Silverdale Lancs....95 K6
Silverdale Staffs....70 E5
Silver End Essex....52 D8
Silverford Abers....159 J5
Silvergate Norfk....76 H6
Silverlace Green Suffk....65 L9
Silverley's Green Suffk....65 K6
Silverstone Nhants....49 J6
Silverstone Kent....38 E9
Silver Street Somset....19 P8
Silverton Devon....9 N4
Silverwell Cnwll....3 J4
Silvington Shrops....57 L9
Simister Bury....89 N9
Simmondley Derbys....83 M6
Simonburn Nthumb....112 C6
Simonsbath Somset....17 P4
Simonsburrow Devon....18 F11
Simonstone Lancs....89 M4
Simonstone N York....96 C2
Simprim Border....129 L11
Simpson M Keyn....49 N7
Simpson Cross Pembks....40 G7
Sinclair's Hill Border....129 L9
Sinclairston E Ayrs....115 J4
Sinderby N York....97 M4
Sinderhope Nthumb....112 B10
Sinderland Green Traffd....82 F7
Sindlesham Wokham....35 L11
Sinfin C Derb....72 A4
Singleborough Bucks....49 L8
Single Street Gt Lon....37 K9
Singleton Kent....26 H3
Singleton Lancs....88 D3
Singleton W Susx....15 N4
Singlewell Kent....37 Q6
Sinkhurst Green Kent....26 D3
Sinnahard Abers....150 D5
Sinnington N York....98 E3
Sinope Leics....72 C7
Sinton Worcs....46 F2
Sinton Worcs....46 F2
Sinton Green Worcs....46 F2
Sipson Gt Lon....36 C5
Sirhowy Blae G....30 F2
Sissinghurst Kent....26 C4
Siston S Glos....32 C9
Sitcott Devon....5 P3
Sithney Cnwll....2 G8
Sithney Common Cnwll....2 G8
Sithney Green Cnwll....2 G8
Sittingbourne Kent....38 F9
Six Ashes Shrops....57 P7
Six Bells Blae G....30 H4
Six Hills Leics....72 G6
Sixhills Lincs....86 G3
Six Mile Bottom Cambs....63 J9
Sixmile Cottages Kent....27 K3
Sixpenny Handley Dorset....21 J11
Six Rues Jersey....11 b1
Sizewell Suffk....65 P9
Skaill Ork....169 e6
Skara Brae Ork....169 b5
Skares E Ayrs....115 K4
Skateraw Abers....151 N9
Skateraw E Loth....129 J5
Skeabost Highld....152 G8
Skeeby N York....103 N10
Skeffington Leics....73 J10
Skeffling E R Yk....93 Q7
Skegby Notts....84 G8
Skegby Notts....85 N7
Skegness Lincs....87 Q8
Skelbo Highld....162 H7
Skelbo Street Highld....162 H8
Skelbrooke Donc....91 N8
Skeldyke Lincs....74 F3
Skellingthorpe Lincs....86 B6
Skellorn Green Ches E....83 K8
Skellow Donc....91 N8
Skelmanthorpe Kirk....90 G8
Skelmersdale Lancs....88 F9
Skelmorlie N Ayrs....124 F4
Skelpick Highld....166 H5
Skelston D & G....108 H3
Skelton C York....98 B9
Skelton Cumb....101 M3
Skelton E R Yk....92 C5
Skelton N York....103 L10
Skelton R & Cl....105 J7
Skelton on Ure N York....97 N7
Skelwith Bridge Cumb....101 K10
Skendleby Lincs....87 M7
Skene House Abers....151 K5
Skenfrith Mons....45 P10
Skerne E R Yk....99 L9
Skerray Highld....165 Q4
Skerricha Highld....164 F6
Skerton Lancs....95 K8
Sketchley Leics....59 P6
Sketty Swans....28 H6
Skewen Neath....29 K5
Skewsby N York....98 C6
Skeyton Norfk....77 J6
Skeyton Corner Norfk....77 K6
Skiall Highld....166 H3
Skidbrooke Lincs....87 M2
Skidbrooke North End Lincs....93 R11
Skidby E R Yk....92 H4
Skigersta W Isls....168 k1
Skilgate Somset....18 C9
Skillington Lincs....73 M5
Skinburness Cumb....109 P9
Skinflats Falk....133 Q11
Skinidin Highld....152 C8
Skinners Green W Berk....34 D11
Skinningrove R & Cl....105 K7
Skipness Ag & B....123 R8
Skipper's Bridge D & G....110 G4
Skiprigg Cumb....110 G11
Skipsea E R Yk....99 P10
Skipsea Brough E R Yk....99 P10
Skipton N York....96 E10
Skipton-on-Swale N York....97 N5
Skipwith N York....91 R3
Skirlaugh E R Yk....93 K3
Skirling Border....116 E3
Skirmett Bucks....35 L6
Skirpenbeck E R Yk....98 E9
Skirwith Cumb....102 B4
Skirwith N York....95 Q6
Skirza Highld....167 Q3

Skitby Cumb....110 H7
Skittle Green Bucks....35 L4
Skokholm Island Pembks....40 D10
Skomer Island Pembks....40 D9
Skulamus Highld....145 L3
Skyborry Green Shrops....56 D10
Skye Green Essex....52 E7
Skye of Curr Highld....148 H3
Skyreholme N York....96 G8
Slack Calder....90 B5
Slackbuie Highld....156 B9
Slackcote Oldham....90 B9
Slack Head Cumb....95 K5
Slackholme End Lincs....87 P6
Slacks of Cairnbanno Abers....159 K8
Slad Gloucs....32 G3
Slade Devon....10 C3
Slade Devon....17 J2
Slade Devon....17 Q6
Slade End Oxon....34 G6
Slade Green Gt Lon....37 M5
Slade Heath Staffs....58 D3
Slade Hooton Rothm....84 H3
Sladesbridge Cnwll....4 G7
Slades Green Worcs....46 F8
Slaggyford Nthumb....111 N10
Slaidburn Lancs....95 Q10
Slaithwaite Kirk....90 D8
Slaley Derbys....84 C9
Slaley Nthumb....112 E9
Slamannan Falk....126 F3
Slapton Bucks....49 P10
Slapton Devon....7 L9
Slapton Nhants....48 H5
Slattocks Rochdl....89 P9
Slaugham W Susx....24 G5
Slaughterford Wilts....32 F10
Slawston Leics....60 G2
Sleaford Hants....23 M7
Sleaford Lincs....86 E11
Sleagill Cumb....101 Q7
Sleap Shrops....69 N9
Sleapford Wrekin....70 A11
Sleapshyde Herts....50 E9
Sleasdairidh Highld....162 E7
Slebech Pembks....41 K7
Sledge Green Worcs....46 F8
Sledmere E R Yk....99 J8
Sleetbeck Cumb....111 K5
Sleight Dorset....12 G5
Sleightholme Dur....103 J8
Sleights N York....105 N9
Slepe Dorset....12 F6
Slickly Highld....167 N3
Sliddery N Ayrs....120 H7
Sligachan Highld....144 G2
Sligrachan Ag & B....131 P9
Slimbridge Gloucs....32 D4
Slindon Staffs....70 E8
Slindon W Susx....15 Q5
Slinfold W Susx....24 D4
Sling Gloucs....31 Q3
Sling Gwynd....79 L11
Slingsby N York....98 D6
Slip End C Beds....50 C7
Slip End Herts....50 G3
Slipton Nhants....61 L5
Slitting Mill Staffs....71 J11
Slockavullin Ag & B....130 G8
Sloley Norfk....77 K7
Sloncombe Devon....8 H7
Sloothby Lincs....87 N6
Slough Slough....35 Q9
Slough Green Somset....19 J11
Slough Green W Susx....24 G5
Slumbay Highld....154 A10
Slyfield Surrey....23 Q4
Slyne Lancs....95 K7
Smailholm Border....118 B3
Smallbridge Rochdl....89 Q7
Smallbrook Devon....9 L7
Smallbrook Gloucs....31 Q4
Smallburgh Norfk....77 L7
Smallburn E Ayrs....115 N2
Smalldale Derbys....83 N9
Smalldale Derbys....83 Q8
Small Dole W Susx....24 F8
Smalley Derbys....72 C2
Smalley Common Derbys....72 C2
Smalley Green Derbys....72 C2
Smallfield Surrey....24 H2
Smallford Herts....50 E9
Small Heath Birm....58 H7
Small Hythe Kent....26 E5
Smallridge Devon....10 G4
Smallthorne C Stke....70 F4
Smallways N York....103 M8
Smallwood Ches E....70 E2
Small Wood Hey Lancs....94 H11
Smallworth Norfk....64 C5
Smannell Hants....22 C5
Smardale Cumb....102 D9
Smarden Kent....26 E3
Smarden Bell Kent....26 E3
Smart's Hill Kent....25 M2
Smeafield Nthumb....119 L3
Smeatharpe Devon....10 D2
Smeeth Kent....27 J4
Smeeton Westerby Leics....60 E2
Smelthouses N York....97 J8
Smerral Highld....167 L10
Smestow Staffs....58 C6
Smethwick Sandw....58 F7
Smethwick Green Ches E....70 E2
Smirisary Highld....138 A2
Smisby Derbys....72 A7
Smith End Green Worcs....46 E4
Smithfield Cumb....110 H7
Smith Green Lancs....95 K9
Smith's End Herts....51 K3
Smith's Green Essex....51 N6
Smith's Green Essex....51 Q2
Smithstown Highld....160 B11
Smithton Highld....156 C8
Smithy Bridge Rochdl....89 Q7
Smithy Green Ches E....82 F10
Smithy Green Stockp....83 J7
Smithy Houses Derbys....84 E11
Smockington Leics....59 Q7
Smoo Highld....165 K3
Smythe's Green Essex....52 F8
Snade D & G....108 H3
Snailbeach Shrops....56 F4
Snailwell Cambs....63 K7

Snainton N York....99 J4
Snaith E R Yk....91 Q6
Snake Pass Inn Derbys....83 P6
Snape N York....97 L4
Snape Suffk....65 M10
Snape Green Lancs....88 D8
Snape Street Suffk....65 M10
Snaresbrook Gt Lon....37 K3
Snarestone Leics....72 A9
Snarford Lincs....86 D4
Snargate Kent....26 G6
Snave Kent....26 H6
Sneachill Worcs....46 H4
Snead Powys....56 E6
Sneath Common Norfk....64 H4
Sneaton N York....105 N9
Sneatonthorpe N York....105 P9
Snelland Lincs....86 E4
Snelson Ches E....82 H10
Snelston Derbys....71 M6
Snetterton Norfk....64 D3
Snettisham Norfk....75 N4
Snibston Leics....72 C8
Snig's End Gloucs....46 E9
Snitter Nthumb....119 K10
Snitterby Lincs....86 C2
Snitterfield Warwks....47 P3
Snitterton Derbys....84 C8
Snitton Shrops....57 K9
Snoadhill Kent....26 F3
Snodhill Herefs....45 L6
Snodland Kent....38 B9
Snoll Hatch Kent....37 Q11
Snowden Hill Barns....90 H10
Snowdon Gwynd....67 L4
Snowdon Kent....39 M11
Snowdonia National Park....67 Q9
Snow End Herts....51 K4
Snowshill Gloucs....47 L8
Snow Street Norfk....64 F5
Soake Hants....15 J4
Soar Cardif....30 E8
Soar Devon....7 J11
Soar Powys....44 D8
Soay Highld....144 F5
Soberton Hants....22 H11
Soberton Heath Hants....14 H4
Sockbridge Cumb....101 N5
Sockburn Darltn....104 B9
Sodom Denbgs....80 F10
Sodylt Bank Shrops....69 K7
Soham Cambs....63 J6
Soham Cotes Cambs....63 J5
Solas W Isls....168 d10
Solbury Pembks....40 G8
Soldon Devon....16 E9
Soldon Cross Devon....16 E9
Soldridge Hants....23 J7
Sole Street Kent....37 Q8
Sole Street Kent....37 Q7
Solihull Solhll....59 J9
Sollas W Isls....168 d10
Sollers Dilwyn Herefs....45 N3
Sollers Hope Herefs....46 B8
Sollom Lancs....88 F7
Solva Pembks....40 F6
Solwaybank D & G....110 F5
Somerby Leics....73 K8
Somerby Lincs....93 J9
Somercotes Derbys....84 F10
Somerford BCP....13 L6
Somerford Keynes Gloucs....33 K5
Somerley W Susx....15 M7
Somerleyton Suffk....65 P2
Somersal Herbert Derbys....71 L7
Somersby Lincs....87 K6
Somersham Cambs....62 E5
Somersham Suffk....53 J2
Somerton Oxon....48 E9
Somerton Somset....19 N9
Somerton Suffk....63 P10
Somerwood Shrops....57 K2
Sompting W Susx....24 E9
Sompting Abbotts W Susx....24 E9
Sonning Wokham....35 L9
Sonning Common Oxon....35 K8
Sonning Eye Oxon....35 K9
Sontley Wrexhm....69 K5
Sopley Hants....13 L5
Sopwell Herts....50 E9
Sopworth Wilts....32 F7
Sorbie D & G....107 M8
Sordale Highld....167 K4
Sorisdale Ag & B....136 H3
Sorn E Ayrs....115 L2
Sornhill E Ayrs....125 N11
Sortat Highld....167 N4
Sotby Lincs....86 H5
Sots Hole Lincs....86 F8
Sotterley Suffk....65 N5
Soughton Flints....81 J11
Soulbury Bucks....49 N9
Souldern Oxon....48 F8
Souldrop Bed....61 L8
Sound Ches E....70 A5
Sound Muir Moray....157 R7
Sourton Devon....8 D6
Soutergate Cumb....94 E4
South Acre Norfk....75 R8
South Alkham Kent....27 M3
Southall Gt Lon....36 D5
South Allington Devon....7 K11
South Alloa Falk....133 P9
Southam Gloucs....47 J9
Southam Warwks....48 D2
South Ambersham W Susx....23 P10
Southampton C Sotn....14 D4
Southampton Airport Hants....22 E11
South Anston Rothm....84 H4
South Ascot W & M....35 P11
South Ashford Kent....26 H3
South Baddesley Hants....14 C7
South Bank C York....98 C9
South Bank R & Cl....104 F6
South Barrow Somset....20 B9
South Beddington Gt Lon....36 G8
South Beer Cnwll....5 N3
South Benfleet Essex....38 C4
South Bockhampton BCP....13 L5
Southborough Gt Lon....37 K7
Southborough Kent....25 N2
Southbourne BCP....13 K6
Southbourne W Susx....15 L5

South Bowood Dorset....11 J5
South Bramwith Donc....91 Q8
South Brent Devon....6 H8
South Brewham Somset....20 D7
South Broomhill Nthumb....119 P11
Southburgh Norfk....76 E10
South Burlingham Norfk....77 M10
Southburn E R Yk....99 K10
South Cadbury Somset....20 B9
South Carlton Lincs....86 B5
South Carlton Notts....85 J2
South Cave E R Yk....92 F4
South Cerney Gloucs....33 K5
South Chailey E Susx....25 J7
South Chard Somset....10 G3
South Charlton Nthumb....119 N6
South Cheriton Somset....20 C10
South Church Dur....103 P5
Southchurch Sthend....38 F4
South Cleatlam Dur....103 M7
South Cliffe E R Yk....92 E3
South Clifton Notts....85 P6
South Cockerington Lincs....87 L3
South Cornelly Brdgnd....29 M8
Southcott Cnwll....5 K2
Southcott Devon....8 D5
Southcott Devon....9 J8
Southcott Devon....16 G8
Southcott Wilts....21 N3
Southcourt Bucks....35 M2
South Cove Suffk....65 P5
South Creake Norfk....76 B4
South Crosland Kirk....90 E8
South Croxton Leics....72 H8
South Dalton E R Yk....99 K11
South Darenth Kent....37 N7
South Dell W Isls....168 j1
South Downs National Park....25 J9
South Duffield N York....92 A4
South Earlswood Surrey....36 G11
Southease E Susx....25 K9
South Elkington Lincs....87 J3
South Elmsall Wakefd....91 M8
Southend Ag & B....120 C10
South End Hants....13 Q7
South End Hants....21 M11
South End Herefs....46 D6
South End N Linc....93 K6
South End Norfk....64 D3
Southend Wilts....33 N10
Southend Airport Essex....38 E4
Southend-on-Sea Sthend....38 E4
Southernby Cumb....101 L3
Southernden Kent....26 E2
Southerndown V Glam....29 N10
Southerness D & G....109 L10
South Erradale Highld....153 N3
Southerton Devon....10 B6
Southery Norfk....63 K2
South Fambridge Essex....38 E3
South Fawley W Berk....34 C8
South Ferriby N Linc....92 G6
South Field E R Yk....92 H5
Southfield Falk....126 E3
Southfleet Kent....37 P6
Southford IoW....14 F11
Southgate Gt Lon....36 G2
Southgate Norfk....76 B4
Southgate Norfk....76 G7
Southgate Norfk....76 G7
Southgate Swans....28 G7
South Godstone Surrey....37 J11
South Gorley Hants....13 L2
South Gosforth N u Ty....113 K7
South Green Essex....37 Q2
South Green Essex....52 H8
South Green Kent....38 E9
South Green Norfk....76 F9
South Green Suffk....64 H6
South Gyle C Edin....127 M3
South Hanningfield Essex....38 B2
South Harting W Susx....23 L11
South Hayling Hants....15 K7
South Hazelrigg Nthumb....119 L4
South Heath Bucks....35 P4
South Heighton E Susx....25 K10
South Hetton Dur....113 N11
South Hiendley Wakefd....91 K8
South Hill Cnwll....5 N7
South Hill Somset....19 M9
South Hinksey Oxon....34 F4
South Hole Devon....16 C7
South Holmwood Surrey....24 E2
South Hornchurch Gt Lon....37 M4
South Horrington Somset....19 Q5
South Huish Devon....6 H10
South Hykeham Lincs....86 B8
South Hylton Sundld....113 N9
Southill C Beds....50 E2
Southington Hants....22 F5
South Kelsey Lincs....92 H11
South Kessock Highld....156 B8
South Killingholme N Linc....93 K6
South Kilvington N York....97 P4
South Kilworth Leics....60 D4
South Kirkby Wakefd....91 L8
South Knighton Devon....7 L4
South Kyme Lincs....86 G11
Southleigh Devon....10 E6
South Leigh Oxon....34 C3
South Leverton Notts....85 N4
South Littleton Worcs....47 L5
South Lopham Norfk....64 E5
South Luffenham Rutlnd....73 N10
South Lynn Norfk....75 M7
South Malling E Susx....25 K8
South Marston Swindn....33 N7
South Merstham Surrey....36 G10
South Middleton Nthumb....119 L4
South Milford N York....91 M4
South Milton Devon....6 H10
South Mimms Herts....50 F10
South Mimms Services Herts....50 F10
Southminster Essex....38 G2
South Molton Devon....17 N6
South Moor Dur....113 J10
Southmoor Oxon....34 C5
South Moreton Oxon....34 G6
Southmuir Angus....142 F7
South Mundham W Susx....15 N6
South Muskham Notts....85 M9
South Newbald E R Yk....92 F3
South Newington Oxon....48 D8
South Newton Wilts....21 L8

South Nitshill C Glas....125 N6
South Normanton Derbys....84 F9
South Norwood Gt Lon....36 H7
South Nutfield Surrey....36 H11
Southoe Cambs....61 Q8
Southolt Suffk....64 H8
South Ormsby Lincs....87 L5
Southorpe C Pete....74 A10
South Ossett Wakefd....90 H7
South Otterington N York....97 N3
Southover Dorset....11 N6
Southover E Susx....25 Q5
South Owersby Lincs....86 E2
Southowram Calder....90 E6
South Park Surrey....36 F11
South Perrott Dorset....11 K3
South Petherton Somset....19 M11
South Petherwin Cnwll....5 N5
South Pickenham Norfk....76 B11
South Pill Cnwll....5 Q10
South Pool Devon....6 K10
South Poorton Dorset....11 L5
Southport Sefton....88 C7
South Queensferry C Edin....127 L2
South Radworthy Devon....17 N5
South Rauceby Lincs....86 D11
South Raynham Norfk....76 B7
South Reddish Stockp....83 J6
Southrepps Norfk....77 K4
South Reston Lincs....87 M4
Southrey Lincs....86 F7
South Ronaldsay Ork....169 d8
Southrop Gloucs....33 N4
Southrope Hants....23 J6
South Runcton Norfk....75 M9
South Scarle Notts....85 P8
Southsea C Port....15 J7
Southsea Wrexhm....69 K4
South Shian Ag & B....138 G9
South Shields S Tyne....113 N7
South Shore Bpool....88 C4
Southside Dur....103 M5
South Somercotes Lincs....87 M2
South Stainley N York....97 M8
South Stifford Thurr....37 N5
South Stoke BaNES....20 D2
South Stoke Oxon....34 G8
South Stoke W Susx....24 B9
South Stour Kent....26 H4
South Street Kent....37 P8
South Street Kent....39 J3
South Street Kent....39 K8
South Tarbrax S Lans....127 J7
South Tawton Devon....8 H5
South Tehidy Cnwll....2 H5
South Thoresby Lincs....87 M5
South Thorpe Dur....103 M8
South Town Hants....23 J7
Southtown Norfk....77 Q10
Southtown Somset....19 K11
South Uist W Isls....168 d14
Southwaite Cumb....110 H11
Southwaite Services Cumb....110 H11
South Walsham Norfk....77 M9
Southwark Gt Lon....36 H5
South Warnborough Hants....23 K5
Southwater W Susx....24 E5
Southwater Street W Susx....24 E5
Southway C Plym....6 D7
Southway Somset....19 P6
South Weald Essex....37 N2
Southwell Dorset....11 P10
Southwell Notts....85 L10
South Weston Oxon....35 K5
South Wheatley Cnwll....5 L3
South Wheatley Notts....85 N3
Southwick Hants....14 H5
Southwick Nhants....61 M2
Southwick Somset....19 L5
Southwick Sundld....113 N9
Southwick W Susx....24 F9
Southwick Wilts....20 F3
South Widcombe BaNES....19 Q3
South Wigston Leics....72 F11
South Willingham Lincs....86 G4
South Wingate Dur....104 D4
South Wingfield Derbys....84 E9
South Witham Lincs....73 N7
Southwold Suffk....65 Q6
South Wonston Hants....22 E7
Southwood Norfk....77 M10
Southwood Somset....19 Q8
South Woodham Ferrers Essex....38 D2
South Wootton Norfk....75 M6
South Wraxall Wilts....20 F2
South Zeal Devon....8 G6
Sovereign Harbour E Susx....25 P10
Sowerby Calder....90 C6
Sowerby N York....97 P4
Sowerby Bridge Calder....90 D6
Sowerby Row Cumb....101 L2
Sower Carr Lancs....88 D2
Sowerhill Somset....18 A10
Sowhill Torfn....31 J4
Sowley Green Suffk....63 M10
Sowood Calder....90 D7
Sowton Devon....6 D5
Sowton Devon....9 N6
Soyland Town Calder....90 C6
Spa Common Norfk....77 K5
Spain's End Essex....51 Q3
Spalding Lincs....74 D6
Spaldington E R Yk....92 C4
Spaldwick Cambs....61 P6
Spalford Notts....85 P7
Spanby Lincs....74 A3
Spanish Green Hants....23 J3
Sparham Norfk....76 F8
Sparhamill Norfk....76 F8
Spark Bridge Cumb....94 G4
Sparket Cumb....101 M5
Sparkford Somset....20 B9
Sparkwell Devon....6 F7
Sparrow Green Norfk....76 C9
Sparrowpit Derbys....83 M8
Sparrows Green E Susx....25 P4
Sparsholt Hants....22 D7
Sparsholt Oxon....34 B7
Spartylea Nthumb....112 C11
Spath Staffs....71 K7
Spaunton N York....98 E3
Spaxton Somset....18 H7
Spean Bridge Highld....146 G11

Spear Hill W Susx............24 D7
Spearywell Hants.............22 B9
Speen Bucks..................35 M5
Speen W Berk.................34 E11
Speeton N York...............99 P6
Speke Lpool..................81 N8
Speldhurst Kent..............25 N2
Spellbrook Herts.............51 L7
Spelmonden Kent..............26 B4
Spelsbury Oxon...............48 B10
Spen Kirk....................90 F5
Spencers Wood Wokham.........35 K11
Spen Green Ches E............70 E2
Spennithorne N York..........96 H3
Spennymoor Dur..............103 Q4
Spernall Warwks..............47 L2
Spetchley Worcs..............46 G4
Spetisbury Dorset............12 F4
Spexhall Suffk...............65 M5
Spey Bay Moray..............157 R4
Speybridge Highld...........149 J2
Speyview Moray..............157 P9
Spilsby Lincs................87 M7
Spindlestone Nthumb.........119 N4
Spinkhill Derbys.............84 G5
Spinningdale Highld.........162 F9
Spion Kop Notts..............85 J7
Spirthill Wilts..............33 J9
Spital Wirral................81 L8
Spital Hill Donc.............85 K2
Spital in the Street Lincs...86 C2
Spithurst E Susx.............25 K7
Spittal E Loth..............128 D4
Spittal E R Yk...............98 F10
Spittal Highld..............167 L6
Spittal Nthumb..............129 Q9
Spittal Pembks...............41 J6
Spittalfield P & K..........141 R9
Spittal of Glenmuick Abers..149 Q10
Spittal of Glenshee P & K...141 R4
Spittal-on-Rule Border......118 A7
Spixworth Norfk..............77 J8
Splatt Cnwll..................4 E6
Splatt Cnwll..................5 L4
Splatt Devon..................8 F3
Splayne's Green E Susx.......25 K6
Splott Cardif................30 H9
Spofforth N York.............97 N10
Spondon C Derb...............72 C3
Spon Green Flints............69 J2
Spooner Row Norfk............64 F2
Sporle Norfk.................76 A9
Spott E Loth................128 H4
Spottiswoode Border.........128 G10
Spratton Nhants..............60 F7
Spreakley Surrey.............23 M6
Spreyton Devon................8 G3
Spriddlestone Devon...........6 E8
Spridlington Lincs...........86 D4
Springburn C Glas...........125 Q4
Springfield D & G...........110 F7
Springfield Essex............52 B10
Springfield Fife............135 J5
Springhill Staffs............58 E4
Springhill Staffs............58 G3
Springholm D & G............108 H6
Springside N Ayrs...........125 K10
Springthorpe Lincs...........85 Q3
Spring Vale Barns............90 H10
Springwell Sundld...........113 L9
Sproatley E R Yk.............93 L4
Sproston Green Ches W........82 F11
Sprotbrough Donc.............91 N10
Sproughton Suffk.............53 K3
Sprouston Border............118 E3
Sprowston Norfk..............77 K9
Sproxton Leics...............73 M6
Sproxton N York..............98 C4
Spunhill Shrops..............69 M8
Spurstow Ches E..............69 Q3
Spyway Dorset................11 L6
Square and Compass
  Pembks....................40 F4
Stableford Shrops............57 P5
Stableford Staffs............70 E7
Stacey Bank Sheff............84 C2
Stackhouse N York............96 B7
Stackpole Pembks.............41 J11
Stackpole Elidor Pembks......41 J11
Stacksford Norfk.............64 F3
Stacksteads Lancs............89 P6
Staddiscombe C Plym...........6 E8
Staddlethorpe E R Yk.........92 D5
Staden Derbys................83 N10
Stadhampton Oxon.............34 H5
Stadhlaigearraidh W Isls....168 c14
Staffield Cumb..............101 P2
Staffin Highld..............152 H4
Stafford Staffs..............70 G10
Stafford Services
  (northbound) Staffs........70 F8
Stafford Services
  (southbound) Staffs........70 F8
Stagsden Bed.................49 Q5
Stainborough Barns...........91 J10
Stainburn Cumb..............100 D5
Stainburn N York.............97 L11
Stainby Lincs................73 N6
Staincross Barns.............91 J8
Staindrop Dur...............103 M6
Staines-upon-Thames
  Surrey....................36 B6
Stainfield Lincs.............74 A6
Stainfield Lincs.............86 F6
Stainforth Donc..............91 Q8
Stainforth N York............96 B7
Staining Lancs...............88 C3
Stainland Calder.............90 D7
Stainsacre N York...........105 P9
Stainsby Derbys..............84 G7
Stainton Cumb................95 L3
Stainton Cumb...............101 N5
Stainton Cumb...............110 G9
Stainton Donc................85 J2
Stainton Dur................103 L7
Stainton Middsb.............104 E8
Stainton N York.............103 M11
Stainton by Langworth
  Lincs.....................86 E5
Staintondale N York.........105 Q11
Stainton le Vale Lincs......86 G2
Stainton with Adgarley
  Cumb......................94 E6
Stair Cumb..................100 H6
Stair E Ayrs................114 H3
Stairfoot Barns..............91 K9

Stairhaven D & G............106 H7
Staithes N York.............105 L7
Stakeford Nthumb............113 L3
Stake Pool Lancs.............95 J11
Stakes Hants.................15 J5
Stalbridge Dorset............20 D11
Stalbridge Weston Dorset.....20 D11
Stalham Norfk................77 M6
Stalham Green Norfk..........77 M7
Stalisfield Green Kent.......38 G11
Stalland Common Norfk........64 E2
Stallen Dorset...............20 B11
Stallingborough NE Lin.......93 L8
Stalling Busk N York.........96 D3
Stallington Staffs...........70 G7
Stalmine Lancs...............94 H11
Stalmine Moss Side Lancs.....94 H11
Stalybridge Tamesd...........83 L5
Stambourne Essex.............52 B4
Stambourne Green Essex.......51 Q3
Stamford Lincs...............73 Q9
Stamford Nthumb.............119 P7
Stamford Bridge Ches W.......81 P11
Stamford Bridge E R Yk.......98 E9
Stamfordham Nthumb..........112 G6
Stamford Hill Gt Lon.........36 H3
Stanah Lancs.................88 D2
Stanborough Herts............50 F8
Stanbridge C Beds............49 Q10
Stanbridge Dorset............12 H4
Stanbury C Brad..............90 C3
Stand Bury...................89 M9
Stand N Lans................126 D4
Standburn Falk..............126 G3
Standeford Staffs............58 D3
Standen Kent.................26 E3
Standen Street Kent..........26 D5
Standerwick Somset...........20 F4
Standford Hants..............23 M8
Standingstone Cumb..........100 E4
Standish Gloucs..............32 E3
Standish Wigan...............88 H8
Standish Lower Ground
  Wigan.....................88 H9
Standlake Oxon...............34 C4
Standon Hants................22 D9
Standon Herts................51 J6
Standon Staffs...............70 E7
Standon Green End Herts......51 J7
Standwell Green Suffk........64 G8
Stane N Lans................126 F6
Stanfield Norfk..............76 C7
Stanford C Beds..............50 E2
Stanford Kent................27 K4
Stanford Shrops..............56 E2
Stanford Bishop Herefs.......46 C4
Stanford Bridge Worcs........57 N11
Stanford Bridge Wrekin.......70 C10
Stanford Dingley W Berk......34 G10
Stanford in the Vale Oxon....34 B6
Stanford le Hope Thurr.......37 Q4
Stanford on Avon Nhants......60 C5
Stanford on Soar Notts.......72 E6
Stanford on Teme Worcs.......57 N11
Stanford Rivers Essex........51 M10
Stanfree Derbys..............84 G6
Stanghow R & Cl.............105 J7
Stanground C Pete............74 D11
Stanhill Lancs...............89 L5
Stanhoe Norfk................75 R3
Stanhope Border.............116 G5
Stanhope Dur................103 J3
Stanhope Kent................26 H3
Stanhope Bretby Derbys.......71 P10
Stanion Nhants...............61 K3
Stanklin Worcs...............58 C10
Stanley Derbys...............72 C2
Stanley Dur.................113 J10
Stanley Notts................84 G8
Stanley P & K...............141 R11
Stanley Shrops...............57 N8
Stanley Staffs...............70 G4
Stanley Wakefd...............91 J4
Stanley Common Derbys........72 C2
Stanley Crook Dur...........103 N3
Stanley Ferry Wakefd.........91 K6
Stanley Gate Lancs...........88 E9
Stanley Moor Staffs..........70 G4
Stanley Pontlarge Gloucs.....47 K8
Stanmer Br & H...............24 H9
Stanmore Gt Lon..............36 E2
Stanmore Hants...............22 E9
Stanmore W Berk..............34 E9
Stannersburn Nthumb.........111 P3
Stanningfield Suffk..........64 B10
Stanningley Leeds............90 G4
Stannington Nthumb..........113 K5
Stannington Sheff............84 D3
Stannington Station
  Nthumb...................113 K4
Stansbatch Herefs............45 L2
Stansfield Suffk.............63 N10
Stanshope Staffs.............71 L4
Stanstead Suffk..............52 D2
Stanstead Abbotts Herts......51 J8
Stansted Kent................37 P8
Stansted Airport Essex.......51 N6
Stansted Mountfitchet
  Essex.....................51 M5
Stanton Derbys...............71 P11
Stanton Gloucs...............47 L8
Stanton Mons.................45 L10
Stanton Nthumb..............112 H4
Stanton Staffs...............71 L5
Stanton Suffk................64 D7
Stanton by Bridge Derbys.....72 B5
Stanton by Dale Derbys.......72 D3
Stanton Drew BaNES...........19 Q2
Stanton Fitzwarren Swindn....33 N6
Stanton Harcourt Oxon........34 D3
Stanton Hill Notts...........84 G8
Stanton in Peak Derbys.......84 B8
Stanton Lacy Shrops..........56 H9
Stanton Lees Derbys..........84 C8
Stanton Long Shrops..........57 K6
Stanton-on-the-Wolds
  Notts.....................72 G4
Stanton Prior BaNES..........20 C2
Stanton St Bernard Wilts.....21 L2
Stanton St John Oxon.........34 G3
Stanton St Quintin Wilts.....32 H9
Stanton Street Suffk.........64 D8
Stanton under Bardon Leics...72 D8
Stanton upon Hine Heath
  Shrops....................69 Q10
Stanton Wick BaNES...........20 B2

Stantway Gloucs..............32 D2
Stanwardine in the Field
  Shrops....................69 M10
Stanwardine in the Wood
  Shrops....................69 M9
Stanway Essex................52 F7
Stanway Gloucs...............47 L8
Stanway Green Essex..........52 G7
Stanway Green Suffk..........65 J7
Stanwell Surrey..............36 C6
Stanwell Moor Surrey.........36 B6
Stanwick Nhants..............61 L6
Stanwick St John N York.....103 N8
Stanwix Cumb................110 H9
Staoinebrig W Isls..........168 c14
Stape N York.................98 F2
Stapehill Dorset.............13 J4
Stapeley Ches E..............70 B5
Stapenhill Staffs............71 P10
Staple Kent..................39 N10
Staple Cross Devon...........18 D10
Staplecross E Susx...........26 C7
Staplefield W Susx...........24 G5
Staple Fitzpaine Somset......19 J11
Stapleford Cambs.............62 G10
Stapleford Herts.............50 H7
Stapleford Leics.............73 L7
Stapleford Lincs.............85 Q9
Stapleford Notts.............72 D3
Stapleford Wilts.............21 L7
Stapleford Abbotts Essex.....37 M2
Stapleford Tawney Essex......51 M11
Staplegrove Somset...........18 H9
Staplehay Somset.............18 H10
Staple Hill Worcs............58 E10
Staplehurst Kent.............26 C3
Staplers IoW.................14 F9
Staplestreet Kent............39 J9
Stapleton Cumb..............111 K6
Stapleton Herefs.............56 E11
Stapleton Leics..............72 C11
Stapleton N York............103 Q8
Stapleton Shrops.............56 H4
Stapleton Somset.............19 N10
Stapley Somset...............10 D2
Staploe Bed..................61 Q8
Staplow Herefs...............46 C6
Star Fife...................135 J7
Star IoA.....................79 J10
Star Pembks..................41 P4
Star Somset..................19 M3
Starbeck N York..............97 M9
Starbotton N York............96 E6
Starcross Devon...............9 N8
Stareton Warwks..............59 M10
Starkholmes Derbys...........84 D9
Starlings Green Essex........51 L4
Starr's Green E Susx.........26 C8
Starston Norfk...............65 J5
Start Devon...................7 L10
Startforth Dur..............103 K7
Startley Wilts...............32 H8
Statenborough Kent...........39 P10
Statham Warrtn...............82 E7
Stathe Somset................19 L9
Stathern Leics...............73 K4
Station Town Dur............104 D3
Staughton Green Cambs........61 P7
Staughton Highway Cambs......61 P8
Staunton Gloucs..............31 Q2
Staunton Gloucs..............46 E9
Staunton in the Vale Notts...73 L2
Staunton on Arrow Herefs.....45 M2
Staunton on Wye Herefs.......45 M6
Staveley Cumb...............101 N11
Staveley Derbys..............84 F6
Staveley N York..............97 N8
Staveley-in-Cartmel Cumb.....94 H3
Staverton Devon...............7 K6
Staverton Gloucs.............46 G10
Staverton Nhants.............60 B8
Staverton Wilts..............20 G2
Staverton Bridge Gloucs......46 G10
Stawell Somset...............19 L7
Stawley Somset...............18 E10
Staxigoe Highld.............167 Q6
Staxton N York...............99 L5
Staylittle Cerdgn............54 E7
Staylittle Powys.............55 K6
Staynall Lancs...............88 D2
Staythorpe Notts.............85 N10
Stead C Brad.................96 H11
Stean N York.................96 G6
Stearsby N York..............98 C6
Steart Somset................19 J5
Stebbing Essex...............51 Q6
Stebbing Green Essex.........51 Q6
Stechford Birm...............58 H7
Stede Quarter Kent...........26 E4
Stedham W Susx...............23 N10
Steel Nthumb................112 D9
Steel Cross E Susx...........25 M4
Steelend Fife...............134 C9
Steele Road Border..........111 K2
Steel Green Cumb.............94 D5
Steel Heath Shrops...........69 P7
Steen's Bridge Herefs........45 Q3
Steep Hants..................23 K9
Steephill IoW................14 F11
Steeple Dorset...............12 F8
Steeple Essex................52 F11
Steeple Ashton Wilts.........20 H3
Steeple Aston Oxon...........48 E9
Steeple Barton Oxon..........48 D10
Steeple Bumpstead Essex......51 Q2
Steeple Claydon Bucks........49 K9
Steeple Gidding Cambs........61 P4
Steeple Langford Wilts.......21 K7
Steeple Morden Cambs.........50 G2
Steep Marsh Hants............23 L9
Steeton C Brad...............90 C2
Stein Highld................152 D6
Stella Gatesd...............113 J8
Stelling Minnis Kent.........27 K2
Stembridge Somset............19 M10
Stenalees Cnwll...............4 G10
Stenhouse D & G.............115 R9
Stenhousemuir Falk..........133 P11
Stenigot Lincs...............86 H4
Stenscholl Highld...........152 H4
Stenson Fields Derbys........72 A4
Stenton E Loth..............128 G5
Steornabhagh W Isls.........168 j4
Stepaside Pembks.............41 M9
Stepford D & G.............109 J4

Stepney Gt Lon...............37 J4
Stepping Hill Stockp.........83 K7
Steppingley C Beds...........50 B3
Stepps N Lans...............126 B4
Sternfield Suffk.............65 M9
Stert Wilts..................21 K3
Stetchworth Cambs............63 K9
Stevenage Herts..............50 F5
Steven's Crouch E Susx.......26 B8
Stevenston N Ayrs...........124 H9
Steventon Hants..............22 F5
Steventon Oxon...............34 E6
Steventon End Essex..........51 N2
Stevington Bed...............49 Q4
Stewartby Bed................50 B2
Stewartfield S Lans.........125 Q6
Stewarton Ag & B............120 C8
Stewarton E Ayrs............125 L8
Stewkley Bucks...............49 N9
Stewley Somset...............19 K11
Stewton Lincs................87 L3
Steyne Cross IoW.............14 H9
Steyning W Susx..............24 E8
Steynton Pembks..............40 H9
Stibb Cnwll..................16 C9
Stibbard Norfk...............76 D6
Stibb Cross Devon............16 G9
Stibb Green Wilts............21 P2
Stibbington Cambs............74 A11
Stichill Border.............118 D3
Sticker Cnwll.................3 P3
Stickford Lincs..............87 L8
Sticklepath Devon.............8 F6
Sticklepath Somset...........18 D7
Stickling Green Essex........51 L4
Stickney Lincs...............87 K9
Stiffkey Norfk...............76 D3
Stifford Clays Thurr.........37 P4
Stifford's Bridge Herefs.....46 D5
Stiff Street Kent............38 E9
Stile Bridge Kent............26 C2
Stileway Somset..............19 N6
Stilligarry W Isls..........168 c14
Stillingfleet N York.........91 P2
Stillington N York...........98 B7
Stillington S on T..........104 C6
Stilton Cambs................61 Q3
Stinchcombe Gloucs...........32 D5
Stinsford Dorset.............11 Q6
Stiperstones Shrops..........56 F4
Stirchley Birm...............58 G8
Stirchley Wrekin.............57 M3
Stirling Abers..............159 R9
Stirling Stirlg.............133 M9
Stirling Castle Stirlg......133 M9
Stirling Services Stirlg....133 N10
Stirtloe Cambs...............61 Q7
Stirton N York...............96 E10
Stisted Essex................52 D7
Stitchcombe Wilts............33 P11
Stithians Cnwll...............3 J6
Stivichall Covtry............59 M9
Stixwould Lincs..............86 G7
St Michaels Fife............135 L3
Stoak Ches W.................81 N10
Stobo Border................116 H3
Stoborough Dorset............12 F7
Stoborough Green Dorset......12 F7
Stobs Castle Border.........117 Q9
Stobswood Nthumb............119 P11
Stock Essex..................51 Q11
Stock N Som..................19 N2
Stockbridge Hants............22 C7
Stockbridge W Susx...........15 N6
Stockbriggs S Lans..........126 D10
Stockbury Kent...............38 D9
Stockcross W Berk............34 D11
Stockdalewath Cumb..........110 G11
Stocker's Head Kent..........38 G11
Stockerston Leics............73 L11
Stock Green Worcs............47 J3
Stocking Herefs..............46 B8
Stockingford Warwks..........59 M6
Stocking Pelham Herts........51 L5
Stockland Devon..............10 E4
Stockland Bristol Somset.....18 H6
Stockland Green Kent.........25 N2
Stockleigh English Devon......9 L3
Stockleigh Pomeroy Devon......9 L4
Stockley Wilts...............33 J11
Stockley Hill Herefs.........45 M7
Stocklinch Somset............19 L11
Stockmoor Herefs.............45 M4
Stockport Stockp.............83 J6
Stocksbridge Sheff...........90 H11
Stocksfield Nthumb..........112 G8
Stockton Herefs..............45 Q2
Stockton Norfk...............65 M3
Stockton Shrops..............56 D4
Stockton Shrops..............57 N5
Stockton Warwks..............48 D2
Stockton Wilts...............21 J7
Stockton on Tees S on T.....104 D7
Stockton Brook Staffs........70 G4
Stockton Heath Warrtn........82 D7
Stockton-on-Tees S on T.....104 D7
Stockton on Teme Worcs.......57 N11
Stockton on the Forest
  C York....................98 D9
Stockwell Gloucs.............32 H2
Stockwell End Wolves.........58 C4
Stockwell Heath Staffs.......71 K10
Stockwood Bristl.............32 B11
Stockwood Dorset.............11 M3
Stock Wood Worcs.............47 K3
Stodday Lancs................95 K9
Stodmarsh Kent...............39 M9
Stody Norfk..................76 F4
Stoer Highld................164 B11
Stoford Somset...............11 M2
Stoford Wilts................21 L7
Stogumber Somset.............18 E7
Stogursey Somset.............18 H6
Stoke Covtry.................59 N9
Stoke Devon..................16 C7
Stoke Hants..................15 K6
Stoke Hants..................22 D4
Stoke Medway.................38 D7
Stoke Abbott Dorset..........11 K4
Stoke Albany Nhants..........60 H3
Stoke Ash Suffk..............64 G7
Stoke Bardolph Notts.........72 G2
Stoke Bliss Worcs............46 C2
Stoke Bruerne Nhants.........49 K5
Stoke-by-Clare Suffk.........52 B3
Stoke-by-Nayland Suffk.......52 G4

Stoke Canon Devon.............9 M5
Stoke Charity Hants..........22 E7
Stoke Climsland Cnwll.........5 P7
Stoke Cross Herefs...........46 B4
Stoke D'Abernon Surrey.......36 D9
Stoke Doyle Nhants...........61 M3
Stoke Dry Rutlnd.............73 M11
Stoke Edith Herefs...........46 B6
Stoke End Warwks.............59 J5
Stoke Farthing Wilts.........21 L9
Stoke Ferry Norfk............75 P10
Stoke Fleming Devon...........7 M9
Stokeford Dorset.............12 E7
Stoke Gabriel Devon...........7 M7
Stoke Gifford S Glos.........32 B9
Stoke Golding Leics..........72 B11
Stoke Goldington M Keyn......49 M5
Stoke Green Bucks............35 Q8
Stokeham Notts...............85 N5
Stoke Hammond Bucks..........49 N9
Stoke Heath Shrops...........70 B9
Stoke Heath Worcs............58 D11
Stoke Holy Cross Norfk.......77 J11
Stokeinteignhead Devon.......7 N4
Stoke Lacy Herefs............46 B5
Stoke Lyne Oxon..............48 G9
Stoke Mandeville Bucks.......35 M2
Stokenchurch Bucks...........35 L5
Stoke Newington Gt Lon.......36 H3
Stokenham Devon...............7 L10
Stoke-on-Trent C Stke........70 F5
Stoke Orchard Gloucs.........46 H9
Stoke Poges Bucks............35 Q8
Stoke Pound Worcs............58 E11
Stoke Prior Herefs...........45 Q3
Stoke Prior Worcs............58 D11
Stoke Rivers Devon...........17 L4
Stoke Rochford Lincs.........73 N5
Stoke Row Oxon...............35 J8
Stoke St Gregory Somset......19 K9
Stoke St Mary Somset.........19 J10
Stoke St Michael Somset......20 C5
Stoke St Milborough Shrops...57 K7
Stokesay Shrops..............56 G8
Stokesby Norfk...............77 N9
Stokesley N York............104 F9
Stoke sub Hamdon Somset......19 N11
Stoke Talmage Oxon...........35 J5
Stoke Trister Somset.........20 D9
Stoke upon Tern Shrops.......70 A9
Stoke-upon-Trent C Stke......70 F5
Stoke Wake Dorset............12 C3
Stoke Wharf Worcs............58 E11
Stolford Somset..............18 H5
Stondon Massey Essex.........51 N10
Stone Bucks..................35 L3
Stone Gloucs.................32 C5
Stone Kent...................37 N6
Stone Rothm..................85 J3
Stone Somset.................19 Q8
Stone Staffs.................70 G8
Stone Worcs..................58 C9
Stonea Cambs.................62 G2
Stoneallerton Somset.........19 L4
Ston Easton Somset...........20 B4
Stonebridge N Som............19 L3
Stonebridge Norfk............64 C3
Stonebridge Warwks...........59 K8
Stone Bridge Corner C Pete...74 E10
Stonebroom Derbys............84 F9
Stone Chair Calder...........90 E6
Stone Cross E Susx...........25 M5
Stone Cross E Susx...........25 P10
Stone Cross E Susx...........25 P11
Stone Cross Kent.............25 M3
Stone Cross Kent.............26 H4
Stone Cross Kent.............27 P10
Stonecross Green Suffk.......63 P9
Stonecrouch Kent.............26 B5
Stone-edge-Batch N Som.......31 N10
Stoneferry C KuH.............93 K4
Stonefield Castle Hotel
  Ag & B...................123 Q5
Stonegate E Susx.............25 Q5
Stonegate N York.............105 L9
Stonegrave N York............98 C5
Stonehall Worcs..............46 G5
Stonehaugh Nthumb...........111 P3
Stonehaven Abers............151 M10
Stonehenge Wilts.............21 M6
Stone Hill Donc..............92 A9
Stonehouse C Plym.............6 D8
Stone House Cumb.............95 R3
Stonehouse Gloucs............32 F3
Stonehouse Nthumb...........111 M4
Stonehouse S Lans...........126 D8
Stone in Oxney Kent..........26 H6
Stoneleigh Warwks............59 M10
Stoneley Green Ches E........69 Q4
Stonely Cambs................61 P7
Stoner Hill Hants............23 K9
Stonesby Leics...............73 L6
Stonesfield Oxon.............48 C11
Stones Green Essex...........53 L6
Stone Street Kent............37 N10
Stone Street Suffk...........52 H3
Stone Street Suffk...........65 M3
Stonestreet Green Kent.......27 J4
Stonethwaite Cumb...........101 J8
Stonewells Moray............157 P4
Stonewood Kent...............37 N6
Stoneybridge W Isls.........168 c14
Stoneybridge Worcs...........58 H5
Stoneyburn W Loth...........126 H5
Stoney Cross Hants...........13 N3
Stoneygate C Leic............72 G10
Stoneyhills Essex............38 G2
Stoneykirk D & G............106 D7
Stoney Middleton Derbys......84 B5
Stoney Stanton Leics.........59 N6
Stoney Stoke Somset..........20 C7
Stoney Stratton Somset.......20 C7
Stoney Stretton Shrops.......56 F3
Stoneywood C Aber...........151 M11
Stoneywood Falk.............133 M11
Stonham Aspal Suffk..........64 G10
Stonnall Staffs..............58 G4
Stonor Oxon..................35 K7
Stonton Wyville Leics........73 J11
Stonybreck Shet.............169 t14
Stony Cross Herefs...........46 D5
Stony Cross Herefs...........57 J11
Stonyford Hants..............22 B11
Stony Houghton Derbys........84 G7
Stony Stratford M Keyn.......49 L6

Stonywell Staffs....................58   G2
Stoodleigh Devon..................17   M5
Stoodleigh Devon..................18   B11
Stop 24 Services Kent.............27   K4
Stopham W Susx...................24   B7
Stopsley Luton......................50   D6
Stoptide Cnwll.......................4   E6
Storeton Wirral.....................81   L8
Storeyard Green Herefs.........46   D6
Storey Arms Powys...............44   D10
Stornoway W Isls.................168   j4
Stornoway Airport W Isls......168   j4
Storridge Herefs...................46   E5
Storrington W Susx................24   C8
Storth Cumb.........................95   K5
Storwood E R Yk...................92   B2
Stotfield Moray.....................157   N3
Stotfold C Beds.....................50   F3
Stottesdon Shrops.................57   M8
Stoughton Leics....................72   G10
Stoughton Surrey..................23   Q4
Stoughton W Susx.................15   M4
Stoulton Worcs.....................46   H5
Stourbridge Dudley...............58   C8
Stourhead Wilts.....................20   E8
Stourpaine Dorset.................12   E3
Stourport-on-Severn Worcs...57   Q10
Stour Provost Dorset.............20   E10
Stour Row Dorset..................20   F10
Stourton Leeds......................91   J4
Stourton Staffs......................58   C8
Stourton Warwks...................47   Q7
Stourton Wilts.......................20   E8
Stourton Caundle Dorset......20   D11
Stout Somset........................19   M8
Stove Shet...........................169   r11
Stoven Suffk..........................65   N5
Stow Border........................117   P2
Stow Lincs............................85   Q4
Stow Bardolph Norfk.............75   M9
Stow Bedon Norfk.................64   D2
Stowbridge Norfk..................75   M9
Stow-cum-Quy Cambs...........62   H8
Stowe Gloucs........................31   Q3
Stowe Shrops........................56   E10
Stowe-by-Chartley Staffs......71   J9
Stowehill Nhants...................60   D9
Stowell Somset.....................20   C10
Stowey BaNES.......................19   Q3
Stowford Devon.......................8   B5
Stowford Devon.......................8   C7
Stowford Devon.....................10   C7
Stowford Devon.....................17   M3
Stowlangtoft Suffk.................64   D8
Stow Longa Cambs................61   P6
Stow Maries Essex................38   D2
Stowmarket Suffk..................64   E10
Stow-on-the-Wold Gloucs.....47   N9
Stowting Kent.......................27   K3
Stowting Common Kent.........27   K3
Stowupland Suffk..................64   F9
Straad Ag & B.......................124   C5
Straanruie Highld.................148   H4
Strachan Abers.....................150   H9
Strachur Ag & B....................131   M7
Stradbroke Suffk...................65   J7
Stradbrook Wilts....................20   H4
Stradishall Suffk....................63   N10
Stradsett Norfk.....................75   N9
Stragglethorpe Lincs............86   B10
Stragglethorpe Notts............72   H3
Straight Soley Wilts...............34   B10
Straiton Mdloth....................127   P4
Straiton S Ayrs....................114   G7
Straloch Abers....................151   M3
Straloch P & K.....................141   P5
Stramshall Staffs...................71   K7
Strang IoM.............................80   e6
Strangeways Salfd.................82   H5
Strangford Herefs.................46   A9
Stranraer D & G..................106   E5
Strata Florida Cerdgn............54   G11
Stratfield Mortimer W Berk....23   J2
Stratfield Saye Hants.............23   J2
Stratfield Turgis Hants...........23   J3
Stratford C Beds....................61   Q11
Stratford Gt Lon....................37   J4
Stratford St Andrew Suffk.....65   M9
Stratford St Mary Suffk.........52   H5
Stratford sub Castle Wilts......21   M8
Stratford Tony Wilts...............21   L9
Stratford-upon-Avon
   Warwks..............................47   P3
Strath Highld......................160   B11
Strathan Highld...................160   H2
Strathan Highld...................165   N4
Strathaven S Lans...............126   C9
Strathblane Stirlg................125   P2
Strathcanaird Highld...........161   K6
Strathcarron Highld.............154   B9
Strathcoil Ag & B.................138   B11
Strathdon Abers..................150   B5
Strathkinness Fife................135   M4
Strathloanhead W Loth........126   G3
Strathmashie House Highld...147   J9
Strathmiglo Fife...................134   G6
Strathpeffer Highld..............155   N6
Strathtay P & K...................141   M7
Strathwhillan N Ayrs............121   K4
Strathy Highld......................166   H3
Strathy Inn Highld...............166   D3
Strathyre Stirlg....................132   H4
Stratton Cnwll.......................16   C10
Stratton Dorset....................11   P6
Stratton Gloucs.....................33   K4
Stratton Audley Oxon............48   H9
Stratton-on-the-Fosse
   Somset...............................20   C4
Stratton St Margaret Swindn...33   N7
Stratton St Michael Norfk......65   J3
Stratton Strawless Norfk.......77   J7
Stream Somset.......................18   E7
Streat E Susx.........................25   J7
Streatham Gt Lon...................36   H6
Streatley C Beds....................50   C5
Streatley W Berk....................34   G8
Street Devon..........................10   D7
Street Lancs..........................95   L10
Street N York........................105   H4
Street Somset........................19   N7
Street Ashton Warwks............59   Q8
Street Dinas Shrops...............69   K7
Street End E Susx...................25   P6
Street End Kent......................39   K11
Street End W Susx.................15   N6
Street Gate Gatesd.................113   K9

Streethay Staffs......................58   H2
Street Houses N York.............98   A11
Streetlam N York...................104   B11
Street Lane Derbys.................84   E11
Streetly Wsall........................58   G5
Streetly End Cambs................63   K11
Street on the Fosse Somset...20   C2
Strefford Shrops.....................56   G7
Strelitz P & K........................142   B10
Strelley Notts..........................72   E2
Strensall C York......................98   C8
Strensham Worcs....................46   H6
Strensham Services
   (northbound) Worcs.............46   G6
Strensham Services
   (southbound) Worcs.............46   H6
Stretcholt Somset...................19   J6
Strete Devon............................7   L9
Stretford Herefs.....................45   N3
Stretford Herefs.....................45   Q3
Stretford Traffd......................82   G6
Stretford Shrops.....................56   G7
Strethall Essex.......................51   L3
Stretham Cambs.....................62   H6
Strettington W Susx...............15   N5
Stretton Ches W.....................69   M4
Stretton Derbys......................84   E8
Stretton Rutlnd......................73   N7
Stretton Staffs........................58   C2
Stretton Staffs........................71   P9
Stretton Warrtn......................82   D8
Stretton en le Field Leics......59   M2
Stretton Grandison Herefs....46   B6
Stretton-on-Dunsmore
   Warwks...............................59   P10
Stretton on Fosse Warwks......47   P7
Stretton Sugwas Herefs........45   P6
Stretton under Fosse
   Warwks...............................59   Q8
Stretton Westwood Shrops.....57   K5
Strichen Abers......................159   M6
Strines Stockp.........................83   L7
Stringston Somset...................18   G6
Strixton Nhants......................61   K8
Stroat Gloucs..........................31   Q5
Strollamus Highld.................145   J2
Stroma Highld.......................167   Q11
Stromeferry Highld...............153   R11
Stromness Ork......................169   b6
Stronaba Highld.....................146   G11
Stronachlachar Stirlg.............132   E5
Stronafian Ag & B..................131   L11
Stronchrubie Highld...............161   L3
Strone Ag & B........................131   P11
Strone Highld........................146   E11
Strone Highld........................147   N2
Stronmilchan Ag & B.............131   P2
Stronsay Ork.........................169   f4
Stronsay Airport Ork............169   f4
Strontian Highld....................138   E5
Strood Kent...........................26   E5
Strood Medway......................38   B8
Strood Green Surrey...............36   F11
Strood Green W Susx..............24   B6
Stroud Gloucs.........................32   G3
Stroud Hants..........................23   K10
Stroude Surrey........................36   B7
Stroud Green Essex................38   E3
Stroud Green Gloucs..............32   F3
Stroxton Lincs.........................73   N4
Struan Highld........................152   E10
Struan P & K.........................141   K4
Strubby Lincs..........................87   N4
Strumpshaw Norfk..................77   L10
Strutherhill S Lans................126   D8
Struthers Fife........................135   K6
Struy Highld..........................155   M9
Stryd-y-Facsen IoA.................78   E8
Stryt-issa Wrexhm..................69   J5
Stuartfield Abers...................159   N8
Stubbers Green Wsall..............58   F4
Stubbington Hants..................14   G6
Stubbins Lancs........................89   M7
Stubbs Cross Kent...................26   G4
Stubbs Green Norfk.................65   K2
Stubhampton Dorset...............12   F2
Stubley Derbys.........................84   D5
Stubshaw Cross Wigan............82   C5
Stubton Lincs...........................85   Q11
Stuckton Hants........................13   L2
Studfold N York.......................96   B7
Stud Green W & M...................35   N9
Studham C Beds......................50   B7
Studholme Cumb....................110   E9
Studland Dorset.......................12   H8
Studley Warwks........................47   L2
Studley Wilts............................33   J10
Studley Common Warwks.......47   L2
Studley Roger N York..............97   L7
Studley Royal N York...............97   L6
Studley Royal Park &
   Fountains Abbey N York......97   L7
Stuntney Cambs.......................63   J5
Stunts Green E Susx................25   P8
Sturbridge Staffs.....................70   E8
Sturgate Lincs.........................85   Q3
Sturmer Essex.........................51   Q2
Sturminster Common
   Dorset.................................12   C2
Sturminster Marshall
   Dorset.................................12   G4
Sturminster Newton Dorset...12   C2
Sturry Kent.............................39   L9
Sturton N Linc.........................92   G10
Sturton by Stow Lincs.............85   Q4
Sturton le Steeple Notts.........85   N4
Stuston Suffk..........................64   G6
Stutton N York........................91   M2
Stutton Suffk...........................53   L5
Styal Ches E............................82   H8
Stydd Lancs.............................89   K3
Stynie Moray.........................157   Q5
Styrrup Notts...........................85   K2
Succoth Ag & B......................132   B6
Suckley Worcs..........................46   D4
Suckley Green Worcs..............46   D4
Sudborough Nhants................61   L4
Sudbourne Suffk......................65   N11
Sudbrook Lincs.........................73   P2
Sudbrook Mons.......................31   P7
Sudbrooke Lincs......................86   D5
Sudbury Derbys........................71   M8
Sudbury Gt Lon.......................36   E3
Sudbury Suffk.........................52   E3
Sudden Rochdl........................89   P8
Sudgrove Gloucs......................32   H3
Suffield N York........................99   J5

Suffield Norfk..........................77   J5
Sugdon Wrekin........................69   R11
Sugnall Staffs...........................70   D8
Sugwas Pool Herefs................45   P6
Suisnish Highld......................145   J4
Sulby IoM.................................80   e3
Sulgrave Nhants......................48   G6
Sulham W Berk.........................34   H10
Sulhamstead W Berk................34   H11
Sulhamstead Abbots W Berk...34   H11
Sulhamstead Bannister
   W Berk.................................34   H11
Sullington W Susx....................24   C8
Sullom Shet...........................169   q6
Sullom Voe Shet....................169   r6
Sully V Glam............................30   G11
Sumburgh Airport Shet........169   q12
Summerbridge N York............97   K8
Summercourt Cnwll..................4   D10
Summerfield Norfk..................75   Q3
Summerfield Worcs.................58   B10
Summer Heath Bucks.............35   K6
Summerhill Pembks................41   N9
Summerhill Staffs....................58   G3
Summer Hill Wrexhm.............69   K4
Summerhouse Darltn.............103   P7
Summerlands Cumb................95   L3
Summerley Derbys...................84   E5
Summersdale W Susx.............15   N5
Summerseat Bury....................89   M8
Summertown Oxon..................34   F3
Summit Oldham.......................89   Q9
Summit Rochdl........................89   Q7
Sunbiggin Cumb....................102   C9
Sunbury-on-Thames Surrey...36   D7
Sundaywell D & G..................108   H4
Sunderland Ag & B.................122   B7
Sunderland Cumb..................100   G3
Sunderland Lancs...................95   J9
Sunderland Sundld................113   N9
Sunderland Bridge Dur..........103   Q3
Sundhope Border...................117   L5
Sundon Park Luton..................50   C5
Sundridge Kent.......................37   L9
Sunk Island E R Yk..................93   N7
Sunningdale W & M.................35   Q11
Sunninghill W & M..................35   P11
Sunningwell Oxon...................34   E4
Sunniside Dur........................103   M3
Sunniside Gatesd...................113   K9
Sunny Brow Dur....................103   N4
Sunnyhill C Derb......................72   A4
Sunnyhurst Bl w D..................89   K6
Sunnylaw Stirlg......................133   M8
Sunnymead Oxon....................34   F3
Sunton Wilts...........................21   P4
Surbiton Gt Lon.......................36   E7
Surfleet Lincs...........................74   E5
Surfleet Seas End Lincs..........74   E5
Surlingham Norfk.....................77   L10
Surrex Essex............................52   E7
Sustead Norfk..........................76   H4
Susworth Lincs.........................92   D10
Sutcombe Devon......................16   E9
Sutcombemill Devon...............16   E9
Suton Norfk.............................64   F2
Sutterby Lincs..........................87   L6
Sutterton Lincs........................74   E3
Sutton C Beds.........................62   B11
Sutton C Pete.........................74   A11
Sutton Cambs..........................62   F5
Sutton Devon............................7   J10
Sutton Devon............................8   H4
Sutton Donc.............................91   P8
Sutton E Susx..........................25   L11
Sutton Gt Lon..........................36   G8
Sutton Kent.............................27   P2
Sutton N York..........................91   M5
Sutton Norfk............................77   M7
Sutton Notts............................73   K3
Sutton Oxon.............................34   D3
Sutton Pembks........................40   H7
Sutton Shrops..........................57   J2
Sutton Shrops..........................57   N7
Sutton Shrops..........................69   L9
Sutton Shrops..........................70   B8
Sutton St Hel..........................82   B6
Sutton Staffs............................70   D10
Sutton Suffk............................53   P2
Sutton Suffk............................23   Q11
Sutton W Susx..........................23   Q11
Sutton Abinger Surrey.............36   D11
Sutton-at-Hone Kent...............37   N7
Sutton Bassett Nhants............60   G2
Sutton Benger Wilts.................32   H9
Sutton Bingham Somset..........11   L2
Sutton Bonington Notts...........72   E6
Sutton Bridge Lincs.................75   J6
Sutton Cheney Leics................72   C10
Sutton Coldfield Birm..............58   H5
Sutton Courtenay Oxon...........34   F6
Sutton Crosses Lincs...............74   H6
Sutton cum Lound Notts..........85   L4
Sutton Fields Notts..................72   D5
Sutton Green Surrey................36   B10
Sutton Green Wrexhm.............69   M5
Sutton Heath Suffk..................53   P2
Sutton Howgrave N York.........97   M5
Sutton-in-Ashfield Notts..........84   G9
Sutton-in-Craven N York.........90   C2
Sutton in the Elms Leics..........60   B2
Sutton Lane Ends Ches E.........83   K10
Sutton Maddock Shrops..........57   N4
Sutton Mallet Somset.............19   L7
Sutton Mandeville Wilts..........21   J9
Sutton Manor St Hel................82   C6
Sutton Marsh Herefs...............45   R6
Sutton Montis Somset.............20   B10
Sutton-on-Hull C KuH.............93   K4
Sutton on Sea Lincs................87   P4
Sutton-on-the-Forest
   N York..................................98   B8
Sutton on the Hill Derbys.......71   N6
Sutton on Trent Notts.............85   N7
Sutton Poyntz Dorset.............11   Q8
Sutton St Edmund Lincs.........74   G8
Sutton St James Lincs............74   G8
Sutton St Nicholas Herefs......45   Q5
Sutton Scotney Hants.............22   E7
Sutton Street Kent..................38   D10
Sutton-under-Brailes
   Warwks...............................48   B7
Sutton-under-
   Whitestonecliffe N York......97   Q4
Sutton upon Derwent E R Yk...98   E11
Sutton Valence Kent...............26   D2
Sutton Veny Wilts....................20   H6

Sutton Waldron Dorset...........20   G11
Sutton Weaver Ches W............82   B9
Sutton Wick BaNES..................19   Q3
Sutton Wick Oxon....................34   E6
Swaby Lincs.............................87   L5
Swadlincote Derbys.................71   P11
Swaffham Norfk.......................75   R9
Swaffham Bulbeck Cambs.......63   J8
Swaffham Prior Cambs............63   J8
Swafield Norfk.........................77   K5
Swainby N York......................104   E10
Swainshill Herefs....................45   P6
Swainsthorpe Norfk.................77   J11
Swainswick BaNES..................32   C11
Swalcliffe Oxon.......................48   C7
Swalecliffe Kent......................39   K8
Swallow Lincs..........................93   L10
Swallow Beck Lincs.................86   B7
Swallowcliffe Wilts...................21   J9
Swallowfield Wokham..............23   K2
Swallownest Rothm.................84   G3
Swallows Cross Essex..............51   P11
Swampton Hants.....................22   D4
Swanage Dorset......................12   H9
Swanbourne Bucks..................49   M9
Swanbridge V Glam.................30   G11
Swancote Shrops.....................57   N6
Swan Green Ches W................82   F10
Swanland E R Yk......................92   G5
Swanley Kent...........................37   M7
Swanley Village Kent...............37   M7
Swanmore Hants.....................22   G11
Swannington Leics..................72   C7
Swannington Norfk.................76   G8
Swanpool Lincs........................86   C7
Swanscombe Kent...................37   P6
Swansea Swans.......................29   J6
Swansea Airport Swans..........28   G6
Swansea West Services
   Swans..................................28   H5
Swan Street Essex...................52   E6
Swanton Abbot Norfk.............77   K6
Swanton Morley Norfk.............76   E8
Swanton Novers Norfk............76   E5
Swanton Street Kent...............38   E10
Swan Valley Nhants.................60   F9
Swan Village Sandw................58   E6
Swanwick Derbys.....................84   F10
Swanwick Hants......................14   F5
Swarby Lincs............................73   Q2
Swardeston Norfk....................77   J11
Swarkestone Derbys................72   B5
Swarland Nthumb...................119   N10
Swarraton Hants......................22   G7
Swartha C Brad........................96   G11
Swarthmoor Cumb...................94   F5
Swaton Lincs............................74   B3
Swavesey Cambs......................62   E7
Sway Hants..............................13   N5
Swayfield Lincs.........................73   P6
Swaythling C Sotn...................22   D11
Sweet Green Worcs.................46   B2
Sweetham Devon........................9   L5
Sweethaws E Susx...................25   M5
Sweetlands Corner Kent..........26   C2
Sweets Cnwll.............................5   K2
Sweetshouse Cnwll....................4   H9
Swefling Suffk..........................65   L9
Swepstone Leics......................72   B8
Swerford Oxon.........................48   C8
Swettenham Ches E.................82   H11
Swffryd Blae G........................30   H5
Swift's Green Kent...................26   E3
Swilland Suffk...........................64   H11
Swillbrook Lancs......................88   F4
Swillington Leeds......................91   K4
Swimbridge Devon...................17   L5
Swimbridge Newland Devon...17   L5
Swinbrook Oxon.......................33   Q2
Swincliffe Kirk..........................90   G5
Swincliffe N York......................97   K9
Swincombe Devon...................17   M3
Swindale Cumb.......................101   P8
Swinden N York........................96   C10
Swinderby Lincs.......................85   Q8
Swindon Gloucs........................46   H9
Swindon Nthumb....................119   J11
Swindon Staffs.........................58   C6
Swindon Swindn......................33   M8
Swine E R Yk............................93   K3
Swinefleet E R Yk.....................92   C6
Swineford S Glos......................32   C11
Swineshead Bed......................61   N7
Swineshead Lincs....................74   D2
Swineshead Bridge Lincs........74   D2
Swiney Highld........................167   M9
Swinford Leics.........................60   C5
Swinford Oxon.........................34   D3
Swingate Notts........................72   E2
Swingfield Minnis Kent...........27   M3
Swingfield Street Kent.............27   M3
Swingleton Green Suffk...........52   G2
Swinhoe Nthumb....................119   P5
Swinhope Lincs........................93   M11
Swinithwaite N York.................96   F3
Swinmore Common Herefs.....46   C6
Swinscoe Staffs........................71   L5
Swinside Cumb.......................100   H6
Swinstead Lincs........................73   Q6
Swinthorpe Lincs.....................86   E4
Swinton Border......................129   L10
Swinton N York........................97   K5
Swinton N York........................98   F6
Swinton Rothm........................91   M11
Swinton Salfd..........................82   G4
Swiss Valley Carmth................28   F4
Swithland Leics........................72   F8
Swordale Highld......................155   Q4
Swordland Highld...................145   N9
Swordly Highld.......................166   B4
Sworton Heath Ches E.............82   E8
Swyddffynnon Cerdgn............54   F11
Swyncombe Oxon....................35   J6
Swynnerton Staffs...................70   F7
Swyre Dorset...........................11   L7
Sycharth Powys........................68   H9
Sychnant Powys........................55   M9
Sychtyn Powys.........................55   M3
Sydallt Wrexhm........................69   K3
Syde Gloucs.............................33   J2
Sydenham Gt Lon....................37   J6
Sydenham Oxon.......................35   K4
Sydenham Damerel Devon.......5   Q6
Sydenhurst Surrey...................23   Q8
Sydling St Nicholas Dorset.....11   N5

Sydmonton Hants....................22   E3
Sydnal Lane Shrops.................57   Q3
Syerston Notts.........................85   M11
Syke Rochdl.............................89   P7
Sykehouse Donc......................91   Q7
Syleham Suffk..........................65   J6
Sylen Carmth...........................28   F3
Symbister Shet......................169   s7
Symington S Ayrs...................125   K11
Symington S Lans..................116   D3
Symondsbury Dorset...............11   J4
Symonds Yat (East) Herefs....45   R11
Symonds Yat (West) Herefs...45   R11
Sympson Green C Brad...........90   F3
Synderford Dorset...................10   H4
Synod Inn Cerdgn...................42   H4
Syre Highld...........................165   Q8
Syreford Gloucs.......................47   K10
Syresham Nhants....................48   H6
Syston Leics............................72   G8
Syston Lincs............................73   N2
Sytchampton Worcs................58   B11
Sywell Nhants.........................60   H7

T

Tabley Hill Ches E....................82   F9
Tackley Oxon............................48   E11
Tacolneston Norfk....................64   G2
Tadcaster N York......................91   M2
Taddington Derbys...................83   P10
Taddington Gloucs...................47   L8
Taddiport Devon......................16   H8
Tadley Hants............................22   H2
Tadlow Cambs..........................62   C11
Tadmarton Oxon......................48   C7
Tadpole Swindn.......................33   M6
Tadwick BaNES........................32   D10
Tadworth Surrey......................36   F9
Tafarnaubach Blae G...............30   F2
Tafarn-y-bwlch Pembks..........41   L4
Tafarn-y-Gelyn Denbgs...........68   G2
Taff's Well Rhondd...................30   F8
Tafolwern Powys......................55   K4
Taibach Neath..........................29   L7
Tain Highld...........................162   H10
Tain Highld...........................167   M3
Tai'n Lôn Gwynd......................66   G4
Tai'r Bull Powys.......................44   D9
Tairgwaith Neath.....................29   K2
Takeley Essex...........................51   N6
Takeley Street Essex................51   M6
Talachddu Powys......................44   F8
Talacre Flints...........................80   G8
Talaton Devon...........................9   Q5
Talbenny Pembks.....................40   F8
Talbot Green Rhondd...............30   D8
Talbot Village BCP...................13   J6
Taleford Devon.........................10   B5
Talerddig Powys.......................55   L4
Talgarreg Cerdgn.....................42   H4
Talgarth Powys.........................44   H8
Talisker Highld......................152   E11
Talke Staffs..............................70   E4
Talke Pits Staffs.......................70   E4
Talkin Cumb...........................111   L9
Talladale Highld.....................154   B3
Talla Linnfoots Border...........116   G6
Tallaminnock S Ayrs..............114   H8
Tallarn Green Wrexhm............69   M6
Tallentire Cumb......................100   F3
Talley Carmth...........................43   M8
Tallington Lincs........................74   A9
Tallwrn Wrexhm.......................69   J5
Talmine Highld......................165   N4
Talog Carmth............................42   F9
Talsarn Cerdgn.........................43   K3
Talsarnau Gwynd......................67   L7
Talskiddy Cnwll..........................4   E8
Talwrn IoA................................78   H9
Talwrn Wrexhm........................69   L5
Tal-y-bont Cerdgn....................54   E7
Tal-y-Bont Conwy.....................79   P11
Talybont Gwynd........................67   K10
Tal-y-bont Gwynd.....................79   L10
Talybont-on-Usk Powys...........44   G10
Tal-y-Cafn Conwy.....................79   P10
Tal-y-coed Mons.......................45   N11
Tal-y-garn Rhondd....................30   D9
Tal-y-llyn Gwynd......................54   G3
Talysarn Gwynd........................66   H4
Tal-y-Waun Torfn......................31   J4
Talywern Powys........................55   J4
Tamar Valley Mining
   District Devon..........................6   C5
Tamer Lane End Wigan............82   D4
Tamerton Foliot C Plym.............6   D6
Tamworth Staffs.......................59   K4
Tamworth Green Lincs.............74   G2
Tamworth Services Warwks....59   K4
Tancred N York........................97   Q9
Tancredston Pembks................40   G5
Tandridge Surrey.....................37   J10
Tanfield Dur...........................113   J9
Tanfield Lea Dur....................113   J10
Tangasdale W Isls..................168   b17
Tangiers Pembks......................41   J7
Tangley Hants..........................22   B4
Tangmere W Susx.....................15   P5
Tan Hill N York.......................102   G9
Tankerness Ork......................169   e6
Tankersley Barns.....................91   J11
Tankerton Kent........................39   K8
Tannach Highld......................167   P7
Tannachie Abers....................151   K11
Tannadice Angus...................142   H6
Tanner's Green Worcs.............58   G10
Tannington Suffk......................65   J8
Tannochside N Lans...............126   C5
Tansley Derbys.........................84   D9
Tansor Nhants..........................61   N2
Tantobie Dur..........................113   J10
Tanton N York........................104   F8
Tanwood Worcs........................58   D10
Tanworth in Arden Warwks.....58   H10
Tan-y-Bwlch Gwynd.................67   M6
Tan-y-fron Conwy.....................68   C2
Tan-y-fron Wrexhm..................69   J4
Tan-y-grisiau Gwynd................67   M5
Tan-y-groes Cerdgn.................42   E5
Taobh Tuath W Isls................168   e9
Taplow Bucks...........................35   P8
Tarbert Ag & B.......................123   Q6
Tarbert Ag & B.......................123   Q6

Tarbert W Isls ... 168 g7
Tarbet Ag & B ... 132 C7
Tarbet Highld ... 145 N9
Tarbet Highld ... 164 E7
Tarbock Green Knows ... 81 P7
Tarbolton S Ayrs ... 114 H2
Tarbrax S Lans ... 127 J6
Tardebigge Worcs ... 58 E11
Tarfside Angus ... 142 H2
Tarland Abers ... 150 D7
Tarleton Lancs ... 88 F6
Tarlscough Lancs ... 88 E8
Tarlton Glouc ... 33 J5
Tarnock Somset ... 19 L4
Tarns Cumb ... 109 P11
Tarnside Cumb ... 95 J2
Tarporley Ches W ... 69 Q2
Tarr Somset ... 17 R5
Tarrant Crawford Dorset ... 12 F4
Tarrant Gunville Dorset ... 12 F2
Tarrant Hinton Dorset ... 12 F2
Tarrant Keyneston Dorset ... 12 F4
Tarrant Launceston Dorset ... 12 F3
Tarrant Monkton Dorset ... 12 F3
Tarrant Rawston Dorset ... 12 F3
Tarrant Rushton Dorset ... 12 F3
Tarring Neville E Susx ... 25 K10
Tarrington Herefs ... 46 B6
Tarskavaig Highld ... 145 J5
Tarves Abers ... 159 L11
Tarvin Ches W ... 81 P11
Tarvin Sands Ches W ... 81 P11
Tasburgh Norfk ... 65 J2
Tasley Shrops ... 57 M6
Taston Oxon ... 48 C10
Tatenhill Staffs ... 71 N10
Tathall End M Keyn ... 49 M5
Tatham Lancs ... 95 N7
Tathwell Lincs ... 87 K4
Tatsfield Surrey ... 37 K9
Tattenhall Ches W ... 69 N3
Tatterford Norfk ... 76 B6
Tattersett Norfk ... 76 A6
Tattershall Lincs ... 86 H9
Tattershall Bridge Lincs ... 86 G9
Tattershall Thorpe Lincs ... 86 H9
Tattingstone Suffk ... 53 K4
Tattingstone White Horse Suffk ... 53 K4
Tatton Park Ches E ... 82 F8
Tatworth Somset ... 10 G3
Tauchers Moray ... 157 R8
Taunton Somset ... 18 H10
Taunton Deane Services Somset ... 18 G10
Taverham Norfk ... 76 H9
Taverners Green Essex ... 51 N7
Tavernspite Pembks ... 41 N8
Tavistock Devon ... 6 D4
Tavistock Devon ... 6 D4
Taw Green Devon ... 8 G5
Tawstock Devon ... 17 K6
Taxal Derbys ... 83 M9
Tay Bridge C Dund ... 135 L2
Taychreggan Hotel Ag & B ... 131 L3
Tay Forest Park P & K ... 141 J5
Tayinloan Ag & B ... 123 L10
Taynton Gloucs ... 46 D10
Taynton Oxon ... 33 P2
Taynuilt Ag & B ... 139 J11
Tayport Fife ... 135 M2
Tayvallich Ag & B ... 130 E10
Tealby Lincs ... 86 G2
Tealing Angus ... 142 G10
Team Valley Gatesd ... 113 K9
Teangue Highld ... 145 L6
Teanord Highld ... 155 Q5
Tebay Cumb ... 102 B10
Tebay Services Cumb ... 102 B9
Tebworth C Beds ... 49 Q9
Tedburn St Mary Devon ... 9 K6
Teddington Gloucs ... 47 J8
Teddington Gt Lon ... 36 E6
Tedstone Delamere Herefs ... 46 C3
Tedstone Wafer Herefs ... 46 C3
Teesport R & Cl ... 104 F6
Teesside Park S on T ... 104 E7
Teeton Nhants ... 60 E6
Teffont Evias Wilts ... 21 J8
Teffont Magna Wilts ... 21 J8
Tegryn Pembks ... 41 P4
Teigh Rutlnd ... 73 M7
Teigncombe Devon ... 8 G7
Teigngrace Devon ... 7 M4
Teignmouth Devon ... 7 N4
Teindside Border ... 117 N9
Telford Wrekin ... 57 M3
Telford Services Shrops ... 57 N3
Telham E Susx ... 26 C9
Tellisford Somset ... 20 F3
Telscombe E Susx ... 25 K10
Telscombe Cliffs E Susx ... 25 K10
Tempar P & K ... 140 G6
Templand D & G ... 109 N3
Temple Cnwll ... 5 J7
Temple Mdloth ... 127 Q6
Temple Balsall Solhll ... 59 K9
Temple Bar Cerdgn ... 43 K4
Temple Cloud BaNES ... 20 B3
Templecombe Somset ... 20 D10
Temple End Suffk ... 63 L10
Temple Ewell Kent ... 27 N3
Temple Grafton Warwks ... 47 M3
Temple Guiting Gloucs ... 47 L9
Temple Herdewyke Warwks ... 48 C4
Temple Hirst N York ... 91 Q6
Temple Normanton Derbys ... 84 F7
Temple of Fiddes Abers ... 151 L11
Temple Sowerby Cumb ... 102 B5
Templeton Devon ... 9 J2
Templeton Pembks ... 41 M8
Templetown Dur ... 112 H10
Tempsford C Beds ... 61 Q10
Tenbury Wells Worcs ... 57 K11
Tenby Pembks ... 41 M10
Tendring Essex ... 53 K7
Tendring Green Essex ... 53 K6
Tendring Heath Essex ... 53 K6
Ten Mile Bank Norfk ... 75 L11
Tenpenny Heath Essex ... 53 J7
Tenterden Kent ... 26 E5
Terling Essex ... 52 C8
Tern Wrekin ... 69 R11
Ternhill Shrops ... 70 A8
Terregles D & G ... 109 K5
Terrington N York ... 98 E6

Terrington St Clement Norfk ... 75 L6
Terrington St John Norfk ... 75 L8
Terry's Green Warwks ... 58 H10
Teston Kent ... 38 B11
Testwood Hants ... 14 C4
Tetbury Gloucs ... 32 G6
Tetbury Upton Gloucs ... 32 G5
Tetchill Shrops ... 69 L8
Tetcott Devon ... 5 N2
Tetford Lincs ... 87 K6
Tetney Lincs ... 93 P10
Tetney Lock Lincs ... 93 P10
Tetsworth Oxon ... 35 J4
Tettenhall Wolves ... 58 C4
Tettenhall Wood Wolves ... 58 C5
Teversal Notts ... 84 G8
Teversham Cambs ... 62 G9
Teviothead Border ... 117 N9
Tewin Herts ... 50 G8
Tewin Wood Herts ... 50 G7
Tewkesbury Gloucs ... 46 G8
Teynham Kent ... 38 G9
Thackley C Brad ... 90 F3
Thackthwaite Cumb ... 100 F6
Thackthwaite Cumb ... 101 M5
Thainstone Abers ... 151 K4
Thakeham W Susx ... 24 D7
Thame Oxon ... 35 K3
Thames Ditton Surrey ... 36 E7
Thamesmead Gt Lon ... 37 L4
Thamesport Medway ... 38 E7
Thanington Kent ... 39 K10
Thankerton S Lans ... 116 D3
Tharston Norfk ... 64 H3
Thatcham W Berk ... 34 F11
Thaxted Essex ... 51 P4
Theakston N York ... 97 M3
Thealby N Linc ... 92 F7
Theale Somset ... 19 N5
Theale W Berk ... 34 H10
Thearne E R Yk ... 93 J3
The Bank Ches E ... 70 E3
The Beeches Gloucs ... 33 K4
Theberton Suffk ... 65 N8
The Blythe Staffs ... 71 J9
The Bog Shrops ... 56 F5
The Bourne Worcs ... 47 J3
The Braes Highld ... 153 J11
The Bratch Staffs ... 58 C6
The Bridge Kent ... 37 M5
The Broad Herefs ... 45 P2
The Broads ... 77 P10
The Brunt E Loth ... 128 H5
The Bryn Mons ... 31 K3
The Bungalow IoM ... 80 e4
The Burf Worcs ... 57 Q11
The Camp Gloucs ... 32 H3
The Chequer Wrexhm ... 69 N6
The City Bed ... 61 P9
The City Bucks ... 35 L5
The Common Oxon ... 47 Q9
The Common Wilts ... 21 P8
The Common Wilts ... 33 K7
The Corner Kent ... 26 B3
The Cronk IoM ... 80 d2
Theddingworth Leics ... 60 E3
Theddlethorpe All Saints Lincs ... 87 N3
Theddlethorpe St Helen Lincs ... 87 N3
The Deep C KuH ... 93 J5
The Den N Ayrs ... 125 J7
The Forge Herefs ... 45 L3
The Forstal Kent ... 26 H4
The Fourells Shrops ... 70 B8
The Green Cumb ... 94 D4
The Green Essex ... 52 C8
The Green N York ... 105 L9
The Green Wilts ... 20 G8
The Grove Dur ... 112 G10
The Grove Worcs ... 46 G6
The Haven W Susx ... 24 C4
The Haw Gloucs ... 46 F9
The Headland Hartpl ... 104 F4
The Hendre Mons ... 31 N2
The Hill Cumb ... 94 D4
The Holt Wokham ... 35 M9
The Hundred Herefs ... 45 Q2
Thelbridge Cross Devon ... 9 J2
The Leacon Kent ... 26 H4
The Lee Bucks ... 35 P4
The Lhen IoM ... 80 e1
Thelnetham Suffk ... 64 E6
The Lochs Moray ... 157 Q5
Thelveton Norfk ... 64 H5
Thelwall Warrtn ... 82 E7
The Marsh Powys ... 56 E5
Themelthorpe Norfk ... 76 F7
The Middles Dur ... 113 K10
The Moor Kent ... 26 C6
The Mumbles Swans ... 28 H7
The Murray S Lans ... 125 Q7
The Mythe Gloucs ... 46 G8
The Narth Mons ... 31 P3
The Neuk Abers ... 151 J8
Thenford Nhants ... 48 F6
Theobald's Green Wilts ... 33 K11
The Quarry Gloucs ... 32 D5
The Quarter Kent ... 26 E3
The Reddings Gloucs ... 46 H10
Therfield Herts ... 50 H3
The Rhôs Powys ... 44 H8
The Ross P & K ... 133 M3
The Sands Surrey ... 23 N5
The Shoe Wilts ... 32 F10
The Smithies Shrops ... 57 M5
The Spring Warwks ... 59 L10
The Square Torfn ... 31 J5
The Stair Kent ... 37 P11
The Stocks Kent ... 26 F6
The Strand Wilts ... 20 H1
Thetford Norfk ... 64 B5
Thetford Forest Park ... 63 P3
Thethwaite Cumb ... 101 L2
The Towans Cnwll ... 2 F6
The Vauld Herefs ... 45 Q5
The Wyke Shrops ... 57 N3
Theydon Bois Essex ... 51 K11
Theydon Mount Essex ... 51 L11
Thicket Priory N York ... 92 A2
Thickwood Wilts ... 32 F10
Thimbleby Lincs ... 86 H6
Thimbleby N York ... 104 D11

Thingwall Wirral ... 81 K8
Thirkleby N York ... 97 Q5
Thirlby N York ... 97 Q4
Thirlestane Border ... 128 F10
Thirn N York ... 97 K3
Thirsk N York ... 97 P4
Thirtleby E R Yk ... 93 L4
Thistleton Lancs ... 88 E3
Thistleton Rutlnd ... 73 N7
Thistley Green Suffk ... 63 L5
Thixendale N York ... 98 G8
Thockrington Nthumb ... 112 E5
Tholomas Drove Cambs ... 74 H9
Tholthorpe N York ... 97 Q7
Thomas Chapel Pembks ... 41 M9
Thomas Close Cumb ... 101 M2
Thomastown Abers ... 158 E10
Thompson Norfk ... 64 C2
Thomshill Moray ... 157 N6
Thong Kent ... 37 Q6
Thongsbridge Kirk ... 90 F9
Thoralby N York ... 96 F3
Thoresby Notts ... 85 K6
Thoresthorpe Lincs ... 87 N5
Thoresway Lincs ... 93 L11
Thorganby Lincs ... 93 M11
Thorganby N York ... 92 A2
Thorgill N York ... 105 K11
Thorington Suffk ... 65 N7
Thorington Street Suffk ... 52 H4
Thorlby N York ... 96 E10
Thorley Herts ... 51 L7
Thorley IoW ... 14 C9
Thorley Houses Herts ... 51 L6
Thorley Street IoW ... 14 C9
Thormanby N York ... 97 Q6
Thornaby-on-Tees S on T ... 104 E7
Thornage Norfk ... 76 F4
Thornborough Bucks ... 49 K8
Thornborough N York ... 97 L5
Thornbury C Brad ... 90 F4
Thornbury Devon ... 16 G10
Thornbury Herefs ... 46 B3
Thornbury S Glos ... 32 B6
Thornby Cumb ... 110 E10
Thornby Nhants ... 60 E5
Thorncliff Staffs ... 71 J3
Thorncombe Dorset ... 10 H4
Thorncombe Street Surrey ... 23 Q6
Thorncott Green C Beds ... 61 Q11
Thorncross IoW ... 14 D10
Thorndon Suffk ... 64 G8
Thorndon Cross Devon ... 8 D7
Thorne Donc ... 92 A8
Thorne Coffin Somset ... 19 P11
Thornecroft Devon ... 7 K5
Thornehillhead Devon ... 16 G8
Thorner Leeds ... 91 K2
Thornes Staffs ... 58 G4
Thornes Wakefd ... 91 J7
Thorne St Margaret Somset ... 18 F10
Thorney Bucks ... 36 B5
Thorney C Pete ... 74 E10
Thorney Notts ... 85 Q6
Thorney Somset ... 19 M10
Thorney Hill Hants ... 13 M5
Thorney Island W Susx ... 15 L6
Thorney Toll Cambs ... 74 F10
Thornfalcon Somset ... 19 J10
Thornford Dorset ... 11 N2
Thorngrafton Nthumb ... 111 Q7
Thorngrove Somset ... 19 L8
Thorngumbald E R Yk ... 93 M5
Thornham Norfk ... 75 P2
Thornham Magna Suffk ... 64 G7
Thornham Parva Suffk ... 64 G7
Thornhaugh C Pete ... 73 R10
Thornhill C Sotn ... 14 E4
Thornhill Caerph ... 30 G6
Thornhill Cumb ... 100 D9
Thornhill D & G ... 116 B7
Thornhill Derbys ... 83 Q8
Thornhill Kirk ... 90 H7
Thornhill Stirlg ... 133 K7
Thornhill Lees Kirk ... 90 G7
Thornhills Calder ... 90 F6
Thornholme E R Yk ... 99 N8
Thornicombe Dorset ... 12 E4
Thornington Nthumb ... 118 G4
Thornley Dur ... 103 M3
Thornley Dur ... 104 C3
Thornley Gate Nthumb ... 112 B9
Thornliebank E Rens ... 125 P6
Thorns Suffk ... 63 L9
Thornsett Derbys ... 83 M7
Thorns Green Ches E ... 82 G8
Thornthwaite Cumb ... 100 H5
Thornthwaite N York ... 97 J9
Thornton Angus ... 142 F8
Thornton Bucks ... 49 K7
Thornton C Brad ... 90 D4
Thornton E R Yk ... 98 F11
Thornton Fife ... 134 H8
Thornton Lancs ... 88 C2
Thornton Leics ... 72 D9
Thornton Lincs ... 86 H7
Thornton Middsb ... 104 E8
Thornton Nthumb ... 129 P10
Thornton Pembks ... 40 H9
Thornton Sefton ... 81 L4
Thornton Curtis N Linc ... 93 J7
Thorntonhall S Lans ... 125 P6
Thornton Heath Gt Lon ... 36 H7
Thornton Hough Wirral ... 81 L8
Thornton-in-Craven N York ... 96 D11
Thornton in Lonsdale N York ... 95 P6
Thornton-le-Beans N York ... 97 N2
Thornton-le-Clay N York ... 98 D7
Thornton-le-Dale N York ... 98 G4
Thornton le Moor Lincs ... 92 H11
Thornton-le-Moor N York ... 97 N3
Thornton-le-Moors Ches W ... 81 N10
Thornton-le-Street N York ... 97 P3
Thorntonloch E Loth ... 129 K5
Thornton Rust N York ... 96 E3
Thornton Steward N York ... 97 J3
Thornton Watlass N York ... 97 K3
Thornwood Common Essex ... 51 L10
Thornydykes Border ... 128 G10
Thornythwaite Cumb ... 101 L4
Thoroton Notts ... 73 K2
Thorp Arch Leeds ... 97 P11
Thorpe Derbys ... 71 M4
Thorpe E R Yk ... 99 K11
Thorpe Lincs ... 87 N4

Thorpe N York ... 96 F8
Thorpe Norfk ... 65 N2
Thorpe Notts ... 85 N11
Thorpe Surrey ... 36 B7
Thorpe Abbotts Norfk ... 64 H6
Thorpe Acre Leics ... 72 E7
Thorpe Arnold Leics ... 73 K6
Thorpe Audlin Wakefd ... 91 M7
Thorpe Bassett N York ... 98 H6
Thorpe Bay Sthend ... 38 F4
Thorpe by Water Rutlnd ... 73 M11
Thorpe Common Rothm ... 91 K11
Thorpe Constantine Staffs ... 59 L3
Thorpe End Norfk ... 77 K9
Thorpe Green Essex ... 53 L7
Thorpe Green Lancs ... 88 G5
Thorpe Green Suffk ... 64 C11
Thorpe Hesley Rothm ... 91 K11
Thorpe in Balne Donc ... 91 P8
Thorpe Langton Leics ... 60 F2
Thorpe Larches Dur ... 104 C5
Thorpe Lea Surrey ... 36 B6
Thorpe le Fallows Lincs ... 86 B5
Thorpe-le-Soken Essex ... 53 L7
Thorpe le Street E R Yk ... 92 D2
Thorpe Malsor Nhants ... 60 H5
Thorpe Mandeville Nhants ... 48 F5
Thorpe Market Norfk ... 77 J4
Thorpe Marriot Norfk ... 76 H8
Thorpe Morieux Suffk ... 64 C11
Thorpeness Suffk ... 65 P10
Thorpe on the Hill Leeds ... 91 J5
Thorpe on the Hill Lincs ... 86 B7
Thorpe Park Surrey ... 36 B7
Thorpe St Andrew Norfk ... 77 K10
Thorpe St Peter Lincs ... 87 N8
Thorpe Salvin Rothm ... 84 H4
Thorpe Satchville Leics ... 73 J8
Thorpe Thewles S on T ... 104 C6
Thorpe Tilney Lincs ... 86 F9
Thorpe Underwood N York ... 97 Q9
Thorpe Underwood Nhants ... 60 G4
Thorpe Waterville Nhants ... 61 M4
Thorpe Willoughby N York ... 91 P4
Thorpland Norfk ... 75 M9
Thorrington Essex ... 53 J8
Thorverton Devon ... 9 M4
Thrales End C Beds ... 50 D7
Thrandeston Suffk ... 64 G6
Thrapston Nhants ... 61 L5
Threapland Cumb ... 100 G3
Threapland N York ... 96 E8
Threapwood Ches W ... 69 N6
Threapwood Staffs ... 71 J6
Threapwood Head Staffs ... 71 J6
Threave S Ayrs ... 114 F6
Three Ashes Herefs ... 45 Q10
Three Bridges W Susx ... 24 G3
Three Burrows Cnwll ... 3 K4
Three Chimneys Kent ... 26 D4
Three Cocks Powys ... 44 H7
Three Crosses Swans ... 28 G6
Three Cups Corner E Susx ... 25 P6
Three Gates Worcs ... 46 C2
Threehammer Common Norfk ... 77 L8
Three Hammers Cnwll ... 5 L4
Three Holes Norfk ... 75 K10
Threekingham Lincs ... 74 A3
Three Leg Cross E Susx ... 25 Q4
Three Legged Cross Dorset ... 13 J3
Three Mile Cross Wokham ... 35 K11
Threemilestone Cnwll ... 3 K5
Threemiletown W Loth ... 127 K2
Three Oaks E Susx ... 26 D9
Threlkeld Cumb ... 101 K5
Threshers Bush Essex ... 51 L9
Threshfield N York ... 96 E8
Thrigby Norfk ... 77 P9
Thringarth Dur ... 102 H6
Thringstone Leics ... 72 C7
Thrintoft N York ... 97 M2
Thriplow Cambs ... 62 G11
Throapham Rothm ... 84 H3
Throckenhalt Lincs ... 74 G9
Throcking Herts ... 50 H4
Throckley N u Ty ... 113 J7
Throckmorton Worcs ... 47 J4
Throop BCP ... 13 K5
Throop Dorset ... 12 D6
Throphill Nthumb ... 112 H3
Thropton Nthumb ... 119 K10
Throsk Stirlg ... 133 P9
Throughgate D & G ... 109 J4
Throwleigh Devon ... 8 G7
Throwley Kent ... 38 G10
Throwley Forstal Kent ... 38 G11
Thrumpton Notts ... 72 E4
Thrumpton Notts ... 85 M4
Thrumster Highld ... 167 P9
Thrunscoe NE Lin ... 93 P9
Thrunton Nthumb ... 119 L9
Thrup Oxon ... 33 Q5
Thrupp Gloucs ... 32 G4
Thrupp Oxon ... 48 E11
Thrushelton Devon ... 8 B7
Thrussington Leics ... 72 H7
Thruxton Hants ... 21 Q5
Thruxton Herefs ... 45 N8
Thrybergh Rothm ... 91 M11
Thulston Derbys ... 72 C4
Thundersley Essex ... 38 C4
Thurcaston Leics ... 72 F8
Thurcroft Rothm ... 84 G3
Thurdon Cnwll ... 16 D9
Thurgarton Norfk ... 76 H5
Thurgarton Notts ... 85 L11
Thurgoland Barns ... 90 H10
Thurlaston Leics ... 72 E11
Thurlaston Warwks ... 59 Q10
Thurlbear Somset ... 19 J8
Thurlby Lincs ... 74 A7
Thurlby Lincs ... 86 B8
Thurlby Lincs ... 87 N5
Thurleigh Bed ... 61 N9
Thurlestone Devon ... 6 H9
Thurloxton Somset ... 19 J8
Thurlstone Barns ... 90 H10
Thurlton Norfk ... 65 N2
Thurlwood Ches E ... 70 E3
Thurmaston Leics ... 72 G9
Thurnby Leics ... 72 G9
Thurne Norfk ... 77 N8
Thurnham Kent ... 38 D10
Thurning Nhants ... 61 N4

Thurning Norfk ... 76 F6
Thurnscoe Barns ... 91 M9
Thurrock Services Thurr ... 37 N5
Thursby Cumb ... 110 F10
Thursden Lancs ... 89 Q4
Thursford Norfk ... 76 D5
Thursley Surrey ... 23 P7
Thurso Highld ... 167 K3
Thurstaston Wirral ... 81 J8
Thurston Suffk ... 64 C8
Thurston Clough Oldham ... 90 B4
Thurstonfield Cumb ... 110 F9
Thurstonland Kirk ... 90 F8
Thurston Planche Suffk ... 64 C9
Thurton Norfk ... 65 M2
Thurvaston Derbys ... 71 N7
Thuxton Norfk ... 76 E10
Thwaite N York ... 102 G11
Thwaite Suffk ... 64 G8
Thwaite Head Cumb ... 94 G2
Thwaites C Brad ... 90 D2
Thwaite St Mary Norfk ... 65 L2
Thwaites Brow C Brad ... 90 D2
Thwing E R Yk ... 99 L6
Tibbermore P & K ... 134 C3
Tibberton Gloucs ... 46 E10
Tibberton Worcs ... 46 H3
Tibberton Wrekin ... 70 B10
Tibenham Norfk ... 64 G4
Tibshelf Derbys ... 84 F8
Tibshelf Services Derbys ... 84 F8
Tibthorpe E R Yk ... 99 K9
Ticehurst E Susx ... 25 Q4
Tichborne Hants ... 22 G8
Tickencote Rutlnd ... 73 P9
Tickenham N Som ... 31 N10
Tickford End M Keyn ... 49 N6
Tickhill Donc ... 85 J2
Ticklerton Shrops ... 56 H6
Ticknall Derbys ... 72 B6
Tickton E R Yk ... 93 J2
Tidbury Green Solhll ... 58 H9
Tidcombe Wilts ... 21 Q3
Tiddington Oxon ... 34 H4
Tiddington Warwks ... 47 P3
Tiddleywink Wilts ... 32 G9
Tidebrook E Susx ... 25 P4
Tideford Cnwll ... 5 P10
Tideford Cross Cnwll ... 5 N9
Tidenham Gloucs ... 31 Q5
Tideswell Derbys ... 83 Q9
Tidmarsh W Berk ... 34 H10
Tidmington Warwks ... 47 Q7
Tidpit Hants ... 21 L11
Tidworth Wilts ... 21 P5
Tiers Cross Pembks ... 40 H7
Tiffield Nhants ... 49 K4
Tigerton Angus ... 143 J5
Tigh a' Ghearraidh W Isls ... 168 c10
Tigharry W Isls ... 168 c10
Tighnabruaich Ag & B ... 124 B3
Tigley Devon ... 7 K6
Tilbrook Cambs ... 61 N7
Tilbury Thurr ... 37 P5
Tilbury Dock Thurr ... 37 P5
Tilbury Green Essex ... 52 B3
Tilbury Juxta Clare Essex ... 52 C2
Tile Cross Birm ... 59 J7
Tile Hill Covtry ... 59 L9
Tilehouse Green Solhll ... 59 J9
Tilehurst Readg ... 35 J10
Tilford Surrey ... 23 N6
Tilgate W Susx ... 24 G4
Tilgate Forest Row W Susx ... 24 G4
Tilham Street Somset ... 19 Q8
Tillers Green Gloucs ... 46 C8
Tillicoultry Clacks ... 133 Q8
Tillietudlem S Lans ... 126 E8
Tillingham Essex ... 52 G11
Tillington Herefs ... 45 P6
Tillington W Susx ... 23 Q10
Tillington Common Herefs ... 45 P5
Tillybirloch Abers ... 150 H6
Tillyfourie Abers ... 150 G5
Tillygreig Abers ... 151 M3
Tillyrie P & K ... 134 E6
Tilmanstone Kent ... 39 P11
Tilney All Saints Norfk ... 75 L7
Tilney High End Norfk ... 75 L7
Tilney St Lawrence Norfk ... 75 K8
Tilshead Wilts ... 21 K5
Tilstock Shrops ... 69 P7
Tilston Ches W ... 69 N4
Tilstone Bank Ches W ... 69 Q3
Tilstone Fearnall Ches W ... 69 Q2
Tilsworth C Beds ... 49 Q10
Tilton on the Hill Leics ... 73 J9
Tiltups End Gloucs ... 32 F5
Tilty Essex ... 51 N5
Timberland Lincs ... 86 F8
Timbersbrook Ches E ... 70 F2
Timberscombe Somset ... 18 C6
Timble N York ... 97 J10
Timewell Devon ... 18 C9
Timpanheck D & G ... 110 F6
Timperley Traffd ... 82 F7
Timsbury BaNES ... 20 C3
Timsbury Hants ... 22 B10
Timsgarry W Isls ... 168 f4
Timsgearraidh W Isls ... 168 f4
Timworth Suffk ... 64 B8
Timworth Green Suffk ... 64 B8
Tincleton Dorset ... 12 C6
Tindale Cumb ... 111 M9
Tingewick Bucks ... 49 J8
Tingley Leeds ... 90 H5
Tingrith C Beds ... 49 Q7
Tingwall Airport Shet ... 169 r9
Tingwell Ork ... 169 d6
Tinhay Devon ... 5 P4
Tinker's Hill Hants ... 22 D5
Tinkersley Derbys ... 84 C8
Tinsley Sheff ... 84 F2
Tinsley Green W Susx ... 24 G3
Tintagel Cnwll ... 4 F4
Tintern Mons ... 31 P4
Tintinhull Somset ... 19 N11
Tintwistle Derbys ... 83 M5
Tinwald D & G ... 109 M4
Tinwell Rutlnd ... 73 Q9
Tippacott Devon ... 17 P2
Tipp's End Norfk ... 75 K11
Tiptoe Hants ... 13 N5
Tipton Sandw ... 58 E6
Tipton Green Sandw ... 58 E6

Tipton St John – Tullynessle 297

Tipton St John Devon 10 B6
Tiptree Essex 52 E8
Tiptree Heath Essex 52 E8
Tirabad Powys 44 B6
Tircoed Swans 28 H4
Tiree Ag & B 136 C7
Tiree Airport Ag & B 136 C7
Tiretigan Ag & B 123 M7
Tirley Gloucs 46 F9
Tiroran Ag & B 137 M10
Tirphil Caerph 30 F4
Tirril Cumb 101 P5
Tir-y-fron Flints 69 J3
Tisbury Wilts 20 H9
Tisman's Common W Susx 24 C4
Tissington Derbys 71 M4
Titchberry Devon 16 C6
Titchfield Hants 14 F5
Titchfield Common Hants 14 F5
Titchmarsh Nhants 61 M5
Titchwell Norfk 75 Q2
Tithby Notts 72 H3
Titley Herefs 45 L2
Titmore Green Herts 50 F5
Titsey Surrey 37 K10
Titson Cnwll 16 C11
Tittensor Staffs 70 F7
Tittleshall Norfk 76 B7
Titton Worcs 58 B11
Tiverton Ches W 69 Q2
Tiverton Devon 9 N2
Tivetshall St Margaret Norfk 64 H4
Tivetshall St Mary Norfk 64 H4
Tivington Somset 18 B5
Tivy Dale Barns 90 H9
Tixall Staffs 70 H10
Tixover Rutlnd 73 P10
Toab Shet 169 q12
Toadhole Derbys 84 E9
Toadmoor Derbys 84 D10
Tobermory Ag & B 137 N4
Toberonochy Ag & B 130 E6
Tobha Mòr W Isls 168 c14
Tocher Abers 158 G11
Tochieneal Moray 158 D4
Tockenham Wilts 33 K9
Tockenham Wick Wilts 33 K8
Tocketts R & Cl 104 H7
Tockholes Bl w D 89 K6
Tockington S Glos 32 B7
Tockwith N York 97 Q10
Todber Dorset 20 E11
Todburn Nthumb 119 M11
Toddington C Beds 50 B5
Toddington Gloucs 47 K8
Toddington Services C Beds 50 B5
Todds Green Herts 50 F5
Todenham Gloucs 47 P7
Todhills Angus 142 G10
Todhills Cumb 110 G8
Todhills Dur 103 P4
Todhills Rest Area Cumb 110 G8
Todmorden Calder 89 Q6
Todwick Rothm 84 G4
Toft Cambs 62 E9
Toft Ches E 82 G9
Toft Lincs 73 R7
Toft Shet 169 r6
Toft Warwks 59 Q10
Toft Hill Dur 103 N5
Toft Hill Lincs 86 H8
Toft Monks Norfk 65 N3
Toft next Newton Lincs 86 D3
Toftrees Norfk 76 B6
Toftwood Norfk 76 D9
Togston Nthumb 119 P10
Tokavaig Highld 145 K5
Tokers Green Oxon 35 K9
Tolastadh bho Thuath W Isls 168 k3
Toldish Cnwll 4 E10
Tolland Somset 18 F8
Tollard Farnham Dorset 21 J11
Tollard Royal Wilts 20 H11
Toll Bar Donc 91 P9
Tollbar End Covtry 59 N9
Toller Fratrum Dorset 11 M5
Toller Porcorum Dorset 11 M5
Tollerton N York 97 R8
Tollerton Notts 72 G4
Toller Whelme Dorset 11 L4
Tollesbury Essex 52 G9
Tolleshunt D'Arcy Essex 52 F9
Tolleshunt Knights Essex 52 F9
Tolleshunt Major Essex 52 F9
Tollingham E R Yk 92 D3
Toll of Birness Abers 159 P11
Tolpuddle Dorset 12 C6
Tolworth Gt Lon 36 E7
Tomatin Highld 148 E2
Tomchrasky Highld 146 H5
Tomdoun Highld 146 F7
Tomich Highld 147 J2
Tomich Highld 155 P8
Tomich Highld 156 B3
Tomich Highld 162 E5
Tomintoul Moray 149 M4
Tomlow Warwks 48 E2
Tomnacross Highld 155 P9
Tomnavoulin Moray 149 N2
Tompkin Staffs 70 G4
Ton Mons 31 K4
Ton Mons 31 L5
Tonbridge Kent 37 N11
Tondu Brdgnd 29 N8
Tonedale Somset 18 F10
Tonfanau Gwynd 54 D4
Tong C Brad 90 G4
Tong Kent 38 G10
Tong Shrops 57 P3
Tong W Isls 168 j4
Tonge Leics 72 C6
Tong Green Kent 38 G11
Tongham Surrey 23 N5
Tongland D & G 108 E10
Tong Norton Shrops 57 P3
Tongue Highld 165 N5
Tongue End Lincs 74 C7
Tongwynlais Cardif 30 F8
Tonmawr Neath 29 M5
Tonna Neath 29 L5
Ton-teg Rhondd 30 E7
Tonwell Herts 50 H7
Tonypandy Rhondd 30 C6
Tonyrefail Rhondd 30 D7
Toot Baldon Oxon 34 G4
Toot Hill Essex 51 M10
Toothill Hants 22 C11
Toothill Swindn 33 M8
Tooting Gt Lon 36 G6
Tooting Bec Gt Lon 36 G6
Topcliffe N York 97 N5
Topcroft Norfk 65 K3
Topcroft Street Norfk 65 K3
Top End Bed 61 M8
Topham Donc 91 Q7
Top of Hebers Rochdl 89 P9
Toppesfield Essex 52 B4
Toprow Norfk 64 H2
Topsham Devon 9 N7
Top-y-rhos Flints 69 J3
Torbeg N Ayrs 120 G6
Torboll Highld 162 H7
Torbreck Highld 156 A9
Torbryan Devon 7 L5
Torcastle Highld 139 L2
Torcross Devon 7 L10
Tore Highld 155 R7
Torfrey Cnwll 5 J11
Torinturk Ag & B 123 P7
Torksey Lincs 85 P5
Torlundy Highld 139 L2
Tormarton S Glos 32 E9
Tormore N Ayrs 120 G5
Tornagrain Highld 156 D7
Tornaveen Abers 150 G6
Torness Highld 147 P2
Toronto Dur 103 N4
Torpenhow Cumb 100 H3
Torphichen W Loth 126 H3
Torphins Abers 150 G7
Torpoint Cnwll 6 C7
Torquay Torbay 7 N6
Torquhan Border 128 C10
Torr Devon 6 F8
Torran Highld 153 K8
Torrance E Duns 125 Q3
Torranyard N Ayrs 125 K9
Torre Somset 18 D7
Torridon Highld 154 B6
Torridon House Highld 153 R6
Torrin Highld 145 J3
Torrisdale Ag & B 120 E4
Torrisdale Highld 165 Q4
Torrish Highld 163 M3
Torrisholme Lancs 95 K8
Torrobull Highld 162 D6
Torry C Aber 151 N6
Torryburn Fife 134 C10
Torteval Guern 10 a2
Torthorwald D & G 109 M5
Tortington W Susx 24 B9
Torton Worcs 58 B10
Tortworth S Glos 32 D6
Torvaig Highld 152 H9
Torver Cumb 94 F2
Torwood Falk 133 N11
Torwoodlee Border 117 P3
Torworth Notts 85 L3
Tosberry Devon 16 D7
Toscaig Highld 153 N10
Toseland Cambs 62 B8
Tosside Lancs 95 R9
Tostock Suffk 64 D9
Totaig Highld 152 C7
Tote Highld 152 G8
Tote Highld 153 J5
Tote Hill W Susx 23 N10
Totford Hants 22 G7
Tothill Lincs 87 M4
Totland IoW 13 P7
Totley Sheff 84 D5
Totley Brook Sheff 84 D4
Totnes Devon 7 L6
Toton Notts 72 E4
Totronald Ag & B 136 F4
Totscore Highld 152 F4
Tottenham Gt Lon 36 H2
Tottenhill Norfk 75 M8
Totteridge Gt Lon 36 F2
Totternhoe C Beds 49 Q10
Tottington Bury 89 M8
Tottleworth Lancs 89 L4
Totton Hants 14 C4
Touchen End W & M 35 N9
Toulston N York 91 M2
Toulton Somset 18 G8
Toulvaddie Highld 163 K10
Tovil Kent 38 C11
Towan Cnwll 3 Q4
Towan Cnwll 4 D7
Toward Ag & B 124 E4
Toward Quay Ag & B 124 E4
Towcester Nhants 49 J5
Towednack Cnwll 2 D6
Tower of London Gt Lon 36 H4
Towersey Oxon 35 K3
Towie Abers 150 C5
Tow Law Dur 103 M3
Town End Cambs 74 H11
Town End Cumb 95 J4
Town End Cumb 101 K9
Town End Cumb 102 B5
Townend W Duns 125 K2
Towngate Cumb 111 K11
Towngate Lincs 74 B8
Town Green Lancs 88 E9
Town Green Norfk 77 M9
Townhead Barns 83 Q4
Townhead Cumb 100 E3
Town Head Cumb 101 M10
Townhead Cumb 102 B4
Townhead D & G 109 M3
Town Head N York 96 B9
Townhead of Greenlaw D & G 108 F8
Townhill Fife 134 E10
Town Kelloe Dur 104 C3
Townlake Devon 5 Q7
Town Lane Wigan 82 E5
Town Littleworth E Susx 25 K7
Town of Lowton Wigan 82 D5
Town Row E Susx 25 N4
Towns End Hants 22 G3
Townsend Somset 10 H2
Townshend Cnwll 2 F7
Town Street Suffk 63 N3
Townwell S Glos 32 D6
Town Yetholm Border 118 F5
Towthorpe C York 98 C9
Towthorpe E R Yk 98 H8
Towton N York 91 M3
Towyn Conwy 80 D9
Toxteth Lpool 81 M7
Toynton All Saints Lincs 87 L8
Toynton Fen Side Lincs 87 L8
Toynton St Peter Lincs 87 M8
Toy's Hill Kent 37 L10
Trabboch E Ayrs 114 H3
Trabbochburn E Ayrs 115 J3
Traboe Cnwll 3 J9
Tracebridge Somset 18 E10
Tradespark Highld 156 F6
Trafford Park Traffd 82 G5
Trallong Powys 44 D9
Tranent E Loth 128 C5
Tranmere Wirral 81 L7
Trantelbeg Highld 166 E6
Trantlemore Highld 166 E6
Tranwell Nthumb 113 J4
Trap Carmth 43 N11
Traprain E Loth 128 F4
Trap's Green Warwks 58 H11
Trapshill W Berk 22 C2
Traquair Border 117 L4
Trash Green W Berk 35 J11
Trawden Lancs 89 Q3
Trawscoed Cerdgn 54 F10
Trawsfynydd Gwynd 67 N7
Trealaw Rhondd 30 D6
Treales Lancs 88 E4
Trearddur Bay IoA 78 D9
Treator Cnwll 4 E6
Tre Aubrey V Glam 30 D10
Trebanog Rhondd 30 D6
Trebanos Neath 29 K4
Trebartha Cnwll 5 M6
Trebarwith Cnwll 4 H4
Trebeath Cnwll 5 M4
Trebetherick Cnwll 4 E6
Treborough Somset 18 D7
Trebudannon Cnwll 4 D9
Trebullett Cnwll 5 N6
Treburgett Cnwll 4 H6
Treburley Cnwll 5 P6
Treburrick Cnwll 4 D7
Trebyan Cnwll 4 H9
Trecastle Powys 44 B9
Trecogo Cnwll 5 N5
Trecott Devon 8 F4
Trecwn Pembks 41 J4
Trecynon Rhondd 30 C4
Tredaule Cnwll 5 L5
Tredavoe Cnwll 2 D8
Tredegar Blae G 30 F3
Tredethy Cnwll 4 H7
Tredington Gloucs 46 H9
Tredington Warwks 47 Q6
Tredinnick Cnwll 4 E7
Tredinnick Cnwll 4 G10
Tredinnick Cnwll 5 K8
Tredinnick Cnwll 5 L10
Tredinnick Cnwll 5 M10
Tredomen Powys 44 G8
Tredrizzick Cnwll 4 F6
Tredunnock Mons 31 L6
Tredustan Powys 44 G8
Treen Cnwll 2 B9
Treen Cnwll 2 C6
Treesmill Cnwll 4 H10
Treeton Rothm 84 F3
Trefasser Pembks 40 G3
Trefdraeth IoA 78 G10
Trefecca Powys 44 G8
Trefechan Myr Td 30 D3
Trefeglwys Powys 55 M6
Trefenter Cerdgn 54 E11
Treffgarne Pembks 41 J6
Treffgarne Owen Pembks 40 G5
Treffynnon Pembks 40 G5
Trefil Blae G 30 F2
Trefilan Cerdgn 43 K3
Trefin Pembks 40 F4
Treflach Shrops 69 J9
Trefnannau Powys 68 H11
Trefnant Denbgs 80 F10
Trefonen Shrops 69 J9
Trefor Gwynd 66 F5
Trefor IoA 78 F8
Treforest Rhondd 30 E7
Trefrew Cnwll 5 J5
Trefriw Conwy 67 P2
Tregadillett Cnwll 5 M5
Tre-gagle Mons 31 P3
Tregaian IoA 78 H8
Tregare Mons 31 M2
Tregarne Cnwll 3 K9
Tregaron Cerdgn 43 N3
Tregarth Gwynd 79 L11
Tregaswith Cnwll 4 D9
Tregatta Cnwll 4 H4
Tregawne Cnwll 4 G8
Tregeare Cnwll 5 L4
Tregeiriog Wrexhm 68 G8
Tregele IoA 78 F6
Tregellist Cnwll 4 G6
Tregenna Cnwll 3 M5
Tregeseal Cnwll 2 B7
Tregew Cnwll 3 L7
Tre-Gibbon Rhondd 30 C3
Tregidden Cnwll 3 K9
Tregiskey Cnwll 3 Q4
Treglemais Pembks 40 F5
Tregole Cnwll 5 K2
Tregolls Cnwll 3 J6
Tregonce Cnwll 4 E7
Tregonetha Cnwll 4 F9
Tregonning & Gwinear Mining District Cnwll 2 F7
Tregony Cnwll 3 N5
Tregoodwell Cnwll 5 J5
Tregorrick Cnwll 3 Q3
Tregoss Cnwll 4 F9
Tregoyd Powys 44 H7
Tregrehan Mills Cnwll 3 Q3
Tre-groes Cerdgn 42 H6
Tregullon Cnwll 4 H9
Tregunna Cnwll 4 F7
Tregunnon Cnwll 5 L5
Tregurrian Cnwll 4 D8
Tregynon Powys 55 P5
Tre-gynwr Carmth 42 H11
Trehafod Rhondd 30 D6
Trehan Cnwll 5 Q10
Treharris Myr Td 30 E5
Treharrock Cnwll 4 G6
Trehemborne Cnwll 4 D7
Treherbert Carmth 43 L5
Treherbert Rhondd 29 P5
Trehunist Cnwll 5 N9
Trekenner Cnwll 5 N6
Treknow Cnwll 4 H4
Trelan Cnwll 3 J10
Trelash Cnwll 5 K3
Trelassick Cnwll 3 M3
Trelawne Cnwll 5 L11
Trelawnyd Flints 80 F9
Treleague Cnwll 3 K9
Treleaver Cnwll 3 K10
Trelech Carmth 41 Q4
Trelech a'r Betws Carmth 42 F9
Treleddyd-fawr Pembks 40 E5
Trelew Cnwll 3 L6
Trelewis Myr Td 30 F5
Treligga Cnwll 4 G5
Trelights Cnwll 4 F6
Trelill Cnwll 4 G6
Trelinnoe Cnwll 5 N5
Trelion Cnwll 3 N3
Trelissick Cnwll 3 L6
Trellech Mons 31 P3
Trelleck Grange Mons 31 N4
Trelogan Flints 80 G8
Trelow Cnwll 4 E8
Trelowarren Cnwll 3 J9
Trelowia Cnwll 5 M10
Treluggan Cnwll 3 M6
Trelystan Powys 56 D4
Tremadog Gwynd 67 K7
Tremail Cnwll 5 K4
Tremain Cerdgn 42 D5
Tremaine Cnwll 5 L4
Tremar Cnwll 5 M8
Trematon Cnwll 5 P10
Trembraze Cnwll 5 M8
Tremeirchion Denbgs 80 F10
Tremethick Cross Cnwll 2 C7
Tremore Cnwll 4 G9
Tre-Mostyn Flints 80 G9
Trenance Cnwll 3 L9
Trenance Cnwll 4 D8
Trenance Cnwll 4 E7
Trenarren Cnwll 3 Q4
Trench Wrekin 57 M2
Trench Green Oxon 35 J9
Trendeal Cnwll 3 M3
Trendrine Cnwll 2 D6
Treneague Cnwll 4 F7
Trenear Cnwll 2 H7
Treneglos Cnwll 5 L4
Trenerth Cnwll 2 G6
Trenewan Cnwll 5 K11
Trenewth Cnwll 4 H6
Trengune Cnwll 5 K3
Treninnick Cnwll 4 C9
Trenowah Cnwll 4 B10
Trenoweth Cnwll 3 K7
Trent Dorset 19 Q11
Trentham C Stke 70 F6
Trentishoe Devon 17 L2
Trentlock Derbys 72 D4
Trent Port Lincs 85 P4
Trent Vale C Stke 70 F6
Trenwheal Cnwll 2 G7
Treoes V Glam 29 P9
Treorchy Rhondd 30 C5
Trequite Cnwll 4 G6
Tre'r-ddol Cerdgn 54 F6
Trerhyngyll V Glam 30 D9
Trerulefoot Cnwll 5 N10
Tresaith Cerdgn 42 E4
Tresawle Cnwll 3 M4
Tresco IoS 2 b2
Trescott Staffs 58 C5
Trescowe Cnwll 2 F7
Tresean Cnwll 4 B10
Tresham Gloucs 32 E6
Treshnish Isles Ag & B 136 G7
Tresillian Cnwll 3 M4
Tresinney Cnwll 5 J5
Treskinnick Cross Cnwll 5 L2
Tresmeer Cnwll 5 L4
Tresparrett Cnwll 5 J3
Tressait P & K 141 K5
Tresta Shet 169 q8
Tresta Shet 169 t4
Treswell Notts 85 N5
Treswithian Cnwll 2 G5
Tre Taliesin Cerdgn 54 F6
Trethevey Cnwll 4 H4
Trethewey Cnwll 2 B9
Trethomas Caerph 30 G7
Trethosa Cnwll 3 N3
Trethurgy Cnwll 4 G10
Tretio Pembks 40 E5
Tretire Herefs 45 Q10
Tretower Powys 44 H10
Treuddyn Flints 69 J3
Trevadlock Cnwll 5 M6
Trevalga Cnwll 4 H3
Trevalyn Wrexhm 69 L3
Trevanger Cnwll 4 F6
Trevanson Cnwll 4 F7
Trevarrack Cnwll 2 D7
Trevarren Cnwll 4 E9
Trevarrian Cnwll 4 D8
Trevarrick Cnwll 3 P5
Trevarth Cnwll 3 J5
Trevaughan Carmth 41 P7
Tre-vaughan Carmth 42 G10
Treveal Cnwll 2 D5
Treveal Cnwll 4 B10
Treveighan Cnwll 4 H6
Trevellas Downs Cnwll 3 J3
Trevelmond Cnwll 5 L9
Trevemper Cnwll 4 C10
Treveor Cnwll 3 P5
Treverbyn Cnwll 3 M4
Treverbyn Cnwll 4 G10
Treverva Cnwll 3 K7
Trevescan Cnwll 2 B9
Trevethin Torfn 31 J4
Trevia Cnwll 4 H5
Trevigro Cnwll 5 N8
Trevilla Cnwll 3 L6
Trevilson Cnwll 4 C10
Treviscoe Cnwll 4 E10
Treviskey Cnwll 3 N5
Trevithick Cnwll 3 P4
Trevithick Cnwll 4 D9
Trevoll Cnwll 4 C10
Trevone Cnwll 4 D6
Trevor Wrexhm 69 J6
Trevorgans Cnwll 2 C8
Trevorrick Cnwll 4 E7
Trevose Cnwll 4 D6
Trew Cnwll 2 G8
Trewalder Cnwll 4 H5
Trewalkin Powys 44 H8
Trewarmett Cnwll 4 H4
Trewassa Cnwll 5 J4
Trewavas Cnwll 2 F8
Trewavas Mining District Cnwll 2 F8
Treween Cnwll 5 L5
Trewellard Cnwll 2 B7
Trewen Cnwll 5 M5
Trewennack Cnwll 2 H8
Trewent Pembks 41 K11
Trewern Powys 56 D2
Trewetha Cnwll 4 G5
Trewethern Cnwll 4 G6
Trewidland Cnwll 5 M10
Trewillis Cnwll 3 K10
Trewint Cnwll 5 L5
Trewint Cnwll 5 M9
Trewithian Cnwll 3 M6
Trewoodloe Cnwll 5 N7
Trewoon Cnwll 2 H10
Trewoon Cnwll 3 P3
Treworga Cnwll 3 M5
Treworgan Cnwll 3 L4
Treworlas Cnwll 3 M6
Treworld Cnwll 5 J3
Treworthal Cnwll 3 M6
Tre-wyn Mons 45 L10
Treyarnon Cnwll 4 D7
Treyford W Susx 23 M11
Trickett's Cross Dorset 13 J4
Triermain Cumb 111 L7
Triffleton Pembks 41 J6
Trillacott Cnwll 5 M4
Trimdon Dur 104 C4
Trimdon Colliery Dur 104 C3
Trimdon Grange Dur 104 C3
Trimingham Norfk 77 K4
Trimley Lower Street Suffk 53 N4
Trimley St Martin Suffk 53 N4
Trimley St Mary Suffk 53 N4
Trimpley Worcs 57 P9
Trimsaran Carmth 28 E4
Trims Green Herts 51 L7
Trimstone Devon 17 J3
Trinafour P & K 140 H5
Trinant Caerph 30 H5
Tring Herts 35 P2
Tringford Herts 35 P2
Tring Wharf Herts 35 P2
Trinity Angus 143 L5
Trinity Jersey 11 b1
Trinity Gask P & K 134 B4
Triscombe Somset 18 G7
Trislaig Highld 139 K3
Trispen Cnwll 3 L3
Tritlington Nthumb 113 K2
Troan Cnwll 4 D10
Trochry P & K 141 N9
Troedrhiwfuwch Caerph 30 F4
Troedyraur Cerdgn 42 F5
Troedyrhiw Myr Td 30 E4
Trofarth Conwy 80 B10
Trois Bois Jersey 11 b1
Troon Cnwll 2 H6
Troon S Ayrs 125 J11
Tropical World Roundhay Park Leeds 91 J3
Trossachs Stirlg 132 G6
Trossachs Pier Stirlg 132 F6
Troston Suffk 64 B7
Troswell Cnwll 5 M3
Trotshill Worcs 46 G3
Trottiscliffe Kent 37 P8
Trotton W Susx 23 M10
Troughend Nthumb 112 C2
Trough Gate Lancs 89 P6
Troutbeck Cumb 101 L5
Troutbeck Cumb 101 M10
Troutbeck Bridge Cumb 101 M10
Troway Derbys 84 E5
Trowbridge Wilts 20 G3
Trowell Notts 72 D3
Trowell Services Notts 72 D2
Trowle Common Wilts 20 F3
Trowley Bottom Herts 50 C8
Trowse Newton Norfk 77 J10
Troy Leeds 90 G3
Trudoxhill Somset 20 D6
Trull Somset 18 H10
Trumfleet Donc 91 Q8
Trumpan Highld 152 C5
Trumpet Herefs 46 C7
Trumpington Cambs 62 F10
Trumpsgreen Surrey 35 Q11
Trunch Norfk 77 K5
Trunnah Lancs 88 C2
Truro Cnwll 3 L5
Truscott Cnwll 5 M4
Trusham Devon 9 L8
Trusley Derbys 71 P7
Trusthorpe Lincs 87 P4
Trysull Staffs 58 C6
Tubney Oxon 34 D5
Tuckenhay Devon 7 L7
Tuckhill Shrops 57 P7
Tuckingmill Cnwll 2 H5
Tuckingmill Wilts 20 H9
Tuckton BCP 13 K6
Tucoyse Cnwll 3 P4
Tuddenham Suffk 53 L2
Tuddenham Suffk 63 M6
Tudeley Kent 37 P11
Tudhoe Dur 103 Q3
Tudorville Herefs 46 A10
Tudweiliog Gwynd 66 C7
Tuesley Surrey 23 Q6
Tuffley Gloucs 32 F2
Tufton Hants 22 E5
Tufton Pembks 41 K5
Tugby Leics 73 K10
Tugford Shrops 57 K7
Tughall Nthumb 119 P5
Tullibody Clacks 133 P8
Tullich Abers 150 B8
Tullich Highld 147 Q2
Tullich Highld 156 F2
Tulliemet P & K 141 P7
Tulloch Abers 159 K11
Tullochgorm Ag & B 131 K8
Tulloch Station Highld 147 K11
Tullymurdoch P & K 142 B7
Tullynessle Abers 150 F4

Tulse Hill Gt Lon ... 36 H6
Tumble Carmth ... 28 F2
Tumbler's Green Essex ... 52 B6
Tumby Lincs ... 86 H9
Tumby Woodside Lincs ... 87 J9
Tummel Bridge P & K ... 141 J6
Tunbridge Wells Kent ... 25 N3
Tundergarth D & G ... 110 C4
Tunga W Isls ... 168 j4
Tungate Norfk ... 77 K6
Tunley BaNES ... 20 C3
Tunstall C Stke ... 70 F4
Tunstall E R Yk ... 93 P4
Tunstall Kent ... 38 E9
Tunstall Lancs ... 95 N6
Tunstall N York ... 103 P10
Tunstall Norfk ... 77 N10
Tunstall Staffs ... 70 D9
Tunstall Suffk ... 65 M10
Tunstall Sundld ... 113 N10
Tunstead Derbys ... 83 P10
Tunstead Norfk ... 77 K7
Tunstead Milton Derbys ... 83 M8
Tunworth Hants ... 23 J5
Tupsley Herefs ... 45 Q6
Turgis Green Hants ... 23 J3
Turkdean Gloucs ... 47 M11
Turleigh Wilts ... 20 F2
Turleygreen Shrops ... 57 P7
Turn Lancs ... 89 N7
Turnastone Herefs ... 45 M7
Turnberry S Ayrs ... 114 D6
Turnchapel C Plym ... 6 D7
Turnditch Derbys ... 71 P5
Turner Green Lancs ... 89 J4
Turner's Green E Susx ... 25 P7
Turner's Green Warwks ... 59 J11
Turners Hill W Susx ... 24 H3
Turners Puddle Dorset ... 12 D6
Turnford Herts ... 51 J10
Turnhouse C Edin ... 127 M3
Turnworth Dorset ... 12 D3
Turriff Abers ... 158 H7
Turton Bottoms Bl w D ... 89 L7
Turves Cambs ... 74 F11
Turvey Bed ... 49 P4
Turville Bucks ... 35 L6
Turville Heath Bucks ... 35 K6
Turweston Bucks ... 48 H7
Tushielaw Inn Border ... 117 L7
Tutbury Staffs ... 71 N9
Tutnall Worcs ... 58 E10
Tutshill Gloucs ... 31 P6
Tuttington Norfk ... 77 J6
Tutts Clump W Berk ... 34 G10
Tutwell Cnwll ... 5 P6
Tuxford Notts ... 85 M6
Twatt Ork ... 169 b4
Twatt Shet ... 169 q8
Twechar E Duns ... 126 B2
Tweedbank Border ... 117 Q4
Tweedmouth Nthumb ... 129 P9
Tweedsmuir Border ... 116 G6
Twelveheads Cnwll ... 3 K5
Twelve Oaks E Susx ... 25 Q6
Twemlow Green Ches E ... 82 G11
Twenty Lincs ... 74 C6
Twerton BaNES ... 20 D2
Twickenham Gt Lon ... 36 E6
Twigworth Gloucs ... 46 F10
Twineham W Susx ... 24 G7
Twineham Green W Susx ... 24 G6
Twinhoe BaNES ... 20 E3
Twinstead Essex ... 52 E4
Twitchen Devon ... 17 P5
Twitchen Shrops ... 56 F9
Twitham Kent ... 39 N10
Two Bridges Devon ... 6 H4
Two Dales Derbys ... 84 C8
Two Gates Staffs ... 59 K4
Two Mile Ash W Susx ... 24 D5
Two Mile Oak Cross Devon ... 7 L5
Two Pots Devon ... 17 J3
Two Waters Herts ... 50 C9
Twycross Leics ... 72 A10
Twycross Zoo Leics ... 59 M3
Twyford Bucks ... 49 J9
Twyford Hants ... 22 E10
Twyford Leics ... 73 J8
Twyford Lincs ... 73 N6
Twyford Norfk ... 76 E7
Twyford Wokham ... 35 L9
Twyford Common Herefs ... 45 Q7
Twyn-carno Caerph ... 30 F3
Twynholm D & G ... 108 E10
Twyning Green Gloucs ... 46 H7
Twynllanan Carmth ... 43 Q10
Twyn-yr-Odyn V Glam ... 30 F10
Twyn-y-Sheriff Mons ... 31 M3
Twywell Nhants ... 61 L5
Tyberton Herefs ... 45 M7
Tyburn Birm ... 58 H6
Tycroes Carmth ... 28 H2
Ty Croes IoA ... 78 E10
Tycrwyn Powys ... 68 F11
Tydd Gote Lincs ... 75 J7
Tydd St Giles Cambs ... 74 H7
Tydd St Mary Lincs ... 74 H7
Tye Hants ... 15 K6
Tye Green Essex ... 51 M6
Tye Green Essex ... 51 N3
Tye Green Essex ... 52 C7
Tyersal C Brad ... 90 F4
Tyldesley Wigan ... 82 E4
Tyler Hill Kent ... 39 K9
Tylers Green Bucks ... 35 P6
Tyler's Green Essex ... 51 M9
Tylers Green Surrey ... 37 J10
Tylorstown Rhondd ... 30 D5
Tylwch Powys ... 55 M8
Ty-nant Conwy ... 68 C6
Ty-nant Gwynd ... 68 B9
Tyncelyn Cerdgn ... 43 M2
Tyndrum Stirlg ... 139 Q11
Ty'n-dwr Denbgs ... 68 H6
Tyneham Dorset ... 12 E8
Tynemouth N Tyne ... 113 N7
Tyne Tunnel S Tyne ... 113 M7
Tynewydd Rhondd ... 29 P5
Tyninghame E Loth ... 128 G4
Tynron D & G ... 115 R9
Ty'n-y-bryn Rhondd ... 30 D7
Ty'n-y-coedcae Caerph ... 30 G7
Tynygongl IoA ... 79 J8
Tynygraig Cerdgn ... 43 F11

Ty'n-y-Groes Conwy ... 79 P10
Tyn-y-nant Rhondd ... 30 E7
Tyrie Abers ... 159 M5
Tyringham M Keyn ... 49 N5
Tyseley Birm ... 58 H8
Tythegston Brdgnd ... 29 N9
Tytherington Ches E ... 83 K9
Tytherington S Glos ... 32 C7
Tytherington Somset ... 20 E6
Tytherington Wilts ... 20 H6
Tytherleigh Devon ... 10 G4
Tytherton Lucas Wilts ... 32 H10
Tyttenhanger Herts ... 50 E9
Tywardreath Cnwll ... 4 H11
Tywardreath Highway Cnwll ... 4 H10
Tywyn Conwy ... 79 P9
Tywyn Gwynd ... 54 D4

U

Ubbeston Green Suffk ... 65 L7
Ubley BaNES ... 19 P3
Uckerby N York ... 103 P10
Uckfield E Susx ... 25 L6
Uckinghall Worcs ... 46 G7
Uckington Gloucs ... 46 H10
Uckington Shrops ... 57 K2
Uddingston S Lans ... 126 B5
Uddington S Lans ... 116 B4
Udimore E Susx ... 26 E8
Udny Green Abers ... 151 M2
Udny Station Abers ... 151 N3
Uffcott Wilts ... 33 M9
Uffculme Devon ... 9 Q2
Uffington Lincs ... 73 R9
Uffington Oxon ... 34 B7
Uffington Shrops ... 57 J2
Ufford C Pete ... 74 A10
Ufford Suffk ... 65 K11
Ufton Warwks ... 48 C2
Ufton Nervet W Berk ... 34 H11
Ugadale Ag & B ... 120 E6
Ugborough Devon ... 6 H7
Uggeshall Suffk ... 65 N5
Ugglebarnby N York ... 105 N9
Ughill Sheff ... 84 C2
Ugley Essex ... 51 M5
Ugley Green Essex ... 51 M5
Ugthorpe N York ... 105 L8
Uibhist A Deas W Isls ... 168 d14
Uibhist A Tuath W Isls ... 168 c10
Uig Ag & B ... 136 F5
Uig Highld ... 152 B7
Uig Highld ... 152 F5
Uig W Isls ... 168 f4
Uigshader Highld ... 152 G8
Uisken Ag & B ... 137 K12
Ulbster Highld ... 167 P8
Ulcat Row Cumb ... 101 M6
Ulceby Lincs ... 87 M6
Ulceby N Linc ... 93 K8
Ulceby Skitter N Linc ... 93 K7
Ulcombe Kent ... 26 D2
Uldale Cumb ... 100 H3
Uley Gloucs ... 32 E5
Ulgham Nthumb ... 113 K2
Ullapool Highld ... 161 J8
Ullenhall Warwks ... 58 H11
Ullenwood Gloucs ... 46 H11
Ulleskelf N York ... 91 N3
Ullesthorpe Leics ... 60 B3
Ulley Rothm ... 84 G3
Ullingswick Herefs ... 46 A5
Ullinish Lodge Hotel Highld ... 152 E10
Ullock Cumb ... 100 E6
Ullswater Cumb ... 101 M6
Ullswater Steamers Cumb ... 101 L7
Ulnes Walton Lancs ... 88 G7
Ulpha Cumb ... 94 D2
Ulpha Cumb ... 95 K4
Ulrome E R Yk ... 99 P9
Ulsta Shet ... 169 r5
Ulting Wick Essex ... 52 D10
Ulva Ag & B ... 137 K4
Ulverley Green Solhll ... 58 H8
Ulverston Cumb ... 94 F5
Ulwell Dorset ... 12 H8
Ulzieside D & G ... 115 Q6
Umberleigh Devon ... 17 L7
Unapool Highld ... 164 F10
Underbarrow Cumb ... 95 K2
Under Burnmouth Border ... 111 J4
Undercliffe C Brad ... 90 F4
Underdale Shrops ... 57 J2
Underling Green Kent ... 26 C2
Underriver Kent ... 37 N10
Underwood Newpt ... 31 L7
Underwood Notts ... 84 G10
Undley Suffk ... 63 L4
Undy Mons ... 31 M7
Union Mills IoM ... 80 e6
Union Street E Susx ... 26 B5
Unst Shet ... 169 s3
Unstone Derbys ... 84 E5
Unstone Green Derbys ... 84 E5
Unthank Cumb ... 101 N3
Unthank Cumb ... 102 B2
Unthank Cumb ... 110 G11
Unthank Derbys ... 84 D5
Unthank Nthumb ... 129 P10
Upavon Wilts ... 21 M4
Up Cerne Dorset ... 11 P4
Upchurch Kent ... 38 D8
Upcott Devon ... 17 P6
Upcott Herefs ... 45 L4
Upend Cambs ... 63 M9
Up Exe Devon ... 9 M4
Upgate Norfk ... 76 G8
Upgate Street Norfk ... 64 F3
Upgate Street Norfk ... 65 K3
Uphall Dorset ... 11 M4
Uphall W Loth ... 127 K3
Upham Devon ... 9 L3
Upham Hants ... 22 F10
Uphampton Herefs ... 45 M2
Uphampton Worcs ... 46 F2
Uphill N Som ... 19 K3
Up Holland Lancs ... 88 G9
Uplawmoor E Rens ... 125 L6
Upleadon Gloucs ... 46 E9
Upleatham R & Cl ... 104 H7
Uplees Kent ... 38 H9
Uploders Dorset ... 11 L6
Uplowman Devon ... 18 D11

Uplyme Devon ... 10 G6
Up Marden W Susx ... 15 L4
Upminster Gt Lon ... 37 N3
Up Mudford Somset ... 19 Q11
Up Nately Hants ... 23 J4
Upottery Devon ... 10 E3
Upper Affcot Shrops ... 56 G7
Upper Arley Worcs ... 57 P8
Upper Arncott Oxon ... 48 H11
Upper Astrop Nhants ... 48 F7
Upper Badcall Highld ... 164 E8
Upper Basildon W Berk ... 34 G9
Upper Batley Kirk ... 90 G5
Upper Beeding W Susx ... 24 E8
Upper Benefield Nhants ... 61 L3
Upper Bentley Worcs ... 58 E11
Upper Bighouse Highld ... 166 E5
Upper Birchwood Derbys ... 84 F9
Upper Boat Rhondd ... 30 F7
Upper Boddington Nhants ... 48 E4
Upper Borth Cerdgn ... 54 E7
Upper Brailes Warwks ... 48 B7
Upper Breinton Herefs ... 45 P6
Upper Broadheath Worcs ... 46 F3
Upper Broughton Notts ... 72 H5
Upper Bucklebury W Berk ... 34 F11
Upper Burgate Hants ... 21 N11
Upper Bush Medway ... 37 Q7
Upperby Cumb ... 110 H10
Upper Caldecote C Beds ... 61 Q11
Upper Canada N Som ... 19 L3
Upper Canterton Hants ... 21 N2
Upper Catesby Nhants ... 60 B9
Upper Catshill Worcs ... 58 E10
Upper Chapel Powys ... 44 E6
Upper Cheddon Somset ... 18 H9
Upper Chicksgrove Wilts ... 21 J9
Upper Chute Wilts ... 21 Q4
Upper Clapton Gt Lon ... 36 H3
Upper Clatford Hants ... 22 C6
Upper Coberley Gloucs ... 47 J11
Upper Cotton Staffs ... 71 K5
Upper Cound Shrops ... 57 K3
Upper Cudworth Barns ... 91 K9
Upper Cumberworth Kirk ... 90 G9
Upper Dallachy Moray ... 157 R5
Upper Deal Kent ... 39 Q11
Upper Dean Bed ... 61 M7
Upper Denby Kirk ... 90 G9
Upper Denton Cumb ... 111 M7
Upper Dicker E Susx ... 25 N9
Upper Dinchope Shrops ... 56 H8
Upper Dounreay Highld ... 166 H3
Upper Dovercourt Essex ... 53 M5
Upper Drumbane Stirlg ... 133 K6
Upper Dunsforth N York ... 97 P8
Upper Eashing Surrey ... 23 Q6
Upper Eathie Highld ... 156 D5
Upper Egleton Herefs ... 46 B6
Upper Elkstone Staffs ... 71 K3
Upper Ellastone Staffs ... 71 L6
Upper End Derbys ... 83 N9
Upper Enham Hants ... 22 C4
Upper Farmcote Shrops ... 57 P6
Upper Farringdon Hants ... 23 K7
Upper Framilode Gloucs ... 32 E2
Upper Froyle Hants ... 23 L6
Upperglen Highld ... 152 E7
Upper Godney Somset ... 19 N6
Upper Gravenhurst C Beds ... 50 D3
Upper Green Mons ... 45 M11
Upper Green Suffk ... 63 M8
Upper Green W Berk ... 22 C2
Upper Grove Common Herefs ... R9
Upper Hackney Derbys ... 84 C8
Upper Hale Surrey ... 23 M5
Upper Halliford Surrey ... 36 C7
Upper Halling Medway ... 37 Q8
Upper Hambleton Rutlnd ... 73 N9
Upper Harbledown Kent ... 39 K10
Upper Hardres Court Kent ... 39 L11
Upper Hardwick Herefs ... 45 N3
Upper Hartfield E Susx ... 25 L4
Upper Hartshay Derbys ... 84 E10
Upper Hatherley Gloucs ... 46 H10
Upper Hatton Staffs ... 70 E7
Upper Haugh Rothm ... 91 L11
Upper Hayton Shrops ... 57 J8
Upper Heaton Kirk ... 90 F7
Upper Helmsley N York ... 98 D9
Upper Hergest Herefs ... 45 K4
Upper Heyford Nhants ... 60 E9
Upper Heyford Oxon ... 48 E9
Upper Hill Herefs ... 45 P4
Upper Hockenden Kent ... 37 M7
Upper Hopton Kirk ... 90 F7
Upper Howsell Worcs ... 46 E5
Upper Hulme Staffs ... 71 J2
Upper Ifold Surrey ... 24 B4
Upper Inglesham Swindn ... 33 P5
Upper Kilcott Gloucs ... 32 E7
Upper Killay Swans ... 28 G6
Upper Kinchrackine Ag & B ... 131 P2
Upper Knockando Moray ... 157 M9
Upper Lambourn W Berk ... 34 B8
Upper Landywood Staffs ... 58 E3
Upper Langford N Som ... 19 N3
Upper Langwith Derbys ... 84 H7
Upper Largo Fife ... 135 L7
Upper Leigh Staffs ... 71 J7
Upper Littleton N Som ... 19 Q2
Upper Lochton Abers ... 150 H8
Upper Longdon Staffs ... 58 G2
Upper Ludstone Shrops ... 57 Q5
Upper Lybster Highld ... 167 N7
Upper Lydbrook Gloucs ... 46 B11
Upper Lyde Herefs ... 45 P6
Upper Lye Herefs ... 56 F11
Upper Maes-coed Herefs ... 45 L8
Upper Marham Norfk ... 75 P9
Upper Midhope Sheff ... 90 G11
Uppermill Oldham ... 90 B9
Upper Milton Worcs ... 57 Q10
Upper Minety Wilts ... 33 K6
Upper Moor Worcs ... 47 J5
Upper Moor Side Leeds ... 90 G4
Upper Mulben Moray ... 157 R7
Upper Netchwood Shrops ... 57 L6
Upper Nobut Staffs ... 71 J7
Upper Norwood W Susx ... 23 P11
Upper Oddington Gloucs ... 47 P9
Upper Padley Derbys ... 84 B5
Upper Pennington Hants ... 13 P5
Upper Pollicott Bucks ... 35 K2
Upper Poppleton C York ... 98 B10

Upper Quinton Warwks ... 47 N5
Upper Ratley Hants ... 22 B10
Upper Rissington Gloucs ... 47 P11
Upper Rochford Worcs ... 57 L11
Upper Ruscoe D & G ... 108 C8
Upper Sapey Herefs ... 46 C2
Upper Saxondale Notts ... 72 H3
Upper Seagry Wilts ... 32 H8
Upper Shelton C Beds ... 49 Q6
Upper Sheringham Norfk ... 76 G3
Upper Skelmorlie N Ayrs ... 124 G4
Upper Slaughter Gloucs ... 47 N10
Upper Soudley Gloucs ... 32 C2
Upper Spond Herefs ... 45 L4
Upper Standen Kent ... 27 M3
Upper Staploe Bed ... 61 P9
Upper Stoke Norfk ... 77 K11
Upper Stondon C Beds ... 50 D3
Upper Stowe Nhants ... 60 D9
Upper Street Hants ... 21 N11
Upper Street Norfk ... 64 H6
Upper Street Norfk ... 77 L8
Upper Street Norfk ... 77 M8
Upper Street Suffk ... 53 K5
Upper Street Suffk ... 53 N10
Upper Street Suffk ... 64 G11
Upper Strensham Worcs ... 46 G7
Upper Sundon C Beds ... 50 B5
Upper Swell Gloucs ... 47 N9
Upper Tankersley Barns ... 91 J11
Upper Tean Staffs ... 71 J7
Upperthong Kirk ... 90 E9
Upperthorpe Derbys ... 84 G4
Upperthorpe N Linc ... 92 C10
Upperton W Susx ... 23 Q10
Uppertown Derbys ... 71 N4
Uppertown Dur ... 103 L3
Uppertown Highld ... 167 Q1
Upper Town N Som ... 31 P11
Upper Town Suffk ... 64 C8
Upper Tumble Carmth ... 28 F2
Upper Tysoe Warwks ... 48 B6
Upper Ufford Suffk ... 65 K11
Upperup Gloucs ... 33 K5
Upper Upham Wilts ... 33 P9
Upper Upnor Medway ... 38 C7
Upper Victoria Angus ... 143 J10
Upper Vobster Somset ... 20 D5
Upper Wardington Oxon ... 48 E5
Upper Weald M Keyn ... 49 M7
Upper Weedon Nhants ... 60 D9
Upper Welland Worcs ... 46 E6
Upper Wellingham E Susx ... 25 K8
Upper Weston BaNES ... 32 D11
Upper Weybread Suffk ... 65 J6
Upper Wick Worcs ... 46 F4
Upper Wield Hants ... 22 H7
Upper Winchendon Bucks ... 35 K2
Upperwood Derbys ... 84 C9
Upper Woodford Wilts ... 21 M7
Upper Woolhampton W Berk ... 34 G11
Upper Wootton Hants ... 22 G4
Upper Wraxall Wilts ... 32 F10
Upper Wyche Worcs ... 46 E6
Uppincott Devon ... 9 M3
Uppingham Rutlnd ... 73 M11
Uppington Dorset ... 12 H3
Uppington Shrops ... 57 K3
Upsall N York ... 97 Q3
Upsettlington Border ... 129 M10
Upshire Essex ... 51 K10
Up Somborne Hants ... 22 C8
Upstreet Kent ... 39 M9
Up Sydling Dorset ... 11 N4
Upthorpe Suffk ... 64 D7
Upton Bucks ... 35 L2
Upton C Pete ... 74 B10
Upton Cambs ... 61 Q5
Upton Ches W ... 81 N11
Upton Cnwll ... 7 M7
Upton Cnwll ... 16 C11
Upton Cumb ... 101 K3
Upton Devon ... 7 J10
Upton Devon ... 10 B4
Upton Dorset ... 12 B8
Upton Dorset ... 12 G6
Upton E R Yk ... 99 N10
Upton Halton ... 81 P7
Upton Hants ... 22 C11
Upton Hants ... 22 C3
Upton Leics ... 72 B11
Upton Lincs ... 85 Q3
Upton Nhants ... 60 F9
Upton Norfk ... 77 M9
Upton Notts ... 85 M10
Upton Notts ... 85 M5
Upton Oxon ... 33 P2
Upton Oxon ... 34 F7
Upton Pembks ... 41 K10
Upton R & Cl ... 105 K7
Upton Slough ... 35 Q9
Upton Somset ... 18 C9
Upton Somset ... 19 N9
Upton Wakefd ... 91 M8
Upton Warwks ... 47 M3
Upton Wilts ... 20 G8
Upton Wirral ... 81 K7
Upton Bishop Herefs ... 46 C9
Upton Cheyney S Glos ... 32 C10
Upton Cressett Shrops ... 57 M6
Upton Crews Herefs ... 46 B9
Upton Cross Cnwll ... 5 M7
Upton End C Beds ... 50 D4
Upton Grey Hants ... 23 J5
Upton Heath Ches W ... 81 N11
Upton Hellions Devon ... 9 K4
Upton Lovell Wilts ... 20 H6
Upton Magna Shrops ... 57 K2
Upton Noble Somset ... 20 D7
Upton Pyne Devon ... 9 M5
Upton St Leonards Gloucs ... 46 G11
Upton Scudamore Wilts ... 20 G5
Upton Snodsbury Worcs ... 46 H4
Upton Towans Cnwll ... 2 F5
Upton-upon-Severn Worcs ... 46 F6
Upton Warren Worcs ... 58 D11
Upwaltham W Susx ... 23 P4
Upware Cambs ... 62 H6
Upwell Norfk ... 75 J9
Upwey Dorset ... 11 P7
Upwick Green Herts ... 51 L6
Upwood Cambs ... 62 C4

Urchfont Wilts ... 21 K3
Urdimarsh Herefs ... 45 Q5
Ure Bank N York ... 97 M6
Urlay Nook S on T ... 104 D8
Urmston Traffd ... 82 G6
Urpeth Dur ... 113 L10
Urquhart Moray ... 157 P5
Urquhart Castle Highld ... 147 N2
Urra N York ... 104 G10
Urray Highld ... 155 P7
Uryside Abers ... 151 K3
Usan Angus ... 143 N7
Ushaw Moor Dur ... 103 P2
Usk Mons ... 31 L4
Usselby Lincs ... 86 E2
Usworth Sundld ... 113 M9
Utkinton Ches W ... 82 B11
Utley C Brad ... 90 D2
Uton Devon ... 9 K5
Utterby Lincs ... 87 K2
Uttoxeter Staffs ... 71 K8
Uwchmynydd Gwynd ... 66 B9
Uxbridge Gt Lon ... 36 C4
Uyeasound Shet ... 169 s3
Uzmaston Pembks ... 41 J8

V

Vale Guern ... 10 c1
Valley IoA ... 78 D9
Valley End Surrey ... 23 Q2
Valley Truckle Cnwll ... 4 H5
Valtos Highld ... 153 J5
Valtos W Isls ... 168 f4
Vange Essex ... 38 B4
Varteg Torfn ... 31 J3
Vatsetter Shet ... 169 s5
Vatten Highld ... 152 D9
Vaynor Myr Td ... 30 D3
Vazon Bay Guern ... 10 b2
Veensgarth Shet ... 169 r9
Velindre Powys ... 44 H7
Vellow Somset ... 18 E7
Velly Devon ... 16 D7
Venngreen Devon ... 16 F9
Vennington Shrops ... 56 E3
Venn Ottery Devon ... 10 B6
Venny Tedburn Devon ... 9 K5
Venterdon Cnwll ... 5 P7
Ventnor IoW ... 14 G11
Venton Devon ... 6 F7
Vernham Dean Hants ... 22 B3
Vernham Street Hants ... 22 B3
Vernolds Common Shrops ... 56 H8
Verwood Dorset ... 13 J3
Veryan Cnwll ... 3 N5
Veryan Green Cnwll ... 3 N5
Vicarage Devon ... 10 E7
Vickerstown Cumb ... 94 D6
Victoria Barns ... 90 F9
Victoria Blae G ... 30 G3
Victoria Cnwll ... 4 F9
Vidlin Shet ... 169 r7
Viewfield Moray ... 157 P5
Viewpark N Lans ... 126 C5
Vigo Kent ... 37 P8
Village de Putron Guern ... 10 c2
Ville la Bas Jersey ... 11 a1
Villiaze Guern ... 10 b2
Vinehall Street E Susx ... 26 C7
Vines Cross E Susx ... 25 N7
Virginia Water Surrey ... 36 B7
Virginstow Devon ... 5 P3
Vobster Somset ... 20 D7
Voe Shet ... 169 r7
Vowchurch Herefs ... 45 M7
Vulcan Village St Hel ... 82 C6

W

Waberthwaite Cumb ... 94 C2
Wackerfield Dur ... 103 N6
Wacton Norfk ... 64 H3
Wadborough Worcs ... 46 H5
Waddesdon Bucks ... 49 K11
Waddesdon Manor Bucks ... 49 K11
Waddeton Devon ... 7 M7
Waddicar Sefton ... 81 M5
Waddingham Lincs ... 92 G11
Waddington Lancs ... 89 L2
Waddington Lincs ... 86 C8
Waddon Devon ... 9 L9
Waddon Dorset ... 11 M7
Waddon Gt Lon ... 36 H8
Wadebridge Cnwll ... 4 F7
Wadeford Somset ... 10 G2
Wadenhoe Nhants ... 61 M4
Wadesmill Herts ... 51 J9
Wadhurst E Susx ... 25 P4
Wadshelf Derbys ... 84 D6
Wadswick Wilts ... 32 F11
Wadworth Donc ... 91 P11
Waen Denbgs ... 68 C2
Waen Denbgs ... 80 G11
Waen Powys ... 68 H11
Waen Fach Powys ... 68 H11
Waen-pentir Gwynd ... 79 K11
Waen-wen Gwynd ... 79 K11
Wagbeach Shrops ... 56 F3
Wainfelin Torfn ... 31 J4
Wainfleet All Saints Lincs ... 87 N9
Wainfleet Bank Lincs ... 87 N9
Wainfleet St Mary Lincs ... 87 N9
Wainford Norfk ... 65 L3
Wainhouse Corner Cnwll ... 16 D3
Wainscott Medway ... 38 B7
Wain's Hill N Som ... 31 L10
Wainstalls Calder ... 90 C5
Waitby Cumb ... 102 E9
Waithe Lincs ... 93 N10
Wakefield Wakefd ... 91 J6
Wake Green Birm ... 58 G8
Wakehurst Place W Susx ... 24 H4
Wakerley Nhants ... 73 N11
Wakes Colne Essex ... 52 E6
Walberswick Suffk ... 65 N7
Walberton W Susx ... 15 Q5
Walbottle N u Ty ... 113 K7
Walbutt D & G ... 108 F7
Walby Cumb ... 110 H9
Walcombe Somset ... 19 Q5
Walcot Lincs ...

Walcot – West Derby 299

Walcot N Linc 92 E6
Walcot Shrops 56 E7
Walcot Shrops 57 K2
Walcot Swindn 33 N8
Walcote Leics 60 C4
Walcote Warwks 47 M3
Walcot Green Norfk 64 G5
Walcott Lincs 86 F9
Walcott Norfk 77 M5
Walden N York 96 F4
Walden Head N York 96 E4
Walden Stubbs N York 91 P7
Walderslade Medway 38 C9
Walderton W Susx 15 L4
Walditch Dorset 11 K6
Waldley Derbys 71 L7
Waldridge Dur 113 L11
Waldringfield Suffk 53 N2
Waldron E Susx 25 M7
Wales Rothm 84 G4
Wales Somset 19 Q10
Walesby Lincs 86 F2
Walesby Notts 85 L6
Walford Herefs 46 A10
Walford Herefs 56 F10
Walford Shrops 69 M10
Walford Staffs 70 E8
Walford Heath Shrops 69 M11
Walgherton Ches E 70 B5
Walgrave Nhants 60 H6
Walhampton Hants 13 P5
Walkden Salfd 82 F4
Walker N u Ty 113 L8
Walkerburn Border 117 M3
Walker Fold Lancs 89 K2
Walkeringham Notts 85 N2
Walkerith Lincs 85 N2
Walkern Herts 50 G5
Walker's Green Herefs 45 Q5
Walker's Heath Birm 58 G9
Walkerton Fife 134 G7
Walkford BCP 13 M6
Walkhampton Devon 6 E5
Walkington E R Yk 92 G3
Walkley Sheff 84 D3
Walk Mill Lancs 89 P5
Walkwood Worcs 47 K2
Wall Nthumb 112 D7
Wall Staffs 58 H3
Wallacetown S Ayrs 114 E7
Wallacetown S Ayrs 114 F3
Wallands Park E Susx 25 K8
Wallasey Wirral 81 K6
Wallasey (Kingsway) Tunnel Wirral 81 L6
Wall End Cumb 94 E4
Wall End Herefs 45 N3
Wallend Medway 38 E6
Waller's Green Herefs 46 C7
Wallhead Cumb 111 J8
Wall Heath Dudley 58 C7
Wall Houses Nthumb 112 F7
Wallingford Oxon 34 H7
Wallington Gt Lon 36 G8
Wallington Hants 14 G5
Wallington Herts 50 G4
Wallington Heath Wsall 58 E4
Wallis Pembks 41 K5
Wallisdown BCP 13 J6
Walliswood Surrey 24 D3
Walls Shet 169 p9
Wallsend N Tyne 113 L7
Wallthwaite Cumb 101 L5
Wall under Haywood Shrops 57 J6
Wallyford E Loth 128 B5
Walmer Kent 39 Q11
Walmer Bridge Lancs 88 F6
Walmersley Bury 89 N8
Walmestone Kent 39 N10
Walmley Birm 58 H6
Walmley Ash Birm 58 H6
Walmsgate Lincs 87 L5
Walney Cumb 94 D7
Walpole Somset 19 K6
Walpole Suffk 65 M7
Walpole Cross Keys Norfk 75 K7
Walpole Highway Norfk 75 K8
Walpole St Andrew Norfk 75 K7
Walpole St Peter Norfk 75 K7
Walrow Somset 19 K5
Walsall Wsall 58 F5
Walsall Wood Wsall 58 F4
Walsden Calder 89 Q6
Walsgrave on Sowe Covtry 59 N8
Walsham le Willows Suffk 64 E7
Walshaw Bury 89 M8
Walshford N York 97 P10
Walsoken Norfk 75 J8
Walston S Lans 127 K8
Walsworth Herts 50 E4
Walter's Ash Bucks 35 M5
Walters Green Kent 25 M2
Walterston V Glam 30 E10
Walterstone Herefs 45 L9
Waltham Kent 27 K2
Waltham NE Lin 93 N10
Waltham Abbey Essex 51 J10
Waltham Chase Hants 14 G4
Waltham Cross Herts 51 J10
Waltham on the Wolds Leics 73 L6
Waltham St Lawrence W & M 35 M9
Waltham's Cross Essex 51 Q4
Walthamstow Gt Lon 37 J3
Walton C Pete 74 C10
Walton Cumb 111 K8
Walton Derbys 84 E7
Walton Leeds 97 P11
Walton Leics 60 C3
Walton M Keyn 49 N7
Walton Powys 45 K3
Walton Shrops 56 H9
Walton Somset 19 N7
Walton Staffs 70 F8
Walton Staffs 70 F9
Walton Suffk 53 N4
Walton W Susx 15 M6
Walton Wakefd 91 K7
Walton Warwks 47 Q4
Walton Wrekin 69 Q11
Walton Cardiff Gloucs 46 H8
Walton East Pembks 41 K6
Walton Elm Dorset 20 E11
Walton Grounds Nhants 48 F8
Walton Highway Norfk 75 J8
Walton-in-Gordano N Som 31 M10
Walton-le-Dale Lancs 88 H5
Walton-on-Thames Surrey 36 D7
Walton-on-the-Hill Staffs 70 H10
Walton-on-the-Hill Surrey 36 F9
Walton-on-the-Naze Essex 53 N7
Walton on the Wolds Leics 72 F7
Walton-on-Trent Derbys 71 N11
Walton Park N Som 31 M10
Walton West Pembks 40 G8
Walwen Flints 80 G9
Walwen Flints 80 H10
Walwen Flints 81 J9
Walwick Nthumb 112 D6
Walworth Darltn 103 P7
Walworth Gt Lon 36 H5
Walworth Gate Darltn 103 P6
Walwyn's Castle Pembks 40 G8
Wambrook Somset 10 F3
Wampool Cumb 110 D10
Wanborough Surrey 23 P5
Wanborough Swindn 33 P8
Wandon End Herts 50 D6
Wandsworth Gt Lon 36 G6
Wangford Suffk 65 P6
Wanlip Leics 72 F8
Wanlockhead D & G 116 B8
Wannock E Susx 25 N10
Wansford C Pete 73 R11
Wansford E R Yk 99 M9
Wanshurst Green Kent 26 C2
Wanstead Gt Lon 37 K3
Wanstrow Somset 20 D6
Wanswell Gloucs 32 C4
Wantage Oxon 34 C7
Wants Green Worcs 46 E3
Wapley S Glos 32 D9
Wappenbury Warwks 59 N11
Wappenham Nhants 48 H5
Warbleton E Susx 25 P7
Warborough Oxon 34 G6
Warboys Cambs 62 D4
Warbreck Bpool 88 C3
Warbstow Cnwll 5 L3
Warburton Traffd 82 F7
Warcop Cumb 102 D7
Warden Kent 38 H7
Warden Nthumb 112 D7
Ward End Birm 58 H7
Warden Street C Beds 50 D2
Ward Green Suffk 64 E9
Ward Green Cross Lancs 89 J3
Wardhedges C Beds 50 C3
Wardington Oxon 48 E5
Wardle Ches E 69 R3
Wardle Rochdl 89 Q7
Wardley Gatesd 113 M8
Wardley Rutlnd 73 L10
Wardley Salfd 82 G4
Wardlow Derbys 83 Q10
Wardsend Ches E 83 K8
Wardy Hill Cambs 62 G4
Ware Herts 51 J8
Wareham Dorset 12 F7
Warehorne Kent 26 G5
Warenford Nthumb 119 M5
Waren Mill Nthumb 119 M4
Warenton Nthumb 119 M4
Wareside Herts 51 J7
Waresley Cambs 62 C10
Waresley Worcs 58 B10
Ware Street Kent 38 C10
Warfield Br For 35 N10
Warfleet Devon 7 M8
Wargate Lincs 74 D4
Wargrave Wokham 35 L9
Warham Herefs 45 P7
Warham Norfk 76 D3
Wark Nthumb 112 C5
Wark Nthumb 118 F3
Warkleigh Devon 17 L7
Warkton Nhants 61 J5
Warkworth Nhants 48 E6
Warkworth Nthumb 119 P9
Warlaby N York 97 M2
Warland Calder 89 Q6
Warleggan Cnwll 5 K8
Warleigh BaNES 20 E2
Warley Town Calder 90 D6
Warlingham Surrey 37 J9
Warmbrook Derbys 71 P4
Warmfield Wakefd 91 K6
Warmingham Ches E 70 C2
Warmington Nhants 61 N2
Warmington Warwks 48 D5
Warminster Wilts 20 G5
Warmley S Glos 32 C10
Warmsworth Donc 91 N10
Warmwell Dorset 12 C7
Warndon Worcs 46 G3
Warner Bros. Studio Tour Herts 50 C10
Warnford Hants 22 H10
Warnham W Susx 24 E4
Warnham Court W Susx 24 E4
Warningcamp W Susx 24 B9
Warninglid W Susx 24 F5
Warren Ches E 83 J10
Warren Pembks 40 H11
Warrenby R & Cl 104 G5
Warrenhill S Lans 116 C3
Warren Row W & M 35 M8
Warren's Green Herts 50 G5
Warren Street Kent 38 F11
Warrington M Keyn 49 N4
Warrington Warrtn 82 D7
Warriston C Edin 127 P2
Warsash Hants 14 E5
Warslow Staffs 71 K3
Warsop Vale Notts 84 H7
Warter E R Yk 98 H10
Warthermaske N York 97 K5
Warthill N York 98 D9
Wartling E Susx 25 Q9
Wartnaby Leics 73 J6
Warton Lancs 88 E5
Warton Lancs 95 K6
Warton Nthumb 119 K10
Warton Warwks 59 L4
Warwick Warwks 59 L11
Warwick Bridge Cumb 111 J9
Warwick Castle Warwks 47 Q2
Warwick-on-Eden Cumb 111 J9
Warwick Services Warwks 48 B3
Warwicksland Cumb 111 J5
Wasbister Ork 169 c3
Wasdale Head Cumb 100 G9
Wash Derbys 83 N8
Washall Green Herts 51 K4
Washaway Cnwll 4 G8
Washbourne Devon 7 K8
Washbrook Somset 19 M4
Washbrook Suffk 53 K3
Washfield Devon 18 B11
Washfold N York 103 L10
Washford Somset 18 E6
Washford Pyne Devon 9 K2
Washingborough Lincs 86 D6
Washington Sundld 113 M9
Washington W Susx 24 D8
Washington Services Gatesd 113 L9
Washwood Heath Birm 58 H7
Wasing W Berk 22 G2
Waskerley Dur 112 F11
Wasperton Warwks 47 Q3
Wasps Nest Lincs 86 E8
Wass N York 98 B5
Wast Water Cumb 100 G9
Watchet Somset 18 E6
Watchfield Oxon 33 P6
Watchfield Somset 19 K5
Watchgate Cumb 101 P11
Watchill Cumb 100 G2
Watcombe Torbay 7 N5
Watendlath Cumb 101 J7
Water Devon 9 J8
Water Lancs 89 N5
Waterbeach Cambs 62 G7
Waterbeach W Susx 15 N5
Waterbeck D & G 110 D5
Waterden Norfk 76 B4
Water Eaton Oxon 34 F2
Water Eaton Staffs 58 D2
Water End Bed 61 P10
Water End Bed 61 P11
Water End C Beds 50 C3
Waterend Cumb 100 F6
Water End E R Yk 92 C3
Water End Essex 51 N2
Water End Herts 50 B8
Water End Herts 50 F10
Waterfall Staffs 71 K4
Waterfoot Ag & B 120 F4
Waterfoot E Rens 125 P6
Waterfoot Lancs 89 N6
Waterford Herts 50 H8
Water Fryston Wakefd 91 M5
Watergate Cnwll 5 J5
Waterhead Cumb 101 L10
Waterheads Border 127 N7
Waterhouses Dur 103 N2
Waterhouses Staffs 71 K4
Wateringbury Kent 37 Q10
Waterlane Gloucs 32 H4
Waterloo Cnwll 5 J7
Waterloo Derbys 84 F8
Waterloo Herefs 45 L5
Waterloo Highld 145 L3
Waterloo N Lans 126 E7
Waterloo Norfk 77 J8
Waterloo P & K 141 Q10
Waterloo Pembks 41 J10
Waterloo Sefton 81 L5
Waterloo Cross Devon 9 Q2
Waterloo Port Gwynd 66 H2
Waterlooville Hants 15 J5
Watermead Bucks 49 M11
Watermillock Cumb 101 M6
Water Newton Cambs 74 B11
Water Orton Warwks 59 J6
Waterperry Oxon 34 H3
Waterrow Somset 18 E9
Watersfield W Susx 24 B7
Waterside Bl w D 89 L6
Waterside Bucks 35 Q4
Waterside Cumb 110 D11
Waterside Donc 91 R8
Waterside E Ayrs 114 H6
Waterside E Ayrs 125 M9
Waterside E Duns 126 B3
Water's Nook Bolton 89 K9
Waterstein Highld 152 A8
Waterstock Oxon 34 H3
Waterston Pembks 40 H9
Water Stratford Bucks 49 J8
Water Street Neath 29 M8
Waters Upton Wrekin 70 A11
Water Yeat Cumb 94 F3
Watford Herts 50 D11
Watford Nhants 60 D7
Watford Gap Services Nhants 60 D7
Wath N York 96 H7
Wath N York 97 M5
Wath upon Dearne Rothm 91 L10
Watlington Norfk 75 M8
Watlington Oxon 35 J6
Watnall Notts 84 H11
Watten Highld 167 M6
Wattisfield Suffk 64 E7
Wattisham Suffk 64 E11
Watton Dorset 11 K6
Watton E R Yk 99 L10
Watton Norfk 76 C11
Watton-at-Stone Herts 50 H7
Watton Green Norfk 76 C11
Wattons Green Essex 51 M11
Wattston N Lans 126 D3
Wattstown Rhondd 30 D6
Wattsville Caerph 30 H6
Wauldby E R Yk 92 G5
Waulkmill Abers 150 G9
Waunarlwydd Swans 28 H5
Waun Fach Powys 44 H9
Waunfawr Cerdgn 54 E8
Waunfawr Gwynd 67 J3
Waungron Swans 28 G4
Waunlwyd Blae G 30 G3
Wavendon M Keyn 49 P7
Waverbridge Cumb 110 D11
Waverton Ches W 69 N2
Waverton Cumb 110 D11
Wawne E R Yk 93 J3
Waxham Norfk 77 N6
Waxholme E R Yk 93 P5
Way Kent 39 P8
Waye Devon 7 K4
Wayford Somset 11 J3
Waytown Dorset 11 K5
Way Village Devon 9 L2
Way Wick N Som 19 L2
Weacombe Somset 18 F6
Weald Oxon 34 B4
Wealdstone Gt Lon 36 E3
Weardley Leeds 90 H2
Weare Somset 19 M4
Weare Giffard Devon 16 H7
Wearhead Dur 102 G3
Wearne Somset 19 M9
Weasdale Cumb 102 C10
Weasenham All Saints Norfk 76 A7
Weasenham St Peter Norfk 76 B7
Weaste Salfd 82 H5
Weatheroak Hill Worcs 58 G10
Weaverham Ches W 82 D10
Weaverslake Staffs 71 L11
Weaverthorpe N York 99 K6
Webbington Somset 19 L3
Webb's Heath S Glos 32 C10
Webheath Worcs 58 F11
Webton Herefs 45 N7
Wedderlairs Abers 159 L11
Wedding Hall Fold N York 96 D11
Weddington Kent 39 N10
Weddington Warwks 59 N6
Wedhampton Wilts 21 L3
Wedmore Somset 19 M5
Wednesbury Sandw 58 E5
Wednesfield Wolves 58 D4
Weecar Notts 85 P7
Weedon Bucks 49 M11
Weedon Bec Nhants 60 D9
Weedon Lois Nhants 48 H5
Weeford Staffs 58 H4
Week Devon 7 K6
Week Devon 17 K6
Week Devon 17 N8
Weeke Devon 9 J3
Weeke Hants 22 E8
Weekley Nhants 61 J4
Week St Mary Cnwll 5 L2
Weel E R Yk 93 J3
Weeley Essex 53 K7
Weeley Heath Essex 53 L7
Weem P & K 141 K8
Weeping Cross Staffs 70 G10
Weethley Warwks 47 L3
Weeting Norfk 63 N3
Weeton E R Yk 93 Q6
Weeton Lancs 88 D4
Weeton N York 97 L11
Weetwood Leeds 90 H3
Weir Lancs 89 P5
Weirbrook Shrops 69 K10
Weir Quay Devon 6 C5
Weisdale Shet 169 q8
Welborne Norfk 76 F9
Welbourn Lincs 86 C10
Welburn N York 98 E7
Welbury N York 104 C10
Welby Lincs 73 P3
Welches Dam Cambs 62 G3
Welcombe Devon 16 C8
Weldon Nhants 61 K3
Weldon Bridge Nthumb 119 M11
Welford Nhants 60 D4
Welford W Berk 34 D10
Welford-on-Avon Warwks 47 M4
Welham Leics 60 G2
Welham Notts 85 M4
Welham Bridge E R Yk 92 C4
Welham Green Herts 50 F9
Well Hants 23 L5
Well Lincs 87 M6
Well N York 97 L4
Welland Worcs 46 E6
Wellbank Angus 142 H10
Well End Bucks 35 N7
Well End Herts 50 F11
Wellesbourne Warwks 47 Q3
Wellesbourne Mountford Warwks 47 Q3
Well Head Herts 50 E5
Well Hill Kent 37 L8
Wellhouse W Berk 34 F10
Welling Gt Lon 37 L5
Wellingborough Nhants 61 J7
Wellingham Norfk 76 B7
Wellingore Lincs 86 C9
Wellington Cumb 100 E10
Wellington Herefs 45 P5
Wellington Somset 18 F10
Wellington Wrekin 57 M2
Wellington Heath Herefs 46 D6
Wellington Marsh Herefs 45 P5
Wellow BaNES 20 D3
Wellow IoW 14 C9
Wellow Notts 85 L7
Wellpond Green Herts 51 K6
Wells Somset 19 P5
Wellsborough Leics 72 B10
Wells Green Ches E 70 B4
Wells Head C Brad 90 D4
Wells-next-the-Sea Norfk 76 C3
Wellstye Green Essex 51 P7
Well Town Devon 9 M3
Welltree P & K 134 B3
Wellwood Fife 134 D10
Welney Norfk 62 H2
Welshampton Shrops 69 M7
Welsh Bicknor Herefs 46 A11
Welsh End Shrops 69 P7
Welsh Frankton Shrops 69 L8
Welsh Hook Pembks 40 H5
Welsh Newton Herefs 45 Q11
Welshpool Powys 56 C3
Welsh St Donats V Glam 30 D9
Welton Cumb 101 L2
Welton E R Yk 92 G5
Welton Lincs 86 D5
Welton Nhants 60 C7
Welton le Marsh Lincs 87 N7
Welton le Wold Lincs 87 J3
Welwick E R Yk 93 P6
Welwyn Herts 50 F7
Welwyn Garden City Herts 50 F8
Wem Shrops 69 P9
Wembdon Somset 19 J7
Wembley Gt Lon 36 E3
Wembury Devon 6 E9
Wembworthy Devon 17 M10
Wemyss Bay Inver 124 F4
Wenallt Cerdgn 54 F10
Wendens Ambo Essex 51 M3
Wendlebury Oxon 48 G11
Wendling Norfk 76 C9
Wendover Bucks 35 N3
Wendron Cnwll 2 H7
Wendron Mining District Cnwll 2 H7
Wendy Cambs 62 D11
Wenfordbridge Cnwll 4 H6
Wenhaston Suffk 65 N6
Wennington Cambs 62 B5
Wennington Gt Lon 37 M4
Wennington Lancs 95 N7
Wensley Derbys 84 C8
Wensley N York 96 G3
Wentbridge Wakefd 91 M7
Wentnor Shrops 56 F6
Wentworth Cambs 62 G5
Wentworth Rothm 91 K11
Wentworth Castle Barns 91 J10
Wenvoe V Glam 30 F10
Weobley Herefs 45 N4
Weobley Marsh Herefs 45 N4
Wepham W Susx 24 B9
Wereham Norfk 75 N10
Wergs Wolves 58 C4
Wern Gwynd 67 J7
Wern Powys 44 G11
Wern Powys 56 D2
Wern Shrops 69 J8
Werneth Low Tamesd 83 L6
Wernffrwd Swans 28 F6
Wern-Gifford Mons 45 L10
Wern-y-gaer Flints 81 J11
Werrington C Pete 74 C10
Werrington Cnwll 5 N4
Werrington Staffs 70 G5
Wervin Ches W 81 N10
Wesham Lancs 88 E4
Wessington Derbys 84 E9
West Aberthaw V Glam 30 D11
West Acre Norfk 75 Q7
West Allerdean Nthumb 129 P10
West Alvington Devon 7 J10
West Amesbury Wilts 21 M6
West Anstey Devon 17 R6
West Appleton N York 97 K2
West Ashby Lincs 87 J6
West Ashling W Susx 15 M5
West Ashton Wilts 20 G3
West Auckland Dur 103 N5
West Ayton N York 99 K4
West Bagborough Somset 18 G8
West Bank Blae G 30 H3
West Bank Halton 81 Q8
West Barkwith Lincs 86 G4
West Barnby N York 105 M8
West Barns E Loth 128 H4
West Barsham Norfk 76 C5
West Bay Dorset 11 K6
West Beckham Norfk 76 G4
West Bedfont Surrey 36 C6
Westbere Kent 39 L9
West Bergholt Essex 52 G6
West Bexington Dorset 11 L7
West Bilney Norfk 75 P7
West Blatchington Br & H 24 G9
West Boldon S Tyne 113 N8
Westborough Lincs 73 M2
Westbourne BCP 13 J6
Westbourne W Susx 15 L5
West Bourton Dorset 20 E9
West Bowling C Brad 90 F4
West Brabourne Kent 27 J3
West Bradenham Norfk 76 C10
West Bradford Lancs 89 L2
West Bradley Somset 19 Q7
West Bretton Wakefd 90 H8
West Bridgford Notts 72 F3
West Briscoe Dur 103 J7
West Bromwich Sandw 58 F6
Westbrook Kent 39 P7
Westbrook W Berk 34 D10
Westbrook Wilts 33 J11
West Buckland Devon 17 M5
West Buckland Somset 18 G10
West Burrafirth Shet 169 p8
West Burton N York 96 F3
West Burton W Susx 15 Q4
Westbury Bucks 48 H7
Westbury Shrops 56 F3
Westbury Wilts 20 G4
Westbury Leigh Wilts 20 G5
Westbury-on-Severn Gloucs 32 D2
Westbury-on-Trym Bristl 31 Q9
Westbury-sub-Mendip Somset 19 P5
West Butsfield Dur 103 M2
West Butterwick N Linc 92 D9
Westby Lancs 88 D4
West Byfleet Surrey 36 B8
West Cairngaan D & G 106 F11
West Caister Norfk 77 Q9
West Calder W Loth 127 J5
West Camel Somset 19 Q10
West Chaldon Dorset 12 C8
West Challow Oxon 34 C7
West Charleton Devon 7 K10
West Chelborough Dorset 11 L3
West Chevington Nthumb 119 P11
West Chiltington W Susx 24 C7
West Chinnock Somset 11 K2
West Chisenbury Wilts 21 M4
West Clandon Surrey 36 B10
West Cliffe Kent 27 P3
Westcliff-on-Sea Sthend 38 E4
West Clyst Devon 9 N5
West Coker Somset 11 L2
West Combe Devon 7 K6
Westcombe Somset 20 C7
West Compton Somset 19 Q6
West Compton Abbas Dorset 11 M6
Westcote Gloucs 47 P10
Westcote Barton Oxon 48 D9
Westcott Bucks 49 K11
Westcott Devon 9 P4
Westcott Surrey 36 D11
Westcott Green N York 92 A2
Westcourt Wilts 21 P2
West Cowick E R Yk 91 Q6
West Cross Swans 28 H7
West Curry Cnwll 5 M3
West Curthwaite Cumb 110 F11
Westdean E Susx 25 M11
West Dean W Susx 15 N4
West Dean Wilts 21 Q9
West Deeping Lincs 74 B9
West Derby Lpool 81 M6

300 West Dereham – Whitrigg

West Dereham Norfk 75 N10
West Ditchburn Nthumb 119 M6
West Down Devon 17 J3
Westdown Camp Wilts 21 K5
Westdowns Cnwll 4 H5
West Drayton Gt Lon 36 C5
West Drayton Notts 85 M6
West Dunnet Highld 167 M2
Wested Kent 37 M7
West Ella E R Yk 92 H5
West End Bed 49 Q4
West End Br For 35 N10
West End Caerph 30 H5
West End Cumb 110 F9
West End E R Yk 92 F4
West End E R Yk 93 L4
West End E R Yk 93 N5
Westend Gloucs 32 E3
West End Hants 14 E4
West End Hants 22 H7
West End Herts 50 G9
West End Herts 50 H9
West End Lancs 89 L5
West End Leeds 90 G3
West End Lincs 93 Q11
West End N Som 31 N11
West End N York 91 N2
West End Norfk 76 C10
West End Norfk 77 Q9
West End Oxon 34 G7
West End S Glos 32 D7
West End Somset 20 C8
West End Surrey 23 P2
West End Surrey 36 D8
West End W & M 35 M9
West End W Susx 24 F7
West End Wilts 20 H10
West End Wilts 21 J10
West End Wilts 33 J9
West End Green Hants 23 J2
Westend Town Nthumb 111 Q7
Westenhanger Kent 27 K4
Wester Aberchalder Highld 147 P3
Westerdale Highld 167 K6
Westerdale N York 105 J9
Westerfield Suffk 53 L2
Westergate W Susx 15 P5
Westerham Kent 37 K10
Westerhope N u Ty 113 J7
Westerland Devon 7 M6
Westerleigh S Glos 32 C9
Western Isles W Isls 168 f8
Wester Ochiltree W Loth 127 J3
Wester Pitkierie Fife 135 P6
Wester Ross Highld 160 F11
Westerton W Susx 15 N5
Westerton of Rossie Angus 143 M7
Westerwick Shet 169 p9
West Ewell Surrey 36 F8
West Farleigh Kent 38 B11
West Farndon Nhants 48 F4
West Felton Shrops 69 K9
Westfield BaNES 20 C4
Westfield Cumb 100 C5
Westfield E Susx 26 D8
Westfield Highld 167 J4
Westfield N Lans 126 C3
Westfield Norfk 76 D10
Westfield Surrey 36 B9
Westfield W Loth 126 G3
Westfields Dorset 12 B3
Westfields Herefs 45 P6
Westfields of Rattray P & K 142 B8
Westfield Sole Kent 38 C9
West Flotmanby N York 99 M5
Westford Somset 18 F10
Westgate Dur 102 H3
Westgate N Linc 92 C9
Westgate Norfk 76 D3
Westgate Hill C Brad 90 G5
Westgate-on-Sea Kent 39 P7
Westgate Street Norfk 76 H7
West Ginge Oxon 34 D7
West Grafton Wilts 21 P2
West Green Hants 23 K3
West Grimstead Wilts 21 P9
West Grinstead W Susx 24 E6
West Haddlesey N York 91 P5
West Haddon Nhants 60 D6
West Hagbourne Oxon 34 F7
West Hagley Worcs 58 D8
Westhall Suffk 65 N5
West Hallam Derbys 72 C2
West Hallam Common Derbys 72 C2
West Halton N Linc 92 F6
Westham Dorset 11 P9
Westham E Susx 25 P10
West Ham Gt Lon 37 J4
Westham Somset 19 M5
Westhampnett W Susx 15 N5
West Handley Derbys 84 E5
West Hanney Oxon 34 D6
West Hanningfield Essex 38 B2
West Harnham Wilts 21 M9
West Harptree BaNES 19 Q3
West Harting W Susx 23 L10
West Hatch Somset 19 J10
West Hatch Wilts 20 H9
West Haven Angus 143 K10
Westhay Somset 19 M6
Westhead Lancs 88 E9
West Head Norfk 75 L9
West Heath Birm 58 F9
West Heath Hants 22 G3
West Helmsdale Highld 163 N3
West Hendred Oxon 34 D7
West Heslerton N York 99 J5
West Hewish N Som 19 L2
Westhide Herefs 46 A6
Westhill Abers 151 L6
West Hill Devon 9 Q6
Westhill Highld 156 C9
West Hoathly W Susx 25 J4
West Holme Dorset 12 E7
Westholme Somset 19 Q6
Westhope Herefs 45 P4
Westhope Shrops 56 H7
West Horndon Essex 37 P3
Westhorp Nhants 48 F4
Westhorpe Lincs 74 D4
Westhorpe Suffk 64 E8
West Horrington Somset 19 Q5
West Horsley Surrey 36 C10
West Horton Nthumb 119 K4
West Hougham Kent 27 N3
Westhoughton Bolton 89 K9
Westhouse N York 95 P6
Westhouses Derbys 84 F9
West Howe BCP 13 J5
West Howetown Somset 18 B8
Westhumble Surrey 36 E10
West Huntingtower P & K 134 D3
West Huntspill Somset 19 K6
West Hyde C Beds 50 D7
West Hyde Herts 36 B2
West Hythe Kent 27 K5
West Ilkerton Devon 17 N2
West Ilsley W Berk 34 E8
West Itchenor W Susx 15 L6
West Keal Lincs 87 L8
West Kennett Wilts 33 M11
West Kilbride N Ayrs 124 G8
West Kingsdown Kent 37 N8
West Kington Wilts 32 F9
West Kirby Wirral 81 J7
West Knapton N York 98 H5
West Knighton Dorset 12 B7
West Knoyle Wilts 20 G8
West Kyloe Nthumb 119 L2
Westlake Devon 6 G8
West Lambrook Somset 19 M11
Westland Green Herts 51 K6
West Langdon Kent 27 P2
West Lavington W Susx 23 N10
West Lavington Wilts 21 K4
West Layton N York 103 M8
West Leake Notts 72 E5
West Learmouth Nthumb 118 F3
West Lees N York 104 E10
West Leigh Devon 8 G3
Westleigh Devon 16 H6
Westleigh Devon 18 E11
West Leigh Somset 18 F8
Westleton Suffk 65 N8
West Lexham Norfk 76 A8
Westley Shrops 56 F3
Westley Suffk 63 P8
Westley Waterless Cambs 63 K9
West Lilling N York 98 C8
Westlington Bucks 35 L2
West Linton Border 127 M7
Westlinton Cumb 110 G8
West Littleton S Glos 32 E9
West Lockinge Oxon 34 D7
West Lulworth Dorset 12 D8
West Lutton N York 99 J7
West Lydford Somset 19 Q8
West Lyn Devon 17 N2
West Lyng Somset 19 K9
West Lynn Norfk 75 M6
West Malling Kent 37 Q9
West Malvern Worcs 46 E5
West Marden W Susx 15 L4
West Markham Notts 85 M6
Westmarsh Kent 39 N9
West Marsh NE Lin 93 N9
West Marton N York 96 C10
West Melbury Dorset 20 G10
West Melton Rothm 91 L10
West Meon Hants 22 H10
West Meon Hut Hants 23 J9
West Meon Woodlands Hants 22 H9
West Mersea Essex 52 H9
Westmeston E Susx 24 H8
West Mickley Nthumb 112 G8
West Midland Safari Park Worcs 57 Q9
Westmill Herts 50 H7
Westmill Herts 51 J5
West Milton Dorset 11 L5
Westminster Gt Lon 36 G5
Westminster Abbey & Palace Gt Lon 36 G5
West Molesey Surrey 36 D7
West Monkton Somset 19 J9
West Moors Dorset 13 J4
West Morden Dorset 12 F5
West Morriston Border 118 B2
West Morton C Brad 90 D2
West Mudford Somset 19 Q10
Westmuir Angus 142 F7
West Ness N York 98 D5
West Newbiggin Darltn 104 C7
Westnewton Cumb 100 F2
West Newton E R Yk 93 M3
West Newton Norfk 75 N5
West Newton Somset 19 J9
West Norwood Gt Lon 36 H6
Westoe S Tyne 113 N7
West Ogwell Devon 7 L4
Weston BaNES 32 D11
Weston Ches E 70 C4
Weston Devon 10 C4
Weston Devon 10 D7
Weston Dorset 11 P10
Weston Halton 81 Q8
Weston Hants 23 K10
Weston Herefs 45 M3
Weston Herts 50 G4
Weston Lincs 74 E6
Weston N York 97 J11
Weston Nhants 48 G5
Weston Notts 85 N7
Weston Shrops 56 E10
Weston Shrops 57 L6
Weston Shrops 69 J9
Weston Staffs 70 H9
Weston Suffk 65 N4
Weston W Berk 34 C10
Weston Beggard Herefs 46 A6
Westonbirt Gloucs 32 G7
Weston by Welland Nhants 60 G2
Weston Colley Hants 22 F7
Weston Colville Cambs 63 K10
Weston Corbett Hants 23 J5
Weston Coyney C Stke 70 G6
Weston Favell Nhants 60 G8
Weston Green Cambs 63 K10
Weston Heath Shrops 57 P2
Weston Hills Lincs 74 E6
Weston in Arden Warwks 59 N7
Westoning C Beds 50 B4
Weston-in-Gordano N Som 31 M10
Westoning Woodend C Beds 50 B4
Weston Jones Staffs 70 D10
Weston Longville Norfk 76 G8
Weston Lullingfields Shrops 69 M10
Weston-on-Avon Warwks 47 N4
Weston-on-the-Green Oxon 48 F11
Weston Park Staffs 57 Q2
Weston Patrick Hants 23 J5
Weston Rhyn Shrops 69 J7
Weston-sub-Edge Gloucs 47 M6
Weston-super-Mare N Som 19 K2
Weston Turville Bucks 35 N2
Weston-under-Lizard Staffs 57 Q2
Weston under Penyard Herefs 46 B10
Weston-under-Redcastle Shrops 69 Q9
Weston under Wetherley Warwks 59 N11
Weston Underwood Derbys 71 P6
Weston Underwood M Keyn 49 N4
Weston-upon-Trent Derbys 72 C5
Westonzoyland Somset 19 L8
West Orchard Dorset 20 F11
West Overton Wilts 33 M11
Westow N York 98 F7
West Panson Devon 5 N3
West Park Abers 151 K8
West Parley Dorset 13 J5
West Peckham Kent 37 P10
West Peeke Devon 5 N3
West Pelton Dur 113 K10
West Pennard Somset 19 P7
West Pentire Cnwll 4 B9
West Pinchbeck Lincs 74 D6
West Porlock Somset 17 R2
Westport Somset 19 L10
West Pulham Dorset 11 Q3
West Putford Devon 16 F8
West Quantoxhead Somset 18 F6
Westquarter Falk 126 G2
Westra V Glam 30 F10
West Raddon Devon 9 L4
West Rainton Dur 113 M11
West Rasen Lincs 86 E3
West Ravendale NE Lin 93 M11
Westray Ork 169 d2
Westray Airport Ork 169 d1
West Raynham Norfk 76 B6
West Retford Notts 85 L4
Westridge Green W Berk 34 G9
Westrigg W Loth 126 G4
Westrop Swindn 33 P6
West Rounton N York 104 D10
West Row Suffk 63 L5
West Rudham Norfk 75 R5
West Runton Norfk 76 H3
Westruther Border 128 G10
Westry Cambs 74 H11
West Saltoun E Loth 128 D6
West Sandford Devon 9 K4
West Sandwick Shet 169 r5
West Scrafton N York 96 G4
West Sleekburn Nthumb 113 L4
West Somerton Norfk 77 P7
West Stafford Dorset 11 Q7
West Stockwith Notts 92 C11
West Stoke W Susx 15 M5
West Stonesdale N York 102 G10
West Stoughton Somset 19 M5
West Stour Dorset 20 E10
West Stourmouth Kent 39 N9
West Stow Suffk 63 P6
West Stowell Wilts 21 M2
West Stratton Hants 22 F6
West Street Kent 38 F11
West Street Kent 39 P11
West Street Medway 38 B6
West Street Suffk 64 D7
West Tanfield N York 97 L5
West Taphouse Cnwll 5 J9
West Tarbert Ag & B 123 Q6
West Tarring W Susx 24 D10
West Thirston Nthumb 119 N11
West Thorney W Susx 15 L6
Westthorpe Derbys 84 G5
West Thorpe Notts 72 G5
West Thurrock Thurr 37 N5
West Tilbury Thurr 37 Q5
West Tisted Hants 23 J9
West Torrington Lincs 86 F4
West Town BaNES 19 P2
West Town Hants 15 K7
West Town Herefs 45 N2
West Town N Som 31 N11
West Town Somset 19 P7
West Town Somset 20 D6
West Tytherley Hants 21 Q9
West Walton Norfk 75 J8
Westward Cumb 101 J2
Westward Ho! Devon 16 G6
Westwell Kent 26 G2
Westwell Oxon 33 P3
Westwell Leacon Kent 26 G2
West Wellow Hants 21 Q11
West Wembury Devon 6 E9
West Wemyss Fife 135 J9
Westwick Cambs 62 F7
Westwick Dur 103 L7
West Wick N Som 19 L2
Westwick Norfk 77 K6
West Wickham Cambs 63 K11
West Wickham Gt Lon 37 J7
West Williamston Pembks 41 K9
West Winch Norfk 75 M7
West Winterslow Wilts 21 P8
West Wittering W Susx 15 L7
West Witton N York 96 G3
Westwood Devon 9 P5
Westwood Kent 37 P6
Westwood Kent 39 Q8
Westwood Notts 84 G10
Westwood Nthumb 111 Q7
Westwood Wilts 20 F3
West Woodburn Nthumb 112 C3
West Woodhay W Berk 22 C2
Westwood Heath Covtry 59 L9
West Woodlands Somset 20 E6
Westwoodside N Linc 92 B10
West Worldham Hants 23 K7
West Worthing W Susx 24 D10
West Wratting Cambs 63 K10
West Wycombe Bucks 35 M6
West Wylam Nthumb 112 H8
West Yatton Wilts 32 G9
West Yoke Kent 37 P7
West Youlstone Cnwll 16 D8
Wetham Green Kent 38 D8
Wetheral Cumb 111 J10
Wetherby Leeds 97 P11
Wetherby Services N York 97 P10
Wetherden Suffk 64 E9
Wetheringsett Suffk 64 G8
Wethersfield Essex 52 B5
Wetherup Street Suffk 64 G9
Wetley Rocks Staffs 70 H5
Wettenhall Ches E 69 R2
Wetton Staffs 71 L3
Wetwang E R Yk 99 J9
Wetwood Staffs 70 D8
Wexcombe Wilts 21 Q3
Wexham Slough 35 Q8
Wexham Street Bucks 35 Q8
Weybourne Norfk 76 G3
Weybourne Surrey 23 N5
Weybread Suffk 65 J5
Weybread Street Suffk 65 J6
Weybridge Surrey 36 C8
Weycroft Devon 10 G5
Weydale Highld 167 L4
Weyhill Hants 22 B5
Weymouth Dorset 11 P9
Whaddon Bucks 49 M8
Whaddon Cambs 62 E11
Whaddon Gloucs 32 F2
Whaddon Wilts 20 G2
Whaddon Wilts 21 N9
Whale Cumb 101 P6
Whaley Derbys 84 H6
Whaley Bridge Derbys 83 M8
Whaley Thorns Derbys 84 H6
Whaligoe Highld 167 P8
Whalley Lancs 89 L3
Whalley Banks Lancs 89 L3
Whalsay Shet 169 s7
Whalton Nthumb 112 H4
Whaplode Lincs 74 F6
Whaplode Drove Lincs 74 F8
Wharf Warwks 48 D4
Wharfe N York 96 A7
Wharles Lancs 88 E3
Wharley End C Beds 49 P6
Wharncliffe Side Sheff 84 C2
Wharram-le-Street N York 98 H7
Wharton Ches W 82 E11
Wharton Herefs 45 Q3
Whashton N York 103 N9
Whasset Cumb 95 L4
Whatcote Warwks 47 Q6
Whateley Warwks 59 K5
Whatfield Suffk 52 H2
Whatley Somset 10 H3
Whatley Somset 20 D5
Whatley's End S Glos 32 C8
Whatlington E Susx 26 C8
Whatsole Street Kent 27 K3
Whatstandwell Derbys 84 D10
Whatton-in-the-Vale Notts 73 J3
Whauphill D & G 107 M8
Whaw N York 103 J10
Wheal Peevor Cnwll 3 J5
Wheal Rose Cnwll 3 J5
Wheatacre Norfk 65 P3
Wheatfield Oxon 35 J5
Wheathampstead Herts 50 E8
Wheathill Shrops 57 L8
Wheathill Somset 19 Q8
Wheatley Hants 23 L6
Wheatley Oxon 34 G3
Wheatley Hill Dur 104 C3
Wheatley Hills Donc 91 P10
Wheatley Lane Lancs 89 N3
Wheaton Aston Staffs 58 C2
Wheddon Cross Somset 18 B7
Wheelbarrow Town Kent 27 K2
Wheeler End Bucks 35 M6
Wheeler's Green Wokham 35 L10
Wheelerstreet Surrey 23 P6
Wheelock Ches E 70 D3
Wheelock Heath Ches E 70 D3
Wheelton Lancs 89 J6
Wheldale Wakefd 91 M5
Wheldrake C York 92 A2
Whelford Gloucs 33 N5
Whelpley Hill Bucks 35 Q4
Whelpo Cumb 101 K3
Whelston Flints 81 J9
Whempstead Herts 50 H6
Whenby N York 98 C7
Whepstead Suffk 64 A10
Wherstead Suffk 53 L3
Wherwell Hants 22 C6
Wheston Derbys 83 P9
Whetsted Kent 37 Q11
Whetstone Gt Lon 36 G2
Whetstone Leics 72 F11
Wheyrigg Cumb 110 C11
Whicham Cumb 94 C4
Whichford Warwks 48 B8
Whickham Gatesd 113 K8
Whiddon Devon 8 C5
Whiddon Down Devon 8 G6
Whigstreet Angus 142 H9
Whilton Nhants 60 D8
Whimble Devon 16 F11
Whimple Devon 9 P5
Whimpwell Green Norfk 77 M6
Whinburgh Norfk 76 E10
Whin Lane End Lancs 88 D2
Whinnieliggate D & G 108 F10
Whinnow Cumb 110 F10
Whinnyfold Abers 159 Q11
Whinny Hill S on T 104 C7
Whippingham IoW 14 F8
Whipsnade C Beds 50 B7
Whipsnade Zoo ZSL C Beds 50 B7
Whipton Devon 9 M6
Whirlow Sheff 84 D4
Whisby Lincs 86 B7
Whissendine Rutlnd 73 L8
Whissonsett Norfk 76 C7
Whistlefield Ag & B 131 Q9
Whistlefield Inn Ag & B 131 N9
Whistley Green Wokham 35 L10
Whiston Knows 81 P6
Whiston Nhants 60 H8
Whiston Rothm 84 F3
Whiston Staffs 58 C2
Whiston Staffs 71 J5
Whiston Cross Shrops 57 P4
Whiston Eaves Staffs 71 J5
Whitacre Fields Warwks 59 L6
Whitbeck Cumb 94 C4
Whitbourne Herefs 46 D3
Whitburn S Tyne 113 P8
Whitburn W Loth 126 G5
Whitby Ches W 81 M9
Whitby N York 105 N8
Whitbyheath Ches W 81 M10
Whitchester Border 129 J8
Whitchurch BaNES 32 B11
Whitchurch Bucks 49 M10
Whitchurch Cardif 30 G9
Whitchurch Devon 6 D4
Whitchurch Hants 22 E5
Whitchurch Herefs 45 R11
Whitchurch Oxon 34 H9
Whitchurch Pembks 40 F5
Whitchurch Shrops 69 P6
Whitchurch Canonicorum Dorset 10 H5
Whitchurch Hill Oxon 34 H9
Whitcombe Dorset 11 Q7
Whitcot Shrops 56 F6
Whitcott Keysett Shrops 56 D8
Whiteacre Kent 27 K2
Whiteacre Heath Warwks 59 K6
Whiteash Green Essex 52 C5
White Ball Somset 18 F11
Whitebridge Highld 147 M4
Whitebrook Mons 31 P3
Whitebushes Surrey 36 G11
Whitecairns Abers 151 N4
Whitechapel Gt Lon 36 H4
White Chapel Lancs 88 H2
Whitechurch Pembks 41 N3
Whitecliff Gloucs 31 Q3
White Colne Essex 52 E6
White Coppice Lancs 89 J7
Whitecraig E Loth 127 Q3
Whitecroft Gloucs 32 B3
Whitecrook D & G 106 G6
Whitecross Cnwll 2 E7
White Cross Cnwll 2 H9
Whitecross Cnwll 4 F7
Whitecross Falk 126 H2
White End Worcs 46 E8
Whiteface Highld 162 G9
Whitefarland N Ayrs 120 G3
Whitefaulds S Ayrs 114 E6
Whitefield Bury 89 N9
Whitefield Devon 17 N4
Whitefield Somset 18 E9
Whitefield Lane End Knows 81 P7
Whiteford Abers 151 J2
Whitegate Ches W 82 D11
Whitehall Hants 23 K4
Whitehall Ork 169 f4
Whitehall W Susx 24 D6
Whitehaven Cumb 100 C7
Whitehill Hants 23 L8
Whitehill Kent 38 H10
Whitehill Leics 72 C8
Whitehills Abers 158 G4
Whitehouse Abers 150 G5
Whitehouse Ag & B 123 P7
Whitehouse Common Birm 58 H5
Whitekirk E Loth 128 F3
White Kirkley Dur 103 K3
White Lackington Dorset 11 Q5
Whitelackington Somset 19 L11
White Ladies Aston Worcs 46 H4
Whiteleaf Bucks 35 M4
White-le-Head Dur 113 J10
Whiteley Hants 14 F5
Whiteley Bank IoW 14 G10
Whiteley Green Ches E 83 K9
Whiteley Village Surrey 36 C8
Whitemans Green W Susx 24 H5
White Mill Carmth 43 J10
Whitemire Moray 156 H7
Whitemoor C Nott 72 E2
Whitemoor Cnwll 4 F10
Whitemoor Derbys 84 E11
Whitemoor Staffs 70 F2
Whiteness Shet 169 q9
White Notley Essex 52 C8
Whiteoak Green Oxon 34 B2
White Ox Mead BaNES 20 D3
Whiteparish Wilts 21 P10
White Pit Lincs 87 L5
Whiterashes Abers 151 M3
White Roding Essex 51 N8
Whiterow Highld 167 Q7
Whiterow Moray 157 J6
Whiteshill Gloucs 32 F3
Whitesmith E Susx 25 M8
White Stake Lancs 88 G5
Whitestaunton Somset 10 F2
Whitestone Devon 9 L6
White Stone Herefs 45 R6
Whitestone Warwks 59 N7
Whitestone Cross Devon 9 L6
Whitestreet Green Suffk 52 G4
Whitewall Corner N York 98 F7
White Waltham W & M 35 M9
Whiteway BaNES 20 D2
Whiteway Gloucs 32 H2
Whitewell Lancs 95 P11
Whiteworks Devon 6 G4
Whitfield C Dund 142 G11
Whitfield Kent 27 P2
Whitfield Nhants 48 H7
Whitfield Nthumb 111 Q9
Whitfield S Glos 32 C6
Whitfield Hall Nthumb 111 Q9
Whitford Devon 10 F5
Whitford Flints 80 G9
Whitgift E R Yk 92 D6
Whitgreave Staffs 70 G9
Whithorn D & G 107 M9
Whiting Bay N Ayrs 121 K6
Whitkirk Leeds 91 K4
Whitland Carmth 41 N7
Whitlaw Border 117 Q8
Whitletts S Ayrs 114 G3
Whitley N York 91 P6
Whitley Readg 35 K10
Whitley Sheff 84 D2
Whitley Wilts 32 G11
Whitley Bay N Tyne 113 N6
Whitley Chapel Nthumb 112 D9
Whitley Heath Staffs 70 E9
Whitley Lower Kirk 90 G7
Whitley Row Kent 37 L10
Whitlock's End Solhll 58 H9
Whitminster Gloucs 32 E3
Whitmore Dorset 13 J3
Whitmore Staffs 70 E6
Whitnage Devon 18 D11
Whitnash Warwks 48 B2
Whitney-on-Wye Herefs 45 K5
Whitrigg Cumb 100 H3
Whitrigg Cumb 110 D9

Whitrigglees – Woodland 301

Whitrigglees Cumb 110 D9
Whitsbury Hants 21 M11
Whitsome Border 129 M9
Whitson Newpt 31 L8
Whitstable Kent 39 K8
Whitstone Cnwll 5 M2
Whittingham Nthumb 119 L8
Whittingslow Shrops 56 G7
Whittington Derbys 84 E5
Whittington Gloucs 47 K10
Whittington Lancs 95 N5
Whittington Norfk 75 P11
Whittington Shrops 69 K8
Whittington Staffs 58 C8
Whittington Staffs 59 J3
Whittington Warwks 59 L5
Whittington Worcs 46 G4
Whittington Moor Derbys 84 E6
Whittlebury Nhants 49 J6
Whittle-le-Woods Lancs 88 H6
Whittlesey Cambs 74 E11
Whittlesford Cambs 62 G11
Whittlestone Head Bl w D 89 L7
Whitton N Linc 92 F6
Whitton Nthumb 119 L10
Whitton Powys 56 D11
Whitton S on T 104 C6
Whitton Shrops 57 K10
Whitton Suffk 53 K2
Whittonditch Wilts 33 Q10
Whittonstall Nthumb 112 G9
Whitway Hants 22 E3
Whitwell Derbys 84 H5
Whitwell Herts 50 E6
Whitwell IoW 14 F11
Whitwell N York 103 Q11
Whitwell Rutlnd 73 N9
Whitwell-on-the-Hill N York 98 E7
Whitwell Street Norfk 76 G7
Whitwick Leics 72 C7
Whitwood Wakefd 91 L6
Whitworth Lancs 89 P7
Whixall Shrops 69 P8
Whixley N York 97 P9
Whorlton Dur 103 M8
Whorlton N York 104 E10
Whyle Herefs 45 R2
Whyteleafe Surrey 36 H9
Wibdon Gloucs 31 Q5
Wibsey C Brad 90 E4
Wibtoft Warwks 59 Q7
Wichelstowe Swindn 33 M8
Wichenford Worcs 46 E2
Wichling Kent 38 F10
Wick BCP 13 L6
Wick Devon 10 D4
Wick Highld 167 Q6
Wick S Glos 32 D10
Wick Somset 18 H6
Wick Somset 19 M9
Wick V Glam 29 P10
Wick W Susx 24 B10
Wick Wilts 21 N10
Wick Worcs 47 J5
Wicken Cambs 63 J6
Wicken Nhants 49 K7
Wicken Bonhunt Essex 51 L4
Wickenby Lincs 86 E4
Wick End Bed 49 Q4
Wicken Green Village Norfk 76 A5
Wickersley Rothm 84 G2
Wicker Street Green Suffk 52 G3
Wickford Essex 38 B3
Wickham Hants 14 G4
Wickham W Berk 34 C10
Wickham Bishops Essex 52 D9
Wickhambreaux Kent 39 M10
Wickhambrook Suffk 63 N10
Wickhamford Worcs 47 L6
Wickham Green Suffk 64 F8
Wickham Green W Berk 34 D10
Wickham Heath W Berk 34 D11
Wickham Market Suffk 65 L10
Wickhampton Norfk 77 N10
Wickham St Paul Essex 52 D4
Wickham Skeith Suffk 64 F8
Wickham Street Suffk 63 N10
Wickham Street Suffk 64 F8
Wickhurst Green W Susx 24 D4
Wick John o' Groats Airport Highld 167 Q6
Wicklewood Norfk 76 F11
Wickmere Norfk 76 H5
Wick St Lawrence N Som 31 L11
Wicksteed Park Nhants 61 J5
Wickstreet E Susx 25 M9
Wickwar S Glos 32 D7
Widdington Essex 51 M4
Widdop Calder 89 Q4
Widdrington Nthumb 119 Q11
Widdrington Station Nthumb 113 K2
Widecombe in the Moor Devon 8 H9
Widegates Cnwll 5 M10
Widemouth Bay Cnwll 16 C11
Wide Open N Tyne 113 K6
Widford Essex 51 Q10
Widford Herts 51 K7
Widham Wilts 33 L7
Widley Hants 15 J5
Widmer End Bucks 35 N5
Widmerpool Notts 72 G5
Widmore Gt Lon 37 K7
Widnes Halton 81 Q7
Widworthy Devon 10 E5
Wigan Wigan 88 H9
Wigborough Somset 19 M11
Wiggaton Devon 10 C6
Wiggenhall St Germans Norfk 75 L8
Wiggenhall St Mary Magdalen Norfk 75 L8
Wiggenhall St Mary the Virgin Norfk 75 L8
Wiggenhall St Peter Norfk 75 M8
Wiggens Green Essex 51 Q2
Wiggenstall Staffs 71 K2
Wiggington Shrops 69 K7
Wigginton C York 98 C9
Wigginton Herts 35 P2
Wigginton Oxon 48 C8
Wigginton Staffs 59 K3
Wigginton Bottom Herts 35 P3
Wigglesworth N York 96 B9
Wiggonby Cumb 110 E10
Wiggonholt W Susx 24 C7
Wighill N York 97 Q11
Wighton Norfk 76 C4
Wightwick Wolves 58 C5
Wigley Derbys 84 D6
Wigley Hants 22 B11
Wigmore Herefs 56 G11
Wigmore Medway 38 C9
Wigsley Notts 85 Q6
Wigsthorpe Nhants 61 M4
Wigston Leics 72 G11
Wigston Fields Leics 72 G10
Wigston Parva Leics 59 Q7
Wigthorpe Notts 85 J4
Wigtoft Lincs 74 E3
Wigton Cumb 110 E11
Wigtown D & G 107 M6
Wigtwizzle Sheff 90 G11
Wike Leeds 91 J2
Wilbarston Nhants 60 H3
Wilberfoss E R Yk 98 E10
Wilburton Cambs 62 G5
Wilby Nhants 61 J7
Wilby Norfk 64 E4
Wilby Suffk 65 J7
Wilcot Wilts 21 M2
Wilcott Shrops 69 L11
Wilcove Cnwll 6 C7
Wilcrick Newpt 31 M7
Wilday Green Derbys 84 D6
Wildboarclough Ches E 83 L11
Wilden Bed 61 N9
Wilden Worcs 58 B10
Wilde Street Suffk 63 M5
Wildhern Hants 22 C4
Wildhill Herts 50 G9
Wildmanbridge S Lans 126 E7
Wildmill Brdgnd 29 P8
Wildmoor Hants 23 J3
Wildmoor Worcs 58 E9
Wildsworth Lincs 92 D11
Wilford C Nott 72 F3
Wilkesley Ches E 70 A6
Wilkhaven Highld 163 L9
Wilkieston W Loth 127 L4
Wilkin's Green Herts 50 F9
Wilksby Lincs 87 J8
Willand Devon 9 P2
Willards Hill E Susx 26 B7
Willaston Ches E 70 B4
Willaston Ches W 81 L9
Willen M Keyn 49 N6
Willenhall Covtry 59 N9
Willenhall Wsall 58 E5
Willerby E R Yk 92 H4
Willerby N York 99 L5
Willersey Gloucs 47 M7
Willersley Herefs 45 L5
Willesborough Kent 26 H3
Willesborough Lees Kent 26 H3
Willesden Gt Lon 36 F4
Willesleigh Devon 17 L5
Willesley Wilts 32 G7
Willett Somset 18 F8
Willey Shrops 57 M5
Willey Warwks 59 Q8
Willey Green Surrey 23 P4
Williamscot Oxon 48 E5
Williamstown Rhondd 30 D6
Willian Herts 50 F4
Willicote Warwks 47 N5
Willingale Essex 51 N9
Willingdon E Susx 25 N10
Willingham Cambs 62 F6
Willingham by Stow Lincs 85 Q4
Willingham Green Cambs 63 K10
Willingham St Mary Suffk 65 N5
Willington Bed 61 P10
Willington Derbys 71 P9
Willington Dur 103 N3
Willington Kent 38 C11
Willington N Tyne 113 M7
Willington Warwks 47 Q7
Willington Corner Ches W 82 B11
Willitoft E R Yk 92 B4
Williton Somset 18 E6
Willoughby Lincs 87 N6
Willoughby Warwks 60 B7
Willoughby Hills Lincs 87 L11
Willoughby-on-the-Wolds Notts 72 G5
Willoughby Waterleys Leics 60 C2
Willoughton Lincs 86 B2
Willow Green Ches W 82 D9
Willows Green Essex 52 B8
Willsbridge S Glos 32 C10
Willsworthy Devon 8 D8
Willtown Somset 19 L10
Wilmcote Warwks 47 N3
Wilmington BaNES 20 C2
Wilmington Devon 10 E5
Wilmington E Susx 25 M10
Wilmington Kent 37 M6
Wilmslow Ches E 82 H8
Wilnecote Staffs 59 K4
Wilpshire Lancs 89 K4
Wilsden C Brad 90 D3
Wilsford Lincs 73 Q2
Wilsford Wilts 21 M3
Wilsford Wilts 21 M7
Wilsham Devon 17 P2
Wilshaw Kirk 90 E9
Wilsill N York 97 J8
Wilsley Green Kent 26 C4
Wilsley Pound Kent 26 C4
Wilson Herefs 45 R10
Wilson Leics 72 C6
Wilsontown S Lans 126 G6
Wilstead Bed 50 C2
Wilsthorpe Lincs 74 A8
Wilstone Herts 35 P2
Wilstone Green Herts 35 P2
Wilton Cumb 100 D8
Wilton Herefs 46 A10
Wilton N York 98 H4
Wilton R & Cl 104 G7
Wilton Wilts 21 L8
Wilton Wilts 21 Q2
Wilton Dean Border 117 P8
Wimbish Essex 51 N3
Wimbish Green Essex 51 P3
Wimbledon Gt Lon 36 F6
Wimblington Cambs 62 F2
Wimboldsley Ches W 70 B2
Wimborne Minster Dorset 12 H5
Wimborne St Giles Dorset 12 H2
Wimbotsham Norfk 75 M9
Wimpole Cambs 62 E11
Wimpstone Warwks 47 P5
Wincanton Somset 20 D9
Winceby Lincs 87 K7
Wincham Ches W 82 E9
Winchburgh W Loth 127 K3
Winchcombe Gloucs 47 K9
Winchelsea E Susx 26 F8
Winchelsea Beach E Susx 26 F8
Winchester Hants 22 E9
Winchester Services Hants 22 F7
Winchet Hill Kent 26 B3
Winchfield Hants 23 L4
Winchmore Hill Bucks 35 P5
Winchmore Hill Gt Lon 36 H2
Wincle Ches E 83 L11
Wincobank Sheff 84 E2
Winder Cumb 100 D7
Windermere Cumb 101 M11
Windermere Jetty Cumb 101 M11
Winderton Warwks 48 B6
Windhill Highld 155 P8
Windlehurst Stockp 83 L7
Windlesham Surrey 23 P2
Windmill Cnwll 4 D7
Windmill Derbys 83 Q9
Windmill Hill E Susx 25 P8
Windmill Hill Somset 19 K11
Windrush Gloucs 33 N2
Windsole Abers 158 E5
Windsor W & M 35 Q9
Windsor Castle W & M 35 Q9
Windsoredge Gloucs 32 F4
Windsor Green Suffk 64 B11
Windygates Fife 135 J7
Windyharbour Ches E 82 H10
Windy Hill Wrexhm 69 K4
Wineham W Susx 24 F6
Winestead E R Yk 93 N6
Winewall Lancs 89 Q2
Winfarthing Norfk 64 G4
Winford IoW 14 G10
Winford N Som 19 P2
Winforton Herefs 45 K5
Winfrith Newburgh Dorset 12 D8
Wing Bucks 49 N10
Wing Rutlnd 73 M10
Wingate Dur 104 D3
Wingates Bolton 89 K9
Wingates Nthumb 119 L11
Wingerworth Derbys 84 E7
Wingfield C Beds 50 B5
Wingfield Suffk 65 J6
Wingfield Wilts 20 F3
Wingfield Green Suffk 65 J6
Wingham Kent 39 M10
Wingland Lincs 75 J6
Wingmore Kent 27 L2
Wingrave Bucks 49 N11
Winkburn Notts 85 M9
Winkfield Br For 35 P10
Winkfield Row Br For 35 N10
Winkhill Staffs 71 K4
Winkhurst Green Kent 37 L11
Winkleigh Devon 17 L10
Winksley N York 97 L6
Winkton BCP 13 L5
Winlaton Gatesd 113 J8
Winlaton Mill Gatesd 113 J8
Winless Highld 167 P6
Winllan Powys 68 H10
Winmarleigh Lancs 95 K11
Winnall Hants 22 E9
Winnersh Wokham 35 L10
Winnington Ches W 82 D10
Winscales Cumb 100 D5
Winscombe N Som 19 M3
Winsford Ches W 82 E11
Winsford Somset 18 B8
Winsham Devon 17 J4
Winsham Somset 10 H3
Winshill Staffs 71 P10
Winshwen Swans 29 J5
Winskill Cumb 101 Q4
Winslade Hants 23 J5
Winsley Wilts 20 E2
Winslow Bucks 49 L9
Winson Gloucs 33 L3
Winsor Hants 13 P2
Winster Cumb 95 J2
Winster Derbys 84 B8
Winston Dur 103 M7
Winston Suffk 64 H9
Winstone Gloucs 33 J3
Winston Green Suffk 64 H9
Winswell Devon 16 H9
Winterborne Came Dorset 11 Q7
Winterborne Clenston Dorset 12 D4
Winterborne Herringston Dorset 11 P7
Winterborne Houghton Dorset 12 D4
Winterborne Kingston Dorset 12 E5
Winterborne Monkton Dorset 11 P7
Winterborne Stickland Dorset 12 D4
Winterborne Tomson Dorset 12 E5
Winterborne Whitechurch Dorset 12 D4
Winterborne Zelston Dorset 12 E5
Winterbourne S Glos 32 B8
Winterbourne W Berk 34 E10
Winterbourne Abbas Dorset 11 N6
Winterbourne Bassett Wilts 33 L10
Winterbourne Dauntsey Wilts 21 N8
Winterbourne Earls Wilts 21 N8
Winterbourne Gunner Wilts 21 N7
Winterbourne Monkton Wilts 33 L10
Winterbourne Steepleton Dorset 11 N7
Winterbourne Stoke Wilts 21 L6
Winterbrook Oxon 34 H7
Winterburn N York 96 D9
Winteringham N Linc 92 F6
Winterley Ches E 70 C3
Wintersett Wakefd 91 K7
Winterslow Wilts 21 P8
Winterton N Linc 92 F7
Winterton-on-Sea Norfk 77 P8
Winthorpe Lincs 87 Q7
Winthorpe Notts 85 P9
Winton BCP 13 J6
Winton Cumb 102 E8
Winton E Susx 25 M10
Winton N York 104 D11
Wintringham Cambs 62 B9
Wintringham N York 98 H6
Winwick Cambs 61 P4
Winwick Nhants 60 D6
Winwick Warrtn 82 D6
Wirksworth Derbys 71 P4
Wirral 81 K7
Wirswall Ches E 69 P6
Wisbech Cambs 75 J9
Wisbech St Mary Cambs 74 H9
Wisborough Green W Susx 24 C5
Wiseman's Bridge Pembks 41 M9
Wiseton Notts 85 M3
Wishanger Gloucs 32 H3
Wishaw N Lans 126 D6
Wishaw Warwks 59 J6
Wisley Surrey 36 C9
Wisley Garden RHS Surrey 36 C9
Wispington Lincs 86 H6
Wissenden Kent 26 F3
Wissett Suffk 65 M6
Wissington Norfk 75 N11
Wissington Suffk 52 G5
Wistanstow Shrops 56 G7
Wistanswick Shrops 70 B9
Wistaston Ches E 70 B4
Wistaston Green Ches E 70 B4
Wisterfield Ches E 82 H10
Wiston Pembks 41 K7
Wiston S Lans 116 D4
Wiston W Susx 24 D8
Wistow Cambs 62 C4
Wistow Leics 72 G11
Wistow N York 91 P3
Wiswell Lancs 89 L3
Witcham Cambs 62 G4
Witchampton Dorset 12 G3
Witchford Cambs 62 H5
Witcombe Somset 19 N10
Witham Essex 52 D9
Witham Friary Somset 20 D6
Witham on the Hill Lincs 73 R7
Witham St Hughs Lincs 85 Q8
Withcall Lincs 87 J4
Withdean Br & H 24 H9
Witherenden Hill E Susx 25 P5
Witheridge Devon 9 K2
Witherley Leics 72 A11
Withern Lincs 87 M4
Withernsea E R Yk 93 P5
Withernwick E R Yk 93 L2
Withersdale Street Suffk 65 K5
Withersfield Suffk 63 L11
Witherslack Cumb 95 J4
Withiel Cnwll 4 F8
Withiel Florey Somset 18 C8
Withielgoose Cnwll 4 G8
Withington Gloucs 47 K11
Withington Herefs 45 R6
Withington Manch 82 H6
Withington Shrops 57 K2
Withington Staffs 71 J7
Withington Green Ches E 82 H10
Withington Marsh Herefs 45 R6
Withleigh Devon 9 M2
Withnell Lancs 89 J6
Withnell Fold Lancs 89 J6
Withybed Green Worcs 58 F10
Withybrook Warwks 59 P8
Withycombe Somset 18 D6
Withyham E Susx 25 L3
Withy Mills BaNES 20 C3
Withypool Somset 17 Q4
Withywood Bristl 31 Q11
Witley Surrey 23 P7
Witnesham Suffk 64 H11
Witney Oxon 34 C2
Wittering C Pete 73 R10
Wittersham Kent 26 F6
Witton Birm 58 G6
Witton Norfk 77 L10
Witton Norfk 77 L5
Witton Gilbert Dur 113 K11
Witton Green Norfk 77 N11
Witton le Wear Dur 103 M4
Witton Park Dur 103 N4
Wiveliscombe Somset 18 E9
Wivelrod Hants 23 J7
Wivelsfield E Susx 24 H6
Wivelsfield Green E Susx 25 J7
Wivelsfield Station W Susx 24 H7
Wivenhoe Essex 52 H7
Wivenhoe Cross Essex 52 H7
Wiveton Norfk 76 E3
Wix Essex 53 L6
Wixams Bed 50 C2
Wixford Warwks 47 L4
Wix Green Essex 53 L6
Wixhill Shrops 69 Q9
Wixoe Suffk 52 B3
Woburn C Beds 49 P8
Woburn Safari Park C Beds 49 Q8
Woburn Sands M Keyn 49 P7
Wokefield Park W Berk 35 J11
Woking Surrey 36 B9
Wokingham Wokham 35 M11
Wolborough Devon 7 M4
Woldingham Surrey 37 J9
Wold Newton E R Yk 99 L6
Wold Newton NE Lin 93 M11
Wolfclyde S Lans 116 E3
Wolferlow Herefs 46 C2
Wolferton Norfk 75 N5
Wolfhampcote Warwks 60 B7
Wolfhill P & K 142 B11
Wolf Hills Nthumb 111 P9
Wolf's Castle Pembks 41 J5
Wolfsdale Pembks 40 H6
Wollaston Dudley 58 C8
Wollaston Nhants 61 K8
Wollaston Shrops 56 E2
Wollaton C Nott 72 E3
Wollaton Hall & Park C Nott 72 E3
Wolleigh Devon 9 K8
Wollerton Shrops 69 R8
Wollescote Dudley 58 D8
Wolseley Bridge Staffs 71 J10
Wolsingham Dur 103 L3
Wolstanton Staffs 70 F5
Wolstenholme Rochdl 89 N8
Wolston Warwks 59 P9
Wolsty Cumb 109 P10
Wolvercote Oxon 34 E2
Wolverhampton Wolves 58 D5
Wolverhampton Halfpenny Green Airport Staffs 58 B6
Wolverley Shrops 69 N8
Wolverley Worcs 58 B9
Wolverton Hants 22 G3
Wolverton Kent 27 N3
Wolverton M Keyn 49 M6
Wolverton Warwks 47 P2
Wolverton Wilts 20 E8
Wolverton Common Hants 22 G3
Wolvesnewton Mons 31 N5
Wolvey Warwks 59 P7
Wolvey Heath Warwks 59 P7
Wolviston S on T 104 E5
Wombleton N York 98 D4
Wombourne Staffs 58 C6
Wombwell Barns 91 L10
Womenswold Kent 39 M11
Womersley N York 91 N7
Wonastow Mons 31 N2
Wonersh Surrey 36 B11
Wonford Devon 9 M6
Wonson Devon 8 G7
Wonston Dorset 12 B3
Wonston Hants 22 E7
Wooburn Bucks 35 P7
Wooburn Green Bucks 35 P7
Wooburn Moor Bucks 35 P7
Woodacott Devon 16 F10
Woodale N York 96 F5
Woodall Rothm 84 G4
Woodall Services Rothm 84 G4
Woodbank Ches W 81 M10
Woodbastwick Norfk 77 L8
Woodbeck Notts 85 N5
Wood Bevington Warwks 47 L4
Woodborough Notts 85 K11
Woodborough Wilts 21 M3
Woodbridge Devon 10 D5
Woodbridge Dorset 20 G11
Woodbridge Suffk 53 N2
Wood Burcote Nhants 49 J5
Woodbury Devon 9 P7
Woodbury Salterton Devon 9 P7
Woodchester Gloucs 32 F4
Woodchurch Kent 26 F5
Woodchurch Wirral 81 K7
Woodcombe Somset 18 C5
Woodcote Gt Lon 36 G8
Woodcote Oxon 34 H8
Woodcote Wrekin 70 D11
Woodcote Green Worcs 58 D10
Woodcott Hants 22 D4
Woodcroft Gloucs 31 P5
Woodcutts Dorset 21 J11
Wood Dalling Norfk 76 F6
Woodditton Cambs 63 L9
Woodeaton Oxon 34 F2
Wood Eaton Staffs 70 E11
Wooden Pembks 41 M9
Wood End Bed 61 M11
Wood End Bed 61 N7
Wood End C Beds 49 Q6
Wood End Cambs 62 E5
Wood End Gt Lon 36 D4
Wood End Herts 50 H5
Woodend Highld 138 D5
Woodend Nhants 48 H5
Woodend Staffs 71 M9
Woodend W Loth 126 G4
Woodend W Susx 15 M5
Wood End Warwks 58 H10
Wood End Warwks 59 K5
Wood End Warwks 59 L7
Wood End Wolves 58 D4
Wood Enderby Lincs 87 J8
Woodend Green Essex 51 N5
Woodfalls Wilts 21 N10
Woodford Cnwll 16 C9
Woodford Devon 7 K8
Woodford Gloucs 32 C5
Woodford Gt Lon 37 K2
Woodford Nhants 61 L5
Woodford Stockp 83 J8
Woodford Bridge Gt Lon 37 K2
Woodford Green Gt Lon 37 K2
Woodford Halse Nhants 48 F4
Woodford Wells Gt Lon 37 K2
Woodgate Birm 58 E8
Woodgate Devon 18 F11
Woodgate Norfk 76 B8
Woodgate Norfk 76 E8
Woodgate W Susx 15 P6
Woodgate Worcs 58 E11
Wood Green Gt Lon 36 H2
Woodgreen Hants 21 N11
Woodgreen Oxon 34 C2
Woodhall N York 96 E2
Woodhall Hill Leeds 90 G3
Woodhall Spa Lincs 86 G8
Woodham Bucks 49 K11
Woodham Dur 103 Q5
Woodham Surrey 36 B8
Woodham Ferrers Essex 38 C2
Woodham Mortimer Essex 52 D11
Woodham Walter Essex 52 D10
Wood Hayes Wolves 58 D4
Woodhead Abers 159 J10
Woodhill Shrops 57 N8
Woodhill Somset 19 L9
Woodhorn Nthumb 113 L3
Woodhorn Demesne Nthumb 113 M3
Woodhouse Leeds 90 H4
Woodhouse Leics 72 E8
Woodhouse Sheff 84 F4
Woodhouse Wakefd 91 K6
Woodhouse Eaves Leics 72 E8
Woodhouse Green Staffs 70 G2
Woodhouselee Mdloth 127 N5
Woodhouselees D & G 110 G6
Woodhouse Mill Sheff 84 F3
Woodhouses Cumb 110 F10
Woodhouses Oldham 83 K4
Woodhouses Staffs 58 G3
Woodhouses Staffs 71 M11
Woodhuish Devon 7 N8
Woodhurst Cambs 62 D5
Woodingdean Br & H 25 J9
Woodkirk Leeds 90 H5
Woodland Abers 151 M3
Woodland Devon 6 G7

Woodland Devon 7 K5
Woodland Dur 103 L5
Woodland Kent 27 K3
Woodland S Ayrs 114 C8
Woodland Head Devon 9 J5
Woodlands Donc 91 N9
Woodlands Dorset 13 J3
Woodlands Hants 13 P2
Woodlands Kent 37 N8
Woodlands N York 97 M10
Woodlands Somset 18 G6
Woodlands of Durris Abers 151 K8
Woodlands Park W & M 35 N9
Woodlands St Mary W Berk 34 B9
Woodland Street Somset 19 P7
Woodland View Sheff 84 D3
Wood Lane Shrops 69 M8
Wood Lane Staffs 70 E5
Woodleigh Devon 7 J9
Woodlesford Leeds 91 K5
Woodley Stockp 83 K6
Woodley Wokham 35 L10
Woodmancote Gloucs 32 E5
Woodmancote Gloucs 33 K3
Woodmancote Gloucs 47 J9
Woodmancote W Susx 15 L5
Woodmancote W Susx 24 F8
Woodmancote Worcs 46 H6
Woodmancott Hants 22 G6
Woodmansey E R Yk 93 J3
Woodmansgreen W Susx 23 N9
Woodmansterne Surrey 36 G9
Woodmanton Devon 9 P7
Woodmarsh Wilts 20 G3
Woodmill Staffs 71 L10
Woodminton Wilts 21 K10
Woodnesborough Kent 39 P10
Woodnewton Nhants 61 M2
Woodnook Notts 84 G10
Wood Norton Norfk 76 E6
Woodplumpton Lancs 88 F4
Woodrising Norfk 76 D11
Wood Row Leeds 91 K5
Woodrow Worcs 58 C9
Wood's Corner E Susx 25 Q7
Woods Eaves Herefs 45 K5
Woodseaves Shrops 70 B8
Woodseaves Staffs 70 D9
Woodsend Wilts 33 P9
Woodsetts Rothm 84 H4
Woodsford Dorset 12 C6
Wood's Green E Susx 25 P4
Woodside Br For 35 P10
Woodside Cumb 100 D4
Woodside Essex 51 L10
Woodside Fife 135 L6
Woodside Gt Lon 36 H7
Woodside Hants 13 P6
Woodside Herts 50 F9
Woodside P & K 142 C10
Woodside Green Kent 38 F11
Woodstock Oxon 48 D11
Woodstock Pembks 41 K5
Woodston C Pete 74 C11
Wood Street Norfk 77 M7
Wood Street Village Surrey 23 Q4
Woodthorpe Derbys 84 G6
Woodthorpe Leics 72 E7
Woodthorpe Lincs 87 M4
Woodton Norfk 65 K3
Woodtown Devon 16 G7
Woodvale Sefton 88 C8
Woodville Derbys 71 Q11
Woodwall Green Staffs 70 D8
Wood Walton Cambs 62 B4
Woodyates Dorset 21 K11
Woody Bay Devon 17 M2
Woofferton Shrops 57 J11
Wookey Somset 19 P5
Wookey Hole Somset 19 P5
Wool Dorset 12 D7
Woolacombe Devon 16 H3
Woolage Green Kent 27 M2
Woolage Village Kent 39 M11
Woolaston Gloucs 31 Q5
Woolaston Common Gloucs 31 Q4
Woolavington Somset 19 K6
Woolbeding W Susx 23 N10
Woolbrook Devon 10 C7
Woolcotts Somset 18 C8
Wooldale Kirk 90 F9
Wooler Nthumb 119 J5
Woolfardisworthy Devon 9 K3
Woolfardisworthy Devon 16 E7
Woolfold Bury 89 M8
Woolfords S Lans 127 J6
Woolhampton W Berk 34 G11
Woolhope Herefs 46 B7
Woolland Dorset 12 C3
Woollard BaNES 20 B2
Woollensbrook Herts 51 J9
Woolley BaNES 32 D11
Woolley Cambs 61 Q6
Woolley Cnwll 16 D8
Woolley Derbys 84 E8
Woolley Wakefd 91 J8
Woolley Bridge Derbys 83 M6
Woolley Edge Services Wakefd 91 J8
Woolley Green W & M 35 M8
Woolmere Green Worcs 47 J2
Woolmer Green Herts 50 G7
Woolmerston Somset 19 J8
Woolminstone Somset 11 J3
Woolpack Kent 26 E4
Woolpit Suffk 64 D9
Woolpit Green Suffk 64 D9
Woolscott Warwks 60 B7
Woolsgrove Devon 9 J4
Woolsington N u Ty 113 J6
Woolstaston Shrops 56 H5
Woolsthorpe by Belvoir Lincs 73 L4
Woolsthorpe-by-Colsterworth Lincs 73 N6
Woolston C Sotn 14 D4
Woolston Devon 7 J10
Woolston Devon 7 J8
Woolston Shrops 56 G7
Woolston Shrops 69 K10
Woolston Somset 18 E7
Woolston Somset 20 C9
Woolston Warrtn 82 D7
Woolstone Gloucs 47 J8
Woolstone M Keyn 49 N7
Woolstone Oxon 33 Q7

Woolston Green Devon 7 K5
Woolton Lpool 81 N7
Woolton Hill Hants 22 D2
Woolverstone Suffk 53 L4
Woolverton Somset 20 E4
Woolwich Gt Lon 37 K5
Woonton Herefs 45 M4
Woonton Herefs 45 R2
Wooperton Nthumb 119 K6
Woore Shrops 70 C6
Wootten Green Suffk 65 J7
Wootton Bed 50 B2
Wootton Hants 13 M5
Wootton Herefs 45 L4
Wootton IoW 14 F8
Wootton Kent 27 M2
Wootton N Linc 93 J7
Wootton Nhants 60 G9
Wootton Oxon 34 E4
Wootton Oxon 48 D11
Wootton Shrops 69 K9
Wootton Staffs 70 E9
Wootton Staffs 71 L6
Wootton Bassett Wilts 33 L8
Wootton Bridge IoW 14 F8
Wootton Broadmead Bed 50 B2
Wootton Common IoW 14 F8
Wootton Courtenay Somset 18 B6
Wootton Fitzpaine Dorset 10 H5
Wootton Rivers Wilts 21 N2
Wootton St Lawrence Hants 22 G3
Wootton Wawen Warwks 47 N2
Worcester Worcs 46 G4
Worcester Park Gt Lon 36 F7
Wordsley Dudley 58 C7
Worfield Shrops 57 P5
Worgret Dorset 12 F7
Workhouse End Bed 61 P10
Workhouse Green Suffk 52 F4
Workington Cumb 100 D5
Worksop Notts 85 J5
Worlaby Lincs 87 K5
Worlaby N Linc 92 H8
Worlds End Bucks 35 N3
Worlds End Hants 14 H4
World's End W Berk 34 E9
Worlds End W Susx 24 H6
Worle N Som 19 L2
Worleston Ches E 70 B3
Worlingham Suffk 65 N4
Worlington Devon 9 J2
Worlington Suffk 63 L6
Worlingworth Suffk 65 J8
Wormald Green N York 97 M7
Wormbridge Herefs 45 N4
Wormegay Norfk 75 N8
Wormelow Tump Herefs 45 P8
Wormhill Derbys 83 P10
Wormhill Herefs 45 N7
Wormingford Essex 52 F5
Worminghall Bucks 34 H3
Wormington Gloucs 47 K7
Worminster Somset 19 Q6
Wormit Fife 135 L2
Wormleighton Warwks 48 E4
Wormley Herts 51 J9
Wormley Surrey 23 P7
Wormleybury Herts 51 J9
Wormley Hill Donc 91 R7
Wormshill Kent 38 E10
Wormsley Herefs 45 N5
Worplesdon Surrey 23 Q4
Worrall Sheff 84 D2
Worrall Hill Gloucs 32 B2
Worsbrough Barns 91 K10
Worsbrough Bridge Barns 91 K10
Worsbrough Dale Barns 91 K10
Worsley Salfd 82 G4
Worstead Norfk 77 L6
Worsthorne Lancs 89 P4
Worston Devon 6 F6
Worston Lancs 89 M2
Worth Kent 39 P10
Worth Somset 19 P5
Worth W Susx 24 H3
Wortham Suffk 64 F6
Worthen Shrops 56 E4
Worthenbury Wrexhm 69 M5
Worthing Norfk 76 D8
Worthing W Susx 24 D10
Worthington Leics 72 C6
Worth Matravers Dorset 12 G9
Worthybrook Mons 31 N2
Worting Hants 22 G4
Wortley Barns 91 J11
Wortley Gloucs 32 E6
Wortley Leeds 90 H4
Worton N York 96 E3
Worton Wilts 21 J3
Wortwell Norfk 65 K5
Wotherton Shrops 56 D4
Wothorpe C Pete 73 Q9
Wotter Devon 6 F2
Wotton Surrey 36 D11
Wotton-under-Edge Gloucs 32 E6
Wotton Underwood Bucks 49 J11
Woughton on the Green M Keyn 49 N7
Wouldham Kent 38 B9
Woundale Shrops 57 P6
Wrabness Essex 53 L5
Wrafton Devon 16 H4
Wragby Lincs 86 F5
Wragby Wakefd 91 L7
Wramplingham Norfk 76 G10
Wrangaton Devon 6 H7
Wrangbrook Wakefd 91 M8
Wrangle Lincs 87 M10
Wrangle Common Lincs 87 M10
Wrangle Lowgate Lincs 87 M10
Wrangway Somset 18 F11
Wrantage Somset 19 K10
Wrawby N Linc 92 H9
Wraxall N Som 31 N10
Wraxall Somset 20 B7
Wray Lancs 95 N7
Wray Castle Cumb 101 L10
Wraysbury W & M 36 B6
Wrayton Lancs 95 N6
Wrea Green Lancs 88 D4
Wreaks End Cumb 94 E3
Wreay Cumb 101 M6
Wreay Cumb 110 H11
Wrecclesham Surrey 23 M6
Wrekenton Gatesd 113 L9
Wrelton N York 98 F3

Wrenbury Ches E 69 Q5
Wrench Green N York 99 K3
Wreningham Norfk 64 H2
Wrentham Suffk 65 P5
Wrenthorpe Wakefd 91 J6
Wrentnall Shrops 56 G4
Wressle E R Yk 92 B4
Wressle N Linc 92 G9
Wrestlingworth C Beds 62 C11
Wretton Norfk 75 N10
Wrexham Wrexhm 69 K4
Wrexham Industrial Estate Wrexhm 69 L4
Wribbenhall Worcs 57 P9
Wrickton Shrops 57 L7
Wrightington Bar Lancs 88 G8
Wright's Green Essex 51 M7
Wrinehill Staffs 70 D5
Wrington N Som 19 N2
Writhlington BaNES 20 C4
Writtle Essex 51 Q9
Wrockwardine Wrekin 57 L2
Wroot N Linc 92 B10
Wrose C Brad 90 F3
Wrotham Kent 37 P9
Wrotham Heath Kent 37 P9
Wroughton Swindn 33 M8
Wroxall IoW 14 G11
Wroxall Warwks 59 K10
Wroxeter Shrops 57 K3
Wroxham Norfk 77 L8
Wroxton Oxon 48 D6
Wyaston Derbys 71 M6
Wyatt's Green Essex 51 N11
Wyberton Lincs 74 F2
Wyboston Bed 61 Q9
Wybunbury Ches E 70 B5
Wychbold Worcs 58 D11
Wych Cross E Susx 25 K4
Wychnor Staffs 71 M11
Wychwood Ches E 70 C4
Wyck Hants 23 L7
Wyck Rissington Gloucs 47 N10
Wycliffe Dur 103 M8
Wycoller Lancs 89 Q3
Wycomb Leics 73 K6
Wycombe Marsh Bucks 35 N6
Wyddial Herts 51 J4
Wye Kent 27 J2
Wyesham Mons 31 P2
Wyfordby Leics 73 K7
Wyke C Brad 90 F5
Wyke Devon 9 L5
Wyke Devon 10 F5
Wyke Dorset 20 E9
Wyke Shrops 57 L4
Wyke Surrey 23 P4
Wyke Champflower Somset 20 C8
Wykeham N York 99 K4
Wyken Covtry 59 N8
Wyken Shrops 57 P5
Wyke Regis Dorset 11 P9
Wykey Shrops 69 L10
Wykin Leics 72 C11
Wylam Nthumb 112 H8
Wylde Green Birm 58 H6
Wylye Wilts 21 K7
Wymeswold Leics 72 G6
Wymington Bed 61 L8
Wymondham Leics 73 L7
Wymondham Norfk 76 G11
Wyndham Brdgnd 29 P6
Wynford Eagle Dorset 11 M5
Wynyard Park S on T 104 D5
Wynyard Village S on T 104 D5
Wyre Piddle Worcs 47 J5
Wysall Notts 72 G5
Wyson Herefs 57 J11
Wythall Worcs 58 G9
Wytham Oxon 34 E3
Wythburn Cumb 101 K8
Wythenshawe Manch 82 H7
Wythop Mill Cumb 100 G5
Wyton Cambs 62 C6
Wyton E R Yk 93 L4
Wyton on the Hill Cambs 62 C6
Wyverstone Suffk 64 E8
Wyverstone Street Suffk 64 E8
Wyville Lincs 73 M5

Y

Yaddlethorpe N Linc 92 E9
Yafford IoW 14 D10
Yafforth N York 97 M2
Yalberton Torbay 7 M7
Yalding Kent 37 Q10
Yanwath Cumb 101 P5
Yanworth Gloucs 33 J2
Yapham E R Yk 98 F10
Yapton W Susx 15 Q6
Yarborough N Som 19 L3
Yarbridge IoW 14 H9
Yarburgh Lincs 87 L2
Yarcombe Devon 10 E3
Yard Devon 17 P7
Yardley Birm 58 H7
Yardley Gobion Nhants 49 L6
Yardley Hastings Nhants 61 J9
Yardley Wood Birm 58 H9
Yardro Powys 45 J3
Yarford Somset 18 H9
Yarkhill Herefs 46 B6
Yarley Somset 19 P6
Yarlington Somset 20 C9
Yarm S on T 104 D8
Yarmouth IoW 14 C9
Yarnacott Devon 17 L5
Yarnbrook Wilts 20 G4
Yarner Devon 9 J9
Yarnfield Staffs 70 F8
Yarnscombe Devon 17 K7
Yarnton Oxon 34 E2
Yarpole Herefs 45 P2
Yarrow Border 117 M5
Yarrow Somset 19 L5
Yarrow Feus Border 117 L5
Yarrowford Border 117 N4
Yarsop Herefs 45 N5
Yarwell Nhants 73 R11
Yate S Glos 32 D8
Yateley Hants 23 M2

Yatesbury Wilts 33 L10
Yattendon W Berk 34 G10
Yatton Herefs 56 G11
Yatton N Som 31 M11
Yatton Keynell Wilts 32 G9
Yaverland IoW 14 H9
Yawl Devon 10 G6
Yawthorpe Lincs 85 Q2
Yaxham Norfk 76 E9
Yaxley Cambs 61 Q2
Yaxley Suffk 64 G7
Yazor Herefs 45 N5
Yeading Gt Lon 36 D4
Yeadon Leeds 90 G2
Yealand Conyers Lancs 95 L6
Yealand Redmayne Lancs 95 L5
Yealand Storrs Lancs 95 K5
Yealmbridge Devon 6 F8
Yealmpton Devon 6 F8
Yearby R & Cl 104 G6
Yearngill Cumb 100 F2
Yearsley N York 98 B6
Yeaton Shrops 69 M11
Yeaveley Derbys 71 M6
Yeavering Nthumb 118 H4
Yedingham N York 98 H5
Yelford Oxon 34 C4
Yell Shet 169 r5
Yelland Devon 16 H5
Yelling Cambs 62 C8
Yelvertoft Nhants 60 C5
Yelverton Devon 6 E5
Yelverton Norfk 77 K11
Yenston Somset 20 D10
Yeoford Devon 9 J5
Yeolmbridge Cnwll 5 N4
Yeo Mill Devon 17 Q6
Yeo Vale Devon 16 G7
Yeovil Somset 19 Q11
Yeovil Marsh Somset 19 P11
Yeovilton Somset 19 P10
Yerbeston Pembks 41 L9
Yesnaby Ork 169 b5
Yetlington Nthumb 119 K9
Yetminster Dorset 11 M2
Yetson Devon 7 L7
Yettington Devon 9 Q7
Yetts o'Muckhart Clacks 134 C7
Yews Green C Brad 90 D4
Yew Tree Sandw 58 F5
Y Felinheli Gwynd 79 J11
Y Ferwig Cerdgn 42 C5
Y Ffôr Gwynd 66 F7
Yielden Bed 61 M7
Yieldingtree Worcs 58 C9
Yieldshields S Lans 126 F7
Yiewsley Gt Lon 36 C4
Y Nant Wrexhm 69 J4
Ynys Gwynd 67 K8
Ynysboeth Rhondd 30 E5
Ynysddu Caerph 30 G6
Ynysforgan Swans 29 J5
Ynyshir Rhondd 30 D6
Ynyslas Cerdgn 54 E6
Ynysmaerdy Rhondd 30 D8
Ynysmeudwy Neath 29 K3
Ynystawe Swans 29 J4
Ynyswen Powys 29 M2
Ynyswen Rhondd 30 C5
Ynysybwl Rhondd 30 E6
Ynysymaengwyn Gwynd 54 D4
Yockenthwaite N York 96 D5
Yockleton Shrops 56 F2
Yokefleet E R Yk 92 D6
Yoker C Glas 125 N4
York C York 98 C10
York Lancs 89 L4
Yorkletts Kent 39 J9
Yorkley Gloucs 32 B3
Yorkshire Dales National Park 96 C5
York Town Surrey 23 N2
Yorton Heath Shrops 69 P10
Youlgreave Derbys 84 B8
Youlthorpe E R Yk 98 F9
Youlton N York 97 Q8
Youngsbury Herts 51 J7
Young's End Essex 52 B8
Yoxall Staffs 71 L11
Yoxford Suffk 65 M8
Y Rhiw Gwynd 66 C9
Ysbyty Cynfyn Cerdgn 54 H9
Ysbyty Ifan Conwy 67 Q5
Ysbyty Ystwyth Cerdgn 54 G10
Ysceifiog Flints 80 H10
Ysgubor-y-Coed Cerdgn 54 F5
Ystalyfera Neath 29 L3
Ystrad Rhondd 30 C5
Ystrad Aeron Cerdgn 43 K3
Ystradfellte Powys 29 P2
Ystrad Ffin Carmth 43 Q5
Ystradgynlais Powys 29 L2
Ystrad Meurig Cerdgn 54 G11
Ystrad Mynach Caerph 30 F6
Ystradowen V Glam 30 D9
Ystumtuen Cerdgn 54 G9
Ythanbank Abers 159 M11
Ythanwells Abers 158 F10
Ythsie Abers 159 L11

Z

Zeal Monachorum Devon 8 H4
Zeals Wilts 20 E8
Zelah Cnwll 3 L3
Zennor Cnwll 2 D6
Zoar Cnwll 3 K10
Zouch Notts 72 E6
ZSL London Zoo Gt Lon 36 G4
ZSL Whipsnade Zoo C Beds 50 B7

Distances and journey times

The mileage chart shows distances in miles between two towns along AA-recommended routes. Using motorways and other main roads this is normally the fastest route, though not necessarily the shortest.

The journey times are shown in hours and minutes. These times should be used as a guide only and do not allow for unforeseen traffic delays, rest breaks or fuel stops.

For example, the 377 miles (607 km) journey between Glasgow and Norwich should take approximately 7 hours 18 minutes.

Journey times

Distances in miles (one mile equals 1.6093 km)